Fourth Edition

Psychology and the Challenges of Life

Adjustment and Growth

Spencer A. Rathus

Department of Psychology
St. John's University
Jamaica, N.Y. 11439

Jeffrey S. Nevid

Department of Psychology
St. John's University
Jamaica, N.Y. 11439

Holt, Rinehart and Winston, Inc.

New York   Chicago   San Francisco   Philadelphia

Montreal   Toronto   London   Sydney   Tokyo

To Jill Rathus, as she undertakes graduate study in psychology

To Eleanor and Marvin Nevid

PUBLISHER *Susan Driscoll*
ACQUISITIONS EDITOR *Eve Howard*
DEVELOPMENTAL EDITOR *Carol Einhorn*
SENIOR PROJECT MANAGER *Françoise Bartlett*
MANAGER OF PRODUCTION *Angelo Puleo*
DESIGN SUPERVISOR *Lou Scardino*
TEXT DESIGN *Caliber Design Planning, Inc.*
COVER PHOTOS Front cover: © *1987 Neil Rabinowitz*
               Back cover: *I. Thoma/The Image Bank*
COVER DESIGN *Fred Pusterla*

Library of Congress Cataloging-in-Publication Data

Rathus, Spencer A.
  Psychology and the challenges of life.

  Rev. ed. of: Adjustment and growth.   3rd ed. c1986.
  Includes indexes.
  Bibliography: p.
  1. Adjustment (Psychology) 2. Psychology.
I. Nevid, Jeffrey S. II. Rathus, Spencer A.
Adjustment and growth. III. Title.
BF335.R28 1989   155.2′4   88-13457

ISBN 0-03-025464-7

Copyright © 1989, 1986, 1983, 1980 by Holt, Rinehart and Winston, Inc.

Printed in the United States of America

9 0 1 2   039   9 8 7 6 5 4 3 2 1

Holt Rinehart and Winston, Inc.
The Dryden Press
Saunders College Publishing

Copyright acknowledgments and photo credits follow References.

■ Preface

Writing *Psychology and the Challenges of Life* was one of the major challenges of our professional careers: describing the theories and methods of the science of psychology and showing how they have revolutionized our abilities to cope with the demands of contemporary life.

To meet our challenge, we decided that the text must be comprehensive, efficient, and balanced. It was written for instructors who require a textbook that is

Comprehensive and balanced
Rigorous and up-to-date
Easily read
Interest arousing
Well-illustrated
Theoretical and applied.

Specifically, *Psychology and the Challenges of Life* balances the following elements:

Information and Applications   Psychological theory and research now extend to elements of our daily lives ranging from doing well in college to adjustment in a new job, from weight control to safe(r) sex in the age of AIDS, from figuring out what to say in social encounters to the quests for values and personal identity. With these issues and others, we report the pertinent psychological theory and research, and then we show readers how to apply theory and research to their own lives.

But a responsible textbook must avoid giving readers the impression that they can handle major psychological problems by themselves. For this reason, we also point out when it is useful to consult a helping professional, and we suggest who the right professional for the problem may be.

Traditional and Innovative Areas in Adjustment
This book discusses the areas found in most psychology of adjustment textbooks, such as stress, sex roles, adult development, marriage, work, anxiety, and prejudice. But it also focuses on areas that have become of major concern to today's readers, but which are found less often in textbooks, or not at all. These innovative areas include student success ("How to Take Charge in College"), alcohol and drug abuse, rape and rape prevention, sexual dysfunctions, aging, job hunting (including using a "job finders' club"), enhancing productivity at work, career decision making, coping with sexual harrassment and sexism, and having and rearing children.

Psychodynamic, Trait, Learning, and Phenomenological Personality Theories   A comprehensive psychology of adjustment textbook cannot be written from a single theoretical perspective. The issues dealt with are too broad to be fully encompassed by one approach. Therefore, we point out how each of the four major psychological approaches to understanding human nature has provided helpful information for personal development. However, we are not naively eclectic; each of these views has shortcomings as well as strengths, and we point them out, as appropriate.

Substance and Readability   It matters little how fine the substance of a textbook is if its style fails to make it accessible to students. Feedback from students and instructors concerning the first three editions suggested that we were highly successful in our efforts to craft every word with the student in mind. Students and instructors appreciated our orderly development of concepts and our interjection of humor. They requested that we maintain our writing style for the fourth edition.

We did.

However, the substance of the current edition has been expanded. We have changed the title of the book to signal this change. The previous edition, entitled *Adjustment and Growth*, suggested that the applications to everyday life take precedence over other considerations. The current edition is entitled *Psychology and the Challenges of Life*, suggesting that psychology is discussed as the rigorous science it is, and that applications are logically derived and empirically based.

Note the following changes in substance.

■ What's New in This Edition
The current edition is divided into three parts.

Part I: Psychological Foundations of Adjustment and Growth
The first part discusses psychology as the science that helps people adjust to the challenges of life and develop as individuals.

Chapter 1, "Psychology and the Challenges of Life." This chapter defines psychology as a science and relates psychology to adjustment and growth. There is a new section on issues in psychology and adjustment, an expanded section on research methods ("How Psychologists Study Adjustment"), and an expanded section on "Student Success: How to Take Charge in College," which addresses ways of planning time, using the SQ4R study method, and of behaving in class.

Chapter 2, "Theories of Personality and Behavior." This chapter explores the four major contemporary approaches to personality. There are new sections on trait theory and George Kelly. The section on social-learning theory is completely revised. The strengths and weaknesses of each approach are evaluated, and the nature of the healthy personality is discussed in terms of each approach.

Chapter 3, "Sex Roles and Sex Differences." This chapter explores sex roles and sex differences in personality and behavior. The section on development of sex differences is expanded to include cognitive-developmental theory and gender-schema theory. There is also a new section on the costs of sex-role stereotyping.

Chapter 4, "Person Perception: How We See Others and Ourselves." This chapter explores the contributions of the psychology of person perception to the ways in which we perceive other people and ourselves. There are new sections on social perception, including schema theory, primacy and recency effects, body language, and attribution theory.

Chapter 5, "Social Influence: Being Influenced By—and Influencing—Others." This chapter explores the contributions of the psychology of social influence to our understanding of the ways in which we and other people attempt to have an impact on each other's behavior.

Part II: Stress, Health, and Coping
The second part explores the links among stress, health, and psychological disorders. Ways of coping are described in step-by-step fashion.

Chapter 6, "Stress: What It Is and What It Does." There is expanded coverage of daily hassles and of the stress-related responses of the sympathetic and endocrine systems. There is new coverage of emotional and cognitive responses to stress, and of moderators of the impact of stress—including the roles of self-efficacy expectancies, psychological hardiness, humor, goal-directedness, predictability, and social support.

Chapter 7, "Psychology and Physical Health." This new chapter covers health psychology—the immune system; the links between stress and physical disorders such as headaches, cardiovascular disorders, and cancer; nutritional patterns (including the roles of fats, vitamins, fiber, and so on in cardiovascular disorders and cancer); activity patterns (for example, the health benefits of exercise); and the psychology of being sick (including factors involved in seeking and complying with medical advice, the conceptualization of illness, and the sick role).

Chapter 8, "Psychological Disorders." There is new coverage of panic disorder, post-traumatic stress disorder, depersonalization, anorexia nervosa, bulimia nervosa, and sexual disorders. The chapter is written from the contemporary perspective of the DMS–III–R, and coverage of etiology is rigorous.

Chapter 9, "Therapies: Ways of Helping." Coverage is generally expanded, especially in the cognitive and biological therapies. There is a rigorous new evaluation of methods of therapy.

Chapter 10, "Active Coping: Ways of Helping Ourselves." This new chapter covers ways of reducing arousal, controlling catastrophizing thoughts, and coping with issues in self-control (weight, smoking, insomnia) and the emotions (anxiety, depression, anger). There is new coverage of methods of alleviating Type A behavior and of enhancing psychological hardiness.

Part III: Adult Life in a Changing World
The third part discusses the challenges that face adults as they develop in a changing world.

Chapter 11, "Adult Development: Passages." There is new material on the physical and cognitive changes that occur during adulthood and on dying with dignity (the hospice movement, euthanasia, and the living will). Coverage of developmental theory is broadened and deepened.

Chapter 12, "The Challenge of the Workplace." Coverage of Super's theory of career development is expanded. There is new coverage of coping styles and vocational types (Holland's theory of career selection), developmental tasks in a new job, cognitive biases in worker appraisal, and organizational theory and adjustment.

Chapter 13, "Interpersonal Attraction: Of Friendship, Love, and Loneliness." There is new coverage of friendship and loneliness.

Chapter 14, "Communication and Intimate Relationships: A Guide on How to Get from Here to There." There is new coverage of stages in a relationship and a new, step-by-step guide to enhancing communication skills.

Chapter 15, "Sexual Behavior: Perspectives, Patterns, Pleasures, and Problems." The discussion of contemporary sexual behavior is fully updated to reflect the relatively conservative trends of the late 1980s. There is a new section on sexually transmitted diseases and a section of concrete advice on "Safe(r) Sex in the Age of AIDS."

Chapter 16, "Having and Rearing Children." There is new material of concern to young adults considering having families: coping with infertility, environmental influences on embryonic and fetal development, methods of childbirth, authoritative child-rearing, breast-feeding, child abuse, and day care.

■ Pedagogical Aids and Features

Most students who take the psychology of adjustment are first- and second-year students. Many of them have not had an introductory course in psychology. We included a number of pedagogical aids and features to help promote learning among students who have little or no background in psychology:

Chapter Outlines

Each chapter opens with a clear chapter outline. Chapter outlines provide students with "advance organizers"—expectations about what is to come that help them integrate the subject matter.

"Truth or Fiction?"

Following the chapter outline is a "Truth or Fiction?" section that stimulates students by challenging folklore and common knowledge. The "Truth or Fiction?" items prompt students to seek the answers within the chapters.

Running Glossary

Research has shown that most students do not take full advantage of a glossary that is tucked away near the end of a book. For this reason, we define key terms in a running glossary that appears in the margins of the two-page spreads on which the terms appear. Thus they are immediately accessible; students need not interrupt their train of thought to go searching at the back of the book.

Key terms are made immediately evident by appering in boldface type in the text. All defined terms are also listed in the subject index, and the pages on which they are defined are also boldfaced, increasing the accessibility of the definitions.

"A Closer Look" Inserts

These inserts are found throughout the text. Some of them provide humorous asides. Others provide in-depth discussions of important studies or of applications. Examples include:

Coping with self-help books
Why young people join religious cults
Pain management
Myths about menopause
Workaholism
Sexual harassment on the job.

"What Do You Say Now?" Inserts

We are particularly proud of this new feature. Each "What Do You Say Now?" section paints a challenging social situation and asks students to write down what they would say in it. Then we present some of our own suggestions, allowing students to compare their thinking with ours. These situations are real and occur quite commonly. We believe that these exercises will help students respond to them—and to similar situations—effectively in their own lives. Examples include:

Handling a sexist remark
Resisting a relative's invitation to eat a fattening dessert
How to make a positive impression at a job interview
Making sex safe(r) in the age of AIDS
Selecting an obstetrician
Selecting a day-care center.

Questionnaires

Questionnaires included throughout the book will further stimulate student interest and also help them satisfy their curiosities about their motives, attitudes, and certain personality traits. For instance, students can gain insight into why they drink or find out how assertive they are as compared to a national sample of college students. They can learn whether or not their expectations of their marriage partners are likely to be highly traditional, and whether or not their views of sex roles are traditional.

Moreover, the presence of questionnaires actually used by psychologists will provide students with additional insight into how psychologists conceptualize research variables and gather data.

Chapter Summaries

End-of-chapter summaries are written in question-and-answer format so as to be consistent with the SQ4R study method outlined in Chapter 1. These summaries help students actively review the subject matter by posing questions and then suggesting answers.

"Truth or Fiction Revisited" Sections

These sections follow the chapter summaries and provide answers to the provocative issues raised at the beginning of the chapter. They also help provide a sense of psychological closure.

Answer Keys to Questionnaires

The answer keys to the questionnaires are placed at the ends of the chapters in which they appear.

Section on "Student Success: How to Take Charge in College"

Chapter 1 includes a section that explains the SQ4R for actively learning textbook material. It is intended to be of help to students not only in their psychology of adjustment course but also throughout their college careers. Other study hints explain the advantages of building study habits, planning ahead, distributing learning, and using other well-documented study techniques.

■ The Ancillaries

Psychology and the Challenges of Life is accompanied by a student Study Guide, an Instructor's Manual/ Test Bank, and Computerized Test Item Files, which are intended to optimize learning and teaching.

Study Guide

The Study Guide is designed to make it easier for students to organize the material in each chapter of the text so that they can learn and remember it more efficiently. Each chapter of the Study Guide contains an Outline, Learning Objectives, Key Terms, and a Self-test section including 25 multi-ple-choice items. An introductory section provides a detailed presentation of study techniques.

Instructor's Manual/Test Bank

For each chapter of the text, the Instructor's Manual provides an Outline, Teaching Objectives, Lecture and Class Activity Suggestions, and Film Suggestions. An introduction explains how best to use these resources.

The Test Bank contains at least 100 multiple-choice test items for each chapter. The questions are designed in part to test knowledge and in part to test students' ability to apply information from the text. The 25 multiple-choice questions in each chapter of the Study Guide are also included in the Test Bank, keyed in the margins for easy recognition. Instructors may choose to include these questions in their exams to reward student review work.

Computerized Test Item Files

Computerized Test Item Files are available for use on the Apple and IBM personal computerized systems.

■ Acknowledgments

At times writing can seem like a solitary task. However, many people participated in the growth and development of *Psychology and the Challenges of Life*. We take this opportunity to express our sincere gratitude to them. First, we must thank our professional colleagues from campuses all across the nation. They painstakingly read the manuscripts for each edition of the textbook and suggested many insightful adjustments. They are:

Bob Arndt
Delta College

Bela Baker
University of Wisconsin–Green Bay

Helene Bakewell
Stephen F. Austin State University

Jacinth Baubitz
Northwood Institute

Nancy Bowers
Pikes Peak Community College

Desmond Cartwright
University of Colorado

David Chance
Central State College

Norma Crews
DeKalb Community College

Jean DeVany
Auburn University

Richard Dienstbier
University of Nebraska

Steve Donahue
Grand Canyon College

William Dugmore
Central Washington University

Thomas Eckle
Modesto Junior College

Richard M. Ehlenz
Rochester Community College

Ron Evans
Washburn University

Jennie Fauchier
Metro Technical Community College

Eugene Fichter
Northern Virginia Community College

Ronnie Fisher
Miami-Dade Community College

Sharon Fisher
El Paso Community College

Lynn Godat
Portland Community College

Peter Gram
Pensacola Community College

Lawrence Grebstein
University of Rhode Island

Myree Hayes
East Carolina University

Gladys Hiner
Rose State College

Gordon M. Kimbrell
University of South Carolina

Clint Layne
Western Kentucky University

Gary Lesniak
Portland Community College

Arnold LeUnes
Texas A&M University

Phyllis McGraw
Portland State University

Louis A. Martone
Miami-Dade Community College

Frederick Medway
University of South Carolina

Roland Miller
Sam Houston State University

Norma Mittenthal
Hillsborough Community College

Patrick Murphy
Spokane Community College

Tony Obradovich
DeVry Institute of Technology

Arne Parma
Massachusetts Bay Community College

Kathy Petrowsky
Southwestern Oklahoma State University

Robert Petty
University of Santa Clara

A. R. Peyman
Mississippi State University

Gary Piggrem
DeVry Institute of Technology

Chris Potter
Harrisburg Area Community College

Jay Pozner
Jackson Community College

James B. Riley
Southeastern Massachusetts University

Suzanne Rucker
Miami-Dade Community College

Claudia Sowa
University of Virginia

Arthur Swanson
University of Missouri—Columbia

Marilyn Thomas
Prince George Community College

Robert Thomlinson
University of Wisconsin—Eau Claire

Deborah Weber
University of Akron

David Weight
Brigham Young University

Robert Wrenn
University of Arizona

We also had the fortune to work with the first-rate staff of publishing professionals at Holt, Rinehart and Winston. We thank Susan Driscoll, Publisher of the Behavioral and Social Sciences group, for her support and encouragement as we deepened the substance and expanded the coverage of the book. Eve Howard, Psychology Editor, was persuaded to surrender the wonders of the Bay Area to move back East and lend this book her expertise. Carol Einhorn, Developmental Editor, made innumerable valuable suggestions for fine-tuning the substance of the manuscript and for finding new ways to make psychology accessible to

students. Lou Scardino, Design Supervisor, is to be credited for the attractive design. Fran Bartlett, Senior Project Manager, once again worked her magic on one of our manuscripts—somehow converting it into the beautiful book you are now holding in your hands. Angelo Puleo, Manager of Production, ably oversaw the book's production.

S.A.R.
Summit, N.J.

J.S.N.
New York, N.Y.

■ Brief Contents

Contents

■ **Features**

■ **What Do You Say Now?**

PART

I

Psychological Foundations of Adjustment and Growth

Psychology and the Challenges of Life

1

Longshoremen have become longshorepersons, and we find ads for Guy Fridays in the "Help Wanted" columns.

Only gay men and intravenous drug abusers are really at risk for being infected by the AIDS virus.

Some people are genetically vulnerable to becoming alcoholics or suffering severe mood swings.

If the risk factors for heart disease are stacked against you, there's nothing you can do about it—you're going to have a heart attack.

Only men are sexually aroused by sexually explicit films.

You are less likely to get a divorce if you live together with your future spouse before getting married.

Sustained exercise is linked to a lower incidence of heart attacks.

There is no experimental evidence, with human beings, that cigarette smoking causes cancer.

You could survey 20 million Americans and still not accurately predict the outcome of a presidential election.

Pretest cramming is more effective than distributed learning.

It is a good idea to participate in every class discussion.

Beth, 22, a fourth-year chemisty major, has been accepted to medical school in Boston. She wants to do cancer research, but this goal means another seven or eight years at the grindstone. Kevin, her fiancé, has landed a solid engineering position in "Silicon Valley," California. He wants Beth to come with him, take a year to start a family, and then go to medical school in California. But Beth hasn't applied to medical school in California, and there's no sure bet that she would "get in" there. If she surrenders her educational opportunity now, another one might not come along. Should she demand that Kevin accompany her to Boston, even though he hasn't been offered work there? Would he go? What if he gives up his golden opportunity and their relationship falters because of resentment? Also, if she has children, she doesn't want to "hand them over to a stranger" all day every day so she can go to school. And how long can she safely put off childbearing? She's "a kid" now, but the biological clock is ticking and she won't be finishing her graduate training—assuming she goes to medical school—until she's 30. And what if having children even then threatens to prevent her from getting established in her career? Beth has just been accepted to medical school—shouldn't she be happy?

John, 21, is a business student who is all business. Every day he reads the *Wall Street Journal* and the business pages of the *New York Times*. He is dedicated to his books and invests most of his energy in trying to construct a solid academic record so that he will get his career off on the right foot. But sometimes he wonders why he bothers; he knows that he is one of those people who "just can't take tests." He begins to shake two days before a test. His thoughts become jumbled when the papers are distributed. By the time the papers are on his desk, his hand is shaking so badly that he can hardly write his name. His grades suffer.

Maria, 19, is a first-year college student. She has seen the TV talk shows and has gone to the R-rated films. She has read the books and the magazine articles about the new sexual openness. But despite the social and sexual pressures, she would prefer to wait for Mr. Right—or at the very least, she'd prefer to have some more time to sort out her feelings. The young man she has been seeing, Mark, has been reasonably "patient," from his point of view, but lately he's been pressuring her, too. He has told Maria they have more than a "fly-by-night" relationship and that other women are more willing to "express their sexual needs." Her girlfriends say they understand her feelings but tell Maria they fear that at some point Mark will turn elsewhere. Quite frankly, Maria is concerned about more than her virginity; she also thinks about diseases such as herpes and AIDS. After all, Mark is 22 years old and she doesn't know every place "he's been." True, they can take some precautions, but these days is even deep kissing completely safe? Maria is sophisticated in many ways, and she often wonders if her concerns are rational or whether she's become a victim of a national hysteria, just as people were hysterical about "Reefer Madness" and syphilis earlier in the century.

Lisa, 20, a hard-working college junior, is popular with faculty, dutiful with relatives. She works out regularly and is proud of her figure. But Lisa also has a secret. When she is sipping her coffee in the morning, she hopes that she won't go off the deep end again, but most of the time she does. She usually starts by eating a doughnut slowly; then she eats another, picking up speed; then she voraciously downs the remaining four in the box. Then she eats two or three bagels with cream cheese. If there is any leftover pizza from the evening before, that goes down too. She feels disgusted with herself, but she hunts through her apartment for food. Down go the potato chips, down go the cookies. Fifteen minutes later she feels as though she will burst and cannot take in anymore. Half nauseated she finds her way to the bathroom and makes herself throw up the contents of her binging. Tomorrow, she tells herself, will be different. But deep inside she suspects that she will buy more

Bulimia nervosa. An eating disorder characterized by cycles of binge eating and a dramatic method for purging, such as vomiting.

doughnuts and more cookies, and that tomorrow might be much the same. She has read about something called **bulimia nervosa.** Does she have it? Does she need professional help?

David, 32, is not sleeping well. He wakes before dawn and cannot get back to sleep. His appetite is off, his energy level is low, he has started smoking again. He has a couple of drinks at lunch and muses that it's lucky that any more alcohol makes him sick to his stomach—otherwise, he'd probably be drinking too much, too. Then he thinks, "So what difference would it make?" Sometimes he is sexually frustrated; at other times he wonders whether he has any sex drive left. Although he's awake, each day it's getting harder to drag himself out of bed in the morning. This week he missed one day of work and was late twice. His supervisor has suggested in an unthreatening way that he "do something about it." David knows that her next warning will not be unthreatening. It's been going downhill since Sue walked out. Suicide has even crossed David's mind. He wonder's if he's going crazy.

Beth, John, Maria, Lisa, David—for them, for millions of others like them and us, life has its joys and its sorrows, its ups and its downs, its victories and its defeats. Life has its challenges.

Beth is experiencing role conflict. She wants to go to medical school but also wants to maintain the relationship with Kevin and start a family. Although she might become a physician, she would probably retain the primary responsibility for child-rearing. In Chapters 3 and 12 we'll see that even women who have become vice presidents and presidents of their companies usually remain the ones who do the laundry and dress the kids. Kevin is not a chauvinist; he accompanies Beth to Boston and looks for work there.

John does have test anxiety, and it has prevented him from performing up to his potential for years. Fortunately, there is a notice on a bulletin board that his college counseling center is running a program to help students with test anxiety. He follows techniques such as those outlined in Chapter 10 and his grades pick up.

Maria is also in conflict—with Mark and with herself. She decides not to be pressured into a sexual relationship, and it happens that Mark turns elsewhere. It hurts, but Maria is confident that dates more to her liking will understand her position and, perhaps, appreciate it.

Lisa does have bulimia nervosa, an eating disorder discussed in Chapter 8. Bulimia is reaching epidemic proportions on college campuses. The causes are unclear, but bulimia might be related to the slender feminine ideal that prevails in our society. It might also reflect snacking on carbohydrates, carbohydrates, and more carbohydrates as a child.

David is depressed. Depression is normal following a loss, such as the end of a relationship, but his feelings have been lingering. His friends tell him that he should start getting out and doing things, but David is so down that he hasn't the motivation. After much prompting David consults a psychologist who, ironically, also pushes him to get out and do things—pleasant events of the sort described in Chapter 10. The psychologist also shows David that part of his problem is that he is viewing himself as a hopeless failure, incapable of making meaningful changes.

Beth, John, Maria, Lisa, and David all need to make *adjustments* to the challenges in their lives.

■ The Challenges of Life

The challenges of life touch us all at one time or another. That is what this book is about: adjusting to challenges as we get on with the business of living— growing, learning, building relationships, establishing careers, making ends meet, and striving to feel good about ourselves. This book portrays our quest for self-development and brings psychological knowledge to bear on some of the problems that may block self-development. Some of these problems, such as anxiety, depression, or obesity, are personal. Some involve intimate relationships and sexuality. Some involve the larger social context—the workplace, natural and technological disasters, pollution, even the problems of city life.

Most challenges offer us an opportunity to grow. Most of the time we solve the problems we encounter by ourselves. But when personal solutions are not at hand, we can often turn to modern psychology for help. In this book you will learn how you can often apply psychological knowledge to your own life. You will also learn about the professional helpers and when and how to seek their intervention. This knowledge is important because life as we approach the twenty-first century has in many ways become more challenging than it has ever been.

In this chapter we first discuss some of the challenges of contemporary life. We define the science of psychology and see that it is well-suited to gathering information about, and suggesting applications for, our own adjustment and growth. We explore some of the major perspectives on adjustment that are held by contemporary psychologists, and we consider some of the issues and controversies that characterize the psychology of adjustment. Then we examine the scientific procedures that psychologists use in gathering knowledge, and we learn that psychologists have very strict rules for separating scientific truth from common sense (or, as some would put it, "common nonsense") and folklore. It is these strict rules that make psychology a science. Finally, we explore what psychologists have learned about making study habits more effective.

Now let us consider the challenges of changing roles, a changing technology, a changing physical environment, and a changing society.

The Challenge of Changing Roles

Only a few short decades ago, women cooked, cleaned, and wiped children's noses, while men engaged in physical labor or sat at desks computing numbers. Women today pilot airplanes and shuttle spacecraft, perform surgery, mine coal, fight fires, and walk the lonely dark beat of the police officer. Longshoremen today are increasingly likely to be longshorepersons. Newspapers carry ads for Gal *and Guy* Fridays. Young male secretaries are opening mail and brewing coffee for women supervisors.

Perhaps some of us would find it comforting to return to the days when men were strong and silent and women were fluffy and dependent. Certainly today's opportunities for self-expression in the worlds of work and the emotional life have led to new problems for both sexes. A number of women fear that by being self-assertive and hardheaded in the business world they are compromising their femininity. Many men are having difficulty adjusting to female bosses and wives who earn more than they do. Today, as we shall see in Chapter 3, some critics are challenging the very concepts of "masculinity" and "femininity" as cultural inventions that perpetuate myths about the sexes and hurt all of us.

The Challenge of Changing Technology

Yesterday's record keepers and clerks have often become today's computer programmers. They read and write several computer languages, such as COBOL and FORTRAN, that did not exist a generation or two ago. Teachers are being trained how to introduce kindergarten students and first-graders to microcomputers.

We used to prefer medical professionals with some gray at the temples and some creases in the brow. But many of today's medical technologies—such as laser-beam surgery and artifical organs—did not exist when older practitioners were in school. Although people who have been in the field for

Today's college students are challenged by rapidly changing technology.

many years can take courses and workshops to catch up, technology overleaps itself at such a pace that years of experience are sometimes balanced by the freshness of being just out of school.

Brilliant scientists are hard pressed to keep up with research findings outside their narrow specialties. Technological needs compel us to rely on young people to plot the paths of our spacecraft, to design efficient marketing and distribution systems for corporations, and literally to hold our hearts in their hands during surgery.

Even as we profit from technological advances, we may fear that we shall not be able to keep pace with them. One of the striking conclusions of *Workforce 2000*, a report issued by the Hudson Institute (1988), is that although the standard of living will continue to rise over the next decade, income distribution will widen because there will be more jobs for most highly skilled members of the work force and fewer jobs for the least-skilled. Jobs in manufacturing will continue to decline as robots replace workers on the assembly line. But there is likely to be an expansion of jobs in education, health care, government, and retailing.

As the pace of change accelerates, we may wonder whether some new invention or procedure will make our own skills and careers obsolete.

The Challenge of a Changing Physical Environment

Changing social roles and a changing technology are, to some degree, dwarfed by the sheer magnitude of some of the environmental changes that are taking place. But, as we shall see, our physical environments are also made up of the littlest things.

Human-Made Environmental Changes   Just as the environment once held humankind in its grip, we now in some ways have a hold on the world at large. For example, the fluorocarbons used in aerosol sprays and industry may be contributing to the erosion of ozone in the upper atmosphere, leaving us more vulnerable to ultraviolet light and skin cancers. The sulfurous emissions from burning coal may be contributing to the acid rain that has struck down life in many lakes and streams.

Changing Resources   The United States stretches vast from ocean to ocean. Once the nation was independent and its resources seemed infinite. We have constructed an industrial plant unmatched in the history of civilization. Our Midwest has been the food factory for the world. But now some shadows creep across the fruited plains of the land of plenty.

Today we import a large amount of the petroleum we use, often from nations with unstable political structures. We really don't know how much natural gas lies below our land and off our shores. We have more than enough coal to meet our fuel needs, if needed, but the burning of large quantities of coal raises environmental problems beyond those of acid rain. One of them is the so-called hothouse effect: The burning of fossil fuels may eventually raise the earth's temperature by a few degrees. Resultant melting of the polar icecaps could flood coastal cities. We also import the great majority of our strategic metals. Thus, problems in international relations today could impair the manufacture of many materials and machines and other goods tomorrow.

In recent years we have made remarkable strides in improving the quality of our air, but industrial wastes still threaten our land and our water. Hazardous and toxic wastes have entered the American consciousness. One of today's challenges, which will affect Americans of future generations, concerns the issue of whether to open public lands to exploration for fuel and metals, or whether to preserve the bits and pieces of wilderness that remain.

Changing Pathogens   And then there are the littlest things—**pathogens,** some of them new, some of them deadly, some of them so far incurable. The frightening sexually transmitted diseases of earlier years, gonorrhea and syphilis, are today usually treated successfully with antibiotics. Although they remain societal problems, they are curable in principle and rarely kill.

Two of today's more disturbing pathogens are the viruses that cause the sexually transmitted diseases genital herpes and **acquired immune deficiency syndrome,** or AIDS. Genital herpes causes blistering and pain, and the AIDS virus—technically termed *HIV,* for "human immunodeficiency virus"—devastates the immune system, leaving the body vulnerable to opportunistic diseases. AIDS to date appears fatal to all who contract full-blown cases of the disorder.* Earlier in the 1980s, AIDS was seen primarily as a scourge of gay men and intravenous drug abusers, but it has been finding its way into the general population. In poverty-stricken areas where drug abuse is also high, such as parts of the Bronx, New York, AIDS **antibodies** have been recently found in the blood of one newborn baby in 43 (*New York Times,* 1988). Of these, it is expected that about 40 percent are actually infected with the virus—as opposed to just receiving antibodies from their mothers' bloodstreams—and hence at risk for developing the disorder. In "safe" upstate New York, only one baby in 749 showed evidence of antibodies. New viral strains also seem to be evolving. We do not mean to be alarmist—we are not arguing that a new plague is upon us. On the other hand, AIDS exists and we all need to be knowledgeable about it and about the behavior patterns that can expose us to it.

The Challenge of a Changing Society

Although most of us have managed to attain adequate standards of living, there remain disadvantaged groups and pockets of poverty. During the 1950s and 1960s we became sensitive to the problems of blacks and other racial minorities who did not share equally in U.S. prosperity. In recent years we have learned to open our ears and minds to the pleas of other disadvantaged groups—women, the elderly, and the handicapped. Women in the work force

Pathogens. Agents that give rise to disease (*generators of pathology*).

Acquired immune deficiency syndrome. A disorder caused by a virus that weakens the immune system, rendering the person vulnerable to opportunistic diseases.

Antibodies. Substances formed by the immune system that combat and eliminate pathogens.

---

*As of this writing, the percentage of those who are infected with the virus who go on to develop "full-blown" cases is unclear.

In recent years we have become more sensitive to the needs of disadvantaged groups. Here a woman signs as an instructor speaks so that deaf students can participate in class discussion.

are demanding equal pay for equal, or comparable, jobs. The aged are struggling to overturn regulations in government and in private industry that mandate retirement at age 65 or 70. The numbers of the aged grow, and, as the age makeup of the population shifts, unused elementary school buildings are converted to house day-care centers and day-care programs for the elderly. The handicapped are demanding access to public transportation and public buildings.

During the 1960s and 1970s young people widely experimented with alternatives to traditional forms of work, marriage, and—through the explosion in drug use—normal states of consciousness. The 1980s witnessed a pendulum swing back toward the popularity of marriage and of the work ethic. A very old drug, alcohol, has reasserted its popularity on campus. Values remain somewhat in flux. During the 1960s and early 1970s, society was struck by the "sexual revolution." Millions of us became more open about sexual feelings and the incidence of premarital sexual activity mushroomed. Even casual, or "recreational," sex became popular in many quarters. Today we retain much of the openness about the expression of sexual feelings, but the threat of AIDS appears to have put a damper on much of the casual sexual activity (*Glamour* magazine, 1988; Wallis, 1987).

Changes in social roles, technology, the physical environment, and the social structure tear at the psychological fabric that provides a sense of security or well-being. Changing roles cloud our senses of identity. New technologies can spawn new riches, but they also challenge us to keep up or become obsolete. A changing physical environment threatens to sweep the green carpet of planet Earth out from under us in more ways than one. A changing society can provide new freedoms and opportunities for some groups while challenging the entrenched interests of others. Change, as we shall see in Chapter 6, is stressful. Some change is necessary for the good of the individual and for the good of society, but too much too soon can lead to physical illness and psychological disorders. Let us now shift our attention to see what psychology is, and how psychology can help us cope with the challenges of life.

■ Psychology and Adjustment

And so contemporary life has its challenges. In this section we shall see that the science of psychology is ideally suited to helping people meet these challenges. We also introduce the concept of adjustment and see how psychology and adjustment are related.

What Psychology Is

Psychology is a scientific approach to the study of behavior. Different sciences have different traditions and explain behavior from different perspectives. The sister science of anthropology, for example, focuses on the physical and cultural characteristics of people, such as their distribution on the planet and their customs and institutions. Sociology, another sister science, focuses on social relationships and social organization. Psychology overlaps with anthropology and sociology to some degree, but psychologists have traditionally attempted to understand or explain behavior in terms of the workings of the nervous system, the interaction of genetic and environmental influences ("nature" and "nurture"), the ways in which we sense and mentally represent the world, the roles of learning and motivation, the nature of personality, and methods of adjustment.

Psychology also has its applied side. Clinical, counseling, and health psychologists—to name but a few—assess individuals' personal strengths and weaknesses through psychological tests and structured interviews, and they help individuals cope with problems and optimize their personal development through methods of **psychotherapy** and **behavior therapy.** Psychiatrists are related to psychologists; they are medical specialists who deal with the diagnosis and treatment of psychological disorders.

Overt Behavior versus Cognitive Processes   As a science, psychology brings carefully controlled methods of observation, such as the experiment and the survey, to bear on its subject matter—behavior. Although psychologists agree that psychology is the science of **behavior,** they do not all agree on what behavior is. Some psychologists limit their definition to **overt** or observable behavior—for example, what people say; muscle contractions; patterns of eating, sleeping, and sexual behavior; and involuntary but directly measurable functions such as heart rate, presence of "stress hormones" in the saliva and urine, blood pressure, and emission of particular brain waves. All these behaviors can be assessed by simple observation or laboratory instruments.

Other psychologists extend the definition of behavior to include subjective **cognitive** processes such as mental images, dreams, fantasies, emotions, thoughts, plans, and the self-concept. The difficulty in studying cognitive processes is that they are private events that cannot be fully verified by laboratory instruments. Sometimes they are assumed present on the basis of the **self-report** of the person experiencing them. However, cognitive processes can at least be partially verified by instrumentation. Dreams, for example, are most likely to occur when particular brain waves are being emitted. Powerful emotions are usually accompanied by dramatic increases in the heart and respiration rates. Tying self-reports to observable behaviors allows psychologists a sort of indirect verification.

Goals of Psychology   Psychology, like other sciences, seeks to *describe, explain, predict,* and *control* the areas of behavior it addresses. Whenever possible, descriptive terms and concepts are interwoven into **theories.** Theories are sets of statements that involve certain assumptions about behavior (for example, we will do things for rewards), and logically derive explanations and predictions from these assumptions (for example, "problem children" will behave

Psychology. The science that studies observable behavior and mental processes.

Psychotherapy. The systematic application of psychological knowledge to the treatment of problem behavior.

Behavior therapy. Application of principles of learning to the direct modification of problem behavior.

Behavior. The observable actions and mental processes of people and lower animals.

Overt. Observable, in the open.

Cognitive. Having to do with mental processes such as the ways in which we sense and mentally represent the world, memory, intelligence, language, thought, and problem solving.

Self-report. A subject's testimony about his or her own thoughts, feelings, or behaviors.

Theory. A formulation of relationships underlying observed events.

Adjustment. Processes by which people respond to environmental pressures and cope with stress.

"properly" in the classroom if we can find ways to reward them for doing so). As another example, eating behavior may be explained in terms of an assumed hunger *drive* (another psychological concept) that increases as the amount of time since eating also increases.

The notion of controlling behavior is controversial. Some people think, erroneously, that psychologists seek ways to make others do their bidding—like puppets dangling on strings. But psychologists are committed to the dignity of the individual. Human dignity demands that people be free to make their own decisions and choose their own behavior. Psychologists are learning more all the time about the factors that influence human behavior, but they apply this knowledge on request only and in ways that will benefit the individual or the institution. In this way, they help people to control, or to take charge of, their own lives.

What Adjustment Is

Adjustment, or coping, is behavior that permits us to meet the demands of the environment. Sometimes the demands are physical. Consider one way in which a group of Eskimos called the Netsilik responded to the challenges of the winter storms and blizzards earlier in this century. As Rasmussen (1931) described it, during the bleakest months the caribou were gone and sealhunts often failed. During two winters the Netsilik lost 25 of their number to the cold and the hunger. This may seem no imposing number, but at their height their population was only 259.

During the harshest years, some of the Netsilik turned to cannibalism. Other Eskimo groups, who also knew of the northern winters, were reluctant to criticize them. Cannibalism, for the Netsilik, was a means to raw survival, the most basic form of adjustment.

When we are cold, we can adjust by dressing warmly, turning up the thermostat, or exercising. Holding down a job to keep the bill collector from our doors, drinking to quench our thirst, meeting the daily needs of our children—these, too, are forms of adjustment.

Sometimes the adjustment demands are more psychological: leaving home for the first time, a major exam, a job interview, the death of a loved one. We may adjust to demands such as these by making new friends, adding up the pluses and minuses of studying versus going to the movies, rehearsing what we'll say in a job interview, or being with supportive relatives.

But we can also make inferior adjustments. For example, we can pretend that problems do not exist—we can avoid thinking about the exam, or we can believe that we'll get that job because we're basically deserving. We can medicate ourselves, dull our anxieties and fears with alcohol or other drugs. We can deceive ourselves that we hurt others for the noblest of reasons—that we have the best of intentions when we're simply reluctant to look within ourselves. We can tell ourselves that our problems are so awful that there's no point to trying to cope with them at all.

We shall see that the strongest, most effective forms of adjustment involve seeing pressures and problems for what they are. Then we can make decisions and plans that will allow us to change them—or, in those cases where they cannot be changed, perhaps we can work to change self-defeating response patterns so that they trouble us less.

■ How Psychologists View Adjustment

There are numerous theories or views of adjustment in psychology, but most psychologists tend to view adjustment from the psychodynamic, trait-theory, learning-theory, or phenomenological perspective.

The Psychodynamic Perspective

Psychodynamic theory, originated by Sigmund Freud, argues that human beings, like lower animals, are basically motivated by primitive impulses, especially sexual and aggressive impulses. Although we are more aware of our conscious thoughts and plans, primitive impulses are more powerful determinants of human behavior. Freud believed that most of our minds were unconscious, a seething cauldron of dark urges and conflicting wishes. We are motivated to gratify these impulses but at the same time seek to avoid social disapproval and self-condemnation. So we often delude ourselves about our true motives.

From a psychodynamic perspective, adjustment implies keeping basic impulses at tolerable levels. It means walking a tightrope—finding partial outlets for these impulses while meeting social and personal standards of behavior. There are prices to pay for adjusting, such as distortion of our actual motives. For example, when our first choices are unavailable, we **displace** our desires onto obtainable objects; when our real reasons for our behavior are unacceptable, we may **rationalize,** or find acceptable but false reasons for it.

Freud believed that the processes of personal adjustment are largely unconscious and that we are unaware of the real reasons for most of our behavior. But it is important to note that "Neo-Freudians," or contemporary adherents of psychodynamic theory, feel that Freud held too bleak a view of human nature. Psychoanalysts such as Erik Erikson, Erich Fromm, Henry Murray, and Karen Horney have argued that some of our functioning is fully conscious and that we can experience constructive, conscious motives as well as basic, gut-level urgings.

The Trait-Theory Perspective

Traits theorists believe that **traits**—such as artistic ability, conventionality, introversion, and enterprising spirit—steer our behavior and account for consistency in behavior. That is, a shy person will tend to withdraw from social interactions; an extraverted person will seek them out. The shy person tends to withdraw from different kinds of social interactions, and the pattern of withdrawal tends to persist over the years.

The thrusts of trait theory lie in the description and measurement of human traits. The origin of traits is less central to trait theory, although it is generally assumed that genetic factors play an important—perhaps the major—role in their development and that they are resistant to change. As such, trait theorists tend to view adjustment in terms of putting people in situations in which there is a good **person–environment fit,** or P–E fit. As we shall see in Chapter 12, a creative person would probably be well advised not to become an accountant. Similarly, the conventional person would probably not be well adjusted as a creative artist.

In Chapter 2 we shall see that there is supportive evidence for a role for genetic factors in the development of traits. Moreover, the wealth of research in personality testing that has been spawned by trait theorists has helped identify and measure the aptitudes and talents of millions of individuals.

Learning-Theory Perspectives

There are a number of learning-theory perspectives, and they could not be more at odds with one another in their views of human nature and adjustment.

Behaviorism   According to **behaviorists,** human beings react mechanically to their environments, almost in the same way a billiard ball reacts to the thrust of the cue. That is, we respond to stimuli. Of course, myriads of stimuli impact upon us at once, as opposed to the single thrust of the cue, and we

Psychodynamic theory. The school of psychology that emphasizes the importance of unconscious motives and conflicts as determinants of human behavior.

Displace. Transfer.

Rationalize. Find a self-deceiving acceptable excuse for unacceptable behavior.

Trait. A personality variable that is inferred from behavior and assumed to account for consistency in behavior from one situation to another.

Person–environment fit. The degree to which a person's traits and environment are compatible.

Behaviorist. A person who adheres to the school of psychology that defines psychology as the study of observable behavior and studies relationships between stimuli and responses.

are capable of learning. That is, after a few "shots," we may learn how to get into the pockets by ourselves.

Behaviorists explain human behavior in terms of the envionmental influences that affect us through two simple forms of learning: classical and operant conditioning. Classical conditioning accounts for the learning of expectations—for example, the mechanical response of salivating at a Whopper commercial on television, or the child's image of Mom being home because of the sound of a car in the driveway. In operant conditioning we learn to respond to specific situations in specific ways because of the effects of our behavior—for example, learning to move fingers so that letters and numbers appear on the screen of the microcomputer, or learning to scratch a certain spot a certain way because our partner says, "Mm, that feels good." *But conditioning occurs mechanically; there is no role for consciousness in explanations of conditioning.*

Social-Learning Theory   **Social-learning theory** supplements conditioning by focusing on cognitive processes and learning by observation. From this perspective, the most important types of learning occur intentionally and are based on observing others, as in books or in "flesh and blood." Social-learning theorists believe that our behavior patterns are not merely shaped by environmental influences, but that our values and conscious decisions come into play. Moreover, our beliefs in our own abilities to achieve desired ends help determine whether we will persist at difficult tasks.

From the behaviorist perspective, adjustment means having accurate expectations about the world and the technical and social skills necessary to attain **reinforcers,** such as food, money, and social approval—considered important in our society. From the social-learning perspective, adjustment also means:

Having a wealth of models to imitate—books, TV and film models, persons
    in real life—so that we learn many ways of influencing the environment
Interpreting experiences in such a way that we perceive solutions to problems
    and do not overly arouse negative emotions such as fear and anger
Believing in our own abilities to achieve desired reinforcers
Being able to regulate our own behavior so that we bring about desired effects
Changing the environment, or creating new environments, so that reinforcers
    become available

Social-learning theorists suggest that maladjustment, as in inappropriate social expectations or excessive anxieties, is also learned through experience. For example, painful experiences (or tales of painful experiences) may cause us to develop habits of avoiding rather than facing the challenges of life.

Phenomenological Perspectives

Phenomenological psychologists are most interested in our subjective, personal experiences. They believe that each of us has a unique perspective on life. We each interpret the world in our own special ways, and we cannot understand other people unless we learn how they look at the world. Our personal views of the world lead us to interpret and evaluate our experiences, and ourselves, in certain ways. Phenomenological psychologists are vitally concerned about whether our ways of perceiving the world, and ourselves, boost or hurt our self-esteem and allow us to engage in effective behavior.

Self-Actualization   The phenomenological psychologists Abraham Maslow and Carl Rogers view people as *actors,* not *reactors.* They believe that we have an inborn tendency, termed **self-actualization,** to strive to become whatever we are capable of being. The biologically well-coordinated child will strive to become an athlete; the child with an aptitude for music will strive to com-

Social-learning theory. A school of psychology in the behaviorist tradition that includes cognitive factors in the explanation and prediction of behavior.

Reinforcer. A stimulus that follows a response and increases the frequency of the response.

Phenomenological. Having to do with subjective, personal experience.

Self-actualization. A hypothesized drive that initiates striving to become whatever we are capable of being.

pose or play an instrument. This view of people is also considered **humanistic.** Humanistic psychologists allow that some sources of motivation may be unconscious, as suggested by Freud, and that we are influenced by environmental stimulation to respond in certain ways, as suggested by behaviorists. But humanists see the essential qualities of being human as self-awareness and the ability to make conscious choices. Whereas trait theorists see our traits as "given," and many learning theorists see our behavior as developed by environmental influences, humanists see us to some degree as the architects of ourselves.

People as Scientists   From George Kelly's perspective, each of us is a scientist. Just as psychologists strive to describe, explain, predict, and control behavior, all of us strive to describe, explain, predict, and control the things that are important to us. To Kelly, that is, we have an inborn tendency to try to make sense of, or **construe,** our environments (describe and explain them) and to predict the future. By so doing, we can adapt and take charge of our lives.

From the phenomenological perspective, we are well adjusted when we accept our unique selves for what we are. We should not attempt to live up to the standards imposed by parents and others; nor should we deny the parts of ourselves that fail to meet these standards. We are well adjusted when we are striving to learn about ourselves and to express our unique talents and aptitudes. To Kelly, we are well adjusted when our ways of perceiving the world, of construing events, allow us to make accurate predictions.

Throughout this book we shall see that each psychological theory has something to contribute to our understanding of human nature and to the creation of strategies for promoting adjustment and growth. Some behavior does seem driven by biological instincts and urges, and at times we do manage to fool ourselves about our reasons for doing things. We do acquire expectations and skills on the basis of rewards and punishments and observing others. But we are also self-aware and can marshal self-awareness to meet life's challenges and to grow from them. In Chapter 2 we shall explore these theories in greater depth and note the strengths and weaknesses of each.

■ Issues in Psychology and Adjustment

There are a number of issues in the psychology of adjustment, and they tend to reflect some of the controversies in the broader field of psychology. They are important because they address the heart of our conceptions of human nature.

Adjustment versus Personal Growth

One of the most basic issues in the psychology of adjustment is what the term *adjustment* addresses. Literally speaking, to adjust is to change so as better to conform to, or meet, the demands of one's environment. Adjustment, in other words, is essentially reactive. The "ball" is perpetually in the environment's "court," and we can only wait to see what forces the environment will unleash upon us next.

However, one of the basic premises of this book is that people are not just reactors to their environments. People are also actors. Not only do things happen to us; we also make things happen. Not only does the environment influence us; we also modify the environment and, now and then, we create novel environments that are better suited to our needs and consistent with our aesthetic tastes.

To accommodate what we see as the active aspects of human nature, we must extend the concept of adjustment to include self-initiated growth and

◼ A CLOSER LOOK

Seaweed, Rocks, Waves, and Personal Growth

On a trip to the West Coast, Carl Rogers, a phenomenological psychologist, became caught up in a drama being enacted on the seashore. It helped reaffirm his personal belief that life forms, including people, do not simply react to the environmental pressures of the moment. Instead, we press through, under even the harshest of circumstances, to become what we are capable of being:

> During a vacation weekend some months ago I was standing on a headland overlooking one of the rugged coves which dot the coastline of northern California. Several large rock outcroppings were at the mouth of the cove, and these received the full force of the great Pacific combers which, beating upon them, broke into mountains of spray before surging into the cliff-lined shore. As I watched the waves breaking over these large rocks in the distance, I noticed with surprise what appeared to be a tiny palm tree on the rocks, no more than two or three feet high, taking the pounding of the breakers. Through my binoculars I saw that these were some type of seaweed, with a slender "trunk" topped off with a head of leaves. As one examined a specimen in the interval between the waves it seemed clear that this fragile, erect, top-heavy plant would be utterly crushed and broken by the next breaker. When the wave crunched down upon it, the trunk bent almost flat, the leaves were whipped into a straight line by the torrent of the water, yet the moment the wave had passed, here was the plant again, erect, tough, resilient. It seemed incredible that it was able to take this incessant pounding hour after hour, day after night, week after week, perhaps, for all I know, year after year, and all the time nourishing itself, extending its domain, reproducing itself; in short, maintaining and enhancing itself in this process which, in our shorthand, we call growth. Here in this palmlike seaweed was the tenacity of life, the forward thrust of life, the ability to push into an incredibly hostile environment and not only hold its own, but to adapt, develop, become itself (1963, pp. 1–2).

In this poetic passage, Rogers clearly paints the distinction between adjustment and personal growth from the humanistic perspective. Adjustment, so to speak, is holding our own in the face of environmental challenges. But personal growth is going farther: it is developing our unique potentials, becoming ourselves, pressing our creative capacities to the farthest limits of the self.

---

development along intellectual, emotional, social, physical, and vocational dimensions. Not only do we react to stress; we also act in order to become.

When we achieve greatness, or when our lives seem filled with meaning, it is not because we have reacted, or adjusted, well. It is because we have acted in order to become; it is because of personal growth.

Nature versus Nurture: Is Biology Destiny?

Psychologists are vitally concerned about the degree to which our traits and behavior patterns reflect our nature, or genetic factors, and our nurture, or environmental influences. We know that physical traits such as height, race, and eye color are biologically transmitted from generation to generation by **genes.** Genes are segments of deoxyribonucleic acid (DNA), the stuff of which our **chromosomes** are composed. Normally speaking, people have 23 pairs of chromosomes in their body cells (with the exception of sperm and ova, which have 23 chromosomes each). Genes—and sometimes combinations of genes—give rise to our biological structures and physical traits.

But genes also broadly determine the limits, or the **reaction ranges,** for a number of psychological traits and behavior patterns (Scarr & Kidd, 1983). Genetic factors are involved to some degree in psychological traits such as intelligence (Plomin & DeFries, 1980), extraversion (Loehlin et al., 1982), emotional instability (Scarr et al., 1981), fearfulness and shyness (Daniels & Plomin, 1985; Kagan, 1984; Plomin, 1982), aggressiveness and social dominance (Goldsmith, 1983), and antisocial behavior (Mednick, 1985).

Gene. The basic unit of heredity, consisting of a segment of DNA.

Chromosome. A strand of DNA that consists of genes.

Reaction range. The potential variation in the expression of a trait, as defined by heredity.

A number of behavior patterns that in part reflect genetic factors are of special interest within the psychology of adjustment. Consider a few examples. There are apparently inheritable predispositions toward problems with anxiety; that is, some of us inherit nervous systems that are readily aroused and appear to place us at greater "risk" than others (Turner, 1987). Recent research with the tightly knit Amish community in Pennsylvania (Egeland et al., 1987) suggests that a gene on chromosome 11 places about half the members of an extended family at risk for bipolar disorder—a psychological disorder characterized by mood swings from elation to severe depression and back. In later chapters we shall explore roles for heredity in obesity and vulnerability to alcoholism. For example, the children of alcoholics seem to be less sensitive to alcohol than other people, making it more difficult for them to know when to stop drinking (Schuckit, 1986, 1987). Moreover, about 30 to 45 percent of Asians are "protected" from alcoholism by responding to alcohol with a reddened face, headaches, or nausea. A gene has been pinpointed that instructs body cells to produce an enzyme that fails to metabolize alcohol properly in these Asians, allowing an aversive alcohol product, acetaldehyde, to build up in their bodies (Monmaney et al., 1988). Health psychologists also recognize that family history places certain individuals at higher risk for physical disorders such as heart attacks and cancer. Researchers are even seeking genetic factors in vulnerability to the AIDS virus in the form of inherited proteins that might help some people resist infection and slow the progress of AIDS, although findings to date are inconsistent (Altman, 1988).

The flip side of the coin is that genetic factors might also contribute to personal strengths. For example, many children, termed "invulnerables," who are reared by single parents or foster parents in harsh, impoverished environments show an uncanny knack for finding other adults to help them and serve as role models, even before the age of 4. They use these outside sources of social support to help them climb out of their quagmires (Farber & Egeland, 1987). Certainly we are talking about complex social behavior patterns that cannot be attributed to a single gene, or even to a small group of genes. Nevertheless, researchers are hard put to find environmental factors that could initiate the upward climbs of these children.

And so it seems clear that genetic factors play a role in issues related to psychological adjustment and effective behavior. However, genetic factors do not in and of themselves give rise to specific behavior patterns; they interact with environmental factors, and apparently with self-determination, to influence behavior. For example, as noted by Dartmouth psychiatrist George Vaillant, peer pressures and other psychological factors are just as important as genes in determining alcoholism: "All the genes do is make it easier for you to become an alcoholic" (Monmaney et al., 1988).

Genetic factors can be powerful influences, but in many cases we can modify their impact through our behavior patterns. Biology is not always destiny. The degree to which you will marshall your inherited resources to adjust and develop your potential is up to you.

The Clinical Approach versus the Healthy-Personality Approach

Over the years, most psychology-of-adjustment textbooks have been written according to one of two major approaches—a clinical approach or a healthy-personality approach. The clinical approach has primarily focused on ways in which psychology can help people correct personal problems and cope with stress. The healthy-personality approach has primarily focused on healthful patterns of personal growth and development, including social and vocational development. Books with a clinical approach have frequently been written

Scientific method. A four-step method for obtaining scientific evidence in which a hypothesis is formed and tested.

Hypothesis. An assumption about behavior that is tested through research.

from psychodynamic and behaviorist perspectives, whereas books with a healthy-personality approach are more likely to have been written from phenomenological perspectives.

The book you are holding in your hands was written with awareness of both approaches to the psychology of adjustment. There is ample discussion of stress and disorder and ways of coping. But there is equal emphasis on optimizing our potentials through preventive and self-actualizing behavior patterns. All in all, we have aimed to be comprehensive and balanced in our approach, to provide ample theory, research, and applications for coping and for optimal development.

■ How Psychologists Study Adjustment

Are women better than men at spelling? Are city dwellers less friendly toward strangers than small-town residents? Do antidiscrimination laws reduce prejudice? Does alcohol cause aggression? Is a drink a day good for you? Is exercise good for your heart? Does pornography trigger violence against women? What are the effects of day care and divorce on children?

Many of us have expressed *opinions* on questions such as these at one time or another, and psychological and medical theories also suggest a number of possible answers. But psychology is a science, and scientific statements about behavior must be supported by *evidence*. Strong arguments, reference to authority figures, celebrity endorsements, even tightly knit theories are not considered adequate as scientific evidence. Scientific evidence is obtained by means of the **scientific method.**

The Scientific Method

There are four basic steps to the sceintific method:

1. *Formulating a research question.* Our daily experiences, psychological theory, Uncle Morris's claim that his sense of humor helped him through his illness, even folklore all help generate questions for research. Daily experience in using day-care centers may motivate us to conduct research to find out whether day care fosters social skills or loosens bonds of attachment between children and mothers.
2. *Developing a hypothesis.* A **hypothesis** is a specific statement about behavior that is tested through research. One hypothesis about day care might be that preschoolers placed in day care will acquire greater social skills in relating to peers than preschoolers cared for in the home.
3. *Testing the hypothesis.* Psychologists test the hypothesis through carefully controlled methods of observation, such as the naturalistic-observation method and the experiment. For example, we could introduce day-care children and non-day-care children to a new child in a college child-research center and observe how each group fares with the new acquaintance.
4. *Drawing conclusions about the hypothesis.* Finally, psychologists draw conclusions about the accuracy of their hypotheses on the basis of their research findings. When findings do not bear out their hypotheses, they may modify the theories from which the hypotheses were derived. Research findings often suggest new hypotheses and, consequently, new studies. In our research on day care, we would probably find that day-care children show somewhat better social skills than children cared for in the home, as we shall see in Chapter 16.

Let us now consider the major research methods used by psychologists: the naturalistic-observation, correlational, experimental, survey, testing, and case-study methods.

The Naturalistic-Observation Method

The next time you visit McDonald's or Burger King for lunch, have a look around. Pick out slender people and overweight people and observe whether they eat their burgers and fries differently. Do the overweight eat more rapidly? Chew less frequently? Leave less food? This is precisely the method psychologists have used to gather knowledge that might help overweight people control their own eating patterns. In fact, if you notice some people at McDonald's peering out over sunglasses and intermittently tapping the head of a partly concealed microphone, perhaps they are recording their observations of other people's eating habits—even as you watch.

This method of scientific investigation is referred to as **naturalistic observation.** Psychologists and other scientists use it to observe behavior in the field, or where it "happens." Every precaution is taken to use **unobtrusive** assessment methods and, in general, not to interfere with the observed behavior. Otherwise, behavior could be distorted by the presence of the observer.

Samples and Populations   In naturalistic observation and other methods, the individuals, or subjects, who are observed are referred to as a **sample.** A sample is a segment of a **population,** and we need to make every effort to ensure that the subjects we observe *represent* our target population, such as residents of the U.S.A., and not subgroups such as southern California Yuppies or Caucasian members of the middle class. Visitors who observed the Times Square area in New York might conclude that only men are sexually excited by pornographic films, since very few women attend these films there, and those who do are usually accompanied by men. In Chapter 15 you will see that observations of people who better represent the population at large lead to different conclusions.

Naturalistic observation can show us *what* people do, but not *why* they do it. For example, men who go to bars and drink are more likely to engage in aggressive behavior than men who do not. But can we conclude that alcohol *causes* aggression? Experimental evidence on the effects of alcohol, to be reported in Chapter 7, suggests that such a conclusion may be unwarranted.

The Correlational Method

In the **correlational method,** one or more variables are related, or linked, to one another. For instance, we may correlate weight and height and find that taller people are usually (but not always) heavier. Or we can correlate depression with weight. In doing so we would probably find that as depression increases appetite slackens, and as a consequence, the weight of the individual decreases. When one variable increases (e.g., weight) as the second variable increases (e.g., height), there is said to be a **positive correlation** between the variables. When one variable increases (e.g., level of physical activity) as the second variable decreases (e.g., incidence of heart disease), there is said to be a **negative correlation** between the variables. Or we may correlate depression with weight and find that depressed people frequently (but not always) lose weight.

Sample Studies

The Swedish Cohabitation Study   A kind of folklore has developed concerning the advantages of premarital cohabitation, or of setting up housekeeping with one's future spouse. Many people believe that a trial period allows them to test their feelings and find out if they can adjust to another's quirks before they make a permanent commitment. And so it is interesting that a recent Swedish study of divorce rates by Yale University sociologist Neil Bennett and his colleagues found that couples who cohabited prior to mar-

Naturalistic observation. A scientific method in which organisms are observed in their natural environments.

Unobtrusive. Not interfering.

Sample. Part of a population selected for research.

Population. A complete group of organisms or events.

Correlational research. A scientific method that studies the relationships between variables.

Positive correlation. A relationship between variables in which one variable increases as the other also increases.

Negative correlation. A relationship between two variables in which one variable increases as the other decreases.

In the naturalistic-observation method, psychologists observe behavior in the field—where it happens. Patrons of fast-food restaurants have been observed in recent years to determine whether normal-weight individuals eat their burgers and fries differently from the overweight.

riage had an 80 percent *higher* chance of getting divorced than couples who chose the traditional route (*New York Times*, 1987).

But do not jump to the conclusion that living together before marriage *causes*, or even heightens the risk of, divorce. We cite the Swedish study because it highlights the fact that correlational research does not show cause and effect. Both variables—the high divorce rate and the choice to live together before marriage—might reflect another factor: liberalism. Liberal attitudes, that is, could contribute to cohabitation and divorce. Similarly, people do not grow taller *because* they weigh more. People do not become depressed, usually, because they lose weight.

Daily Hassles, Activity Patterns, and Physical Illness   Let us consider a couple of examples of correlational research that are particularly pertinent to the psychology of adjustment: they involve the links between daily hassles, or sources of aggravation, and physical illness and between physical activity levels and cardiovascular disorders. In Chapter 6 we shall see that people who encounter greater amounts of aggravation and annoyance are also more likely to become physically ill. And in Chapter 7 we shall see that studies of British postal workers, U.S. longshoremen, and Harvard University alumni concur that men who have higher levels of physical activity (e.g., sustained exercise) are less likely to fall prey to heart attacks.

With these studies, too, it is tempting to assume that cause and effect are revealed—that an accumulation of aggravation causes illness and that exercise reduces the likelihood of heart attacks. But these correlational studies, too, do not show cause and effect. Concerning the link between hassles and illness, it could also be that a third factor accounts both for exposure to hassles and illness. For example, people who are not in control of their own lives could find themselves exposed to greater aggravation from day to day and also to physical illnesses. Concerning the link between activity levels and heart attacks, it could be that people who are already healthier, and less likely to incur heart disease, also feel more up to engaging in physical activity.

Cigarette Smoking and Illness   Also consider the research links between cigarette smoking, cardiovascular disease, and cancer. In Chapter 7 we shall see that people who smoke run higher risks of heart attacks and several kinds of cancer. But even here it is possible that people who are less in control over their lives are more likely to fall into smoking and also to become physically ill. Correlational research is not logically sufficient to reveal cause and effect.

However, there is a form of research that reveals cause and effect—the experiment. Whereas correlational research does not show cause and effect, it frequently suggests experiments that will provide better information on cause-effect relationships. For example, we know that certain pleasant events, such as being with friends or exercising, are linked to a positive mood. As we shall see in Chapter 10, this correlational evidence has led to experiments that suggest that engaging in pleasant events might elevate the moods of many depressed people. Correlational research on the links between activity levels and heart disease, and between smoking and cancer, has led to experiments with animals, as we shall see in the following section.

The Experimental Method

Most psychologists agree that the preferred method for determining cause and effect—for answering questions such as whether physical activity lowers the incidence of heart disease, smoking causes cancer, alcohol causes aggression, or psychotherapy relieves feelings of anxiety—is the **experiment.** In an experiment, a group of participants, or subjects, receives a **treatment,** for example, eight weeks of fast walking around a track, smoking the equivalent

Experiment. A scientific method that seeks to discover cause-and-effect relationships by introducing independent variables and observing their effects on dependent variables.

Treatment. In experiments, a condition received by participants so that its effects may be observed.

■ A CLOSER LOOK

Coping with Self-Help Books

How To Be Your Own Best Friend; Don't Say Yes When You Want To Say No; The Art of Sensual Massage; Don't Be Afraid; Mind Power; Dianetics; Dr. Atkins' Diet Revolution; Our Bodies, Our Selves; Toilet Training in a Day; The Relaxation Response; Treating Type A Behavior and Your Heart; Becoming Orgasmic; The Scarsdale Diet; Looking Out for Number One—these are a bare shelf-ful of the hundreds of self-help books that have flooded the marketplace in recent years. Shy people, anxious people, depressed people, heavy people, stressed people, and confused people scan the bookstores and the check-out counter racks of supermarkets every day in hopes of finding the one book that will hold the answer.

How are we to know what to buy? How can we separate the helpful wheat from the useless and sometimes harmful chaff? How can we be intelligent consumers of these works?

The fact of the matter is that there are no easy answers. Many of us are used to believing most of the things we see in print, and anecdotes about how John lost 60 pounds in 60 days and how Joni blossomed from a wallflower into a social butterfly in one month have a powerful allure—especially when we are needy. Moreover, in a nation where self-help books are displayed one aisle over from the U.S. government-inspected meats, the books might have the aura of a government stamp as well.

Not so. The price we pay for the protection of the First Amendment of the Constitution is that nearly anything can wind up in print. Authors can make the most extravagant claims without fear of imprisonment. They can lie about the effectiveness of the newest fad diet without fear of prosecution just as easily as they can lie about their latest communion with the departed Elvis Presley or their most recent kidnapping by the occupants of a U.F.O.

With so many self-help books on the market, it can be difficult to sort out the scientifically based wheat from the off-the-cuff chaff. But readers can avoid books that make extravagant claims and can check out authors' credentials.

So how can you protect yourself? How would you be able to tell, for example, that *Don't Be Afraid, Toilet Training in a Day,* and *Mind Power* were authored by respected psychologists, whereas *Looking Out for Number One* was written by a professional writer and book publisher? How would you know that *The Relaxation Response* is well researched, whereas *Dr. Atkins' Diet Revolution* is not?

---

of a pack a day, a half ounce of alcohol, or three months of therapy. Then the subjects are observed carefully to determine whether the treatment makes a difference in their behavior.

Experimental and Control Subjects   Ideal experiments randomly assign subjects to experimental and control groups. **Experimental subjects** receive some amount of the experimental treatment—alcohol in the above example. **Control subjects** do not. Every effort is made to hold all other conditions constant for both groups. In this way the experimenters can be reasonably sure that it was the experimental treatment, and not uncontrolled factors such as room temperature or time of day, that influenced the outcome.

Random Assignment   Why should subjects be assigned to experimental treatments at random? If we allow subjects to determine for themselves

Experimental subjects. Subjects receiving a treatment in an experiment.

Control subjects. Experimental participants who do not receive the experimental treatment but for whom all other conditions are comparable to those of experimental subjects.

We don't have all the answers, but here are some helpful hints:

1. First of all, don't judge the book by its cover or its title. Good books as well as bad books tend to have catchy titles and exciting covers. After all, dozens, perhaps hundreds of books are competing for your attention, so all publishers try to do something "snazzy" with the covers.
2. Avoid books that make extravagant claims. No method helps everyone who tries it. Also, very few methods work overnight (*Toilet Training in a Day* might be an exception). No healthful diet, for example, allows you to lose a pound or more a day. Unfortunately, as noted by William D. Phillips, editor-in-chief at Little, Brown, "People want the instant cure. A book that guarantees you will lose 10 pounds in two days will sell faster than one that says it will take six months" (Hinds, 1988).
3. Check authors' educational credentials. Be suspicious if the author's title is just "Dr.," and it is placed before the name. The degree could be a phony doctorate purchased through the mail; it could be issued by a religious cult rather than a university or professional school. It is better if the "doctor" puts Ph.D., Psy.D., Ed.D., or M.D. after his or her name rather than "Dr." in front of it.
4. Check authors' current affiliations. Again there are no guarantees, but psychologists who are affiliated with colleges and universities and physicians who are affiliated with medical schools might have more to offer than those who are not.
5. Consider authors' complaints about the conservatism of professional groups a red flag. If authors boast about how they are ahead of their time and berate the psychological and medical "establishments" for reactionary pigheadedness, be suspicious. Although it's true that great discoveries are now and then met with opposition, such as the discovery that the Earth revolves around the sun, most psychologists and physicians are committed to change and advancement of their sciences. They are open to new ideas, as long as the ideas are supported by scientific evidence.
6. Check the evidence reported in the book. Bad books usually use anecdotal evidence, or superficially reported case studies. By and large, the techniques that authors claim will help should have been tested by experiments with many subjects. Moreover, the subjects should have been assigned at random to treatment groups and control groups, and measures should have been taken to control for subjects' expectations.
7. Check the reference citations for the evidence. Solid, legitimate psychological and medical research is reported in the journals found in the reference list of this textbook. To get published in these journals, research reports must be submitted to peer reviewers—respected psychologists and physicians—and judged valid. If the publications in the book's reference list are suspicious, or if there is no bibliography, you be suspicious, too.
8. Another strategy is to ask your instructor for advice. A faculty member in an academic department is likely to be able to point out which books can help and which can hurt.
9. Read textbooks and professional books, such as this book, instead of self-help books. For knowledge about healthful dieting, read a health psychology or nutrition textbook used in a course in your college. For exercise advice, read a textbook used in teaching physical education courses. Roam the college bookstore for appropriate textbooks and professional books. Don't be scared by technical terms—these books usually have helpful glossaries.
10. You can also consult a member of a respected helping profession for ideas and for help. If you're thinking of consulting a professional, check our suggestions in Chapter 9 or ask your instructor how to go about it.

There are no guarantees and no quick fixes. But by exercising a few precautions you can become a more sophisticated consumer of self-help books.

---

whether they would like to drink the alcohol or not, we could not determine the effects of alcohol. For example, subjects who chose to drink might also be more aggressive to begin with than the nondrinkers. Certainly their expectations about the effects of alcohol would differ from those of the nondrinkers; otherwise they, too, would choose not to drink.

Controlling for Subjects' Expectations   The effects of treatments usually stem from the treatments and our expectations about the treatments. And so, in well-designed experiments, researchers also try to control for the effects of subjects' expectations about the treatments. In doing so, they often create conditions in which subjects are **blind** as to whether or not they have received the treatment. For instance, people could behave aggressively after drinking alcohol because they *believe* that alcohol causes aggression, not because of the alcohol itself. Thus, if subjects do not *know* whether they have drunk alcohol,

Blind. In experimental terminology, unaware of whether one has received a treatment.

Placebo. A bogus treatment that has the appearance of being genuine.

we can control for this expectation. In Chapter 7 we shall learn how researchers made subjects blind as to whether they had drunk vodka by mixing it with tonic water.

Control subjects are very often given a "sugar pill," or **placebo** treatment, to control for the effects of expectations. For example, in a study on the effects of therapy method A on mood, it would be inadequate to randomly assign a single treatment group to therapy A and the control group to a no-treatment waiting list. The therapy-A group might show improvement because group membership leads them to expect improvement. For this reason it would be wise to randomly fill a placebo-treatment group, one in which subjects also expect to improve. In such studies, the placebo-treatment groups frequently have general discussions of problems, or general education about problems, instead of specific therapies. And sometimes it's difficult to find a "placebo" that doesn't do some good!

Sample Studies   Let us examine experimental methods in greater depth by applying them to some of the research issues we have raised.

The Swedish Cohabitation Study
In the section on correlational research it was noted that Swedish cohabitors had a higher divorce rate than couples who had not cohabited prior to marriage. However, cause-and-effect relationships in that study were obscured by the probability that more liberal Swedes would be likely both to choose to cohabit and, after marriage, to seek divorce. If we were to run a scientific experiment to gather more information on the effects of cohabitation, we would have to assign some couples *at random* to premarital cohabitation and others to maintaining separate living quarters. By using random assignment, we could control for the effects of liberalism— that is, we could assume that fairly even numbers of liberals and conservatives would fall into the cohabitation and noncohabitation groups. And this "ideal" experiment brings us face to face with the limitations of research with human subjects: For ethical and practical reasons, we could not assign some couples to cohabitation and others to living apart. People must be allowed to make their own decisions about their life-styles.

Effects of Activity and Nutritional Patterns on Cardiovascular Disease
As we shall see in Chapter 7, researchers have randomly assigned groups of *monkeys* to sedentary life-styles or to sustained exercise on a treadmill and have carefully observed them for more than three years. The monkeys were also placed on high-fat diets. We can report that the monkeys assigned to exercise showed a lower incidence of heart attacks and a lower mortality rate. This procedure raises two questions: One, can we generalize the results to human beings? (Perhaps we can; the physiology of monkeys is not all that far removed from our own.) Two, would it be ethical to give human subjects a high-fat diet in order to observe the results? (We think not.)

Is It Ethical to Withhold Promising Experimental Treatments for Illness?
The flip side of the coin is that experimental treatments for illnesses are sometimes intentionally withheld from randomly chosen human subjects so that true comparisons can be made between experimental subjects and control subjects. Here, too, there are ethical issues. For example, AIDS patients and their advocates argue that they should not be denied experimental treatments that offer any hope of improvement or cure just for the sake of better research designs.

Effects of Smoking Revisited
And let us return to the question of whether smoking cigarettes causes cardiovascular disorders and cancer. There is no experimental research on this question with humans because it would

be unethical and cruel to randomly assign people to smoke cigarettes. Moreover, imagine the practical problems of monitoring subjects' behavior over the 10 to 30 years such an experiment might entail. Not only would we have to ensure that experimental subjects kept up their cigarette consumption; we would also have to ascertain that control subjects did not "sneak" cigarettes. For all these reasons such an experiment has not been run, and it will not be run. However, researchers have randomly assigned laboratory animals to smoking or nonsmoking conditions and controlled their long-term smoke intake with precision. The experimental animals develop higher rates of heart disease and cancer, dovetailing with the correlational research with humans. Together they make a powerful case, one that is denied only by tobacco company executives and a handful of smokers.

The Survey Method

In **surveys,** psychologists administer interviews or questionnaires or examine public records to learn about people's behavior, attitudes, feelings, or opinions. Many people, perhaps thousands, can be surveyed at a time.

The "Kinsey Studies"   In the 1940s and 1950s Indiana University researcher Alfred Kinsey and his colleagues published two surveys of sexual behavior, based on interviews, that shocked the nation: *Sexual Behavior in the Human Male* (1948) and *Sexual Behavior in the Human Female* (1953). Kinsey found that masturbation was virtually universal in his male sample at a time when masturbation was widely believed to impair physical and mental health. He also reported that one of three single women had engaged in premarital intercourse by the age of 25. (Today this figure has about doubled.)

The survey was the appropriate method for attaining these data, since Kinsey wished to focus on what was happening in the U.S.A. rather than study the causes of sexual behavior in depth. And if Kinsey had tried to use the naturalistic-observation method, he and his colleagues might have landed in jail as Peeping Toms.

Interviews and questionnaires are not foolproof, of course. People may inaccurately recall their behavior or purposefully misrepresent it. Some people try to ingratiate themselves with their interviewers by giving what they consider socially desirable answers. The Kinsey studies have been criticized because all the interviewers were men. Women respondents might have felt more free to open up to female interviewers on some issues (Rathus, 1983). The nearby questionnaire on social desirability will afford you some insight concerning your own tendencies to behave in socially desirable ways. Problems can also occur when interviewers and respondents are of different racial or socioeconomic backgrounds. Some respondents falsify attitudes and exaggerate bizarre behavior patterns to draw attention to themselves, or just to foul up the results.

Sampling Methods   Survey samples, like samples attained for other research methods, must accurately represent the population they are intended to reflect. One way to attain a representative sample is by **random sampling.** In a random sample, each member of the target population has an equal chance of being selected for participation. Researchers can also use a **stratified sample,** which is drawn so that identified subgroups in the population are represented proportionately. For example, about 12 percent of the U.S. population is black. Therefore, a racially stratified survey sample would be about 12 percent black. As a practical matter, a large randomly selected sample will show reasonably proportionate stratification. For example, a randomly selected nationwide sample of about 1,500 represents the general U.S. population quite well. But a haphazardly drawn sample of 20 million might not.

Survey. A scientific method in which large samples of people are questioned.

Random sample. A sample drawn such that every member of a population has an equal chance of being selected.

Stratified sample. A sample drawn such that known subgroups within a population are represented in proportion to their numbers in the population.

The Kinsey studies on sexual behavior did not adequately represent blacks, poor people, the elderly, and other groups. Large-scale magazine surveys of sexual behavior run by *Redbook* (Tavris & Sadd, 1977) and *Cosmopolitan* (Wolfe, 1981) asked hundreds of thousands of readers to return questionnaires. Although several thousand responded in each case, did they represent the general U.S. population? Probably not. For one thing, readers of these magazines tend to be more affluent than the general population. Second, respondents represented a subgroup of readers who were willing to fill out candid questionnaires about their sexual behavior. It seems that they would have been more liberal than those who did not. Similarly, Shere Hite (1976, 1981, 1987) distributed over 100,000 questionnaires for each of her surveys on sexual behavior and male–female relationships. She had returns of about 3,000 for the 1976 report, 7,000 for the 1981 report, and 4,500 for the 1987 report. Did respondents accurately represent all recipients of the questionnaires? What do you think?

The Testing Method

Psychologists also use psychological tests, such as intelligence, aptitude, personality, and interests tests, to measure individual differences and the presence of various traits and characteristics among samples of populations. In Chapter 3 we shall see how psychologists have compared the cognitive abilities of males and females with tests of overall intelligence, verbal abilities, math skills, and spatial-relations skills. In Chapter 12 we shall see how psychologists use tests to help people choose satisfying careers.

Reliability and Validity   To be useful psychological tests must be reliable and valid. The **reliability** of a test is its consistency. For example, a reliable psychological test will yield very similar results on different testing occasions, as long as the individual has not made significant changes in the trait or traits being measured between testings. The **validity** of a test is the degree to which it measures what it is supposed to measure. The validity of intelligence tests is usually studied by comparing, or correlating, test scores with academic achievement or teacher ratings of student intellectual abilities. A test of musical aptitude would be expected to predict how well an individual learns to play a musical instrument. The interest tests that are widely used in career selection are frequently validated in terms of whether people who are well adjusted in a vocation score high on scales that show an interest in that vocation.

Sources of Error   Psychological test results, like the results of surveys, can be distorted by test takers who answer in the socially desirable direction or exaggerate personal problems. The nearby questionnaire on social desirability assesses the extent to which people tend to respond to tests in what they believe to be the socially desirable direction.

The Case-Study Method

Sigmund Freud developed psychodynamic theory largely on the basis of **case studies,**0 or carefully drawn biographies of the lives of individuals. In this method the psychologist studies one or a handful of individuals in great depth, seeking the factors that contribute to notable behavior patterns. Freud studied some patients for many years, meeting with them several times a week.

Sources of Error   Of course there are bound to be gaps in memory when people are interviewed. People also distort their pasts, even to themselves, because of social desirability and other factors. Interviewers might unintentionally encourage their subjects to fill in gaps in ways that are consistent with their theoretical perspectives. Psychoanalysts have been criticized, for example, for guiding patients into viewing their own lives from the psychodynamic perspective (e.g., Bandura, 1986). No wonder, then, that many patients offer "evidence" consistent with psychodynamic theory. But interviewers who hold other perspectives run the risk of subtly prodding subjects into saying what they expect to hear as well.

Psychologists, then, use many types of research to gather knowledge that can be applied to the processes of adjustment. Throughout this book we shall refer extensively to this body of research to learn how we can enhance our own adjustment and personal growth. But first let us note some strategies for studying that may enhance our adjustment to college and the growth of our grade point averages.

■ Student Success: How to Take Charge in College

When he first went off to college, your first author had little idea of what to expect. (Your second author was never surprised by anything.) New faces, a new locale, responsibility for doing his own laundry, new courses—it added up to an overwhelming assortment of changes. Perhaps the most stunning change of all was his new-found freedom. It was completely up to him to plan ahead to get his coursework completed but somehow to manage to leave time for socializing and his addiction to the game of bridge.

Another big surprise was that it was not enough for him just to enroll in a course and sit in the class. To see what we mean, take a moment to participate in a simple experiment. Imagine that you put some water into a bathtub and then sit in the tub. Wait a few moments, then look around. Unless strange things are happening, you'll notice that the water is still there, even though you may have displaced it a bit. You are not a sponge, and you will not simply soak up the water. You have to take active measures to get it inside—perhaps a straw and patience would help.

Taking an Active Approach to Learning— We Don't Really "Soak Up" Knowledge

The problems of soaking up knowledge from this and other textbooks are not entirely dissimilar. You won't accomplish much by sitting on it, except, perhaps, looking an inch taller. But psychological theory and research have taught us that an active approach to learning results in better grades than a passive approach. It is more efficient to look ahead and seek the answers to specific questions than to just flip through the pages "like a good student." It is also helpful not to try to do it all in one sitting, as in cramming before tests—especially when a few bathtubsful of academic material are floating around you.

Plan Ahead Begin your active approach to studying by assessing the amount of material you must master during the term and considering your rate of learning. How long does it take you to learn the material in a chapter or in a book? How many hours do you spend studying each day? How much material is there? Does it add up right? Will you make it? It may be that you will not be able to determine the answers until you have gotten into your textbooks for a week or two. But once you have, be honest with yourself about the mathematics of how you are doing. Be willing to revise initial estimates.

Once you have determined the amount of study time you will need for each course, try to space it out fairly evenly. For most of us, spaced or distributed learning is more efficient than massed learning or cramming. So outline a study schedule that will provide nearly equal time periods each weekday. But leave weekends relatively open so that you can have some time

Going off to college can add up to an overwhelming assortment of changes. Although most of us anticipate college with positive excitement, college requires us to make new friends, adjust to a new locale, do our own laundry, and take an active approach to learning.

▪ Q U E S T I O N N A I R E ▪

The Social-Desirability Scale

Do you say what you think, or do you tend to misrepresent your beliefs to earn the approval of others? Do you answer questions honestly, or do you say what you think other people want to hear?

Telling others what we think they want to hear is making the socially desirable response. Falling prey to social desirability may cause us to distort our beliefs and experiences in interviews or on psychological tests. You can complete the following test devised by Crowne and Marlowe (1960) to gain insight into whether you have a tendency to produce socially desirable responses. Read each item and decide whether it is true (T) or false (F) for you. Try to work rapidly and answer each question by placing a T or an F on the appropriate blank to the right of each item. Then turn to the scoring key at the end of the chapter to interpret your answers.

	TRUE	FALSE
1. Before voting I thoroughly investigate the qualifications of all the candidates.	____	____
2. I never hesitate to go out of my way to help someone in trouble.	____	____
3. It is sometimes hard for me to go on with my work if I am not encouraged.	____	____
4. I have never intensely disliked anyone.	____	____
5. On occasions I have had doubts about my ability to succeed in life.	____	____
6. I sometimes feel resentful when I don't get my way.	____	____
7. I am always careful about my manner of dress.	____	____
8. My table manners at home are as good as when I eat out in a restaurant.	____	____
9. If I could get into a movie without paying and be sure I was not seen I would probably do it.	____	____
10. On a few occasions, I have given up something because I thought too little of my ability.	____	____
11. I like to gossip at times.	____	____
12. There have been times when I felt like rebelling against people in authority even though I knew they were right.	____	____

for yourself and your friends and some extra hours to digest topics or assignments that are not going down so smoothly.

The following scheduling suggestions are derived from psychologists Tim Walter and Al Siebert (1987, pp. 47–48, 77):

1. Determine where and when the next test will be and what material will be covered.
2. Ask your instructor what will be most important for you to know, and check with students who have already taken the course to determine the sources of test questions—chapters in the text, lecture notes, student study guides, old exams, and so on.
3. Determine the number of chapters to be read between now and the test.
4. Plan to read a specific number of chapters each week and try to "psych out" your instructor by generating possible test questions from the chapters.

13. No matter who I'm talking to, I'm always a good listener.   _____   _____
14. I can remember "playing sick" to get out of something.   _____   _____
15. There have been occasions when I have taken advantage of someone.   _____   _____
16. I'm always willing to admit it when I make a mistake.   _____   _____
17. I always try to practice what I preach.   _____   _____
18. I don't find it particularly difficult to get along with loud-mouthed, obnoxious people.   _____   _____
19. I sometimes try to get even rather than forgive and forget.   _____   _____
20. When I don't know something I don't mind at all admitting it.   _____   _____
21. I am always courteous, even to people who are disagreeable.   _____   _____
22. At times I have really insisted on having things my own way.   _____   _____
23. There have been occasions when I felt like smashing things.   _____   _____
24. I would never think of letting someone else be punished for my wrong-doings.   _____   _____
25. I never resent being asked to return a favor.   _____   _____
26. I have never been irked when people expressed ideas very different from my own.   _____   _____
27. I never make a long trip without checking the safety of my car.   _____   _____
28. There have been times when I was quite jealous of the good fortune of others.   _____   _____
29. I have almost never felt the urge to tell someone off.   _____   _____
30. I am sometimes irritated by people who ask favors of me.   _____   _____
31. I have never felt that I was punished without cause.   _____   _____
32. I sometimes think when people have a misfortune they only got what they deserved.   _____   _____
33. I have never deliberately said something that hurt someone's feelings.   _____   _____

Source: D. P. Crowne and D. A. Marlowe, A new scale of social desirability independent of pathology, *Journal of Consulting Psychology* 24 (1960): 351. Copyright 1960 by the American Psychological Association. Reprinted by permission.

5. In generating possible test questions, keep in mind that good questions often start with phrases such as:

Give several examples of . . .
Which of the following is an example of . . .
Describe the functions of . . .
What is most important about . . .
List the major . . .
Compare and contrast . . .
Describe the structure of . . .
Explain how psychologists have determined that . . .
Why do psychologists advise clients to . . .
Identify the parts of . . .

6. Plan specific study periods each week during which you will generate questions from lecture notes, old exams, the student study guide, and so on.

7. Plan for weekly study periods during which you will compose and take practice tests.
8. Take the practice quizzes in the student study guide. Many instructors reinforce use of the study guide by occasionally taking some exam questions directly from them.
9. Keep a diary or log in which you record your progress, including when, where, and how long you study and how well you perform on practice tests.

Study a Variety of Subjects Each Day   Also remember that variety is the spice of life—that is, we are more responsive to novel stimulation. Don't study the psychology of adjustment all day Monday, physics all day Tuesday, and literature all day Wednesday. Study each for a little while each day so that you won't feel bored or dulled by too lengthy an immersion in one subject.*

"Accept Your Humanness" Concerning Your Concentration Span
If you can't push yourself at first into studying enough each day, start at a more comfortable level and build toward the amount of study time you'll need by adding a few minutes every day. As noted by Walter and Siebert (1987), "accept your humanness." See what your concentration span is like for your subjects—how long you can continue to focus on coursework without your attention slipping away and, perhaps, lapsing into daydreaming. Plan to take brief study breaks before you reach your limit. Get up and stretch. Get a sip of water.

Cope with Distractions   Find a study place that is comfortable and free from distractions. To better understand how distractions work, consider the case of Benita:

> Benita is like most students. She has created a comfy nest for herself in her study area. As she closes the door to the den, the wonderful family pictures covering one wall draw her attention. Benita takes several minutes to gaze nostalgically at the photos of herself and Bill at the ocean. The next thing she knows, she's ready to pull out the slides and not bother with studying. Walking to her desk, she spots a pile of magazines she hasn't had a chance to read. There's the television in the corner. Why not turn it on and catch the last half of the special she wanted to watch? "I can read and watch TV at the same time," she thinks to herself. Everything in the room has a pull for Benita. She feels as though magnetic forces are drawing her to every item in the room.
>
> And that's the trouble. Before she knows it, 20 minutes have slipped away. She glances at the clock and suddenly thinks, "Why have I wasted so much time? Okay, I'll get to work. That's the last time I'll be distracted." That's what she thinks (Walter & Siebert, 1987, p. 68).

Avoid Benita's pitfalls by letting your spot for studying—your room, a study lounge, a place in the library—come to mean studying to you. Do nothing but study there—no leafing through magazines, no socializing, no snacking. But after you have met a goal, such as finishing half of your studying, you may want to reward yourself with a break, and do something like people watching in a busier section of the library.

Use Self-Reward   Use rewards for meeting daily study goals. Don't be a martyr and try to postpone all pleasures until the end of the term. Some people can do this, but it isn't necessary. And if you have never spent that

---

*Here, of course, we are referring to those other subjects. Obviously, you could study this book for several hours every day without ever becoming bored.

SQ4R method. An active study method in which the student *surveys* the subject matter, formulates *questions*, *reads* the material, *writes* notes, *recites* answers to questions, and *reviews* the material regularly.

much time in nonstop studying, you may be demanding too much from yourself. In fact, when you meet your daily study goals, you may want to select one or two of the activities from the Pleasant Events Schedule (pp. 381–383) to reward yourself the following day or on the weekend. Note these examples from Beverly's reward list (Walter & Siebert, 1987, p. 52). Whenever she successfully completed an important task, such as meeting her daily study goal, Beverly would choose from the following:

1. Listen to record
2. Take nap
3. Eat snack
4. Jog
5. Watch "The People's Court"
6. Play video game
7. Watch music video
8. Call boyfriend
9. Ride bike
10. Go to movie
11. Lunch date
12. Read favorite magazine

SQ4R: Survey, Question, Read, Write, Recite, and Review

Don't question some of your instructors' assignments. Question all of them. By so doing, you can follow the active **SQ4R** study technique originated by educational psychologist Francis Robinson (1970). In SQ4R, that is, you phrase questions about your assignments as you go along, and then seek to answer them. SQ4R has helped students raise their grades at several colleges (Benecke & Harris, 1972; Walter & Siebert, 1987). There are six steps to SQ4R: surveying, questioning, reading, writing, reciting, and reviewing.*

Survey   Skipping through the pages of a "whodunit" to identify the killer is a sure-fire way to destroy the impact of a mystery novel, but it can help you learn textbook material. In fact, many textbooks are written with devices that stimulate you to survey the material before reading it. This book has chapter outlines, "Truth or Fiction?" sections, major and minor section heads throughout each chapter, and chapter summaries. If drama and suspense are your goals, begin the chapters with the "Truth or Fiction?" sections and then read them page by page. But if learning the facts comes first, it may be more effective (sigh), first to examine the chapter outlines, skim the minor heads not covered in the outlines, and read the summaries—before you get to the meat of the chapters. Familiarity with the skeletons or advance organizers of the chapters will provide you with frameworks for learning the meat of the chapters.

Question   Phrase questions for each head in the chapter and write them down in a notebook. Some questions can also be based on material within sections. For courses in which the textbooks do not have helpful major and minor heads, get into the material page by page and do the best you can at phrasing questions as you go along. You will develop questioning skills with practice, and your questions will help you perceive the underlying structure of each chapter, even when the authors do not use heads. Most of the following questions are recastings of the major and minor heads on the first several pages of Chapter 7. Notice that they are indented according to the outlined chapter structure, providing an immediate sense of how the material is organized:

*Yes, we confess: "Writing" begins with a *w*. But sacrifices must be made for catchy titles such as SQ4R.

A. What is health psychology?
A. What is the immune system?
   B. What are the functions of the immune system?
   B. What are the effects of stress on the immune system?
A. What are the relationships between stress and physical disorders?
   B. How are headaches related to stress?
      C. What are muscle-tension headaches?
      C. What are migraine headaches?
      C. How do psychologists help people cope with headaches?

. . . .

B. What are cardiovascular disorders? What kinds of cardiovascular disorders are there?
   C. What are the risk factors for cardiovascular disorders?
   C. How can we modify our behavior to reduce the risk of cardiovascular disorders?

The questions you would have phrased from these heads might have been different, but they might have been as useful as these, or more useful. As you study, you will learn what works best for you.

Read and Write   Once you have phrased questions, read the subject matter with the purpose of answering them. This sense of purpose will help you focus on the essential points of the material. As you answer each question, write down a few key words in your notebook that will telegraph that answer to you when you recite and review later on. Many students find it helpful to keep two columns in their notebooks: questions in the column to the left, and key words (to the answer) in the column to the right.

If the material you are reading happens to be fine literature, you may wish to read it once just to appreciate its poetic features. But when you reread it, use SQ4R in order to tease out the essential information it contains.

Recite   Once you have read a section and jotted down the key words to the answer, recite each answer aloud if possible. (Your ability to do so may depend on where you are, who's around, and your level of concern over how you think they'll react to you.) Reciting answers aloud helps us to remember them and provides an immediate check on the accuracy of the key words.

Review   Review the material according to a reasonably regular schedule, such as once weekly. Cover the answer column and read the questions as though they were a quiz. Recite your answers and then check them against the key response words. Reread the subject matter when you forget an answer. Forgetting too many answers may mean that you haven't phrased the questions efficiently for your own use or that you haven't reviewed the material frequently enough. By taking a more active approach to studying, you may find that you are earning higher grades and gaining more pleasure from the learning process.

Ways to Frustrate Instructors and Jeopardize Progress in Class

Now that we've given you some ideas about things you can do to learn more and improve your grades, it seems that we should also provide a list of things *not* to do. Why should you avoid the following behavior patterns? Because you will annoy your instructors, interfere with class instruction, and jeopardize your own grade. Most instructors grade students on their academic performance in class and on tests. By behaving foolishly in class, your class-performance grade may suffer. Even when instructors grade students only on the basis of written performances, there might be "judgment calls" on essay questions and term papers that will go against the obnoxious student— not because the instructor is intentionally punishing the student, but because the instructor conceptualizes the student as uncommitted or "out in left field."

Here are the aggravating behavior patterns, as listed by Walter and Siebert (1987, pp. 153–157), and a number of suggested alternatives:

1. *You argue angrily with instructors, especially over exams.* Angry arguments may arouse feelings of mutual dislike. Alternative: Present your ideas clearly and back them up with evidence, but not with anger.
2. *You treat classes as social hours or as unwanted obligations.* Yawning, sleeping, chatting, leaving early, making faces—all are guaranteed to make instructors think that you do not belong in the class.
3. *You are a know-it-all student.* Fellow students as well as instructors are annoyed by know-it-all students. Alternative: Assume that others also have valuable things to say. Try listening to, and acknowledging, the contributions of others.
4. *You tell emotional and personal stories leading to nowhere.* Alternative: Before going off on a personal tangent, ask yourself, "Will my remarks add to the class discussion, or do I just want to tell everyone about myself?" If you have nothing to add to the class discussion, fight the temptation.
5. *You expect your instructors to be outstanding every day.* With the exception of your authors, most instructors have days when they haven't had enough time to prepare for class; now and then a personal problem might also be distracting them. Rather than getting frustrated yourself, and letting the instructor know about it, show some compassion. Be attentive and

One of the ways students can frustrate instructors and jeopardize progress in class is to argue angrily, especially over exams. It is wiser to present ideas clearly and back them with evidence—not with anger.

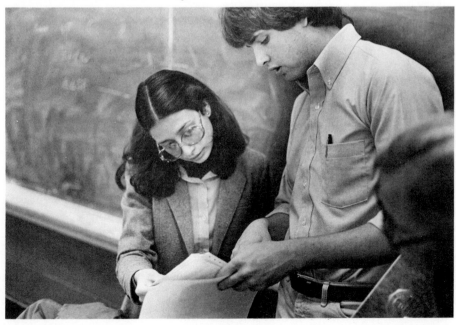

ask good questions when your instructor is having a hard time of it; don't look out the window and snicker to friends.

6. *You tell other students what you dislike about the instructor—you never go directly to the instructor.* Actually, such complaints may interfere with other students' efforts to get the most out of a course and are of no value to the instructor.

7. *You are irritating to an instructor who irritates you.* Some students read magazines, scowl and sneer, sit back with their arms crossed, even knit (clicking needles loudly!) to "get to" instructors who irritate them. Don't blame other people, even poor instructors, for your own misbehavior. If you are not determined to learn what you can from the course, you might be better advised to withdraw or transfer to another class.

8. *You talk down to instructors you think are "losers."* Some students are sarcastic with, and even show open contempt for, the occasional instructor who strikes them as a "loser." Alternative: Try complimenting the instructor for a better-than-average class; maybe you'll be offering helpful hints as to what works.

9. *You ask your instructors to be personal counselors.* It's fine to be friendly with your instructors, to stop by their offices and chat. Most instructors enjoy informal contacts with their students; in fact, some believe that that is what teaching is all about. But don't take advantage of your instructors' friendliness by monopolizing all their time and telling them your life's history and all your problems. Alternative: Spend your informal contacts with instructors discussing your mutual interests in the subject matter, and talk to personal friends or a professional at the college counseling center about your personal problems.

10. *You demand that your instructors give you special favors and consideration.* Some students miss half their classes and then go to their instructors to get the missing information. Some ask if it will be okay to go on vacation a week early or to take the final at a more convenient time. Others fail the quizzes but claim to know the subject matter inside out—just not to do well on the instructor's tests. (Such claims are usually wildly inaccurate.) Requests such as these usually only serve to get across the message that you don't take the course seriously and are not willing to invest yourself as much as other students do. But if a true emergency arises and you need an important favor, ask for it. If you have worked steadily all along and have a solid reputation with the instructor, he or she will probably be willing to meet you halfway.

■ Summary

1. **What are some of the challenges of contemporary life?** Some of today's challenges include changing roles, a changing technology, a changing physical environment, and a changing society.

2. **What is psychology?** Psychology is a scientific approach to the study of behavior. The goals of psychology are the description, explanation, prediction, and control of behavior.

3. **What is adjustment?** Adjustment is behavior that permits us to meet the challenges of life.

4. **How do psychodynamic theorists view adjustment?** From a psychodynamic view, adjustment implies finding outlets for basic impulses while avoiding social disapproval and self-condemnation.

5. **How do trait theorists view adjustment?** Trait theorists view adjustment in terms of placing people in situations where there is a good person–environment fit.

6. **How do learning theorists view adjustment?** Learning theorists view

adjustment in terms of having accurate expectations and the skills to manipulate and even create environments.

7. **How do phenomenologists view adjustment?** Phenomenologists view adjustment in terms of self-actualizing unique potentials and having useful ways of construing the world.

8. **What is the difference between adjustment and personal growth?** Adjustment is reactive—meeting the challenges of life. Personal growth is conscious, active self-development.

9. **Is biology destiny?** Not necessarily. Genes (nature) determine the reaction ranges for the expression of traits, but our chosen behavior patterns can minimize genetic risk factors and maximize genetic potential.

10. **What is the difference between the clinical and healthy-personality approaches to the psychology of adjustment?** The clinical approach focuses on ways in which problems can be corrected, whereas the healthy-personality approach focuses on optimizing our development along personal, social, physical, and vocational lines.

11. **What is the scientific method?** This method is a systematic approach used by psychologists to gather scientific evidence. It involves formulating a research question, developing a hypothesis, testing the hypothesis, and drawing conclusions.

12. **What are the various research methods used by psychologists?** The naturalistic-observation method studies behavior where it happens—in the field. The correlational method allows psychologists to determine the relationships between variables, such as daily hassles and illness. The experimental method tests a treatment in an effort to determine cause and effect. Survey methods use interviews and questionnaires to assess overt behavior and attitudes. The case-study method is an in-depth study of an individual or a small group of individuals.

13. **What are some of the sources of error in research?** One is assuming that a biased sample represents a population. Another is assuming that self-reports accurately reflect overt behavior and attitudes. Still another is interpreting correlation as cause and effect. And yet another is failure to control for subjects' expectations in experiments.

14. **What are some of the ways in which students can optimize learning?** Students can plan ahead to distribute learning, find quiet places for studying, vary the subjects they study, try to figure out what questions will appear on tests, reward themselves for meeting goals, use the SQ4R method.

15. **What is the SQ4R method?** SQ4R stands for survey, question, read, write, recite, and review. It is an active study method in which students survey the material, phrase questions about it, read in order to answer the questions, and review the material in various ways.

16. **Why does the text include ways for students to annoy their instructors and jeopardize their progress?** The heading for this material was written in tongue-in-cheek fashion, and this is a list of behavior patterns for students to *avoid*. By and large, they include ways in which students show that they are not serious about learning and impede class interaction.

■ **TRUTH OR FICTION REVISITED**

Longshoremen have become longshorepersons, and we find ads for Guy Fridays in the "Help Wanted" columns. True. Changing sex roles provide new opportunities for, but also pose new challenges to, both men and women.

Only gay men and intravenous drug abusers are really at risk for being infected by the AIDS virus. False. Even newborn babies whose mothers are infected by the AIDS virus may be infected.

Some people are genetically vulnerable to becoming alcoholics or suffering severe mood swings. True. For example, children of alcoholics are more tolerant of alcohol.

If the risk factors for heart disease are stacked against you, there's nothing you can do about it—you're going to have a heart attack. Not necessarily. A few people might not be able to do anything about it, but many of us can reduce the risk of cardiovascular disorders by changing high-risk behavior patterns such as smoking cigarettes and eating high-fat diets.

Only men are sexually aroused by sexually explicit films. False, as we shall see in Chapter 15. However, naturalistic-observation studies in New York's Times Square area might lead to an erroneous impression.

You are less likely to get a divorce if you live together with your future spouse before getting married. False. A recent Swedish study showed that cohabitors are *more* likely eventually to get divorces.

Sustained exercise is linked to a lower incidence of heart attacks. True. Several studies have shown this correlation.

There is no experimental evidence, with human beings, that cigarette smoking causes cancer. True. The evidence with humans is correlational.

You could survey 20 million Americans and still not accurately predict the outcome of a presidential election. True. For example, surveying mostly Democrats or Republicans would yield biased results. A random sample of 1,500 would serve better.

Pretest cramming is more effective than distributed learning. False. Distributed, or spaced, learning is more effective than massed learning (cramming).

It is a good idea to participate in every class discussion. False. If you don't have something useful to say, you may just irritate your instructors and fellow students.

■ Scoring Key for the Social Desirability Scale

Place a check mark on the appropriate line of the scoring key each time your answer agrees with the one listed in the scoring key. Add the check marks and record the total number of check marks below.

1. T _____	**12.** F _____	**23.** F _____
2. T _____	**13.** T _____	**24.** T _____
3. F _____	**14.** F _____	**25.** T _____
4. T _____	**15.** F _____	**26.** T _____
5. F _____	**16.** T _____	**27.** T _____
6. F _____	**17.** T _____	**28.** F _____
7. T _____	**18.** T _____	**29.** T _____
8. T _____	**19.** F _____	**30.** F _____
9. F _____	**20.** T _____	**31.** T _____
10. F _____	**21.** T _____	**32.** F _____
11. F _____	**22.** F _____	**33.** T _____

Interpreting Your Score

Low Scorers (0–8)   About one respondent in six earns a score between 0 and 8. Such respondents answered in a socially *undesirable* direction much of the time. It may be that they are more willing than most people to respond to tests truthfully, even when their answers might meet with social disapproval.

Average Scorers (9–19).   About two respondents in three earn a score from 9 through 19. They tend to show an average degree of concern for the social desirability of their responses, and it may be that their general behavior represents an average degree of conformity to social rules and conventions.

High Scorers (20–33).   About one respondent in six earns a score between 20 and 33. These respondents may be highly concerned about social approval and respond to test items in such as way as to avoid the disapproval of people who may read their responses. Their general behavior may show high conformity to social rules and conventions.

Theories of Personality and Behavior

According to psychodynamic theory, the human mind is like a vast submerged iceberg, only the tip of which rises above the surface into awareness.

Biting one's fingernails or smoking cigarettes as an adult is a sign of conflict during very early childhood.

It is normal for boys to be hostile toward their fathers.

Psychologists have studied human personality by reading the dictionary.

Human behavior is largely consistent from situation to situation.

Traits such as emotional responsiveness and sociability show genetic influences.

According to behaviorists, we may believe that we have freedom of choice, but our preferences and choices are actually forced upon us by the environment.

Psychologists helped a young boy overcome his fear of rabbits by having him eat cookies as a rabbit was brought nearer.

Reinforcement is essential if learning is to occur.

We are more motivated to tackle difficult tasks if we believe that we shall succeed at them.

You can learn to raise your heart rate or to lower your blood pressure by being hooked up to a machine that "bleeps" when you make the desired response.

We all have unique ways of looking at ourselves and at the world outside.

There is an ancient Islamic tale about the first time three blind men encounter an elephant. Each touches a different part of the elephant, but each is stubborn and claims that he alone has grasped the true nature of the beast. One grabbed the elephant by the legs and described it as firm, strong, and upright, like a pillar. To this the blind man who had touched the ear of the elephant objected. From his perspective, the animal was broad and rough, like a rug. The third man had become familiar with the trunk. He was astounded at the gross inaccuracy of the others. Clearly the elephant was long and narrow, he declared, like a hollow pipe.

Each of this trio had come to know the elephant from a different perspective. Each was blind to the beliefs of his fellows and to the real nature of the beast—not only because of his physical limitations, but also because his initial encounter had led him to think of the elephant in a certain way.

So it is that different ways of encountering people lead scientists to view us from different perspectives. Biologists view us in terms of biological and chemical processes. Medical researchers view us in terms of sickness and health. Psychologists tend to view us in terms of **personality** and behavior. By and large, biological and chemical processes can be observed and measured directly. But personality is not something that can be touched directly, and so theories of personality and behavior may differ as widely as the blind men's concepts of the elephant.

Nor do people agree on what the term *personality* means. Some equate personality with liveliness, as in, "She's got a lot of personality." Others characterize a person's personality as consisting of the most striking or dominant traits, as in a "shy personality," or a "happy-go-lucky personality." Psychologists tend to define personality as the reasonably stable patterns of behavior, including thoughts and emotions, that distinguish people from one another (Mischel, 1986; Phares, 1984). These behavior patterns reflect a person's characteristic ways of adapting to the challenges of life. Personality, therefore, deals with the ways in which people differ in behavior. Theories of personality and behavior may include discussion of internal variables such as thoughts and emotions, as well as overt behavior.

Psychologists seek to explain how people develop distinctive patterns of behavior, and to predict how people with certain patterns will respond to the demands of a changing world. In this chapter we explore four major approaches to the understanding of personality and behavior: psychodynamic theories, trait theories, learning theories, and phenomenological theories. We shall see what each of them has to say about human nature, and what each suggests about our abilities to cope with the challenges of life and to develop as individuals.

Personality. The distinct patterns of behaviors, including thoughts and feelings, that characterize a person's adaptation to life. (From the Latin *persona*, meaning "actor's face mask.")

Psychodynamic. Descriptive of Freud's view that various forces move through the personality and determine behavior.

■ Psychodynamic Theories

There are several **psychodynamic** theories of personality, but they have a number of things in common. Each teaches that personality is characterized by a dynamic struggle. Drives such as sex, aggression, and the need for superiority come into conflict with laws, social rules, and moral codes. The laws and social rules become internalized. We make them parts of ourselves. After doing so, the dynamic struggle becomes a clashing of opposing *inner* forces. At a given moment our observable behaviors, as well as our thoughts and emotions, represent the outcome of these inner clashes.

Each psychodynamic theory also owes its origin to the thinking of Sigmund Freud.

Sigmund Freud's Theory of Psychosexual Development

In 1856, in a Czechoslovakian village, an old woman told his mother that she had given birth to a great man. The child was reared with great expectations.

In manhood, Sigmund Freud himself would be cynical about this notion. Old women, after all, would earn greater favors by forecasting good tidings than doom. But the prophecy about Freud was not pure fantasy. Few have shaped our thinking about human nature so deeply.

Freud was trained as a physician. Early in his practice, he was astounded that some people apparently experienced loss of feeling in a hand or paralysis of the legs in the absence of any medical disorder. These strange symptoms often disappeared once patients had recalled and discussed distressful events and feelings of guilt or anxiety that seemed to be associated with the symp-toms. For a long time these events and feelings were hidden beneath the surface of awareness. Even so, they had the capacity to influence patients' behavior.

From this sort of clinical evidence, Freud concluded that the human mind was like an iceberg (Figure 2.1). Only the tip of an iceberg rises above the surface of the water, while the great mass of it darkens the deep. Freud came to believe that people, similarly, were only aware of a small number of the ideas and the impulses that dwelled within their minds. Freud argued that the greater mass of the mind, our deepest images, thoughts, fears, and urges, remained beneath the surface of conscious awareness, where little light illuminated them. He labeled the region that poked through into the light of awareness the **conscious** part of the mind. He called the regions that lay below the surface the preconscious and the unconscious.

The **preconscious** mind contains elements of experience that are pres-ently out of awareness, but can be made conscious simply by focusing on them. The **unconscious** mind is shrouded in mystery. It contains biological instincts such as sex and aggression. Some unconscious urges cannot be ex-perienced consciously because mental images and words could not portray them in all their color and fury. Other unconscious urges may be kept below the surface by repression.

FIGURE 2.1 The Iceberg of the Human Mind—According to Psychoanalytic Theory

According to Freud's view of human nature, only the tip of the human mind rises above the surface, into the light of conscious awareness. Material in the precon-scious can become conscious if we direct our attention to it, but the impulses and ideas in the unconscious tend to remain shrouded in mystery.

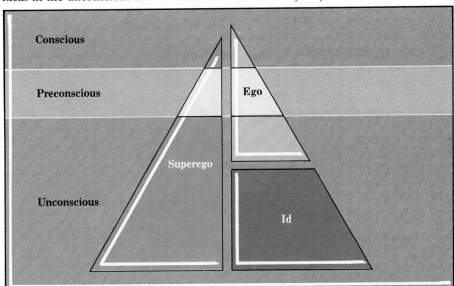

Sigmund Freud.

Repression. In psychodynamic theory, a defense mechanism that protects the person from anxiety by ejecting anxiety-evoking ideas and impulses from awareness.

Psychoanalysis. In this usage, Freud's method of exploring human personality.

Self-insight. In psychodynamic theory, accurate awareness of one's motives and feelings.

Resistance. In psychodynamic theory, a blocking of thoughts whose awareness could cause anxiety; a reflection of the defense mechanism of repression.

Psychic structure. In psychodynamic theory, a hypothesized mental structure that helps explain different aspects of behavior.

Id. The psychic structure, present at birth, that represents physiological drives and is fully unconscious. (A Latin word meaning "it.")

Pleasure principle. The governing principle of the id—the seeking of immediate gratification of instinctive needs.

Ego. The second psychic structure to develop, characterized by self-awareness, planning, and the delay of gratification. (A Latin word meaning "I.")

Repression is the automatic ejection of anxiety-evoking ideas from awareness. Repression protects us from recognizing impulses we would consider inappropriate in light of our moral values.

The unconscious is the largest part of the mind. Here the dynamic struggle between biological drives and social rules is most fierce. As drives seek expression, and internalized values exert counterpressures, the resultant conflict can give rise to various psychological disorders and behavioral outbursts. Since we cannot view the unconscious mind directly, Freud developed a method of mental detective work called **psychoanalysis.** In psychoanalysis people are prompted to talk about anything that "pops" into their minds while they remain comfortable and relaxed. People may gain **self-insight** by pursuing some of the thoughts that pop into awareness. But they are also motivated to avoid discussing threatening subjects. The same repression that has ejected unacceptable thoughts from awareness prompts **resistance,** or the desire to avoid thinking about or discussing them. Repression and resistance can make psychoanalysis a tedious process that lasts for years, or decades.

The Structure of Personality

When is a structure not a structure? When it is a mental or **psychic structure.** Sigmund Freud labeled the clashing forces of personality psychic structures. They could not be seen or measured directly, but their presence was suggested by observable behavior, expressed thoughts and emotions. Freud hypothesized the existence of three psychic structures: the *id, ego,* and *superego.*

The **id** is present at birth. It represents physiological drives and is fully unconscious. Freud described the id as "a chaos, a cauldron of seething excitations" (1964, p. 73). The conscious mind might find it inconsistent to love and hate the same person at the same time, but Freud believed that conflicting emotions could dwell side by side in the id. In the id we could experience hatred for our mothers for failing to immediately gratify all of our needs, even at the same time we loved them.

The id follows what Freud termed the **pleasure principle.** It demands instant gratification of instincts without consideration of law, social custom, or the needs of others.

The **ego** begins to develop during the first year of life, largely because not all of a child's demands for gratification can be met immediately. The ego "stands for reason and good sense" (Freud, 1964, p. 76), for rational ways of coping with frustration. It curbs the appetites of the id and makes plans that are in keeping with social convention, so that a person can find gratification yet avoid the disapproval of others. The id lets you know that you are starving. The ego creates the idea of walking to the refrigerator, heating up some tacos, and pouring a glass of milk.

The ego is guided by the **reality principle.** It takes into account what is practical and possible, as well as what is urged. Within Freudian theory, it is the ego that provides the conscious sense of self.

Although most of the ego is conscious, some of its business is carried out unconsciously. For instance, the ego also acts as a watchdog or censor that screens the impulses of the id. When the ego senses that socially unacceptable impulses are rising into awareness, it may use psychological defenses to prevent them from surfacing. Repression is one such psychological defense, or **defense mechanism.** We shall discuss a number of other important defense mechanisms in Chapter 6.

The **superego** develops throughout middle childhood, usually incorporating the moral standards and values of parents and significant members of the community through **identification.** The superego functions according to the **moral principle.** The superego can hold forth shining examples of an ideal self and also acts like the conscience, an internal moral guardian. Throughout life, the superego monitors the intentions of the ego and hands out judgments of right and wrong. It floods the ego with feelings of guilt and shame when the verdict is in the negative.

The ego hasn't an easy time of it. It stands between id and superego, braving the arrows of each. It strives to satisfy the demands of the id and the moral sense of the superego. The id may urge, "You are sexually aroused!" But the superego may warn, "You're not married." The poor ego is caught in the middle.

Stages of Psychosexual Development
Freud stirred controversy within the medical establishment of his day by arguing that sexual impulses, and

Reality principle. Consideration of what is practical and possible in gratifying needs—characteristic of the ego.

Defense mechanism. In psychodynamic theory, an unconscious function of the ego that protects it from anxiety-evoking material by preventing accurate recognition of this material.

Superego. The third psychic structure, which functions as a moral guardian and sets forth high standards for behavior.

Identification. In psychodynamic theory, the unconscious assumption of the behavior of another person, usually the parent of the same sex.

Moral principle. The governing principle of the superego, which sets moral standards and enforces adherence to them.

Childhood Sexuality?
Freud shocked the medical establishment of his day by asserting that even young children have sexual instincts and motives. Many of Freud's own followers (ego analysts) also believe that Freud may have placed too much emphasis on sexual motivation.

their gratification, were central factors in personality development, even among children. Freud saw children's basic ways of relating to the world, such as sucking their mothers' breasts and moving their bowels, as involving sexual feelings.

Freud believed that there was a major instinct to preserve and perpetuate life, which he termed **Eros.** Eros contained a certain amount of energy, which Freud labeled **libido.** This energy was psychological in nature and involved sexual impulses, so Freud considered it *psychosexual.* Libidinal energy would be expressed through sexual feelings in different parts of the body, or **erogenous zones,** as the child developed. To Freud, human development involved the transfer of libidinal energy from one zone to another. He hypothesized five stages of **psychosexual development:** oral, anal, phallic, latency, and genital.

During the first year of life, a child experiences much of its world through the mouth. If it fits, into the mouth it goes. This is the **oral stage.** Freud argued that oral activities such as sucking and biting bring the child sexual gratification as well as nourishment.

Freud believed that children would encounter conflicts during each stage of psychosexual development. During the oral stage, conflict would center around the nature and extent of oral gratification. Early **weaning** could lead to frustration. Excessive gratification, on the other hand, could lead an infant to expect it would automatically be handed everything in life. Inadequate or excessive gratification in any stage could lead to **fixation** in that stage, and the development of traits characteristic of that stage. Oral traits include dependency, gullibility, and optimism or pessimism.

Freud theorized that adults with an **oral fixation** could experience exaggerated desires for "oral activities," such as smoking, overeating, alcohol abuse, and nail biting. Like the infant whose very survival depends on the mercy of an adult, adults with oral fixations may be disposed toward clinging, dependent interpersonal relationships.

Note that according to **psychoanalytic theory,** people are largely at the mercy of events that occurred long before they can weigh alternatives and make decisions about how to behave. Freud's own "oral fixation," cigar smoking, seems to have contributed to the cancer of the mouth and jaw that killed him in 1939.

During the **anal stage,** sexual gratification is attained through contraction and relaxation of the muscles that control elimination of waste products. Elimination, which was controlled reflexively during most of the first year of life, comes under voluntary muscular control, even if such control at first is not reliable. The anal stage is said to begin in the second year of life.

During the anal stage, children learn to delay the gratification of eliminating as soon as they feel the urge. The general issue of self-control may become a source of conflict between parent and child. **Anal fixations** may stem from this conflict and lead to two sets of anal traits. So-called **anal retentive** traits involve excessive use of self-control. They include perfectionism, a strong need for order, and exaggerated neatness and cleanliness. **Anal-expulsive** traits, on the other hand, "let it all hang out." They include carelessness, messiness, even **sadism.**

Children enter the **phallic stage** during the third year of life. During this stage the major erogenous zone is the phallic region (the **clitoris** in girls). Parent-child conflict is likely to develop over masturbation, which parents may treat with punishment and threats. During the phallic stage children may develop strong sexual attachments to the parent of the opposite sex and begin to view the same-sex parent as a rival for the other parent's affections. Boys may want to marry Mommy, and girls may want to marry Daddy.

Feelings of lust and jealousy are difficult for children to handle. Home

---

Eros. In psychodynamic theory, the basic instinct to preserve and perpetuate life.

Libido. (1) In psychoanalytic theory, the energy of Eros; the sexual instinct. (2) Generally, sexual interest or drive.

Erogenous zone. An area of the body that is sensitive to sexual sensations.

Psychosexual development. In psychodynamic theory, the process by which libidinal energy is expressed through different erogenous zones during different stages of development.

Oral stage. The first stage of psychosexual development, during which gratification is hypothesized to be attained primarily through oral activities, like sucking and biting.

Weaning. Accustoming the child to surrender sucking the mother's breast or a baby bottle.

Fixation. In psychodynamic theory, arrested development. Attachment to objects of a certain stage when one's development should have advanced so that one is attached to objects of a more advanced stage.

Oral fixation. Attachment to objects and behaviors characteristic of the oral stage.

Psychoanalytic theory. Sigmund Freud's perspective, which emphasizes the importance of unconscious motives and conflicts as determinants of behavior.

Anal stage. The second stage of psychosexual development, when gratification is attained through anal activities, such as eliminating wastes.

Anal fixation. Attachment to objects and behaviors characteristic of the anal stage.

Anal retentive. Descriptive of behaviors and traits that have to do with "holding in," or with the expression of self-control. A Freudian personality type.

Anal expulsive. Descriptive of behaviors and traits that have to do with unregulated self-expression, such as messiness. A Freudian personality type.

life would be tense indeed if they were aware of them. So these feelings remain unconscious, although their influence is felt through fantasies about marriage and hostility toward the same-sex parent. Freud labeled this conflict in boys the **Oedipus complex,** after the legendary Greek king who unwittingly killed his father and married his mother. Similar feelings in girls give rise to the **Electra complex.** According to Greek legend, Electra was the daughter of the king Agamemnon. She longed for him after his death and sought revenge against his slayers—her mother and her mother's lover.

The Oedipus and Electra complexes become resolved by about the ages 5 or 6. Children then repress their hostilities toward and identify with the parent of the same sex. Identification leads to playing the social and sexual roles of the same-sex parent, and internalizing that parent's values. Sexual feelings toward the opposite-sex parent are repressed for a number of years. When they emerge during adolescence, they are **displaced** onto socially appropriate members of the opposite sex.

By the age of 5 or 6, Freud believed that children would have been in conflict with their parents over sexual feelings for several years. The pressures of the Oedipus and Electra complexes would motivate them to repress all sexual urges. In so doing they would enter the **latency stage,** a period of life during which sexual feelings would remain unconscious.

Freud wrote that we enter the final stage of psychosexual development, or **genital stage,** at puberty. Adolescent males again experience sexual urges toward their mothers, and adolescent females toward their fathers. But the **incest taboo** provides ample motivation for keeping these impulses repressed and displacing them onto other adults or adolescents of the opposite sex. But boys might still seek girls "just like the girl that married dear old Dad." Girls might still be attracted to men who resemble their fathers.

People in the genital stage prefer, by definition, to find sexual gratification through intercourse with a member of the opposite sex. In Freud's view, oral or anal stimulation, masturbation, and homosexual activity would all represent **pregenital** fixations and immature forms of sexual conduct. They would not be in keeping with the life instinct Eros.

Other Psychodynamic Views

A number of personality theorists are intellectual descendants of Sigmund Freud. Their theories, like Freud's, include roles for unconscious motivation, for motivational conflict, and for defensive responses to anxiety that involve repression and cognitive distortion of reality (Wachtel, 1982). In other respects, they differ markedly.

Carl Jung (1875–1961) was a Swiss psychiatrist who had been a member of Freud's inner circle. He fell into disfavor with Freud when he developed his own psychodynamic theory. Jung downplayed the importance of the sexual instinct. He saw it as but one of several important instincts. Jung also believed in the **Self,** a unifying force of personality that gives direction and purpose to human behavior. According to Jung, heredity dictates that the Self will persistently strive to achieve wholeness or fullness. Jung believed that an understanding of human behavior must incorporate self-awareness and self-direction as well as knowledge of unconscious impulses.

Alfred Adler (1870–1937), another follower of Freud, also believed that Freud had placed too much emphasis on sexual impulses. Adler believed that people are basically motivated by an **inferiority complex.** In some people feelings of inferiority may be based on physical problems and the need to compensate for them. But Adler believed that all of us encounter some feelings of inferiority because of our small size as children, and that these feelings give rise to a **drive for superiority.** Adler, like Jung, believed that self-awareness plays a major role in the formation of personality. Adler spoke of a

---

Sadism. Attaining gratification from inflicting pain on or humiliating others. (After the French Marquis de Sade.)

Phallic stage. The third stage of psychosexual development, characterized by a shift of libido to the phallic region. (From the Greek *phallos*, meaning "image of the penis.")

Clitoris. An external female sexual organ which is highly sensitive to sexual stimulation. (From the Greek *kleitoris*, meaning "hill.")

Oedipus complex. A conflict of the phallic stage in which the boy wishes to possess his mother sexually and perceives his father as a rival in love.

Electra complex. A conflict of the phallic stage in which the girl longs for her father and resents her mother.

Displaced. Transferred.

Latency stage. The fourth stage of psychosexual development, characterized by repression of sexual impulses.

Genital stage. The mature stage of psychosexual development, characterized by preferred expression of libido through intercourse with an adult of the opposite sex.

Incest taboo. The cultural prohibition against marrying or having sexual relations with a close blood relative.

Pregenital. Characteristic of stages less mature than the genital stage.

Self. According to Jung, a unifying force of personality that provides people with direction and purpose.

Inferiority complex. Feelings of inferiority hypothesized by Adler to serve as a central motivating force in the personality.

Drive for superiority. Adler's term for the desire to compensate for feelings of inferiority.

◼ A CLOSER LOOK

Do Women Who Compete with Men Suffer from Penis Envy?

Psychoanalytic theory in many ways has been a liberating force, allowing people to admit the importance of sexuality in their lives. But it has also been argued that Freud's views are repressive toward women. Freud's **penis-envy** hypothesis, in particular, has stigmatized women who compete with men in the business world as having failed to resolve the Electra complex.

Freud believed that little girls envy boys their penises. Why, they would feel, should boys have something that they do not? As a consequence of this jealousy, girls would resent their mothers for bringing them into the world so "ill-equipped," as Freud wrote in *New Introductory Lectures on Psychoanalysis*. They would then develop the wish to marry their fathers as a substitute for not having penises of their own.

Through a series of developmental transformations, the wish to marry the father would evolve into the desire to marry another man and bear children. A baby, especially a male child, would at least partially gratify the unconscious need to have something growing from the genital region. Freud also equated the penis with power and declared that the well-adjusted woman would also accept her husband's authority, symbolically surrendering the wish to have a penis of her own. Freud warned that retaining the wish for a penis would cause maladjustment. Persistent jealousy would cause women to develop masculine-typed traits such as competitiveness and self-assertiveness—at worst, female homosexuality.

These views have been attacked strongly by women and by many modern-day psychoanalysts. Karen Horney, for example, contended that little girls do not feel inferior to boys, and that the penis-envy hypothesis was not confirmed by observations of children. Horney argued that Freud's views reflected a Western cultural prejudice against women, and not good psychological theory. Horney believed that cultural expectations played a greater role than penis envy in shaping women's self-images. Because of her outspoken opposition to the ways in which the psychoanalytic establishment conceptualized and treated women, Horney was expelled from the staid New York Psychoanalytic Institute early in this century (Quinn, 1987).

Many people want women to remain passive and submissive, emotional, and dependent on men. In Freud's day oppression of women was even more extreme. Psychoanalytic theory, in its original form, supported the belief that motherhood and family life are the only proper avenues of fulfillment for women.

---

creative self, a self-aware aspect of personality that strives to overcome obstacles and develop the individual's potential.

Karen Horney (1885–1952) agreed with Freud that childhood experiences played a major role in the development of adult personality, but, like many other neoanalysts, she believed that sexual and aggressive impulses took a back seat in importance to social relationships. Moreover, she disagreed with Freud that anatomical differences between the sexes led girls to feel inferior to boys.

Horney, like Freud, saw parent-child relationships to be of paramount importance. On the other hand, it should be noted that Horney was more optimistic than Freud concerning the effects of early childhood traumatic experiences. She believed that genuine and consistent love could mitigate the effects of even the most traumatic childhoods (Quinn, 1987).

Erik Erikson also believed that Freud had placed undue emphasis on sexual instincts, and he asserted that social relationships are more crucial determinants of personality. To Erikson, the general climate of the mother–infant relationship is more important than the details of the feeding process or the sexual feelings that might be stirred by contact with the mother. Erikson also argued that to a large degree we are the conscious architects of our own personalities—a view which grants more powers to the "ego" than Freud had allowed. Within Erikson's theory it is possible for us to make real choices; within Freud's theory we might think that we are making choices, but we are probably only rationalizing the compromises forced upon us by intrapsychic warfare.

Erikson, like Freud, is known for devising a comprehensive develop-

Penis envy. In psychodynamic theory, jealousy of the male sexual organ attributed to girls in the phallic stage.

Creative self. According to Adler, the self-aware aspect of personality that strives to achieve its full potential.

Karen Horney.

TABLE 2.1   Erik Erikson's Stages of Psychosocial Development

Time Period	Life Crisis	The Developmental Task
Infancy (0–1)	Trust vs. mistrust	Coming to trust the mother and the environment—to associate one's surroundings with feelings of inner goodness
Early childhood (2–3)	Autonomy vs. shame and doubt	Developing the wish to make choices and the self-control to exercise choice
Preschool years	Initiative vs. guilt	Adding planning and "attacking" to choice, becoming active and on the move
Grammar-school years (6–12)	Industry vs. inferiority	Becoming eagerly absorbed in skills, tasks, and productivity; mastering the fundamentals of technology
Adolescence	Identity vs. role diffusion	Connecting skills and social roles to formation of career objectives
Young adulthood	Intimacy vs. isolation	Committing the self to another; engaging in sexual love
Middle adulthood	Generativity vs. stagnation	Needing to be needed; guiding and encouraging the younger generation; being creative
Late adulthood	Integrity vs. despair	Accepting the timing and placing of one's own life cycle; achieving wisdom and dignity

Source: Erikson, 1963, pp. 247–269.

mental theory of personality. But whereas Freud proposed stages of psycho*sexual* development, Erikson proposed stages of psycho*social* development. In other words, rather than labeling a stage after an erogenous zone, Erikson labeled stages after the traits that might be developed during that stage (Table 2.1). Each stage is named according to the possible outcomes, which are polar opposites. For example, the first stage of **psychosocial development** is named the stage of trust versus mistrust because of the two possible major outcomes. (1) A warm, loving relationship with the mother (and others) during infancy might lead to a sense of basic trust in people and the world. (2) A cold, nongratifying relationship might lead to a pervasive sense of mistrust. Erikson believed that most of us would wind up with some combination of trust and mistrust—hopefully with more trust than mistrust. But a basic sense of mistrust could impair the development of relationships for a lifetime unless we came to recognize its presence and challenge its appropriateness.

Erikson's Views on Adolescent and Adult Development
One of Erikson's most important accomplishments is his extension of Freud's five developmental stages to eight. Whereas Freud's developmental theory ends with adolescence, in the form of the genital stage, Erikson's theory includes the changing concerns of adulthood.

For Erikson, the goal of adolescence is the attainment of **ego identity,** not genital sexuality. Adolescents who attain ego identity develop a firm sense of who they are and what they stand for. One aspect of ego identity is learning how to "connect the roles and skills cultivated [during the elementary school years] with the occupational prototypes of the day" (Erikson, 1963, p. 261)—that is, with jobs. But ego identity extends to sexual, political, and religious

■ A CLOSER LOOK

Cognitive vs. Psychodynamic Views of Religious Conversion: Do We Suddenly See the Light, or Do We Strive to Keep a Lid on the Id?

Each year thousands of U.S. parents are shocked to learn that their children have become Hare Krishnas or "Moonies," or joined some other religious cult. They cannot fathom why their children have foredsaken not only their early religious teachings, but also their families. Now and then we hear of children who have their own children kidnapped and "deprogrammed" in an effort to return them to the family and fold.

Why do people undergo the travail of religious conversion? Cognitive and psychodynamic perspectives offer very different explanations. From the cognitive perspective, religious conversion reflects a conscious effort to end uncertainty about the nature of man and the universe. A person ripe for conversion might be expected to show concern about basic religious and political questions during adolescence. From a psychodynamic perspective, religious conversion represents a defense against an upsurge of unconscious Oedipal hatred directed toward the father (Freud, 1927/1964). By converting to a new religion, a person is submitting to a powerful father figure (God), and keeping the lid on impulses from the id. The psychodynamic view suggests that converts would have encountered more traumatic events during childhood and adolescence, giving rise to feelings of hostility which can be better controlled through conversion.

In a study of the cognitive and psychodynamic views of religious conversion, Chana Ullman (1982) in-terviewed 40 religious converts and 30 nonconverts. Ullman had anticipated that her findings would support the cognitive perspective, and so she expected that converts would show less tolerance for uncertainty and greater concern about basic religious issues than nonconverts. To her surprise, the converts and nonconverts could not be distinguished according to these variables.

Instead, in keeping with the psychodynamic view, Ullman found that 77 percent of the religious converts, as compared with 23 percent of nonconverts, reported problematic relationships with their fathers, including frequent father absence. Consider these excerpts from interviews with converts: "My relationship with [my father] was to keep from antagonizing him or causing any trouble," and "He did not understand anything you did, you could do nothing right [and] I started hating him" (Ullman, 1982, p. 192). Converts were also more likely than nonconverts to report traumatic and stressful events during childhood and adolescence.

In addition, 80 percent of the converts reported emotional turmoil before converting, in statements such as "I thought I was going crazy" and "I had suicidal thoughts." The same percentage reported that conversion provided relief from anxiety, anger, or depression.

Ullman concludes that stress and anxiety can precipitate religious conversion. Of course her study cannot directly reveal "unconscious" processes in her subjects, but it strongly suggests that childhood trauma and a rejecting or absent father figure contribute to the likelihood of conversion. As Ullman writes, "In many religious conversion cases, the experience may be seen as an attempt to gain the approval, protection, or guidance of an authority figure, as suggested by the original psychoanalytic hypothesis" (1982, pp. 191–192).

---

beliefs and commitments. According to Erikson, adolescents who do not develop a firm sense of identity are especially subject to peer influences and short-sighted hedonism. In Chapter 11's discussion of young, middle, and late adulthood, we shall explore Erikson's sixth, seventh, and eighth stages of psychosocial development.

Psychodynamic theories have had tremendous appeal. By and large, they are "rich" theories; that is, they involve many concepts and they explain many varieties of human behavior and traits. Let us begin this section by cataloguing some of the strengths of psychodynamic theories. Then we shall focus on their shortcomings.

Strengths of Psychodynamic Approaches

Psychic Determinism: Toward a More Scientific View of Behavior

One of the basic tenets of psychodynamic theory is that behavior is determined by the outcome of intrapsychic conflict. Concepts such as "intrapsychic conflict" and "psychic energy" have struck many psychologists as unscientific, and so it is somewhat ironic that in his day Freud fought for the ideas that

Erikson named the first stage of psychosocial development the stage of trust versus mistrust. During the first year, a warm, loving relationship with one's mother and other people might lead to a basic sense of trust in people and in the world.

human personality and behavior were subject to scientific analysis. Freud believed that by understanding the forces within people, we could understand and predict their behavior. Moreover, we could find ways to foster adjustment and personal development.

The Importance of Childhood   Freud's psychoanalytic theory also focused the attention of scientists and helping professionals on the far-reaching effects of childhood experiences. As noted by Rathus (1988), children over the centuries have generally been treated—for better or worse—as "little adults." Freud's studies helped show how different children are from adults, and the developmental theories of Freud and Erikson suggest ways in which early childhood traumas can color our perceptions and influence our behavior for a lifetime.

The Importance of "Primitive" Impulses   Freud can be credited for "getting people talking" about the importance of sexuality in their lives and about the prevalence of aggressive impulses and urges. Freud has helped us recognize that the experience of sexual and aggressive urges is commonplace, and that there is a difference between recognizing these urges and acting on them.

The Role of Cognitive Distortion   Freud also noted that people have defensive ways of looking at the world, and he developed a list of so-called defense mechanisms that have become a part of everyday parlance. Regardless of whether we attribute these cognitive distortions to unconscious ego functioning, it would seem that our thinking can be distorted by our efforts to defend ourselves against anxiety and guilt.

Innovation of Methods of Psychotherapy   In Chapter 9 we shall describe the methods of therapy originated by Freud and other psychodynamic theorists, and we shall see that they have probably helped many thousands of people to adjust to the challenges of life and to develop as individuals.

Weaknesses of Psychodynamic Approaches
But despite their richness, psychodynamic theories, particularly the original psychoanalytic views of Sigmund Freud, have met with extensive criticism.

Overemphasis on Sexuality and Underemphasis on Social Relationships   Some followers of Freud, such as Karen Horney and Erik Erikson, have argued that Freud placed too much emphasis on human sexuality and neglected the relative importance of social relationships. Other followers, such as Alfred Adler and Erich Fromm, have argued that Freud placed too much emphasis on unconscious motives. Adler and Fromm assert that people consciously seek self-enhancement and intellectual pleasures. They do not just try to gratify the dark demands of the id.

The Lack of Substance of "Psychic Structures"   A number of critics note that "psychic structures" such as the id, ego, and superego have no substance. They are little more than useful fictions, poetic ways to express inner conflict.

Resistance to **Disproof**   Sir Karl Popper (1985) has argued that Freud's hypothetical mental processes fail as scientific concepts because they cannot be observed. Nor do they predict observable behavior with precision. They only "explain" behavior after the fact. For example, we can speculate that a client "repressed" (forgot about) an appointment because "unconsciously" he did not want to attend the session, but we cannot accurately predict when such "repression" will occur.

Also, scientific propositions must be capable of being proven false. As noted by Popper, Freud's statements about mental structures are unscientific, precisely because no imaginable type of evidence can disprove them; any behavior can be explained in terms of these hypothesized (but unobservable) "structures."

Inaccuracies in Developmental Theories   Nor have the stages of psychosexual development escaped criticism. Children begin to masturbate as early as the first year, not in the "phallic stage." As parents know from observing their children play "doctor," the latency stage is not so sexually latent as Freud believed. Much of Freud's thinking concerning the Oedipus and Electra complexes remains speculation.

Possible Biases in the Gathering of Evidence   As noted by philosopher Adolph Grünbaum (1985), Freud's method of gathering evidence from the clinical session is also suspect. Therapists may subtly influence clients to produce what they expect to find. Therapists may also fail to separate reported facts from their own interpretations.

Also, Freud and many other psychodynamic theorists restricted their evidence gathering to case studies with individuals who sought treatment for adjustment problems. Persons seeking therapy do not represent the population at large. Also, they are likely to have more problems than the general population.

The Healthy Personality
Psychodynamic theories were developed by working with troubled individuals, and so the theoretical emphasis has been on the development of psychological

Trait. An aspect of personality that is inferred from behavior and assumed to give rise to behavioral consistency.

disorders, not a healthy personality. Nevertheless, the thinking of the major theorists can be combined to form a solid picture of what is meant by psychological health:

The Abilities to Love and to Work   Freud is noted to have equated psychological health with the abilities *lieben und arbeiten*—that is, "to love and to work." That is, the healthy individual is capable of caring deeply for other people, engaging in sexual love within an intimate relationship, and leading a productive work life. In order to accomplish these ends, sexual impulses must be allowed expression in a relationship with an adult of the opposite sex, and other impulses must be channeled into socially productive directions.

Ego Strength   The ego of the healthy individual has the strength to control the instincts of the id and to withstand the condemnation of the superego. The presence of acceptable outlets for the expression of some primitive impulses decreases the pressures within the id, and, at the same time, lessens the burdens of the ego in repressing the remaining impulses. Being reared by reasonably tolerant parents might prevent the superego from becoming overly harsh and condemnatory.

A Creative Self   Jung and Adler both spoke of a self (or Self)—a unifying force that provides direction to behavior and helps develop a person's potential. The notion of a guiding self, as we shall see, provides bridges between psychodynamic theories, social-learning theory (which speaks of self-regulatory processes), and phenomenological theories (which also speak of a self and the fulfillment of potential).

Compensation for Feelings of Inferiority   None of us can be "good at everything." According to Adler, we attempt to compensate for feelings of inferiority by excelling in one or more of the arenas of human interaction. So choosing productive arenas in which to contend—finding out what we are good at and developing our talents—constitutes healthful behavior from Adler's perspective.

Erikson's Positive Outcomes   A positive outcome within each of Erik Erikson's psychosocial stages also contributes to the healthy personality. That is, it is healthful to develop a basic sense of trust during infancy, to develop a sense of industry during the grammar school years, to develop a sense of who we are and what we stand for during adolescence, to develop intimate relationships during young adulthood, to be productive during middle adulthood, and so on.

■ Trait Theories

The notion of **traits** is very familiar. If we asked you to describe yourself, you would probably mention one or more of your traits. In everyday usage, we also tend to describe other people in terms of traits. If you describe a friend as "shy," it may be because you observed some social anxiety or withdrawal in early meetings. Traits, that is, are elements of personality that are inferred from behavior. Psychologist Gordon Allport (1937, 1961) saw traits as enduring and as accounting for consistent behavior in various situations. You are likely to expect your "shy" friend to be somewhat withdrawn in all or most social encounters—"all across the board," as the saying goes. The concept of traits also finds a place in other approaches to personality. Recall that Freud linked development of certain traits to children's experiences throughout his stages of psychosexual development.

More than 50 years ago Allport and Odbert (1936) catalogued some

18,000 human traits from a search through word lists of the sort found in dictionaries. Some were physical traits, such as short, white, and brunette. Others were behavioral traits, such as shy and emotional. Still others were moral traits, such as honesty. This exhaustive list has served as the basis for personality research by many other psychologists, including Raymond Cattell.

Surface and Source Traits

Psychologists such as Cattell (1965) have used statistical techniques to reduce this universe of traits to smaller lists that show commonality in meaning. Cattell also distinguished between surface traits and source traits. **Surface traits** describe characteristic ways of behaving, i.e., cleanliness, stubbornness, thrift, and orderliness. We may observe that these traits tend to form meaningful patterns that are suggestive of underlying traits. (Cleanliness, stubbornness, and so on were all referred to as *anal retentive* traits by Freud.)

Cattell refined the Allport catalogue by removing unusual terms and grouping the remaining traits into **source traits**—the underlying traits from which surface traits are derived. Cattell argued that psychological measurement of a person's source traits would enable us to predict his or her behavior in various situations. Cattell's research led him to suggest the existence of 16 source traits, which can be measured by means of his Sixteen Personality Factors Scale. Figure 2.2 shows the differences between airline pilots, creative artists, and writers, according to this scale. Notice that the pilots are more stable, conscientious, tough-minded, practical, controlled, and relaxed than the other two groups. But artists and writers are more intelligent, sensitive, and imaginative. You might prefer to have artists at a cocktail party, but pilots—at least those tested by Cattell—seem to have the stable and self-disciplined personality profile you might prefer to have in charge in the cockpit.

It is fascinating to note that the pilots seem "better adjusted" than the writers and artists, from a superficial point of view. That is, they are more "stable," more "self-controlled," and less "tense." Yet writers and artists make indispensable contributions to society and, by and large, are willing to "pay the emotional price" for their more sensitive and apprehensive personalities.

Raymond Cattell.

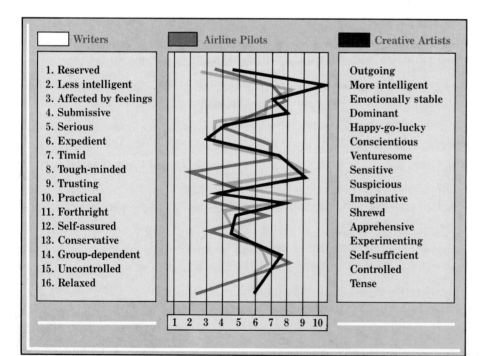

	Writers	Airline Pilots	Creative Artists	
1. Reserved				Outgoing
2. Less intelligent				More intelligent
3. Affected by feelings				Emotionally stable
4. Submissive				Dominant
5. Serious				Happy-go-lucky
6. Expedient				Conscientious
7. Timid				Venturesome
8. Tough-minded				Sensitive
9. Trusting				Suspicious
10. Practical				Imaginative
11. Forthright				Shrewd
12. Self-assured				Apprehensive
13. Conservative				Experimenting
14. Group-dependent				Self-sufficient
15. Uncontrolled				Controlled
16. Relaxed				Tense

1 2 3 4 5 6 7 8 9 10

FIGURE 2.2 Three Personality Profiles According to Cattell's Personality Factors

How do the traits of writers, pilots, artists compare? Where would you place yourself along these sixteen personality dimensions?

Introversion–Extraversion and Emotional Stability

British psychologist Hans J. Eysenck (1960; Eysenck & Eysenck, 1985) has focused much of his research on the relationships between two very important traits: **introversion–extraversion** and emotional stability–instability, otherwise called **neuroticism.** His research suggests that these basic traits are independent dimensions, as shown in Figure 2.3, and that our combinations of these traits place us along these dimensions. Figure 2.3 shows a number of surface traits (such as "touchy" and "restless" in the upper-right quadrant) and how they reflect combinations of the two basic source traits or personality dimensions.

Eysenck has catalogued a number of personality traits according to where they are "situated" along these dimensions (refer to Figure 2.3). For instance, an anxious person would be high both in introversion and neuroticism—that is, preoccupied with his or her own thoughts and emotionally unstable.

Where would you place athletes and artists in terms of the dimensions of introversion–extraversion and neuroticism? Where would you place yourself? Trait theories are often ignored by psychologists who write about adjustment and personal growth. The reason is that trait theories offer few, if any, direct suggestions for fostering individual development. It could even be argued that the trait theories are generally pessimistic about our capacities for change and improvement. After all, if traits are relatively stable, and if they account for consistent behavior, it would seem that we are "stuck"—for better or worse—with the traits we have.

But on closer inspection, we find that trait theories have made many direct and indirect contributions to the psychology of adjustment.

Strengths of Trait-Theory Approaches

Development of Psychological Tests   Psychologists have focused a good deal of their attention on the development of tests to measure traits. These include the Sixteen Personality Factors Scale and the California Psychological

Introversion. A source trait characterized by intense imagination and the tendency to inhibit impulses.

Extraversion. A source trait characterized by tendencies to be socially outgoing and to express feelings and impulses freely.

Neuroticism. Eysenck's term for emotional instability.

Surface traits. Cattell's term for characteristic, observable ways of behaving.

Source traits. Cattell's term for underlying traits from which surface traits are derived.

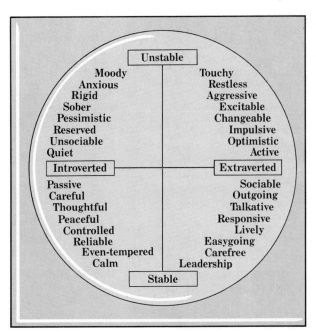

FIGURE 2.3   Eysenck's Personality Dimensions

Various personality traits fall within the two major dimensions of personality suggested by Hans Eysenck.

Can measurement of our traits predict behavior in certain situations? What traits would you attribute to the people in this photo?

Inventory, for assessing traits common to all of us, and the Minnesota Multiphasic Personality Inventory, for assessing psychological disorders.

Spawning of Theories Concerning the Fit Between Personality and Jobs   Since most of us spend some 40 hours a week on the job—and a good deal of the rest of the time thinking about our work!—it is important to our well-being that we "fit" our jobs. As we shall see in Chapter 12, the qualities that suit us for various kinds of work can be expressed in terms of our abilities and our personalities—that is, our personality traits and our interests. By using interviews and tests to learn about our abilities and our traits, testing and counseling centers can make valuable suggestions about our likelihoods for success and fulfillment in various kinds of jobs.

Hans J. Eysenck.

Identification of Basic Traits   Sigmund Freud spoke theoretically of traits linked to his stages of psychosexual development—such as oral traits, anal-retentive traits, and anal-expulsive traits. However, trait theorists have administered broad personality tests to thousands of people and used sophisticated statistical techniques to identify the basic traits, or factors, that tend to describe us.

Numerous empirical studies (e.g., Digman & Inouye, 1986; Noller et al., 1987) suggest that there may be five basic personality factors, including a number of those suggested by Eysenck and Cattell. These include the two found by Eysenck: (1) introversion–extraversion and (2) emotional stability ("neuroticism"). The others are (3) self-control or conscientiousness, (4) tough-mindedness versus sensitivity, as suggested by Cattell, and (5) openness to new experience, which is similar to Cattell's experimenting–conservative dimension.

Pointing Out That Traits Are Reasonably Stable (Longitudinal Studies)   Research has shown that a number of personality traits seem to possess remarkable stability over the years. James Conley (1984, 1985), for example, studied psychological tests taken by a sample of adults during the 1930s, the 1950s, and again during the 1980s. Their scores on the traits of extraversion, neuroticism, and impulsiveness showed significant consistency across five decades. Ravenna Helson and Geraldine Moane (1987) analyzed personality test results of college women taken at age 21 and at ages 27 and 43. There was a good deal of stability over the decades in some traits, such as social dominance and self-control. Some traits, such as independence, increased over the years; other traits, such as flexibility, decreased. All in all, there were significant relationships over the years in most of the traits that were assessed, although the magnitude of the relationships tended to be moderate rather than strong.

Pointing Out a Role for Heredity in Traits   Psychodynamic theories seem to suggest that most traits develop in response to early childhood experiences. Oral traits develop in response to trauma encountered during the first year of life, and so on. However, many contemporary psychologists (e.g., Daniels & Plomin, 1985; DeFries et al., 1987; Scarr & Kidd, 1983) argue that basic traits such as activity level, emotional responsiveness, sociability, and impulsivity reflect strong genetic influences.

Weaknesses of Trait-Theory Approaches

Trait Theory as Descriptive, Not Explanatory   Trait theory is more descriptive than explanatory. It focuses on describing existing traits rather than tracing their origins or investigating how they may be modified.

Circular Explanations   The "explanations" provided by trait theory are often criticized as **circular explanations.** That is, they simply restate what is observed, and do not explain what is observed. Saying that John failed to ask Marsha on a date *because* of shyness is an example of a circular explanation; all we have done is to restate John's (shy) behavior as a trait (shyness).

Situational Variability in Behavior   We noted that there is a good deal of stability in several personality traits, as measured by personality tests, over the years. This is important because the concept of stability is essential to trait theory. It is a basic assumption of trait theory that human behavior tends to be largely consistent over time and from one situation to another.

But some research suggests that behavior varies more from situation to situation—at least for some people—than trait theory would allow (Bem & Allen, 1974; Mischel, 1977, 1986). People who are high in **private self-consciousness**—who carefully monitor their own behavior, even when others are not observing them—also try to show consistent behavior from situation to situation (Fenigstein et al., 1975; Scheier et al., 1978; Underwood & Moore, 1981). Other people show more variability in behavior.

The Healthy Personality

The concept of a healthy personality, from a trait-theory perspective, is expressed in terms of traits. Persons with healthy personalities are reasonably "balanced" in some traits, possess a number of traits that permit them to govern their own lives, and show reasonably few disturbing traits.

Being "Balanced"   Within Eysenck's theory, it would be healthy for individuals to be reasonably well-balanced between the extremes of introversion and extraversion. Balanced individuals would have the rich inner life necessary for contemplation and creative activity, but they would also be responsive and easy-going in their relations with other people. Well-adjusted individuals might also be somewhat balanced in terms of personality dimensions such as serious–happy-go-lucky and practical–imaginative.

Being balanced can also mean showing traits that permit one to emotionally experience the world, such as a certain degree of sensitivity and openness to new experience, and traits that permit self-direction.

Possessing Self-Regulatory Traits   Psychologically healthy individuals might possess traits such as conscientiousness, self-control, emotional stability, and self-sufficiency. These traits permit us to apply ourselves to the challenges of life and to direct our development in spite of obstacles.

Suiting Situations to One's Traits   Well-adjusted persons are also likely to seek jobs and social situations that are compatible with their traits. For example, a submissive individual is not likely to fare well in athletic contests. An imaginative, intelligent, and talented individual is likely to fare better as a creative artist than an accountant.

Changing the Unchangeable?   Let us return to the issue of the stability of traits so that we can consider what a healthful response might be for a person who has a number of counterproductive traits, such as shyness and tenseness. Is it healthful to simply be accepting and say, "That's me—that's my personality," and then settle for what your "traits" will allow? Or is it more healthful to try to change self-defeating behavior patterns, such as social withdrawal and tenseness?

In answering this question, let us recall the study by Ravenna Helson and Geraldine Moane (1987). Helson and Moane found that some people change dramatically over the years to meet the requirements of emerging

Radical behaviorist. A person who does not believe in "mind" or other mentalistic concepts.

situations. Also, some personality traits seem easier to change than others. Given that many people do, in fact, make major changes in the ways in which they respond to the demands in life, it seems most adaptive to assume that many changes are possible—if we work at them.

Rather than thinking in terms of changing embedded traits, we can think about changing, or modifying, our *behavior.* Traits, after all, are inferred from behavior. Rather than changing social withdrawal, we can work on modifying socially withdrawn *behavior.* Rather than eliminating *tenseness,* we can modify the body responses and thoughts that we associate with tenseness. If we acquire consistent new behavior patterns, aren't we, in effect, changing our traits? Even when a trait is "deeply imbedded," it might only mean that we need to work a bit harder to respond to challenges more effectively.

This is a perfect time to consider learning-theory approaches to understanding personality and behavior. Learning theories suggest that if we practice hard enough—if we work at them—new, adaptive behavior patterns can become habits. And the research on substituting socially skillful behavior for socially withdrawn behavior is encouraging. So is the research on reducing tension. Once new, adaptive behavior patterns are habitual, they might as well be new traits. Perhaps they are.

■ Learning Theories

There are a number of learning-theory approaches to understanding personality and behavior. We focus on two of them: behaviorism and social-learning theory. Behaviorism is important for its historical significance and still has many followers. But today most learning-theory-oriented psychologists identify with social-learning theory.

Behaviorism

At Johns Hopkins University in 1924, psychologist John B. Watson announced the battle cry of the **radical behaviorist** movement:

> Give me a dozen healthy infants, well-formed, and my own specified world to bring them up in and I'll guarantee to take any one at random and train him to become any type of specialist I might suggest—doctor, lawyer, merchant-chief and, yes, even beggar-man and thief, regardless of his talents, penchants, tendencies, abilities, vocations, and the race of his ancestors (p. 82).

So it was that Watson sounded the behaviorist cry that situational variables, or environmental influences—and not internal variables such as intrapsychic forces, traits, and conscious choice—shape our preferences and our behavior. Watson argued that if psychology were to be accepted as a science, unseen, undetectable mental structures must be rejected in favor of that which can be seen and measured. In the 1930s, Watson's hue and cry was taken up by B. F. Skinner, who suggests that we focus on the impact that reinforcers have upon behavior.

The radical behaviorist outlooks of John B. Watson and B. F. Skinner largely discard concepts of personal freedom, choice, and self-direction. Most of us tend to assume that our wants originate within us. But Skinner suggests that environmental influences, such as parental approval and social custom, shape us into *wanting* certain things and *not wanting* others. To Watson and Skinner, even our telling ourselves that we have free will is determined by the environment as surely as is our becoming startled at a sudden noise.

We shall return to a critical examination of the philosophical views of Watson and Skinner later. But now let us turn our attention to two basic types of learning proposed by behaviorists: classical conditioning and operant conditioning. We shall not pretend that these simple forms of learning tell the

John B. Watson.

whole story about people. However, we *can* learn by means of conditioning, and we shall see how knowledge of these types of learning has led to many innovations in helping us adjust.

Classical Conditioning

Classical conditioning, like so many other important scientific principles, was discovered by accident. The Russian physiologist Ivan Pavlov (1849–1936) was studying the biological pathways of laboratory dogs' salivation glands, but the dogs botched his results by what, at first, looked like random salivation. Upon investigation, Pavlov noticed that the dogs were actually salivating in response to things such as his assistants' entering the lab or the inadvertent clanking of metal on metal. And so Pavlov initiated an ingenious series of experiments to demonstrate that the dogs salivated in response to these things because they had been *associated* with being fed.

If you place meat on a dog's tongue, it will salivate. Salivation in response to food is a reflex—a simple form of unlearned behavior. We, too, have many reflexes, such as the well-known knee jerk in response to a tap below the knee and the eye blink in response to a puff of air.

Within learning theory, a change in the environment, such as placing meat on a dog's tongue or tapping below the knee, is called a **stimulus.** A reflex is one kind of **response** to a stimulus. Reflexes are unlearned, but they can also be associated with, or *conditioned* to, different stimuli.

Pavlov (1927) strapped a dog into a harness (see Figure 2.4). He placed meat powder on the dog's tongue, and the dog salivated. He repeated the process several times, with one difference. Each time he preceded the meat with the ringing of a bell. After several pairings of bell and meat, Pavlov rang the bell but did not present the meat. What did the dog do? It salivated anyway. The dog had learned to salivate in response to the bell because the bell had been repeatedly paired with the meat.

In this experiment, meat is an **unconditioned stimulus** (US), and salivation in response to meat is an **unconditioned response** (UR). "Unconditioned" means unlearned. At first the bell is a meaningless, or neutral, stimu-

Classical conditioning. A simple form of learning in which one stimulus comes to bring forth the response usually brought forth by a second stimulus as a result of being paired repeatedly with the second stimulus.

Stimulus. (1) A change in the environment that leads to a change in behavior (a response). (2) Any form of physical energy, like light or sound, that impinges on the sensory receptors of an organism.

Response. In behavioral theory, a movement or other observable reaction to a stimulus.

Unconditioned stimulus. A stimulus that elicits a response from an organism without learning.

Unconditioned response. An unlearned response. A response to an unconditioned stimulus.

FIGURE 2.4   Pavlov's Demonstration of Conditioned Reflexes in Laboratory Dogs

From behind this two-way mirror, a laboratory assistant rings a bell and then places meat powder on the dog's tongue. Eventually the dog salivates to the bell alone. Saliva is collected through a tube and passed to a vial, where the amount of saliva is taken as a measure of the strength of the animal's response.

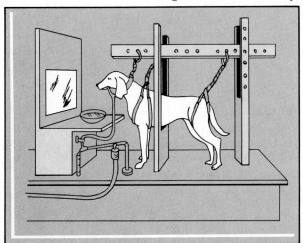

Ivan Pavlov and his staff demonstrate conditioned responses.

lus. But by being paired repeatedly with the US (meat), the bell becomes a learned or **conditioned stimulus** (CS), and it becomes capable of evoking, or eliciting, the salivation response. Salivation to the bell is a learned or **conditioned response** (CR).

Conditioning of Fears   Can you identify classical conditioning in your own life? Perhaps you automatically cringe or grimace in the waiting room when you hear the dentist's drill. The sound of the drill may have become a conditioned stimulus (CS) for conditioned responses (CRs) of muscle tension and fear. John Watson and his future wife Rosalie Rayner (1920) demonstrated how fears could be conditioned by presenting an 11-month-old lad, "Little Albert," with a laboratory rat and then clanging steel bars behind his head. At first the boy reached out to play with the animal, but after several pairings of animal and clanging, the boy cried when he saw the rat and attempted to avoid it.

Adjustment often requires responding appropriately to conditioned stimuli—stimuli that have taken on the meaning of other events. After all, if we did not learn to fear touching a hot stove after one or two pairings of seeing the reddened burner and experiencing pain, we would suffer many needless burns. If we did not learn to avoid the taste of food that nauseates us, we might become poisoned.

But adjustment can also require coping with excessive or irrational conditioned fears. If the sound, or the thought, of the drill is enough to keep you away from the dentist's office, you may wish to consider one of the fear-reduction techniques we'll discuss below and in Chapters 9 and 10.

Extinction and Spontaneous Recovery   Conditioned responses (CRs) may become "extinguished" when conditioned stimuli (CSs) are presented repeatedly but no longer paired with unconditioned stimuli (USs). Pavlov found that **extinction** of the salivation response (CR) would occur if he presented the bell (CS) repeatedly but no longer followed it with the meat (US). Extinction, too, is adaptive. After all, if your dentist becomes more skillful or uses an effective painkiller, why should the sound of the drill continue to make you cringe? If you acquire effective social skills, why should you continue to experience anxiety at the thought of meeting new people or asking someone out on a date?

However, extinguished responses may return simply as a function of the passage of time; that is, they may show **spontaneous recovery.** After Pavlov extinguished his dogs' salivation in response to a bell, they would again salivate if they heard a bell a few days later. You might cringe again in the office of the (recently painless) dentist if a year has passed between check-ups. If you haven't dated for several months, you might experience anxiety at the thought of asking someone out. Is spontaneous recovery adaptive? It seems so; as time passes, situations may change again.

Applications of Classical Conditioning: Some Methods for Reducing Fears   Principles of conditioning have led to the development of a number of innovations in solving human problems. Among these are a number of so-called *behavior-therapy* methods for reducing acquired fears.

The first method, flooding, is based on the principle of extinction. In **flooding,** a person is exposed to a fear-evoking, but harmless, stimulus until fear responses are extinguished. Watson and Rayner did not extinguish Little Albert's fear of the laboratory rat, but they might have been able to reduce or eliminate his fear by placing him in contact with the rat until fear of the animal became fully extinguished. Technically speaking, the CS (in this case, the rat) would be presented repeatedly in the absence of the US (clanging of the steel bars) until the CR (fear) became extinguished.

Although flooding is usually effective, it is unpleasant: When you are fearful of rats, being placed in a small room with one is not a holiday. For this reason, behavior therapists frequently prefer to use a second method, **systematic desensitization,** in which people are gradually exposed to fear-evoking stimuli under circumstances in which they remain relaxed. Systematic desensitization is described more fully in Chapters 9 and 10. Here let us note that systematic desensitization, like flooding, is highly effective; it takes longer to work than flooding, but the tradeoff is that it is not unpleasant.

However, psychologists are not agreed on their explanations of why systematic desensitization works. Some suggest that fear is extinguished gradually, in progressive amounts. Others explain it in terms of **counterconditioning.** Here the idea is that by remaining relaxed in the presence of fear-evoking stimuli, we are actually associating, or conditioning, the feelings of relaxation to these stimuli. The feelings of relaxation then *counteract* our fear responses—hence the term *counter*conditioning.

The principle of counterconditioning is to pair a pleasant stimulus with a fear-evoking object in order to counteract the fear response. Consider a historic application of this principle. Eating sweets is a pleasant activity for most of us (sigh), and psychologists discovered early in the century that a rabbit could be gradually introduced into a room where a boy, Peter, who feared rabbits was eating cookies (Jones, 1924). The pleasure from the cookies counteracted fear and apparently generalized to, or "rubbed off on," the rabbit, so that the animal could be brought closer gradually without causing discomfort. Eventually Peter played with it.

In classical conditioning we learn to associate stimuli, so that a simple, usually passive response evoked by one is then evoked by the other. In the

Extinction. In classical conditioning, repeated presentation of the conditioned stimulus in the absence of the unconditioned stimulus, leading to suspension of the conditioned response.

Spontaneous recovery. In classical conditioning, the eliciting of an extinguished conditioned response by a conditioned stimulus after some time has elapsed.

Flooding. A behavior-therapy technique for extinguishing fear in which a person is continuously exposed to fear-evoking, but harmless, stimulation.

Systematic desensitization. A method for reducing fears in which images of fear-evoking stimuli are presented while the person is deeply relaxed, thus leading to cessation of the fear response.

Counterconditioning. The pairing of a pleasant stimulus with a fear-evoking stimulus in order to counteract the fear response.

case of Little Albert, clanging noises were associated with a rat, so that the rat came to elicit the fear response brought forth by the noise. Let us now turn our attention to operant conditioning, in which we learn to engage in certain behavior patterns because of their effects. After classical conditioning took place, Albert's avoidance of rats would be an example of voluntary, or operant, behavior that has desired effects—in this case, allowing the boy to avoid a dreaded object and, by so doing, to avert discomforting sensations of fear. Similarly, the sight of a hypodermic syringe might elicit an involuntary fear response because a person once had a painful injection. But subsequent avoidance of injections is voluntary, operant behavior. It has the effect of reducing fear. In other cases we engage in operant behavior to attain rewards, not to avert unpleasant outcomes.

Operant Conditioning

In **operant conditioning,** an organism learns to engage in certain behavior because of the effects of that behavior. Behavior that operates upon, or manipulates, the environment in order to attain desired consequences is referred to as operant behavior.

Operant conditioning can take place mechanically with lower organisms. B. F. Skinner (1938) showed that hungry pigeons will learn to peck buttons when pecking is followed by food pellets dropping into their cages. It may take the pigeons a while to happen upon the first response (button-pecking) that is followed by food, but after the pecking–food association has occurred a few times, pecking will become fast and furious until the birds have eaten their fill. Similarly, hungry rats will learn to press levers to attain food, or for a burst of electrical stimulation in the so-called pleasure center of the brain. Later we shall see that rats will even learn to accelerate or decelerate their heart rates, when the change in rate leads to a good shot of electricity in these brain centers.

In operant conditioning, organisms are said to acquire responses or skills that lead to **reinforcment.** A reinforcement is a change in the environment (that is, a stimulus) that increases the frequency of the behavior that precedes it. A **reward,** by contrast, is defined as a *pleasant* stimulus that increases the frequency of behavior. Skinner preferred the concept of reinforcement to that of reward because it is fully defined in terms of observable behaviors and environmental contingencies. The definition of reinforcement does not rely on "mentalistic" assumptions about what another person or lower organism finds pleasant or unpleasant. However, some psychologists use the terms *reinforcement* and *reward* interchangeably.

Types of Reinforcers   Psychologists speak of various kinds of reinforcers, and it is useful to be able to distinguish among them.

Positive reinforcers increase the frequency of behavior when they are applied. Money, food, opportunity to mate, and social approval are common examples of positive reinforcers. **Negative reinforcers** increase the frequency of behavior when they are removed. Pain, anxiety, and social disapproval usually function as negative reinforcers. That is, we will usually learn to do things that lead to the removal or reduction of pain, anxiety, or the disapproval of other people.

Adjustment requires learning responses or skills that enable us to attain positive reinforcers and to avoid negative reinforcers. In the examples given, adjustment means acquiring skills that allow us to attain money, food, and social approval, and to avoid pain, anxiety, and social disapproval. *When we do not have the capacity, the opportunity, or the freedom to learn these skills, our ability to adjust is impaired.*

We can also distinguish between primary and secondary, or conditioned, reinforcers. **Primary reinforcers** have their values because of the biological

Operant conditioning. A simple form of learning in which the frequency of behavior is increased by means of reinforcement or rewards.

Reinforcement. A stimulus that increases the frequency of behavior.

Reward. A pleasant stimulus that increases the frequency of behavior.

Positive reinforcer. A reinforcer that increases the frequency of behavior when it is presented—e.g., food and approval.

Negative reinforcer. A reinforcer that increases the frequency of behavior when it is removed—e.g., pain, anxiety, and social disapproval.

Primary reinforcer. An unlearned reinforcer, such as food, water, warmth, or pain.

B. F. Skinner.

Secondary reinforcer. A stimulus that gains reinforcement value as a result of association with established reinforcers. Money and social approval are secondary reinforcers.

Punishment. An unpleasant stimulus that suppresses behavior.

makeup of the organism. We seek primary reinforcers such as food, liquid, affectionate physical contact with other people, sexual excitement and release, and freedom from pain because of our biological makeup. Conditioned reinforcers, or **secondary reinforcers,** acquire their value through association with established reinforcers. We may learn to seek money because money can be exchanged for primary reinforcers such as food and heat (or air conditioning). Or we may learn to seek social approval—another secondary reinforcer—because approval may lead to affectionate embraces or the meeting of various physical needs.

Punishment   **Punishments** are painful, or aversive, events that suppress or decrease the frequency of the behavior they follow. *Recall that* negative reinforcers *are defined in terms of increasing the frequency of behavior, although the increase occurs when the negative reinforcer is removed.*

Punishment can rapidly suppress undesirable behavior. For this reason it may be warranted in emergencies, such as when a child tries to run out into the street. But many learning theorists suggest that punishment is most often undesirable, especially in rearing children. They list reasons such as the following (Rathus, 1989):

1. Punishment does not in and of itself suggest an alternate, acceptable form of behavior. *If you must use punishment, be certain that the recipient is aware of, and has the skills to perform, alternative behaviors.*
2. Punishment tends to suppress undesirable behavior only under circumstances in which delivery is guaranteed. It does not take children long to learn that they can "get away with murder" with one parent, or one teacher, but not with another.
3. Punishments may induce people to withdraw from the situation. Severely punished children may run away, cut class, or drop out of school. Adults in punishing jobs or marriages may find it difficult to get out of bed in the morning. Or they may get a new job or a divorce.
4. Punishment can create anger and hostility. Adequate punishment will almost always suppress unwanted behavior, but at what cost? A child may express accumulated feelings of anger toward other children. A hostile employee may find subtle ways of cutting into the profit margins of the company.
5. Punishment may generalize too far. The child who is punished severely for bad table manners may stop eating altogether. Overgeneralization is more likely to occur when children do not know exactly why they are being punished, or when they have not been shown alternative, acceptable behaviors.
6. Punishment may be imitated as a way of solving problems or of coping with stress. We shall see that children learn by observing other people. Even though children may not immediately perform the behavior they observe, they may perform it later on, when they are under stress, with their own children as targets.
7. Finally, people learn responses that are punished. Whether or not children choose to perform punished responses, punishment draws their attention to them. For this reason, adults might be well-advised to ignore children's misbehavior—when possible.

It is usually preferable to focus on rewarding children and adults for desirable behavior than to punish them for misbehavior. But rewarding desirable behavior means that we must pay attention to people when they are doing what is desired, not just when they are doing things that displease us. Ironically, some children can gain the attention of the important adults in their lives only by misbehaving. In such cases, punishment may function as a positive reinforcer—that is, children may learn to misbehave in order to gain the attention of the people they care about.

We must also be certain that people know how to perform the behavior we desire. It is not enough to "expect" good behavior from children. Instead, we need to show children how to engage in behavior that we consider good, and then to reinforce them generously.

Applications of Operant Conditioning: Socialization, Biofeedback Training, and Aversive Conditioning

Operant conditioning is not just a laboratory procedure. It is used every day in the real world. Consider the **socialization** of young children. As we shall see in Chapter 3, parents and peers influence children to acquire "sex-appropriate" behavior patterns through the elaborate use of rewards and punishments. Parents also tend to praise their children for sharing and to punish them for being too aggressive. Peers participate in the socialization process by playing with children who are generous and nonaggressive and, often, by avoiding those who are not (Rathus, 1988).

The therapy techniques of biofeedback training and aversive conditioning are also based on the principle of operant conditioning. **Biofeedback training** (BFT) has been an important innovation in the treatment of health-related problems and has allowed people to gain control over **autonomic** functions, such as blood pressure and heart rate.

In a landmark series of experiments on BFT, Neal E. Miller (1969) placed electrodes in the "pleasure centers" of rats' brains. Electrical stimulation of these centers is reinforcing. The heart rates of the rats were monitored. One group of rats received electrical stimulation (reinforcement) when their heart rates increased. Another group received stimulation when their heart rates decreased. After a single 90-minute training session, the rats had altered their heart rates by as much as 20 percent in the targeted direction. Somehow laboratory rats had learned to manipulate their heart rate—an autonomic function—because of reinforcement. Human beings can also gain control over autonomic functions such as heart rate and blood pressure by means of BFT. Moreover, they can improve control over voluntary health-related functions, such as muscle tension in various parts of the body.

When people receive BFT, reinforcement takes the form of information, not electrical stimulation of the brain. The targeted biological function is monitored, by instruments such as the electroencephalograph (EEG) for brain waves, the electromyograph (EMG) for muscle tension, and the blood pressure cuff.

A "bleep" on an electronic console can change in pitch or frequency to signal a bodily change in the desired direction. Brain waves referred to as **alpha waves** tend to be emitted when we are relaxed. By pasting or taping electrodes to our scalps, and providing us with feedback about the brain waves we are emitting, we can learn to emit alpha waves more frequently—and, as a result, to feel more relaxed. The "bleep" can be sounded more frequently whenever alpha waves are emitted, and the biofeedback instructor can simply instruct clients to "make the bleep go faster." Muscle tension in the forehead or the arm can be monitored by the EMG, and people can learn to lower tension by means of "bleeps" and instructions. But lessened muscle tension is usually signaled by a slower rate of bleeping. Lowered muscle tension also induces feelings of relaxation.

Aversive conditioning has been used to help people control harmful habits, such as smoking or excessive drinking. In this method, which will be elaborated on in Chapter 9, undesired behaviors (smoking, drinking alcohol, etc.) are suppressed as a result of being paired with offensive stimuli. Classical and operant conditioning are usually conceptualized as mechanical in nature. They reflect environmental demands on the individual—what many learning theorists refer to as situational variables. They do not originate from

Socialization. The process of fostering socially acceptable behavior by means of rewards and punishments.

Biofeedback training. An operant conditioning technique in which an organism gains control over body functions as a result of receiving a flow of information about those functions.

Autonomic. Automatic. Of the autonomic nervous system. (See Chapter 6.)

Alpha waves. Brain waves associated with feelings of relaxation.

Aversive conditioning. A form of conditioning in which previously desirable objects (e.g., cigarettes, alcohol) become repugnant as a result of being paired repeatedly with aversive stimulation. The objects are then perceived as punitive rather than rewarding.

within. Let us now turn our attention to social-learning theory, which focuses on the mental, or cognitive, aspects of learning, including intentional learning by means of observing others.

Social-Learning Theory

Social-learning theory is a contemporary view of learning developed by Albert Bandura (1977, 1986) and other psychologists. It focuses on the importance of learning by observation and on the role of cognitive activity in human behavior. Social-learning theorists see people as influencing the environment, just as the environment influences them (Figure 2.5). Social-learning theorists agree with behaviorists that discussions of human nature should be tied to observable experiences and behaviors, but assert that variables within the person—person variables—must also be considered if we are to understand human personality and behavior.

In Chapter 1 it was noted that one goal of psychological theory is the prediction of behavior. Psychologist Julian B. Rotter (1972) argues that we cannot predict behavior from situational variables alone. Whether or not a person will behave in a certain way also depends upon the person's **expectancies** concerning the outcome of that behavior and the perceived or **subjective values** of those outcomes. **Generalized expectancies** are broad ex-

Social-learning theory. A cognitively oriented learning theory in which observational learning, values, and expectations play major roles in determining behavior.

Expectancies. Personal predictions about the outcomes of potential behaviors. "If-then" statements.

Subjective value. The desirability of an object or event, based upon the reinforcement history of the individual.

Generalized expectancies. Broad expectations that reflect extensive learning and are relatively resistant to change.

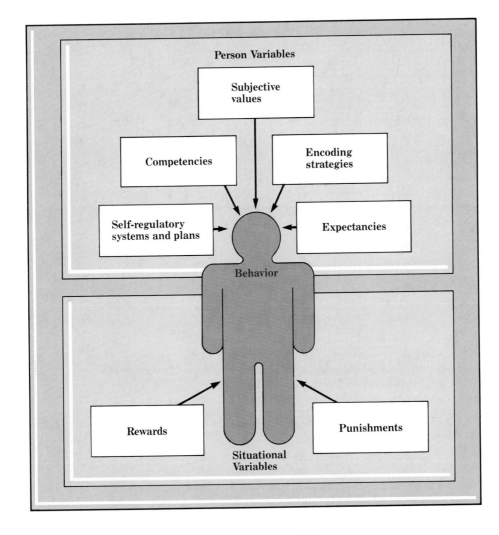

FIGURE 2.5 Person and Situational Variables

According to social-learning theory, person and situational variables interact to determine behavior.

pectations that reflect extensive learning and are relatively enduring. Their consistency and stability make them the equivalent of "traits" within social-learning theory.

To social-learning theorists, people are self-aware and intentionally engage in learning. People are not simply at the mercy of the environment. Instead, people seek to learn about their environments. People even modify and create environments so that reinforcers will be made available.

Social-learning theorists also note the importance of rules and symbolic processes in learning. Our children, for example, learn more effectively how to behave in specific situations when we as parents state the rules that are involved. In so-called **inductive** methods of discipline, parents use the specific situation to teach children about general rules and social codes that should govern their behavior. Inductive methods have also been shown to be more effective in disciplining children than punishment alone (Rathus, 1988).

Observational Learning   Observational learning (also termed **modeling)** refers to acquiring knowledge by observing others. For operant conditioning to occur, an organism (1) must engage in a response and (2) that response must be reinforced. But observational learning occurs even when the learner does not perform the observed behavior pattern, and, therefore, direct reinforcement is not required either. "Observing" others extends to reading about them or perceiving what they do and what happens to them in media such as radio, television, and film.

Our expectations of what will happen if we do something stem from our observations of what happens to others as well as our own experiences. For example, teachers are more accepting of "calling out" in class from boys than girls (Sadker & Sadker, 1985). As a result, boys frequently expect to be rewarded for calling out in class; girls, however, are more likely to expect to be reprimanded for behaving in what traditionalists might refer to as an "unladylike" manner.

Let us now consider a number of the person variables that account for individual differences in behavior in social-learning theory.

Person Variables in Social-Learning Theory   Social-learning theorists view behavior as stemming from a fluid, ongoing interaction between person and **situational variables. Person variables** include competencies, encoding strategies, expectancies, subjective values, and self-regulatory systems and plans. Our discussion of these variables follows that of Walter Mischel (1986, pp. 308–312; see Figure 2.5).

Competencies: What Can You Do?   **Competencies** include knowledge of rules that guide conduct; concepts about ourselves and other people; and skills. Our abilities to actively use information to constuct plans and plan overt behavior depend on our competencies.

Competencies include knowledge of the physical world, of cultural codes of conduct, and of the behavior patterns expected in certain situations. They include academic skills such as reading and writing; athletic skills such as swimming and tossing a football properly; social skills such as knowing how to ask someone out on a date; job skills; and many others.

There are individual differences in our competencies, based on genetic variation, nourishment, differences in learning opportunities, and other environmental factors.

Encoding Strategies: How Do You See It?   Different people **encode** (symbolize or represent) the same stimuli in different ways, and their encoding strategies are an important factor in their overt behavior. One person might encode a tennis game as a chance to bat the ball back and forth and have

Inductive. Going from the particular to the general. Descriptive of a disciplinary technique in which the individual is taught the principle involved and not merely punished.

Model. In social-learning theory, an organism that exhibits behaviors that others will imitate, or acquire, through observational learning.

Situational variables. In social-learning theory, determinants of behavior that lie outside the person.

Person variables. In social-learning theory, determinants of behavior that lie within the person.

Competencies. Knowledge and skills.

Encode. Interpret; tranform.

Self-efficacy expectations.
Beliefs to the effect that one
can handle a task.

some fun; another might encode the same game as a demand to perfect his or her serve. One person might encode a date that doesn't work out as a sign of his social incompetence; another might encode the dating experience as reflecting the fact that people are not always "made for each other." Similarly, a person who missed the opportunity to buy IBM at $50 a share may encode a current price of $120 a share as a symbol of a loss that will never be made up. A newcomer to the market may encode the price of $120 a share as an excellent buying opportunity based on projected earnings.

In Chapter 9 we shall see how people can make themselves miserable by encoding stimuli in self-defeating ways. For example, the linebacker encodes an average day on the field as a failure because he didn't get any sacks. A college student encodes one refusal to accept a date as a disaster that reflects upon his basic worth as a human being. Cognitive and behavior therapists help foster adjustment by challenging their clients to encode stimuli in more productive ways.

Expectancies: What Will Happen?   Expectancies are "if-then" statements or personal predictions about the outcome (or reinforcement contingencies) of engaging in a response. The unique human abilities to manipulate symbols and to ponder events allow us to foresee the potential consequences of our behavior. Expectancies as to what will happen if we behave in certain ways are based on our observations of others and on our own experiences in similar situations.

Competencies influence expectancies, and expectancies, in turn, influence motivation to perform. People who believe that they have the competencies required to perform effectively are more likely to try difficult tasks than people who do not believe that they can master them. Albert Bandura (1982) refers to beliefs that one can handle a task as **self-efficacy expectations.** As noted by Bandura and his colleagues Linda Reese and Nancy Adams:

> In their daily lives people must make decisions about whether to attempt risky courses of action or how long to continue, in the face of difficulties, those they have undertaken. Social-learning theory posits that . . . people tend to avoid situations they believe exceed their coping capabilities, but they undertake and perform assuredly activities they judge themselves capable of managing. . . .
>   Self-judged efficacy also determines how much of an effort people will make and how long they will keep at a task despite obstacles or adverse experiences. . . . Those who have a strong sense of efficacy exert greater effort to master the challenges . . . (1982, p. 5).

Bandura also suggests that one of the helpful aspects of psychotherapy is that it frequently changes clients' self-expectancy expectations from "I can't" to "I can." As a result, clients are motivated to try out new—and more adaptive—patterns of behavior.

Albert Bandura.

Subjective Values: What Is It Worth?   Because of our different learning histories, we may each place a different value on the same outcome. What is frightening to one person may entice another. What is desirable to one may be irresistible to another. From the social-learning perspective, as contrasted with the behaviorist perspective, we are not controlled by stimuli. Instead, stimuli have various meanings for us, and these meanings influence our behavior.

The subjective value of a particular stimulus or reward is related to experience with it or similar rewards. Experience may be direct or observational. Because of experience, our feelings about the outcome may be positive or negative. If you became nauseated the last time you drank a glass of iced tea, its subjective value as an incentive may diminish, even on a hot day.

QUESTIONNAIRE

The Expectancy for Success Scale

Life is filled with opportunities and obstacles. What happens when you are faced with a difficult challenge? Do you rise to meet it, or do you back off?

Social-learning theorists note the importance of our expectancies in influencing our behavior. Of particular importance, according to Albert Bandura, are our self-efficacy expectations. When we believe that we are capable of accomplishing difficult things through our own efforts, we marshall our resources and apply ourselves. When we believe that our efforts will pay off, we are more likely to persist.

The following scale, created by Hale and Fibel (1978) can provide you with insight as to whether you believe that your own efforts are likely to meet with success. You can compare your own expectancies for success with those of other undergraduates taking psychology courses by taking the questionnaire and turning to the scoring key at the end of the chapter.

Directions: Indicate the degree to which each item applies to you by circling the appropriate number, according to this key:

1 = highly improbable
2 = improbable
3 = equally improbable and probable, not sure
4 = probable
5 = highly probable

In the future I expect that I will

1. find that people don't seem to understand what I'm trying to say   1 2 3 4 5
2. be discouraged about my ability to gain the respect of others   1 2 3 4 5
3. be a good parent   1 2 3 4 5
4. be unable to accomplish my goals   1 2 3 4 5
5. have a stressful marital relationship   1 2 3 4 5
6. deal poorly with emergency situations   1 2 3 4 5
7. find my efforts to change situations I don't like are ineffective   1 2 3 4 5
8. not be very good at learning new skills   1 2 3 4 5
9. carry through my responsibilites successfully   1 2 3 4 5
10. discover that the good in life outweighs the bad   1 2 3 4 5
11. handle unexpected problems successfully   1 2 3 4 5
12. get the promotions I deserve   1 2 3 4 5
13. succeed in the projects I undertake   1 2 3 4 5
14. not make any significant contributions to society   1 2 3 4 5
15. discover that my life is not getting much better   1 2 3 4 5
16. be listened to when I speak   1 2 3 4 5
17. discover that my plans don't work out too well   1 2 3 4 5
18. find that no matter how hard I try, things just don't turn out the way I would like   1 2 3 4 5
19. handle myself well in whatever situation I'm in   1 2 3 4 5
20. be able to solve my own problems   1 2 3 4 5
21. succeed at most things I try   1 2 3 4 5
22. be successful in my endeavors in the long run   1 2 3 4 5
23. be very successful working out my personal life   1 2 3 4 5
24. experience many failures in my life   1 2 3 4 5
25. make a good first impression on people I meet for the first time   1 2 3 4 5
26. attain the career goals I have set for myself   1 2 3 4 5
27. have difficulty dealing with my superiors   1 2 3 4 5
28. have problems working with others   1 2 3 4 5
29. be a good judge of what it takes to get ahead   1 2 3 4 5
30. achieve recognition in my profession   1 2 3 4 5

Source: Reprinted with permission from Hale and Fibel, 1978, p. 931.

Self-Regulatory Systems and Plans: How Can You Achieve It? Social-learning theory recognizes that one of the features of being human is that we tend to regulate our own behavior, even in the absence of observers and external constraints. We set goals and standards for ourselves, construct plans for achieving them, and congratulate or criticize ourselves, depending on whether we reach them.

Self-regulation amplifies our opportunities for influencing our environments. We can select the situations to which we expose ourselves. We can select the arenas in which we shall contend. Based on our expectancies, we may choose to enter the academic or athletic worlds. We may choose marriage or the single life. And when we cannot readily select our environments, we can to some degree select our responses within an environment—even an aversive one. For example, if we are undergoing an uncomfortable medical procedure, we may try to focus on something else—the cracks in the tiles on the ceiling or an inner fantasy—to reduce the stress.

There is little doubt that learning theorists have made monumental contributions to the scientific understanding of behavior. There is equally little doubt that they have left a number of psychologists dissatisfied. Let us examine some of the strengths and weaknesses of learning-theory approaches.

Strengths of Learning-Theory Approaches

Focus on Observable Behavior Psychodynamic theorists and trait theorists propose the existence of psychological structures that cannot be seen and measured directly. Learning theorists—particularly behaviorists—have dramatized the importance of referring to publicly observable variables, or behaviors, if psychology is to be accepted as a science.

Focus on the Situation Psychodynamic theorists and trait theorists focus on internal variables, such as intrapsychic conflict and traits, in the explanation and prediction of behavior. Learning theorists have emphasized the importance of environmental conditions, or situational variables, as determinants of behavior.

Outlining of the Conditions of Learning Learning theorists have also elaborated on the conditions that foster learning—even automatic kinds of learning. They have shown that involuntary responses, including fear responses, may be conditioned, and at early ages. They have also shown how we can learn to do, and not to do, things because of environmental contingencies, or reinforcements. Moreover, social-learning theorists have shown that many broad behavior patterns are acquired by observing others.

Innovation of Behavior-Therapy and Cognitive-Therapy Methods Learning theorists have devised methods for helping individuals solve adjustment problems that probably could not have been derived from any other theoretical perspective. Consider the behavioral, extinction-based fear-reduction method of flooding and systematic desensitization, and the operant-conditioning methods of biofeedback training. Moreover, social-learning theorists have focused on the ways in which we encode our experiences and regulate our own behavior—which are cognitive issues. We shall learn more about behavior-therapy and cognitive-therapy methods in Chapter 9.

General Impact on Psychology Learning theories have probably had a broader impact on psychology than any other set of theories. They address issues ranging from learning per se, animal behavior, and motivation to child development, psychological disorders, therapy methods, and even attitude formation and change. Moreover, only learning theories overlap the psychology of human beings and lower organisms. While most forms of social learning are limited to people, conditioning applies to lower animals as well.

Weaknesses of Learning-Theory Approaches

Shortcomings of Radical Behaviorism   Radical behaviorism, which has led to many helpful innovations, cannot describe or explain the richness of human behavior. We all have the experiences of thought, of complex inner maps of the world, and behaviorism in a sense deprives us of the right to search for ways to scientifically discuss what it means to us to be human. Behaviorism also seems at a loss to explain how it is that many of us will strive, against all hardships, to fulfill distant inner visions. If we only repeat behaviors that have been reinforced, how is it that we struggle—without reinforcers—to create new works and ideas? How is it that mathematicians and composers sit motionless for hours, then suddenly write new formulas and symphonies?

Shortcomings of Social-Learning Theory   Critics of social-learning theory do not accuse its supporters of denying the import of cognitive activity. But they might contend that social-learning theory has not derived satisfying statements about the development of traits and accounted for self-awareness. Social-learning theory—like its intellectual forebear, radical behaviorism—has also not always paid sufficient attention to genetic variation in explaining individual differences in behavior. Learning theories do very little to account for the development of traits or personality types.

Social-learning theorists seem to be working on a number of these theoretical issues. Today's social-learning theorists view people as active, not as mechanical reactors to environmental pressures (as Watson saw them). Cognitive functioning is clearly considered an appropriate area of study by social-learning theorists (Bandura, 1986; Wilson, 1982). In the area of psychological disorders, social-learning theorists Gerald Davison and John Neale (1986) may speak for many of their fellows when they suggest that inherited or physiological factors often interact with situational stress to give rise to abnormal behavior.

The Healthy Personality

Learning theorists do not usually speak in terms of a healthy personality, since a personality cannot be observed or measured directly. They prefer to speak in terms of behavior, and behavior tends to be viewed as "adaptive" or "productive," rather than "healthy." Nevertheless, learning theory is rich with concepts that describe adaptive and productive behavior. Some of them are noted below.

Learning of Appropriate Emotional Responses   Ideally, we should learn to anticipate positive events with pleasure and potentially harmful events with fear. In this way we shall be motivated to approach desirable stimuli and to avoid noxious stimuli. Fears should be sufficient to warn of real danger, but not excessive, such that they inhibit necessary exploration of the self and the environment.

Rich Opportunities for Observational Learning   Since most human learning occurs by observing others, it is desirable for us to be exposed to a diversity of models. In this way we can form complex, comprehensive views of the social and physical world.

Learning of Competencies   Getting along and getting ahead require competencies—that is, knowledge and skills. Competencies are acquired by combinations of observational learning and operant conditioning. We require accurate, efficient models and the opportunities to practice and improve skills.

Accurate Encoding of Events We need to encode events accurately and productively. One failure should not be magnified as a sign of total incompetence; a social provocation may be better encoded as a problem to be solved than an injury that must be avenged.

Accurate Expectations and Positive Self-Efficacy Expectancies Accurate expectancies enhance the probability that our efforts will pay off. Positive self-efficacy expectancies increase our motivation and persistence in tackling difficult challenges.

Subjective Values It is useful for the subjective values we assign objects to be proportionate to our needs. Then we shall pursue the things we need, and we shall not dissipate our efforts by running after those that we do not.

Methodical and Efficient Self-Regulatory Systems Methodical, efficient self-regulatory systems facilitate our performances. For example, thoughts such as "One step at a time" and "Don't get bent out of shape" help us to cope with difficulties and pace ourselves.

And so, learning theories, despite their focus on behavior rather than personality, offer numerous suggestions for fostering a "healthy personality." Now let us turn our attention to phenomenological theories, which, like social-learning theory, emphasize cognitive processes and conscious experience.

■ Phenomenological Theories

In this section we discuss three **phenomenological** approaches to personality: the theories of Abraham Maslow, Carl Rogers, and George Kelly. They have a number of things in common: each proposes that the personal, or subjective, experiencing of events is the most important aspect of human nature. Each proposes that we as individuals are our own best experts on ourselves. Each proposes that we have unique ways of looking at the world.

Abraham Maslow and the Challenge of Self-Actualization

Maslow's views owe much to the European school of philosophy called **existentialism,** which holds that we are free to choose and so adaptable that human nature is whatever we believe it to be. Existentialists asserted that the main task of life is to come to grips with the experiences of being mortal and free to choose. It is up to us to make our lives meaningful by exercising free will and seeking goals and values that lead to individual fulfillment.

Maslow believed that we each have needs for **self-actualization**—to become whatever we are capable of being. He also believed that each of us is unique, and thus no two people can follow exactly the same path to self-actualization. Expressing our unique potentials, finding fulfillment, requires setting out to some degree on our own—taking risks. Otherwise, our lives may degenerate into the drab and the routine.

On Becoming a Self-Actualizer: How About You? Maslow attributed the following eight characteristics to the self-actualizing individual. How many of them are characteristic of you? Why not check them and undertake some honest self-evaluation? Self-actualizers:

1. *Fully experience life in the present—the here and now.* They do not focus excessively on the lost past or wish their lives away as they stride down the path toward distant goals.

Phenomenological. Having to do with subjective experience

Existentialism. A philosophical view which holds that people are free to make choices and are responsible for their own behavior.

Self-actualization. In humanistic theory, the innate tendency to strive to realize one's potential. Self-initiated striving to become all one is capable of being.

Boston Celtic star Larry Bird wins a trophy. Maslow believed that we are all unique, but that we each have a need for self-actualization—to become all we are capable of being. Bird's accomplishments on the court reflect his genetically based talents and his drive to develop them.

Peak experience. In humanistic theory, a brief moment of rapture that stems from the realization that one is on the path to self-actualization.

Hierarchy of needs. Maslow's progression from basic, physiological needs to social needs to aesthetic and cognitive needs.

2. *Make growth choices rather than fear choices.* Self-actualizers take reasonable risks to develop their unique potentials. They do not bask in the dull life of the status quo. They do not "settle."

3. *Acquire self-knowledge.* Self-actualizers look inward; they search for values, talents, and meaningfulness. (The questionnaires in this book offer a decent jumping-off point for getting to know yourself. It might also be enlightening to take an "interest inventory"—a test frequently used to help make career decisions—at the college testing and counseling center.)

4. *Strive toward honesty in interpersonal relationships.* Self-actualizers strip away the social facades and games that stand in the way of self-disclosure and the formation of intimate relationships.

5. *Become self-assertive and express their own ideas and feelings, even at the risk of occasional social disapproval.*

6. *Strive toward new goals and strive to become the best in a chosen life role.* Self-actualizers do not live by the memory of past accomplishments; nor do they give second-rate efforts.

7. *Become involved in meaningful and rewarding life activities in order to experience brief moments of actualization referred to as* **peak experiences.** Peak experiences are brief moments of rapture filled with personal meaning. Examples might include completing a work of art, falling in love, redesigning a machine tool, suddenly solving a complex problem in math or physics, or having a baby. Again, we differ as individuals, and one person's peak experience might bore another person silly.

8. *Remain open to new experiences.* Self-actualizers do not hold themselves back for fear that novel experiences might shake their views of the world, or of right and wrong. Self-actualizers are willing to revise their expectations, values, and opinions.

The Hierarchy of Needs: What Do You Do When You're No Longer Hungry?

Phenomenological psychologists accuse Freud of getting stuck in the basement of the human condition by focusing so heavily on the roles of primitive drives, such as sex and aggression. Maslow believed that there was an order, or **hierarchy of needs,** that ranges from basic biological needs, such as hunger and thirst, to self-actualization (see Figure 2.6).

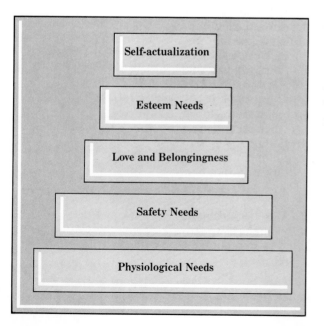

FIGURE 2.6   Maslow's Hierarchy of Needs

Maslow believed that we progress toward higher psychological needs once basic survival needs have been met. Where do you fit in this picture?

Gestalt. In this usage, a quality of wholeness.

Frame of reference. One's unique patterning of perceptions and attitudes, according to which one evaluates events.

Freud saw all motivation as stemming from the id, and he argued that our ideas that we have conscious and noble intentions were defensive and self-deceiving. By contrast, Maslow saw all levels of needs as equally valid and real. Maslow believed that once we had met our lower-level needs, we would be motivated to fulfill higher-order needs for personal growth. We do not simply snooze away the hours until lower-order needs stir us to act again. In fact, some of us—as in the stereotype of the "struggling artist"—will sacrifice basic comforts in order to devote ourselves to higher-level needs.

Maslow's hierarchy of needs includes:

1. *Biological needs.* Water, food, elimination, warmth, rest, avoidance of pain, sexual release, and so forth.
2. *Safety needs.* Protection from the physical and social environment by means of clothing, housing, and security from crime and financial hardship.
3. *Love and belongingness needs.* Love and acceptance through intimate relationships, social groups, and friends. Maslow believed that in a well-fed and well-housed society, a principal source of maladjustment lay in the frustration of needs at this level.
4. *Esteem needs.* Achievement, competence, approval, recognition, prestige, status.
5. *Self-actualization.* Personal growth, the development of our unique potentials. At the highest level are also found needs for cognitive understanding (as found in novelty, understanding, exploration, and knowledge) and aesthetic experience (as found in order, music, poetry, and art).

How far have your personal growth and development proceeded up through the hierarchy of needs? At what levels have you adequately met your needs? What levels are you attacking now?

Carl Rogers' Self Theory

"My experience in therapy and in groups makes it impossible for me to deny the reality and significance of human choice. To me it is not an illusion that man is to some degree the architect of himself," wrote Carl Rogers (1974, p. 119). According to Rogers, people tend to shape themselves through freedom of choice and action.

Rogers' views are labeled "self theory" because of his focus on the self as an "organized, consistent, conceptual **gestalt** composed of perceptions of the characteristics of the 'I' or 'me' and the perceptions of the relationships of the 'I' or 'me' to others and to various aspects of life, together with the values attached to these perceptions" (1959, p. 200). Your self is your center of experience. It is your ongoing sense of who and what you are, your sense of how and why you react to the environment, and how you choose to act upon the environment. Your choices are made on the basis of your values, and your values are also parts of your self.

To Rogers the sense of self is inborn, or innate. The self provides the experience of being human in the world. It is the guiding principle behind personality structure and behavior. One of the most important aspects of the self is the self-concept.

The Self-Concept and Frames of Reference   Our self-concepts are our impressions of ourselves and our evaluations of our adequacy.

Rogers stated that we all have unique ways of looking at ourselves and the world, or unique **frames of reference.** It may be that we each use a different set of dimensions in defining ourselves, and that we judge ourselves according to different sets of values. To one person achievement–failure may be the most important dimension. To another person the most important dimension may be decency–indecency. A third person may not even think in terms of decency.

Self-Esteem and Positive Regard Rogers assumes that we all develop a need for self-regard or **self-esteem** as we develop and become self-aware. Self-esteem at first reflects the esteem others hold us in. Parents help children develop self-esteem when they show them **unconditional positive regard**—accept them as having intrinsic merit regardless of their behavior of the moment. But when parents show children **conditional positive regard**—accept them only when they behave in a desired manner—they may learn to disown the thoughts, feelings, and behaviors that parents have rejected. Conditional positive regard may lead children to develop **conditions of worth,** to think that they are worthwhile only if they behave in certain ways.

Rogers, like Maslow, saw each of us as having a unique potential. Therefore, children who develop conditions of worth must wind up somewhat disappointed in themselves. We cannot fully live up to the wishes of others and remain true to ourselves. This does not mean that the expression of the self inevitably leads to conflict. In fact, Rogers—in contrast to Freud—was optimistic about human nature. Rogers believed that we hurt others or act in antisocial ways only when we are frustrated in our efforts to develop our potential. But when parents and others are loving and tolerant of our differentness, we, too, shall be loving—even if some of our preferences, abilities, and values differ from those of our parents.

But children in some families learn that it is bad to have ideas of their own, especially about sexual, political, or religious matters. When they perceive their parents' disapproval, they may come to see themselves as rebels and label their feelings as selfish, wrong, or evil. If they wish to retain a consistent self-concept, and self-esteem, they may have to deny many of their genuine feelings, or disown parts of themselves. In this way the self-concept becomes distorted. According to Rogers, anxiety often stems from partial perception of feelings and ideas that are inconsistent with the distorted self-concept. Since anxiety is unpleasant, we may deny that these feelings and ideas exist.

According to Rogers, the path to self-actualization requires getting in touch with our genuine feelings, accepting them as ours, and acting upon them. This is the goal of Rogers' method of psychotherapy, person-centered therapy, which we shall discuss in Chapter 9. Here suffice it to say that person-centered therapists provide an atmosphere in which clients can cope with the anxiety that may attend focusing on disowned parts of the self.

Rogers also believes that we have mental images of what we are capable of becoming, or **self-ideals.** We are motivated to reduce the **discrepancy** between our self-concepts and our self-ideals. But as we undertake the process of actualizing ourselves, our self-ideals may gradually grow more complex. Our goals may become higher or change in quality. The self-ideal is something like a carrot dangling from a stick strapped to a burro's head. The burro strives to reach the carrot, as though it were a step or two away, without recognizing that its own progress also causes the carrot to advance. Our own forward movement creates more distant goals. It may be that we are happiest when our goals seem attainable, almost within our grasp, and we are striving with confidence to achieve them. We may never be completely satisfied with what we attain, but, according to Rogers, the process of striving to meet meaningful goals, the good struggle, yields happiness.

George Kelly's Psychology of Personal Constructs

Psychodynamic theorists view personality in terms of motives and internal conflicts. Trait theorists view personality in terms of, well, traits. Learning theorists view personality in terms of overt behavior and ways of learning. Phenomenological theorists view personality in terms of the ways in which people view their own experiences. George Kelly (1955, 1958), a phenomenologist, believed that people view their experiences in terms of their **personal**

Self-esteem. One's evaluation and valuing of oneself.

Unconditional positive regard. A persistent expression of esteem for the value of a person, but not necessarily an unqualified acceptance of all of the person's behaviors.

Conditional positive regard. Judgment of another person's value on the basis of the acceptability of that person's behaviors.

Conditions of worth. Standards by which the value of a person is judged.

Discrepancy. Lack of agreement, inconsistency.

Self-ideal. A mental image of what we believe we ought to be.

Personal construct. A psychological dimension according to which we categorize ourselves and others.

Carl Rogers.

constructs. A personal construct is a psychological dimension according to which we categorize ourselves and others. Extraversion–introversion is a construct of importance to Eysenck. In Chapter 3 we shall see that strong–weak is a construct of more relevance to males than females in our culture.* According to Kelly, people are motivated to understand, anticipate, and control the events in their lives. People try to use constructs that allow them to anticipate and control events.

Unique
According to Maslow and Rogers, each of us is unique. Each of us has a unique potential, and no two of us can follow the same path to self-actualization.

Alternate Constructions   To know the individual, wrote Kelly, we must learn how the individual categorizes and interprets experience—how the individual construes events. People construe the same event in different ways, as in the example offered by Walter Mischel:

> A boy drops his mother's favorite vase. What does it mean? The event is simply that the vase has been broken. Yet ask the child's psychoanalyst and he may point to the boy's unconscious hostility. Ask the mother and she tells you how "mean" he is. His father says he is "spoiled." The child's teacher may see the event as evidence of the child's "laziness" and chronic "clumsiness." Grandmother calls it just as "accident." And the child himself may construe the event as reflecting his "stupidity" (1986, pp. 207–208).

Different ways of construing the same event—that is, alternate constructions of the event—lead to different emotional reactions and, perhaps, to different courses of action. In Chapter 8 we shall see why the boy's construing the event as evidence of his "stupidity" could well be linked to depression. Whereas some psychoanalyst might wonder whether the dropping of the vase reflected unconscious motives, George Kelly might try to point out to the boy that his way of construing the event is not *convenient* for him. Kelly did not believe that there is one absolutely true way of construing events. Instead, he believed that when our constructions of events make us miserable and do not lead to productive behavior, we might be well advised to seek an alternative construction.

Role Playing   Psychoanalysts see our characters as formed by early life experiences. Trait theorists see our traits as generally stable and steering us to behave in similar ways in different situations. Some learning theorists view us as creatures of habit; others suggest that "generalized expectancies" might lead to stability in behavior in many situations. Kelly, by contrast, saw people as capable of continuous change, as capable of enacting different roles. If the roles we have assumed in life are making us miserable, Kelly believed that we can make broad, sweeping changes in the ways in which we construe the world and behave from day to day.

The construct of strong–weak is central to the self-evaluations of many men and, today, to a number of women as well.

Phenomenological theories usually have tremendous appeal for college students because of their optimistic views of human nature and their focus on the importance of personal experience. Phenomenological ideas sort of "invaded" the popular culture during the 1970s, which has been referred to by some as the "Me Decade." These views gave birth to the so-called human-potential movement, which was especially well-received in centers such as California and New York. A spate of phenomenologically oriented therapies and groups entered our consciousness, including movements based on Maslow and Rogers' ideas, Gestalt therapy, transactional analysis (TA), encounter groups, microgroups, marathon groups, and so on. Hundreds of thousands

*Women are also likely to use the construct strong–weak in making some evaluations, but their own self-esteem is less likely to be wrapped up in how strong they are. One of the reasons that women body-builders are looked upon by some people as "strange" is that the construct strong–weak is extremely important to their self-evaluations and their evaluations of other women.

of people went off in a flurry of directions in order to "get in touch" with their "genuine" feelings and talents and to actualize their potentials.

But the same factors that account for the appeal of phenomenological approaches have led to their criticism by many psychologists as unscientific. Let us examine some of the strengths and weaknesses of these approaches and then see what phenomenological theorists have to say about the healthy personality.

Strengths of Phenomenological Approaches

Focus on Conscious Experience   The things we are likely to treasure most in the world are our conscious experiences (our "selves") and those (the "selves") of the people whom we care about. For lower organisms, to be alive is to move, to process food, to exchange oxygen and carbon dioxide, and to reproduce one's kind. But for human beings, the essential aspect of being alive is having conscious experience—the sense of one's self as progressing through space and time. Only phenomenological theorists grant consciousness the central role it seems to occupy in our daily lives, and there is some merit to finding such a "fit" between psychology and the experiences of people.

Phenomenological Theory Sets Us Free   Psychodynamic theories see us largely as victims of our childhoods, whereas learning theories, to some degree, see us as "victims of circumstances"—or, at least, as victims of situational variables. Some trait theorists seem to see us as victims of our genetic codes. But phenomenological theorists envision us as free to make choices. Psychodynamic theorists and learning theorists wonder whether a sense of freedom is merely an illusion; phenomenological theorists begin with an assumption of personal freedom.

Innovations in Therapy Methods   Some of the peripheral approaches that were so popular during the 1970s may have, so to speak, come and gone. However, each of the phenomenological theorists we have discussed has made important innovations and contributions to the practice of psychotherapy. Of these the best-known and most influential innovation is undoubtedly **person-centered therapy,** the type of therapy originated by Carl Rogers.

In person-centered therapy, as we shall see in Chapter 9, the person "undergoing treatment" takes the lead. The "therapist" essentially provides a warm, encouraging atmosphere so that the person will feel free to engage in self-exploration and make choices.

Elements of Kelly's thinking have found their way into cognitive theories of psychological disorders (see Chapter 8) and into cognitive-therapy approaches (see Chapter 9). As in the example of the boy who broke the vase, it has been shown that the ways in which we construe our failures and shortcomings are linked to our emotional responses.

Weaknesses of Phenomenological Approaches

Focus on Conscious Experience   It is ironic that the primary strength of the phenomenological approaches—their focus on conscious experience—is also their primary weakness. Conscious experience is private and subjective. It cannot be detected by direct observation and measurement. From the viewpoint of outsiders, consciousness is what consciousness does. That is, my consciousness can only be known to you in terms of your observation of my behavior. Therefore, as the behaviorists pointed out many years ago, it can be unscientific to formulate theories in terms of consciousness.

The Concept of Self-Actualization   The concept of self-actualization—so important to Maslow and Rogers—cannot be proved or disproved. Like an id, or a trait, a self-actualizing force cannot be observed or measured directly. It must be inferred from its supposed effects.

Failure to Account for Traits   Phenomenological theories, like learning theories, have little to say about the development of traits and personality types. Maslow and Rogers assume that we are all unique, but do not predict the sorts of traits, abilities, and interests we shall develop.

The Healthy Personality

Phenomenological theorists have literally spoken volumes about the healthy personality. In fact, their focus has been on the functioning of the psychologically healthy individual. Let us consider a number of the qualities shown by psychologically healthy people. According to the phenomenological theorists we have discussed, persons with a healthy personality:

Experience Life Here and Now   They do not dwell excessively on the past or wish their days away as they strive toward future happiness. (Maslow, Rogers)

Are Open to New Experience   They do not turn away from ideas and ways of life that might challenge their own perceptions of the world and values. (Maslow, Rogers)

Express Their Feelings and Ideas   They assert themselves in interpersonal relationships and are honest about their feelings. They show integrity or congruence: There is a fit between their ideas, feelings, and behavior. (Maslow, Rogers)

Trust Their Intuitive Feelings   They believe in their own inner goodness and are not afraid of their urges and impulses. (Maslow, Rogers)

Engage in Meaningful Acitivities   They strive to live up to their self-ideals, to enact fulfilling roles. As a result, they may have "peak experiences"—moments of rapture that tell them they are on the right path. (Maslow, Rogers, Kelly)

Are Capable of Making Major Changes in Their Lives   They can find more convenient ways to interpret experiences, strive toward new goals, and act with freedom. (Maslow, Rogers, Kelly)

Are Their Own Persons   They have developed their own values and their own ways of construing events. As a consequence they take risks and can anticipate and control events.

And so each of the major approaches to understanding personality and behavior has a number of strengths to recommend it, and a number of drawbacks, or at least questionmarks. These approaches continue to evolve and, in some cases, to test their boundaries with other approaches.

■ Some Concluding Thoughts about Theories of Personality and Behavior

The phenomenological approach is usually preferred by students. It reflects our beliefs that we are aware of ourselves and the world around us, and it places self-awareness at the heart of things. For another, phenomenological theory seems to suggest that we can become whatever we want to be. Phenomenological theory seems to assert that we are in full command of our selves and our futures.

But the facts of human life suggest that we are not always in full command of ourselves and our futures. We might generally attribute far too much control to the individual, as we shall see in Chapter 4. Under unusual and stressful circumstances, we might find ourselves behaving in ways that are alarming to us, as we shall see in Chapter 5. In that chapter, which explores social influences on behavior, we shall see that we sometimes are victims of circumstances, even when we assume that we remain in charge.

And so, despite their diversity, each personality theory might touch on meaningful aspects of human nature. What if we were simply to put together a list of some of the basic ideas set forth by these theories? Each item on the list might not apply equally to everyone, but such a list might reflect something of what we see in ourselves and others. Let's try it out:

1. We make assumptions about personality traits based on the behavior we see in ourselves and others.
2. Our behavior is reasonably consistent under run-of-the-mill circumstances, but can differ markedly in extreme situations.
3. Early childhood experiences can have lasting influences upon us.
4. Our cognitive processes can be distorted, so that we see what we want to see and hear what we want to hear.
5. We are influenced by our circumstances as well as by inner preferences, talents, and emotional conflicts.
6. Our experiences can lead us to anticipate events with pleasure or apprehension.
7. We generally seek rewards and avoid punishments.
8. We model much of our behavior after that of people we observe.
9. We are more likely to persevere in difficult tasks when we believe that our efforts will pay off.
10. Our conceptions of who we are and what we can do have powerful influences on our behavior.
11. Life can seem gray and dismal to us when we are involved in humdrum, meaningless activities.
12. Each of us has something unique to offer, although it may not seem very important to other people.
13. We are to some degree the architects of ourselves.
14. When we close ourselves off to new experiences, we are less likely to find things that are of value to us and to develop as individuals.
15. We try to become like our mental images of what we are capable of being.
16. We try to anticipate and control events.
17. Our responses to events are influenced by the ways in which we interpret events.
18. Developing as an individual can mean taking risks—moving beyond "the tried and the true."

If it strikes you that there is truth in each of these statements, then perhaps each approach to understanding personality and behavior tells us something of value. Each theory views the "elephant" from a different perspective, but each might shed some valuable light on aspects of human nature.

In the next chapter we shall explore the contributions of gender to the understanding of personality and behavior—and to the fostering of adjustment and personal growth. We don't want to "give the chapter away" at this point, but it might be worth mentioning that we shall conclude that assuming the stereotypical masculine and feminine roles does *not* necessarily guarantee the development of a healthy personality. In fact, overly masculine men and overly feminine women might be somewhat handicapped.

■ Summary

1. **What does *personality* mean?** Personality can be defined as the reasonably stable patterns of behavior that distinguish people from one another and characterize a person's ways of adjusting to the demands of life.

2. **What are the major features of the psychodynamic view of personality and behavior?** Sigmund Freud's psychodynamic view of personality suggests that our behavior is determined by the outcome of internal and largely unconscious conflict. Conflict is inevitable as the primitive instincts of sex and aggression come up against social pressures to follow laws, rules, and moral codes.

3. **What are the three psychic structures and how do they function?** The unconscious id represents psychological drives and operates according to the pleasure principle. The ego is the sense of self, or "I," and operates according to the reality principle. So-called defense mechanisms protect the ego from anxiety by repressing unacceptable ideas or distorting reality. The superego operates according to the moral principle. The superego acts like a conscience, handing out judgments of right and wrong.

4. **What are the stages of psychosexual development?** People undergo psychosexual development as psychosexual energy, or libido is transferred from one erogenous zone to another. There are five stages of psychosexual development: the oral, anal, phallic, latency, and genital stages.

5. **What important events take place during each stage?** Freud believed that each stage would bring conflict. During the oral stage, conflict would center on the nature and extent of oral gratification, and issues such as weaning. Conflict during the anal stage would concern toilet training and the general issue of self-control. Fixation in a stage may lead to the development of traits associated with that stage. An oral fixation is revealed by traits such as dependency and gullibility. Anal fixation may result in extremes of cleanliness vs. messiness, or of perfectionism vs. carelessness.

6. **What are the Oedipus and Electra complexes?** The Oedipus and Electra complexes are conflicts of the phallic stage. In these conflicts, children long to possess the parent of the opposite sex and resent the parent of the same sex. Under normal circumstances, these complexes eventually become resolved by identifying with the parent of the same sex. The latency stage is a period of life during which Freud believed sexual feelings remain largely unconscious. Freud believed that we enter the genital stage at puberty, and during this stage, the incest taboo motivates us to displace sexual impulses onto adults or adolescents of the opposite sex.

7. **How do Carl Jung's views differ from Freud's?** Jung downplayed the importance of the sexual instinct. He also believed in the Self, a unifying force in the personality that provides us with direction and purpose.

8. **How do Alfred Adler's views differ from Freud's?** Adler believed that people are basically motivated by an inferiority complex, and that this complex gives rise to a compensating drive for superiority.

9. **How do Karen Horney's views differ from Freud's?** Horney, like Freud, saw parent-child relationships as paramount in importance, but was more optimistic that children can overcome early emotional hardships.

10. **What are the basic ideas in Erik Erikson's theory of psychosocial development?** Erikson highlights the importance of early social relationships rather than the gratification of childhood sexual impulses. Erikson extended Freud's five developmental stages to eight.

11. **What are traits?** Traits are personality elements that are inferred from behavior. Traits account for consistent behavior.

12. **How did Raymond Cattell distinguish between surface traits and source traits?** According to Cattell, surface traits are characteristic ways of behaving that seem linked in an orderly manner. Source traits are underlying traits from which surface traits are derived.

13. **What are Hans Eysenck's dimensions of personality?** Eysenck has focused on the relationship between two source traits: introversion–extraversion and emotional stability.

14. **What are the views of the behaviorists?** John B. Watson, the father of modern behaviorism, rejected notions of mind and personality altogether. Watson and B. F. Skinner discarded notions of personal freedom, and argued that environmental contingencies can shape people into wanting to do the things that the physical environment and society require of them. Behaviorists explain behavior in terms of classical conditioning and operant conditioning.

15. **How does social-learning theory differ from behaviorism?** Social-learning theory has a strong cognitive orientation and focuses on the importance of learning by observation. Social-learning theorists do not consider only situational rewards and punishments important in the prediction of behavior. They also consider the roles of person variables. Person variables include competencies, encoding strategies, expectancies, subjective values, and self-regulatory systems and plans. Self-efficacy expectancies concern the degree to which we believe our efforts will result in a positive outcome, and they have an impact on our motivation to try the difficult.

16. **What do phenomenological theories of personality have in common?** They each propose that the personal, or subjective, experiencing of events is the most important aspect of human nature. They also propose that we each have unique ways of perceiving the world.

17. **What are the major ideas of Abraham Maslow's phenomenological theory?** Maslow believed that we are motivated by self-actualization—the urge to become everything we are capable of being. He stated that people traveled up through a hierarchy of needs, with biological needs at the bottom and self-actualization at the top.

18. **What are the major ideas of Carl Rogers' self theory?** According to Rogers, the self is an innate, organized, and consistent way in which a person perceives his or her "I" to relate to others and the world. The self attempts to develop its unique potential when the person receives unconditional positive regard.

19. **What are the major ideas of George Kelly's theory of personal constructs?** According to Kelly theory, we all function as scientists; we all attempt to explain and predict behavior. Kelly believed that we view our experiences in terms of personal constructs. To understand people, we must know how they construe events.

■ TRUTH OR FICTION REVISITED

According to psychodynamic theory, the human mind is like a vast submerged iceberg, only the tip of which rises above the surface into awareness. True. This statement in consistent with Freud's psychodynamic theory, which proposes the existence of an unconscious psychic structure (the id) and a partly unconscious psychic structure (the ego). However, empirical evidence does not confirm the existence of these structures.

Biting one's fingernails or smoking cigarettes as an adult is a sign of conflict during very early childhood. Probably not. This statement is consistent with the psychodynamic view that adult problems can reflect fixations during early stages of psychosexual development. But again, empirical evidence does not confirm this view.

It is normal for boys to be hostile toward their fathers. Probably not. We have another statement consistent with Freud's views—in this case, his views concerning the Oedipus complex. However, as pointed out by neoanalyst Karen Horney, Freud's views on the Oedipus complex are speculative.

Psychologists have studied human personality by reading the dictionary. True. Allport, for example, used the dictionary to derive a preliminary list of personality traits.

Human behavior is largely consistent from situation to situation. Not necessarily. However, people high in private self-consciousness attempt to behave consistently.

Traits such as emotional responsiveness and sociability show genetic influences. True. Their patterns of appearance are closely related to patterns of kinship.

According to behaviorists, we may believe that we have freedom of choice, but our preferences and choices are actually forced upon us by the environment. True. This statement is consistent with the behaviorist view that behavior, including preferences, is situationally determined, but social-learning theorists argue that people modify and create environments in addition to simply conforming to environmental demands.

Psychologists helped a young boy overcome his fear of rabbits by having him eat cookies as a rabbit was brought nearer. True. In this way University of California psychologist Mary Cover Jones counterconditioned fear of rabbits in a lad named Peter.

Reinforcement is essential if learning is to occur. False. Observational learning occurs in the absence of reinforcement.

We are more motivated to tackle difficult tasks if we believe that we shall succeed at them. True. Positive self-efficacy expectancies motivate us to take on challenges.

You can learn to raise your heart rate or lower your blood pressure by being hooked up to a machine that "bleeps" when you make the desired response. True. The method described is referred to as biofeedback training.

We all have unique ways of looking at ourselves and at the world outside. Since all of us, with the exception of identical twins, are genetically unique, this assertion is probably accurate. It is also consistent with phenomenological theories of personality.

■ Scoring Key for the Expectancy-for-Success Scale

In order to calculate your total score for the expectancy-for-success scale, first reverse the scores for the following items: 1, 2, 4, 6, 7, 8, 14, 15, 17, 18, 24, 27, and 28. That is, change a 1 to a 5; a 2 to a 4; leave a 3 alone; change a 4 to a 2; and a 5 to a 1. Then add the scores.

The range of total scores can vary from 30 to 150. The higher your score, the greater your expectancy for success in the future—and, according to social-learning theory, the more motivated you will be to apply yourself in facing difficult challenges.

Fibel and Hale administered their test to undergraduates taking psychology courses and found that women's scores ranged from 65 to 143 and men's from 81 to 138. The average score for each gender was 112 (112.32 for women and 112.15 for men).

Sex Roles and
Sex Differences

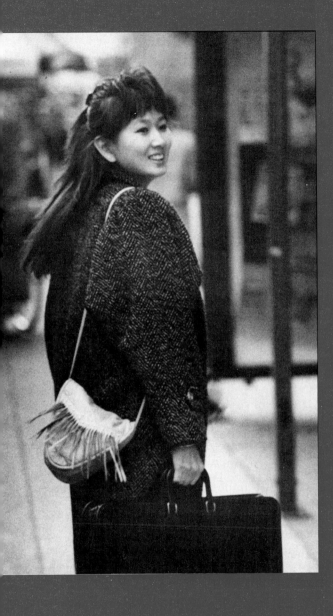

Women are expected to be more vain than men.

An essay written by a woman is poorer in quality than an essay written by a man—even when it is the same essay.

Teachers are more likely to accept calling out in class from boys than from girls.

Women are superior to men in verbal abilities.

Men have greater math and spatial-relations abilities than women do.

Men behave more aggressively than women do.

Men are more likely than women to curse.

Women prefer to sit next to their friends, whereas men prefer to sit across from them.

Adolescents who reach sexual maturity early tend to have greater verbal skills than those who reach sexual maturity at later ages.

Parents treat sons and daughters differently, even when they are under one year of age.

A 2½-year-old may know that he is a boy but think that he can grow up to be a mommy.

Five- and 6-year-olds tend to distort their memories so that they "remember" boys playing with trains and sawing wood—even when these activities were actually carried out by girls.

Throughout most of human history, girls were considered unsuited to education.

The children of working women are less well adjusted than the children of women who remain in the home.

Working women remain more likely than their husbands to do the cooking and take care of the laundry, even when the women are presidents or vice presidents of their companies.

Adolescent girls who show a number of masculine traits are more popular than girls who thoroughly adopt the traditional feminine sex role.

Two children were treated at Johns Hopkins University Hospital for the same disorder. But the treatments and the outcomes were vastly different. Each child was genetically female, and each had the internal sex organs of a girl. But because of excessive exposure to male sex hormones while they were being carried by their mothers, each had developed external sex organs that resembled a boy's (Money & Ehrhardt, 1972).

The problem was identified in one child (let's call her Deborah) at a very early age. The masculinized sex organs were surgically removed when she was 2 years old. Like many other girls, Deborah was tomboyish during childhood, but she was always feminine in appearance and had a female **gender identity.** She dated boys, and her fantasies centered around marriage to a man.

The other child (let's call him Mitch) was at first mistaken for a genetic male whose external sex organs were stunted. This error was discovered at the age of 3½. But by then Mitch had a firm male gender identity. So instead of undergoing surgery to remove his external sex organs, Mitch had surgery to further masculinize them. At puberty, hormone therapy fostered the development of body hair, male musculature, and other male **secondary sex characteristics.**

As an adolescent, Mitch did poorly in school. Possibly in an effort to compensate for his poor grades, he joined a gang of semidelinquents. He was accepted as one of the boys. In contrast to Deborah, Mitch was sexually attracted to women.

Deborah and Mitch both had **androgenital syndrome.** In this hormonal disorder, prenatal exposure to androgens masculinizes the sex organs of genetic females. In the case of Deborah, the child was assigned to the female gender and reared as a girl. The other child, Mitch, was labeled male and raised as a boy. Each child acquired the gender identity of the assigned sex.

The problems encountered by Deborah and Mitch are rare. Still, they raise questions about what it means to be male or female in our society. For all of us, our knowledge of being male or being female is one of the most obvious and important aspects of our self-definitions and self-images. Our gender identities in contemporary society provide us with a sense of certain opportunities and also a number of limitations. But perhaps we do not all share equal opportunities, and perhaps some of us sense more limitations than others. And so, the whole issue of sex roles is of major importance to the psychology of adjustment and to our development as individuals.

Let us explore these issues further by first defining the masculine and feminine sex-role stereotypes as they exist today. We shall see how sharp stereotyping has been linked to sexism directed, in particular, against women. Then we examine research on sex differences in cognitive functioning and personality and explore how we develop "masculine" and "feminine" traits. We explore the costs of traditional stereotyping to adjustment in several spheres—in education, in activities and career choices, and in interpersonal relationships. We consider the particular burdens placed on working women and the question as to whether the children of working mothers encounter special difficulties. Finally, we examine the concept of psychological androgyny. *Physical androgyny,* or the possession of the sex organs of both sexes, can pose towering adjustment problems and is usually corrected medically at an early age—when it can be. But *psychological androgyny* might be desirable because it places a wider range of traits and adjustment strategies at the disposal of the individual.

Gender identity. One's concept of being male or female.

Secondary sex characteristics. Characteristics such as voice and distribution of body hair that distinguish the sexes but are not directly involved in reproduction.

Androgenital syndrome. A disorder in which genetic females become masculinized as a result of prenatal exposure to male hormones.

■ Sex Roles and Stereotypes

"Why Can't a Woman Be More Like a Man?" You may remember this song from the musical *My Fair Lady.* In the song, Henry Higgins laments that women are emotional and fickle, whereas men are logical and dependable. The emotional woman is a **stereotype**—a fixed conventional idea about a group. The logical man is also a stereotype. Stereotypes shape our expectations so that we assume that unknown individuals who belong to the group share the stereotypes we attribute to the group.

Cultural expectations of men and women encompass more traits than emotionality and logic. They also involve complex clusters of stereotypes that define the ways in which men and women are expected to behave and that are called **sex roles.** Lay persons tend to see the traditional feminine stereotype as dependent, gentle, helpful, kind, mild, patient, and submissive (Cartwright et al., 1983). The typical masculine sex-role stereotype is perceived as tough, protective, gentlemanly (Myers & Gonda, 1982). Females are more often viewed as warm and emotional, whereas males are more frequently seen as independent and competitive. Women are more often expected to care for the kids and cook the meals (Deaux & Lewis, 1983). Men are more frequently expected to head the family and put bread on the table.

In a well-known study of the cultural conception of masculine and feminine sex roles, Inge Broverman and her colleagues (1972) first had undergraduate psychology students list traits and behaviors that they thought differentiated men from women. A list of 122 traits, each of which was mentioned at least twice, was generated. Each trait was made into a bipolar scale, such as:

Not at all aggressive. . . . . .very aggressive

Another group of students indicated which pole of the scale was more descriptive of the "average" man or woman. Only 41 of the 122 traits achieved a 75 percent agreement rate, and they are shown in Table 3.1.

Further analysis broke the list down into two broad factors. One centered around competency in the realm of objects, including the business world (which we label "instrumentality"). The second involved emotional warmth and expression of feelings (the Brovermans' "warmth-expressiveness cluster"). Other samples then rated the items as more desirable for men or women. In general, masculine traits in the instrumentality cluster were rated as more desirable for men, while feminine traits in this cluster were rated as more desirable for women. The people in this study felt it was desirable for women to be less rational than men, less aggressive, less competitive, and less dominant, but more emotional and dependent. The ideal woman was also seen as neater, gentler, more empathetic, and more emotionally expressive than a man.

As pointed out by Alice Eagly and Valerie Steffen (1984), these stereotypes largely reflect the traditional distribution of men into breadwinning roles and women into homemaking roles. When the wife works, she is less likely to be perceived as sharing stereotypical feminine traits—that is, so long as she works because of choice, and not because of financial necessity (Atkinson & Huston, 1984).

■ Sexism

All of us have encountered the effects of **sexism**—the prejudgment that a person, because of gender, will possess negative traits. These traits may be assumed to prevent adequate performance in certain types of jobs or social situations. Until recently, sexism excluded women from many occupations, with medicine and law being the most visible examples.

Sexism may lead us to interpret the same behavior in different ways when shown by women or by men. We may see the male as "self-assertive," but the female as "pushy." We may view him as "flexible," but her as "fickle" and "indecisive." He may be "rational," when she is "cold." He is "tough"

TABLE 3.1   Stereotypical Sex-Role Traits

Instrumentality Cluster (Masculine Role Perceived as More Desirable)

Feminine	Masculine
Not at all aggressive	Very aggressive
Not at all independent	Very independent
Very emotional	Not at all emotional
Does not hide emotions at all	Almost always hides emotions
Very subjective	Very objective
Very easily influenced	Not at all easily influenced
Very submissive	Very dominant
Dislikes math and science very much	Likes math and science very much
Very excitable in a minor crisis	Not at all excitable in a minor crisis
Very passive	Very active
Not at all competitive	Very competitive
Very illogical	Very logical
Very home-oriented	Very worldly
Not at all skilled in business	Very skilled in business
Very sneaky	Very direct
Feelings easily hurt	Feelings not easily hurt
Not at all adventurous	Very adventurous
Has difficulty making decisions	Can make decisions easily
Cries very easily	Never cries
Almost never acts as a leader	Almost always acts as a leader
Not at all self-confident	Very self-confident
Very uncomfortable about being aggressive	Not at all uncomfortable about being aggressive
Not at all ambitious	Very ambitious
Unable to separate feelings from ideas	Easily able to separate feelings from ideas
Very dependent	Not at all dependent
Very conceited about appearance	Never conceited about appearance
Thinks women are always superior to men	Thinks men are always superior to women
Does not talk freely about sex with men	Talks freely about sex with men

Warmth-Expressiveness Cluster (Feminine Pole Perceived as More Desirable)

Feminine	Masculine
Doesn't use harsh language at all	Uses very harsh language
Very talkative	Not at all talkative
Very tactful	Very blunt
Very gentle	Very rough
Very aware of feelings of others	Not at all aware of feelings of others
Very religious	Not at all religious
Very interested in own appearance	Not at all interested in own appearance
Very neat in habits	Very sloppy in habits
Very quiet	Very loud
Very strong need for security	Very little need for security
Enjoys art and literature	Does not enjoy art and literature at all
Easily expresses tender feelings	Does not easily express tender feelings

Source: Adapted from I.K. Broverman et al., Sex-role stereotypes: A current appraisal, *Journal of Social Issues* 28(2): 63.

when necessary, but she is "bitchy." When the businesswoman dons stereotypical masculine behaviors, the sexist reacts negatively by branding her abnormal or unhealthy.

Sexism can also make it difficult for men to show stereotypical feminine behaviors. A "sensitive" woman is simply sensitive, but a sensitive man may be seen as a "sissy." A woman may seem "polite," when a man showing the same behavior is labeled "passive" or "weak." Only recently have men begun to enter occupational domains restricted largely to women in this century, such as nursing, secretarial work, and teaching elementary school.

Let us examine some studies of the power of sexism. For example, what happens once women have gained footholds in traditional male preserves such as medicine and engineering? Do sexists say, "I guess I was wrong about women's abilities, after all"? Not according to a study at the University of Tulsa (Touhey, 1974). The Touhey study suggests, rather, that sexists downgrade the value of the profession, as if the profession must be lowering its standards when women are admitted. College students downgraded the prestige of architecture, college teaching, medicine, and science when they received exaggerated reports that these professions were being flooded by women. Women students, products of the same culture, shared men's sexist expectations; they also downgraded these fields.

In another study, Sandra and Daryl Bem (1973) had college students rate the quality of professional articles in several fields. When the same article was attributed to a woman, it received lower ratings than when it was attributed to a man. As in the Touhey study, women raters were as guilty as men at assuming male superiority. This rating pattern was maintained with works of art as well as essays.

Rachel Hare-Mustin (1983) argues that women are misunderstood by mental-health professionals. Women, for example, are more frequently depressed than men, which has been traditionally interpreted as meaning that women more often show a psychological problem than men do. But, suggests Hare-Mustin, women more often than men are forced to live with low social status, discrimination, and helplessness. Their depression is often an appropriate response to their more stressful situations. The appropriate "treatment" of women whose depression stems from these problems is social and economic change—not psychotherapy.

School Days, School Days—Dear Old Sexist School Days?

Now that society has been aware of the existence of sexism for nearly two decades, you might expect that the practice would have greatly diminished, especially among schoolteachers. Schoolteachers, after all, are generally well educated and fair-minded. They have also been trained to be sensitive to the needs of their young charges in today's changing society.

But recent studies by investigators such as Myra and David Sadker (1985) suggest that we are far from hearing the last of sexism. Field researchers enlisted by the Sadkers observed students in fourth-, sixth-, and eighth-grade classes in four states and in the District of Columbia. Teachers and students were drawn from various racial backgrounds and from urban, suburban, and rural settings. But in almost all cases, the findings were similar across the board.

Boys generally dominated classroom communication, whether the subject was math (a traditionally "masculine" area) or language arts (a traditionally "feminine" area). Boys were eight times more likely than girls to call out answers to questions without raising their hands. So far it could be argued we have evidence for a sex difference—not for sexism. But teachers were not impartial in their responses to children who called out. Teachers, male and female, were significantly more likely to accept boys' responses when they called out. Girls were significantly more likely to—as the song goes—receive "teacher's dirty looks," or to be reminded that they should raise their hands and wait their turn. Boys, it seems, are expected to be "boys"—that is, impetuous—but girls are reprimanded for unladylike behavior.

Despite boys' dominance of classroom communication, the Sadkers (1985) found that teachers unwittingly adhere to the stereotype that girls talk more often than boys. In a clever experiment, the researchers showed teachers and administrators films of classroom discussions. Then they asked who did more talking, boys or girls. Most teachers reported that the girls were more talkative, even though the boys actually spent three times as much time talking.

The Sadkers also report these instances of sexism in the classroom:

At the preschool level, teachers praise boys more often than girls and are more likely to give them detailed instructions.

Girls are less likely to take courses in math and science, even when their aptitude in these areas equals or exceeds that of boys. (We shall talk more about this later.)

Girls, as a group, begin school with greater skills in basic computation and reading, but have lower SAT scores in quantitative and verbal subtests by the time they have graduated from high school. It seems unlikely that girls carry genetic instructions that cause academic potential to self-destruct as the years progress. Instead, it would seem that the educational system does relatively more to encourage boys to develop academic skills.

The irony is that our educational system has lifted generation upon generation of the downtrodden into the mainstream of U.S. life. Sad to say, the system appears to be doing more for males than for females—even in our "enlightened" time.

■ Sex Differences: Vive La Différence or Vive La Similarité?

If the sexes were not clearly anatomically different, this book might have been about the development of regional differences in Chinese cooking. But there are serious questions about differences in cognition and personality between the sexes, especially in the light of the controversy over sex-role stereotypes. Let us now examine what is known of these differences.

Differences in Cognitive Abilities

It was once believed that males were more intelligent than females, because of their greater knowledge of world affairs and their skill in science and industry. We now recognize that greater male knowledge and skill reflected not differences in intelligence, but the systematic exclusion of females from world affairs, science, and industry. Whereas there are no overall differences in cognitive abilities between the sexes, Eleanor Maccoby and Carol Nagy Jacklin (1974) found persistent suggestions that females are somewhat superior to males in verbal ability. Males, on the other hand, seem somewhat superior in visual-spatial and math abilities (Table 3.2).

Verbal Abilities   Girls seem to acquire language somewhat faster than boys. Some investigators have found that girls make more prelinguistic vocalizations and utter their first word about half a month sooner—at 11.4 as compared to 12 months (Harris, 1977). Girls acquire additional words more rapidly, and their pronunciation is clearer, making them easier to understand (Nelson, 1973; Schachter et al., 1978).

Between the ages of 5 and 11 girls show greater word fluency. They can name letters, colors, and objects more rapidly than their male age-mates (Denckla & Rudel, 1974). Larger sex differences in verbal abilities are found at about the age of 11, and differences continue to increase throughout the high school years (Maccoby & Jacklin, 1974). Female high school students

TABLE 3.2   Vive la Différence? Just How Different Are Boys and Girls?

Differences Borne Out by Some Research Studies	Differences about Which There Is Great Doubt	Assumed Differences That Research Has Shown to Be False
Boys tend to be more aggressive than girls.	Girls are more timid and anxious than boys.	Boys are more logical and analytical than girls.
Girls have greater verbal ability than boys.	Boys are more active than girls.	Girls are more suggestible than boys.
Boys have greater visual-spatial ability than girls.	Boys are more competitive than girls.	Boys have higher self-esteem than girls.
Boys have greater ability in math than girls.	Boys are more dominant than girls.	Girls lack achievement motivation.
	Girls are more sociable than boys.	

It has been commonly assumed that there are great cognitive and personality differences between males and females, and that these differences represent heredity or the natural order of things. But psychological research has found that certain assumed differences do not exist, and that others are smaller than expected. Those differences that remain, such as greater verbal ability in females and greater math ability in males, may reflect cultural expectations and not heredity.

Source: Based on data from Maccoby & Jacklin, 1974.

excel in spelling, punctuation, reading comprehension, solving verbal analogies (such as "Washington:one::Lincoln:?"), and solving anagrams (scrambled words).

Spatial Abilities   Beginning in adolescence, boys usually outperform girls on tests of spatial ability. These tests assess skills such as mentally rotating figures in space and finding figures embedded within larger designs (Maccoby & Jacklin, 1974; Petersen, 1980).

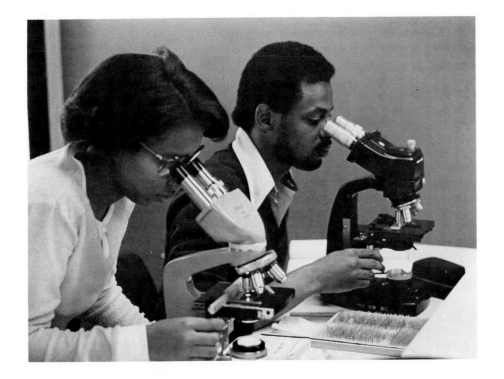

Are there cognitive differences between the sexes? Females appear to excel in language abilities, whereas males seem to excel in math and spatial-relations skills. Do these differences reflect biological factors or cultural expectations?

Mathematics Abilities   Maccoby and Jacklin (1974) found that boys and girls show similar math ability until late childhood. However, boys outperform girls in high school mathematics (Feingold, 1988; Meece et al., 1982).

There are also sex differences on the mathematics test of the Scholastic Aptitude Test (SAT) (Feingold, 1988). The mean score is 500, and about two-thirds of the test-takers receive scores between 400 and 600. Twice as many boys as girls attain scores over 500 (Benbow & Stanley, 1980). *Thirteen* times as many boys as girls attain scores over 700 (Benbow & Stanley, 1983).

A Cautionary Note   In sum, it does appear that within our culture girls show greater verbal abilities than boys, whereas boys show greater spatial and math abilities than girls. However, three factors should caution us not to attach too much importance to these sex differences. First, in most cases they are small (Deaux, 1984; Hyde, 1981). For example, whereas one study of 440,000 high school students found that boys did outperform girls on math tests (Fox et al., 1979), *the average girl missed only 0.6 of an item more than the average boy.*

Second, these sex differences are *group* differences. Variation in these skills is larger *within,* than between, the sexes. Despite group differences, millions of males exceed the "average" female in writing and spelling skills. Millions of females outdistance the "average" male in math and spatial abilities. Males have produced their Shakespeares and females their Madame Curies.

Third, the small differences that appear to exist may largely reflect cultural expectations and environmental influences (Tobias, 1982). Reading ability is stereotyped as feminine in our culture, whereas spatial and math abilities are stereotyped as masculine. Female introductory psychology students given just three hours of training in various visual-spatial skills, such as rotating geometric figures, showed no performance deficit in these skills when compared to men (Stericker & LeVesconte, 1982).

Differences in Play and School Activities

Boys and girls develop stereotypical preferences for toys and activities early. Even within their first year, boys are more explorative and independent. Girls

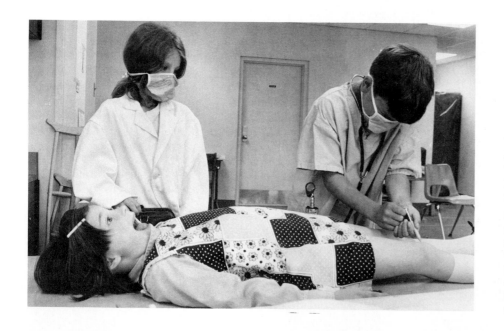

Although you would not know it from this photo, boys and girls show dramatically different play preferences. For example, 7- to 11-year-old boys are more likely to enjoy rough-and-tumble sports and making and fixing things, whereas girls of this age are more likely to enjoy cooking, caring for children, sewing, dancing, and playing with dolls.

are relatively more quiet, dependent, and restrained (Goldberg & Lewis, 1969). By 18 to 36 months, girls are more likely to play with soft toys and dolls and to dance. Eighteen- to 36-month-old boys are more likely to play with hard objects, blocks, and toy cars, trucks, and airplanes (Fagot, 1974).

Sex-typed preferences extend to school activities and team sports. Table 3.3 shows some of the results of a national survey of more than 2,000 children aged 7 to 11 (Zill, 1985).

Differences in Aggressiveness

In almost all cultures, with a couple of fascinating exceptions (Ford & Beach, 1951; Mead, 1935), it is the males who march off to war and who battle for glory and shaving-cream-commercial contracts. Most psychological studies of aggression have found that males behave more aggressively than females, whether the subjects are under 6 years of age (Maccoby & Jacklin, 1980; White, 1983) or older.

Ann Frodi and her colleagues (1977) reviewed 72 studies concerning sex differences in aggression. Their findings show that females are more likely to act aggressively (or to report acting aggressively) under some circumstances than others.

1. Males are more likely than females to report physical aggression in their behavior, intentions, and dreams. (Matlin [1987] notes that self-reports are notoriously vulnerable to distortion in the culturally expected direction and that males in these studies may have been trying to live up to their sex-role stereotypes.)
2. Males and females are about equally likely to approve of violence.
3. Males and females both appreciate hostile humor.
4. Females are more likely to feel anxious or guilty about behaving aggressively. These feelings tend to inhibit aggression.
5. Females behave as aggressively as males when they have the means to do so and believe that their behavior is justified. For example, women act as aggressively as men in experiments in which they are given the physical capacity to do so and believe that they should act aggressively.

TABLE 3.3   Rankings of Activities Favored By Boys and Girls

	Boys	Girls
LOVE	1. Team sports 2. Watching TV 3. Caring for pets 4. Going to parties	1. Going to parties 2. Watching TV 3. Caring for pets 4. Going to school 5. Going to church
LIKE	5. Making things 6. Fixing things 7. Going to school 8. Going to church 9. Boxing 10. Reading 11. Playing with guns 12. Caring for kids 13. Cooking	6. Cooking 7. Reading 8. Caring for kids 9. Team sports 10. Sewing 11. Dancing 12. Playing with dolls 13. Making things 14. Fixing things
DON'T LIKE	14. Going to doctor 15. Dancing 16. Sewing 17. Playing with dolls	15. Going to doctor 16. Boxing 17. Playing with guns

Source: Zill, 1985.

Personal space. A psychological boundary that permits one to maintain a comfortable distance from others.

6. Females are more likely to empathize with the victim—to put themselves in the victim's place.
7. Sex differences in aggression decrease when the victim is anonymous. Anonymity may prevent females from empathizing with their victims.

Differences in Communication Styles: "He's Just an Old Chatterbox"

Despite the stereotype of women as gossips and "chatterboxes," research in communication styles suggests that males in many situations spend more time talking than women. Males are also more likely to introduce new topics and to interrupt (Brooks, 1982; Deaux, 1985; Hall, 1984). During early childhood, girls frequently do more talking than boys (Haas, 1979), which may reflect their greater verbal ability. However, boys dominate discussion by the time they enter the classroom (Sadker & Sadker, 1985). Moreover, as girls grow up, they appear to learn to let boys do the talking. Girls take a back seat to boys in mixed-sex groups (Haas, 1979; Hall, 1984).

Yet females do seem more willing to reveal their feelings and personal experiences (Cozby, 1973). Females are less likely than males to curse—with the exception of women who are bucking sex-role stereotypes. As noted in Table 3.1, use of harsh language is considered a masculine trait.

Let us now consider sex differences in two aspects of nonverbal communication—personal space and body posture.

Differences in Personal Space: "Are You Sitting Next to Me?"   How do you react when a stranger sits at your table in the library or the cafeteria—when someone "invades" your **personal space?**

Women appear to require less personal space than boys and men do. They tend to stand and sit closer to one another than men do, as noted both in naturalistic observation of window shoppers and visitors to art exhibits (Fisher et al., 1984), and in experiments (Sussman & Rosenfeld, 1982). Women also prefer to have friends sit next to them, whereas boys prefer friends to sit across from them (Sommer, 1969; Fisher & Byrne, 1975).

Differences in seating preferences and personal-space requirements might reflect greater male competitiveness. Males might perceive close encounters as confrontations in which they face potential adversaries. Thus, they need to keep an eye on them from a safe distance.

Body Posture   Just as they seem to require more personal space, males occupy more space with their bodies. They sit or stand with their legs apart, and their hands tend to reach out. Females are more likely to sit or stand with their legs together and with their hands folded in front of them or at their sides (Davis & Weitz, 1981; Hall, 1984).

There are also a number of sex-typed mannerisms found among girls and boys as young as age 4 (Rekers et al., 1977). Girls, for example, are more likely than boys to show fluttering arms, bent elbows, and limp wrists.

And so, there appear to be a number of differences between males and females. Some of them are first shown during infancy. Others emerge during middle childhood or adolescence. These include minor differences in cognitive functioning, and differences in play, school activities, aggressiveness, and communication styles. In the next section we consider the development of these differences.

■ On Becoming a Man or a Woman: Theoretical Views

Like mother, like daughter; like father, like son—at least often, if not always. Why is it that little boys (often) grow up to behave according to the cultural stereotypes of what it means to be male? That little girls (often) grow up to behave like female stereotypes? Let us have a look at biological and psychological factors that appear to contribute to the development of sex differences.

Biological Influences

Biological views on sex differences tend to focus on two issues: brain organization and sex hormones.

Brain Organization   A number of studies suggest that we can speak of "left brain" versus "right brain" functions. Language skills seem to depend more on left-brain functioning, whereas right-brain functioning may be more involved in spatial relations and aesthetic and emotional responses. The brain hemispheres may be even more specialized in males than in females (Bryden, 1982).

Evidence for this view derives from adults who receive brain injuries. Men with damage to the left hemisphere are more likely to show verbal deficits than women with similar damage (McGlone, 1980). Men with damage to the right hemisphere are more likely to show spatial-relations deficits than similarly injured women.

Sex differences in brain organization might in part explain why women exceed men in verbal skills that require some spatial organization, such as reading, spelling, and crisp articulation of speech. But men might be superior at more specialized spatial-relations tasks, such as interpreting road maps and visualizing objects in space.

But let us retain a note of caution. Brain research is in its infancy, and, as noted earlier, the differences *within* the sexes remain greater than the differences *between* the sexes.

Prenatal Sex Hormones   Sex hormones are responsible for prenatal differentiation of sex organs. At the beginning of the chapter we noted that the sex organs of genetic females who are prenatally exposed to excess androgens may become masculinized. Prenatal sex hormones might also "masculinize" or "feminize" the brain by creating predispositions that are consistent with some sex-role stereotypes (Diamond, 1977; Money, 1977, 1987).

Diamond takes an extreme view. She suggests that **in-utero** brain masculinization can cause tomboyishness and assertiveness—even preferences for trousers over skirts and for playing with "boys' toys." Money agrees that predispositions may be created in utero, but argues that social learning plays a stronger role in the development of gender identity, personality traits, and preferences. Money claims that social learning is powerful enough to counteract many prenatal predispositions.

Sex Hormones at Puberty   Sex hormones also spur sexual maturation during adolescence, and there are some interesting suggestions that sexual maturation is linked to development of cognitive skills. Girls usually reach sexual maturity earlier than boys. Researchers have found that late maturers, whether boys or girls, show the "masculine pattern" of exceeding early maturers on math and spatial-relations tasks (Sanders & Soares, 1986; Sanders et al., 1982; Waber et al., 1985). Early-maturing boys exceed late-maturing boys in verbal skills, and also show the "feminine pattern" of higher verbal than math and spatial-relations skills (Newcombe & Bandura, 1983). And so early maturation would seem to favor development of verbal skills, whereas late maturation might favor development of math and spatial-relations skills. Since females usually mature earlier than boys, their verbal skills would usually be favored. The opposite would hold true for males.

Let us now consider psychological views of the development of sex differences.

Psychodynamic Theory

Sigmund Freud explained the acquisition of sex roles in terms of **identification.** In psychodynamic theory, identification is the process of incorporating within ourselves the behaviors and our perceptions of the thoughts and feelings of others. Freud believed that gender identity remains flexible until the resolution of the Oedipus and Electra complexes at about the age of 5 or 6. Appropriate sex-typing requires that boys identify with their fathers and surrender the wish to possess their mothers. Girls would have to surrender the wish to have a penis and identify with their mothers. But, as noted earlier, children display stereotypical sex-role behaviors long before the arrival of the hypothetical conflicts of the phallic stage.

Let us consider the ways in which social-learning and cognitive theories account for sex-typing.

Social-Learning Theory

Social-learning theorists explain the acquisition of sex roles and sex differences in terms such as observational learning, identification,* and socialization.

Children learn much of what is considered masculine or feminine by observational learning, as suggested by an experiment conducted by David Perry and Kay Bussey (1979). In this study, children learned how behaviors are sex-typed by observing the *relative frequencies* with which men and women performed them. However, the adult role models expressed arbitrary preferences for one of each of 16 pairs of items—pairs such as oranges vs. apples, and toy cows vs. toy horses—as 8- and 9-year-old boys and girls observed. Then the children were asked to show their own preferences. Boys selected an average of 14 of 16 items that agreed with the "preferences" of the men. Girls selected an average of only three of 16 items that agreed with the choices of the men.

Social-learning theorists view identification as a broad, continuous learning process in which children are influenced by rewards and punishments to imitate adults of the same sex—particularly the parent of the same gender (Bronfenbrenner, 1960; Kagan, 1964; Storms, 1979). In identification as opposed to imitation, children not only imitate a certain behavior pattern. They also try to become broadly like the model.

Socialization also plays a role. Parents and other adults—even other children—inform children as to how they are expected to behave. They reward children for behavior they consider sex-appropriate. They punish (or fail to reinforce) children for behavior they consider inappropriate. Girls, for example, are given dolls while they still sleep in cribs. They are encouraged to rehearse care-taking behaviors in preparation for traditional feminine adult roles.

The Role of the Parents   Mothers more so than fathers have the major responsibility for the day-to-day nurturance of children (Belsky et al., 1984; Feldman et al., 1984). Mothers tend to provide the supportive and empathic functions—the "emotional glue"—that keeps the family integrated as a unit (Johnson, 1983; Orlofsky, 1983). Fathers are more likely to interact playfully with their children and communicate norms for sex-typed behaviors (Lamb, 1981; Power, 1985). Mothers share fathers' cultural expectations concerning "sex-appropriate" behavior patterns, but do not usually make so sharp a distinction in expressing their attitudes to their sons and daughters (McHale & Huston, 1984).

Identification. In psychodynamic theory, the process of incorporating within the personality elements of others. (In social-learning theory, a broad, continuous process of learning by observation and imitation.

Socialization. The fostering of "sex-appropriate" behavior patterns by providing children with information and using rewards and punishments.

---

*But the social-learning concept of identification differs from the psychoanalytic concept, as noted in this section.

■ A CLOSER LOOK

What's Sweet for Jack Is Often Sour for Jill

Many parents may believe that they treat their children reasonably equally, regardless of whether they are boys or girls. But observational studies and experiments suggest that boys are more equal than girls, especially when they try to engage in vigorous physical activity or to explore their environments.

In several observational studies, Beverly Fagot (e.g., 1974, 1978, 1982) found that boys and girls are treated quite differently, even when they show the same behavior. Mothers are more likely, for example, to encourage their young daughters to follow them around the house, while boys of the same age are pushed to be independent. Boys are told to run errands outside the home at earlier ages than girls (Saegert & Hart, 1976). Both parents are more likely to reinforce sons for exploring the environment and manipulating objects. Girls are more likely to be criticized for the same behavior, or warned about the prospects of getting hurt.

In a fascinating experiment, Hannah Frisch (1977) found that parents treated 14-month-old boys and girls significantly differently. The gender of the infants was visually concealed and the parents were told at random that they were boys or girls. Parents who believed that the infants were boys were more likely to encourage them to play with blocks and tricycles. Parents who believed that the children were girls spent more time talking to them and were more likely to encourage them to play with dolls and baby bottles.

Caroline Smith and Barbara Lloyd (1978) found that Frisch's results could be replicated with infants as young as 6 months. Mothers who were told that the infant was a girl were more likely to cuddle "her." Mothers who were told that the infant was a boy were more likely to encourage and reinforce motor activities such as crawling and playing with toys, including a hammer.

In general, boys are given athletic equipment, cars, and guns from early ages, and are encouraged to compete aggressively. Boys are handled more frequently than girls. Girls are spoken to more often. There may be biological predispositions for boys to act more aggressively and for girls to show greater verbal skills. However, early socialization also fosters stereotypical sex-role development.

Fathers tend to encourage instrumental behavior in their sons and warm, expressive behavior in their daughters. Fathers encourage sons to be active and dominant. Girls are encouraged to comfort others and show affection (Block, 1979). Fathers toss their sons into the air and use hearty expressions with them such as "How're yuh doin', Tiger?" and "Hey you, get your keester over here" (Jacklin et al., 1984; Power & Parke, 1982). By contrast, fathers are likely to cuddle their daughters gently. The first author went out of his way to toss his young daughters up into the air, and the relatives yelled at him for being too rough. Of course, he modified his behavior. He learned to toss them up into the air when they were alone—not in front of the relatives.

Effects of Father Absence Research has also shown that boys from father-absent families show a weaker preference for the traditional masculine sex role, are more dependent, and perform less well in school than boys reared in two-parent homes. A study of 2½-year-old nursery-school children by Rachel Levy-Shiff (1982) found that boys from father-absent homes were also less-well socially adjusted and more likely to encounter problems in relating to peers than boys from intact homes.

But boys from father-absent homes with older brothers are relatively more "masculine" and less dependent. They also earn higher grades in school (Santrock, 1970; Sutton-Smith et al., 1968; Wohlford et al., 1971). Boys with older sisters are more likely than boys with older brothers or no siblings to show a number of feminine-typed behaviors (Sutton-Smith & Rosenberg, 1970). Girls with older brothers are also more likely to show masculine-typed behaviors than girls with older sisters or no siblings.

The Levy-Shiff (1982) study found that girls from father-absent homes were more independent and assertive than girls from intact homes. However, there was no indication that greater independence and assertiveness was linked to social problems. While independence and assertiveness may be stereotyped as masculine, they are valuable traits for both sexes in the academic and vocational worlds.

The Role of Peers   Children are also motivated to engage in "sex-appropriate" behaviors in order to earn the approval, and avoid the disapproval, of their peers. In one study, the researchers (Serbin et al., 1979) observed children in a playroom under three conditions: alone, with a peer of the same sex, or with an opposite-sex peer. Many toys were available in the room. When peers of either sex were present, the children were significantly more likely to restrict their play to toys that were consistent with the stereotypes for their sex.

Research by Michael Lamb and his colleagues (Lamb & Roopnarine, 1979; Lamb et al., 1980) suggests that children have good reason to select "sex-appropriate" toys in the presence of their peers. Three-year-old children, for example, frequently stop playing with boys who play with dolls or tea sets, or with girls who play with toy guns, firetrucks, and hammers. Most 5-year-olds are openly critical of children who choose "inappropriate toys" and guide them into playing with "appropriate toys."

The Role of Schools   Schools also spur the socialization process. Girls are usually expected to outperform boys in English and language arts, whereas boys are expected to excel in math and science. Stereotypical socialization messages are even found in nursery schools. In one school that proclaimed a commitment to breaking down traditional sex-role stereotypes, girls were still complimented on their clothing more frequently than boys were, particularly when they wore dresses (Joffee, 1971). In high school, girls are more likely to be assigned courses in homemaking, secretarial work, and dancing. Boys are more frequently guided into shop courses and preprofessional studies (Naffziger & Naffziger, 1974).

One study highlights the power of teacher praise in sex-typing (Serbin et al., 1977). Over a two-week baseline period, the researchers recorded the frequency with which children engaged in cooperative play activities that were usually preferred by children of the opposite sex. During the next two weeks, teachers praised children for engaging in cross-gender play, and the frequency of such play increased significantly. However, when the teachers discontinued their reinforcement, cross-gender play fell back to baseline levels.

The Social Learning of Sex Differences in Aggressive Behavior
Concerning the greater aggressiveness of boys, Maccoby and Jacklin note that:

> Aggression in general is less acceptable for girls, and is more actively discouraged in them, by either direct punishment, withdrawal of affection, or simply cognitive training that "that isn't the way girls act." Girls then build up greater anxieties about aggression, and greater inhibitions against displaying it (1974, p. 234).

As noted earlier, girls frequently learn to respond to social provocations by feeling anxious about the possibility of acting aggressively, whereas boys are generally encouraged to retaliate (Frodi et al., 1977). Parents usually squelch aggression in their daughters (Sears et al., 1957). Boys are likely to be permitted to express some aggression toward their parents. Many boys are encouraged to fight with peers, when necessary, in order to defend themselves and their property.

Several experiments also highlight the importance of social-learning factors in female aggressiveness. Studies by Albert Bandura and his colleagues (1963) found that boys are more likely than girls to imitate film-mediated aggressive models, because the social milieu more often frowns upon aggressiveness in girls (Figure 3.1). Other investigators find that the development

Sex norm. An expectation about what sort of behavior is considered appropriate in social interactions between males and females.

of aggressive behavior in females is influenced by situational variables, such as the nature of the provocation and the possibility that someone will disapprove of them (Taylor & Epstein, 1967; Richardson et al., 1979).

In the Taylor and Epstein study, aggressive behavior was measured by the strength of the electric shock selected for delivery to another person. Subjects used a fearsome looking console (Figure 3.2) to take turns shocking other participants in the study when they failed to respond quickly enough to a stimulus. Subjects could select the strength of the shock themselves. When men set low or moderate shock levels for women subjects, the women generally chose somewhat lower shock levels for the men when their turn came. In this way, they adhered to the feminine stereotype of nonaggressiveness. But when the men violated the **sex norm** of treating women favorably by setting high levels of shock for them, the women retaliated by setting shock levels that were equally high. Apparently the women decided that what was sauce for the gander was sauce for the goose. If men could violate sex norms and treat women aggressively, women, too, could violate sex norms and respond just as aggressively.

The development of aggressive behavior in girls is also influenced by the responses of those who monitor their behavior and reward or punish them. In the Richardson study, college women competed with men in responding quickly to a stimulus over four blocks of trials, with six trials in each block. They could not see their opponents. The loser of each trial received an electric shock whose intensity was set by the opponent. Women competed under one of three experimental conditions: "public," "private," or with a

FIGURE 3.1 A Classic Experiment in the Imitation of Aggressive Models

Children will imitate the behavior of adult models in certain situations, as shown in these pictures from a classic study by Albert Bandura and his colleagues (1963). In the top row, an adult model strikes a clown doll. The next two rows show a boy and a girl imitating the aggressive behavior.

FIGURE 3.2

In the Taylor and Epstein study on aggressive behavior, subjects pressed levers on this console to deliver electric shocks to other participants in the study.

"supportive other." In the public condition, another woman observed her silently. In the private condition, there was no observer. In the supportive-other condition, another woman urged her to retaliate strongly when her opponent selected high shock levels. As shown in Figure 3.3, women in the private and supportive-other conditions selected increasingly higher levels of shock in retaliation. Presumably, the women in the study assumed that an observer—though silent—would frown on aggressive behavior. This assumption is likely to reflect their own early socialization experiences. Women who were unobserved or urged on by a supportive-other apparently felt free to violate the sex norm of nonaggressiveness when their situations called for aggressive responses.

If the Richardson experiment were replicated with boys, is it possible that boys in a room with a silent observer would also be highly aggressive? After all, their early socialization experiences might lead them to expect that an observer would disapprove of them for *failing* to respond aggressively to a provocation. Why not run such an experiment and tell us about the results?

In sum, social-learning theory has done an admirable job of outlining the ways in which rewards, punishments, and modeling foster "sex-appropriate" behavior patterns. Critics of social-learning theory do not challenge the validity of experiments such as those we have reported. Instead, they focus on theoretical issues such as, *How do reinforcers influence us?* Do reinforcers mechanically increase the frequency of behavior, or do reinforcers provide us with information that we process in making decisions? Let us consider two cognitive-theory approaches to sex-typing that will shed some light on this matter: cognitive-developmental theory and gender-schema theory.

Cognitive-Developmental Theory

Harvard University psychologist Lawrence Kohlberg (1966) has proposed a cognitive-developmental view of sex-typing. Cognitive-developmental theory views children as active participants in the development of sex roles and sex differences. These developments are seen as occurring in stages and as entwined with the child's general cognitive development.

Rewards and punishments influence children's choice of toys and activities, but from the cognitive perspective, rewards do not mechanically strengthen stimulus–response connections. Instead, rewards provide children with information as to when they are behaving in ways that other people desire. For this reason, even at the ages of 21 to 25 months, girls respond more positively to rewards from other girls. Boys at this age respond more positively to rewards from other boys (Fagot, 1985a). Rewards are a source of information that is processed in terms of the gender of the "rewarder"; their effects are not mechanical.

Gender identity. One's concept of being male or female. (The first stage in the cognitive-developmental theory of the assumption of sex roles.)

Gender stability. The concept that one's gender is a permanent feature.

Gender constancy. The concept that one's gender remains the same, despite superficial changes in appearance or behavior.

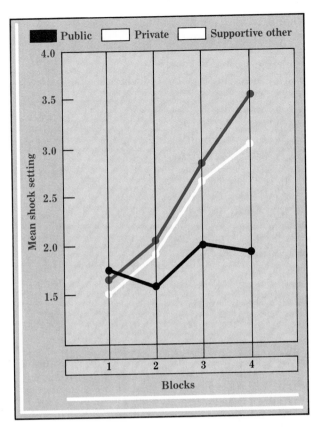

Public   Private   Supportive other

Mean shock setting

Blocks

FIGURE 3.3   **Mean Shock Settings Selected by Women to Retaliate Against Male Opponents in the Richardson Study**

Women in this study behaved more aggressively when they were alone (private) or encouraged to do so (by a supportive other). They acted least aggressively when accompanied by a silent observer (public). Perhaps they feared the condemnation of the silent observer because aggression is inconsistent with the female sex-role stereotype.

And so there is a role for rewards and punishments in cognitive theories: They provide information. But Kohlberg views the essential aspects of sex-typing to be the emergence of three concepts: *gender identity, gender stability,* and *gender constancy.*

The first step in sex-typing is attaining **gender identity,** or knowledge of being male or female. Gender identity appears to begin with sexual assignment, or the labeling of the child a boy or girl. Sexual assignment reflects the child's anatomic sex and usually occurs at birth. Gender identity is so important to parents that they usually want to know "Is it a boy or a girl?" before they begin to count fingers and toes.

Most children acquire a firm gender identity by the age of 36 months (Marcus & Corsini, 1978; McConaghy, 1979; Money, 1977). By this age most children can also tell anatomic sex differences (Ruble & Ruble, 1980).

At 4 or 5 most children develop the concept of **gender stability.** They recognize that people retain their genders for a lifetime. Girls no longer believe that they will grow up to be daddies, and boys no longer think they can become mommies. According to cognitive-developmental theory, the emergence of gender stability contributes to the organization of sex-typed behavior (Siegal & Robinson, 1987).

By 7 or 8 most children develop the more sophisticated concept of **gender constancy.** Children with gender constancy recognize that gender does not change, even if people modify their dress or their behavior patterns. Gender, that is, remains constant despite rearrangement of superficial appearances. A woman who crops her hair short remains a woman. A man who cries remains a man.

A number of studies have found that the concepts of gender identity, gender stability, and gender constancy do emerge in the order predicted by

Kohlberg (Slaby & Frey, 1975). The order of emergence is confirmed in cross-cultural studies of the United States, Samoa, Nepal, Belize, and Kenya (Munroe et al., 1984).

According to cognitive-developmental theory, once children have established concepts of gender stability and constancy, they will be motivated to behave in ways that are consistent with their genders. Once girls understand that they will remain female, they will show a preference for "feminine" activities. As shown by Perry and Bussey (1979), children do appear to actively seek information as to which behavior patterns are "masculine" and which are "feminine." They are then significantly more likely to imitate the "sex-appropriate" patterns.

However, there are problems with the ages at which sex-typed play emerges. Numerous studies have shown that many children prefer sex-typed toys such as cars and dolls at the age of 2 (Huston, 1983). At this age, children are likely to have a sense of gender identity, but gender stability and gender constancy remain some years away (Fagot, 1985b). Therefore, gender identity alone seems to provide a child with sufficient motivation to assume sex-typed behavior patterns.

Cornell University psychologist Sandra Bem (1983) notes that Kohlberg's theory also does not explain why children focus on gender as a crucial factor in classifying people and behavior patterns. Another cognitive view, gender-schema theory, attempts to address these shortcomings.

Gender-Schema Theory: An Information-Processing Approach

Gender-schema theory holds that children use gender as one way of organizing their perceptions of the world (Bem, 1981, 1985; Martin & Halverson, 1981). Gender has a great deal of prominence, even to young children. And so children mentally group people of the same gender together.

Gender-schema theory borrows elements from social-learning theory and from cognitive-developmental theory. As in social-learning theory, sex-typing is viewed as largely learned from experience. Children learn "appropriate" behavior patterns by observation. But children's active cognitive processing of information also contributes to their sex-typing.

Consider the example of strength and weakness. Children learn that strength is linked to the male sex-role stereotype, and weakness to the fe-

Gender-schema theory. The view that one's knowledge of the gender schema in one's society (the distribution of behavior patterns that are considered appropriate for men and women) guides one's assumption of sex-typed preferences and behavior patterns.

According to cognitive theories of sex typing, children are motivated to behave in ways that are consistent with their views of their genders. Boys are motivated to assume the behavior patterns that they perceive as typical of men, and girls are motivated to assume the behavior patterns that they perceive as typical of women.

male's. But they also learn that some traits, such as strong–weak, are more relevant to one gender than the other—in this case, for males.* Bill will learn that the strength he displays in weight training or wrestling has an impact on the way others perceive him. But most girls do not find this trait so important, unless they are competing in sports such as gymnastics, tennis, or swimming. Even so, boys are expected to compete in these sports, and girls are not. Jane is likely to find that her gentleness and neatness are more important in the eyes of others than her strength.

And so children learn to judge themselves according to the traits, or constructs, considered relevant to their genders. In so doing, their self-concepts become blended with the gender schema of their culture. The gender schema provides standards for comparison. Children whose self-concepts are consistent with their society's gender schema are likely to have higher self-esteem than children whose self-concepts are not.

From the viewpoint of gender-schema theory, gender identity would be sufficient to prompt "sex-appropriate" behavior. As soon as children understand the labels *boy* and *girl*, they have a basis for blending their self-concepts with the gender schema of their society. Children with gender identity will actively seek information concerning the gender schema. Their self-esteem will soon become wrapped up in the ways in which they measure up to the gender schema.

A number of recent studies support the view that children process information according to the gender schema (Cann & Newbern, 1984; List et al., 1983). Boys, for example, show better memory for "masculine" toys and objects, whereas girls show better memory for "feminine" objects and toys (Bradbard & Endsley, 1984).

In one study, Carol Martin and Charles Halverson (1983) showed 5- and 6-year-old boys and girls pictures of actors engaged in "sex-consistent" or "sex-inconsistent" activities. The sex-consistent pictures showed boys in activities such as playing with trains or sawing wood and girls in activities such as cooking and cleaning. Sex-inconsistent pictures showed actors of the opposite sex engaged in these sex-typed activities. Each child was shown a randomized collection of pictures that included only one picture of each activity. One week later, the children were asked who had engaged in a pictured activity, a male or a female. Boys and girls both replied incorrectly significantly more often when the picture they had seen showed sex-inconsistent activity. As in the Bradbard and Endsley (1984) study, the processing of information had been distorted to conform to the gender schema.

In sum, brain organization and sex hormones may contribute to sex-typed behavior patterns. They may play at least minor roles in math skills and aggressive behavior patterns. But there is also evidence that the effects of social-learning may be strong enough to counteract most prenatal biological influences. Social-learning theory does an excellent job of outlining the environmental factors that influence children to assume "sex-appropriate" behavior patterns. But social-learning theory may pay insufficient attention to children's active role in acquiring sex-role information and to the role of developing concepts of masculinity and femininity. Cognitive-developmental theory views children as active seekers of information, but may overestimate the roles of gender stability and gender constancy in sex-typing. Gender-schema theory integrates the strengths of social-learning theory and cognitive-developmental theory and also highlights the ways in which children process information, so as to blend their self-concepts with the gender schema of their culture.

---

*George Kelly, discussed in Chapter 2, would have said that the "construct" strong–weak is more relevant for males.

■ Costs of Sex-Role Stereotyping

And so we have seen that in our society there are rather clear concepts of a traditional masculine and a traditional feminine sex role. These stereotypes are learned early and they influence the child's active efforts to develop into a competent person. Although biology seems to play a role in sex-typing, it is unclear where biological influences leave off and psychological influences begin.

Yet it is deeply ingrained in our society that sex differences in cognition and personality are biological in nature—or "natural." It is also ingrained, at least in traditionalists, that when we "buck" our "natural" sex roles, we endanger male–female relationships and the fabric of society at large.

These deeply ingrained ideas have their costs. Put succinctly, they have left millions of individuals confused and frustrated. In many, many cases our self-concepts do not quite fit the gender schema of our society, and it is asking quite a lot for individuals who are unacquainted with psychological theory and research to realize that in many ways the gender shema might be arbitrary. Many people who are uncomfortable with the stereotypical social demands being made of them are likely to doubt themselves rather than society. This is just one of the many costs of sex-role stereotyping. There are more concrete costs, in terms of educational channeling, limitations placed on activities and career choices, and problems in interpersonal relationships.

Costs in Terms of Education

The educational costs of stereotyping and sexism have been enormous. Stereotyping has historically worked to the disadvantage of women. In past centuries girls were considered unsuited to education. Even the great Swiss-French philosopher Jean-Jacques Rousseau, who was in the forefront of an open approach to education, believed that girls were basically irrational and naturally disposed to child-rearing and homemaking tasks—certainly not commerce, science, and industry. Although the daughters of royal or sophisticated families have always managed to receive some tutoring, it is only in the twentieth century that girls have been fully integrated into public school systems. But we have seen that even as members of these systems, they receive different treatment from boys (Sadker & Sadker, 1985). Boys seem to receive more encouragement and more direct instruction, and certain courses still seem to be considered part of the "male domain."

In the U.S.A. today, boys and girls are looked upon as about equal in **aptitude** for learning. Yet there remain some differences in expectations, and these stereotypes limit the horizons of both sexes.

Reading   Consider the issue of reading. Reading is one of the most basic educational skills. Reading opens doorways to all academic subjects, and problems in reading generalize to nearly every area of academic life. It turns out that far more U.S. boys than girls have reading problems, simply reading below grade level or the much more severe problem of **dyslexia.** Girls appear to attend more carefully to the details that allow discrimination among letters (Smith, 1985).

Psychologists have many hypotheses as to why girls, as a group, read better than boys. Many of these hypotheses involve biological factors, such as different patterns of specialization of the hemispheres of the brain in boys and girls. But it might also be that cultural factors, and stereotyping in particular, play a role in sex differences in reading. Evidence for this view is found in that fact that sex differences in reading tend to disappear or be reversed in other cultures (Matlin, 1987). Reading is stereotyped as a feminine activity in the United States and Canada, and girls surpass boys in reading skills in these countries. But boys score higher than girls on most tests of

Aptitude. A specific ability or talent, such as aptitude for music or for writing.

Dyslexia. Severe impairment of reading ability, characterized, for example, by inability to recall vowel sounds and reversals of letters such as small *b* and small *d*.

reading in Nigeria and England, where boys have traditionally been expected to outperform girls in academic pursuits, including reading.

Spatial Relations The sex difference that is found in spatial ability may similarly be related to stereotyping, because spatial ability is linked to the number of math courses taken. Children are likely to practice spatial skills in geometry and related courses, and boys take more math courses in high school than girls (Meece et al., 1982). One study found no sex differences in spatial ability when the number of math courses taken was considered (Fennema & Sherman, 1977).

Mathematics Boys, as noted, are more likely to take math courses in high school than girls. Math courses open doorways for boys to occupations in the natural sciences, engineering, and economics, among many others. There are several reasons why U.S. boys are more likely than U.S. girls to feel "at home" with math:

1. Fathers are more likely than mothers to help children with math homework (Meece et al., 1982; Raymond & Benbow, 1986).
2. Advanced math courses are more likely to be taught by men (Fox, 1982).
3. Teachers often show higher expectations for boys in math courses (Meece et al., 1982). *And, of course, the expectancies of others tend to translate into our own self-efficacy expectancies.*
4. Teachers of math courses spend more time instructing and interacting with boys than girls (Meece et al., 1982).

Given these typical experiences with math, we should not be surprised that:

1. By junior high, boys view themselves as more competent in math than girls do, even when they receive identical grades (Meece et al., 1982). *Recall, from our discussion of social-learning theory in Chapter 2, that high self-efficacy expectancies foster motivation and perseverance in difficult tasks. Girls, therefore, who view themselves as less competent in math, are less likely than boys to "work hard" at math. Expectancies of success lead to hard work, and hard work often leads to success. And so, with boys, it is often the case that "success breeds success" in math.*
2. By high school, students perceive math as part of the male domain (Fox, 1980).
3. By junior high, boys are more likely than girls to perceive math as useful (Meece et al., 1982).
4. Boys are more likely to have positive feelings about math. Girls are more likely to have math anxiety (Tobias & Weissbrod, 1980).
5. It becomes increasingly difficult to convince high school and college women to take math courses, even when they show superior math ability (Eccles, 1985; Fox et al., 1985; Paulsen & Johnson, 1983).

Julia Sherman (1981, 1982, 1983) found several factors related to girls' decisions to take math courses in high school. First, traits stereotyped as "masculine" were associated with mathematics and apparently dissuaded some girls from exploring it. These traits included ambition, independence, self-confidence, and spatial ability. Girls choosing to take math were less likely to view math as a male domain, and they had had positive early experiences with math.

Now let us consider the limitations that stereotyping tends to impose upon our choices of activities and careers.

Costs in Terms of Activities and Careers

As noted, children show preferences for sex-stereotyped activities and toys by the ages of 2 or 3. Then, if they should stray from sex-typed activities, their peers are sure to let them know of the "errors of their ways." How many little girls are dissuaded from thinking about professions such as engineering and architecture because they are given dolls, not firetrucks and blocks? How many little boys are dissuaded from child-care and nursing professions because others look askance at them when they reach for dolls?

Occupational Stereotypes and Career Choices   Children not only develop stereotypical attitudes toward play activities at an early age; they also acquire clear ideas as to what is "man's work" and what is "woman's work."

Consider a study on 2- and 3-year-olds' stereotypes about the workplace. In order to learn about the children's ideas, the researchers Gettys and Cann (1981) showed them male and female dolls and asked them to point to the one that held a particular job. Even by this age, 78 percent of the children thought that the male doll was the construction worker. By contrast, only 23 percent pointed to the male doll as a teacher.

Although it is women who have been historically excluded from certain "male occupations," boys by and large seem to be more restricted in their occupational stereotypes. Shepard and Hess (1975) gave children a list of jobs and asked respondents to indicate whether each should be performed by a man or a woman, or whether it could be performed by either. Except for kindergartners, the youngest age group, girls were more likely than boys to choose "either."

Boys are also more rigid in their own career aspirations. Lavine (1982) asked 7- to 11-year-olds what they wanted to do as adults. She coded responses according to census information that indicated the proportion of men in each position. The jobs mentioned by boys were occupied by men 89 percent of the time. The jobs chosen by girls were occupied by men 41 percent of the time. Boys chose male-sex-typed positions significantly more often than girls did. However, if we view the average "neutral" position as being occupied by men 50 percent of the time, girls' responses were more neutral. Girls, that is, were willing to accept nonstereotyped positions more often.

A recent study by Linda Dunlap and Joseph Canale (1987) of Marist College appears to clarify some of the issues involved in choosing nontraditional careers. Dunlap and Canale assessed career aspirations among second-, fifth-, eighth-, and twelfth-graders in upstate New York. As in the Lavine (1982) study, boys chose masculine-typed jobs more often than girls did. But boys' "rigidity" peaked at the fifth grade, then declined. Seventy-eight percent of second-grade boys chose masculine-typed jobs, as compared to 100 percent of fifth-graders, 92 percent of eighth-graders, and 69 percent of twelfth-graders. The pattern for girls also showed ascent then decline. Only 20 percent of second-grade girls chose masculine-typed careers, as compared to 41 percent of fifth-grade girls, 59 percent of eighth-grade girls, and 39 percent of twelfth-grade girls.

This developmental trend may reflect increasing awareness of nontraditional career opportunities among girls through eighth grade. *But at some point during high school, girls' aspirations may become tempered by real-world opportunities and accumulating years of socialization as well as by changes in actual preferences. An overwhelming majority of the parents of the girls in this study wanted them to enter traditional feminine-typed jobs. And so many previously adventurous girls might have begun to focus on traditional occupations as they approached entry into the work force or selection of a college major.*

Dunlap and Canale also found that the prestige of the mother's job influenced children's job choices. The children of mothers with highly prestigious jobs were more likely to choose highly prestigious jobs for themselves. As more women attain highly prestigious jobs, perhaps their daughters will become more likely to aspire to them as well.

Evidence is mixed as to whether adolescent girls select careers that are as prestigious as those chosen by boys. Dunlap and Canale (1987) found that their sample of upstate New York boys generally aspired to higher-prestige jobs than girls did. But in a study of 1,234 Illinois ninth- and twelfth-graders, girls chose more prestigious careers than boys (Farmer, 1983).

All in all, Farmer found that the career aspirations of today's male and female adolescents were more similar than different, although the girls remained more committed to homemaking than the boys. As noted earlier, *the double commitment of girls to homemaking and the business world all too often reflects the role overload awaiting them in adulthood.*

Inequities in the Workplace Once we enter the workplace, we also find inequities that are based on gender. And here too, it is women who suffer most. We shall explore the workplace for women in Chapter 12 in depth, but here let us briefly note a number of costs to women—and the rest of us:

1. *Pay.* Women earn less than men for comparable work.
2. *Promotions.* Women are less likely than men to be promoted into responsible managerial positions.
3. *"Toughness."* Once in managerial positions, women often feel pressured to be "tougher" than men in order to seem as tough.
4. *Being "businesslike."* Women managers who are strict and businesslike with employees are often accused of being cold or "unwomanly" by their employees—male and female—whereas men showing the same behavior might be considered "matter-of-fact," or not even be noticed.
5. *Dress.* Once in managerial positions, women feel pressured to pay more attention to their appearance than men do, because co-workers pay more attention to what they wear, how they crop their hair, and so forth. If they don't look crisp and tailored every day, others will think that they are unable to exert the force to remain in command. Yet if they dress up "too much," they are accused of being fashion plates rather than serious workers!
6. *Perils of friendliness.* Women can feel pressured to pay more attention to their interpersonal behavior than men do, because women who act friendly are often misinterpreted as being seductive (Abbey, 1982). And, of course, the friendly female manager might also be perceived as a potential doormat.
7. *Decision making.* Once in managerial positions, women who do not reach rapid decisions (even if they are poor decisions) may stand accused of being "wishy-washy."
8. *Flexibility.* If women managers change their minds, they run the risk of being labeled fickle and indecisive, rather than flexible and willing to consider new information.
9. *Sexual harrassment.* Women are subject to sexual harrassment on the job. Many male superiors expect sexual favors in return for advancement on the job.
10. *"Feminine" tasks.* Women are expected to engage in traditional feminine tasks, such as making the coffee or cleaning up after the conference lunch, as well as the jobs they were hired to do.
11. *Role overload.* Women usually have the dual responsibility of being the major caretaker for the children.

This has been a partial list, not an exhaustive list, but it helps indicate some of the costs of stereotyping in terms of careers. All this, of course, adds up to a big headache for women. In many cases, stereotyping discourages highly qualified female individuals from making their highest possible contributions to the work force and to the nation.

In case it is not self-evident, let us note that men also have a stake in reversing these pressures on women. Mistreatment of women by men hurts

▓ WHAT DO YOU SAY NOW?

Handling a Sexist Remark

You have "arrived." You are out of college for only a dozen years, and you have become a vice president for sales at your computer firm. Your letterheads use your initials, "J. T. Hernandez," rather than your first name, so sometimes your correspondents are surprised to learn that you're a woman.

One of them has called on you at your office. He walks in and raises his eyebrows as you rise to meet him. You hold out your hand, and he takes it in both of his. He gives you a great big grin, winks, and says, "What's a nice girl like you doing in a job like this?"

He is being friendly, but you are fuming. This is a business call and not a blind date.

What do you say now? Write down some possible responses and then check the discussion below.

1. _____
   _____
   _____

2. _____
   _____
   _____

3. _____
   _____

Let us note first that male readers have probably learned at least one thing *not* to say to businesswomen, unless they purposefully want to sabotage their business relationships with them. Women may wish to consider responses such as the following.

1. "My hand's not cold, Mr. Harbinger. Perhaps we can talk about why you're here." (This is a very negative response to his holding your hand within his own, and may be linked to another response as well.)
2. "We've found out that men just aren't tough enough for this job." (This comment can be made in a pleasant, humorous voice if the goal is to "proceed as

normal," or in a biting voice, if the expression of displeasure is the sole goal.)
3. "This is a busy day, Mr. Harbinger. Perhaps you'd care to discuss your reasons for coming here." (This lets your visitor know that he is taking your time and that he is on your "territory." It can be said matter-of-factly, in which case there is the possibility for exploring a business relationship further, or it can be said in a way to let your visitor know that the meeting is perilously close to an end. Either way, it puts you in the driver's seat.)
4. "This is the twentieth century, Mr. Harbinger. We refer to adult females as women, not girls." (This points up the fact that "girl" is a demeaning way of addressing an adult, and it can be linked with responses such as 2 or 3.)
5. A suggestion about what *not* to say: It's probably wise not to take your visitor up on the adjective *nice*—that is, avoid saying anything to suggest that you are not, or are, "nice." The word *nice* in this context has an old-fashioned degrading connotation that you need not deal with.

Some of the suggested responses may at first seem like an overreaction. After all, one could argue that Mr. Harbinger was nonplussed and did not know exactly what to say. Perhaps his remark was "innocent," and not an effort at "one-ups-person-ship." If you suspect that he meant no harm, you could make a remark such as one suggested in a more friendly voice, but it might be an error to just let his sexist remark go. It gives him an advantage on your territory, and it might be that no profitable business can be transacted with him while he retains this advantage. In other words, by saying nothing you lose in terms of business as well as self-esteem. By saying something, there is a chance of coming out ahead in business, and you'll certainly feel better about yourself.

women who are loved and cared about by other men. Also, misery in the workplace does not stop at 5:00 P.M. It carries over into home life. Men are married to women, and men have women as mothers and daughters. So mistreatment on the job impairs the quality of home life. And again, there is the larger picture. If we as a society utilize the best talents of all of our people, we produce more, we invent more, and we increase our standard of living.

Costs in Terms of Psychological Well-Being and Interpersonal Relationships

Educational frustrations and problems on the job are sources of the stress that can make us anxious and depressed and interfere with our abilities to function in our relationships with others. In Chapter 6 we shall learn more about stress and the ways in which stress influences our behavior and even our physical health. We have noted the ways in which sex-role stereotyping has an impact on our educations and on our functioning in the workplace.

Here let us note a number of the ways in which stereotyping interferes with our psychological well-being and our interpersonal relationships:

1. Women who fully accept the traditional feminine sex role appear to have lower self-esteem than women who also show some masculine-typed traits (Flaherty & Dusek, 1980; Spence et al., 1975).
2. Women who fully accept the traditional feminine sex role find stressful events more aversive than women who also show some masculine-typed traits (Shaw, 1982).
3. Women who fully accept the traditional feminine sex role are less capable of bouncing back from failure experiences that women who also show some masculine-typed traits (Baucom & Danker-Brown, 1979).
4. Women who fully accept the traditional feminine sex role are likely to believe that women are to be seen and not heard. Therefore, they are unlikely to assert themselves by making their needs and wants known. As a consequence, they are likely to encounter frustration.
5. Women who accept the traditional feminine sex role are more likely to conform to group pressure (Bem, 1975; Cooper, 1979).
6. Men who accept the traditional masculine sex role are more likely to be upset if their wives earn more money than they do!
7. Men who accept the traditional masculine sex role are less likely to feel comfortable performing the activities involved in caring for children, such as bathing them, dressing them, and feeding them (Bem, 1975; Bem et al., 1976; Helmreich et al., 1979).
8. Men who accept the traditional masculine sex role are less likely to ask for help—including medical help—when they need it (Rosenstock & Kirscht, 1979).
9. Men who accept the traditional masculine sex role are less likely to be sympathetic and tender and to express feelings of love in their marital relationships (Coleman & Ganong, 1985).
10. Men who accept the traditional masculine sex role are less likely to be tolerant of their wives' or lovers' faults (Coleman & Ganong, 1985).

Again, we have attempted to suggest just a few of the ways in which sex-role stereotyping interferes with our personal happiness and well-being and intrudes into our interpersonal relationships. We have not provided an exhaustive list. But later in the chapter we shall see how these problems might be ameliorated if we are open to adopting a number of nontraditional behavior patterns. First let us consider some of the particular conflicts and questions faced by working mothers.

■ On the Adjustment of Working Wives and Their Children

The numbers of women in the work force have changed dramatically in recent years. According to the U.S. Bureau of Labor Statistics, during the 12-year span between 1973 and 1985, the percentage of working wives with children under age 18 jumped by 20 points—from 42 to 62 (Lublin, 1984; *New York Times*, 1985). In 1985, even 50 percent of women with children younger than 3 were in the labor force.

Working wives, especially mothers, are in situations that can create role conflict. Sometimes the conflict is internal or in the marriage; the stereotype that "a woman's place is in the home" can lead women or their husbands to wonder whether working women are doing the right thing. Sometimes conflict is caused by role overload as mothers and workers. Working women cannot be in two places at once—at home with their children and at work. Marital (and internal) conflict can also occur when women earn more than their husbands, especially when their husbands feel that their traditional role as breadwinner is being compromised. But despite all these sources of potential conflict, it is instructive to note that women are more likely to feel that they are overloaded and are being pulled in different directions in the role of mother than in the role of paid worker (Barnett & Baruch, 1985).

Since so many of today's women are bucking tradition, let us examine what is known about how working affects a woman's marital happiness and general life satisfaction. Let us also see how working influences her relationship with her children.

In terms of personal satisfaction, it seems that the reasons why a wife is working are more important than the simple fact of her being in the labor force. (Hofferth & Moore, 1979). Wives who choose to work, who have the support of their husbands, who work part-time, or who enter the work force when their children have begun school seem more satisfied than women who are under pressure to work or who would rather have remained in the home with very young children.

The Wall Street Journal/*Gallup Survey* Women still account for the majority of secretaries (99%) and school teachers (71%), but they have also made recent gains in the professions, now accounting, for example, for about 16 percent of lawyers and 37 percent of bank officials and financial managers (Rathus, 1987).

The Wall Street Journal and the Gallup Organization recently ran a joint survey of 772 women executives, all of whom had reached a position of vice president, or higher, in their firms. Of this group, the married women executives were more satisfied with their lives than the unmarried women executives (Rogan, 1984a). However, 57 percent of the executives who were earning *less* than their husbands were totally satisfied with their lives, as compared with only 38 percent of the women executives who brought home *more* than their husbands. It may be that husbands of women who outearn them feel insecure or threatened by their wives' success, or that very high earners spend more energy bringing home the bacon than enjoying it with their spouses.

The Ferree Study A frequently cited study by sociologist Myra Marx Ferree (1976) surveyed 135 predominantly working-class wives who had children

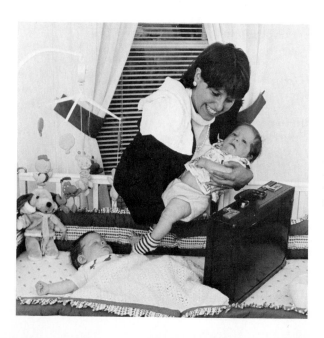

Although the woman in this picture seems well enough adjusted, many working mothers experience role overload as workers and mothers. However, research shows that the children of working mothers adjust as well as the children of non-working mothers, and that they have more egalitarian views concerning sex roles.

in the first or second grade. Forty-five percent of them were housewives. Twenty-six percent held full-time jobs, and 29 percent held part-time jobs. There were no group differences in marital happiness, but the working women were more satisfied with themselves and with their lives in general. Part-time workers were happiest. Their jobs apparently offered the social and psychological benefits of employment, while also allowing them more time for family life.

The working wives in the Ferree study did not hold glamorous occupations. Most filled stereotypical female positions such as typist, waitress, cashier, or office-machine operator. But even these jobs apparently provided the benefits of a paycheck, a sense of accomplishment, and expanded social contacts.

Ferree attributes the dissatisfaction of many full-time homemakers to a breaking down of the supportive family and social network as people have emigrated to the suburbs or followed the breadwinners' jobs to new towns and cities. Nowadays there may be little companionship for a woman at home during the day other than TV game shows or soap operas. Some homemakers complained, "I feel like I'm going crazy staying home," "I feel like I'm in jail," or "I don't see anything but four walls a day."

Must Women Be Superwomen to Be Happy? Women have traditionally subordinated career interests to child-rearing and homemaking. But contemporary values have to some degree devalued the homemaking role, and expectations for a meaningful career have led some women to believe that they must "do it all." They feel pressured to be superwives, super career women, and super mothers—in short, Superwomen (Shreve, 1982).

Despite the new Superwoman ethic, a study of relatively affluent California women suggests that homemaking can still be fulfilling (Tavris, 1976). Work for these women was not a necessity. In contrast to the full-time homemakers in the Ferree study, most of these women had the resources to meet their homemaking responsibilities and still develop personal interests. Working wives in the Tavris study expressed greater feelings of self-esteem and competence, but full-time housewives were more satisfied with their marriages. The least satisfied wives wanted to work but did not. They felt trapped in a role they could not change.

And so it seems that wives' happiness does not hinge on whether they work inside or outside the home. The central issues in their life satisfaction seem to be whether they can choose their life roles, whether they have or can develop enjoyable social contacts, and whether they become involved in activities that enhance their feelings of competence and self-esteem.

Working Mothers and Their Children The major reason that women have been expected to remain in the home is so that they can "be there" for their children. What are the effects of maternal employment on children? Must mother be available for round-the-clock love and attention if her children are to thrive? Not necessarily.

Developmental psychologists (e.g., Easterbrooks & Goldberg, 1985; Hoffman, 1985) have found no consistent evidence that maternal employment is harmful to children. Generally speaking, the children of working women do not differ from those of full-time housewives in terms of anxiety, incidence of antisocial behavior, dependence, or complaints of stress-related disorders such as headaches and upset stomachs. In fact, the children of working women see their mothers as more competent and hold fewer stereotypical sex-role attitudes (Gold & Andres, 1978a, 1978b, 1978c). Children of working women are more helpful with the housework. The daughters of working women are more achievement oriented and set themselves higher career goals than do the daughters of nonworking women.

In some cases, the stereotypical sex roles are reversed and the father stays at home (serves as "househusband"), whereas the mother takes the morning trek to the factory or the office. Children in these families also show fewer stereotypical sex-role attitudes, higher intelligence-test scores, and a greater internal locus of control (Radin, 1982; Russell, 1982). But we cannot necessarily attribute these findings to the father's remaining in the home. It may be that the egalitarian or nontraditional attitudes that endorsed the parental role-reversal also fostered the differences in the children.

All in all, working women spend half as much time caring for their infant children as housewives do, but these children develop normal attachments to them (Moore & Hofferth, 1979). The quality of the time parents and children spend together, along with the making of adequate child-care arrangements, apparently outweighs the importance of the number of hours (Bralove, 1981; Easterbrooks & Goldberg, 1985). When mothers choose to work and find their work fulfilling, they are happier with their lives. They and their husbands are more egalitarian in the distribution of chores in the home as well as in the breadwinning role (Gold & Andres, 1978a, 1978b, 1978c). Perhaps working mothers' feelings of competence and high self-esteem transfer into more productive relationships with their children in the home.

So Now That Women Are Running Companies, Who Does the Laundry? (You Guessed It.)   However, despite the greater egalitarianism found in homes where mothers work, the *Wall Street Journal*/Gallup survey found that married women executives were still much more likely than their husbands to have the major responsibility for certain traditional household chores (Rogan, 1984b): For example, 52 percent of the women executives saw that the laundry got done, as compared to 7 percent of their husbands. Women executives were also more likely than their husbands to plan meals and shop for food (47% vs. 8%), shop for the children's clothes (70% vs. 3%), and stay home with their children when they got ill (30% vs. 5%).* These women, remember, were all vice presidents or presidents in their companies!

Now that we have seen some of the things that happen when women take on traditional masculine chores, let us consider what happens when women taken on traditional masculine personality traits. We also consider the effects, on men, of assuming stereotypical feminine traits.

■ Adjustment and Psychological Androgyny: The More Traits the Merrier?

Most of us think of masculinity and femininity as opposite poles of one continuum (Storms, 1980). We assume that the more masculine people are, the less feminine they are, and vice versa. And so a man who shows the "feminine" traits of nurturance, tenderness, and emotionality might be considered less masculine than other men. Women who compete with men in the business world are not only seen as more masculine than other women, but also as less feminine.

Are Masculinity and Femininity Opposites on the Same Continuum or Independent Dimensions?   But today many psychologists assert that masculinity and femininity make up independent personality dimensions. That is, people (male or female) who score high on measures of masculine traits need not score low on feminine traits. People who show stereotypical masculine *instrumentality* can also show stereotypical feminine *warmth-expressiveness* (see Table 3.1). People who have both intrumentality and warmth-

---

*These percentages do not add up to 100 because in many cases the responsibilities were shared.

Psychological androgyny.
Possession of instrumental
and warmth–expressiveness
traits.

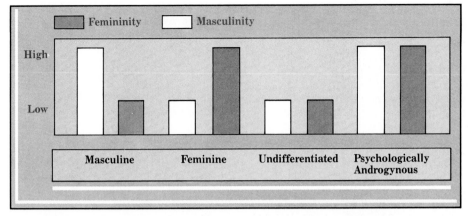

FIGURE 3.4   Masculinity, Femininity, and Psychological Androgyny
Many psychologists conceptualize "masculinity" (instrumentality) and "femininity"
(warmth-expressiveness) as independent dimensions of personality. Psychologically
androgynous individuals show both instrumentality and warmth-expressiveness.
People high in instrumentality only are stereotypically masculine. People high in
warmth-expressiveness only are stereotypically feminine. People low in both clusters
of traits are considered "undifferentiated."

expressiveness traits are said to show **psychological androgyny** (see Figure
3.1). People high in instrumentality *only* are stereotypically masculine. People
high in warmth-expressiveness *only* are stereotypically feminine. People who
are low in both instrumentality and warmth-expressiveness are "undifferentiated" according to the stereotypical sex-role dimensions.

   Before discussing the impact of psychological androgyny on adjustment,
let us note that undifferentiated people seem to encounter distress. Undifferentiated women, for example, are viewed less positively than either more
feminine or more masculine women, even by their friends (Baucom &
Danker-Brown, 1983). And undifferentiated women are less satisfied with
their marriages (Baucom & Aiken, 1984). However, psychologically androgynous people, as we shall see, may be more resistant to stress.

*Contributions of Psychological Androgyny to Well-Being, Adjust-
ment, and Personal Development*   Now let us consider research findings
considering the ways in which psychological androgyny contributes to our
well-being, our adjustment, and our development as individuals. First of all,
research is mixed as to whether psychologically androgynous people are physically healthier than highly masculine or feminine people (Hall & Taylor,
1985). But there is a good deal of evidence that androgynous people are
relatively well-adjusted, apparently because they can summon both "masculine" and "feminine" traits to express their talents and desires and to meet
the demands of their situations.

   In terms of Erik Erikson's concepts of **ego identity** and intimacy, androgynous college students are more likely than feminine, masculine, and
undifferentiated students to show a combination of "high identity" and "high
intimacy" (Schiedel & Marcia, 1985). That is, they are more likely to show a
firm sense of who they are and what they stand for (identity), and they have
a greater capacity to form intimate, sharing relationships.

   Psychologically androgynous people of both sexes show "masculine" independence under group pressures to conform and "feminine" nurturance
in interactions with a kitten or a baby (Bem, 1975; Bem et al., 1976). They
feel more comfortable performing a wider range of activities, including (the
"masculine") nailing of boards and (the "feminine") winding of yarn (Bem &

Q U E S T I O N N A I R E

The ANDRO Scale: A Measure of Psychological Androgyny

What about you? Do you adhere to strict, traditional sex roles? Are you, in the words of Cornell University psychologist Sandra Bem, a "chesty" male or a "fluffy" female? Or is psychological androgyny—the expression of both "masculine" and "feminine" traits—more your style?

To find out, indicate whether the following items from the ANDRO scale are mostly true or mostly false for you by placing a checkmark (√) in the appropriate blank space. Then use the tables at the end of the chapter to compare your score to those of a national sample of men and women.

Then you may have other people in your life take the test. How many chesty males and fluffy females are there in your life?

		TRUE	FALSE
1.	I like to be with people who assume a protective attitude toward me.	____	____
2.	I try to control others rather than permit them to control me.	____	____
3.	Surfboard riding would be dangerous for me.	____	____
4.	If I have a problem I like to work it out alone.	____	____
5.	I seldom go out of my way to do something just to make others happy.	____	____
6.	Adventures where I am on my own are a little frightening to me.	____	____
7.	I feel confident when directing the activities of others.	____	____
8.	I will keep working on a problem after others have given up.	____	____
9.	I would not like to be married to a protective person.	____	____
10.	I usually try to share my problems with someone who can help me.	____	____
11.	I don't care if my clothes are unstylish, as long as I like them.	____	____
12.	When I see a new invention, I attempt to find out how it works.	____	____
13.	People like to tell me their troubles because they know I will do everything I can to help them.	____	____
14.	Sometimes I let people push me around so they can feel important.	____	____
15.	I am only very rarely in a position where I feel a need to actively argue for a point of view I hold.	____	____
16.	I dislike people who are always asking me for advice.	____	____
17.	I seek out positions of authority.	____	____
18.	I believe in giving friends lots of help and advice.	____	____
19.	I get little satisfaction from serving others.	____	____
20.	I make certain that I speak softly when I am in a public place.	____	____
21.	I am usually the first to offer a helping hand when it is needed.	____	____
22.	When I see someone I know from a distance, I don't go out of my way to say "Hello."	____	____
23.	I would prefer to care for a sick child myself rather than hire a nurse.	____	____

24. I prefer not being dependent on anyone for assistance.   _____ _____

25. When I am with someone else, I do most of the decision making.   _____ _____

26. I don't mind being conspicuous.   _____ _____

27. I would never pass up something that sounded like fun just because it was a little hazardous.   _____ _____

28. I get a kick out of seeing someone I dislike appear foolish in front of others.   _____ _____

29. When someone opposes me on an issue, I usually find myself taking an even stronger stand than I did at first.   _____ _____

30. When two persons are arguing, I often settle the argument for them.   _____ _____

31. I will not go out of my way to behave in an approved way.   _____ _____

32. I am quite independent of the people I know.   _____ _____

33. If I were in politics, I would probably be seen as one of the forceful leaders of my party.   _____ _____

34. I prefer a quiet, secure life to an adventurous one.   _____ _____

35. I prefer to face my problems by myself.   _____ _____

36. I try to get others to notice the way I dress.   _____ _____

37. When I see someone who looks confused, I usually ask if I can be of any assistance.   _____ _____

38. It is unrealistic for me to insist on becoming the best in my field of work all of the time.   _____ _____

39. The good opinion of one's friends is one of the chief rewards for living a good life.   _____ _____

40. If I get tired while playing a game, I generally stop playing.   _____ _____

41. When I see a baby, I often ask to hold him.   _____ _____

42. I am quite good at keeping others in line.   _____ _____

43. I think it would be best to marry someone who is more mature and less dependent than I.   _____ _____

44. I don't want to be away from my family too much.   _____ _____

45. Once in a while I enjoy acting as if I were tipsy.   _____ _____

46. I feel incapable of handling many situations.   _____ _____

47. I delight in feeling unattached.   _____ _____

48. I would make a poor judge because I dislike telling others what to do.   _____ _____

49. Seeing an old or helpless person makes me feel that I would like to take care of him.   _____ _____

50. I usually make decisions without consulting others.   _____ _____

51. It doesn't affect me one way or another to see a child being spanked.   _____ _____

52. My goal is to do at least a little bit more than anyone else has done before.   _____ _____

53. To love and to be loved is of greatest importance to me.   _____ _____

54. I avoid some hobbies and sports because of their dangerous nature.   _____ _____

55. One of the things which spurs me on to do my best is the realization that I will be praised for my work.   _____ _____

56. People's tears tend to irritate me more than to arouse my sympathy.   _____ _____

Lenney, 1976; Helmreich et al., 1979). In adolescence, they report greater interest in pursuing nontraditional occupational roles (Motowidlo, 1982). They show greater maturity in moral judgments, greater self-esteem (Flaherty & Dusek, 1980; Spence et al., 1975), and greater ability to bounce back from failure (Baucom & Danker-Brown, 1979). They are more likely to try to help others in need. Androgynous people are more willing to share the leadership in mixed-sex groups; masculine people attempt to dominate such groups and feminine people tend to be satisfied with taking a back seat (Porter et al., 1985). Androgynous women rate stressful life events as less undesirable than do feminine women (Shaw, 1982).

In adolescence it appears that "masculinity" and androgyny are associated with popularity and higher self-esteem in both boys and girls (Lamke, 1982b). Given the prevalence of sexism, it is not surprising that young men fare better than their peers when they show masculine-typed traits. It is of greater interest that young women also fare better when they exhibit masculine-typed, instrumental traits. Apparently these traits do not compromise their "femininity" in the eyes of others—providing more evidence that so-called masculinity and femininity are independent clusters of traits.

A Challenge to Androgyny: Does Masculinity Account for Greater Self-Esteem?   These findings on adjustment have not gone unchallenged. Self-esteem is an important factor in our psychological well-being. On the basis of an analysis of 35 studies on the relationship between sex roles and self-esteem, Bernard Whitley (1983) argues that the self-esteem benefits of psychological androgyny do *not* derive from the combination of masculine and feminine traits. Instead, they reflect the presence of "masculine" traits, whether they are found in males or females. That is, traits such as independence and assertiveness contribute to high self-esteem in both sexes.

Does Femininity—in Men as Well as Women—Contribute to Marital Happiness?   The Whitley study does not address all the correlates of psychological androgyny, of course. Nor does it suggest that it is disadvantageous for either sex to show stereotypical feminine traits, such as nurturance. Other research, in fact, suggests that "feminine" traits contribute to marital happiness. Antill (1983) found not only that husbands' happiness was positively related to their wives' femininity, but also that wives' happiness was positively related to their husbands' femininity. Wives of psychologically androgynous husbands were far happier than women whose husbands adhered to a strict, stereotypical masculine sex role. Androgynous men are more tolerant of their wives' or lovers' faults and more likely to express loving feelings than are "macho" males (Coleman & Ganong, 1985), and women, like men, appreciate spouses who are sympathetic, warm, tender, and who love children.

The Feminist Critique of the Concept of Psychological Androgyny
Criticism of the view that psychological androgyny is a worthwhile goal has also been voiced by some feminists—for quite a different reason. The problem, from the feminist perspective, is that psychological androgyny is defined as the possession of both masculine and feminine personality traits. However, this very definition relies upon the presumed rigidity of masculine and feminine sex-role stereotypes. Feminists such as Bernice Lott (1981, 1985) would prefer to see the dissolution of these stereotypes.

In any event, Sandra Bem (1974) has found that about 50 percent of her samples of college students have adhered to their own sex-role stereotypes on her own test for measuring psychological androgyny—the Bem Sex Role Inventory. About 15 percent have been cross-typed (described by traits stereotypical of the opposite sex), and 35 percent have been androgynous. Other studies (e.g., by Lamke, 1982a) show that the incidence of androgyny among the high school population is lower—about 25 percent. Yet at least one-quarter of our young people seem to be challenging stereotypical sex roles and deciding that they are free both to show competence in the realm of objects and to express feelings of warmth and tenderness.

Since larger numbers of college students are androgynous, and since college students more so than other groups are likely to shape our future as a society, it may be that stereotypes will become less rigid as we progress toward the twenty-first century. Perhaps opportunities for self-expression will expand both for men and women.

Sex roles are just one of the shapers of the ways in which we perceive ourselves and other people. There are others, as we shall see in Chapter 4.

■ Summary

1. **What is meant by a sex-role stereotype?** A stereotype is a fixed, conventional idea about a group, and a sex role is a cluster of stereotypes attributed to one of the sexes.

2. **What are the stereotypical masculine and feminine roles in our society?** In our society, the masculine sex-role stereotype includes aggressiveness, independence, logic, and competence in the business world or the realm of objects ("instrumentality"). The feminine sex-role stereotype includes nurturance, passivity, and dependence ("warmth–expressiveness" traits).

3. **What is sexism?** Sexism is the prejudgment that a person, because of gender, will possess negative traits, and is usually directed against women. Sexism causes people to evaluate the performance of males as superior to that of females.

4. **What cognitive sex differences are there?** Girls generally excel in verbal abilities, while boys excel in math and spatial-relations abilities. Girls talk somewhat earlier than boys, expand their vocabularies faster, and their pronunciation is clearer. Boys develop more reading problems. However, cognitive sex differences are generally small, abilities within the sexes vary more greatly than abilities between the sexes, and cognitive sex differences may reflect cultural expectations.

5. **What sex differences are there in play and school activties?** Preferences for sex-typed toys develop by 15 to 36 months. Boys prefer transportation toys, and girls prefer dolls and soft toys. During middle childhood, boys like rough-and-tumble sports; girls do not. Girls like dancing and sewing; boys do not. Boys like making and fixing things more than girls do.

6. **What sex differences are there in aggression?** Boys are more aggressive than girls under most circumstances. Aggressiveness in girls may be inhibited by lesser physical strength, by anxiety (caused by aggression's inconsistency with the feminine sex-role stereotype), and by empathy with the victim.

7. **Are there any other sex differences in personality or behavior?** In group settings, men talk and interrupt more often than women do. Boys are more likely to make demands and curse. Girls require less personal space than boys do, and they prefer to sit next to companions, while boys prefer to sit across from them. Boys' postures take up more space than girls'.

8. **What biological influences contribute to sex differences in personality and behavior?** Greater brain lateralization in boys might be associated with differences in cognitive abilities. Prenatal influences of male sex hormones may increase activity level and masculine sex-typed preferences.

9. **What is the psychodynamic view of sex typing?** According to psychodynamic theory, sex typing stems from resolution of the conflicts of the phallic stage. However, children assume sex roles at much earlier ages than the theory would suggest.

10. **What is the social-learning view of sex typing?** Social-learning theory explains sex-typing in terms of observational learning, identification, and socialization. Observational learning may largely account for children's knowledge of "gender-appropriate" preferences and behavior patterns. Children generally identify with adults of the same sex and attempt to broadly imitate their behavior, but only when they perceive it as gender-appropriate. Children are also guided into stereotypical sex-role behaviors by early socialization messages and reinforcement.

11. **What is the cognitive-developmental view of sex typing?** Cognitive-developmental theory views sex typing in terms of the emergence of gender identity, gender stability, and gender constancy. Gender identity is one's sense of being male or being female, and develops by about 18–36 months of age. It is thought that the development of gender stability fosters the organization of sex-typed behavior. However, children usually show sex-typed preferences and behavior patterns upon the emergence of gender identity.

12. **What is the gender-schema view of sex typing?** Gender-schema theory includes elements from social-learning theory and cognitive-developmental theory. Gender-schema theory proposes that children use the gender schema of their society to organize their perceptions, and that children attempt to blend their self-concepts with the gender schema. Evidence in support of gender-schema theory shows that children process information according to the gender schema.

13. **What are the costs of sex-role stereotyping in terms of education?** A sampling of the educational costs include the following: Math is more likely to be considered a male domain, while reading is viewed as a female domain in our society. It is difficult to convince even highly capable girls to take math courses in high school, and boys read more poorly than girls.

14. **What are the costs of sex-role stereotyping in terms of activities and careers?** For one thing, children tend to think of some kinds of jobs as men's jobs and others as women's jobs. For another, women earn less pay, must dress and behave more carefully on the job, and are subject to sexual harrassment on the job.

15. **What are the costs of sex-role stereotyping in terms of psychological well being and interpersonal relationships?** Women who accept the feminine sex role have lower self-esteem and adapt to stress less well than women who do not. Men who accept the masculine sex role are less likely to express warm feelings and are more rigid in the activities they will permit themselves.

16. **How well adjusted are married women who work?** Married female workers who *choose* to work are more satisfied with their lives. There are social and psychological benefits to employment as well as the paycheck.

17. **How well adjusted are the children of working mothers?** There is no consistent evidence that maternal employment is harmful to children. Children of working mothers hold fewer stereotypical sex-role attitudes and see their mothers as more competent.

18. **What is psychological androgyny?** Psychological androgyny is the possession of the clusters of traits referred to as instrumentality and warmth-expressiveness.

19. **Does psychological androgyny foster adjustment and personal development?** Apparently so. Psychologically androgynous people show high "identity" and "intimacy"—using the concepts of Erik Erikson. They show both independence and nurturance, depending on the situation. They have higher self-esteem and greater ability to bounce back from failure. Wives of psychologically androgynous husbands are happier than wives of husbands who adhere to a strict stereotypical masculine sex role.

■ **T R U T H   O R   F I C T I O N   R E V I S I T E D**

Women are expected to be more vain than men. True. Being conceited about one's appearance is considered part of the traditional feminine sex-role stereotype.

An essay written by a woman is poorer in quality than an essay written by a man—even when it is the same essay. False. However, research into sexism found that the same essay was rated as poorer in quality when authorship was attributed to a woman.

Teachers are more likely to accept calling out in class from boys than from girls. True. Teachers seem to have the attitude that "boys will be boys," but that girls should be shaped into "ladylike" behavior.

Women are superior to men in verbal abilities. True. The questions are how much and why.

Men have greater math and spatial-relations abilities than women do. True. Again, the questions are how much and why.

Men behave more aggressively than women do. True. However, women can also act aggressively when they are provoked, when they have the means, and when they believe that the social milieu will tolerate aggressive behavior from them.

Men are more likely than women to curse. True.

Women prefer to sit next to their friends, whereas men prefer to sit across from them. True. This sex difference might stem from socializing women into cooperation and men into competition.

Adolescents who reach sexual maturity early tend to have greater verbal skills than those who reach sexual maturity at later ages. True. Time of sexual maturation appears to play a role in the development of "feminine" or "masculine" patterns of cognitive skills.

Parents treat sons and daughters differently, even when they are under one year of age. True. They encourage exploratory behavior in boys and tend to be protective of girls.

A 2½-year-old may know that he is a boy but think that he can grow up to be a mommy. True. Children do not realize that gender is permanent until they develop gender constancy at about the age of 4 or 5.

Five- and 6-year-olds tend to distort their memories so that they "remember" boys playing with trains and sawing wood—even when these activities were actually carried out by girls. True. Such patterns of processing information lend support to the gender-schema theory of sex-typing.

Throughout most of human history, girls were considered unsuited to education. True. Not until this century did girls attend schools in large numbers.

The children of working women are less well adjusted than the children of women who remain in the home. False. No consistent differences between these groups of children have been found.

Working women remain more likely than their husbands to do the cooking and take care of the laundry, even when the women are presidents or vice presidents of their companies. True, according to a poll taken by *The Wall Street Journal* and the Gallup organization.

Adolescent girls who show a number of masculine traits are more popular than girls who thoroughly adopt the traditional feminine sex role. True. Apparently the presence of some masculine-typed, instrumental traits does not compromise their "femininity."

■ Scoring Key for the ANDRO Scale

People who score high on masculinity alone on this scale endorse traditionally masculine attitudes and behaviors, whereas people who score high on femininity alone hold traditionally feminine ways of relating to the world. Many psychologists now believe that you will experience life more fully and be better adjusted if you score relatively high on both masculinity and femininity. Scoring high on both suggests that you are psychologically androgynous and can summon up characteristics attributed to both sexes, as needed. That is, you can be assertive but caring, logical but emotionally responsive, strong but gentle.

You can determine your own masculinity and femininity scores by seeing how many of your answers agree with those on the key in Table 3.4.

Use Table 3.5 to compare your masculinity and femininity scores to those of 386 male and 723 female University of Kentucky students. Your percentile score (%) means that your own score equaled or excelled that of the percentage of students shown. Then look at Figure 3.5 to compare your score with those of people from many walks of life.

TABLE 3.4   Key for Determining Total Masculinity and Femininity Scores

	Masculinity			Femininity	
Item No.	Key	Score: 1 if same as key, 0 if not	Item No.	Key	Score: 1 if same as key, 0 if not
2.	T	____	1.	T	____
3.	F	____	5.	F	____
4.	T	____	9.	F	____
6.	F	____	13.	T	____
7.	T	____	14.	T	____
8.	T	____	16.	F	____
10.	F	____	18.	T	____
11.	T	____	19.	F	____
12.	T	____	20.	T	____
15.	F	____	21.	T	____
17.	T	____	22.	F	____
25.	T	____	23.	T	____
26.	T	____	24.	F	____
27.	T	____	28.	F	____
29.	T	____	32.	F	____
30.	T	____	36.	T	____
31.	T	____	37.	T	____
33.	T	____	39.	T	____
34.	F	____	41.	T	____
35.	T	____	43.	T	____
38.	F	____	44.	T	____
40.	F	____	45.	T	____
42.	T	____	49.	T	____
46.	F	____	51.	F	____
47.	T	____	53.	T	____
48.	F	____	55.	T	____
50.	T	____	56.	F	____
52.	T	____			
54.	F	____			

Total Masculinity Score: ____   Total Femininity Score: ____
Maximum Score = 29   Maximum Score = 27

To determine your masculinity and femininity scores on the ANDRO Scale, place a 1 in the appropriate blank space each time your answer agrees with the answer (T or F) shown on the key. Place a 0 in the space each time your answer disagrees with the answer shown on the key. Then add up the totals for each.
Source of data: Berzins et al., 1977.

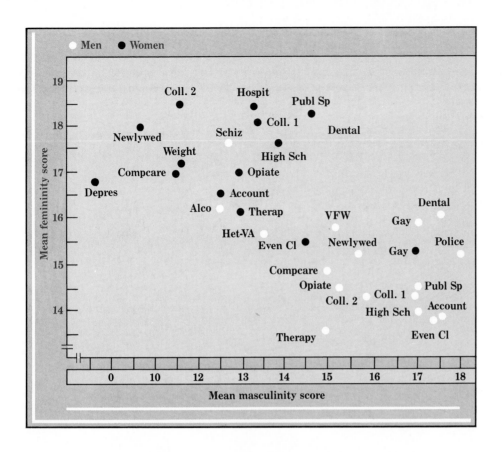

FIGURE 3.5 Distribution of Mean Masculinity and Femininity Scores for 20 Samples.

Legend Account = college students in accounting classes, N^* = 105 ALCO = hospitalized Veterans Administration alcoholics, N = 760 Coll.1 & Coll.2 = college students in introductory psychology classes N = 2,547, and 986, respectively Compcare = community mental health center outpatients, N = 134 Dental = dental school students, N = 54 Depres = hospitalized clinically depressed patients, N = 20 Even CL = college students in evening and day psychology classes, N = 185 Gay = homosexual volunteers, N = 71 Het-VA = heterogeneous, nonschizophrenia group of Veterans Administration outpatients, N = 33 High sch = high school students, N = 700 Hospit = hospitalized nonpsychiatric medical patients, N = 20 Newlywed = newlywed couples, N = 198 Opiate = civilly committed opiate addicts, N = 216 Police = municipal police, N = 25 Publ sp = college students in public speaking classes, N = 166 Schiz = schizophrenic Veterans Administration outpatients, N = 20 Therapy = psychotherapists and trainees, N = 276 VFW = Veterans of Foreign Wars, N = 57 Weight = participants in a hospital weight-reducing program, N = 54

TABLE 3.5 Percentile Rankings of Masculinity and Femininity Scores of College Student Sample

Masculinity Scores				Femininity Scores			
Raw Score	Males (%)	Females (%)	Combined (%)	Raw Score	Males (%)	Females (%)	Combined (%)
29	99	99	99	27	99	99	99
28	99	99	99	26	99	99	99
27	99	99	99	25	99	99	99
26	99	99	99	24	99	99	99
25	98	99	99	23	99	98	99
24	96	98	97	22	99	94	96
23	92	96	94	21	98	87	92
22	88	96	92	20	95	78	86
21	80	94	87	19	91	65	78
20	73	93	83	18	85	53	69
19	63	88	75	17	76	42	59
18	54	83	68	16	65	32	48
17	47	78	60	15	56	24	40
16	39	72	56	14	47	17	32
15	30	65	48	13	37	12	25
14	23	58	40	12	28	6	17
13	17	50	33	11	20	4	12
12	13	41	27	10	14	3	8
11	10	34	22	9	7	2	4
10	6	28	17	8	4	1	3
9	4	21	13	7	3	0	2
8	2	16	9	6	2	0	1
7	2	11	6	5	2	0	1
6	1	9	5	4	1	0	0
5	1	5	3	3	0	0	0
4	0	2	1	2	0	0	0
3	0	1	0	1	0	0	0
2	0	0	0	0	0	0	0
1	0	0	0				
0	0	0	0				

Source of data: Berzins et al., 1977.

Person Perception: How We See Others and Ourselves

First impressions last.

Waitresses who touch their patrons while making change receive higher tips.

We tend to divide the social world into "us" and "them."

Children who have been victims of discrimination are less likely to practice discrimination themselves.

Contact between members of different racial groups can reduce feelings of prejudice.

One way of combatting prejudice is to seek compliance with the law.

An identity crisis is a sign of maladjustment.

A rose by any other name, contrary to William Shakespeare, could smell just plain awful.

Psychology Today readers are generally satisfied with their eyes and ears, but less happy with their teeth and their behinds.

U.S. residents place more value on pleasure and excitement than on peace and freedom.

The self-esteem of an average student may exceed that of a scholar.

Children with strict parents have higher self-esteem than children with permissive parents.

We can build our self-esteem by becoming good at something.

We hold other people responsible for their misdeeds, but we tend to see ourselves as victims of circumstances.

We tend to attribute our successes to our abilities and hard work, but we attribute our failures to external factors such as lack of time or obstacles placed in our paths by others.

So you think you've had trouble getting from place to place? You complain you've waited in lines at airports, or you've been stuck in freeway traffic? These experiences are frustrating, to be sure, but according to Greek mythology, some ancient travelers had a tougher time of it. They met up with a highwayman named Procrustes (pronounced pro-CRUSS-tease).

Now this Procrustes had a quirk. Not only was he interested in travelers' pocketbooks, but also in their height. He had a concept—a **schema**—of just how tall people should be, and when people did not fit his schema, they were in for it. You see, Procrustes also had a very famous bed, a bed that comes down to us in history as a "Procrustean bed." He made his victims lie down in the bed, and when they were too short for it, he stretched them to make them fit. When they were too long for it, he is said to have practiced surgery on their legs. Many unfortunate passersby failed to survive.

■ On Perception and Schemas: An Information-Processing Approach

The myth of Procrustes may sound absurd, but it reflects a quirky truth about each of us. We all carry our cognitive Procrustean beds around with us—our unique ways of perceiving the world—and we try to make things and people fit. In Chapter 3 we saw how many of us carry around the Procrustean beds of sex-role stereotypes—an example of a **role schema**—and how we try to fit men and women into them. For example, when the career woman oversteps the bounds of the male chauvinist's role schema, he metaphorically chops off her legs.

We carry many other kinds of schemas* around with us, and they influence our adjustment and personal development. Some are **person schemas,** as formed, for example, by first impressions. We shall see that our first impressions of others often form schemas, or kinds of cognitive anchors, that color our future observations. Other schemas concern our ways of "reading" body language. As noted in Chapter 2, we infer personality traits from behavior; in this chapter we shall see how we draw a number of conclusions about other people's feelings and attitudes from the ways in which they carry themselves and look at one another. Still other schemas concern groups of people; they involve prejudices concerning racial and ethnic groups. We shall examine the origins of prejudice and make a number of suggestions as to what you can do about prejudice when it affects you.

We shall also see that we carry inward-directed schemas, or **self-schemas,** in the form of self-concepts and self-ideals. Self-schemas have powerful impacts on our feelings about ourselves and influence our behavior. Finally, we shall see that we carry schemas that influence the ways in which we interpret the successes and shortcomings of other people and ourselves. These particular schemas are called "attributions," and they have a major impact on our relationships with others.

As we progress, a continuing theme will emerge: We do not perceive other people and ourselves directly. Instead, we process information about others and ourselves through our schemas. We perceive the social and the personal worlds as through a glass—and sometimes darkly. And when other people do not quite fit our schemas, we have a way of perceptually stretching them or of chopping off their legs. And, ironically, we do not spare ourselves this cognitive pruning.

Schema. An organized collection of beliefs and feelings about a thing, such as a stereotype, a preconception, or a generalization.

Role schema. A schema about how people in certain roles (e.g., boss, spouse, teacher) are expected to behave.

Person schema. A schema about how a particular individual is expected to behave.

Self-schema. The set of beliefs, feelings, and generalizations we have about ourselves.

*Many psychologists prefer to use the Greek plural, *schemata,* as opposed to the English *schemas.*

Primacy effect. The tendency to evaluate others in terms of first impressions.

Recency effect. The tendency to evaluate others in terms of the most recent impression.

■ Perception of Others

Let us begin by seeing how first impressions prompt the development of schemas that resist change. Then we shall discuss our schemas concerning body language and prejudice.

Primacy and Recency Effects: The Importance of First Impressions

Why do you wear your best outfit to an interview for an attractive job? Why do defense attorneys dress their clients immaculately before they go before the jury? Because first impressions are important.

First impressions often make or break us. This is the **primacy effect.** As noted in Chapter 2, we tend to infer traits, or to form person schemas, from behavior. If we act considerately at first, we are labeled considerate. The trait of considerateness is used to explain and predict our future behavior. If, after being labeled considerate, one keeps a date out past curfew, this behavior is likely to be seen as an exception to a rule—as justified by circumstances or external factors. But if at first one is seen as inconsiderate, several months of considerate behavior may be perceived as a cynical effort to "make up for it" or to camouflage one's "real personality."

In a classic experiment on the primacy effect, SUNY at Albany psychologist Abraham Luchins (1957) had subjects read different stories about "Jim." The stories consisted of one or two paragraphs. One-paragraph stories portrayed Jim as friendly or unfriendly. These paragraphs were also used in the two-paragraph stories, but presented to different subjects in opposite order. Of subjects reading only the "friendly" paragraph, 95 percent rated Jim as friendly. Of those who read just the "unfriendly" paragraph, 3 percent rated him as friendly. Seventy-eight percent of those who read two-paragraph stories in the "friendly-unfriendly" order labeled Jim as friendly. But when they read the paragraphs in the reverse order, only 18 percent rated Jim as friendly.

How can we encourage people to pay more attention to more recent impressions? Luchins accomplished this by allowing time to elapse between presenting the paragraphs. In this way, fading memories allowed more recent information to take precedence. We call the phenomenon in which the most recent impressions govern the formation of the person schema the **recency effect.** Luchins found a second way to counter first impressions: He simply counseled subjects to avoid snap judgments and to weigh all the evidence.

First Impressions, Person Schemas, and Adjustment: What to Do

And so, the first impressions you make on others, and the first impressions others make on you, are quite important to your interpersonal relationships. There are a number of things that we can do concerning first impressions:

1. First, be aware of the first impressions you make on others. When you meet people for the first time, remember that they are forming person schemas about you. Once these schemas are formed, they are resistant to change.
2. When you apply for a job, your first impression may reach your prospective employer before you walk in the door. It is in the form of your vita or résumé. Make sure that it is neat and that some of your more important accomplishments are presented right at the beginning.
3. There's no harm in planning and rehearsing your first few remarks for a date or a job interview. Imagine the situation and, in the case of a job interview, things you are likely to be asked. If you have some relatively smooth statements prepared, along with a nice smile, you are more likely

to be thought of as socially competent, and competence is respected. (We'll give you some specific ideas of things to say and do in Chapter 12.)

4. Smile. As you'll see in Chapter 13, you're more attractive when you smile.

5. Be well dressed for job interviews, college interviews, first dates, or other appointments that are of importance. It's not even a bad idea to be well dressed when you go to the doctor's office with a physical complaint! The appropriate dress to make an impression on a first date might differ from that you would wear to a job interview. But in each case ask yourself, What type of dress is expected for this occasion? What's the best I can do to make a positive first impression?

6. When you write answers to essay questions, be concerned about your penmanship. It is the first thing your instructor notices when looking at your paper. Try also to present relevant knowledge in the first sentence or paragraph of the answer, or restate the question by writing something like, "In this essay I shall show how . . ."

7. In class, seek eye contact with your instructors and look interested. That way, if you do poorly on a couple of quizzes, your instructor might think of you as a "basically good student who made a couple of errors" rather than "a poor student who is revealing his/her shortcomings." (Don't tell your instructor that this paragraph is in this book. Maybe he/she won't notice.)

8. The first time you talk to your instructor outside of class, be reasonable and sound interested in his/her subject.

9. When you pass someone in a race, put on a huge burst of speed. That way the other guy may think that trying to catch you will be futile.

10. Ask yourself if you are being fair to other people in your life. If your date's parents are a bit cold toward you the evening of your first date, maybe it's because they don't know you and are concerned about their son/daughter's welfare. If you show them that you are treating their son/daughter decently, they may very well come around. Don't assume that they're basically prunefaces.

11. Before you eliminate people from your life on the basis of first impressions, ask yourself, "Is the first impression the 'real person,' or is it just one instance of that person's behavior?" Give other people more than one chance and you may find that you they have something to offer. After all, would you want to be held accountable for everything you've ever said and done? Haven't you changed for the better as time has gone on? Haven't you become more sophisticated and knowledgeable? (You're reading this book, aren't you?) People are not always at their best. Don't create person schemas that are carved in stone on the basis of one social exchange.

12. When you meet people after a number of years have passed, give them a fresh chance. You might be surprised by how much they have changed—and by how much your own social needs and interests have changed. You just might hit it off.

Body Language

Body language is another important source of information in our perceptions of other people's thoughts and feelings. They make a major contribution to the development of our person schemas.

On Being "Uptight" and "Hanging Loose"   At an early age we learn that the ways that people carry themselves provide cues as to how they feel and are likely to behave. You may have noticed that when people are "uptight," their bodies are also often rigid and straight-backed. People who are relaxed are more likely to literally "hang loose." It seems that various combinations of eye contact, posture, and distance between people provide

WHAT DO YOU SAY NOW?

On Overcoming Negative First Impressions

You are waiting for a job interview in the outer office. You and the secretary are exchanging banter and you make a playful remark that you hope you do not get the job because if you do, you'll have to work for a living. In the middle of your conversation, your interviewer, Mr. Grim, marches in and catches the tail end of your remarks. He gives you a rather peevish glance and marches into the inner office. His secretary says "Uh oh" and then the intercom sounds. Mr. Grim is ready for you.

You walk into the inner office and Mr. Grim—his facial expression living up to his name—rises to meet you. After the formal introductions, he says "I'm not sure I caught everything you were saying to my secretary. Would you care to elaborate?"

What do you say now? How do you overcome the first impression you have made? Jot down some possible responses and then compare them with the ideas that follow.

1. _____
   _____
2. _____
   _____
3. _____
   _____

So, what do you say after you remove your foot from your mouth? Here are some thoughts:

1. Rather than deny what you were saying, and appear evasive, why not repeat the remark—recast slightly, but then point out that it was only banter. You can say something like, "I was saying that the negative aspect to attaining a job is that it means that one must work. But your secretary and I were only exchanging banter, Mr. Grim. If my character has a flaw concerning my diligence, it's actually in the opposite direction. I am a very hard worker."

2. You can go on to assertively express a feeling: "Interviews tend to induce anxiety, Mr. Grim, and I was trying to break the tension with a bit of humor."

3. Or you could say something like, "Frankly, I hope you won't jump to conclusions concerning my character from one remark made in jest. I hope you'll consider everything we discuss and my past employment (or college) record." Then mention a couple of sterling achievements. By taking this approach, you are inviting your interviewer to consider all the evidence, not just his first impression.

4. If Mr. Grim continues to focus on your remark and becomes contentious, it is clear that you are unlikely to be offered the job. However, you can retain your self-respect and take charge of the situation by saying something like, "It seems to me that you are hesitant to look beyond my remark to your secretary. Unless you are willing to recognize that my comments were made in jest, and that the full weight of my record suggests that I have a great deal to offer, I think that it is probably pointless for us to pursue this discussion further." You have clearly taken charge of the situation and shown that you are willing to depart at once; however, you have also "left the door open a crack" if Mr. Grim realizes that he should reopen it.

---

broadly recognized cues as to their moods and as to their feelings toward their companions (Schwartz et al., 1983).

When people face us and lean toward us, we may assume that they like us or are interested in what we are saying. If we are privy to a conversation between a couple and observe that the woman is leaning toward the man but that he is sitting back and toying with his hair, we may rightly infer that he is not having any of what she is selling (Clore et al., 1975; DePaulo et al., 1978).

Touching Touching also communicates. Women are more likely than men to touch other people when they are interacting with them (Stier & Hall, 1984). In one touching experiment, Kleinke (1977) showed that appeals for help can be more effective when the distressed person engages in physical contact with people being asked for aid. A woman received more dimes for phone calls when she touched the arm of the person she was asking for money. In another experiment, women about to undergo operations reported lower anxiety and showed lower blood pressure when nurses explaining the procedures touched them on the arm (Whitcher & Fisher, 1979). But men who were touched while the procedures were explained reported higher anxiety and showed elevated blood pressure. How do we account for this sex difference? Female patients may have perceived touching as a sign of warmth, whereas male patients might have perceived touching as a threatening sign of the nurse's superior status in the hospital.

Body language can also be used to establish and maintain territorial control (Brown & Altman, 1981), as anyone who has had to step aside because a football player was walking down the hall can testify. Werner and her colleagues (1981) found that players in a game arcade used touching as a way of signaling others to keep their distance. Solo players engaged in more touching than did groups, perhaps because they were surrounded by strangers.

Gazing and Staring: The Eyes Have It   We also tend to make a number of inferences about other people's eye contact with us. When other people are looking at us "squarely in the eye," we are more likely to assume that they are being assertive, direct, and open with us. When other people avert their gaze, we often infer that they are shy, deceptive, or depressed (Knapp, 1978; Siegman & Feldstein, 1977). In a study designed to validate a scale to measure romantic love, Brandeis University psychologist Zick Rubin (1970) found that couples who attained higher "love scores" also spent more time gazing into each other's eyes.

Gazes are different, of course, from persistent "hard" stares. Hard stares are interpreted as provocations or signs of anger (Ellsworth & Langer, 1976). When the first author was in high school, adolescent males often engaged in "staring contests" as an assertion of dominance.* The adolescent who looked away first "lost."

In a series of field experiments, Phoebe Ellsworth and her colleagues (1972) subjected drivers stopped at red lights to hard stares from riders of motor scooters (see Figure 4.1). Recipients of the stares crossed the intersection more rapidly than nonrecipients when the light changed. Greenbaum and Rosenfeld (1978) found that recipients of hard stares from a man seated near an intersection also drove off more rapidly after the light turned green. Other research shows that recipients of hard stares show higher levels of physiological arousal than people who do not receive the stares (Strom & Buck, 1979). It may be that many of us rapidly leave situations in which we are stared at in order to return to comfortable levels of arousal and avoid the threat of danger.

On Body Language and Adjustment: What to Do   There are a number of ways in which we can use information about body language to foster adjustment and social relationships:

1. Be aware of what other people are telling you with their body language. If they are looking away as you are telling them something, perhaps you are "turning them off." If they are leaning toward you, nodding, and meeting your gaze, they are probably agreeing with you. Make mental notes of their reactions to get a fix on their attitudes and feelings about you.
2. Pay attention to your own body language as a way of helping to make the desired impressions on other people. Are you maintaining eye contact and nodding "yes" when you want to say "no"? If so, you can't be very happy with yourself. Would you like to be encouraging but wear a perpetual frown? If so, you may be pushing other people away without intending to.
3. Pay attention to your own body language as a way of learning about yourself—as a way of getting "in touch" with your own feelings. If you are agreeing to something, but you are leaning away from the other person and your back is rigid, perhaps you would like to rethink your assent. Or

---

*Of course, the author was too sophisticated to participate in such nonsense.

We infer a great deal about people's feelings from their "body language." What does the body language of this couple suggest about their feelings toward one another?

perhaps you are staring when you think you might be gazing. Could it be that you are more upset by something than you had imagined? As we shall see in Chapter 9, Gestalt therapists encourage their clients to pay very close attention to what their bodies are "telling them" about their genuine feelings.

Prejudice

Iowa schoolteacher Jane Elliot taught her all-white class of third-graders some of the effects of prejudice. She divided the class into blue-eyed and brown-eyed children. The brown-eyed children were labeled inferior, made to wear collars that identified their group, and denied classroom privileges. After a few days of discrimination, the brown-eyed children lost self-esteem and earned poorer grades. They cried often and expressed the wish to stay at home.

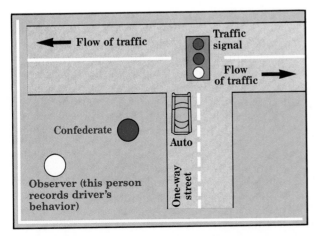

FIGURE 4.1   Diagram of an Experiment in Hard Staring and Avoidance

In the Greenbaum and Rosenfeld study, the confederate of the experimenter stared at some drivers and not at others. Those stared at drove across the intersection more rapidly once the light turned green. Why?

Then the pattern was reversed. Blue-eyed children were assigned the inferior status. After a few days they, too, learned how painful it is to be victims of prejudice.

Prejudice is an attitude toward a group that leads people to evaluate members of that group negatively. As a person schema, prejudice is linked to expectations that the target group will behave badly, in the workplace, say, or by engaging in criminal activity. On an emotional, or **affective,** level, prejudice is associated with negative feelings such as dislike or hatred. Behaviorally, prejudice is associated with avoidance behavior, aggression, and discrimination.

Sexism, Racism, and Ageism   In Chapter 3 it was noted that women are often expected to produce inferior work. This form of prejudice is called sexism. In **racism,** one race or ethnic group holds negative person schemas of, or attitudes toward, the other. For example, many white people are more likely than blacks to assume that blacks are guilty of crimes of violence, whereas many blacks are more likely to attribute guilt for such crimes to whites (Ugwuegbu, 1979).

In recent years, we have become more aware of the effects of a form of prejudice called **ageism.** "Ageists" assume that the elderly are less capable of performing on the job, that they will hold "old-fashioned" moral and political views, and that they are easily irritated, or "crotchety." Many ageists even believe that senior citizens cannot (or should not) engage in sexual activity (Rathus, 1983). None of these schemas necessarily conforms to the facts, but senior citizens may also aquire them and disqualify themselves from productive work or enjoyable sexual activity.

There is an interaction between our cognitions, affects, and behaviors. Consider a recent study in which white people had appeared to adopt new egalitarian norms. In an experimental situation in which they had the opportunity to respond aggressively toward other people, they acted less aggressively toward blacks than toward other whites. But when anger was induced in the white subjects by experimental means, the pattern was reversed and they acted more aggressively toward blacks than whites. It seems that underlying prejudices had persisted and could be evoked by stressful circumstances (Rogers & Prentice-Dunn, 1981).

Discrimination   **Discrimination** is one form of negative behavior that results from prejudice. Many groups have been discriminated against from time to time in the U.S.A. They include, but are not limited to, Jews, Catholics, blacks, Native Americans, Hispanic Americans, homosexuals, the aged, and women. Discrimination takes many forms, including denial of access to jobs, housing, even the voting booth. Many people have forgotten that U.S. blacks gained the right to vote several decades before it was obtained by U.S. women.

Stereotypes   Are women emotional? Are Jews shrewd? Are blacks musical? Are Orientals inscrutable? If you believe such ideas, you are falling for stereotyped person schemas—prejudices about a group that can lead us to process information about members of these groups in a biased fashion. For example, in one experiment, subjects who watched videotapes of a child taking an academic test rated her performance as superior when told that she came from a high socioeconomic background. Other subjects were told that she came from a low socioeconomic background. They watched the same videotape, but rated her performance as below grade level (Darley & Gross, 1983).

In recent studies of stereotypes (Sagar & Schofield, 1980; Smedley & Bayton, 1978), whites viewed middle-class blacks as ambitious, intelligent, conscientious, and responsible, but saw *lower-class* blacks as ignorant, rude, dangerous, and self-pitying. Blacks shared whites' negative impressions of lower-class individuals of the other race. But blacks also negatively evaluated

Prejudice. The belief that a person or group, on the basis of assumed racial, ethnic, sexual, or other features, will possess negative characteristics or perform inadequately.

Affective. Emotional.

Racism. The preconception that a person, on the basis of race, will perform inadequately or have negative characteristics.

Ageism. The preconception that a person, on the basis of age, will perform inadequately or have negative characteristics.

Discrimination. The denial of privileges to a person or group on the basis of prejudice.

Holocaust. The name given the Nazi murder of millions of Jews during World War II.

Scapegoat. A person or group upon whom the blame for the mistakes or crimes of others is cast.

Authoritarianism. Belief in the importance of unquestioning obedience to authority.

middle-class whites as biased, sly, and deceitful, even though they also considered middle-class whites conscientious and ambitious.

Despite the persistence of some stereotypes, white children in recent years seem more willing to work with and befriend blacks than they were during the 1960s (Moe et al., 1981).

Sources of Prejudice The sources of prejudice are many and varied. Let us briefly consider several possible contributors.

1. *Attitudinal differences.* As we shall see in Chapter 13, we are prone to feeling attracted to and liking people who share our attitudes. In forming impressions of others, we are influenced by attitudinal similarity and dissimilarity as well as by race (Goldstein & Davis, 1972; Rokeach et al., 1960). People of different religions and races often have different backgrounds and values, giving rise to dissimilar attitudes. But even when people of different races share important values, they are likely to assume that they will not.

2. *Social conflict and economic competition.* There is also a lengthy history of social and economic conflict between people of different races and religions. Conflict and competition lead to negative attitudes (Sherif, 1966). In their description of a lynching, Miller and Dollard (1941) argue that the hatred of whites for blacks in the South of the Great Depression stemmed, in part, from fear that blacks would take low-level jobs and deprive many whites of an income. There are updated examples. Similar fears in more recent years have, for example, led some Floridians—including blacks—to develop negative attitudes toward Hispanic immigrants, and some Texans to develop negative attitudes toward Vietnamese immigrants. In some locales black U.S. citizens have developed negative attitudes toward black immigrants from Jamaica.

3. *Authoritarianism and scapegoating.* Based on psychoanalytic theory and their interpretation of the **holocaust,** some social scientists (e.g., Adorno et al., 1950) have argued that racial and religious minorities serve as **scapegoats** for majority groups. The Germans, for instance, submitted to Nazi **authoritarianism,** because they had been reared to submit to authority figures. They then displaced unconscious hostility toward their fathers onto Jews. These Freudian concepts have been criticized by many psychologists, but authoritarian people do appear to harbor more prejudices than nonauthoritarians (e.g., Stephan & Rosenfield, 1978).

4. *Social learning.* Children tend to acquire many attitudes from others, especially parents, through identification and socialization. Children often broadly imitate their parents, and parents often reinforce their children for doing so. In this way, prejudices are likely to be transferred from generation to generation.

5. *Information processing.* An information-processing view of prejudice suggests that the origins of prejudice and stereotyping are frequently more cognitive than affective. Stereotypes make it easier to process information about unknown individuals (Taylor, 1978). In other words, if one needs an architect and assumes that men make the best architects, women architects are excluded from the search—making the search more efficient (although not likely to culminate in a superior outcome!). Similarly, one might only hire female babysitters if he or she believed that only women possess nurturant qualities. Or one might seek a (presumably shrewd) Jewish lawyer or a (presumably musical) black entertainer.

Of course, this sort of information processing frequently leads us to exclude qualified people as candidates for various jobs. The people we exclude suffer, and we suffer also—by narrowing our choices and maintaining our ignorance.

From another information-processing perspective, we can note that people often divide the social world into two categories—"us" and "them"—as a way of trying to understand their own behavior and the behavior of others. People also usually view those who belong to their own groups—the "ingroup"—more favorably than those who do not—the "outgroup" (Hemstone & Jaspars, 1982; Wilder & Thompson, 1980). Moreover, there is a tendency for us to assume that outgroup members are more alike (homogeneous) in their attitudes and behaviors than members of our own groups (Park & Rothbart, 1982). Our relative isolation from outgroups does not encourage us to break down our stereotypes.

Coping with Prejudice and Discrimination: What to Do   Prejudice has existed throughout history and we doubt that "miracle cures" are at hand to eradicate it fully. However, as we shall see, a number of measures have met with success. In many cases, it is easier to deal with discrimination, the behavioral manifestation of prejudice. For example, laws now prohibit denial of access to jobs, housing, and other social necessities on the basis of race, religion, handicaps, and related factors.

Let us consider a number of things that can be done:

1. *Role reversal: An immunization technique?* A study by Weiner and Wright (1973) tested the implications of Jane Elliot's informal demonstration with blue- and brown-eyed children. White third-graders were assigned at ranom to "Green" or "Orange" groups and identified with armbands. First, the "green" people were labeled inferior and denied social privileges. After a few days, the pattern was reversed. Children in a second class did not receive the "Green–Orange treatment" and served as a control group.

    Following this treatment, children from both classes were asked whether they wanted to go on a picnic with black children from another school. Ninety-six percent of the "Green–Orange" group expressed desire to go on the picnic, as compared with 62 percent of the controls. The experience of prejudice and discrimination apparently led the "Green–Orange" children to think that it is wrong to discriminate on the basis of color. Perhaps being discriminated against made the children more mindful of the sensitivities and feelings of members of outgroups. Unless we are encouraged to actively consider our attitudes toward others, we may automatically rely upon previously conceived ideas, and these ideas are very often prejudiced (Langer et al., 1985).

2. *Intergroup contact.* A stereotype is a fixed, conventional schema about a *group* of people. Negative stereotypes can lead us to avoid other groups, but intergroup contact can break down stereotypes. Contact reveals that groups consist of individuals who are not, after all, homogeneous. They have different abilities, interests, personalities, attitudes, and even prejudices (Amir, 1976; Stephan, 1978).

    Research has shown that intergroup contact can reduce prejudice when it is handled in a certain way (Clore et al., 1978; Kennedy & Stephan, 1977; Wilder & Thompson, 1980; Worchel et al., 1977). First, the individuals should work toward common goals rather than compete. Competition can stir up feelings of antipathy. Second, the individuals should come from similar socioeconomic backgrounds so that they have a number of things in common. Third, contacts should be informal. Highly structured contacts cause participants to feel distant from one another. Finally, prolonged contact is more effective than brief contact. Brief contacts might be insufficient to induce lasting change of person schemas, and so our memories of events might be distorted by previously existing schemas (Skrypnek & Snyder, 1982). With prolonged contact, it is more likely that our reconstructions (memories) of the events that took place will be accurate and unbiased.

3. *Seeking compliance with the law.* On a more personal level, it may sometimes be more appropriate to demand legal support if we have been discrimi-

nated against on the basis of race, religion, or other ethnic factors. It has been said that "We can't legislate morality"—that is, we cannot compel people to change their values and innermost feelings. True, perhaps, but people can be compelled by the law to modify illegal behavior. Furthermore, as we shall see in Chapter 5, being compelled to behave in a certain way *can* foster attitudes consistent with that behavior.

4. *Self-examination.* Very often we say or do things that remind us that we have certain prejudices. Recently a Catholic acquaintance of the first author said "That damned Jew" when someone disappointed him. He was asked if he had ever been disappointed by a Catholic, and, of course, the answer was yes. He was then asked, "Did you call him 'That damned Catholic'?" Of course, he hadn't. The thought had not even occurred to him. Individuals of all groups have done, or might do, things that disappoint or disturb us. In such cases we need not deny the harm, but we should remember to attribute the behavior to them as *individuals*, not as *group representatives*.

■ Self-Perception

Some of our most important person schemas are directed inward. These schemas are called *self-schemas*. Our self-schemas have a powerful impact on our behavior and on the ways that we feel about ourselves, as noted in this true story, reported by Erik Erikson.

For the U.S.A., World War II in the Pacific meant island hopping and a bloody miniature war on each island. Ever nearing the Japanese home islands, U.S. marines landed on hostile sands, drew enemy fire, gained difficult beachheads, and gradually cleared the islands of the enemy. During this war, as during other wars, some chose to make their contribution through the medical corps, to follow the battles and try to minimize the human wreckage, rather than add to it themselves.

One young medical corpsman, strongly opposed to the bloodshed, was stuck one night on such a beachhead. Soldiers around him struggled through the night to prevent them all from being swept back into the ocean as enemy fire raged. Shells burst into light, illuminating the corpses and the embattled. The air around them was punctured by the crack of enemy bullets whistling by before whacking into sand—or flesh—with dead thuds. Promised air and naval support failed to arrive. Soldiers cursed their commanders, the navy, the island, the human species. Resentments combined with fear, and the medical corpsman's agitation grew until that his perceptions and memories became clouded and unreal.

Later he recalled that he had been required to unload ammunition rather than tend to the sick and wounded. He recalled a superior officer screaming profanities. His last memory of that night was of someone handing him an automatic rifle.

When he awoke in the field hospital the next day, he was plagued by jumpiness, anxiety, and vicious headaches. No physical ailments could be found, but his condition worsened. Finally he was sent stateside and referred for treatment to the Mount Zion Veterans' Rehabilitation Clinic in San Francisco, where he was treated by Erikson.

Erikson worked with this soldier and many others suffering from was then called *battlefield neurosis* and is today referred to as *post-traumatic stress disorder (PTSD).** They had all recently returned from the battlefields of the Pacific theater. They experienced intense anger and anxiety, especially when startled or awakened from recurrent battlefield nightmares.

Erikson (1963) gradually learned our medical corpsman's history. Parental violence and maternal drinking had wracked his childhood. During one

*PTSD is discussed fully as a diagnostic category in Chapter 8.

drunken rage, his mother had threatened him with a gun. He took it from her and threw it out the window. He left home that day and vowed never to drink, curse, or carry a gun. He confirmed his own sense of identity by rejecting these aspects of his mother's behavior. Nonviolence, sobriety, self-control, clean speech—all became central aspects of the corpsman's **self-identity,** or self-schema—his sense of who he was and what he stood for.

That night in the Pacific his nerves had been taut. He had been confronted with the cursing of a respected officer. A rifle had been thrust into his hands. He had spun out of control, and his self-identity as a good and honorable person had been shaken.

His disorder had little to do with fear or cowardice. Erikson sensed that many such soldiers had engaged in behavior incompatible with their **values** and self-identities. They had lost touch with who and what they were. Successful adjustment to stress requires maintaining a stable sense of self. When self-identity is threatened by disease, tragedy, or awareness that our behavior is incompatible with our self-schemas, we may encounter anxiety, panic, and **alienation.** We may feel cut adrift from life's purposes and meaning.

In this section we define what is meant by the self and explore the parts of the self: the physical, social, and personal selves. We see that aspects of our personal selves include our names, values, self-concepts, even our self-efficacy expectancies—all of which can contribute to, and reflect, our adjustment and personal growth.

The Self as a Guiding Principle of Personality

In 1890, William James, one of the founders of modern psychology, wrote that the newborn baby must sense the world as "one great booming, buzzing confusion." As newborn babies, we emerge from being literally suspended in a temperature-controlled environment to being—again, in James' words—"assailed by eyes, ears, nose, skin, and entrails at once." But gradually we organize our perceptions and sort things out. We come to understand that there is a point at which we end and the rest of the world—the world of other things—begins. As time goes on, we develop a sense of being persons. Our impressions, thoughts, and feelings take on a totality that makes up our conscious senses of being, or our selves.

Many psychologists have written about the **self.** As noted in Chapter 2, the psychodynamic theorists Carl Jung and Alfred Adler both spoke of a self (or Self) that serves as a guiding principle of personality. Erik Erikson and Carl Rogers spoke of ways in which we are, to some degree, the conscious architects of ourselves. Your self is your ongoing sense of who and what you are, your sense of how and why you react to the environment, and, more important, how you choose to act on your environment. To Rogers, the sense of self is innate—a "given." It is an essential part of the experience of being human in the world, and the guiding principle behind personality structure and behavior.

Now let us turn our attention to some "parts" of the self.

The Parts of the Self

In this section we discuss the physical self, the social self, and the personal self.

The Physical Self   The physical person you carry around with you plays an enormously influential role in your self-concept. You may tower above others or always have to look up to them—literally. Because of your physical appearance, others may smile and seek your gaze, or they may pretend that you do not exist. Your health and conditioning may be such that you assume that you will be up to new athletic challenges or that the sporting life is not for you. *The New Our Bodies, Ourselves* (Boston Women's Health Book Collective, 1984) emphasizes repeatedly how intertwined the business of having

Self-identity. Our sense of who we are and what we stand for.

Value. A social principle, standard, or goal in which a person believes.

Alienation. Deatchment, separation; feelings of being cast adrift from our values.

Self. The totality of our impressions, thoughts, and feelings, such that we have a conscious, continuous sense of being in the world.

Transsexual. An individual who feels trapped in the body of the wrong sex.

female features and sex organs is with the identity of women. Men's features and organs are no less major a contribution to their self-concepts.

Whereas some aspects of the physical self, such as hair length and weight, change as we grow, sex and race are permanent features of our physical identities . . . or are they?

Some people, called **transsexuals,** feel trapped in the body of the wrong sex. As a result of sex-reassignment surgery and hormone treatments, many transsexuals take on the physical appearance of the opposite sex and are better able to live lives that are consistent with their self-images. Former tennis professional Renée Richards recently coached Martina Navratilova. Renée was born Richard Raskin and underwent sex-reassignment several years ago.

In *Black Like Me,* John Howard Griffin (1960) recounted his experiences in the South of the 1950s after he darkened his skin color by dyes, drugs, and ultraviolet rays. He was soon being called "nigger" and "boy," and he was denied the use of "white" rest rooms, hotels, and cafeterias. Within a few days, he felt that his identity as a black man had penetrated more than skin deep.

For most of us, adjustment to traits such as height, sex, and race involves self-acceptance. But other physical traits, such as weight, athletic condition, and hair style, can be modified. Our determination, behavior, and choices can be more influential than heredity in shaping these latter aspects of the self.

The Social Self   The social self refers to the various masks we wear, or social roles we play—suitor, student, worker, husband, wife, mother, father, citizen, leader, follower. Roles and masks are adaptive responses to the social world. In a job interview you might choose to project enthusiasm, self-confidence, and commitment to hard work but not to express self-doubts or serious reservations about the company. You may have prepared a number of such roles for different life situations.

The Physical Self. The physical person we carry around with us plays an enormously influential role in our self-concept. Because of our physical appearance, others may smile at us and seek our gaze, or they may act as though we do not exist. The social responses we receive can foster very different patterns of self-esteem.

Are social roles and masks merely deceptions and lies? Usually not. Our roles and masks often reflect different features within us. The job hunter has strengths and weaknesses but logically decides to project the strengths. You may perceive yourself to be something of a rebel, but it would be understandable if you were respectful when stopped by a highway patrol officer. This is not necessarily dishonesty; it is an effort to meet the requirements of a particular situation. If you did not understand what respect is, or did not have the social skills to act respectfully, you would not be able to enact a respectful role—even when one was required.

But when our entire lives are played behind masks, it may be difficult for others, and us, to discover our inner selves. Partners tend to be reasonably genuine with one another in a mature intimate relationship. They drop the masks that protect and separate them. Without an expression of genuine feelings, life can be the perpetual exchange of one cardboard mask for another.

The Personal Self In Mark Twain's *The Prince and the Pauper,* a young prince is sabotaged by enemies of the throne. He seeks to salvage the kingdom by exchanging places with Tom Canty, a pauper who happens to look just like him. It is a learning experience for both of them. The pauper is taught social graces and learns how the powerful are flattered and praised. The prince learns what it means to stand or fall on the basis of his own behavior, not his royalty.

Toward the end of the tale, there is a dispute. Which is the prince and which is Tom Canty? The lads are identical in appearance and behavior, even highly similar in experience. Does it matter? Both, perhaps, can lead the realm as well. But court officials seek the one whose personal self—whose *inner identity*—is that of the prince. The tale ends happily. The prince retakes the throne and Tom earns the permanent protection of the court.

Your personal self is visible to you and you alone. It is the day-to-day experience of being you, a changing display of sights, thoughts, and feelings to which you hold the only ticket of admission.

There are many aspects of our personal selves, or self-schemas. In the following section we discuss some of them, including our names, values, and self-concepts.

Aspects of the Self-Schema: Names, Values, and Self-Concept

Names: Labels for the Self

> ALICE: Must a name mean something?
> HUMPTY-DUMPTY: Of course it must. . . . My name means the shape I am. . . .
> With a name like yours, you might be any shape, almost.
> Lewis Carroll, *Through the Looking Glass*

What's in a name? Possibly quite a lot. The voyages of the *Starship Enterprise* are more dynamic with Captain Kirk and Mr. Spock at the helm than they would be with Captain Milquetoast and Mr. Anderson. Marilyn Monroe was sexier than Norma Jean Baker. "Dr. J" was a wizard on the basketball court: Julius Irving sounds more like a lawyer. Richard Starkey might well be a factory worker in Liverpool, but Ringo Starr is, well, a star.

Names even have an influence on perceptions of physical attractiveness. In one experiment, photographs of women who had been rated equal in attractiveness were assigned various names at random (Garwood et al., 1980). They were then rated by a new group of subjects with the assigned names in view. Women given names such as Jennifer, Kathy, and Christine were rated as significantly more attractive than women assigned names such as Gertrude,

B.C.

Q U E S T I O N N A I R E

How Content Are You with Your Physical Self?

Imagine a future society in which cosmetic surgery and other methods allowed you to have your entire body sculpted to your exact specifications. You might leaf through a "Whole Human Catalogue" and select your preferred dimensions of face and form. Then your physical self would spring forth custom made.

But could satisfaction be guaranteed? Would nonclassic forms such as Barbra Streisand's nose or Clark Gable's ears be tolerated in this mix-and-match society? Would there be one perfect body and one perfect face, or would some people select less than "ideal" features to lend their physical selves an air of individuality? And when everyone is beautiful, does the allure of beauty fade away?

How satisfied are you with your physical features? Why not complete the following questionnaire and then turn to the end of the chapter to compare your satisfaction with your physical self to that expressed by a nationwide sample of 2,000 *Psychology Today* readers?

Directions: For each of the following, place a checkmark (√) in the column that indicates your degree of satisfaction or dissatisfaction.

Body Part	Quite or Extremely Dissatisfied	Somewhat Dissatisfied	Somewhat Satisfied	Quite or Extremely Satisfied
My overall body appearance	____	____	____	____
FACE				
overall facial attractiveness	____	____	____	____
hair	____	____	____	____
eyes	____	____	____	____
ears	____	____	____	____
nose	____	____	____	____
mouth	____	____	____	____
teeth	____	____	____	____
voice	____	____	____	____
chin	____	____	____	____
complexion	____	____	____	____
EXTREMITIES				
shoulders	____	____	____	____
arms	____	____	____	____
hands	____	____	____	____
feet	____	____	____	____
MID-TORSO				
size of abdomen	____	____	____	____
buttocks (seat)	____	____	____	____
hips (upper thighs)	____	____	____	____
legs and ankles	____	____	____	____
HEIGHT, WEIGHT, AND TONE				
height	____	____	____	____
weight	____	____	____	____
general muscle tone or development	____	____	____	____

Source: Berscheid, Walster, and Bohrnstedt, 1973.

Glamorous movie star Marilyn Monroe was born Norma Jean Baker. What do our names suggest about us? Why do so many film stars change their names? And by the way, who is Richard Starkey?

Ethel, and Harriet. There are two messages in this: First, names do not really serve as an index to beauty. But second, if your name is a constant source of dismay, there might be little harm to using a more appealing nickname.*

Our names and nicknames can also reflect our attitudes toward ourselves. Although we may have one legal given name, the variations or nicknames we select say something about our self-schemas. For example, are you a Bob, Bobby, or Robert? An Elizabeth, Betty, or Liz? Shakespeare wrote that a rose by any other name would smell as sweet, but perhaps a rose by the name of skunkweed would impress us as smelling just plain awful.

According to Berne (1976b), the names our parents give us, and the ways in which they refer to us, often reflect their expectations about what we are to become:

> Charles and Frederick were kings and emperors. A boy who is steadfastly called Charles or Frederick by his mother, and insists that his associates call him that, lives a different life style from one who is commonly called Chuck or Fred, while Charlie and Freddie are likely to be horses of still another color (p. 162).

Berne offers another example, the names of two famous neurologists— H. Head and W. R. Brain.

Unusual names may create childhood problems, but seem linked to success in adulthood. In a U.S. study, men with names such as David, John, Michael, and Robert were rated more positively than men with names such as Ian, Dale, and Raymond (Marcus, 1976). Children with common names tend to be more popular (McDavid & Harari, 1966). But college professors and upper-level army brass frequently have unusual names: *Omar* Bradley, *Dwight* Eisenhower. There are high frequencies of odd, even unique, names in *Who's Who*. In a survey of 11,000 North Carolina high school students, boys and girls with unusual first names earned more than their fair share of academic achievements (Zweigenhaft, 1977). In another study, no personality differences were found between men with common or unusual names, but women with unusual names scored more optimally than their counterparts with common names on several personality scales of the California Psychological Inventory (Zweigenhaft et al., 1980).

The Zweigenhaft group (1980) found no differences in personality between students with common names and students with sexually ambiguous

---

*Yes, we are being inconsistent. Remember Ralph Waldo Emerson's remark, "A foolish consistency is the hobgoblin of little minds."

■ A CLOSER LOOK

What's in a Name? Sign on the Dotted Line and See

Sign your name here:

_____

Now sign your name as though you were the President of the U.S.A.:

_____

What do we reveal about ourselves through our signatures? Were your signatures as yourself and as president equal in size? Psychologist Richard Zweigenhaft (1970) asked Wesleyan University students to sign both ways, and found that 75 percent wrote their names larger as president. The presidential signatures were also often less legible. Status, perhaps, is associated with larger signatures and less felt the need to make them readable. Witness the scratchings of many physicians on prescription pads. Zweigenhaft also found that Wesleyan professors signed their names larger than people of lesser status, such as students and blue-collar university employees.

Now try another experiment. Consider your name to be either John David Smith or Jane Debra Smith. Now use your (assumed) name either in full or in whatever abbreviated form (e.g., J. D. Smith, John or Jane Smith, etc.) appeals to you for signing each of the following:

a job application

_____

a note to your teacher

_____

a petition

_____

a personal letter to a friend

_____

a check

_____

a note to your work supervisor

_____

a love letter

_____

a letter to the president

_____

a complaint to the city about collection of refuse

_____

a letter-to-the-editor of your newspaper

_____

What form or forms did you use most often? J. D. Smith? John (Jane) Smith? J. Smith? J. David (Debra) Smith? Just John (Jane)?

In a New Zealand study with the name John David Smith, J. D. Smith was used most frequently, followed by J. Smith and John Smith (Boshier, 1973). Different forms reflected personality differences. For example, John Smiths were more liberal than J. or J. D. Smiths.

Zweigenhaft (1975) replicated the New Zealand study with community college students in California. The majority (61 percent) preferred John Smith, 30 percent used J. D. Smith, and the other 9 percent of styles were mixed. Zweigenhaft found no links between personality and signature, but males and older respondents were more likely to use their middle names.

(e.g., Ronnie and Leslie) or misleading (e.g., boys named Marion or Robin) names. But another study found that college women with masculine names (such as Dean or Randy)—who _used_ them—were less anxious, more culturally sophisticated, and had greater leadership potential than women with masculine names who chose to use feminine nicknames (Ellington et al., 1980). The women who used their masculine names showed no signs of maladjustment. A woman who uses a given masculine name may be asserting that she possesses instrumental traits, as defined in Chapter 3. Discomfort in using one's (masculine) given name might be linked to more complete acceptance of the stereotypical feminine sex role. According to the stereotype, as discussed in Chapter 3, women take a back seat to men.

Values   Our values involve the importance we place on objects and things. If we're hot, we may value air conditioning more than pizza. We may value love more than money, or money more than love. How many of us are in conflict because our values do not mesh fully with those of our friends, our spouses, or our employers?

▪ Q U E S T I O N N A I R E ▪

Ranking Your Values: What Is Important to You?

Freedom, recognition, beauty, eternal salvation, a world without war—which is most important to you? Are people who put pleasure first likely to behave differently from people who rank salvation, wisdom, or personal achievement number 1?

Milton Rokeach devised a survey of values that allows us to rank our life goals according to their relative importance to us. How will you rank yours?

Directions: Eighteen values are listed below in alphabetical order. Select the value that is most important to you and write a 1 next to it in Column I. Then select your next most important value and place a 2 next to it in the same column. Proceed until you have ranked all 18 values. By turning to the key at the end of the chapter, you can compare your rankings to those of a recently-drawn national sample of U.S. adults (Ball-Rokeach et al., 1984).

Now would you like to participate in a brief experiment? If so, imagine how someone very close to you, perhaps an old trusted friend or relative, would rank the 18 values. Place his or her rankings in Column II. Then think of someone with whom you have had a number of arguments, someone whose way of life seems at odds with your own. Try to put yourself in his or her place, and rank the values as he or she would in Column III. Now compare your own ranking to the rankings of your friend and your adversary. Are your own values ranked more similarly to those in Column II or in Column III? Do you and your good friend or close relative have rather similar values? Is it possible that you and the person represented in Column III do not get along, in part, because your values differ?

As a class exercise, compare your rankings to those of classmates, or to the class average rankings. Do class members share similar values? Do they fall into groups with characteristic values? Does the behavior of different class members reflect differences in values?

Value	I	II	III
A Comfortable Life a prosperous life	___	___	___
An Exciting Life a stimulating, active life	___	___	___
A Sense of Accomplishment lasting contribution	___	___	___
A World at Peace free of war and conflict	___	___	___

Our values give rise to our personal goals and tend to place limits on the means we shall use to reach them. The medical corpsman's values caused him to renounce violence and adopt the goal of seeking to aid the wounded. His psychological problems developed when he was compelled to engage in behavior that was inconsistent with his values.

We all have unique sets of values, but we probably get along best with people whose values resemble our own. Values are often derived from parents and other childhood influences. But we may also derive values and **ethics,** our standards of conduct or behavior, through logic and reasoning. According to psychologist Lawrence Kohlberg (1981), the highest level of moral functioning requires us to use ethical principles to define our own moral standards and then to live in accord with them.

Determining our values is an essential aspect of self-development. If we do not have personal values, our behavior seems meaningless, without purpose. During some periods of life, especially during adolescence, our values

Ethics. Standards for behavior. A system of beliefs from which one derives standards for behavior.

Value	I	II	III
A World of Beauty beauty of nature and the arts	——	——	——
Equality brotherhood, equal opportunity for all	——	——	——
Family Security taking care of loved ones	——	——	——
Freedom independence, free choice	——	——	——
Happiness contentedness	——	——	——
Inner Harmony freedom from inner conflict			
Mature Love sexual and spiritual intimacy	——	——	——
National Security protection from attack	——	——	——
Pleasure an enjoyable, leisurely life	——	——	——
Salvation saved, eternal life	——	——	——
Self-respect self-esteem	——	——	——
Social Recognition respect, admiration	——	——	——
True Friendship close companionship	——	——	——
Wisdom a mature understanding of life	——	——	——

may be in flux. For most of us, this is an unsettling experience, or crisis in self-identity, and we are motivated to make our beliefs consistent and meaningful. But until we do, we may be subject to the whims and opinions of others—concerned about risking social disapproval because we have not yet established stable standards for self-approval.

Self-concept. One's perception of oneself, including one's traits and an evaluation of these traits. The self-concept includes one's self-esteem and one's ideal self.

The Self-Concept Your **self-concept** is your impression or concept of yourself. It includes your own listing of the personal traits (fairness, competence, sociability, and so on) you deem important, and your evaluation of how you rate according to these traits.

You can get in better touch with your own self-concept as follows. First, think of your personal traits as what phenomenological psychologist George Kelly referred to as constructs—that is, as existing along bipolar dimensions of the kind shown in Figure 4.2. Use the constructs in Figure 4.2 so that you and your classmates will have a common reference point. We have purpose-

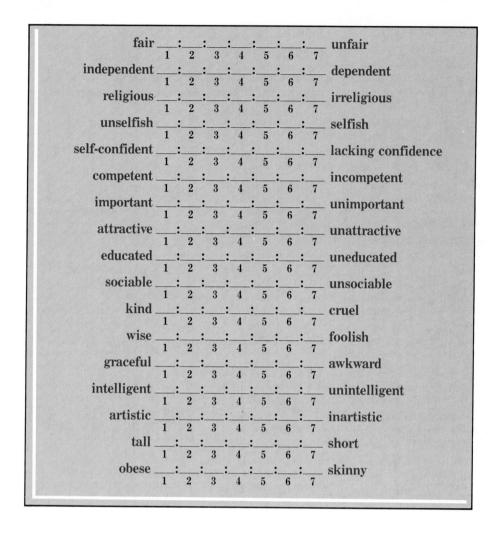

FIGURE 4.2 Rating Scales for Measurement of the Self-Concept

fully omitted a number of constructs, such as strong–weak, that are sex-typed. Recall from the discussion of gender-schema theory in Chapter 3, for example, that stereotyped masculine men might find the construct strong–weak of relevance, whereas stereotyped feminine women might not. And so, in Figure 4.2 we have listed a number of trait-constructs considered important by many people, even though a list constructed by you would no doubt be different.

Now, you can define your own self-concept, at least in regard to these dimensions, by placing a checkmark (√) in one of the seven spaces for each dimension. Use the number code of 1–7 as your guide, as in the following example for the trait of fairness:

1 = extremely fair
2 = rather fair
3 = somewhat fair
4 = equally fair and unfair; or not sure
5 = somewhat unfair
6 = rather unfair
7 = extremely unfair

The self-concept is multifaceted. In addition to your self-evaluation it includes your sense of personal worth (or self-esteem), your sense of who and

Self-esteem. Self-approval. One's self-respect or favorable opinion of oneself.

Ideal self. One's perception of what one ought to be and do. Also called the self-ideal.

what you would like to be (or ideal self), and your sense of your competence to meet your goals (your self-efficacy expectancies). We shall see that self-esteem depends on many factors, including social approval, competence, and the discrepany between the way you see yourself and what you think you ought to be.

Self-Esteem

> Oh, that God the gift would give us
> To see ourselves as others see us.
> ROBERT BURNS

Actually, despite Robert Burns' poetry, we do largely see ourselves as others see us. That is, **self-esteem** appears to begin with parental love and approval. Children who are loved and cherished by their parents usually come to see themselves as being worthy of love. They are likely to learn to love and accept themselves.

Coopersmith (1967) studied self-esteem patterns among fifth- and sixth-grade boys and found that boys with high self-esteem more often came from homes with strict but not harsh or cruel parents. Such parents were highly involved in their sons' activities. Parents of boys low in self-esteem were generally more permissive, but tended to be harsh when they did administer discipline.

The boys with higher self-esteem had parents who were more demanding, but they were also more involved in their lives. Involvement communicates worthiness. The encouragement of children to develop competence not only contributes to self-esteem as an expression of love and caring. Resultant behavioral competencies in intellectual tasks (Flippo & Lewinsohn, 1971) or in physical activities, such as swimming (Koocher, 1971), heighten self-esteem in their own right.

Once self-esteem is established, it seems to endure. Coopersmith (1967) found high similarities between his subjects' self-esteem at three-year intervals. We may all fail at our endeavors now and then, but if our self-esteem is initially high, perhaps we shall retain belief in our ability to master adversity. But low self-esteem may become a self-fulfilling prophecy: people with low self-esteem may carve out little to boast of in life.

As noted earlier, our self-concepts may be described according to our perceptions of our positions along dimensions like those shown in Figure 4.2. But our self-esteem tends to depend on our approval of our self-positioning. It is related to the discrepancy between where we place ourselves along these dimensions and where our values suggest that we ought to be. That is, self-esteem is based on the discrepancy between our self-descriptions and our ideal selves.

The Ideal Self Our concepts of what we ought to be are called our **ideal selves,** or self-ideals. How about you? What "oughts" and "shoulds" are you carrying around about your ideal self? You can gain some insight into the nature of your ideal self through the following exercise. Return to Figure 4.2. Use a pencil of a different color or make another kind of mark, perhaps an x instead of a checkmark. This time around, mark the spaces that indicate where you think you *ought* to be, not where you think you are. Try not to be influenced by the first set of marks.

Now look at Table 4.1, which is a summary of the list of traits in Figure 4.2. Select a few traits (perhaps four or five) that make you feel good about yourself and place a plus sign (+) in the blank space in front of them. Then select an equal number of traits about which you feel somewhat disappointed,

TABLE 4.1   Summary List of Traits Shown in Figure 4.2

_____ fair–unfair
_____ independent–dependent
_____ religious–irreligious
_____ unselfish–selfish
_____ self-confident–lacking confidence
_____ competent–incompetent
_____ important–unimportant
_____ attractive–unattractive
_____ educated–uneducated
_____ sociable–unsociable
_____ kind–cruel
_____ wise–foolish
_____ graceful–awkward
_____ intelligent–unintelligent
_____ artistic–inartistic
_____ tall–short
_____ obese–skinny

and place a minus sign (−) in front of each. What, you have only one "bad" trait?* Then select only one good trait as well.

Now return to Figure 4.2 and make some comparisons. Compare your self-concept with your ideal self. Observe that the mark that describes your ideal self is usually placed closer to the end of the dimension that *you* value more positively. (For example, some people wish that they were taller, but others would prefer that they were shorter.)

Now let us note the discrepancies, or differences, between your self-description and your ideal self for the dimensions to which you assigned pluses and minuses. For instance, let's say that you are 5 feet 9 inches tall but would like to be a star center in basketball. The discrepancy between your self-description (S) and your ideal self (I) might be illustrated like this:

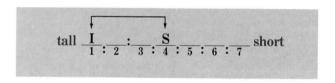

Mathematically, the discrepancy between your self-description and your ideal self on the tallness dimension is $4 - 1 = 3$. Or, more generally,

Discrepancy = Ideal Self − Self-Description

Now figure out the discrepancies for each trait that pleased you and displeased you, as listed in Table 4.1. For instance, if you placed plus signs in front of fairness, kindness, and sociability, add the discrepancies for these three dimensions. If you placed minus signs before the dimensions of competence, education, and wisdom, also add these three numbers together. Now compare the total discrepancy scores for the positive and negative clusters of traits. We would be pleased to take bets that the total for the traits that disappoint you is *larger* than the total for the traits that please you.

Why are we so confident? Simply because the *reason* that certain trait-constructs please you is that there is little or no discrepancy between your ideal self and where you perceive yourself to be on them. These are the traits that are likely to contribute to your self-esteem. (Whenever you feel a bit low,

_____
*Of course it's difficult for your authors to empathize with people who have even one bad trait, since we haven't been able to find any of our own.

why not sit back for a moment and think of how you sparkle along these constructs!) In general, the closer your self-description is in keeping with your ideal self, the higher your self-esteem will be. The farther away you are, the bleaker your self-description will look to you.

Enhancing Self-Esteem

Now that we have reviewed theory and research concerning the self-schema, we can focus on a number of applications—ways in which you can raise your own self-esteem.

Improve Yourself   This is not an absurd suggestion of the sort that one of our (less well-liked!) literature professors made when he told a student, "Get a new brain." Here we are talking about undertaking strategies that can lead to improvement in specific areas of life.

You can begin, for example, by thinking about reducing some of the discrepancies between your self-description and your ideal self. Consider again the traits in Figure 4.1. Are you miserable because of overdependency on another person? Perhaps you can enhance your social skills (e.g., through assertiveness training, as discussed in the next chapter) or your vocational skills (as discussed in Chapter 12) in an effort to become more independent. Are you too heavy? Perhaps you can follow some of the suggestions in Chapter 10 for losing weight.

Challenge the Realism of Your Ideal Self   In later chapters we shall discuss at length how our "oughts" and "shoulds" can create such perfectionistic standards that we are constantly falling short and experiencing frustration. But here let us briefly note that one way of adjusting to perfectionistic self-demands is to challenge them and, when appropriate, to revise them. It may be harmful to abolish worthy and realistic goals, even if we do have trouble measuring up now and then. However, some of our goals or values may not stand up under our close scrutiny, and it is always healthful to be willing to consider them objectively.

Substitute Realistic, Attainable Goals for Unattainable Goals   It may just be that we shall never be as artistic, or as tall, or as graceful as we would like to be. We can certainly work to enhance our drawing skills, but if it becomes clear that we shall not become Michelangelos, perhaps we can just enjoy our scribblings for what they are and also look to other fields for satisfaction.* We cannot make ourselves taller (once we have included our elevator shoes or heels, that is), but we can take off five pounds and we can cut our time for running the mile by a few seconds. We can also learn to whip up a great fetuccini Alfredo.

Build Self-Efficacy Expectancies   As noted in Chapter 2, social-learning theorist Albert Bandura (1986) argues that our self-efficacy expectancies are a major factor in our willingness to take on the challenges of life and persist in meeting them. Our self-efficacy expectancies define the degree to which we believe that our efforts will bring about a positive outcome. We can build self-efficacy expectancies by selecting tasks that are consistent with our interests and abilities and then working at them. In Chapter 12 we shall see that many tests have been devised to help us focus in on our interests and abilities. They are often available at your college testing and counseling center. But we can also build self-efficacy expectancies by working at athletics and on hobbies.

*Somewhere along the line, the first author discovered that he would never write the "great American novel," but he found that he could achieve a great deal of personal satisfaction by writing college textbooks.

Remember: realistic self-assessment, realistic goals, and a reasonable schedule for improvement are the keys to building self-efficacy expectancies. The chances are that you will not be able to run a four-minute mile, but after a few months of reasonably taxing workouts under the advice of a skilled trainer, you might be able to put a few seven-minute miles back to back. You might even enjoy them!

In the following section, we shall see that the ways in which we explain our successes and failures to ourselves also have a great deal to do with our self-esteem.

■ Attribution Theory

At the age of 3, one of the first author's daughters believed that a friend's son was a boy because he *wanted* to be a boy. Since she was 3 at the time, this error in my daughter's **attribution** for the boy's gender is charming and understandable. But we as adults tend to make somewhat similar attribution errors. No, we do not usually believe that people's preferences have much to do with their gender, but as we shall see, we may tend to exaggerate the role of conscious choice in other aspects of their behavior.

An assumption as to why people do things is called an attribution for behavior. Our inference of the motives and traits of others through the observation of their behavior is called the **attribution process.** We now focus on attribution theory, or the processes by which people draw conclusions about the factors that influence one another's behavior. Attribution theory is very important to adjustment because our attributions lead us to perceive other people, and ourselves, either as purposeful actors or as victims of circumstances.

Dispositional and Situational Attributions

As this section is being written, the first author's wife Lois is having a huge dispute with her sister Cindy, who is attempting to toilet train her son "Mikey," who just turned 2. Lois and I let our children become toilet trained according to their own schedule. We assumed that they would toilet train themselves in time for college, or else they'd have some explaining to do. Anyhow, poor Mikey is failing miserably at the task imposed on him, and Lois and I hate to see him pressured so much.

I didn't dare say a word, of course, but why, Lois asked Cindy the other day, why was she so insistent that Mikey be trained right now? If Cindy had answered, "Because I believe that it is right and proper for children to control their bowels when they turn 2," she would have been making a **dispositional attribution** for her behavior. That is, she would have been attributing her behavior to internal causes, such as her own attitudes, beliefs, and goals. However, Cindy said that she was pressuring Mikey because her husband Michael wanted it that way. Why did Michael want it that way? Because *his parents* told him that *he* was toilet-trained at 13 months! So Cindy actually made a **situational attribution** for her harsh toilet training. That is, she explained it in terms of external causes, in this case because of pressure from Michael. Note that she also made a situational attribution for Michael's placing pressure on her; he did it because *his* parents had placed pressure on him!

This story is continuing and, if I have the courage, I may write more about it later on—so long as you promise not to tell my wife to read the book. But it does serve to illustrate the difference between dispositional and situational attributions for behavior. Our attributions for behavior are very important, in part because they indicate whether we are taking responsibility for our own behavior. As we shall see over and over again throughout this book, proper adjustment and personal development require that we take responsibility for the things we do—or don't do.

Attribution. A belief concerning why people behave in a certain way.

Attribution process. The process by which people draw inferences about the motives and traits of others.

Dispositional attribution. An assumption that a person's behavior is determined by internal causes, such as personal attitudes or goals.

Situational attribution. An assumption that a person's behavior is determined by external circumstances, such as the social pressure found in a situation.

Fundamental attribution error. The tendency to assume that others act predominantly on the basis of their dispositions, even when there is evidence suggestive of the importance of their situations.

Actor-observer effect. The tendency to attribute our own behavior to situational factors but to attribute the behavior of others to dispositional factors.

Also, our perceptions of why people do things are a factor in whether we hold them responsible for what they do. Our holding or not holding them responsible for things we don't like affects our relationships with them. In effect, Cindy was saying, "Hey, don't blame me! I'm being pressured into this!" That is, Cindy saw herself as a victim of circumstances. Lois wasn't buying it, of course. She believed Cindy *chose* to be a victim of circumstances as a way of evading responsibility for her behavior.

My wife's conflict with her sister helps point out some of the biases that are found in the attribution process. Let us begin by considering the so-called fundamental attribution error.

The Fundamental Attribution Error

A colleague brought to our attention a recent newspaper article, "Experts Say Women at Risk Are Well-Informed on AIDS." He showed us the article's points that

> Inner-city women at high risk of AIDS infections are now well-informed of their risk, but few are changing their behavior as a result [as by using condoms], according to experts here for a federally sponsored conference on AIDS and women.
> More than 90 percent of all drug users in New Jersey know that AIDS can be transmitted by shared needles and more than 80 percent know that it can be transmitted heterosexually and from infected mothers to their unborn children, according to a recent survey by Joyce Jackson of the New Jersey State Department of Health (Kolata, 1987, p. A18).

He went on to lambaste the women in the article for their "stupidity" and their "irresponsibility." That is, he made a dispositional attribution for their behavior. We noted that the same article mentioned that "opposition from men was discouraging women from changing sexual practices" and that the women had overwhelming feelings of helplessness and powerlessness: "According to Dr. Judith Cohen of San Francisco General Hospital, many women fear that if they broach the subject of safe sex with their drug-using partners, 'they will be laughed at, left, or beaten up' " (Kolata, 1987, p. A18). That is, situational factors were clearly implicated.

It turns out that we frequently attribute too much of other people's behavior to internal, dispositional factors. In fact, this bias in the attribution process is what social psychologists refer to as the **fundamental attribution error.** Our colleague's making of a dispositional attribution for the inner-city women's behavior led him to believe that education and government intervention would be wasted. However, the article's own situational attributions pointed to some appropriate targets for inducing behavioral change, including the rigid negative attitudes of many inner-city men toward condoms.

The fundamental attribution error is linked to another bias in the attribution process: the actor-observer effect.

The Actor-Observer Effect

When we see ourselves and others engaging in behavior that we do not like, we tend to see the others as willful, but to perceive ourselves as victims of circumstances. The tendency to attribute the behavior of others to internal, dispositional factors, and our own behavior to external, situational influences is called the **actor-observer effect** (Jellison & Green, 1981; Jones, 1979; Reeder, 1982; Safer, 1980).

Let us consider an example of the actor-observer effect that may hit home. Surely you have dated someone whom your parents thought should be placed in an institution. When parents and children argue about the children's choice of friends or dates, the parents infer traits from behavior and tend to perceive their children as stubborn, difficult, and independent. But

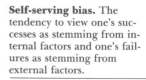

In this father–daughter disagreement, each tends to see the other as willful and stubborn, but himself/herself as a victim of circumstances. This perceptual tendency is an example of the actor–observer effect— one source of bias in the attribution process.

the children also infer traits from behavior and may perceive their parents as bossy and controlling. Parents and children alike attribute the others' behavior to internal causes. That is, they make dispositional attributions about the behavior of others.

But how do the parents and children perceive themselves? The parents probably see themselves as forced into combat by their children's foolishness. If they become insistent, it is in response to their children's stubbornness. The children probably see themselves as responding to peer pressures, and, perhaps, to sexual urges that may come from within but do not seem "of their own making." The parents and the children both tend to see their own behavior as motivated by external factors. That is, they make situational attributions for their own behavior.

The Self-Serving Bias

There is also a **self-serving bias** in the attribution process. We are more likely to attribute our successes to internal, dispositional factors, but our failures to external, situational influences (Baumgardner et al., 1986; O'Malley & Becker, 1984; Van der Plight & Eiser, 1983). When we have done well on a test or impressed a date, we are more likely to attribute these outcomes to our intelligence and charm. But when we fail, we are more likely to attribute these outcomes to bad luck, an unfairly difficult test, or our date's "bad mood."

There are some exceptions to the self-serving bias. As noted in Chapter 8, for example, depressed people are more likely than nondepressed people to attribute their failures to internal factors, even when dispositional attributions are not justified.

Another interesting bias in attribution is a sex difference in attributions for friendly behavior. Men are more likely than women to interpret a woman's friendliness toward men as a sign of promiscuity or seductiveness (Abbey, 1982). Traditional sex-role expectations apparently still lead men to believe that "decent" women are socially passive.

Attribution Theory and Conflict Resolution: Seeing Where the Other Person Is "Coming From"

And so we have seen that there are many biases in the attribution process. These biases interfere with our ability to understand other people's motives for their behavior. As a result, we may blame them when blame is undue, and we may engender conflict. At times these errors even cloud our perceptions of ourselves.

Our review of theory and research concerning the attribution process leads to a number of suggestions for enhancing adjustment and personal development:

Avoid Jumping to the Conclusion That Others Are Always to Blame for Their Behavior

It might seem ironic that we are suggesting that other people are not always responsible for their behavior. After all, one of the primary goals of this textbook is to encourage readers to take responsibilty for their own behavior as a prelude to effective behavioral change. Still, we are biased to attribute too much of other people's behavior to dispositional factors (i.e., to make the fundamental attribution error), and people are influenced by situational variables as well as by dispositional, person variables. Just a handful of these include financial hardship, physical illness, social pressures, academic stresses and strains, role models, the promise of reward, and the threat of punishment.

And so, when we do not like other people's behavior, we might try to empathize with them and imagine the pressures that are impacting upon them from their own perspective. As results, we might understand them better, and we might also find factors that can be changed in an effort to induce more appropriate behavior. For example, concerning the inner-city women who feel helpless to change their risky sexual behavior patterns, we might focus on the financial and social pressures that ensnare them.

Avoid Jumping to Conclusions That We Are Never to Blame for Our Behavior

We have also seen that we tend to be highly aware of the situational forces that act upon us and influence our behavior. We tend to focus on external factors to the point that we often ignore the roles of our own dispositional factors—for example, the role of decision making in our own behavior.

As noted earlier, the first author's sister-in-law was focusing on the situational factors that contributed to harshly toilet training her son. It is as if she were saying, "How can you expect me to do anything about it? Talk to my husband, instead. If he changes his mind about things, he won't pressure me into it." And so all of us from time to time have a way of placing the responsibility for our own behavior—and our own behavioral changes—in the hands of others.

Do you do the same thing? Do you ever say to yourself, "How can I be expected to relax and unwind when I'm going to this pressure cooker of a college?" "How can I be happy when John/Mary treats me this way?" "How can I enjoy myself when I'm broke?" "How can I get out from under when my boss treats me this way?" "John/Mary will never understand me." Situational and dispositional variables may interact to influence our behavior patterns, but when we focus on the situational variables, we may lose sight of our own involvement in maladaptive behavior.

Recognize That Other People May Tend to Blame You for Things That Are Not Your Fault

Other people, not only we, are subject to biases in the attribution process. For example, they may attribute too much of our behavior to dispositional, internal factors. Our parents, employers, professors, lovers, and friends may think that we are being stubborn, mean, or even stupid when we do not accede to their requests. In conflict situations, it is useful for us to explain the forces that we perceive to be acting upon us—to give other people the information that will permit them to empathize with us. It is pointless to say things such as "You'll never understand" or "You don't give a damn" and then to walk away from them.

Recognize That Other People Often See Themselves as Coerced into Their Behavior

Remember that to some degree we tend to see ourselves

as victims of circumstances, as compelled by our situations. Consider our involvement in Vietnam. The U.S.A. perceived itself as coming to the aid of South Vietnamese friends who valued democracy and sought protection from the invaders from North Vietnam. But many North Vietnamese perceived themselves as attempting to unify their country and resist the influence of a superpower from the other side of the world.

It is helpful to try to perceive events from the perspective of one's adversary. When we realize that other people can feel forced into their behavior, just as we can, we can begin to focus on the forces that compel us all—not just on our own injuries.

In the next chapter we focus on many of the kinds of situations that compel us to behave in certain ways. In that chapter we talk about the psychology of social influence and how we can resist social influence by becoming more assertive as individuals.

■ Summary

1. **How do schemas influence our perception of ourselves and others?** Schemas are expectations that influence our perceptions of other people (person schemas), social roles (role schemas), and ourselves (self-schemas). Schemas bias us to see things in certain ways.

2. **Do first impressions matter?** Very much so. According to the primacy effect, we tend to interpret people's behavior in terms of our first impressions of them. However, we may also focus on our most recent impressions of people (the so-called recency effect), especially when we are advised to weigh all the evidence in impression formation.

3. **How shall we read other people's body language?** People who are anxious are usually rigid in posture, whereas people who are relaxed usually "hang loose." When people lean toward one another they are usually interested in each other. Gazing is a sign of interest, and sometimes of love; hard staring is an aversive challenge.

4. **What is prejudice?** Prejudice is an attitude toward a group that leads us to evaluate group members negatively. Prejudice is associated with negative feelings and with disciminatory behavior.

5. **Where does prejudice come from?** Possible sources of prejudice include attitudinal differences (real or assumed) between groups, social conflict, authoritarianism, and social learning. Prejudices in the form of stereotypes also make it easier to process information about unknown individuals.

6. **What happens to us when we are coerced into behavior that is inconsistent with our self-identity?** We may experience anxiety, despair, and feelings of alienation, as Erik Erikson found among soldiers with "battlefield neurosis."

7. **What is the self?** The self is a guiding principle of personality. The self is an organized, consistent way of perceiving our "I" and our perceptions of the ways in which we relate to the world.

8. **What are the parts of the self?** The self has physical, social, and personal aspects. Our social selves are the masks and social roles we don to meet the requirements of our situations. Our personal selves are our private inner identities.

9. **What is the relationship between our names and our self-identities?** Names are linked to expectations by parents and society at large. People with common names are usually rated more favorably, but people with unusual names often accomplish more. People of higher status often sign their names larger and less legibly.

10. **What do our values imply about us?** Our values indicate the importance we place on objects and behavior. Values give rise to goals and set limits

on behavior. We are more subject to social influences when we do not have personal values or when our values are in flux.

11. **What is the self-concept?** Our self-concept is our self-description in terms of bipolar traits, or constructs.

12. **What is self-esteem?** Our self-esteem is our sense of self-worth. Our self-esteem rests on our self-approval of our placement along the constructs we use to describe ourselves. The smaller the discrepancy between our self-concepts and our ideal selves, the higher our self-esteem.

13. **How can we build self-esteem?** We can boost self-esteem by self-improvement; by challenging the realism of our ideal selves; by substituting realistic, attainable goals for unattainable goals; and by building self-efficacy expectancies.

14. **What is the attribution process?** The attribution process refers to our inferences of the motives and traits of others through observing their behavior.

15. **What kinds of attributions are there?** There are dispositional and situational attributions. In dispositional attributions, we attribute people's behavior to internal factors, such as personality traits and choice. In situational attributions, we attribute people's behavior to their circumstances, or external forces.

16. **What is the fundamental attribution error?** This error is the tendency to attribute too much of other people's behavior to dispositional factors.

17. **What is the actor-observer effect?** According to this effect, we tend to attribute the negative behavior of others to internal, dispositional factors, but we tend to attribute our own shortcomings to our situations.

18. **What is the self-serving bias?** This bias is the tendency to attribute our successes to dispositional factors, such as talent and hard work, but our failures to our situations.

■ TRUTH OR FICTION REVISITED

First impressions last. True, but they are not "engraved in stone." New information, or advice to focus on all the evidence, can modify person schemas.

Waitresses who touch their patrons while making change receive higher tips. True. Touching often induces positive behavior.

We tend to divide the social world into "us" and "them." True. This information-processing phenomenon leads to (usually favorable) perceptions of an ingroup and (not-so-favorable) perceptions of an outgroup.

Children who have been victims of discrimination are less likely to practice discrimination themselves. True. Role reversal heightens their awareness of the unfairness of, and pain induced by, discrimination.

Contact between members of different racial groups can reduce feelings of prejudice. True, especially when contact involves working toward common goals.

One way of combatting prejudice is to seek compliance with the law. True. Laws prohibit discrimination in hiring and housing, and changing behavior often leads to changes in attitudes as well.

An identity crisis is a sign of maladjustment. Not necessarily. An identity crisis provides an opportunity for self-examination and decision making.

A rose by any other name, contrary to William Shakespeare, could smell just plain awful. Probably so. Names influence our perceptions.

Psychology Today **readers are generally satisfied with their eyes and ears, but less happy with their teeth and their behinds.** True. What about you?

U.S. residents place more value on pleasure and excitement than on peace and freedom. False. A recently drawn national sample of U.S. adults ranked peace and freedom as second and third in importance, whereas they ranked pleasure and excitement as sixteenth and seventeenth.

The self-esteem of an average student may exceed that of a scholar. True. The average student may not value scholarship and may be very pleased with his or her other attributes and accomplishments; the scholar, meanwhile, may be perfectionistic and fault his or her scholary achievements.

Children with strict parents have higher self-esteem than children with permissive parents. True. Children whose parents demand more accomplish more, and accomplishment is linked to self-esteem.

We can build our self-esteem by becoming good at something. True. Competence boosts self-esteem.

We hold other people responsible for their misdeeds, but we tend to see ourselves as victims of circumstances. True. This bias in the attribution process is referred to as the actor-observer effect.

We tend to attribute our successes to our abilities and hard work, but we attribute our failures to external factors such as lack of time or obstacles placed in our paths by others. True. This perceptual bias is referred to as the self-serving bias.

Results of the *Psychology Today* Poll on Satisfaction with Body Parts

Table 4.2 suggests that most respondents to the *Psychology Today* poll had a positive image of their physical selves. Women were generally less satisfied with their bodies than men, perhaps because society tends to focus more on women's bodies than on men's. In Chapter 5 you will see that depictions of women in photographs and art usually focus more on their bodies than do depictions of men. In Chapter 6 you will see that when we meet a woman for the first time, we are more likely to immediately notice her body than if she were a man.

In the poll, both sexes reported general approval of their sexual features (*not* shown in Table 4.2), with only one woman in four expressing dissatisfaction with her breasts, and an even smaller percentage of men (15 percent) expressing dissatisfaction with the size of their sex organs.

When the investigators compared responses from people of various age groups, they found no major declines in body satisfaction with advancing age. Older men, in fact, were more satisfied with their mid-torsos than younger men. Older respondents of both sexes were more satisfied with their complexions—presumably because adolescent-type acne problems were no longer a source of concern. However, older respondents were less satisfied with their teeth, and older women voiced dissatisfaction with the objects of so many detergent commercials: their hands.

Responses of a National Sample to the Survey of Values

Table 4.3 shows the average rankings assigned the values by a national sample of adults. The sample ranked security, peace, and freedom at the top of the list. Beauty, pleasure, and excitement—factors that stimulate the senses—were ranked near the bottom of the list. Accomplishment and physical comfort were placed about halfway down the list. Apparently we're an idealistic bunch who place hard work ahead of physical pleasure—or so it seems from the survey of values. There are a number of interesting response patterns. In one, peace and freedom were ranked second and third on the list, but it appears that peace and freedom were not perceived as being linked to national security, which was ranked thirteenth. Friendship was also considered more valuable than love.

TABLE 4.2 **Results of the *Psychology Today* Poll on Satisfaction with Body Parts (in Percents)**

Body Part/Area	Quite or Extremely Dissatisfied		Somewhat Dissatisfied		Somewhat Satisfied		Quite or Extremely Satisfied	
	Women	Men	Women	Men	Women	Men	Women	Men
Overall Body Appearance	7	4	16	11	32	30	45	55
FACE								
overall facial attractiveness	3	2	8	6	28	31	61	61
hair	6	6	13	14	28	22	53	58
eyes	1	1	5	6	14	12	80	81
ears	2	1	5	4	10	13	83	82
nose	5	2	18	14	22	20	55	64
mouth	2	1	5	5	20	19	73	75
teeth	11	10	19	18	20	26	50	46
voice	3	3	15	12	27	27	55	58
chin	4	3	9	8	20	20	67	69
complexion	8	7	20	15	24	20	48	58
EXTREMITIES								
shoulders	2	3	11	8	19	22	68	67
arms	5	2	11	11	22	25	62	62
hands	5	1	14	7	21	17	60	75
feet	6	3	14	8	23	19	67	70
MID-TORSO								
size of abdomen	19	11	31	25	21	22	29	42
buttocks (seat)	17	6	26	14	20	24	37	56
hips (upper thighs)	22	3	27	9	19	24	32	64
legs and ankles	8	4	17	7	23	20	52	69
HEIGHT, WEIGHT, AND TONE								
height	3	3	10	10	15	20	72	67
weight	21	10	27	25	21	22	31	43
general muscle tone or development	9	7	21	18	32	30	38	45

Source: Berscheid, Walster, and Bohrnstedt, 1973.

TABLE 4.3 **Responses of a National Sample to the Survey of Values**

Family security	1	Salvation	10
A world at peace	2	Inner harmony	11
Freedom	3	Equality	12
Self-respect	4	National security	13
Happiness	5	Mature love	14
Wisdom	6	A world of beauty	15
A sense of accomplishment	7	Pleasure	16
A comfortable life	8	An exciting life	17
True friendship	9	Social recognition	18

Source: Ball-Rokeach et al., 1984.

Social Influence: Being Influenced by —and Influencing —Others

5

Admitting your product's weak points in an ad is the death knell for sales.

Most of us are swayed by ads that offer useful information, not by emotional appeals or celebrity endorsements.

People who are highly worried about what other people think of them are likely to be low in sales resistance.

We appreciate things more when we have to work hard for them.

Coercing people into behavior that contradicts their values can actually change their values.

Most people would refuse to deliver painful electric shock to an innocent party, even under powerful social pressure.

Many people are late to social gatherings because they are conforming to a social norm.

Nearly 40 people stood by and did nothing while a woman was being stabbed to death.

Most of us would be reluctant to wear blue jeans to a funeral, to walk naked on city streets, or, for that matter, to wear clothes at a nudist colony. Other people and groups can exert enormous pressure on us to behave according to their wishes or according to group norms. **Social influence** is the area of social psychology that studies the ways in which people alter the thoughts, feelings, and behavior of other people.

In Chapter 4 we saw that we sometimes attribute people's behavior to internal, or dispositional, factors and sometimes to external, or situational, factors. In this chapter we elaborate on some of the situational factors that affect our behavior—in particular, the influences of other people. In doing so, we explore some rather fascinating topics, such as the power of TV commercials to persuade us to buy and the possibility that most if not all of us can be pressured to do things that are repugnant to us. Moreover, it seems that being coerced into doing things that contradict our values sometimes actually changes our values—as in the case of Patty Hearst.

But this chapter offers much more than a "warning." We finally suggest a way in which you can prevent yourself from being unduly pressured by other people: the adoption of assertive behavior. Assertive behavior, as we shall see, allows you to express your genuine feelings and to say no to unreasonable requests. Assertive behavior is multifaceted. Not only does it help you to avert the unwanted demands of other people; it also helps you to express positive feelings of appreciation, liking, and love.

■ Persuasion

To get some quick insight into the topic of persuasion, let's go back in history to the year 1741 when Jonathan Edwards, a Puritan minister, delivered a famous sermon, "Sinners in the Hands of an Angry God," to his Connecticut congregation. As you can see from this excerpt, he wanted his audience to shape up:

> The God that holds you over the pit of hell, much as one holds a spider or some loathesome insect over the fire, abhors you and is dreadfully provoked. He looks upon you as worthy of nothing else but to be cast into the fire . . . You are ten thousand times so abominable in his eyes as the most hateful venemous serpent is in ours . . . Oh, sinner! Consider the fateful danger you are in . . . You hang by a slender thread, with the flames of divine wrath flashing about it, and ready every moment to singe it and burn it asunder.

We're sure you get the message, so we'll cut the sermon short. It's getting a bit warm around here. Through his highly charged appeals, Edwards was hoping to return his congregation to the orthodoxy of the generation that had settled Massachusetts. If logic would not persuade them to rededicate themselves, perhaps the **emotional appeal**—*fear*, that is—would do the job.

Richard Petty and John Cacioppo (1986) have devised the **elaboration-likelihood model** for understanding the processes by which people examine the information presented in persuasive messages. According to this view, there are at least two routes to persuading others to change their attitudes and behavior—two ways of responding to, or elaborating, persuasive messages. With the first, or central, route, change results from careful consideration of arguments and evidence. The second, or peripheral, route involves associating objects or proposed behavioral change with positive or negative "cues." These cues include rewards (such as McDonald's french fries) and punishments (such as parental disapproval), positive and negative emotional reactions (such as the fear generated by Jonathan Edwards' harangue), and factors such as the trustworthiness and attractiveness of the communicator.

Advertisements, which are a form of persuasive communication, also rely on central and peripheral routes. Some advertisements focus on the qual-

Social influence. The area of social psychology that studies the ways in which people influence the thoughts, feelings, and overt behavior of other people.

Emotional appeal. A type of persuasive communication that influences behavior on the basis of feelings that are aroused instead of rational analysis of the issues.

Elaboration-likelihood model. The view that persuasive messages are evaluated (elaborated) on the basis of central and peripheral cues.

ity of the product (central route), whereas others attempt to associate the product with appealing images (peripheral route) (Fox, 1984). Ads for Total cereal, which emphasize its nutritional benefits, provide information about the quality of the product (Snyder & DeBono, 1985). So too do the "Pepsi challenge" taste-test ads, which claim that Pepsi-Cola tastes better than Coca-Cola. The Marlboro cigarette ads, by contrast, focused on the masculine, rugged image of the "Marlboro man," and offered no information about the product itself (Snyder & DeBono, 1985).

The success of most persuasive communications often relies on a combination of central and peripheral cues, such as speech content and voice quality (O'Sullivan et al., 1985). In this section we examine a central factor in persuasion—that is, the nature of the message itself—and three peripheral factors: (1) the person delivering the message; (2) the context in which the message is delivered; and (3) the audience. We also examine two methods of persuasion used frequently, for example, by persons seeking charitable contributions and by salespersons: the foot-in-the-door technique and low-balling.

The Persuasive Message: Say What? Say How? Say How Often?

How do we respond when TV commercials are repeated until we have memorized every dimple on the actors' faces? Research suggests that familiarity breeds content, not contempt.

Consider the zabulon and the afworbu—whatever they are. You might not be crazy about them at first, but Zajonc (1968) found that people began to react favorably toward these bogus Turkish words on the basis of repeated exposure. Political candidates who become highly familiar to the public through frequent TV commercials attain more votes (Grush, 1980). People respond more favorably to abstract art (Heingartner & Hall, 1974), classical music (Smith & Dorfman, 1975), photographs of black people (Hamm et al., 1975) and of college students (Moreland & Zajonc, 1982) simply on the basis of repetitive viewing. Love for classical art and music may begin through exposure in the nursery—not the college appreciation course. The more complex the stimuli, the more likely it is that frequent exposure will have favorable effects (Saegert & Jellison, 1970; Smith & Dorfman, 1975). The one-hundredth repetition of a Bach concerto may be less tiresome than the one-hundredth repetition of a pop tune.

Two-sided arguments, in which the communicator recounts the arguments of the opposition in order to refute them, can be especially effective when the audience is at first uncertain about its position (Hass & Linder, 1972). Theologians and politicians sometimes expose their followers to the arguments of the opposition. By refuting them one by one, they give their followers a sort of psychological immunity to them. Swinyard found that two-sided product claims, in which advertisers admitted their product's weak points as well as highlighting its strengths, were most believable (in Bridgwater, 1982).

It would be nice to think that we are too sophisticated to be persuaded by an emotional appeal. However, grisly films of operations on cancerous lungs are more effective than matter-of-fact presentations at changing smoking attitudes (Leventhal et al., 1972). Films of bloodied gums and decayed teeth are also more effective than logical discussions aimed at increasing toothbrushing (Dembroski et al., 1978). Fear appeals are most effective when they are strong, when the audience believes the dire consequences, and when the recommendations offered seem practical (Mewborn & Rogers, 1979). Induced feelings of guilt as well as of fear facilitate persuasion (Regan et al., 1972; Wallington, 1973).

Experiments suggest that food and pleasant music increase acceptance of persuasive messages.

Audiences also tend to believe arguments that appear to run counter to the personal interests of the communicator (Wood & Eagly, 1981). People may pay more attention to a whaling-fleet owner's claim, than to a conservationist's, that whales are becoming extinct. If the president of Chrysler or General Motors admitted that Toyotas and Hondas were superior, you can bet that we would prick up our ears.

Selective avoidance. Diverting one's attention from information that is inconsistent with one's attitudes.

Selective exposure. Deliberate seeking of and attending to information that is consistent with one's attitudes.

The Persuasive Communicator: Whom Do You Trust?

Would you buy a used car from a person convicted of larceny? Would you attend weight-control classes run by a 350-pound leader? Would you leaf through fashion magazines featuring clumsy models? Probably not. Research shows that persuasive communicators show expertise (Hennigan et al., 1982), trustworthiness, attractiveness, or similarity to their audiences (Baron & Byrne, 1987).

Health professionals enjoy high status in our society and are considered experts. It is not coincidental that toothpaste ads boast that their products have the approval of the American Dental Association.

Even though we are reared not to judge books by their covers, we are more likely to find attractive people persuasive. Corporations do not gamble millions on the physically unappealing to sell their products. Some advertisers seek out the perfect combination of attractiveness and plain, simple folksiness with which the audience can identify. Ivory Soap commercials sport "real" people with attractive features who are so freshly scrubbed that you might think you can smell Ivory Soap emanating from the TV set.

TV news anchorpersons also enjoy high prestige. One study (Mullen et al., 1987) found that before the 1984 presidential election, Peter Jennings of ABC News had shown significantly more favorable facial expressions when reporting on Ronald Reagan than when reporting on Walter Mondale. Tom Brokaw of NBC and Dan Rather of CBS had not shown measurable favoritism. The researchers also found that viewers of ABC News voted for Reagan in greater proportions than viewers of NBC or CBS News. It is tempting to conclude that viewers were subtly persuaded by Jennings to vote for Reagan. However, Sweeney and Gruber (1985) have shown that viewers do not simply absorb like a sponge whatever the tube feeds them. Instead, they show **selective avoidance** and **selective exposure.** They tend to switch channels when they are faced with news coverage that seems to run counter to their own attitudes, and they seek communicators whose attitudes coincide with their own. And so, whereas Jennings might have had an influence on his audience's attitudes toward Reagan, it might also be that Reaganites preferred Jennings to Brokaw and Rather.

The Context of the Message: "Get 'Em in a Good Mood"

You are too clever and insightful to allow someone to persuade you by buttering you up, but perhaps someone you know would be influenced by a sip of wine, a bite of cheese, and a sincere compliment. Seduction attempts usually come at the tail end of a date—after the Szechuan tidbits, the nouveau Fresno film, the disco party, and the wine that was sold at its time. An assault at the outset of a date would be viewed as . . . well, an assault. Experiments suggest that food and pleasant music increase acceptance of persuasive messages (Janis et al., 1965; Galizio & Hendrick, 1972).

It is also counterproductive to call your dates fools when they disagree with you—even though their views are bound to be foolish if they do not coincide with yours. Agreement and praise are more effective at encouraging others to accept your views (Baron, 1971; Byrne, 1971). Appear sincere, or else your compliments will look manipulative. It seems a bit unfair to give out this information.

Foot-in-the-door technique. A method for inducing compliance in which a small request is followed with a larger request.

The Persuaded Audience: Are You a Person Who Can't Say No?

Why do some people have "sales resistance," whereas others enrich the lives of every door-to-door salesperson? For one thing, people with high self-esteem might be more likely to resist social pressure than people with low self-esteem (Santee & Maslach, 1982). However, Baumeister and Covington (1985) challenge the view that persons with low self-esteem are more open to persuasion. Persons with high self-esteem may be persuaded as readily, but people with high self-esteem may be less willing to admit that others have persuaded them.

Santee and Maslach (1982) also suggest that people high in social anxiety are more readily persuaded than people with low social anxiety. A study by Schwartz and Gottman (1976) reveals the cognitive nature of the "social anxiety" that can make it hard for some of us to say no to requests. Schwartz and Gottman found that people who comply with unreasonable requests are more likely to report thinking: "I was worried about what the other person would think of me if I refused"; "It is better to help others than to be self-centered"; or "The other person might be hurt or insulted if I refused." People who did not comply reported thoughts like "It doesn't matter what the other person thinks of me"; "I am perfectly free to say no"; or "This request is an unreasonable one" (p. 916).

Broad knowledge of the areas that a communicator is discussing also tends to decrease persuadability (Wood, 1982). If we know a great deal about cars, we are less open to the unrealistic claims of salespersons.

The Foot-in-the-Door Technique

You might think that giving money to door-to-door solicitors for charity will get you off the hook. That is, they'll take the cash and leave you alone for a while. Actually, the opposite is true: The next time the organization mounts a campaign, they are more likely to call on generous you. In fact, they may even recruit you to go door to door! Giving an inch apparently encourages others to try to take a yard. They have gotten their "foot in the door."

In order to gain insight into the **foot-in-the-door technique,** consider a classic experiment by Freedman and Fraser (1966). In this study, groups of women received phone calls from a consumer group who asked whether they would allow a six-man crew to drop by their homes to inventory every product they used. It could take several hours to complete the chore. Only 22 percent of one group acceded to this rather troublesome request. But 53 percent of another group of women agreed to a visit from this wrecking crew. Why was the second group more compliant? The more compliant group had been phoned a few days earlier and had agreed to answer a few questions about the soap products they used. They had been primed for the second request. The caller had gotten his "foot in the door." The foot-in-the-door technique has also been shown to be effective in persuading people to make charitable contributions (Pliner et al., 1974) and to sign petitions (Baron, 1973).

The results of one study (Snyder & Cunningham, 1975) suggest that people who have acceded to a small request become more likely to accede to a larger one, because they come to view themselves as the "type of person" who helps others by acceding to requests. Regardless of how the foot-in-the-door technique works, if you want to say no, it may be easier to say no (and stick to your guns) the first time a request is made, and not later. And organizations have learned that they can compile lists of persons they can rely on.

Low-Balling

Have you ever had a salesperson promise you a low price for merchandise, committed yourself to buy at that price, and then had the salesperson tell you that he or she had been in error, or that the manager had not agreed to the price? Have you then cancelled the order or stuck to your commitment?

You might have been a victim of **low-balling,** a sales method also referred to as "throwing the low ball." In low-balling, you are persuaded to make a commitment on favorable terms; the persuader then claims that he or she must revise the terms. Perhaps the car you agreed to buy for $9,400 did not have the automatic transmission and air conditioning you both assumed it had. Perhaps the yen or the mark has just gone up against the dollar, and the price of the car has to be raised proportionately.

Low-balling is an aggravating technique, and there are few protections against it. One possibility is to ask the salesperson whether he or she has the authority to make the deal, and then to have him or her write out the terms and sign the offer. Unfortunately, the salesperson might later confess to misunderstanding what you meant by his or her having the "authority" to make the deal. Perhaps the best way to combat low-balling is to be willing to take your business elsewhere when the salesperson tries to back out of an arrangement.

Low-balling places us in cognitive conflict because we have made a commitment to buy the merchandise but the terms have been altered. Perhaps we also fear that we are being suckered, and we perceive our self-esteem to be on the line. Let us examine the role of cognitive conflict further by considering the things that happen when we perceive our own attitudes to be inconsistent.

Cognitive-Dissonance Theory

According to **cognitive-dissonance theory,** which was originated by Leon Festinger (Festinger, 1957; Festinger & Carlsmith, 1959), people dislike inconsistency. We do not like to think that our attitudes (cognitions) are inconsistent or that our attitudes are inconsistent with our behavior. Awareness that two cognitions are dissonant, or that our cognitions and our behavior are inconsistent, appears sufficient to motivate us to reduce the discrepancy. Cognitive dissonance is an unpleasant state (Fazio & Cooper, 1983) that is accompanied by heightened physiological arousal (Croyle & Cooper, 1983). That is, our heart rate, respiration rate, and blood pressure are all higher when we are in a state of cognitive dissonance. And so a physiological motive for eliminating cognitive dissonance might be to reduce our body arousal to more comfortable levels.

In the first and one of the best-known studies on cognitive dissonance, one group of subjects received $1.00 for telling someone else that a just-completed boring task was very interesting (Festinger & Carlsmith, 1959). A second group of subjects received $20.00 to describe the task positively. Both groups were paid to engage in **attitude-discrepant behavior**—that is, behavior that ran counter to their actual thoughts and feelings. After "selling" the task to others, the subjects were asked to rate their own liking for the task. Ironically, the group paid *less* rated the task as significantly more interesting. *Why?*

From a learning-theory point of view, this result would be confusing. After all, shouldn't we learn to like that which is highly rewarding? But cognitive-dissonance theory would predict this "less-leads-to-more effect" for the following reason: The cognitions "I was paid very little" and "I told someone that this task was interesting" are dissonant. You see, another concept in cognitive-dissonance theory is **effort justification,** and subjects in studies such as these are helped to justify their behavior by concluding that their attitudes might not have been as discrepant with their behavior as they had originally believed.*

***

*The notion that we have greater appreciation for the things for which we must work hard is another example of effort justification.

Low-balling. A method in which extremely attractive terms are offered to induce a person to make a commitment. Once the commitment is made, the terms are revised.

Cognitive-dissonance theory. The view that people have a need to organize their perceptions, opinions, and beliefs in a consistent manner.

Attitude-discrepant behavior. Behavior that runs counter to one's thoughts and feelings.

Effort justification. The tendency to seek justification (reasons) for strenuous efforts.

WHAT DO YOU SAY NOW?

Responding to "Low-Balling"

Imagine that you're shopping for a new stereo set. You know just what you want and you see it advertised by a discount store at the excellent price of $350. You rush to the store and find a salesperson.

"Uh-oh," says the salesperson, shaking his head. "These sets have been going fast. I'll have to check on whether it's in stock. Give me a couple of minutes." Then he disappears into the back.

Fifteen minutes pass and you're getting fidgety. But then the salesperson returns—looking more upbeat. You are optimistic.

"I looked everywhere," he says, "and we're all out of the speakers." You have a sinking feeling. "But I checked with my manager," he continues, "and he says we can give you the same amplifier and turntable with more powerful speakers for $425. That's a bargain when you consider the sound you'll be getting."

You're no sucker, so you ask, "Won't you be getting them in stock again?"

"Sure," says the salesperson, "but not at $350. The dollar's been going down against the yen, and Japanese electronics are going up every day. Look, we don't want you to be unhappy. Believe me, at $425, the set with bigger speakers is a very good deal."

You want the set, but you don't need bigger speakers. And the price in the paper was $350 with the speakers you wanted.

What do you say now? Consider a number of possible responses, and write them here. Then check below:

1. _____

2. _____

3. _____

So what did you say?

You have probably been a victim of low-balling. In this kind of low-balling, the customer is lured into the store by a good price on unavailable merchandise and then offered substitute goods at a higher price. Sad to say, this is not a rare sales practice. What kinds of things might you have said? There is no single right answer, but here are some possibilities:

1. "I think you had better let me talk to that manager myself. Please show me the way." (If the salesperson hems and haws, or if he says he'll "bring the manager out to you" in a few minutes, it might be that he had not spoken to the manager but was following a preplanned tactic.)

2. "It's illegal to advertise merchandise that's unavailable. Why don't you recheck with the manager and go through the storeroom again?" (If the salesperson—or the manager—is concerned about your veiled threat of a legal suit, he might be able to come up with the advertised merchandise.)

3. "Thank you for looking. I'll find the set I want at a decent price elsewhere." (This lets the salesperson know you're not going to be suckered, and perhaps you will find that set elsewhere—at a good price.)

4. Or you could simply walk out.

Consider another situation. Cognitive dissonance would be created if we were to believe that our preferred candidate were unlikely to win the U.S. presidential election. One cognition would be that our candidate is better for the country, or, at an extreme, would "save" the country from harmful forces. A second and dissonant cognition would be that our candidate does not have a chance to win. Research shows that in the presidential elections from 1952–1980, people by a four-to-one margin helped reduce such dissonance by expressing the belief that their candidate would win (Granberg & Brent, 1983). They frequently held these beliefs despite lopsided polls to the contrary. Among highly involved but poorly informed people, the margin of self-deception was still higher.

Return for a moment to the low-balling technique. You have agreed to buy a car for the (excellent!) price of $9,400, but your salesperson tells you that the price did not include air conditioning, even though you assumed that it did. However, the salesperson admits that it was his error, and offers to throw in the air conditioning "at cost," for just another $450. Perhaps one of your cognitions is that you had made a deal. Another is that you are being "suckered." Some people apparently reduce dissonance by deciding that the salesperson's error was an "honest mistake" and that they are not being suckered after all!*

Let us now consider an even more powerful application of cognitive-dissonance theory: the case study of the kidnapping of newspaper heiress Patty Hearst. It provides graphic evidence of the ways in which attitude-discrepant behavior might be able to change our basic sense of who we are and what we stand for.

Can One's Self-Identity Be Converted Through Attitude-Discrepant Behavior? The Strange Case of Patty Hearst

In February, 1974, newspaper heiress Patty Hearst, an undergraduate student at Berkeley, was abducted by a revolutionary group known as the Symbionese Liberation Army (SLA). Early messages from the SLA directed the Hearst family to distribute millions of dollars' worth of food to the poor if they wished their daughter to live. There was no suggestion that Patty was a willing prisoner.

But a couple of months later, SLA communiqués contained statements by Patty that she had willingly joined them. Patty declared her revolutionary name Tania and sent a photograph in which she wore a guerrilla outfit and held a machine gun. She expressed contempt for her parents' capitalist values and referred to them as pigs. But her family did not believe that Patty's attitudes had really changed. They had reared her for 20 years, and she had been under the influence of the SLA for only two months. Surely her statements were designed to earn favorable treatment by her captors.

In April, Patty and other SLA members robbed a San Francisco bank. Patty was videotaped brandishing a rifle. She was reported to have threatened a guard. But the Hearsts maintained that the rifle could have been unloaded. Patty might still have been acting out of fear of losing her life. Then Patty became involved in another incident. She acted as a cover for SLA members William and Emily Harris, firing an automatic rifle as they fled from a store they had robbed. Patty seemed unsupervised at the time.

Patty and the Harrises were captured in San Francisco late in 1975. At first Patty was defiant. She gave a revolutionary salute and identified herself as Tania. But once she was in prison, her identity appeared to undergo another transformation. She asked to be called Patty again. At her trial she seemed quite remorseful. The defense argued that had it not been for the social influence of the SLA, Patty would never have engaged in criminal behavior or adopted revolutionary values. When President Jimmy Carter signed an order for Patty's early release from prison in 1979, he was operating under an admission from Patty's original prosecutors that they, too, believed that Patty would not have behaved criminally without being abducted by the SLA and experiencing dread in the days that followed.

How is it that a college undergraduate with typical American values came to express attitudes that were opposed to her lifelong ideals? How is it that other people, when they come under the influence of "Moonies" or other cults, show conversion in some of their most basic attitudes and behavior patterns?

According to Erik Erikson, as noted in Chapter 3, our basic sense of who we are and what we stand for is our *ego identity*. It may be that some conversions in ego identity can be explained through cognitive-dissonance theory. After Patty's kidnapping, she was exposed to fear and fatigue and forced into attitude-discrepant behavior. She was coerced into expressing agreement with SLA values, engaging in sexual activity with SLA members,

---

*Of course, in such a situation you can take you business elsewhere or insist that the salesperson stick to the deal, since it was his "error" and not yours. Sad to say, if the salesperson refuses to stick to the deal and you want the dealership to stick to the original price, you might need an attorney to follow through, not a psychologist.

Patty Hearst and Cognitive-Dissonance Theory
Patty Hearst as the "urban guerrilla" Tania (left), and in manacles as she arrives for
sentencing in court. After her kidnapping by a revolutionary group, Patty was influenced to commit armed robbery and other acts that were inconsistent with her sense
of self-identity. After a while, it appears that she came to view herself as a revolutionary. How can any of us know where our "real selves" leave off and the social
influences of others begin?

and training for revolutionary activity. So long as she clung firmly to her self-
identity as Patty, these repugnant acts created great cognitive dissonance. But
by adopting the suggested revolutionary identity of Tania, Patty could look
upon herself as "liberated" rather than as a frightened captive or as a criminal.
Not only was her fear of her captors reduced. Her cognitive dissonance was
reduced as well because her behavior was not inconsistent with her newly
adopted values.

 Of course, Patty Hearst's story provides us with a case study. We cannot
be certain as to what led to what. Nor can we share directly in the private
events of Patty's mind. We are dependent on her self-reports. Still, well-con-
trolled research shows that we do tend to draw conclusions about our attitudes
from our decisions to engage in particular behavior (Fazio et al., 1982; Nisbett
& Ross, 1980). Also, we have no reason to believe that Patty misrepresented
her recollections of her frightening experiences. Reports of her overt behavior
were corroborated by reports from SLA members who were captured, and
her self-reports are consistent with her participation in SLA activities and her
behavior before and afterward.

 And so, cognitive-dissonance theory leads to the hypothesis that we can
change people's attitudes by getting them somehow to behave in a manner
consistent with the attitudes we wish to promote. Research does show that
people may indeed change attitudes when attitude-discrepant behavior is rewarded (Calder et al., 1973; Cooper, 1980). It is at once a frightening and
promising concept. For instance, it sounds like a prescription for totalitari-
anism. Yet it also suggests that prejudiced individuals who are prevented from
discriminating—who are compelled, for example, by open-housing laws to
allow people from different ethnic backgrounds to buy homes in their neighborhoods—may actually become less prejudiced.

Patty Hearst obeyed the SLA because she feared for her life. Her desire to ingratiate herself with her threatening captors is understandable, even if some questions remain unanswered concerning the exact nature of her conversion in ego identity. Let us now explore the phenomenon of obedience in some more detail, and here we happen upon some aspects of human nature that are equally disturbing—the tendency to obey immoral commands of authority figures, even when we are *not* in danger.

■ Obedience to Authority

Richard Nixon resigned the presidency of the United States in August, 1974. For two years the business of the nation had almost ground to a halt while Congress investigated the 1972 burglary of a Democratic party campaign office in the Watergate office and apartment complex. It turned out that Nixon supporters had authorized the break-in. Nixon himself might have been involved in the cover-up of this connection later on. For two years Nixon and his aides had been investigated by the press and by Congress. Now it was over. Some of the bad guys were thrown in jail. Nixon was exiled to the beaches of Southern California. The nation returned to work. The new President, Gerald Ford, declared "Our national nightmare is over."

But was it over? Have we come to grips with the implications of the Watergate affair?

According to Stanley Milgram *(APA Monitor,* January 1978), a prominent Yale University psychologist, the Watergate cover-up, like the Nazi slaughter of the Jews, was made possible through the compliance of people who were more concerned about the approval of their supervisors than about their own morality. Otherwise they would have refused to abet these crimes. The broad questions are: How pressing is the need to obey authority figures at all costs? What can we do to ensure that we follow the dictates of our own consciences and not the immoral commands of authority figures?

The Milgram Studies: Shocking Stuff at Yale

Stanley Milgram also wondered how many of us would resist authority figures who made immoral requests. To find out, he ran a series of experiments at Yale University. In an early phase of his work, Milgram (1963) placed ads in New Haven, Connecticut, newspapers for subjects for studies on learning and memory. He enlisted 40 men ranging in age from 20 to 50—teachers, engineers, laborers, salespeople, men who had not completed elementary school, men with graduate degrees. The sample was a cross section of the population of this Connecticut city.

Let us suppose you had answered an ad. You would have shown up at the university for a fee of $4.50, for the sake of science, and for your own curiosity. You might have been impressed. After all, Yale was a venerable institution that dominated the city. You would not have been less impressed by the elegant labs where you would have met a distinguished behavioral scientist dressed in a white laboratory coat and another newspaper recruit—like you. The scientist would have explained that the purpose of the experiment was to study the *effects of punishment on learning.* The experiment would require a "teacher" and a "learner." By chance you would be appointed the teacher, and the other recruit the learner.

You, the scientist, and the learner would enter a laboratory room with a rather threatening chair with dangling straps. The scientist would secure the learner's cooperation and strap him in. The learner would express some concern, but this was, after all, for the sake of science. And this was Yale University, was it not? What could happen to a person at Yale?

You would follow the scientist to an adjacent room from which you would do your "teaching." This teaching promised to be effective. You would punish the "learner's" errors by pressing levers marked from 15 to 450 volts on a fearsome looking console (see Figure 3.2, p. 94). Labels described 28 of the 30 levers as running the gamut from "Slight Shock" to "Danger: Severe Shock." The last two levers resembled a film unfit for anyone under age 17: They were rated simply "XXX." Just in case you had no idea what electric shock felt like, the scientist gave you a sample 45-volt shock. It stung. You pitied the fellow who might receive more.

Your learner was expected to learn word pairs. Pairs of words would be read from a list. After hearing the list once, the learner would have to produce the word that was paired with the stimulus word. He would do so by pressing a switch that would signify his choice from a list of four alternatives. The switch would light one of four panels in your room (see Figure 5.1). If it was the correct panel, you would proceed to the next stimulus word. If not, you would deliver an electric shock. With each error, you would increase the voltage of the shock.

You would probably have some misgivings. Electrodes had been strapped to the learner's wrists (see Figure 5.2), and the scientist had applied electrode paste to "avoid blisters and burns." You were also told that the shocks would cause "no permanent tissue damage," although they might be extremely painful. Still, the learner was going along, and, after all, this was Yale.

The learner answered some items correctly and then made some errors. With mild concern you pressed the levers up through 45 volts. You had tolerated that much yourself. Then a few more mistakes were made. You pressed the 60-volt lever, then 75. The learner made another mistake. You paused and looked at the scientist. He was reassuring: "Although the shocks may be painful, there is no permanent tissue damage, so please go on." Further errors were made, and quickly you were up to a shock of 300 volts. But now the learner was pounding on the other side of the wall! Your chest tightened and you began to perspire. Damn science and the $4.50! you thought. You hesitated and the scientist said, "The experiment requires that you continue." After the delivery of the next stimulus word, there was no answer at all. What were you to do? "Wait for five to ten seconds," the scientist instructed, "and then treat no answer as a wrong answer." But after the next shock, there was again that pounding on the wall! Now your heart was racing and you were convinced that you were causing extreme pain and discomfort. Was it possible that no lasting damage was being done? Was the experiment that important, after all? What to do? You hesitated again. The scientist said, "It is absolutely essential that you continue." His voice was very convincing. "You have no other choice," he said, "you *must* go on." You could barely think straight, and for some unaccountable reason you felt laughter rising in your throat. Your finger shook above the lever. What were you to do?

On Truth at Yale

Milgram (1963, 1974) found out what most people would do. Of the 40 men in this phase of his research, only 5 refused to go beyond the 300-volt level, at which the learner first pounded the wall. Nine more teachers defied the scientist within the 300-volt range. But 65 percent of the participants complied with the scientist throughout the series, believing that they were delivering 450-volt, XXX-rated shocks.

Were these newspaper recruits simply unfeeling? Not at all. Milgram was impressed by their signs of stress. They trembled, they stuttered, they bit their lips. They groaned, they sweated, they dug their fingernails into their flesh. There were fits of laughter, though laughter was inappropriate. One salesperson's laughter was so convulsive that he could not continue with the experiment.

Milgram wondered if college students, heralded for independent think-

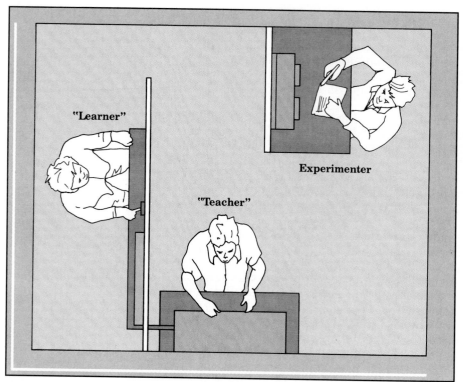

FIGURE 5.1 **The Experimental Setup in the Milgram Studies on Obedience**
When the learner makes an error, the experimenter prods the teacher to deliver an electric shock.

FIGURE 5.2 **A Learner**
This man could be in for quite a shock. He was designated as a learner in the Milgram studies on obedience.

ing, would show more defiance. But a replication of the study with Yale undergraduates yielded similar results. What about women, who were supposedly less aggressive than men? Women, too, shocked the "learners"—and all of this in a nation that values independence and the free will of the individual. Our "national nightmare" may not be over at all.

On Deception at Yale

You are probably skeptical enough to wonder whether the "teachers" in the Milgram study actually shocked the "learners" when they pressed the levers on the console. They didn't. The only real shock in this experiment was the 45-volt sample given the teachers. Its purpose was to lend credibility to the procedure.

The learners in the experiment were actually confederates of the experimenter. They had not answered the newspaper ads, but were in on the truth from the start. "Teachers" were the only real subjects. Teachers were led to believe that they were chosen at random for the teacher role, but the choosing was rigged so that newspaper recruits would always become teachers.

The Big Question: Why?

We have shown that most people obey the commands of others, even when pressed to immoral tasks. But we have not answered the most pressing question: *Why?* Why did Germans "just follow orders" and commit atrocities? Why did "teachers" obey orders from the experimenter? We do not have all the answers, but we can offer a number of hypotheses:

1. *Socialization.* Despite the expressed U.S. ideal of independence, we are socialized to obey others (such as parents and teachers) from the time we are little children.

2. *Lack of Social Comparison.* In Milgram's experimental settings, experimenters showed command of the situation, whereas teachers (subjects) were on the experimenter's ground and very much on their own. Being on their own, teachers did not have the opportunity to compare their ideas and feelings with those of people in the same situation. And so, they were less likely to have a clear impression of what to do. Ironically, in Nazi Germany, the average citizen was taught that all decent Germans revile Jews, blacks, and other "foreign" peoples. In Germany bigotry was the social norm.

3. *Perception of Legitimate Authority.* The phase of Milgram's research described above took place within the hallowed halls of Yale University. Subjects there might be overpowered by the reputation and authority of the setting. An experimenter at Yale might appear very much the legitimate authority figure—as might a government official or a high-ranking officer in the military. Further research showed that the university setting contributed to compliance, but was not fully responsible for it. The percentage of subjects complying with the experimenter's demands dropped from 65 percent to 48 percent when Milgram (1974) replicated the study in a dingy storefront in a nearby town. In the less prestigious setting, slightly fewer than half of the subjects were willing to administer the highest levels of shock.

   At first glance this finding might seem encouraging. But the main point of the Milgram studies is precisely that most of us remain willing to engage in morally reprehensible acts at the behest of a legitimate-appearing authority figure. Hitler and his henchmen were very much the legitimate authority figures in Nazi Germany. Nixon was the authority figure in the White House of the early 1970s. "Science" and Yale University legitimized the authority of the experimenters in the Milgram studies. The problem of acquiescence to authority figures remains.

4. *The Foot-in-the-Door Technique.* The foot-in-the-door technique might also have contributed to the obedience of the teachers (Gilbert, 1981). That is, after teachers had begun the process of delivering graduated shocks to learners, perhaps they found it progressively more difficult to extricate themselves from the project. Soldiers, similarly, are first taught to obey unquestioningly in innocuous matters such as dress and drill. By the time they are ordered to risk their lives and storm that hill, they have been saluting smartly and following commands for quite some time.

5. *Inaccessibility of Values.* People are more likely to behave in ways that are consistent with their values and other attitudes when their attitudes are readily accessible, or "come to mind" (Fazio, 1986; Fazio et al., 1986). But we become subject to confused and conflicting thoughts and motives as our levels of anxiety shoot up. As teachers in the Milgram experiments

became more and more aroused, their values might have become less accessible. As a consequence, it might have become progressively more difficult for them to behave in ways that were consistent with their moral values.

6. *Buffers.* Social psychologist Daryl Bem (1987) also notes that several buffers decreased the immediate impact of the teachers' violence. Learners (confederates of the experimenter), for example, were in another room. When learners were in the same room with teachers—that is, when subjects had full view of their victims—the compliance rate dropped from 65 to 40 percent. Moreover, when the subject was given the task of holding the learner's hand on the shock plate, the compliance rate dropped to 30 percent. Similarly, many bomber pilots during World War II said that they could not have carried out their missions if they had seen the faces of their victims. In modern warfare, opposing soldiers tend to be separated by great distances. It is one thing to press a button to launch a missile, or to aim a piece of artillery at a distant troop carrier or a distant ridge. It is another thing to hold the weapon to the throat of the victim.

And so, there are numerous theoretical explanations for obedience. Regardless of the exact nature of the forces that acted upon the teachers in the Milgram studies, his research has alerted us to a real and present danger—the tendency of most people to obey authority figures, even when the figures' demands contradict their own moral attitudes and values. It has happened before. Unhappily, unless we remain alert, it may happen again. Who are the authority figures in your life? How do you think you would have behaved if you had been a "teacher" in the Milgram studies? Are you sure?

■ Group Behavior

To be human is to belong to groups. Families, classes, religious groups, political parties, circles of friends, bowling teams, sailing clubs, conversation groups, therapy groups—to how many groups do you belong? How do groups influence the behavior of individuals?

In this section we have a look at two important aspects of group behavior: mob behavior and the bystander effect.

Mob Behavior and Deindividuation

Gustave Le Bon (1960), the French social thinker, branded mobs and crowds irrational, like a "beast with many heads." Mob actions such as race riots and lynchings sometimes seem to operate on a psychology of their own. Do mobs elicit the beast in us? How is it that mild-mannered people will commit mayhem as members of a mob? In seeking an answer, let us examine a lynching and the baiting type of crowd that often seems to attend threatened suicides.

The Lynching of Arthur Stevens In *Social Learning and Imitation,* Neal Miller and John Dollard (1941) vividly described a southern lynching. Arthur Stevens, a black man, was accused of murdering his lover, a white woman, when she wanted to break up with him. Stevens was arrested and confessed to the crime. The sheriff feared violence and moved Stevens to a town 200 miles distant during the night. But his location was uncovered. The next day a mob of a hundred persons stormed the jail and returned Stevens to the scene of the crime.

Outrage spread from person to person like a plague bacillus. Laborers, professionals, women, adolescents, and law-enforcement officers alike were infected. Stevens was tortured and killed. His corpse was dragged through the streets. Then the mob went on a rampage in town, chasing and assaulting

Deindividuation. The process by which group members may discontinue self-evaluation and adopt group norms and attitudes.

Diffusion of responsibility. The spreading or sharing of responsibility for a decision or behavior among a group.

Conform. To change one's attitudes or overt behavior to adhere to social norms.

Social norms. Explicit and implicit rules that reflect social expectations and influence the ways people behave in social situations.

other blacks. The riot ended only when troops were sent in to restore law and order.

Deindividuation   When we act as individuals, fear of consequences and self-evaluation tend to prevent antisocial behavior. But as members of a mob, we may experience **deindividuation**, a state of reduced self-awareness and lowered concern for social evaluation (Mann et al., 1982). Many factors lead to deindividuation, including anonymity, **diffusion of responsibility,** arousal due to noise and crowding (Zimbardo, 1969), and focusing of individual attention on the group process (Diener, 1980). Individuals also tend to adopt the emerging norms and attitudes of the group (Turner & Killian, 1972). Under these circumstances, crowd members behave more aggressively than they would as individuals.

Police know that mob actions are best averted early, by dispersing the small groups that may gather into a crowd. On an individual level, perhaps we can resist deindividuation by instructing ourselves to stop and think whenever we begin to feel highly aroused as group members. If we dissociate ourselves from such groups when they are in the formative process, we shall be more likely to retain critical self-evaluation and avoid behavior that we shall later regret.

The Baiting Crowd in Cases of Threatened Suicide   As individuals, we often feel compassion when we observe people so distressed that they are considering suicide. Why is it, then, that when people who are considering suicide threaten to jump from a ledge the crowd often baits them, urging them on?

Such baiting occurred in 10 of 21 cases of threatened suicide studied by Leon Mann (1981). Analysis of newspaper reports suggested a number of factors that might have contributed to baiting. The crowds were large and it was dark out (past 6 P.M.), and so baiters were likely to be anonymous. Also, the victim and the crowd were distant from one another, with the victim, for example, on a high floor. Distance might have served as a buffer between the baiting crowd and the victim, just as separate rooms seemed to serve as a buffer between the "teacher" and the "learner" in the Milgram studies on obedience. Baiting by the crowd was also linked to high temperatures (the summer season) and long duration of the episode, suggestive of stress and fatigue among crowd members.

Once a couple of individuals in a crowd begin baiting the person threatening to jump, others join in, as though they are conforming to the emerging group norm of callousness. Let us now turn our attention to the subject of conformity.

Conformity

Earlier we noted that most of us would be reluctant to wear blue jeans to a funeral or to walk naked on city streets. Such behavior would fly in the face of social norms, and other people would show us disapproval for it. We are said to **conform** when we change our behavior in order to adhere to social norms. **Social norms** are widely accepted rules that indicate how we are expected to behave under certain circumstances (Moscovici, 1985). Rules that require us to whisper in libraries and to slow down when driving past a school are examples of explicit, or openly stated, social norms. Other social norms are unspoken, or implicit (Zuckerman et al., 1983). One unspoken social norm is to be fashionably late for social gatherings.

There are a couple of unspoken social norms that operate in elevators. One is to face the front. The other is to mind one's own business, especially when the elevator is crowded. The first author likes to test the second elevator norm now and then by making friendly comments to strangers. The strangers usually smile briefly and say as little as possible.

The tendency to conform to social norms is often a good thing. Many norms have evolved because they favor comfort and survival. In the tight confines of the elevator people seem to hold on to dignity in the face of others pressing against them and literally breathing down their necks by pretending that they are not there. The pretense works as long as everyone plays the same game. Given the discomfort of being crowded in with strangers, the distance provided by minding one's own business seems adaptive. But group norms can also promote maladaptive behavior, as in pressuring business people to wear coats and ties in summer in buildings cooled only, say, to 78 degrees Fahrenheit. At that high temperature the only motive for conforming to a dress code may be to show that we have been adequately socialized and are not threats to social rules.

Let us have a look at a classic experiment on conformity run by Solomon Asch in the early 1950s. Then we shall examine some of the factors that promote conformity.

Seven Line Judges Can't Be Wrong: The Asch Study

Do you believe what you see with your own eyes? Seeing is believing, is it not? Not if you were a participant in the Asch (1952) study.

You would enter a laboratory room with seven other subjects for an experiment on visual discrimination. If you were familiar with psychology experiments, you might be surprised: There were no rats and no electric-shock apparatus in sight, only a man at the front of a room with some cards with lines drawn on them (Figure 5.3).

The eight of you would be seated in a series. You would be given the seventh seat, a minor fact at the time. The man would explain the task. There was a single line on the card on the left. Three lines were drawn on the card at the right (Figure 5.4). One line was the same length as the line on the

FIGURE 5.3 The Asch Experiment on Conformity

The experimenter is to the right, and the unsuspecting subject is seated second from the right.

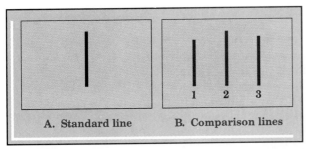

A. Standard line   B. Comparison lines

FIGURE 5.4   Cards Used in the Asch Study on Conformity
Which line on card B—1, 2, or 3—is the same length as the line on card A? Line 2, right? But would you say "2" if you were a member of a group and six people answering ahead of you all said "3"? Are you sure?

other card. You and the other subjects need only call out, one at a time, which of the three lines—1, 2, or 3—was the same length. Simple.

You would try it out. Those to your right spoke out in order: "3," "3," "3," "3," "3," "3." Now it was your turn. Line 3 was clearly the same length as the line on the first card, so you said "3." Then the fellow after you chimed in "3." That's all there was to it. Then two other cards were set up in the front of the room. This time line 2 was clearly the same length as the line on the first card. "2," "2," "2," "2," "2," "2." Your turn again. "2," you said, and perhaps your mind began to wander. Your stomach was gurgling a bit. That night you would not even mind dorm food particularly. "2," said the fellow after you.

Another pair of cards was held up. Line 3 was clearly the correct answer. The six people on your right spoke in turn: "1," "1 . . ." Wait a second! ". . . 1," "1—" You forgot about dinner and studied the lines briefly. No, 1 was too short, by a good half an inch. ". . . 1," "1," and suddenly it was your turn. Your hands had quickly become sweaty and there was a lump in your throat. You wanted to say 3, but was it right? There was really no time and you had already paused noticeably. "1," you said. "1," the last fellow confirmed matter-of-factly.

Now your attention was riveted on the task. Much of the time you agreed with the other seven line judges, but sometimes you did not. And for some reason beyond your understanding, they were in perfect agreement, even when they were wrong—assuming that you could trust your eyes. The experiment was becoming an uncomfortable experience, and you began to doubt your judgment.

The discomfort in the Asch study was caused by the pressure to conform. Actually, the other seven recruits were confederates of the experimenter. They prearranged a number of incorrect responses. The sole purpose of the study was to see whether you would conform to the erroneous group judgments.

How many of Asch's subjects caved in? How many went along with the crowd rather than assert what they thought to be the right answer? Seventy-five percent. *Three of four agreed with the majority wrong answer at least once.*

What about you? Would you wear blue jeans if everyone else wore slacks and skirts? A number of more recent experiments (Wheeler et al., 1978) show that the tendency to conform did not go out with the Fabulous Fifties.

Factors That Influence Conformity   Several personal and situational factors prompt conformity to social norms. Personal factors include the desires to be liked by other members of the group and to be right (Insko, 1985), low self-esteem, high self-consciousness, social shyness (Krech et al., 1962; Santee

& Maslach, 1982), gender, and familiarity with the task. Situational factors include group size and social support.

There has been a great deal of controversy as to whether women conform to social norms more so than men do. Old-fashioned stereotypes portray men as rugged individualists and women as "civilizing" influences upon them, so it is not surprising that women have been generally perceived as more conformist. Experimental findings over the past several decades have at first glance tended to support this view. A sophisticated statistical analysis of the literature up through the middle 1970s, for example, suggested that women by and large were more conformist than men (Cooper, 1979).

On the other hand, there have been a number of studies suggestive that sex differences are complex and not quite so predictable. For example, an experiment run by Sandra Bem (1975) of Cornell University found that women who accept the sex-role stereotype of the passive, dependent female are more likely than men to conform. But other women can be as self-assertive and independent as men. Another fascinating experiment on sex differences was run by social psychologist Alice Eagly and her colleagues (1981). The Eagly group found that men conform to group opinions as frequently as women do when their conformity or independence will be private. But when their conformity would be made known to the group, they conform less often than women do, apparently because nonconformity is more consistent with the masculine sex-role stereotype of independence. Ironically enough, men may be motivated to act independently in order to conform to the male sex-role stereotype of rugged individualism. It's a little bit like "doublethink" in the Orwell novel *1984:* "Nonconformity is conformity." (As with experiments showing that we are more "altruistic" when we are rewarded for being altruistic, sometimes you just can't win.)

Social psychologists Robert Baron and Donn Byrne (1987) take issue with Cooper's (1979) findings and assert that "it now seems clear that there are no important differences between males and females in terms of the tendency to conform" (p. 233). But Baron and Byrne admit that many people still perceive women as being easier to "push around." They offer the explanation that we usually see people of lower social status as being more conformist, and that women, sad to say, are often afforded lower social standing in the U.S.A.—in society at large and especially in the work force. In other words, the view of women as lower in social standing often stems from the traditional distribution of men into breadwinning roles and women into homemaking roles (Eagly & Steffen, 1984). And women in the work force as a group earn less than men.

Familiarity with the task at hand promotes self-reliance (Eagly, 1978). In one experiment, for example, Sistrunk and McDavid (1971) found that women were more likely to conform to group pressure on tasks involving identification of tools (such as wrenches) that were more familiar to men. But men were more likely to conform on tasks involving identification of cooking utensils, with which women, in our society, are usually more familiar.

Situational factors include the number of people who hold the majority opinion and the presence of at least one other who shares the discrepant opinion. Probability of conformity, even to incorrect group judgments, increases rapidly as a group grows to five members. Then it increases at a slower rate up to eight members (Gerard et al., 1968; Wilder, 1977), at which point maximum probability of conformity is reached.

But finding just one other person who supports your minority opinion is apparently enough to encourage you to stick to your guns (Morris et al., 1977). In a variation of the Asch experiment, recruits were provided with just one confederate who agreed with their minority judgments (Allen & Levine, 1971). Even though this confederate seemed to have a visual impairment, as evidenced by thick glasses, his support was sufficient to lead actual subjects not to conform to incorrect majority opinions.

Helping Behavior and the Bystander Effect: Some Watch While Others Die

We are all part of vast social networks—schools, industries, religious groups, communities, and society at large. Although we may have individual pursuits, in some ways our adjustment and personal development are intertwined. To some degree we depend on one another. What one person produces, another consumes. Goods are available in stores because other people have transported them, sometimes halfway around the world. A medical discovery in Boston saves a life in Taiwan. An assembly-line foul-up in Detroit places an accident victim in a hospital in Florida.

Because of such mutual dependency, one might think that we would come to the aid of others in trouble—especially when their lives are threatened. And sometimes we do, even at risk to ourselves. But now and then we let others down, as in the murder of 28-year-old Kitty Genovese in New York City in 1964. Murder was not unheard of in the "Big Apple," but Kitty had screamed for help as her killer had repeatedly stabbed her. Nearly 40 neighbors had heard the commotion. Many watched. Nobody helped. Why? Are we a callous bunch who would rather watch than help others who are in trouble? Penn State Psychologist R. Lance Shotland notes that by the 1980s more than 1,000 books and articles had been written attempting to explain the behavior of bystanders in crises (Dowd, 1984). According to Stanley Milgram, the Genovese case "touched on a fundamental issue of the human condition. If we need help, will those around us stand around and let us be destroyed or will they come to our aid?" (in Dowd, 1984).

Social psychologists refer to helping behavior as **altruism.** Let us consider some of the factors that determine whether we will come to the aid of others who are in trouble.

The Helper: Who Helps?   With some exceptions, we are more likely to be altruistic and help others when we are in a good mood (Berkowitz, 1987; Manucia et al., 1984; Rosenhan et al., 1981). Yet we may help others when we are miserable ourselves, if our own problems work to increase our empathy or sensitivity to the plights of others (Batson et al., 1981; Thompson et al., 1980). People with a high need for approval may help others in order to earn approval from others (Satow, 1975). People who are empathic, who can take the perspective of others, are also likely to help (Archer et al., 1981).

Highly masculine people might be expected to try to "take charge" of most situations, and thus be expected to be more likely to come to the aid of others in emergencies. However, Dianne Tice and Roy Baumeister (1985) found that highly masculine subjects, as measured by Sandra Bem's Sex Role Inventory, were *less* likely than others to help others in distress. The researchers suggest that highly masculine people may have a greater fear of potential embarrassment and loss of poise than most people—that is, they have a "tougher" image to protect. Such fears might inhibit them from intervening in emergencies.

There are other reasons why bystanders might not come to the aid of people in distress. For example, if bystanders do not fully understand what they are seeing, they may not recognize that an emergency exists. That is, the more ambiguous the situation, the less likely it is that bystanders will try to help (Shotland & Heinold, 1985). Second, the presence of others may lead to diffusion of responsibility, so that no one assumes responsibility for helping others (as we shall see in a following section). Third, if bystanders are not certain that they possess the competencies to take charge of the situation, they may also stay on the sidelines for fear of making a social blunder and being subject to ridicule (Pantin & Carver, 1982)—or for fear of getting hurt themselves.

Bystanders who believe that others "get" what they deserve may rationalize not helping by thinking that a person would not be in trouble unless this outcome was just (Lerner et al., 1975). And so a homeless person is allowed to lie in the gutter, as passers-by assume that he or she "belongs" there.

A sense of personal responsibility or commitment increases the likelihood of helping. People whose jobs involve bringing homeless people in from the cold of winter do come to their aid. Of course, we could say that people who help others in their work are not being altruistic in the sense of showing "unselfish" concern for the welfare of others—that is, they are also earning their paychecks. In any event, we usually help others when we have been designated as responsible for them (Maruyama et al., 1982). A sense of responsibility for others may also stem from having made a verbal commitment to help. For example, in an experiment by Moriarty (1975), people at a beach blanket intervened to prevent robbery of articles from a neighboring beach blanket—when they had been asked to watch these objects by their owners and had agreed to do so. Otherwise, they "minded their own business."

The Victim: Who Is Helped?   Although sex roles have been changing, it is traditional for men to help women in our society. Latané and Dabbs (1975) found that women were more likely than men to receive help, especially from men, when they dropped coins in Atlanta (a southern city) than in Seattle or Columbus (northern cities). The researchers explain this difference by noting that traditional sex roles persevere more strongly in the South.

Women are also more likely than men to be helped when their cars have broken down on the highway or they are hitchhiking (Pomazal & Clore, 1973). There may be sexual overtones to some of this "altruism." Women are most likely to be helped by males when they are attractive and when they are alone (Snyder et al., 1974; Benson et al., 1976).

Similarity between helper and person in distress also seems to promote helping behavior. Poorly dressed people are more likely to succeed in requests for a dime with poorly dressed strangers, whereas well-dressed people are more likely to get money from well-dressed strangers (Hensley, 1981).

Situational Determinants of Helping: "Am I the Only One Here?"
It may seem logical that a group of people would be more likely to have come to the aid of Kitty Genovese than would a lone person. After all, a group could more effectively have overpowered her attacker. Yet an experiment by Darley and Latané (1968) suggests that a lone person might have been more likely to try to help her.

In the Darley and Latané study, male subjects were performing meaningless tasks in cubicles when they heard a (convincing) recording of a person apparently having an epileptic seizure. When the subjects thought that four other persons were immediately available to help, only 31 percent made an effort to help the victim. But when they thought that no one else was available, 85 percent of them tried to offer aid. As in other areas of group behavior, it seems that diffusion of responsibility inhibits helping behavior in groups or crowds. When we are in a group, we are often willing to let George (or Georgette) do it. When George isn't around, we are more willing to help others ourselves.

Note that the bystanders in most studies on the bystander effect are strangers (Latané & Nida, 1981). Research shows that bystanders who are acquainted with victims are more likely to respond to the social norm of helping others in need (Rutkowski et al., 1983). After all, aren't we more likely to give to charity when asked directly by a co-worker or supervisor in the socially exposed situation of the office, as compared to in response to a letter received in the privacy of our own homes?

We are more likely to help others when we can clearly see what is happening (for instance, if we can see clearly that the woman whose car has broken down is alone), and when the environment is familiar to us (for instance, when we are in our home town rather than a strange city).

And so, being a member of a group can inhibit helping behavior rather than facilitate it. What will you do the next time you pass by someone who is obviously in need of aid? Will you help or will you be a bystander?

■ Becoming an Assertive Person: How to Win *Respect* and Influence People

In this chapter we have reviewed some of the pitfalls of social influence. We have seen how we can be persuaded to buy things or engage in immoral behavior against out better judgment. We have seen how—in the extreme—attitude-discrepant behavior might convert our self-identity. We have seen how social influence can give rise to unquestioning obedience and blind conformity. We have seen how group processes can subvert decision making by diffusion of responsibility, and how crowds prompt tragic behavior by deindividuation. We have even seen how group membership can give rise to harmful *inaction* in the case of the bystander effect.

There is no simple, single answer to the adjustment problems that are brought about by social influence. Running off to an island on the other side of the world would be a poor, if not impossible, solution for most of us. Other people provide us with exciting and needed stimulation, and so averting social influence by avoiding social contact is a punitive prospect for most of us. But there are a number of things we can do about social influence, and one of them is to become more self-assertive.

Assertive behavior involves many things—the expression of your genuine feelings, standing up for your legitimate rights, and refusing unreasonable requests (Rathus, 1978). It means withstanding undue social influences, disobeying *arbitrary* authority figures, and refusing to conform to *arbitrary* group standards. Since many of our feelings are positive, such as love and admiration, assertive behavior also means expressing them.

Assertive people also use the power of social influence to achieve desired ends. That is, they influence others to join them in worthwhile social and political activities. They may become involved in political campaigns, consumer groups, conservationist organizations, and other groups to advance their causes.

Alternatives to assertive behavior include submissive, or *nonassertive,* behavior and *aggressive* behavior. When we are submissive, our self-esteem plummets. Unexpressed feelings sometimes smolder as resentments and then catch fire as socially inappropriate outbursts. Aggressive behavior includes physical and verbal attacks, threats, and insults. Sometimes we get our way through aggression, but we also earn the condemnation of others. And, unless we are unfeeling, we condemn ourselves for bullying others.

It may be that you can't become completely assertive overnight, but you can decide *now* that you have been nonassertive long enough and construct a plan for change from the following guidelines. There may be times when you want to quit and revert to your nonassertive ways. Expressing your genuine beliefs may lead to some immediate social disapproval. Others may have a stake in your remaining a doormat, and the people we wind up confronting are sometimes those who are closest to us: parents, spouses, supervisors, and friends.

QUESTIONNAIRE

The Rathus Assertiveness Schedule

How assertive are you? Do you stick up for your rights, or do you allow others to walk all over you? Do you say what you feel, or what you think other people want you to say? Do you initiate relationships with attractive people, or do you shy away from them?

One way to gain insight into how assertive you are is to take the following self-report test of assertive behavior. Once you have finished, turn to the end of the chapter to find out how to calculate your score. A table at the end of the chapter will also allow you to compare your assertiveness to that of a sample of 1,400 students drawn from 35 college campuses across the U.S.A.

Directions: Indicate how well each item describes you by using this code:

    3 = very much like me
    2 = rather like me
    1 = slightly like me
   −1 = slightly unlike me
   −2 = rather unlike me
   −3 = very much unlike me

_____ **1.** Most people seem to be more aggressive and assertive than I am.*

_____ **2.** I have hesitated to make or accept dates because of "shyness."*

_____ **3.** When the food served at a restaurant is not done to my satisfaction, I complain about it to the waiter or waitress.

_____ **4.** I am careful to avoid hurting other people's feelings, even when I feel that I have been injured.*

_____ **5.** If a salesperson has gone to considerable trouble to show me merchandise that is not quite suitable, I have a difficult time saying "No."*

_____ **6.** When I am asked to do something, I insist upon knowing why.

_____ **7.** There are times when I look for a good, vigorous argument.

_____ **8.** I strive to get ahead as well as most people in my position.

_____ **9.** To be honest, people often take advantage of me.*

You can use the following four methods to become more assertive: (1) self-monitoring, (2) challenging irrational beliefs, (3) modeling, and (4) behavior rehearsal.

Self-Monitoring: Following Yourself Around the Block

Self-monitoring of social interactions can help you pinpoint problem areas and increase your motivation to behave more assertively. Keep a diary for a week or so. Jot down brief descriptions of any encounters that lead to negative feelings such as anxiety, depression, or anger. For each encounter, record:

The situation
What you felt and said or did
How others responded to your behavior
How you felt about the behavior afterward

Here are some examples of self-monitoring.* They involve an office worker (Jane), a teacher (Michael), and a medical student (Leslie), all in their 20s:

*Adapted from Rathus and Nevid (1977).

_____ **10.** I enjoy starting conversations with new acquaintances and strangers.

_____ **11.** I often don't know what to say to attractive persons of the opposite sex.*

_____ **12.** I will hesitate to make phone calls to business establishments and institutions.*

_____ **13.** I would rather apply for a job or for admission to a college by writing letters than by going through with personal interviews.*

_____ **14.** I find it embarrassing to return merchandise.*

_____ **15.** If a close and respected relative were annoying me, I would smother my feelings rather than express my annoyance.*

_____ **16.** I have avoided asking questions for fear of sounding stupid.*

_____ **17.** During an argument I am sometimes afraid that I will get so upset that I will shake all over.*

_____ **18.** If a famed and respected lecturer makes a comment which I think is incorrect, I will have the audience hear my point of view as well.

_____ **19.** I avoid arguing over prices with clerks and salespeople.*

_____ **20.** When I have done something important or worthwhile, I manage to let others know about it.

_____ **21.** I am open and frank about my feelings.

_____ **22.** If someone has been spreading false and bad stories about me, I see him or her as soon as possible and "have a talk" about it.*

_____ **23.** I often have a hard time saying "No."*

_____ **24.** I tend to bottle up my emotions rather than make a scene.*

_____ **25.** I complain about poor service in a restaurant and elsewhere.

_____ **26.** When I am given a compliment, I sometimes just don't know what to say.*

_____ **27.** If a couple near me in a theater or at a lecture were conversing rather loudly, I would ask them to be quiet or to take their conversation elsewhere.

_____ **28.** Anyone attempting to push ahead of me in a line is in for a good battle.

_____ **29.** I am quick to express an opinion.

_____ **30.** There are times when I just can't say anything.*

Reprinted from Rathus, 1973, pp. 398–406.

Jane: Monday, April 6 9:00 A.M. I passed Artie in the hall. I ignored him. He didn't say anything. I felt disgusted with myself. NOON Pat and Kathy asked me to join them for lunch. I felt shaky inside and lied that I still had work to do. They said all right, but I think they were fed up with me. I felt miserable, very tight in my stomach. 7:30 P.M. Kathy called me and asked me to go clothes shopping with her. I was feeling down and I said I was busy. She said she was sorry. I don't believe she was sorry—I think she knows I was lying. I hate myself. I feel awful.

Jane's record reveals a pattern of fear of incompetence in social relationships and resultant avoidance of other people. Her avoidance may once have helped her to reduce the immediate impact of her social anxieties, but has led to feelings of loneliness and depression. Now, because of Jane's immediate self-disgust, her defensive avoidance behavior doesn't even seem to help her in the short run.

Michael: Wednesday, December 17 8:30 A.M. The kids were noisy in homeroom. I got very angry and screamed my head off at them. They quieted down, but sneaked looks at each other as if I were crazy. My face felt red and hot, and my stomach was in a knot. I wondered what I was doing. 4:00 P.M. I was driving home from school. Some guy cut me off. I followed him closely for two blocks, leaning on my horn but praying he wouldn't stop and get out of his car. He didn't. I felt shaky as hell and thought someday I'm going to get myself killed. I had to pull over and wait for the shakes to pass before I could go on driving. 8:00 P.M. I was writing lesson plans for tomorrow. Mom came into the room and started crying—Dad was out drinking again. I yelled it was her problem. If she didn't want him to drink, she could confront him with it, not me, or divorce him. She cried harder and ran out. I felt pain in my chest. I felt drained and hopeless.

Michael's record showed that he was aggressive, not assertive. The record pinpoints the types of events and responses that had led to higher blood pressure and many painful bodily sensations. The record also helped him realize that he was living with many ongoing frustrations instead of making decisions—as to where he would live, for example—and behaving assertively.

Leslie was a third-year medical student whose husband was a professor of art and archaeology:

Leslie: Tuesday, October 5 10:00 A.M. I was discussing specialization interests with classmates. I mentioned my interest in surgery. Paul smirked and said, "Shouldn't you go into something like pediatrics or family practice?" I said nothing, playing the game of ignoring him, but I felt sick and weak inside. I was wondering if I would survive a residency in surgery if my supervisors also thought that I should enter a less-pressured or more "feminine" branch of medicine.

Thursday, October 7 7:30 P.M. I had studying to do, but was washing the dinner dishes, as per usual. Tom was reading the paper. I wanted to scream that there was no reason I should be doing the dishes just because I was the woman. I'd worked harder that day than Tom, my career was just as important as his, and I had studying to do that evening. But I said nothing. I felt anxiety or anger—I don't know which. My face was hot and flushed. My heart rate was rapid. I was sweating.

Even though Leslie was competing successfully in medical school, men apparently did not view her accomplishments as important as their own. It may never have occurred to Tom that he could help her with the dishes, or that they could rotate responsibility for household tasks. Leslie resolved that she must learn to speak out—to prevent male students from taunting her and to enlist Tom's cooperation around the house.

Confronting Irrational Beliefs: Do Your Own Beliefs Lead to Nonassertive or Aggressive Behavior?

While you are monitoring your behavior, try to observe irrational beliefs that may lead to nonassertive or to aggressive behavior. These beliefs may be fleeting and so ingrained that you no longer pay any attention to them. But by ignoring them, you deny yourself the opportunity to evaluate them, and to change them if they are irrational.

Jane feared social incompetence. Several irrational beliefs heightened her concerns. She believed, for example, that she must be perfectly competent in her social interactions or else avoid them. She believed that it would be awful if she floundered at a social effort and another person showed disapproval of her, even for an instant. She also believed that she was "naturally shy," that heredity and her early environment must somehow have forged a fundamental shyness that she was powerless to change. She also told herself that she could gain greater happiness in life through inaction and "settling" for other-than-social pleasures like reading and television—that she could achieve a contentment even if she never confronted her avoidance behavior.

When shown Albert Ellis's list of ten basic irrational beliefs (pp. 321–323), even Jane had to admit that she had unknowingly adopted nearly all of them.

Many of Michael's frustrations stemmed from a belief that life had singled him out for unfair treatment. How *dare* people abuse him? The *world* should change. With the world so unfair and unjust, why should he have to search out his *own* sources of frustration and cope with them? For many reasons: For example, Michael was attributing his own miseries to external pressures and hoping that if he ignored them they would go away. With an alcoholic father and a weak mother, he told himself, how could *he* be expected to behave appropriately?

Women and Assertive Behavior: Problems Caused by Early Socialization Messages   Leslie failed to express her feelings because she harbored subtle beliefs to the effect that women should not be "pushy" and cause resentments when they compete in areas traditionally reserved for men. She kidded herself that she could "understand" and "accept" the fact that Tom had simply been reared in a home atmosphere in which women carried out the day-to-day household chores. She kidded herself that it was easier for her to remain silent on the issue instead of making a fuss and expecting Tom to modify lifelong attitudes.

Women like Leslie have typically received early socialization messages that underlie many of their adult irrational beliefs (Wolfe & Fodor, 1975). Among these messages are the following: "I need to rely on someone stronger than myself—a man," "Men should handle large amounts of money and make the big decisions," "It is awful to hurt the feelings of others," "A woman does not raise her voice," and "I should place the needs of my husband and children before my own." In the area of sexual behavior, women have frequently received these early socialization messages: that they need to be guided by men to achieve satisfaction; that only men should initiate sexual activity; that sexually assertive women are sluttish or castrating; and that women must use artifical means such as makeup and scented sprays to make themselves attractive. Beliefs such as these endorse the stereotypical feminine sex role, and traits like dependence, passivity, and nurturance (at all costs). In short, they deny women *choice*.

Changing Irrational Beliefs   Do any of Jane's, Michael's, or Leslie's irrational beliefs also apply to you? Do they prevent you from behaving assertively? From making the effort to get out and meet people? From expressing your genuine feelings? From demanding your legitimate rights? Do they sometimes prompt aggressive rather than assertive behavior?

If so, you may decide to challenge your irrational beliefs. Ask yourself if they strike you as logical or simply as habit? Do they help you behave assertively or give you excuses for being submissive or aggressive? What will happen if you try something new? What if your new behavior has a few rough edges at first? Will the roof cave in if someone disapproves of you? Will the Ice Age be upon us if you try to speak up and flub it once or twice? Will the gods descend from Mount Olympus and strike you with lightning if you question an authority figure who makes an unreasonable request?

Modeling: Creating the New (Well, Almost New) You

Much of our behavior is modeled after those of people we respect and admire, people who have seemed capable of coping with situations that posed some difficulty for us. Here and there we adopt a characteristic, a gesture, a phrase, a tone of voice, a leer, a sneer.

Therapists who help clients become more assertive use extensive modeling. They may provide examples of specific things to say. When we are

Feedback. In assertiveness training, information about the effectiveness of behavior.

Behavior rehearsal. Practice of a skill.

Role playing. Showing the behavior appropriate in a certain social role.

In assertiveness training, psychologists help individuals learn how to express their genuine feelings and stand up for their legitimate rights.

interacting with other people, our degrees of eye contact, our postures, and our distances from them also communicate strong messages (Schwarz et al., 1983). Direct eye contact, for example, suggests assertiveness and honesty. So therapists help clients shape nonverbal behaviors as well—whether to lean toward the other person, how to hold one's hands, how far away to stand, and so on. Then the client tries it. The therapist provides **feedback**—tells the client how well he or she did.

Behavior Rehearsal: Practice Makes Much Better

At first it is a good idea to try out new assertive behaviors in nonthreatening situations, such as before your mirror or with trusted friends. This is **behavior rehearsal.** It will accustom you to the sounds of assertive talk as they are born in your own throat.

Therapists have clients rehearse assertive responses in individual or group sessions. They may use **role playing,** in which they act the part of a social antagonist or encourage you or other group members to take the roles of important people in your life. They alert you to posture, tone of voice, and the need to maintain eye contact.

Joan was a recently divorced secretary in her twenties. She returned home to live with her parents, and six months later her father died. Joan offered support as her mother, in her fifties, underwent several months of mourning. But Joan eventually realized that her mother had become excessively dependent on her. She no longer drove or went anywhere alone. Joan felt she must persuade her mother to regain some independence—for both their sakes.

Joan explained her problem in an assertiveness-training group. The therapist and group members suggested things that Joan could say. A group member then role played her mother while Joan rehearsed responses to her mother's requests. Her goal was to urge independent behavior in such a way

Fogging. Paraphrasing a social antagonist's point of view to show understanding, followed by disagreeing.

Broken-record technique. Persistent repetition of one's position to wear down the opposition.

that her mother would eventually see that Joan was interested in her welfare. Joan showed that she understood her mother's feelings by using the technique of **fogging,** or by paraphrasing them. But she clung to her basic position through the **broken-record technique,** as in this sample dialogue:

MOTHER ROLE: Dear, would you take me over to the market?

JOAN: Sorry, Mom, it's been a long day. Why don't you drive yourself?

MOTHER ROLE: You know I haven't been able to get behind the wheel of that car since Dad passed away.

JOAN: I know it's been hard for you to get going again (fogging), but it's been a long day (broken record) and you've got to get started doing these things again sometime.

MOTHER ROLE: You know that if I could do this for myself, I would.

JOAN: I know that you believe that (fogging), but I'm not doing you a favor by driving you around all the time. You've got to get started sometime (broken record).

MOTHER ROLE: I don't think you understand how I feel. *(Cries.)*

JOAN: You can say that, but I think I really do understand how awful you feel (fogging). But I'm thinking of your own welfare more than my own, and I'm not doing you a favor when I drive you everywhere (broken record).

MOTHER ROLE: But we need a few things

JOAN: I'm not doing you any favor by continuing to drive you everywhere (broken record).

MOTHER ROLE: Does that mean you've decided not to help?

JOAN: It means that I'm *not* helping you by continuing to drive you everywhere. I'm thinking of your welfare as well as my own, and you have to start driving again sometime (broken record).

Joan's task was difficult, but she persisted. She and her mother reached a workable compromise in which Joan at first accompanied her mother while her mother drove. But after an agreed-upon amount of time, her mother began to drive by herself.

We can use modeling on our own by carefully observing friends; business acquaintances; characters on television, in films, and in books; and noting how effective they are in their social behavior. If their gestures and words seem effective and believable in certain situations, we may try them out. Ask yourself whether the verbal and nonverbal communications of others would fit you if you trimmed them just a bit here and there. Sew bits and pieces of the behavior patterns of others together; then try them on for size. After a while you may find that they need a bit more altering. But if you wear them for a while once they have been shaped to fit you, you may come to feel as if you have worn them all your life.

■ Summary

1. **What is the elaboration-likelihood model of persuasion?** According to the elaboration-likelihood model, people can be persuaded to change attitudes by central and peripheral routes. The central route involves change by consideration or arguments and evidence. The peripheral route involves associating the objects of attitudes with positive or negative cues, such as attractive communicators.

2. **How does the nature of the message influence whether or not it will be persuasive?** Repeating messages also makes them more persuasive. Messages that are too discrepant with audience views, however, may fail to persuade.

3. **What peripheral factors influence whether or not a message will be persuasive?** We tend to be persuaded by communicators who appear to

have expertise, trustworthiness, and attractiveness. Emotional appeals are more effective with most people than are logical presentations. We are more likely to be persuaded by people who compliment and agree with us. Food and music also create an atmosphere in which we are more compliant.

4. **Are some people more readily persuaded than others?** Yes. People who feel inadequate, or who believe that it is awful to earn the disapproval of others, show less sales resistance.

5. **What is the foot-in-the-door technique?** This is a method for inducing compliance with requests in which another person makes a small request to which you are likely to accede. Having gotten his or her "foot in the door," he or she follows with a larger request. You become likely to comply because you conceptualize yourself as complying with, or helping, this individual.

6. **What is low-balling?** This is a persuasive, or sales, technique in which you are induced to make a commitment (such as to buy a product) by being offered extremely favorable terms. Then the persuader, or salesperson, alters the terms in hopes that you will retain your commitment.

7. **What is cognitive-dissonance theory, and how does it account for changes in attitudes?** Cognitive-dissonance theory suggests that people are made uncomfortable by inconsistent attitudes and are motivated to bring them into harmony. Cognitive-dissonance theory also suggests that people can be induced to change their attitudes by being coerced into attitude-discrepant behavior. Patty Hearst apparently underwent a conversion in self-, or ego-, identity and adopted revolutionary beliefs because she was forced into revolutionary attitude-discrepant behavior. She might have been able to reduce the dissonance caused by the behavior by changing her beliefs and attitudes to conform to her behavior.

8. **What happened during the Milgram studies on obedience, and what factors are thought to account for the behavior of the subjects?** In the Milgram studies, most subjects gave electric shock to an innocent person in obeying an authority figure. Factors that heighten the tendency to obey other people include socialization, lack of social comparison, perception of a legitimate authority figure, the foot-in-the-door technique, inaccessibility of values, and buffers between the actor and the victim.

9. **How does our behavior as members of the crowd differ from our behavior as individuals? Why?** As members of crowds, many people engage in behavior they would find unnacceptable if they were acting alone, to some degree because of high arousal and anonymity. In doing so, they set aside their own values and adopt the norms of the group. The adoption of group norms is called deindividuation, and once people have become deindividuated, their responsibility for their own behavior becomes diffused.

10. **What factors contribute to conformity to social norms?** In the Asch studies on conformity, 75 percent of subjects bent to social pressure and conformed to incorrect group judgments at least once. Studies have shown that women who uncritically adopt the stereotypical feminine sex role are more likely to conform than men. For men, however, it seems that "rugged individualism" is, in a sense, conformity to the stereotypical masculine sex role.

11. **Why do we sometimes help people in trouble and at other times stand by and do nothing?** When we are members of groups or crowds, we may ignore people in trouble because of diffusion of responsibility. We are more likely to help others when we think we are the only ones available to help, when we understand the situation, when we believe that our efforts will succeed, and when we feel responsible for helping.

12. **What is assertive behavior?** Assertive behavior helps us withstand social influence. It is assertive to express our genuine feelings and stand up for our legitimate rights. It is aggressive, not assertive, to insult, threaten, or attack verbally or physically. Women may find it more difficult than men to behave assertively, because nonassertive submissive behavior is more consistent with the stereotypical feminine sex role.

13. **How can we become more assertive?** We can become more assertive through techniques such as self-monitoring, challenging irrational beliefs that prevent us from speaking up, modeling, and behavior rehearsal. In doing so, we should attend to nonverbal communications such as eye contact, posture and gestures, and distance from others, as well as to the things we say.

■ TRUTH OR FICTION REVISITED

Admitting your product's weak points in an ad is the death knell for sales. Not necessarily. It lends the communicator credibility and may be used to foster persuasiveness.

Most of us are swayed by ads that offer useful information, not by emotional appeals or celebrity endorsements. False. Emotional appeals and endorsements work quite well, especially when we are not experts on the products being advertised.

People who are highly worried about what other people think of them are likely to be low in sales resistance. True. They may be overly concerned about what the disappointed salesperson will be thinking.

We appreciate things more when we have to work hard for them. True. This phenomenon is referred to as effort justification, one of the concepts in cognitive-dissonance theory.

Coercing people into behavior that contradicts their values can actually change their values. True. Attitude-discrepant behavior causes dissonance, which people find unpleasant and are motivated to reduce—sometimes by changing their attitudes.

Most people would refuse to deliver painful electric shock to an innocent party, even under powerful social pressure. False. Sad to say, the Milgram studies on obedience suggest the contrary.

Many people are late to social gatherings because they are conforming to a social norm. True. Being "fashionably late" is an implict (unspoken) social norm.

Nearly 40 people stood by and did nothing while a woman was being stabbed to death. True. Kitty Genovese was the victim, and there has been much research into the so-called bystander effect since this incident.

■ Scoring Key for the Rathus Assertiveness Schedule

Tabulate your score as follows: For those items followed by an asterisk (*), change the signs (plus to minus; minus to plus). For example, if the response to an asterisked item was 2, place a minus sign (−) before the two. If the response to an asterisked item was −3, change the minus sign to a plus sign (+) by adding a vertical stroke. Then add up the scores of the 30 items.

Scores on the assertiveness schedule can vary from +90 to −90. The table on page 178 will show you how your score compares to those of 764 college women and 637 men from 35 campuses across the U.S.A. For example, if you are a woman and your score was 26, it exceeded that of 80

percent of the women in the sample. A score of 15 for a male exceeds that
of 55–60 percent of the men in the sample.

Women's Scores	Percentile	Men's Scores
55	99	65
48	97	54
45	95	48
37	90	40
31	85	33
26	80	30
23	75	26
19	70	24
17	65	19
14	60	17
11	55	15
8	50	11
6	45	8
2	40	6
−1	35	3
−4	30	1
−8	25	−3
−13	20	−7
−17	15	−11
−24	10	−15
−34	5	−24
−39	3	−30
−48	1	−41

Source: Nevid and Rathus (1978).

Stress: What It Is and What It Does

6

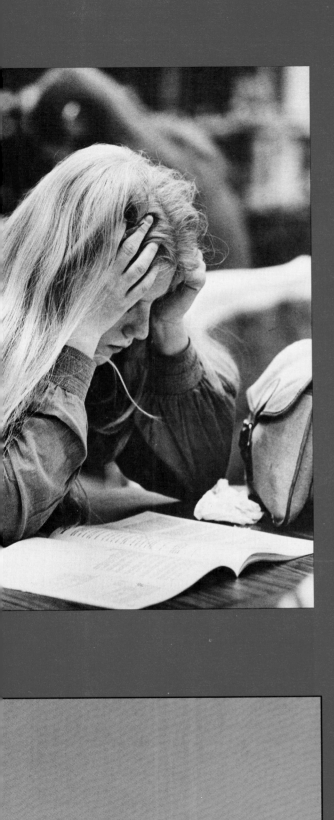

Too much of a good thing can make you ill.

Commuting on the freeway elevates our blood pressure.

Many people create their own sources of stress.

Our own bodies produce chemicals that are similar in function to the narcotic morphine.

Video games help children cancer patients cope with the side effects of chemotherapy.

Children in noisy classrooms do not learn to read as well as children in quiet classrooms.

Hot temperatures make us hot under the collar—that is, they prompt aggression.

We leave larger tips at restaurants when the sun is streaming through the windows.

Auto fumes may lower your children's IQ's.

Crowding a third roommate into a dorm room built for two usually makes somebody unhappy.

If quarterbacks get too "psyched up" for a big game, their performance on the field may suffer.

Fear can give you indigestion.

Some people drink alcohol in order to provide themselves with a handicap in their ability to cope with stress.

The belief that we can handle stress is linked to lower levels of adrenalin in the bloodstream.

Some people are psychologically hardier than others.

A sense of humor helps buffer the effects of stress.

Single men live longer.

■ Sources of Stress

Did you know that too much of a good thing can make you ill? Yes, you might think that marrying Mr. or Ms. Right, finding a prestigious job, and moving to a better neighborhood all in the same year would propel you into a state of bliss. It might. But the impact of all these events, one on top of the other, could also lead to headaches, high blood pressure, and asthma. As pleasant as they may be, they all involve major life changes, and life changes are one source of **stress** (Holmes & Rahe, 1967).

In the science of physics, stress is defined as a pressure or force exerted on a body. Tons of rock pressing against the earth, one car smashing into another, a rubber band stretching—all are types of physical stress. Psychological forces, or stresses, also "press," "push," or "pull." We may feel "crushed" by the "weight" of a big decision, "smashed" by misfortune, or "stretched" to the point of "snapping."

In psychology, stress is the demand made on an organism to adapt, to cope, or to adjust. Some stress is necessary to keep us alert and occupied (Selye, 1980). But stress that is too intense or prolonged can overtax our adjustive capacity, dampen our moods (Eckenrode, 1984; Stone & Neale, 1984), and have harmful physical effects. Types of stress include daily hassles, life changes, pain and discomfort, frustration, conflict, Type A behavior, the need for power, and environmental factors such as natural disasters, noise, and crowding.

Daily Hassles

It is the "last" straw that will break the camel's back—so goes the saying. Similarly, stresses can pile atop each other until we can no longer cope. Some stresses take the form of **daily hassles,** or notable daily conditions and experiences that are threatening or harmful to a person's well-being (Lazarus, 1984); others are life changes. Lazarus and his colleagues (1985) analyzed a scale that measures daily hassles and their opposites—**uplifts**—and found that hassles could be grouped as follows:

1. *Household hassles.* For example, preparing meals, shopping, and home maintenance
2. *Health hassles.* For example, physical illness, concern about medical treatment, and the side effects of medication
3. *Time-pressure hassles.* For example, having too many things to do, too many responsibilities, and not enough time
4. *Inner-concern hassles.* For example, being lonely and fear of confrontation
5. *Environmental hassles.* For example, crime, neighborhood deterioration, and traffic noise
6. *Financial-responsibility hassles.* For example, concern about owing money, such as mortgage payments and loan installments
7. *Work hassles.* For example, job dissatisfaction, not liking one's work duties, and problems with co-workers, and
8. *Future-security hassles.* For example, concerns about job security, taxes, property investments, stock-market swings, and retirement

These hassles were linked to psychological symptoms such as nervousness, worrying, inability to get going, feelings of sadness, feelings of aloneness, and so on.

Life Changes: "Going Through Changes"

Researchers have also focused on the impact of life changes on us. Life changes differ from daily hassles in two important ways: (1) Many life changes are positive and desirable, whereas all hassles, by definition, are negative. (2) The hassles referred to tend to occur on a daily basis, whereas life changes

Stress. An event that exerts physical or psychological force or pressure on a person. The demand made on an organism to adjust.

Daily hassles. Lazarus's term for routine sources of annoyance or aggravation that have a negative impact on health.

Uplifts. Lazarus's term for regularly occurring enjoyable experiences.

What kinds of daily
hassles add stress to
your life?

are relatively more isolated events, such as a change in financial state or living
conditions.

It may seem reasonable enough that hassles and life changes—especially
negative life changes—will have a psychological effect on us, that they may
cause us to worry and may generally dampen our moods. But a number of
researchers suggest that hassles and life changes (even positive life changes)
can also lead to physical illness.

Richard Lazarus and his colleagues (e.g., Kanner et al., 1981) assess
exposure to hassles by listing 117 daily hassles and having subjects indicate
which they have encountered and how intense they were, according to a three-
point scale. Thomas Holmes and Richard Rahe (1967) constructed a scale to
measure the impact of life changes by assigning marriage an arbitrary weight
of 50 "life-change units." Then they asked people from all walks of life to
assign units to other life changes, using marriage as the baseline. Most events
were rated as less stressful than marriage, but a few were considered more
stressful, for example, death of a spouse (100 units) and divorce (73 units).
Positive life changes such as an outstanding personal achievement (28 units)
and going on vacation (13 units) also made the list.

Hassles, Life Changes, and Illness Both daily hassles (e.g., Kanner et
al., 1981) and life changes appear to be predictors of physical illness. Holmes
and Rahe, for example, found that people who "earned" 300 or more life-
change units within a year according to their scale were at greater risk for
illness. Eight of ten developed medical problems, as compared with only one
of three people whose life-change-unit totals for the year were below 150.
Other researchers have found that high numbers of life-change units amassed
within a year are linked to a host of physical and psychological problems,
ranging from heart disease and cancer to accidents, school failure, and re-
lapses among persons who show psychological disorders, such as schizophrenia (Lloyd et al., 1980; Perkins, 1982; Rabkin, 1980; Thoits, 1983).

Although uplifts are defined by Lazarus (1984) as the opposite of hassles,
research has not shown that they are necessarily beneficial in terms of health.
That is, people who experience greater numbers of daily uplifts have not
been shown to have fewer health problems (DeLongis et al., 1982; Zarski,
1984).

▢ Q U E S T I O N N A I R E ▢

Social Readjustment Rating Scale

Life changes can be a source of stress. How much stress have you experienced in the past year as a result of life changes? In order to compare the amount of change-related stress you have encountered with that of other college students, fill out the following questionnaire.

Directions: Indicate how many times ("frequency") you have experienced the following events during the past 12 months. Then multiply the frequency (do not enter a number larger than 5) by the number of life-change units ("value") associated with each event. Write the product in the column to the right ("total"). Then add up all the points and check the key at the end of the chapter.

EVENT	VALUE	FREQUENCY	TOTAL
1. Death of a spouse, lover, or child	94	_____	_____
2. Death of parent or sibling	88	_____	_____
3. Beginning formal higher education	84	_____	_____
4. Death of a close friend	83	_____	_____
5. Miscarriage or stillbirth of pregnancy of self, spouse, or lover	83	_____	_____
6. Jail sentence	83	_____	_____
7. Divorce or marital separation	82	_____	_____
8. Unwanted pregnancy of self, spouse, or lover	82	_____	_____
9. Abortion of unwanted pregnancy of self, spouse, or lover	80	_____	_____
10. Detention in jail or other institution	79	_____	_____
11. Change in dating activity	79	_____	_____
12. Death of a close relative	79	_____	_____
13. Change in marital situation other than divorce or separation	78	_____	_____
14. Separation from significant other whom you like very much	77	_____	_____
15. Change in health status or behavior of spouse or lover	77	_____	_____
16. Academic failure	77	_____	_____
17. Major violation of the law and subsequent arrest	76	_____	_____
18. Marrying or living with lover against parents' wishes	75	_____	_____
19. Change in love relationship or important friendship	74	_____	_____
20. Change in health status or behavior of a parent or sibling	73	_____	_____
21. Change in feelings of loneliness, insecurity, anxiety, boredom	73	_____	_____
22. Change in marital status of parents	73	_____	_____
23. Acquiring a visible deformity	72	_____	_____
24. Change in ability to communicate with a significant other whom you like very much	71	_____	_____
25. Hospitalization of a parent or sibling	70	_____	_____
26. Reconciliation of marital or love relationship	68	_____	_____

EVENT	VALUE	FREQUENCY	TOTAL
27. Release from jail or other institution	68	———	———
28. Graduation from college	68	———	———
29. Major personal injury or illness	68	———	———
30. Wanted pregnancy of self, spouse, or lover	67	———	———
31. Change in number or type of arguments with spouse or lover	67	———	———
32. Marrying or living with lover with parents' approval	66	———	———
33. Gaining a new family member through birth or adoption	65	———	———
34. Preparing for an important exam or writing a major paper	65	———	———
35. Major financial difficulties	65	———	———
36. Change in the health status or behavior of a close relative or close friend	65	———	———
37. Change in academic status	64	———	———
38. Change in amount and nature of interpersonal conflicts	63	———	———
39. Change in relationship with members of your immediate family	62	———	———
40. Change in own personality	62	———	———
41. Hospitalization of yourself or a close relative	61	———	———
42. Change in course of study, major field, vocational goals, or work status	60	———	———
43. Change in own financial status	59	———	———
44. Change in status of divorced or widowed parent	59	———	———
45. Change in number or type of arguments between parents	59	———	———
46. Change in acceptance by peers, identification with peers, or social pressure by peers	58	———	———
47. Change in general outlook on life	57	———	———
48. Beginning or ceasing service in the armed forces	57	———	———
49. Change in attitudes toward friends	56	———	———
50. Change in living arrangements, conditions, or environment	55	———	———
51. Change in frequency or nature of sexual experiences	55	———	———
52. Change in parents' financial status	55	———	———
53. Change in amount or nature of pressure from parents	55	———	———
54. Change in degree of interest in college or attitudes toward education	55	———	———
55. Change in the number of personal or social relationships you've formed or dissolved	55	———	———
56. Change in relationship with siblings	54	———	———
57. Change in mobility or reliability of transportation	54	———	———
58. Academic success	54	———	———
59. Change to a new college or university	54	———	———

(continued)

EVENT	VALUE	FREQUENCY	TOTAL	
60. Change in feelings of self-reliance, independence, or amount of self-discipline	53	____	____	*(continued)*
61. Change in number or types of arguments with roommate	52	____	____	
62. Spouse or lover beginning or ceasing work outside of the home	52	____	____	
63. Change in frequency of use of amounts of drugs other than alcohol, tobacco, or marijuana	51	____	____	
64. Change in sexual morality, beliefs, or attitudes	50	____	____	
65. Change in responsibility at work	50	____	____	
66. Change in amount or nature of social activities	50	____	____	
67. Change in dependencies on parents	50	____	____	
68. Change from academic work to practical fieldwork experience or internship	50	____	____	
69. Change in amount of material possessions and concomitant responsibilities	50	____	____	
70. Change in routine at college or work	49	____	____	
71. Change in amount of leisure time	49	____	____	
72. Change in amount of in-law trouble	49	____	____	
73. Outstanding personal achievement	49	____	____	
74. Change in family structure other than parental divorce or separation	48	____	____	
75. Change in attitude toward drugs	48	____	____	
76. Change in amount and nature of competition with same sex	48	____	____	
77. Improvement of own health	47	____	____	
78. Change in responsibilities at home	47	____	____	
79. Change in study habits	46	____	____	
80. Change in number or type of arguments or conflicts with close relatives	46	____	____	

Criticisms of the Research Links Between Hassles, Life Changes, and Illness

Although the links between daily hassles, life changes, and illness seem to have been supported by a good deal of research, there are a number of limitations, such as the following.

Correlational Evidence   The links that have been uncovered between hassles, life changes, and illness are correlational rather than experimental (Dohrenwend et al., 1982; Monroe, 1982). It may seem logical that the hassles and life changes caused the disorders, but the hassles and life changes were not manipulated experimentally. Rival explanations of the data are therefore possible. One possibility is that people who are predisposed toward medical or psychological problems encounter more hassles and amass more life-change units. For example, before medical disorders are diagnosed, the disorders may contribute to sexual problems, arguments with one's spouse or in-laws, changes in living conditions and personal habits, changes in sleeping habits, and so on. So in many cases it may be that the physical and psycho-

EVENT	VALUE	FREQUENCY	TOTAL
81. Change in sleeping habits	46	———	———
82. Change in frequency of use or amounts of alcohol	45	———	———
83. Change in social status	45	———	———
84. Change in frequency of use or amounts of tobacco	45	———	———
85. Change in awareness of activities in external world	45	———	———
86. Change in religious affiliation	44	———	———
87. Change in type of gratifying activities	43	———	———
88. Change in amount or nature of physical activities	43	———	———
89. Change in address or residence	43	———	———
90. Change in amount or nature of recreational activities	43	———	———
91. Change in frequency of use or amounts of marijuana	43	———	———
92. Change in social demands or responsibilities due to your age	43	———	———
93. Court appearance for legal violation	40	———	———
94. Change in weight or eating habits	39	———	———
95. Change in religious activities	37	———	———
96. Change in political views or affiliations	34	———	———
97. Change in driving pattern or conditions	33	———	———
98. Minor violation of the law	31	———	———
99. Vacation or travel	30	———	———
100. Change in number of family get-togethers	30	———	———

Source: Peggy Blake, Robert Fry, & Michael Pesjack, *Self-assessment and behavior change manual* (New York: Random House, 1984), pp. 43–47. Reprinted by permission of Random House, Inc.

logical problems precede rather than result from hassles and life changes (Dohrenwend et al., 1984; Dohrenwend & Shrout, 1985; Monroe, 1983).

Positive versus Negative Life Changes   Other aspects of the research into the relationship between life changes and illness have also been challenged. For instance, positive life changes may be less disturbing than hassles and negative life changes, even when their number of life-change units is high (Lefcourt et al., 1981; Perkins, 1982; Thoits, 1983). That is, a change for the better in the health of a family member is usually less stressful than a change for the worse—a change for the better is a change, but it is also less of a "hassle."

The Need for Novel Stimulation   In a similar vein, keep in mind the saying that "variety is the spice of life." People seem motivated to seek change, or novel stimulation. Stress researcher Hans Selye (1980) also noted that a certain amount of stress was necessary, even healthful. He referred to healthful stress as *eustress* (pronounced yoo-stress, and derived from the Greek *eu*, meaning "good" or "well"). Stress is apparently sometimes in the eye of the beholder. That is, one person's stress might be another person's eustress, because the second person encodes experiences in a different way.

Personality Differences   Another problem with the Holmes and Rahe approach is that different kinds of people respond to life stresses in different ways. For example, people who are "easy-going" and people who are "psychologically hardy"—as we shall see later in the chapter—are less likely than their opposites to become ill under the impact of stress. Factors such as self-confidence and support from family members can also alleviate many of the potential effects of life stresses (Holahan & Moos, 1985).

A Role for Cognitive Appraisal   The degree of stress linked to an event will also reflect the meaning the event has for the individual. Pregnancy, for example, can be a positive or negative life change, depending on whether one wants and is prepared to have a child. We cognitively appraise hassles and life changes (Lazarus et al., 1985). In responding to them, we take into account our values and goals, our beliefs in our coping ability, our social support, and so on. The same kind of event will be less taxing for people who have greater coping ability and support. Later in the chapter we shall see how our appraisal of stressors and many other psychological factors moderate the impact of stressors upon us.

Still, hassles and life changes do require adjustments, and it seems wise for us to be aware of the hassles and life changes associated with our styles of life.

Pain and Discomfort

Pain and discomfort impair performance and coping ability. Athletes report that pain interferes with their ability to run, swim, and so forth, even when the source of the pain does not directly weaken them.

What Pain Is   Pain is a signal that something is wrong in the body. Pain is adaptive in the sense that it motivates us to do something about it. But for some of us, chronic pain—pain that lingers once injuries or illnesses have otherwise cleared up—saps our vitality and the pleasures of everyday life.

As shown in Figure 6.1, pain originates at the point of contact, as with a stubbed toe. At the site of injury, a number of chemicals are released, including **prostaglandins.** The pain message is carried to the central nervous system, which consists of the spinal cord and brain, by way of cells called **neurons.** Prostaglandins facilitate transmission of the pain message to the brain and heighten circulation to the injured area, causing the redness and swelling we refer to as inflammation. Inflammation attracts infection-fighting blood cells to the area to protect against invading bacteria. **Analgesic** drugs such as aspirin and ibuprofen (brand names Motrin, Advil, Medipren, Nuprin) work by inhibiting the production of prostaglandins and thus decreasing fever, inflammation, and pain.

Endorphins   In response to pain, the brain triggers the release of **endorphins,** a kind of chemical messenger, or **neurotransmitter,** that is involved in transmitting messages from neuron to neuron. The make-up of neurons is described in the nearby "A Closer Look" box. The word *endorphin* is the contraction of *endogenous morphine. Endogenous* means "developing from within." Endorphins, then, are similar to the narcotic morphine in their functions and we produce them in our own bodies. They occur naturally in the brain and the bloodstream. Endorphins act by "locking into" the receptor sites on neurons for chemicals that transmit pain messages to the brain. Once the

Prostaglandins. Substances derived from fatty acids that are involved in body responses such as inflammation and menstrual cramping.

Neuron. A nerve cell.

Analgesic. Not feeling pain, although fully conscious.

Endorphin. A neurotransmitter that is composed of chains of amino acids and is functionally similar to morphine.

Neurotransmitter. A chemical substance involved in the transmission of "messages" from one neuron to another.

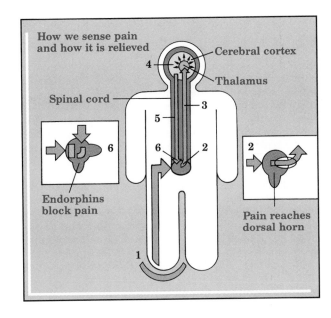

How we sense pain and how it is relieved

Cerebral cortex

Thalamus

Spinal cord

Endorphins block pain

Pain reaches dorsal horn

FIGURE 6.1 Perception of Pain

Pain originates at the point of contact, and the pain message to the brain is initiated by the release of prostaglandins, bradykinin, and substance *P*.

endorphin "key" is in the "lock," pain-causing chemicals are prevented from transmitting their messages.

The Richter Experiment In a classic experiment, psychiatrist Curt Richter (1957) dramatized the effects of pain on behavior. First, Richter obtained baseline data by recording the amount of time rats could swim to stay

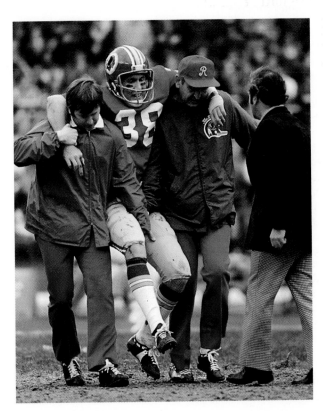

Pain is a signal that something is wrong in the body. This football player cannot continue to perform in this game, but athletes report that pain interferes with their ability to run, swim, and so on, even when the source of pain does not directly weaken them.

■ A CLOSER LOOK

On Neurons and Neurotransmitters

Neurons are the cells which serve as building blocks of the nervous system. For example, our brains and spinal cords are made up of neurons. Neurons also extend into our limbs, carrying instructions from the brain and spinal cord that cause muscles to contract, and messages from our limbs that tell the brain when muscles are contracted or when there has been an injury. Neurons also extend into organs such as the heart, liver, and sex organs, regulating the heart rate, the release of sugar from the liver, and sexual response.

As you can see in Figure 6.2, neurons have cell bodies, which contain the nucleus; dendrites, which receive messages from other neurons; and axons, which are involved in transmission of messages to other neurons. Neurons are microscopic, but their axons may vary in length from a few thousandths of an inch, which is typical of neurons in the brain, to several feet, which is typical of neurons that run down your back to your toes. A message is usually received from one neuron by means of dendrites, and then conducted along the axon of the receiving neuron. Axons with myelin sheaths conduct messages more efficiently, because myelin insulates axons from the surrounding body fluid. The axon then typically splits into smaller, branching structures called terminals. At the ends of axon terminals are bulbs, or knobs, which have sacs containing neurotransmitters. We know of the functions of a few dozen neurotransmitters, including acetylcholine, which controls muscle contractions and is involved in memory (in Chapter 11, we shall see that Alzheimer's disease has been linked to deficiencies of acetylcholine), and endorphins, which decrease pain.

The rectangular insert in Figure 6.2 shows a synapse, which is the junction between a transmitting neuron and a receiving neuron. A synapse consists of an axon terminal of a transmitting neuron; a small, fluid-filled gap between the neurons (the synaptic cleft); and a dendrite of a receiving neuron. Sacs in axon terminals release neurotransmitters into the synaptic cleft. From there they are taken up by receptor sites they fit (or "lock into") on the receiving neuron. Neurotransmitters that do not lock into receptor sites may remain for a while in the synaptic cleft, may be broken down by chemicals (enzymes) in the cleft, or may be "re-uptaked" by the transmitting neuron.

Endorphins help fight pain by "locking into" receptor sites that would otherwise receive chemicals transmitting messages of pain. (So do molecules of morphine.) Another link between neurotransmitters and adjustment is found with norepinephrine and serotonin. As we shall see in Chapter 8, deficiencies of these neurotransmitters have been linked to depression. Drugs that help fight depression act by increasing the availability of these neurotranmitters.

FIGURE 6.2 The Anatomy of a Neuron

"Messages" enter neurons through dendrites, are transmitted along the trunklike axon, and then are sent through axon terminals to muscles, glands, and other neurons. A neuron relays its message to another neuron across a junction called a synapse, which consists of an axon terminal from the transmitting neuron, a dendrite of the receiving neuron, and a small gap between the neurons referred to as the synaptic cleft. Axon terminals contain sacs of chemicals called neurotransmitters. Neurotransmitters are released by the transmitting neuron into the synaptic cleft, and many of them are taken up by receptor sites on the dendrites of the receiving neuron. Some neurotransmitters (called "excitatory") influence receiving neurons in the direction of firing; others (called "inhibitory") influence them in the direction of *not* firing. To date, a few dozen possible neurotransmitters have been identified.

---

afloat in a tub of water. In water at room temperature, most rats could keep their noses above the surface for about 80 hours. But when Richter blew noxious streams of air into the animal's faces, or kept the water uncomfortably hot or cold, the rats could remain afloat for only 20 to 40 hours.

When rats were traumatized before their dunking by having their whiskers noisily cropped off, some managed to remain afloat for only a few minutes. Yet the clipping itself had not weakened them. Rats that were allowed several minutes to recover from the clipping before being launched swam for the usual 80 hours. Psychologists also recommend that we space aggravating tasks or chores, so that discomfort does not build to the point where it compounds stress and impairs our performance.

Frustration

You may wish to play the line for the varsity football team, but you may weigh only 120 pounds or you may be a woman. You may have been denied a job

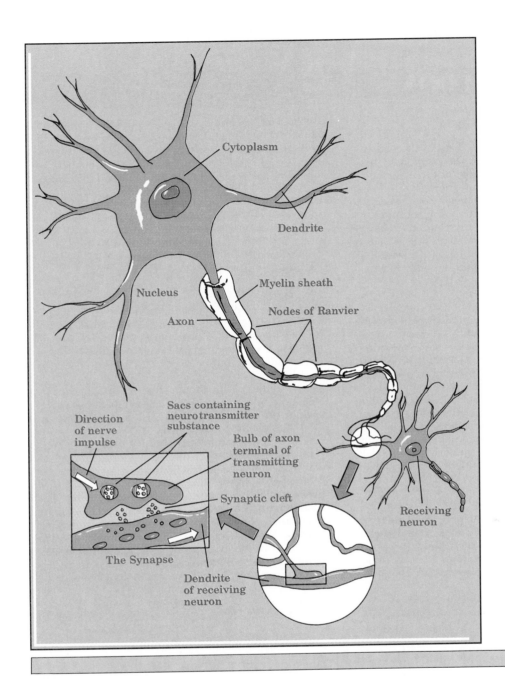

or educational opportunity because of your ethnic background or favoritism. We all encounter **frustration,** the thwarting of a motive to attain a goal (see Figure 6.3, Part A). Frustration is another source of stress.

Many sources of frustration are obvious. Adolescents are used to being too young to wear makeup, drive, go out, engage in sexual activity, spend money, drink, or work. Age is the barrier that requires them to delay gratification. We may frustrate ourselves as adults if our goals are set too high, or if our self-demands are irrational. As Albert Ellis (1977, 1987) notes, if we try to earn other people's approval at all costs, or insist on performing perfectly in all of our undertakings, we doom ourselves to failure and frustration.

The Frustrations of Commuting   One of the common frustrations of contemporary life is commutation. Distance, time, and driving conditions are some of the barriers that lie between us and our work or schooling. How

Frustration. (1) The thwarting of a motive. (2) The emotion produced by the thwarting of a motive.

■ A CLOSER LOOK

Pain Management

Psychologists have been of major help in the management of pain. Pain management has traditionally been a medical issue, with the main type of treatment being chemical, as in the use of analgesic drugs. But drugs are not always effective. Moreover, patients can develop tolerance for many analgesic drugs, such as morphine or demerol, so that increased doses are required to achieve the same effects. Because of limitations and problems such as these, health psychologists have increasingly focused their efforts on psychological methods for managing pain.

Accurate Information

One psychological method for pain management is the provision of accurate and thorough information. Most people try not to think about their symptoms (and their implications!) during the early phases of an illness. However, when it comes to administering painful or discomforting treatments, as with chemotherapy for cancer, knowledge of the details of the treatment, including how long it will last and how much pain will be entailed, often helps patients cope—particularly patients who prefer to receive high levels of information in an effort to maintain control over their situations (Martelli et al., 1987). Accurate information even helps small children cope with painful procedures (Jay et al., 1983).

Distraction and Fantasy

Although it appears generally helpful for patients to have accurate and detailed explanations of painful procedures, psychologists have also been studying ways of minimizing discomfort once these procedures are under way. A number of such methods involve the use of distraction or fantasy. For example, patients can distract themselves from pain by focusing on environmental details, as by counting ceiling tiles, the hairs on the back of a finger, or describing the clothing of medical personnel or passers-by (Kanfer & Goldfoot, 1966; McCaul & Haugvedt, 1982). We are also less sensitive to pain when we try to recall lists of meaningless words (Farthing et al., 1984; Spanos et al., 1984). Studies with children ranging in age from 9 into their teens have found that playing video games diminishes the pain and discomfort of the side effects of chemotherapy (Kolko & Rickard-Figueroa, 1985; Redd et al., 1987).

Hypnosis

Hypnosis is used by thousands of professionals to manage pain in dentistry, childbirth, even some forms of surgery. Hundreds of case studies and experiments attest that hypnosis often, although not always, significantly reduces pain (see reviews by Barber, 1982; Turk et al., 1983; Turner & Chapman, 1982b).

Hypnosis is an altered state of consciousness that is induced by having people focus on repetitious stimuli, such as the voice of the hypnotist, and follow suggestions, frequently to the effect that their limbs are becoming warmer and heavier and that they are "going to sleep." They do not sleep during hypnosis, but they usually interpret these instructions as an invitation to become passive, follow directions, and adopt a what-will-happen-will-happen attitude. Historically, it had been assumed that hypnotism induced a special "trance" state, but contemporary psychologists downplay this concept. Ernest Hilgard (1978), for example, a leading researcher in the study of hypnosis, attributes the pain-reducing effects of hypnosis to relaxation, narrowed attention, and heightened suggestibility. Theodore X.

---

many of us fight the freeways or crowd ourselves into train cars or buses for an hour or more *before* the workday begins? For most people, the stresses of commuting are mild but persistent (Stokols & Novaco, 1981). Still, lengthy drives on crowded highways are linked to increases in heart rate, blood pressure, and other physical signs of stress, including reports of chest pains. Noise, humidity, and air pollution all contribute to the frustration involved in driving to work.

If you must drive, try to pick times and roads that provide lower volumes of traffic. It may be worth your while to take a longer, more scenic route that has less stop-and-go traffic. Such routes are linked to lower blood pressure and heart rates (Littler et al., 1973).

Emotional Barriers   Anxiety and fear may serve as emotional barriers that prevent us from acting effectively to meet our goals. A high-school senior who wishes to attend an out-of-state college may be frustrated by fear of leaving home. A young adult may not ask an attractive person out on a date because of fear of rejection.

Hypnosis. A condition in which people appear highly suggestible and behave as though they are in a trance.

Hypnosis helps many people cope with pain, although psychologists do not fully agree as to why. Hilgard attributes the pain-relieving effects of hypnosis to relaxation, narrowed attention, and heightened suggestibility.

Barber (1982), another specialist in the field, attributes many of the benefits of hypnosis to suggestions of comfort and well-being given by a prestigious authority figure, such as a psychologist or physician. Moreover, suggestions that limbs are becoming warmer and heavier do tend to have relaxing effects: They encourage the flow of blood to the periphery of the body and decrease activity of the sympathetic branch of the autonomic nervous system (Pennebaker & Skelton, 1981).

Relaxation Training

If hypnosis does not involve a special trance state, might it be possible to achieve similar benefits by intentionally inducing some of the body effects brought about by hypnosis? It appears so. **Relaxation training** refers to a number of psychological techniques that relax muscles and lower sympathetic activity. As we shall see in detail in Chapter 10, some relaxation methods focus on relaxing muscle groups. Some involve breathing exercises. Some focus on guided imagery, including suggestions that limbs are becoming warmer and heavier. However, none of them claims to induce a trance, and their benefits are explained by theories that link behavior to human physiology. These methods appear to be as effective as hypnosis in managing pain (Moore & Chaney, 1985; Turner & Chapman, 1982a).

Coping with Irrational Beliefs

Irrational beliefs about pain have been shown to heighten pain. For example, telling oneself that the pain is unbearable and will never cease increases discomfort, as found in a study relating knee pain and beliefs about pain (Keefe et al., 1987). Cognitive methods aimed at modifying irrational patient belief systems (see Chapter 10) would also thus seem to be of promise.

Social Support

Supportive social networks also seem to help us cope with discomfort. And so, having friends visit the patient and encourage a return to health is as consistent with psychological findings as it is with folklore (Rook & Dooley, 1985).

Tolerance for Frustration Getting ahead is often a gradual process that demands that we must be able to live with some frustration and delay gratification. Yet our **tolerance for frustration** may fluctuate. Stress heaped upon stress can lower our tolerance, just as Richter's rats, stressed from their close shaves, sank quickly to the bottom of the tub. We may laugh off a flat tire on a good day. But if it is raining, or if we have just waited for an hour in a gas line, the flat may seem like the last straw. People who have encountered frustration, but learned that it is possible to surmount barriers or find substitute goals, are more tolerant of frustration than those who have never experienced it, or those who have experienced excesses of frustration.

Conflict

Have you ever felt "damned if you did and damned if you didn't"? Regretted that you couldn't do two things, or be in two places, at the same time? Wanted to go to a film but had to study for a test? This is **conflict**—being torn in two or more directions by opposing motives. Conflict is frustrating and stressful.

Relaxation training. Methods for inducing relaxation that focus on systematic relaxation of muscle groups, relaxing imagery, and so on.

Tolerance for frustration. Ability to delay gratification, to maintain self-control when a motive is thwarted.

Conflict. A condition characterized by opposing motives, in which gratification of one motive prevents gratification of the other.

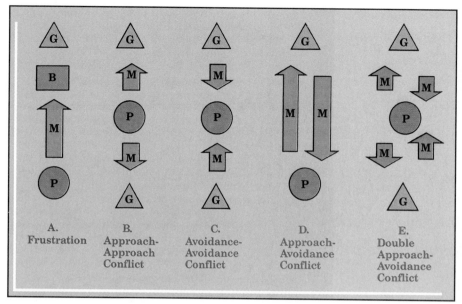

FIGURE 6.3   Models for Frustration and Conflict

Part A is a model for frustration in which a person (P) has a motive (M) to reach a goal (G), but is frustrated by a barrier (B). Part B shows an approach-approach conflict, in which the person cannot approach two positive goals simultaneously. Part C is an avoidance-avoidance conflict, in which avoiding one undesirable goal requires approaching another undesirable goal. Part D shows an approach-avoidance conflict, in which the same goal has both positive and negative features. Part E is a model for a double approach-avoidance conflict, in which the various goals perceived by the individual have their positive and negative features.

Conflict may also be looked at as a type of frustration in which the barrier to achieving a goal is an opposing impulse or motive. Psychologists often break conflicts down into four types:

Approach-approach conflict   An **approach-approach conflict** (Figure 6.3, Part B) is the least stressful form of conflict. Here each of two goals is positive and within reach. You may not be able to decide between pizza or tacos, Tom or Dick, or a trip to Nassau or Hawaii. Conflicts are usually resolved by making decisions. People in conflict may **vacillate** until they make a decision, and afterward, there may be some regrets, especially if one's choice falls short of expectations.

Avoidance-avoidance conflict   An **avoidance-avoidance conflict** (Figure 6.3, Part C) is more stressful, because you are motivated to avoid each of two negative goals. However, avoiding one requires approaching the other. You may be fearful of visiting the dentist, but also fear that your teeth will decay if you do not. You may not want to contribute to the Association for the Advancement of Lost Causes, but fear that your friends will consider you cheap or uncommitted if you do not. Each goal is negative in an avoidance-avoidance conflict. When an avoidance-avoidance conflict is highly stressful, and no resolution is in sight, some people withdraw from the conflict by focusing their attention on other matters or by suspending behavior altogether. For example, some highly conflicted people refuse to get out of bed in the morning and start the day.

Approach-avoidance conflict   The same goal can produce both approach and avoidance motives, as in the **approach-avoidance conflict** (Figure 6.3, Part D). People and things have their pluses and minuses, their good points and their bad points. Cream cheese pie may be delicious, but oh, the calories! Why are so many attractive goals immoral, illegal, or fattening?

Multiple approach-avoidance conflict   The most complex form of conflict is the **multiple approach-avoidance conflict,** in which each of several alternative courses of action has its promising and distressing aspects. Consider the example in which there are two goals, as in Figure 6.3, Part E. This sort of conflict might arise on the evening of an examination, when you are faced with the choice of studying or, say, going to a film. Each alternative has its positive and negative aspects: "Studying's a drag, but I won't have to worry about flunking. I'd love to see the movie, but I'd just be worrying about how I'll do tomorrow."

Similarly, should you take a job or go on for advanced training when you complete your college program? This is another double approach-avoidance conflict. If you opt for the job, cash will soon be jingling in your pockets, but later you might wonder if you have the education to reach your potential. By furthering your education you may have to delay the independence and gratification that are afforded by earning a living, but you may find a more fulfilling position later on.

All forms of conflict entail motives that aim in opposite directions. When one motive is much stronger than the other—as when you feel "starved" and are only slightly concerned about your weight—it will probably not be too stressful to act in accord with the powerful motive and, in this case, eat. But when each conflicting motive is powerful you may encounter high levels of stress and confusion about the proper course of action. At such times you are faced with the need to make a decision, although making decisions can also be stressful, especially when there is no clear correct choice. In the nearby box, we see how psychologists have helped a number of people make decisions with the use of the balance sheet.

■ A CLOSER LOOK

Using the Balance Sheet to Make Decisions

Making decisions involves choosing among various goals or courses of action to reach goals. In order to make rational decisions, we carefully weigh the pluses and minuses of each possible course of action. We need to clarify the subjective values of our goals, our ability to surmount the obstacles in our paths, and the costs of surmounting them. Frequently, we need to gather information about the goals and about our abilities to do so.

There is nothing new in the general concept of "weighing the pluses and minuses," but Janis and Mann (1977) have found that use of a balance sheet can help us make sure that we have considered the information available to us. The balance sheet also helps highlight gaps in information. Experiments with the balance sheet show that it has helped high-school students select a college and adults decide whether to go on diets and attend exercise classes. Balance sheet users show fewer regrets about the option they did not select and are more likely to stick to their decisions.

Balance sheets help us list the pluses and minuses of any course of action. To use the balance sheet, jot down the following information for each choice (see Table 6.1): (1) projected tangible gains and losses for oneself; (2) projected tangible gains and losses for others; (3) projected self-approval or self-disapproval; and (4) projected approval or disapproval of others.

Consider the following case from our files. Meg was a 34-year-old woman whose husband, Bob, beat her. She had married Bob at 27, and for two years life had run smoothly. But she had been bruised and battered, fearful of her life, for the past five. She sought psychotherapy to cope with Bob, her fears, her resentments,

and her disappointments. The therapist asked if Bob would come for treatment too, but Bob refused. Finally, unable to stop Bob from abusing her, Meg considered divorce. But divorce was also an ugly prospect, and she vacillated.

Table 6.1 shows the balance sheet, as filled out by Meg, for the alternative of divorce. Meg's balance sheet supplied Meg and her therapist with a clear agenda of concerns to work out. It also showed that Meg's anticipations were incomplete. Would she really have no positive thoughts about herself if she got a divorce from Bob? Would no one other than her mother applaud the decision? (And did she have an irrational need to avoid the disapproval of others?) Meg's list of negative anticipations pointed to the need to develop financial independence by acquiring job skills. Her fears about undertaking a new social life also seemed overblown. Yes, making new acquaintances might not be easy, but it was not impossible. And what of Meg's feelings about herself? Wouldn't she be pleased that she had done what she thought was necessary, even if divorce also entailed problems?

Meg concluded that many of her negative anticipations were exaggerated. Many fears could be collapsed into an umbrella fear of change. Fear of change had also led her to underestimate her need for self-respect. Meg did get a divorce, and at first she was depressed, lonely, and fearful. But after a year she was working and dating regularly. She was not blissful, but had regained a sense of forward motion. She took pride in being independent and no longer dwelled in fear. It is fortunate that this story has a relatively happy ending. Otherwise, we would have had to look for another.

Are you now putting off making any decisions in your own life? Could using the balance sheet be of any help?

Type A Behavior

Some of us behave as though we were dedicated to the continuous creation of our own stress through the **Type A behavior** pattern. Type A people are highly driven, competitive, impatient, and aggressive (Matthews et al., 1982; Holmes & Will, 1985). They feel rushed and under pressure and keep one eye glued firmly to the clock. They are not only prompt, but frequently early for appointments (Strahan, 1981). They eat, walk, and talk rapidly, and become restless when they see others working slowly (Musante et al., 1983). They attempt to dominate group discussions (Yarnold et al., 1985). Type A people find it difficult to surrender control or to share power (Miller et al., 1985; Strube & Werner, 1985). As a consequence, they are often reluctant to delegate authority in the workplace, and in this way they increase their own workloads. Type A people also "accentuate the negative": they are merciless in their self-criticism when they fail at a task (Brunson & Matthews, 1981), and they seek negative information about themselves in order to better themselves (Cooney & Zeichner, 1985).

Type A people find it difficult just to go out on the tennis court and bat the ball back and forth. They watch their form, perfect their strokes, and

Type A behavior. Stress-producing behavior, characterized by aggressiveness, perfectionism, unwillingness to relinquish control, and a sense of time urgency.

TABLE 6.1   Meg's Balance Sheet for the Alternative of Getting a Divorce from Bob

	Positive Anticipations	Negative Anticipations
Tangible gains and losses for me	1. Elimination of fear of being beaten or killed	1. Loneliness 2. Fear of starting a new social life 3. Fear of not having children owing to age 4. Financial struggle 5. Fear of personal emotional instability
Tangible gains and losses for others	1. Mother will be relieved	1. Bob might harm himself or others (he has threatened suicide if I leave)
Self-approval or self-disapproval		1. I might consider myself a failure because I could not help Bob or save our marriage
Social approval or social disapproval		1. Some people will complain marriage is sacred and blame me for "quitting" 2. Some men may consider me an easy mark

When making a decision, weighing up the pluses and minuses for the various alternatives can lead to more productive choices and fewer regrets. Meg's balance sheet for the alternative of getting a divorce from an abusive husband showed her psychologist that her list of positive anticipations was incomplete.

Type A people create much of their own stress with their high drive level, competitiveness, impatience, and aggressiveness.

QUESTIONNAIRE

Are You Type A or Type B?

Are you Type A or Type B? Type A's are ambitious, hard driving, and chronically discontent with their current achievements. Type B's, by contrast, are more relaxed, more involved with the quality of life, and—according to cardiologists Meyer Friedman and Ray Rosenman—less prone to heart attacks.

The following checklist was developed from descriptions of Type A people by Friedman and Ulmer (1984), Matthews and her colleagues (1982), and Musante et al. (1983). The checklist will help give you insight into whether you are closer in your behavior patterns to the Type A or the Type B individual. Simply place a checkmark under the Yes if the behavior pattern is typical of you, and under the No if it is not. Try to work rapidly and leave no item blank. Then turn to the scoring key at the end of the chapter.

DO YOU:

	YES	NO
1. Strongly accent key words in your everyday speech?	___	___
2. Eat and walk quickly?	___	___
3. Believe that children should be taught to be competitive?	___	___
4. Feel restless when watching a slow worker?	___	___
5. Hurry other people to get on with what they're trying to say?	___	___
6. Find it highly aggravating to be stuck in traffic or waiting for a seat at a restaurant?	___	___
7. Continue to think about your own problems and business even when listening to someone else?	___	___
8. Try to eat and shave, or drive and jot down notes at the same time?	___	___
9. Catch up on your work on vacations?	___	___
10. Bring conversations around to topics of concern to you?	___	___
11. Feel guilty when you spend time just relaxing?	___	___
12. Find that you're so wrapped up in your work that you no longer notice office decorations or the scenery when you commute?	___	___
13. Find yourself concerned with getting more *things* rather than developing your creativity and social concerns?	___	___
14. Try to schedule more and more activities into less time?	___	___
15. Always appear for appointments on time?	___	___
16. Clench or pound your fists, or use other gestures, to emphasize your views?	___	___
17. Credit your accomplishments to your ability to work rapidly?	___	___
18. Feel that things must be done *now* and quickly?	___	___
19. Constantly try to find more efficient ways to get things done?	___	___
20. Insist on winning at games rather than just having fun?	___	___
21. Interrupt others often?	___	___
22. Feel irritated when others are late?	___	___
23. Leave the table immediately after eating?	___	___
24. Feel rushed?	___	___
25. Feel dissatisfied with your current level of performance?	___	___

demand regular self-improvement. The irrational belief that they must be perfectly competent and achieving in everything they undertake seems to be their motto.

Type B people, by contrast, relax more readily and focus more on the quality of life. They are less ambitious, less impatient, and pace themselves. Type A's perceive time as passing more rapidly than do Type B's, and they work more quickly (Yarnold & Grimm, 1982). Type A's earn higher grades and more money than Type B's of equal intelligence (Glass, 1977). Type A's also seek greater challenges than Type B's (Ortega & Pipal, 1984).

Type A Behavior and Cardiovascular Risks   There is an irony in the Type A person's seeking of difficult challenges: Type A's respond to challenge with higher blood pressure than Type B's do (Holmes et al., 1984). In addition, Type B's smoke less and have lower **serum cholesterol** levels. Many studies have also shown that Type A people are at greater risk for heart disease than Type B's (e.g., DeBacker et al., 1983; French-Belgian Collaborative Group, 1982; Haynes et al., 1980). Some researchers even claim that Type A behavior is a stronger predictor of heart disease than smoking, lack of exercise, poor diet, or obesity (Friedman & Rosenman, 1974).

On the other hand, some studies have found no difference in the incidence of heart attacks and death rates between Type A and Type B men (Brody, 1988; Fischman, 1987). The so-called Multiple Risk Factor Intervention Trial (MRFIT), which followed 12,700 men from 1973 to 1982 is one such study. In fact, a study published by David Ragland and Richard Brand in the January 1988 issue of *The New England Journal of Medicine* reported that Type A men were actually at *lower risk* for recurrent heart attacks than Type B men (Brody, 1988). Ragland and Brand followed the survival patterns of 257 heart attack victims over a dozen years and found that five Type B's died for every three Type A's who died.

We cannot satisfactorily explain the discrepancies in studies of the cardiovascular risks of Type A behavior. Meyer Friedman, one of the originators of the Type A concept, argues that the MRFIT study did a poor job of interviewing subjects and assigning them to Type A or Type B categories (Fischman, 1987). We can also note that the Ragland and Brand research addresses only recurrent heart attack victims, not initial victims.

Because the global concept of Type A behavior has not been satisfactorily linked to cardiovascular disease, a number of investigators are looking into the cardiovascular risks of various components of the Type A behavior pattern, such as hostility (Barefoot et al., 1982; Chesney & Rosenman, 1985; Fischman, 1987; Friedman et al., 1985; Shekelle et al., 1983; Wright, 1988). Some of these researchers suggest that a factor related to hostility—expecting the worst from people, or cynicism—is the culprit. Others point to the possible cardiovascular consequences of holding in rather than expressing anger (e.g., Dembroski et al., 1985; Spielberger et al., 1985). Of course, there is no one-to-one relationship between any behavior pattern and heart disease. The cardiovascular systems of different people react to stress differently. Some people termed **hot reactors** by Eliot and Buell (1983), for example, respond to stress with accelerated heart rate and constriction of blood vessels in peripheral areas of the body, whereas others do not. And some people, including some Type A's, moderate the effects of stress successfully through psychological means, as we shall see later in the chapter.

And so we must conclude that research concerning the Type A–heart disease link is somewhat in disarray. However, in Chapter 10 we shall describe research suggesting that alleviating Type A behavior patterns seems to reduce the risk of *recurrent* heart attacks significantly (Friedman & Ulmer, 1984). We shall also offer some suggestions for alleviating Type A behavior which are based on Friedman and Ulmer's research.

Environmental Stressors

The impact of environmental stressors is one of the major stimulators of the development of the psychology of adjustment. Among these stressors are natural disasters, technological disasters, noise, air pollution, extremes of temperature, and crowding.

Natural Disasters: Of Fire and Ice

> Some say the world will end in fire,
> Some say in ice.
> ROBERT FROST

Blizzards, hurricanes, tornadoes, wind storms, ice storms, monsoons, floods, earthquakes, mudslides, avalanches, and volcanic eruptions—these are a sampling of the natural disasters to which we are prey. In some cases we are warned of natural disasters. For example, we may know that we live in an area that is prone to earthquakes or flooding. But in others cases we are stunned by their suddenness and left numb.

There may be some degree of panic during a disaster, but the survivors usually behave with relative calmness. Perhaps 25–30 percent of survivors report stress-related problems such as anxiety and depression for a number of months following the disaster (Logue et al., 1979). People who have lost more are more likely to show distress (Parker, 1977). Natural disasters are not only dangerous as they occur; they may also cause life changes to suddenly pile atop one another by disrupting or destroying community life for months or years afterward. Services that had been taken for granted, such as electric power and the delivery of water, may be lost temporarily. Businesses and homes may be destroyed, causing people to have to rebuild or relocate (Fisher, Bell, & Baum, 1984).

Technological Disasters: When High-Tech Fails

We owe our dominance over the natural environment to technological advance, but technology can sometimes fail or backfire, causing another type of disaster. The 1984 leakage of poisonous gas at Bhopal, India; the 1983 collapse of a bridge along the Connecticut Turnpike; the 1979 nuclear accident at Three Mile Island; the 1976 collapse of the dam at Buffalo Creek; the 1977 Beverly Hills Supper Club fire (Green et al., 1983); airplane accidents, blackouts, and the leakage of toxic chemicals—these are a sampling of the technological disasters that befall us. When they do, we feel as though we have lost control of things and suffer stress (Davidson et al., 1982).

After the dam burst at Buffalo Creek in February 1976, thousands of tons of water poured onto the small town of Saunders, West Virginia. The flood lasted only 15 minutes, but 125 people were killed and over 5,000 left homeless. Reactions to the flood included anxiety; withdrawal or numbness; depression; bodily signs of stress; unfocused feelings of anger (Hargreaves, 1980); regression among children; nightmares and other sleep disturbances (Gleser et al., 1981). Many survivors felt guilty that they had been spared by the waters while family members and friends had died (Titchener & Kapp, 1976).

For many days after the 1979 leakage of radioactive gases and liquids at the Three Mile Island nuclear plant in Pennsylvania, it was feared that there might be a nuclear explosion, a meltdown, or massive releases of radiation. Evacuation was advised, contributing to fears. Local residents experienced the greatest stress (Bromet, 1980; Houts et al., 1980). The psychological and physical effects of stress lingered 15–22 months after the accident (Baum et al., 1982, 1983; Schaeffer & Baum, 1982).

Technological disasters differ from natural disasters in that in the former there is someone to blame (Baum, 1988). As a consequence, there may be

Decibel. A unit expressing the loudness of a sound.

legal suits. Suits tend to go on for years, and they provide a continuing source of stress both to the victims and to those identified as responsible for the disaster.

Noise: The Worse to Hear You With
How do you react when a neighbor's stereo is too loud, when an airplane screeches low overhead, or when the instructor scratches chalk across the blackboard? If you are like most of us, you find loud noises aversive.

The **decibel** (dB) is the unit that expresses the loudness of noises (see Figure 6.4). The hearing threshold is rated at 0 dB. The hushed tones of your school library probably register at about 30–40 dB. Rapid transit trains in New York City expose hundreds of thousands of residents to 85–100 dB, while people living in third-floor apartments by Los Angeles freeways are exposed to 90-dB levels (Raloff, 1982). This is rather disconcerting because persistent exposure to 90-dB levels for only eight hours can impair hearing. A discotheque rocks in at 110–120 dB. We find 140 dB painfully loud, and 150 dB can rupture the eardrums.

High levels of noise can lead to increases in blood pressure (Cohen et al., 1979); neurological and gastrointestinal disorders (National Academy of Science, 1981); and an assortment of stress-related illnesses, such as ulcers (Colligan & Murphy, 1982; Doring et al., 1980). In an industrial setting, workers over age 55 who had suffered hearing loss, presumably from prolonged exposure to workplace noise, showed significantly higher blood pressure than agemates who had not suffered hearing loss (Talbott et al., 1985). In noisy surroundings, such as the midtown area during heavy traffic, people appear less concerned with the distress of others and are less inclined to offer help (Bell & Doyle, 1983; Matthews & Canon, 1975). High noise levels also seem to impair learning, a particular problem for inner-city children.

Children who attend schools beneath the flight paths at Los Angeles International Airport show performance deficits and give up at solving problems more quickly than children at less noisy schools who are matched for ability, age, and ethnic background (Cohen et al., 1980). Time to adjust and subsequent noise abatement do not seem to reverse their cognitive and perceptual deficits (Cohen et al., 1981).

FIGURE 6.4   Decibel Ratings of Some Familiar Sounds

Excessive noise is an environmental stressor that may raise blood pressure and interfere with learning and performance.

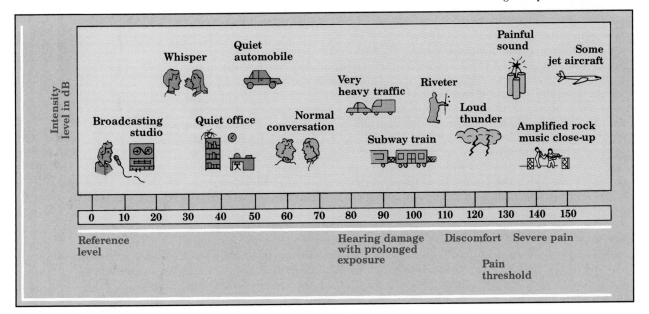

High noise levels are a source of stress that can raise the blood pressure and lead to hearing loss and stress-related disorders. Children who attend school beneath the flight paths at Los Angeles International Airport show performance deficits, including giving up at trying to solve problems relatively early.

Noise levels also influence feelings of attraction and aggressive behavior. Dating couples may interpret the high dB levels at the disco as enjoyable, but, as measured by the interpersonal distance they maintain, attraction decreases in the psychologists's laboratory when they are exposed to unpleasant noises of 80 dB. If you and your date have had a fight and are then exposed to the sudden explosion of a blowout, watch it! Angry people are more likely to behave aggressively when they are exposed to an unexpected noise of 95 dB, as compared to an unexpected noise of 55 dB (Donnerstein & Wilson, 1976).

And as noted, loud noises may cause us to turn a deaf ear on those in need. People are less likely to pick up a dropped package when the background noise created by a construction crew is at 92 dB, as compared to 72 dB (Page, 1977). They are even less likely to permit themselves to be troubled to make change for a quarter.

Air Pollution: Fussing and Fuming   Auto emissions, industrial smog, cigarette smoke, smoke from fireplaces and burning leaves—these are some of the air pollutants that affect us. Carbon monoxide, the most common air pollutant, combines with the substance in the blood that carries oxygen, thus preventing organs such as the brain and heart from receiving adequate oxygen. Prolonged exposure to high concentrations of carbon monoxide can contribute to headaches, memory disturbances, fatigue, even epilepsy. Carbon monoxide also impairs learning ability and the judgment of the passage of time (Beard & Wertheim, 1967). Since high concentrations of carbon monoxide can interfere with information processing (Lewis et al., 1970) and make it harder to attend to several things at once (Putz, 1979), they may very well contribute to the epidemic of highway accidents.

Air pollution can kill more directly. In December 1952, stagnation of industrial smog over London was held responsible for 3,500 deaths, with sulfur dioxide the specific culprit (Goldsmith, 1968). On the positive side, it is heartening to note that the air quality of New York City today is better than that of the 1960s because apartment buildings now heat with fuels that are low in sulfur content.

Extremes of temperature are aversive events that heighten arousal. Extreme cold causes the metabolism to increase and taxes our adjustment capacities.

The lead in auto fumes may impair children's intellectual functioning in the same way that chewing lead paint does (Fogel, 1980). But here, too, there are heartening signs. With stricter auto-emission requirements and the switch of many consumers to unleaded gasolines, Los Angeles' air has also shown major improvements in quality over the past several years. But Los Angeles residents are still advised to avoid jogging and remain indoors during occasional atmospheric inversions, when smog accumulates at low levels for days at a time.

There is also some evidence that malodorous air pollutants, like other forms of aversive stimulation, can decrease feelings of attraction between people and heighten the likelihood of aggression (Rotton et al., 1978, 1979). When there is a stink, some people are more likely to . . . make a stink.

Extremes of Temperature   A hot car engine makes great demands on the circulatory system. The water can overheat and the radiator can pop its cap. Excesses of heat also make demands on our own circulatory systems and can cause dehydration, heat exhaustion, heat stroke, and, in severe enough cases, a heart attack.

When it is too cold, the body responds by attempting to generate and retain heat. The metabolism increases; we shiver; and blood vessels in the skin constrict, decreasing flow of blood to the periphery of the body, where its warmth can be transmitted more easily to the outside. Members of a native tribe who live near the South Pole manage to keep their body temperatures warm through an elevated metabolism (Bell & Greene, 1982).

Hot and cold temperatures are aversive events with similar consequences, the first of which is increased arousal. In other words, heat and cold get your attention (Bell, 1981, 1982). Relatively moderate shifts in temperature may facilitate learning and behavior, increase feelings of attraction, and have largely positive effects, but extreme temperature variations tax our adjustment capacities, and our performance and activity levels tend to deteriorate.

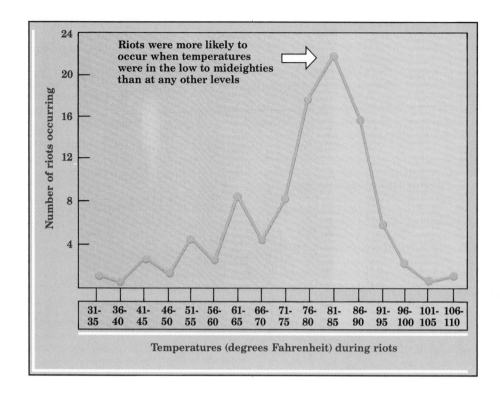

FIGURE 6.5 The "Long, Hot Summer Effect"

Most riots of the 1960s occurred when temperatures were in the uncomfortable mid-80s. There was a rapid decrease in the incidence of rioting as temperatures increased further. When the heat is really on, perhaps people "cool it" by themselves.

We find this sort of relationship between temperature and aggressive behavior (Bell & Baron, 1981). Consider Figure 6.5, which describes the so-called "Long, Hot Summer Effect." During the summers of the tumultuous 1960s, campus and race riots were most likely to break out as temperatures soared into the 80s Fahrenheit. However, their frequency diminished as temperatures then edged up into the sweltering and usually humid 90s Fahrenheit (U.S. Riot Commission, 1968).

Crowding: Life in Rat City and Beyond Sometimes you do everything you can for rats. You give them all they can eat, sex partners, a comfortable temperature, and protection from predators such as owls and pussycats. And how do they reward you. By acting like, well, rats.

John Calhoun (1962) allowed rats to reproduce with no constraints but for the limited space of their laboratory environment (Figure 6.6). At first, all was bliss in rat city. The males scurried about, gathered females into harems, and defended territories. They did not covet their neighbors' wives. They rarely fought. The females, unliberated, built nests and nursed their young. They resisted the occasional advance of the passing male.

But unrestricted population growth proved to be the snake in rat paradise. Beyond a critical population, the mortality rate rose. Family structure broke down. Packs of delinquent males assaulted inadequately defended females. Other males shunned all social contact. Some females avoided all sexual advances and huddled with the fearsome males. There were even instances of cannibalism. Upon dissection, many rats showed changes in organs that were characteristic of stress.

High density can be a source of stress in people, too. People who live in crowded institutional settings, such as prisons, hospitals, and college dormitories, may share some of the problems encountered by Calhoun's rats. Crowded prison inmates, for example, show higher blood pressure, more

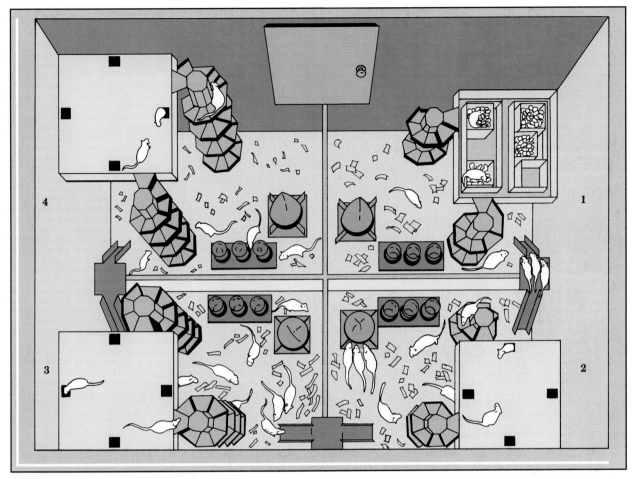

FIGURE 6.6   The "Rat Universe"

In Calhoun's "rat universe," an unlimited food supply and easy access between compartments (with the exception of compartments 1 and 4, between which there was no direct access) caused compartments 2 and 3 to become a "behavioral sink." The "sink" was characterized by overpopulation, breakdown of the social order, and a higher mortality rate. Do some human cities function as behavioral sinks?

psychiatric illness, and a higher mortality rate than uncrowded prisoners (D'Atri, 1975; Paulus et al., 1975; McCarthy & Saegert, 1979).

You may have been shoehorned with other roommates into a dorm room intended only for two. Students in high-density living situations sometimes adjust by withdrawing from social interaction whenever possible (Baum & Valins, 1977; Paulus, 1979). Crowded students are more likely to complain about roommates and label them uncooperative (Baron et al., 1976). They are less likely to show social responsibility; they more frequently fail to return lost letters (Bickman et al., 1973).

There is also a "tripling" effect. When three students live together, a coalition frequently forms between two of them so that the third feels isolated. The isolate reports the crowding to be more aversive than the pair who have formed the coalition (Aiello et al., 1981; Reddy et al., 1982). Findings such as these suggest that with humans it is not crowding *per se* that is so aversive. Instead, it is the sense that one does not have *control* over the situation. We shall learn more about the importance of a sense of control in coping with stress in the section on psychological hardiness.

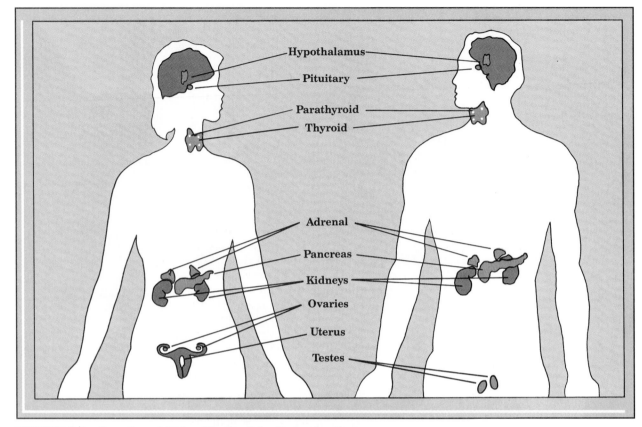

FIGURE 6.7   Location of Major Glands of the Endocrine System

■ Responses to Stress

And so the sources of stress are complex and varied. No less varied and complex are our responses to stress. In this section we review a number of physiological, emotional, cognitive, and behavioral responses to stress.

Physiological Responses

How is it that too much of a good thing, or that anxiety, frustration or conflict can make us ill? Why do Type A people run a greater risk of heart attacks than Type B's? We do not yet have all the answers, but those we have suggest that the body, under stress, is like a clock with an alarm system that does not shut off until its energy is dangerously depleted.

General Adaptation Syndrome   The body's response to different stressors shows some similarities, whether the stressor is a bacterial invasion, a perceived danger, a major life change, an inner conflict, or a wound. Selye (1976) has labeled this response the **general adaptation syndrome** (GAS). The GAS consists of three stages: an alarm reaction, a resistance stage, and an exhaustion stage.

The Alarm Reaction   The **alarm reaction** is triggered by perception of a stressor. It mobilizes or arouses the body in preparation for defense. Cannon (1929) had earlier termed this alarm system the **fight-or-flight reaction.** The alarm reaction involves a number of body changes that are initiated by the brain and further regulated by the endocrine system and the sympathetic

General adaptation syndrome. Selye's term for a hypothesized three-stage response to stress. Abbreviated GAS.

Alarm reaction. The first stage of the GAS, which is "triggered" by the impact of a stressor and characterized by sympathetic activity.

Fight-or-flight reaction. Cannon's term for a hypothesized innate adaptive response to the perception of danger.

division of the autonomic nervous system. Let us consider the roles of these two body systems.

The Role of the Endocrine System

The **endocrine system** consists of ductless glands, such as those shown in Figure 6.7. Glands such as tear glands send their secretions (in this case, tears) to their destinations (the eyes) by ducts (tear ducts). But the ductless glands of the endocrine system pour their secretions directly into the bloodstream. Like neurotransmitters, hormones have specific receptor sites. And so, although they are poured into the bloodstream and circulate throughout the body, they only act upon hormone receptors in certain locations. For example, some hormones released by the hypothalamus influence only the pituitary gland. Some hormones released by the pituitary gland influence the adrenal cortex, others influence the testes and ovaries, and so on.

The hypothalamus, a pea-sized structure in the brain, is essential to the alarm reaction. The hypothalamus secretes corticotrophin-releasing hormone (CRH), which stimulates the pituitary gland (frequently referred to as the "master gland") to secrete adrenocorticotrophic hormone (ACTH). ACTH, in turn, acts upon the outer part of the adrenal glands (the adrenal cortex), causing it to release a number of hormones, referred to as **corticosteroids,** which help the body respond to stress by fighting inflammation and allergic reactions (such as difficulty breathing). Cortisol is an important corticosteroid. Steroids also cause the liver to release stored glucose (sugar), making energy available. The names of these hormones are a "mouthful," but note the logic to them: the *cortico-* in each one refers to the adrenal *cortex,* indicating that they act, in a sort of domino effect, to cause the adrenal cortex to secrete steroids. Moreover, *cortex* is the Latin word for "bark," or outer covering.

Two hormones that play a major role in the alarm reaction are secreted by the adrenal medulla, or inner part (*medulla* means "marrow") of the adrenal glands. These are the **catecholamines** adrenalin (also known as epinephrine) and noradrenalin (also known as norepinephrine). *Ad-renal* is Latin for "near the kidneys," and *epi-nephros* has the same meaning in Greek. Figure 6.7 shows that the adrenal glands are located on top of the kidneys. Adrenalin is manufactured exclusively by the adrenal glands, but norepinephrine is also produced at other sites in the body.* Adrenalin acts on the sympathetic branch of the autonomic nervous system to arouse the body in preparation for coping with threats and stress. Norepinephrine raises the blood pressure and, in the nervous system, it acts as a neurotransmitter.

Since cortisol and adrenalin are secreted in response to stress, the amount of these substances in the body serves as an objective measure of stress. For example, psychologists frequently use the amount of cortisol in the saliva and the amount of adrenalin in the urine as biological measures of stress.

Since adrenalin acts on the autonomic nervous system, let us now consider the role of that system in the alarm reaction.

The Role of the Autonomic Nervous System

Autonomic means "automatic." The **autonomic nervous system,** or ANS, regulates the glands and involuntary activities such as heartbeat, digestion, and dilation of the pupils of the eyes.

The ANS has two branches or divisions, the **sympathetic** division and the **parasympathetic** division (see Figure 6.8). These branches of the ANS have largely opposing effects; when they work at the same time, their effects can average out to some degree. Many organs and glands are stimulated by both branches. In general, the sympathetic division is stimulated by adrenalin

---

Endocrine system. The body's system of ductless glands that secrete hormones and release them directly into the bloodstream.

Corticosteroids. Hormones produced by the adrenal cortex that increase resistance to stress in ways such as fighting inflammation and causing the liver to release stores of sugar. Also called *cortical steroids.*

Catecholamines. The amino acid derivatives adrenalin and noradrenalin (also referred to as epinephrine and norepinephrine), which heighten the activity of the sympathetic division of the autonomic nervous system.

Autonomic nervous system. The part of the nervous system that regulates glands and involuntary activities such as heartbeat, respiration, digestion, and dilation of the pupils of the eyes. Abbreviated ANS.

Sympathetic. The division of the ANS that is most active during activities and emotional responses—such as anxiety and fear—that spend the body's reserves of energy.

Parasympathetic. The division of the ANS that is most active during processes that restore the body's reserves of energy, such as digestion.

---

*We shall use the names adrenalin and norepinephrine from this point forward, but epinephrine and noradrenalin would be equally correct.

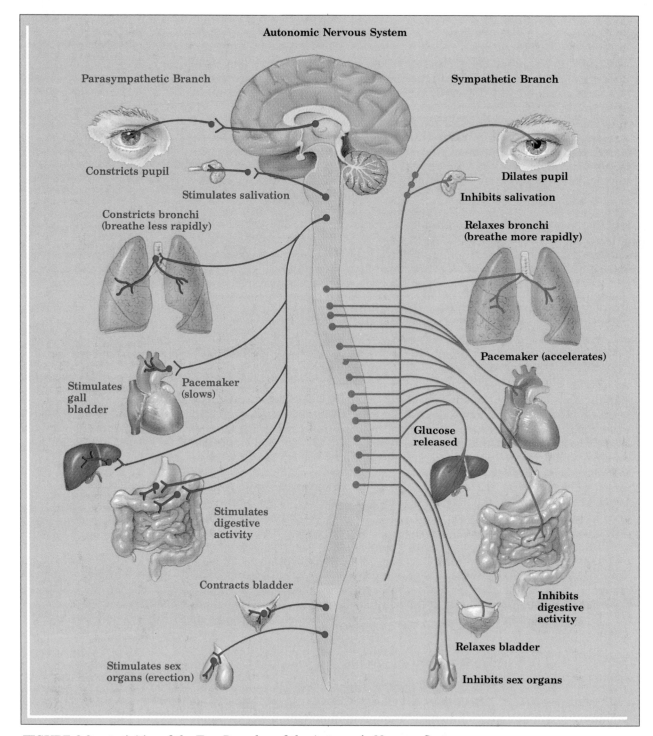

FIGURE 6.8   Activities of the Two Branches of the Autonomic Nervous System

The parasympathetic branch of the ANS is generally dominant during activities that replenish the body's stores of energy, such as eating and relaxing. The sympathetic branch is most active during activities that spend energy, such as fighting or fleeing from an enemy, and when we experience emotions such as fear and anxiety. For this reason, most of the organs shown are stimulated to heightened activity by the sympathetic branch of the ANS. Digestive processes are an exception; they are inhibited by sympathetic activity.

and is most active during processes that spend body energy from stored re-serves, such as when you chafe at the bit in stop-and-go traffic or when you find out that your mortgage payment is going to be increased. Adrenalin increases the heart and respiration rates, the blood sugar level, and so on.

The parasympathetic division is most active during processes that re-plenish reserves of energy, as during eating (Arms & Camp, 1987). For in-stance, when we are anxious, the sympathetic division of the ANS accelerates the heart rate. But when we relax, it is the parasympathetic division that decelerates the heart rate. The parasympathetic division stimulates digestion, but the sympathetic branch inhibits digestion. Since the sympathetic division predominates when we feel anxiety or fear, fear or anxiety can give you indigestion.

The sympathetic division of the ANS provides more energy for muscular activity, which can be used to fight or flee from a source of danger, and decreases the body's vulnerability to wounds. These and other changes are outlined in Table 6.2. The fight-or-flight reaction is inherited from a long-ago time when many stressors were life-threatening. It was triggered by a predator at the edge of a thicket or by a sudden rustling in the undergrowth. Once the threat is removed, the body returns to a lower state of arousal.

Our ancestors lived in situations in which the alarm reaction would not be activated for long. They fought or ran quickly or, to put it bluntly, they died. Sensitive alarm reactions contributed to survival.

Are sensitive alarm reactions still an advantage? Our ancestors did not spend years in the academic grind or carry 30-year mortgages. Contemporary pressures may activate our alarm systems for hours, days, or months at a time. For this reason, highly sensitive systems may now be a handicap. Pardine and Napoli (1983) administered a life-events questionnaire to college undergrad-uates. Students who reported high levels of recent stress showed higher levels of heart rate and blood pressure in response to an experimentally-induced stressor than did students reporting low levels of stress. That is, students with more sensitive alarm reactions recover less rapidly from stressors and find their lives generally more stressful. We cannot change our heredity—sensitive alarm systems will tend to remain sensitive to some degree. But in Chapter 10 we shall explore methods for directly lowering our levels of arousal (turn-ing the alarm system down or off), and for getting in touch with irrational ideas that may contribute to the activity of our alarm systems.

The Resistance Stage   In any event, if the alarm reaction mobilizes the body and the stressor is not removed, we enter the adaptation stage, or **re-sistance stage,** of the GAS. The levels of endocrine and sympathetic activity are not as high as in the alarm reaction, but it is still greater than normal. In this stage the body attempts to restore lost energy and repair whatever damage has been done.

The Exhaustion Stage   If the stressor is still not adequately dealt with, we may enter the final stage, or **exhaustion stage,** of the GAS. Our individual

Resistance stage. The sec-ond stage of the GAS, char-acterized by prolonged sym-pathetic activity in an effort to restore lost energy and re-pair damage. Also called the *adaptation stage.*

Exhaustion stage. The third stage of the GAS, char-acterized by weakened resist-ance and possible deteriora-tion.

TABLE 6.2   Components of the Alarm Reaction

Corticosteroids are secreted	Muscles tense
Adrenalin is secreted	Blood shifts away from the skin
Respiration rate increases	Digestion is inhibited
Heart rate increases	Sugar is released from the liver
Blood pressure increases	Blood coagulability increases

The alarm reaction is triggered by various types of stressors. It is defined by release of corticosteroids and adrenalin, and activity of the sympathetic nervous system. It prepares the body to fight or flee from a source of danger.

capacities for resisting stress vary, but all of us, as even the strongest of Richter's rats, eventually become exhausted when stress persists indefinitely. Our muscles become fatigued and we deplete our bodies of resources required for combatting stress. With exhaustion, the parasympathetic division of the ANS may become predominant. As a result, our heartbeats and respiration rates slow down, and many of the body responses that had characterized sympathetic activity are reversed. It might sound as if we would profit from the respite, but remember that we are still under stress—and, possibly, an external threat. Continued stress in the exhaustion stage may lead to what Selye terms "diseases of adaptation"—from allergies and hives to ulcers and coronary heart disease—and, ultimately, to death. In Chapter 7 we shall explore a number of stress-related illnesses.

Emotional Responses

Emotions color our lives. We are green with envy, red with anger, blue with sorrow. The poets paint a thoughtful mood as a brown study. Positive emotions such as love and desire can fill our days with pleasure, but negative emotions, such as those induced by stress, can fill us with dread and make each day an intolerable chore.

An **emotion** is a state of feeling that has situational, physiological, and cognitive components. Different kinds of stressful situations lead to different kinds of emotional responses. Although no two people experience emotions in exactly the same way, we can make some generalizations. Let us consider three of the most important emotional responses to stress: anxiety, anger, and depression.

Anxiety Anxiety tends to occur in response to *threats* of stressors such as physical danger, loss of valuable things or of a significant other person, and failure. Anxiety is a stressor in its own right as well as an emotional response to stress.

Psychologists frequently distinguish between trait anxiety and state anxiety. **Trait anxiety** is a personality variable. People with trait anxiety have persistent feelings of dread and foreboding—cognitions that something terrible is about to happen. They are chronically worried and concerned. **State anxiety** is a temporary condition of arousal that is triggered by a specific situation, such as the eve of a final exam, a big date, a job interview, or a visit to the dentist.

On a physiological level, anxiety of either type involves predominantly sympathetic arousal (rapid heartbeat and breathing, sweating, muscle tension, and so on).

Anger Anger is an emotional state that usually occurs in response to stressors such as frustration and social provocation. Hostility differs from anger in that it is an enduring trait. Physiologically, anger can involve both sympathetic and parasympathetic arousal (Funkenstein, 1955). Anger usually involves cognitions to the effect that the world has no right to be the way it is (in the case of frustration) or that another person has no right to treat us in a certain way (in the case of a social provocation).

Depression Depression is an emotional state that usually occurs in response to stressors such as the loss of a close friend, lover, or relative; to failure; to inactivity or lack of stimulation; and to prolonged stress of any source. Why does depression sometimes stem from inactivity and lack of stimulation? Remember that people have needs for stimulation, and that some "stress," which Selye referred to as eustress, is desirable and healthful. Why does depression stem from prolonged exposure to stress? On a physiological level, depression

Emotion. A state of feeling that possesses physiological, situational, and cognitive components.

Trait anxiety. Anxiety as a personality variable, or persistent trait.

State anxiety. A temporary condition of anxiety that may be attributed to a situation.

is characterized by parasympathetic dominance, and parasympathetic activity is characteristic of the exhaustion stage of the GAS.

As we shall see in Chapter 8, depression is linked to cognitions that we are worthless or helpless to make changes. In Chapters 8 and 9 we shall also see that depressed people tend to interpret their experiences in stress-evoking, self-defeating ways. For example, they tend to minimize their accomplishments, to focus on negative life events, and to attribute their shortcomings to factors that are resistant to change.

Emotions and Behavior   Emotions tend to motivate us to behave in certain ways. Negative emotions such as anxiety, anger, and depression can motivate us to behave in maladaptive ways, as we shall see in the section on defensive coping. For example, anxiety tends to motivate escape behavior; anger, aggressive behavior; and depression, withdrawal.

It is helpful for us to perceive negative emotional responses as signs that something is wrong, to study our environments to learn what we can about the sources of stress, and then to plan behavior that will enable us to remove stressors or to react to them in ways that buffer their impact. But when our emotions "run too high," they can disrupt our cognitive processes and interfere with adaptive behavior. In Chapter 10 we shall outline a number of ways of handling anxiety, anger, and depression.

Cognitive Responses

Although psychologists speak of physiological, emotional, and cognitive behaviors or responses, they also recognize that people are not to be carved up into convenient compartments. There are continuous interactions between the physiological, the emotional, and the cognitive aspects of human nature. Emotions, as we have seen, include physiological and cognitive "components." High levels of physiological arousal in response to stress heighten our emotional responses and also influence our cognitions.

Effects of High Arousal on Behavior   It appears that we are motivated to seek *optimal* levels of arousal at which we feel best and function most efficiently. By and large, our levels of arousal are determined by the levels of activity of the sympathetic and parasympathetic divisions of the ANS. Most of us seek a balance between the two divisions—preferring to avoid the extremes characterized by, say, anxiety (sympathetic dominance) and depression and inactivity (parasympathetic dominance).

According to the **Yerkes-Dodson law,** there is also a relationship between our levels of arousal and our abilities to function effectively. Note Figure 6.9. As suggested by part A, a high level of arousal facilitates performance of relatively simple behavior patterns, whether these patterns involve playing linebacker in a football game, performing simple math calculations, fleeing from a predator, or attacking a social provocateur.

However, as suggested by part C, we perform complex, difficult behavior patterns most efficiently under relatively low levels of arousal. Whereas a linebacker can afford to get "worked up" before a big game, it is probably to the advantage of the quarterback, who must integrate rapidly changing information about the movements and positions of many offensive and defensive players simultaneously, to "keep a cool head"—even when being tackled is imminent. Whereas high levels of arousal facilate fleeing and fighting, lower levels of arousal are useful in helping us consider various alternatives to environmental threats and social provocations.

Evocation of Dominant Cognitions and Overt Behavior Patterns
And so, strong physiological and emotional responses to stress, which are

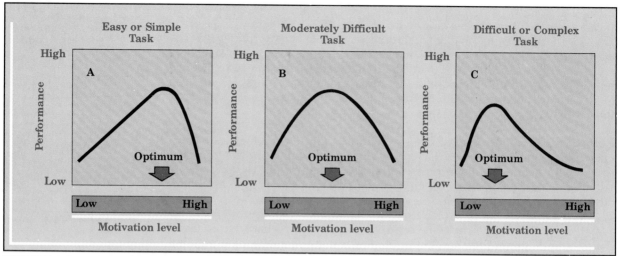

FIGURE 6.9   The Yerkes-Dodson Law

An easy or simple task may be facilitated by a high level of arousal or motivation. A highly aroused 118-pound woman is reported to have lifted the front end of a two-ton Cadillac in order to rescue a child. But a complex task, such as quarterbacking a football team or attempting to solve a math problem, requires attending to many variables at once. For this reason, a complex task is usually carried out more efficiently at a lower level of arousal.

characterized by high levels of arousal, can impair cognitive activity and interfere with our problem solving ability. One way in which this occurs is that our dominant cognitions and overt behavior patterns are evoked by high levels of arousal. And so, if we have been working to find more adaptive ways of responding to threats and social provocations, we may revert to earlier fleeing or fighting under conditions of high arousal.

What Do We Focus On When the Adrenalin Is Pumping?   Another way in which high arousal impairs cognitive functioning is by distracting us from the tasks at hand. That is, we focus on our body responses—and, as a result, cognitions to the effect that perhaps we need to escape or are doomed to failure—rather than on the problems to be solved.

In later chapters we shall see that adaptive coping methods include ways of lowering arousal and maintaining a task orientation.

Behavioral Responses to Stress: Ways of Coping

Many techniques for coping with stress are essentially defensive. They reduce the immediate impact of the stressor, but at some cost. This cost includes socially inappropriate behavior (as in alcoholism, aggression, or regression), avoidance of problems (as in withdrawal), or self-deception (as in rationalization or denial). **Defensive coping** grants us time to marshall our resources, but it does not deal with the source of stress or improve the effectiveness of our response to stress. In the long run, defensive methods can be harmful if we do not use the chance they provide to find more active ways of coping.

Direct, or **active, coping** methods aim to manipulate the environment—in socially acceptable ways—or to change the response patterns of the individual so that a stressor is permanently removed or its harmfulness is buffered. We explored a number of active coping methods in the sections on pain management and conflict (decision making). We shall explore active coping methods further in Chapter 10 and elsewhere throughout the book. They include measures such as lowering our levels of arousal, perceiving stressors as problems to be solved rather than unsurmountable hurdles, challenging irrational beliefs and self-demands, and acquiring various skills.

Defensive coping. A response to stress that reduces the immediate impact of the stressor, but does not change the environment or the self to permanently remove, or modify the effects of, the stressor.

Active coping. A response to stress that manipulates the environment, or changes the response patterns of the individual, to permanently remove the stressor or to buffer its harmfulness.

Defense mechanisms. In psychodynamic theory, unconscious functions of the ego that protect it from anxiety by preventing accurate recognition of anxiety-evoking ideas and impulses.

In this section we discuss ways of defensive coping: use of alcohol and other drugs, aggression, withdrawal, fantasy, and the defense mechanisms of regression, denial, repression, rationalization, reaction formation, projection, intellectualization, displacement, and sublimation. Freud labeled the latter group **defense mechanisms** in keeping with the trend of his day to think of human functions in machinelike terms. He believed that defense mechanisms operated unconsciously to protect the ego from the anxiety that might stem from recognition of unacceptable ideas and impulses. But Freud's mechanisms may also be viewed as not necessarily unconscious ways of responding to stress that become habits because their reduction of discomfort, anxiety, or frustration is reinforcing.

Defense mechanisms are used by normal and abnormal people alike. They become problems when they are the only means used to cope with stress.

Alcohol and Other Drugs   Alcohol and a number of other drugs, including tranquilizers, act as central nervous system depressants that can directly blunt feelings of tension, anxiety, and frustration. Alcohol can also lower self-awareness (Hull, 1981), reducing the negative feelings that might otherwise stem from recognizing that one's behavior has fallen short of one's values or morals.

People also often attribute their inappropriate aggressive or sexual behavior to alcohol. Tucker and his colleagues (1981) found that subjects used alcohol consumption as a "self-handicapping strategy." Subjects involved in a difficult experimental task drank more when they were denied access to materials that could have aided them in the task. It may well be that they drank in order to provide themselves with an external, or situational, attribution for failure: "It wasn't me—it was the alcohol." An external reason for failure may also have allowed them to maintain their self-esteem.

Consistent use of alcohol to cope with stress constitutes psychological dependence on alcohol. People may become dependent on many drugs in order to blunt awareness of stress or distort perception of what has become—for them—an unpleasant reality.

Aggression   Violence is often used to cope with social provocations and, sometimes, as a response to frustration. In warfare and in self-defense, aggressive behavior is usually positively valued. But most violence in our society is frowned upon, and its benefits are usually short-lived. Attacking a police officer who is writing you a traffic ticket will not earn a judge's understanding approval. Aggressive behavior, except for rare instances, heightens rather than reduces interpersonal conflict by creating motives for retaliation.

Withdrawal   When you are intensely frightened, or feel helpless, or believe that any decision would be futile, you may feel pressed to withdraw from the situation. Withdrawal can be emotional, as in showing loss of interest, or physical, as in moving or changing one's lifestyle. For example, victims of rape frequently move to a new location in order to avoid painful memories and future threats (Rathus, 1983). Also, city dwellers tend to withdraw from social contacts with strangers as ways of protecting themselves from crime and from the stimulus overload created by crowding (Lavrakas, 1982; Milgram, 1977). City dwellers are less likely than small-town residents to shake the extended hand of a stranger (Milgram, 1977), to respond to a cheerful "Hello" from a stranger (Amato, 1980), or to meet the gaze of a stranger (Newman & McCauley, 1977). City dwellers are even less likely than small-town residents to help children who pretend to be lost (Milgram, 1977).

Temporary withdrawal can be healthful; it can provide the chance to find better methods of coping. Withdrawal may also be the appropriate course when there is no succesful way to cope with a stressful situation. But withdrawal from social interaction and social responsibility is harmful to the social fabric and accounts for some of the more troublesome aspects of contemporary urban life.

Fantasy   Fantasy is not for children only. Have you ever daydreamed about the future, testing career and marital choices through cognitive trial and error? Fantasy serves many functions and is useful so long as it does not become an indefinitely prolonged substitute for effective action.

Defense Mechanisms

Regression   You may have been trying to explain a fine point in physics to your roommate for an hour. Then your roommate, who had "yessed" you all during the explanation, asks a question that shows that nothing you said was understood. You slam your book on the desk, shout "Jerk!" and stamp out of the room.

If you are 6 years old, this behavior is normal. For a college student, it is **regression**—returning to an earlier way of behaving under stress. You may know people who quit smoking or biting their nails but have returned to these habits before a big exam or after a fight with a date. These, too, are examples of regression. A psychoanalyst might consider them regression to the oral stage.

Denial   Many people simply deny sources of danger. Many smokers refuse to believe that they risk cancer. A person may vaguely perceive that the company is going downhill, but maintain a complacent attitude until the layoff notice arrives. Hackett and Cassem (1970) found that many cardiac patients respond with an "It can't happen to me" attitude when the patient in the next bed dies. Kübler-Ross (1969) found that many terminally ill patients greet news of impending death with **denial.** Women who find lumps in their breasts* sometimes put off seeing a physician for fear of consequences—diagnosis of cancer and surgery (Stillman, 1977).

Denial reduces the immediate impact of stressors, but denies us the chance to take effective action to ward off real threats.

Repression   Repression is the thrusting out of awareness of unacceptable ideas or urges that are often sexual or aggressive. Repression occurs unconsciously; we are not aware of when we are repressing unacceptable ideas. Freud theorized that repression is a normal aspect of personality development, which permits us to place certain conflicts behind us and move ahead. But repressing the fact that an important paper is due in two weeks is not adjustive.

Repression must be contrasted with **suppression**—the conscious decision not to focus on a distressing topic. When you are aware that you are avoiding focusing on unacceptable ideas or threatening impulses, you are engaging in suppression, not repression.

Rationalization   The smoker justifies his or her habit by saying, "I just can't quit." The prostitute says, "Why condemn me? I'd be out of business if wives were doing their job." These are **rationalizations**—ways of explaining unacceptable behavior that exonerate us from blame and guilt. We may also rationalize to cut our losses: "So the date didn't work out—we were too different to develop a relationship anyhow." Rationalization may also be used to

---

*Most of the time such lumps are benign, but early detection of cancer is an important factor in cure. Women are therefore encouraged to have regular medical checkups and to learn how to engage in self-breast examination.

Regression. Return, under stress, to a form of behavior characteristic of an earlier stage of development.

Denial. A defense mechanism in which threatening events are misperceived to be harmless.

Suppression. The conscious placing of stressful or threatening events or ideas out of awareness.

Rationalization. A defense mechanism in which an individual engages in self-deception, finding justifications for unacceptable ideas, impulses, or behaviors.

Regression is defined as returning to an earlier way of behaving under stress. Do any of the people you know show "infantile" behavior when they are under stress?

Reaction formation. A defense mechanism in which unacceptable ideas and impulses are kept unconscious through the exaggerated expression of opposing ideas and impulses.

Projection. A defense mechanism in which unacceptable ideas and impulses are cast out, or attributed, to others.

Intellectualization. A defense mechanism in which threatening events are viewed with emotional detachment.

justify criminal behavior. Maital (1982) found that people who cheat on their income tax returns often rationalize that government programs cost more than they're worth or that they pay more than their fair share of taxes. And muggers have been known to blame their victims: "Don't look at me. He was dumb for walking down that street alone with all that cash."

Reaction Formation   Have you ever thought that someone who was sickeningly sweet and overpolite might be sitting on a hotbed of hostility? Has anyone denied feelings so strongly that you suspected they were actually present? Perhaps so. Freud theorized that another avenue for dealing with unacceptable impulses is **reaction formation**—taking an exaggerated position that opposes our true feelings.

Projection   Freud suggested that we sometimes deal with our own unacceptable impulses through **projection**—attributing them to other people, and disowning them as parts of ourselves. An angry person may perceive the world as a hostile place. A sexually frustrated person who believes that sex is evil may interpret the innocent gestures of others as sexual advances.

Intellectualization   Physicians who become emotionally involved with patients may not be able to undertake painful diagnostic and surgical procedures to save their lives. Instead, they try to distance themselves from their patients' immediate discomfort so that they can apply their knowledge and skills without excessive arousal. Similarly, psychologists who become as upset as a client over a family dispute would not be effective at suggesting coping behavior. **Intellectualization** is cognitive focusing on stress that permits emotional detachment.

While intellectualization permits us to solve problems rationally, excessive intellectualization may prevent us from experiencing life fully. Constant intellectualizers may impress us as cold, distant, or machinelike.

Displacement   Freud considered **displacement** an essential aspect of developing mature sexual relationships. He argued that we develop lasting attachments to adults of the opposite sex by transferring onto them, or displacing, emotions first experienced toward our own parents. Displacement is adjustive because it permits us to substitute attainable goals for unattainable goals.

Aggressive impulses may be displaced onto targets less threatening than the person who provoked us. There is the old tale about the man who was scolded by his boss and took it out on his wife. She then scolded the child who, in turn, kicked the dog. The dog chased the cat, the cat chased the mouse, and so on. Some microscopic form of life may still be bearing the brunt of the boss's wrath.

Sublimation   Why do we build cities, sculpt statues, write poems and novels? Are our motives noble, or do they have a darker basis?

Freud suggested that these creative acts represented **sublimation**—the channeling of socially unacceptable impulses into socially productive behavior. Sublimation permits one to escape self-criticism from recognition of, or acting out on, primitive impulses. An artist, for example, may gratify sexual impulses by working with nude models while also earning a high income and critical acclaim.

This dim view of human creativity has sparked much criticism. Even contemporary followers of Freud—neo-Freudians—believe that motives can stem from the (conscious) ego as well as from the (unconscious) id.

■ Psychological Moderators of the Impact of Stress

As noted, there is no one-to-one relationship between the amount of stress we experience and dependent variables such as physical disorders or psychological distress. Physical factors account for some of the variability in our responses. For example, as we shall see in Chapters 7 and 8, some people apparently inherit predispositions toward certain physical and psychological disorders. But psychological factors also play a role. That is, psychological factors can influence, or *moderate,* the impact of sources of stress.

In this section we discuss a number of psychological moderators of stress: self-efficacy expectancies, psychological hardiness, a sense of humor, goal-directedness versus playfulness, predictability, and social support.

Self-Efficacy Expectancies

Social-learning theorists (e.g., Bandura, 1982) argue that our self-efficacy expectancies—that is, our perceptions of our capacities to bring about change—have important influences on our abilities to withstand stress. For example, when we are faced with fear-inducing objects, it has been shown experimentally that high self-efficacy expectancies are accompanied by *low* levels of adrenalin and norepinephrine in the bloodstream (Bandura et al., 1985). Adrenalin, as we saw earlier in the chapter, is secreted by the adrenal medulla when we are under stress, and it arouses the body by stimulating the sympathetic division of the ANS. As a result, we may experience shakiness, "butterflies in the stomach," and feelings of nervousness. And so, people with higher self-efficacy expectancies have biological as well as psychological reasons for remaining calmer.

Further evidence of the importance of self-efficacy expectancies to psychological well-being is found in research that shows that normal people have higher levels of perceived self-efficacy than do psychiatric subjects (Rosenbaum & Hadari, 1985).

Displacement. A defense mechanism in which ideas or impulses are transferred from a threatening or unsuitable object to an acceptable object.

Sublimation. A defense mechanism in which primitive impulses—usually sexual and aggressive—are channeled into positive, constructive activities.

People in whom high self-efficacy expectancies are experimentally induced complete tasks more successfully than people of comparable ability but lower self-efficacy expectancies. Moreover, subjects with high self-efficacy expectancies show lower emotional arousal as they work, allowing them to maintain more of a task orientation. A combination of high self-efficacy expectancies *and a detailed plan* help overweight college students lose weight (Schifter & Ajzen, 1985). People with higher self-efficacy expectancies are less likely to relapse after they have lost weight or quit smoking (Condiotte & Lichtenstein, 1981; Marlatt & Gordon, 1980). They are more effective in athletic competition (Weinberg et al., 1980), and they are more likely to seriously consider nontraditional and challenging career options (Betz & Hackett, 1981). They are also more likely to profit from psychotherapy for problems such as depression (Steinmetz et al., 1983). Women with higher self-efficacy expectancies are more likely to persist without medication in controlling pain during childbirth (Manning & Wright, 1983).*

When intelligence and aptitudes are held constant, it appears that people with higher self-efficacy expectancies regulate problem-solving behavior more effectively and bounce back more readily from failure. In these ways it seems that life's challenges may be less stressful for them.

The relationship between self-efficacy expectancies and performance also appears to be a two-way street. Although self-efficacy expectancies contribute to successful performances, Feltz (1982) found that improved performance (in women who were back-diving) also heightens self-efficacy expectancies.

Psychological Hardiness

Psychological hardiness is another factor that apparently helps people resist stress. The research on psychological hardiness is largely indebted to the pioneering work of Suzanne Kobasa (1979) and her colleagues who studied business executives who resisted illness despite heavy loads of stress. In one phase of her research, Kobasa administered a battery of psychological tests to hardy and nonhardy executives and found that the hardy executives differed from the nonhardy in three important ways (Kobasa et al., 1982, pp. 169–170):

1. Hardy individuals were high in *commitment.* That is they showed a tendency to involve themselves in, rather than experience alienation from, whatever they were doing or encountering.
2. Hardy individuals were high in *challenge.* They believed that change rather than stability was normal in life. They appraised change as an interesting incentive to personal growth, and not as a threat to security.
3. Hardy individuals were also high in perceived *control* over their lives. They felt and behaved as though they were influential rather than helpless in facing the various rewards and punishments of life. In terms suggested more than two decades ago by social-learning theorist Julian Rotter (1966), psychologically hardy people tend to have an internal **locus of control.**

According to Kobasa, hardy people are more resistant to stress because they see themselves as *choosing* to be in their stress-producing situations. They also interpret, or encode, the stress impacting upon them as making life more interesting, not as compounding the pressures to which they are subjected. Their activation of control allows them to regulate to some degree the amount of stress they will encounter at any given time (Maddi & Kobasa, 1984). Of the three aspects of psychological hardiness that help people resist stress, Hull

Psychological hardiness. A cluster of traits that buffer stress and are characterized by commitment, challenge, and control.

Locus of control. The place (locus) to which an individual attributes control over the receiving of reinforcers—either inside or outside the self.

---

*We are not promoting natural childbirth, but merely illustrating the point that people with high self-efficacy expectancies generally show greater willingness than others to persist in an endeavor, despite discomfort.

▌QUESTIONNAIRE▐

Locus of Control Scale

Psychologically hardy people tend to have an internal locus of control. They believe that they are in control of their own lives. Persons with an external locus of control, by contrast, tend to see their fates as being out of their hands.

Are you more of an "internal" or more of an "external"? To learn more about your perception of your locus of control, respond to the following questionnaire developed by Nowicki and Strickland (1973).

Place a checkmark in either the Yes or the No column for each question, and, when you have finished, turn to the answer key at the end of the chapter.

	YES	NO
1. Do you believe that most problems will solve themselves if you just don't fool with them?	___	___
2. Do you believe that you can stop yourself from catching a cold?	___	___
3. Are some people just born lucky?	___	___
4. Most of the time do you feel that getting good grades means a great deal to you?	___	___
5. Are you often blamed for things that just aren't your fault?	___	___
6. Do you believe that if somebody studies hard enough he or she can pass any subject?	___	___
7. Do you feel that most of the time it doesn't pay to try hard because things never turn out right anyway?	___	___
8. Do you feel that if things start out well in the morning it's going to be a good day no matter what you do?	___	___
9. Do you feel that most of the time parents listen to what their children have to say?	___	___
10. Do you believe that wishing can make good things happen?	___	___
11. When you get punished does it usually seem it's for no good reason at all?	___	___
12. Most of the time do you find it hard to change a friend's opinion?	___	___
13. Do you think that cheering more than luck helps a team to win?	___	___
14. Did you feel that it was nearly impossible to change your parents' minds about anything?	___	___
15. Do you believe that parents should allow children to make most of their own decisions?	___	___
16. Do you feel that when you do something wrong there's very little you can do to make it right?	___	___
17. Do you believe that most people are just born good at sports?	___	___
18. Are most of the other people your age stronger than you are?	___	___

and his colleagues (1987) argue that commitment and control are the ones that make the most difference.

Kobassa and Pucetti (1983) suggest that psychological hardiness helps individuals resist stress by providing buffers between themselves and stressful life events. Buffering allows people the opportunity to draw upon social supports (Ganellen & Blaney, 1984) and to use successful coping mechanisms, such as controlling what they will be doing from day to day. And Type A

	YES	NO

19. Do you feel that one of the best ways to handle most problems is just not to think about them?

20. Do you feel that you have a lot of choice in deciding who your friends are?

21. If you find a four-leaf clover, do you believe that it might bring you good luck?

22. Did you often feel that whether or not you did your homework had much to do with what kinds of grades you got?

23. Do you feel that when a person your age is angry with you, there's little you can do to stop him or her?

24. Have you ever had a good-luck charm?

25. Do you believe that whether or not people like you depends on how you act?

26. Did your parents usually help you if you asked them to?

27. Have you felt that when people were angry with you it was usually for no reason at all?

28. Most of the time, do you feel that you can change what might happen tomorrow by what you did today?

29. Do you believe that when bad things are going to happen they are just going to happen no matter what you try to do to stop them?

30. Do you think that people can get their own way if they just keep trying?

31. Most of the time do you find it useless to try to get your own way at home?

32. Do you feel that when good things happen they happen because of hard work?

33. Do you feel that when somebody your age wants to be your enemy there's little you can do to change matters?

34. Do you feel that it's easy to get friends to do what you want them to do?

35. Do you usually feel that you have little to say about what you get to eat at home?

36. Do you feel that when someone doesn't like you there's little you can do about it?

37. Did you usually feel that it was almost useless to try in school because most other children were just plain smarter than you were?

38. Are you the kind of person who believes that planning ahead makes things turn out better?

39. Most of the time, do you feel that you have little to say about what your family decides to do?

40. Do you think it's better to be smart than to be lucky?

individuals who show psychological hardiness are more resistant to illness, including coronary heart disease, than Type A individuals who do not (Booth-Kewley & Friedman, 1987; Friedman & Booth-Kewley, 1987; Kobasa et al., 1983; Rhodewalt & Agustsdottir, 1984).

As noted, a sense of control is one of the essential factors in psychological hardiness. You may wish to take the nearby questionnaire on locus of control to see whether you tend to believe that you are in charge of your own life.

Control as an Adjustment Strategy for Coping with Crowding

Many examples from everyday life suggest that a sense of control over the situation—a sense of making choices—fosters adjustment. Consider the role of control in our responses to crowding. When we are at a concert, a disco, or a sports event, we may experience greater crowding than we do in those frustrating registration lines. But we may be having a wonderful time. Why? Because we have *chosen* to be at the concert and are focusing on our good time (unless a tall or noisy person sits in front of us). We feel that we are in control.

So how can we handle the registration lines? First, challenge the irrational idea that we have no choice about being in the registration lines. When we know that we will encounter frustration but choose to attend, we do so because we have decided that the pluses of waiting outweigh the negatives—for example, by waiting we are less likely to get closed out of desired courses. We can also plan ahead and bring an enjoyable novel to read in line, or wait with a friend and chat.

Sense of Humor: "Doeth a Merry Heart Good Like a Medicine?"

The idea that humor lightens the burdens of the day and helps us cope with stress has been with us for millenia (Lefcourt & Martin, 1986). Consider the biblical maxim "a merry heart doeth good like a medicine" (Proverbs 17:22).

Sigmund Freud regarded humor as "the highest of [the] defensive processes" (1960, p. 233). According to Freud, "The essence of humor is that one spares oneself the [emotional responses] to which the situation would naturally give rise and overrides with a jest the possibility of such an emotional display" (1959, p. 216). Rollo May, a phenomenological psychotherapist, suggested that humor has the function of "preserving the sense of self. [Humor] is the healthy way of feeling a distance between one's self and the problem, a way of standing off and looking at one's problem with perspective" (1953, p. 61).

The well-known writer and editor Norman Cousins (1979) recently recovered from a lengthy bout with a painful illness. He reported that ten minutes of belly laughter had a powerful anesthetic effect, allowing him to sleep for at least two hours without analgesic medication. Laughter also appeared to reduce his inflammation, a finding that has led some writers to speculate that laughter might stimulate the output of endorphins within the body. But the benefits of humor might also be explained in terms of the sudden cognitive shifts they entail and the emotional changes that accompany them (Dixon, 1980). Levine (1977) simply notes that humor provides pleasure and affords us a way of enjoying things and expressing ideas that might otherwise be forbidden.

Until recently, the benefits of humor were largely speculative and anecdotal. But an important psychological study of the moderating effects of humor on stress was run by Canadian psychologists Rod Martin and Herbert Lefcourt (1983). The researchers administered a negative-life-events checklist and a measure of mood disturbance to college students. The mood-disturbance measure also yielded a stress score. In addition, the students were given self-report scales concerning their sense of humor and behavioral assessments of their ability to produce humor under stressful conditions. Overall, there was a significant relationship between negative life events and stress scores; that is, high accumulations of negative life events predicted higher levels of stress. However, students with a greater sense of humor and who produced humor in difficult situations were less affected by negative life events than other students. Humor, that is, apparently played its assumed historic stress-buffering role.

Goal-Directedness versus Playfulness

Research by Rod Martin and his colleagues (1987) suggests that the same amounts of stress that may disturb us during the workweek may be perceived as pleasant on the weekend, or vice versa! The issue is whether we are in a goal-directed or playful frame of mind. When we are focusing on achieving goals, we tend also to be serious-minded and avoidant of arousal. In such a state, moderate and high levels of body arousal are perceived as interfering with goal attainment; as a consequence, they are stressful, as measured by the amount of cortisol (a corticosteroid secreted by the adrenal cortex) in the saliva (Martin et al., 1987). But when we are oriented toward playfulness, our behavior is more spontaneous and we tend to seek at least moderate levels of arousal. The same person who finds moderate levels of arousal stressful when goal-directed can find low levels of arousal stressful when in a playful mode.

Many of us switch back and forth between goal-directed and playful modes, depending on our situations. But a number of individuals tend to seek moderate to high levels of arousal most of the time. They are referred to as sensation seekers.

Sensation Seeking Cliff is a couch potato, content to watch TV shows for most of the day, but P. J. loves the tightness in his throat when he pushes his motorcycle across back trails at breakneck speeds. Ally enjoys jogging a couple of miles, but Liz is at her peak when she's catching the big wave or diving freefall from airplanes. P. J. and Liz are sensation seekers.

Whereas the same person may move back and forth between goal-directed and playful states, sensation seekers generally aim to achieve moderate to high levels of body arousal. They are comfortable at levels of arousal that would be perceived as stressful by other people.

Zuckerman and his colleagues (1978) find four factors involved in sensation seeking:

1. Seeking of thrill and adventure,
2. Disinhibition (that is, the tendency to act out on impulses),
3. Seeking of experience, and
4. Susceptibility to boredom.

Other studies show that high-sensation seekers are less tolerant of sensory deprivation. They are also more likely to become involved in drugs and sexual experiences, to show public drunkenness, and to volunteer for high-risk activities and unusual experiments (Kohn et al., 1979; Malatesta et al., 1981; Zuckerman, 1974).

Consider some of the adjustment problems encountered by married couples who differ markedly in the levels of arousal they seek. Couch-potato Cliff would bore Liz to distraction, and Liz would have Cliff's "heart in his mouth" perpetually. Also consider the importance of Cliff and Liz being placed in the proper work environments. Cliff would not fare well as an air-traffic controller, and Liz would wither in a routine office job.

Do you have sensation-seeking tendencies? The nearby items from Marvin Zuckerman's sensation-seeking scale may afford you some insight.

Predictability

It appears that being able to predict the onset of a stressor moderates its impact upon us. Predictability allows us to brace ourselves for the inevitable and, in many cases, permits us to plan ways of coping with it. As we saw in the section on pain management, people who have accurate knowledge of medical procedures and what they will feel cope with pain more effectively than people who do not (e.g., Shipley et al., 1978; Staub et al., 1971). Experiments also show that crowding is less aversive when we are forewarned

QUESTIONNAIRE

Are You a Sensation Seeker?

Are you content reading or watching TV all day, or must you catch the big wave or bounce the bike across the dunes of the Mohave Desert? For a number of years, University of Delaware psychologist Marvin Zuckerman (1980) has been working with sensation-seeking scales that measure the level of stimulation or arousal a person will seek.

To gain insight into your own sensation-seeking tendencies, try this shortened version of one of Zuckerman's sensation-seeking scales. For each of the thirteen items, circle the choice, A or B, that best describes your behavior, tastes, or attitudes. Then compare your responses to those in the answer key at the end of the chapter.

1. A. I would like a job that requires a lot of traveling.
   B. I would prefer a job in one location.
2. A. I am invigorated by a brisk, cold day.
   B. I can't wait to get indoors on a cold day.
3. A. I get bored seeing the same old faces.
   B. I like the comfortable familiarity of everyday friends.
4. A. I would prefer living in an ideal society in which everyone is safe, secure, and happy.
   B. I would have preferred living in the unsettled days of our history.
5. A. I sometimes like to do things that are a little frightening.
   B. A sensible person avoids activities that are dangerous.
6. A. I would not like to be hypnotized.
   B. I would like to have the experience of being hypnotized.
7. A. The most important goal in life is to live it to the fullest and experience as much as possible.
   B. The most important goal in life is to find peace and happiness.
8. A. I would like to try parachute jumping.
   B. I would never want to try jumping out of a plane, with or without a parachute.
9. A. I enter cold water gradually, giving myself time to get used to it.
   B. I like to dive or jump right into the ocean or a cold pool.
10. A. When I go on a vacation, I prefer the comfort of a good room and bed.
    B. When I go on a vacation, I prefer the change of camping out.
11. A. I prefer people who are emotionally expressive even if they are a bit unstable.
    B. I prefer people who are calm and even-tempered.
12. A. A good painting should shock or jolt the senses.
    B. A good painting should give one a feeling of peace and security.
13. A. People who ride motorcycles must have some kind of unconscious need to hurt themselves.
    B. I would like to drive or ride a motorcycle.

as to how crowding might make us feel (Baum et al., 1981; Fisher & Baum, 1980; Paulus & Matthews, 1980; Langer & Saegert, 1977).

On the other hand, there is a relationship between personality factors, such as the desire to assume control over one's situation, and the usefulness of information about impending stressors (Lazarus & Folkman, 1984). It seems that predictability is of greater benefit to **"internals"**—that is, to people who desire exercise of control over their situations—than to **"externals."**

Animal Research   Animal research tends to support the view that there are advantages to predictability, especially when predictability allows one to exercise direct control over a stressor (Weinberg & Levine, 1980). For example, Weiss (1972) found that providing laboratory rats with a signal that a stressor was approaching apparently buffered its impact.

"Internals." People who perceive the ability to attain reinforcements as largely within themselves.

"Externals." People who perceive the ability to attain reinforcements as largely outside themselves.

Weiss placed three sets of rats matched according to age and weight into individual soundproof cages, as shown in Figure 6.10. The rat on the left received electric shock following a signal. It could then terminate the shock by turning the wheel. The rat in the center was shocked in tandem with the rat to the left, but it received no warning signal and could do nothing to terminate the shock. The rat to the right received no signal and no electric shock. However, it was placed in the identical apparatus, including having electrodes attached to its tail, to control for any effects of this unnatural environment.

As shown in Figure 6.11, shock led to ulceration in the rats—the definition of stressful experience in this study. The rats to the right, which received no signal and no shock, showed hardly any ulceration. Rats that received shock without warning showed greatest ulceration. Rats given warning signals and allowed to terminate the shock also developed ulcers, but to a significantly lesser degree.

The Weiss study suggests that inescapable stressors may be less harmful to us when they are predictable and when we act purposefully upon their arrival. The predictability of a stressor is to some degree a situational variable. But if we learn what we can about the sources of stress in our lives—concurrent and impending—and commit ourselves to regulating them as best we can, we may, like Weiss's warned subjects, be able to brace ourselves and plan effective responses. We may not avert stress completely, but we may buffer its impact.

Social Support

Social support, like psychological hardiness, seems to buffer the effects of stress (Cohen & Wills, 1985; Pagel & Becker, 1987; Rook & Dooley, 1985). Although social support is a situational variable, it should be noted that we can make the choice of actively seeking such support. As a matter of fact, children who thrive despite environmental hardships show an uncanny knack

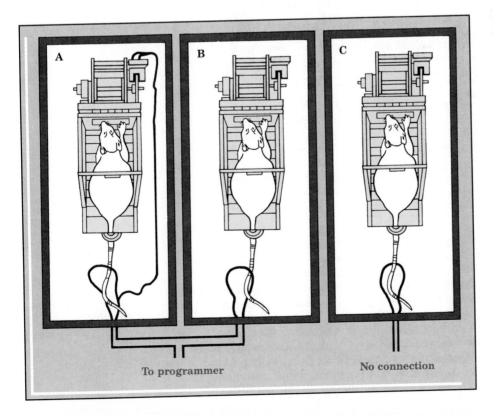

FIGURE 6.10   The Weiss Study

The rat on the left is signaled prior to delivery of an electric shock, and may terminate the shock by turning the wheel. The rat in the center receives shocks of the same duration and intensity as the rat on the left, but is not signaled prior to shock or capable of taking any action to terminate the shock. The rat on the right receives no signals and no shocks.

A   B   C

To programmer   No connection

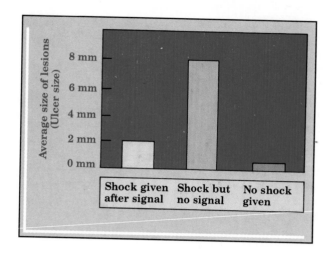

FIGURE 6.11 The Stressful Effect of Unpredictability on Ulcer Formation in Rats

for seeking out the support of adults—before their fourth birthdays (Farber & Egeland, 1987). Social support, in turn, helps the child behave more resiliently.

Writing in the context of handling stress on the job, James House (1981, 1984) identifies four kinds of social support that can help us cope with stress. Fiore (1980) adds a fifth. Altogether, these forms of social support include:

1. *Emotional concern.* Emotional concern involves listening to people's problems and expressing feelings of sympathy, caring, understanding, and reassurance.
2. *Instrumental aid.* Instrumental aid includes the material supports and services that make adaptive behavior possible. For example, after a disaster the government may arrange for low-interest loans so that survivors can rebuild. Foodstuffs, medicines, arrangement for temporary living quarters are further examples.
3. *Information.* This form of support involves giving people cognitive guidance and advice that will enhance their abilities to cope. Seeking of information as to how to cope is a primary motivation for undertaking psychotherapy or talking with experienced grandparents and religious personnel.
4. *Appraisal.* Appraisal is the provision of feedback from others on how one is doing. This kind of support involves helping people interpret, or "make sense of," what has happened to them. As noted by psychologist George Kelly (see Chapter 2), there may not always be one correct way of construing events, but some ways are more useful or convenient than others.
5. *Socializing.* Beneficial effects are derived from socializing itself, even in ways that are not oriented toward solving problems (Fiore, 1980). Examples include simple conversation, recreation, even going shopping with another person.

Research shows that social support moderates the impact of stress in situations ranging from problems at work to technological disasters. Consider the "nuclear accident" at the Three Mile Island nuclear plant in Pennsylvania. Nearby residents who had solid networks of social support—close relatives and friends with whom they could share the experience—reported less stress than those who did not (Fleming et al., 1982).

Psychologists know that it is useful for people who encounter stress to get together and talk about their ideas and feelings so that they can give one another support. Let us return once more to the effects of crowding. When compared with men who are crowded in with other men, women find being crowded in with women less aversive. An experiment by Karlin suggests that the effects of the stress of crowding are moderated for women because women feel freer to talk to one another and share their feelings about noxious events (Karlin et al., 1976). Men who conform to the tough, independent masculine stereotype tend to keep a "stiff upper lip." Women are thus more likely to form supportive social networks that provide advantages for adjustment.

It also seems that people who receive social support may live longer, as was found in studies of Alameda County, California (Berkman & Syme, 1979; Berkman & Breslow, 1983) and Tecumseh, Michigan (House, Robbins, & Metzner, 1982). In the Tecumseh study, 2,754 adults were followed from 1967 through 1979. Over this 12-year period, the mortality rate was significantly lower for men who were married, who regularly attended meetings of voluntary associations, and who frequently engaged in social leisure activities. Women with lower mortality rates frequently attended church and watched *less television* than their shorter-lived counterparts! Before jumping to the conclusions that marriage saves lives and that television kills, remember that these findings are correlational. It might be that men who get married are also in some ways more stable or more likely to take care of themselves. Similarly, women who are "addicted" to "the tube" might be more sedentary than other women, and activity and exercise have a number of healthful benefits. And what of church-going? Does church attendance itself benefit women or do the factors that contribute to regular church-going (social involvement and personal stability might be two) add on the years? What other hypotheses can you develop?

In this chapter we have explored the nature of stress, our responses to stress, and factors that moderate the impact of stress. In the next chapter we expand some of these ideas in our discussion of stress-related illnesses. In Chapter 8 we examine the ways in which stress apparently contributes to a number of psychological disorders, and in Chapters 9 and 10 we discuss various psychological methods for coping with stress actively and effectively.

■ Summary

1. **What is stress? What are some of the sources of stress?** Stress is the demand made on an organism to adjust. Whereas some stress is desirable ("eustress") to keep us alert and occupied, too much stress can tax our adjustive capacities and contribute to physical illness. Sources of stress include daily hassles, life changes, pain, frustration, conflict, and Type A behavior.

2. **What is the difference between daily hassles and life changes?** Daily hassles are regularly encountered sources of aggravation or annoyance. Life changes occur on an intermittent basis and may be positive (such as a major achievement or a vacation) as well as negative

3. **How do daily hassles and life changes affect us?** Hassles and life changes require adjustment, although negative life changes are more taxing than positive life changes. People who "earn" more than 300 life-change units within a year, according to the Holmes and Rahe scale, are at high risk for medical and psychological disorders.

4. **What are the limitations of the data on daily hassles, life changes, and illness?** The data on these relationships are correlational, however, and not experimental. Therefore, it is possible that people about to develop illnesses encounter more hassles or lead life-styles characterized by more life changes. Also, the degree of stress imposed by an event is linked to the individual's cognitive appraisal of that event.

5. **What are pain and discomfort, and how do they affect us?** Pain originates at a source of body injury and is transmitted to the brain. Pain and discomfort impair our ability to perform, especially when severe demands are made on the heels of a traumatic experience.

6. **What are some psychological methods of pain management?** These methods include provision of accurate information about the source, intensity, and duration of the pain; distraction and fantasy; hypnosis; relaxation training; coping with irrational beliefs; and social support.

7. **What is frustration?** Frustration results from having unattainable goals or from barriers to reaching our goals.

8. **What kinds of conflict are there?** Conflict results from opposing motives. We often vacillate when we are in conflict. Approach-approach conflicts are least stressful. Multiple approach-avoidance conflicts are most complex. Making decisions is often the way out of conflict. We can use the balance sheet to help list and weigh the pluses and minuses for the alternatives available to us.

9. **What is Type A behavior, and how does it affect us?** Type A behavior is characterized by aggressiveness, a sense of time urgency, and competitiveness. Type A people are more aggressive and more reluctant to relinquish control or power than are Type B's. Type A people also respond to challenge with higher blood pressure than Type B's, and evidence at to whether Type A's are at greater risk for heart attacks is mixed.

10. **What are some environmental stressors?** Environmental stressors include natural disasters, technological disasters, high noise levels, air pollution, extremes of temperature, and crowding.

11. **What is the general adaptation syndrome (GAS)?** Hans Selye suggested that the general adaptation syndrome is triggered by perception of a stressor and consists of three stages: alarm, resistance, and exhaustion stages.

12. **What is the role of the endocrine system in the body's response to stress?** In response to stress, the hypothalamus and pituitary glands secrete hormones which stimulate the adrenal cortex to release cortisol and other corticosteroids. Corticosteroids help the body resist stress by fighting inflammations and allergic reactions. Adrenalin and norepinephrine are also secreted by the adrenal medulla, and adrenalin arouses the body by activating the sympathetic division of the autonomic nervous system.

13. **What is the role of the autonomic nervous system (ANS) in the body's response to stress?** The sympathetic division of the ANS is highly active during the alarm and resistance stages of the GAS, and is characterized by rapid heartbeat and respiration rate, release of stores of sugar, muscle tension, and other responses that spend the body's stores of energy. The parasympathetic division of the ANS predominates during the exhaustion stage of the GAS and is characterized by responses, such as digestive processes, that help restore the body's reserves of energy.

14. **What are some of our emotional responses to stress?** Emotional responses to stress include anxiety, anger, and depression. Anxiety involves sympathetic ANS activity. Trait anxiety is a personality variable, while state anxiety is situational. Anger is a response to frustration and social provocations. Depression involves predominantly parasympathetic ANS activity and is a response to a loss, to failure, or to prolonged stress.

15. **What are some of our cognitive responses to stress?** According to the Yerkes-Dodson law, high levels of arousal—as due to stress—can impair cognitive functioning on complex tasks but facilitate cognitive performance on simple tasks. Stress can also distract us from focusing on the tasks at hand.

16. **What are our behavioral responses to stress?** Behavioral responses to stress are referred to as coping. Defensive coping methods decrease the immediate impact of a stressor and may grant us time to marshall our resources. However, there is usually a personal or social cost to defensive coping, as found in socially inappropriate behavior, withdrawal, or self-deception. Direct or active coping methods manipulate the environment

to reduce or remove sources of stress, or else they involve changing our cognitive or physiological responses to unavoidable stress so that the harmfulness of the stress is decreased.

17. **How do self-efficacy expectancies moderate the impact of stress?** Self-efficacy expectancies—our beliefs that we can cope successfully—encourage us to persist in difficult tasks and to endure pain and discomfort.

18. **What is psychological hardiness, and how does it help us cope with stress?** Psychological hardiness is characterized by commitment, challenge, and control. Persons with an internal locus of control ("internals") endure stress more successfully than people with an external locus of control ("externals"). Internals seek information about their situations, which increases the chances of coping successfully.

19. **Does humor help us cope with stress?** Yes. A sense of humor, and particularly the ability to produce humor under stress, buffer the impact of negative life events.

20. **Are there times when we *seek* stress, or is stress always aversive?** Yes, we may seek stress from time to time. When we are in a goal-directed mode of functioning, we tend to be serious-minded and to try to decrease the stress impinging on us by lowering our levels of arousal. However, when we are in a playful mode, we may seek to increase the amount of arousal we experience.

21. **How does predictability moderate the impact of stress?** Predictability buffers stress by allowing us to brace ourselves for stressors and, sometimes, to plan effective ways of coping.

22. **How does social support moderate the impact of stress?** Social support buffers the impact of stress in five ways: expression of emotional concern, instrumental aid, provision of information, appraisal, and socialization activities.

■ TRUTH OR FICTION REVISITED

Too much of a good thing can make you ill. This may often be the case. An excessive number of life changes, even positive life changes, can be stressful, and stress is related to physical illness.

Commuting on the freeway elevates our blood pressure. True—especially when traffic is heavy.

Many people create their own sources of stress. True. As a couple of examples, some do through irrational perfectionistic attitudes, and others by means of Type A behavior.

Our own bodies produce chemicals that are similar in function to the narcotic morphine. True. They are called *endorphins*—the contraction of endogenous morphine.

Video games help children cancer patients cope with the side effects of chemotherapy. True. The games distract them from unpleasant body sensations.

Children in noisy classrooms do not learn to read as well as children in quiet classrooms. True, according to research carried out near an airport in Los Angeles.

Hot temperatures make us hot under the collar—that is, they prompt aggression. True—up to a point. But it may be that when temperatures rise into the high 90s and the 100s, we "cool it" by ourselves.

We leave larger tips at restaurants when the sun is streaming through the windows. True. Sunshine, temperature, and humidity all influence our moods, and our generosity.

Auto fumes may lower your children's IQ's. True. Auto exhaust contains chemicals that can impair learning, memory, and other cognitive functions.

Crowding a third roommate into a dorm room built for two usually makes somebody unhappy. True. According to the "tripling effect," two frequently form an alliance against the third.

If quarterbacks get too "psyched up" for a big game, their performance on the field may suffer. True. Quarterbacks have a complex job to do, and high levels of arousal impair performance on complex tasks.

Fear can give you indigestion. True. Fear is characterized by sympathetic arousal, and sympathetic arousal inhibits digestive processes.

Some people drink alcohol in order to provide themselves with a handicap in their ability to cope with stress. True. By doing so they provide themselves with an external attribution for failure.

The belief that we can handle stress is linked to lower levels of adrenalin in the bloodstream. True. As a result, we are likely to feel less nervous.

Some people are psychologically hardier than others. True. Psychological hardiness is characterized by commitment, challenge, and control.

A sense of humor helps buffer the effects of stress. True, according to research by Martin and Lefcourt.

Single men live longer. False. According to a long-term study carried out in Tecumseh, Michigan, married men outlive their unmarried peers.

■ Answer Key for Social Readjustment Rating Scale

Add all the scores in to Total column to arrive at your final score.

Interpretation

Your final score is indicative of the amount of stress you have experience during the past 12 months:

From 0 to 1500 = Minor stress
1501–3500 = Mild stress
3501–5500 = Moderate stress
5501 and above = Major stress

Research has shown that the probability of enountering physical illness within the *following* year is related to the amount of stress experiences during the *past* year. That is, college students who experienced minor stress have a 28 percent chance of becoming ill; mild stress, a 45 percent chance; moderate stress, a 70 percent chance; and major stress, an 82 percent chance. Moreover, the seriousness of the illness also increases with the amount of stress.

It should be recognized that these percentages reflect previous research with college students. Do not assume that if you have encountered a great deal of stress you are "doomed" to illness. Also keep in mind that a number of psychological factors moderate the impact of stress, as described in this chapter. For example, psychologically hardy college students would theoretically withstand the same amount of stress that could enhance the risk of illness for nonhardy individuals.

■ Answer Key for "Are You Type A or B?" Questionnaire

Yesses suggest the Type A behavior pattern, which is marked by a sense of time urgency and constant struggle. In appraising your "type," you need not be overly concerned with the precise number of "yes" answers; we have no normative data for you. But as Friedman and Rosenman (1974, p. 85) note, you should have little trouble spotting yourself as "hard core" or "moderately afflicted"—that is, if you are honest with yourself.

■ Answer Key for the "Locus of Control Scale"

Place a checkmark (√) in the blank space in the scoring key, below, each time your answer agrees with the answer in the key. The number of checkmarks is your total score.

Interpreting Your Score

Low Scorers (0–8).   About one respondent in three earns a score of from 0 to 8. Such respondents tend to have an internal locus of control. They see themselves as responsible for the reinforcements they attain (and fail to attain) in life.

Average Scorers (9–16).   Most respondents earn from 9 to 16 points. Average scorers may see themselves as partially in control of their lives. Perhaps they see themselves as in control at work, but not in their social lives—or vice versa.

High Scorers (17–40).   About 15 percent of respondents attain scores of 17 or above. High scorers tend largely to see life as a game of chance, and success as a matter of luck or the generosity of others.

■ Answer Key for Sensation-Seeking Scale

Since this is a shortened version of a questionnaire, no norms are available. However, the following answers are suggestive of sensation seeking:

1. A	**6.** B	**10.** B
2. A	**7.** A	**11.** A
3. A	**8.** A	**12.** A
4. B	**9.** B	**13.** B
5. A		

Psychology and Physical Health

7

At any given moment, myriads of microscopic warriors within our bodies are carrying out search-and-destroy missions against foreign agents.

Most headaches are caused by muscle tension.

Stress can influence the course of cancer.

Some people inherit a predisposition toward becoming dependent on alcohol.

Heroin was once used as a cure for addiction to morphine.

Coca-Cola once "added life" by using cocaine.

Cigarette smokers are less aware than nonsmokers of the perils of smoking.

Cigarette smokers tend to smoke more when they are under stress.

LSD-users can have flashbacks at any time.

Your diet can influence the likelihood that you will contract cancer.

Obese people have more fat cells than normal-weight people.

Obese people are more responsive to their stomach contractions than normal-weight people.

People who sleep nine hours or more a night tend to be lazy and happy-go-lucky.

We tend to act out our forbidden fantasies in our dreams.

Young people aged 18–29 are more likely to exercise than senior citizens.

Medical patients should be told as little as possible about their illnesses and why they are being given certain medicines.

Patients are more likely to comply with "doctor's orders" when they are issued by an authoritarian physician.

Mark Twain once quipped that it was easy to give up smoking—he had done it a dozen times. The other day, your authors sat down and tried to catalogue some of the behavioral changes they and their spouses had made over the years—including giving up smoking—in order to enhance their physical health. We won't admit which of the four of us did what or when, but we'll try to give you the flavor of things.

Two of us have quit smoking cigarettes in order to reduce the chances of coronary heart disease and the threat of cancers of the lungs, pancreas, bladder, larynx, and esophagus. The other two never took up smoking. The two of us who smoked gave it up Mark Twain's dozen times—between us.

One of us took up running in order to foster cardiovascular fitness, decrease the probability of coronary heart disease, take off a few pounds, and firm muscles. He started out huffing and puffing to get up to a single ten-minute mile. After about a year he was running twelve seven-and-one-half minute miles. Then he developed sharp knee pain from abrading cartilege, suspended running for a few months, and now runs five eight-minute miles about four times per week—unless the weather is bad, in which case he remains indoors and feels guilty.

One of us took up weight lifting to build muscles and enhance his sense of self-efficacy. To assure himself of the best, he splurged $3,500 on Universal equipment. He rapidly worked up to four one-hour workouts a week and built up his chest and arms. Then a new baby forced him to consign his equipment to the basement. Despite the best of intentions to go down to the dungeon to work out, there the grand investment sits, gathering dust.

One of us took up exercise cycling in order to foster cardiovascular fitness, decrease the probabilities of coronary heart disease, take off a few pounds, and firm muscles. She spent $1,500 on a Lifecycle. She progressed gradually from three-minute workouts at a difficulty factor of one (the easiest level) to twelve-minute workouts at a moderate difficulty factor of three.

One of us bought Jane Fonda **aerobic** workout video tapes, Raquel Welch aerobic workout video tapes, and—why not?—Debbie Reynolds workout video tapes in order to foster cardiovascular fitness, decrease the probabilities of coronary heart disease, take off a few pounds, and firm muscles. After the tapes were memorized and a spot from running in place was worn out on the living room carpet, the tapes started collecting dust.

Three of us go for regular medical checkups. (No comment on the fourth.)

Two of us decreased their intake of fats and increased their intake of fiber and vitamins in order to decrease the risk of cancers of the digestive tract.

One of us stopped eating food with nitrate preservatives, such as frankfurters. Nitrates form nitrites, a suspected **carcinogen.** Nitrites, in turn, form nitrosamines, considered potent carcinogens. Another of us learned that ascorbic acid (vitamin C) scavenges nitrites, preventing formation of nitrosamines. And so he pops a couple of vitamin C pills whenever he eats hot dogs, even though evidence as to the effectiveness of vitamin C as a cancer preventative is fairly weak (Newberne & Suphakarn, 1983). The other two of us think that the first two are fanatics and down their occasional hot dogs with abandon.

Two of us upped their milk intake after learning that calcium might serve to protect against **osteoporosis** later in life and against certain kinds of cancers of the digestive tract.

One of us became a carrot and sweet-potato "freak" after learning that vitamin A and beta-carotene (a form of vitamin A found in plentiful supply in these and some other vegetables) was linked to a "slightly lower than average incidence of cancer" (Peto et al., 1981, p. 207). More recent studies (e.g., by Hinds et al., 1984; Stehr et al., 1985) suggest that moderate amounts of

Aerobic. Referring to exercise that requires sustained increase in oxygen consumption.

Carcinogen. An agent that gives rise to cancerous changes.

Osteoporosis. A condition caused by calcium deficiency and characterized by brittleness of the bones.

these vitamins afford some protection against stomach and lung cancers—particularly in men.

Three of us have counted calories. Counted and counted.

The one of us who avoids foods with nitrate preservatives also took up aerobic exercise, increased fiber intake (via fruits and vegetables and whole-grain breads), decreased fats, and swallows moderate doses of multivitamins. She has lost weight, is very firm, seems to have fewer colds than the rest of us, and has developed a strong sense of self-efficacy. One of her former friends remarked, "At least she doesn't enjoy much of what she eats."

And so it goes.

In recent years knowledge of the benefits of exercise and the hazards of various substances has been amassed. Healthfood stores have opened in every shopping mall. The fitness craze is upon us. Large numbers of us have taken to exercise and modified our diets in an effort to enhance our physical well-being and attractiveness. Some of us have even kept to our regimens.

■ Health Psychology

During the last several years a new field of psychology has also emerged. It is dedicated to issues such as encouraging exercise and proper nutrition. It is called **health psychology,** and it studies the relationships between psychological factors (e.g., overt behavior patterns, emotions, stress, beliefs, and attitudes) and the prevention and treatment of physical illness. Health psychologists have investigated the ways in which stress affects the body's immune system, helping pave the way for the development of physical disorders ranging from hypertension to ulcers. They have examined the ways in which our behavior patterns—such as smoking, drinking, and exercise—can help us prevent or cope with physical disorders, including cardiovascular disorders and cancer. They have also explored the psychology of being sick—factors that induce us to seek medical advice, how we conceptualize illness, and how we "play" the sick role. They have also identified many of the factors that enter into a good physician–patient relationship and those that foster compliance with medical advice.

These are the topics that we pursue in this chapter.

■ The Immune System

Given the complexities of our bodies and the fast pace of scientific change, it is common for us to think of ourselves as highly dependent on trained professionals, such as physicians, to cope with illness. But we actually do a great deal for ourselves by means of our **immune system.**

Functions of the Immune System

One way in which we combat physical disorders is by producing white blood cells that routinely engulf and kill **pathogens** such as bacteria, fungi, and viruses; wornout body cells; even cells that have changed into cancerous cells. White blood cells are technically termed **leucocytes.** Leucocytes carry on microscopic warfare. They engage in search-and-destroy missions in which they "recognize" and then eliminate foreign agents and unhealthy cells.

A second function of the immune system is to "remember" foreign agents to facilitate future combat. The foreign agents that are recognized and destroyed by leucocytes are called **antigens.** While some leucocytes kill antigens, others operate by producing **antibodies,** or specialized proteins, that bind to their antigens and mark them for destruction. The immune system "remembers" how to battle these antigens by maintaining antibodies in the bloodstream, often for many years.

Health psychology. The field of psychology that studies the relationships between psychological factors (e.g., attitudes, beliefs, situational influences, and overt behavior patterns) and the prevention and treatment of physical health.

Immune system. The system of the body that recognizes and destroys foreign agents (antigens) that invade the body.

Pathogen. A microscopic organism (e.g., bacterium or virus) that can cause disease.

Leucocytes. (LOO-co-sites). White blood cells. (Derived from the Greek words *leukos,* meaning "white," and *kytos,* literally meaning "a hollow," but used to refer to cells.)

Antigen. A substance that stimulates the body to mount an immune-system response to it. (The contraction for *anti*body *gen*erator.)

Antibodies. Substances formed by white blood cells that recognize and destroy antigens.

Vaccination involves the introduction of a weakened form of an antigen (usually a bacteria or a virus) into the body, stimulating the production of antibodies. Antibodies can confer immunity for many years, in some cases for a lifetime. Smallpox has been eradicated by means of vaccination, and scientists are searching for a vaccine against the AIDS virus, which has so far proved resistant to medical treatment and nearly 100 percent fatal.

Inflammation is a third function of the immune system. When injury occurs, blood vessels in the area first contract (stemming bleeding) but then dilate. Dilation increases the flow of blood to the damaged area, causing the redness and warmth that characterize inflammation. The increased blood supply also brings in large numbers of white blood cells to combat invading microscopic life forms, such as bacteria, that might otherwise use the local damage as a point of entry into the body.

Vaccination. Purposeful infection with a small amount of an antigen so that in the future the immune system will recognize and efficiently destroy the antigen.

Inflammation. Increased blood flow to an injured area of the body, resulting in redness, warmth, and increased supply of white blood cells.

Psychoneuroimmunology. The field that studies the relationships between psychological factors (e.g., attitudes and overt behavior patterns) and the functioning of the immune system.

Effects of Stress on the Immune System

Health psychologists along with biologists and medical researchers have recently been exploring a new field of study that addresses the relationships between psychological factors and the immune system: **psychoneuroimmunology** (Schindler, 1985). One of the major concerns of psychoneuroimmunology is the effects of stress on the immune system.

In Chapter 6 it was noted that persistent stress can lead to exhaustion and loss of capacity to cope with the stressor. One of the reasons that stress eventually exhausts us is that it stimulates us to produce corticosteroids such as cortisol. Cortisol and related hormones suppress the functioning of the immune system. This suppression has negligible effects when corticosteroids are secreted intermittently, but persistent secretion impairs the immune system by decreasing inflammation and interfering with the formation of antibodies. As a consequence, susceptibility to illness increases.

Empirical Findings Concerning Stress–Immune-System Relationships Research supports the hypothesized links between stress and the immune system and also demonstrates the moderating effects of the psychological factors such as control and social support.

An experiment with laboratory rats and electric shock, for example, mirrored the method of Weiss (1972), as discussed in the previous chapter. But this time the dependent variable was activity of the immune system, not ulcer formation (Laudenslager et al., 1983). The rats were exposed to inevitable electric shocks, but, as in the Weiss study, one group of rats could engage in behavior that would terminate the shock. Rats who could *not* exert control over the stressor showed immune-system deficits, but the rats who could terminate the shock showed no decline in immune-system functioning.

One study with people focused on dental students (Jemmott et al., 1983). Students showed lower immune-system functioning, as measured by lower levels of antibodies in the saliva, during stressful school periods than immediately following vacations. Student with many friends showed relatively less suppression of the immune system. Social support, that is, apparently buffered school stresses.

Another study with students found that the stress of examinations depressed immune-system response to the Epstein-Barr virus, which causes fatigue and other physical problems (Kiecolt-Glaser et al., 1984). Moreover, students who were lonely showed greater suppression of the immune system than students who had more social support. In a study of elderly people it was found that relaxation training, which decreases sympathetic activity, and training in coping skills *improve* immune-system functioning (Kiecolt-Glaser et al., 1985). We shall detail training in relaxation and coping skills in Chapters 9 and 10.

A question remains as to whether there is any relationship between the *type* of stressor encountered and the physical disorder that is developed. That is, do stressors generally suppress the immune system so that we are more susceptible to any and all disorders? Or do particular stressors tend to give rise to specific disorders? As we shall see in our discussion of physical disorders and stress, the evidence is not always clear.

■ Physical Disorders and Stress

Headaches

Headaches are among the most common stress-related physical disorders. According to Bonica (1980), 45 million U.S. residents suffer from severe headaches.

Muscle-Tension Headache   The single most frequent kind of headache is the muscle-tension headache. We are likely to contract muscles in the shoulders, neck, forehead, and scalp during the first two stages of the GAS. Persistent stress can lead to persistent contraction of the muscles of the scalp, face, neck, and shoulders, giving rise to persistent muscle-tension headaches. Such headaches uually come on gradually. They are most often characterized by dull, steady pain on both sides of the head and feelings of tightness or pressure.

Migraine Headaches   Most other headaches, including the severe migraine headache, are vascular in nature—stemming from changes in the blood supply to the head. **Migraine headaches** have preheadache phases, during which the arteries that supply the head with blood are constricted, decreasing blood flow, and headache phases, during which the arteries are dilated, increasing the flow of blood. Migraine attacks are frequently accompanied by exaggerated sensitivity to light; loss of appetite, nausea, and vomiting; sensory and motor disturbances, such as loss of balance; and changes in mood. The so-called common migraine headache is identified by sudden onset and throbbing on one side of the head. The so-called classic migraine is known by sensory and motor disturbances that precede the pain. The origins of migraine headaches are not fully clear, but it is believed that they can be induced by barometric pressure; pollen; specific drugs; the chemical monosodium glutamate (MSG), which is often used to enhance the flavor of food; red wine (Dean, 1988); and the hormonal changes of the period prior to and during menstruation.

Regardless of the original source of the headache, we can unwittingly propel ourselves into a vicious cycle: Headache pain is a stressor that can lead us to increase, rather than relax, muscle tension in the neck, shoulders, scalp, and face. In this way we may compound headache pain.

Treatment   As noted in Chapter 6, aspirin and ibuprofen frequently decrease pain, including headache pain, by inhibiting the production of the prostaglandins that help initiate transmission of pain messages to the brain. Behavioral methods can also help. Progressive relaxation (described in Chapter 10), which focuses on decreasing muscle tension, has been shown to be highly effective in relieving the pain of muscle-tension headaches (Blanchard et al., 1985, 1987; Teders et al., 1984). Biofeedback training that alters the flow of blood to the head has been used effectively to treat migraine headache (Blanchard et al., 1980, 1982, 1985, 1987). People who are sensitive to MSG or red wine can ask that MSG be left out of their dishes and can switch to a white wine.

Why, under stress, do some of us develop ulcers, others develop hypertension, and still others suffer no bodily problems? In the following sections we see that there may be an interaction between stress and predisposing biological and psychological differences between individuals (Davison & Neale, 1986; Walker, 1983).

Hypertension

Ten to 30 percent of U.S. residents are afflicted by **hypertension,** or abnormally high blood pressure (Seer, 1979). When high blood pressure has no identifiable causes, it is referred to as *essential hypertension.* Arousal of the sympathetic division of the ANS heightens the blood pressure, and, when we are very stressed, we may believe that we can feel our blood pressure "pounding through the roof." But these ideas are usually misleading. Although most people believe that they would be able to recognize symptoms of hypertension, most of the time we cannot (Baumann & Leventhal, 1985; Meyer et al., 1985). For this reason, it is important to have our blood pressure checked regularly.

Hypertension predisposes victims to other cardiovascular disorders such as arteriosclerosis, heart attacks, and strokes (Berkman et al., 1983). Blood pressure rises in situations in which people must be constantly on guard against threats, whether in combat, in the work place, or in the home. Blood pressure appears to be higher among blacks than whites, and also higher among people who hold in, rather than express, feelings of anger (Diamond, 1982; Harburg et al., 1973).

Treatment High blood pressure can frequently be controlled by means of medicine, but because of the lack of symptoms, many patients do not take their medication reliably. Dietary components, particularly sodium (salt), can heighten blood pressure.

Behavioral methods such as progressive relaxation also show promise in the treatment of hypertension (Agras et al., 1983). Meditation is another psychological method (to be described in Chapter 10) that seems to lower the blood pressure of many hypertensive individuals (Benson et al., 1983). Meditators focus on a pleasant stimulus, such as the odor of incense or a special word or "mantra" that is mentally repeated; this allows concerns of the day to be placed on the back burner.

One study highlighted the powerful potential of dietary behavior modification in the treatment of hypertension with a group of 496 patients whose blood pressure had been normalized by medication for five years (Langford et al., 1985). The patients were taken off their medication and assigned to either a general weight-loss diet or a sodium-restricted diet; 72 percent of those in the weight-loss group and 78 percent of those in the sodium-restricted group were able to maintain their blood pressure at normal levels without medication.

Cardiovascular Disorders

Cardiovascular disorders cause nearly half the deaths in the U.S.A. (U.S. Department of Health and Human Services, 1984). Cardiovascular diseases include heart disease and disorders of the circulatory system, the most common of which is stroke.

There are basically four risk factors for cardiovascular disease:

1. *Family history.* People whose families show a history of cardiovascular disease are more likely to develop cardiovascular disease themselves (Feist & Brannon, 1988). It was surprising when running enthusiast James Fixx died a few years ago because he had been in such excellent condition. However, his family history of heart disease was against him, and it might be that his running had staved off death for many years.
2. *Physiological conditions.* Such conditions include hypertension and high levels of serum cholesterol.

3. *Behavior patterns.* Such patterns include smoking, overeating, and eating of food high in cholesterol, such as animal fats and coconut oils.
4. *Type A behavior.* Evidence is mixed as to whether the Type A behavior pattern—or one or more of its components—places people at risk for cardiovascular disorders. Still, it is worthy of consideration.

Eight- and ten-year longitudinal studies of people in Framingham, Massachusetts, found that men and women who showed the Type A behavior pattern were overall about twice as likely as their Type B counterparts to develop coronary heart disease (Haynes et al., 1980, 1983). Male Type A white-collar workers were about three times as likely as male Type B white-collar workers to develop coronary heart disease. An exception was found among older (65 to 74) male blue-collar workers; Type B's among this age and occupational-status group were at higher risk than Type A's. For women the white-collar–blue-collar distinction was not evident. Younger Type A women showed about 2.5 times the risk for coronary heart disease as compared with young Type B women, but the Type A–Type B difference in risk declined with age. There were no differences in incidence of coronary heart disease between working women and women who remained in the home.

Behavior Modification for Reducing Risk Factors   Once cardiovascular disease has been diagnosed, there are a number of medical treatments, including surgery and medication. However, persons who have not encountered cardiovascular disease, and those who have, can profit from behavior modification that is intended to reduce the risk factors. These methods include:

1. *Stopping smoking.* Methods will be described in Chapter 10.
2. *Weight control.* Methods will be described in Chapter 10.
3. *Reducing hypertension.*
4. *Lowering serum cholesterol.*
5. *Modifying Type A behavior.* Methods described in Chapter 10 can modify Type A behavior patterns and decrease the risk of heart attacks, even for people who have previously suffered heart attacks (Friedman & Ulmer, 1984; Roskies et al., 1986).

We can end this section with some encouraging news. A number of the risk factors involved in cardiovascular disorders, such as smoking and dietary factors, have been known for 25 years or more. It seems that the U.S. public has responded to this knowledge by making a number of changes in their lifestyles, so that the incidence of coronary heart disease has declined in recent years (Pell & Fayerweather, 1985; Stamler, 1985a, 1985b). Stamler also found that better-educated individuals are more likely to modify health-impairing behavior patterns and reap the benefits of change.

Ulcers

Ulcers may afflict one person in ten and cause as many as 10,000 deaths each year in the United States (Whitehead & Bosmajian, 1982). People who develop ulcers under stress often have higher pepsinogen levels than those who do not (Weiner et al., 1957), and heredity may contribute to pepsinogen level (Mirsky, 1958). Research with laboratory rats suggests that intense approach-avoidance conflict may also contribute to ulcers (Sawrey et al., 1956; Sawrey & Weisz, 1956).

Asthma

Asthma is a respiratory disorder which is often the result of an allergic reaction in which the main tubes of the windpipe—the bronchi—contract, making it difficult to breathe. Asthma has been linked to stress, but the link is controversial. In one study, for example, efforts to induce asthma attacks in sufferers by subjecting them to stress led to a slightly decreased air flow, but not to an actual attack (Weiss et al., 1976). Other evidence suggests that asthma sufferers can experience attacks in response to the suggestion that their air flow will become constricted (Luparello et al., 1971). In any event, in most cases the initial asthma attack follows on the heels of a respiratory infection (Alexander, 1981). Such evidence again suggests an interaction between the psychological and the physiological. There are some reports (e.g., by Rathus, 1973b) in which asthma sufferers have been helped by cognitive-behavioral methods in which they modify their self-efficacy expectancies concerning their ability to cope with asthma and engage in relaxed, regular breathing regimens.

Cancer

The term *cancer* refers not just to one illness, but to a number of disorders that afflict plants and animals as well as people. These disorders show the common feature of the development of abnormally changed, or mutant, cells that reproduce rapidly and rob the body of nutrients. Cancerous cells may take root anywhere, such as the blood (leukemia), bones, digestive tract, lungs, and genital organs. If not controlled early, the cancerous cells may metastasize—that is, establish colonies elsewhere in the body.

With all the talk of environmental toxins and the assorted hazards of contemporary life, one might expect that cancer rates have been skyrocketing. This is not the case. According to the National Institutes of Health (1985), cancers of the bladder, prostate, colon, and rectum have been stable since the 1940s. Cancer of the stomach has been declining. Lung cancer increased markedly between the 1940s and 1980, but has recently leveled off. However, a recent rise in cases among women has offset a decline among men. Smoking would seem to be the culprit. As women have entered the work force and taken managerial positions, they have increased their smoking. Men, meanwhile, have been smoking less.

Risk Factors   As with cardiovascular and many other disorders, people can inherit dispositions toward developing cancer (Moolgavkar, 1983). However, many behavior patterns markedly heighten the risk for cancer, such as smoking, drinking alcohol (especially in women), the ingestion of animal fats, sunbathing (which because of ultraviolet light causes skin cancer [Levy, 1985]), and, apparently, stress.

Stress and Cancer   In recent years, researchers have begun to uncover links between stress and cancer. For example, a study of children with cancer by Jacob and Charles (1980) revealed that a significant percentage had encountered severe life changes within a year of the diagnosis, often involving the death of a loved one or the loss of a close relationship. There are also numerous studies that connect stressful life events to the onset of cancer among adults. However, this research has been criticized in that it tends to be retrospective (Krantz et al., 1985). That is, cancer patients tend to be interviewed after their diseases have been diagnosed about events preceding their diagnoses and about their psychological well-being prior to the onset of the disease. Self-reports are confounded by problems in memory and other inaccuracies. Moreover, as noted earlier in the chapter, the causal relationships in such research are clouded. For example, development of the illness might have precipitated many of the stressful events. Stress, in other words, might have been the result of the illness rather than the cause.

As in so many other areas of psychology, experimental research has been conducted with rats and other animals that could not be conducted with humans. In one type of study, animals are injected with cancerous cells or with viruses that cause cancer and then exposed to a variety of conditions, so that we can determine whether or not these conditions influence the likelihood that the animals' immune systems will be able to fend off the antigens. Such experiments with rodents suggest that once cancer has affected the individual, stress can influence its course. In one study, for example, rats were implanted with small numbers of cancer cells so that their own immune systems would have a chance to successfully combat them (Visintainer et al., 1982). Some of the rats were then been exposed to inescapable shocks, whereas others were exposed to escapable shocks or to no shock. The rats exposed to the most stressful condition—the inescapable shock—were half as likely as the other rats to reject the cancer, and two times as likely to die from it.

In a study of this kind with mice, Riley (1981) studied the effects of a cancer-causing virus that can be passed from mothers to offspring by means of nursing. This virus usually produces breast cancer in 80 percent of female offspring by the time they have reached 400 days of age. Riley placed one group of female offspring at risk for cancer in a stressful environment of loud noises and noxious odors. Another group was placed in a less stressful environment. At the age of 400 days, 92 percent of the mice who developed under stressful conditions developed breast cancer, as compared to 7 percent of the controls. Moreover, the high-stress mice showed increases in "stress hormone," which depresses the functioning of the body's immune system, and lower blood levels of disease-fighting antibodies. However, the "bottom line" in this experiment is of major interest: By the time another 200 days had elapsed, the "low-stress" mice had nearly caught up to their "high-stress" peers in the incidence of cancer. Stress appears to have hastened the inevitable for many of these mice, but the ultimate outcomes for the high-risk rodents were not overwhelmingly influenced by stress.

And so it may be that while stress influences the timing of the onset of certain diseases, such as cancer, genetic predispositions toward disease and the presence of powerful antigens will in many or most cases eventually do their damage. An extreme expression of this position was recently expressed in *The New England Journal of Medicine*: "The inherent biology of [cancer] alone determines the prognosis, overriding the potentially mitigating influence of psychosocial factors" (Cassileth et al., 1985, p. 1555). Even if this pessimistic view is largely accurate, we can still do these things:

1. We can control our exposure to behavioral risk factors for cancer,
2. We can go for regular medical checkups so that we catch cancer early,
3. We can regulate the amount of stress impacting upon us, and,
4. If we are struck by cancer, we can "fight like hell."

Health psychologists have also found that the stressful feelings of depression and helplessness that often accompany the diagnosis of cancer can interfere with recovery among humans (Goldberg & Tull, 1984; Levy et al., 1985), perhaps by depressing the responsiveness of the patient's immune system. For example, a ten-year follow-up of breast cancer patients found a significantly higher survival rate for patients who met their diagnosis with anger and a "fighting spirit" rather than helplessness or stoic acceptance (Pettingale et al., 1985). Hospitalization itself is highly stressful because it reduces the patient's sense of control over his or her own fate (Peterson & Raps, 1984), and, if handled insensitively, it might further depress the patient's own ability to fight illnesses.

Health psychologists are also investigating the role of chronic stress in inflammatory diseases, such as arthritis; premenstrual distress; digestive diseases, such as colitis; even metabolic diseases such as diabetes and hypoglycemia. The relationships between behavior patterns, attitudes, and illness are complex and under intense study. With some stress-related illnesses, it may be that stress determines whether or not the person will contract the disease at all. In others, it may be that an optimal environment merely delays the inevitable, or that a stressful environment merely hastens the onset of the inevitable. Then, too, in different illnesses stress may have different effects on the patient's ability to recover. Let us now focus more on health-related behavior patterns per se.

■ Health-Related Behavior Patterns

Some of us are our own best friends. We pay attention to what we eat, we exercise regularly, and we monitor the sources of stress in our lives so that we can regulate their impact.

But some of us are our own worst enemies. Some of us share contaminated needles or engage in reckless sexual behavior despite knowledge that AIDS can be transmitted in these manners (Kolata, 1987). Many of us continue to eat foods high in cholesterol and fats despite our knowledge that we heighten the risk of developing coronary heart disease or cancer (Burros, 1988). Many teenagers engage in dangerous behaviors such as smoking, drinking, and reckless driving in the belief that they are invulnerable to harm (Goleman, 1987). And, of course, many of us continue to smoke even though we know full well that we are *not* invulnerable.

In this section we examine a number of our health-related behavior patterns. We begin our discussion with substance abuse (including smoking cigarettes). Then we consider nutritional patterns, sleep patterns, and activity patterns, and we see that there are ways in which we can do ourselves much more good than harm.

Substance Abuse and Dependence

The world is a supermarket of **psychoactive** substances, or drugs. The U.S.A. is flooded with hundreds of drugs that distort perceptions and change mood—drugs that take you up, let you down, and move you across town. Some people use drugs because their friends do, or because their parents tell them not to. Some are seeking pleasure, others are seeking inner truth.

Following a dropoff in popularity during the 1960s, alcohol has reasserted its dominance among drugs used on college campuses. Most college students have tried marijuana, and perhaps one in five smokes it regularly. Many U.S. residents take **depressants** to get to sleep at night and **stimulants** to get going in the morning. Heroin may literally be the opium of the lower classes. Cocaine was until recently the toy of the well-to-do, but price breaks have brought it into the lockers of high school students. Despite laws, moral pronouncements, medical warnings, and an occasional horror story, drugs are very much with us.

The American Psychiatric Association considers use of a substance abusive when it is continued for a period of at least one month despite the fact that it is causing or compounding a social, occupational, psychological, or physical problem (1987, p. 169). If you are missing school or work because you are drunk, or "sleeping it off," your behavior fits the definition of **substance abuse.** The amount of the drug you use is not the crucial factor. It is whether your pattern of use interferes with other areas of life.

Substance dependence is more severe than substance abuse. Dependence is shown by signs such as increased usage despite knowledge that the substance is interfering with your life and despite desire or efforts to cut down. Dependence is also characterized by orienting your life toward getting and using the substance, by tolerance, by frequent intoxication, and by withdrawal symptoms (American Psychiatric Association, 1987, pp. 166–168). **Tolerance** is the body's habituation to a drug, so that with regular usage higher doses are required to achieve similar effects. Dependence is physiological; there are characteristic withdrawal symptoms, or an **abstinence syndrome,** when the

Psychoactive. Having psychological effects.

Depressant. A drug that lowers the rate of activity of the nervous system.

Stimulant. A drug that increases the rate of activity of the nervous system.

Substance abuse. Continued use of a substance despite knowledge that it is dangerous or that it is linked to social, occupational, psychological, or physical problems.

Substance dependence. Dependence is shown by signs such as persistent use despite efforts to cut down, marked tolerance, and withdrawal symptoms.

Tolerance. Habituation to a drug, with the result that increasingly higher doses of the drug are needed to achieve similar effects.

Abstinence syndrome. A characteristic cluster of symptoms that results from sudden decrease in the level of usage of an addictive drug.

level of usage suddenly drops off. The abstinence syndrome for alcohol includes anxiety, tremors, restlessness, weakness, rapid pulse, and high blood pressure.

When doing without a drug, people who are *psychologically* dependent on it show signs of anxiety (shakiness, rapid pulse, and sweating are three) that overlap abstinence syndromes. And so they may believe that they are physiologically dependent on a drug when they are psychologically dependent. Still, symptoms of abstinence from certain drugs are unmistakably physiological. One is **delirium tremens** ("the DT's"), encountered by some chronic alcoholics when they suddenly lower intake. The DT's are characterized by heavy sweating, restlessness, general **disorientation,** and terrifying **hallucinations**—often of creepy, crawling animals.

Causal Factors in Substance Abuse and Dependence There are many reasons for substance abuse and dependence. Just a handful include curiosity, conformity to peer pressure, rebelliousness, and escape from boredom or pressure (Brook et al., 1980; Conger & Petersen, 1984; Hollister, 1983; Kandel, 1980; Mittelmark et al., 1987). Another is self-handicapping, as noted in Chapter 6; that is, if we use alcohol or another drug when faced with a difficult task, we can blame failure on the alcohol, not ourselves. Similarly, alcohol and other drugs have been used as excuses for behaviors such as aggression, sexual forwardness, and forgetfulness.

Psychodynamic Views Psychodynamic explanations of substance abuse propose that drugs help people control or express unconscious needs and impulses. Alcoholism, for example, may reflect the need to remain dependent on an overprotective mother, or the effort to reduce emotional conflicts, or to cope with unconscious homosexual impulses.

Learning-Theory Views Social-learning theorists suggest that first use of tranquilizing agents such as Valium and alcohol usually results from observing others or from a recommendation. Expectancies about the effects of a substance are powerful predictors of the use of that substance (Wilson, 1987). But subsequent usage may be reinforced by the drug's positive effects on mood and its reduction of unpleasant sensations such as anxiety, fear, and tension. For people who are physiologically dependent, avoidance of withdrawal symptoms is also reinforcing. Carrying the substance around is reinforcing, because then one need not worry about having to go without it. Some people, for example, will not leave the house without taking Valium along.

Children whose parents use drugs such as alcohol, tranquilizers, and stimulants are more likely to turn to drugs themselves. Modeling increases children's knowledge of drugs and shows them when to use them—for example, when they are anxious or depressed.

Genetic Factors There is growing evidence that people can have a genetic predisposition toward physiological dependence on certain substances (Goodwin, 1985; Schuckit, 1987; Vaillant, 1982). The biological children of alcoholics who are reared by adoptive parents are more likely to develop alcohol-related problems than are the natural children of the adoptive parents (Goodwin, 1985). Alcoholics (and their children) inherit bodily reactions to alcohol that provide greater tolerance of alcohol. For example, college-age children of alcoholics show better muscular control and visual-motor coordination when they drink (Kolata, 1987). They feel less intoxicated when they drink large quantities of alcohol, and they show lower hormonal response to alcohol.

Let us now consider the effects of some frequently used depressants, stimulants, and hallucinogenics.

Delirium tremens. A condition characterized by sweating, restlessness, disorientation, and hallucinations. The "DT's" occurs in some chronic alcohol users when there is a sudden decrease in usage.

Disorientation. Gross confusion. Loss of sense of time, place, and the identity of people.

Hallucinations. Perceptions in the absence of sensation that are confused with reality.

Effects of Depressants

Depressant drugs act by slowing the activity of the central nervous system, although there are a number of other effects specific to each drug. In this section we consider the effects of alcohol, opiates and opioids, barbiturates, and methaqualone.

Alcohol　No drug has meant so much to so many as alcohol. Alcohol is our dinnertime relaxant, our bedtime sedative, our cocktail-party social facilitator. We celebrate holy days, applaud our accomplishments, and express joyous wishes with alcohol. The young assert their maturity with alcohol. The elderly use it to stimulate circulation in peripheral areas of the body. Alcohol kills germs on surface wounds. Some pediatricians even swab the painful gums of teething babies with alcohol.

No drug has been so abused as alcohol. Ten to 20 million U.S. residents are **alcoholics.** By contrast, 200,000 use heroin regularly, and 300,000 to 500,000 abuse sedatives. Excessive drinking has been linked to lower productivity, loss of employment, and downward movement in social status (Baum-Baicker, 1984; Mider, 1984; Vaillant & Milofsky, 1982). Yet half of all U.S. residents use alcohol, and despite widespread marijuana use, alcohol remains the drug of choice among adolescents.

People believe that alcohol reduces tension, diverts one from worrying, enhances pleasure, increases social ability, and transforms experiences for the better (Brown et al., 1980, 1985; Christiansen et al., 1982; Rohsenow, 1983). What *does* alcohol do?

As a depressant, alcohol slows the activity of the central nervous system. It can also induce feelings of **euphoria,** which is one of its major attractions. Regular alcohol use over a year or more may contribute to feelings of depression, although short-term use may lessen feelings of depression (Aneshensel & Huba, 1983). Alcohol relaxes and deadens minor aches and pains. Alcohol also intoxicates: It impairs cognitive functioning, slurs the speech, and reduces motor coordination. Alcohol is implicated in about half of our auto accidents.

Alcohol and Aggression　A solid link has been established between alcohol and aggressive behavior; that is, when people drink moderate to high doses of alcohol, they are more likely to behave aggressively—in the laboratory setting and *in vivo*, or in real life (Taylor & Leonard, 1983). However, this

Alcoholic. A person whose drinking persistently impairs his or her personal, social, or physical well-being.

Euphoria. Feelings of well-being, elation.

Two Facets of Drinking in U.S. Society
No drug has meant so much to so many as alcohol. Alcohol is our dinnertime relaxant and cocktail-party social facilitator (see photo at left). Yet alcohol has also been linked to loss of employment and downward movement in social status (see photo at right).

research does not show that alcohol *causes* aggressive behavior. In our society, alcohol is conceptualized as liberating primitive impulses, and so drinking alcohol might suggest to people that they behave more aggressively (Marlatt & Rohsenow, 1981). Also, they can later attribute their aggressive behavior to the alcohol, escaping blame.

In some studies, such as one run by Alan Lang and his colleagues (1975), social drinkers have been given alcohol (vodka) but led to believe that they are drinking tonic water only, whereas other subjects have been given tonic water only but led to believe that they are drinking alcohol (Figure 7.1). In these studies subjects who believe they have drunk alcohol behave more aggressively, whereas subjects who actually drink alcohol, but are unaware of it, do not—providing evidence for the view that expectations concerning the effects of alcohol, and not alcohol itself, probably account for aggressive behavior.

Alcohol and Sex   In Shakespeare's *Macbeth,* a minor character notes that drink provokes three things—nosepainting (rupture of small blood vessels in the nose, turning the nose reddish), sleep, and urine. "Lechery," the character adds, "it provokes and unprovokes; it provokes the desire, but takes away the performance." *Does alcohol stir the sexual appetite? Does alcohol inhibit sexual response (i.e., "take away the performance")?*

Studies of the effects of alcohol on sexual response, as measured by response to sexually explicit films, are similar to those of the Lang group's study on alcohol and aggression. For example, men who *believe* they have drunk alcohol, when they have not, show increased sexual arousal, as measured by size of erection and reported subjective feelings of sexual arousal. But men who have actually drunk alcohol, without knowing it, show decreased sexual response—which is not all that surprising, since alcohol is a nervous system depressant (Briddell & Wilson, 1976). Such studies are made possible by the inability to taste vodka when mixed with tonic water. In this way subjects can be led to believe that they have drunk vodka when they have not, and vice versa. Research using this technique also shows that alcohol decreases women's sexual response to sexually explicit films (Wilson & Lawson, 1978).

And so our beliefs about the effects of alcohol may diverge markedly from its actual effects. The "sexy" feeling we may experience after a few drinks may stem from general feelings of euphoria, decreased sympathetic activity, and our expectations—not from the alcohol itself.

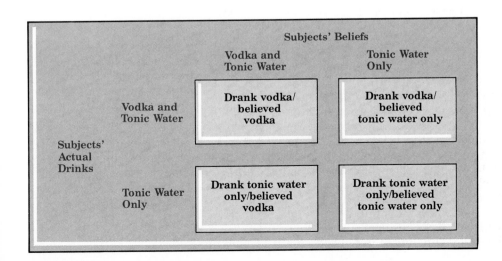

FIGURE 7.1   The Experimental Conditions in the Lang Study

The taste of vodka cannot be discerned when vodka is mixed with tonic water. For this reason, it was possible for subjects in the Lang study on the effects of alcohol to be kept "blind" as to whether or not they had actually drunk alcohol. Blind studies allow psychologists to control for the effects of subject expectations.

Drinkers might do things they would not do if sober (Lang et al., 1980; Lansky & Wilson, 1981), such as linger over sexually explicit pictures in the presence of researchers. One possible reason for the "liberating" effects of alcohol is that it might impair the information-processing needed to inhibit impulses (Hull et al., 1983; Steele & Southwick, 1985). That is, when intoxicated, people may be less able to foresee the negative consequences of misbehavior and may also be less likely to focus on social and personal standards for behavior. Another reason is that the feelings of elation and euphoria induced by alcohol may also help wash away self-doubts and self-criticism. But do not forget that alcohol is associated with a liberated social role in our culture and that it provides an external excuse (a situational attribution) for otherwise unacceptable behavior.

Alcohol and Physical Disorders

As a food, alcohol is fattening. Yet chronic drinkers may be malnourished. Though high in calories, alcohol does not contain nutrients such as vitamins and proteins. Moreover, alcohol can interfere with the body's absorption of a number of vitamins, particularly thiamine, a B vitamin. And so chronic drinking can lead to a number of disorders, such as **cirrhosis of the liver,** which has been linked to protein deficiency, and to **Wernicke-Korsakoff syndrome,** which has been linked to vitamin B deficiency (Eckhardt et al., 1981). In cirrhosis of the liver, connective fibers replace active liver cells, impeding circulation of the blood. Wernicke-Korsakoff syndrome is a specific brain dysfunction that is characterized by gross confusion and disorientation, memory loss for recent events (that is, problems in storage of new information), and visual problems.

When alcohol is metabolized in the body, there are increases in lactic and uric acids. Lactic acid has been correlated with anxiety attacks, although there is little reason to think that alcohol causes anxiety. Uric acid can cause gout. Chronic drinking has also been linked to coronary heart disease and high blood pressure (Eckhardt et al., 1981).

Heavy use of alcohol has been linked with cancer of the pancreas (Heuch et al., 1983) and stomach (Gordon & Kannel, 1984; Popham et al., 1984), although light to moderate drinking has not been shown to heighten the risk of stomach cancer. The question has also been raised as to whether alcohol is linked to breast cancer. According to one study reported in the *New England Journal of Medicine,* women who have one or two alcoholic drinks a day raise the risk of developing breast cancer from about 7 percent to about 11 percent (Stipp, 1987), but other studies find no increased risk of breast cancer for women who drink (Kolata, 1988). *Any* drinking by a pregnant woman might be harmful to the embryo (see Chapter 16 and, also, Rathus, 1988).

Possible Benefits of Alcohol: Moderation in All Things?

Having noted these problems with alcohol, it might seem ironic that a number of studies suggest that light to moderate drinking *benefits* many people—but they appear to do just that.

An often-cited Kaiser-Permanente study followed 2,015 Hayward, California, residents for ten years and found that light drinkers—defined as people who had no more than two drinks a day, or up to 60 ounces of alcohol a month—had a significantly lower mortality rate than heavier drinkers and, surprisingly, nondrinkers (Klatsky et al., 1981). In a study carried out in Alameda County, California, moderate drinkers showed a lower mortality rate than nondrinkers, light drinkers, and heavy drinkers—although the apparent benefits of alcohol were much stronger for men than women (Berkman et al., 1983). Another study followed thousands of residents of Framingham, Massachusetts, for 22 years and found that moderate drinking of 20–30 ounces of alcohol per week reduced the risk of incidence of coronary heart disease among men by about 40 percent (Friedman & Kimball, 1986). A study in

Cirrhosis of the liver. A disease caused by protein deficiency in which connective fibers replace active liver cells, impeding circulation of the blood. Alcohol does not contain protein; therefore, persons who drink excessively may be prone to this disease.

Wernicke-Korsakoff syndrome. A disorder associated with heavy drinking and characterized by severe memory problems concerning recent events and disorientation.

Albany County, New York, followed civil service employees for a period of 18 years and found that men who consumed 10–29 ounces of alcohol a month had lower mortality rates than male nondrinkers, occasional drinkers, and heavy drinkers (Gordon & Doyle, 1987). Again, the correlational links were weaker for women. Still another study found that male light drinkers are apparently at lower risk for strokes than nondrinkers and heavy drinkers (Gill et al., 1986).

As you can imagine, observers have scrutinized these studies carefully, because they would appear to encourage light to moderate drinking. These studies also seem to contradict other kinds of research that have suggested that alcohol is harmful. Moreover, since one can become dependent on alcohol, many people who drink have trouble limiting themselves to light or moderate drinking.

Perhaps the important thing to keep in mind is that these studies have been correlational, not experimental. And so it might be that light to moderate drinking does not *induce* positive body changes, but rather that the same factors that lead to light or moderate drinking can also enhance physical health. For example, it is possible that light to moderate drinkers, as compared to nondrinkers, are more relaxed, more willing to "let go." And, when compared to heavy drinkers, it might also be that light to moderate drinkers—that is, people who control their alcohol intake—are in generally greater control of their lives.

Treatment of Alcoholism   Treatment of alcoholism has been a frustrating endeavor. *Detoxification,* or helping a physiologically dependent alcoholic safely through the abstinence syndrome, is a generally straightforward medical procedure, requiring about one week (Rada & Kellner, 1979). But assisting the alcoholic to learn to cope with life's stresses through measures other than drinking is the heart of the problem. Several treatments have been tried, most with little documented success.

Medication. The drug *disulfuram* (brand name Antabuse) has been used most widely with alcoholics. Mixing Antabuse with alcohol can cause feelings of illness. However, current maintenance doses of Antabuse are usually too low to have this result, and there is little convincing evidence of the drug's effectiveness (Miller & Hester, 1980).

Alcoholics Anonymous. Many people consider Alcoholics Anonymous (AA), a nonprofessional organization, to offer the most effective treatment for alcoholics. At AA, alcoholics undergo a conversion in identity to that of a "recovering alcoholic." Conversion requires confession of one's drinking problems before a group of alcoholics, and the making of a public commitment not to touch another drop. The new identity becomes confirmed with the passing of each sober day, and recovering alcoholics often help other alcoholics undergo a similar conversion.

While AA commonly cites a success rate in the neighborhood of 75 percent (Wallace, 1985), critics note that figures this high usually include only persons who remain in treatment. As many as 90 percent of those who attend AA meetings drop out after a handful of meetings (Miller, 1982).

Behavior Therapy. Behavior therapy is proving helpful to many alcoholics. A variety of methods to be explained in depth in Chapter 12 show promising success rates: aversion therapy, relaxation training, covert sensitization, instruction in social skills, and self-monitoring (Elkins, 1980; Miller & Mastria, 1977; Olson et al., 1981).

▓ Q U E S T I O N N A I R E ▓

Why Do You Drink?

Do you drink? If so, why? To enhance your pleasure? To cope with your problems? To help you in your social encounters? Because you will feel withdrawal symptoms if you don't? Half of all U.S. residents use alcohol, and as many as one user in ten is an alcoholic. College students who expect that alcohol will help them reduce tension are more likely than other students to encounter alcohol-related problems (Brown, 1985).

To gain insight into your reasons for using alcohol, respond to the following items by circling the *T* if an item is true or mostly true for you, or the *F* if an item is false or mostly false for you. Then turn to the answer key at the end of the chapter.

T   F

_____ _____   **1.** I find it very unpleasant to do without alcohol for some time.
_____ _____   **2.** Alcohol makes it easier for me to talk to other people.
_____ _____   **3.** I drink to appear more grown up and more sophisticated.
_____ _____   **4.** When I drink, the future looks brighter to me.
_____ _____   **5.** I like the taste of what I drink.
_____ _____   **6.** If I go without a drink for some time, I am not bothered or uncomfortable.
_____ _____   **7.** I feel more relaxed and less tense about things when I drink.
_____ _____   **8.** I drink so that I will fit in better with the crowd.
_____ _____   **9.** I worry less about things when I drink.
_____ _____   **10.** I have a drink when I get together with the family.
_____ _____   **11.** I have a drink as part of my religious ceremonies.
_____ _____   **12.** I have a drink when a toothache or some other pain is disturbing me.
_____ _____   **13.** I feel much more powerful when I have a drink.
_____ _____   **14.** You really can't blame me for the things I do when I have been drinking.
_____ _____   **15.** I have a drink before a big test, date, or interview when I'm afraid of how well I'll do.
_____ _____   **16.** I find I have a drink for the taste alone.

Opiates and Opioids   **Opiates** are a group of **narcotics** derived from the opium poppy. The opiates include morphine, heroin, codeine, demerol, and similar drugs whose major medical application is analgesia, or control of pain. Opiates appear to stimulate centers in the brain that lead to pleasure and to physiological dependence (Goeders & Smith, 1984; Ling et al., 1984). Opioids are similar to opiates in chemical structure and effect, but are artificial (synthesized in the laboratory).

Heroin and morphine are powerful depressants that can provide a euphoric "rush." Users of heroin claim it is so pleasurable it can eradicate any thought of food or sex. Although regular users develop tolerance for heroin, high doses can cause drowsiness, stupor, altered time perception, and impaired judgment.

The opioid **methadone** has been used to treat dependence on heroin. Methadone is slower acting than heroin and does not provide the thrilling rush. Most people treated with it simply swap dependence on one drug for

Opiates. A group of addictive drugs derived from the opium poppy that provide a euphoric "rush" and depress the nervous system.

Narcotics. Drugs used to relieve pain and induce sleep. The term is usually reserved for opiates.

Methadone. An artificial narcotic that is slower acting than, and does not provide the "rush" of, heroin. Methadone use allows heroin addicts to abstain from heroin without experiencing an abstinence syndrome.

T   F

_____ _____ 17. I've found a drink in my hand when I can't remember putting it there.

_____ _____ 18. I'll have a drink when I feel "blue" or want to take my mind off my cares and worries.

_____ _____ 19. I can do better socially and sexually after having a drink or two.

_____ _____ 20. Drinking makes me do stupid things.

_____ _____ 21. Sometimes when I have a few drinks, I can't get to work.

_____ _____ 22. I feel more caring and giving after having a drink or two.

_____ _____ 23. I drink because I like the look of a drinker.

_____ _____ 24. I like to drink more on festive occasions.

_____ _____ 25. When a friend or I have done something well, we're likely to have a drink or two.

_____ _____ 26. I have a drink when some problem is nagging away at me.

_____ _____ 27. I find drinking pleasurable.

_____ _____ 28. I like the "high" of drinking.

_____ _____ 29. Sometimes I pour a drink without realizing I still have one that is unfinished.

_____ _____ 30. I feel I can better get others to do what I want when I've had a drink or two.

_____ _____ 31. Having a drink keeps my mind off my problems at home, at school, or at work.

_____ _____ 32. I get a real gnawing hunger for a drink when I haven't had one for a while.

_____ _____ 33. A drink or two relaxes me.

_____ _____ 34. Things look better when I've had a drink or two.

_____ _____ 35. My mood is much better after I've been drinking.

_____ _____ 36. I see things more clearly when I've been drinking.

_____ _____ 37. A drink or two enhances the pleasure of sex and food.

_____ _____ 38. When I'm out of alcohol, I immediately buy more.

_____ _____ 39. I would have done much better on some things if it weren't for alcohol.

_____ _____ 40. When I have run out of alcohol, I find it almost unbearable until I can get some more.

Sources: Items adapted from (1) general discussion of expectancies about alcohol in Christiansen et al. (1982) and (2) smokers' self-testing items analyzed by Leventhal and Avis (1976).

dependence on another. Because they are unwilling to undergo withdrawal symptoms, or to contemplate a life-style devoid of drugs, they must be maintained indefinitely on methadone.

Overdoses of opiates and opioids depress body functioning and are capable of killing. But the effects of "normal" doses are less than clear (Davison & Neale, 1986). Some of the apparent ill effects of the drugs stem from substances that contaminate them. Consider New York's South Bronx. This is a neighborhood of high unemployment and extreme poverty. As many as one in five young men are infected by the AIDS virus here, and the vast majority of them are intravenous drug users who have become infected by sharing contaminated needles (Bakeman et al., 1986; Lambert, 1987).

Barbiturate. An addictive depressant used to relieve anxiety or induce sleep.

Barbiturates and Methaqualone

Barbiturates such as amobarbital, phenobarbital, pentobarbital, and secobarbital are depressants with a number

■ A CLOSER LOOK

The Sobell Experiment

For years the gospel had been that alcoholics must abstain completely from their habit if they were to recover—one drink and they would lose control. Linda and Mark Sobell committed heresy. They argued that through behavior modification, alcoholics could learn self-control techniques that would allow them to engage in something called *controlled social drinking*. That is, they could have a drink or two in the company of others without necessarily falling off the wagon.

The Sobells' critics generally support the AA goal of total abstinence. They argue that controlled social drinking is an impossible dream. They claim that if an alcoholic, or a recovering alcoholic, has just one drink, he or she is likely to go off on a binge.

The critics were astounded when the Sobells published the results of their experiment with 20 alcoholic subjects who were taught behavioral self-control methods at Patton State Hospital in San Bernardino, California. Eighty-five percent of the subjects were reported by the Sobells (1973, 1976, 1984) as engaging in successful controlled social drinking at a two-year follow-up.

But psychologist Mary Pendery believed that the Sobells had made extravagant claims. As a result, she attempted to track down the men in the experiment to get their own stories. After many years of investigation,

Pendery, Maltzman, and West (1982) published a more recent follow-up of the Sobells' subjects in *Science*. Pendery and her colleagues reported that despite the Sobells' claims, most subjects had returned to uncontrolled drinking on several occasions, and that only *one* had successfully continued to moderate his drinking. Four of the original 20 had died from alcohol-related causes.

According to psychologist Alan Marlatt, there were shortcomings in both the studies run by the Sobells and by the Pendery group (Fisher, 1982). In each case, for example, the follow-ups may have been biased because they were conducted by investigators who had an interest in showing a particular outcome.

Other investigators (e.g., Miller & Muñoz, 1983; Peele, 1984; Sanchez-Craig et al., 1984) do claim that the goal of controlled social drinking remains possible, at least for people on the road to alcoholism. The research group headed by M. Sanchez-Craig, for example, assigned 35 "early-stage problem drinkers" to controlled social drinking. After two years they reported that "Six months after treatment drinking had been reduced from an average of about 51 drinks per week to 13, and this reduction was maintained throughout the second year" (1984, p. 390).

The goal of controlled social drinking remains controversial (Foy et al., 1984; McCrady, 1985; Marlatt, 1985), and the final chapter has not yet been written.

---

of medical uses, including relief of anxiety and tension, deadening of pain, and treatment of epilepsy, high blood pressure, and insomnia. Barbiturates lead rapidly to dependence. **Methaqualone,** sold under the brand names Quaalude and Sopor, is a depressant similar in effect to barbiturates.

Methaqualone. An addictive depressant. Often referred to as "ludes."

Psychologists generally oppose using barbiturates and methalqualone for anxiety, tension, and insomnia, since they lead rapidly to dependence and do nothing to teach the individual how to alter disturbing patterns of behavior. Many physicians, too, have become concerned about barbiturates.

Barbiturates and methaqualone are popular as street drugs, because they relax the muscles and produce a mild euphoric state. High doses of barbiturates result in drowsiness, motor impairment, slurred speech, irritability, and poor judgment. A dependent person who is withdrawn abruptly may experience severe convulsions and die. High doses of methaqualone may cause internal bleeding, coma, and death. Because of additive effects, it is dangerous to mix alcohol and other depressants at bedtime, or at any time.

Effects of Stimulants

Stimulants act by increasing the activity of the nervous system. The other effects of stimulants vary somewhat from drug to drug, and some seem to contribute to feelings of euphoria and self-confidence.

Amphetamines   Amphetamines were first used by soldiers during World War II to help them remain alert through the night. Truck drivers have used them to drive through the night. But amphetamines have become more widely known through students who have used them for all-night cram sessions, and through dieters who use them because they reduce hunger.

Amphetamines and a related stimulant, Ritalin (methylphenidate), increase self-control in hyperactive children, increase their attention span, decrease fidgeting, and lead to academic gains (Abikoff & Gittelman, 1985; Barkley et al., 1984; Kavale, 1982; Rapport, 1984; Whalen et al., 1987). The paradoxical calming effect of stimulants on hyperactive children may be explained by assuming that a cause of hyperactivity is immaturity of the cerebral cortex. Amphetamines might stimulate the cortex to exercise control over more primitive centers in the lower brain.

Called speed, uppers, bennies (for Benzedrine), and dexies (for Dexedrine), these drugs are often used for the euphoric "rush" they can produce, especially in high doses. Regular users may stay awake and "high" for days on end. Such highs must come to an end. People who have been on prolonged highs sometimes "crash," or fall into a deep sleep or depression.

People can become psychologically dependent on amphetamines, especially when they are using them to cope with depression. Tolerance develops rapidly, but opinion is mixed as to whether they lead to physiological dependence. High doses may cause restlessness, insomnia, loss of appetite, and irritability. In the so-called amphetamine psychosis, there are hallucinations and delusions that mimic the symptoms of paranoid schizophrenia, a psychological disorder that is discussed in the next chapter.

Cocaine   No doubt you've seen commercials claiming that Coke adds life. Given its caffeine and sugar content, Coca-Cola should provide quite a lift. But Coca-Cola hasn't been "the real thing" since 1906. At that time the manufacturers discontinued use of the coca leaves from which the soft drink derived its name. Coca leaves contain **cocaine,** a stimulant that produces a state of euphoria, or high, reduces hunger, deadens pain, and bolsters self-confidence.

Cocaine is brewed from coca leaves as a "tea," breathed in ("snorted") in powder form, and injected ("shot up") in liquid form. The potent deriva-

Cocaine. A powerful stimulant that provides feelings of euphoria and bolsters self-confidence.

The stimulant cocaine produces a state of euphoria, deadens pain, and bolsters self-confidence. On a physiological level, cocaine stimulates sudden rises in blood pressure, dangerously constricts the blood vessels, and quickens the heart rate.

tives, "crack" and "bazooka," have recently received great attention in the media. These derivatives are inexpensive because they are unrefined; bazooka, in particular, which can be purchased for as little as one dollar a dose, tends to be contaminated with heavy metals, which can damage the brain and lead to other problems. Cocaine has grown in popularity in recent years, and one survey of young adults (aged about 25) found that 37 percent of males and 24 percent of females had tried it (Kandel et al., 1986). Five million Americans use cocaine regularly (Altman, 1988).

Cocaine—also called *snow* and *coke,* like the slang term for the soft drink—has been used as a local anesthetic since the early 1800s. It came to the attention of one Viennese neurologist in 1884, a young chap named Sigmund Freud, who used it to fight his own depression and published a supportive article, "Song of Praise."

Despite media claims that cocaine is addictive, there remains some question as to whether cocaine does cause physiological dependence. For example, it is not clear that there is a specific abstinence syndrome for cocaine (Van Dyke & Byck, 1982). On the other hand, there is no doubt that users can readily become psychologically dependent.

On a physiological level, cocaine stimulates sudden rises in blood pressure, tightening of the blood vessels (with associated decrease of the oxygen supply to the heart), and quickening of the heart rate (Altman, 1988). Overdoses can lead to restlessness and insomnia, tremors, headaches, nausea, convulsions, hallucinations, delusions, and—as with recent cases of athletes who have died following cocaine use—respiratory and cardiovascular collapse. Robert Post of the National Institute of Mental Health and his colleagues have reported that cocaine gradually lowers the brain threshold for seizures in laboratory rats (Bales, 1986). That is, individual moderate doses of cocaine had no apparent harmful effect, but there was a cumulative "kindling effect" for brain seizures and, in some cases, sudden death.

Repeated "snorting" constricts blood vessels in the nose, drying the skin and, at times, exposing cartilege and perforating the nasal septum. These problems require cosmetic surgery. Of course, people who take cocaine intravenously and share contaminated needles risk becoming infected by the AIDS virus (e.g., Lambert, 1987). Cocaine remains the anesthetic of choice for surgery on the nose and throat.

Cigarettes   All cigarette packs sold in the U.S.A. carry messages such as: "Warning: The Surgeon General Has Determined That Cigarette Smoking Is Dangerous to Your Health." Cigarette advertising has been banned on the radio and television. In 1982, Surgeon General C. Everett Koop declared that "Cigarette smoking is clearly identified as the chief preventable cause of death in our society and the most important public health issue of our time."

In that year, 430,000 people would die from cancer, and the Surgeon General's report argued that 30 percent of these deaths were attributable to smoking. The average life reduction for smokers, depending on dosage, is estimated at about five to eight years (Fielding, 1985). Cigarette smoking can cause cancer of the lungs, larynx, oral cavity, and esophagus, and may contribute to cancer of the bladder, pancreas, and kidneys. Cigarette smoking is also linked to death from heart disease, chronic lung and respiratory diseases, and other illnesses.

Once it was thought that smokers' ills tended to focus on men, and, to be sure, the smoking-attributable mortality rate in a recent year was more than twice as high for men (192 deaths per 100,000) as women (68 per 100,000) (*New York Times,* 1987). But today women smokers also have a 30 percent greater risk of dying from cancer than women nonsmokers. Pregnant women who smoke risk miscarriage, premature birth, low birth weight, res-

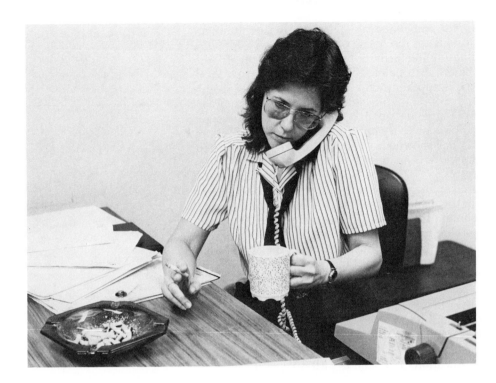

It is widely known that smoking cigarettes is one of the risk factors for contracting cardiovascular disorders and cancer, yet millions of us continue to smoke. In recent years, in fact, increasing numbers of women have undertaken smoking, even as the number of male smokers has decreased.

piratory ailments, and birth defects. In 1984, 2,000 U.S. infants died before their first birthdays for reasons attributable to maternal smoking during pregnancy (*New York Times*, 1987).

Because of the noxious effects of second-hand smoke, smoking has been banished from many public places, like elevators. Many restaurants now reserve sections for nonsmokers. So it's no secret that cigarette smoking is dangerous. In fact, today only about 27 percent of adult Americans smoke, as compared to 40 percent in 1964 (*New York Times, 1987*). But that's still 50 million or so of us who are betting our lives that our smoking will not do us in.

Tobacco smoke contains carbon monoxide, hydrocarbons (or "tars"), and nicotine. Oxygen is carried through the blood stream by a substance called hemoglobin. But when carbon monoxide combines with hemoglobin, it impairs the blood's ability to supply the body with oxygen. One result: shortness of breath.

A number of the "tars" found in cigarette smoke have been shown to cause cancer in laboratory animals. Tars are assumed by most researchers to have the same effect in humans, although cigarette companies argue that it has never been proved that cigarettes cause cancer because human-subjects experiments in which some people have been randomly assigned to smoking and others to nonsmoking have never been carried out. And of course it will not be. Ethical and practical considerations prevent us from recruiting human subjects and assigning some at random to years of smoking cigarettes. Nor could we be certain that those assigned to nonsmoking would live up to their experimental task. And so, the argument that the "ideal" experiment has never been run is, technically speaking, correct. However, the weight of the evidence from correlational studies with humans and experimental studies with laboratory animals seems solid enough to satisfy nearly everyone with the exception of the management of the cigarette companies.

Hallucinogenic. Giving rise to hallucinations.

Marijuana. A hallucinogenic substance made up of the dried vegetable matter of the *Cannabis sativa* plant.

Psychedelic. Causing hallucinations and delusions or heightening perceptions.

Nicotine and Physiological Dependence Nicotine is the stimulant found in cigarettes. Nicotine stimulates discharge of the hormone adrenalin. Adrenalin creates a burst of autonomic activity, including rapid heart rate and release of sugar into the blood. Adrenalin accounts for the mental "kick" provided by cigarettes. Nicotine is apparently the agent that creates dependence. The withdrawal symptoms from smoking cigarettes (nervousness, drowsiness, energy loss, headaches, fatigue, irregular bowels, lightheadedness, insomnia, dizziness, cramps, palpitations, tremors, and sweating) mimic an anxiety state. Schachter (1977) has shown that regular smokers adjust their smoking in order to maintain fairly even levels of nicotine in their bloodstream.

Nicotine is excreted more rapidly when the urine is highly acid. Stress increases the amount of acid in the urine, and so smokers may need to smoke more when under stress to maintain the same blood nicotine level. They may *believe* that smoking is helping them cope with stress, but the "calming effect" attributed to cigarette smoking may only be suspension of the withdrawal symptoms of physiologically dependent smokers (Silverstein, 1982). The only source of stress with which smokers may be "coping" is the stress of withdrawal.

In Chapter 10 we shall describe a number of strategies for cutting down and quitting smoking. Although quitting can be difficult for many people, there is encouragement in the fact that about 29 million U.S. residents have quit and remained abstinent within the 15-year period from 1964 to 1979 (U.S. Department of Health, Education, and Welfare, 1979).

Effects of Hallucinogenics

Hallucinogenic drugs are named as such because they produce hallucinations—that is, sensations and perceptions in the absence of external stimulation. But hallucinogenic drugs may also have additional effects, such as relaxing the individual, creating a sense of euphoria, or, in some cases, causing panic. We shall focus on the effects of marijuana and LSD.

Marijuana **Marijuana** is produced from the *cannabis sativa* plant, which grows wild in many parts of the world. Marijuana helps some people relax and can elevate the mood. It also sometimes produces mild hallucinations, and so is classified as a **psychedelic** or hallucinogenic drug. The major psychoactive substance in marijuana is delta-9-tetrahydrocannabinol, or THC.

Marijuana smokers report different sensations at different levels of intoxication. The early stages of intoxication are frequently characterized by restlessness, which gives way to calmness. Fair to strong intoxication is linked to reports of heightened perceptions, and increases in self-insight, creative thinking, and empathy for the feelings of others. Strong intoxication is linked to perceiving time as passing more slowly and to increased awareness of bodily sensations, such as heartbeat. Smokers also report that strong intoxication heightens sexual sensations and that a song might seem to last an hour rather than a few minutes. Strong intoxication may cause disorientation. High levels of intoxication occasionally induce nausea and vomiting. Needless to say, smokers with such experiences smoke infrequently, or just once.

Some people report that marijuana helps them socialize at parties. But the friendliness characteristic of early stages of intoxication may give way to self-absorption and social withdrawal as the smoker becomes higher (Fabian & Fishkin, 1981).

In the nineteenth century, marijuana was used almost as aspirin is used today for headaches and minor aches and pains. It could be bought without prescription in any drugstore. Today marijuana use and possession are illegal in most states, but medical applications are being explored. Marijuana is known to decrease nausea and vomiting among cancer patients receiving

Amotivational syndrome. Loss of ambition or motivation to achieve.

LSD. Lysergic acid diethylamide. A hallucinogenic drug.

Flashbacks. Distorted perceptions or hallucinations that occur days or weeks after LSD usage but mimic the LSD experience.

chemotherapy (Grinspoon, 1987). It appears to help glaucoma sufferers by reducing fluid pressure in the eye. It may even offer some relief from asthma. But there are also causes for concern, as noted in 1982 by the Institute of Medicine of the National Academy of Sciences. For example, marijuana impairs motor coordination and perceptual functions used in driving and the operation of other machines. It also impairs short-term memory and slows learning. Although it causes positive mood changes in many people, there are also disturbing instances of anxiety, confusion, and occasional reports of psychotic reactions. Marijuana increases the heart rate up to 140–150 beats per minute and, in some people, raises blood pressure. This rise in workload poses a threat to persons with hypertension and cardiovascular disorders.

It has also been feared that marijuana causes **amotivational syndrome**—that is, destroys achievement motivation, melts away ambition, and causes difficulty in concentrating on task-oriented activities, such as work. These fears have been fueled by correlational evidence that heavy smokers in the college ranks do not strive to succeed as strenuously as do nonsmoking or infrequently smoking classmates. But we cannot confuse correlation with cause and effect. Other studies suggest that people who choose to smoke heavily may already differ from those who do not (Maugh, 1982). For instance, heavy smokers may be more concerned with emotional experience and fantasy than intellectual performance and self-control. Their approach to life could underlie both relative lack of ambition and regular use of marijuana. Still other research finds no cognitive effects from heavy use of marijuana over a seven-year period (Schaeffer et al., 1981).

Marijuana's entire story has not yet been told. While certain horror stories about marijuana may have been exaggerated, we cannot assume that marijuana smoke, which contains 50 percent more carcinogenic hydrocarbon than tobacco smoke, is harmless.

LSD **LSD** is the abbreviation for lysergic diethylamide acid, a synthetic hallucinogenic drug. Users of "acid" claim that it "expands consciousness" and opens new worlds. Sometimes people believe they achieved great insights while using LSD, but when it wears off they usually cannot apply or recall these discoveries.

As a powerful hallucinogenic, LSD produces vivid and colorful hallucinations or "trips" that can be somewhat unpredictable. Some regular users have only "good trips." Others have one bad trip and swear off. Regular users who have had no bad trips argue that people with bad trips were psychologically unstable prior to using LSD. Barber's review of the literature (1970) does suggest that psychotic symptoms are rare and usually limited to people with a history of psychological problems.

Some LSD users report **flashbacks**—distorted perceptions or hallucinations that occur long after usage. It has been speculated that flashbacks stem from chemical changes in the brain produced by LSD, but Heaton and Victor (1976) and Matefy (1980) offer a psychological explanation for flashbacks. Heaton and Victor (1976) found that users who have flashbacks are more oriented toward fantasy, allowing their thoughts to wander, and focusing on internal sensations. When they experience sensations similar to a trip, they label them flashbacks and allow themselves to focus on them, causing a replay of the experience to unfold. Matefy (1980) found that users who have flashbacks show greater capacity to become fully engrossed in role-playing, and hypothesized that flashbacks may be nothing more than enacting the role of being on a trip. Users who do not have flashbacks prefer to be more in charge of their thought processes and have greater concern for meeting the demands of daily life.

Other hallucinogenic drugs include mescaline (derived from the peyote cactus) and phencyclidine (PCP). Regular use of hallucinogenics may lead to tolerance and psychological dependence. But hallucinogenics are not known to lead to physiological dependence. High doses can induce frightening hallucinations, impaired coordination, poor judgment, mood changes, and paranoid delusions.

Let us now turn our attention to another groups of substances—foods. We shall see that many of our nutritional patterns are cause for concern and that people can "abuse" foodstuffs as well as psychoactive drugs.

Nutritional Patterns

Since much of our knowledge about the importance of proper nutrition has been accumulated in recent years, you might think that young people would pay more attention to what they eat than their elders do. But according to a *New York Times* poll reported by Marian Burros (1988), you would be wrong. Of the 1,870 people aged 18 and above who were contacted by telephone, respondents at least 30 years of age reported better eating habits than those aged 18–29. As shown in Table 7.1, women also reported paying significantly more attention to their diets than men.

Why do young people pay less attention to their nutritional patterns than their elders? Bonnie Liebman, director of nutrition at the Washington Center for Science in the Public Interest, notes that "Instead of teaching good nutrition in schools, we subject our kids to television commercials that push fast foods, soft drinks, candy bars, and sugary cereals. And then we wonder why kids don't ask for fruits and vegetables" (Burros, 1988, pp. C1, C6). Fabian Linden, executive director of the consumer research center of the Conference Board, a marketing information service, adds that "Youth has a magic feeling that they are invulnerable. They don't pay attention to the medical wisdom we have accumulated" (Burros, 1988, p. C6). Lewis Lipsitt, a developmental psychologist at Brown University, notes that things that seem dangerous to adults may seem safe, or safe enough, to teenagers (Goleman, 1987, pp. C1, C17). Teenagers are particularly unrealistic in their evaluation of risk.

In *The New York Times* poll, there were also discrepancies between what respondents knew about nutrition, how they thought their eating habits had changed over the years, and what they were actually eating. For example, although some respondents claimed to "pay attention" to cholesterol at every meal, many of them reported that they had eaten meals heavy in eggs and red meat—foods high in cholesterol—during the past 24 hours. Moreover, the majority of us still prefer french fries (high in fats) to baked potatoes, red meat (high in fats again) to poultry and fish, and soft drinks (high in sugar content and lacking vitamins) to fruit juices.

TABLE 7.1   Percentage of Respondents to *The New York Times* Poll Who Pay Attention to These Dietary Components at Every Meal

Dietary Component	Men	Women	Ages 18–29	Ages 30 and above
Cholesterol	19	31	13	30
Salt	43	60	39	57
Fats	31	46	26	44
Additives and preservatives	20	25	16	25
Sugar and sweets	34	42	30	42
Calories	16	36	21	29
Fiber	12	21	10	19
Caffeine	21	30	20	28

Source of data: *The New York Times*, January 6, 1988, p. C6.

Nutritional Patterns and Physical Illness   Some of the relationships between nutritional patterns and physical illness have grown clearer in recent years. For example, Simone (1983) estimates that about 60 percent of the cases of cancer in men and 40 percent in women can be linked to dietary practices. Food preservatives, high levels of fat intake, and vitamin deficiencies pose particular risks. High levels of cholesterol heighten the risks of cardiovascular disorders (Stamler et al., 1986). On the other hand, vitamins, calcium, fruits and vegetables, and nonfatty fish (Kromhaut et al., 1985) appear to reduce the risk of cancer.

Of course, one of the basic components of the diet is calories. The intake of excessive quantities of calories often leads to what might well be our number one nutrition-related problem—obesity.

Obesity   We need food to survive, but food means more than survival to many of us. Food is a symbol of family togetherness and caring. We associate food with the nurturance of the parent-child relationship, with visits home during the holidays. Friends and relatives offer food when we enter their homes. Saying no may be interpreted as a personal rejection. Bacon and eggs, coffee with cream and sugar, meat and mashed potatoes, all seem part of sharing U.S. values and agricultural abundance.

But many of us are paying the price of abundance:

Forty percent of U.S. residents consider themselves overweight (Burros, 1988), and 35 percent want to lose at least 15 pounds (Toufexis et al., 1986).

One out of five U.S. adults is obese—that is, weighs more than 20 percent above the recommended weight (Wallis, 1985).

Eleven million U.S. adults are severely obese (Wallis, 1985), exceeding their desirable body weight by at least 40 percent.

Twenty-one percent of us are on diets (Burros, 1988), and the number of women on diets exceeds the number of male dieters significantly (Toufexis et al., 1986).

Within a few years, at least two-thirds of "successful" dieters regain every pound they have lost—and then some (Toufexis et al., 1986).

This nation idealizes slender heroes and heroines. For many of us who measure more-than-up to TV and film idols, food may have replaced sex as the central source of guilt. The obese also encounter more than their fair share of illnesses, including cardiovascular diseases, diabetes, gout, and even certain types of cancer (Feist & Brannon, 1988; Sorlie et al., 1980; Wallis, 1985). The pattern of fat accumulation is also significant. Studies in the U.S.A. (Hartz et al., 1984) and Sweden (Smith, 1985) have found that men and women who accumulate fat around the waistline (referred to by some researchers as "apples") are more likely to encounter coronary heart disease, hypertension, diabetes, and gall bladder problems than people who accumulate fat in the hips and thighs ("pears"). Since men are relatively more likely than women to accumulate fat around the middle, they are also at higher risk for these disorders. Large weight changes over the years also heighten the risk for coronary heart disease, and so some professionals have suggested that a few extra pounds might do less damage in the long run than "yo-yo dieting" (Borkan et al., 1986).

Why do so many of us overeat? Is obesity a physiological problem, a psychological problem, or both? Research suggests that psychological and physiological factors both play a role in obesity.

Heredity   It is well-known that obesity runs in families. It used to be the conventional wisdom that obese parents encouraged their children to be overweight by having fattening foods in the house and setting poor examples.

Fat cells. Cells that contain fat; adipose tissue.

Set point. A theoretical setting in the hypothalamus that governs when we feel satiated.

However, a recent study of Scandinavian adoptees by University of Pennsylvania psychiatrist Albert J. Stunkard and his colleagues (1986) found that children bear a closer resemblance in weight to their biological parents than their adoptive parents. However, we shall see that environmental factors also play a role.

Fat Cells   The efforts of obese people to maintain a slender profile might be sabotaged by microscopic units of life within their own bodies: **fat cells.** No, fat cells are not overweight cells. They are adipose tissue, or cells that store fat. Hunger might be related to the amount of fat stored in these cells. As time passes after a meal, the blood sugar level drops. Fat is then drawn from these cells to provide further nourishment. At some point, referred to as the **set point,** the hypothalamus is signaled of the fat deficiency in these cells, triggering the hunger drive.

People with more adipose tissue than others feel food-deprived earlier, even though they may be equal in weight. This might be because more signals are being sent to the brain. Obese people, and *formerly* obese people, tend to have more adipose tissue than people of normal weight. For this reason, many people who have lost weight complain that they are always hungry when they try to maintain normal weight levels. Psychologist Richard Keesey (1986) notes that people who are dieting and people who have lost significant amounts of weight usually do not eat enough to satisfy the set points in their hypothalamuses. As a consequence, compensating metabolic forces are set in motion; that is, fewer calories are burned.

The Perils of Yo-Yo Dieting   Repeated cycles of dieting and regaining lost weight—"yo-yo dieting"—might be particularly traumatic to the set point. Psychologist Kelly Brownell (1986) points out that such cycles might teach the body that it will be intermittently deprived of food, slowing the metabolism whenever future food intake is restricted. For this reason, *to maintain a slim profile, formerly obese people must usually eat much less than people of the same weight who have always been slender.*

Brownell suggests a second effect of yo-yo dieting that hampers repeated dieting efforts:

> Consider a hypothetical dieter, Christine, who drops from 140 pounds down to 120 pounds. She might lose 15 pounds of fat and 5 pounds of muscle. If she regains the 20 pounds, will she replace all 5 pounds of muscle? [Animal studies] suggest that she won't, so Christine may replace 18 pounds of fat and only 2 pounds of muscle. She may be the same weight before and after this cycle, but her metabolic rate would be lower after the cycle because she has more fat, which is less metabolically active than muscle (Brownell, 1988, p. 22).

In other words, it will be more difficult for Christine to merely maintain the 140 pounds the second time around. In fact, if she eats as many calories as she had eaten earlier at 140 pounds, she will probably go above 140. Moreover, now that her body is overall somewhat "less metabolically active," it will be harder for her to lose the same 20 pounds again.

Responsiveness to Internal and External Sources of Stimulation: Out of Sight, Out of Mouth?   During the late evening news, just as your first author is settling in for sleep, a fast-food hamburger or frozen-pizza ad assaults him from the TV set. Visions of juicy meat, gooey cheese, and drippy sauce threaten to do him in. His stomach growlings are all the evidence he needs that hunger can be triggered by external stimuli, such as the sight of food, as well as by chemical imbalances in the body.

Although food commercials might stir most of us, the overweight seem more responsive than the normal-weight to external stimulation, such as the aroma of food or the approach of the dinner hour (Schachter & Gross, 1968).

Normal-weight people are relatively more influenced by internal sensations, such as those produced by stomach contractions, or "hunger pangs" (Stunkard, 1959).

Why are obese people more responsive than the normal-weight to external stimulation? In considering this question, Stanley Schachter (1971) drew behavioral parallels between obese people and rats subjected to a laboratory procedure in which a section of the hypothalamus thought to serve as a "stop-eating center" is destroyed. These rats become **hyperphagic;** they overeat until they level off at about five times their normal body weight (see Figure 7.2). The eating patterns of many obese people are remarkably similar to those of hyperphagic rats. For example, obese people (like hyperphagic rats) are more sensitive than normal-weight people to the taste of food (Schachter, 1971; Schachter & Rodin, 1974). Obese people (like hyperphagic rats) eat relatively larger quantities of sweet foods, such as vanilla milkshakes, but lower quantities of bitter foods. Obese people, like hyperphagic rats, also take larger mouthfuls, chew less, and finish their meals more rapidly than normal-weight people (LeBow et al., 1977; Marston et al., 1977). For all these reasons, Schachter speculated that many obese people may be troubled by faulty neural regulation of hunger because of problems in the hypothalamus.

Other factors, such as emotional state, may also play a role in obesity. Dieting efforts might be impeded by negative emotional states such as depression (Baucom & Aiken, 1981; Ruderman, 1985) and anxiety (Pine, 1985).

But now, some good news for people who would like to lose a few pounds. Psychological research has led to a number of helpful suggestions for people who would like to lose some weight and keep it off. Following a self-help manual can be successful (Wing et al., 1982), and we shall provide just such a manual in Chapter 10.

Sleep Patterns

Sleep has always been a fascinating topic. We spend about one-third of our adult lives sleeping. Most animals relax their muscles and collapse when they

FIGURE 7.2   A Hyperphagic Rat

This rodent winner of the basketball look-alike contest went on a binge after it received a lesion in the ventromedial nucleus (VMN) of the hypothalamus. It is as if the lesion pushed the "set point" for body weight up several notches, and the rat's weight is now about five times normal. But now it eats only enough to maintain its pleasantly plump stature, so you need not be concerned that it will eventually burst. If the lesion had been made in the lateral hypothalamus, the animal might have become the "Twiggy" of the rat world.

Rapid-eye-movement sleep. A stage of sleep characterized by rapid eye movements, which have been linked to dreaming. Abbreviated REM sleep.

sleep, but birds and horses sleep upright. Their antigravity muscles are at work all night long. Most of us complain when we have not gotten several hours of sleep, but some people sleep for an hour or less a day and appear to lead otherwise normal lives.

Why do we sleep? Why do we dream? Why do some of us have trouble getting to sleep, and what can we do about it?

Functions of Sleep   One outdated theory of sleep suggested that sleep allowed the brain to rest and recuperate from the stresses of "being on" all day. But research with the electroencephalograph (EEG), an instrument that measures the electrical activity of the brain, has shown that brain cells are active all night long. Moreover, at least during **rapid-eye movement sleep,** or REM sleep, the brain waves resemble those of light sleep and the waking state. So the power isn't switched off at night.

But what of sleep and the rest of the body? Sleep apparently helps us to rejuvenate a tired body (Levitt, 1981) and to recover from stress (Hartmann, 1973). Most of us have gone without sleep for a night and felt "wrecked" the following day. Perhaps the following evening we went to bed early to "get our sleep back."

There is also the question as to how much sleep we need. According to sleep researcher Wilse Webb, experiments with people who remain sleepless for several consecutive days result in few serious disturbances. Most often, participants show temporary problems in attention, confusion, or misperception (Goleman, 1982). These cognitive lapses may reflect brief episodes of borderline sleep.

What if we were to decide that we want to spend more of our lives in the walking state—to work, to play, perchance to daydream? Would any ill effects attend curtailing our sleep to, say, five and a half hours a night? To find out, Webb followed 15 college men who restricted their sleep to five and a half hours a night for 60 days. Over this time period, they showed little dropoff in cognitive functioning, as measured, for example, by the abilities to remember and compute numbers (Goleman, 1982). The men reported falling asleep in class or feeling drowsy during the day only during the first week of the study. After that they reported less drowsiness than prior to the study. Did the lack of harmful effects of sleep depirvation encourage the men to permanently curtail their hours of sleep so that they could experience more each day? No. All participants returned to their normal seven or eight hours when the study was completed.

So far, we have discussed experiments in which people have been deprived of the amount of sleep they normally obtain. We have not yet dealt with whether or not there are differences between people who normally sleep different numbers of hours. In one study along these lines, Hartmann (1973) compared people who slept nine hours or more a night ("long sleepers") with people who slept six hours or less ("short sleepers"). He found that short sleepers tended to be more happy-go-lucky. They spent less time ruminating and were energetic, active, and relatively self-satisfied. The long sleepers were more concerned about personal achievement and social causes. They tended to be more creative and thoughtful, but were also more anxious and depressed. We generally require more sleep during periods of change and stress, such as during a change of jobs, an increase in work load, or an episode of depression. So perhaps sleep does help us recover from life's stresses.

Hartmann also found that long sleepers spend proportionately more time in REM sleep than do short sleepers. Subtracting the amount of time spent in REM sleep by both types of sleepers largely closed the gap between them. Perhaps REM sleep is at least partially responsible for the restorative function. Animals and people deprived of REM sleep seem to learn more slowly and forget what they have learned more rapidly (Hartmann & Stern,

A Nap—the Pause That Refreshes? Sleep helps us to rejuvenate a tired body and to recover from stress. But researchers have not determined how much sleep we need.

1972; Greenberg et al., 1983). And people deprived of REM sleep tend to spend more time in REM sleep the following night. They catch up. Since much REM sleep is spent in dreaming, it has been speculated that dreams might somehow contribute to the benefits of sleep.

Dreams Just what is the stuff of dreams? Some dreams are so realistic and well organized that they seem real. Others are disorganized and unformed.

Dreams are most vivid during REM sleep. Then they are most likely to have clear imagery and coherent plots, even if some of the content is fantastic. Plots are vaguer and images more fleeting during non-REM sleep. You might dream every time you are in REM sleep, which occurs about five times during a typical eight-hour sleep period. Dreams tend to take place in "real time": 15 minutes of events fills about 15 minutes of dreaming. Your dream theater is quite flexible: you can dream in black and white and in full color.

Now and then dreams involve fantastic adventures, but according to Calvin Hall (1966), who has interviewed hundreds of dreamers, most dreams are extensions of the activities and concerns of the day. Hall links dreams to life stresses. If we are preoccupied with illness or death, sexual or aggressive urges, or moral dilemmas, we are likely to dream about them. The characters in our dreams are more often friends and neighbors than spies, monsters, and princes.

Sigmund Freud, the founder of psychodynamic theory, theorized that dreams reflect unconscious wishes and urges. He argued that through dreams we express impulses that we would censor during the day. Moreover, to Freud the content of dreams symbolizes unconscious fantasized objects and activities, such as genital organs and sexual activity. As we shall see in Chapter 9, Freudian psychoanalysts engage in dream analysis as part of the process of psychotherapy. Freud also believed that dreams "protect sleep" by providing imagery that would help keep disturbing, repressed thoughts out of awareness. But disturbing events tend to be followed by related disturbing dreams— not protective imagery. Our behavior in dreams is also generally consistent with our waking behavior. Most dreams, then, are unlikely candidates for the expression (even disguised) of repressed urges. Moralistic people generally do not run wild in their dreams.

J. Allan Hobson and Robert McCarley (1977; Hobson, 1987) suggest that dreams reflect random stimulation of parts of the brain involved in vision, hearing, and memory. From this perspective, dreams reflect biological rather than psychological activity. A time-triggered mechanism deep in a primitive part of the brain (the pons) stimulates three kinds of responses: One arouses neural activity in the parts of the cerebral cortex involved in vision, hearing, and memory, but not to the point of waking. Second, the eye muscles are aroused, showing the rapid eye movement associated with dreaming. Third, there is general inhibition of motor (muscle) activity, so that we don't thrash about as we dream, saving ourselves, and our bed partners, wear and tear. From this perspective, there would also be a greater than chance tendency to dream about the events and concerns of the day, since these would have been represented more recently in the neural circuits of the brain. From this biological perspective, it might not seem that there would be much psychological purpose to analyzing our dreams, but Hobson (1987) suggests that our dreams contain "unique stylistic features and concerns" and can provide some information about our "life strategies."

A third theory of dreams, proposed by Francis Crick and Graeme Mitchison, suggests that REM sleep helps the brain flush out excessive information, helping free it for new information the following day (Schmeck, 1987).

In sum, it has not been demonstrated that dreams in and of themselves serve necessary functions, but REM sleep appears to be linked strongly to the restorative functions of sleep, although we do not know exactly why. A few days without sleep are not known to be particularly harmful. When people lose REM sleep, they tend to spend proportionately more time the following night in REM sleep—sort of making up for the loss. And so loss of sleep for a night or two, or relatively little sleep over a period of several nights, might do no measurable harm.

Insomnia The term **insomnia** refers to three types of sleep problems: difficulty falling asleep (sleep-onset insomnia), difficulty remaining asleep through the night, and awakening prematurely in the morning. As many as 30 million Americans suffer from insomnia (Clark et al., 1981), with women complaining of the problem more frequently than men.

As a group, insomnia sufferers show higher levels of sympathetic nervous system activity as they try to get to sleep and while they sleep (Haynes et al., 1981). Poor sleepers are more depressed and ruminative than good sleepers, more concerned about physical complaints, and more shy and retiring (Freedman & Sattler, 1982; Marks & Monroe, 1976; Monroe & Marks, 1977). Insomnia comes and goes with many people, and tends to increase during periods of anxiety and major life changes.

Insomniacs tend to compound their sleep problems through their efforts to force themselves somehow to get to sleep (Kamens, 1980; Youkilis & Bootzin, 1981). Their concern heightens sympathetic nervous system activity and muscle tension. The fact is that you cannot force yourself to get to sleep. You can only set the stage for sleep by lying down and relaxing when you are tired. If you focus on sleep too closely, it might elude you. Yet millions of us go to bed each night dreading the prospect of sleep-onset insomnia. In Chapter 10 we shall provide a number of suggestions for getting to sleep and sleeping through the night.

Activity Patterns: Run for Your Life?

You might expect that young people are more likely to exercise than the elderly. After all, their bodies are likely to be firmer and more supple; the years have not yet had their chance to take their toll in wear and tear. And so it was not surprising when a *New York Times* poll found that people aged 18–29 were more likely than people over 64 to say that they exercise and exercise often (Burros, 1988). But when respondents were asked whether they had exercised *the day before,* the elderly reported that they had done so more often than the young! So as in the case of our nutritional patterns, there is often a discrepancy between what we think we do and what we actually do.

In this section we discuss types of exercise, the physiological effects of exercise, the health benefits (and hazards!) of exercise, the psychological effects of exercise, and, for those of you who remain couch potatoes, some hints on getting started.

Types of Exercise There are many different kinds of exercise, but for our purposes we shall distinguish between **aerobic exercise** and anaerobic exercise. Aerobic exercise is any kind of exercise that requires a sustained increase in the consumption of oxygen. Kenneth Cooper (1982, 1985), the originator of the term *aerobic,* suggests that at least 5 minutes of continued effort is required to obtain the "training effects" of aerobic exercise—that is, to promote cardiovascular fitness. Aerobic exercises include but are not limited to running and jogging, running in place, walking (at more than a "leisurely pace"), aerobic dancing, jumprope, swimming, bicycle riding, basketball, raquetball, and cross-country skiing.

Anaerobic exercises, by contrast, involve short bursts of muscle activity. Examples of anaerobic exercises are weight training, use of Nautilus-type equipment, calisthenics (which usually allow rest periods between exercises),

Insomnia. A term for three types of sleeping problems: (1) difficulty falling asleep, (2) difficulty remaining asleep, and (3) waking early.

Aerobic exercise. Exercise that requires sustained increase in oxygen consumption, such as jogging, swimming, or riding a bicycle.

Anaerobic exercise. Exercise that does not require sustained increase in oxygen consumption, such as weight lifting.

and sports such as baseball, in which there are infrequent bursts of strenuous activity.

The cardiovascular benefits of exercise we shall describe are obtained from aerobic exercise, although anaerobic exercises can strengthen muscles and improve flexibility.

Physiological Effects of Exercise   The major physiological effect of exercise is the promotion of *fitness*. Fitness is a complex concept (Kuntzleman, 1978) that includes muscle strength; muscle endurance; suppleness or flexibility; cardiorespiratory, or aerobic, fitness; and changes in body composition such that the ratio of muscle to fat is increased, usually as a result of both building muscle and reducing fat.

Muscle strength is usually promoted by contracting muscles—often by pressing against a source of resistance—and then returning gradually to the starting position. Weight training, use of Nautilus equipment, and calisthenics such as push-ups and chin-ups are based on this principle. Flexibility can be improved by slow, sustained stretching exercises. Flexibility is desirable in its own right and also because it helps prevent injuries from other types of exercises; this is why many people stretch before running. Stretching exercises can be incorporated into the warm-up and cool-down phases of an aerobic exercise program (Kuntzleman, 1978).

Cardiovascular fitness, or "condition," means that the body can use greater amounts of oxygen during vigorous activity and pump more blood with each heartbeat (Pollock et al., 1978). Since the conditioned athlete pumps more blood with each beat, he or she usually has a slower pulse rate—that is, fewer heart beats per minute. However, during aerobic exercise, the person may double or even triple his or her resting heart rate for many minutes at a time.

Exercise raises the metabolic rate and burns more calories than we burn in a resting state. Sustained exercise practiced at least four times weekly has been shown to foster weight loss, whereas less frequent exercise might not (Epstein & Wing, 1980). Exercise appears to promote weight loss in ways other than just burning calories while it is being performed. Recall from our discussion of obesity that the body often compensates when we eat less by slowing the metabolic rate, frustrating dieters; failure to reach the "set point" in the brain may also trigger persistent feelings of hunger. Concerning the first problem faced by would-be weight losers, an important recent experiment showed that regular aerobic exercise caused dieters to maintain their metabolic rates at normal predieting levels throughout the day (Donahoe et al., 1984). Concerning the second (set-point) problem, it has been speculated that sustained exercise can lower the set point in the hypothalamus (Bennett & Gurin, 1982), so that dieters who exercise would feel less hungry. However, this contention has not yet received strong empirical support.

Exercise and Health   Not only does sustained activity foster cardiovascular fitness, it also appears to reduce the risks of cardiovascular disorders, as measured by incidence of heart attacks and mortality rates. A well-known early English study by Jeremy Morris and his colleagues (1953) correlated the incidence of cardiovascular disorders and physical activity among transportation and postal workers. It was found that conductors aboard London's double-decker buses, who constantly moved about the buses in order to collect fares, had about half the heart attacks of the more sedentary bus drivers. Among the postal workers, mail carriers had significantly fewer heart attacks than clerks in their stations.

A few years later, Ralph Paffenbarger (1972) and his colleagues surveyed some 3,700 San Francisco longshoremen and found that those who sustained strenuous cargo handling had only about 60 percent as many heart attacks

Aerobic Exericse
Aerobic exercise promotes cardiovascular fitness, muscle strength and endurance, and a higher muscle-to-fat ratio. It also burns calories, decreases the likelihood of heart attacks, and has psychological benefits.

as longshoremen engaged in less strenuous activity. In more recent years, Paffenbarger and his colleagues (1978, 1984, 1986) have been tracking some 17,000 Harvard University alumni by means of university records and questionnaires. The Paffenbarger group has correlated incidence of heart attacks with level of physical activity and finds that the incidence of heart attacks declines as the activity level rises to "burning" about 2,000 calories a week by means of physical activity—the exercise equivalent of jogging some 20 miles a week (see Figure 7.3). But above 2,000 calories a week, the incidence of heart attacks begins gradually to climb again, although not steeply. Inactive alumni run the highest risks of heart attacks, and alumni who burn at least 2,000 calories a week live two years longer, on the average, than their less active counterparts.

Of course there is an important limitation to the Morris and Paffenbarger studies: They are correlational, not experimental. It is possible that persons in better health to begin with choose to engage in, and enjoy, higher levels of physical activity. If such is the case, then their lower incidence of heart attacks and their lower mortality rates would be attributable to their initial superior health, and not to physical activity.

However, an experiment with monkeys appears to confirm the cardiovascular benefits of sustained activity (Kramsch et al., 1981). Three groups of nine monkeys each were assigned at random to the following conditions: (a) a sedentary group who received a low-fat diet; (b) another sedentary group switched to a diet high in fats and cholesterol after 12 months; and (c) an active group who gradually worked up to an hour of exercise on a treadmill three times weekly, and who were also switched to the diet high in fats and cholesterol. The animals were monitored over a 42-month period. Now, to

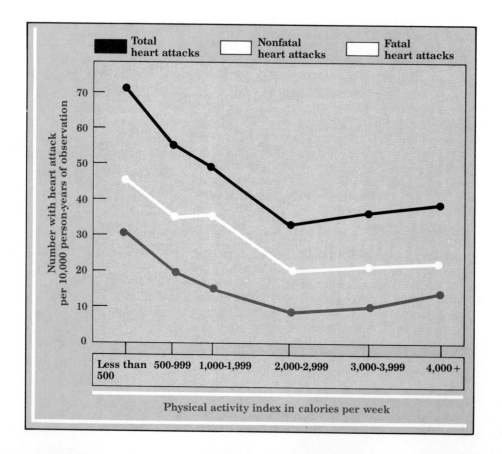

FIGURE 7.3   The Relationship between Exercise and Heart Attacks

A longitudinal study of Harvard University alumni finds that the probability of having a heart attack declines as the number of calories expended in exercise increases up to about 2,000 calories per week. Then the incidence of heart attacks increases gradually along with the number of calories expended. We expend about 2,000 calories a week by jogging three miles a day or walking for about an hour a day.

fully understand the results of this study, we must first point out that there are two types of cholesterol—"good" cholesterol, which contains high-density lipoprotein (HDL) and is linked to cardiovascular health; and "bad" cholesterol, which contains low-density lipoprotein (LDL) and is linked to cardiovascular disorders. It turns out that the monkeys who exercised on the treadmill had higher levels of "good" cholesterol and lower levels of "bad" cholesterol than their sedentary counterparts. Morover, atherosclerosis and sudden death were significantly more frequent occurrences among the sedentary groups.

Hazards of Exercise   Exercise can also have its hazards. Perhaps the most obvious of these are injuries. Jogging, for example, places severe pressures on joints, and soreness and minor injuries are accepted as run-of-the-mill by most enthusiasts. Proper equipment helps protect against injury in many sports. In other words, the higher price of better running shoes is often justified, although, as recent issues of *Consumer Reports* attest, the very highest-priced shoes may have little marginal advantage other than snob appeal. (It's worth a trip to the library.)

Our discussion must now return to James Fixx, who was running about ten six-minute miles daily when he collapsed from a heart attack and died. There is no question that physically active people with cardiovascular problems are more likely to die from them *while engaged in vigorous activity* (Siscovick et al., 1982, 1984). Most cases of sudden death while exercising stem from cardiovascular collapse, and the major predictor of collapse is a preexisting condition of atherosclerosis—narrowing of the arteries (Thompson, 1982). Unfortunately (or fortunately, depending on your point of view), atherosclerosis can be present even when there are no symptoms, such as chest pain. But cardiovascular risks can usually be detected during so-called stress tests, and testing is strongly recommended for people who have not exercised vigorously in the recent past. It is especially recommended for people over 40. If they smoke, are overweight, or have family histories of cardiovascular disorders, testing should be considered mandatory.

But maintain a proper perspective: People *with preexisting cardiovascular conditions* are at risk for sudden death when they undertake strenuous exercise programs *without expert medical guidance*. For most other people, a regular exercise schedule, developed gradually, provides more cardiovascular benefits than hazards (Siscovick et al., 1982, 1984).

Psychological Effects of Exercise: "Running Therapy"?   Psychologists have been keenly interested in the effects of exercise, particularly aerobic exercise, on psychological variables such as depression. Articles have been appearing on exercise as "therapy"—for example, "running therapy" (Greist, 1984).

Depression is characterized by inactivity and feelings of helplessness. Aerobic exercise is, in a sense, the "opposite" of inactivity, and success at it might also help alleviate feelings of helplessness. In a notable experiment, McCann and Holmes (1984) assigned mildly depressed college women at random to aerobic exercise, a progressive-relaxation placebo, and a no-treatment control group. The relaxation group showed some improvement, but aerobic exercise made dramatic inroads on students' depression.

Other experiments also suggest that aerobic exercise alleviates feelings of depression, at least among mildly and moderately depressed individuals (Buffone, 1984). Buffone (1980) found that eight weeks of treatment combining cognitive-behavioral methods and running helped clinically depressed patients. Reuter and Harris (1980) found that a combination of running and counseling alleviates feelings of depression more effectively than counseling alone. Greist (1984) assigned depressed subjects at random to aerobic exercise, relaxation training, or group therapy. All three treatments helped, but the exercise and relaxation groups had outpaced the verbal therapy patients at a three-month follow-up.

Still other research suggests that sustained exercise alleviates feelings of anxiety (Long, 1984) and boosts feelings of self-esteem (Sonstroem, 1984). However, Sonstroem points out that in all these studies it might not be the exercise itself that is reponsible for the psychological benefits. Sonstroem (1984) notes that the apparent benefits of exercise might also be attributed to

a. feelings of physical well-being,
b. improved physical health,
c. achievement of (exercise) goals,
d. an enhanced sense of control over one's body,
e. the social support of fellow exercisers, or even
f. the attention of the researchers.

Of course, reasons a–e still provide very good reasons for exercising.

Starting to Exercise   And so, how about you? Are you considering climbing aboard the exercise bandwagon? If so, consider the following suggestions:

1. Unless you have engaged in sustained and vigorous exercise recently, seek the advice of a medical expert. If you smoke, have a family history of cardiovascular disorders, are overweight, or are over 40, get a stress test.
2. Consider joining a beginners aerobics class. Group leaders are not usually experts in physiology, but at least they "know the steps." You'll also be among other beginners and derive the benefits of social support.
3. Get the proper equipment to facilitate performance and help avert injury.
4. Read up on the activity you are considering. There are many excellent books on the market, such as the recent Kenneth Cooper (1982, 1985) books on aerobic exercise that will give you an idea of how to get started and how fast you can expect to progress.
5. Try to select activities that you can sustain for a lifetime. Don't worry about building yourself up rapidly. Enjoy yourself and your strength and endurance will progress on their own. If you do not enjoy what you're doing, you're not likely to stick to it.
6. Keep a diary or log and note your progress. If running, note the paths or streets you follow, the distance you run, the weather conditions, and any remarkable details that come to mind. Check your notes now and then to remind yourself of enjoyable paths and experiences.
7. If you feel severe pain, don't try to exercise "through" it. Soreness is to be expected for beginners (and some old-timers now and then). In that sense, soreness, at least when intermittent, is normal. But sharp pain is abnormal and a sign that something is wrong.
8. Have fun!

■ The Psychology of Being Sick

Individual differences truly hit home when it comes to our illness behavior. Some of us refuse to go to the doctor unless we are incapable of moving; others rush off to the doctor at the drop of a hat. Some of us deny pain and other symptoms; others of us exaggerate pain. Some of us view chronic disorders such as essential hypertension and diabetes as temporary setbacks; others see them as the lingering problems that they are. Some of us make good use of visits to the doctor; some do not. Some of us comply with medical advice; some do not.

In this section we first review factors that determine whether we shall seek help when we feel ill and the ways in which we conceptualize illness. Then we consider "the sick role" that is enacted in our society. Next we discuss patient–physician interactions and the issues involved in whether or not we comply with medical advice.

Factors That Determine Willingness to Seek Health Care

You've heard the expression, "Do as I say, not as I do." This saying applies perfectly to illness behavior, because people are much more willing to advise others to go to the doctor when they are ill than they are to go themselves (Feldman, 1966). Reluctance to seek health care is related to fear of what the doctor might find; to social and demographic factors, such as gender, socioeconomic status, and ethnic background; to characteristics of the symptoms; and to the ways in which we tend to conceptualize illness.

Women, for example, are more likely to seek medical help than men, even when we take into account visits for pregnancy and childbirth (Rosenstock & Kirscht, 1979). The gender difference may reflect the traits associated with the rugged, independent stereotypical masculine sex role in our society, as we saw in Chapter 3. Men, that is, are expected to be self-sufficient. According to a U.S. Department of Health, Education, and Welfare (1979) report, people of higher socioeconomic status are more willing than persons of lower status to seek medical help, even though poor people are more likely to become ill and eventually get hospitalized. Also note these ethnic factors found by Mechanic (1978): Irish Americans are more likely than most other U.S. groups to stoically deny pain; Mexican Americans frequently deny serious symptoms and exaggerate others; and Jewish Americans tend to engage in preventive behavior, seek medical help when needed, and exaggerate pain.

Mechanic (1978) found that four symptom characteristics also help determine whether or not we shall seek medical help (see Figure 7.4):

1. *Visibility of the symptom.* For example, everything else being equal, a rash or a cut on the face is more likely to cause concern than a rash or a cut on the torso or the legs.

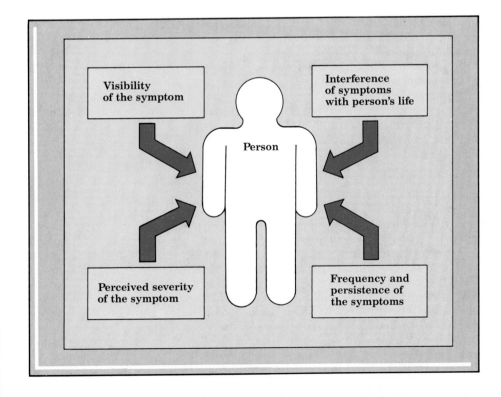

FIGURE 7.4 Symptom Characteristics That Determine Whether We Shall Seek Medical Advice

Four symptom characteristics influence the likelihood that we shall seek medical help: visibility of the symptoms, perceived severity of the symptoms, the degree to which the symptoms interfere with our lives, and the frequency and persistence of the symptoms.

2. *Perceived severity of the symptom.* More severe symptoms prompt greater concern and are more likely to induce a visit to the doctor.
3. *Interference of symptoms with the person's life.* We are more likely to see the doctor when symptoms, say, make it difficult to eliminate, engage in sexual activity, eat, or move around.
4. *Frequency and persistence of the symptoms.* Symptoms that come on frequently and persist are more likely to prompt a visit to the doctor than intermittent symptoms.

Ways in Which We Conceptualize Illness

The ways in which we conceptualize illness are important because they, too, influence whether or not we will behave in health-enhancing ways. Howard Leventhal and his colleagues (1980, 1984; Meyer et al., 1985) have identified four components of our conceptualizations of illness:

1. *Identity of the illness.* Our ideas about what is wrong with us provide a framework for the interpretation of symptoms. Severe chest pains, for example, can be symptoms of a heart attack, a spasm of the esophagus (the muscular tube through which food passes on the way to the stomach), indigestion, and other problems. We have a tendency to attribute symptoms to minor, common illnesses because such illnesses are more likely to be within our experiences (Lau & Russell, 1983). A proper label is the basis for proper illness behavior, such as seeking help or complying with treatment.
2. *Time Course of the Illness and the Treatment.* Accurate conceptualization of the course of a disease is important to maintaining an adequate treatment regimen. Even though professionals may tell them otherwise, people tend to erroneously view hypertension, diabetes, and bipolar affective disorder (see Chapter 8) as acute, temporary problems. Each of these and many other disorders can require staying on a therapeutic regimen over an extended period of time.
3. *Consequences of the Illness.* Sometimes we do not seek medical advice for symptoms because the illnesses they suggest are minor, as in the case of cold symptoms. But we might also avoid seeking advice about symptoms such as a lump in the breast or blood in the urine because they suggest the possibility of life-threatening disorders.
4. *Causal Attributions for the Illness.* Causal attributions for illnesses are important because they influence preventive behavior as well as seeking of proper treatment. For example, if we overattribute cardiovascular disorders and cancer to genetic factors, we might throw up our hands in despair at being able to influence their onsets and ignore our nutritional and activity patterns. But recognition that there are multiple risk factors for such illnesses can motivate us to engage in daily healthful behavior patterns.

The Sick Role

And so there are a number of factors that enter into our determinations as to whether we are sick and, if so, what type of illness we have. Sociologist Talcott Parsons (1978) has noted that once we label ourselves as sick, we tend to enact "the sick role." The sick role is based on three assumptions: first, that we are not to blame for being sick; second, that being sick relieves us of our normal responsibilities; and three, that sick people do what is required to get well.

The notion that we are not to blame for being sick is complex and in many cases at least partially inaccurate. For example, if we are struck by a pathogen such as the AIDS virus, do we attribute subsequent problems to the virus *or to our own behavior which exposed us to the virus and which, in many cases, might have been prevented?* Before the AIDS virus was isolated, people could not be expected to behave in a manner that would lessen the likelihood of

☐ WHAT DO YOU SAY NOW?

Encouraging a Friend to Seek Help

You have a friend who has been complaining of chest pains for a few days but who has not gone to have them evaluated by a physician. There may be nothing serious wrong, but you are becoming concerned. What do you say now?

Write some possible responses in the following spaces. Then look below for the authors' suggestions.

1. _____
   _____ .
2. _____
   _____ .
3. _____
   _____ .

Your friend might be avoiding medical evaluation for fear of the possible consequences of whatever illness he or she might have. Note the following suggestions:

1. Your friend might have told you what he or she suspects the symptoms might mean, but if not you can say something like, "You've been having these pains now for at least a week. Do you have any idea what they might be from?" This is a relatively nonthreatening way of drawing your friend out to find out how he or she conceptualizes the symptoms. You can get an impression of whether he or she is minimizing them, as many of us do, or assuming "the worst"— that is, something like a life-threatening cardiovascular disorder.

2. If your friend has been minimizing symptoms and says, "Oh, they're nothing," you can follow up with something like, "Yes, they might mean nothing at all, but they could mean something. I care about you and it would make me very happy if you would get looked at." You can add an offer to go with your friend to the doctor; correcting minimization and social support are of help.

3. If your friend has been catastrophizing the symptoms and is afraid to seek medical advice, you can say something like, "I understand your concern. I'm no doctor, but I understand that lots of the time chest pains mean something like indigestion. Why don't you get looked at? It's probably something you can take care of and at least it'll put your mind at ease." Again, you can follow up by offering to go along with your friend.

exposure to it. But today, when pathways such as sharing contaminated needles and unsafe sexual practices have been widely publicized, we can say that the pathogen and the behavior of the person are jointly responsible. With cancer and cardiovascular disorders there are certainly genetic risk factors, but our nutritional and activity patterns can also play a role.

Depending on the illness, sick people may not be expected to go to school, work, mow the grass, or care for the children. Some people find it difficult to take on this aspect of the sick role and insist on continuing to work as much as they can. Others are all too willing to be relieved of their responsibilities! This aspect of the sick role sometimes backfires in the case of psychological disorders. As we shall see in Chapter 9, many persons with psychological disorders are helped rather than hurt by remaining in the community and not being hospitalized; living at home and staying at their jobs keeps them in touch with the realities of daily life and bolsters their self-efficacy expectancies. The responsibility-relieving aspect of the sick role is also one of the reasons that many psychologists object to the so-called medical model of psychological disorders, which includes the elements of the sick role.

The desire to get well is expected of sick people. And in order to get well, people must frequently interact with medical experts and comply with medical advice. Let us now turn our attention to physician–patient interactions and to the issue of compliance.

Talking to the Doctor: Enhancing Physician–Patient Interactions

Psychologists have found many ways in which physicians and patients can increase the effectiveness and satisfaction of their interactions. One area involves the so-called bedside manner of the physician. In an experiment to determine which aspects of a physician's nonverbal behavior contributed to patient satisfaction, Harrigan and Rosenthal (1983) manipulated behaviors such as leaning forward versus sitting back. It was found that patients evaluated physicians most positively when they leaned forward rather than sat back, nodded their heads in response to patient verbalizations, and kept their arms open rather than folded.

As noted, because of the anxiety they provoke, most people try not to think about the symptoms of illnesses when they first appear (Suls & Fletcher, 1985). By the time they visit the physician, they are frequently quite anxious about them. Anxiety during the physician–patient interview sometimes causes patients to forget to mention certain symptoms and to forget to ask questions that had been on their minds. Roter (1984) found that having patients take ten minutes before the visit with the physician to jot down concerns and questions led to asking more questions and greater satisfaction with the interview.

Complying with Medical Instructions and Procedures

Once we have been to see the doctor, how many of us comply with medical instructions and procedures? In a review of the literature, Sackett and Snow (1979) concluded that about 75 percent of us keep appointments we have made with health professionals, but only about half of us keep appointments scheduled by the professional. More of us will take medicines to cure illnesses than to prevent them: 77 percent of us will take medicine over the short term

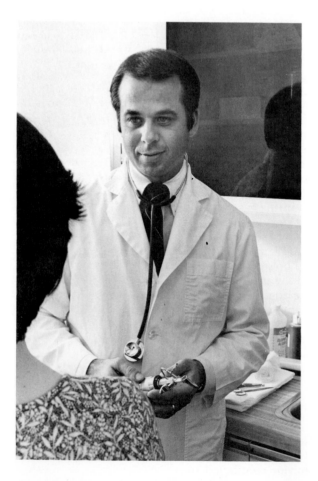

A Physician–Patient Interaction
Anxiety during the physician–patient interview can cause patients to forget to mention symptoms and to forget to ask questions that had been on their minds. How can you make the best use of a visit to the doctor? How can you be sure to get the information you need to enhance your health behavior?

WHAT DO YOU SAY NOW?

Enhancing Patient–Physician Interactions

You have had eye pain for several weeks. Rubbing the eye makes it worse, not better, and over-the-counter eyedrops have not been very helpful. You finally go to an ophthalmologist—a physician who specializes in eye disorders—and he makes a few mm-hmm's as he examines you.

Finally he says, "Well, there's no doubt about it. You have some irritation. I'm going to prescribe an ointment that has a steroid in it that should give you some relief, and I'd like you to come back in a month for another look."

You say, "Will you please tell me what the diagnosis is?" and the physician replies, quite amiably, "I'll be glad to tell you, but what's the point of my throwing technical terms at you? The steroid ought to help with the irritation; I'm sure you'll be feeling better."

What do you say now? Write some possible responses in the following spaces. Then look below for the authors' suggestions

1. _____
_____ .
2. _____
_____
3. _____
_____

In posing your comments and questions, keep in mind that accurate conceptualization of your disorder—including knowledge of the diagnosis—will help you to maintain an appropriate treatment regimen. And you are entitled to accurate information about your condition. Moreover, you are likely to discontinue treatment if you do not perceive it to be effective, or if there are uncomfortable side effects and you do not expect them.

So consider the following possibilities:

1. In order to obtain information that will allow you to conceptualize your illness, say something like, "Well, I was going to ask for an explanation of the diagnosis. I would like very much to know where my condition came from—whatever it is—and what its course is." You have a need to know whether you have been engaging in behavior patterns that brought on the eye condition, whether it means that there are genetic eye problems in your family, and how long the condition is likely to persist.
2. In order to help you remain on the medication successfully, you may want to say something like, "Please explain to me how the ointment—with the steroid, I think you said—will help me." An explanation will heighten your expectations concerning the efficacy of the treatment.
3. Many medical treatments, including medications, have discomforting, or potentially discomforting, side effects. In order to help brace yourself for possible discomfort, you can say something like, "What are the side effects of the treatment (or ointment)? What can I expect?"
4. If, in response to your request for information about side effects, the physician says, "Oh, most people don't experience side effects," you might say something like, "It would be of help to me to know what might happen, especially the circumstances under which I should call you or stop using the ointment."

In most cases, you can expect that the physician will be pleased to answer all of your questions. Physicians sometimes have a hard time gauging just how much information will be of help to each patient. In a sense, you are providing the physician with the information he or she needs in order to make that decision.

to cure an illness, whereas 63 percent of us will take the medicine to prevent it. Over the long term, compliance drops to about 50 percent, which is especially troublesome for disorders such as hypertension, in which there can be no symptoms and persistent treatment is usually required. Similarly, it has been found that only about 50 percent of patients stick to clinical exercise programs following the first six months (Dishman, 1982)

Some factors that determine compliance reside with the physician. Patients are more likely to adhere to advice from physicians who are perceived as competent, friendly, warm, and concerned about their patients (DiNicola & DiMatteo, 1984). On the other hand, patients are less likely to comply with instructions from physicians whom they perceive as authoritarian and condescending (Gastorf & Galanos, 1983). There was a time when medical training was almost completely technical, but research findings such as these have prompted medical schools to train students in ways of relating to patients as people.

Health psychologists have found that patients are more likely to comply with medical instructions when illness is severe (Becker & Maiman, 1980), and when they believe that the instructions will work. Women, for example, are more likely to engage in breast self-examination when they believe that they will really be able to detect abnormal growths (Alagna & Reddy, 1984). Diabetes patients are more likely to use insulin regularly to control their blood sugar levels when they believe that their regimens will be of help (Brownlee-Duffeck et al., 1987).

Physicians often prescribe drugs and other treatment regimens without explaining to patients the purposes of the treatments and their possible complications. This approach can backfire. When it comes to taking prescribed drugs, patients frequently tend not to take them or to take them incorrectly (Haynes et al., 1979). Patients are particularly likely to discontinue medications when they encounter side effects, especially when they are unexpected. Therefore, specific instructions coupled with accurate information about potential side effects would appear to be most useful in inducing compliance (Baron & Byrne, 1987; Keown et al., 1984).

Cultural factors are also involved in compliance. It has been shown, for example, that Hispanic Americans are more likely to comply with medical instructions when they are issued by personnel who have an understanding of Hispanic-American culture. A study in Zimbabwe, Africa, points out that some people do not comply with medical regimens because of belief in nonscientific but traditional methods of healing (Zyazema, 1984).

As in so many other areas of life, social support is of help in fostering compliance with medical instructions and procedures. One study, for example, found that men whose spouses are supportive are more likely than men with less supportive spouses to make changes in nutritional and activity patterns in an effort to avert cardiovascular disorders (Doherty et al., 1983).

In this chapter we have dealt primarily with matters of physical health. In the following chapter we turn our attention to psychological disorders.

■ Summary

1. **What is health psychology?** Health psychology is an emerging field of psychology that studies the relationships between psychological factors (e.g., overt behavior, emotions, stress, beliefs, and attitudes) and the prevention and treatment of physical illness.

2. **What are the functions of the immune system?** The first function of the immune system is to engulf and kill pathogens, wornout body cells, and cancerous cells. The second function of the immune system is to "remember" pathogens to facilitate future combat against them. The third function is inflammation, which increases the numbers of white blood cells brought to a damaged area.

3. **What are the effects of stress on the immune system?** By stimulating the release of corticosteroids, stress depresses the functioning of the immune system. (E.g., steroids counter inflammation.)

4. **What kinds of headaches are there, and how are they related to stress?** The most common kinds are muscle-tension headaches and migraine headaches. Stress causes and compounds headache pain by stimulating muscle tension.

5. **What is hypertension, and how is it related to stress?** Hypertension is elevated blood pressure; persistent hypertension in the absence of external stressors is called essential hypertension. Stress increases the blood pressure by activating the sympathetic division of the ANS.

6. **What are the risk factors for cardiovascular disorders?** There are four basic risk factors for cardiovascular disorders: family history, physiological conditions such as hypertension and high levels of serum cholesterol, behavior patterns such as smoking and eating fatty foods, and Type A behavior.

7. **What behavioral measures contribute to the prevention and treatment of cardiovascular disorders?** The following measures do: stopping smoking, controlling one's weight, reducing hypertension, lowering serum cholesterol, and modifying Type A behavior.

8. **What are the risk factors for cancer?** Risk factors for cancer include: family history, smoking, drinking alcohol, eating animal fats, sunbathing, and stress.

9. **What behavioral measures contribute to the prevention and treatment of cancer?** The following measures do: controlling our exposure to behavioral risk factors for cancer; going for regular medical checkups; regulating the amount of stress impacting upon us; and vigorously fighting cancer, if we are afflicted.

10. **What is the difference between substance abuse and substance dependence?** Substance abuse is continued use of a substance despite the fact that abuse is causing social, occupational, or other problems. Dependence is characterized by inability to control use, by tolerance, and by withdrawal symptoms.

11. **What are the effects of alcohol?** Alcohol is a depressant that can induce feelings of euphoria. Alcohol does not cause aggression, but gives people an aggressive social role to play. Similarly, alcohol depresses sexual response but provides people with a liberated sexual role. Alcohol can lead to cirrhosis of the liver, Wernicke-Korsakoff syndrome, cardiovascular disorders, and cancer. There is correlational evidence that light to moderate drinking may lower the incidence of heart attacks, especially in men.

12. **What are the effects of smoking cigarettes?** Smoking heightens the risks of cancer, cardiovascular disorders, lung and respiratory disorders, miscarriage, and—in the offspring of pregnant smokers—premature birth, low birth weight, respiratory ailments, and birth defects.

13. **How do nutritional patterns influence our health?** Cholesterol, fats, and obesity heighten the risk of cardiovascular disorders. Salt raises the blood pressure. Fats and preservatives heighten the risk of cancer. Diets high in fiber, vitamins, fruits and vegetables, and fish are apparently healthful.

14. **What factors contribute to obesity?** Risk factors for obesity include family history, overeating, and a low level of activity. Obese people have more fat cells than normal-weight people and seem more responsive to external cues for hunger.

15. **How do sleeping patterns influence our health?** Sleep appears to serve a general restorative function, although the mechanisms are unclear. REM sleep also seems required. Sleep deprivation over a few days does not appear particularly harmful, although there are some cognitive lapses and some drowsiness during the day.

16. **How do activity patterns influence our health?** Physical inactivity is a risk factor for cardiovascular disorders. Exercise has the benefits of promoting muscle strength, muscle endurance, flexibility, cardiorespiratory fitness, and a higher body muscle-to-fat ratio. Burning about 2,000 calories per week by means of exercise seems ideal for lowering the risk of cardiovascular disorders. Exercise also appears to lower feelings of depression and anxiety and to boost self-esteem.

17. **What factors influence willingness to seek health care when we are ill?** Factors that influence willingness to bring symptoms to the attention of a health professional include visibility of the symptoms, perceived severity

of the symptoms, interference of the symptoms with our lives, and frequency and persistence of the symptoms.

18. **How do we conceptualize illness?** There are four components to our conceptualization of illness: the identity of the illness, the time course of the illness and the treatment, the consequences of the illness, and our causal attributions for the illness. Our conceptualization of the illness influences whether we will seek medical attention and comply with medical advice.

19. **What are the components of the sick role in our society?** The sick role has three components: first, that we are not to be blamed for being sick; second, that sickness relieves us of responsibilities; and third, that we should desire to get well and take steps in that direction.

20. **What factors influence compliance with medical instructions and procedures?** Factors that influence compliance include the "bedside manner" of the physician (we are more likely to comply with advice from competent, friendly, concerned physicians), belief that the advice will be effective, ability to cope with side effects, cultural factors, and social support.

■ TRUTH OR FICTION REVISITED

At any given moment, myriads of microscopic warriors within our bodies are carrying out search-and-destroy missions against foreign agents. True. They are white blood cells.

Most headaches are caused by muscle tension. True. Muscle tension can also increase the pain of headaches that stem from other causes.

Stress can influence the course of cancer. True. Stress seems to hasten the progress of the disease.

Some people inherit a predisposition toward becoming dependent on alcohol. True. Such people appear to have a higher tolerance for alcohol.

Heroin was once used as a cure for addiction to morphine. True. Today many heroin addicts are treated with the narcotic methadone.

Coca-Cola once "added life" by using cocaine. True. In fact, Coca-Cola derives its name from the cocoa plant.

Cigarette smokers are less aware than nonsmokers of the perils of smoking. False. However, there is often a discrepancy between our knowledge and our health-related behavior patterns.

Cigarette smokers tend to smoke more when they are under stress. True. Stress speeds up the elimination of nicotine from the body, and dependent smokers attempt to maintain a certain nicotine level.

LSD users can have flashbacks at any time. False. Flashbacks are more common among users who are willing to let themselves go and focus on fantasy.

Your diet can influence the likelihood that you will contract cancer. True. Vitamin deficiencies and fats, for example, heighten the risk of cancer.

Obese people have more fat cells than normal-weight people. True. As a result, they may feel hungry sooner after meals than normal-weight people.

Obese people are more responsive to their stomach contractions than normal-weight people. False. Normal-weight individuals are actually more sensitive to internal hunger-related sensations.

People who sleep nine hours or more a night tend to be lazy and happy-go-lucky. False. Actually, they are more anxious and ruminative than people who sleep six hours a night or less.

We tend to act out our forbidden fantasies in our dreams. False. People do not usually "let go" in their dreams any more than they do during their waking hours.

Young people aged 18–29 are more likely to exercise than senior citizens. False.

Medical patients should be told as little as possible about their illnesses and why they are being given certain medicines. False. Accurate information promotes compliance to medical instructions and procedures.

Patients are more likely to comply with "doctor's orders" when they are issued by an authoritarian physician. False. They resent authoritarian physicians and tend to resist them.

■ Scoring Key for the "Why Do You Drink?" Questionnaire

Why do you drink? Score your questionnaire by seeing how many items you answered in accord with the following reasons for drinking. Consider the key suggestive only. For example, if you answered several items in such a way that you scored on the *addiction* factor, it may be wise to seriously examine what your drinking means to you. However, a few test items cannot be interpreted as binding evidence of addiction.

Addiction (Physiological dependence)

1. T	38. T
6. F	40. T
32. T	

Anxiety/Tension Reduction

7. T	18. T
9. T	26. T
12. T	31. T
15. T	33. T

Pleasure/Taste

2. T	28. T
5. T	35. T
16. T	37. T
27. T	

Transforming Agent

2. T	28. T
4. T	30. T
19. T	34. T
22. T	36. T

Social Reward

3. T	23. T
8. T	

Celebration

10. T	25. T
24. T	

Religion

11. T

Social Power

2. T	19. T
13. T	30. T

Scapegoating (Using alcohol as an excuse for failure or social misconduct)

14. T	21. T
15. T	39. T
20. T	

Habit

17. T	29. T

Psychological Disorders

8

A man shot the president of the United States in front of millions of television witnesses, yet was found not guilty by a court of law.

Some people are suddenly flooded with feelings of panic, even when there is no external threat.

Some people have irresistible urges to wash their hands—over and over again.

Stressful experiences can lead to recurrent nightmares.

Some people have not one, but two or more distinct personalities dwelling within them.

People have lost the use of their legs or eyes under stress, even though there was nothing medically wrong with them.

Dieting has become the normal way of eating for women in the United States.

Some college women control their weight by going on cycles of binge eating followed by self-induced vomiting.

It is abnormal to feel depressed.

Some people ride an emotional roller-coaster, with cycles of elation and depression.

People who threaten suicide are only seeking attention.

In some mental disorders, people see and hear things that are not actually there.

Some people persistently injure others and violate their rights without feeling guilty.

Thousands of U.S. citizens have changed their sex through surgery.

Strip-teasers are exhibitionists.

The Ohio State campus lived in terror throughout the long fall of 1978. Four college women were abducted, forced to cash checks or obtain money with their instant-cash cards, and then raped. A mysterious phone call led to the arrest of a 23-year-old drifter, William, who had been dismissed from the Navy.

William was not the boy next door.

Several psychologists and psychiatrists who interviewed William concluded that ten personalities resided within him, eight male and two female (Keyes, 1982). His personality had been "fractured" by an abusive childhood. The personalities showed distinct facial expressions, vocal patterns, and memories. They even performed differently on personality and intelligence tests.

Arthur, the most rational personality, spoke with a British accent. Danny and Christopher were normal, quiet adolescents. Christene was a 3-year-old girl. It was Tommy, a 16-year-old, who had enlisted in the Navy. Allen was 18 and smoked. Adelena, a 19-year-old lesbian personality, had committed the rapes. Who had made the mysterious phone call? Probably David, aged 9, an anxious child personality.

The defense claimed that William was suffering from **multiple personality.** Several distinct personalities dwelled within him. Some were aware of the others; some believed that they were the sole occupants. Billy, the core personality, had learned to sleep as a child to avoid the abuse of his father. A psychiatrist asserted that Billy had also been "asleep," in a "psychological coma," during the abductions. Therefore Billy should be found innocent by reason of **insanity.**

On December 4, 1978, Billy was found not guilty by reason of insanity. He was committed to an institution for the mentally ill and released in 1984.

In 1982, John Hinckley, was also found not guilty of the assassination attempt on President Reagan by reason of insanity. Expert witnesses testified that he was suffering from **schizophrenia.** Hinckley, too, was committed to an institution for the mentally ill.

Multiple personality and schizophrenia are two types of psychological disorders, or abnormal behavior patterns. In this chapter we first define psychological disorder. Next we examine various broad explanations for, or "models" of, such disorders. Then we discuss various kinds of psychological disorders, including *anxiety disorders, dissociative disorders, somatoform disorders, eating disorders, mood disorders, schizophrenia, personality disorders, and sexual disorders.*

■ What Are Psychological Disorders?

There is quite a range of psychological disorders. Some are characterized by anxiety or depression, but many of us are anxious or depressed now and then, without having psychological disorders. It is "normal" to be anxious before a big date or on the eve of a midterm examination. It is appropriate to be depressed if a friend is upset with you or if you have done poorly on a test or in a job.

Anxiety and depression might be abnormal, or signs of psychological disorders, when they are not appropriate for our situations. It is normal to be depressed because of a poor performance on a test, but not when everything is going well. It is normal to be anxious before a job interview, but not when one is looking out a fourth-story window or about to receive a harmless vaccination. The magnitude of the problem might also suggest psychological disorder. Whereas some anxiety is to be expected before going on an important job interview, feeling that your heart is pounding so severely that it might leap out of your chest—and then avoiding the interview—are not. Nor is sweating so profusely that your clothing becomes literally soaked.

Multiple personality. A disorder in which a person appears to have two or more distinct personalities, which may alternate in controlling the person.

Insanity. A legal term descriptive of a person judged to be incapable of recognizing right from wrong or of conforming his or her behavior to the law.

Schizophrenia. A psychotic disorder characterized by loss of control of thought processes and inappropriate emotional responses.

Hallucination. A perception in the absence of sensory stimulation that is confused with reality.

Ideas of persecution. Erroneous beliefs that one is being victimized or persecuted.

Medical model. The view that abnormal behavior is symptomatic of mental illness.

Most psychologists agree that we are showing a psychological disorder when our behavior meets some combination of the following criteria:

1. *Our behavior is unusual.* Although people who show serious psychological disorders are in a minority, being different is not sufficient cause to assume that the person has a disorder. There is only one president of the United States at a given time, yet that person is not considered disordered (usually). Only one person holds the record for running or swimming the fastest mile. That person is different from you and me, but he or she is not abnormal.

2. *Our behavior is socially unacceptable.* Each society has standards or norms for acceptable behavior in a given context. In our society, walking naked is normal in a locker room, but abnormal on a crowded boulevard. Similarly, what is abnormal for one generation can be normal for another. Living together without benefit of marriage was almost unheard of a generation ago, but raises few eyebrows today.

3. *Our perception or interpretation of reality is faulty.* We've heard it said that it's all right to say that you talk to God through prayer, but if you say that God talks back, you may be committed to a mental institution. Our society considers it normal to be inspired by religious beliefs, but abnormal to believe that God is literally speaking to you. "Hearing voices" and "seeing things" are considered **hallucinations.** Similarly, **ideas of persecution,** such as believing that the Mafia or the CIA or the communists are "out to get you"—all are considered signs of disorder. (Unless they *are* out to get you, of course.)

4. *We are in severe personal distress.* Anxiety, depression, exaggerated fears, and other psychological states cause personal distress, and severe personal distress can be a sign of disorder. But, as noted, anxiety and depression are appropriate responses to a real threat or a loss. In such cases they are not abnormal unless they persevere long after the source of distress has been removed, or after most people would have adjusted.

5. *Our behavior is self-defeating.* Behavior that leads to misery rather than happiness and fulfillment may be considered disordered. From this perspective, chronic drinking that interferes with work and family life, and cigarette smoking that impairs health, are examples of disordered behavior.

6. *Our behavior is dangerous.* Behavior that is dangerous to the self or others is considered abnormal or disordered. People who threaten or attempt suicide may be considered abnormal, as may people who threaten or attack others.

■ Contemporary Models of Psychological Disorders

There are a number of contemporary views or models of psychological disorders: the medical, psychodynamic, social-learning, and cognitive models.

The Medical Model

According to the **medical model,** psychological disorders reflect underlying biological or biochemical problems. In 1883 Emil Kraepelin published a textbook of psychiatry in which he argued that there were specific kinds of psychological disorders which, within the medical model, are often referred to as mental illnesses. (See Table 8.1 for a list of many of the commonly used terms concerning psychological disorders that reflect the widespread influence of the medical model.) Each mental illness is believed to have specific biological origins. Throughout history researchers have looked to various parts of the body as possible sites for the abnormalities that might contribute to psychological disorders.

TABLE 8.1   Some Commonly Used Terms Concerning Psychological Disorders That Are Derived from the Medical Model

Mental Illness	Mental Hospital
Mental Health	Prognosis
Symptoms	Treatment
Syndrome	Therapy
Diagnosis	Cure
Mental Patient	Relapse

Syndrome. A cluster or group of symptoms suggestive of a particular disorder.

DNA. Deoxyribonucleic acid. The substance which carries the genetic code and makes up genes and chromosomes.

Kraepelin argued that each mental illness, just like each physical illness, was typified by its own cluster of symptoms, or **syndrome.** Each mental illness or psychological disorder had a specific outcome, or course, and would presumably respond to a characteristic form of treatment, or therapy.

Contemporary supporters of the medical model point out various sources of evidence. For one thing, a number of mental disorders run in families, and might therefore be transmitted from generation to generation by way of **DNA,** which is the material that contains our genetic codes. For another, chemical imbalances in the brain and elsewhere produce behavioral effects such as those found in disorders like severe depression and schizophrenia, as we shall see later in the chapter.

According to the medical model, treatment requires medical expertise and involves controlling or curing the underlying biological or biochemical problem. The biological therapies discussed in Chapter 9 are largely based on the medical model.

There are some problems with the medical model. For one thing, biological causes have not been found for each psychological disorder. For another, the model suggests that the mentally ill, like the physically ill, may not be responsible for their problems and limitations. In the past, this view often led to hospitalization and suspension of responsibility (as in work and maintenance of a family life) among the mentally ill. Thus removed from the real world, the ability of the mentally ill often declined further instead of returning to normal. But today even most adherents to the medical model encourage patients to remain in the community and maintain as much responsibility as they can. Finally, treatments derived from other models have been shown to be of help with several psychological disorders, as we shall see in Chapter 9.

The Psychodynamic Model

Whereas the medical model suggests that psychological disorders reflect underlying biological problems, Sigmund Freud's psychodynamic model argues that they are symptomatic of underlying psychological problems or conflicts. In keeping with Freud's theory of psychosexual development, the underlying problem is usually assumed to be unconscious conflict of childhood origins. The disordered behavior patterns are viewed as "symptoms" of the underlying conflict. Frequently, as in the case of persistent anxiety, they are assumed to be symptomatic of difficulty in repressing primitive sexual and aggressive impulses. According to psychodynamic theory, treatment (other than a sort of "band-aid" therapy) requires resolving the unconscious conflicts that underlie the disordered behavior.

The Social-Learning Model

From a social-learning point of view, psychological disorders are not necessarily symptomatic of anything. Rather, the disordered behavior is itself the problem. To a large degree, abnormal behavior is believed to be acquired in the same way normal behaviors are acquired—for example, by means of conditioning and observational learning. Why, then, do some people show disordered behavior? One reason is found in situational variables; that is, their learning or reinforcement histories might differ from those of most of us. But differences in person variables such as competencies, encoding strategies, self-efficacy expectations, and self-regulatory systems might also make the difference.

A person who lacks social skills may never have had the chance to observe skillful models. Or it might be that a minority subculture reinforced behaviors that are not approved by the majority. Punishment for early exploratory behavior, or childhood sexual activity, might lead to adult anxieties over independence or sexuality. Inconsistent discipline (haphazard rewarding of desirable behavior and unreliable punishing of misbehavior) might lead to antisocial behavior. Children whose parents ignore or abuse them might come to pay more attention to their fantasies than the outer world, leading to schizophrenic withdrawal and inability to distinguish reality from fantasy. Deficits in competencies, encoding strategies, and self-regulatory systems may heighten schizophrenic problems. Since social-learning theorists do not believe that behavior problems necessarily reflect biological problems or unconscious conflict, they often try to change or modify them directly, as by means of behavior therapy (see Chapter 9).

The Cognitive Model

Cognitive theorists focus on the cognitive events—such as thoughts, expectations, and attitudes—that accompany and in some cases underlie psychological disorders.

One cognitive approach to understanding disordered behavior involves information processing. Schizophrenic individuals, for example, frequently jump from topic to topic in a disorganized fashion, which information-processing theorists might explain as problems in manipulation of information.

Other cognitive theorists (Albert Ellis [1977, 1987] is one) view anxiety problems as stemming from irrational beliefs and attitudes, such as overwhelming desires for social approval and perfectionism. Aaron Beck attributes many cases of depression to "cognitive errors" such as self-devaluation, interpretion of events in a negative light, and general pessimism (Beck et al., 1979). Some cognitive psychologists, as we shall see, attribute many cases of depression to cognitions to the effect that one is helpless to change things for the better.

Social-learning theorists such as Albert Bandura (1986) and Walter Mischel (1986) straddle the border between the behavioral and the cognitive. As noted, they place primary importance on encoding strategies, self-regulatory systems, and expectancies in explaining and predicting behavior. For example, expectancies that we shall not be able to carry out our plans (low self-efficacy expectancies) sap motivation and lead to feelings of hopelessness—two aspects of depression (Bandura, 1982).

Many psychologists look to more than one model to explain and treat psychological disorders. They are considered **eclectic.** For example, many social-learning theorists believe that some psychological disorders stem from biochemical factors or the interaction of biochemistry and learning. They are open to combining behavior therapy with drugs to treat problems such as schizophrenia and **bipolar disorder.** Psychoanalysts may also be eclectic. Some believe that schizophrenic disorganization reflects control of the personality by the id and argue that only long-term psychotherapy can help the ego achieve supremacy. But they may still be willing to use drugs to calm agitation on a temporary basis.

Now let us consider the major types of psychological disorders. In doing so, we shall use the classification system of the American Psychiatric Association (1987), as compiled in the Diagnostic and Statistical Manual of the Mental Disorders, third edition, revised version—in short, the DSM–III–R. We refer to the DSM–III–R because it is the most widely used system in the United States. However, psychologists criticize the DSM–III–R on many grounds, such as adhering too strongly to the medical model. So our use of the DSM–III–R is a convenience, not an endorsement. In future years psychologists may publish their own system for classifying psychological disorders.

■ Anxiety Disorders

Anxiety disorders are characterized by nervousness, fears, feelings of dread and foreboding, and signs of sympathetic overarousal that include rapid heartbeat, sweating, elevated blood pressure, muscle tension, and shakiness. Anxiety itself is an appropriate response to threatening situations, but anxiety is suggestive of psychological disorder when the amount of anxiety experienced is out of proportion to the threat, or when it "comes out of the blue"— that is, when its occurrence is not in response to environmental changes. The anxiety disorders include phobic, panic, generalized anxiety, obsessive-compulsive, and post-traumatic stress disorders.

Phobias

There are several types of phobias, including *simple phobia, social phobia,* and *agoraphobia.* According to the DSM–III–R (American Psychiatric Association, 1987), **simple phobias** are excessive, irrational fears of specific objects or situations. **Social phobias** are persistent fears of scrutiny by others and of doing something that will be humiliating or embarrassing. Stage fright and speech anxiety are examples of common social phobias.

One simple phobia is fear of elevators. Some people will not enter them, despite the hardships they suffer (such as walking six flights of steps) as a result. Yes, the cable *could* break. The ventilation *could* fail. One *could* be stuck

Anxiety disorders are characterized by nervousness, fears, feelings of dread and foreboding, and bodily signs such as rapid heartbeat, sweating, elevated blood pressure, muscle tension, and shakiness.

Claustrophobia. Fear of tight, small places.

Acrophobia. Fear of high places.

Agoraphobia. Fear of open, crowded places.

Panic disorder. The recurrent experiencing of attacks of extreme anxiety in the absence of external stimuli that usually elicit anxiety.

Generalized anxiety disorder. Feelings of dread and foreboding and sympathetic arousal of at least one month's duration.

Obsession. A recurring thought or image that seems beyond control.

in midair waiting for repairs. But these problems are infrequent, and it does not make sense for most of us to repeatedly walk flights of stairs to avoid them. Similarly, some people with simple phobias for hypodermic needles will not receive injections, even when they are the recommended treatment for serious illness. Injections can be painful, but most people with phobias for needles would gladly suffer a pinch that would cause still greater pain if it would help them fight illness. Other simple phobias include **claustrophobia** (fear of tight or enclosed places), **acrophobia** (fear of heights), and fear of mice, snakes, and other creepy-crawlies.

Phobias can seriously interfere with one's life. A person may know that a phobia is irrational, yet still experience intense anxiety and avoid the phobic object or situation.

Agoraphobia is among the most widespread phobias of adults (Mahoney, 1980). Agoraphobia is derived from the Greek meaning "fear of the marketplace," or of being out in open, busy areas. Persons with agoraphobia fear being in places from which it might be difficult to escape, or in which help might be unavailable if they become distressed. In practice, people who receive this label are frequently afraid of venturing out of their homes, especially when they are alone. They find it difficult or impossible to hold jobs or to carry out a normal social life.

Panic Disorder

Panic disorder is an unexpected attack of intense anxiety that is not triggered by a specific object or situation. Panic sufferers experience symptoms such as shortness of breath, heavy sweating, trembling, and pounding of the heart (Anderson et al., 1984; Barlow et al., 1985; Norton et al., 1985). According to the DSM–III–R, there may also be choking sensations, nausea, numbness or tingling, flushes or chills, chest pain, and fear of dying, going crazy, or losing control. There is a stronger bodily component to the anxiety experienced by people with panic disorders than to that encountered by people with other anxiety disorders (Barlow et al., 1985). Panic attacks may last from a minute or two to an hour or more, and afterward victims usually feel exhausted.

Forty to 50 percent of us experience panic now and then (Norton & Rhodes, 1983), but the DSM–III–R diagnoses panic disorder when there have been four attacks in a four-week period or an attack has been followed by months of dread of another attack. When we use these criteria, panic disorders affect only about 1 percent of the population (Meyers et al., 1984).

Because panic attacks seem to descend from nowhere, some sufferers remain in the home most of the time, for fear of succumbing to an attack in public. In such cases, sufferers are diagnosed as having *panic disorder with agoraphobia.*

Generalized Anxiety Disorder

The central feature of **generalized anxiety disorder** is persistent anxiety of at least one month's duration. As in the panic disorder, the anxiety cannot be attributed to a phobic object, situation, or activity. Rather, it seems free-floating. Symptoms may include motor tension (shakiness, inability to relax, furrowed brow, fidgeting, etc.); autonomic overarousal (sweating, dry mouth, racing heart, light-headedness, frequent urinating, diarrhea, etc.); feelings of dread and foreboding; and excessive vigilance, as shown by distractibility, insomnia, and irritability.

Obsessive-Compulsive Disorder

An **obsession** is a recurring thought or image that seems irrational and beyond control. Obsessions are so strong and frequent that they interfere with daily life. They may include doubts as to whether one has locked the doors

■ Q U E S T I O N N A I R E ■

The Temple Fear Survey Inventory

Loud noises? Cars? Being alone? Tests? Needles and knives? Illness? Blood? High or tight places? Making a speech? Creepy-crawlies? What do you fear? What objects or situations give you pause?

To compare your fears to those of undergraduates at Temple University, write in a number from 1 to 5 for each of the following items, according to this code:

1 = None
2 = Some
3 = Much
4 = Very Much
5 = Terror

Then turn to the answer key at the end of the chapter for the norms for college men and college women.

_____	1. Noise of vacuum cleaners	_____	21. Being teased
_____	2. Being cut	_____	22. Dentists
_____	3. Being alone	_____	23. Cemeteries
_____	4. Speaking before a group	_____	24. Strangers
_____	5. Dead bodies	_____	25. Being physically assaulted
_____	6. Loud noises	_____	26. Failing a test
_____	7. Being a passenger in a car	_____	27. Not being a success
_____	8. Driving a car	_____	28. Losing a job
_____	9. Auto accidents	_____	29. Making mistakes
_____	10. People with deformities	_____	30. Sharp objects (knives, razor blades, scissors)
_____	11. Being in a strange place	_____	31. Death
_____	12. Riding a roller coaster	_____	32. Death of a loved one
_____	13. Being in closed places	_____	33. Worms
_____	14. Thunder	_____	34. Imaginary creatures
_____	15. Falling down	_____	35. Dark places
_____	16. One person bullying another	_____	36. Strange dogs
_____	17. Being bullied by someone	_____	37. Receiving injections
_____	18. Loud sirens	_____	38. Seeing other people injected
_____	19. Doctors	_____	39. Illness
_____	20. High places	_____	40. Angry people

and shut the windows; impulses, such as the wish to strangle one's spouse; and images, such as one mother's recurrent fantasy that her children had been run over by traffic on the way home from school. In other cases, a 16-year-old boy found "numbers in my head" whenever he was about to study or take a test. A housewife became obsessed with the notion that she had contaminated her hands with Sani-Flush and that the contamination was spreading to everything she touched.

A **compulsion** is a seemingly irresistible urge to engage in an act, often repeatedly, such as lengthy, elaborate washing after using the bathroom. The impulse is frequent and forceful, interfering with daily life. Some men, called _exhibitionists,_ report experiencing the compulsion to expose their genitals to women strangers. The woman who felt contaminated by Sani-Flush engaged in elaborate hand-washing rituals. She spent three to four hours daily at the sink and complained, "My hands look like lobster claws."

Compulsion. An apparently irresistible urge to repeat an act or engage in ritualistic behavior, such as hand-washing.

_____ 41. Mice and rats

_____ 42. Fire

_____ 43. Ugly people

_____ 44. Snakes

_____ 45. Lightning

_____ 46. Sudden noises

_____ 47. Swimming alone

_____ 48. Witnessing surgical operations

_____ 49. Prospects of a surgical operation

_____ 50. Deep water

_____ 51. Dead animals

_____ 52. Blood

_____ 53. Seeing a fight

_____ 54. Being in a fight

_____ 55. Being criticized

_____ 56. Suffocating

_____ 57. Looking foolish

_____ 58. Being a passenger in an airplane

_____ 59. Arguing with parents

_____ 60. Meeting someone for the first time

_____ 61. Being misunderstood

_____ 62. Crowded places

_____ 63. Being a leader

_____ 64. Losing control

_____ 65. Being with drunks

_____ 66. Being self-conscious

_____ 67. People in authority

_____ 68. People who seem insane

_____ 69. Boating

_____ 70. God

_____ 71. Being with a member of the opposite sex

_____ 72. Stinging insects

_____ 73. Crawling insects

_____ 74. Flying insects

_____ 75. Crossing streets

_____ 76. Entering a room where other people are already seated

_____ 77. Bats

_____ 78. Journeys by train

_____ 79. Journeys by bus

_____ 80. Feeling angry

_____ 81. Dull weather

_____ 82. Large open spaces

_____ 83. Cuts

_____ 84. Tough-looking people

_____ 85. Birds

_____ 86. Being watched while working

_____ 87. Guns

_____ 88. Dirt

_____ 89. Being in an elevator

_____ 90. Parting from friends

_____ 91. Feeling rejected by others

_____ 92. Odors

_____ 93. Feeling disapproved of

_____ 94. Being ignored

_____ 95. Premature heart beats

_____ 96. Nude men

_____ 97. Nude women

_____ 98. Unclean silverware in restaurants

_____ 99. Dirty restrooms

_____ 100. Becoming mentally ill

Fear survey inventory reprinted from P. R. Braun and D. J. Reynolds (1969). A factor analysis of a 100-item fear survey inventory, *Behaviour Research and Therapy*, 7: 399–402.

Post-Traumatic Stress Disorder

Post-traumatic stress disorder (PTSD) is defined as intense and persistent feelings of anxiety and helplessness that are caused by a traumatic experience, such as a physical threat to oneself or one's family, destruction of one's community, or witnessing the death of another person. PTSD has troubled many Vietnam war veterans, victims of rape, and persons who have seen their homes and communities destroyed by natural disasters such as floods or tornadoes. In some cases, PTSD occurs six months or more after the event.

The precipitating event is persistently reexperienced as in the form of intrusive memories, recurrent dreams, and the sudden feeling that the event is actually recurring (as in "flashbacks" to the event). Typically the sufferer attempts to avoid thoughts and activities associated with the traumatic event. He or she may also display sleep problems, irritable outbursts, difficulty concentrating, excessive vigilance, and a heightened "startle" response. When

Post-traumatic stress disorder. A disorder which follows a psychologically distressing event that is outside the range of normal human experience, and which is characterized by symptoms such as intense fear, avoidance of stimuli associated with the event, and reliving of the event.

Prepared conditioning.
The view that people are biologically "prepro-grammed" to learn to fear stimuli that are potentially harmful.

Many soldiers relive their combat experiences by way of post-traumatic stress disorder (PTSD). In PTSD, war veterans, rape victims, and victims of disasters may encounter intrusive memories of the traumatic events, recur-rent nightmares about them, even the sudden feeling that the events are recurring.

traumatic events take place, it appears that being part of a supportive social network can mitigate their impact (Stretch, 1985, 1987).

Theoretical Views

According to the psychodynamic model, phobias symbolize conflicts of child-hood origin. Psychodynamic theory explains generalized anxiety as persistent difficulty in maintaining repression of primitive impulses. Psychoanalysts view obsessions as the leakage of unconscious impulses, and compulsions as acts that allow people to keep such impulses partly repressed.

A number of learning theorists suggest that phobias may be conditioned fears that were acquired in early childhood, and whose origins are beyond memory. Avoidance of feared stimuli is reinforced by reduction of anxiety. In the case of rape victims, evidence suggests that exposure to situations (e.g., the neighborhood, one's place of employment) in which the attack occurred, in the absence of further attack, can extinguish some of the post-traumatic distress (Wirtz & Harrell, 1987).

Seligman and Rosenhan (1984) suggest that there is an interaction be-tween organic factors and conditioning that biologically predisposes us to acquire phobias to certain classes of stimuli. We are genetically prepared to be conditioned to certain stimuli, and, for this reason, this view is termed **prepared conditioning.** We would not inherit specific fears, according to this view, but evolutionary forces would have favored the survival of individuals who were biologically *prepared* to acquire fears of large animals, snakes, heights, entrapment, sharp objects, and strangers. In laboratory experiments, people have been shown photographs of various objects and then been given electric shock (Hugdahl & Ohman, 1977; Ohman et al., 1976). Subjects do seem to have been more "prepared" to acquire fear reactions to some stimuli (e.g., spiders and snakes) than others (e.g., flowers and houses), as measured by galvanic skin response to subsequent presentations of these stimuli.

Similarly, a number of social-learning theorists have noted the role of observational learning in acquiring fears (Bandura et al., 1969). If parents squirm, grimace, and shudder at mice, blood, or dirt on the kitchen floor, children may encode these stimuli as awful and imitate their behavior. Social-learning theorists suggest that generalized anxiety is often nothing more than fear that has been associated with situations so broad that they are not readily identified, such as social relationships or personal achievement. Social-learning and cognitive theorists suggest that anxiety can be maintained by thinking that one is in a terrible situation and is helpless to change it. Psychoanalysts and social-learning theorists broadly agree that compulsive behavior reduces anxiety, but social-learning theorists suggest that obsessions and compulsions serve the purpose of diverting attention from more important and threatening issues, such as "What am I to do with my life?"

Cognitive theorists note that when anxieties are acquired at a young age, we may later interpret them as enduring traits and label ourselves as "people who fear . . . (you fill in the blank)." Then we live up to the labels. We also entertain thoughts that heighten and perpetuate anxiety (Meichenbaum & Jaremko, 1983), such as "I've got to get out of here," or "My heart is going to leap out of my chest." Such thoughts heighten physical anxiety responses, interfere with planning, magnify the aversiveness of stimuli, motivate avoidance, and decrease self-efficacy expectations concerning the ability to control the situation. Belief that we shall not be able to handle a threat heightens anxiety (Bandura, 1981; Bandura et al., 1982), whereas belief that we are in control lessens anxiety (Miller, 1980).

Organic factors might play a role in anxiety disorders. For one thing, anxiety disorders tend to run in families (Turner et al., 1987). The **concordance** rate for anxiety disorders is higher among pairs of identical than fraternal twins (Torgersen, 1983). And so, a predisposition toward anxiety—perhaps in the form of a highly reactive autonomic nervous system—might be inherited.

■ Dissociative Disorders

The DSM–III–R lists four major **dissociative disorders:** *psychogenic amnesia, psychogenic fugue, multiple personality,* and *depersonalization.* In each case there is a disturbance in the normal functions of identity, memory, or consciousness that make the person feel whole.

Psychogenic Amnesia

In **psychogenic amnesia,** there is sudden inability to recall important personal information. Memory loss cannot be attributed to organic problems, such as a blow to the head or alcoholic intoxication. Thus it is *psycho*genic. In the most common example, the person cannot recall events for a number of hours after a stressful incident, as in warfare or as in the case of the uninjured survivor of an accident. In generalized amnesia, people forget their entire lives. Amnesia may last for hours or years. Termination of amnesia is also sudden.

Psychogenic Fugue

In **psychogenic fugue,** the person shows loss of memory for the past, travels suddenly from his or her home or place of work, and assumes a new identity. Either the person does not think about the past, or reports a past filled with bogus memories that are not recognized as false. Following recovery, the events that occurred during the fugue are not recalled.

Multiple Personality Disorder

Multiple personality is the name given William's disorder, as described in the beginning of the chapter. In this disorder, two or more "personalities," each with distinct traits and memories, "occupy" the same person, with or without awareness of the others. Different personalities may even have different eyeglass prescriptions (American Psychiatric Association, 1987).

Dissociative disorders. Disorders in which there are sudden, temporary changes in consciousness or self-identity.

Psychogenic amnesia. A dissociative disorder marked by loss of memory or self-identity. Skills and general knowledge are usually retained.

Psychogenic fugue. A dissociative disorder in which one experiences amnesia, then flees to a new location and establishes a new life style.

In the celebrated case that became the subject of the film *The Three Faces of Eve,* a timid housewife named Eve White harbored two other personalities: Eve Black, a sexually aggressive, antisocial personality, and Jane, an emerging personality who was able to accept the existence of her primitive impulses, yet show socially appropriate behavior (Figure 8.1). Finally, the three faces merged into one: Jane. Ironically, Jane (Chris Sizemore, in real life) reportedly split into 22 personalities later on. Another publicized case is that of Sybil, a woman with 16 personalities, played by Sally Field in a recent film.

Depersonalization Disorder

Depersonalization is the persistent feeling that one is not real. Persons with the disorder may feel detached from their own bodies, as if they are observing their thought processes from the outside. Or they may feel that they are functioning on automatic pilot, or as if in a dream.

Theoretical Views

According to psychoanalytic theory, dissociative disorders involve massive use of repression to prevent recognition of unacceptable impulses. In psychogenic amnesia and fugue, the person forgets a profoundly disturbing event or impulse. In multiple personality, people express unacceptable impulses through alternate personalities. In depersonalization, the person stands outside—removed from the turmoil within.

Social-learning theorists generally regard dissociative disorders as conditions in which people learn *not to think* about disturbing acts or impulses in order to avoid feelings of guilt and shame. Technically speaking, *not thinking about these matters* is reinforced by *removal* of the aversive stimuli of guilt and shame.*

Social-learning theory also suggests that many people come to role-play people with multiple personality through observational learning. This is not exactly the same thing as faking a disorder, because people can "forget to tell themselves" that they have assumed a role. Reinforcers are made available by role-playing individuals with multiple personality: drawing attention to oneself and escaping responsibility for unacceptable behavior are two (Spanos et al., 1985; Thigpen & Cleckley, 1984).

One cognitive perspective explains dissociative disorders in terms of deployment of attention. Perhaps all of us are capable of dividing our awareness so that we become unaware, at least temporarily, of events that we usually focus more attention on. Perhaps the marvel is *not* that attention can be divided, but that human consciousness normally integrates experience into a meaningful whole.

■ Somatoform Disorders

In **somatoform disorders,** people show or complain of physical problems, such as paralysis, pain, or the persistent belief that they have a serious disease, yet no evidence of a physical abnormality can be found. In this section we shall discuss two somatoform disorders: *conversion disorder* and *hypochondriasis.*

Conversion Disorder

Conversion disorder is characterized by a major change in or loss of physical functioning, although there are no medical findings to support the loss of functioning. The symptoms are not intentionally produced; that is, the person is not faking.

Depersonalization disorder. Persistent or recurrent feelings that one is not real or is detached from one's own experiences or body.

Somatoform disorders. Disorders in which people complain of physical (somatic) problems, although no physical abnormality can be found.

Conversion disorder. A disorder in which anxiety or unconscious conflicts are "converted" into physical symptoms that often have the effect of helping the person cope with anxiety or conflict.

---

*This is an example of negative reinforcement, because the frequency of behavior—in this case, the frequency of diverting one's attention from a certain topic—is reinforced by *removal* of a stimulus—in this case, by removal of feelings of guilt or shame.

FIGURE 8.1   Multiple Personality
In the film *The Three Faces of Eve*, Joanne Woodward played three personalities in the same woman: the shy, inhibited Eve White (above); the flirtatious, promiscuous Eve Black (top, right); and a third personality, Jane (bottom, right), who was healthy enough to accept her sexual and aggressive impulses and still maintain her sense of identity.

If you lost the ability to see at night, or if your legs became paralyzed, you would show understandable concern. But some victims of conversion disorder show indifference to their symptoms, a remarkable feature referred to as **la belle indifférence.** Conversion disorder is so named because it appears to "convert" a source of stress into a physical problem. Instances are rare and of short duration, but their existence led the young Sigmund Freud to believe that subconscious processes were at work in people.

During World War II a number of bomber pilots developed night blindness. They could not carry out their nighttime missions, although no damage to the optic nerves was found. In rare cases, women with large families have been reported to become paralyzed in the legs, again with no medical findings.

Conversion disorder, like dissociative disorders, seems to serve a purpose. The "blindness" of the pilots may have afforded them temporary relief from stressful missions, or allowed them to avoid the guilt of bombing civilian populations. The paralysis of a woman who prematurely commits herself to a large family and a life at home may prevent her from doing housework or from engaging in sexual intercourse and becoming pregnant again. She "accomplishes" certain ends without having to recognize them or make decisions.

Hypochondriasis

Persons with **hypochondriasis,** hold the persistent belief that they are suffering from a serious disease, although no medical evidence can be found for it. Sufferers often become preoccupied with minor physical sensations and maintain an unrealistic belief that something is wrong despite medical reassurance. "Hypochondriacs" may go from doctor to doctor, seeking the one who will find the cause of the sensations. Fear may impair work or home life.

Some hypochondriacs use their complaints as a self-handicapping strategy (Smith et al., 1983). That is, they are more likely to complain of

La belle indifférence. A French term descriptive of the lack of concern sometimes shown by people with conversion disorders.

Hypochondriasis. Persistent belief that one has a medical disorder despite lack of medical findings.

feeling ill in situations in which illness can serve as an excuse for poor performance. In other cases, focusing on physical sensations and possible problems may serve the function of taking the person's mind off other life problems. However, every effort should be made to uncover real medical problems. Now and then a supposed hypochondriac dies from something all too real.

■ Eating Disorders

Did you know that today the eating habits of the "average" U.S. woman are characterized by dieting? For this reason, efforts to restrict the intake of food have become the norm. However, the eating disorders that we discuss in this section are characterized by gross disturbances in patterns of eating. They include *anorexia nervosa* and *bulimia nervosa*.

Anorexia Nervosa

There is a saying that you can never be too rich or too thin. Excess money may be pleasant enough, but one certainly can be too thin, as in the case of **anorexia nervosa.** Anorexia is a life-threatening disorder characterized by refusal to maintain a healthful body weight, intense fear of being overweight, a distorted body image, and, in females, **amenorrhea.** Anoretic persons usually weigh less than 85 percent of their expected body weight.

By and large, anorexia afflicts girls and young women. Nearly one in 200 school-aged girls has trouble gaining or maintaining weight (Crisp et al., 1976), and the incidences of anorexia nervosa and bulimia nervosa have increased markedly since the 1950s (Boskind-White & White, 1986; Strober, 1986). Anoretic females outnumber anoretic males by estimates of 9:1 to 20:1. Onset is most often between the ages of 12 and 18.

Anoretic girls may be full height but weigh 60 pounds or less. They may drop 25 percent or more of their body weight in a year. Severe weight loss triggers amenorrhea. The girl's general health declines, and she may experience slowed heart rate, low blood pressure, constipation, dehydration, and a host of other problems (Kaplan & Woodside, 1987). About 5 percent of anoretic girls die from weight loss (Hsu, 1986; Szmukler & Russell, 1986).

In the typical pattern, girls notice some weight gain after menarche and decide that it must come off. However, dieting and, often, exercise continue at a fever pitch. They go on long after girls reach normal body weights, even after family and others have told them that they are losing too much. Anoretic girls almost always adamantly deny that they are wasting away. They may point to their fierce exercise regimens as proof. Their body images are distorted. Whereas others perceive them as "skin and bones," they frequently sit before the mirror and see themselves as getting where they want to be. Or they focus on nonexistent "remaining" pockets of fat.

Although the thought of eating can be odious to anoretic girls, now and then they may feel quite hungry. Many anoretics become obsessed with food and are constantly "around it." They may engross themselves in cookbooks, take on the family shopping chores, and prepare elaborate dinners for others.

Bulimia Nervosa

Consider the case of Nicole:

> Nicole awakens in her cold dark room and already wishes it was time to go back to bed. She dreads the thought of going through this day, which will be like so many others in her recent past. She asks herself the question every morning, "Will I be able to make it through the day without being totally obsessed by thoughts of food, or will I blow it again and spend the day on a binge"? She tells herself that today she will begin a new life, today she will start to live like a normal human being. However, she is not at all convinced that the choice is hers. (Boskind-White & White, 1983, p. 29.)

Anorexia nervosa. An eating disorder characterized by maintenance of an abnormally low body weight, intense fear of weight gain, a distorted body image, and, in females, amenorrhea.

Amenorrhea. Absence of menstruation.

Bulimia nervosa. An eating disorder characterized by recurrent episodes of binge eating followed by purging, and persistent overconcern with body shape and weight.

Fitness model and actress Jane Fonda recently revealed that as an adolescent she suffered from bulimia nervosa.

It turns out that this day Nicole begins by eating eggs and toast. Then she binges on cookies; doughnuts; bagels smothered with butter, cream cheese, and jelly; granola; candy bars; and bowls of cereal and milk—all within 45 minutes. Then she cannot take in any more food and turns her attention to purging what she has eaten. She goes to the bathroom, ties back her hair, turns on the shower to mask any noise she will make, drinks a glass of water, and makes herself vomit. Afterward she vows, "Starting tomorrow, I'm going to change." But she knows that tomorrow it will probably be the same story.

Nicole has **bulimia nervosa.** Bulimia nervosa is defined as recurrent cycles of binge eating, especially of foods rich in carbohydrates,* and the taking of dramatic measures to purge the food, once consumed. These measures include self-induced vomiting, fasting or strict dieting, use of laxatives, and vigorous exercise. As with anorexia, there is overconcern about body shape and weight. The disorder usually begins in adolescence or early adulthood, and afflicts women more so than men by about a 10:1 ratio (American Psychiatric Association, 1987).

Bulimia is even more common than anorexia. It has been estimated to affect 5 percent of the general population (Nagelman et al., 1983). Foreyt (1986) estimates that as high as 15 percent of the college-age female population could be considered bulimic!

Theoretical Views

It has been speculated that a number of eating disorders might reflect problems in the hypothalamus. For example, when the neurotransmitter norepinephrine acts upon a segment of the hypothalamus, it stimulates animals to eat, and these animals show preference for carbohydrates (Kaplan & Woodside, 1987; Leibowitz, 1986; Mitchell & Eckert, 1987). The neurotransmitter serotonin, by contrast, appears to induce feelings of satiation, thereby suppressing the appetite, and particularly the desire for carbohydrates (Halmi et al., 1986; Kaplan & Woodside, 1987). Therefore, a biological condition that would increase the impact of serotonin could have a negative impact on the

---

*For example, candy, cookies, cakes. Meats contain protein and fat, and are of relatively less interest to bulimic bingers.

desire to eat, as in anorexia. One could also speculate that a biological condition that decreased the impact of serotonin, which normally suppresses appetite for carbohydrates, could result in periodic carbohydrate binging, as found in bulimia. These hypotheses are under intense study, as are hypotheses concerning a possible role for still another transmitter—dopamine (Kaplan & Woodside, 1987). It is of major interest that "antidepressant" medications, which work by increasing the quantities of norepinephrine and serotonin available to the brain, have increased the appetite in a number of anoretic individuals. They have also controlled cycles of binge eating and vomiting (Halmi et al., 1986; Hughes et al., 1986; Walsh et al., 1984). However, antidepressants have not helped all anoretic and bulimic patients who try them.

Of course, the question comes about, how do we account for the current epidemic of possible problems with the hypothalamus? We must consider a possible interaction of biological and behavioral factors. For example, as noted in our discussion of obesity in Chapter 7, it could be that dieting affects the weight-regulating functions of the hypothalamus. Early and repeated dieting could have particularly severe effects. Why all this dieting, and at tender ages? An irrational fear of gaining weight might reflect cultural idealization of the slender female. As noted by psychologists Janet Polivy and C. Peter Herman (1987), this cultural ideal has become so ingrained that "normal" eating for U.S. women today is characterized by dieting! This ideal may contribute to distortion of the body image. Women college students generally see themselves as significantly heavier than the figure that is most attractive to males and as heavier, still, that the "ideal" female figure (Fallon & Rozin, 1985). College men actually prefer women to be heavier than women expect—about halfway between the girth of the average woman and what the woman thinks is most attractive.

Other psychological hypotheses concerning the origins of anorexia nervosa and bulimia nervosa have also been advanced. For example, the frequent link between anorexia and **menarche** has led psychoanalysts to suggest that anorexia may represent an effort by the girl to remain **prepubescent.** Anorexia allows the girl to avoid growing up, separating from the family, and assuming adult responsibilities. Severe weight loss also prevents the rounding of the breasts and the hips. And so, some investigators hypothesize that anoretic girls are conflicted about their sexuality, and the possibility of pregnancy in particular.

Other theorists note that self-starvation has a brutal effect on parents (Bemis, 1978). They suggest that adolescents may use the refusal to eat as a weapon when family relationships become disturbed.

■ Mood Disorders

The mood disorders are characterized by disturbance in expressed emotions and generally involve depression or elation. As noted earlier, most instances of depression are normal. If you have failed an important test, if a business investment has been lost, or if your closest friend becomes ill, it is appropriate for you to feel depressed. As with the anxiety disorders, feelings of depression are abnormal when they are magnified beyond one's circumstances, or when there is no apparent situational basis for them. In this section we discuss two mood disorders: *major depression* and *bipolar disorder,* which involves feelings of elation as well as depression.

Major Depression

Depression is the "common cold" of psychological problems, according to Seligman (1973)—the most common psychological problem we face. People with "run-of-the-mill" depression may feel sad, blue, or "down in the dumps." They may complain of lack of energy, loss of self-esteem, difficulty in concentrating, loss of interest in other people and usually enjoyable activities, pessimism, crying, and thoughts of suicide.

People with **major depression** may share most or all of these feelings, but they tend to be more severe. In addition, people with major depression may show poor appetite and significant weight loss, agitation or severe **psychomotor retardation,** inability to concentrate and make decisions, complaints of "not caring" anymore, and they may have recurrent thoughts of death or make suicide attempts.

Persons with major depression may also show faulty perception of reality, or psychotic symptoms such as delusions of unworthiness, guilt for imagined great wrongdoings, even ideas that one is rotting away from disease. There may also be hallucinations, as of the Devil administering just punishment or of strange sensations in the body.

Bipolar Disorder

In bipolar disorder, formerly known as manic-depression, there are mood swings from elation to depression. These cycles seem unrelated to external events. In the elated, or **manicky**, phase, people may show excessive excitement or silliness, carrying jokes too far. They may show poor judgment, sometimes destroying property, and may be argumentative (Depue et al., 1981). Roommates may avoid them, finding them abrasive. Manicky people often speak rapidly ("pressured speech") and jump from topic to topic, show-

Major depression. A depressive disorder more severe than dysthymic disorder in which the person may show loss of appetite, psychomotor symptoms, and impaired reality testing.

Psychomotor retardation. Slowness in motor activity and (apparently) in thought.

Manicky. Elated, showing excessive excitement.

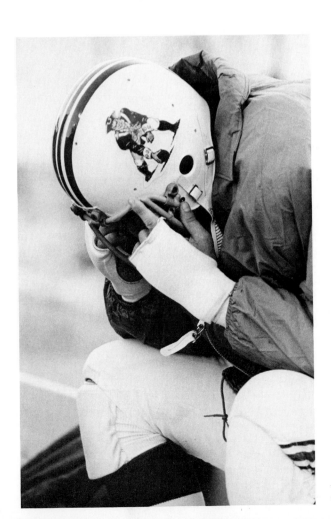

Cognitive Factors in Depression

This depressed football player has done poorly on the last play and is now rehashing it. Unfortunately, he's telling himself that he's generally no good and that there's nothing he can do to improve his play. In this way, he is pushing himself down into the pits of depression and is likely to be of little use the next time he is on the field. But if he had told himself, instead, that his foul-up was an exception to the rule and that anyone has to be allowed a mistake now and then, his mood would be better and he would probably perform better during his next opportunity.

ing **rapid flight of ideas.** It is hard to "get a word in edgewise." They may show extreme generosity by making unusually large contributions to charity or giving away expensive possessions. They may not be able to sit still or to sleep restfully.

Depression is the other side of the coin. Bipolar depressed people often sleep more than usual and are lethargic. People with major (or "unipolar") depression are more likely to show insomnia and agitation (Davison & Neale, 1986). Bipolar depressed individuals show social withdrawal and irritability.

Some persons with bipolar disorder attempt suicide "on the way down" from the elated phase of the disorder. They report that they will do almost anything to escape the depths of depression that they realize lie ahead.

Theoretical Views

As noted, depression is a normal reaction to loss or to exposure to unpleasant events. Negative life events such as marital discord, physical discomfort, incompetence, failure at work, and pressure at work all contribute to feelings of depression (Coyne et al., 1987; Eckenrode, 1984; Lewinsohn & Amenson, 1978; Stone & Neale, 1984). We are most likely to be depressed by undesirable events when we feel responsible for them (Hammen & Mayol, 1982). But many people recover from losses less readily than the rest of us. When compared to nondepressed people, depressed individuals are less likely to use problem solving to alleviate the stresses acting upon them, and they have fewer supportive relationships to draw upon (Asarnow et al., 1987; Billings et al., 1983; Nezu & Ronan, 1985; Pagel & Becker, 1987; Schotte & Clum, 1987).

Most researchers, as we shall see, believe that bipolar disorder has an organic basis (Klein & Depue, 1985).

Psychodynamic Views Psychoanalysts suggest various explanations for depression. In one, depressed people are overly concerned about hurting others' feelings or losing their approval. As a result, they hold in rather than express feelings of anger. Anger becomes turned inward and is experienced as misery and self-hatred.

Social-Learning Views Social-learning theorists note similarities in behavior between people who are depressed and laboratory animals who are not reinforced for instrumental behavior. Inactivity and loss of interest result in each. Lewinsohn (1975) theorizes that many depressed people lack skills that might lead to rewards. Some depressed people are nonassertive (Gotlib, 1984); others do have the social skills of nondepressed people, but they do not reinforce (credit) themselves as much for showing them (Gotlib, 1982).

Learned Helplessness Research has also found links between depression and **learned helplessness.** In one study, Seligman (1975) taught dogs that they were helpless to escape an electric shock by preventing them from leaving a cage in which they received repeated shock. Later a barrier to a safe compartment was removed, allowing the animals a way out. But when they were shocked again, the dogs made no effort to escape. Apparently they had learned that they were helpless. Seligman's dogs were also, in a sense, reinforced for doing nothing. That is, the shock *eventually* stopped when the dogs were showing helpless behavior—inactivity and withdrawal. "Reinforcement" may have increased the likelihood of repeating their "successful behavior"— that is, doing nothing—in a similar situation. This helpless behavior resembles that of depressed people.

Cognitive Factors Learned helplessness bridges social-learning and cognitive approaches in that it is an attitude, an expectancy. There are other

Rapid flight of ideas. Rapid speech and topic changes, characteristic of manicky behavior.

Learned helplessness. Seligman's model for the acquisition of depressive behavior, based on findings that organisms in aversive situations learn to show inactivity when their operants are not reinforced.

cognitive factors in depression. For example, "perfectionists" set themselves up for depression through irrational self-demands. They are likely to fall short of their (unrealistic) expectations and, as a consequence, to feel depressed (Vestre, 1984).

Attributional Styles   Seligman and his colleagues note that we can attribute our failures to *internal* or *external, stable* or *unstable,* and *global* or *specific* causes. Let us explain these various **attributional styles** through the example of having a date that does not work out. An internal attribution involves self-blame, as in "I really loused it up," whereas an external attribution places the blame elsewhere (as in "Some couples just don't take to each other," or, "She was the wrong sign for me"). A stable attribution ("It's my personality") suggests a problem that cannot be changed, whereas an unstable attribution ("It was the head cold") suggests a temporary condition. A global attribution of failure ("I have no idea what to do when I'm with people") suggests that the problem is quite large. A specific attribution ("I have problems making small talk at the very outset of a relationship") chops the problem down to a manageable size. Research shows that depressed people are more likely than non-depressed people to attribute the causes of their failures to internal, stable, and global factors—factors which lead them to see themselves as more helpless to change things for the better (Blumberg & Izard, 1985; Miller et al., 1982; Peterson et al., 1981; Pyszczynski & Greenberg, 1985; Raps et al., 1982; Seligman et al., 1979, 1984).

Organic Factors   Researchers are also searching for organic factors in the mood disorders. Mood swings tend to run in families, and there is a higher concordance rate for bipolar disorder among identical than fraternal twins (Klein et al., 1985; Smith & Winokur, 1983). A recent study of the Amish community in Pennsylvania by Janice Egeland and her colleagues (1987) traced the distribution of bipolar disorder among the members of an extended family with a high incidence of the problem. The group isolated a segment of DNA (gene) on chromosome 11, which was transmitted to children half the time and apparently present in all family members who showed bipolar disorder. However, only about 80 percent of those who possessed this "genetic vulnerability" actually displayed the disorder. And so genetic factors probably create a predisposition for bipolar disorder but do not, in and of themselves, guarantee its appearance. Perhaps depressive cognitions and other stressors heighten the probability that the disorder will be manifested.

Perhaps the genetic vulnerability manifests itself in terms of the actions of neurotransmitters. Much research has focused on the role of the neurotransmitter norepinephrine. Rats with lowered levels of norepinephrine show behavior similar to that of depressed people (Ellison, 1977). They are less aggressive than colony-mates and appear apathetic and withdrawn. They lie around listlessly in their burrows. Their appetites decrease and they lose weight.

As will be noted in Chapter 9, people whose depression has reached psychotic proportions often respond to antidepressant drugs. One effect of these drugs is to raise norepinephrine levels; another might be to enhance the sensitivity of norepinephrine receptors. And so the apparent actions of antidepressant drugs suggest further evidence of a role for norepinephrine in depression. Moreover, the metal lithium, which is the major chemical treatment for bipolar disorder, apparently flattens out manic-depressive cycles by moderating levels of norepinephrine.

Other researchers argue that the neurotransmitter serotonin also plays a role in mood disorders (e.g., Berger, 1978). It has been speculated that deficiencies in serotonin may create a general disposition toward mood disorders. A deficiency of serotonin *combined with* a deficiency of norepinephrine

WHAT DO YOU SAY NOW?

Suicide Prevention

You are having a heart-to-heart talk with one of your best friends on campus, Jamie. Things haven't been going well, you know. Jamie's grandmother died a month ago, and they were very close. Jamie's coursework has been suffering, and things have also been going downhill with the person Jamie has been seeing regularly. But you are not prepared when Jamie looks you straight in the eye and says, "I've been thinking about this for days, and I've decided that the only way out is to kill myself."

What do you say now? Write down three possible responses, and then check below for our suggestions.

1. _____
   _____.
2. _____
   _____.
3. _____
   _____.

If someone tells you that he or she is considering suicide, you may feel frightened and flustered, or that an enormous burden has been placed on you. It has. In such cases, your objective should be to encourage the person to consult a professional mental health worker, or to consult a worker yourself as soon as possible. But if the person refuses to talk to anyone else and you feel that you can't break free for a consultation, there are a number of things you can do:

1. **Draw the person out.** Edwin Shneidman suggests asking questions such as "What's going on?" "Where do you hurt?" "What would you like to see happen?" (1985, p. 11). Questions such as these may encourage people to express frustrated psychological needs and provide some relief. They also give you time to assess the danger and think.
2. **Be empathetic.** Show that you understand how upset the person is. Do *not* say, "Don't be silly."
3. **Suggest that measures other than suicide may be found to solve the problem,** even if they are not evident at the time. Shneidman (1985) suggests that suicidal people can typically see only two solutions

---

may be linked with depression. But a deficiency of serotonin combined with excessive levels of norepinephrine might produce manicky behavior.

The relationships between the mood disorders and organic factors are complex and under intense study. Moreover, even if people can be biologically predisposed toward depression, it seems that self-efficacy expectations and attitudes—particularly attitudes as to whether or not one can change things for the better—may also play a role. Although the exact causes of depression remain clouded to some degree, we know all too well that for some people suicide is one of the possible outcomes of depression. We discuss that distressing topic next.

Suicide

Consider a number of facts about suicide:

Suicide is more common among college students than among nonstudents. About 10,000 college students attempt suicide each year.
Suicide is the second leading cause of death among college students.
Nearly 200,000 people attempt suicide each year in the United States. About one in ten succeeds.
Three times as many women as men attempt suicide, but three times as many men succeed.
Men prefer to use guns or hang themselves, but women prefer to use sleeping pills.
Young blacks and native Americans are more than twice as likely as whites to commit suicide.
Suicide is especially common among physicians, lawyers, and psychologists, although it is found among all occupational groups and at all age levels.
No other cause of death leaves such feelings of guilt, distress, and puzzlement in friends and relatives.

Why do people take their own lives? It seems that the great majority of suicides are linked to depression (Leonard, 1977; Schotte & Clum, 1982).

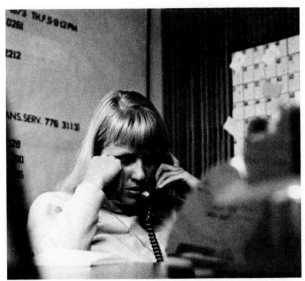

A Suicide Hotline.
What do you say when a person threatens to commit suicide? What would you do if a friend confided suicidal intentions to you?

to their problems—either death or a magical resolution of their problems. Therapists thus attempt to "widen the mental blinders" of suicidal people.

4. Ask how the person intends to commit suicide. People with concrete plans and the weapon are at greater risk. Ask if you may hold on to the weapon for a while. Sometimes the person says yes.

5. Suggest that the person go *with you* to obtain professional help *now*. The emergency room of a general hospital, the campus counseling center or infirmary, the campus or local police will do. Some campuses have "hot lines" you can call. Some cities have suicide prevention centers with hot lines that people can use anonymously.

6. Extract a promise that the person will not commit suicide before seeing you again. Arrange a concrete time and place to meet. Get professional help as soon as you are apart.

7. Do *not* tell people threatening suicide that they're silly or crazy. Do *not* insist on contact with specific people, like parents or a spouse. Conflict with these people may have led to the suicidal thinking.

But above all, please remember that your primary objective is to consult a helping professional. Don't "go it alone" for one moment more than you have to.

Although most people who attempt suicide show hopelessness and despair, they do not appear out of touch with reality (Leonard, 1974).

Strongly suicidal people report finding life more dull, empty, and boring than do less suicidal or nonsuicidal people. They feel more anxious, excitable, submissive, angry, guilt-ridden, helpless, and inadequate than others (Mehrabian & Weinstein, 1985; Neuringer, 1982). According to psychologist Edwin Schneidman (1985) of the UCLA Neuropsychiatric Institute, people who attempt suicide are usually experiencing unendurable psychological pain and are attempting to bring consciousness of their suffering to an end. In a Boston University study, college women who had attempted suicide were more likely than their peers to implicate their parents as a source of the pain that led to the attempt (Cantor, 1976). They were also less likely to feel able to ask parents or others for help when they felt desperate or under great stress. Thus a major source of social support was lost to them.

Suicide attempts are more frequent following stressful life events, especially "exit events" (Slater & Depue, 1981). Exit events involve loss of social support—as in the death of a spouse, close friend, or relative; divorce or separation; a family member's leaving home; or the loss of a close friend. People who consider suicide in response to stress have also been found less capable of solving problems than those who do not consider suicide (Schotte & Clum, 1987). That is, they are less likely to find ways of changing the stressful circumstances.

Now let us consider a number of myths about suicide—and the realities.

Myths About Suicide   Some believe that people who threaten suicide are only seeking attention. The serious just "do it." Actually 70 to 80 percent of suicides give clear clues concerning their intentions prior to the act (Cordes, 1985; Leonard, 1977).

Some believe that those who fail at suicide attempts are only seeking attention. But 75 percent of successful suicides had made prior attempts (Cohen et al., 1966). Contrary to myth, discussion of suicide with a depressed

Autism. Self-absorption. Absorption in daydreaming and fantasy.

Delusions. False, persistent beliefs that are uunsubstantiated by sensory or objective evidence.

person does not prompt suicide. In fact, extracting a promise that the person will not commit suicide before calling or visiting a mental-health worker seems to have prevented suicides.

Some believe that only "insane" people (meaning people who are out of touch with reality) would take their own lives. However, Shneidman points out that suicidal thinking is not necessarily a sign of psychosis, neurosis, or personality disorder; instead, the contemplation of suicide reflects a narrowing of the range of options that people think are available to them (Cordes, 1985). Finally, most people with suicidal thoughts, contrary to myth, will *not* act on them. Suicidal thoughts at a time of great stress are not uncommon.

■ Schizophrenia

Joyce was 19. Her boyfriend Ron brought her into the emergency room because she had slit her wrists. When she was interviewed, her attention wandered. She seemed distracted by things in the air, or something she might be hearing. It was as if she had an invisible earphone.

She explained that she had cut her wrists because the "hellsmen" had told her to. Then she seemed frightened. Later she said that the hellsmen had warned her not to reveal their existence. She had been afraid that they would punish her for talking about them.

Ron told the emergency-room physician that Joyce had been living with him for about a year. At first they had been together in a small apartment in town. But Joyce did not want to be near other people and had convinced him to rent a bungalow in the country. There she would make fantastic drawings of goblins and monsters during the days. Now and then she would become agitated and act as if invisible things were giving her instructions.

"I'm bad," Joyce would mutter, "I'm bad." She would begin to jumble her words. Ron would then try to convince her to go to the hospital, but she would refuse. Then the wrist cutting would begin. Ron thought he had made the cottage safe by removing knives and blades. But Joyce would always find something.

Then Joyce would be brought to the hospital, have stitches put in, be kept under observation for a while, and medicated. She would explain that she cut herself because the hellsmen had told her that she was bad and must die. After a few days she would deny hearing the hellsmen, and she would insist on leaving the hospital.

Ron would take her home. The pattern continued.

When the emergency-room physician examined Joyce's wrists and heard that she believed she had been following the orders of "hellsmen," he began to suspect that she was suffering from schizophrenia. Schizophrenia touches every aspect of victims' lives. Schizophrenia is characterized by disturbances in (1) thought and language; (2) perception and attention; (3) motor activity; (4) mood; and by (5) withdrawal and **autism.**

Schizophrenia is known primarily by disturbances in thought, which are inferred from verbal and other overt behavior. Schizophrenic persons may show *loosening of associations.* Unless we are daydreaming or deliberately allowing our thoughts to wander, our thinking is normally tightly knit. We start at a certain point and the things that come to mind (the associations) tend to be logically and coherently connected. But schizophrenics often think in an illogical, disorganized manner. Their speech may be jumbled, combining parts of words or making rhymes in a meaningless fashion. Schizophrenics may also jump from topic to topic, conveying little useful information. Nor do they usually have insight that their thoughts and behavior are abnormal.

Schizophrenics often have **delusions,** for example, delusions of grandeur, persecution, or reference. In the case of delusions of grandeur, people may believe they are Jesus or people on a special mission, or they may have grand, illogical plans for saving the world. Delusions tend to be unshakable,

The "Son-of-Sam Killer"
David Berkowitz, the "Son-of-Sam killer," smiles benignly upon his arrest in 1977. Does his response to arrest seem appropriate? Because of his inappropriate emotional responses and his claim that a dog had urged him to commit his crimes, many mental-health professionals considered him schizophrenic.

despite disconfirming evidence. Persons with delusions of persecution may believe that they are sought by the Mafia, CIA, FBI, or some other group or agency. A woman with delusions of reference expressed the belief that national news broadcasts contained coded information about her. A man with such delusions complained that neighbors had "bugged" his walls with "radios." Other schizophrenics may have delusions to the effect that they have committed unpardonable sins, that they are rotting away from a hideous disease, or that they or the world do not really exist.

The perceptions of schizophrenics often include hallucinations—imagery in the absence of external stimulation that the schizophrenic cannot distinguish from reality. Joyce believed she heard "hellsmen." Others may see colors or even obscene words spelled out in midair. Auditory hallucinations are most common.

Motor activity may become wild and excited or slow to a **stupor.** There may be strange gestures and peculiar facial expressions. Emotional response may be flat or blunted, or inappropriate—as in giggling at bad news. Schizophrenics tend to withdraw from social contacts and become wrapped up in their own thoughts and fantasies.

It should be understood that many people diagnosed as schizophrenic show only a few of these symptoms. The DSM–III–R takes the view that schizophrenics at some time or another show delusions, problems with associative thinking, and hallucinations, but not necessarily all at once. There are also different kinds or types of schizophrenia, and different symptoms predominate with each type.

Types of Schizophrenia
The DSM–III–R lists three major types of schizophrenia: *disorganized, catatonic,* and *paranoid*.

Disorganized Type   **Disorganized schizophrenics** show incoherence, loosening of associations, disorganized behavior, disorganized delusions and vivid, abundant hallucinations that are often sexual or religious. One 23-three-year-old female disorganized schizophrenic remarked "I see 'pennis' " when one of us interviewed her. She pointed vaguely into the air before her. Asked to spell *pennis,* she replied irritatedly: "P-e-n-i-s." Apparently her social background was so inhibited that she had never heard the word for the male sex organ spoken aloud; and so she mispronounced it. Extreme social impairment is common among disorganized schizophrenics. They also often show silliness and giddiness of mood, and giggle and speak nonsensically. They may neglect their appearance and hygiene, and lose control of their bladder and their bowels.

Catatonic Type   **Catatonic schizophrenics** show striking impairment in motor activity. Impairment is characterized by slowing of activity to a stupor, which may change suddenly into an agitated phase. Catatonic individuals may hold unusual, even difficult postures for hours, even as their limbs grow swollen or stiff. A striking symptom is **waxy flexibility,** in which they maintain positions into which they have been manipulated by others. Catatonic individuals may also show **mutism,** but afterward they usually report that they heard what others were saying at the time.

Paranoid Type   **Paranoid schizophrenics** have systematized delusions and, frequently, related auditory hallucinations (American Psychiatric Association, 1987). They usually show delusions of grandeur and persecution, but may also show delusions of jealousy, in which they believe that a spouse or lover has been unfaithful. They may show agitation, confusion, and fear, and experience vivid hallucinations that are consistent with their delusions. The paranoid schizophrenic often constructs a complex or systematized delusion involving themes of wrongdoing or persecution.

A rarely used, related diagnostic category is **paranoia** (or "delusional [paranoid] disorder," according to the DSM–III–R). People may receive this diagnosis if they show a permanent, "unshakable" delusional system that does not have the bizarreness typical of schizophrenia. Persons with the disorder do not show the confused, jumbled thinking suggestive of schizophrenia. Hallucinations, when present, are not prominent. Daily functioning in paranoia and in some cases of paranoid schizophrenia may be minimally impaired, or not impaired at all, so long as the person does not act on the basis of his or her delusions.

Theoretical Views

Psychologists have investigated various factors that may contribute to schizophrenia.

Psychodynamic Views   According to the psychodynamic model, schizophrenia is the overwhelming of the ego by sexual or aggressive impulses from the id. The impulses threaten the ego and cause intense intrapsychic conflict. Under this threat, the person regresses to an early phase of the oral stage in which the infant has not yet learned that it and the world are separate. Fantasies become confused with reality, giving birth to hallucinations and delusions. Primitive impulses may carry more weight than social norms.

Critics point out that schizophrenic behavior is not that similar to infantile behavior. Moreover, psychoanalysts have not been able to predict a schizophrenic outcome on the basis of theoretically predisposing early experiences.

Social-Learning Views   Social-learning theorists explain schizophrenia through conditioning and observational learning. From this perspective, people show schizophrenic behavior when it is more likely than normal behavior to be reinforced. This may occur when the person is reared in a socially nonrewarding or punitive situation; inner fantasies then become more reinforcing than social realities.

In the mental hospital, patients may learn what is "expected" of them by observing other patients. Hospital staff may reinforce schizophrenic behavior by paying more attention to patients who behave bizarrely. This view is consistent with folklore that the child who disrupts the class earns more attention from the teacher than the "good" child.

Catatonic schizophrenics. Schizophrenics who show striking impairment in motor activity.

Waxy flexibility. A symptom of catatonic schizophrenia in which persons maintain postures into which they are placed.

Mutism. Refusal to talk.

Paranoid schizophrenia. A type of schizophrenia characterized primarily by delusions—commonly of persecution—and by vivid hallucinations.

Paranoia. A major but rare disorder in which a person shows a persistent delusional system, but not the confusion of the schizophrenic.

Critics note that many of us grow up in socially punitive settings but seem to show immunity to extinction of socially appropriate behavior. Others acquire schizophrenic behavior patterns without having had the opportunity to observe other schizophrenics.

Genetic Factors Schizophrenia, like many other psychological disorders, runs in families. Children of schizophrenic parents are at greater than average risk for showing certain problems at early ages (Watt et al., 1982). Schizophrenic persons constitute about 1 percent of the population, but children with two schizophrenic parents have about a 35 percent chance of becoming schizophrenic (Rosenthal, 1970). Twin studies also find a higher concordance rate for the diagnosis among pairs of identical twins, whose genetic codes are the same, than among pairs of fraternal twins, who are no more closely related genetically than other siblings. Studies of adopted children have been undertaken to determine whether their natural or adoptive parents exert a greater influence on the likelihood of their being judged schizophrenic (e.g., Heston, 1966; Wender et al., 1974). In such studies, the biological parent typically places the child at greater risk than the adoptive parent—even though the child has been reared by the adoptive parent.

Whereas evidence for a genetic role in schizophrenia seems strong, heredity cannot be the sole factor. If it were, there would be a 100 percent concordance rate for schizophrenia between pairs of identical twins. Genetic factors probably create a predisposition toward schizophrenia that interacts with other factors to produce schizophrenic behavior. Heredity might transmit biochemical factors, such as those discussed in the following section.

The Dopamine Theory of Schizophrenia Over the years numerous substances have been thought to play a role in schizophrenic disorders. Much current theory and research focus on the neurotransmitter **dopamine.**

The dopamine theory of schizophrenia evolved from observation of the effects of **amphetamines,** a group of stimulants. Researchers are confident that amphetamines act by increasing the quantity of dopamine in the brain. High doses of amphetamines lead to behavior that mimics paranoid schizophrenia in normal people, and even low doses exacerbate the symptoms of schizophrenics (Snyder, 1980). A second source of evidence for the dopamine theory lies in the effects of a class of drugs called **phenothiazines.** Research suggests that the phenothiazines, which are often effective in treating schizophrenia, work by blocking the action of dopamine receptors (Creese et al., 1978; Turkington, 1983).

It does not appear that schizophrenic persons produce more dopamine than others, but that they *utilize* more of the substance. Why? It could be that they have a greater number of dopamine receptors in the brain or that their dopamine receptors are hyperactive (Lee & Seeman, 1977; Mackay et al., 1982; Snyder, 1984).

Future research may suggest that schizophrenia can have multiple causes. In some cases it may be that genetic biochemical factors predispose borderline individuals to develop schizophrenic disorders in response to stressors. In such cases, biological predispositions would interact with situational factors to produce the disorder. But other people may be so severely handicapped by biochemical factors that they will develop schizophrenia under even the most positive environmental conditions.

■ Personality Disorders

Personality disorders, like personality traits, are characterized by enduring patterns of behavior. Personality disorders, however, are inflexible and maladaptive. They impair personal or social functioning and are a source of distress to the individual or to others.

Dopamine. A neurotransmitter implicated in schizophrenia.

Amphetamines. Stimulants whose abuse can trigger symptoms that mimic schizophrenia.

Phenothiazines. A family of drugs that are effective in treatment of many cases of schizophrenia.

Personality disorders. Enduring patterns of maladaptive behavior that are a source of distress to the individual or others.

There are a number of personality disorders, including the *paranoid, schizotypal, schizoid,* and *antisocial personality disorders.* The defining trait of the **paranoid personality disorder** is the tendency to interpret other people's behavior as deliberately threatening or demeaning. Although persons with the disorder do not show grossly disorganized thinking, they are mistrustful of others, and their social relationships suffer for it. They may be suspicious of coworkers and supervisors, but they can generally hold onto jobs.

Schizotypal personality disorder is characterized by pervasive peculiarities in thought, perception, and behavior, such as excessive fantasy and suspiciousness, feelings of being unreal, or odd usage of words (American Psychiatric Association, 1987, pp. 340–342). The bizarre psychotic behaviors that characterize schizophrenia are absent, and so this disorder is schizo*typal* instead of schizophrenic. Because of their oddities, persons with the disorder are often maladjusted on the job.

Schizoid personality disorder is defined by indifference to social relationships and flatness in emotional responsiveness. Schizoid personalities are "loners" who do not develop warm, tender feelings for others. They have few friends and rarely get married. Some schizoid personalities do very well on the job, so long as continuous social interaction is not required. Hallucinations and delusions are absent.

Paranoid personality disorder. A disorder characterized by persistent suspiciousness, but not the disorganization of paranoid schizophrenia.

Schizotypal personality disorder. A disorder characterized by oddities of thought and behavior, but not involving bizarre psychotic symptoms.

Schizoid personality disorder. A disorder characterized by social withdrawal.

Antisocial personality disorder. The diagnosis given a person who is in frequent conflict with society, yet is undeterred by punishment and experiences little or no guilt and anxiety.

The Antisocial Personality

Persons with **antisocial personality disorders** persistently violate the rights of others, show indifference to commitments, and encounter conflict with the law (see Table 8.2). In order for the diagnosis to be used, the person must be at least 18 years old (American Psychiatric Association, 1987). Cleckley (1964) notes that persons with antisocial personalities often show a superficial charm and are at least average in intelligence. Perhaps their most striking feature, given their antisocial behavior, is their lack of guilt and low level of anxiety. They seem largely undeterred by punishment. Though they have usually received punishment from parents and others for their misdeeds, they continue their impulsive, irresponsible styles of life.

Theoretical Views   Various factors appear to contribute to antisocial behavior, including an antisocial father, parental lack of love and rejection during childhood, and inconsistent discipline.

Antisocial personalities tend to run in families. Studies of adoptees have found higher incidences of antisocial behavior among the biological than the adoptive relatives of persons with the disorder (Cadoret, 1978; Hutchings & Mednick, 1974; Mednick, 1985).

TABLE 8.2   Characteristics of the Antisocial Personality

Persistent violation of the rights of others
Irresponsibility
Lack of formation of enduring relationships or loyalty to another person
Failure to maintain good job performance over the years
Failure to develop or adhere to a life plan
History of truancy
History of delinquency
History of running away
Persistent lying
Sexual promiscuity
Substance abuse
Impulsivity
Inability to tolerate boredom
At least 18 years of age
Onset of antisocial behavior by age 15

Source: DSM–III–R (1987).

One promising avenue of research concerns the observation that antisocial personalities are unlikely to show guilt for their misdeeds or be deterred by punishment. It is suggested that low levels of guilt and anxiety reflect lower-than-normal levels of arousal, which, in turn, have at least a partial genetic basis (Lykken, 1957, 1982). Experiments on this issue show, for example, that antisocial subjects do not learn as rapidly as others equal in intelligence when the payoff is avoidance of impending electric shock. But when the levels of arousal of the antisocial subjects are increased by injections of adrenalin, they learn to avoid punishment as rapidly as others (Schachter & Latané, 1964; Chesno & Kilmann, 1975).

A lower-than-normal level of arousal would not guarantee the development of an antisocial personality. It might also be necessary that a person be reared under conditions that do not foster the self-concept of a person who abides by law and social custom. Punishment for deviation from the norm would then be unlikely to induce feelings of guilt and shame. The individual might be "undeterred" by punishment.

■ Sexual Disorders

The DSM–III–R lists a number of sexual disorders, including *paraphilias and sexual dysfunctions*. We shall also discuss the **gender-identity disorder** of transsexualism in this section.* In a gender-identity disorder, one's assigned sex (as based on anatomic sex and recorded on the birth certificate) is inconsistent with one's gender identity (one's psychological sense of being male or being female). In the **paraphilias,** people show sexual arousal in response to unusual or bizarre objects or situations. **Sexual dysfunctions** are characterized by lack of sexual "appetite" or problems in becoming sexually aroused and reaching orgasm. We shall discuss sexual dysfunctions in Chapter 15.

Transsexualism

About 30 years ago headlines were made when an ex-GI, now known as Christine Jorgensen, had a "sex-change operation" in Denmark. Since that time some 2,500 American transsexuals, including tennis player Dr. Renée Richards, have undergone sex-reassignment surgery. Sex-reassignment surgery is cosmetic. It does not actually change gender by implanting reproductive organs of the opposite sex. Instead, it creates the appearance of the external genitals of the opposite sex—more successfully with male-to-female than female-to-male transsexuals. After these operations, transsexuals can engage in sexual activity and reach orgasm, but they cannot have children.

Transsexualism is a towering adjustment problem, because it is the persistent feeling that one is of the wrong sex. Transsexuals wish to be rid of their own genitals and to live as members of the opposite sex.

The causes of transsexualism are unclear. Socialization patterns might affect transsexuals who are reared by parents who had wanted children of the opposite sex and who thus encourage cross-sex dressing and patterns of play. But it is also possible that some transsexuals have been influenced by prenatal hormonal imbalances. It may be that the brain can be "masculinized" or "feminized" by sex hormones during certain stages of prenatal development. Perhaps the brain is influenced in one direction, even as the genitals are being differentiated in the other direction (Money, 1987).

Results are mixed concerning transsexuals who undergo sex reassignment. Female-to-male transsexuals are somewhat better adjusted than male-to-female transsexuals (Abramowitz, 1986). Most female-to-male transsexuals rate their adjustment as positive, and are solid workers and taxpayers (Person

Gender-identity disorder. A disorder in which a person's anatomic sex is inconsistent with his or her gender identity (or sense of being male or female).

Paraphilias. Disorders in which people show sexual arousal in response to unusual or bizarre objects or situations.

Sexual dysfunctions. Persistent problems in achieving or maintaining sexual arousal or in reaching orgasm.

Transsexualism. A gender-identity disorder in which a person feels trapped in the body of the wrong sex.

---

*The DSM–III–R classifies transsexualism as a "disorder usually first evident in infancy, childhood, or adolescence."

& Ovesey, 1974; Randall, 1969). Despite difficulties in surgically constructing structures that serve as external male sex organs, a group of 22 postoperative female-to-male transsexuals were generally satisfied with their new bodies (Fleming et al., 1982). A follow-up study of 116 transsexuals (both female-to-male and male-to-female) at least one year after surgery found that most were pleased with the results and that the majority were acceptably adjusted (Blanchard et al., 1985). One study of 42 postoperative male-to-female transsexuals found that all but one would repeat the surgery, and the great majority found sexual activity more pleasurable as a "woman" (Bentler, 1976). However, about 10 percent of male-to-female transsexuals seem to encounter serious adjustment problems (Abramowitz, 1986).

Paraphilias

Paraphilias are characterized by sexual response to unusual objects or situations. The American Psychiatric Associations (1987) uses the following diagnoses when people act on these urges, or—if they do not act on them—when they are markedly distressed by them.

Fetishism **Fetishism** is sexual response to an inanimate object, such as an article of clothing, or to a body part, such as the feet. Sexual gratification is often achieved through masturbating in the presence of the object. Fetishes for undergarments and for objects made of leather, rubber, or silk are not uncommon.

Transvestic Festishism **Transvestic fetishism** is recurrent, persistent dressing in clothing usually worn by a woman in order to achieve sexual excitement in a heterosexual male. Transvestism may range from wearing a single female undergarment in private to sporting full dress at a transvestite club. Most transvestites are married and engage in sexual activity with their wives, but they seek additional sexual gratification through dressing as women.

Zoophilia **Zoophilia,** or *bestiality*, is sexual contact with animals as a preferred or exclusive means of achieving sexual arousal. Thus, a child or adolescent who shows some sexual response to an episode of rough-and-tumble play with the family pet is not likely to be showing zoophilia.

Pedophilia **Pedophilia** is actual or fantasized sexual activity with children as a preferred means of becoming sexually aroused. Most episodes are not coerced and involve exhibitionism or fondling rather than sexual intercourse.

Exhibitionism **Exhibitionism** is the repetitive act of exposing one's genitals to a stranger in order to surprise or shock, rather than sexually arouse, the victim. The exhibitionist is usually not interested in actual sexual contact with the victim. He may masturbate while fantasizing about or actually exposing himself.

Professional strip-teasers and scantily clad swimmers do not fit the definition of exhibitionist. Both groups might seek to sexually arouse, but usually not to shock, observers. In fact, the central motive of the strip-teaser might be simply to earn a living.

Voyeurism **Voyeurism** is repetitive watching of unsuspecting strangers while they are undressing or engaging in sexual activity as the preferred or exclusive means of achieving sexual arousal. We may enjoy observing spouses undress, or even the nudity in an R-rated film, without being diagnosed as voyeurs. In voyeurism, the "victim" does not know that he or she is being watched, and the voyeur prefers looking to doing.

Fetishism. A variation of choice in sexual object in which a bodily part (e.g., a foot) or an inanimate object (e.g., an undergarment) elicits sexual arousal and is preferred to a person.

Transvestic fetishism. Recurrent, persistent dressing in clothing worn by the opposite sex for purposes of sexual excitement.

Zoophilia. Sexual contact with animals as the preferred source of sexual excitement. Also called *bestiality*.

Pedophilia. Sexual contact with children as the preferred source of sexual excitement.

Exhibitionism. The compulsion to expose one's genitals in public.

Voyeurism. Attainment of sexual gratification through observing others undress or engage in sexual activity.

Masochism. Attainment of sexual gratification by means of receiving pain or humiliation.

Sadism. Attainment of sexual gratification by means of inflicting pain or humiliation on sex partners.

Sexual Masochism   **Masochism** is named after the Austrian storyteller Leopold von Sacher-Masoch, who portrayed sexual satisfaction as deriving from pain or humiliation. The sexual masochist must receive pain or humiliation in order to achieve sexual gratification. It has been suggested that many masochists experience guilt about sex, but can enjoy sex so long as they see themselves as being appropriately punished for it.

Sexual Sadism   **Sadism** is named after the infamous Marquis de Sade, a Frenchman who wrote stories about the pleasures of achieving sexual gratification by inflicting pain or humiliation on others. In sadism, the person may not be able to become sexually excited unless he inflicts pain on his partner.

Theoretical Views   According to psychodynamic theory, paraphilias are defenses against anxiety. The exhibitionist, for example, has unconscious castration anxiety. His victim's shock at his exposure reassures him that he does, after all, have a penis. Fetishism, pedophilia, and so on protect him from fear of failure in adult heterosexual relationships and provide him with sexual outlets.

Rathus (1983) offers a social-learning view of fetishism and other paraphilias. First, a fantasized or actual event—such as becoming excited when a woman happens upon a boy who is urinating behind a bush—prompts the person to encode the unusual object or situation as sexually arousing. As a consequence, second, the person acquires the expectancy that the object or situation will increase the pleasure of sexual activity. Expectancies concerning an outcome can be powerful influences on behavior, and so, third, the object is used in actuality or fantasy to heighten sexual arousal. Fourth, recognition of the deviance of the fantasy or act causes feelings of anxiety or guilt. These feelings, if not extreme, enhance emotional arousal in the presence of the deviant object or activity. Heightened emotional response is then *attributed* to the deviant object or activity. Fifth, orgasm reinforces the preceding behaviors and fantasies. Sixth, orgasm also confirms the stimulating properties attributed to the deviant object or activity. Seventh, in cases in which a person is anxious about normal sexual relationships, the deviant object or activity becomes the major or sole sexual outlet.

Although the causes of many psychological disorders remain in dispute, a number of therapies have been devised to deal with them. Those methods are the focus of Chapter 9.

■ Summary

1. **What are psychological disorders?** Behavior is likely to be labeled disordered when it is unusual, socially unacceptable, involves faulty perception of reality, is personally distressful, dangerous, or self-defeating.

2. **What are the major models of psychological disorders?** These are the medical, psychodynamic, learning-theory, and cognitive models. Adherents to the medical model view psychological disorders as symptomatic of underlying organic disorders. Psychodynamic theorists view them as symbolizing psychological conflicts. Social-learning theorists see psychological disorders as acquired through principles of learning, or as problems in person variables. Cognitive theorists tend to explain them as problems in processing information, or as reflecting self-defeating beliefs and attitudes.

3. **What are the anxiety disorders?** Anxiety disorders are characterized by motor tension, feelings of dread, and overarousal of the sympathetic branch of the ANS. Anxiety disorders include irrational, excessive fears, or phobias; panic disorder, which is characterized by sudden attacks in which people typically fear that they may be losing control or going crazy;

generalized, or "free-floating," anxiety; obsessive-compulsive disorders, in which people are troubled by intrusive thoughts or impulses to repeat some activity; and post-traumatic stress disorder (PTSD), in which a stressful event is followed by persistent fears and intrusive thoughts about the event.

4. **What are the dissociative disorders?** Dissociative disorders are characterized by a sudden temporary change in consciousness or self-identity. They include psychogenic amnesia, or "motivated forgetting" of personal information; psychogenic fugue, which involves forgetting plus fleeing and adopting a new identity; multiple personality, in which a person behaves as if distinct personalities occupied the body; and depersonalization, which is characterized by feelings that one is not real, or that one is standing outside one's body and observing one's thought processes.

5. **What are the somatoform disorders?** In somatoform disorders, people show or complain of physical problems, although no evidence of a medical abnormality can be found. The somatoform disorders include conversion disorder and hypochondria. In a conversion disorder, there is loss of a body function with no organic basis. Some people with conversion disorder show la belle indifférence, or lack of concern about their disorder. Hypochondriacs insist that they are suffering from illnesses, although there are no medical findings.

6. **What is anorexia nervosa?** Anorexia nervosa is an eating disorder characterized by dramatic weight loss and intense fear of being overweight. Anoretic females also show amenorrhea; that is, they stop menstruating. Anoretic women have a distorted body image in which they view themselves as overweight when others perceive them as dangerously thin.

7. **What is bulimia nervosa?** In bulimia nervosa, the individual also fears becoming overweight, but goes on eating binges, especially of carbohydrates. Binging is followed by severe weight-loss methods such as fasting or self-induced vomiting.

8. **What are the mood disorders?** Mood disorders are characterized by disturbance in expressed emotions. Major depression is characterized by persistent feelings of sadness, loss of interest, feelings of worthlessness or guilt, inability to concentrate, and physical symptoms that may include disturbances in the regulation of eating and sleeping. Feelings of unworthiness and guilt may be so excessive that they are considered delusional. In bipolar disorder there are mood swings from elation to depression and back. Manicky people also tend to show pressured speech and rapid flight of ideas.

9. **Who is likely to commit suicide?** Suicide is more common among college students than nonstudents, more common among minority groups and among physicians, lawyers, and psychologists. More women than men attempt suicide; more men "succeed."

10. **Why do people commit suicide?** Most suicides reflect feelings of depression and hopelessness, and they tend to follow "exit events," such as loss of a spouse, close friend, divorce, or a family member's leaving home.

11. **What is schizophrenia?** Schizophrenia is characterized by disturbances in thought and language, such as loosening of associations and delusions; perception and attention, as found in hallucinations; motor activity, as shown by a stupor or by excited behavior; mood, as in flat or inappropriate emotional responses; and by withdrawal and autism.

12. **What are the subtypes of schizophrenia?** There are three major types of schizophrenia: disorganized, catatonic, and paranoid. Disorganized schizophrenia is characterized by disorganized delusions and vivid, abundant hallucinations. Catatonic schizophrenia is characterized by impaired motor activity, as in a stupor, and by waxy flexibility. Paranoid schizophrenia is characterized by paranoid delusions.

13. **What are the personality disorders?** Personality disorders are inflexible, maladaptive behavior patterns that impair personal or social functioning and are a source of distress to the individual or others. The defining trait of the paranoid personality is suspiciousness. Persons with schizotypal personality disorders show oddities of thought, perception, and behavior. Social withdrawal is the major characteristic of the schizoid personality. Persons with antisocial personality disorders persistently violate the rights of others and encounter conflict with the law. They show little or no guilt or shame over their misdeeds and are largely undeterred by punishment.

14. **What is transsexualism?** In transsexualism, the person feels trapped in the body of the wrong sex and seeks surgery so that his or her external genitals will take on the appearance of those of the opposite sex. Transsexualism is considered a gender identity disorder.

15. **What are the paraphilias?** In the paraphilias, people are sexually aroused by unusual or bizarre objects or situations. The paraphilias include fetishism; transvestic fetishism, or cross-dressing; pedophilia, or sexual preference for children; exhibitionism; voyeurism; sexual masochism, in which gratification involves personal experiencing of pain or humiliation; and sexual sadism, in which gratification involves hurting or humiliating one's partner.

■ TRUTH OR FICTION REVISITED

A man shot the president of the United States in front of millions of television witnesses, yet was found not guilty by a court of law. True. The man's name is John Hinckley and he was found not guilty by reason of insanity.

Some people are suddenly flooded with feelings of panic, even when there is no external threat. True. They are said to have panic disorder.

Some people have irresistible urges to wash their hands—over and over again. True. They are said to have a compulsion.

Stressful experiences can lead to recurrent nightmares. True. Recurrent nightmares are one of the symptoms of post-traumatic stress disorder.

Some people have not one, but two or more distinct personalities dwelling within them. Perhaps—we cannot be certain. There are many convincing case studies of multiple personality, but personalities are inferred from behavior, not observed directly. Therefore, our investigative methods do not absolutely rule out the possibility that people have convincingly faked multiple personality.

People have lost the use of their legs or eyes under stress, even though there was nothing medically wrong with them. True. They are said to have conversion disorder, in which stress is converted into loss or disturbance of a bodily function.

Dieting has become the normal way of eating for women in the United States. True. Surveys show that the majority of women diet at one time or another.

Some college women control their weight by going on cycles of binge eating followed by vomiting. True. Cycles of binging and purging define the disorder of bulimia.

It is abnormal to feel depressed. False. Depression is an appropriate response to a loss or failure.

Some people ride an emotional roller-coaster, with cycles of elation and depression. True. They are said to have bipolar mood disorder.

People who threaten suicide are only seeking attention. False. Most people who commit suicide have informed others of their intentions.

In some mental disorders, people see and hear things that are not actually there. True. This occurs in schizophrenia, for example.

Some people persistently injure others and violate their rights without feeling guilty. True. Persons with antisocial personalities feel little or no guilt over their misdeeds.

Thousands of U.S. citizens have changed their sex through surgery. False. Transsexuals have undergone sex-reassignment surgery, which provides the *appearance* of the external genitals of the opposite sex, but internal sex organs cannot be altered to function as those of the opposite sex.

Strip-teasers are exhibitionists. False. Exhibitionists attempt to surprise and shock their victims. Strip-teasers attempt to make a living by sexually arousing their audiences.

■ Normative Data for the Temple Fear Survey Inventory

When you have completed the Temple Fear Survey Inventory, you can compare your answers to those of a sample of 435 introductory psychology students at Temple University by referring to the following table. Note that some items such as the noise from vacuum cleaners (item 1) and dull weather (81) evoke very little fear. Others such as death of a loved one (32) and prospects of a surgical operation (49) elicit quite a bit. There are also some sex differences. For example, being physically assaulted (25), worms (33), and guns (87) evoke more fear from women, whereas men are somewhat more fearful of not being a success (27). Where do you fit in?

Item	Mean Score Male	Mean Score Female	Item	Mean Score Male	Mean Score Female
1	1.1	1.0	32	3.0	3.4
2	2.2	2.2	33	1.2	1.8
3	1.5	1.7	34	1.2	1.4
4	2.4	2.6	35	1.5	2.0
5	2.0	2.8	36	1.8	2.0
6	1.5	1.7	37	1.8	1.9
7	1.3	1.2	38	1.5	1.7
8	1.2	1.5	39	1.8	1.9
9	2.5	2.9	40	1.7	1.9
10	1.5	1.6	41	1.6	2.6
11	1.6	1.8	42	1.8	2.7
12	2.0	2.1	43	1.3	1.3
13	1.5	1.6	44	2.0	2.8
14	1.1	1.5	45	1.4	1.9
15	1.6	1.8	46	1.8	2.1
16	1.7	1.8	47	1.6	1.8
17	2.0	2.0	48	1.9	2.7
18	1.3	1.7	49	2.5	2.7
19	1.5	1.6	50	1.7	2.1
20	2.0	2.1	51	1.4	2.0
21	1.6	1.6	52	1.6	1.8
22	1.9	2.1	53	1.5	1.9
23	1.4	1.7	54	2.2	2.6
24	1.4	1.6	55	2.0	2.1
25	2.2	3.1	56	2.5	2.6
26	2.6	2.7	57	2.3	2.3
27	2.7	2.4	58	1.5	1.7
28	2.1	2.0	59	1.6	1.6
29	2.2	2.1	60	1.6	1.7
30	1.7	1.7	61	1.7	1.9
31	2.4	2.7	62	1.4	1.4

Item	Mean Score		Item	Mean Score	
	Male	*Female*		*Male*	*Female*
63	1.5	1.7	82	1.1	1.1
64	1.7	1.7	83	1.7	1.8
65	1.7	2.2	84	1.7	2.0
66	1.9	2.1	85	1.1	1.2
67	1.4	1.5	86	1.8	1.9
68	2.1	2.3	87	1.6	2.2
69	1.3	1.5	88	1.1	1.2
70	1.6	1.5	89	1.1	1.4
71	1.4	2.1	90	1.7	1.9
72	2.0	2.4	91	2.2	2.4
73	1.7	2.3	92	1.4	1.3
74	1.6	2.1	93	2.3	2.3
75	1.1	1.1	94	2.0	2.1
76	1.6	1.7	95	1.6	1.5
77	1.9	2.7	96	1.1	1.7
78	1.1	1.1	97	1.1	1.2
79	1.1	1.1	98	1.8	1.9
80	1.4	1.4	99	1.9	2.1
81	1.1	1.1	100	2.1	2.0

Therapies: Ways of Helping

9

The terms *psychotherapy* and *psychoanalysis* are interchangeable.

In order to be of significant help, psychotherapy must be undertaken for months, perhaps years.

If you were in traditional psychoanalysis, your major tasks would be to lie back, relax, and say whatever pops into your mind.

Some psychotherapists interpret clients' dreams.

Some psychotherapists encourage their clients to take the lead in the therapy session.

Other psychotherapists tell their clients precisely what to do.

Still other psychotherapists purposefully argue with clients.

A goal of psychotherapy is to help clients solve problems.

Some clients in psychotherapy delve into their pasts as a way to avoid confronting the problems they have today.

You might be able to gain control over bad habits merely by keeping a record of where and when you practice them.

Lying around in your reclining chair and fantasizing can be an effective way of confronting your fears.

Smoking cigarettes can be an effective treatment for helping people to . . . stop smoking cigarettes.

Individual therapy is preferable to group therapy, for people who can afford it.

Drugs are never a solution to abnormal behavior problems.

There is a treatment for severe depression in which an electric current strong enough to induce seizures is passed through the head.

The originator of a surgical technique intended to reduce violence learned that it was not always successful—when one of his patients shot him.

Brad is having an uplifting experience—literally. Six people who minutes ago were perfect strangers have cradled him in their arms and raised him into midair. His eyes are closed. Gently they rock him back and forth and carry him about the room.

Brad is no paralyzed hospital patient. He has just joined an encounter group. He hopes to be able to learn to relate to other people as individuals, not as passing blurs on the street or as patrons asking him to cash payroll checks at the bank where he works as a teller. The group leader had directed that Brad be carried about in order to help him break down his defensive barriers and establish trust in others.

Brad had responded to a somewhat flamboyant ad in the therapy section of the classifieds in New York's *Village Voice*:

Come to life! Stop being a gray automaton in a mechanized society! Encounter yourself and others. New group forming. First meeting free. Call 212–555–0599. Qualified therapist.

Like many who seek personal help, Brad had little idea how to go about it. His group experience might or might not work out. For one thing, he has no idea about the qualifications of the group leader and did not know to ask. If he had answered other ads in the *Voice*, including some placed by highly qualified therapists, his treatment might have looked quite different. Brad could have been:

Lying on a couch talking about anything that pops into awareness and exploring the hidden meanings of a recurrent dream.
Sitting face to face with a gentle, accepting therapist who places the major burden for what happens during therapy directly on Brad's shoulders.
Listening to a frank, straightforward therapist insist that his problems stem from self-defeating attitudes and beliefs, such as an overriding need to be liked and approved of.
Initiating a social relationship, through role-play, in which he smiles at a new acquaintance, makes small talk, and looks the person squarely in the eye.

These methods, although quite different from one another, all represent various kinds of psychotherapies. In order to make sense of what is happening to Brad—and of all the things that are not happening to him—in this chapter we first define psychotherapy. We talk about who goes for therapy and see who conducts therapy. Then we describe and evaluate several of the major psychotherapies, including psychodynamic, phenomenological, cognitive, behavior, and group therapies. After exploring these approaches to psychotherapy, we shall turn our attention to *biological therapies*, such as the use of drugs. Although biological therapies are most appropriately used with some of the more severe psychological disorders, such as schizophrenia, major depression, and biolar disorder, Brad might also have been given drugs, especially if he had seemed very upset about his situation. The biological therapies include drug therapy (also called chemotherapy), electroconvulsive shock therapy, and psychosurgery.

Psychotherapy. A systematic interaction between a therapist and a client that brings psychological principles to bear on influencing the client's thoughts, feelings, or behavior in order to help that client overcome abnormal behavior or adjust to problems in living.

■ Overview: What Is Therapy? Who Goes for Therapy? Who Does Therapy?

The form of psychotherapy practiced by a psychologist or another helping professional is related to that practitioner's theory of personality or theoretical model of psychological disorders. Treatment is not, or ought not be, a matter of chance. Let us now define what is meant by psychotherapy.

Definitions and Clients
Although there are many different kinds of psychotherapy, they have a number of things in common. **Psychotherapy** is defined as a systematic interaction

between a therapist and a client that brings psychological principles to bear on influencing the client's thoughts, feelings, or behavior in order to help the client overcome psychological disorders, adjust to problems in living, or develop as an individual.

Quite a mouthful? True. But note the essentials:

Systematic Interaction   Psychotherapy is a systematic interaction between a client and a therapist. The client's needs and goals and the therapist's theoretical point of view interact to determine how the therapist and client will relate to one another.

Psychological Principles   Psychotherapy brings psychological principles to bear on the client's problems or goals. Psychotherapy is based on principles concerning human personality, learning, motivation and emotion. Psychotherapy is not based on, say, religious or biological principles, although there is no reason why psychotherapy cannot be compatible with both.

Thoughts, Feelings, and Behavior   Psychotherapy influences clients' thoughts, feelings, and behavior. Psychotherapy can be aimed at any or all of these aspects of human psychology.

Psychological Disorders, Adjustment Problems, and Personal Growth   Psychotherapy helps the client overcome psychological disorders, adjust to problems in living, or develop as an individual.

Types of Clients   Psychotherapy is used with at least three types of clients. First there are people who have been diagnosed as having psychological disorders, such as anxiety disorders, mood disorders, or schizophrenia. When these disorders are severe, as in the case of major depression or schizophrenia, biological therapies can play a major role in treatment. But still, psychotherapy may be used to help the individual in areas of personal, social, or vocational concern.

Then there are people who seek help in adjusting to problems such as social shyness, weight problems, loss of a spouse, or career confusion. In such cases there is usually no need for biological approaches. Finally, many individuals use psychotherapy, especially psychodynamic and phenomenological therapies, not because they are seeking help in solving problems, but because they want to learn more about themselves and to reach their full potential as individuals, creative artists, parents, members of social groups, and so on.

The Helping Professions

Throughout history people in many roles have helped others to adjust, including priests and ministers, grandparents, witch doctors, palm readers, and wise men (and women). Today qualified professionals in these roles include psychologists, counselors, psychiatrists, social workers, and psychiatric nurses, among others.

Unfortunately, most states allow almost anyone to use the label *therapist*. This label indicates nothing about one's education and experience. People seeking effective therapy should never be shy about asking helping professionals about their education and supervised experience. Here are some of the professions that are genuinely qualified to help:

Psychology   Psychologists have at least a master's degree and in most states must have a doctoral degree (Ph.D, Ed.D., Psy.D.), in order to use the label *psychologist*. The state will typically weigh the adequacy of the individual's education and supervised experience in psychology before granting a license to practice psychology. Psychologists use interviews, behavioral observations, and psychological tests to diagnose psychological disorders and adjustment problems, and they use psychotherapy to treat them. Most psychologists have been trained extensively in research methods. They are more likely than other helping professionals to be critically acquainted with psychological theory. Psychologists work with people with various disorders and adjustment problems, and also help clients develop as individuals.

There are many different kinds of psychologists, and although their functions overlap, there are also some differences. Clinical psychologists, for example, are more likely than other psychologists to focus on psychological disorders. Health psychologists might focus on helping people control weight, quit smoking, and undertake styles of life that lower the risk for heart disease. Counseling psychologists, like counselors, frequently focus on adjustment problems and career development. Community psychologists often focus on helping school systems and community agencies foster mental health and prevent problems such as drug abuse and teen-age pregnancies.

Counseling   Counselors usually have degrees in education, such as the Ed.M. (Master of Education) or Ed.D. (Doctor of Education). Their graduate programs will have included supervised counseling experience, and in many states counselors are licensed. Counselors are frequently found in school settings, such as college and university testing and counseling centers. Many counselors specialize in areas such as academic, vocational, marriage, and family counseling or therapy. Counselors typically specialize in adjustment problems or career development and do not work with individuals with severe psychological disorders.

Psychiatry   A psychiatrist is a licensed physician. Psychiatrists earn medical degrees such as the M.D. (Doctor of Medicine) or D.O. (Doctor of Osteopathy), and then they undertake a psychiatric residency during which time they learn to apply medical skills, such as prescribing drugs, to treat psychological disorders. Psychiatrists, like psychologists, may practice psychotherapy. Most psychiatrists rely on interviews for diagnostic purposes, but may refer patients to psychologists for psychological testing.

Psychiatric Social Work   Psychiatric social workers have an M.S.W. (Master of Social Work) or D.S.W. (Doctor of Social Work) degree and supervised experience in helping people adjust. Many offer psychotherapy, but social workers do not use psychological tests or prescribe medical treatments. Like counselors, many specialize in marital or family problems.

Psychoanalysis   Once only physicians were admitted to psychoanalytic training, but today many psychologists and social workers also practice this form of therapy, which was originated by Sigmund Freud. The practice of psychoanalytic therapy typically requires years of training beyond the doctoral level and completion of one's own psychoanalysis. Psychoanalysts usually focus on problems such as anxiety, depression, and difficulties in forming and maintaining productive social relationships.

■ Psychodynamic Therapies

Psychodynamic therapies are based on the thinking of Sigmund Freud, the founder of psychoanalytic theory. Broadly speaking, they are based on the view that our problems largely reflect early childhood experiences and internal conflicts. According to Freud, as noted in Chapter 2, this internal conflict involves the shifting of psychic, or libidinal, energy among the three psychic structures—id, ego, and superego. The sway of psychic energy determines our behavior and, when primitive urges threaten to break through from the id, or when the superego floods us with excessive guilt, it prompts the establishment of defenses and creates distress. Freud's psychodynamic therapy method—**psychoanalysis**—aims to modify the flow of energy among these structures, largely to bulwark the ego against the torrents of energy loosed by the id and the superego. With impulses and feelings of guilt and shame placed under greater control, clients are emotionally freed to develop more adaptive behavior patterns.

But not all psychodynamically oriented therapists view internal conflict in terms of unconscious forces. In this section we first outline Freud's psychoanalytic methods for shoring up the ego, frequently referred to as "traditional" psychoanalysis. Then we examine more modern psychoanalytic approaches, and we see that their concepts of conflict and their methods differ from those of Freud.

Traditional Psychoanalysis: Where Id Was, There Shall Ego Be

> Canst thou not minister to a mind diseas'd,
> Pluck out from the memory a rooted sorrow,
> Raze out the written troubles of the brain,
> And with some sweet oblivious antidote
> Cleanse the stuff'd bosom of that perilous stuff
> Which weighs upon the heart?
> —SHAKESPEARE, *MACBETH*

In this passage from *Macbeth*, Macbeth asks a physician to minister to Lady Macbeth after she has gone mad. In the play, her madness is in part caused by current events, namely her guilt for participating in murders designed to seat her husband on the throne of Scotland. But there are also hints of more deeply rooted and mysterious problems that might involve infertility.

If Lady Macbeth's physician had been a traditional psychoanalyst, he might have asked her to lie down on a couch in a slightly darkened room. He would have sat just behind her and encouraged her to talk about anything that popped into her mind, no matter how trivial, no matter how personal. In order to avoid interfering with her self-exploration, he might have said little or nothing for session after session. That would have been par for the course. A traditional psychoanalysis, you see, can extend for months, or years.

Psychoanalysis is the clinical method devised by Freud for plucking "from the memory a rooted sorrow," for razing "out the written troubles of the brain." Psychoanalysis is the method used by Freud and his followers to "cleanse . . . that perilous stuff which weighs upon the heart"—to provide insight into the conflicts presumed to lie at the roots of a person's problems. Insight involves a number of things: knowledge of the experiences that lead to conflicts and maladaptive behavior; identification and labeling of feelings and conflicts that lie below conscious awareness; and objective evaluation of one's beliefs and ideas, feelings, and overt behavior.

Psychoanalysis also seeks to allow the client to express emotions and impulses that are theorized to have been dammed up by the forces of repression. Freud was fond of saying, "Where id was, there shall ego be." In part he meant that psychoanalysis could shed light on the inner workings of the mind. But Freud did not believe that we ought, or needed to, become conscious of all of our conflicts and primitive impulses. Instead, he sought to replace impulsive and defensive behavior with coping behavior. He believed that impulsive behavior reflected the urges of the id. Defensive behavior, such as timidly avoiding confrontations, represented the ego's compromising efforts to protect the client from these impulses and the possibility of retaliation. Coping behavior would allow the client to partially express these impulses, but in socially acceptable ways. In so doing, the client would find gratification but avoid social disapproval and self-condemnation.

In this way a man with a phobia for knives might discover that he had been repressing the urge to harm someone who had taken advantage of him.

Abreaction. In psychoanalysis, expression of previously repressed feelings and impulses to allow the psychic energy associated with them to spill forth.

Catharsis. Another term for *abreaction*.

Free association. In psychoanalysis, the uncensored uttering of all thoughts that come to mind.

Compulsion to utter. The urge to express ideas and impulses—in psychoanalytic theory, a reflection of the urge to seek expression of impulses within the id.

A View of Freud's Consulting Room at Berggasse 19 in Vienna
While his patient lay on the couch free-associating, Freud would sit quietly at the head of the couch, so as not to interfere.

He might also find ways to confront his antagonist verbally. A woman with a conversion disorder—for example, paralysis of the legs—could see that her disability allowed her to avoid unwanted pregnancy without guilt. She might also taste her resentment at being pressed into a stereotypical feminine sex role and decide to expand her options.

Freud also believed that psychoanalysis permitted the client to spill forth the psychic energy theorized to have been repressed by conflicts and guilt. He called this spilling forth **abreaction,** or **catharsis**. Abreaction would provide feelings of relief by alleviating some of the forces assaulting the ego.

Free Association   Early in his career as a therapist, Freud found that hypnosis allowed his clients to focus on repressed conflicts and talk about them. The relaxed "trance state" provided by hypnosis seemed to allow clients to break through to topics of which they were otherwise unaware. But Freud also found that many clients denied the accuracy of this material once they were out of the trance. Other clients found these revelations premature and painful. And so Freud turned to **free association**—a more gradual method of breaking down the walls of defense that blocked insight into unconscious processes.

In free association, the client is made comfortable, as by lying on a couch, and asked to talk about any topic that comes to mind. No thought is to be censored—that is the cardinal rule. Psychoanalysts ask their clients to wander "freely" from topic to topic, but they do not believe that the process *within* the client is fully free. Repressed impulses press for release. On a verbal level, they lead to a **compulsion to utter.** A client may begin to free-associate with meaningless topics, but eventually the compulsion to utter will cause pertinent repressed material to surface.

But the ego persists in trying to repress unacceptable impulses and threatening conflicts. As a result, clients may show **resistance** to recalling and discussing threatening ideas. Clients may claim "My mind is blank" when they are about to entertain such a thought. They may accuse the analyst of being demanding or inconsiderate. They may "forget" their appointment when threatening material is due to be uncovered.

The therapist observes the dynamic struggle between the compulsion to utter and resistance. Through discreet remarks, the analyst subtly tips the balance in favor of uttering. A gradual process of self-discovery and self-insight ensues. Now and then the analyst offers an **interpretation** of an utterance, showing how it suggests resistance or deep-seated feelings and conflicts.

Dream Analysis   Freud considered dreams the "royal road to the unconscious." The psychoanalytic theory of dreams holds that they are determined by unconscious processes as well as the remnants or "residues" of the day. Unconscious impulses tend to be expressed in dreams as a form of **wish fulfillment.**

But unacceptable sexual and aggressive impulses are likely to be displaced onto objects and situations that reflect the era and culture of the client. These objects become symbols of the unconscious wishes. For example, long, narrow dream objects might be **phallic symbols,** but whether the symbol takes the form of a spear, rifle, "stick shift," or spacecraft partially reflects one's cultural background.

Freud often asked clients to jot down their dreams upon waking so that they could be interpreted during the psychoanalytic session.

Transference   Freud found that his clients responded not only to his appearance and behavior, but also according to what they meant to clients. A young woman might see Freud as a father figure and displace, or transfer, her feelings toward her own father onto Freud. Another woman might view him as a lover and act seductively or suspiciously. Men also showed **transference.** A man, like a woman, might view Freud as a father figure, but a man might also respond to Freud as a competitor.

Freud discovered that transference was a two-way street. Freud could also transfer his feelings onto his clients—perhaps viewing a woman as a sex object or a young man as a rebellious son. He called this placing of clients into roles in his own life **countertransference.**

Transference and countertransference lead to unjustified expectations of new people and can foster maladaptive behavior. We might relate to our spouses as to our opposite-sex parents and demand too much (or too little) from them. Or we might accuse them unfairly of harboring wishes and secrets we attribute to our parents. We might not give new friends or lovers "a chance," when we have been mistreated by someone who played a similar role in our lives or our fantasies.

In any event, psychoanalysts are trained to be **opaque** concerning their own behavior and feelings, so that they will not encourage client transference or express their own feelings of countertransference. Then, when the client acts accusingly, seductively, or otherwise inappropriately toward the analyst, the analyst can plead not guilty of encouraging the client's behavior and suggest that it reflects historical events and fantasies. In this way, transference behavior becomes grist for the therapeutic mill.

Analysis of client transference is an important element of therapy. It provides client insight and encourages more adaptive social behavior. But it might take months or years for transference to develop fully and be resolved, which is one reason that psychoanalysis can be a lengthy process.

Resistance. The tendency to block the free expression of impulses and primitive ideas—a reflection of the defense mechanism of repression.

Interpretation. An explanation of a client's utterance according to psychoanalytic theory.

Wish fulfillment. A primitive method used by the id to attempt to gratify basic instincts.

Phallic symbol. A sign that represents the penis.

Transference. In psychoanalysis, the generalization to the analyst of feelings toward a person in the client's life.

Countertransference. In psychoanalysis, the generalization to the client by the analyst of feelings toward a person in the analyst's life.

Opaque. In psychoanalysis, descriptive of the analyst, who hides personal feelings.

Modern Psychodynamic Approaches

A number of psychoanalysts still adhere faithfully to Freud's traditional techniques. In recent years, however, briefer, less intense forms of psychodynamic therapy have been devised (Koss et al., 1986; Zaiden, 1982). Briefer methods make it possible for therapists to practice "psychoanalytically oriented" therapy with clients who cannot afford protracted therapy, or whose schedules will not permit it. Also, frankly, many of these therapists believe that protracted therapy simply isn't needed or justifiable in terms of the ratio of cost to benefits.

Some modern psychodynamic therapies continue to focus on revealing unconscious material and on breaking through psychological defenses or resistance, but even so there are a number of differences from traditional psychoanalysis. One of them is that client and therapist usually sit face to face, as opposed to the client's reclining on a couch. The therapist is also usually more directive than the traditional psychoanalyst. Modern psychoanalytically oriented therapists frequently suggest productive behavior patterns, besides fostering self-insight. Finally, there is usually more focus on the ego and the ways in which the ego acts as the "executive" of personality; accordingly, there is less emphasis on the role of the id. For this reason, many modern psychodynamic therapists are considered **ego analysts.**

And so today there are many psychodynamic therapies, many approaches that show the influence of Sigmund Freud. Let us now turn our attention to phenomenological approaches to therapy.

■ Phenomenological Therapies

Whereas psychodynamic therapies focus on internal conflicts and unconscious processes, phenomenological therapies focus on the quality of clients' subjective, conscious experience. Whereas psychodynamic therapies tend to focus on the past, and particularly on early childhood experiences, phenomenological therapies usually focus on what clients are experiencing today—in "the here and now."

Having noted these differences, we must point out that they are frequently differences in *emphasis*. The happenings of the past have a way of influencing the mental activity and overt behavior of the present. Carl Rogers, the originator of person-centered therapy, recognized that early childhood experiences tended to give rise to the conditions of worth that troubled his clients in the here and now. Rogers and Fritz Perls, the originator of Gestalt therapy, recognized that early incorporation of the values of other people often leads clients to "disown" parts of their own personalities in the here and now.

Let us now consider person-centered therapy, transactional analysis, and Gestalt therapy and discuss some of these ideas in more detail.

Person-Centered Therapy: Removing Roadblocks to Self-Actualization

Person-centered therapy, as noted, was originated by Carl Rogers (1951), who was rated as the most influential psychotherapist in the Smith (1982) survey. As noted in Chapter 2, Rogers saw us as basically free to make choices and control our destinies, despite the burdens of our pasts.

Rogers also believed that we have natural tendencies toward health, growth, and fulfillment. Given this view, Rogers wrote that psychological disorders stem largely from roadblocks placed in the path of our own self-actualization. Because others show us selective approval when we are young, we learn to disown the disapproved parts of ourselves. We don masks and façades to earn social approval. We might learn to be seen but not heard—not even heard, or examined fully, by ourselves. As a result we might expe-

Ego analyst. A psychodynamically oriented therapist who focuses on the conscious, coping behavior of the ego instead of the hypothesized unconscious functioning of the id.

Person-centered therapy. Carl Rogers' method of psychotherapy, which emphasizes the creation of a warm, therapeutic atmosphere that frees clients to engage in self-exploration and self-expression.

Unconditional positive regard. Acceptance of the value of another person, although not necessarily acceptance of all of that person's behaviors.

rience stress and discomfort and the feeling that we—or the world—are not real.

Person-centered therapy aims to provide insight into parts of us that we have disowned, so that we can feel whole. It stresses the importance of a warm, therapeutic atmosphere that encourages client self-exploration and self-expression. Therapist acceptance of the client is thought to lead to client self-acceptance and self-esteem. Self-acceptance frees the client to make choices that foster development of his or her unique potential.

Person-centered therapy is nondirective. The client takes the lead, listing and exploring problems. The therapist reflects or paraphrases expressed feelings and ideas, helping the client get in touch with deeper feelings and to follow the strongest leads in the quest for self-insight.

It should also be noted that person-centered therapy is practiced widely in college and university counseling centers, not just to help students experiencing, say, anxieties or depression, but also to help them make decisions. Many college students have not yet made career choices, for example, or they wonder whether to become involved with certain people or in sexual activity. Person-centered therapists, like other therapists, may facilitate career decision making by providing clients with accurate information, and also by providing an encouraging atmosphere in which clients can verbally explore various choices and paths. The point is that person-centered therapists do not tell clients what to do. Instead, they help clients arrive at their own decisions.

The effective person-centered therapist also shows four qualities: *unconditional positive regard, empathetic understanding, genuineness,* and *congruence.* In showing **unconditional positive regard** for clients, person-centered therapists respect clients as important human beings with unique values and goals. Clients are provided with a sense of security that encourages them to follow their own feelings. Psychoanalysts might hesitate to encourage clients to freely express their impulses because of the fear that primitive sexual and aggressive forces might be unleashed. But person-centered therapists believe that people are basically *pro*social. If people follow their own feelings, rather than act defensively, they should not be abusive or *anti*social.

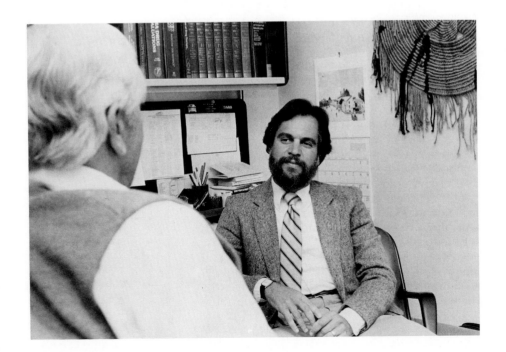

Person-Centered Therapy
The qualities of the effective person-centered therapist include unconditional positive regard for clients, empathetic understanding, genuineness, and congruence.

Empathetic understanding is shown by accurately reflecting the client's experiences and feelings. Therapists try to view the world through their clients' **frames of reference** by setting aside their own values and listening closely.

Whereas psychoanalysts are trained to be opaque, person-centered therapists are trained to show **genuineness.** Person-centered therapists are open about their feelings. It would be harmful to clients if their therapists could not truly accept and like them, even though their values might differ from those of the therapists. Rogers admitted that he sometimes had negative feelings about clients, usually boredom; he usually expressed these feelings rather than hold them in (Bennett, 1985). Person-centered therapists must also be able to tolerate differentness, because they believe that every client is different in important ways.

Person-centered therapists also try to show **congruence,** or a fit between their thoughts, feelings, and behavior. Congruence gives us access to inner experience (Kahn, 1985). Person-centered therapists serve as models of integrity to their clients.

Transactional Analysis: Who's OK?

Although **Transactional Analysis** (TA) is considered a phenomenological therapy because of its focus on clients' subjective experiences, it is also rooted in the psychoanalytic tradition. According to Thomas Harris, author of *I'm OK—You're OK* (1967), many of us suffer from inferiority complexes of the sort described by the psychoanalyst Alfred Adler. Even though we have become adults, we might continue to see ourselves as dependent children. We might think other people are "OK," but not see ourselves as "OK."

Within TA, *I'm not OK—You're OK* is one of four basic "life positions," or ways of perceiving relationships with others. A major goal of TA is to help people adopt the life position *I'm OK—You're OK,* in which they accept others and themselves. Unfortunately, people tend to adopt "games," or styles of relating to others that are designed to confirm one of the unhealthy life positions: I'm OK—You're not OK, I'm not OK—You're OK, or I'm not OK—You're not OK.

Psychiatrist Eric Berne, the originator of TA and author of the well-known book *Games People Play* (1976), described our personalities as containing three "ego states": **Parent, Child,** and **Adult.** The "parent" is a moralistic ego state. The "child" is an irresponsible and emotional ego state. The "adult" is a rational ego state. It is easy to confuse the "child" ego state with the id, the "adult" ego state with the ego, and the "parent" ego state with the superego. But note that these are three hypothesized *ego states,* or ways of coping. As we saw in Chapter 2, the id is unconscious and so is some of the functioning of the superego. However, we are capable of being fully conscious of the child and parent ego states, which is another reason why TA is considered a phenomenological rather than psychodynamic therapy.

Many interpersonal troubles occur because people tend to relate to each other as parents, children, or adults. A social exchange between two people is called a **transaction.** A transaction is said to fit, or be **complementary,** when a social exchange follows the same lines. In one type of complementary transaction, people relate as adults. But a transaction can also be complementary, even if upsetting, when two people relate as parent and child (Parent: "You shouldn't have done that"; Child: "I'm sorry, I promise it won't happen again"). Communication breaks down when the social exchange between the parties does not follow complementary lines (as in Figure 9.1). Note these examples:

Empathetic understanding. Ability to perceive a client's feelings from the client's frame of reference. A quality of the effective person-centered therapist.

Frame of reference. One's unique patterning of perceptions and attitudes, according to which one evaluates events.

Genuineness. Recognition and open expression of the therapist's own feelings.

Congruence. A fit between one's self-concept and behaviors, thoughts, and emotions.

Transactional Analysis. A form of psychotherapy that deals with how people interact and how their interactions reinforce attitudes, expectations, and "life positions." Abbreviated TA.

Parent. In TA, a moralistic ego state.

Child. In TA, an irresponsible, emotional ego state.

Adult. In TA, a rational, adaptive ego state.

Transaction. In TA, an exchange between two people.

Complementary. In TA, descriptive of a transaction in which the ego states of two people interact harmoniously.

FIGURE 9.1   A Crossed Transaction

Natalie asks Hal, "Did you have a good time tonight?" Hal replies, "Why do you wanna know?" Communication is thus broken off.

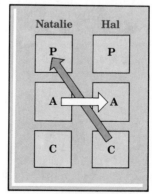

Gestalt therapy. Fritz Perls' form of psychotherapy, which attempts to integrate conflicting parts of the personality through directive methods designed to help clients perceive their whole selves.

NATALIE (adult to adult): Did you have a good time tonight?

    HAL (child to parent): Why do you wanna know?

Or:

    BILL (adult to adult): Nan, did you see the checkbook?

NAN (parent to child): A place for everything and everything in its place!

    TA is often carried out with couples who complain of communication problems. It encourages people to relate to each other as adults.

    TA also attempts to put an end to game playing. The most commonly played marital game is "If It Weren't for You" (Berne, 1976). People who play this game marry domineering mates who prevent them from going into things they would not have the courage to do anyhow, such as taking a more challenging job or moving to a new city. By playing "If It Weren't for You," they can blame their mates for their shortcomings and excuse their own timidity.

    TA is one of the types of psychotherapy that focuses on the present—the "here and now"—rather than the past. It is assumed that we have the capacity to change, despite painful incidents in the past, and that excessive focusing on the past is a diversion. Berne (1976) noted that some clients play a psychoanalytically oriented game which he called "Archaeology." Archaeologists dig in the ruins of ancient civilizations. In this game, people dig into the ruins of their pasts to unearth the one crucial event that they assert will explain why they are having problems today. Why? Craig DeGree and C. R. Snyder (1985) of the University of Kansas have found that many of us emphasize the adversity of our early experiences when we are faced with the possibility of failure today, and a traumatic background might serve as a suitable excuse for failure.

    In therapy groups, Berne noted, some clients take advantage of the Freudian view that no thought is to be censored by playing the game of "Self-Expression." In this game, a client uses vulgar language and paints a lurid scene, while other group members play "liberated" roles and applaud his or her "honesty." One might ask, of course, why a "liberated" person need be vulgar. Some of the other games people play have intriguing and reasonably self-explanatory titles:

"Look How Hard I've Tried"

"I'm Only Trying to Help You"

"Why Does This Always Happen to Me?"

"Now I've Got You, You Son of a Bitch!"

"See What You Made Me Do"

"You Got Me into This"

"Kick Me"

Gestalt Therapy: Getting It Together

Like Rogers' person-centered approach, **Gestalt therapy,** originated by Fritz Perls (1893–1970), aims to help individuals integrate conflicting parts of the personality. Perls used the term *Gestalt* to signify his interest in providing the conflicting parts of the personality an integrated form or shape. He aimed to have his clients become aware of inner conflict, accept the reality of conflict rather than deny it or keep it repressed, and make productive choices despite misgivings and fear.

    Although Perls' ideas about conflicting personality elements owe much to psychoanalytic theory, his form of therapy, unlike psychoanalysis, focuses on the here and now. In Gestalt therapy, clients undergo exercises to heighten awareness of current feelings and behavior, rather than explore the past. Perls also believed, along with Carl Rogers, that people are free to make choices and to direct their personal growth; but unlike person-centered therapy, Ge-

Fritz Perls

stalt therapy is highly directive. The therapist leads the client through planned experiences.

One Gestalt technique that increases awareness of internal conflict is the **dialogue.** Clients undertake verbal confrontations between opposing wishes and ideas. An example of these clashing personality elements is "top dog" and "underdog." One's top dog may conservatively suggest, "Don't take chances. Stick with what you have or you may lose it all." One's frustrated underdog may then rise up and assert, "You never try anything. How will you ever get out of this rut if you don't take on new challenges?" Heightened awareness of the elements of conflict can clear the path toward resolution, perhaps through compromise.

Body language also provides insight into conflicting feelings. Clients may be instructed to attend to the ways in which they furrow their eyebrows and tense their facial muscles when they express ideas that they think they support. In this way they often find that their body language asserts feelings that they have been denying.

In order to increase clients' understanding of opposing points of view, Gestalt therapists may encourage them to argue in favor of ideas opposed to their own. They may also have clients role-play people who are important to them in order to get more in touch with their points of view.

Whereas psychodynamic theory views dreams as the "royal road to the unconscious," Perls saw the stuff of dreams as disowned parts of the personality. He would often ask clients to role-play the elements in their dreams to get in touch with these parts. In *Gestalt Therapy Verbatim,* Perls—known to clients and friends alike as Fritz—describes a session in which a client "Jim" is reporting a dream:

> JIM: I just have the typical recurring dream which I think a lot of people might have if they have a background problem, and it isn't of anything I think I can act out. It's the distant wheel—I'm not sure what type it is—it's coming towards me and ever-increasing in size. And then finally, it's just above me and it's no height that I can determine, it's so high. And that's—
>
> FRITZ: If you were this wheel, . . . what would you do with Jim?
>
> JIM: I am just about to roll over Jim. (1971, p. 127)

■ Cognitive Therapies: "There Is Nothing Either Good or Bad, But Thinking Makes It So"

Cognitive therapies are the newest kinds of therapies presented in this book. Although there are many cognitively oriented therapists and more than one type of cognitive therapy, cognitive therapists would in general agree with Carl Rogers that people are free to make choices and develop in accord with their concepts of what they are capable of becoming. Cognitive therapists would also agree with Fritz Perls that it is appropriate for clients to focus on the "here and now." Cognitive therapists, like Perls, are also reasonably directive in their approaches.

Cognitive therapists tend to focus on the beliefs, attitudes, and automatic types of thinking that create and compound their clients' problems. Cognitive therapists, like psychodynamic and phenomenological therapists, are interested in fostering client self-insight, but they aim to heighten clients' insight into their *current cognitions,* and not the distant past. Cognitive therapists also aim to directly *change* maladaptive cognitions to reduce negative feelings, to provide more accurate perceptions of the self and others, and to orient the client toward solving problems.

Let us have a look at some of the major cognitive therapists and at some of their approaches and methods.

Dialogue. A Gestalt therapy technique in which clients verbalize confrontations between conflicting parts of their personality.

Cognitive therapy. A form of therapy that focuses on how clients' cognitions (expectations, attitudes, beliefs, etc.) lead to distress and may be modified to relieve distress and promote adaptive behavior.

Rational-emotive therapy. Albert Ellis' form of cognitive psychotherapy, which focuses on how irrational expectations create anxiety and disappointment and encourages clients to challenge and correct these expectations.

Catastrophizing. Exaggerating, making into a catastrophe; blowing out of proportion.

Albert Ellis's Rational-Emotive Therapy: Ten Doorways to Distress

New York psychologist Albert Ellis is the founder of **rational-emotive therapy** and the second most influential psychotherapist in the Smith (1982) survey. Ellis (1977, 1985, 1987) notes that our beliefs about events, as well as the events themselves, fashion our reactions to them. Consider a case in which one is fired from a job and is anxious and depressed about it. It might seem logical that losing the job is responsible for all the misery, but Ellis points out how beliefs about the loss compound misery.

Let us examine this situation according to Ellis's A–B–C approach: Losing the job is an *activating event* (A). The eventual outcome, or *consequence* (C), is misery. But between the activating event (A) and the consequences (C) lies a set of *beliefs* (B), such as the following: "This job was the most important thing in my life," "What a no-good failure I am," "My family will starve," "I'll never find a job as good," "There's nothing I can do about it." Beliefs such as these compound misery, foster helplessness, and divert us from planning and deciding what to do next. For example, the belief "There's nothing I can do about it" fosters helplessness. The belief "What a no-good failure I am" internalizes the blame and is also an exaggeration that might be based on perfectionism. The belief "My family will starve" is also probably an exaggeration.

We can diagram the situation like this:

Activating events → Beliefs → Consequences

Anxieties about the future and depression over a loss are quite normal and to be expected. However, the beliefs of the person who lost the job tend to **catastrophize** the extent of the loss and to contribute to anxiety and depression. By heightening emotional reaction to the loss and fostering feelings of helplessness, these beliefs also impair coping ability. They lower people's self-efficacy expectations and divert their attention from attmpting to solve their problems.

Ellis proposes that most of us harbor a number of the following ten irrational beliefs. We carry them around with us everywhere as our personal doorways to distress. These beliefs can give rise to problems in and of themselves, and, when problems assault us from other sources, these beliefs can magnify their impact on us. How many of these beliefs do you harbor? Are you sure?

Irrational Belief #1. You must have sincere love and approval almost all the time from the people who are important to you. (One study found that the irrational belief that one must be loved by, and earn the approval of, practically everyone was endorsed by 65 percent of anxious subjects, as compared with only 2 percent of nonanxious subjects [Newmark et al., 1973].)

Irrational Belief #2. You must prove yourself thoroughly competent, adequate, and achieving. Or you must at least have real competence or talent at something important.

Irrational Belief #3. Things must go the way you want them to go. Life proves awful, terrible, and horrible when you don't get your first choices in everything. (College men who believe that it is awful to be turned down for a date show more social anxiety than men who are less likely to catastrophize rejection [Gormally et al., 1981].)

Irrational Belief #4. Other people must treat everyone fairly and justly. When people act unfairly or unethically, they are terrible and rotten.

Irrational Belief #5. When there is danger or fear in your world, you must be preoccupied with it and upset by it.

Irrational Belief #6. People and things should turn out better than they do. It's awful and horrible when you don't find quick solutions to life's hassles.

QUESTIONNAIRE

Irrational Beliefs Questionnaire

Are you making yourself miserable? Are your attitudes and beliefs setting you up for distress? Do you expect that other people are obligated to put you first? Do you make such great demands of yourself that you must fall short? Do you think that you can be happier by sliding along than by applying yourself? Do you feel like dirt when other people disapprove of you?

Albert Ellis points out that our own attitudes and beliefs can make us miserable just as surely as failing that test or not getting that job. Following are a number of irrational beliefs that serve as examples of Ellis's ten basic irrational beliefs. Place a checkmark to the left of each one that might apply to you. (If you're in doubt, check it—nobody's going to fault you for having more checkmarks than the person sitting next to you and it'll give you something to think about!) Recognizing irrational beliefs is not the same as overcoming them, but it's a valuable first step. It will enhance your self-knowledge and give you some things to work on.

_____ 1. Since your parents don't approve of your date, you must give him/her up.

_____ 2. Since your date doesn't approve of your parents, you must give them up.

_____ 3. It's awful if your teacher doesn't smile at you.

_____ 4. It's awful when your boss passes you in the hall without saying anything.

_____ 5. You're a horrible parent if your children are upset with you.

_____ 6. How can you refuse to buy the vacuum cleaner when the salesperson will be disappointed?

_____ 7. Unless you have time to jog 5 miles, there's no point in going out at all.

_____ 8. You must get A's on all your quizzes and tests; a B+ now and then is a disaster.

_____ 9. Your nose (mouth, eyes, chin, etc.) should be (prettier/more handsome) or else your face is a mess.

_____ 10. Since you are 15 pounds overweight, you are totally out of control and must be sickened by yourself.

_____ 11. Since you can't afford a Mercedes, how can you possibly enjoy your Mazda?

_____ 12. Every sexual encounter should lead to a huge orgasm.

_____ 13. You can't just go out on the courts and bat the ball back and forth a few times, you have to perfect your serves, returns, and volleys.

_____ 14. You can't be happy with your life from day to day when people who are no more talented or hard-working make more money than you do.

_____ 15. The cheerleader/quarterback won't go out with you, so why go out at all?

_____ 16. Your boss is awful because a co-worker got a promotion and you didn't.

_____ 17. White people are awful because they'd usually rather associate with whites.

Irrational Belief #7. Your emotional misery comes almost completely from external pressures that you have little or no ability to control. Unless these external pressures change, you must remain miserable.

Irrational Belief #8. It is easier to evade life's responsibilities and problems than to face them and undertake more rewarding forms of self-discipline.

Irrational Belief #9. Your past influenced you immensely and must therefore continue to determine your feelings and behavior today.

_____ **18.** Black people are awful because they'd usually rather associate with blacks.

_____ **19.** Since there is the possibility of nuclear war, you must spend all your time worrying about it—and, of course, there's no point to studying.

_____ **20.** How can you be expected to do your best on the job after you didn't get the raise?

_____ **21.** Given all your personal problems, how can your teachers expect you to study?

_____ **22.** Since the quizzes are hard, why should you study for them?

_____ **23.** How can your spouse expect you to be nice to him/her when you've had an awful day on the job?

_____ **24.** Your spouse (boyfriend, girlfriend, etc.) should know what's bugging you and should do something about it.

_____ **25.** It should be possible to get A's in your courses by quick cramming before tests.

_____ **26.** Since you have the ability, why should you have to work at it? (That is, your teacher/boss should appraise you on the basis of your talents, not on your performance.)

_____ **27.** You should be able to lose a lot of weight by dieting for just a few days.

_____ **28.** Other people should be nicer to you.

_____ **29.** How can you be expected to learn the subject matter when your instructor is a bore? (Note: This belief couldn't possibly apply to this course.)

_____ **30.** Your spouse (boyfriend, girlfriend, mother, father, etc.) is making you miserable, and unless your spouse changes, there's nothing you can do about it.

_____ **31.** Since you didn't get the promotion, how can you be happy?

_____ **32.** How can you be expected to relax unless college gets easier?

_____ **33.** Since college is difficult, there's a bigger payoff in dropping out than in applying yourself for all those years.

_____ **34.** You come from a poor background, so how can you ever be a success?

_____ **35.** Your father was rotten to you, so how can you ever trust a man?

_____ **36.** Your mother was rotten to you, so how can you ever trust a woman?

_____ **37.** You had a deprived childhood, so how can you ever be emotionally adjusted?

_____ **38.** You were abused as a child, so you are destined to abuse your own children.

_____ **39.** You come from "the street," so how can you be expected to clean up your act and stop cursing with every other word?

_____ **40.** It's more fulfilling just to have fun than to worry about college or a job.

_____ **41.** You can be happier dating a bunch of people than by investing yourself in meaningful relationships.

Irrational Belief #10. You can achieve happiness by inertia and inaction, or by just enjoying yourself from day to day.

Ellis points out that it is understandable that we would want the approval of others, but it is irrational to believe we cannot survive without it. It would be nice to be competent in everything we do, but it's unreasonable to expect it. Sure, it would be nice to serve and volley like a tennis pro, but most of us haven't the time or natural ability to perfect the game. Demanding self-perfection prevents us from going out on the courts on weekends and just batting the ball back and forth for fun. Belief #5 is a prescription for perpetual emotional upheaval. Beliefs #7 and #9 lead to feelings of helplessness and demoralization. Sure, Ellis might say, childhood experiences can explain the origins of irrational beliefs, but it is our own cognitive appraisal—here and now—that causes us misery.

People whose marriages are distressed are also more likely than people with functional marriages to harbor a number of irrational beliefs (Eidelson & Epstein, 1982). They are more likely to believe that any disagreement is destructive, that their partners should be able to read their minds (and know what they want), that their partners cannot change, that they must be perfect sex partners, and that men and women differ dramatically in personality and needs. It is rational, and adjustive to a marriage, for partners to recognize that no two people can agree all the time, to express their wishes rather than depend on "mind-reading" (and a gloomy face) to get the message across, to believe that we all can change (although change may come slowly), to tolerate some sexual blunders and frustrations, and to treat each other as equals.

Rather than sitting back like the traditional psychoanalyst and occasionally offering an interpretation, Ellis actively urges clients to seek out their irrational beliefs, which are sometimes fleeting and hard to catch. He then shows clients how their beliefs lead to misery and directly challenges them to change their beliefs. According to Ellis, we need less misery and less blaming, but more action.

Aaron Beck's Cognitive Therapy: Correcting Cognitive Errors

Psychiatrist Aaron Beck (1976, 1985) also focuses on clients' cognitive distortions. He questions patients in a manner that will encourage them to see the irrationality of their own ways of thinking—how, for example, their minimizing of their accomplishments and their pessimistic assuming that the worst will happen heightens feelings of depression. Beck, like Ellis, notes that our cognitive distortions can be fleeting and automatic, difficult to detect. His therapy methods help clients pin down these self-defeating thoughts.

Beck notes in particular the pervasive influence of four basic types of cognitive errors that contribute to clients' miseries:

1. Clients may *selectively perceive* the world as a harmful place and ignore evidence to the contrary;
2. Clients may *overgeneralize* on the basis of a few examples. For example, they may perceive themselves as worthless because they were laid off at work or as grossly unattractive because they were refused a request for a date;
3. Clients may *magnify,* or blow out of proportion, the significance of negative events. As noted in the discussion of Ellis's views, clients may catastrophize flunking a test by assuming they will flunk out of college, or catastrophize losing a job by believing that they will never work again and that serious harm will befall their families;
4. Clients may engage in *absolutist thinking,* or looking at the world in black and white rather than in shades of gray. In doing so, a rejection on a date takes on the meaning of a lifetime of loneliness; a discomforting illness takes on life-threatening proportions.

The concept of pinpointing and modifying errors may become more clear from an excerpt from a case in which a 53-year-old engineer was treated with cognitive therapy for severe depression. The engineer had left his job and become inactive. As reported by Beck and his colleagues, the first treatment goal was to foster physical activity—even things like raking leaves and preparing dinner—because activity is incompatible with depression. Then:

> [The engineer's] cognitive distortions were identified by comparing his assessment of each activity with that of his wife. Alternative ways of interpreting his experiences were then considered.
>
> In comparing his wife's resumé of his past experiences, he became aware that he had (a) undervalued his past by failing to mention many previous accomplishments, (2) regarded himself as far more responsible for his "failures" than she did, and (3) concluded that he was worthless since he had not succeeded in attaining certain goals in the past. When the two accounts were contrasted, he could discern many of his cognitive distortions. In subsequent sessions, his wife continued to serve as an "objectifier."
>
> In midtherapy, [he] compiled a list of new attitudes that he had acquired since initiating therapy. These included:
>
> (1) I am starting at a lower level of functioning at my job, but it will improve if I persist.
>
> (2) I know that once I get going in the morning, everything will run all right for the rest of the day.
>
> (3) I can't achieve everything at once.
>
> (4) I have my periods of ups and downs, but in the long run I feel better.
>
> (5) My expectations from my job and life should be scaled down to a realistic level.
>
> (6) Giving in to avoidance [e.g., staying away from work and social interactions] never helps and only leads to further avoidance.
>
> He was instructed to re-read this list daily for several weeks even though he already knew the content (Rush et al., 1975).

Rereading the list of productive attitudes is a variation of a very common cognitive therapy technique—having clients rehearse or repeat accurate and rational ideas so that they come to replace cognitive distortions and irrational beliefs. The engineer became gradually less depressed in therapy and returned to work and an active social life. Along the way he learned to combat inappropriate self-blame for problems, perfectionistic expectations, magnifications of failures, and overgeneralizations from failures.

Becoming aware of cognitive errors and modifying catastrophizing thoughts helps provide us with coping ability under stress. In the discussion of depression in Chapter 8, it was noted that internal, stable, and global attributions of failure lead to depression and feelings of helplessness. Cognitive therapists also alert clients to cognitive errors such as these so that they can change their attitudes and pave the way for more effective overt behavior.

Cognitive Restructuring: "No, No, Look at It This Way"

In cognitive restructuring, clients are shown how their interpretations of events lead to maladaptive responses and are then helped to rethink their situations so that they can generate more adaptive overt behavior (Goldfried, 1988; Meichenbaum & Deffenbacher, 1988). Consider the example of aggressive people who see themselves as "simply exploding" at the slightest provocation. To them, the explosion is an automatic response to another person's insult. But the fact is that in people, aggressive behavior is not automatic, even when they are sorely annoyed—it involves thought processes and decision making (Berkowitz, 1983).

Still, many people claim that they "just explode" and are unaware of the thoughts that mediate provocations and their reactions. Cognitive therapists have devised a number of methods to help people get in touch with fleeting thoughts, such as "running movies." Consider this example, as found in the nearby "What-Do-You-Say-Now?" box: Close your eyes. Imagine that you are pushing a cart down an aisle in a supermarket. Someone pushes into you, so hard that it seems purposeful, and then says, "What the hell's the matter with you? Why don't you watch where you're going!"

What would you think? Would you think, "This so-and-so can't treat me this way! People can't be allowed to act like that!" If so you would have made the cognitive errors of taking this person's rudeness personally and expecting others to live up to your own standards. Irrational beliefs and cognitive errors intensify negative feelings and prompt maladaptive behavior. They might prompt you to violence, to behavior you might regret afterward.

In running a movie about the supermarket incident, a client would relive this upsetting experience in the imagination to search out fleeting thoughts that might otherwise barely be noticed. In an important experiment, Novaco (1974) showed how running movies, cognitive restructuring, and relaxation training helped explosive men and women deal with the supermarket-type of provocation more effectively. His strategy included three phases: education, planning, and application training. In phase 1, participants were shown how anger is intensified by the irrational beliefs that one must expect flawless behavior from others, and that an insult is a threat to one's self-esteem. In phase 2, they were taught relaxation skills* and alternatives for their irrational beliefs. In phase 3, participants imagined provocations and practiced using rational beliefs and relaxation to arrive at adaptive, nonviolent responses. Subjects made dramatic gains in coping with provocations in socially acceptable ways. Many attributed their gains to reconceptualizing provocations as problems demanding a solution, rather than as threats requiring a violent response.

In Chapter 10 we shall see how psychologists and educators have used cognitive restructuring to help students cope with test anxiety. Cognitive restructuring modifies attitudes toward test taking, thereby decreasing feelings of discomfort and actually raising grades.

Problem-Solving Training

Another cognitive-therapy approach, problem-solving training, encourages clients to use the stages of problem solving to enhance their control over their lives. There are four stages in problem solving (Rathus, 1989):

1. Preparation: studying all aspects of a problem, so that the problem is well understood and you develop goals for a solution (e.g., the goals for marital conflict might include greater expression of affection and fewer personal insults)
2. Production: generating multiple solutions to the problem
3. Trying out the possible solutions
4. Evaluation: evaluating the effectiveness of the possible solutions, and then selecting the one that best meets your goals.

Subjects receiving problem-solving training for preventing angry outbursts are encouraged to study sample provocations, to generate various behavioral solutions (alternatives to violence), and to try out and evaluate the most promising ones. Subjects in a study by Moon and Eisler (1983) learned to control their anger and respond to provocations with socially skillful (non-aggressive) behavior.

Before leaving our discussion of cognitive therapy, it should be noted that many theorists consider cognitive therapy to be a collection of techniques that belong within the province of behavior therapy, which is discussed in the following section. Some members of this group prefer the name "cognitive *behavior* therapy"; others argue that the term *behavior therapy* is broad enough

---

*Relaxation training is usually considered a behavior-therapy technique, but it has been adopted by therapists of many orientations.

WHAT DO YOU SAY NOW?

Responding to a Social Provocation

Cognitive therapists sometimes help clients get in touch with their feelings and beliefs by having them "run movies," or place themselves in imaginary situations. For example, picture yourself in this situation: You are pushing a cart down an aisle in a supermarket, looking at the containers on the shelves. Maybe you're not paying attention to other people and you wander out into the middle of the aisle. Suddenly, someone pushes into you, so hard that it seems purposeful. He then says, "What the hell's the matter with you? Why don't you watch where you're going!"

What do you say now? Write down a number of responses you might make and then check the suggested responses below.

1. _____
   _____.
2. _____
   _____.
3. _____
   _____.

As noted in the nearby text, cognitive therapists believe that your responses will reflect the way in which you interpret your antagonist's behavior. For example, would you perceive his behavior as a challenge to your "honor" or as a problem to be solved?

We suggest responses such as the following:

1. Say *nothing*. Perhaps it will be dropped if you let it pass. (This person might be angry at the world because of personal failures and shortcomings and might be spoiling for a fight. Or for some reason, he might really think that *you* bumped into *him* and that *you* are looking for trouble. How can you know what is motivating him or how dangerous he is?)
2. Say something like, "No harm intended." (It might not be necessary to actually apologize in order to avert a fight. This remark, or one like it, is almost neutral in terms of affixing blame, but might help diffuse your antagonist's feelings of outrage.)
3. If your antagonist will accept nothing short of an apology, you might strongly consider apologizing. He might be carrying a weapon, or he might be so enraged that he is not thinking clearly about the consequences of trying to hurt you severely. You might be able to fight him off, but is it worth risking your life to find out? Why should your self-esteem suffer for making a wise decision? And why should *your antagonist* be in control of *your* behavior? If you allow him to press you into a fight, he is.

Of course, our suggestions assume that you will be motivated not to get into a fight with a stranger over this silly business. If you do think that the bump is worth fighting about, we suggest that you closely examine your beliefs about it and ask yourself why.

---

to include cognitive techniques. However, there is a difference in focus between many cognitive therapists and behavior therapists. To behavior therapists, the purpose of dealing with client cognitions is to change *overt* behavior. Cognitive therapists agree that cognitive change leads to overt behavioral change and also see the value of tying treatment outcomes to observable behavior. But cognitive therapists tend to assert that cognitive change is in and of itself an important goal.

Behavior therapy. Systematic application of the principles of learning to the direct modification of a client's problem behaviors.

■ Behavior Therapy: Adjustment Is What You Do

Behavior therapy—also called *behavior modification*—is the systematic application of principles of learning in the promotion of desired behavioral changes. As suggested in the section on cognitive therapy, behavior therapists incorporate cognitive processes in their theoretical outlook and cognitive procedures in their methodology (Wilson, 1982). For example, techniques such as systematic desensitization, covert sensitization, and covert reinforcement ask clients to focus on visual imagery. But behavior therapists insist that their methods be established by experimentation (Wolpe, 1985) and that therapeutic outcomes be assessed in terms of observable, measurable behavior.

Behavior therapists rely heavily on principles of classical and operant conditioning and observational learning. They help clients discontinue self-defeating behavior patterns, such as overeating, smoking, and phobic avoidance of harmless stimuli. They also help clients acquire adaptive behavior patterns, such as the social skills required to initiate relationships and to say no to insistent salespeople. Now and then they also lead "personal growth groups" in activities such as assertiveness training.

Behavior therapists might help clients gain "insight" into maladaptive behavior in the sense of fostering awareness of the circumstances in which the behavior occurs. But they do not foster insight in the psychoanalytic sense of unearthing the early childhood origins of problems and the symbolic meanings of maladaptive behavior patterns. Behavior therapists, like psychoanalysts and person-centered therapists, may also build warm, therapeutic relationships with clients, but they see the special efficacy of behavior therapy as deriving from specific learning-based procedures (Wolpe, 1985).

About 17 percent of the clinical and counseling psychologists surveyed by Smith (1982) labeled themselves behavioral or cognitive-behavioral in orientation—the largest group of therapists who identified with a specific orientation. Behavior therapists Joseph Wolpe and Arnold Lazarus were ranked fourth and fifth among the ten most influential psychotherapists (Smith, 1982, p. 807).

Let us look at a number of behavior-therapy techniques.

Systematic Desensitization

Adam has a phobia for receiving injections. His behavior therapist treats him as he reclines in a comfortable padded chair. In a state of deep muscular relaxation, Adam observes slides projected on a screen. A slide of a nurse holding a needle has just been shown three times, 30 seconds at a time. Each time Adam has shown no anxiety. So now a slightly more discomforting slide is shown: the nurse aiming the needle toward someone's bare arm. After 15 seconds our armchair adventurer notices twinges of discomfort and raises a finger as a signal (speaking might disturb his relaxation). The projector operator turns off the light, and Adam spends two minutes imagining his "safe scene"—lying on a beach beneath the tropical sun. Then the slide is shown again. This time Adam views it for 30 seconds before feeling anxiety (see Figure 9.2).

Adam is undergoing **systematic desensitization,** a method originated by psychiatrist Joseph Wolpe (1958, 1973) for reducing phobic responses. Systematic desensitization is a gradual process. Clients learn to handle increasingly disturbing stimuli as anxiety to each one is counterconditioned. About 10 to 20 stimuli are arranged in a sequence, or hierarchy, according to their capacity to elicit anxiety. In imagination, or by being shown photos, the client travels gradually up through this hierarchy, approaching the target behavior. In Adam's case the target behavior was the ability to receive an injection without undue anxiety.

Joseph Wolpe developed systematic desensitization on the assumption that maladaptive anxiety responses, such as other behaviors, are learned or conditioned. He reasoned that they can be unlearned by **counterconditioning** or by extinction (see Chapter 2). In counterconditioning, a response that is incompatible with anxiety is made to appear under conditions that usually elicit anxiety. Muscle relaxation is incompatible with anxiety. For this reason Adam's therapist is teaching Adam to experience relaxation in the presence of (usually) anxiety-evoking slides of needles. (Muscle relaxation is usually achieved by means of *progressive relaxation,* which will be discussed in Chapter 10.)

Remaining in the presence of phobic imagery, rather than running from it, is also likely to enhance our self-efficacy expectations (Galassi, 1988). Self-efficacy expectations are negatively correlated with levels of adrenalin in the bloodstream (Bandura et al., 1985). Thus raising clients' self-efficacy expectations may help lower their adrenalin levels, counteract feelings of nervousness, and lessen the physical signs of anxiety.

Systematic desensitization. Wolpe's method for reducing fears by associating a hierarchy of images of fear-evoking stimuli with deep muscle relaxation.

Counterconditioning. The repeated pairing of a stimulus that elicits a certain response (say, fear) with a stimulus that elicits an antagonistic response (say, relaxation instructions) in such a way that the first stimulus loses the capacity to elicit the problematic (fear) response.

Systematic Desensitization
In systematic desensitization, clients engage in deep muscle relaxation while the therapist presents a hierarchy of fear-evoking stimuli. Systematic desensitization has been successfully carried out in groups as well as on an individual basis.

The Symptom-Substitution Controversy   Psychoanalysts have argued that phobias are symptoms of unconscious conflicts, and that systematic desensitization of a "symptom" might only lead to the appearance of another symptom—that is, to **symptom substitution.** To behavior therapists, maladaptive behavior *is* the problem, not just a symptom of the problem. Evidence suggests that systematic desensitization is effective in 80 to 90 percent of cases (Paul, 1969a; Smith & Glass, 1977; Marks, 1982), and symptom substitution has not been found to be a problem (Deffenbacher & Suinn, 1988).

Participant Modeling   A behavioral alternative to systematic desensitization is **participant modeling,** which relies on observational learning. In this method, clients observe and then imitate people who do approach and cope with the objects or situations they fear. Bandura and his colleagues (1969) found that participant modeling worked as well as systematic desensitization, and more rapidly, in reducing fear of snakes (see Figure 9.3). Participant modeling, like systematic desensitization, is likely to increase self-efficacy expectations in coping with feared stimuli.

In any event, systematic desensitization is a largely "painless" way to confront fears.

Aversive Conditioning

You might have read or seen the filmed version of the futuristic Anthony Burgess novel, *A Clockwork Orange.* Alex, the antisocial "hero," finds violence and rape superb pastimes. When he is caught, he is given the chance to undergo an experimental reconditioning program rather than serve a prison term. In this program, he watches films of violence and rape while vomiting under the influence of a nausea-inducing drug. After his release, he feels ill whenever he contemplates violence. Unfortunately, Beethoven's music, which he had enjoyed, accompanies the films and feelings of nausea. So Alex acquires an aversion for Beethoven as well.

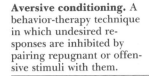
Aversive conditioning. A behavior-therapy technique in which undesired responses are inhibited by pairing repugnant or offensive stimuli with them.

Aversive conditioning is a behavior-therapy method for helping clients discontinue unwanted behavior patterns. In this example, overexposure to cigarette smoke renders smoke aversive rather than pleasurable, decreasing the smoker's desire for cigarettes.

In the novel, Alex undergoes a program of **aversive conditioning**—also called *aversion therapy*—which is actually used quite frequently today, although not in prisons. It is one of the more controversial procedures in behavior therapy. In aversive conditioning, painful or aversive stimuli are paired with unwanted impulses—such as desire for a cigarette or desire to engage in antisocial behavior—in order to make the goal less appealing. For example, in order to help people control alcohol intake, tastes of different alcoholic beverages can be paired with drug-induced nausea and vomiting, or with electric shock (Wilson et al., 1975).

Aversive conditioning has been used with some success in treating problems as divergent as paraphilias (Rathus, 1983), cigarette smoking (Lichtenstein, 1982; Walker & Franzoni, 1985), and retarded children's self-injurious behavior. In one large-scale study of aversive conditioning in the treatment of alcoholism, 63 percent of the 685 people treated remained abstinent for one year afterward, and about a third remained abstinent for at least three years (Wiens & Menustik, 1983). It might seem paradoxical to use punitive aversive stimulation to stop children from punishing themselves, but people sometimes hurt themselves to obtain sympathy and attention from others. If self-injury leads to more pain than anticipated, and no sympathy, it might be discontinued.

A number of aversive-conditioning techniques are used to help people quit smoking. In one, rapid smoking, the would-be quitter inhales every six seconds. In another, the hose of an everyday hair dryer is hooked up to a chamber with several lit cigarettes. Smoke is blown into the quitter's face as he or she also smokes a cigarette. In a third, branching pipes are used so that the smoker draws in smoke from two or more cigarettes simultaneously. In all of these methods, overexposure renders once-desirable cigarette smoke aversive. The quitter becomes motivated to avoid, rather than seek, cigarettes, and stops smoking on a preplanned date. Many reports have shown a quit rate of 60 percent or higher at six-month follow-ups.

Rapid smoking is the most widely researched aversion method for treating cigarette smoking (Lichtenstein, 1982). Rapid smoking is popular, because it is as effective as other methods and the apparatus is readily available—the quitter's own cigarettes. But in addition to producing discomfort, rapid smoking raises the blood pressure, decreases the blood's capacity to carry oxygen, and produces heart abnormalities, as shown by the electrocardiogram (Lichtenstein & Glasgow, 1977). Nevertheless, a two-year follow-up study of cardiac and pulmonary patients found no negative effects from rapid smoking (Hall et al., 1984)—and, when we consider the positive benefits of quitting smoking for these patients, rapid smoking elicits hope.

Operant Conditioning

We usually prefer to relate to people who smile at rather than ignore us, and to take courses in which we do well rather than fail. We tend to repeat behavior that is reinforced. Behavior that is not reinforced tends to become extinguished. Behavior therapists have applied these principles of operant conditioning with psychotic patients as well as clients with milder problems.

The staff at one mental hospital were at a loss as to how to encourage withdrawn schizophrenic patients to eat regularly. Ayllon and Haughton (1962) observed that the staff were exacerbating the problem by coaxing patients into the dining room, even feeding them. Increased staff attention apparently reinforced the patients for uncooperativeness. Some rules were changed. Patients who did not arrive at the dining hall within 30 minutes after serving were locked out. Staff could not interact with patients at mealtime. With uncooperative behavior no longer reinforced, patients quickly changed their eating habits. Patients were then required to pay one penny to enter the dining hall. Pennies were earned by interacting with other patients and showing other socially appropriate behaviors. These target behaviors also increased in frequency.

Many psychiatric wards and hospitals now use **token economies** in which tokens, such as poker chips, must be used by patients to purchase TV-viewing time, extra visits to the canteen, or private rooms. The tokens are reinforcements for productive activities such as making beds, brushing teeth, and socializing. Whereas token economies have not eliminated all symptoms of schizophrenia, they have enhanced patient activity and cooperation. Tokens have also been used successfully in programs designed to modify the behavior of children with conduct disorders. For example, Schneider and Byrne (1987) gave children tokens for helpful behaviors such as volunteering, and removed tokens for behaviors such as arguing and inattention.

We can often use the operant-conditioning method of **successive approximations** in building good habits. Let us use a (not uncommon!) example: You wish to study three hours an evening, but can only maintain concentration for half an hour. Rather than attempting to increase study time all at once, you could do so gradually, say by five minutes an evening. After every hour or so of studying, you could reinforce yourself with five minutes of people watching in a busy section of the library.

Assertiveness Training

Are you a person who can't say no? Do people walk all over you? Brush off those footprints and get some assertiveness training! Over the years large numbers of people have done just that. Assertiveness training helps clients decrease social anxieties, but it is also one of the therapy methods that has been used to optimize the functioning of individuals without problems.

Assertive behavior can be contrasted with both *nonassertive* (submissive) behavior and *aggressive* behavior. Assertive people express their genuine feelings, stick up for their legitimate rights, and refuse unreasonable requests. But they do not insult, threaten, or belittle. Assertive people also do not shy away from meeting and constructing relationships with new people, and they express positive feelings such as liking and love.

As noted in Chapter 5, assertiveness training decreases social anxiety and builds social skills through techniques such as self-monitoring, modeling, and behavior rehearsal. Assertiveness training is also effective in groups.

Functional analysis. A systematic study of behavior in which one identifies the stimuli that trigger it and the reinforcers that maintain it.

Group members can role-play important people in the lives of other members, such as parents, spouses, or potential dates.

Self-Control Techniques

Does it sometimes seem that mysterious forces are at work? Forces that delight in wreaking havoc with your New Year's resolutions and other efforts to take charge of bad habits? Just when you go on a diet, that juicy Big Mac stares at you from the TV set. Just when you resolve to balance your budget, that sweater goes on sale. Behavior therapists have developed a number of self-control techniques to help people cope with such temptations.

Functional Analysis of Behavior   Behavior therapists usually begin by doing a **functional analysis** of the problem behavior. In this way, they help determine the stimuli that trigger problem behavior and the reinforcers that maintain it. In a functional analysis, you use a diary to jot down each instance of the behavior. You note the time of day, location, your activity (including your thoughts and feelings), and reactions (yours and others').

Functional analysis serves a number of purposes. For example, it makes you more aware of the environmental context of your behavior and can increase your motivation to change. In studies with highly motivated people, functional analysis alone has been found to increase the amount of time spent studying (Johnson & White, 1971) and talking in a therapy group (Komaki & Dore-Boyce, 1978), and to decrease cigarette consumption (Lipinski et al., 1975).

Brian used functional analysis to learn about his nail biting. Table 9.1 shows a few items from his notebook. He discovered that boredom and humdrum activities seemed to serve as triggers for nail biting. He began to watch out for feelings of boredom as signs to practice self-control. He also made some changes in his life, so that he would feel bored less often.

There are a number of self-control strategies aimed at (1) the stimuli that trigger behavior; (2) the behaviors themselves; and (3) reinforcers.

Strategies Aimed at Stimuli that Trigger Behavior

Restriction of the stimulus field. Gradually exclude the problem behavior from more environments. For example, for a while first do not smoke while driving, then extend not smoking to the office. Or practice the habit only outside the environment in which it normally occurs. Psychologist J. Dennis Nolan's (1968) wife had tried quitting smoking several times—to no avail. Finally the Nolans applied restriction of the stimulus field by limiting her smoking to one place—a "smoking chair." The rule was

TABLE 9.1   Excerpts from Brian's Diary of Nail Biting for April 14

Incident	Time	Location	Activity (Thoughts, Feelings)	Reactions
1	7:45 AM	Freeway	Driving to work, bored, not thinking	Finger bleeds, pain
2	10:30 AM	Office	Writing report	Self-disgust
3	2:25 PM	Conference	Listening to dull financial report	Embarrassment
4	6:30 PM	Living room	Watching evening news	Self-disgust

A functional analysis of problem behavior, like nail biting, increases awareness of the environmental context in which it occurs, spurs motivation to change, and, in highly motivated people, may lead to significant behavioral change.

that Ms. Nolan could smoke as much as she wanted to, but only in that chair. Also, smoking was the only activity permitted in the chair. The chair was set in a "stimulus-deprived" corner of the basement, so that smoking would become dissociated from its usual triggers, such as watching television, reading, and conversing. Ms. Nolan's awareness of the details of her habit increased, and she had more opportunity to reflect on her reasons for cutting down. Her smoking fell off, and, after a few weeks of humiliating trips to the basement, she quit altogether.

Avoidance of powerful stimuli that trigger habits. Avoid obvious sources of temptation. People who go window-shopping often wind up buying more than windows. If eating at The Pizza Glutton tempts you to forget your diet, eat at home or at The Celery Stalk instead.

Stimulus control. Place yourself in an environment in which desirable behavior is likely to occur. Maybe it's difficult to lift your mood directly at times, but you can place yourself in the audience of that uplifting concert or film. It may be difficult to force yourself to study, but how about rewarding yourself for spending time in the library?

Strategies Aimed at Behavior

Response prevention. Make unwanted behavior difficult or impossible. Impulse buying is curbed when you shred your credit cards, leave your checkbook home, and carry only a couple of dollars. You can't reach for the strawberry cream cheese pie in your refrigerator if you have left it at the supermarket (that is, have not bought it).

Competing responses. Engage in behaviors that are incompatible with the bad habits. It is difficult to drink a glass of water and a fattening milkshake simultaneously. Grasping something firmly is a useful competing response for nail biting or scratching.

Chain breaking. Interfere with unwanted habitual behavior by complicating the process of engaging in it. Break the chain of reaching for a readily available cigarette and placing it in your mouth by wrapping the pack in aluminum foil and placing it on the top shelf in the closet. Rewrap the pack after taking one. Put your cigarette in the ashtray between puffs, or put your fork down between mouthfuls of dessert. Ask yourself if you really want more.

Successive approximations. Gradually approach targets through a series of relatively painless steps. Increase studying by only five minutes a day. Decrease smoking by pausing for a minute when the cigarette is smoked halfway, or by putting it out a minute before you would wind up eating the filter. Decrease your daily intake of food by 50 to 100 calories every couple of days, or else cut out one type of fattening food every few days.

Strategies Aimed at Reinforcements

Reinforcement of desired behavior. Why give yourself something for nothing? Make pleasant activities, like going to films, walking on the beach, or reading a new novel, contingent upon meeting reasonable, daily behavioral goals. Put one dollar away toward that camera or vacation trip each day you remain within your calorie limit.

Response cost. Heighten awareness of the long-term reasons for dieting or cutting down smoking by punishing yourself for not meeting a daily goal or for practicing a bad habit. Make out a check to your least favorite cause and mail it at once if you bite your nails or inhale that cheesecake.

"Grandma's method." Remember Grandma's method for inducing children to eat their vegetables? Simple: No veggies, no dessert. In this method, desired behaviors, like studying and toothbrushing, can be increased by insisting that they be done before you carry out a favored or frequent

activity. For example, don't watch television unless you have studied first. Don't leave the apartment until you've brushed your teeth. You can also place reminders of new attitudes you're trying to acquire on little cards and read them regularly. For example, in quitting smoking, you might write "Every day it becomes a little easier" on one card and "Your lungs will turn pink again" on another, place these cards and others in your wallet, and read them like clockwork before you leave the house.

Covert sensitization. Create imaginary horror stories about problem behavior. Psychologists have successfully reduced overeating and smoking by having clients imagine that they become acutely nauseated at the thought of fattening foods, or that a cigarette is made from vomit. Some horror stories are not so "imaginary." Deliberately focusing on heart strain and diseased lungs every time you overeat or smoke, rather than ignoring these long-term consequences, might also promote self-control.

Covert reinforcement. Create rewarding imagery for desired behavior. When you have achieved a behavioral goal, fantasize about how wonderful you are. Imagine friends and family patting you on the back. Fantasize about the *Playboy* or *Playgirl* centerfold for a minute.

In Chapter 10 we shall apply some of these self-control methods to problems such as weight control, smoking, and insomnia.

■ Group Therapy

When a psychotherapist has several clients with similar problems—whether stress management, adjustment to divorce, lack of social skills, or anxiety—it often makes sense to treat them in groups of 6 to 12 rather than conduct individual therapy. The methods and characteristics of the group will reflect the needs of the members and the theoretical orientation of the leader. In a psychoanalytic group, clients may interpret one anothers' dreams. In a person-centered group, they may provide an accepting atmosphere for self-exploration. Clients in a TA group may comment on the games played by others. Behavior-therapy groups may undergo joint desensitization to anxiety-evoking stimuli or model and rehearse social skills.

There are several advantages to group therapy:

1. Group therapy is economical. It allows the therapist to work with several clients seen simultaneously. Since good therapists are usually very busy, the group format allows them to see people who may otherwise have to be placed on a waiting list.

2. As compared with one-to-one therapy, group therapy provides a greater fund of information and experience for clients to draw upon. The helping professionals who lead groups may have greater group skills and psychological knowledge than individual group members, but the group will have a large fund of life experiences. When a group member explains how something worked out (or didn't work out) for him or her, it may have more impact than a theoretical discussion or a "second-hand" story from the leader.

3. Appropriate behavior receives group support. Clients usually appreciate approval from their therapists, but a spontaneous pouring out of approval from peers may seem more appropriate in that they will attain future approval from peers, not a therapist. Also, approval from several people usually has a greater impact than approval from one person.

4. When we run into troubles, it is easy to imagine that we are different from other people, and possibly inferior. Group members frequently learn that other people have had similar problems, similar self-doubts, similar failure experiences. Social psychologists have demonstrated that "misery loves company," but even more so when the company has similar problems

(Schachter, 1959). Affiliating with people who have similar problems is reassuring.

5. Group members who show improvement provide hope for other members.
6. Many individuals seek therapy because of problems in relating to other people; and people who seek therapy for other reasons are also frequently socially inhibited. Members of therapy groups have the opportunity to rehearse social skills with one another in a relatively nonthreatening atmosphere. In a group consisting of men and women of different ages, group members can role-play one another's employers, employees, spouses, parents, children, and friends. A 20-year-old can practice refusing unreasonable requests from a 47-year-old as a way of learning how to refuse such requests from a parent. Members can role-play asking one another out on dates, saying no (or yes) to sexual requests, and so on.

Although there are advantages to group treatment, many clients prefer individual therapy, and they may have quite valid reasons. For example, they may not wish to disclose their problems to a group. They may be inhibited in front of others, or they may desire individual attention. Because many clients who are willing to enter groups also share these concerns, it is the responsibility of the therapist to insist that group disclosures be kept confidential, to establish a supportive atmosphere, and to see that group members receive the attention they need.

Many types of therapy can be conducted either individually or in groups. Encounter groups and family therapy can be conducted in group-format only.

Encounter Groups

Encounter groups are not appropriate for treating serious psychological problems. Rather, they are intended to promote personal growth by heightening awareness of one's own needs and feelings and those of others. This goal is sought through intense confrontations, or encounters, between strangers. Like ships in the night, group members come together out of the darkness, touch one another briefly, then sink back into the shadows of one anothers' lives. But something is thought to be gained from the passing.

Encounter groups stress interactions between group members in the here and now. Discussion of the past may be outlawed. Interpretation is out. Expression of genuine feelings toward others is encouraged. When group members think that a person's social mask is phony, they may descend en masse to rip it off.

Professionals recognize that encounter groups can be damaging when they urge overly rapid disclosure of intimate matters, or when several members attack one member in unison. Responsible leaders do not tolerate these abuses and try to keep groups moving in growth-enhancing directions.

Family Therapy

In **family therapy,** one or more families constitute the group. Family therapy may be undertaken from various theoretical viewpoints. One is the "systems approach," for which much credit is to be given family therapist Virginia Satir (1967). In Satir's method, the family system of interaction is studied and modified to enhance the growth of family members and of the family unit as a whole.

It is often found that family members with low self-esteem cannot tolerate different attitudes and behaviors from other family members. Faulty family communications also create problems. It is also not uncommon for the family to present an "identified patient"—that is, the family member who has *the* problem and is *causing* all the trouble. But family therapists usually assume that the identified patient is a scapegoat for other problems within and among

Encounter group. A type of group that aims to foster self-awareness by focusing on how group members relate to each other in a setting that encourages open expression of feelings.

Family therapy. A form of therapy in which the family unit is treated as the client.

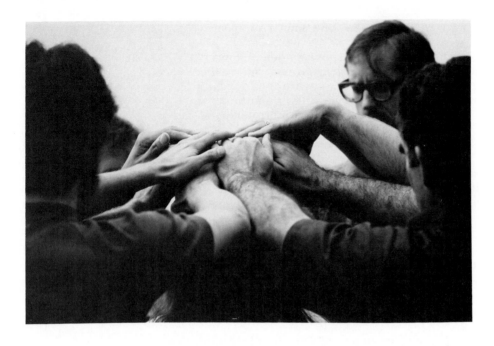

Some groups use touching exercises to help members grow comfortable with one another. Touching encourages them to be open about their feelings toward one another and to try out new, adaptive behavior patterns.

family members. It is a sort of myth: Change the bad apple, or identified patient, and the barrel, or family, will be functional once more.

The family therapist—who is often a specialist in this field—attempts to teach the family to communicate more effectively and to encourage growth and the eventual autonomy, or independence, of each family member. In doing so, the family therapist will also show the family how the identified patient has been used as a focus for the problems of other members of the group.

There are many other types of groups: couples groups, marathon groups, sensitivity-training groups, and psychodrama groups, to name just a few.

■ Evaluation of Methods of Psychotherapy

Now that we have explored a number of the types of psychotherapy in use today, we must tackle a very important issue: Does psychotherapy *work*? Many of us know people who "swear by" the therapy they have received, but very often the evidence they provide is shaky—for example, "I was a wreck before, but now . . . ," or "I feel so much better now." Anecdotes such as these may be encouraging, but we have no way of knowing what would have happened to these same people if they had not gone for help. As was pointed out by psychologist Hans Eysenck (1952) in an evaluation that "shook up" psychotherapists, many people feel better about their problems as time goes on, with or without therapy; sometimes problems just go away (believe it or not!), and at other times people find solutions to their problems on their own. Then, too, we hear many stories of how therapy was to no avail, and sometimes we hear of people hopping fruitlessly from therapist to therapist.

Let us now consider some of the problems in evaluating therapy methods scientifically.

Problems in Running Experiments on Psychotherapy   As noted in Chapter 1, the ideal method for evaluating the effectiveness of a treatment— such as a method of therapy—is the experiment. But it is not always easy to run experiments in the realm of therapy. Consider the case of psychoanalysis.

In well-run experiments, subjects are assigned to experimental and control groups at random. And so it could be argued that a sound experiment to evaluate psychoanalysis would require randomly assigning people seeking therapy to psychoanalysis and to a control group or to a number of other kinds of therapy for comparison. Also, a subject might have to remain in traditional psychoanalysis for years in order to attain results, but how could control subjects be kept in briefer forms of therapy or in a no-treatment control group for a comparable period of time? Moreover, some people seek psychoanalysis per se rather than psychotherapy in general. Would it be ethical to assign them at random to other treatments or to a no-treatment control group? Clearly not (Basham, 1986; Parloff, 1986). Could it even be done? That is, could clients requesting psychoanalysis be deceived into thinking that a cognitive or behavioral form of therapy is psychoanalysis? Probably not, and no ethical helping professional would want to deceive a client in such a manner. So we run into obstacles with the subjects we can place in our experimental and control groups, just as we do when we try to define a comparable duration of treatment for various kinds of therapies.

Recall also that in an ideal experiment subjects are blind as to the treatment they receive. In the Lang (1975) experiment on the effects of alcohol discussed in Chapter 7, subjects were blind as to whether or not they had received the treatment—alcohol. In this way, the researchers could control for subjects' expectations about the effects of alcohol. And so, in a perfect experimental world, subjects would be blind as to the type of therapy they are receiving—or whether they are receiving a placebo. But again, can we always conceal from clients the type of therapy they are receiving? And would we want to?

Problems in Measuring the Outcomes of Therapy Also consider the problems we run into in measuring the outcomes of various kinds of therapies. Since behavior therapists define their goals in behavioral terms—such as a formerly phobic individual being able to receive an injection or look out of a twentieth-story window—behavior therapists do not encounter too many problems in this area. But what of the cognitive therapist who seeks to alter the ways in which clients interpret the world, or to replace irrational beliefs with rational beliefs? We cannot directly measure a mental picture of the world or the presence of a rational belief; instead, we must assess what clients say and do.

Also, consider the problems we can encounter with therapies such as psychoanalysis and person-centered therapy. The goals for such therapies include fostering self-insight, becoming one's own person, and actualizing one's unique talents. As a matter of fact, many well-adjusted individuals undertake psychoanalysis and person-centered therapy in order to learn about themselves, not to "get better." Since each person's self-insights and growth potentials are by nature unique, it may be impossible in principle to measure just how much insight has been gained or just how well clients have separated their perceptions and values from those of others.

Are Clinical Judgments Valid? Because of problems such as these, many psychodynamically and phenomenologically oriented therapists claim—understandably so—that clinical judgment must be the basis for evaluating the effectiveness of therapy. Unfortunately, therapists have a stake in believing that their clients profit from treatment, and so they are not unbiased judges, even though they may try to be.

Analyses of Therapy Effectiveness Despite these evaluation problems, research into the effectiveness of psychodynamic, person-centered, and other therapies has been reasonably encouraging (Lambert et al., 1986; Smith et al., 1980). The largest gains from therapy occur within the first few months (Howard et al., 1986), and these gains appear to be lasting (Nicholson & Berman, 1983).

In an averaging technique referred to as *meta-analysis,* for example, Mary Lee Smith and Gene Glass analyzed the results of dozens of outcome studies on types of therapies and concluded that people who receive psychodynamic therapy show greater well-being, on the average, than 70 to 75 percent of those who are left untreated (Smith & Glass, 1977; Smith et al., 1981). Similarly, nearly 75 percent of the clients receiving person-centered therapy were better off than people who were left untreated. There also seems to be a consensus that psychodynamic and person-centered therapies are most effective with well-educated, highly verbal, and strongly motivated clients who report problems with anxiety, depression (of light to moderate proportions), and interpersonal relationships (Abramowitz et al., 1974; Luborsky & Spence, 1978; Wexler & Butler, 1976). Neither form of therapy appears successful with psychotic disorders such as major depression, bipolar disorder, and schizophrenia. Smith and Glass (1977) found that people who receive TA are better off than about 72 percent of those left untreated, and people who receive Gestalt therapy show greater well-being than about 60 percent of those left untreated. In sum, the effectiveness of psychoanalysis, person-centered therapy, and TA is reasonably comparable; Gestalt therapy falls somewhat behind.

Does Therapy Help Because of the Method or Because of the Therapist?

Despite the positive findings of Smith and Glass, critics of psychoanalysis and person-centered therapy, such as behavior therapist Joseph Wolpe (1985), assert that it has not been shown that their benefits can be attributed to the therapy methods per se. There are common factors in many types of therapy, such as showing warmth, encouraging exploration, and combating feelings of hopelessness and helplessness (Klein & Rabkin, 1984; Rounsaville et al., 1987). And so benefits could stem purely from the relationship with the therapist. If so, the method itself might have little more value than the famed "sugar-pill" placebo does in combatting physical ailments.

What Is the Experimental Treatment in Psychotherapy Outcome Studies?

This point raises another important issue in the evaluation of psychotherapeutic methods: What, exactly, is the experimental "treatment" being evaluated? Several therapists might say that they are practicing psychoanalysis but they differ as individuals and in their training. Moreover, no clients present precisely the same set of problems. Treatment techniques interact with client problems so that no two clients receive exactly the same treatment from the same therapist. For all these reasons, it is difficult to specify just what is happening in the therapeutic session (Luborsky & De-Rubeis, 1984; Vallis et al., 1986). In sum, many of the positive outcomes found by Smith and Glass could be attributed to the benefits of a close client–therapist relationship—benefits that could be derived from almost any sort of therapy. These considerations extend to the evaluation of other types of psychotherapy.* For reasons such as these, psychologists in recent years have been introducing detailed treatment manuals into their therapy-outcome studies (e.g., Luborsky & DeRubeis, 1984), but even so, there remains some variability in the practitioners who use the manuals and in the clients themselves.

---

*Even behavior therapists, who tend to stick closer to the therapeutic "script" than many other therapists, establish relationships with clients and combat demoralization, encouraging them to take charge of their own lives.

In any event, during the 1940s and 1950s, psychotherapy was almost synonymous with psychoanalysis. Few other approaches to psychotherapy had an impact on psychologists or on public awareness (Garfield, 1981, 1982). But today, according to a survey of clinical and counseling psychologists, only 14 percent of psychotherapists have a psychoanalytic orientation (Smith, 1982). Sigmund Freud, once the model for almost all therapists, is currently rated third in influence, following Carl Rogers and Albert Ellis. The largest group of psychotherapists (41 percent) consider themselves eclectic (Smith, 1982, p. 804).

Evaluation of Cognitive Therapies There is an increasing body of evidence that cognitive factors play an important role in psychological disorders and adjustment problems (e.g., Blackburn et al., 1981; DeRubes, 1983; Murphy et al., 1984; Rush et al., 1982; Simons et al., 1986). They are especially pertinent to feelings of anxiety and depression that are acquired through experience. This is abundantly clear in phobias, in which the client believes that an object or situation is awful and must be avoided at all costs, and in depressive reactions that are linked to cognitive distortions.

Smith and Glass (1977) did not include cognitive therapies in their meta-analysis because, as noted earlier, these approaches are relatively new. Also, behavior therapists incorporate many of them, and so it can be difficult to sort out which aspects—cognitive or otherwise—of behavior-therapy treatments are most effective. Nonetheless, a number of studies show that modification of irrational beliefs decreases emotional distress (Lipsky et al., 1980; Smith, 1983). Also, researchers who have analyzed the recent studies that compare cognitive, psychodynamic, and phenomeonological approaches to the treatment of anxiety and depression have generally found that cognitive approaches foster greater improvements (Andrews & Harvey, 1981; Shapiro & Shapiro, 1982). In fact, there is some evidence that cognitive therapy is helpful in severe cases of depression that are usually considered responsive only to biological therapies (Simons et al., 1986).

Evaluation of Behavior Therapy Behavior therapy has provided a number of strategies for treating anxiety, mild depression, social-skills deficits, and problems in self-control. They have proved effective for most clients in terms of quantifiable behavioral change. Behavior therapists have also been innovative with a number of problems, such as phobias and sexual dysfunctions, for which there had not previously been effective treatments. Overall, Smith and Glass (1977) found behavior-therapy techniques somewhat more effective than psychodynamic or phenomenological methods. About 80 percent of those receiving behavior-therapy treatments, such as systematic desensitization and strategies for self-control, showed greater well-being than people who were left untreated (as compared to percentages in the low to middle 70s for psychodynamic and phenomenological approaches).

In analyses of studies that directly compare treatment techniques, behavior-therapy, psychodynamic, and phenomenological approaches have been found about equal in overall effectiveness (Berman et al., 1985; Smith et al., 1980). However, psychodynamic and phenomenological approaches seem to foster greater self-understanding, whereas behavior-therapy techniques (including cognitive-behavioral techniques) show superior results in problems such as phobias and sexual problems. Behavior therapy has also been effective in helping manage institutionalized populations, including schizophrenics and the mentally retarded. However, there is little evidence that behavior therapy alone is effective in treating the thought disorders involved in severe psychotic disturbance (Wolpe, 1985).

So it is not enough to ask which type of therapy is most effective. We must ask, instead, which type of therapy is most effective for a particular

Minor tranquilizer. A drug that relieves feelings of anxiety and tension.

Chemotherapy. The use of drugs to treat disordered behavior.

problem? What are its advantages? What are its limitations? Clients may successfully use systematic desensitization to overcome stagefright, as measured by actual ability to get up and talk before a group of people. But if clients also want to know why they have stagefright, behavior therapy alone will not be fully satisfactory. (Behavior therapists would counter that insight-oriented therapists would merely construct a tale, consistent with their theory, about the origins of the problem but that truth would elude them [and their clients] anyhow.)

There is also some question as to *why* behavior therapy works. Is it because clients replace self-defeating habits with adaptive habits? Or is it because they cognitively reappraise disturbing stimuli and relationships and use their reappraisals to confront their problems and solve them? Since behavioral change in humans usually does not occur in the absence of cognitive awareness, no broad, simple answer to this question is possible. Furthermore, many behavioral and cognitive methods overlap, so that much of the efficacy attributed to behavior therapy may have to be extended to cognitive therapy. Nevertheless, behavior therapists can point with pride to a wide and growing body of experimental evidence that their techniques are effective with the behavior problems of the vast majority of the clients they treat.

Moreover, the treatment manuals for behavioral techniques tend to be more specific than those for psychodynamic and phenomenological methods. For this reason, it may be that the benefits of behavior therapy are more attributable to the techniques themselves than to the personal qualities and general skills of the therapist. But this is a relative and not an absolute issue: As Wolpe (1985) noted, behavior therapists generally establish at least a warm working relationship with clients, and so the usefulness of the techniques themselves cannot be totally divorced from therapist factors.

Overall, the results of the various kinds of psychotherapies are encouraging. Individuals who feel that they may profit from professional help are well advised to become familiar with different therapeutic approaches so that they can select those that are most appropriate for their situations.

■ Biological Therapies

In the 1950s Fats Domino popularized the song "My Blue Heaven." Fats was singing about the sky and happiness. But today "blue heavens" is the street name for the ten-milligram dose of one of the more widely prescribed drugs in the world: Valium. The **minor tranquilizer** Valium became popular because it reduces feelings of anxiety and tension. The manufacturer also once claimed that people could not become addicted to Valium nor readily kill themselves with overdoses. Today Valium looks more dangerous. Some people who have been using high doses of Valium are reported to go into convulsions when use is suspended. And now and then someone dies from mixing Valium with alcohol, or someone shows unusual sensitivity to the drug.

Psychiatrists and other physicians prescribe Valium and other drugs as chemical therapy, or **chemotherapy,** for various forms of abnormal behavior. In this section we discuss chemotherapy, *electroconvulsive therapy,* and *psychosurgery,* three biological or medical approaches to treating abnormal behavior.

Chemotherapy

Minor Tranquilizers Valium is but one of many (many!) minor tranquilizers. Some of the others are Librium, Miltown, Atarax, Serax, and Equanil. These drugs are usually prescribed for outpatients who complain of anxiety or tension, although many people also use them as sleeping pills.

Valium and other tranquilizers are theorized to depress the activity of parts of the central nervous system. The CNS, in turn, decreases sympathetic activity, reducing the heart rate, respiration rate, and feelings of nervousness and tension (Caplan et al., 1983).

With regular usage, unfortunately, people come to tolerate small dosages of these drugs very quickly. Dosages must be increased in order for the drug to remain effective.

Major Tranquilizers   Schizophrenic patients are likely to be treated with **major tranquilizers** or "antipsychotic" drugs. Many of them, including Thorazine, Mellaril, and Stelazine, belong to the chemical class of **phenothiazines** and are thought to act by blocking the action of dopamine in the brain. Research along these lines supports the dopamine theory of schizophrenia (see Chapter 8).

Unfortunately, in many cases the blocking of dopamine action leads to symptoms such as those of Parkinson's disease, including tremors and muscular rigidity (Calne, 1977; Levitt, 1981). These side effects can usually be

Major tranquilizer. A drug that decreases severe anxiety or agitation in psychotic patients or in violent individuals.

Phenothiazines. A family of drugs that act as major tranquilizers and are effective in treating many cases of schizophrenic disorders.

"It's no use, Marvin. We tried tenderness and we tried Valium and you're still impossible."

■ A CLOSER LOOK

Coffee: Chemotherapy for Depression?

Millions of Americans assault the morning blahs and the midafternoon doldrums by downing cups of coffee, that tasty drink that also happens to contain the stimulant caffeine. Millions of Britishers ritualistically down their afternoon tea, another beverage containing caffeine. Legend has it that shepherds at an Arabian monastery watched as their goats chewed on the beans (which, botanically, are berries) of the *Coffea arabica* plant and then proceeded to frisk sleepless through the night. The abbot, sensing a way to remain awake through the evening prayers, experimented with brewing a beverage from the berries. Today the coffee plant is cultivated on many continents, and coffee and tea joust for worldwide supremacy.

We need no proof of the lift provided by coffee, but Emory University anthropologist/physician Melvin Konner suggests that millions of us might also be self-medicating ourselves for depression by imbibing. Physicians have long used 5 to 10 cups (500 to 1,000 milligrams of caffeine) a day to help in treatment of low blood pressure and asthma, but many of us may also use these "therapeutic dosages" to help cope with lethargy and feelings of sadness.

How does caffeine work? Research by Solomon Snyder at Johns Hopkins Medical School shows that molecules of caffeine are similar in structure to molecules of adenosine, a naturally occurring substance in the nervous system (Konner, 1988). Adenosine, it seems, fits into receptor sites on, and suppresses the activity of, neurons that would normally elevate the mood and increase alertness. Caffeine molecules also fit into these receptor sites, and by doing so they lock adenosine out. But caffeine molecules do not suppress the activity of these cells. Caffeine, that is, lets these neurons "do their thing," and keeps adenosine, the "party pooper," out the door.

Are there dangers to the caffeine high? Are depressing side effects found in the stimulant's clothing? Perhaps. For one thing, some of us are more susceptible to "coffee jitters" than others. Coffee is also acidic and so can be harmful to the digestive tract and contribute to ulcers. (Antacid medications help.) Coffee raises the blood pressure, and persons with cardiovascular conditions are advised to consult their physicians about it. Moreover, there are some unresolved questions about drinking coffee—or "too much" coffee—during pregnancy. (Check with your obstetrician.)

But for most of us, two to four cups of coffee a day pose no documented risks, and millions of us are apparently going to continue to fight the blahs with caffeine.

---

controlled by drugs that are used for Parkinsonism. But in some patients, long-term use of phenothiazines leads to motor problems that are not readily controlled (Jus et al., 1976).

Antidepressants   So-called **antidepressant** drugs are often given patients with major depression, but, as noted in Chapter 8, they are also helpful with some individuals who suffer from anorexia nervosa and bulimia nervosa. The reason for this seems to be that problems in the regulation of norepinephrine and serotonin may be involved in eating disorders as well as depression. Antidepressants are believed to work by increasing the amount of these neurotransmitters available in the brain, which can have an impact on both kinds of disorders.

Antidepressants tend to alleviate the physical aspects of depression. For example, they tend to increase the patient's activity level and to reduce eating and sleeping disturbances (Lyons et al., 1985; Weissman et al., 1981). In this way patients may become more receptive to psychotherapy, which addresses the cognitive and social aspects of depression. Research suggests that a combination of chemotherapy and psychotherapy is more effective in treating depression than is chemotherapy alone (Beckham & Leber, 1985; Conte et al., 1986). However, it should be noted that some researchers (e.g., Simons et al., 1986) argue that psychotherapy is more effective than chemotherapy for even severe cases of depression. As of this writing, this issue remains unresolved.

Antidepressant. Acting to relieve depression.

Lithium   In a sense, the ancient Greeks and Romans were among the first to use the metal lithium as a psychoactive drug. They would prescribe mineral water for patients with bipolar disorder. They had no inkling as to why this treatment sometimes helped, but it may have been because mineral water contains lithium. A salt of the metal lithium (lithium carbonate), in tablet form, flattens out cycles of manicky behavior and depression for most sufferers, apparently by moderating the level of norepinephrine available to the brain.

It may be necessary for persons with bipolar disorder to use lithium indefinitely, just as a medical patient with diabetes must continue insulin to control the illness. Lithium has also been shown to have the side effects of impairing memory and depressing motor speed (Shaw et al., 1987). Memory impairment is reported as the primary reason that patients discontinue lithium (Jamison & Akiskal, 1983).

Electroconvulsive Therapy

Electroconvulsive therapy (ECT) was introduced by Italian psychiatrist Ugo Cerletti in 1939 for use with psychiatric patients. Cerletti had noted that some slaughterhouses used electric shock to render animals unconscious. The shocks also produced convulsions, and Cerletti erroneously believed, as did other European researchers of the period, that convulsions were incompatible with schizophrenia and other major disorders.

After the advent of major tranquilizers, use of ECT was generally limited to treatment of people with major depression. The discovery of antidepressants has limited use of ECT even further—to patients who do not respond to these drugs. But even as a therapy of last resort, ECT is still used with about 60,000 to 100,000 people a year in the United States (Sackeim, 1985).

ECT patients typically receive one treatment three times a week for several weeks. Electrodes are attached to the temples and an electrical current strong enough to produce a convulsion is passed between them. The shock induces unconsciousness, and so patients do not recall it. Still, patients are usually put to sleep with a sedative prior to treatment. In the past, ECT patients flailed about wildly during the convulsions, sometimes breaking bones. Today they are given muscle-relaxing drugs, and convulsions are barely perceptible to onlookers. ECT is not given patients with high blood pressure or heart ailments.

ECT is controversial for many reasons. First, many professionals are distressed by the thought of passing electric shock through the head and producing convulsions, even if they are suppressed by drugs. Second are the side effects. ECT disrupts recall of recent events. Although memory functioning usually seems near normal for most patients a few months after treatment, some patients appear to suffer permanent memory impairment (Roueche, 1980). Third, nobody knows *why* ECT works.

Psychosurgery

Psychosurgery is more controversial than ECT. The best-known modern technique, the **prefrontal lobotomy,** has been used with severely disturbed patients. In this method, a picklike instrument is used to crudely sever the nerve pathways that link the prefrontal lobes of the brain to the thalamus. The prefrontal lobotomy was pioneered by the Portuguese neurologist Antonio Egas Moniz and was brought to the United States in the 1930s. It was performed on more than a thousand mental patients by 1950. Although the prefrontal lobotomy often reduces violence and agitation, it is not universally successful. One of Dr. Moniz's failures shot him, leaving a bullet lodged in his spine and causing paralysis in the legs.

The prefrontal lobotomy also has a host of side effects, including hyperactivity and distractibility, impaired learning ability, overeating, apathy and withdrawal, epileptic-type seizures, reduced creativity, and, now and then, death. Because of these side effects, and because of the advent of major tranquilizers, the prefrontal lobotomy has been largely discontinued.

Evaluation of the Biological Therapies

There is little question that major tranquilizers, antidepressants, and lithium help many persons with severe psychiatric disorders. They enable thousands of formerly hospitalized patients to enter or return to the community and lead productive lives. Moreover, their potential for helping persons with eating disorders looks promising. Drug-related problems usually concern dosage and side effects.

Minor tranquilizers are frequently abused by overuse. Many people request them to dull the arousal that stems from anxiety-producing life-styles or interpersonal problems. Rather than make the often painful decisions required to confront their problems and change their lives, they find it easier to pop a pill. At least for a while. Then the dosage must be increased if the drug is to remain effective, and substance dependence becomes a possibility. Another problem is that many family physicians, even some psychiatrists, find it easier to prescribe minor tranquilizers than to help patients examine their lives and change anxiety-evoking conditions. The physician's lot is not eased by the fact that many patients want pills, not conversation.

In spite of the controversies that surround ECT, there is evidence that this treatment brings many immobilized patients out of their depression when antidepressant drugs fail (Janicak et al., 1985; NIMH, 1985; Scovern & Kilmann, 1980). There are also suggestions that memory impairment might be minimized by giving patients the lowest dose of electricity required to produce seizures (Daniel & Crovitz, 1983a; Sackeim et al., 1985). Also encouraging is the development of unilateral ECT in which the electrodes are attached to only one side of the brain. With unilateral ECT, there seems to be no decrease in effectiveness, but the side effects, such as memory impairment, are lessened (Daniel & Crovitz, 1983b; Squire, 1977; Squire & Slater, 1978).

In sum, biological forms of therapy, particularly chemotherapy, seem desirable for some major psychiatric disorders that do not respond to psychotherapy or behavior therapy alone. But common sense as well as research evidence suggest that psychological methods of therapy are preferable with problems such as anxiety, mild depression, and interpersonal conflict. No chemical can show a client how to change an idea or to solve an interpersonal problem.

In this chapter we explored the ways in which the helping professions come to the aid of people with psychological disorders and adjustment problems. In the following chapter, we examine a number of the ways in which we can apply these techniques to help ourselves cope with the challenges of life.

■ Summary

1. **What are psychotherapy and behavior therapy?** Psychotherapy is a systematic interaction between a therapist and client that brings psychological principles to bear in helping the client overcome psychological disorders or adjust to problems in living. Behavior therapy is a kind of therapy that relies on psychological principles of learning (e.g., conditioning and observational learning) to help clients directly develop adaptive behavior patterns and discontinue maladaptive behavior patterns.

2. **What are the goals of traditional psychoanalysis?** Goals are to provide self-insight, allow the spilling forth (catharsis) of psychic energy, and replace defensive behavior with coping behavior.

3. **What are the methods of traditional psychoanalysis?** Methods include free association, dream analysis, and resolution of the transference relationship between the therapist and client.

4. **How do modern psychodynamic approaches differ from traditional psychoanalysis?** Modern approaches are briefer and more directive, and the therapist and client usually sit face to face.

5. **What are the goals and traits of the person-centered therapist?** The person-centered therapist uses nondirective methods to help clients overcome obstacles to self-actualization. Therapists show unconditional positive regard, empathetic understanding, genuineness, and congruence.

6. **What are the goals and methods of Transactional Analysis (TA)?** TA helps people adopt healthy life positions ("I'm OK—You're OK"); fosters complementary transactions, or exchanges; encourages people to interact as adults rather than children or parents; and alerts people to the "games" they play in order to retain self-defeating life positions.

7. **What are the goals and methods of cognitive therapies?** Cognitive therapies aim to provide clients with insight into irrational beliefs and cognitive distortions, and to replace these cognitive errors with rational beliefs and accurate perceptions. Ellis notes that clients often show one or more of his ten irrational beliefs, including excessive needs for approval and perfectionism. Beck notes that clients may become depressed because of minimizing accomplishments, catastrophizing failures, and general pessimism. Problem-solving training shows clients how to use the stages of problem solving (preparation, production, and evaluation) to solve personal problems.

8. **What is systematic desensitization?** This is a behavior-therapy method that counterconditions fears by gradually exposing clients to a hierarchy of fear-evoking stimuli while they remain deeply relaxed.

9. **What is aversive conditioning?** This is a behavior-therapy method for discouraging undesirable behavior by repeatedly pairing the goals (e.g., alcohol, cigarette smoke, deviant sex objects) with aversive stimuli so that the goals become aversive rather than tempting.

10. **What is operant conditioning?** This is a behavior-therapy method that fosters adaptive behavior through successive approximations and reinforcement and extinguishes maladaptive behavior, usually by ignoring it.

11. **What is assertiveness training?** This is a behavior-therapy method for fostering social skills and decreasing social anxieties that uses techniques such as modeling, role playing, feedback, and behavior rehearsal.

12. **What are self-control methods?** These are behavior-therapy methods for adopting desirable behavior patterns and breaking bad habits; these methods focus on modifying the antecedents (stimuli that act as triggers) and consequences (reinforcers) of behavior and on modifying the behavior itself.

13. **What are the advantages of group therapy?** Group therapy is more economical than individual therapy. Moreover, group members profit from one another's social support and experiences.

14. **Does psychotherapy work?** Apparently it does. Complex statistical analyses show that people receiving most forms of psychotherapy fare better than people left untreated. Psychodynamic and person-centered approaches are particularly helpful with highly verbal and motivated individuals. Cognitive and behavior therapies are probably most effective, and behavior therapy also helps in the management of retarded and severely disturbed populations.

15. **What are the uses of chemotherapy?** Major tranquilizers often help schizophrenic individuals, apparently by blocking the action of dopamine. Antidepressants often help severely depressed people, apparently by raising the levels of norepinephrine and serotonin available to the brain. Lithium often helps persons with bipolar disorder, apparently by moderating levels of norepinephrine. The text criticizes the use of minor tranquilizers for daily tensions and anxieties because people rapidly build tolerance, drugs do not solve personal or social problems, and people attribute resultant calmness to the drugs and not to their own self-efficacy.

16. **What is electroconvulsive therapy (ECT)?** ECT passes an electrical current through the temples, inducing a seizure and frequently relieving severe depression. ECT is controversial because of side effects, such as loss of memory, and because nobody knows why it works.

17. **What is psychosurgery?** Psychosurgery is an extremely controversial method for alleviating severe agitation by severing nerve pathways in the brain. The best-known psychosurgery technique, the prefrontal lobotomy, has been largely discontinued because of side effects.

■ TRUTH OR FICTION REVISITED

The terms **psychotherapy** *and* **psychoanalysis** *are interchangeable.* False. Psychotherapy is a generic term, and psychoanalysis is the name of Freud's method of psychotherapy.

In order to be of significant help, psychotherapy must be undertaken for months, perhaps years. Not necessarily. Brief methods have been shown to be of help.

If you were in traditional psychoanalysis, your major tasks would be to lie back, relax, and say whatever pops into your mind. True. This is the method of free association.

Some psychotherapists interpret clients' dreams. True. Psychoanalysts and Gestalt therapists do, for example.

Some psychotherapists encourage their clients to take the lead in the therapy session. True. Person-centered therapists do.

Other psychotherapists tell their clients precisely what to do. True. Gestalt therapists do, for example.

Still other psychotherapists purposefully argue with clients. True. Cognitive therapists might do so in pointing out that clients' beliefs are irrational and self-defeating.

A goal of psychotherapy is to help clients solve problems. True. In fact, one cognitive approach is termed *problem-solving training.*

Some clients in psychotherapy delve into their pasts as a way to avoid confronting the problems they have today. True. Berne referred to this as playing the game of "Archaeology."

You might be able to gain control over bad habits merely by keeping a record of where and when you practice them. True. Self-monitoring and functional analysis heighten our motivation to change.

Lying around in your reclining chair and fantasizing can be an effective way of confronting your fears. True. These behaviors are elements of the behavior-therapy method of systematic desensitization.

Smoking cigarettes can be an effective treatment for helping people to . . . stop smoking cigarettes. True, as when one uses the aversive-conditioning method of rapid smoking.

Individual therapy is preferable to group therapy, for people who can afford it. Not necessarily. Groups give clients social support and the benefits of the experience of the other members.

Drugs are never a solution to abnormal behavior problems. False. Antipsychotic and antidepressant drugs and lithium can be of help.

There is a treatment for severe depression in which an electric current strong enough to induce seizures is passed through the head. True. It is electroconvulsive therapy.

The originator of a surgical technique intended to reduce violence learned that it was not always successful—when one of his patients shot him. True. His name was Moniz and he was the originator of the prefrontal lobotomy.

Active Coping: Ways of Helping Ourselves

10

The best way to modify catastrophizing thoughts is to . . . modify them.

Meditation can help people with hypertension lower their blood pressure.

If you tell people just to allow their muscles to relax, many will have no idea what to do.

You can decrease feelings of anxiety by regulating your breathing.

Modification of Type A behavior helps prevent recurrent heart attacks.

Visiting museums and art galleries is one of the methods for treating Type A behavior.

Telling someone you love them is another method for treating Type A behavior.

When your spouse insists on getting a divorce, learning to ski can help you cope.

A 220-pound person burns more calories running around the track than a 125-pound person.

In quitting smoking, it is helpful to tell relatives and friends of plans to quit.

One way of coping with test anxiety is not to allow it to distract us from the test items.

Psychologists have put together scientifically derived lists of turn-ons that can elevate your mood without your popping pills.

Wearing clean clothes and breathing clean air can help lift us out of feelings of depression.

We cannot be expected to stand still for it when someone insults us or threatens our honor.

■ Stress Management

What do you do when the pressures of work or school begin to get to you? What do you do when you feel that your instructor or your supervisor doesn't appreciate your performance? When your steady date finds someone else? When you want to take off a few pounds? When you're losing sleep? When you're uptight before a test or irritated because you're stuck in traffic?

In Chapter 9 we saw how psychologists and other health professionals use methods of therapy to help people in distress. In this chapter we explore various methods of active coping—ways of helping ourselves manage stress.

Stress management is not just one technique. The term refers to a number of methods that have been devised and adapted by contemporary psychologists and other professionals. In managing stress you might find people doing things as diverse as repeating aloud, "Easy—stop and think"; sitting quietly while thinking the word *one*; learning how to ski; walking around the block when struck by temptation to light up a cigarette; imagining receiving an injection; and informing their roommates that it's their turn to clean up the place.

If there is a common thread in all these methods, it is the theme of personal *control*. It is the fact that all of these involve ways of taking charge of your own life, not just letting things happen to you.

We begin the chapter by discussing ways of controlling irrational and catastrophizing thoughts that compound, and sometimes create, stressors. In Chapter 6 we described how our physiological responses to stress are characterized by arousal of the sympathetic division of the autonomic nervous system (ANS). In this chapter we examine a number of methods for lowering arousal, from meditation and progressive relaxation to biofeedback and regulation of our patterns of breathing. We describe methods originated by physicians and psychologists for coping with Type A behavior. We look at experimental ways of increasing psychological hardiness, a moderator of the impact of stress. Then we address specific ways of managing the self-control problems of overeating, smoking cigarettes, and insomnia. Finally we consider ways of coping with the three basic emotional responses to stress—anxiety, depression, and anger.

You will see that there is overlap among these methods, but that is fine. The overlapping will help you see how to apply the methods you have learned to other areas of life. This is a skill that will come in handy in your future, because the script has not yet been written for your life. One of the wonderful (and somewhat anxiety-evoking) aspects of life is that you cannot foresee everything that will happen to you.

And certainly there is "academic material" in this chapter, plenty of it. But also think of this chapter as a personal resource—something you can draw upon, as needed, to help you cope with the stressors in your life.

Stress management. A generic term for a number of techniques that moderate the effects of stress by, for example, lowering arousal, increasing one's sense of control, and reconceptualizing one's situation.

■ Methods for Controlling Irrational and Catastrophizing Thoughts

Have you had any of these experiences?

1. You have difficulty with the first item on a test and become absolutely convinced that you will flunk.
2. You want to express your genuine feelings but think that you might make another person angry or upset.
3. You haven't been able to get to sleep for 15 minutes and assume that you will lie awake the whole night and feel "wrecked" in the morning.
4. You're not sure what decision to make, so you try to put your conflicts out of your mind by going out, playing cards, or watching TV.

5. You decide not to play tennis or go jogging because your form isn't perfect and you're in less than perfect condition.

If you have had these or similar experiences, it may be because you harbor a number of the irrational beliefs identified by Albert Ellis (see page 321). These beliefs may make you overly concerned about the approval of others (experience 2, above) or perfectionistic (experience 5). They may lead you to think that you can best relieve yourself of certain dilemmas by pretending that they do not exist (experience 4), or that a minor setback will invariably lead to greater problems (experiences 1 and 3).

How, then, do we change irrational or catastrophizing thoughts? The answer is deceivingly simple: We change these thoughts by changing them. However, change may require some work, and before we can change our thoughts we must first be, or become, aware of them.

Meichenbaum's Three Steps for Controlling Catastrophizing Thoughts

Cognitive psychologist Donald Meichenbaum (1976, 1983) suggests a three-step procedure for controlling the irrational and catastrophizing thoughts that often accompany feelings of pain, anxiety, frustration, conflict, or tension:

1. Develop awareness of these thoughts through careful self-examination. Study the examples at the beginning of this section or in Table 10.1 to see if these experiences and thought patterns apply to you. (Also read Ellis's irrational beliefs carefully and ask yourself whether any of them tend to govern your behavior.) When you encounter anxiety or frustration, pay careful attention to your thoughts. Are they helping to point toward a solution, or are they compounding your problems?

TABLE 10.1 Controlling Irrational, Catastrophizing Beliefs and Thoughts

Irrational, Catastrophizing Thoughts	Incompatible (Coping) Thoughts
"Oh my God, I'm going to lose all control!"	"This is painful and upsetting, but I don't have to go to pieces."
"This will never end."	"This will come to an end, even if it's hard to see right now."
"It'll be awful if Mom gives me that look."	"It's more pleasant when Mom's happy with me, but I can live with it if she isn't."
"How can I get out there? I'll look like a fool."	"So you're not perfect; it doesn't mean you'll look stupid. And if someone thinks you look stupid, you can live with that too. Just stop worrying and have some fun."
"My heart's going to leap out of my chest! How much can I stand?"	"Easy—hearts don't leap out of chests. Stop and think! Distract yourself. Breathe slowly, in and out."
"What can I do? There's nothing I can do!"	"Easy—stop and think. Just because you can't think of a solution right now doesn't mean there's nothing you can do. Take it a minute at a time. Breathe easy."

Do irrational beliefs and catastrophizing thoughts compound the stress you experience? Cognitive psychologists suggest that we can cope with stress by becoming aware of self-defeating beliefs and thoughts and replacing them with rational, calming beliefs and thoughts.

2. Prepare thoughts that are **incompatible** with the irrational and catastrophizing thoughts, and practice saying them firmly to yourself. (If nobody is nearby, why not say them firmly aloud?)
3. Reward yourself with a mental pat on the back for effective changes in beliefs and thought patterns.

Controlling catastrophizing thoughts along with lowering the arousal of your alarm reaction—which we shall discuss next—serves to reduce significantly the impact of the stressor, whether it is pain, anxiety, or feelings of frustration. It gives you the chance to develop a plan for effective action. When effective action is not possible, controlling our thoughts and our levels of arousal dramatically increases our capacity to tolerate discomfort.

■ Methods for Lowering Arousal

One reason that a squash does not become as aroused as a person when it is assaulted is that it does not catastrophize. Another reason is that it does not have an autonomic nervous system, or ANS. And so it has no alarm reaction.

Once you are aware that a stressor is acting on you, and have developed a plan to cope with it, it is no longer helpful to have blood pounding so fiercely through your arteries. Psychologists and other scientists have developed many methods for teaching people to lower excessive bodily arousal. They include meditation, biofeedback, progressive relaxation, and diaphragmatic breathing.

Meditation
It is a well-known fact of life that the rare individuals who have gained inner harmony with the mysteries of the universe wear flowing robes, have long beards streaked with white, and set up shop on some distant mountaintop. These sages are tough to meet. You've got to wait for the end of the monsoon season, or for a thaw, to make the trip. Then you've got to bribe one of the few remaining guides who know the route.

So it's not surprising that psychologist Robert Ornstein's (1972) recounting of such a journey by U.S. travelers is filled with perilous details of scrambling and stumbling across the Himalayan Mountains. Of course the trip was long and arduous. Many would have turned back. But these rugged travelers were seeking the scoop on heightened consciousness—for the key to peace and harmony.

Finally, the travelers found themselves at the feet of the venerable **guru.** They told him of the perils of their journey and of the importance they attached to this audience. They implored the guru to share his wisdom, to help them open their inner pathways.

In response, the guru said, "Sit, facing the wall, and count your breaths."

This was it? The secret of the ages? The wisdom of several lifetimes? The prize for which our seekers had risked limb, life, and bank account?

Yes, in a sense it was. Counting your breaths is one method of **meditation**—one way of narrowing the focus of your consciousness so that the stresses of the outside world fade away. The Yogis stare at a pattern on a vase or mandala. The ancient Egyptians gazed upon an oil-burning lamp—the origin of the fable of Aladdin's magic lamp. Islamic mystics of Turkey, referred to as "whirling dervishes," concentrate on their body movements and the rhythms of their breathing.

Although methods of meditation vary, they seem to share a common thread: Through passive observation, the normal person–environment relationship is altered. Problem-solving, planning, worry, the concerns of the day are all suspended. Focusing on relaxing, repetitive stimuli, and thereby narrowing consciousness, is also one way of lowering our levels of sympathetic ANS arousal. Meditators may report that they have "merged" with the object

Incompatible. Not capable of occurring simultaneously.

Guru. A spiritual adviser or teacher.

Meditation. As a method for coping with stress, a systematic narrowing of attention that slows the metabolism and helps produce feelings of relaxation.

Meditation
Meditation is one way of reducing the arousal that accompanies stress, tension, and anxiety. In meditation the person focuses on a pleasant, repetitive stimulus, such as a mantra, and allows the concerns of the day to fade.

of meditation (the vase or a repeated phrase, for example) and then transcended it, leading to "oneness" with the universe, rapture, or some great insight. Psychologists have no way of measuring "oneness with the universe," and so such claims are unscientific, but psychologists can measure body changes, as we shall see—and meditation does lead to measurable body changes, as we shall see.

Thousands of Americans regularly engage in **transcendental meditation,** or TM, a simplified form of meditation brought to the U.S.A. from India by the Maharishi Mahesh Yogi in 1959. TM is practiced by repeating **mantras**—relaxing words or sounds such as *ieng* and *om*.

Effects of Transcendental Meditation

Herbert Benson (1975) of Harvard Medical School studied practitioners of TM ranging in age from 17 to 41—business people, students, artists. His subjects included people who had practiced TM anywhere from a few weeks to nine years. Benson found that TM produces what he labels a **relaxation response** in many people, which is characterized by a lower rate of metabolism, as measured by oxygen consumption. The blood pressure of people with hypertension decreases. In fact, people who meditate twice daily tend to show normalized blood pressure throughout the day (Benson et al., 1973). Meditators also produce more frequent and intense alpha waves, the brain waves that are associated with relaxation.

Other researchers agree that meditation lowers a person's level of arousal, but argue that the same relaxing effects can be achieved by engaging in other relaxing activities (West, 1985), or even by resting quietly for the same amount of time (Holmes et al., 1983; Holmes, 1984, 1985). The Holmes group (1983) found no differences between experienced meditators and novice "resters" in heart rate, respiration rate, blood pressure, and sweat in the palms of the hands (that is, galvanic skin response, or GSR). Most critics of meditation do not argue that meditation is useless, but rather that meditation may have no special effects as compared with a restful break from a tension-producing routine.

Meditation appears to facilitate adjustment to stress without decreasing awareness. In this way it does not reduce perception of potential threats. In one experiment, Orne-Johnson (1973) exposed meditators and nonmeditators to unpredictable loud noises. Meditators stopped showing a stress reaction, as measured by GSR, earlier than nonmeditators. In another experiment, Goleman and Schwartz (1976) used heart rate and GSR to measure stress reactions to a film that explicitly portrayed accidents and death. Meditators showed a greater alarm reaction than nonmeditators when the contents of the film were announced, but recovered normal levels of arousal more rapidly during the showings. Meditators in this study thus showed greater alertness to potential threat—a factor that could allow them to develop a plan for dealing with a stressor more rapidly—but also more ability to control arousal.

How to Meditate

If you want to try out meditation for yourself, the following measures may be of help:

1. Begin by meditating once or twice daily for 10 to 20 minutes.
2. What you *don't* do is more important than what you do do: Adopt a passive, "what happens, happens" attitude.
3. Create a quiet, nondisruptive environment. For example, don't directly face a light.
4. Do not eat for an hour beforehand; avoid caffeine for at least two.
5. Assume a comfortable position. Change it as needed. It's okay to scratch or yawn.
6. For a concentrative device, you may focus on your breathing or seat yourself before a calming object such as a plant or burning incense. Ben-

---

Transcendental meditation. The simplified form of meditation brought to the U.S. by the Maharishi Mahesh Yogi. Abbreviated TM.

Mantra. A word or sound that is repeated in TM.

Relaxation response. Benson's term for a group of responses which can be brought about by meditation. They involve lowered activity of the sympathetic branch of the autonomic nervous system.

son suggests "perceiving" (rather than "mentally saying") the word *one* on every outbreath. This means thinking the word, but "less actively" than usual (good luck). Carrington (1977) suggests thinking or perceiving the word *in* as you are inhaling and *out*, or *ah-h-h*, as you are exhaling. Carrington also suggests mantras such as *ah-nam*, *shi-rim*, and *ra-mah*.

7. If you are using a mantra, you can prepare for meditation and say the mantra out loud several times. Enjoy it. Then say it more and more softly. Close your eyes and think only the mantra. Allow the thinking to become "passive" so that you sort of "perceive," rather than actively think, the mantra. Again, adopt a passive, "what happens, happens" attitude. Continue to perceive the mantra. It may grow louder or softer, disappear for a while and then return.

8. If disruptive thoughts come in as you are meditating, you can allow them sort of to "pass through." Don't get wrapped up in trying to squelch them, or you may raise your level of arousal.

9. Above all, "take what you get." You cannot force the relaxing effects of meditation. You can only set the stage for it and allow it to happen.

10. Allow yourself to drift. (You won't go too far.) What happens, happens.

Biofeedback

Through **biofeedback training** (BFT), people (and lower animals) have learned to voluntarily regulate many functions, such as heart rate and blood pressure, that were previously thought to be beyond conscious control. BFT can also make us more aware of body responses we can normally influence, such as our level of muscle tension.

As noted in Chapter 2, it was in the 1960s that reports first appeared of laboratory rats being trained by biofeedback to raise or lower their heart rates (Miller, 1969). Since then people, too, have learned to gain control of their heart rates and other bodily functions through BFT—not for a "reward" of electric shock, but simply for a "bleep" or other electronic signal that indicates a change in the desired direction. Some people have gained control over their blood pressure; others over the sweat in the palm of the hand (an index of sympathetic ANS activity). The electroencephalograph (EEG) is used in BFT to teach people how to produce alpha waves, which are associated with relaxation, and the electromyograph (EMG), which monitors muscle tension, is used in BFT for control of muscle tension in the forehead and the rest of the body. Some people attach a *thermister*, an instrument that provides feedback about temperature, to a finger in order to cope with migraine headaches. By learning to raise the temperature in the finger, they alter the pattern of blood flow throughout the body and frequently relieve their headaches.

In research on BFT and stress, Sirota and his colleagues (1976) trained college women to slow their heart rates voluntarily, after which they reported a painful electric shock to be less stressful. College students at another campus reduced speech anxiety through BFT; this taught them to control their heart rates (Gatchel & Proctor, 1976).

Progressive Relaxation

University of Chicago physician Edmund Jacobson (1938), the originator of progressive relaxation, noted that people tense their muscles when they are under stress, compounding their discomfort. However, they are often unaware of these contractions. Jacobson reasoned that if people could learn to relax these contractions, they could directly lower the tension they experienced. But when he asked clients to focus on relaxing muscles, they often had no idea what to do.

Jacobson developed the method of **progressive relaxation** to teach people how to relax these tensions. In this method, people purposefully tense a muscle group before relaxing it. This sequence allows them to (1) develop

Biofeedback training. The systematic feeding back to an organism of information about a bodily function so that the organism can gain control of that function. Abbreviated BFT.

Progressive relaxation. A method for lowering arousal in which the individual alternately tenses then relaxes muscle groups throughout the body.

Biofeedback
Biofeedback is a system that provides, or "feeds back," information about a bodily function. Psychologists often use biofeedback to help clients relax. Clients can use biofeedback to gain better control over muscle tension, blood pressure, sweating, and other bodily responses that are related to stress.

awareness of their muscle tensions and (2) differentiate between feelings of tension and relaxation. The method is "progressive" because people move on, or progress, from one muscle group to another. Since its beginnings in the 1930s, progressive relaxation has undergone development by several behavior therapists, including Joseph Wolpe and Arnold Lazarus (1966).

You can practice progressive relaxation with the following instructions. Why not tape them or have a friend read them aloud?

Hanging Loose through Progressive Relaxation: A Manual   Before you relax, create a conducive setting. Settle down on a reclining chair, a couch, or a bed with a pillow. Pick a time and place where you're not likely to be interrupted. Be sure that the room is warm and comfortable. Dim the lights. Loosen any tight clothing.

Use the instructions given below, which were written by Joseph Wolpe and Arnold Lazarus (1966, pp. 177–180). Tighten each muscle group about two-thirds as hard as you could if you were using maximum strength. If you feel that a muscle could go into spasm, you are tensing too hard. When you let go of your tensions, do so completely.

The instructions can be memorized (slight variations from the text will do no harm), tape-recorded, or read aloud by a friend. An advantage to having someone read them is that you can signal the person to speed up or slow down by, say, lifting either one or two fingers.

After you have practiced alternate tensing and relaxing for a couple of weeks, you can switch to relaxing muscles only.

Relaxation of Arms (time: 4–5 minutes)

Settle back as comfortably as you can. Let yourself relax to the best of your ability. . . . Now, as you relax like that, clench your right fist, just clench your fist tighter and tighter, and study the tension as you do so. Keep it clenched and feel the tension in your right fist, hand, forearm . . . and now relax. Let the fingers of your right hand become loose, and observe the contrast in your feelings. . . . Now, let yourself go and try to become more relaxed all over. . . . Once more, clench your right fist really tight . . . hold it, and notice the tension again. . . . Now let go, relax; your fingers straighten out, and you notice the difference once more. . . . Now repeat that with your left fist. Clench your left fist while the rest of your body relaxes; clench that fist tighter and feel the tension . . . and now relax. Again enjoy the contrast. . . . Repeat that once more, clench the left fist, tight and tense. . . . Now do the opposite of tension—relax and feel the difference. Continue relaxing like that for a while. . . . Clench both fists tighter and together, both fists tense, forearms tense, study the sensations . . . and relax; straighten out your fingers and feel that relaxation. Continue relaxing your hands and forearms more and more. . . . Now bend your elbows and tense your biceps, tense them harder and study the tension feelings . . . all right, straighten out your arms, let them relax and feel that difference again. Let the relaxation develop. . . . Once more, tense your biceps; hold the tension and observe it carefully. . . . Straighten the arms and relax; relax to the best of your ability. . . . Each time, pay close attention to your feelings when you tense up and when you relax. Now straighten your arms, straighten them so that you feel most tension in the triceps muscles along the back of your arms; stretch your arms and feel that tension. . . . And now relax. Get your arms back into a comfortable position. Let the relaxation proceed on its own. The arms should feel comfortably heavy as you allow them to relax. . . . Straighten the arms once more so that you feel the tension in the triceps muscles; straighten them. Feel that tension . . . and relax. Now let's concentrate on pure relaxation in the arms without any tension. Get your arms comfortable and let them relax further and further. Continue relaxing your arms even further. Even when your arms seem fully relaxed, try to go that extra bit further; try to achieve deeper and deeper levels of relaxation.

Relaxation of Facial Area with Neck, Shoulders and Upper Back (time: 4–5 minutes)

Let all your muscles go loose and heavy. Just settle back quietly and comfortably. Wrinkle up your forehead now; wrinkle it tighter. . . . And now stop wrinkling your forehead, relax and smooth it out. Picture the entire forehead and scalp becoming smoother as the relaxation increases. . . . Now frown and crease your brows and study the tension. . . . Let go of the tension again. Smooth out the forehead once more. . . . Now close your eyes tighter and tighter . . . feel the tension . . . and relax your eyes. Keep your eyes closed, gently, comfortably, and notice the relaxation. . . . Now clench your jaws, bite your teeth together; study the tension throughout the jaws. . . . Relax your jaws now. Let your lips part slightly. . . . Appreciate the relaxation. . . . Now press your tongue hard against the roof of your mouth. Look for the tension . . . All right, let your tongue return to a comfortable and relaxed position. . . . Now purse your lips, press your lips together tighter and tighter. . . . Relax the lips. Note the contrast between tension and relaxation. Feel the relaxation all over your face, all over your forehead and scalp, eyes, jaws, lips, tongue, and throat. The relaxation progresses further and further. . . . Now attend to your neck muscles. Press your head back as far as it can go and feel the tension in the neck; roll it to the right and feel the tension shift; now roll it to the left. Straighten your head and bring it forward, press your chin against your chest. Let your head return to a comfortable position, and study the relaxation. Let the relaxation develop. . . . Shrug your shoulders, right up. Hold the tension. . . . Drop your shoulders and feel the relaxation. Neck and shoulders relaxed. . . . Shrug your shoulders again and move them around. Bring your shoulders up and forward and back. Feel the tension in your shoulders and in your upper back. . . . Drop your shoulders once more and relax. Let the relaxation spread deep into the shoulders, right into your back muscles; relax your neck and throat, and your jaws and other facial areas as the pure relaxation takes over and grows deeper . . . deeper . . . ever deeper.

Relaxation of Chest, Stomach and Lower Back (time: 4–5 minutes)

Relax your entire body to the best of your ability. Feel that comfortable heaviness that accompanies relaxation. Breathe easily and freely in and out. Notice how the relaxation increases as you exhale . . . as you breathe out just feel that relaxation. . . . Now breathe right in and fill your lungs; inhale deeply and hold your breath. Study the tension. . . . Now exhale, let the walls of your chest grow loose and push the air out automatically. Continue relaxing and breathe freely and gently. Feel the relaxation and enjoy it. . . . With the rest of your body as relaxed as possible, fill your lungs again. Breathe in deeply and hold it again. . . . That's fine, breathe out and appreciate the relief. Just breathe normally. Continue relaxing your chest and let the relaxation spread to your back, shoulders, neck and arms. Merely let go . . . and enjoy the relaxation. Now let's pay attention to your abdominal muscles, your stomach area. Tighten your stomach muscles, make your abdomen hard. Notice the tension. . . . And relax. Let the muscles loosen and notice the contrast. . . . Once more, press and tighten your stomach muscles. Hold the tension and study it . . . And relax. Notice the general well-being that comes with relaxing your stomach. . . . Now draw your stomach in, pull the muscles right in and feel the tension this way. . . . Now relax again. Let your stomach out. Continue breathing normally and easily and feel the gentle massaging action all over your chest and stomach. . . . Now pull your stomach in again and hold the tension. . . . Now push out and tense like that; hold the tension . . . once more pull in and feel the tension . . . now relax your stomach fully. Let the tension dissolve as the relaxation grows deeper. Each time you breathe out, notice the rhythmic relaxation both in your lungs and in your stomach. Notice thereby how your chest and your stomach relax more and more. . . . Try and let go of contractions anywhere in your body. . . . Now direct your attention to your lower back. Arch up your back, make your lower back quite hollow, and feel the tension along your spine . . . and settle down comfortably again relaxing the lower back. . . . Just arch your back up and feel the tensions as you do so. Try to keep the rest of your body as relaxed as possible. Try to localize the tension throughout your lower back area. . . . Relax once more, relaxing further and further. Relax your lower back, relax your upper back, spread the relaxation to your stomach, chest, shoulders, arms and facial area. These parts relax further and further and further and ever deeper.

Relaxation of Hips, Thighs and Calves Followed by Complete Body Relaxation (time: 4–5 minutes)

Let go of all tensions and relax. . . . Now flex your buttocks and thighs. Flex your thighs by pressing down your heels. . . . Relax and note the difference. . . . Straighten your knees and flex your thigh muscles again. Hold the tension. . . . Relax your hips and thighs. Allow the relaxation to proceed on its own. . . . Press your feet and toes downwards, away from your face, so that your calf muscles become tense. Study that tension. . . . Relax your feet and calves. . . . This time, bend your feet towards your face so that you feel tension along your shins. Bring your toes right up. . . . Relax again. Keep relaxing for a while. . . . Now let yourself relax further all over. Relax your feet, ankles, calves and shins, knees, thighs, buttocks and hips. Feel the heaviness of your lower body as you relax still further. . . . Now spread the relaxation to your stomach, waist, lower back. Let go more and more. Feel the relaxation all over. Let it proceed to your upper back, chest, shoulders and arms and right to the tips of your fingers. Keep relaxing more and more deeply. Make sure that no tension has crept into your throat; relax your neck and your jaws and all your facial muscles. Keep relaxing your whole body like that for a while. Let yourself relax.

Now you can become twice as relaxed as you are merely by taking in a really deep breath and slowly exhaling. With your eyes closed so that you become less aware of objects and movements around you and thus prevent any surface tensions from developing, breathe in deeply and feel yourself becoming heavier. Take a long, deep breath and let it out very slowly . . . Feel how heavy and relaxed you have become.

In a state of perfect relaxation you should feel unwilling to move a single muscle in your body. Think about the effort that would be required to raise your right arm. As you *think* about raising your right arm, see if you can notice any tensions that might have crept into your shoulder and your arm. . . . Now you decide not to lift the arm but to continue relaxing. Observe the relief and the disappearance of the tension. . . .

Just carry on relaxing like that. When you wish to get up, count backwards from four to one. You should then feel fine and refreshed, wide awake and calm.

Letting Go Only   Once you have practiced progressive relaxation through alternate tensing and letting go, you may be able to relax fully by letting go only. Simply focus on the muscle groups in your arms and allow them to relax. Just keep letting go. Allow the sensations of relaxation, warmth, and heaviness to develop on their own. Repeat for your facial area, neck, shoulders, and upper back; chest, stomach, and lower back; hips, thighs, and calves.

You will find that you can skip over some areas. Relaxation from one area can be allowed to "flow" into relaxation in another. Tailor instructions to your own needs.

You can probably achieve deep relaxation by letting go only in about five minutes. Continue to relax and enjoy the sensations for another 10 to 20 minutes. Now and then you can take "mind trips" through your body for pockets of residual tension and let them go also. But you may want to return to the full-length instructions every few months to maintain sharp relaxation skills.

Once you have learned how to relax, you can call on your skills as needed, letting go of bodily tensions when you want that alarm turned down.

You can also relax once or twice daily to reduce high blood pressure throughout the working day (Agras et al., 1983) and to cut down on Type A behavior.

One may also acquire muscle relaxation skills and control of breathing in preparation for childbirth. They are basic elements of the Lamaze method.

Diaphragmatic Breathing

Diaphragmatic breathing tends to lower arousal by slowing down the respiration rate and, possibly, by stimulating the parasympathetic division of the ANS (Harvey, 1978). And so it may also develop feelings of relaxation.

To use diaphragmatic breathing, lie on your back. Place your hands lightly on your stomach. Breathe so that you can see your stomach rise as you inhale and lower with every outbreath. You are now breathing "through" your diaphragm. The following methods help maintain slow, regular breathing:

1. Breathe through the nose only.
2. Take the same amount of time to inhale and exhale.
3. Make inhaling and exhaling continuous and leisurely. You can count ("one thousand one, one thousand two, one thousand three," etc.) as you breathe in and out.
4. To breathe diaphragmatically as you sit in a chair, monitor your chest movements with one hand so that you prevent it from rising and falling. Monitor your abdomen with your other hand to see that it does rise and fall.

When you are tense, anxious, or in pain, diaphragmatic breathing may also help distract you from your discomfort. It keeps your hands occupied and you can use mental arithmetic to monitor breaths and block out catastrophizing thoughts.

■ Methods for Coping with the Type A Behavior Pattern

Type A behavior, as noted in Chapter 6, is identified by characteristics such as a sense of time urgency, hostility, and hard-driving, self-destructive behavior patterns. Cardiologist Meyer Friedman, one of the originators of the Type A concept, and registered nurse Diane Ulmer reported in 1984 on some of the results of the San Francisco Recurrent Coronary Prevention Project (RCPP). The RCPP was designed to help Type A heart-attack victims modify their behavior in an effort to avert future attacks. After three years, participants placed in a treatment group in which they learned to reduce Type A behavior patterns had only one-third as many recurrent heart attacks as participants placed in a control group.

Readers who desire a complete description of the treatment program are referred to Friedman and Ulmer's *Treating Type A Behavior and Your Heart* (1984). Here we shall note the broad guidelines and some of the specifics of the behavioral program. The three broad RCPP guidelines were alleviating participants' sense of time urgency, their hostility, and their self-destructive tendencies. Of course, subjects were also counseled to give up smoking, eat a low-fat diet, and establish a peaceful environment. The buffering effects of a sense of humor were also noted.

Alleviating Your Sense of Time Urgency

Stop driving yourself—get out and walk. Too often we jump out of bed to an abrasive alarm, hop into a shower, fight commuter crowds, and arrive at class or work with no time to spare. Then we first become involved in our hectic "day." For Type A people, the day begins urgently and never lets up.

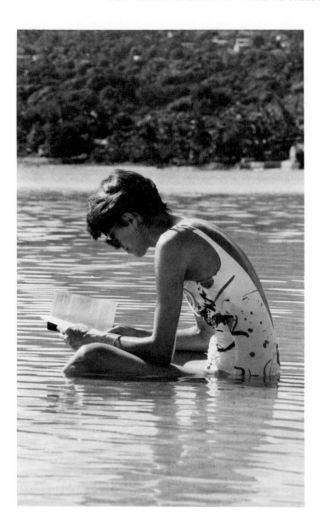

Alleviating the Sense of Time Urgency
Methods for coping with the Type A behavior pattern include engaging in more social activities, reading entertaining books, visiting museums and art galleries, and taking the time to write letters to friends.

The first step in coping with a sense of time urgency is confronting and replacing the beliefs that support it. Friedman and Ulmer (1984) note that Type A individuals tend to harbor the following beliefs:

1. "My sense of time urgency has helped me gain social and economic success" (p. 179). *The idea that impatience and irritation contribute to success, according to Friedman and Ulmer, is absurd.*
2. "I can't do anything about it" (p. 182). Of course, the belief that we cannot change ourselves is also one of Albert Ellis's irrational beliefs, as noted in Chapter 9. *Even in late adulthood, note Friedman and Ulmer, old habits can be discarded and new habits can be acquired.*

Friedman and Ulmer (1984) also use many exercises to help combat the sense of time urgency. The following are but a sampling:

1. Engage in more social activities with family and friends.
2. Spend a few minutes each day recalling events from the distant past. Check old photos of family and friends.
3. Read books—literature, drama, politics, biographies, science, nature, science fiction. (Not books on business or on climbing the corporate ladder!)
4. Visit museums and art galleries for their aesthetic value—not for speculation on the price of paintings.
5. Go to the movies, ballet, and theater.
6. Write letters to family and friends.

7. Take a course in art, or begin violin or piano lessons.
8. Remind yourself daily that life is by nature unfinished and you do not need to have all your projects finished on a given date.
9. Ask a family member what he or she did that day, and actually *listen* to the answer.

Colorado State University psychologist Richard Suinn (1976, 1982) adds the following suggestions for alleviating the sense of time urgency:

10. Get a nice-sounding alarm clock!
11. Move about slowly when you awake. Stretch.
12. Drive more slowly. This saves energy, lives, and traffic citations. It's also less stressful than racing the clock.
13. Don't wolf lunch. Get out; make it an occasion.
14. Don't tumble words out. Speak more slowly. Interrupt less frequently.
15. Get up earlier to sit and relax, watch the morning news with a cup of tea, or meditate. This may mean going to bed earlier.
16. Leave home earlier and take a more scenic route to work or school. Avoid rush-hour jams.
17. Don't car-pool with last-minute rushers. Drive with a group that leaves earlier or use public transportation.
18. Have a snack or relax at school or work before the "day" begins.
19. Don't do two things at once. Avoid scheduling too many classes or appointments back to back.
20. Use breaks to read, exercise, or meditate. Limit intake of stimulants like caffeine. Try decaffeinated coffee (tasty when brewed, not instant).
21. Space chores. Why have the car and typewriter repaired, work, shop, and drive a friend to the airport all in one day?
22. If rushed, allow unessential work to go to the next day. Friedman and Ulmer add, "Make no attempt to get everything finished by 5:00 P.M. if you must pressure yourself to do so" (1984, p. 200).
23. Set aside some time for yourself: for music, a hot bath, exercise, relaxation. (If your life will not permit this, get a new life.)

Alleviating Your Hostility

Friedman and Ulmer (1984) note that hostility, like time urgency, is supported by a number of irrational beliefs. And so it is up to us to begin again by recognizing our irrational beliefs and replacing them with new beliefs. Irrational beliefs that support hostility include:

1. "I need a certain amount of hostility to get ahead in the world" (p. 222). *Becoming readily irritated, aggravated, and angered does not contribute to getting ahead.*
2. "I can't do anything about my hostility" (p. 222). Need we comment?
3. "Other people tend to be ignorant and inept" (p. 223). Surely some of them are, but the world is what it is, and, as Ellis points out, we just expose ourselves to aggravation by demanding that other people be what they are not.
4. "I don't believe I can ever feel at ease with doubt and uncertainty" (p. 225). There are ambiguities in life; certain things remain unpredictable. Becoming irritated and aggravated doesn't make things less uncertain.
5. "Giving and receiving love is a sign of weakness" (p. 228). This belief is rugged individualism carried to the extreme, and it can isolate us from social support.

Friedman and Ulmer (1984) also offer a number of suggestions in addition to replacing irrational beliefs:

1. Tell your spouse and children that you love them.
2. Make some new friends.

3. Let friends know that you stand ready to help them.
4. Get a pet. (Take care of it!)
5. Don't talk to another person about subjects on which you know that the two of you hold divergent and fixed opinions.
6. When other people do things that fall short of your expectations, consider the situational factors such as level of education or cultural background that may limit or govern their behavior. Don't assume that they "will" the behavior that distresses you.
7. Look for the beauty and joy in things.
8. Stop cursing so much.
9. Express appreciation for the help and encouragement of others.
10. Play to lose, at least some of the time. (Ouch?)
11. Say "Good morning" in a cheerful manner.
12. Look at your face in the mirror at various times during the day. Search for signs of aggravation and anger and ask yourself if you need to look like that.

Alleviating Your Self-Destructive Tendencies

Friedman and Ulmer (1984) assert that Type A individuals harbor (frequently unconscious) wishes to destroy themselves. We cannot accept this view without evidence, but there is no doubt that many of us overeat, gorge high-fat foods, drink heavily, fail to exercise, and work 16-hour workdays month after month with full knowledge that such behavior can be harmful.

We do not have a list of irrational beliefs and exercises for this category. Here we are advised to monitor our behavior throughout the day and to determine whether it is health-enhancing or health-impairing. Having come this far in the book, we have developed some ideas about what is good for us and what is not. If we are doing things that are health-impairing, are we going to continue them or modify them? If not, why not? Are we going to tell ourselves we cannot change? Do we think so little of ourselves that we do not think it is worth it to change our behavior?

A little honest self-reflection is in order.

■ Methods for Enhancing Psychological Hardiness

Psychological hardiness, as explained in Chapter 6, buffers the effects of stress and is characterized by the "three C's"—commitment, challenge, and control. Psychologist Salvatore Maddi, who along with Susanne Kobasa originated the concept of psychological hardiness, maintains that hardiness can be enhanced by teaching people three coping strategies: situational reconstruction, focusing, and compensatory self-improvement. These methods, that is, heighten our sense of commitment and control and give us meaningful challenges.

In a pilot study of this approach, Maddi met with small groups of male and female Illinois Bell managers over 15 weeks, during which their problems were discussed and they were shown how to use these strategies (Fischman, 1987). At the end of the treatment period participants showed significant gains on paper-and-pencil tests of hardiness constructed by Maddi. They reported greater job satisfaction, fewer headaches, and improved sleep patterns. Moreover, their blood pressure dropped from a pretreatment average of 130/92 to 120/87. These findings appear exceptionally promising, but there are some methodological limitations. For example, there has not yet been a follow-up to determine whether the training has reduced the incidence of illness. Moreover, since Maddi taught all participants, we cannot really say whether the benefits of the treatment can be attributed to hardiness training per se or to Maddi's (unquestioned) expertise as a therapist.

Although questions remain unanswered about the empirical support for these techniques as improvers of hardiness, let's have a look at them. They are consistent with other methods presented in this book and, whether or not they enhance hardiness, they will certainly foster self-insight and suggest additional coping strategies.

Situational Reconstruction: "It's Not So Bad, But How Can You Make It Better?"

Situational reconstruction aims to place stressful situations in a broad perspective by alerting people to their assumptions (frequently irrational) about their situations. The method is also designed to enhance problem-solving skills.

Consider the case of Arthur, who was upset by a mediocre appraisal of his work that gave him a salary increase but cost him a promotion (Fischman, 1987). Maddi had Arthur imagine outcomes that would have been worse, such as not getting any raise or being fired, and outcomes that would have been better, such as upper-level management promoting him despite the evaluation. Since Arthur hadn't been fired and had been given a raise, he realized that his performance hadn't been all that bad, enhancing his sense of competence and self-esteem. Also, the promotion was not likely to come about unless upper-level management became aware of him and his work. Arthur realized that he could foster management's awareness of him by taking on more challenging assignments, and he initiated conferences with his much-surprised supervisor (took control of the situation) to explore ways of enhancing his value to Illinois Bell.

Focusing: "What's Really Bothering You?"

Focusing is aimed at providing insight for people who are unhappy or distressed but unable to locate the causes of their feelings. Maddi has such people focus on their negative body sensations, such as tightness in the chest, and reflect on the circumstances in which they usually occur. By using focusing, Roger, another Illinois Bell executive, realized that tightness in the chest and churning in the stomach had originated in elementary school when he had not done his homework and was consequently afraid of failure. Now he had similar feelings when he feared that there would not be enough time to meet his work assignments.

According to Maddi, Roger's recognition of the origins of his problem challenged him to work on something specific—not just a nameless feeling. As a result, his sense of control was restored.

Compensatory Self-Improvement: "If Love Eludes You, Take Up Skiing?"

Barbara, another Illinois Bell manager, was up against a genuine roadblock in her personal life—her husband's insistence upon getting a divorce. Nothing she could do would change his mind, and so she saw herself as a failure and became depressed. Also, her failure to win back her husband seemed emblematic, to her, of general inability to control her life.

After discussion back and forth, Maddi suggested to Barbara that she go out and learn how to ski. Skiing may seem irrelevant when one's marriage is in a shambles, but the sport was important in the area of the country where Barbara lived, and she had always seen herself as too timid and incompetent to learn.

And so Barbara signed up for skiing lessons. At first with her heart in her mouth, she gingerly descended the slopes. Gradually, as her skills increased, she began to look forward to her lessons and to assault the slopes. Not only did she enhance her skiing skills, she also made new acquaintances on the slopes and had something to share with them. She also felt that she was taking charge of her life once more, not just letting things happen to her.

And isn't that the trick to things?

Calories. Food energy; scientifically, units expressing the ability to raise temperature or give off body heat.

■ Methods for Controlling Weight

There is no mystery about it. Successful weight-control programs do not involve sometimes dangerous fad diets (Brownell, 1988), such as fasting, eliminating carbohydrates, or eating excessive amounts of grapefruit or rice. Instead, psychologists (Epstein et al., 1985; Israel et al., 1985; Stalonas & Kirschenbaum, 1985) have found that successful diets tend to involve major changes in life-style that include improving nutritional knowledge, decreasing calorie intake, exercise, and behavior modification.

Improving Nutritional Knowedge

Because eating fewer **calories** is the central method for decreasing weight, it is important for us to have adequate nutritional knowledge. Knowledge helps assure that we will not deprive ourselves of essential food elements and suggests strategies for losing weight without feeling overly deprived. For example, taking in fewer calories doesn't only mean eating smaller portions. It includes switching to some lower-calorie foods—relying more on fresh, unsweetened fruits and vegetables (eating apples rather than apple pie); lean meats; fish and poultry; and skim milk and cheese products. It means cutting down on, or eliminating, butter, margarine, oils, and sugar.

It turns out that the same foods that help us control our weight also tend to be high in vitamins and fiber and low in fats. And so they also lower our risk of developing cardiovascular disorders, cancer, and a number of other illnesses.

Calories One pound of body weight is roughly equivalent to 3,500 calories. As a rule of thumb, if you eat 3,500 more calories than your body requires in order to maintain its proper weight, you will gain a pound or so.* If you eat 3,500 fewer calories than you burn, you will lose a pound or so. How many calories do *you* burn in a day? As you can see from Table 10.2, your calorie expenditure is a function of your activity level and, yes, of your weight. Sex and age figure in somewhat, but not as much.

Fuel for the Fire—How Many Calories Do You Burn? You can use the guidelines in Table 10.2 to arrive at an estimate. Let's follow Paul, a rather sedentary office worker, through his day. He weighs 150 pounds. First, he records eight hours of sleep a night. As we see in Table 10.3, that's 8 × 60, or 480 calories. He spends about six hours a day at the desk, for another 900

TABLE 10.2 Calories Expended in One Hour According to Activity and Body Weight

Activity	Body Weight (in pounds)				
	100	*125*	*150*	*175*	*200*
Sleeping	40	50	60	70	80
Sitting quietly	60	75	90	105	120
Standing quietly	70	88	105	123	140
Eating	80	100	120	140	160
Driving, housework	95	119	143	166	190
Desk work	100	125	150	175	200
Walking slowly	133	167	200	233	267
Walking rapidly	200	250	300	350	400
Swimming	320	400	480	560	640
Running	400	500	600	700	800

*Actually, you may gain a bit less because the body makes some effort to compensate for excess calories by using more of them to digest excess food. But you will gain weight.

TABLE 10.3 **Approximate Number of Calories Burned by Paul on a Typical Weekday***

Activity	Hours/Day		Calories/Hour		Subtotal
Sleeping	8	×	60	=	480
Desk work	6	×	150	=	900
Driving	1	×	143	=	143
Eating	1	×	120	=	120
Sitting quietly	5	×	105	=	525
Hobbies	2	×	150	=	300
Walking rapidly	1	×	300	=	300
Totals	24				2,768

*Based on a body weight of 150 pounds.

calories. He eats for about an hour (120 calories) and drives for an hour (143 calories). He admits to himself that he spends about five hours a day in quiet sitting, watching television and reading (525 calories). He has begun an exercise program of walking rapidly for an hour a day—that's 300 calories. Another couple of hours of desk work at home—working on his stamp collection and other hobbies (300 calories)—accounts for the remainder of the day. In this typical weekday, Paul burns up about 2,768 calories.

If you weigh less than Paul, your calorie expenditure will probably be less than his, unless you are more active.

Burning Up More Fuel Than You Consume   You can use the information provided in Table 10.2 to estimate the number of calories you burn each day. To lose weight you will have to take in fewer calories, burn more, or do both.

Decreasing Calorie Intake

To get started decreasing calorie intake, you need a calorie book and a physician. The book will suggest what to eat and what to avoid and enable you to track your calorie intake. The physician will tell you how extensively you may restrict your calorie intake.

Establishing Daily Calorie Intake Goals   It is a good idea to establish specific weight-loss plans (Stuart, 1978), including daily calorie intake goals. If the daily goal sounds forbidding—such as eating 500 calories a day fewer than you do now—you can gradually approach the goal by reducing daily intake, say, by 100 calories for a few days or a week, then 200 calories, and so on.

Tracking Calories   Behavior-modification programs frequently employ self-monitoring or tracking, as noted in Chapter 9. In weight control it is usually better to track calorie intake than weight. Temporary fluctuations, such as water retention, can make the daily tracking of weight a frustrating experience. Counting calories is more reliable and effective (Romanczyk et al., 1973).

Determining Your Calorie-Intake Baseline   Before cutting down, determine your calorie-intake baseline. Record the calories you consume throughout the day *and* the sorts of encounters that that make it difficult to exercise self-control.* Keep a notebook and jot down:

What you have eaten
Estimated number of calories (use the calorie book)
Time of day, location, your activity, and your reactions to eating

*If it is difficult to continue to overeat while engaging in tracking of calories, feel free to cut down and thereby sacrifice the integrity of the record somewhat.

Your record may suggest foods that you need to cut down on or to eliminate; places you should avoid; and times of day, such as midafternoon or late evening, when you are particularly vulnerable to snacking. Planning small, low-calorie snacks (or distracting activities) for these times will prevent you from feeling deprived and from inhaling two shelves of the refrigerator.

Once you have established your baseline, maintain a daily record of calories consumed throughout the weight-loss program. Weigh yourself as often as you wish, but use calories, not weight, as your guiding principle.

Exercise

Why exercise? For many reasons, as noted in Chapter 7. First of all, exercise burns calories (Epstein et al., 1984b). This is one reason that dieting plus exercise is more effective than dieting alone (Epstein et al., 1984a). But remember that when we restrict calories our metabolic rates decrease (Apfelbaum, 1978; Polivy & Herman, 1985). This decrease can frustrate dieters severely. Some dieters justly complain that they reach "plateaus" from which they cannot shed additional pounds unless they literally starve themselves (Brownell, 1988). Exercise helps by increasing the metabolic rate throughout the day, even though we are restricting calories (Donahoe et al., 1984). Of course, aerobic exercise also confers cardiorespiratory fitness, a higher body muscle-to-fat ratio, and psychological benefits.

Behavior Modification

The self-monitoring of calorie intake is a behavior-modofication method. Now let us expand your use of behavior modification by adding a number of self-control strategies, as applied to lowering calorie intake. Pick ones that sound right for you. If they work, continue to use them. If not, discard them and try others.

Restricting the Stimulus Field

Eat in the dining area only. Break the habit of eating while watching television or studying.

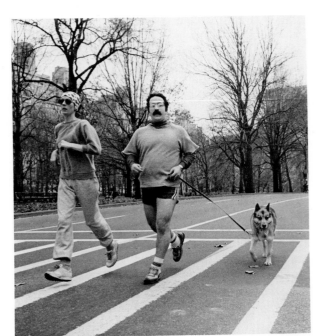

Exercise
Exercise helps dieters because it burns calories while they are exercising and also keeps the metabolism at a higher rate throughout the rest of the day.

Avoiding Powerful Triggers for Eating

Avoid trouble spots identified in your baseline record. Shop at the mall with the Alfalfa Sprout Restaurant, not the Gushy Gloppy Shoppe.

Use smaller plates. Remove or throw out leftover foods quickly.

Don't starve yourself—deprivation may lead to binging.

Don't read that appetizing restaurant menu. Order according to prearranged plan.

Pay attention to your own plate only—not the sumptuous dish at the next table.

Shop from a list. Walk briskly through the market, preferably after dinner, when you're no longer hungry. Don't browse. The colorful, appetizing packages may stimulate you to make unwise purchases.

Keep out of the kitchen. Study, watch television, write letters elsewhere.

Response Prevention

Keep fattening foods out of the house.

Prepare only enough food to remain within the restrictions of your diet.

Using Competing Responses

Stuff your mouth with celery, not ice cream or candy.

Eat premade, low-calorie snacks instead of losing control and binging on a jar of peanuts.

Try jogging for half an hour instead of eating an unplanned snack.

Reach for your mate, to coin a phrase—not for your plate.

Chain Breaking—Making Emily Post Happy

Always make a place setting before eating, even a snack.

Take small bites. Chew slowly and thoroughly.

Put down your utensils between bites.

Take a five-minute break during the meal to allow your blood sugar level to rise and cause bodily mechanisms to signal that you're no longer famished. Ask yourself if you really need to finish *every* bite when you return.

Building Desired Habits by Successive Approximations

Increase your daily calorie deficit by 100 calories each week so that you won't feel deprived by a sudden plunge.

Schedule frequent, low-calorie snacks as dieting gets under way. Gradually space them farther apart and eliminate one or two.

Build your daily exercise routine by just a few minutes each week.

Eliminate fattening foods from your diet one by one.

Making Rewards Contingent on Desired Behavior

Do not eat dinner unless you have exercised during the day.

Do not go to see that great new film unless you have met your weekly calorie-intake goal.

Each time you meet your weekly calorie-intake goal, put cash in the bank toward a vacation or new camera.

Response Cost

Keep a dollar bill in a stamped envelope addressed to your least favorite cause. If the cheesecake wins, mail it at once.

Dock yourself a dollar toward the camera every time the cheesecake wins.

WHAT DO YOU SAY NOW?

Resisting an Invitation To Eat

Part of the challenge of following a self-control program for losing weight is maintaining control in a social environment. It's relatively easy to rid your own house of fattening foods, but what do you do when you're at the relatives over the holidays, or at a party, and your host brings out the Boston Cream pie, "made especially for you"?

"Look at what I've got!" your host exclaims. "Your favorite. I baked it just for you, and I know you're going to love it."

What do you say now? Write down the responses that come to mind in the spaces below, and then note some of the following suggestions.

1. _____
   _____

2. _____
   _____

3. _____
   _____

What a dilemma! It's not easy to disappoint a close relative or friend, yet you have been doing such an excellent job of maintaining control. It is helpful if you have anticipated situations such as this—they're bound to arise—and prepared responses for them, such as the following:

1. "That looks great, Uncle Andy! I really appreciate your going to all this trouble for me, but I've been on a diet for three months now, and it's important to me. So I'll have to be content with that marvelous turkey you served!"
2. "That looks wonderful, but I've been feeling so much better since I've cut back on desserts. I'll feel good while I'm eating it, but then I'll feel terrible for days, so I have to pass."
3. "I'd love a piece, but I'm determined to fit into my bikini this July."
4. If Uncle Andy says, "Don't be silly, this is Thanksgiving—come on, now," you can say something like, "Yes, and I want to have something to be thankful about, like staying on my diet!" (If it's Christmas, you can say, "Yes, and I'd like to have something to be merry about," etc.)
5. If Uncle Andy says, "Oh, just have a mouthful. I made it especially for you," you can say something like, "I really appreciate it, but it will be torture for me to just have one mouthful, especially of your delicious pie. Have mercy!"
6. If Uncle Andy says, "Don't be silly, you're already skinny as a rail," you can say something like, "Thanks for the compliment, but I've still got a way to go." By the way, if many people are telling you that you're skinny and should stop dieting, perhaps it wouldn't hurt to get an impartial medical opinion on the subject.

Note, too, that it's possible to make occasional exceptions when you are dieting—so long as you continue to conceptualize yourself as being on a diet and do not catastrophize the exception. If you believe that the possibility of making exceptions will be of help to you, include it as part of your original dieting plan—make a note of it. But if your experiences lead you to believe that it would do you more harm than good to make exceptions and eat the pie, or a few mouthfuls, "stick to your guns."

And if you still eat the pie, notice that the world hasn't caved in on you. Try not to catastrophize; return to your diet right after you brush the taste of the pie out of your mouth—which it would be advisable to do quickly.

Covert Reinforcement and Covert Sensitization

Imagine reaching for something fattening—Stop! and congratulate yourself for doing so. Imagine your pride; imagine friends patting you on the back.

Imagine how wonderful you're going to look in that brief swimsuit on the beach next summer.

Mentally rehearse your next visit to parents, in-laws, or other relatives who usually try to stuff you like a pincushion. Imagine how you will politely but firmly refuse seconds. Think of how proud of yourself you'll be.

Tempted by a fattening dish? Imagine that it's rotten, that you would be nauseated by it and have a sick taste in your mouth for the rest of the day.

Tempted to binge? Strip before the mirror and handle a fatty area of your body. Ask yourself if you *really* want to make it larger or would prefer to exercise self-control?

When tempted you can also think of the extra work your heart must do for every pound of extra weight. Imagine your arteries clogging up with dreaded substances (not far off base!).

Keep 6 to 10 business-size cards in your wallet. On half of them print pro-reducing statements such as "I'll be able to fit in that new swimsuit if I'm careful," "I can get rid of this awful roll of fat," and "I'll be sexually appealing." Print anti-overeating statements on the others, such as "Think of the way you look in a mirror," "Think of how sick you feel after you binge on cake," and so on. Shuffle the cards and read them each time you're about to leave home or engage in another frequent activity. Keep them fresh by rotating them one by one with alternate messages. The benefits of losing and the perils of gaining will tend to remain in your mind.

■ Methods for Quitting and Cutting Down Smoking

When it comes to stopping smoking, common sense is also good psychology. People who successfully cut their cigarette use by half or more are more highly motivated and committed to cutting down than would-be reducers (Perri et al., 1977). For successful quitters, the cons of smoking significantly outweigh the pros (Velicer et al., 1985). Premack (1970) believes that humiliation is also a prime motivator for those who succeed. At some point we become humiliated by our inability to quit. Perhaps we torch a hole into a favorite piece of clothing or see our children fiddling with cigarettes and decide that we have finally had it with cigarettes. Our self-efficacy expectancies that we can cut down or quit are also important (Blittner et al., 1978). Once we have quit, belief in our ability to remain abstinent correlates positively with abstinence at three- and six-month follow-ups (McIntyre et al., 1983).

Evidence is mixed as to whether it is more effective to cut down gradually or quit all at once. Going cold turkey (quitting all at once) is more effective for some smokers (Flaxman, 1978), but cutting down gradually is more effective for others (Glasgow et al., 1984). Although it is most healthful to quit smoking entirely, some smokers, unable to quit, have learned to reduce their cigarette consumption by at least half, and have stuck to their lower levels for up to two and a half years (Glasgow et al., 1983, 1985).

Suggestions for Quitting Cold Turkey

Psychologists have compiled suggestions such as the following for helping people quit smoking:

1. Tell your family and friends that you're quitting—make a public commitment.
2. Think of specific things to tell yourself when you feel the urge to smoke: how you'll be stronger, free of fear of cancer, ready for the marathon, etc., etc.
3. Tell yourself that the first few days are the hardest—after that, withdrawal symptoms weaken dramatically.
4. Remind yourself that you're "superior" to nonquitters.
5. Start when you wake up, at which time you've already gone eight hours without nicotine.
6. Go on a smoke-ending vacation to get away from places and situations in which you're used to smoking.
7. Throw out ashtrays and don't allow smokers to visit you at home for a while.
8. Don't carry matches or light other people's cigarettes.
9. Sit in nonsmokers' sections of restaurants and trains.
10. Fill your days with novel activities—things that won't remind you of smoking.

One strategy for cutting down or quitting smoking is to place yourself in an environment in which smoking is not possible.

11. Use sugar-free mints or gum as substitutes for cigarettes (don't light them).*
12. Interpret withdrawal symptoms as a sign that you're winning and getting healthier. After all, you wouldn't have withdrawal symptoms if you were smoking.
13. Buy yourself presents with all that cash you're socking away.

Suggestions for Cutting Down Gradually

Psychologists have compiled suggestions such as the following for people who would rather try to cut down than quit altogether:

1. Count your cigarettes to establish your smoking baseline.
2. Set concrete goals for controlled smoking. For example, plan to cut down baseline consumption by at least 50 percent.
3. Gradually restrict the settings in which you allow yourself to smoke.
4. Get involved in activities where smoking isn't allowed or practical.
5. Switch to a brand you don't like. Hold your cigarettes with your nondominant hand only.
6. Keep only enough cigarettes to meet the (reduced) daily goal. Never buy more than a pack at a time.
7. Use sugarfree candies or gum as a substitute for a few cigarettes each day.
8. Jog instead of having a cigarette. Or walk, swim, or make love.
9. Pause before lighting up. Put the cigarette in an ashtray between puffs. Ask yourself before each puff if you really want more. If not, throw the cigarette away.
10. Put the cigarette out before you reach the end. (No more eating the filter.)
11. Gradually lengthen the amount of time between cigarettes.
12. Imagine living a prolonged, noncoughing life. Ah, freedom!
13. As you smoke, picture blackened lungs, coughing fits, the possibilities of cancer and other lung diseases.

Using strategies such as the above, many individuals have gradually cut down their cigarette consumption and eventually quit. It's true that there is a high relapse rate for quitters. Be on guard: We are most likely to relapse—that is, return to smoking—when we feel highly anxious, angry, or depressed (Shiffman, 1982). But when you are tempted, you can decrease the chances of relapsing by using almost any of the strategies outlined above (Hall et al., 1984; Shiffman, 1982, 1984), like reminding yourself of reasons for quitting, having a mint, or going for a walk. And also keep in mind a note of encouragement: Despite high relapse "rates," millions of Americans have quit and been able to stay away from cigarettes permanently (Schachter, 1982).

■ Methods for Coping with Insomnia

As noted in Chapter 7, insomniacs tend to compound their sleep problems by trying to force themselves to get to sleep. Their concern heightens, rather than lowers, autonomic activity and muscle tension. You cannot force yourself to get to sleep. You can only set the stage for sleep by relaxing when you are tired.

Our most common method for fighting insomnia is popping sleeping pills. Pill popping is often effective—for a while. Sleeping preparations work by reducing arousal, and lowered arousal can induce sleep. At first, focusing

---

*There is a nicotine gum available that may be of use to some smokers who are heavily physiologically dependent on nicotine, especially when combined with behavioral techniques (Hall et al., 1985). The gum decreases withdrawal symptoms by providing a source of nicotine, but does not contain harmful hydrocarbons or carbon monoxide.

on changes in arousal may also distract you from efforts to get to sleep. Expectancies of success may also help.

But there are problems with sleeping pills. First, you attribute your success to the pill and not yourself. And so you do nothing to enhance your self-efficacy expectancies, and you are at risk for becoming dependent on the pills. Second, you develop tolerance for sleeping pills and must increase the dose if they are to continue to work. Third, high doses of these chemicals can be dangerous, especially if mixed with an alcoholic beverage or two.

Let us now consider psychological strategies for coping with insomnia. They include using relaxation to reduce tension, challenging irrational beliefs that otherwise heighten tension, distraction from the task of somehow *getting* to sleep, and stimulus control.

Lowering Arousal

Muscle relaxation methods reduce tension directly and reduce the time needed to fall asleep (Woolfolk & McNulty, 1983). They increase the number of hours slept and leave us feeling more rested in the morning (Haynes et al., 1974; Weil & Gottfried, 1973).

In a typical experiment, Lick and Heffler (1977) used newspaper ads to enlist people with a **sleep-onset latency** of at least 50 minutes. Participants were assigned to one of four conditions: (1) progressive relaxation; (2) progressive relaxation plus taped relaxation instructions; (3) a placebo (phony) treatment group; and (4) a no-treatment control group. Participants who received only progressive relaxation training decreased their "sleep-onset latency"—the amount of time it took them to get to sleep—by an average of more than 32 minutes. They also increased the amount of time spent sleeping by more than an hour. Subjects who received relaxation training plus tape recordings of their therapist's voice reduced sleep-onset latency by a mean of 23 minutes and slept three-quarters of an hour longer. Placebo and no-treatment control groups showed no improvement.

In many procedures, people gain facility with progressive relaxation and then achieve relaxation at bedtime by letting go muscle tensions only. Biofeedback training for relaxation of the muscles in the forehead has been shown to be as effective as progressive relaxation for university students and others (Haynes et al., 1977). **Autogenic training** has also been found to help people cope with insomnia (Nicassio & Bootzin, 1974). In autogenic training, one reduces muscle tension by focusing on suggestions that the limbs are growing warm and heavy and that the breathing is becoming regular. All these methods also provide one with something on which to focus other than trying to fall asleep.

Challenging Irrational Beliefs

You need not be an expert on insomnia to realize that thinking that the following day will be ruined unless you get to sleep *right now* will increase, rather than decrease, body arousal at bedtime. Still, we often catastrophize the problems that will befall us if we do not sleep. Table 10.4 lists some irrational beliefs that are reported by many insomniacs, and suggests some rational alternatives.

Using Fantasy: Taking Nightly Mind Trips

Mind trips have advantages over real trips. They're less expensive and you conserve energy. In bed at night, mind trips may also distract you from what you may see as your nightly burden—confronting insomnia and forcing yourself to somehow get to sleep. You may be able to ease yourself to sleep by focusing on pleasant images, such as lying on a sun-drenched beach and listening to waves lapping on the shore, or walking through a summer meadow high among the hills.

TABLE 10.4 Some Irrational Beliefs about Sleep and Rational Alternatives

Irrational Belief	Rational Alternative
"If I don't get to sleep, I'll feel wrecked tomorrow."	"Not necessarily. If I'm tired, I can go to bed early tomorrow night."
"It's unhealthy for me not to get more sleep."	"Not necessarily. Some people get only a few hours of sleep each night and lead apparently normal lives. I may not need eight hours at all."
"I'll wreck my sleeping schedule for the whole week if I don't get to sleep very soon."	"Not at all. I don't need a schedule for the week. I'll just get up in time to do what I have to do in the morning. I can catch up by going to bed tomorrow night early, if I'm tired."
"If I don't get to sleep, I won't be able to concentrate on that big test/conference in the morning."	"Possibly, but my fears may also be exaggerated. I may just as well relax, or get up and do something enjoyable. There's no point to just lying here and worrying."

Irrational thoughts increase our tensions at bedtime, contributing to insomnia. Rational alternatives tend to lower our tensions by granting us a proper perspective.

Using Stimulus Control

A number of methods are based on the principle of stimulus control, as defined in Chapter 9 (Bootzin & Nicassio, 1978; Morin & Azrin, 1987). Stimulus control can be used, for example, to convert your bed from an arena for a nightly contest between you and insomnia to a place where you can relax and escape the tensions of the day.

One way to make your bed a friendlier place is to think or ruminate about tomorrow's responsibilities elsewhere. When you lie down, you may allow yourself a few moments to organize your thoughts about the day's events and the morrow. But then allow yourself to relax and, perhaps, to engage in fantasy. If an important thought or plan comes to you, don't fight it or lose it—jot it down on a pad you can keep nearby. But if thoughts persist, get up and go elsewhere. Let your bed be a place to collect yourself and sleep—not your study. Even a waterbed is not a think tank.

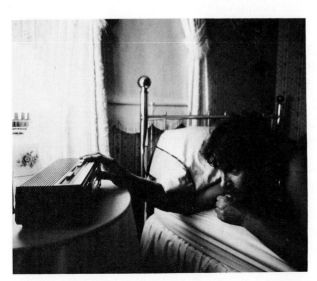

Insomnia
Psychological methods for alleviating insomnia include lowering arousal, challenging irrational beliefs about sleep, using fantasy, and using stimulus control.

Similarly, it may help to avoid studying or snacking in bed throughout the day. These activities could also give your bed meanings that are incompatible with sleeping.

Stimulus control can also be made to work to your advantage by establishing a regular routine, at least during weeknights. Set your alarm for the same time each morning and get up, regardless of how much sleep you have had. Oversleeping in the morning to compensate for a long sleep-onset latency the night before means that you will be less ready to go to sleep at a "normal" bedtime the following evening. Also avoid napping if you can; napping also sets back the time when you will be ready to go to sleep in the evening.

Above all: Try to accept the idea that it really doesn't matter if you don't get to sleep early *this night*. You will survive. (You really will, you know.) In fact, you'll do just fine.

■ Methods for Coping with Emotional Responses to Stress

The emotional responses to stress discussed in Chapter 6 include fear, depression, and anger. Let us explore a number of methods devised by contemporary psychologists for coping with each of them.

Coping with Fears and Phobias

Adjustment often requires that we learn to approach and master the objects and situations that frighten us. Maintaining our physical health can require mastering our fear of what the doctor may tell us. Getting ahead in school or in business can require speaking before groups, and so it may be necessary for some of us to cope with stagefright. And getting better grades on tests may require mastering test anxiety.

Contemporary methods for mastering fears tend to reverse the natural tendency to avoid feared objects. Of course in "an emergency" we can simply "do what we have to" despite fear—for example, have a dreaded injection—and we can control our body sensations by relaxing, by reminding ourselves that injections don't last forever, and, perhaps, by thinking about lying on a beach somewhere. If continued exposure to frightening objects, such as hypodermic needles, is necessary, some fear may actually become extinguished.* But the techniques suggested by most psychologists involve approaching feared objects and situations *under nondistressing circumstances*. Lack of discomfort gives us the opportunity to reappraise dreaded objects. Examples of these methods include gradual approach and systematic desensitization.

Gradual Approach   One can reduce fears by gradually approaching, or behaviorally confronting, the feared object or situation (Biran & Wilson, 1982).

To use this method, define the feared object or situation as the target. Then list specific behaviors that allow you to make a gradual approach of the target. Options include gradually decreasing the distance between yourself and the target, first approaching it with a friend and then approaching it alone, and gradually increasing the amount of time you remain in contact with the target. In order to be certain that the behaviors are listed in order of increasing difficulty, many people write 10 to 20 steps down on index cards, mixing the three strategies. Then they order and reorder the cards until they are satisfied that they are placed in a hierarchy. If there seems to be too great a jump between steps, one or two intermediary steps can be added.

*Refer to discussion of "flooding" in Chapter 2 for an explanation.

Fear-stimulus hierarchy.
The arrangement of fear-evoking objects or situations in order from least to most aversive. (Used in fear-reduction methods such as gradual approach and systematic desensitization.)

Kathy experienced fear of driving, which made her dependent on family and friends for commuting to work, shopping, and recreation. Driving 30 miles back and forth to work was identified as the target. She constructed this hierarchy of steps to gradually approach the target (Rathus & Nevid, 1977):

1. Sitting behind the wheel of her car with an understanding friend
2. Sitting alone behind the wheel of her car
3. Driving around the block with her friend
4. Driving around the block alone
5. Driving a few miles back and forth with her friend
6. Driving a few miles back and forth alone
7. Driving the route to work and back on a nonworkday with her friend
8. Driving the route to work and back on a nonworkday alone
9. Driving the route to work and back on a workday with her friend
10. Driving the route to work and back on a workday alone

Kathy repeated each step until she experienced no discomfort. As the procedure progressed, Kathy became aware of how her cognitive appraisal of driving first created and compounded her fears, and, later, how cognitive *reappraisal* aided her coping efforts. At first she found herself catastrophizing: "What a baby I am! Marian is being so understanding and here I am ruining her day with my stupidity."

After discussing her self-defeating thoughts with a helping professional, Kathy learned to forgive herself for imperfect performances, to recognize her growing self-efficacy, and to reward herself for progress. As time went on, she entertained thoughts such as, "I don't like my fears, but I didn't get them on purpose and I'm working to overcome them. I am grateful to Marian, but I don't have to feel guilty about inconveniencing her because, in the long run, this will make things easier for her, too. Now, this isn't so bad—you're sitting behind the wheel without going bananas, so give yourself a pat on the back for that and stop condemning yourself. You're gradually gaining control of the situation. You're taking charge and mastering it, bit by bit."

Systematic Desensitization Joseph Wolpe (1958, 1973), the originator of systematic desensitization, theorized that we cannot experience fear or anxiety and deep muscle relaxation at the same time. If a person could relax while perceiving dreaded stimuli, the stimuli should lose their sting. So Wolpe combined Jacobson's method of progressive relaxation with gradual movement up a hierarchy of *imagined* or *symbolized* (as with photographic slides) objects or situations that induce fear. A hierarchy of fear-evoking stimuli is called a **fear-stimulus hierarchy.**

It even appears that we can engage in systematic desensitization on our own, as suggested by studies in the treatment of acrophobia (Baker et al., 1973) and other fears (Dawley et al., 1973; Marks, 1982; Rosen et al., 1976). Wolpe believes that systematic desensitization is effective because relaxation counterconditions anxiety, but the procedure also gives clients the chance to reappraise the phobic object or situation and shows clients that they can master it.

In order to use systematic desensitization, first develop facility with progressive relaxation (see pp. 355–357). Learn to relax yourself in a few minutes through abbreviated instructions or by letting go only. Prepare a vividly imagined "safe scene," such as lying on the beach or walking in the woods, that you can focus on when you encounter anxiety. Use index cards to construct a fear-stimulus hierarchy. The first item should elicit only the slightest anxiety. If you cannot progress from one item to another, try placing one or two in between.

Relax in a recliner or on a couch. Imagine hierarchy items vividly, or project slides onto a screen. Control the projector yourself or have a friend help. Focus on each item until it produces some anxiety. Then imagine the safe scene until you regain complete relaxation. Focus on the item again. When you can focus on a hierarchy item without anxiety for 30 seconds three times in a row, move on to the next item. Once you have completed the hierarchy, approach the target in vivo—that is, in real life—gradually if necessary.

The following case is taken from Rathus and Nevid (1977, pp. 52–54).

David, a 25-year-old art teacher, was scheduled to begin his first full-time teaching job in a month and a half. During the prior weeks he had begun to ruminate about his shaky student teaching the spring before. He was growing more and more fearful of going before his classes. He had even considered resigning before he began. He had developed shakiness, light-headedness, cold hands, loose bowels, and "spells" during which he forgot what he was going to do. A friend who had taken a few psychology courses told David that he was "really" afraid that if he became a competent teacher he would run out of excuses for continuing to live with his mother. Sad to say, neither this "insight" nor David's haphazard attempts to medicate himself with beer were useful.

When David consulted a professional, it was suggested that systematic desensitization might help him overcome his fear of teaching within the few weeks remaining before the school year began. David received two weeks of intensive relaxation training. A hierarchy of fear-inducing stimuli was constructed along two dimensions: time left to go before teaching and amount of threat in various teaching situations. He listed the items on index cards and sorted them until he was satisfied that they were in the proper order. In a couple of cases, an item from one dimension induced as much anxiety as an item from another, and their order was randomized. The list was as follows:

1. It is four weeks before classes begin
2. It is three weeks before classes begin
3. Talking after school with a student about the possibility of a career in art
4. It is two weeks before classes begin
5. Supervising a student's art project after class
6. It is ten days before classes begin
7. Supervising one student during class while other students work independently in the classroom
8. It is one week before classes begin
9. Supervising two students working on a project while other students work independently in the classroom
10. Supervising a group of three students working on a project while other students work independently in the classroom
11. It is five days before classes begin
12. Asking a class involved in independent projects if there are any questions
13. It is two days before classes begin
14. Preparing a lesson plan for the first day of classes
15. It is the night before classes begin
16. Driving to work the first morning of classes
17. Greeting a new class, talking about the course, and fielding questions

So that he would not worry about how to greet his classes, David prepared concrete initial talks for his students. He rehearsed them until they seemed "natural." Parts of clinical sessions were spent in behavior rehearsal, during which David delivered pieces of lessons. Now and then the therapist role-played difficult students, asking confusing questions or making sarcastic remarks. David rehearsed responses to these students in the nonthreatening therapeutic situation.

When David appeared before his classes, he experienced mild anxiety. He took a deep breath, told himself to relax, and exhaled. The effect was calming. By the time David introduced himself to his last class, he was enjoying his first day as a teacher. He had increased his perceived self-efficacy by learning that he could control his level of arousal and focus on his teaching rather than on his fear.

Coping with Test Anxiety

Have you had or heard these complaints? "I just know I'm going to flunk." "I study hard and memorize everything, but when I get in there my mind goes blank." "I don't know what's wrong with me—I just can't take tests." "The way I do on standardized tests, I'll never get into graduate school."

Some students may complain of test anxiety as an excuse for performing poorly (Smith et al., 1982), but for others test anxiety is a frustrating handicap. When we study diligently, test anxiety seems a particularly cruel obstacle.

Why Do Some of Us Encounter Test Anxiety?   We are not born with test anxiety. Test anxiety appears to reflect a combination of high arousal of the sympathetic division of the ANS and self-defeating thoughts, including critical self-evaluations. People with high test anxiety show high levels of arousal during tests and are likely to report bodily sensations such as dryness in the mouth and rapid heart rate (Galassi et al., 1981). On a cognitive level, they have more negative thoughts and are more self-critical than people with low or moderate test anxiety, even when they are performing just as well (Galassi et al., 1984; Holroyd et al., 1978; Meichenbaum & Butler, 1980). Moreover, they allow their self-criticisms, and negative thoughts of the sort shown in Table 10.5, to *distract* them from working effectively on their tests (Arkin et al., 1982; Bandura, 1977; Sarason, 1984). As you can see in Table 10.5, many of these thoughts catastrophize the test-taking situation, and, in many instances, they are irrational.

Cognitive Restructuring of Test Taking   Test anxiety is often linked to catastrophic, irrational thoughts that distract the test-taker from the tasks at hand. Therefore, it is appropriate to cope with test anxiety by challenging such thoughts and returning one's attention to the test itself (Goldfried, 1988). College students on several campuses have reduced test anxiety and improved their test grades through such a method—cognitive restructuring.

Participants in one study of this method (Goldfried et al., 1978) selected 15 anxiety-evoking items from the Suinn Test Anxiety Behavior Scale (STABS). Three of the items were presented for four one-minute trials during

TABLE 10.5   Percent of Positive and Negative Thoughts for University Students with Low or High Test Anxiety

Thought	Low Test Anxiety *Percent*	High Test Anxiety *Percent*
POSITIVE THOUGHTS		
Will do all right on test	71	43
Mind is clear, can concentrate	49	26
Feel in control of my reactions	46	23
NEGATIVE THOUGHTS		
Wish I could get out or test was over	46	65
Test is hard	45	64
Not enough time to finish	23	49
Work I put into studying won't be shown by my grade	16	44
Stuck on a question and it's making it difficult to answer others	13	34
Mind is blank or can't think straight	11	31
Going to do poorly on test	11	28
Think how awful it will be if I fail or do poorly	11	45

High test-anxious students report fewer positive thoughts and more negative thoughts while taking tests. Moreover, their negative thoughts are linked to bodily sensations like dryness in the mouth and rapid heart rate. Source of data: Galassi, Frierson, & Sharer, 1981, pp. 56, 58.

QUESTIONNAIRE

The Suinn Test Anxiety Behavior Scale

How about you? Do you look upon tests as an opportunity to demonstrate your knowledge and test-taking ability, or do you drive yourself bananas by being overly self-critical and expecting the worst? How does your level of test anxiety compare to that of others? To find out, take the Suinn Test Anxiety Behavior Scale (STABS) items listed below. Then compare your results to those of others by turning to the key at the end of the chapter.

The items in the questionnaire refer to experiences that may cause fear or apprehension. For each item, place a checkmark (√) under the column that describes how much you are frightened by it nowadays. Work quickly but be sure to consider each item individually.

	Not at All	A Little	A Fair Amount	Much	Very Much
1. Rereading the answers I gave on the test before turning it in.	___	___	___	___	___
2. Sitting down to study before a regularly scheduled class.	___	___	___	___	___
3. Turning in my completed test paper.	___	___	___	___	___
4. Hearing the announcement of a coming test.	___	___	___	___	___
5. Having a test returned.	___	___	___	___	___
6. Reading the first question on a final exam.	___	___	___	___	___
7. Being in class waiting for my corrected test to be returned.	___	___	___	___	___
8. Seeing a test question and not being sure of the answer.	___	___	___	___	___

each of five treatment sessions. During these trials, subjects first pinpointed the irrational or catastrophizing thoughts that were evoked. Then they restructured their responses to them by constructing rational alternative thoughts.

One student's irrational thoughts included, "I'm going to fail this test, and then everyone's going to think I'm stupid." Restructuring of these catastrophizing ideas might be as follows: "Chances are I probably won't fail. And even if I do, people probably won't think I'm stupid. And even if they do, that doesn't mean I *am* stupid" (Goldfried et al., 1978, p. 34).

You can use these four steps to restructure your own cognitions concerning test-taking:

1. Pinpoint irrational, catastrophizing thoughts
2. Construct incompatible, rational alternatives
3. Practice thinking the rational alternatives
4. Reward yourself

You can pinpoint irrational thoughts by taking the STABS (see the nearby questionnaire). Jot down several items that cause you concern. Feel

	Not at All	A Little	A Fair Amount	Much	Very Much
9. Studying for a test the night before.	___	___	___	___	___
10. Waiting to enter the room where a test is to be given.	___	___	___	___	___
11. Waiting for a test to be handed out.	___	___	___	___	___
12. Waiting for the day my corrected test will be returned.	___	___	___	___	___
13. Discussing with the instructor an answer I believed to be right but which was marked wrong.	___	___	___	___	___
14. Seeing my standing on the exam relative to other people's standing.	___	___	___	___	___
15. Waiting to see my letter grade on the test.	___	___	___	___	___
16. Studying for a quiz.	___	___	___	___	___
17. Studying for a midterm.	___	___	___	___	___
18. Studying for a final.	___	___	___	___	___
19. Discussing my approaching test with friends a few weeks before the test is due.	___	___	___	___	___
20. After the test, listening to the answers my friends selected.	___	___	___	___	___

Source: © 1971 by Richard M. Suinn. The Suinn Test Anxiety Behavior Scale is available from Rocky Mountain Behavioral Science Institute, Inc., P.O. Box 1066, Ft. Collins, CO 80522.

free to include similar items that come to mind as you review the STABS items. Sit back, relax, imagine yourself in each situation. After a minute or so, jot down the irrational thoughts that have come to mind.

Examine each thought carefully. Is it rational and accurate, or is it irrational? Does it catastrophize? Construct incompatible rational alternatives for each thought that is irrational, as in Table 10.6.

Arrange practice tests that resemble actual tests. Time yourself. If the tests are GRE's or civil service exams, buy the practice tests and make testing conditions as realistic as possible.

Attend to your thoughts while you take the practice tests. Can you find additional irrational thoughts? If so, prepare additional rational alternatives.

Whenever an irrational thought comes to mind, say the rational alternative to yourself firmly. If you are alone, say it out loud. If no irrational thoughts "pop" into mind, say to yourself, one by one, the ones that you usually think in such a situation. For each one, say the rational alternative to yourself firmly.

Reward yourself for thinking rational alternatives. Say to yourself, for example, "That's better, now I can return to the test," or, "See, I don't have

Overlearning. Continuing to study academic material that has already been learned adequately.

TABLE 10.6   **Rational Alternatives to Irrational Cognitions Concerning Test Taking**

Irrational, Catastrophizing Thoughts	Incompatible, Rational Alternatives
"I'm the only one who's going so bananas over this thing."	"Nonsense, lots of people have test anxiety. Just don't let it take your mind off the test itself."
"I'm running out of time!"	"Time is passing, but just take it item by item and answer what you can. Getting bent out of shape won't help."
"This is impossible! Are all the items going to be this bad?"	"Just take it item by item. They're all different. Don't assume the worst."
"I just can't remember a thing!"	"Just slow down and remember what you can. Take a few moments and some things will come back to you. If not, go on to the next item."
"Everyone else is smarter than I am!"	"Probably not, but maybe they're not distracting themselves by catastrophizing. Just do the best you can and take it easy."
"I've got to get out of here! I can't take it anymore!"	"Even if I feel that way now and then, I don't have to act on it. Just focus on the items, one by one."
"I just can't do well on tests."	"That's only true if you believe it's true. Back to the items, one by one."
"There are a million items left!"	"Quite a few, but not a million. Just take them one by one and answer as many as you can."
"Everyone else is leaving. They're all finished before me."	"Fast work is no guarantee of good work. Even if they do well, it doesn't mean you *won't* do well. Just take all the time you need."
"If I flunk, everything is ruined!"	"You won't be happy if you fail, but it won't be the end of the world either. Just take it item by item and don't let worrying distract you."

In order to restructure your cognitions concerning test taking, prepare rational alternatives to your irrational thoughts and rehearse them. Don't let catastrophizing distract you from the test items.

Test Anxiety
Psychologists have found that people with test anxiety have high levels of arousal during tests and negative thoughts about their performance. Moreover, they allow their levels of arousal and self-defeating thoughts to distract them from the test items.

to be at the mercy of irrational thoughts. I can decide what I'm going to say to myself." When the test is over, think something like, "Well, I did it. What's done is done, but I certainly got through that feeling much better, and I may have done better as well."

Additional hints: Practice progressive relaxation. If you feel uptight during a test, allow feelings of relaxation to drift in, especially into your shoulders and the back of your neck. Take a deep breath, tell yourself to relax, and let the breath out (Suinn & Deffenbacher, 1988). See if you can't become twice as relaxed as you were before. Also, try **overlearning** the material you're studying. That is, study it once more after you feel you know it fully. Overlearning aids retention of material and increases your belief in your ability to recall it. Finally, when a test is over, *let it be over*. Check answers to help master important material, if you wish, but not just to check your score. Do something

enjoyable. If you don't, you may find yourself opening the door to depression—which is our next topic.

Coping with Depression

In this section, we discuss methods for coping with the inactivity, feelings of sadness, and cognitive distortions that characterize depression. People who feel that their situations may fit the picture of a major depressive episode or bipolar disorder, as described in Chapter 8, are advised to talk over their problems with their instructors or with a helping professional. However, there are many strategies that we can use to cope with lingering feelings of depression that accompany losses, failures, or persistent pressures. These include using pleasant events, modifying depressing thoughts, exercise, and assertive behavior.

Using Pleasant Events to Lift Your Mood Becky's romance had recently disintegrated, and she was now at a low ebb, weepy and withdrawn. Depression is an appropriate emotional response to a loss, but after weeks of moping, Becky's friends became concerned. After much argument, they finally prevailed on her to accompany them to a rock concert. It took Becky a while to break free from her own ruminations and begin to focus on the music and the electricity of the crowd, but then Becky found herself clapping and shouting with her friends. Depressive feelings did not return until the following morning. At that time Becky thought, "Well, what could I expect? I was really depressed *underneath it all.*"

Becky's thoughts were understandable, if irrational. She had a right to feel sad that her romance had ended. But after several weeks had passed, her belief that sadness was the only emotion she ought to feel was irrational. (She also seemed to believe that her feelings were subject to the whims of others, and that there was nothing she could do to elevate her mood so long as her love life was in a shambles.) For Becky, the rock concert was incompatible with depression. She could not listen to the punk rock group, The Naked and the Dead, and remain miserable.* Although her friends were helpful, it is unfortunate that they, and not Becky, were responsible for placing her in the audience. Becky eventually profited from the experience, but she attributed her improvement to good friends, and not her own resources. Again, her own mood was attributed to, and dependent upon, the behavior of others.

In any event, there is a significant relationship between our moods and our activities. In Chapter 8 we saw that pressures and failures can trigger feelings of depression. It seems that the opposite also holds true; feelings of happiness and joy can be generated by pleasant events. Peter Lewinsohn and his colleagues (Lewinsohn & Graf, 1972; Lewinsohn & Libet, 1972) had subjects track their activities and feelings of depression for 30 days, using checklists they mailed to the researchers on a daily basis. Lewinsohn and Graf (1973) found 49 items from 160-item checklists that contributed to a positive mood in at least 10 percent of subjects. Several are listed in Table 10.7. The researchers classify them into three groups: (1) activities that counteract depression by producing positive, or incompatible, emotional responses; (2) social interactions; and (3) ego-supportive activities or events. "Ego-supportive" activities help raise self-efficacy expectancies.

Will pleasant events do the trick for you? Experiments in using pleasant events with the purpose of lifting one's mood have shown mixed results. Reich and Zautra (1981) found that engaging in pleasant activities enhanced feelings of well-being, but relieved distress only for people under considerable stress. In another study (Biglan & Craker, 1982), pleasant activities increased the activity level of four depressed women, but did not improve self-reports of

*Your authors, however, would be able to accomplish this feat.

TABLE 10.7   Activities Linked to Positive Feelings in the Lewinsohn and Graf Study

ACTIVITIES PRODUCING INCOMPATIBLE EMOTIONAL RESPONSES
Thinking about something good in the future
Listening to music
Being relaxed
Wearing clean clothes
Breathing clean air
Sitting in the sun
Watching wild animals
Seeing beautiful scenery

SOCIAL INTERACTIONS
Being with happy people
Having a frank and open conversation
Having coffee, tea, a Coke with friends
Watching people
Being told I am loved
Meeting someone new of the same sex
Being with friends
Smiling at people
Expressing my love to someone
Having a lively talk
Kissing
Having sexual relations
Complimenting or praising someone

EGO-SUPPORTIVE ACTIVITIES OR EVENTS
Doing a project in my own way
Planning trips or vacations
Reading stories, novels, poems, or plays
Planning or organizing something
Doing a job well
Learning to do something new

mood. Research involving athletic activities is more encouraging, as we shall see below.

If you have been down in the dumps for a while, it may also help you to engage in activities that are incompatible with depression. You can systematically use pleasant events to lift your mood—or enrich the quality of your daily life—through the following steps:

1. Check off items that appeal to you on the Pleasant Events Schedule (see the nearby questionnaire).
2. Engage in at least three pleasant events each day.
3. Record your pleasant activities in a diary. Add other activities and events that struck you as pleasant, even if they were unplanned.
4. Toward the end of each day, rate your response to each activity using a scale like

   +3 Wonderful
   +2 Very nice
   +1 Somewhat nice
    0 No particular response
   −1 Somewhat disappointing
   −2 Rather disappointing
   −3 The pits

5. After a week or so, check the activities and events in the diary that received positive ratings.
6. Make a point of repeating highly positive activities and continue to experiment with new ones.

Q U E S T I O N N A I R E

The Pleasant Events Schedule—A List of Turn-Ons

Walking, loving, reading, collecting, redecorating—different people enjoy different things. Here is a list of 116 activities and events enjoyed by many. One hundred fourteen are derived from research by MacPhillamy and Lewinsohn (1971). The last two are a contemporary update. You can use the 116 items to get in touch with what turns you on by rating them according to the scale given below. Then you may want to enrich the quality of your daily life by making sure to fit one or more of them in.

> 2 = very pleasant
> 1 = pleasant
> 0 = not pleasant

_____   **1.** Being in the country
_____   **2.** Wearing expensive or formal clothes
_____   **3.** Making contributions to religious, charitable, or political groups
_____   **4.** Talking about sports
_____   **5.** Meeting someone new
_____   **6.** Going to a rock concert
_____   **7.** Playing baseball, softball, football, or basketball
_____   **8.** Planning trips or vacations
_____   **9.** Buying things for yourself
_____   **10.** Being at the beach
_____   **11.** Doing art work (painting, sculpture, drawing, moviemaking, etc.)
_____   **12.** Rock climbing or mountaineering
_____   **13.** Reading the Scriptures
_____   **14.** Playing golf
_____   **15.** Rearranging or redecorating your room or house
_____   **16.** Going naked
_____   **17.** Going to a sports event
_____   **18.** Going to the races
_____   **19.** Reading stories, novels, poems, plays, magazines, newspapers
_____   **20.** Going to a bar, tavern, club
_____   **21.** Going to lectures or talks
_____   **22.** Creating or arranging songs or music
_____   **23.** Boating
_____   **24.** Restoring antiques, refinishing furniture
_____   **25.** Watching television or listening to the radio
_____   **26.** Camping
_____   **27.** Working in politics
_____   **28.** Working on machines (cars, bikes, radios, television sets)
_____   **29.** Playing cards or board games
_____   **30.** Doing puzzles or math games
_____   **31.** Having lunch with friends or associates
_____   **32.** Playing tennis
_____   **33.** Driving long distances
_____   **34.** Woodworking, carpentry
_____   **35.** Writing stories, novels, poems, plays, articles
_____   **36.** Being with animals

(continued)

QUESTIONNAIRE: The Pleasant Events Schedule
(continued)

_____ **37.** Riding in an airplane

_____ **38.** Exploring (hiking away from known routes, spelunking, etc.)

_____ **39.** Singing

_____ **40.** Going to a party

_____ **41.** Going to church functions

_____ **42.** Playing a musical instrument

_____ **43.** Snow skiing, ice skating

_____ **44.** Wearing informal clothes, "dressing down"

_____ **45.** Acting

_____ **46.** Being in the city, downtown

_____ **47.** Taking a long, hot bath

_____ **48.** Playing pool or billiards

_____ **49.** Bowling

_____ **50.** Watching wild animals

_____ **51.** Gardening, landscaping

_____ **52.** Wearing new clothes

_____ **53.** Dancing

_____ **54.** Sitting or lying in the sun

_____ **55.** Riding a motorcycle

_____ **56.** Just sitting and thinking

_____ **57.** Going to a fair, carnival, circus, zoo, amusement park

_____ **58.** Talking about philosophy or religion

_____ **59.** Gambling

_____ **60.** Listening to sounds of nature

_____ **61.** Dating, courting

_____ **62.** Having friends come to visit

_____ **63.** Going out to visit friends

_____ **64.** Giving gifts

_____ **65.** Getting massages or backrubs

_____ **66.** Photography

_____ **67.** Collecting stamps, coins, rocks, etc.

_____ **68.** Seeing beautiful scenery

_____ **69.** Eating good meals

_____ **70.** Improving your health (having teeth fixed, changing diet, having a checkup, etc.)

_____ **71.** Wrestling or boxing

_____ **72.** Fishing

_____ **73.** Going to a health club, sauna

_____ **74.** Horseback riding

_____ **75.** Protesting social, political, or environmental conditions

_____ **76.** Going to the movies

_____ **77.** Cooking meals

_____ **78.** Washing your hair

_____ **79.** Going to a restaurant

_____ **80.** Using cologne, perfume

_____ **81.** Getting up early in the morning

_____ **82.** Writing a diary

_____ **83.** Giving massages or backrubs

_____ **84.** Meditating or doing yoga

_____ **85.** Doing heavy outdoor work

_____ **86.** Snowmobiling, dune buggying

_____ **87.** Being in a body-awareness, encounter, or "rap" group

_____ **88.** Swimming

_____ **89.** Running, jogging

_____ **90.** Walking barefoot

_____ **91.** Playing frisbee or catch

_____ **92.** Doing housework or laundry, cleaning things

_____ **93.** Listening to music

_____ **94.** Knitting, crocheting

_____ **95.** Making love

_____ **96.** Petting, necking

_____ **97.** Going to a barber or beautician

_____ **98.** Being with someone you love

_____ **99.** Going to the library

_____ **100.** Shopping

_____ **101.** Preparing a new or special dish

_____ **102.** Watching people

_____ **103.** Bicycling

_____ **104.** Writing letters, cards, or notes

_____ **105.** Talking about politics or public affairs

_____ **106.** Watching attractive women or men

_____ **107.** Caring for houseplants

_____ **108.** Having coffee, tea, or Coke, etc., with friends

_____ **109.** Beachcombing

_____ **110.** Going to auctions, garage sales, etc.

_____ **111.** Water skiing, surfing, diving

_____ **112.** Traveling

_____ **113.** Attending the opera, ballet, or a play

_____ **114.** Looking at the stars or the moon

_____ **115.** Using a microcomputer

_____ **116.** Playing videogames

Source of first 114 items: Adapted from D. J. MacPhillamy & P. M. Lewinsohn, *Pleasant Events Schedule, Form III-S*, University of Oregon, Mimeograph, 1971.

Challenging Irrational, Depressing Thoughts

> Public opinion is a weak tyrant compared with our own private opinion. What a man thinks of himself, that it is which determines, or rather indicates his fate.
>
> Henry David Thoreau, *Walden*

Depressed people tend to have excessive needs for social approval and to be perfectionistic in their self-demands (Vestre, 1984). They also tend to blame themselves for failures and problems, even when they are not at fault. They *internalize* blame and see their problems as *stable* and *global*—as all but impossible to change. Depressed people also make the cognitive errors of tending to *catastrophize* their problems and to *minimize* their accomplishments (Beck, 1976).

Consider Table 10.8. Column 1 illustrates a number of (often) irrational, depressing thoughts. How many of them have you had? Column 2 indicates the type of cognitive error being made (such as internalizing or catastrophizing), and column 3 shows examples of more rational, less depressing alternatives.

You can pinpoint your own irrational, depressing thoughts by focusing on what you are thinking whenever you feel low. Try to pay particular attention to the rapid, fleeting thoughts that can trigger mood changes. It helps to jot down the negative thoughts. Then challenge their accuracy. Do you characterize difficult situations as impossible and hopeless? Do you expect too much from yourself and therefore minimize your achievements? Do you internalize more than your fair share of blame?

You can use the guidelines in Table 10.8 to classify your own cognitive errors. Also use the table as a guide in constructing rational alternatives to your own depressing thoughts. Jot down the rational alternatives next to each irrational thought, and review them now and then. When you are alone, read the irrational thought aloud, then follow it by saying, firmly, "No, that's irrational!" Then read aloud the rational alternative twice, *emphatically*.

After you have thought or read aloud the rational alternative, think or say things like, "That makes a bit more sense! That's a more accurate view of things! It feels better now that I have things in proper perspective."

Irrational thoughts do not just happen; nor are you stuck with them. You can learn to exert control over your thoughts and, in this way, to exert a good deal of control over your feelings—whether the feelings are of anxiety, depression, or anger.

Exercise   Exercise, particularly sustained exercise, frequently has a positive effect on the moods of depressed people, as noted in Chapter 7. Aerobic exercises such as running, jogging, swimming, bicycle riding, or fast walking appear to alleviate feelings of depression in many cases (Doyne et al., 1983; Folkins & Sime, 1981; Klein et al., 1985). As noted in Chapter 8, depression may be linked to deficiencies in norepinephrine, serotonin, even endorphins. It has been speculated that sustained exercises may achieve mood-enhancing effects by increasing levels of these substances (Dimsdale & Moss, 1980; Carr et al., 1981), although these hypotheses have not yet been borne out empirically.

In any event, in a University of Kansas study, one group of depressed women attended twice-weekly classes in which they danced, jogged, and ran. They also continued these exercises outside of the classroom. After ten weeks, these women showed fewer symptoms of depression than women who practiced progressive relaxation or who had had no treatment (McCann & Holmes, 1984).

A Pleasant Event
One way for people to fight depression is to push themselves to engage in events that they have usually experienced as pleasant. Pleasant events can be incompatible with feelings of depression.

TABLE 10.8   Irrational, Depressing Thoughts and Rational Alternatives

Irrational Thought	Type	Rational Alternative
"There's nothing I can do."	Catastrophizing, minimizing, stabilizing	"I can't think of anything to do right now, but if I work at it, I may."
"I'm no good."	Internalizing, globalizing, stabilizing	"I did something I regret, but that doesn't make me evil or worthless as a person."
"This is absolutely awful."	Catastrophizing	"This is pretty bad, but it's not the end of the world."
"I just don't have the brains for college."	Stabilizing, globalizing	"I guess I really need to go back over the basics in that course."
"I just can't believe I did something so disgusting!"	Catastrophizing	"That was a bad experience. Well, I won't be likely to try that again soon."
"I can't imagine ever feeling right."	Stabilizing, catastrophizing	"This is painful, but if I try to work it through step by step, I'll probably eventually see my way out of it."
"It's all my fault."	Internalizing	"I'm not blameless, but I wasn't the only one involved. It may have been my idea, but he/she went into it with his/her eyes open."
"I can't do anything right."	Globalizing, stabilizing, catastrophizing, minimizing	"I sure screwed this up, but I've done a lot of things well, and I'll do other things well."
"I hurt everybody who gets close to me."	Internalizing, globalizing, stabilizing	"I'm not totally blameless, but I'm not responsible for the whole world. Others make their own decisions and live with the results, too."
"If people knew the real me, they would have it in for me."	Globalizing, minimizing (the positive in yourself)	"I'm not perfect, but nobody's perfect. I have positive as well as negative features, and am entitled to self-interests."

Many of us create or compound feelings of depression because of cognitive errors such as those in this table. Have you had any of these irrational, depressing thoughts? Are you willing to challenge them?

Assertive Behavior   Since we humans are social creatures, our social interactions are very important to us. Nonassertive behavior patterns, as measured by scores on the Rathus Assertiveness Schedule (see Chapter 5), are linked to feelings of depression (Gotlib, 1984). Learning to express our feelings and relate effectively to others, on the other hand, has been shown to alleviate feelings of depression (Hersen et al., 1984). Assertive behavior permits more effective interactions with our families, friends, co-workers, and strangers—thereby removing sources of frustration and increasing the social support we receive. Expressions of positive feelings—saying you love someone or simply saying "Good morning" brightly—help reduce feelings of hostility and paves the way for further social involvement.

In Chapter 5 we suggested many ways in which readers can become more socially effective in demanding their just rights and expressing their genuine feelings, and in Chapter 14 we shall note a number of ways in which readers can become more effective in their attempts to establish rewarding intimate relationships.

Coping with Anger

Anger is a common emotional response to frustration and to social provocations, such as insults or threats, as noted in Chapter 6. Anger can be adaptive when it motivates us to surmount obstacles in our paths or to defend ourselves against aggressors. But anger can be troublesome when it leads to excessive arousal or self-defeating aggression. Prolonged arousal is stressful and may lead to diseases of adaptation such as high blood pressure (see Chapter 6). Insulting, threatening, or physically attacking strangers, supervisors, co-workers, or family members can cause problems such as getting fired, being expelled from school, getting into legal trouble, being physically hurt, and hurting people we care about.

A Rational-Emotive Analysis of Anger and Aggression   Why do we respond aggressively when we are frustrated or provoked? Many of us make decisions to act aggressively under such circumstances, and, in these cases, we can weigh the effects of our aggression to determine whether we should change our behavior. But others of us feel that our aggressive responses occur automatically when others insult or argue with us, and that there is little we can do to take charge of them.

Not so. Aggressive responses may occur with lower animals when they are subjected to aversive stimulation, but aggressive behavior in humans involves thought processes (Berkowitz, 1983). But as noted by cognitive therapists, our thoughts are sometimes so automatic and fleeting that we are not in touch with them. Still we can be influenced by them. At an extreme, no injury may have been done us at all, but because of automatic thoughts we might still blow up if a parent asks if we had a nice time on a date or when a supervisor offers a helping hand.

It turns out that many of these automatic thoughts (see Table 10.9) are irrational and reflect persistent sources of frustration, such as ongoing conflicts and fears. Conflicts over independence, sexual behavior, and personal competence may plague us persistently, yet we may be barely aware of them (Beck, 1976). In such cases, we have to work to tune in to them.

In a rational-emotive analysis, a parent's inquiry about a date, or a supervisor's offer to help, serves as an *activating event*. Subtle, ongoing frustrations—say, frustrated wishes to be independent of parents or to be recognized as competent on the job—lead to irrational *beliefs*. For instance, we may interpret a parent's or supervisor's innocent expression of interest as an effort to control or undermine us. Such irrational beliefs, in turn, trigger the *consequences* of intense feelings of anger and, perhaps, aggressive behavior. But since we are not usually fully aware of the *beliefs* in this chain, our aggressive *consequences* may seem a mystery to us. We may wonder why we become so

**TABLE 10.9   How Frustrations Set the Stage for Activating Events
to Trigger Irrational Thoughts and Consequences
of Anger and Aggression**

Possible Sources of Frustration	Activating Event →	Irrational Beliefs →	Possible Consequences
Unresolved dependence-independence conflict Need for privacy from parents	Your mother asks, "Did you see a nice movie?"	"Why does she always ask me that?" "That's my business!"	"I don't want to talk about it!" You walk away angrily. You make a noncommital grunt and then walk way.
Concern about your worth as a person Concern about competent behavior (work, date, athletics, etc.) at destination	You are caught in a traffic jam.	"Who the hell are they to hold me up?" "I'll never get there! It'll be a mess!"	You lean on the horn. You weave in and out of traffic. You curse at drivers who respond to the jam nonchalantly.
Frustration with sex-role expectatons Concern with your adequacy as a parent	Your husband says, "The baby's crying pretty hard this time."	"Are you blaming me for it?" "So do something about it!"	"So what the hell do you want from me?" "Just leave me alone, will you?"
Concern with your adequacy as a student Competition (social, academic, etc.) with a roommate	Your roommate asks, "How's that paper of yours coming?"	"He's got nothing to do tonight, has he?" "Wouldn't he love it if I failed!"	"Why do you ask?" "I don't feel like talking about it, okay?" "Mind your own damn business."
Concern with your adequacy on the job Concern that your boss is acting like a parent—thwarting needs for independence and privacy	Your boss asks, "So how did that conference turn out?"	"I can handle conferences by myself!" "Always checking up on me!" "Dammit, I'm an adult!"	You get flustered and feel your face reddening. You are so enraged that you can barely speak. You excuse yourself. When alone, you kick your desk.
Conflict over expression of sexual needs Concerns about sexual adequacy	Your fiancé asks, "Did you have a good time tonight?"	"He's always testing me!" "Didn't *he* have a good time?"	"You feel your face redden. You scream, "Why do you always have to talk about it?"

Ongoing frustrations may cause us to respond to innocent activating events with irrational thoughts, anger, and inappropriate social behaviors.

Anger
Anger is a common emotional response to frustration and social provocations that can lead to aggressive behavior. One way of combating feelings of anger is to challenge the irrational beliefs that can give rise to or heighten them. We can also substitute assertive behavior for aggressive behavior.

upset or explode. Our behavior may seem inauthentic and we may disown it. We wind up feeling alienated and disappointed in ourselves.

Table 10.9 provides a number of examples of how ongoing frustrations can set the stage for the irrational *beliefs* behind the *consequences* of anger and aggression.

Using Rational Alternatives to Enraging Beliefs Since anger often stems from frustration, an ideal method for coping with anger is to remove sources of frustration. This may require creating plans for surmounting barriers or finding substitute goals. But when we choose to, or must, live with our frustrations we can still get in touch with our irrational beliefs, challenge them, and replace them with rational alternatives.

As with anxiety-evoking and depressing beliefs, we can pinpoint enraging beliefs by closely attending to our fleeting thoughts when we feel ourselves becoming angry. Or we can get in touch with them by "running a movie" (see Chapter 9). Once we have noted our automatic thoughts, let us consider: Are we jumping to conclusions about the motives of others? Are we overreacting to our own feelings of frustration? If so, we can construct and rehearse rational alternatives to our irrational beliefs, as in the examples in Table 10.10.

The rational alternatives in Table 10.10 have several functions:

1. They help you focus on your fleeting cognitive responses to an activating event and to weigh them.
2. They help you control your level of arousal.

TABLE 10.10   Irrational Thoughts That Intensify Feelings of Anger and Rational Alternatives

Activating Event	Irrational Thoughts	Rational Alternatives
Your mother asks, "Did you see a nice movie?"	"Why does she always ask me that?"	"She probably just wants to know if I had a good time."
	"That's my business!"	"She's not really prying. She just wants to share my pleasure and make conversation."
You are caught in a traffic jam.	"Who the hell are they to hold me up?"	'They're not doing it on purpose. They're probably as frustrated by it as I am."
	"I'll never get there! It'll be a mess!"	"So I'm late. It's not my fault and there's nothing I can do. When I get there, I'll just have to take a few minutes to get things straightened out. That's all."
Your husband says, "The baby's crying pretty hard this time."	"Are you blaming me for it?"	"Don't jump to conclusions. It's a statement of fact."
	"So do something about it!"	"Stop and think. Why not ask Mr. Macho to handle it this time?"
Your roommate asks, "How's that paper of yours coming?"	"He's got nothing to do tonight, has he?"	"The paper is difficult, but that's not his fault."
	"Wouldn't he love it if I failed?"	"I shouldn't assume I can read his mind. Maybe it's a sincere question. And if it's not, why should I let him get me upset?"
Your boss asks, "So how did that conference turn out?"	"I can handle conferences by myself!"	"Cool it! Relax. Of course I can handle them. So why should I get bent out of shape?"
	"Always checking up on me!"	"Maybe she's just interested, but checking up is a part of her job, after all."
	"Dammit, I'm an adult!"	"Of course you are. So why get upset?"
Your fiancé asks, "Did you have a good time tonight?"	"He's always testing me!"	"Stop and think! Maybe it's an innocent question—and if he is checking, maybe it's because he cares about my feelings."
	"Didn't *he* have a good time tonight?	"Stop reaching and digging for reasons to be upset. He only asked if I had a good time."

By replacing irrational, enraging thoughts with rational alternatives, we can avert uncalled-for feelings of anger and aggressive outbursts.

3. They help prevent you from jumping to conclusions about other people's intentions. Some people, of course, may have ulterior motives when they make "innocent" remarks, but we learn who they are and can handle them differently. We need not assume that everyone has such motives.
4. They help you focus on what is happening *now,* rather than on misinterpreting events because of years of ongoing frustration.

Sometimes you may feel yourself becoming angered by what someone says or does, but not be able to grasp the fleeting beliefs that are intensifying your feelings. In such a situation you can say things to yourself like "Stop and think!" "Don't jump to conclusions," or "Wait a minute before you do anything." Here are some suggestions from Novaco (1977):

"I can work out a plan to handle this. Easy does it."
"As long as I keep my cool, I'm in control of the situation."
"You don't need to prove yourself. Don't make more out of this than you have to."
"There's no point in getting mad. Think of what you have to do."
"Muscles are getting tight. Relax and slow things down."
"My anger is a signal of what I need to do. Time for problem solving."
"He probably wants me to get angry, but I'm going to deal with it constructively."

Other Methods for Coping with Anger
Other strategies for coping with feelings of anger include relaxation training, assertive behavior, and self-reward for self-control.

Using Relaxation
You can use one of the relaxation methods described earlier to counteract directly the arousal that accompanies feelings of anger. If you have practiced progressive relaxation, try the following: When you feel angry take a deep breath, tell your self to relax, and exhale. Allow the bodily sensations of relaxation to "flow in" and replace feelings of anger. If you are stuck in midtown traffic, take a breath, think "Relax," exhale, and then think about some of the pleasant activities or events you checked off earlier in the chapter. (But continue to pay some attention to other cars.)

Using Assertive Behavior Instead of Exploding
Assertive behavior involves expressing your genuine feelings and sticking up for your rights. Assertive behavior does *not* include insulting, threatening, or attacking. However, it is assertive (not aggressive), to express strong disapproval of another person's behavior and to ask that person to change his or her behavior.

In Table 10.11, we review some of the situations noted earlier, but now we suggest assertive responses as a substitute for aggressive responses to activating events. In Table 10.12, we present some new situations and compare potential assertive and aggressive responses to them.

Using Self-Reward
When you have coped with frustrations or provocations without becoming enraged and aggressive, pat yourself on the back. Tell yourself you did a fine job. Think, "This time I didn't say or do anything I'll regret later," or "This time I caught myself, and I'm proud of the way I handled things." Novaco (1977) suggests some additional self-rewarding thoughts:

"I handled that one pretty well. That's doing a good job."
"I could have gotten more upset than it was worth."
"My pride can get me into trouble, but I'm doing better at this all the time."
"I actually got through that without getting angry."

TABLE 10.11 Assertive Responses to Activating Events

Activating Event	Assertive Responses
You are caught in a traffic jam.	You admit to yourself, "This is damned annoying." But you also think, "But it is *not* a tragedy. *I* will control the situation rather than allow the situation to control me. *Relax.* Let those muscles in the shoulders go. When I arrive, I'll just take things step by step. If it works out, fine. If not, getting bent out of shape won't make things better.
Your roommate asks, "How's that paper of yours coming?"	You say, "It's a pain! I absolutely hate it! I can't wait till it's over and done with. So what're you up to?"

Assertive responses involve expression of genuine feelings.

Note the difference in your feelings when you have handled a frustration or a provocateur without becoming enraged or aggressive. When we commit ourselves to monitoring and working on our negative feelings, we take direct charge of our emotional lives rather than condemning ourselves to passively riding out the winds of whatever emotion is driving us from moment to moment.

In a sense, that is what this chapter has been about—taking charge of our lives rather than riding out the winds of our situations and our emotional responses.

TABLE 10.12 A Comparison of Aggressive and Assertive Responses to Provocative Activating Events

Provocation (Activating Event)	Aggressive Response	Assertive Response
Your supervisor says, "I would have handled that differently."	"Well, that's the way I did it! If you don't like it, fire me."	"What is your concern?" If the supervisor becomes argumentative, say, "I believe that I handled it properly because . . .". If you think that you were wrong, admit it straightforwardly."
A co-worker says, "You are a fool."	"Drop dead."	"That's an ugly thing to say. It hurts my feelings and I'd like an apology."
A provocateur says, "So what're yuh gonna do about it?"	You push or strike the provocateur.	You say "Goodbye" and leave.
Your roommate has not cleaned the room.	"Dammit! You're a pig! Living with you is living in filth."	"It's your turn to clean the room. You agreed to clean it, and I expect you to stick to it. Please do it before dinner."

■ Summary

1. **What are Meichenbaum's methods of controlling irrational and catastrophizing thoughts?** Meichenbaum suggests pinpointing irrational thoughts, replacing them with rational thoughts, and rewarding ourselves for doing so.
2. **What is meditation, and how does it help us lower arousal?** Meditation is a method of becoming relaxed by reducing awareness of the surrounding world and the problems of the day. To meditate, we relax in a calming setting and focus on a pleasant, repetitive stimulus, such as a mantra.
3. **How is biofeedback used to help us lower arousal?** We can use biofeedback to reverse various aspects of sympathetic nervous system arousal. For example, we can decrease muscle tension, slow our heart rates, or decrease the amount of sweat forming on our hands.
4. **What is progressive relaxation, and how does it help us lower arousal?** Progressive relaxation is Jacobson's method for alternately tensing then relaxing muscle groups in sequence. Progressive relaxation reverses the muscle tension associated with arousal and may also help through its suggestions of warm and heavy limbs.
5. **What is diaphragmatic breathing?** This is a method for breathing regularly and calmly "through" the diaphragm which may inhibit sympathetic activity by promoting parasympathetic activity.
6. **What methods are used to help alleviate the Type A behavior pattern?** Friedman and Ulmer suggest various methods for alleviating one's sense of time urgency, such as visiting museums and reading books; for alleviating hostility, such as complimenting people (when deserved); and for alleviating "self-destructive tendencies," such as stopping smoking, controlling heavy drinking, and reducing fat intake.
7. **What methods have been devised for enhancing psychological hardiness?** Maddi and Kobasa suggest techniques that enhance our senses of commitment, challenge, and control over our situations. In situational reconstruction, we consider how the situation could be worse and how we can improve it. In focusing we gain insight into underlying causes of our frustrations. We can use compensatory self-improvement when we can do nothing to regain losses in another area.
8. **What psychological methods of weight control are there?** Psychologists focus on improving nutritional knowledge (e.g., substituting healthful food for fattening, harmful foods); decreasing calorie intake; exercise in order to raise the metabolic rate; and behavior modification to help us avoid temptations and eat less.
9. **What methods of quitting and cutting down smoking are suggested by psychologists?** Quitting cold turkey is aided by making a public commitment, removing cues for smoking, and reinterpreting withdrawal symptoms as signs that we are winning. Suggestions for cutting down gradually include self-monitoring, chain breaking, and setting concrete reduced-smoking goals.
10. **Why are psychologists opposed to using sleeping pills to get to sleep?** We develop tolerance for sleeping pills so that we need progressively larger doses. Moreover, we attribute getting to sleep to the pills, not our self-efficacy.
11. **What are some psychological methods of coping with insomnia?** Psychological methods include lowering arousal, challenging irrational beliefs (such as the thought that something awful will happen if you don't get enough sleep tonight), using fantasy to distract yourself from the "task" of getting to sleep, and using stimulus control so that your bed comes to mean "sleep" to you.

12. **What are some psychological methods of coping with fears and phobias?** Methods include gradual approach and systematic desensitization. In each case we have the opportunity to reappraise fear-evoking stimuli.

13. **How do psychologists help students cope with test anxiety?** They help students pinpoint irrational beliefs that heighten anxiety and distract them from the tasks at hand. The irrational beliefs are challenged, and students learn other ways of lowering arousal. Also, students remain task-oriented.

14. **What are some psychological methods for coping with depression?** One is to pinpoint and challenge erroneous attributions for failure and cognitive distortions (e.g., minimization of achievements). Engaging in pleasant events (events incompatible with depression) and exercise also help.

15. **What are some psychological methods for coping with anger?** Psychological methods for coping with anger include a rational-emotive analysis of anger, in which social provocations are interpreted as activating events that trigger irrational beliefs—beliefs that frequently reflect ongoing frustrations. Challenging these beliefs, lowering arousal, and replacing aggressive behavior with assertive behavior are recommended.

■ TRUTH OR FICTION REVISITED

The best way to modify catastrophizing thoughts is to . . . modify them. True. Practicing rational alternatives is one method for doing so.

Meditation can help people with hypertension lower their blood pressure. True, as shown by Benson's research.

If you tell people just to allow their muscles to relax, many will have no idea what to do. True. This is why Jacobson devised the method by which people alternately tense then relax muscles.

You can decrease feelings of anxiety by regulating your breathing. True. Diaphragmatic breathing is one method for doing so, but we can also regulate our breathing by practicing meditation and progressive relaxation.

Modification of Type A behavior helps prevent recurrent heart attacks. True, according to research reported by Friedman and Ulmer.

Visiting museums and art galleries is one of the methods for treating Type A behavior. True. It helps alleviate the sense of time urgency.

Telling someone you love them is another method for treating Type A behavior. True. It helps alleviate feelings of hostility.

When your spouse insists on getting a divorce, learning to ski can help you cope. True. Learning to ski is an example of compensatory self-improvement.

A 220-pound person burns more calories running around the track than a 125-pound person. True. The heavier person is doing more work.

In quitting smoking, it is helpful to tell relatives and friends of plans to quit. True. Making a public commitment can help.

One way of coping with test anxiety is not to allow it to distract us from the test items. True. One of the ways in which test anxiety impairs test performance is by distracting us from the task at hand.

Psychologists have put together scientifically derived lists of turn-ons that can elevate your mood without your popping pills. True. They are pleasant events.

Wearing clean clothes and breathing clean air can help lift us out of feelings of depression. True. This is one of the many pleasant events that can help alleviate feelings of depression.

We cannot be expected to stand still for it when someone insults us or threatens our honor. False—sure we can! Why let someone else control our behavior, especially when we don't like what they are doing?

■ Scoring Key for the Suinn Test Anxiety Behavior Scale (STABS)

To attain your total STABS score, first assign points to your checkmarks according to the following code:

Not at all = 1
A little = 2
A fair amount = 3
Much = 4
Very much = 5

Add the numbers to find your total score. (You may want to include items on which you scored a 4 or a 5 in your cognitive restructuring program.)

The following norms for the 20-item STABS were attained with Northeastern University students. There were no sex differences.

Raw Stabs Score	Percentile
68	95
61	80
57	75
52	60
49	50
45	35
41	25
38	20
32	10

Adult Life in the World of Today

Adult Development: Passages

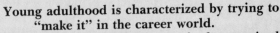

Young adulthood is characterized by trying to "make it" in the career world.

Men's early adult development is characterized by a shift from restriction to control, whereas women's development is more likely to be characterized by a shift from being cared for to caring for others.

Women experience a midlife crisis earlier than men do.

At about age 40 there is psychological shift from viewing our ages in terms of how many years have elapsed since we were born to how many years we have left.

There is a dramatic decline in physical strength and ability during middle adulthood.

Women at menopause encounter debilitating hot flashes.

Women tend to lose their sexual desire at menopause.

Most parents suffer from the "empty-nest syndrome" when the youngest child leaves home.

Women in their 50s tend to be more assertive than they are at earlier ages.

As people become older, they become more homogeneous—more alike in their attitudes and their behavior patterns.

Most of the elderly live with children, in institutions, or in retirement communities.

Retired people frequently become disenchanted with their new-found freedom.

The terminally ill undergo a predictable sequence of emotional and cognitive responses.

So, what now? You've been through the early childhood years of utter dependency on adults. You've come through elementary school and high school. You're developing plans about the career world and you may be thinking about marriage and a family. Maybe you've already got a good part of your early career laid out. Maybe you're already involved in an enduring intimate relationship or a marriage.

But what's going to happen as you journey through the years of your adult life? Is everything going to progress smoothly, right on course? What are some of the typical life experiences of 40-, 50-, and 60-year-olds? Do you ever think about the years of middle and late adulthood? Is it almost impossible to imagine that they will ever arrive? Given the alternative, let us hope that they do. And if you hold some fears or negative stereotypes of what it will be like to be a 45-year-old or a 55-year-old, let us also hope that this chapter will help to replace some of your prejudices with accurate information and positive expectations.

As your authors, we must admit that we cannot fully foresee what your life will be like in 20 years or in 40 years. As we noted in the Chapter 1, changes are occurring at ever accelerating paces, and it may be that our homes and our work lives will bear little resemblance to what they are today. But psychologists in recent years have made enormous strides in cataloguing and accounting for many of the psychological changes that we undergo as we travel through young, middle, and late adulthood. They have found that although we are unique as individuals, we also have a number of common experiences. Common experiences are beneficial in that they allow us to have some predictive power concerning our own futures. And, so to speak, "forewarned is forearmed." That is, when our futures are somewhat predictable, we can exert a good deal of control over our destinies: we can brace ourselves for inevitable negative life changes, and we can prepare ourselves to take advantage of our opportunities.

We think that the weight of the theory and research concerning adult development reinforces the view that there is a great deal of future to look forward to. Yes, there are alligators in the streams, and occasionally some of the strands of our rope bridges get frayed. Yes, accidents, illnesses, and failures can foreclose opportunities at any time. But for most of us the outlook is reasonably bright—in terms of our physical, cognitive, and personality development.

■ Young Adulthood

Young or early adulthood covers the two decades from the ages of 20 to 40.

Physical Development

Although Olympic gymnasts are frequently in their early teens, most of us reach our physical peaks during the 20s. Everything else being equal, it is during that decade and the early 30s that we are faster, stronger, better coordinated, and have more endurance than we ever had or will have again. Experience interacts with physical development so that many professional athletes, such as football players and golfers, come into their own after they have been in the league or on the circuit for a few years.

Cognitive Development

Longitudinal studies in which people are given intelligence tests repeatedly over the years suggest that we are also at the height of our cognitive powers during early adulthood (Rebok, 1987). Many professionals show the broadest knowledge of their fields at about the time they are graduating from college or graduate school. At this time their coursework is "freshest," and, often, they have just recently studied for comprehensive examinations. Once they

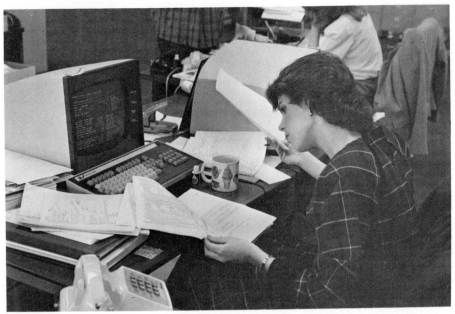

Beginning a career is one of the so-called developmental tasks of young adulthood.

Intimacy versus isolation.
Erikson's life crisis of young adulthood, which is characterized by the task of developing abiding intimate relationships.

Ego identity. According to Erikson, a firm sense of who one is and what one stands for.

enter their fields they often specialize. As a result, their knowledge becomes deeper in certain areas, but understanding of peripherally related areas may become relatively superficial.

Personality Development and Adjustment

Personality development concerns the ways in which we adapt to the challenges of our lives at various ages. We shall primarily discuss personality development according to the views of Erik Erikson, Robert Havighurst, Daniel Levinson and his colleagues, and the journalist Gail Sheehy. But there are other noted views, such as Roger Gould's "transformations" and Carol Gilligan's insights into the factors that influence women, and we shall refer to them as well.

Erikson's Stages of Psychosocial Development

According to Erik Erikson (1963), whose theory of psychosocial development was outlined in Chapter 2, young adulthood is the stage of **intimacy versus isolation.** Erikson saw the establishment of intimate relationships as a central task of young adulthood. Young adults who have evolved a firm sense of identity during adolescence are now ready to "fuse" their identities with those of other people through relationships such as marriage and the establishment of abiding friendships.

Erikson warns that we may not be capable of committing ourselves to others in a meaningful way until we have achieved **ego identity,** or established stable life roles. Achieving ego identity in Erikson's theory is the central task of adolescence. Lack of personal stability may be one reason that teenage marriages suffer a much higher divorce rate than those formed in adulthood.

A recent study found suggestions of Erikson's predicted relationships between ego identity and the achievement of intimacy (Kahn et al., 1985). Men who develop a strong sense of ego identity by young adulthood get married earlier than men who do not. Women with well-developed senses of identity, on the other hand, *maintain* more stable marriages. The discrepancy may be explained by the fact that women in our society encounter greater pressure than men to get married—ready or not, so to speak (Gilligan, 1982).

For women, then, the test of stability is more likely to be whether they endure in relationships, not whether they enter them (Kahn et al., 1985).

In any event, Erikson argues that people who do not reach out to develop intimate relationships may risk retreating into isolation and loneliness.

Havighurst's Developmental Tasks

Developmental psychologist Robert Havighurst (1972) lists a number of tasks for each stage of development, beginning in childhood. As we grow older, the tasks that apply to us broaden our social worlds and increase in complexity. As in Erikson's theory, successful achievement of a developmental task at one stage brings feelings of fulfillment and facilitates achievement of tasks during subsequent stages.

Havighurst's developmental tasks for young adulthood include:

1. Selecting and courting a mate
2. Learning to live contentedly with one's partner
3. Starting a family and becoming a parent
4. Rearing children
5. Assuming the responsibilities of managing a home
6. Beginning a career or job
7. Assuming some civic responsibilities
8. Establishing a social network

It is immediately evident that Havighurst's tasks exclude many of us—those who remain single, those who postpone (or forego) childbearing, those who prefer to be and live by themselves, and those who are not civic-minded, to name but a few. Havighurst admitted that his list was culture-specific and sort of "all-American"—that is, strongly influenced by American ideals and explicit social norms.

We think that there is danger in believing that Havighurst's tasks ought to apply to each of us equally. Such an interpretation gives us many "oughts" and "shoulds" to live up to, and they may not fit all of us very well. Perhaps the best use of Havighurst's lists is as a reminder of stereotypical expectations for each stage of development. That is, they inform us of what many people expect. With this rationale, we shall list Havighurst's tasks for each stage of adult development.

Levinson's Seasons

According to Daniel Levinson's in-depth study of 40 men, which was published in 1978 as *The Seasons of a Man's Life*, we enter the adult world in our early 20s (see Figure 11.1). Upon entry we are faced with the tasks of exploring adult roles (in terms of careers and intimate relationships, for example) and of establishing some stability in the roles we choose. At this time we also often adopt a **dream**, which serves as a tentative blueprint for our lives and is characterized by the drive to "become" someone, to leave our mark on history.

Sheehy's Passages

U.S. surveys show that adults in their 20s tend to be fueled with ambition as they strive to establish their pathways in life (Gould, 1975; Sheehy, 1976). In her popular book *Passages*, Gail Sheehy (1976) labeled the 20s the **Trying 20s**—a period during which people strive basically to advance themselves in the career world.

In one phase of her work, reported in *Passages*, Sheehy interviewed 115 people drawn largely from the middle and upper classes, including many managers, executives, and other professionals. In another phase, she examined 60,000 questionnaires filled out by readers of *Redbook* and *Esquire* magazines, reported in her 1981 book *Pathfinders*. The young adults in her samples were concerned about establishing their pathways in life, finding their places in the world. They were generally responsible for their own support, made their own choices, and were largely free from parental influences.

Dream. In this usage, Levinson's term for the overriding drive of youth to become someone important, to leave one's mark on history.

Trying 20s. Sheehy's term for the third decade of life, when people are frequently occupied with advancement in the career world.

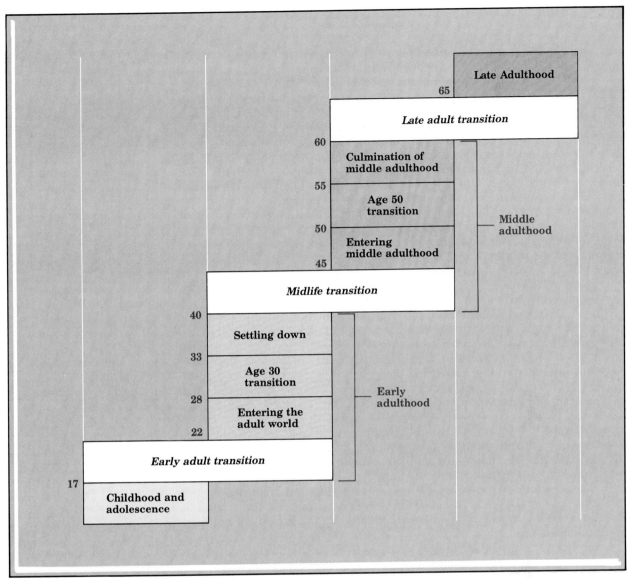

FIGURE 11.1   The Seasons of a Man's Life

Daniel Levinson and his colleagues (1978) further break down young, middle, and late adulthood into a number of developmental periods, including transitions. Our major tasks as we enter the adult world are to explore, and to establish some stability in, our adult roles. During the age 30 transition we reevaluate our earlier choices. How does women's adult development differ from men's?

Sheehy noted that during the 20s we often feel "buoyed by powerful illusions and belief in the power of the will [so that] we commonly insist . . . that what we have chosen to do is the one true course in life" (1976, p. 33). This "one true course" usually turns out to have many swerves and bends. As we develop, what seemed important one year can lose some of its allure in the next. That which we hardly noted can gain prominence. We can also be influenced in unpredictable ways by chance encounters with people who gain sudden prominence in our lives (Bandura, 1982).

Sex Differences   On the basis of his samples drawn from psychiatric clinics, psychiatrist Roger Gould (1975) suggested that men's development seems generally guided by needs for **individuation** and **autonomy**. Psychologists

Individuation. The process by which one separates from others and gathers control over his or her own behavior.

Autonomy. Self-direction.

Age 30 transition. Levinson's term for the ages from 28 to 33, which are characterized by reassessment of the goals and values of the 20s.

who have focused on the development of women, such as Judith Bardwick (1980) and Carol Gilligan (1982) have found that women are relatively more guided by changing patterns of attachment and caring (Bardwick, 1980; Gilligan, 1982). In becoming adults men are likely to undergo a transition from restriction to control. But women, as pointed out by Gilligan in her 1982 book *In a Different Voice,* are relatively more likely to undergo a transition from being cared for to caring for others.

Levinson has recognized that he was remiss in studying only men in his earlier years, and he has recently become involved in research into the "seasons" of women's lives. One of his findings is that many young successful businesswomen differ from their male counterparts in that they do not have long-term goals: "They want to be independent but they are conflicted about ambition" (cited in Brown, 1987). Some of the conflict stems from concerns as to whether ambition is compatible with femininity. Other conflicts stem from practical concerns about balancing a career with a home life and child rearing.

Although there are very important differences in the development of women and men, a study by Ravenna Helson and Geraldine Moane (1987) of the University of California found that between the ages of 21 and 27, college women do develop in terms of individuation and autonomy. That is, they tend increasingly to assert control over their own lives. They come to accept the differences between romanticized visions of the way the world ought to be and the way it really is, and they broaden their psychological understanding of the people who matter to them. On the other hand, they also become more introspective and vulnerable.

Separation from Parents

In his developmental theorizing, Gould tends to focus on "transformations" in people's ideas about, and relationships with, their parents. He also notes common, but not universal, "false assumptions" we tend to have at certain ages. For example, between the ages of 16 to 22, many of us believe, "My parents will always be my parents. I'll always believe in them." Gould considers the major developmental tasks of these years as including moving away from home and abandoning the idea that one's parents are always right.

Between the ages of 22 to 28, Gould notes additional false assumptions about parents—first, that we must do things the ways our parents do if we want to be successful; and second, that our parents will be there to rescue us if things don't work out. According to Gould, it is our task to become increasingly independent of parents during these years. Optimal development means exploring adult roles, abandoning the notion that imitating our parents is right for us, and learning to pick ourselves up if we fall down.

During the 30s, many women are concerned about nearing the end of the fertile years, the closing down of opportunities, and heightened responsibilities at home and work.

The Age 30 Transition

Levinson labeled the ages of 28 to 33 the **age 30 transition.** This is for many a period of reassessment of the choices made during the early 20s. A number of researchers have noted that women frequently encounter a crisis that begins between the ages of 27 and 30 (Reinke et al., 1985). During the early 30s many of the women studied by Helson and Moane (1987) felt exploited by others, alone, weak, limited, and as if they would "never get myself together." Concerns about nearing the end of the fertile years, opportunities closing down, and heightened responsibilities at home and work all contribute to these feelings of inadequacy. Levinson notes that women also have cause for fearing success:

> By and large the image of a highly successful career woman is a single woman. But there is a flip side. The image of the single, childless career woman sitting alone by the fire at night is a powerful image today, one that is frightening to a lot of women, particularly businesswomen. Very few women get to their late 30s without strongly wanting to have children (Brown, 1987).

Catch 30s. Sheehy's term for the fourth decade of life, when many people undergo major reassessments of their accomplishments and goals.

Menopause. The cessation of menstruation.

For men and women, the late 20s and early 30s are commonly characterized by self-questioning: "Where is my life going?" "Why am I doing this?" Sheehy (1976) labeled the 30s the **Catch 30s** because of such reassessment. During the 30s we often find that the life styles we adopted during the 20s do not fit so comfortably as we had anticipated.

One response to the disillusionments of the 30s, according to Sheehy,

is the tearing up of the life we have spent most of our 20s putting together. It may mean striking out on a secondary road toward a new vision or converting a dream of "running for president" into a more realistic goal. The single person feels a push to find a partner. The woman who was previously content at home with children chafes to venture into the world. The childless couple reconsiders children. And almost everybody who is married . . . feels a discontent (1976, p. 34).

Many people make major life changes in their 30s, 40s, and even later in life (Sheehy, 1981). Making successful life changes requires risk taking, but risk taking in itself is no guarantee of success. Successful "life-changers" also show foresight, psychological androgyny, and strong belief in their purpose.

Settling Down   According to Levinson, the ages of about 33 to 40 are characterized by settling down. Men during this period still strive to forge ahead in their careers, their interpersonal relationships, and their communities. During the latter half of their 30s, men are also concerned about "becoming one's own man." That is, they desire independence and autonomy in their careers and adult relationships. Promotions and pay increases are important as signs of success.

Sheehy similarly found that young adults who had successfully ridden out the storm of reassessments of the Catch 30s begin the process of "rooting" at this time. They feel a need to plant roots, to make a financial and emotional investment in their homes. Their concerns become more focused on promotion or tenure, career advancement, and long-term mortgages.

■ Middle Adulthood

Middle adulthood spans the years from 40 to 60 or 65. Some authors, such as Levinson and his colleagues (1978), consider the years from 60 to 65 separately as a transition to late adulthood. Let us consider some of the physical and cognitive changes that take place in middle adulthood. Then we turn our attention once more to personality development.

Physical Development

In terms of physical development, at age 40 we do not possess quite the strength, coordination, and stamina that we had during our 20s and early 30s. This decline is most obvious in the professional ranks where peak performance is at a premium. Gordie Howe still played hockey at 50 and George Blanda was still kicking field goals at that age, but most professionals at these ages can no longer keep up with the "kids."

But the years between 40 and 60 are reasonably stable. There is some gradual physical decline, but it is minor and only likely to be of concern if we insist on competing with young adults—or with idealized memories of ourselves at younger ages. On the other hand, a great many of us first find or make the time to develop our physical potentials during middle adulthood. The 20-year-old couch potato occasionally becomes the 50-year-old marathon runner. By any reasonable standard, we can maintain excellent cardiorespiratory condition throughout middle adulthood.

Menopause   **Menopause,** or the cessation of menstruation, usually occurs during the late 40s or early 50s, although there are wide variations. Menopause is the final stage of a broader female experience, the **climacteric,** which is caused by a falling off in the secretion of the hormones estrogen and progesterone. The climacteric begins with irregular periods and ends with menopause.* With menopause, **ovulation** and reproductive capacity also draw to an end. There is also some atrophy of breast tissue and a decrease in the elasticity of the skin. There can also be a loss of bone density which leads to **osteoporosis** in late adulthood.

During the climacteric some 50 to 85 percent of women encounter symptoms such as hot flashes (uncomfortable sensations characterized by heat and perspiration), insomnia, fatigue, labored breathing, and mood changes as a result. However, in most cases these symptoms are relatively mild, and menopause does not signal the end of a woman's sexual interests (Sarrell & Sarrell, 1984; Skalka, 1984). Physical changes that stem from falloff in hormone production are frequently controlled by estrogen-replacement therapy—although this treatment has side effects and is not used universally. Perhaps a more important issue is the meaning of menopause to the individual. Women who equate menopause with loss of femininity are likely to encounter more distress than those who do not (Rathus, 1983). Highly traditional women who have tied their self-esteem to their reproductive and child-rearing capacities are likely to find menopause most stressful and depressing. Some women, however, greet menopause with relief. As with other major life events and potential sources of stress, acccurate information (which enhances predictability and allows women to choose how they will respond) and social support help (Turner & Helms, 1987). Adjustment is also influenced by the woman's perceptions of the ways in which women in her family, particularly her mother, and her peers respond to menopause (Millette & Hawkins, 1983).

Cognitive Development

Cognitive development is reasonably stable during middle adulthood (Rebok, 1987). There may be gradual falling off of skills and knowledge in areas that we have largely ignored since school days. However, we may have enhanced our skills and knowledge in the areas in which we are regularly involved, as at work and in our leisure activities.

Again, our adjustment is advanced by modifying our self-expectations. Although we may have lost some skills that we had at an earlier age, there is no reason to assume that it will be difficult for us to learn to handle new technologies—such as acquiring capacity to use microcomputers or statistics. The task is to undertake our learning in an orderly manner and allow ourselves time to learn. Learning takes time at any age, but as we become older we sometimes erroneously attribute "not getting it the first time" to age and not to the difficulty of the subject matter or the quality of instruction.

Personality Development and Adjustment

Erikson's Stages of Psychosocial Development   Erikson (1963) labels the life crisis of the middle years as that of **generativity versus stagnation.** In other words, are we still striving to produce or to rear our children well, or are we marking time, treading water? Generativity by and large requires doing things that we believe are worthwhile. In so doing we enhance and maintain our self-esteem. Generativity also involves the Eriksonian ideal of helping shape the new generation. This shaping may involve rearing our own children, or generally working to make the world a better place. And many of us find great satisfaction in these tasks.

Climacteric. The multiyear process triggered by falloff in production of sex hormones in which menstrual periods become irregular and finally cease.

Ovulation. The releasing of an ovum (egg cell) from an ovary.

Osteoporosis. A condition characterized by porosity, and hence brittleness, of the bones, more common among women.

Generativity versus stagnation. Erikson's term for the crisis of middle adulthood, characterized by the task of being productive and contributing to younger generations.

*There are many other reasons for irregular periods, and women who encounter them are advised to discuss them with their doctors.

■ A CLOSER LOOK

Myths About Menopause

We are better able to adjust to life's changes when we have accurate information about them. Menopause is a major life change for most women, and many of us harbor misleading and maladaptive ideas about it. Consider the following myths and realities about menopause (Turner & Helms, 1987):

Myth 1. *Menopause is abnormal.* The reality is that menopause is a normal developmental event in women's lives.

Myth 2. *The medical establishment defines menopause as a disease.* No longer. Today menopause is conceptualized as a "deficiency syndrome," in recognition of the dropoff in secretion of estrogen and progesterone. Unfortunately, the term *deficiency* also has negative and possibly harmful meanings.

Myth 3. *After menopause, women need complete replacement of estrogen.* Not necessarily. Some estrogen is still produced by the adrenal glands, fatty tissue, and the brain, and the pros and cons of estrogen-replacement therapy are still being debated.

Myth 4. *Menopause is accompanied by depression and anxiety.* Not necessarily. Much of the emotional response to menopause reflects its meaning to the individual rather than physiological changes themselves.

Myth 5. *At menopause, women suffer debilitating hot flashes.* Many women do not have them at all, and for those who do, these symptoms are usually mild.

Myth 6. *A woman who has had a hysterectomy will not undergo menopause afterward.* It depends on whether the ovaries, which are the major producers of estrogen, were removed along with the uterus. If they were left in, menopause should proceed as usual.

Myth 7. *Menopause signals an end to women's sexual interests.* Not at all. In fact, many women feel freed by the final severing of the links between sexual expression and reproduction.

Myth 8. *A woman's general level of activity is lower after menopause.* Research actually shows that many women tend to become peppier and more assertive at this time of life.

Myth 9. *Men are not affected by their wives' menopause.* Many of them are, of course. But men could become more supportive if they knew more about menopause and if their wives felt freer to communicate about it with them.

Havighurst's Developmental Tasks Havighurst's tasks for middle adulthood include:

1. Facilitating our children's transition from home life to "making it" in the outside world
2. Developing engrossing leisure activities
3. Relating to one's spouse as a person
4. Assuming important social and civic responsibilities
5. Maintaining satisfactory performance in one's career
6. Adjusting to the physical changes that attend middle age
7. Adjusting to aging parents

According to Erikson, one of the major challenges of middle adulthood is the shaping of the younger generation. These parents are helping their daughter get started in college.

We remind you of the "disclaimer" made in the section on young adulthood: Havighurst's tasks in many cases reflect ideals more than realities, and we urge readers not to consider them standards by which they should judge themselves.

Levinson's Seasons   According to Levinson, there is a **midlife transition** at about 40 to 45 that is characterized by a dramatic shift in psychological perspective. Previously we had thought of our ages largely in terms of the number of years that have elapsed since birth. But once the midlife transition takes place, there is a tendency to think of our ages in terms of the number of years we have left.

Men in their 30s still think of themselves as part of the Pepsi Generation, older brothers to "kids" in their 20s. But at about 40 to 45, some marker event—illness, a change on the job, the death of a friend or of a parent, or being beaten at tennis by one's child—leads men to realize that they are a full generation older than 20-year-olds.

During this transition it strikes men that life may be more than halfway over. There may be more to look back upon than forward to. It dawns on men that they'll never be president or chairperson of the board. They'll never play shortstop for the Dodgers. They mourn their own youth and begin to adjust to the specter of old age and the finality of death.

The Midlife Crisis   The midlife transition may trigger a crisis referred to as the **midlife crisis.** The middle-level, middle-aged businessperson looking ahead to another 10 to 20 years of grinding out accounts in a Wall Street cubbyhole may encounter severe depression. The housewife with two teenagers, an empty house from 8:00 to 4:00, and a 40th birthday on the way may feel that she is coming apart at the seams. Both feel entrapment and loss of purpose. Some people are propelled into extramarital affairs at this time by the desire to prove to themselves that they remain attractive.

The Dream: Inspiration or Tyrant?   Until midlife, the men studied by the Levinson group were largely under the influence of their dream—the overriding drive of youth to "become," to be the great scientist or novelist, to leave one's mark on history. At midlife we must come to terms with the discrepancies between our dream and our actual achievements. Middle-aged people who free themselves from their dream find it easier to enjoy the passing pleasures of the day.

Sheehy's Passages   Remember that Levinson's study was carried out with men. Women, as suggested by Sheehy and other writers (e.g., Reinke et al., 1985), might undergo a midlife transition a number of years earlier. Sheehy (1976) writes that women enter midlife about 5 years earlier than men, at about 35 rather than 40. Entering midlife triggers a sense of urgency, of a "last chance" to do certain things.

What is so special about the mid-30s for women? Sheehy notes that:

35 is the average age at which women send the youngest child off to school
35 is the beginning of the so-called age of infidelity
35 is the average age at which married women who had stayed in the home to rear a family reenter the work force
34 is the average age at which divorced women get remarried
35 is the age at which wives most frequently run away
35 brings nearer the end of the childbearing years

Let us add that at age 35 women are usually first advised to have their fetuses routinely tested for Down syndrome and other chromosomal disorders (see Chapter 16). At age 35 women also enter high-risk categories for side

Midlife transition. Levinson's term for the ages from 40 to 45, which are characterized by a shift in psychological perspective from viewing ourselves in terms of years lived to viewing ourselves in terms of the years we have left.

Midlife crisis. A crisis experienced by many people during the midlife transition when they realize that life may be more than halfway over and reassess their achievements in terms of their dreams.

During the midlife transition, people realize that life may be more than halfway over. It dawns on men that they'll never be president or play shortstop for the Dodgers. They mourn their own youth and begin to adjust to the specter of advanced age.

effects of birth-control pills. In any event, Sheehy refers to the years between 35 and 45 as the **Deadline Decade.** This decade is characterized by recognition of one's own mortality in women and men. There is reevaluation of youthful illusions and, often, there is turmoil.

The study of college women by Helson and Moane (1987) suggests that many women in their early 40s may already be emerging from some of the fears and uncertainties that are first confronting men. For example, they found that women at age 43 are more likely than women in their early 30s to feel confident; to exert an influence on their communities; to feel secure and committed; to feel productive, effective, and powerful; and to extend their interests beyond their own families.

The Comeback Decade After the midlife crisis, many middle-aged people experience a new sense of commitment to their families and their work. Sheehy refers to the years of 46 to 55 as the **Comeback Decade,** suggesting that we can emerge from the "Deadline Decade" (35–45) in good psychological shape. We can improve our balancing of work and play, adjust to our middle placement among the generations, and become more accepting of our mortality. Of course, there can be new problems as well, especially if our evaluation of how far we have come, in relation to our dream, falls miserably short.

Some of the advice of cognitive therapists, as noted in Chapter 9, can help us adjust when our self-evaluations are harsh. For example, we can ask ourselves whether we are being overly perfectionistic, minimizing our accomplishments, and catastrophizing our shortcomings. And if we still fall short, we can enhance our psychological hardiness by aiming toward compensatory self-improvement, as suggested by Salvatore Maddi (see Chapter 10). Why not take up skiing, or scuba diving, or photography?

The Freestyle Fifties For those of us who come through the 40s in reasonably good shape, the 50s can be much more relaxed and productive. Sheehy refers to this decade as the **Freestyle 50s,** in recognition that we can reach our peak productivity and immensely enjoy our social relationships. The 50s can mark especially significant changes for women.

The Empty-Nest Syndrome In earlier decades psychologists placed great emphasis on a concept referred to as the **empty-nest syndrome** that applied to women in particular. It was assumed that women experienced a profound sense of loss when the youngest child went off to college, got married, or moved into an apartment. As noted by Harbeson (1971), "Many married women arrive at middle age without having looked and planned far enough ahead, and experience difficulties in making the transition from motherhood to socially useful occupations" (p. 139). Because of overcommitment to rearing a family and lack of planning for a productive life once the "nest" is empty, women were thought to lose their sense of meaningfulness and to become depressed.

However, research findings have shown a much more mixed and, frankly, optimistic picture. Certainly there can be problems, and these apply to both parents. Perhaps the largest of these is letting go of one's children after so many years of mutual interdependence (Bell, 1983). The stresses of letting go can be compounded when the children are also ambivalent about becoming independent.

But we must also note that many mothers report increased marital satisfaction and personal changes such as greater mellowness, self-confidence, and stability after the children have left home (Reinke et al., 1985). One study of life satisfaction among Americans found that both men and women with children over 17 reported more general life satisfaction and more positive

Deadline Decade. Sheehy's term for the ages of 35 to 45, which are characterized by recognition of mortality, turmoil, and reassessment of youthful dreams.

Comeback Decade. Sheehy's term for the ages of 46 to 55 which can be characterized by development of new coping strategies.

Freestyle 50s. Sheehy's term for the decade that can be characterized by peak productivity and enjoyment of social relationships.

Empty-nest syndrome. A sense of depression and loss of purpose experienced by some parents when the youngest child leaves home.

feelings than parents of younger children (Campbell, 1975). A number of studies have found that middle-aged women show increased dominance and assertiveness, an orientation toward achievement, and greater influence in the worlds of politics and work (Serlin, 1980; Sheehy, 1976). It is as if they are cut free from traditional shackles by the knowledge that their childbearing years are behind them. In fact, this is a time of increased freedom for both parents (Dyer, 1983). They have frequently become free of financial worries and are now also free to travel. They have the opportunity to experiment with new activities, which is one of the reasons that the 50s can be characterized as "freestyle." Slightly more than half the women whose children have left the nest are now in the work force. Some have returned to college.

Of course there is wide variation. But it is highly encouraging that the stage of adulthood that frequently begins with such a sense of time urgency, of "deadlines," frequently develops into a stage of new freedoms and self-development.

■ Late Adulthood

> Most people say that as you get old you have to give up things. I think you get old because you give up things.
> Senator Theodore Francis Green, age 87, *Washington Post,* June 18, 1954

> The idea that society can provide only a limited number of jobs, and that the elderly are the logical ones to be left out, is no longer tenable. There are unlimited goods and services needed and desired in American society. Among the greatest resources that could be channeled toward these ends are the experience, skill and devotion of America's elderly millions.
> Mae Rudolph, *Family Health,* March 1970

> How old would you be if you didn't know how old you was?
> Satchel Paige, ageless baseball pitcher

> The true test of maturity is not how old a person is but how he reacts to awakening in the midtown area in his shorts.
> Woody Allen, *Without Feathers*

Late adulthood begins at age 65. One reason that developmental psychologists have become concerned about the later years is the so-called demographic imperative (Swensen, 1983). That is, more of us are swelling the ranks of the nation's elderly all the time. More Americans than ever before are 65 or older because of improved health care and knowledge of the importance of diet and exercise. In 1900 only one American in 30 was over 65, as compared to one in nine in 1970. By the year 2020, perhaps one American in five will be 65 or older (Eisdorfer, 1983).

Another reason for the increased interest in aging is the recognition that, in a sense, *all* development involves aging. Developmental psychologist Bernice Neugarten (1982) suggests that development and aging are similar, perhaps synonymous, terms.

A third reason for studying the later years is to learn how we can further promote the health and psychological well-being of the elderly. The later years provide opportunities to do things other than setting the stage for dying.

Physical Development

A number of changes—some of them problematic—do occur during the later years. Changes in calcium metabolism lead to increased brittleness in the bones and heightened risk of breaks from accidents like falls. The skin becomes less elastic, subject to wrinkles and folds.

The senses become less acute. The elderly see and hear less acutely (Belsky, 1984), and because of a decline in the sense of smell, they may use more spice to flavor their food. The elderly require more time, or **reaction**

Late adulthood. The last stage of life, beginning at age 65.

Reaction time. The amount of time required to respond to a stimulus.

▉ Q U E S T I O N N A I R E ▉

Attitudes toward Aging

What are your assumptions about late adulthood? Do you see the elderly as basically different from the young in their behavior patterns and their outlooks, or just as a few years more mature?

To evaluate the accuracy of your attitudes toward aging, mark each of the following items true (T) or false (F). Then turn to the answer key at the end of the chapter.

T F **1.** By age 60 most couples have lost their capacity for satisfying sexual relations.

T F **2.** The elderly cannot wait to retire.

T F **3.** With advancing age people become more externally oriented, less concerned with the self.

T F **4.** As individuals age, they become less able to adapt satisfactorily to a changing environment.

T F **5.** General satisfaction with life tends to decrease as people become older.

T F **6.** As people age they tend to become more homogeneous—that is, all old people tend to be alike in many ways.

T F **7.** For the older person, having a stable intimate relationship is no longer highly important.

T F **8.** The aged are susceptible to a wider variety of psychological disorders than young and middle-aged adults.

T F **9.** Most older people are depressed much of the time.

T F **10.** Church attendance increases with age.

T F **11.** The occupational performance of the older worker is typically less effective than that of the younger adult.

T F **12.** Most older people are just not able to learn new skills.

T F **13.** When forced to make a decision, elderly persons are more cautious and take fewer risks than younger persons.

T F **14.** Compared to younger persons, aged people tend to think more about the past than the present or the future.

T F **15.** Most elderly people are unable to live independently and reside in nursing home-like institutions.

time, to respond to stimuli. Elderly drivers need more time to respond to traffic lights, other vehicles, and changing road conditions.

As we grow older, our immune systems also function less effectively, leaving us more vulnerable to disease.

Cognitive Development

The elderly show some decline in general intellectual ability as measured by scores on intelligence tests. The drop-off is most acute on timed items, such as those on many of the "performance" scales of the Wechsler Adult Intelligence Scale. Performance items contain tasks such as putting puzzles together, copying designs with blocks, and learning to associate meaningless symbols with numbers—all of them to be completed within time limits.

Although changes in reaction time, intellectual functioning, and memory are common, we understand very little about *why* they occur (Storandt,

1983). Loss of sensory acuity and of motivation to do well may contribute to lower scores. Elderly psychologist B. F. Skinner (1983) argues that much of the fall-off is due to an "aging environment" rather than an aging person. That is, in many instances the behavior of elderly people goes unreinforced. Note that nursing home residents who are rewarded for remembering recent events show improved scores on tests of memory (Langer et al., 1979; Wolinsky, 1982). Skinner (1983) suggests many strategies that the elderly can adopt to enhance their sensory and motor functioning, memory, and even to cope with mental fatigue.

In some cases, supposedly "irreversible cognitive changes" may also reflect psychological problems such as depression (Albert, 1981). Such changes are neither primarily cognitive nor irreversible. If the depression is treated effectively, intellectual performance may also improve.

However, the elderly often combine years of experience with high levels of motivation on the job. In these cases, forced retirement can be an arbitrary and painful penalty for no sin other than turning 65 or 70. According to Kimmel,

> Up to the age of 65 there is little decline in learning or memory ability; factors of motivation, interest, and lack of recent educational experience are probably more important in learning complex knowledge than age per se. Learning may just take a bit longer for the elderly and occur more at the individual's own speed instead of at an external and fast pace (1974, p. 381).

Theories of Aging

Although it may be hard to believe that it will happen to us, everyone who has so far walked the Earth has aged—which may not be a bad fate, considering the alternative. Why do we age? Various factors, some of which are theoretical, apparently contribute to aging.

Heredity plays a role. **Longevity** runs in families. People whose parents and grandparents lived into their eighties and nineties have a better chance of reaching these years themselves.

Environmental factors influence aging. People who exercise regularly appear to live longer. Disease, stress, obesity, and cigarette smoking can contribute to an early death. Fortunately, we can exert control over some of these factors.

According to psychologist Judith Rodin, elderly people show better health and psychological well-being when they do exert control over their own lives (Rodin & Langer, 1977; Wolinsky, 1982). Unfortunately, some elderly people are placed in nursing homes and surrender independence because of a decline in health and finances. But even in the nursing home, they fare better when they are kept well-informed and allowed to make decisions on matters that affect them.

There are several biological theories of aging. The **cellular-aging theory** suggests that the DNA within cells, which carries the genetic code of the individual, suffers damage from external factors (like ultraviolet light) and random internal changes. As the person ages, the ability to repair DNA decreases. Damage and other changes eventually accumulate to the point where affected cells can no longer reproduce or serve their bodily functions. Another view is that waste products within cells eventually accumulate so that many cells are poisoned and no longer capable of functioning. These views are currently somewhat speculative.

Alzheimer's Disease

Alzheimer's disease, which may afflict 2 to 5 percent of elderly persons (Sloane, 1983), rarely afflicts persons in middle adulthood. The disease is associated with the degeneration of cells in an area of the brain (the hippocampus) that normally produces large amounts of the neurotransmitter **acetylcholine,** or ACh. The brain cells, or neurons, that are involved collect plaques (dark areas of cellular "garbage") and die off in large numbers.

Longevity. A long span of life.

Cellular-aging theory. The view that aging occurs because bodily cells lose the capacity to reproduce and maintain themselves.

Alzheimer's disease. A disorder caused by falloff in production of acetylcholine and degeneration of brain cells and characterized by memory loss and disorientation.

Acetylcholine. A neurotransmitter involved in memory formation and other functions.

Ego integrity versus despair. Erikson's term for the crisis of late adulthood, characterized by the task of maintaining one's sense of identity despite physical deterioration.

The affected area of the brain and ACh are involved in the formation of new memories. For this reason, one of the cardinal symptoms of Alzheimer's disease is progressive memory loss and disorientation. But memories for remote events may remain reasonably intact. The older the individual, the greater the risk of Alzheimer's disease. The causes of Alzheimer's are unclear, but they may involve some combination of genetic factors, early viral infections, and accumulations of metals such as zinc and aluminum in the brain (Turkington, 1987).

Alzheimer's usually comes on gradually among the elderly, over a period of 8 to 20 years. At first victims note memory loss and frequently get lost—even in their own homes. Eventually they may become highly disoriented; fail to recognize other people, including family members; show childish emotions; and lose the ability to take care of their own hygiene and dress.

Researchers are investigating ways of controlling Alzheimer's disease, ranging from diets low in metals to the transplanting of ACh-producing cells into the affected areas of the brain. Elderly people with Alzheimer's or with less dramatic memory problems can make behavioral adjustments as well. All of us, not only the elderly, profit from keeping pads and pencils near the phone so that we can readily record messages. We can keep calendars and mark down scheduled events, even routine daily events. Persons with memory loss can mark off each day as it passes. Medicine containers with compartments for each day of the week are available at pharmacies. The establishment of daily routines and environmental prompts is of great value to the elderly (Skinner, 1983).

Personality Development and Adjustment

Erikson's Stages of Psychosocial Development   According to Erikson, late adulthood is the stage of **ego integrity versus despair.** The basic conflict is to maintain the belief that life is meaningful and worthwhile in the face of the inevitability of death. Ego integrity derives from wisdom, from the acceptance of one's life span as occurring at a certain point in the sweep of

Erikson was optimistic about late adulthood. Research finds, too, that most of the elderly are reasonably well satisfied with their lives.

history and as being limited. We spend most of our lives accumulating things and relationships. Erikson also argues that adjustment in the later years requires the wisdom to be able to let go.

Erikson was optimistic. He believed that we can maintain a sense of trust through life and avoid feelings of despair. And research does suggest that most of the elderly are reasonably well satisfied with their lives, as we shall see below.

Peck's Extension of Erikson's Views

According to Robert Peck (1968), who has extended Erikson's views, a number of psychological shifts aid us in adjusting to late adulthood:

1. Coming to value wisdom more than physical strength and power
2. Coming to value friendship and social relationships more than sexual prowess*
3. Retaining emotional flexibility so that we can adjust to changing family relationships and the ending of a career
4. Retaining mental flexibility so that we can form new social relationships and undertake new leisure-time activities
5. Keeping involved and active and concerned about others so that we do not become preoccupied with physical changes or the approach of death
6. Shifting interest from the world of work to retirement activities

Havighurst's Developmental Tasks

Havighurst's developmental tasks for late adulthood include:

1. Adjusting to physical changes
2. Adjusting to retirement and to changes in financial status
3. Establishing satisfying living arrangements
4. Learning to live with one's spouse in retirement (e.g., coping with being home much of the time)
5. Adjusting to the death of one's spouse
6. Forming new relationships with aging peers
7. Adopting flexible social roles

Levinson's Seasons

Because his subjects were predominantly middle-aged, Levinson had relatively little to say about late adulthood, although he did suggest the existence of a late adult transition between the ages of 60 and 65 (see Figure 11.1), which is characterized by new reevaluation of our progress in relation to the dreams formed at earlier ages.

Sheehy's Passages

Sheehy (1976), on the other hand, noted some commonalities among her subjects in the 60s, 70s, and 80s. She labeled the 60s the **Selective 60s** because during this decade we are better able to sort out the truly important from the trivial. During the 60s our personalities can reach the height of development, becoming most distinct. We may also retain the high level of excitement about life that is often experienced during the "freestyle" 50s.

Sheehy refers to the 70s as the **Thoughtful 70s,** recognizing that during this decade many of us have surmounted the problems and concerns of the day and have the opportunity to sit back and reflect. Most of us continue to enjoy our cognitive capacities and are independent, healthy, and happy.

Sheehy's sample did not extend beyond the 80s, and she labels this decade the **Proud-to-Be 80s.** Many of her subjects who had reached this

Selective 60s. Sheehy's term for the decade in which we can separate the important from the trivial.

Thoughtful 70s. Sheehy's term for the decade in which we are independent and involved and plan ahead.

Proud-to-Be 80s. Sheehy's term for the decade in which we take pride in continued survival and competence.

---

*However, most of us continue, or can continue, to enjoy sexual expression for a lifetime, and we should not fall prey to the stereotype of the elderly as asexual (Rathus, 1983). See Chapter 15.

decade take pride in their continuing competence at meeting the challenges of their lives. Although they may need help and comfort from others, they can also give help and comfort to their children, grandchildren, and peers. Those who are well adjusted have managed somewhat to transcend physical concerns by remaining involved and mentally active.

Adjustment Among the Elderly   Sheehy's "passages"—her characterizations of the 60s, 70s, and 80s—are filled with cause for optimism. Does research bear out her point of view? By and large, it seems to do just that.

Despite the changes that occur with aging, one survey of people aged 70 to 79 found that 75 percent were generally satisfied with their lives (Neugarten, 1971). A more recent study of people retired for from 18 to 120 months found that 75 percent rated retirement as mostly good (Hendrick et al., 1982). Over 90 percent were generally satisfied with life, and more than 75 percent reported their health as good or excellent.

Adjustment among the elderly, as at any age, is related to our financial security and our physical health. That is, the sicker we are, the less likely we are to be well adjusted. Also, there is a link between financial status and physical health: poor elderly people are more likely to report ill health than are the financially secure (Birren, 1983). This finding would seem to call for better health care for the aged, and it does. But it may also be that people who have been healthier over the years are also better able to provide for their own financial security.

Among the elderly, as among younger people, there remains a relationship between social support and adjustment. Elderly couples are less lonely and more happy than the single or the widowed (Barrow & Smith, 1983). In Chapter 16 we shall see that widows with children are also better adjusted than other widows, a prospect that contributes to some people's desire for children. Once retired, couples tend to spend more time together and their relationship tends to improve and take on greater importance (Atchley, 1980; Harris & Cole, 1980).

Living Arrangements   There are some stereotypes concerning living arrangements for the elderly. One has them living with children; another in institutions. Still another has them buying recreational vehicles and taking off for condominiums or retirement communities in the sunbelt.

First let us put to rest the stereotype that elderly people are dependent on others in their living arrangements. According to the U.S. Bureau of the Census (1985), nearly 70 percent of heads of households aged at least 65 own their own homes. Also, only about 10 percent of the elderly reside in institutions (Turner & Helms, 1987). The populations of nursing homes are disproportionately old, with most residents aged 80 or above.

And despite the stereotype of taking off for the sunbelt, the majority of the elderly remain in their home towns and cities. Moving is stressful at any age, and apparently most of the elderly prefer to remain in familiar locales. However, when elderly people do decide to move, it appears that carefully made plans and adequate financial resources markedly decrease the stressfulness of moving (Hendrick et al., 1982).

Economics   Here, too, there are some stereotypes. Often the elderly are portrayed as living in poverty or at the mercy of their children and external forces, such as government support. Unfortunately, some of these stereotypes are based on reality. People who no longer work are usually dependent on savings and fixed incomes such as pensions from their places of work and social security payments. The flip side of the coin is that nationwide only about 13 percent of those aged 65 and above live below the official poverty level (Schultz, 1982; U.S. Census of the Bureau, 1985). But the financial status of elderly black people is worse: Two out of three live below the poverty level.

Kinship and Grandparenthood   There is a saying that grandparents have more relaxed relationships with their grandchildren than they did with their own children. Perhaps. Certainly their perspectives have grown broader over the years. Whereas parents may fret and worry, grandparents may have learned that children will turn out to be all right most of the time. Also, they can reap the enjoyment of grandchildren without bearing the brunt of the responsibility for caring for them.

More than 80 percent of elderly people have children and interact with them regularly (Lee, 1980). They frequently pass power to the family's middle generation and sometimes allow their children to manage their finances. They frequently attempt to balance their own needs for maintaining independence with their needs for continuing involvement with their children and grand-children. How often they see the children and grandchildren and whether they have the right to make "suggestions" become very important issues. Although many elderly people worry that their families might no longer need them or want them around, the elderly are not usually alienated from, or rejected by, their children (Francis, 1984).

Grandparents are frequently valued by their children for the roles they play with their grandchildren. On a very practical level, having retired grand-parents available for babysitting and picking the children up at school is ex-tremely valuable, especially with more and more mothers working outside the home. Many adults regret that the need to move to new locales to climb the corporate ladder has separated their children from their grandparents. Grandparents also often serve as special sources of wisdom, love, and under-standing. As noted, they are frequently more relaxed and less demanding with their grandchildren than with their own children.

Retirement   Although major life changes can be stressful, research shows that retirement can be a positive step. According to psychologist Joan Crow-ley, who analyzed U.S. Department of Labor data on 1,200 elderly men, "most people are perfectly happy not to have to get up each morning to go to work" (1985, p. 80). Many retirees enjoy their leisure, and some continue to engage in part-time labor, paid or voluntary (see Figure 11.2). Crowley argues that most people who deteriorate rapidly after retirement were unhealthy prior to retirement.

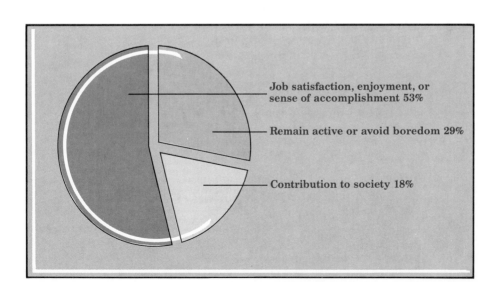

Job satisfaction, enjoyment, or sense of accomplishment 53%

Remain active or avoid boredom 29%

Contribution to society 18%

FIGURE 11.2   Why Retired People Return to Work

As reported in *The Wall Street Journal,* one third of a surveyed group of re-tired senior executives re-turned to full-time work within eighteen months of retirement. The rea-sons are shown in the chart.

Atchley's Phases of Retirement   Robert Atchley (1985) has theorized that many elderly people undergo a six-phase developmental sequence of retirement:

1. *The Preretirement Phase.* This phase involves fantasies about retirement—positive and negative. Company preretirement programs and retired friends can foster adjustment by providing accurate information about financial realities and postretirement life-styles.
2. *The Honeymoon Phase.* This phase often involves the euphoria that accompanies new-found freedom. It is a busy period during which people do the things they had fantasized doing once they had the time—as financial resources permit.
3. *The Disenchantment Phase.* As one's schedule slows down and one discovers that fantasized activities are less stimulating than anticipated, disenchantment can set in.
4. *The Reorientation Phase.* Now a more realistic view of the possibilities of retirement develops. Now retirees frequently join volunteer groups and increase civic involvements.
5. *The Stability Phase.* Now the retirement role has been mastered. Routine and stability set in; there is more accurate self-awareness of one's needs and strengths and weaknesses.
6. *The Termination Phase.* Retirement can come to an end in different ways. One is death; another is the assumption of the sick role because of disability. Still another is return to work.

As noted in Figure 11.2, a number of people do return to some form of work after retiring. For them, the benefits of employment apparently outweigh the lure of leisure.

■ On Death and Dying

Death is the last great taboo. Psychiatrist Elisabeth Kübler-Ross comments on our denial of death in her landmark book *On Death and Dying:*

> We use euphemisms, we make the dead look as if they were asleep, we ship the children off to protect them from the anxiety and turmoil around the house if the [person] is fortunate enough to die at home, [and] we don't allow children to visit their dying parents in the hospitals (1969, p. 8).

In this section we explore a number of aspects of death and dying. First we consider the pioneering theoretical work of Kübler-Ross and the writings of more recent theorists. Then we examine issues concerning dying with dignity, the funeral, and the process of bereavement.

Theoretical Perspectives

Kübler-Ross's Theory   From her work with terminally ill patients, Kübler-Ross found some common responses to news of impending death. She identified five stages of dying through which many patients pass, and she suggests that elderly people who suspect that death is approaching may undergo similar emotional and cognitive responses. The stages are:

1. *Denial.* In the denial stage, people feel, "It can't be me. The diagnosis must be wrong." As noted by Carroll (1985), denial can be flat and absolute, or it can fluctuate so that now the patient accepts the medical verdict, now the patient starts chatting animatedly about distant plans.
2. *Anger.* Denial usually gives way to anger and resentment toward the young and healthy, and, sometimes, toward the medical establishment—"It's unfair. Why me?"

3. *Bargaining.* Next people may try to bargain with God to postpone death, promising, for example, to do good deeds if they are given another six months, another year.
4. *Depression.* With depression come feelings of loss and hopelessness—grief at the specter of leaving loved ones and life itself.
5. *Final acceptance.* Ultimately an inner peace may come, a quiet acceptance of the inevitable. Such "peace" does not resemble contentment; it is nearly devoid of feeling.

Shneidman's Theory   Psychologist Edwin Shneidman (1984) acknowledges the presence of feelings such as those described by Kübler-Ross, but he does not perceive them to be linked in sequence. Instead, Shneidman suggests that people show a variety of emotional and cognitive responses that tend to be fleeting or relatively stable, to ebb and flo, and to reflect pain and bewilderment. He also points out that the kinds of responses shown by individuals reflect their personality traits and their philosophies of life.

Research is more supportive of Shneidman's views than Kübler-Ross's. Reactions to nearing death turn out to be quite varied. For example, Robert Kastenbaum (1977) found that some people are reasonably accepting of the inevitable; others are despondent; still others are terrorized. Some people show a rapid shifting of emotions, ranging from rage to surrender, from envy of those who are younger and healthier to moments of yearning for the inevitable (Shneidman, 1984). Richard Kalish and David Reynolds (1976) questioned several hundred young adults, middle-aged persons, and elderly people in the Los Angeles area about their feelings concerning death. Generally speaking, the elderly thought more about death, but death was somewhat less frightening for them than it was for the younger groups.

Pattison's Theory   E. Mansell Pattison (1977) agrees with Shneidman that people respond in different ways to impending death, but believes that the process of dying can be described in terms of three overall phases:

1. *The acute phase.* The acute phase immediately follows awareness of imminent death and is characterized by a crisis involving strong feelings of anxiety. Powerful feelings of anger and resentment may also be present.
2. *The chronic living-dying interval.* The chronic living-dying interval follows and is characterized by a reduction in the initial anxiety. However, various combinations of other feelings rise to the fore and may be no less unpleasant. These include fear of the unknown; loneliness; sorrow; feelings of shame and inadequacy that may stem from loss of control over body functions; suffering and pain; and loss of identity. Overall, there is a sense of loss of human contact, self-control, and self-esteem.
3. *The terminal phase.* The final phase is characterized by emotional and cognitive withdrawal from people and the events of the day. Other strongly felt emotions may persist, but they seem overwhelmed by the central phenomenon of withdrawal.

Pattison suggests a number of guidelines for helping dying people, such as

Providing social support
Providing accurate information as to what might be experienced in terms of pain and loss of body functions and control
Acknowledging the reality of the impending loss of family and other people
Helping the person make final financial and legal arrangements
Allowing the person to experience grief

Hospice. A homelike environment in which the staff help a dying person and his or her family adjust to impending death.

Euthanasia. Mercy killing.

Assuming maintenance of necessary body functions in a way that allows the person to maintain dignity, and

Pointing out that the person should not engage in self-blame for the loss of control over body functions

Dying with Dignity

Dying people, like other people, have needs for self-confidence, security, and dignity. They may also need relief from pain, and a medical controversy is raging concerning the advisability of providing them with powerful, addictive pain-killing drugs (e.g., narcotics) that are unavailable to the general public. We believe that the dignity and immediate pain of dying people should take precedence over broader political issues in making such decisions. We also agree with Gray (1984) that the medical staff should anticipate and prevent extremes of pain rather than simply respond to patients' requests. Finally, the dying patient should have the right to decide how much pain-killing medicine is enough.

The dying also often need to share their emotional pain (Hendin, 1984; Turner & Helms, 1987). Sometimes it is helpful to encourage the dying to feel free to talk about what they are feeling. It can also be helpful just to be there with them—not to withdraw from them when they may be so afraid themselves of withdrawing from everything that they value and hold dear.

The Hospice Movement   The word **hospice** derives from the same root that has given rise to the words *hospital* and *hospitality*. It has come to refer to homelike environments in which terminally ill people can face death with physical and emotional supports that provide them with dignity.

In contrast to hospitals, hospices do not restrict visiting hours. Family and friends work with a specially trained staff to provide emotional support. Again, as in contrast to hospital procedures, patients are given as much control over their lives as they can handle. So long as their physical conditions permit, patients are encouraged to make decisions as to what they will eat, how they will spend the day, and what medication they will receive—including a "cocktail" that consists of sugar, narcotics, alcohol, and a tranquilizer (Holden, 1982). The goal of the cocktail is to reduce pain and anxiety without clouding awareness and cognitive functioning—although this goal cannot usually be perfectly met. Relatives and friends frequently maintain contact with staff in order to work through their bereavement once the patient has died (Kübler-Ross & Magno, 1983; Saunders, 1984).

Euthanasia   The term **euthanasia** derives from the Greek roots *eu,* meaning "well," and *thanatos,* meaning "death." In Chapter 6 we saw that *eustress* was coined by Selye to refer to healthful stress. *Thanatos* was adopted by Sigmund Freud as the name of his theoretical death instinct, and "Thanatopsis" is the name of Bryant's poem about death, to which we shall refer in the following pages. If the hospice cocktail is controversial, euthanasia is much more so.

Euthanasia is also referred to as "mercy killing." Euthanasia is likely to be considered when there is no hope for a patient's recovery and the patient is either unconscious (as in a coma) or in relentless pain and requests death. It can be brought about in two broad ways. In positive or active euthanasia, the patient is given high doses of drugs, such as the narcotic morphine, that will induce death painlessly. As of this writing, positive euthanasia is illegal throughout the United States. Negative or passive euthanasia, by contrast, refers to *not* preventing death. Negative euthanasia is sometimes practiced by

Living will. A document that expresses the wish not to be kept alive by extraordinary support systems in the event of terminal illness and inability to express this decision at the time.

denying comatose patients medicine, food, or access to life-support systems such as respirators. The legal status of negative euthanasia varies somewhat from locale to locale.

Perhaps the best-known case of negative euthanasia involved Karen Anne Quinlan, who lapsed into a coma in 1975. When the medical community agreed that there was no hope for her recovery, the New Jersey Supreme Court in 1976 granted permission to have her life-supporting respirator removed, although Quinlan would continue to be fed intravenously. Remarkably Quinlan "lived"* until 1985.

The Living Will   The **living will** is a recently conceived legal document in which people request that they not be kept "alive" by artificial support systems, such as respirators, when there is no hope for recovery. The goals of the living will are to spare individuals the indignity of being kept "alive" by "tubes" and complex medical equipment and to spare their families the misery of visiting them in the hospital setting and coping with their states. The living will is intended to bring the inevitable to a conclusion so that people can deal with it and get on with their lives.

The Funeral

The funeral is an organized, ritualistic way of responding to death in which a community acknowledges that one of its members has died. When as individuals we might not know how to cope with the passing of a family member, the funeral provides us with customary behavior patterns. In part we are adhering to religious beliefs and cultural formalities. But we are also enlisting professionals to carry on when our grief would impair our own attendance to details.

In a sense, we also become somewhat prepared for the loss of our own family members when we attend the funerals of people who are further removed from us. And especially for people who are religious, the funeral cognitively ties in a family member's death to the ongoing progress of time and the universe.

Raether and Slater (1977) have found that funerals tend to have five common phases:

1. *Separation of the dead from the living.* The dead person is physically removed and prepared for final disposition.
2. *Visitation.* Many religions provide for defined periods of time during which people come to the funeral home (or comparable setting) to see the body and socially support the family of the deceased. If the deceased person is a public figure, he or she may "lie in state" for a defined period, allowing the public to come by and adjust.
3. *The funeral rite.* This is the ceremony that recounts the life of the deceased person, testifying as to its meaning. In the United States, most funeral rites are defined by religious customs.
4. *The procession.* The people who attend the funeral follow the body to the place of disposition, such as the cemetery. Moving *to* the cemetery is thought to help family and friends accept the loss. Later, moving *away from* the cemetery is symbolic of family and friends beginning to get on with their lives.
5. *Committing the body to its final resting place.* In this act the finality of death is again underscored. And again, the need for the survivors to go on is suggested.

*That is, her heart continued to beat although she had been considered "brain dead."

Bereavement. The saddened, lonely state of those who have experienced the death of a loved one.

Bereavement

Those who are left behind, as those who learn of impending death, undergo a complex range of powerful emotions. The term **bereavement** refers to the state of the survivors. It implies feelings of sadness and loneliness, and a process of mourning.

There are so many aspects to bereavement: sorrow, emptiness and numbness, anger ("Why did he or she have to die?" "How could they let this happen?" "What do I do now?"), loneliness—even relief, as when the deceased person has suffered over a prolonged period and we feel that we have reached the limits of our abilities to help sustain him or her. Death also makes us mindful of our own mortality (Kalish, 1985).

Investigators have also derived stages or phases of grief and mourning—for example numbness and shock, followed by preoccupation with the loved one and acute expressions of grief, and, finally, acceptance of the loss and return to functioning within society (Parkes & Weiss, 1983).

Many mourners apparently find it helpful to "rework" the events leading up to the loss, such as the details of what happened in the hospital. You may listen to the spouse of the deceased describe these events for nearly an hour and then be surprised to hear him or her go through it again, with equal intensity, when another person comes to visit.

Usually, the most intense grief is encountered after the funeral, when the relatives and friends have gone home and the bereaved person is finally alone. Then he or she may have to finally come to grips with the reality of an empty house, of being truly alone. For this reason, it is helpful to space one's social support over a period of time, not to do everything at once. We are not suggesting that expressions of concern are artificial and to be preplanned; we are merely pointing out that mourning takes time and that support is helpful throughout the process, not just at the beginning.

The bereaved do usually "come back" from their losses. They may never forget the deceased person, but they become less preoccupied with him or her. They resume certain routines at work or in the home. They may never be as happy or satisfied with life as they were, but most of the time they resume functioning. And sometimes they grow in compassion because of their loss. They gain a deeper appreciation of the value of life.

"Lying Down to Pleasant Dreams . . ."

The American poet William Cullen Bryant is best known for his poem "Thanatopsis," which he composed at the age of 18. "Thanatopsis" expresses Erik Erikson's goal of ego integrity, Erikson's optimism that we can maintain a sense of trust through life. By meeting squarely the challenges of our adult lives, perhaps we can take our leave with dignity. When our time comes to "join the innumerable caravan"—the billions who have died before us—perhaps we can depart life with integrity.

Live, wrote the poet, so that

> . . . when thy summons comes to join
> The innumerable caravan that moves
> To the pale realms of shade, where each shall take
> His chamber in the silent halls of death,
> Thou go not, like the quarry-slave at night,
> Scourged to his dungeon, but, sustained and soothed
> By an unfaltering trust, approach thy grave
> Like one who wraps the drapery of his couch
> About him, and lies down to pleasant dreams.

Bryant, of course, wrote "Thanatopsis" at 18, not 85, the age at which he died. At that advanced age his feelings, his pen, might have differed. But literature and poetry, unlike science, need not reflect reality. They can serve to inspire and warm us.

■ Summary

1. **How are the stages of adulthood divided?** Most researchers divide adulthood into young adulthood (ages 20 to 40), middle adulthood (ages 40 to 60 or 65), and late adulthood (age 65 and above).

2. **What happens to cognitive and physical development during young adulthood?** Cognitive and physical development are at their peaks during young adulthood.

3. **Who are the major theorists of adult personality development?** They include Erik Erikson, who theorized stages of psychosocial development; Robert Havighurst, who catalogued developmental tasks; Daniel Levinson, who described the "seasons" of men's lives; journalist Gail Sheehy, who proposed various "passages" we go through. Psychologists such as Judith Bardwick and Carol Gilligan have focused on the development of women.

4. **How do these theorists describe the major events of young adulthood?** Erikson sees the establishment of intimate relationships as the central task. Other theorists focus on striving to advance in the career world. Many suggest some sort of reassessment at about age 30, and Levinson proposes that we settle into our roles at about 35.

5. **What sex differences are there in the development of personality during young adulthood?** Men's development seems to be characterized by a transition from restriction to control, and women's development, according to Gilligan, is characterized by a transition from being cared for to caring for others. Many women are conflicted about success in the career world because of a career's impact on family life.

6. **What cognitive and physical changes take place during middle adulthood?** There is a slight and gradual decline in overall cognitive abilities and in physical functioning. Because of falloff in estrogen production, women usually encounter the climacteric in the 40s and menopause in the late 40s or early 50s.

7. **What is menopause, and how does it affect women?** Menopause is a normal process whose symptoms are mild for most women. Menopause is cessation of menstruation. Since it signals the end of reproductive capacity, menopause can have complex and powerful meanings for women. But despite stereotypes of middle-aged women as irritable and depressed, women are frequently peppier and more assertive following menopause.

8. **What is the midlife transition, and why does it affect women and men at different ages?** The midlife transition is a shift in psychological perspective from self-perception in terms of how many years we have lived to how many years we have left. In men it usually arrives at about age 40 and is triggered by a marker event, such as death of a parent or peer. According to Sheehy, women undergo a midlife transition about five years earlier than men do, at age 35. It is triggered by awareness of the nearing of the end of the childbearing years.

9. **What is the midlife crisis?** The midlife crisis is a period of major reassessment during which we evaluate the discrepancies between our achievements and our youthful dreams. We recognize our limits, including our mortality.

10. **What is the empty-nest syndrome?** This is a cluster of symptoms including depression and loss of purpose which is theorized to affect parents,

especially mothers, when the last child leaves home. Although an "empty nest" requires adjustment and the ability to let go, many parents enjoy new-found freedoms at this time.

11. **Why does Sheehy refer to the 50s as the Freestyle 50s?** This is because many of us reach our peaks of productivity, a measure of financial freedom, and are also "over the hump" in terms of child-rearing.

12. **What physical and cognitive changes take place during late adulthood?** The elderly show less sensory acuity, and reaction time increases. Some presumed cognitive deficits may actually reflect declining motivation or psychological problems such as depression. There is continued decline in strength and stamina—also in the immune system, increasing vulnerability to disease.

13. **What theories of aging are there?** Heredity plays a role in longevity. We do not know exactly why people age, although one possibility is that cells lose the abilities to maintain themselves and reproduce adequately. But environmental factors such as exercise, proper diet, and the maintenance of responsibility can apparently delay aging.

14. **How do personality theorists characterize the major challenges and changes of late adulthood?** Tasks of late adulthood include adjusting to retirement and maintaining one's ego identity and self-concept in the face of physical decline.

15. **How well adjusted are the elderly?** Most elderly people rate their life satisfaction and their health as generally good. Retirement can be a positive step, so long as it is voluntary. Having adequate financial resources is a major contributor to satisfaction among the elderly.

16. **What theories are there concerning death and dying?** Kübler-Ross identifies five stages of dying among the terminally ill: denial, anger, bargaining, depression, and final acceptance. However, research by other investigators, such as Shneidman, shows that psychological reactions to approaching death are more varied and more closely related to the individual's personality and philosophy of life.

17. **How can people be helped to die with dignity?** Others can help them discuss their anxieties and fears, make legal and financial arrangements, provide social support, allow them to spend their last days as they wish, and provide sufficient pain-killing medication. The living will permits people to state that they do not want to be sustained by life-support systems if because of illness their daily existence is painful or meaningless.

18. **How does the funeral affect adjustment to death of a loved one?** The funeral provides community rituals that relieve the bereaved of the need to plan and take charge during the crisis of death. The rituals help the bereaved accept the finality of death and point to their eventual return to communal functioning.

19. **What is bereavement?** Bereavement is a normal process of grieving or mourning that begins with sadness and preoccupation with images of the deceased and gradually leads to return to communal functioning.

■ TRUTH OR FICTION REVISITED

Young adulthood is characterized by trying to "make it" in the career world. True, according to Sheehy, Gould, and other investigators.

Men's early adult development is characterized by a shift from restriction to control, whereas women's development is more likely to be characterized by a shift from being cared for to caring for others. True, according to Gould, Gilligan, and other investigators.

Women experience a midlife crisis earlier than men do. True, according to Sheehy's research.

At about age 40 there is psychological shift from viewing our ages in terms of how many years have elapsed since we were born to how many years we have left. True. This phenomenon in part defines the midlife transition.

There is a dramatic decline in physical strength and ability during middle adulthood. False. Actually, the decline is quite gradual.

Women at menopause encounter debilitating hot flashes. False. Some women do not have them at all, and for most women these flashes are mild.

Women tend to lose their sexual desire at menopause. False. In fact some women feel sexually liberated because of the separation of sexual expression and reproduction.

Most parents suffer from the "empty-nest syndrome" when the youngest child leaves home. False. There can be some conflicts concerning letting go, but for most parents this is a period of new-found freedom.

Women in their 50s tend to be more assertive than they are at earlier ages. True. Perhaps menopause helps free them from traditional feminine, passive social roles.

As people become older, they become more homogeneous—more alike in their attitudes and their behavior patterns. False. Older people may share some common concerns, but they retain their stamps as unique individuals.

Most of the elderly live with children, in institutions, or in retirement communities. False. Most of the elderly own their own homes in the communities where they had previously lived and worked.

Retired people frequently become disenchanted with their new-found freedom. True. Many of them return to work.

The terminally ill undergo a predictable sequence of emotional and cognitive responses. False. This statement is consistent with Kübler-Ross's theory but is not borne out by psychological research.

■ Answer Key to Attitudes toward Aging

1. False. Most healthy couples continue to engage in satisfying sexual activities into their 70s and 80s.
2. False. This is too general a statement. Those who find their work satisfying are less desirous of retiring.
3. False. In late adulthood we tend to become more concerned with internal matters—our physical functioning and our emotions.
4. False. Adaptability remains reasonably stable throughout adulthood.
5. False. Age itself is not linked to noticeable declines in life satisfaction. Of course, we may respond negatively to disease and losses, such as death of a spouse.
6. False. Although we can predict some general trends for the elderly, we can also do so for the young. The elderly remain heterogeneous in personality and behavior patterns.
7. False. Elderly people with stable intimate relationships are more satisfied.
8. False. We are susceptible to a wide variety of psychological disorders at all ages.
9. False. Only a minority are depressed.
10. False. Actually church attendance declines, although there is no difference in verbally expressed religious beliefs.
11. False. Although reaction time may increase and general learning ability may undergo a slight decline, the elderly usually have little or no difficulty at familiar work tasks. In most jobs experience and motivation are more important than age.

12. False. Learning may just take a bit longer.
13. False.
14. Elderly people do not direct a higher proportion of thoughts toward the past than younger people do; but we may spend more time daydreaming at any age if we have more time on our hands.
15. Only about 10 percent of the elderly require some form of institutional care (Turner & Helms, 1987).

The Challenge of the Workplace

12

Many million-dollar lottery winners feel aimless and dissatisfied if they quit their jobs after striking it rich.

Successful salespeople have a need for honesty.

Anybody who has the ability to get ahead would be satisfied with prestigious vocations such as college professor, psychologist, physician, or lawyer.

Women who wear perfume to interviews are more likely to get the job

It's a good idea to ask for the lowest salary you can get by on at a job interview.

In dual-career marriages, today's couples consider the woman's work as important as the man's.

Hard work is the most powerful predictor of who gets ahead in the United States.

Efficient, skillful employees are evaluated more highly than hard-working employees who must struggle to get the job done.

Allowing employees to piece together their own work schedules is demoralizing to workers and interferes with productivity.

Stressed workers have more accidents on the job.

Apathetic workers are most likely to experience job burnout.

Most workaholics have severe adjustment problems.

Women in the United States account for 99 percent of secretaries, but only 2 percent of mechanics.

Women average only about 60 percent of the earnings of men.

Extrinsic. External, coming from outside.

Intrinsic. Internal, coming from within.

At the turn of the century, British playwright George Bernard Shaw pronounced, "Drink is the greatest evil of the working class." Upon sober reflection, he added that "Work is the greatest evil of the drinking class."

Humor aside, work for most in Shaw's day involved back-breaking physical labor or mind-numbing factory work, sunrise to sunset, six days a week. In this chapter we shall see that most of today's workers, living in a more affluent, technologically advanced society, are less likely to abide being just another cog—even a highly paid cog—in the industrial machine.

In this chapter we first examine motives for working and see how workers' values have changed over the years. Then we follow the stages of vocational development and see how knowledge of our coping styles can enhance the vocational decision-making process. We discuss adjustment in the workplace. We find out who gets ahead in America and see how industrial/organizational psychologists have contributed to our knowledge of factors that enhance job satisfaction—from biases in the process of worker appraisal to organizational structure. Then we look at women on the job and explore issues such as the earnings gap between the sexes, sexual harrassment, and the adjustment of men who work for women supervisors. Finally, we turn our attention to the stresses of unemployment and note some innovative methods for finding new jobs.

■ Seeking Self-Fulfillment in the Workplace

In Chapter 1 we noted that the workplace is in flux and that many workers fear that they will become obsolete. In this section we explore motives for working and values concerning the workplace, and we see that some time-honored motives and values may be headed toward obsolescence.

Extrinsic versus Intrinsic Motives for Working

There is no doubt that one of the major reasons, if not *the* major reason, for working is economic. Work provides us with the financial means for paying our bills. The paycheck, fringe benefits, security in old age—all these are external or **extrinsic** motives for working. But work also satisfies many internal or **intrinsic** motives, including the opportunity to engage in stimulating and satisfying activities. It is not totally surprising that many million-dollar lottery winners who quit their jobs encountered feelings of aimlessness and dissatisfaction (Kaplan, 1978). Other intrinsic reasons for working include the work ethic, self-identity, self-fulfillment, self-worth, the social values of work, and social roles:

1. *The Work Ethic.*

> In works of labor, or of skill,
>   I would be busy too;
> For Satan finds some mischief still
>   For idle hands to do.
>   ISAAC WATTS

The so-called work ethic is the belief that we are morally obligated to engage in productive labor, to avoid idleness or laziness. Adherents to the work ethic view life without work as unthinkable and perhaps immoral, even for people who are financially independent.

2. *Self-Identity.* Our occupational identities become intertwined with our self-identities. We are likely to think, "I *am* a nurse" or "I *am* a lawyer" rather than "I assist in operations and bathe patients" or "I plea bargain with the district attorney and write last wills and testaments." Psychological bonds to work permit us to think of ourselves as *having careers* or occupations, not as simply *holding jobs*.

We work for many reasons—for extrinsic benefits such as money and fringe benefits and for intrinsic motives, such as the work ethic, doing what is consistent with our self-identities, seeking self-fulfillment, enhancing our self-worth, extending our social contacts, and carrying out our social roles in the community.

3. *Self-Fulfillment.* We often express our personal needs, interests, and values through our work. We may choose a profession that allows us to express these interests. Your authors entered psychology because they were interested in learning about other people and themselves. The self-fulfilling values of the work of the astronaut, scientist, and athlete may seem obvious. But factory workers, plumbers, police officers, and fire fighters can also find self-enrichment as well as cash rewards for their work.

4. *Self-Worth.* Recognition and respect for a job well done contribute to our self-esteem. For some, self-worth may ride on accumulating money. For a writer, self-worth may hinge upon acceptance of a poem or article by a magazine. When we fail at work, our self-esteem plummets as sharply as the bank account.

5. *Social Values of Work.* The workplace extends our social contacts. It introduces us to friends, lovers, even challenging adversaries. At work we are likely to meet others who share our interests and goals, and to form supportive social networks that in our highly mobile society must sometimes substitute for family.

6. *Social Roles.* Work roles help define our functions in the community. Communities have their public identities: druggist, shoemaker, teacher, doctor. Family roles are also influenced by members' roles in the social fabric. Traditionally, men have been the breadwinners and women the homemakers, but these stereotypical patterns have been changing. Today both spouses are likely, as one television commercial phrased it, "to bring home the bacon and fry it in a pan."

Traditional versus "New Breed" Values Concerning the Workplace

Americans once held many job-related values sacred. These included the central importance of money and loyalty to one's company. But since the turbulent 1960s and 1970s, a new generation of workers has matured. Many of them possess values that set these standards topsy-turvy. Yankelovitch (1981) labels today's workers a "new breed." Their values are contrasted with those of traditional workers in Table 12.1.

A survey of 23,000 *Psychology Today* readers (Renwick & Lawler, 1978) illustrates these shifting patterns of values. The *Psychology Today* sample was overrepresented by affluent, professional, well-educated, and female workers. But this is all to the good because readers of this book are also overrepresented by these groups. The sample may thus be quite relevant. In any event, survey respondents specified that the opportunity for self-growth was the most important factor in working. Two of three reported that they would *not* take a higher-paying, less interesting job. But four out of ten (41 percent) would accept a lower-paying, more interesting job in preference to their current position. Opportunities to acquire new skills and enhance feelings of self-worth excelled traditional incentives such as fringe benefits, promotional opportunities, physical conditions, and the friendliness of coworkers in importance.

Some traditional outlooks related to stereotypical sex-role divisions remained strong. In dual-career marriages, the husband's career was rated as more important by most husbands and by a significant minority (40 percent) of wives. One-third of working wives rated both careers as equally important. A scant 9 percent of working wives reported that their careers came first when decisions affecting both had to be made.

Now that we have an idea of motives for working and of the values of many contemporary workers, let us follow the course of vocational development and see how we make (and, too often, fail to make) career decisions.

TABLE 12.1   Comparison of Traditional versus New Breed Values

Traditional Values	New Breed Values
1. Women who can afford not to work and to stay at home should remain in the home.	2. Work is an opportunity for self-fulfillment, and women should have equal access to career opportunities.
2. Extrinsic rewards such as money and job status are sufficient to motivate workers.	2. The "carrot and stick" types of traditional work incentives (financial rewards and threat of deprivation) may still carry weight, but they are no longer sufficient compensation for workers who are seeking self-fulfillment.
3. Loyalty should bind workers to their companies.	3. We owe our allegiance to ourselves and our families. When opportunity knocks, we should "hop jobs" with no more regret than the company would show if financial exigency required layoffs.
4. Workers' personal identities stem chiefly from their work roles. Other life interests, such as recreation and self-fulfillment, take a back seat.	4. Workers define themselves in terms of who they are, not what they do. Leisure is more important than work. One's individuality is based on one's values, attitudes, interests, and abilities.
5. We should put up with our jobs no matter what, so long as they provide a decent wage and allow us to support our families.	5. Work must do more than allow us to put meat on the table. Work should provide opportunities for self-development and self-fulfillment. If our current job does not, then another one will.

■ Vocational Development

> . . . if one advances confidently in the direction of his dreams, and endeavors to live the life which he has imagined, he will meet with a success unexpected in common hours.
>
> Henry David Thoreau, *Walden*

"Any child can grow up to be President." "My child—the doctor." "You can do anything, if you set your mind to it." America—land of opportunity. America—land of decision anxiety.

In societies with caste systems, such as Old England or India, children grew up to do what their parents did. They assumed that they would follow in their parents' footsteps. The caste system saved people the necessity of deciding what they would "do" with themselves. Unfortunately, it also squandered special talents and made a mockery of personal freedom.

And what we "do" is most important. *"What* do you do?" is a more important question at social gatherings than *"How* do you do?" It is usually the first question raised in small talk. Occupational prestige is central to general social standing.

Some young people still aspire to their parents' occupations. But this goal is usually limited to cases in which parents are proud of their work. In a study of occupational choice among 76,000 first-year college students, Werts (1968) found that many sons of physicians, scientists, and teachers leaned toward their parents' professions.

Career Counseling
Career counselors use various sources of information about clients and occupations to help clients find a career that "fits" their personalities—including their personal traits, their interests, and their aptitudes.

But in many cases there is a bewildering array of career possibilities. For example, the current edition of *The Dictionary of Occupational Titles,* published by the U.S. Department of Labor, lists about 20,000 different occupations. Now of course most of us do not select careers by leafing through the dictionary. In fact, most of us make our choices from a relatively narrow group of occupations (Shertzer, 1985). On the other hand, about a third of us postpone career decisions so that when we have graduated from college we are no closer to settling on a career than when we began college (Shertzer, 1985). Many of us "fall into" careers after college, not because of particular skills and interests, but because of what is available at the time, family pressures, or the lure of high income or a certain style of life (Rice, 1985). We make no commitment to an occupation. Sometimes we simply take the first job that comes along after graduation. Sometimes we are lucky and things work out. Sometimes we are not and we hop from job to job.

One of the central purposes to writing this chapter was to demonstrate that we need not rely on luck in finding a career. There are a number of stages in vocational development to be aware of, and there are ways of finding out what kinds of occupations are likely to "fit" us.

Stages of Vocational Development

There are a number of theories concerning the stages of vocational development, although they overlap to a considerable degree. We shall orient our discussion around the five-stage theory of Donald Super (1957; Super & Hall, 1978), but we shall also refer to the concepts of other theorists.

Super's stages are as follow:

1. The first stage involves the child's unrealistic conception of self-potential and of the world of work. Eli Ginzberg (1972) refers to this stage as the **fantasy stage,** which dominates from early childhood until about age 11. Young children focus on the glamour professions, such as acting, medicine, sports, and law enforcement. They show little regard for practical considerations, such as the fit between these occupations and their abilities, or the likelihood of "getting anywhere" in them. For example, the first author's daughter Allyn, at age 6, was thoroughly committed to becoming a "rock star." Her sister Jordan, 4 at the time, intended with equal intensity to become a ballerina. But they also intended to become teachers, authors, psychologists, art historians (like their mother), and physicians.

2. During the second of Super's stages, children narrow down their choices and begin to show some realism in self-assessment and expectations about occupations. Ginzberg refers to this stage as the **tentative stage,** referring to the tentative nature of children's career choices during this stage. From about 11 through high school, children base tentative choices on their interests, abilities, and limitations, as well as glamour.

3. Following is what Super and Ginzberg refer to as a **realistic-choice stage.** Beyond the age of 17 or so, choices become narrowed or more realistic. Students weigh job requirements, rewards, even the futures of occupations. They appraise themselves more accurately. Ideally, they try to mesh their interests, abilities, and values with a job, and they may also direct their educations toward supplying the general and specific kinds of competencies—knowledge and skills—that they will need to enter the chosen occupation. But keep in mind that many of us never make realistic choices and sort of "fall into" our occupations.

4. Next is Super's **maintenance stage.** Maintenance is characterized by "settling into" the vocational role, which Daniel Levinson (see Chapter 11) suggested often characterizes the second half of the 30s. Although the individual may change positions within a company, or within a broad career (such as "publishing" or "education"), there is frequently a sense of

Fantasy stage. The first stage in vocational development, dominated by imagination and little or no concern for person–environment fit.

Tentative stage. The second stage of vocational development, in which preliminary choices are somewhat consistent with one's aptitudes and needs.

Realistic-choice stage. The third stage of vocational development, in which career selection is based on knowledge of one's aptitudes, needs, and interests and the requirements of occupations.

Maintenance stage. The fourth stage of vocational development, usually characterized by settling into an occupation.

logical development and forward movement. But individuals can also get "trapped" during this stage into dead-end jobs and fail to find fulfillment. Their employers may come to view them as cogs in the wheel and only pay attention to them when and if something goes wrong.

5. Fifth is the **retirement stage,** during which the individual severs bonds with the workplace and may encounter the kinds of adjustment problems described in the previous chapter.

Retirement stage. The fifth of Super's stages of vocational development.

Coping style. Holland's term for the way in which one approaches occupational demands: realistic, investigative, artistic, social, enterprising, conventional, or a combination of these.

Coping Styles and Career Selection: Vocational "Types"

In making realistic career decisions, we try to select careers that will fit us. In our discussion of trait theory in Chapter 2, we noted that one of the strengths of this point of view is that it has given rise to ways of thinking about "person–environment fit." A "proper fit," in terms of our aptitudes, our interests, and our personality traits, will enhance our satisfaction from day to day.

Put it another way: it might matter little that we are bringing home a good salary if we feel trapped in our jobs and hate getting up in the morning to face them. Also, if we do not have a good person–environment fit with our jobs, we will find them more stressful and we are unlikely to be motivated to do our best in them (Chemers et al., 1985). And when our performance is poor or mediocre, we are not likely to get ahead. Although our starting income might be decent enough, our income might not keep pace with that of peers who fit better in the same job environment. Our self-esteem might also plummet as we observe our peers being promoted ahead of us. We might become alienated from the job; we might even get fired.

There are a number of different approaches to predicting whether or not we are likely to adjust well to various job environments, or occupations. By and large, they all involve some kind of matching of our traits to the job. John Holland (1975) has developed a theory of matching in which various **coping styles** are linked to a fit in certain kinds of occupations (Figure 12.1). In his research, Holland has identified six coping styles:

1. *Realistic.* Persons with a realistic coping style tend to be concrete in their thinking, mechanically oriented, and interested in jobs that involve motor activity. Examples include farming; unskilled labor, such as attending gas stations; and skilled trades, such as construction and electrical work.
2. *Investigative.* Investigative people tend to be abstract in their thinking, creative, and introverted. They are frequently well adjusted in research and college and university teaching.
3. *Artistic.* Artistic individuals tend to be creative, emotional, interested in subjective feelings, and intuitive. They tend to gravitate toward the visual arts and the performing arts.
4. *Social.* Socially oriented people tend to be extraverted and socially concerned. They frequently show high verbal ability and strong needs for

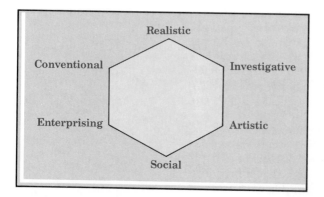

FIGURE 12.1   Holland's Coping Styles
Holland has found that there is a relationship between our coping styles and our adjustment in various occupations. What about you? Are you enterprising, artistic, or investigative? Or are you a combination of the three? What kinds of occupations would fit your coping style?

■ A CLOSER LOOK

Making Millions in Sales: "A Dirty Job But Someone's Got to Do It"

What is the stereotype of the salesperson that crosses your mind? Someone with fallen arches standing behind a counter at a department store? A sleazy individual swearing that the former owner of a used car was a little old lady who only drove it to church on Sundays? A door-to-door salesperson with squashed toes (from having the door slammed on them)?

Of course there are some salespersons who fit these images—more or less. But then there are the salespersons who are hardworking experts in their fields—salespersons who help people solve their problems and meet their needs. Salespersons do not just sell used cars or the proverbial vacuum cleaners—although there is nothing necessarily wrong with selling these products. After all, we do need them and appreciate finding ones that do the job and are affordable. But salespersons also sell word-processing systems, financial advice, wind turbines, commercial and industrial real estate, computers, high-tech hospital equipment, and airplanes. And successful salespersons in many fields have become multimillionnaires.

Do you have what it takes to be a winner in sales? Psychologists have studied the personalities of thousands of highly successful salespersons, and have found that many of them show the following seven needs (Moine, 1984):

1. *Status:* The best salespersons are highly aware of their reputations and seek recognition for their success.
2. *Control:* Successful salespersons like and enjoy other people, and take delight in influencing others. However, they do not have a strong need to be liked by others, which allows them to handle rejection. (Yes, even the best salespersons are frequently rejected.)
3. *Respect:* Top salespersons see themselves as interested in helping others meet their needs. They see themselves as deserving of respect for their expertise—for the wealth of accurate information they can dispense.
4. *Routine:* Successful sellers are highly disciplined, hardworking, and tend to stick to routines that work for them.
5. *Accomplishment:* Top salespeople are initially motivated by material goals—a fine house, a prestigious car, fine clothing. But after they become financially successful, they frequently create challenges such as "impossible sales" to inspire themselves.
6. *Stimulation:* Successful salespersons have a high level of physical energy and thrive on stimulation from challenging encounters.
7. *Honesty.* This one may surprise you. However, the most successful salespeople believe in their products. They are not rigidly moralistic, but they earn money and make reputations by helping buyers fulfill their needs.

affiliating with others. Jobs such as social work, counseling, and teaching children often fit them well.

5. *Enterprising.* Enterprising individuals tend to be adventurous and impulsive, domineering, and extraverted. They gravitate toward leadership and planning roles in industry, government, and social organizations. The successful real-estate developer or tycoon is usually enterprising.
6. *Conventional.* Conventional people tend to enjoy routines. They show high self-control, needs for order, and the desire for social approval; they are not particularly imaginative. Jobs that suit them include banking, accounting, and clerical work.

Note, of course, that many occupations call for combinations of these coping styles. For example, a copywriter in an advertising agency might be both artistic and enterprising. Clinical and counseling psychologists tend to be investigative, artistic, and socially oriented. Military people and beauticians tend to be realistic and conventional. (But military leaders who plan major operations and form governments are also enterprising; and individuals who create new hair styles and fashions are also artistic.)

Holland has created the Vocational Preference Inventory in order to assess these coping styles, but these styles are also measured by more widely used vocational tests, such as the Strong/Campbell Interest Inventory.

Now that we have seen the value of making realistic career choices—that is, of finding a good "person–environment fit" in our occupations—let us turn our attention to ways in which psychology can help us make effective choices. Two of them involve using the balance sheet, which was introduced in Chapter 6, and using psychological tests.

Using the Balance Sheet to Make Career Decisions

We first discussed the balance sheet in the context of making personal decisions, and saw how Meg used it in deciding whether or not to get a divorce from an abusive husband. Balance sheets can also be applied to career decisions. Seniors at Yale found that the balance sheet helped heighten awareness of gaps in information they needed to make wise career decisions (Janis & Wheeler, 1978). The balance sheet can also help you weigh your goals, pinpoint potential sources of frustration, and plan how to get more information or to surmount obstacles.

Gloria, a first-year liberal arts major, wondered whether she should strive to become a physician. There were no physicians in her family with whom to discuss the idea. A psychologist in her college counseling center advised her to fill out the balance sheet shown in Table 12.2 in order to help weigh the pluses and minuses of medicine.

Gloria's balance sheet helped her see that she needed dozens of pieces of information to decide. For example, how would she react to intense, prolonged studying? What were her chances of being accepted by a medical school? How did the day-to-day nitty-gritty of medical work fit her coping style and her psychological needs? Could she handle the taunts of others who thought that medicine should remain a male preserve?

Gloria's need for information is not peculiar to those contemplating medicine. The types of questions that we must consider about any career are shown in Table 12.3.

Using Psychological Tests to Make Career Decisions

As part of her information-gathering process, Gloria's career counselor used a number of psychological tests. Most career counselors rely on testing to some degree, and combine test results with interview information and knowledge of their clients' personal histories. In this way, they attain a rounded picture of their clients' interests, abilities, personalities, and degrees of motivation (Rice, 1985).

TABLE 12.2   Gloria's Balance Sheet for the Alternative of Taking Premedical Studies

Areas of Consideration	Positive Anticipations	Negative Anticipations
Tangible gains and losses for Gloria	1. Solid income	1. Long hours studying 2. Worry about acceptance by medical school 3. High financial debt
Tangible gains and losses for others	1. Solid income for benefit of family	1. Little time for family life
Self-approval or self-disapproval	1. Pride in being a physician	
Social approval or disapproval	1. Other people admire doctors	1. Some people frown on women doctors

Gloria's balance sheet for the alternative showed that although she knew that other people admired physicians, she had not considered how she would feel about herself as a physician. It encouraged her to seek further information about her personal psychological needs.

TABLE 12.3 Types of Information Needed to Make Satisfying Career Decisions

1. *Intellectual and Educational Appropriateness: Is your intended career compatible with your own intellectual and educational abilities and background?*

   Have you taken any ("preprofessional") courses that lead to the career? Have you done well in them? What level of intellectual functioning is shown by people already in the career? Is your own level of intellectual functioning comparable? What kinds of special talents and intellectual skills are required for this career? Are there any psychological or educational tests that can identify where you stand in your possession of these talents, or in the development of these skills? If you do not have these skills, can they be developed? How are they developed? Is there any way of predicting how well you can do at developing them? Would you find this field intellectually demanding and challenging? Would you find the field intellectually sterile and boring?

   Information Resources: College or university counseling or testing center, college placement center, private psychologist or vocational counselor, people working in the field, professors in or allied to the field.

2. *Intrinsic Factors: Is your intended career compatible with your coping style, your psychological needs, and your interests?*

   Does the job require elements of the realistic coping style? Of the investigative, artistic, social, enterprising, or conventional coping styles? What is your coping style? Is there a good "person–job-environment fit"?

   Is the work repetitious, or is it varied? Do you have a marked need for change (perpetual novel stimulation), or do you have a greater need for order and consistency? Would you be working primarily with machinery, with papers, or with other people? Do you prefer manipulating objects, doing paper work, or interacting with other people? Is the work indoors or outdoors? Are you an "indoors" or an "outdoors person"? Do you have strong needs for autonomy and dominance, or do you prefer to defer to others? Does the field allow you to make your own decisions, permit you to direct others, or require that you closely take direction from others? Do you have strong aesthetic needs? Is the work artistic? Are you Type A or Type B, or somewhere in between? Is this field strongly competitive or more relaxed?

   Information Resources: Successful people in the field. (Do you feel similar to people in the field? Do you have common interests? Do you like them and enjoy their company?) Written job descriptions. Psychological tests of personality (e.g., coping style and psychological needs) and interests.

3. *Extrinsic Factors: What is the balance between the investment you would have to make in the career and the probable payoff?*

   How much time, work, and money would you have to invest in your educational and professional development in order to enter this career? Do you have the financial resources? If not, can you get them? (Do the sacrifices you would have to make to get them—such as long-term debt—seem worthwhile?) Do you have the endurance? The patience? What will the market for your skills be like when you are ready to enter the career? In 20 years? Will the financial rewards adequately compensate you for your investment?

   Information Resources: College financial aid office, college placement office, college counseling center, family, people in the field.

Intelligence Tests One of the tests Gloria took was a Wechsler Adult Intelligence Scale (WAIS). The WAIS and the Stanford-Binet Intelligence Scales are the most widely used intelligence tests (Figure 12.2), and the WAIS is the most widely used with adults. The WAIS consists of 11 subtests, which are grouped into verbal subtests and performance subtests. Verbal subtests, as shown in Table 12.4, require knowledge of verbal concepts, such as the meanings of words or ways in which concepts are alike, and performance subtests require familiarity with spatial-relations concepts.

TABLE 12.4   Subtests from the Wechsler Adult Intelligence Scale (WAIS)

Verbal Subtests:

1. *Information:* "What is the capital of the United States?" "Who was Shakespeare?"
2. *Comprehension:* "Why do we have zip codes?" "What does the saying *A stitch in time saves nine* mean?"
3. *Arithmetic:* "If 3 candybars cost 25 cents, how much will 18 candybars cost?"
4. *Similarities:* "How are *good* and *bad* alike?"
5. *Digit span:* Repeating series of numbers backwards and forwards.
6. *Vocabulary:* "What does *duct* mean?"

Performance Subtests:

7. *Digit symbol:* Learning and drawing meaningless figures that are associated with numbers.
8. *Picture completion:* Pointing to the missing parts in a series of pictures.
9. *Block design:* Copying pictures of geometric designs using multicolored blocks.
10. *Picture arrangement.* Arranging cartoon pictures in sequence so that they tell a meaningful story.
11. *Object assembly:* Putting pieces of a puzzle together so that they make up a meaningful object.

FIGURE 12.2   Items Resembling Those in the Performance Subtests of the Wechsler Adult Intelligence Scale

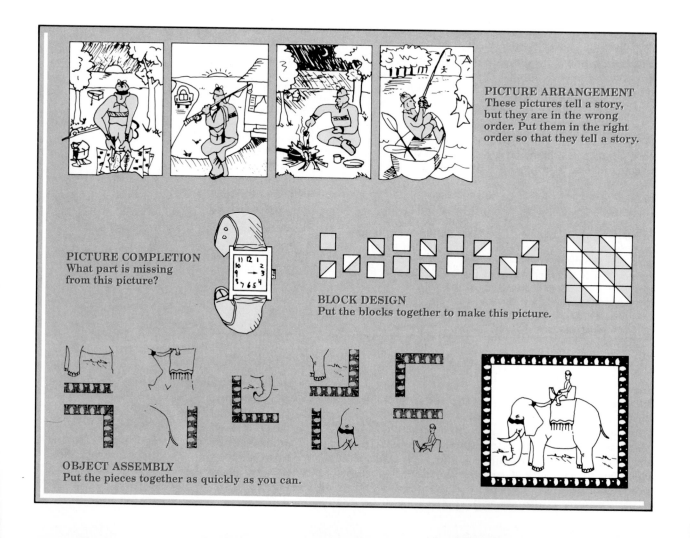

PICTURE ARRANGEMENT
These pictures tell a story, but they are in the wrong order. Put them in the right order so that they tell a story.

PICTURE COMPLETION
What part is missing from this picture?

BLOCK DESIGN
Put the blocks together to make this picture.

OBJECT ASSEMBLY
Put the pieces together as quickly as you can.

Intelligence is a complex and controversial concept. David Wechsler (1975), developer of the Wechsler scales, defined it as the capacity to understand the world and the resourcefulness to cope with its challenges. Many people think of intelligence as completely innate, a broad ability to learn that makes adjustment and achievement possible. But most psychologists and educational experts believe that intelligence involves genetic and environmental factors (Snyderman & Rothman, 1987), so that children who are reared with early advantages not only achieve more but actually become more intelligent.

Intelligence tests such as the WAIS also yield **intelligence quotients,** or IQ's, that are determined by comparing test takers' scores with those of their peers. The **mean** IQ is defined as an IQ of 100. Fifty percent of the population attain IQ scores within the broad average range of 90 to 110. Only about 2 percent of the population attain scores above 130, and they are labeled "very superior" by Wechsler. Only about 2 percent of the population attain scores below 70, and Wechsler labeled them "intellectually deficient."

Gloria's WAIS score was in the 130s, and so she learned that her general level of intellectual functioning was on a par with that of people who performed well in medicine. Her verbal, mathematical, and spatial-relations skills showed no deficiencies. Thus, any academic problems would more likely reflect lack of motivation or of specific prerequisites than general ability. But her counselor also told Gloria that "The best predictor of future behavior is past behavior." Since premedical programs are dominated by chemistry, Gloria's solid performance in high school chemistry was promising.

The balance sheet suggested that Gloria had only superficially asked herself about how she would enjoy being a physician. She had recognized that physicians are generally admired, and assumed that she would have feelings of pride. But would the work of a physician be consistent with her coping style? Would her psychological needs be met? The counselor provided helpful personality information through the Strong/Campbell Interest Inventory (SCII) and the Edwards Personal Preference Schedule (EPPS).

Interest Inventories   The Strong/Campbell Interest Inventory (SCII) is used with college students and other adults and is the most widely used test in college counseling and testing centers (Lubin et al., 1985). Most items on the SCII require that test takers indicate whether they like, are indifferent to, or dislike various occupations (e.g., actor/actress, architect); school subjects (algebra, art); activities (adjusting a carburetor, making a speech); amusements (golf, chess, jazz or rock concerts); and types of people (babies, nonconformists). The preferences of test takers are compared with those of people in various occupations. Areas of general interest (e.g., sales, science, teaching, agriculture) and specific interest (e.g., mathematician, guidance counselor, beautician) are derived from these comparisons. Test takers also gather information about their coping styles, according to Holland's model.

Other Personality Tests   Interest inventories are one kind of personality test. Personality tests are frequently used by psychologists to help understand personal problems. But they are also used with well-adjusted individuals in order to heighten the chances of finding the right person–environment fit in the workplace. One commonly used test for measuring personality traits is the California Psychological Inventory. Another is the Edwards Personal Preference Schedule (EPPS).

The EPPS pairs a number of statements expressive of psychological needs, and test takers indicate which of each pair of statements is more descriptive of them. In this way it can be determined, for example, whether test takers have a stronger need for dominance than for deference (taking direction from others), or a strong need for order or to be helped by others. All in all, the relative strength of 15 psychological needs is examined.

Intelligence. A complex, controversial concept characterized by the ability to form an accurate cognitive representation of the world and the resourcefulness to cope with its challenges.

Intelligence quotient. A score on an intelligence test. Abbreviated IQ.

Mean. A kind of average derived by adding scores and then dividing the sum by the number of scores.

WHAT DO YOU SAY NOW?

How to Make a Positive Impression at a Job Interview

After you have chosen and prepared for a career, you will be applying for a job. And at some point you will be invited to a job interview.

The interview is a combination of a social occasion and a test. First impressions and neatness count, so dress well and look your best. When other things are held equal, people who look their best usually get the job (Cash & Kilcullen, 1985). You're probably best advised not to wear perfume or cologne unless you know that your interviewer is a woman. Social psychologist Robert A. Baron (1983) found that women interviewers rate applicants who wear perfume or cologne more positively, but that male interviewers rate fragrant applicants—male and female alike—more negatively. Perhaps male interviewers are more rigid than female interviewers and hold the idea that serious things do not come in fragrant packages.

Maintain direct eye contact with your interviewer, but look alert, cooperative, and friendly—don't stare. Recall from Chapter 4 that a hard stare is perceived as an aversive challenge.

As noted in Chapter 1, one good way to prepare for an academic test is to try to anticipate your instructor's questions. Similarly, anticipating an interviewer's questions will help prepare you for the interview—just

What do you say in a job interview? Your interviewer wants to hear that you are familiar with his or her organization and that you have concrete goals that are consistent with organizational needs.

as anticipating reporters' questions helps prepare the president for press conferences. Once you have arrived at a list of potential questions, rehearse answers to them. Practice them aloud, perhaps recruiting a friend to role-play the interviewer.

And, as noted in Chapter 1, a good student doesn't necessarily have to say something during every class. Similarly, a good job candidate doesn't have to do all the talking in the interview. Be patient: Allow the interviewer to tell you about the job and the organization without feeling that you must jump in. Look interested. Nod now and then. Don't champ at the bit.

Now, back to the questions. Some of the interviewer's questions will be specific to your field, and we cannot help you anticipate those. But others are more likely to be found in any interview, and some of them follow. But note that we are using a slightly different format in this "What-Do-You-Say-Now" segment: We ask the question, then provide room for just one possible answer. Next we offer our thoughts on the subject and try to alert you as to what your interviewer is looking for; we don't always supply a specific answer. The specific words will have to be consistent with the nature of your field, the organization to which you have applied, your geographical setting, and so on.

All right, the person ahead of you leaves and it's your turn for an interview! Here are the questions? What do you say now?

1. *How are you today?*

_____

_____

Our recommendation: *Don't* get cute or fancy. Say something like, "Fine, thank you. How're you?"

2. *How did you learn about the opening?*

_____

_____

Don't say, "I indicated that in my application." Yes, you probably did specify this on your application or in the cover letter for your résumé, but your interviewer may not be familiar with the letter or may want to follow standard procedure anyhow. So answer concisely.

3. *What do you know about our organization?*

_____

_____

Your interviewer wants to learn whether you actually know something about the organization or applied everywhere with equal disinterest. Do your homework and show that you know quite a bit about the organization. Suggest how the organization is an ideal setting for you to reach your vocational goals.

4. *What are you looking for in this job?*

_____

_____

This is another opportunity to show that you have concrete goals, and that's what interviewers are looking for. Mention things like the opportunity to work with noted professionals in your field, the organizational personality (organizations, like people, can be conceptualized as having personalities), the organization's leadership in its field, etc. *Don't* say "It's close to home." You can say that you know that salaries are good, but also refer to opportunities for personal growth and self-fulfullment.

5. *What do you plan to be doing ten years from now?*

_____

_____

Your interviewer wants to hear that you have a clear cognitive map of the corporate ladder and that your career goals are consistent with company needs. Preplan a coherent answer, but also show flexibility—perhaps that you're interested in exploring a couple of branches of the career ladder. This will show your interviewer that you're not rigid and that you recognize that the organization will affect your concept of your future.

6. *Are you willing to relocate after a year or two if we need you in another office/plant?*

_____

_____

Your interviewer wants to hear that you would be willing—that your ties to the company would be more important than your geographical ties. *Don't* say that your fiancé or spouse is flexible; it implies that he or she really is not, and you just don't want to get into this.

7. *What are your salary needs?*

_____

_____

Entry-level salaries in many positions are fixed, especially in large organizations. But if this question is asked, *don't* fall into the trap of thinking you're more likely to get the job if you ask for less. Mention a reasonably high—not ridiculously high—figure. You can also mention the figure "with an explanation"—reemphasizing your experience and training. Good things don't come cheap, and organizations know this. And why should they think more of you than you think of yourself?

8. *What is the first thing you would do if you were to take the job?*

_____

_____

Your interviewer probably wants to know (a) if you're an active, take-charge type of person and (b) whether you do have an understanding of what is required. *Don't* say you'd be shocked or surprised. Say something like, "I'd get to know my supervisors and coworkers to learn the details of the organization's goals and expectations for the position." Or it might be appropriate to talk about organizing your workspace, or evaluating and ordering equipment, depending on the nature of the occupation.

9. *Do you realize that this is a very difficult (or time-consuming) job?*

_____

_____

It is or it isn't, but the interviewer doesn't want to hear that you think the job's a snap. The interviewer wants to hear that you will dedicate yourself to your work and that you have boundless energy. One legitimate response is to ask your interviewer to amplify a bit on the remark so that you can fine-tune your eventual answer.

10. *What do you see as your weaknesses?*

_____

_____

Trap time! *Don't* make a joke and say that can't get along with anyone or know nothing about the job! Your interviewer is giving you a chance to show that you are arrogant by denying weaknesses or to drop some kind of bombshell—that is, admit to a self-disqualifying problem. Don't do either. Turn the question into an opportunity for emphasizing strengths. Say something like, "I think my weakness is that I have not already done this job (or worked for your organization), and so we cannot predict with certainty what will happen. But I'm a fast learner and pretty flexible, so I'm confident that I'll do a good job."

11. *Do you have any questions?*

_____

_____

Having intelligent questions is a sign that you are interested and can handle the job. Prepare a few good questions before the interview. In the unlikely event that the interviewer manages to cover them all during his or her presentation, you can say something like, "I was going to ask such and such, but then you said that such and such. Could you amplify on that a bit?"

12. Finally, what do you say when the interview is over?

_____

_____

Say something like, "Thank you for the interview. I look forward to hearing from you."

The SCII suggested that Gloria would enjoy investigative work, science—including medical science—and mathematics. However, she was not particularly socially oriented. Well-adjusted physicians usually show a combination of investigative and social coping styles.

The EPPS showed relatively strong needs for achievement, order, dominance, and endurance. All these factors meshed well with premedical studies—the long hours, the willingness to delay gratification, and the desire to learn about things—to make them fit together and work properly. The EPPS report dovetailed with the SCII's report to the effect that Gloria was not particularly socially oriented in her coping style: The EPPS suggested that Gloria had a low need for **nurturance,** for caring for others and promoting their well-being.

With this information in hand, Gloria recognized that she really did not sense any strong desire to help others through medicine. Her medical interests might be purely academic. But after some reflection, she chose to pursue premedical studies, and to expand her college work in chemistry and other sciences in order to lay the groundwork for alternative careers in medically related sciences. The courses promised to be of interest even if she did not develop a strong desire to help others or was not accepted by medical school. Contingency plans such as these are useful for all of us. If we can consider the available alternatives, even as we head down the path toward a concrete goal, we are better equipped to deal with unanticipated problems and frustrations.

Developmental Tasks in Taking a Job

You've got it! The job you've been dreaming about! Your academic work has paid off, and you did brilliantly at the interview. Good salary, solid opportunities for advancement, and the promise of self-development in a field that you enjoy—all of these are yours. From here on in, it's smooth sailing, right? Not necessarily.

If the job you have landed fits your education, experience, and coping style, the chances are that you will do well indeed. But there are a number of developmental tasks that we undertake when we take a new job (Faux, 1984b; Okun, 1984; Turner & Helms, 1987), and it is useful to be aware of them:

1. *Making the transition from school to the workplace.* You have already mastered the school world, and change can be threatening as well as exciting. You are also going from the "top" of the school world (graduation) to a relatively low position in the organizational hierarchy. Moreover, you are moving from a system in which there is measurable progress, including courses completed each term and movement up the educational ladder each year. In a job one can go for years without a promotion.
2. *Learning how to carry out the job tasks.* Job tasks include executing occupational skills and also meshing your own attitudes and values with those of the organization. Simply learning the organization's explicit (written) and implicit (unwritten) rules is a job in itself.
3. *Accepting responsibility for your job tasks and functions.*
4. *Accepting your subordinate status within the organization or profession.* Despite your sterling qualities, you are a newcomer.
5. *Learning how to get along with your coworkers and supervisor.*
6. *Showing that you can maintain the job, make improvements, and show progress.*
7. *Finding a sponsor or mentor to help "show you the ropes."*
8. *Defining the boundaries between the job and other areas of life.* Where do work and concerns about work end? Where do your personal interests and social relationships begin?
9. *Evaluating your occupational choice in the light of supervisor appraisal and measurable outcomes of your work.* Is the job really for you?

Nurturance. A psychological trait or need characterized by caring for people (or other living organisms) and/or rearing them.

10. *Learning to cope with daily hassles on the job, frustrations, and successes and failure.*

Career Shifts

Even the best laid plans of young adulthood often go astray later in life. As noted in Chapter 11, the "one true course" at age 20 often develops bumps and curves during the reassessments of the 30s and 40s. We may decide to switch careers because of boredom or lack of personal fulfillment. We may find that our jobs are incompatible with our values, or that adult experience has opened new doors.

Workers in dead-end jobs switch most frequently (Sommers & Eck, 1977). More than half the busboys, stock clerks, and gas station attendants surveyed by the U.S. Census Bureau had switched occupations within the previous five years. However, only 22 percent of professional or technical workers had done so. There was also considerable variability among professions. Only 5 percent of physicians and 8 percent of lawyers reported changes, as compared to 33 percent of economists, 23 percent of social workers, 21 percent of accountants, and 36 percent of surveyors. Perhaps the greater the career investment we make in terms of time and money, the less likely we are to switch.

If you are considering switching careers, in addition to the stresses of career selection you might feel guilt about the years you have "wasted." But cognitive therapists might suggest that job experiences—even in the "wrong" job—serve the valuable functions of fine-tuning our self-identities. That is, they help teach us who we are and what we want and need.

Persistent "job-hopping" may be a sign that we have difficulty making lasting commitments. However, recognition at age 28 that the choice we made at age 18 might not lead to a lifetime of fulfillment is perfectly normal and understandable. Go easy on yourself. And remember that the same resources (e.g., testing and counseling) that you used or could have used at age 18 are still available.

■ Adjustment in the Workplace

Work provides a major opportunity for personal growth and may also demand major adjustments. In this section we have a look at who gets ahead in the U.S. workplace and factors that contribute to satisfaction on the job.

Getting Ahead in America

In their book *Who Gets Ahead: The Determinants of Economic Success in America*, sociologist Christopher Jencks and his colleagues (1979) synthesize the findings of 11 national surveys of men. The major predictor of economic success?—*family background.* Nearly half the differences in occupational status, and about one-third of the differences in earnings, could be attributed to the status and income of their families. Sons from familes on the *top* fifth of the economic ladder earned 150–186 percent of the national average. Sons of families from the bottom fifth earned 56–67 percent of the national average.

How do we interpret this finding? A genetic hypothesis would be that talented individuals genetically transmit the traits that lead to academic performance and occupational achievement to their children. But an environmental hypothesis is as persuasive: Affluent families tend to have fewer children (and, therefore, to focus more resources on each), to live in communities with better schools, and to communicate an achievement ethic to their children. Children from affluent families may also gain easier access to prestigious colleges and universities (Yankelovitch, 1979), even though equal-opportunity laws may prevent the systematic exclusion of minority groups. The truth doubtless lies somewhere in between—a combination of genetic and environmental factors.

Second in importance as a predictor of success was completion of college. High school graduates earned 15–25 percent more than nongraduates. College graduates earned 30–40 percent more. Academic majors, grades, and prestige of institution contributed little to financial success. The diploma seems to have been more essential than the specifics of the education. Perhaps the traits that led to the *decision* to attend college and the *persistence* to remain in college until graduation were more important than the courses themselves (with the exception of courses such as the one you are now taking, of course).

If we hold family and educational background constant, only then are scores from standardized intelligence and achievement tests taken earlier in school linked to differences in income. Men who were identified as gifted as early as the sixth grade earned more than men with lower test scores.

Leadership ability in the sixth to tenth grades, as measured by self-assessments and teacher ratings, was also linked to economic success. But students who rated themselves higher on sociability than on assiduous study habits, and who might have spent more time dating or "out with the guys," earned less later in life than more serious students.

What does it all mean? We cannot do anything about our family backgrounds and we certainly cannot go back and modify the abilities and skills we showed during the sixth to tenth grades. But we can decide to develop persevering study and work habits now, and do what is necessary to bring college to a successful conclusion. In this way we may eventually also be able to do something about the family backgrounds of *our* children.

Satisfaction on the Job

Surveys consistently show that most workers in every job category report that they like their jobs (Jahoda, 1981). Still, large numbers are dissatisfied.

Talk is rife about dissatisfaction on the assembly line. Some refer to feelings of alienation and dissatisfaction among factory workers as "blue-collar blues." Some factory workers find their work boring or dehumanizing. They complain that supervisers treat them with disrespect and fail to use them as resources for learning how to improve working conditions and productivity.

As pointed out in *Theory Z* (Ouchi, 1981), Japanese managers frequently involve workers with their companies by requesting and acting upon their opinions. Managers also eat in the same cafeterias as line workers. Everyone feels "in it together." In the United States, there is usually an adversary relationship between labor and management. Each side feels the other is "out for all they can get" and willing to exploit the opposition in any way they can. Japanese workers are also often given lifetime jobs—a "gift" that can create great loyalty to the company, but one that frequently prevents upward mobility.

How to Enhance Job Satisfaction *and Productivity:* Improving the Quality of Work Life Is Also Good Business

For some of us, the responsibility for our job satisfaction is in our own hands. Many professionals open their own practices and charge competitive fees for their services. We can form partnerships and corporations, or open shops or industrial plants. Our lots, in essence, are what we make of them.

For others, such as factory workers, the responsibility for the quality of their work life often appears to be in the hands of supervisors and managers. In a sense this is illusory; except in situations of extreme deprivation, workers usually choose to work in a certain plant in a certain location. When there is choice, plants that offer more in the way of extrinsic and intrinsic rewards will attract and keep better workers.

Increasing the quality of work life turns out to be very good business for everyone. First, increased job satisfaction decreases employee turnover

■ A CLOSER LOOK

The Work Junkies

When Marilyn Machlowitz was 24 years old, she tried to take a vacation. Packing up her sexiest sun dress and a new maillot, she headed for Martinique's Club *Mediterrané*—a holiday camp that pursues hedonism. But once on the beach, she realized something was wrong. Around her, Club Med voluptuaries laughed and flirted, frolicked and romped, while Machlowitz, an attractive brunette, checked statistics from a computer print-out. Odder still, she was having a wonderful time.

Machlowitz is a workaholic. The print-out was one step toward a Yale Ph.D. dissertation that has finally put workaholism on the academic map. "To date, alienated workers have received most of the scholarly attention," explains Machlowitz. "I thought we could learn about work from people who like it, too."

That's putting things mildly. Workaholics don't just like to work; they *live* to work. At stake, say mental-health experts, is a self-esteem based on meeting purely self-imposed standards. When a workaholic has paid the mortgage or conquered a deadline, he or she creates new excuses for nonstop toil. Mental-health workers who recognize workaholism as a syndrome are divided on its significance. Some cite the workaholics' damaging neglect of their families, while others rue the shakiness of their egos. Still others deplore hard-core workaholics as burnt-out drones who drive their subordinates crazy with incessant demands. But to Machlowitz, workaholics are neither good nor bad—simply "frustrated or fulfilled."

Workaholism often masquerades virtuously as the good old American work ethic. But in the 1960s, along with other time-honored ideas, the notion of work-centered lives took a drubbing. And the 1970s' remorseless pursuit of leisure steadily reduced the number of hours on the job per wage earner, making workaholics increasingly conspicuous.

Mental-health workers view workaholics as obsessive-compulsives who dread inactivity. The universal worry of workaholics, according to Machlowitz, is lack of time. Even as youngsters they are afraid of wasting it and literally never learn to play. Instead of chasing butterflies or collecting baseball cards, they sell vegetables from Mommy's garden and run penny-pitch games. While some adult workaholics may be bullied into vacations, which often turn into tightly scheduled frenzies of tennis or sightseeing, the true workaholic shuns even Sundays away from the job. Machlowitz found that all workaholics cited work as a key factor in broken marriages, a conclusion which makes her wonder if workaholics might be best off wed to each other.

But for all their rushing around, and potential family conflict, Machlowitz found that workaholics, as a group, were generally happy, well adjusted, and satisfied with their lives. Two factors which contributed to their adjustment were meaningful work and the support of family members.

Workaholics are among the world's most productive people—so what's so awful about being one? Expert opinion differs. Machlowitz is troubled by the emotional cost to their children. To Dr. Clinto Weiman, medical director of Citibank, the real victim may be the work junkie himself or herself, who sometimes pays in high blood pressure, ulcers, and migraines. Yet the corporations Machlowitz called to check on specific measures for aiding workaholics all replied incredulously, like Polaroid, "Where can we find more of them?"

---

and absenteeism—two expensive measures of job dissatisfaction. Second, there is a link between enhanced productivity and the quality of work life. Many of the methods for increasing productivity also contribute to the satisfaction of the worker (Katzell & Guzzo, 1983). These include but are not limited to the following:

Improved Recruitment and Placement   Part of the satisfaction/productivity issue is solved by using appropriate application forms, interviews, and tests to recruit the right person for the job (Hunter & Schmidt, 1983). Adequate recruitment requires careful specification of the skills and personal attributes that are needed in a position. Just as individuals can take tests to learn about the relationships among their abilities, interests, coping styles, and potential careers, so, too, can organizations develop tests to help identify the traits that predict success in the occupations that they offer. As an example, IBM administers tests to determine whether former assembly-line workers are good candidates for retraining as computer programmers. As another, many firms have tests that suggest whether job candidates have the outgoing and persuasive characteristics that are linked to success in sales.

Training and Instruction   Training and instruction are the most commonly reported methods for enhancing productivity (Katzell & Guzzo, 1983). Adequate training provides workers with appropriate skills. It also reduces the stresses on workers by equipping them to solve the problems they will face. Capacity to solve challenging problems enhances worker feelings of self-worth.

Unbiased Appraisal of Workers' Performance   Workers fare better and productivity is enhanced when workers receive individualized guidance and reinforcers based on an accurate appraisal of their performance.

In an ideal world, appraisal of workers' performances would be based solely on how well workers do their jobs. And it does turn out, by and large, that managers give the greatest salary increments to workers whose objective performances are rated as most positive (Alexander & Barrett, 1982). However, research into appraisal of performance shows that a number of cognitive biases are at work in the appraisal process.

Biases in the Appraisal Process   First, there is a tendency for supervisors to focus on the *worker* rather than the worker's performance. Raters form general impressions of workers and may then evaluate them on the basis of these impressions and not on how well specific tasks are performed (Williams, 1986). The tendency to rate workers according to general impressions (e.g., of liking or disliking) can apparently be overcome much of the time when raters are asked to focus on how well the worker carries out specific tasks.

Learning theorists have suggested that the criteria for appraisal be totally objective—based on publicly observable behaviors and outlined to workers and supervisors prior to performance. Ideally, workers would be rated according to whether or not they engage in targeted behavior patterns. Workers would not be penalized for intangibles such as "poor attitude."

In order to appraise workers objectively, it is sometimes necessary to undertake a **task analysis** of the job. Teachers know that other teachers are sometimes evaluated as excellent by administrators because their classrooms are quiet and parents do not complain about them. Of course, quiet rooms and lack of complaints characterize vacant houses as well as schools. It would be more pertinent—although more difficult—to undertake a task analysis of the job of teaching and then to find ways of measuring whether the components of the task are actually being carried out.

Another bias in the appraisal process is the tendency to evaluate workers according to how much effort they put into their work (Knowlton & Mitchell, 1980). Hard work is not necessarily good work. (Do you think that students who work harder than you should be given higher grades on tests, even when you get all the answers right and they make many errors?) It is fairer, again, to focus on how well workers perform targeted behaviors and to evaluate them on this basis.

Goal Setting   Workers should know exactly what is demanded of them. Too often goals are vague. Workers are told that they should "work hard" or "be serious" about their jobs, but hard work and seriousness are ill defined. Workers do not know exactly what is expected of them, and lack of knowledge creates anxiety and contributes to poor performance. **Industrial/organizational psychologists,** or I/O psychologists, point out that when workers know exactly what is expected of them, they can better conform their behavior to supervisors' expectations. Setting concrete goals at high but attainable levels can render work challenging but keep stress within acceptable limits.

Financial Compensation   When possible, performance should be linked to financial reward. In many instances it is demoralizing when productive

The Assembly Line Industrial/organizational psychologists understand the stresses that many assembly-line workers encounter because of repetitive work and lack of a sense of pride in the finished product. In one experiment in work redesign, assembly-line workers move down the line with the product, particpating in its development in a variety of ways.

workers receive no more pay than nonproductive workers. If financial incentives for productivity are to be used, the assessment of productivity must be made in an absolutely fair, objective manner. If objective assessment is not possible, workers may become demoralized because of actual or suspected favoritism.

A number of I/O psychologists suggest that supervisors handle problem performances in a manner consistent with principles of **behavior modification.** For example, as noted in Chapter 2, punishment of unacceptable behavior does not in and of itself teach acceptable behavior and can also create hostility. It is preferable, through careful assessment and training, to provide workers with the skills to perform adequately, and then to reinforce the targeted work behaviors.

Behavior modification. Application of principles of learning to changing behavior.

Quality circle. A regularly scheduled meeting in which a group of workers discuss problems and suggest solutions in order to enhance the quality of products.

Work Redesign I/O psychologists understand the importance of creating settings in which workers can feel pride and a sense of closure. An assembly-line worker may repeat one task hundreds of times a day and never see the finished product. To make factory work more meaningful, workers at one Volvo assembly plant in Sweden have been organized into small groups that elect leaders and distribute tasks among themselves. In another work-redesign program, workers move along the assembly line with "their" truck chassis, giving them the satisfaction of seeing their product take shape (Blackler & Brown, 1978). In an experiment at Motorola, one worker builds an entire pocket radio pager and signs the product when finished. The janitorial staff at a Texas Instruments worksite meets in small groups to set goals and distribute cleaning tasks among themselves. Texas Instruments reports a cleaner plant, lowered costs, and decreased turnover (Dickson, 1975).

The concept of the **quality circle,** practiced widely in Japan, has also been catching on in the U.S.A. Ironically, this method, in which workers meet regularly to discuss problems and suggest solutions, was brought to Japan after World War II by H. Edwards Deming, an American. I/O psychologists note that quality circles give workers a greater sense of control over their jobs and increase their commitment to the company (Lawler & Mohrman, 1985; Marks, 1986); control and commitment enhance psychological hardiness, as noted in Chapters 6 and 10. Moreover, it seems likely that workers are in the best position to understand some of the problems that prevent them from performing optimally.

Work Schedules When there is no company reason for maintaining a rigid 9:00-to-5:00 schedule, workers frequently profit from **flextime,** or being able to modify their own schedules to meet their personal needs. In one variation on flextime, workers put in four ten-hour workdays, rather than five eight-hour days (Ronen, 1981). One study found that flextime lowered absenteeism (Narayanan & Nath, 1982).

At Honeywell, a "mothers' shift" allows women to coordinate their work schedules with their children's school hours. Mothers may also have college students fill in for them during their children's summer vacations. Are we ready for a "fathers' shift"?

Our perspective on enhancing job satisfaction has so far focused on the individual worker within the organization. But in their efforts to enhance efficiency and productivity, I/O psychologists also focus on the broader nature of organizations themselves, as we shall see in our discussion of organizational theory.

Organizational Theory and Adjustment in the Workplace

Organizations have formal characteristics, such as chains of command; channels of communication; and policies concerning hiring, compensation, retirement, and so on. Organizations also have informal characteristics, such as "personalities," which may be impersonal and cold, warm and familylike, authoritarian, or relatively permissive.

In Chapter 2 we saw that individuals are thought of as having *traits*—relatively stable ways of responding to the challenges of life. The formal and informal characteristics of organizations serve as "traits" too—relatively stable ways in which organizations respond to economic, political, and other challenges. As with individuals, we also speak of corporations as adjusting or failing to adjust to environments—such as "economic environments"—and as growing and thriving or as acting "sick" and dying or disintegrating.

As with other areas of psychology, there are different theoretical approaches to organizing businesses. Landy (1985) suggests that three broad approaches have a major impact today: *classic organization theories, contingency theories,* and *human-relations theories.*

Classic Organization Theories **Classic organization theories** propose that there is one best way to structure an organization—from the skeleton outward. That is, organization is based on the required levels of authority and supervision.

Classic organization theories frequently rely on a **bureaucracy,** which ideally frees workers from the injustices of favoritism and nepotism and enables them to make long-range plans. Other elements of classic organization theories include the division of labor and the delegation of authority. The computer firm Texas Instruments has the classic organization and "sends down orders from the top" (*New York Times,* 1987, p. D8).

Contingency Theories of Organization **Contingency theories** take issue with the view that there is one best way to structure an organization. They hold, instead, that there are many valid ways to structure organizations, and that organizational approaches are *contingent on* factors such as organizational goals, workers' characteristics, and the overall political or economic environment. For example, a classic bureaucracy might make sense when timeliness and accuracy in production are central corporate objectives. When scientific innovation is the major goal, however, a less centralized, and less authoritarian organization might be facilitative.

Flextime. A modification of one's work schedule from the standard 9:00 to 5:00 to meet personal needs.

Classic organization theories. Theories that hold that organizations should be structured from the skeleton (governing body) outward.

Bureaucracy. An administrative system characterized by departments and subdivisions whose members frequently are given long tenure and inflexible work tasks.

Contingency theories. Theories that hold that organizational structure should depend on factors such as goals, workers' characteristics, and the overall economic or political environment.

Human-Relations Theories of Organization   **Human-relations theories** begin their structuring with the individual—the worker. They argue that the behavior of the organization cannot be predicted or controlled without taking into account the characteristics and needs of the individual. From this perspective, efficient organizational structure will reflect the cognitive processes of individuals as these processes are applied to problem solving, decision making, and the quests for self-expression and self-fulfillment. Let us consider three human-relations approaches: McGregor's *Theory Y*, Argyris' developmental theory, and Ouichi's *Theory Z*.

Douglas McGregor's (1960) **Theory Y** is based on the assumption that workers are motivated to take responsibility for their work behavior and that worker apathy and misbehavior stem from shortcomings of the organization. Theory Y holds that the central task of management is to structure the organization so that organizational goals will be congruent with workers' goals. Workers cannot be expected to be productive if their personal goals are at odds with those of the organization.

Chris Argyris (1972) notes a number of developmental principles and suggests that organizations are structured efficiently when they allow their workers to develop. For example, Argyris notes that workers develop in the following ways:

Workers develop from passive to active organisms
Workers develop from dependent to independent organisms
Workers develop from organisms capable of dealing with concrete issues to organisms capable of dealing with abstract issues
Workers develop from organisms with few abilities to organisms with many abilities

Because of these broad developmental processes, certain kinds of work environments are basically flawed—at least for most workers. For example, assembly-line work does not allow workers to function independently and to express a variety of abilities. As a consequence, tension is created on the job, leading to apathy and high absenteeism and turnover rates. As noted earlier, methods such as work redesign have been instituted by many companies in an effort to allow workers to experience some sense of control and self-development.

Ouichi's (1981) **Theory Z** combines some of the positive features of the Japanese workplace with some of the realities of the U.S. workplace in an effort to foster loyalty to the company and heighten productivity. Perhaps the most salient feature of many Japanese workplaces is their *paternalism*—that is, offering security through lifetime employment, involvement of workers' families in company activities, and subsidizing of housing and education for workers' families. Many U.S. firms, by contrast, lay off workers with every economic downturn. Ouichi's theory "compromises" by suggesting that U.S. firms offer long-term employment when possible. Restructuring to avoid layoffs would enhance workers' loyalty.

Traditionally there is high division of labor and specialization in the U.S. workplace, leading to feelings of being "cubbyholed" and lack of a sense of control over the whole product. Japanese career paths tend to be relatively nonspecialized, allowing for sideways movement and variety. Again, the compromise of a "moderately specialized" career path is suggested. In the traditional U.S. workplace, decision making and responsibility are in the hands of a relatively few supervisors, whereas in Japan decision making tends to be consensual and responsibility collective. In Japan, moreover, managers often eat with laborers and share their bathrooms. The importing of the quality circle and the creation of other methods for enhancing employees' senses of participation in the decision-making process are also consistent with the compromises of Theory Z. Although the Japanese are highly competitive in the

Human-relations theories. Theories that hold that organizations are best structured according to the characteristics and needs of the individual worker.

Theory Y. McGregor's view that organizational goals should be congruent with workers' goals.

Theory Z. Ouichi's view that adapts positive features of the Japanese workplace to the U.S. workplace.

world marketplace, managers within given firms tend to reach decisions by means of consensus, as contrasted to the usual U.S. "winner-take-all" approach. And so, another Theory-Z Japanese import is a consensus management system, in which managers tend to feel that "nobody has lost," as encouraged within the ranks at Houston-based Compaq, another U.S. computer firm (*New York Times,* 1987).

Professional psychologists are highly concerned with the dignity of the individual. For this reason, they tend to gravitate toward organizational structures that allow for the self-development and satisfaction of the individual worker. In many cases, this leaning also heightens productivity. However, as noted by Baron and Byrne (1987), it is also widely accepted that job satisfaction should be maximized for its own sake.

In the next section we shall examine an issue in which health psychology and I/O psychology overlap: stress in the workplace. We shall also see some of the ways in which work stresses are addressed, both by the individual and by the organization.

Stress and Work

Work for most of us involves more than 40 hours a week. When we figure in commutation, preparation, lunchtime, continuing education, and just thinking about the job, many of us put at least half our waking hours into our work.

Stress at work also spills over into stress at home. Frustrations and resentments about the workplace can make us tired and short-tempered, and they can contribute to arguments with spouse and family (Gibson et al., 1985). In a vicious cycle, marital conflict may then compound problems in the workplace.

Causes of Stress in the Workplace   The left-hand part of Figure 12.3 shows how various features of the workplace can contribute to stress (Matteson & Ivancevich, 1987). Among the aspects of the physical environment that can produce stress are poor lighting, air pollution (including cigarette or cigar smoke produced by coworkers and clients), crowding, noise, and extremes of temperature. Individual stressors include work overload, boredom, conflict about one's work (e.g., a lawyer's being asked by superiors to defend a person who seems guilty, or politicians' having to seek the support of groups whose values are inconsistent with their own in order to get elected), excessive responsibility, and lack of forward movement. Group stressors include bothersome relationships with supervisors, subordinates, and peers.

Organizational stressors include lack of opportunity to participate in decision making, ambiguous or conflicting company policies, too much or too little organizational structure, low pay, racism, and sexism. There are many others (Holt, 1982).

The Role of the Worker   The central part of Figure 12.2 shows the worker and the sources of stress that may be acting on him or her. For example, marital or inner conflict may compound any conflicts encountered in the workplace. A Type A personality may turn the easiest, most routine task into a race to beat the clock. Irrational needs for excessive approval may minimize the impact of most rewards.

Effects of Stress in the Workplace   The right-hand side of the figure suggests a number of subjective, behavioral, cognitive, physiological, and organizational outcomes from the interaction of these sources of stress.

On a subjective level, stressed workers can experience anxiety, depression, frustration, fatigue, boredom, loss of self-esteem (Gibson et al., 1985), and **job burnout.**

Job burnout. A three-phase response to job stress encountered by competent, idealistic workers and characterized by exhaustion, cynicism, and, when possible, a change of jobs.

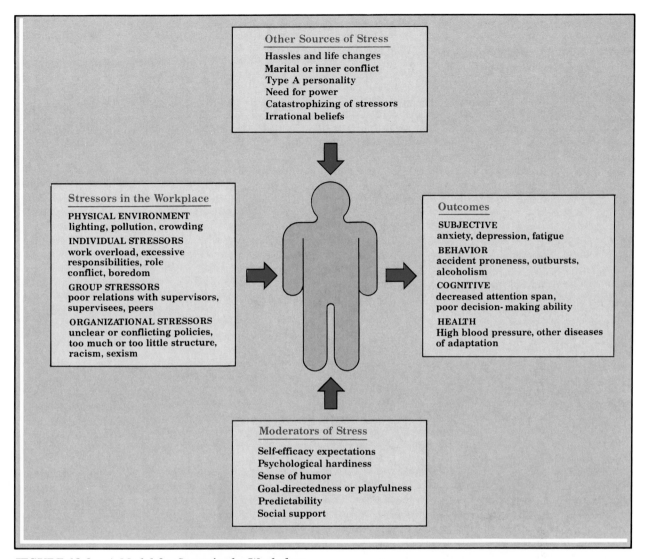

FIGURE 12.3   A Model for Stress in the Workplace
Various factors in the workplace, such as the physical environment and organizational stressors, have their impact on the worker. Workplace stressors can also interact with stresses from home and factors in the personality to produce a number of negative outcomes.

Job Burnout   The signs of burnout include apathy, loss of efficiency, and, occasionally, despair (Perlman & Hartman, 1982). Maslach (1976) has identified three common phases of job burnout:

1. Feelings of being drained, used up, and emotionally exhausted
2. A phase of cynicism, insensitivity, and callousness toward the people they deal with in their work
3. The conclusion that their efforts have been in vain and that their careers are pointless. People in this phase frequently shift careers

People are most likely to experience burnout when they enter their fields with idealistic fervor and dedication, and then find that they are "banging their heads against brick walls" (Farber, 1983; Shinn et al., 1984). Typically, burnout victims are competent, efficient people who become overwhelmed by the demands of their jobs and the recognition that they are unlikely to have the impact that they had anticipated. Teachers, nurses, mental-health workers, police officers, social workers, and criminal and divorce lawyers seem particularly prone toward job burnout.

Behaviorally, stressed workers may become accident-prone, engage in excessive eating or smoking, turn to alcohol or other drugs (Bensinger, 1982; Milam & Ketcham, 1981; Peyser, 1982), and show temperamental outbursts.

The cognitive effects of excessive stress on the job include decreased attention span, poor concentration, and inability to make sound decisions.

Physiological effects include high blood pressure and the "diseases of adaptation" discussed earlier.

The organizational effects of excessive stress include absenteeism, alienation from coworkers, decreased productivity, high turnover rate, and loss of commitment and loyalty to the organization (Gibson et al., 1985; McKenna et al., 1981).

Coping with Stress on the Job   Fortunately, psychologists have found that many measures can be taken to decrease stress in the workplace. One can begin with an objective analysis of the workplace to determine whether physical conditions are hampering rather than enhancing the quality of life. A good deal of job stress arises from a mismatch between job demands and

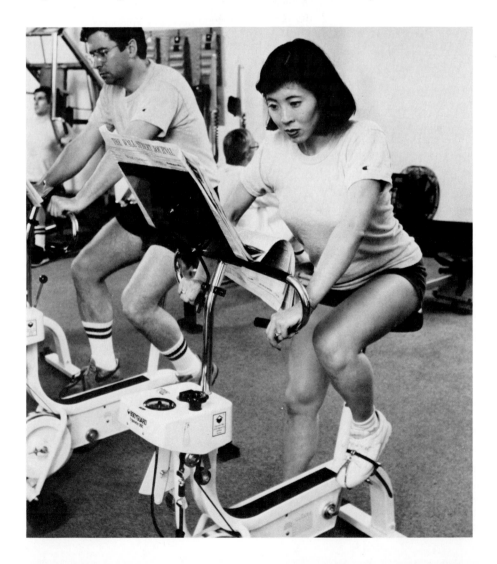

Stress Management in the Workplace
Many organizations help workers manage stress by offering counseling and supportive therapy, education about health, and fitness programs.

the abilities and needs of the employee (Chemers et al., 1985). To prevent mismatches, companies can use more careful screening measures (e.g., interviewing and psychological testing) to recruit employees whose personalities are compatible with job requirements and then provide the training and education needed to impart the specific skills that will enable workers to perform effectively. Job requirements should be as specific and clear as possible.

Workers need to feel they will find social support from their supervisors if they have complaints or suggestions (Gottlieb, 1983; Rocco et al., 1980). Companies can also help workers manage stress by offering counseling and supportive therapy, education about health, and gyms. Kimberly-Clark, Xerox, Pepsi-Cola, Weyerhauser, and Rockwell International, for example, have all made significant investments in gyms that include jogging tracks, exercise cycles, and other equipment.

Workers whose companies do not help them manage stress can tackle this task on their own by using methods such as relaxing, examining whether perfectionism or excessive needs for approval are heightening the tension they encounter at work, or attempting to enhance their psychological hardiness, along the lines suggested by Salvatore Maddi in Chapter 10. Of course, they can always consult psychologists for additional ideas. If these measures are not sufficient, they may wish to carefully weigh the pluses and minuses and decide whether to change their jobs or shift careers.

■ Working Women

From every hamlet, town, and city they came. They came by the millions to fill the jobs left vacant by the men fighting on the foreign battlefields of World War II. They manned the drill presses and the assembly lines. They cranked out weapons and ammunition to support the war effort. They did the skilled labor expected of men.

The new breed of female worker—collectively called "Rosie the Riveter"—filled many jobs closed to women before the war. Because of the war, the percentage of women in the work force grew from under 26 percent in 1940–1941 to 37 percent by 1945 (David, 1957). But when the men came home, millions of women were laid off. Others were shunted from skilled blue-collar work and trades into clerical and service positions. Between 1945 and 1947, public pressures forced 3 million American women back into their "beloved kitchens" (Baker et al., 1980).

But since 1950, women have returned to the work force in record numbers. The U.S. Department of Labor reported in 1980 that 60 percent of women aged 18–64 were at work, as compared with 88 percent of the men in this age group. Working women include 62 percent of mothers of children under 18, and 50 percent of mothers of preschool children (Lublin, 1984; *New York Times*, 1985). Economist Ralph Smith (1979) labels the women's work movement a "subtle revolution," which he believes may have an impact on the quality of life equal to that of the earlier Industrial Revolution.

Why Do Women Work?

Women work for the same reasons as men: first to earn money, but also to meaningfully structure their time, to meet people, and to find self-fulfillment. According to the U.S. Department of Labor (1987), nearly two out of three female workers are single, separated, divorced, widowed, or have husbands whose income is below the national average. Among lower-income families, the wife's earnings often lift the total income above the poverty level. And according to the U.S. Census Bureau (1984), millions of wives earn more than their husbands.

Nevertheless, it is sometimes heard that women are less committed than men to their jobs. Employers who have denied women equal access to training and promotional opportunities have justified their discrimination by citing higher quit rates for women. However, women and men in the same job categories show comparable quit rates (U.S. Department of Labor, 1987). Women are overrepresented in lower-echelon and dead-end jobs; and workers of both sexes in dead-end jobs have higher quit rates than workers in higher-paying, challenging positions. The job role, not the sex of the worker, seems to be the predictor of commitment.

The Workplace for Women

Despite some recent breaking down of traditional sex-segregation, many occupations largely remain "men's work" or "women's work." Women still account for 99 percent of secretaries and 70 percent of school teachers. But women only account for 7 percent of police officers and 2 percent of mechanics (Rathus, 1987). On the other hand, in 1972 women accounted for only 2 to 3 percent of police officers. The percentage of women in first-year medical-school classes has risen from 9 percent in 1969 to 37 percent in 1987 (Klass, 1988).

A recent report on women lawyers adds some insight to the statistics (Goldstein, 1988). In the last two decades, the ranks of lawyers have doubled to 800,000, and overall about 15 to 20 percent are women. Yet a larger proportion of women are now entering lawschools and legal firms. Forty percent of Harvard Law School's students are women, and in the last two years, 40 percent of the new associates in the 250 largest U.S. legal firms were women. All that sounds promising enough, but here's the rub. New legal associates aspire to becoming partners in these firms. Partners share in the profits and have "arrived" in the profession. Associates are usually considered for partnership after about 10 years. Although 40 percent of new associates are women, only one partner in 13 is a woman.

There has also been an expansion of the numbers of women in engineering in recent years, from about 4 percent of engineering graduates in 1976 to about 14 percent of graduates in 1986. Women engineers are readily hired but find "subtle discrimination" in the firms for which they work: for example, they are likely to be passed over for promotions in favor of men (Adelson, 1988). And so in both law and engineering, women get hired; however, they do not get to join the upper echelons of their firms as readily as men do. This fact contributes to the earnings gap between the sexes, as we shall see.

But first, we should note one more thing about women lawyers. A survey of 2,000 Boston area lawyers found that women lawyers were significantly more likely than men lawyers to be single, divorced, and without children (Goldstein, 1988). Is it any wonder that the stereotype of the successful career woman is of a social isolate?

The Earnings Gap According to the U.S. Department of Labor (1987), women overall earn about 60 percent of the income of men (see Table 12.5). Even 70 percent of a sample of women executives with the title of vice president, or higher, reported that they had at one time or another felt that they were being paid less than men of equal ability (Rogan, 1984a)—although not necessarily in their present positions. Note these sad but fascinating examples of the earnings gap:

The average female high school graduate earns less than the average male grade-school *dropout.*
Men with only an eighth-grade education earn more than the average female *college graduate.*

Why this gap in earnings? Much of it can be explained by the fact that most women still work in traditionally low-paying occupations such as wait-

TABLE 12.5   Weekly Earnings of Women and Men,
                          1986

	Women	Men
Professional, technical workers	$428	$599
Managers and administrators	395	620
Sales workers	239	447
Clerical workers	284	403
Craft workers	277	418
Operatives	225	332
Services workers	191	284
Nonfarm laborers	226	271
Private household workers	119	—

Source: U.S. Department of Labor, 1987.

ress, housekeeper, clerk, sales, and light factory and plant work. Even in the same job area, such as sales, men are usually given higher-paying, more responsible positions. Men in sales are more likely to vend high-ticket items such as automobiles, microcomputers, and appliances, whereas women usually sell less-costly goods (Blau, 1975).

Entry into unions and crafts guilds has been generally reserved for the *sons* of current members (Basow, 1980), and so women in a recent year comprised only about 6 percent of our craft workers and filled only about 3 percent of apprenticeships. It is sometimes argued that women are not strong enough for physically taxing work in construction and other fields, but many women can fill these positions, especially when they involve use of machines and tools (Baker et al., 1980).

But the U.S. Census Bureau (1984) reports that in 1980 women with two years of experience earn only 83 percent of the income of men with similar experience *in the same job*. Moreover, this was not an improvement. Women in the same category in 1970 earned 86 percent of men's incomes. And even when women enter the same job as a man, at the same pay, they are unlikely to advance as quickly (Goldstein, 1988).

Reducing the Earnings Gap   The Equal Pay Act of 1963 requires equal pay for equal work. The Civil Rights Act of 1964 prohibits discrimination in hiring, firing, or promotion on the basis of race, ethnic origin, or sex. But women's progress in eliminating discrimination has been impeded by the overburdening of federal enforcement agencies with discrimination cases and the lack of effective enforcement powers (Seidman, 1978; Barrett, 1979). Barrett recommends several measures for improving the quality of work life and reducing the earnings gap for women:

1. *More Realistic Career Planning.* The average woman today spends about 28 years in the work force, but plans for a much shorter tenure. Young women should assume that they will be working for several decades so that they will avail themselves of opportunities for education and training.
2. *Providing Employers with Accurate Information about Women in the Work Force.* If more employers recognized that women spend so many years in the work force, and that commitment to a job reflects the type of work rather than the sex of the worker, they might be more motivated to open the doors to women.
3. *Heightening Awareness of the Importance of the Woman's Career in Dual-Career Marriages.* Husbands may also hold stereotypes that damage their wives' chances for career advancement and fulfillment. A couple should not blindly assume that the man's career always comes first. The man can share child-rearing and housekeeping chores so that each may reap the benefits of employment.

■ A CLOSER LOOK

Resisting Advances: Employers Act to Curb Sexual Harassment on the Job

The Hewlett-Packard Co. sales managers kidded around as they waited to see "The Workplace Hustle," a movie on sexual harassment of employees. "Hey, we're going to see a film on sex. This is going to be a fun way to spend a morning," one of the men joked.

Afterward, he stopped joking. "I wasn't aware this was such a problem," he soberly told Woodrow Clark, the president of Clark Communications Inc., a San Francisco film producer that made the movie.

Sexual harassment on the job no longer is a laughing matter. The federal government and the courts insist that sexual harassment is illegal discrimination in employment; some major employers have lost lawsuits charging them with failure to act against harassment. And several surveys suggest that unwelcome physical or verbal sexual advances, usually directed by men at women, pervade the workplace and increase employee absenteeism and turnover.

As a result, hundreds of corporations, colleges, hospitals, unions and government agencies are scrambling to mitigate the problem and protect themselves against lawsuits. Many are issuing formal policies denouncing sexual harassment. Some are also making employees more sensitive to the problem through training, strengthening internal grievance procedures, and reprimanding or firing known harassers.

Many Companies Involved

The Equal Opportunity Employment Commission is stirring much of the employer concern over sexual harassment. The federal job-bias agency threatens to sue employers for any sexual harassment by bosses, coworkers, and even nonemployees such as suppliers or customers that create an "offensive work environment." The EEOC also urged employers "to take all the steps necessary," including employee training and stricter sanctions, to prevent sexual harassment.

Sexual harassment encompasses not only requested sexual favors but also off-color jokes, sexual leers, pats on the rear, and requirements for sexually revealing uniforms.

Victims' Victories

At the same time, harassment victims are seeking and winning unemployment insurance, workers' compensation, and extensive damages for assault and emotional distress.

In addition to concern about potential legal liability, many executives feel uncomfortable about policing so sensitive and nebulous an area as male–female relationships. They worry about invading privacy, about being dragged into mere lovers' quarrels, and about unfairly damaging a man's reputation because of what often is essentially an unproved and perhaps unprovable allegation.

The subjective nature of many such incidents is notorious. What sounds to one woman like a compliment strikes another as harassment. As a result, some men believe that the new vigilance will end even innocent flirtation.

To provide greater guidance, some employers' policies spell out "no-no's" extending well beyond hiring, firing, or promotion decisions based on demands for sexual favors. AT&T is warning its employees that they can be fired for "repeated, offensive flirtations," using "sexually degrading words" to describe someone, or putting up "sexually suggestive" pictures or objects at work.

The U.S. Army goes further. Among other things, it recently ordered officers to end soldiers' use of catcalls, whistles, terms such as "honey" or "baby" around women, and the wearing of T-shirts imprinted with "sexual language."

4. *Maintaining Employment Continuity and Stability.* Promotions and entry into training programs are usually earned by showing a stable commitment to a career and, often, one's employer. Many couples permit both partners to achieve these benefits by postponing childbearing or sharing child-rearing tasks (Gallese, 1981).

5. *Increasing Job Flexibility and Providing Child-Care Facilities.* Employers can also assist women workers through flextime, providing on-site child-care facilities, and granting extended maternity and *paternity* leaves. By 1984, for example, nearly 20 U.S. hospitals were operating around-the-clock child-care centers for employees (Lublin, 1984). Still, according to the U.S. Census Bureau (1985), only 9 percent of American women who work can make arrangements for their children at their work sites. Forty percent leave their children in another family's home; 31 percent arrange for ba-

bysitters in their own homes; and 15 percent leave their children at daycare centers (not operated at the work site).

6. *Recruiting Qualified Women into Training Programs and Jobs.* Educational institutions, unions, and employers can actively recruit qualified women for positions that have been traditionally held by men.

■ Unemployment: Problems and Coping

When we consider the extrinsic and intrinsic rewards derived from work, it is understandable that unemployment can be a major source of stress. Unemployment has been linked to increased criminal behavior, alcoholism, and admissions to mental hospitals. The financial strain imposed by unemployment is obvious, but unemployment also has less obvious psychological effects, such as loosening our "ties to social reality" (Jahoda, 1981).

Work demands that we deal with social reality. We must rise every morning and prepare ourselves to face the world. We must maintain a daily schedule, relate to other workers, and assume our public roles as accountant, teacher, druggist, and bus driver. We also focus on communal goals, such as the aims of the company or the needs of society as a whole.

The unemployed are cut off from these realities. They may narrow their attention to personal fantasies and problems. Cut off from public life, the unemployed may encounter aimlessness, despair, and a precipitous drop in self-esteem. Although unemployment benefits may provide an adequate standard of living, at least for a while, the unemployed may also see themselves as tossed onto society's scrap heap.

Phases of Unemployment

Powell and Driscoll (1973) studied the responses of 75 professional men, mostly scientists and engineers, who were laid off during a business slowdown, and found that most of them experienced a response pattern that involved four phases:

1. *The Period of Relaxation and Relief.* Most men had noted the company's downhill slide and had feared being laid off for quite a while. Although being laid off can cause immediate mental anguish (Dooley & Catalano, 1980), many of these men actually reported feeling relieved that the inevitable had finally happened. They felt confident that they would find other jobs, and so they took the opportunity to spend a few weeks relaxing. Family relationships remained on an even keel. They postponed job hunting and puttered around the house.
2. *The Period of Concerted Effort.* After about a month, most men became edgy to return to work and instituted a systematic job hunt. They phoned friends, combed want ads, contacted their college placement centers and employment agencies, and sent out résumés. They maintained a sense of confidence and optimism for about three months. During this period they avoided the company of other unemployed men, as if to say, "I'm not one of them. They're losers, but I'll get a call from Boeing any day now."
3. *The Period of Vacillation and Doubt.* After a few months of frustration and disappointment, job hunting became sporadic for many men who did not find jobs. Self-confidence gave way to waves of anxiety, depression, anger, and self-doubt. Family relationships became strained, with wives frequently pushing husbands to remain active in the job market. Some men returned to school or changed careers. Some over 35 complained that companies only wanted younger men. After about 3–4 weeks of vacillation and doubt, many searches skidded to near or total halts. Many men drifted into the fourth phase.

4. *The Period of Malaise and Cynicism.* In Phase IV, hopelessness and despair sapped the vitality from further aggressive job hunting. Protecting the remnants of self-esteem became more important than continued job hunting to many. They frequently excluded most possibilities by narrowing their searches to jobs that fit their skills and backgrounds perfectly. Now they lost their sense of being in control over their own fates. One cynical job hunter said, "No matter what I do, it just doesn't make any difference. It's just a throw of the dice, whether I'll get the job or not." In Phase IV, anger and anxiety gave way to hopelessness, resignation, and cynicism. Marital roles shifted as many wives returned to the work force to make ends meet. Marital relations sometimes improved as many wives stopped prodding their spouses. But the men commonly avoided contacts with friends and the extended family because their own lives were so different.

Using a Job-Finding Club to Land a Job

Despite the thoughts of some "Phase IV" people, finding a job is not a matter of luck. Job hunters can profit from persistent effort, developing concrete job-seeking skills, and maximizing potential and actual resources.

Nathan Azrin and his colleagues (1975) recruited 120 job seekers mainly in their mid-20s, with an average of 14 years of education, for research on an experimental job-finding club. They were matched into pairs according to the probability that they would land a job. Then one member of each pair was randomly assigned to the club or a no-treatment control group in which they were simply encouraged to find work on their own. Club members were further paired off into a buddy system for mutual support and advice.

Club members sought work on a full-time basis. They contacted relatives and friends about possible openings. They wrote letters, made phone calls, and attended interviews. They also received daily counseling and support in small groups. These sessions encouraged them to broaden their vistas to seek various positions, not just one job. Groups discussed dress and grooming and daily progress. Buddies gave partners feedback about their appearance.

Since the "personal touch" often influences potential employers, club members were urged to see employers in person whenever possible. If they could not see employers, they tried to speak to them on the phone. They used names of referring parties, included photographs and lists of personal interests in résumés.

The club itself became a referral source. Members shared leads that weren't right for themselves. Job finders notified the club when other jobs became available at their places of employment. Family and friends were encouraged to be on the lookout for leads. Members also listed themselves in "Situation Wanted" ads and included desirable personal characteristics, such as "likes to work with people."

Other techniques included (1) training in résumé writing, (2) creating a file of open letters of recommendation that could be sent with applications, (3) behavior rehearsal, role playing, and feedback to improve telephoning and interviewing skills, (4) callbacks to potential employers to learn of new openings, (5) record keeping of leads and callbacks, and (6) sharing of transportation resources to ferry applicants to interviews.

Club members found jobs in an average of 14 days, as compared with 53 days for control subjects. After two months, 90 percent of club members had landed jobs, as compared to 55 percent of controls. Club members also found relatively more professional positions than controls, and their starting income was 36 percent higher.

Other projects with the job-finding club have shown encouraging results with alcoholics (Hunt & Azrin, 1973) and with welfare recipients (Richman et al., 1980). How would such a club profit a college graduating class?

■ Summary

1. **Why do we work?** Workers are motivated both by extrinsic rewards (money, status, security) and intrinsic rewards (the work ethic, self-identity, self-fulfillment, self-worth, and the social values of work).

2. **How have attitudes toward work changed in recent years?** Traditional values such as belief that one should work for extrinsic rewards and be bound by loyalty to one's company have been replaced to some degree by "new breed" values that emphasize the right to self-fulfillment and loyalty to the self and one's family.

3. **What are the stages of vocational development?** Super identifies five stages of vocational development: the fantasy, tentative, realistic-choice, maintenance, and retirement stages.

4. **What is the relationship between a person's "coping style" and adjustment in an occupation?** Holland identified six coping styles: realistic, investigative, artistic, social, enterprising, and conventional. Persons with certain coping styles better fit, or are better adjusted in, certain occupations. For example, scientists are investigative and beauticians are realistic and conventional.

5. **How can we use the balance sheet to help make career decisions?** Use of the balance sheet helps us weigh the pluses and minuses of following a particular career path, and also helps us identify gaps in the information we need to make a decision.

6. **How can we use psychological tests to help us make career decisions?** Psychological tests measure our intelligence, specific aptitudes (such as in music), interests, and personality traits. We can then compare our performance on these measures to those of people who are well adjusted in various occupations.

7. **What are the developmental tasks in taking a new job?** These include making the transition from school to the workplace, learning the job tasks, accepting responsibility and subordinate status, and learning how to cope with coworkers, supervisors, successes, and failures.

8. **Why do people shift careers?** People in low-paying, dead-end occupations are more likely to shift occupations than are people in better-paying, more challenging positions. But sometimes we find out that our occupations do not "fit" our abilities or personalities and seek more suitable work.

9. **What factors contribute to getting ahead in America?** Family background best predicts who will earn most in the United States. College completion and standardized academic test scores are the runner-up predictors.

10. **What is workaholism?** Workaholics work compulsively and are governed by a sense of lack of time. Yet they are not necessarily dissatisfied or maladjusted.

11. **What measures can be taken to enhance job satisfaction?** It happens that many of the measures that contribute to the quality of work life also enhance productivity. These measures include careful recruitment and selection, training and instruction, unbiased appraisal and feedback, goal setting, linking financial compensation to productivity, work redesign, allowing workers to make appropriate decisions, and innovative work schedules (such as flextime).

12. **What does organizational theory have to contribute to adjustment in the workplace?** Oganizations have formal and informal characteristics, and we can fit in with them or not. For example, some organizations follow classic organization patterns, with rigid bureaucracies. Others are more flexible and attempt to help workers develop as individuals. Some

organizations make their approach contingent on changing goals, business environments, and worker characteristics.

13. **What sources of stress do we find in the workplace, and what can we do about them?** There are physical, individual, group, and organizational stressors. We can cope with them by evaluating our appraisal of them, enhancing our person–environment fit, and managing stress in ways elaborated on in Chapter 7.

14. **Why do women work?** Women work for the same reasons men do—for a combination of extrinsic rewards (e.g., the paycheck) and intrinsic rewards (e.g., self-identity and the social rewards of work).

15. **What can be done to improve the workplace for women?** Women today work for an average of 28 years but average only 60 percent of the income of men. Women profit from more realistic career planning, maintaining employment continuity, child-care facilities, training programs—and from putting an end to sexual harassment in the workplace.

16. **What is sexual harassment?** Sexual harassment includes requiring women to engage in sexual activity in order to be hired or promoted, unwanted flirting, use of sexually degrading words, even hanging up sexually suggestive pictures in the workplace.

17. **What happens when we become unemployed?** Unemployment not only brings financial strain, but also loosens our ties to social reality. Many unemployed people undergo a four-phase process: relaxation and relief, concerted job hunting, vacillation and doubt, and malaise and cynicism.

18. **How does a job-finding club help people find work?** Job-finding clubs help members land jobs by providing motivation, developing job-seeking skills, and maximizing the use of resources.

■ TRUTH OR FICTION REVISITED

Many million-dollar lottery winners feel aimless and dissatisfied if they quit their jobs after striking it rich. True. We work not only for extrinsic rewards such as the paycheck and financial security, but also for intrinsic rewards, such as the opportunity to engage in challenging activities and broaden social contacts.

Successful salespeople have a need for honesty. True. They make their reputations by helping clients meet their needs.

Anybody who has the ability to get there would be satisfied with prestigious vocations such as college professor, psychologist, physician, or lawyer. False. We could be miserable in an occupation that is inconsistent with our coping styles and other psychological attributes.

Women who wear perfume to interviews are more likely to get the job. This is true only if their interviewers are women. Male interviewers frown on female applicants who wear perfume—and also on male applicants who wear cologne.

It's a good idea to ask for the lowest salary you can get by on at a job interview. False. Quote a relatively high but reasonable figure. Show that your work is valuable.

In dual-career marriages, today's couples consider the woman's work as important as the man's. False. The majority of men and a sizable minority of women still consider the man's job more important.

Hard work is the most powerful predictor of who gets ahead in the United States. False. Family background is the major predictor.

Efficient, skillful employees are evaluated more highly than hard-working employees who must struggle to get the job done. False. The hard-working strugglers get rated more positively.

Allowing employees to piece together their own work schedules is demoralizing to workers and interferes with productivity. Not necessarily. Flextime can help workers cope with parenthood, for example, and as a result boost their morale on the job.

Stressed workers have more accidents on the job. True.

Apathetic workers are most likely to experience job burnout. False. Burnout afflicts the most dedicated workers.

Most workaholics have severe adjustment problems. False. It may be that their families suffer from their devotion to work, but they seem to be generally well adjusted as individuals.

Women in the United States account for 99 percent of secretaries, but only 2 percent of mechanics. True. Despite recent gains in occupations traditionally reserved for men, women are still overrepresented in "traditional female occupations."

Women average only about 60 percent of the earnings of men. True. Women are usually found in lower-paying positions, but even women in comparable work generally earn less than their male counterparts.

Interpersonal Attraction: Of Friendship, Love, and Loneliness

13

Beauty is in the eye of the beholder.

Tallness is an attractive feature in men, but not in women.

College men prefer college women to be thinner than the women expect.

People are perceived as more attractive when they are smiling.

Physical attractiveness is the most important trait we seek in our partners for long-term, meaningful relationships.

During telephone conversations attractive people are more likely than unattractive people to be rated as likable and socially skillful by the person to whom they are talking—*even though they cannot be seen.*

"Opposites attract": We are more likely to be attracted to people who disagree with our attitudes than to people who share them.

Juries are less likely to find attractive individuals guilty of burglary or of cheating on an exam.

The most sought-after quality in a friend is warmth.

It is possible to be in love with someone who is not also a friend.

Romantic love is found around the world.

Male college students are more likely than females to play games in their love relationships—for example, to keep lovers a bit up in the air and to misrepresent their genuine level of commitment.

College students consider selflessness one of the attributes of love.

Taking a date to a horror film or for a roller coaster ride may stimulate feelings of passion.

Many lonely people report that they have as many friends as people who are not lonely do.

Many people are lonely because they fear being rejected in social relationships.

Candy and Stretch. A new technique for controlling weight gains? No, these are the names Bach and Deutsch (1970) give two people who have just met at a camera club that doubles as a meeting place for singles.

Candy and Stretch stand above the crowd—literally. Candy, an attractive woman in her early 30s, is almost six feet tall. Stretch is more plain-looking, but wholesome, in his late 30s, and six feet, five inches.

Stretch has been in the group for some time. Candy is a new member. Let's listen in on them as they make conversation during a coffee break. As you will see, there are some differences between what they say and what they are thinking:

THEY SAY	THEY THINK
STRETCH: Well you're certainly a welcome addition to our group.	(Can't I ever say something clever?)
CANDY: Thank you. It certainly is friendly and interesting.	(He's cute.)
STRETCH: My friends call me Stretch. It's left over from my basketball days. Silly, but I'm used to it.	(It's safer than saying my name is David Stein.)
CANDY: My name is Candy.	(At least my nickname is. He doesn't have to hear Hortense O'Brien.)
STRETCH: What kind of camera is that?	(Why couldn't a girl named Candy be Jewish? It's only a nickname, isn't it?)
CANDY: Just this old German one of my uncle's. I borrowed it from the office.	(He could be Irish. And that camera looks expensive.)
STRETCH: May I? (He takes her camera, brushing her hand and then tingling with the touch.) Fine lens. You work for your uncle?	(Now I've done it. Brought up work.)
CANDY: Ever since college. It's more than being just a secretary. I get into sales, too.	(So okay, what if I only went for a year. If he asks what I sell, I'll tell him anything except underwear.)
STRETCH: Sales? That's funny. I'm in sales, too, but mainly as an executive. I run our department.	(Is there a nice way to say used cars? I'd better change the subject.)
I started using cameras on trips. Last time it was in the Bahamas. I took—	(Great legs! And the way her hips move—)
CANDY: Oh! Do you go to the Bahamas, too? I love those islands.	(So I went just once, and it was for the brassiere manufacturers convention. At least we're off the subject of jobs.)
STRETCH:	(She's probably been around. Well, at least we're off the subject of jobs.)
I did a little underwater work there last summer. Fantastic colors. So rich in life.	(And lonelier than hell.)
CANDY:	(Look at that build, He must swim like a fish. I should learn.)
I wish I'd had time when I was there. I love the water.	(Well, I do. At the beach, anyway, where I can wade in and not go too deep.)

And so begins a relationship. Candy and Stretch have a drink and talk. They share their likes and their dislikes. Amazingly, they seem to agree on everything—from cars to clothing to politics. The attraction is very strong, and neither is willing to risk turning the other off by seeming disagreeable.

They spend the weekend together and feel that they have fallen in love.

They still agree on everything they discuss, but they scrupulously avoid one topic: religion. Their religious differences became apparent when they exchanged last names. But that doesn't mean they have to talk about it.

They also put off introducing each other to their parents. The O'Briens and the Steins are narrow-minded about religion. If the truth be known, so are Candy and Stretch. Candy errs when she tells Stretch, "You're not like the other Jews I know." Stretch also allows his feelings to be voiced now and then. After Candy has nursed him through a cold, he remarks, "You know, you're very Jewish." But Candy and Stretch manage to continue playing the games that are required to maintain the relationship. They tell themselves that the other's remarks were mistakes, and, after all, anyone can make mistakes.

Both avoid bringing in old friends. Friends and acquaintances might say embarrassing things about religion or provide other sources of disruption. Their relationships thus become narrowed. So does their conversation; in order to avoid fights, they do not discuss certain topics. They are beginning to feel isolated from other people and alienated from their genuine feelings.

One of the topics they avoid discussing is birth control. Because of her religious beliefs, Candy does not use contraception, and she becomes pregnant. Stretch claims that he had assumed that Candy was on the pill, but he does not evade responsibility. Candy and Stretch weigh the alternatives and decide to get married. Although physical intimacy came to them quickly, only gradually do they learn to disclose their genuine feelings to one another—and they need professional counseling to help them do so. And on many occasions their union comes close to dissolving.

How do we explain this tangled web of deception? Candy and Stretch pretended to agree on most subjects. They kept each other removed from their families in order to maintain feelings of attraction. In this chapter we explore the meaning of *attraction* and the factors that contribute to feelings of attraction. We shall see how many of us adjust to fear of rejection by potential dating partners, to parental opposition, and to other difficulties.

Two of the outcomes of interpersonal attraction are friendship and love. Candy and Stretch "fell in love." What is *love?* When the first author was a teenager, the answer was, "Five feet of heaven in a ponytail," but this answer may be somewhat deficient in scientific merit. In this chapter we also attempt to define the enigmatic concept of love. We shall see that we sometimes use the term *love* to justify feelings of sexual arousal, and that we sometimes ignore the shortcomings of those we love.

Attraction and love also have a way of leading to the formation of intimate relationships, a subject we explore in Chapter 14. But not everyone develops friendships or love relationships. Some of us remain alone, and lonely. Loneliness is that final topic of this chapter, and we shall have a number of suggestions for overcoming loneliness.

■ Attraction

Whether we are discussing the science of physics, a pair of magnetic toy dogs, or a couple in a singles bar, **attraction** is a force that draws bodies together. In psychology and sociology, attraction is also thought of as a force that draws bodies, or people, together. Attraction can be positive or negative, as in liking or disliking others. Magnetic "kissing" dogs are usually constructed so that the heads attract one another, but—unlike their flesh-and-blood counterparts—a head and tail repel one another. We shall see that when there is a matching of the heads—that is, a meeting of the minds—people are also attracted to one another. And, as with the toy dogs, when we believe another person's opinions are, well, asinine, we are repelled.

Social psychologist Ellen Berscheid (1976) defines **positive attraction** and **negative attraction** (liking and disliking) as attitudes toward another person. According to the **ABC model** of attitudes, attitudes have *A*ffective (emotional), *B*ehavioral, and *C*ognitive components. Attitudes of liking and disliking also involve affective components (good or bad "vibes"), behavioral tendencies (to approach or to avoid), and cognitions (positive or negative evaluations). Many factors influence our attitudes of liking and disliking others. A partial list includes their physical attractiveness, attitudinal similarity, complementarity, reciprocity, propinquity, parental opposition, our general feelings in their presence, and whether they seem to be "hard to get."

Physical Attractiveness: How Important Is Looking Good?

You might like to think that we are all so intelligent and sophisticated that we rank physical appearance low on the roster of qualities we seek in a date—below sensitivity and warmth, for example. But in experimental "Coke dates" and computer dates, physical appearance has been found the central factor in attraction and consideration of partners for future dates, sexual activity, and marriage (Byrne et al., 1970; Green et al., 1984; Hatfield & Sprecher, 1986).

What determines physical attractiveness? Are our standards subjective, or is there broad agreement on what is attractive?

Is Beauty in the Eye of the Beholder? It may be that there are no universal standards for beauty (Ford & Beach, 1951), but there are some common standards for physical attractiveness in our culture. Tallness is an asset for men in our culture, although college women prefer dates who are medium in height (Graziano et al., 1978). Tall women tend to be viewed less positively. Undergraduate women prefer their dates to be about six inches taller than they are, whereas undergraduate men, on the average, prefer women who are about four and a half inches shorter (Gillis & Avis, 1980).

Stretch and Candy were quite tall. Since we tend to associate tallness with social dominance, many women of Candy's height are concerned that their stature will compromise their femininity. Some fear that shorter men are discouraged from asking them out. A few walk with a slight hunch, trying to minimize their height.

Plumpness is valued in many cultures. Grandmothers who worry that their granddaughters are starving themselves often come from cultures in which plumpness is considered acceptable or a positive feature.* But in contemporary Western society, both sexes find slenderness attractive (Lerner & Gellert, 1969). Women generally prefer men with a V-taper, whose backs and shoulders are medium wide, but whose waists, buttocks, and legs taper from medium thin to thin (Lavrakas, 1975; Horvath, 1981).

Both sexes perceive obese people as unattractive (Harris et al., 1982), but there remain some sex differences in perceptions of the most desirable body shape. Male college undergraduates as a group believe that their current physique is similar to the ideal male physique and to the physique women will find most appealing (Fallon & Rozin, 1985). Women undergraduates, by contrast, generally see themselves as significantly heavier than the figure that is most attractive to males, and heavier still than the ideal female figure (see Figure 13.1). But both sexes err in their estimates of the preferences of the opposite sex. Men actually prefer women to be heavier than women expect—about halfway between the girth of the average woman and what the woman thinks is most attractive. And women prefer their men to be somewhat thinner than the men assume.

*But as we saw in the discussion of anorexia nervosa in Chapter 8, some granddaughters are literally starving themselves today.

Positive attraction. An attitude of liking

Negative attraction. An attitude of disliking.

ABC model. The model that views attitudes in terms of affective, behavioral, and cognitive components.

Ellen Berscheid.

Kim Basinger (left) and Ted Danson epitomize standards for physical attractiveness in contemporary American culture. Are attractive people more successful? Do they make better spouses and parents?

A flat-chested look was a hallmark of the attractive profile of the 1920s era of the "flapper," but ample busts are considered more attractive today. Men desire women with larger-than-average breasts, medium-length legs, and small to medium buttocks (Wiggins et al., 1968).

How Behavior Patterns Influence Perceptions of Physical Attractiveness
It turns out that both men and women are perceived as being more attractive when they are attempting to pose "happy" faces as opposed to "sad" faces (Mueser et al., 1984). Thus there is ample reason to, as the song goes, "put on a happy face" when you are meeting people or looking for a date.

Other aspects of behavior also play a role in impressions of physical attractiveness. Women viewing videotapes of prospective dates preferred men who acted outgoing and self-expressive. Men viewing videotapes responded negatively to women who role-played the same behavior patterns (Riggio & Wolf, 1984). College men who showed "dominance" (defined in this experiment as control over a social interaction with a professor) in a videotape were rated as more attractive by female viewers than men who did not. But women showing dominance were not rated as more attractive by male viewers (Sadalla et al., 1987). Despite the liberating forces in recent years, the cultural stereotype of the ideal woman still finds a place for demureness. Of course we are not suggesting that self-assertive, expressive women mend their ways to make themselves more appealing to traditional men; assertive women might find nothing but perpetual conflict with traditional men anyhow.

As noted in Chapter 4, names also influence perceptions of physical attractiveness. Women assigned names such as Jennifer, Kathy, and Christine were rated as more attractive than women assigned the names Gertrude, Ethel, and Harriet (Garwood et al., 1980). Here we have two comments: First, this is another example of overattribution of "behavior" (that is, name selection) to the dispositions of the individual. Parents name us; we usually do not name ourselves. Second, if you dislike your own name, why not select a more appealing nickname? Starting off in college or in a new work setting is an

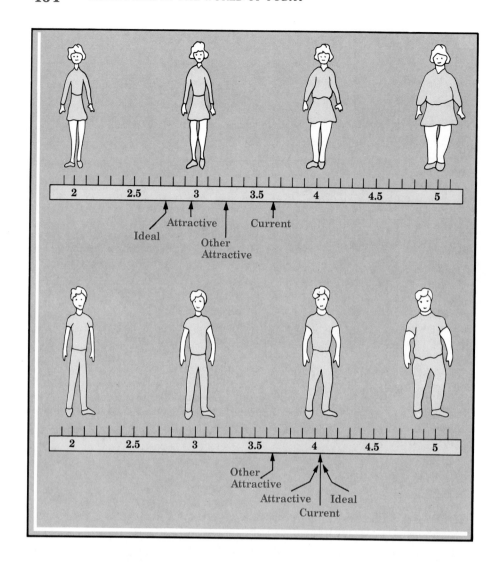

FIGURE 13.1 **Can You Ever Be Too Thin?**

Research suggests that most college women believe that they are heavier than they ought to be. However, men actually prefer women to be a bit heavier than women assume they would like them to be.

ideal time to do so. This suggestion is intended for male readers as well as women. On the other hand, if you have an unusual or unappealing name and are happy with it, stick with it! Remember that many people who accomplish great things have unusual names (see Chapter 4).

What Do You Look for in a Long-Term, Meaningful Relationship?

Your second author ran a survey of college men and women and found that they are relatively more concerned about their dating partners' attractiveness when they are involved in a relationship that they perceive as predominantly sexual (Nevid, 1984). When they are involved in long-term, meaningful relationships, psychological traits such as honesty, fidelity, warmth, and sensitivity are rated as playing relatively more prominent roles. Overall, however, men were relatively more swayed than women by the physical characteristics of their partners, both for sexual and meaningful relationships. Women placed relatively greater emphasis on personal qualities such as warmth, assertiveness, need for achievement, and wit. What was the most important quality that college men and women claimed to want in long-term partners? Honesty.

Nevid's findings sound admirable, in a way, but remember that they are based on self-report. Although personal qualities take on more prominence in long-term relationships, physical attractiveness probably plays at least a filtering role. That is, unless the prospective partner measures up to minimal physical standards, most of us are probably unwilling to look "beneath the surface" for the "more meaningful" personality traits and behavior patterns.

Nevid's findings are replicated in studies on mate selection. Women tend to place greater emphasis than men on characteristics such as professional status, consideration, dependability, kindness, and fondness for children. Men place relatively greater emphasis on physical attractiveness, cooking ability (can't men turn on the microwave oven themselves?), and even thriftiness (Buss & Barnes, 1986; Howard et al., 1987).

"Reproductive Investment Theory"   On the surface, the sex differences in characteristics that influence perceptions of attractiveness sound unbearably sexist—and, probably, ultimately they are. But it is interesting to note that some theorists believe that evolutionary forces have favored the survival of men and women with such preferences because these traits provide certain reproductive advantages. For example, according to "reproductive investment theory," a woman's attractiveness is linked strongly to her age and health, both of which are suggestive of reproductive capacity. But the value of men as reproducers is less clearly suggested by physical appearance. Factors that contribute to the provision of a stable home atmosphere—such as community standing and dependability—might have become relatively more appealing in the eyes of women over the millenia. But, as noted, such theorizing is largely speculative and not fully consistent with all the evidence. For example, despite the stereotype that men can physically father healthy children at any age, aging men, like aging women, place their children at greater risk for chromosomal abnormalities, as we shall see in Chapter 16. And what of cultures in which women do the fighting and hunting while men remain in the home to rear the children? Reproductive investment theory might do little more than provide a pseudoscientific rationale for sexist beliefs, such as the view that a woman's place is in the home.

■ A CLOSER LOOK

What Do You Look at First?

When you first meet someone of the opposite sex, what do you look at first? Are you impressed by an even-featured face? Do you search for sensitive eyes? Do bright teeth snap up your attention? Or, for you, do clothes tend to make the man, or woman?

According to a poll by the Roper Organization (*Psychology Today*, 1984), the largest number of women (35 percent) first notice how a man is dressed, while 29 percent of men are initially influenced by a woman's clothing. The largest group of men (45 percent) immediately responds to the woman's figure or build, while 29 percent of women share this interest in what is happening below the neck. Other things that men and women tend to notice first include the eyes (30 percent of women; 22 percent of men), the face (27 percent of women; 34 percent of men), smile (27 percent of women; 24 percent of men), and hair (16 percent of both sexes). The teeth, height, hands, and legs earn our less immediate interest, if we focus on them at all.

What do we look at first when meeting a person of the same sex? Women (41 percent) and men (39 percent) are both most likely to note how the person is dressed. Women and men are about equally impressed by the person's face (26 percent of women; 28 percent of men) and figure (20 percent of women; 16 percent of men). Women pay more attention to the new person's hair (27 percent of women; 13 percent of men), while men are more likely to rapidly focus in on the new person's height (15 percent of men; only 2 percent of women).

Is there a message in all this? Perhaps. Although we are brought up not to judge books by their cover, clothing apparently makes a significant contribution to our first impressions on others. There may be limits to what we can do about our faces, but our figures are also important and we may be able to maximize their presentability through diet, exercise, and—yes—strategic dressing. That's two (clothing and figure) out of three, and that isn't too bad.

Stereotypes of Attractive People: Do Good Things Come in Pretty Packages? By and large, we rate what is beautiful as good. We expect physically attractive people to be poised, sociable, popular, mentally healthy, and fulfilled. We expect them to be persuasive and hold prestigious jobs. We even expect them to be good parents and have stable marriages. Physically unattractive individuals are more likely to be rated as outside of the main-stream—for example, politically radical, homosexual, or psychologically disordered (Berscheid & Walster, 1974; Brigham, 1980; Dion et al., 1972; O'Grady, 1982; Unger et al., 1982). Unattractive college students are even more likely to rate themselves as prone toward developing problems and psychological disorders.

These stereotypes seem to have some basis in reality. For one thing, it seems that more attractive individuals are less likely to develop psychological disorders, and that the disorders of unattractive individuals are more severe (e.g., Archer & Cash, 1985; Farina et al., 1986; Burns & Farina, 1987). For another, physical attractiveness is positively correlated with educational achievement, occupational prestige, and income (Umberson & Hughes, 1984).

One way to interpret the data on the correlates of physical attractiveness is to assume that these links are all innate—in other words, we can believe that beauty and competence genetically go hand in hand. We can believe that biology is destiny and throw up our hands in despair. But a more useful way to interpret this data is to assume that we can do things to make ourselves more attractive and also more successful and fulfilled. Recall that smiling (and a popular name!) are linked to attractiveness. So is having a decent physique or figure (which is something we can work on), good grooming, and attending to the ways in which we dress. So don't give up the ship.

Then, too, we can make us mere mortals feel better by pointing out that attractive people are seen as more vain and self-centered, and more likely to have extramarital affairs (Dermer & Thiel, 1975). Yet even these "negative" assumptions have a positive side. After all, don't they mean that we think attractive people have more to be self-centered about, and that their affairs reflect their greater sexual opportunities?

Attractive people are also more likely to be found innocent of burglary and cheating in mock jury experiments. When found guilty, they are handed down less severe sentences (Efran, 1974). Perhaps we assume that more attractive people are less likely to need to resort to deviant behavior to achieve their goals. Even when they have erred, perhaps they will have more opportunity for personal growth and be more likely to change their evil ways.

The beautiful are also perceived as more talented. In one experiment, students rated essays as higher in quality when their authorship was attributed to a more attractive woman (Landy & Sigall, 1974).

Attractive children learn early of the high expectations of others. Even during the first year of life, adults tend to rate physically attractive babies as good, smart, likeable, and unlikely to cause their parents problems (Stephan & Langlois, 1984). Parents, teachers, and other children expect attractive children to do well in school and be popular, well behaved, and talented. Since our self-esteem reflects the admiration of others, it is not surprising that the physically attractive have higher self-esteem (Maruyama & Miller, 1975).

Physical Attractiveness in Social Interaction: Do Good Looks Somehow Translate into Social Skills? If we are given to expecting that "good things come in pretty packages," we shall probably treat pretty packages—that is, physically attractive people—as if they are good things. That is, we will respond to them more favorably. We expect more from physically attractive people (Adams, 1977), and they, in turn, have higher self-expectations and more positive self-images. More positive self-images perhaps give them confidence (positive self-efficacy expectations) in interpersonal behavior, and high self-efficacy expectations motivate them to develop social skills and persist in difficult undertakings.

In one experiment, Snyder, Tanke, and Berscheid (1977) informed some men telephone callers at random that a woman to whom they were speaking was physically attractive. Other callers, also selected at random, were informed that she was unattractive. The woman had actually been rated as equal in attractiveness. Judges who heard the woman's side of the conversation only rated the women who had been labeled as attractive more likeable, sociable, and friendly. Apparently, male callers who believed their telephone partners were attractive somehow elicited more competent social behavior from them.

In another study, Goldman and Lewis (1977) found that attractive people were more likely to be rated by telephone partners as socially skillful and likeable, even though their conversants were blind as to their appearance. Physically attractive people appear to acquire and maintain the socially competent behavior that is fostered in them.

Reis and his colleagues (1980, 1982) surveyed college undergraduates concerning their social interactions. In one phase of their research, they had college undergraduates maintain records of social interactions for four ten-day periods. Photos of the students were then rated for physical attractiveness at another university. It was found that attractive college men engage in more social interaction with women, but less interaction with men, than their less attractive peers. Their increased contacts with women appear to be at the expense of relationships with men. There is no such link between attractiveness and social interactions among college women. More attractive college women spend more time on dates and at parties than their less attractive peers, but increased heterosexual interactions do not spill over into other areas of social contact. The satisfaction derived from opposite-sex interactions is positively related to attractiveness for both sexes.

Women whose attractiveness ratings were highly variable were more likely to find satisfaction in their social encounters than women whose ratings were more consistent. It may be that women with variable ratings possess an idiosyncratic appeal that is highly attractive to some, but not at all to others. Thus they may feel that they are liked for their character traits rather than just for their physical features. Their more idiosyncratic appeal may also cause them to think that they are capable of being "special" to people who also appeal to them. What kinds of idiosyncratic appeal can you focus on developing?

The Matching Hypothesis: Who Is "Right" for You?

Have you ever refrained from asking out an extremely attractive person for fear of rejection? Do you feel more comfortable when you approach someone who is a bit less attractive? If so, you're not alone. But make no mistake: classical studies suggest that physical attractiveness may be the major factor that motivates us to develop relationships with people of the opposite sex.

Donn Byrne and his colleagues (1970) brought couples together for a brief "Coke date." Each participant was rated for attractiveness before the experiment began. After a 30-minute date, subjects were rated by their partners as to desirability as a future date, a sex partner, or a prospective spouse. More attractive dates achieved consistently higher ratings. Students were also more likely to pursue postexperiment relationships with more attractive dates, and more readily recalled the names of attractive dates at the end of the semester.

In another study, Walster and her colleagues (1966) arranged computer dates for a dance for university first-year students. Participants were rated for attractiveness when they bought their tickets. Students rated their dates as to likability and appropriateness for future dates halfway through the dance.

Donn Byrne.

Physical attractiveness was the major determinant of liking and desire for further contact. Intelligence, academic achievement, and personality variables had no bearing on ratings.

But do not despair if you see yourself as less than exquisite in physical attractiveness. Although we may rate highly attractive people as most desirable, we shall not necessarily be left to blend in with the wallpaper. According to the **matching hypothesis,** we actually tend to ask out people who are similar to ourselves in physical attractiveness rather than the local Tom Selleck or Kim Basinger lookalike (Berscheid et al., 1971).

The major motive for asking out "matches" seems to be fear of rejection by more attractive people. Shanteau and Nagy (1979) asked female undergraduates to choose between two possible male dates on the basis of physical attractiveness (as suggested by a photograph) and probability that the man would accept the date request (as suggested by statements attached to the photographs, varying from "Sure thing" to "No chance"). Women preferred not to pursue men who were either very unattractive or very unlikely to accept the date. Moderately attractive men who were "highly likely" to accept the date were chosen most often. In a second phase of the experiment, women were asked to choose a date on the basis of the photograph alone. Again, most women chose moderately attractive men, suggesting that they *assumed* that the more attractive a man was, the less likely he would be to accept the date.

People also tend to select mates more or less equal in attractiveness to themselves (Murstein, 1972; Murstein & Christy, 1976). Yet we tend to rate our mates as slightly more attractive than ourselves—as if we had somehow "gotten the better of the deal" (Murstein, 1972). This is not too surprising. Later in the chapter we shall see that we tend to idealize loved ones. It may also be that by focusing on our mates' positive features we shall feel happier with our marriages. Too, we may be aware of our own struggles to present ourselves to the world each day, but take our mates' appearance more or less for granted. Remember the biases in the attribution process: Although our mates may labor to make themselves attractive, we are likely to attribute their attractiveness as "coming from within." But when we perceive ourselves we tend to focus on all the external influences (exercise, hair shaping, makeup, etc.) that add to our appeal.

Matching hypothesis. The view that people generally seek to develop relationships with people who are similar to themselves in attractiveness and other attributes, such as attitudes.

According to the matching hypothesis, we usually ask out people who are similar to ourselves in physical attractiveness, attitudes, and background. People similar in attractiveness are less likely to reject us than people who are better looking than we are.

▉ A CLOSER LOOK

"Let's Make a Deal": On Lonely Hearts Ads and the Matching Hypothesis

All the lonely people—where will they all be found? Some of them are found in personal ads on the back pages of newspapers. Some samples:

> Born-again Christian woman, 33, 4'9", queen-size, loves children, quiet home life, sunsets. Seeks marriage-minded man, 33 or over. Children, handicap, any height or weight welcome.

> Horseman, handsome, wealthy, 48, 5'10", 180 lbs, likes dancing, traveling. Seeking beautiful, slender girl, under 35, sweet, honest, neat, without dependents. Send full-length photo, details.

> Single, 28, 5'7", 128 lbs with strawberry-blond hair, blue eyes. Wants to meet secure, sincere gentleman, 32–48, who loves the outdoors and dancing. Preferably Taurus. No heavy drinker need reply. Send photo and letter first.

> Tall male, 40, slim, divorced, nice-looking, hardworking nondrinker, owns home and business. Seeks attractive, plump gal, 25–35, not

extremely heavy, but plump, kind, sweet, for a lasting relationship. Photo, phone.

Harrison and Saeed (1977) examined 800 such lonely hearts ads. They scored each for the self-suggested attractiveness of the advertiser and the requested attractiveness of the respondent. Consistent with the matching hypothesis, more attractive advertisers generally sought more attractive respondents. But women were more likely to advertise themselves as physically attractive, and men were more likely to tout financial security as a selling point. Attractive women were more likely to demand financial security, and wealthy men demanded greater physical appeal. At first glance, this finding may seem to run counter to the matching hypothesis, but wealth and physical beauty are both highly desirable. And so the overall desirability of advertiser and respondent tended to remain constant—good looks were up for sale, and a "deal" could be made.

The researchers also found that women sought older men and men sought younger women. Men, you may be surprised to learn, more often than women expressed an interest in marriage. *Are* men actually more interested in women than marriage? Perhaps. But it could also be that men assumed that expressing a willingness to marry would be a strong selling point for them and that women feared that they might scare off potential matches by requesting marriage.

There are exceptions. Now and then we find a beautiful woman married to a plain man, or vice versa. How do we explain it? According to Bar-Tal and Saxe (1976), we may assume that such men are wealthy—as in the Jackie Kennedy–Aristotle Onassis match—highly intelligent, or otherwise successful. We seek an unseen factor that will maintain the sense of balance in the match.

The matching hypothesis does not only apply to physical attractiveness. We are also more likely to get married to people who are similar to us in their psychological needs (Meyer & Pepper, 1977), personality traits (Buss, 1984; Lesnik-Oberstein & Cohen, 1984), and attitudes, as we shall see below.

Now let us turn our attention to other factors, including attitudinal similarity, that influence feelings of attraction.

Attraction and Attitudinal Similarity: Birds of a Feather Flock Together

In this land of free speech, we do respect the right of others to reveal their ignorance by disagreeing with us, don't we? Perhaps. But it has been observed since ancient times that we tend to like people who agree with us (Jellison & Oliver, 1983). The more dogmatic we are, the more likely we are to reject people who disagree with us (Palmer & Kalin, 1985). Attitudinal similarity is a powerful contributor to the formation of both friendships and love relationships.

The strong physical attraction Candy and Stretch felt for one another motivated them to pretend that their preferences, tastes, and opinions coincided. They entered a nonspoken agreement not to discuss their religious differences. Research also suggests that birds of a feather flock together—especially when they are good-looking. College students are most attracted to dates who are physically appealing and express similar attitudes (Byrne et al., 1970). In the Byrne study, ratings of physically attractive dates with dissimilar attitudes approximated those of unattractive dates with similar attitudes. Unattractive dates who held dissimilar attitudes were least desirable.

But there is also evidence that we may tend to *assume* that physically attractive people share our attitudes (Marks et al., 1981). Can this be a sort of wish fulfillment? When physical attraction is very strong, as it was with Candy and Stretch, perhaps we like to think that all the kinks in a relationship will be small, or capable of being ironed out. Similarly, we tend to assume that preferred presidential candidates share our political and social attitudes (Brent & Granberg, 1982). We may even fail to remember statements they make that conflict with our attitudes (Johnson & Judd, 1983). Then, once they are in office, we may become disillusioned when they swerve from our expectations.

Not all attitudes are necessarily equal. Men on computer dates at the University of Nevada were more influenced by sexual than religious attitudes (Touhey, 1972). But women were more attracted to men whose religious views coincided with their own. These findings suggest that women may have been less interested than men in a physical relationship but more concerned about creating a family with cohesive values. Studies show that attitudes toward religion and children are more important in mate selection than characteristics such as kindness and professional status (e.g., Buss & Barnes, 1986; Howard et al., 1987).

Similarity in tastes and distastes is also important in the development of relationships, including friendships. For example, May and Hamilton (1980) found that college women rate photos of male strangers as more attractive when they are listening to music that they like (in most cases, rock) as compared to music that they don't like (in this experiment, "avant-garde classical"). If a dating couple's taste in music does not overlap, one member may look more appealing at the same time the second is losing appeal in the other's eyes—and all because of what is on the stereo. Are we suggesting that you find out what music your date likes and make sure to play it when you're together? Certainly not if you're interested in a long-term relationship! It could be rather distressing to wind up with music you hate blaring from the stereo for the next 50 years.

Candy and Stretch used common but maladaptive methods to avoid having to cope with attitudinal dissimilarity. They initially allowed themselves to misperceive the others' religious background. When they realized that they were wrong, they tried to push the issue out of their minds. When ignoring differences also failed, they misrepresented or hid their genuine feelings.

There are other ways of trying to cope with dissimilar attitudes. We can try to convince others to change their attitudes, or, perhaps, to convert to our own religions. We can reevaluate our attitudes and explore the possibility of changing them. We can also choose to end the relationship. But Candy and Stretch were unwilling to do any of these because they took their religious feelings seriously and were strongly attracted to one another on a physical level.

Complementarity: Every Comic Needs a Straight Man, or Woman

There are some occasions on which opposites do attract. In terms of sex roles, the historical attraction between man and woman has been viewed as a natural

Complementarity. A feature of a relationship, or a source of attraction, that is characterized by the reinforcement value of opposing traits.

Reciprocity. The tendency to return feelings and attitudes that are expressed about one.

Propinquity. Nearness.

intermingling of the active and the passive, the dominant and the submissive. Now that stereotypical sex roles are fading, it is no longer easy to predict whether someone will be active or dominant on the basis of gender. But a dominant person may still often be attracted to someone who is submissive. A needy person may be attracted to someone who is giving. These are examples of **complementarity,** in which opposing traits reinforce each other so that each person benefits from the interaction.

Although dominant people might be more comfortable with friends and lovers who let them take the lead, the evidence that people form relationships on this basis is sketchy (Nias, 1979). Social psychologist Zick Rubin (1973) suggests that friends and lovers may be more likely to develop complementary relationships as they interact over the years.

In any event, relationships characterized by dominance–submissiveness may run aground when the submissive party decides that he or she is tired of playing the doormat. The formerly submissive wife of a domineering husband may decide that the times are a-changing and begin to assert herself. Similarly, the "student" in a student–teacher type of romance may eventually mature and decide that he or she can think things out and make decisions. In each case, the dominant person is likely to find the other suddenly disagreeable, and the relationship will encounter friction.

Reciprocity: If You Like Me, You Must Have Excellent Judgment

Has anyone told you how good-looking, brilliant, and mature you are? That your taste is refined? That all in all, you are really something special? If so, have you been impressed by his or her fine judgment?

In his 1937 classic *How to Win Friends and Influence People,* Dale Carnegie advised that we could make others like us by greeting them with enthusiasm and pouring on the praise. When we feel admired and complimented, we tend to return these feelings and behaviors. This is **reciprocity.** Carnegie's advice was based on his own personal observations, but research also suggests that we are prone to liking people who do favors for us, compliment us, and tell us that they like us (Baron, 1971; Byrne, 1971). Men tend to be attracted to women who engage them in conversation, maintain eye contact, and lean toward them while speaking, even when their attitudes are dissimilar (Gold et al., 1984).

Perhaps we can thank the reciprocity effect for the fact that so many couples do seem to be happy and reasonably well adjusted. With encouragement, formerly neutral or mild feelings are sometimes capable of turning into powerful, positive feelings of attraction. But it may be that we should also be wary of people who compliment too quickly, who seem enthusiastic about us before they get to really know us. They may be aware of the power of reciprocity and be attempting to influence us to do things that are beneficial for them, but not necessarily for us.

Propinquity: "Simply Because You're Near Me"

Why did Sarah Abrams walk down the aisle with Allen Ackroyd and not Danny Schmidt? Sarah and Danny actually had more in common. But Sarah and Al exchanged smoldering glances all throughout 11th-grade English because their teacher had used an alphabetical seating chart. Danny sat diagonally across the room and had to content himself with passing romantic notes to Andrea Sugarman. Sarah Abrams, to him, was only a name he heard called when attendance was taken.

Attraction is more likely to develop between people who are placed in frequent contact with one another. This is the effect of nearness, or **propinquity.** The development of friendships as well as romances is influenced by propinquity. Students are more likely to develop friendships when they sit next to one another (Segal, 1974). Homeowners are most likely to become friendly with next-door neighbors, especially those with adjacent driveways (Whyte, 1956). Apartment dwellers tend to find friends among those who live nearby on the same floor (Nahemow & Lawton, 1975). Even infants respond more positively to strangers after a few meetings (Levitt, 1980). Adults report increased liking for a photograph of a stranger simply as a result of being exposed to the picture several times (Moreland & Zajonc, 1982).

When Parents Say No: The "Romeo and Juliet Effect"

> They longed to marry but their parents forbade it. Love, however, cannot be forbidden. The more the flame is covered up, the hotter it burns.
>
> Edith Hamilton, 1942, on the myth of Pyramus and Thisbe

Would parental opposition drive a wedge between you and your love, or would you fight to maintain the relationship? In the Shakespearean play, the young lovers, Romeo and Juliet, drew closer against the bloody backdrop of a family feud. But that was literature. What about real life?

Psychologists sought an answer through a survey of dating and married couples at the University of Colorado (Driscoll et al., 1972). Student questionnaires suggested that parental opposition intensified feelings of love between couples during the first six to ten months of the relationship. But parental opposition did not affect feelings between married couples. There was an important footnote: Although parental opposition intensified feelings of love during the early stages of a relationship, it also lowered feelings of trust and increased faultfinding within the couple.

During the early stages of a relationship, parental opposition may intensify needs for security within a couple so that they cling together more strongly. But for couples who have already made a strong commitment, as in a lengthy courtship or a marriage, parental opposition may become irrelevant. And in those cases in which seeds of mistrust are sewn, the relationship may eventually suffer even when feelings of love have been intensified. Couples should probably frankly discuss the possible motives of oppositional parents. In this way they can lay potential problems on the table and have the chance to cope with them before they negatively influence the relationship.

Emotions and Attraction: "Get 'Em in a Good Mood"

Attempts at seduction usually come at the tail end of a date—after the dinner, the film, the wine, and all that witty commentary on contemporary mores, politics, and the horrible state of our _____ (you fill it in—there is no shortage of topics). An "assault" at the beginning of a date might be viewed as . . . well, as an assault. But in a number of experiments, food and pleasant music have been found to increase acceptance of persuasive messages—that is, of what the other person is trying to sell (Janis et al., 1965; Galizio & Hendrick, 1972). General good feelings and positive emotions can help increase our feelings of attraction toward our companions.

In an instructive study, Veitch and Griffit (1976) had college students wait in an office to participate in an experiment while a "radio" delivered a newscast in the background. Some students were exposed to positive stories: There was a breakthrough in cancer research. Food prices were falling. Students could now use faculty parking lots! Others heard bleaker tales. An apparent cancer breakthrough had failed. Food prices were soaring. New student parking lots were being built in Outer Mongolia.

The news stories were phony tapes, of course. They set the stage for the second stage of the experiment in which students rated the likability of others whom they believed to have similar or dissimilar attitudes. As in other experiments, students were more attracted to people who seemed to possess similar attitudes. But the news stories also had an effect. Good news was good news for attraction: Students who heard positive stories expressed greater feelings of attraction than those who heard negative ones, regardless of similarity in attitudes.

In another study, female undergraduates who were shown a slapstick comedy were more attracted to new acquaintances than women who had just seen a depressing documentary about the career and assassination of John F. Kennedy (Gouaux, 1971). However, going to a horror film could have a different effect, as we shall see in the section on love.

Playing "Hard to Get": Is Hard to Get Hard to Forget?

We tend to reciprocate feelings of attraction, but what if a person who professes to be attracted to you is equally attracted to everybody? Are you more impressed when the other person has eyes for you only?

Elaine Walster and her colleagues (1973) recruited male subjects for an experiment in which they were given the opportunity to rate and select dates. They were given phony initial reactions of their potential dates to them and to the other men in the study. One woman was generally hard to get. She reacted indifferently to all the men. Another woman was uniformly easy to get. She responded positively to all male participants. A third showed the fine judgment of being attracted to the rater only. Men were overwhelmingly more attracted to this woman—the one who had eyes for them only. She was selected for dates 80 percent of the time.

We do not have the outcome of a comparable study with women subjects, but women would also probably be more attracted to men who show special interest in them. In the film *Play It Again, Sam*, Woody Allen (upon the advice of a fantasized Humphrey Bogart) tells Diane Keaton, "I have met a lot of dames in my life, but you are something special." She is delighted. Before using this line, first ask whether your date has seen *Play It Again, Sam*.

■ Friendship

Friendship, friendship,
What a perfect blendship . . .

Development of Friendships

Friends play a major role in our lives from the time we are children through late adulthood. For young children, friendships are based largely on propinquity (Berndt & Perry, 1986; Rathus, 1988). For 5- to 7-year-olds, "friends" are our classmates and those with whom we do things and have fun. Between the ages of 8 and 11, similarity enters the picture: Children now say that they share interests as well as toys with their friends. And at about the age of 12, having someone with whom one can share intimate feelings is mentioned (Damon, 1977).

By the early teens it becomes important that friends keep our confidences. We want to be able to tell our friends "everything" without worrying that they will spread stories around town (Berndt & Perry, 1986). Teenaged girls report intimacy as more important in their friendships than boys do, and girls also report that their friendships are more intimate (Berndt, 1982).

Are friendships, as the song goes, "perfect blendships"? By and large our friends tend to be similar to us in race, social class, and values.

In high school and college, we tend to belong to **cliques** and **crowds**. A clique is a small number of close friends who share confidences. A crowd is a larger, loosely knit group of friends who share activities. The "crowd" may go to the football game together or to a party. But we tend to share our innermost feelings about people at the party within the "clique."

Friends can also play an important role during late adulthood. The

Elaine Walster.

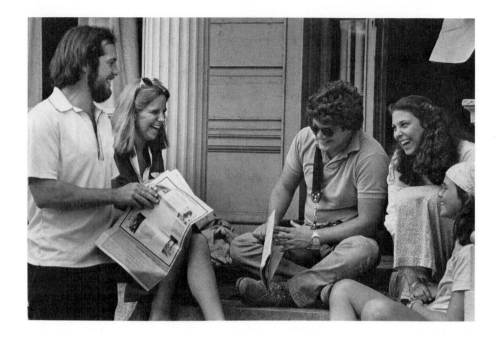

Friends
What roles do friends play in your life? What qualities do you look for in friends?

quality of friendliness is associated with psychological well-being among the elderly (Costa & McCrae, 1984; Lowenthal & Haven 1981). Having a confidant heightens morale even in the face of tragic events such as serious illness or the death of a spouse (Lowenthal & Haven, 1981). People with confidants are also less depressed and lonely.

Qualities of Good Friends

As noted, the qualities we attribute to friends varies with our ages, but at some point during adolescence sharing and keeping confidences becomes crucial.

In 1979, *Psychology Today* magazine reported the results of a survey of readers on friendship. As noted in Chapter 1, magazine surveys are notorious for yielding biased results. First of all, readers of any one magazine do not represent the general population. Second, readers who respond to surveys very often are the most interested in making or selling their points of view; representative surveys somehow get the rest of us to respond. We are not disturbed by the first objection, since *Psychology Today* readers are likely to be similar to readers of this book—better educated than average and interested in what psychology has to offer them in their daily lives.

In any event, some 40,000 readers responded to the survey. To these readers, keeping confidences and loyalty were the most sought-after qualities in a friend (Parlee, 1979). Overall, the qualities deemed important in friends were:

1. Ability to keep confidences (endorsed by 89% of respondents)
2. Loyalty (88%)
3. Warmth and affection (82%)
4. Supportiveness (75%)
5. Honesty and frankness (73%)
6. Humor (72%)
7. Willingness to set aside time for me (62%)
8. Independence (61%)
9. Conversational skills (59%)
10. Intelligence (58%)
11. Social conscience (49%)

And so, among sophisticated young adults loyalty (keeping confidences is one aspect of loyalty) appears to be the prime requisite for friendship. Also important are the social-supportive aspects of the relationship (including warmth, humor, and willingness to set aside time for the relationship). General positive traits also figure in—honesty, independence, intelligence, and so on.

On Friendship and Love

If we can return to Stretch and Candy for a moment, let us note that their relationship lacked a quality associated with the most frequently endorsed qualities of friendship—trust and the sharing of confidences. In fact, their relationship was so superficial (despite the physical intimacy) that they hadn't even exchanged information about their religious beliefs and attitudes.

The trials of Candy and Stretch highlight the fact that it is possible to be "in love" even when we are not friends. Friendship and love, in other words, do not necessarily overlap. However, we shall see that the most lasting love relationships combine the two.

■ Love

What makes the world go round? **Love,** of course. Love is one of the most deeply stirring emotions, the ideal for which we will make great sacrifice, the emotion that launched a thousand ships in the Greek epic *The Iliad*.

For thousands of years, poets have sought to capture love in words. A seventeenth-century poet wrote that his love was like "a red, red rose." In Sinclair Lewis's novel *Elmer Gantry*, love is "the morning and the evening star." Love is beautiful and elusive. It shines brilliantly and heavenly. Passionate love—**romantic love**—can also be earthy and sexy, involving a solid dose of sexual desire.

Models of Love

Psychologists today find that love is a complex concept, involving many areas of experience—emotional, cognitive, and motivational (Sternberg & Grajek, 1984). Psychologists also speak of different kinds of love and different styles of love. Let's have a look at how the concept of love evolved in our Western culture.

The Greek Heritage of Four Types of Love   The concept of love can be traced back at least to the classical Greeks, who had four concepts related to the modern concept of love: *storge, agape, philia,* and *eros*. **Storge** (pronounced STORE-gay) is translated as attachment and nonsexually oriented affection, the emotion that binds friends and parents and children together. **Agape** (AH-gah-pay) is similar to generosity and charity. It implies the wish to share one's bounty, and is epitomized by anonymous donations to charity. **Philia** (FEEL-yuh), like storge, is close in meaning to friendship. It is based on liking and respect and involves the desire to do and share things with another person.

Eros is closest in meaning to passionate, or romantic, love. Sigmund Freud used the concept *eros* to describe a basic life instinct, which he thought motivated most human behavior (see Chapter 2). Freud believed, literally, that *eros* "makes the world go round." Our own concept of romantic love does not imply any basic life instinct. Still, romantic love can be an important determinant of behavior—in societies that believe in the concept.

Styles of Love   Other psychologists speak of contemporary styles of love. For example, Clyde and Susan Hendrick (1986) of Texas Tech University developed a love-attitude scale that suggests the existence of six styles of love

Love. An intense, positive emotion that involves feelings of affection and desire to be with and to help another person.

Romantic love. A type of love that is characterized by passion. An intense, positive emotion that involves arousal, the presence of a person one finds attractive, a cultural setting that idealizes romance, and the belief that one is "in love."

Storge. In ancient Greece, a type of love similar to attachment and affection.

Agape. In Greek, a type of love similar to generosity; selfless love.

Philia. In Greek, a type of love similar to liking and respect.

Eros. In Greek, a type of love similar to romantic love.

There are many different styles of love, including romantic love, game-playing love, and logical love. What styles of love characterize your relationships?

among college students. Following is a list of the styles, with items that identify the style and are similar to the actual items on the love-attitude scale. As you will see, current conceptions of love still owe a debt to the ancient Greeks:

1. *Eros,* or romantic love. "My lover fits my ideal," "My lover and I were attracted to one another immediately."
2. ***Ludus,*** or game-playing love. "I keep my lover up in the air about my commitment," "I get over love affairs pretty easily."
3. *Storge,* or friendship-love. "The best love grows out of an enduring friendship."
4. ***Pragma;*** pragmatic or logical love. "I consider a lover's potential in life before committing myself," "I consider whether my lover will be a good parent."
5. *Mania,* or possessive, excited love. "I get so excited about my love that I cannot sleep," "When my lover ignores me I get sick all over."
6. *Agape,* or selfless love. "I would do anything I can to help my lover," "My lover's needs and wishes are more important than my own."

Most people who are "in love" combine a number of these "styles of love" in their feelings. Using these six styles of love, the Hendricks (1986) found some interesting sex differences. Male college students are significantly more "ludic" (i.e., game-playing) than females. Female college students are significantly more "storgic" (friendly), pragmatic (long-term-relationship oriented), and manic* (possessive) than males. However, there were no sex differences in terms of eros (passion) or agape (selflessness).

Romantic Love in Contemporary Western Culture: A Role-Playing Approach

In order to experience romantic love, in contrast to attachment or sexual arousal, one must be exposed to a culture that idealizes the concept. In Western culture, romantic love blossoms with the fairy tales of Sleeping Beauty, Cinderella, Snow White, and all their princes charming. It matures with romantic novels, television tales and films, and the personal tales of friends and relatives about dates and romances (Udry, 1971).

Romantic love may not reflect any natural inner state. A person must have experience with a culture that idealizes the concept of love in order to successfully play the role of a person who is "in love." This does not mean that we are being "phony" when we enact the role of someone in love—any more than subjects of hypnosis are necessarily being phony when they behave as though they are in a "trance." It simply means that we require a clear concept of what a behavior pattern is supposed to be like before we can enact it.

We retain much of a double standard toward sexual behavior. Women often justify sexual experiences as involving someone they love. Men usually need not justify sexual desires, and so need not attribute passion to love. A number of college students have found that their experiences have not lived up to their fantasized expectations for romantic love, and so they reject the concept altogether (Dion & Dion, 1975).

Romantic Love: A Definition

Definitions of romantic love vary. Psychoanalysts generally speak in global concepts, such as Erich Fromm's "craving for complete fusion . . . with one other person. [Love] is by its very nature exclusive" (1956, p. 44). Erik Erikson also sees love as the merging of two identities. To Erikson, mature love is possible only after one has established ego identity (see Chapters 2 and 11).

*Not to be confused with manic-depression, the disorder discussed in Chapter 8.

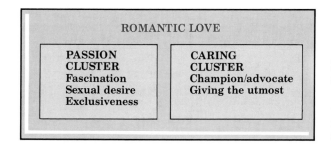

FIGURE 13.2   Passion and Caring
Romantic love is characterized by two clusters of feelings—a passion cluster and a caring cluster.

Others have avoided unmeasurable concepts like the merging or fusing of identities, and define romantic love in terms of the behavior of lovers. According to psychologist Keith Davis (1985), romantic love is characterized by two clusters of behavior patterns: a passion cluster and a caring cluster (see Figure 13.2). The passion cluster contains feelings of fascination, as shown by preoccupation with the loved one; sexual arousal or desire; and the desire for exclusiveness (a special relationship with the loved one). The caring cluster includes agape—championing the interests of the loved one and giving one's utmost to or for the loved one, including sacrificing one's own interests, if necessary. College undergraduates see the desire to help or care for the loved one as more central to the concept of love than concern about how the loved one can meet one's own needs (Steck et al., 1982). Romantic lovers also idealize one another (Driscoll et al., 1972). They magnify each other's positive features and overlook their flaws.

Social psychologists Ellen Berscheid and Elaine Hatfield (Berscheid & Walster, 1978; Walster & Walster, 1978) define love in terms of physiological response and cognitive appraisal of that response. Love, to them, involves intense arousal and some reason to label that arousal love.

Let us define romantic love as an intense, positive emotion that involves (1) arousal in the form of sexual attraction; (2) a cultural setting that idealizes love; (3) the actual or fantasized presence of a person considered attractive; (4) caring; and (5) the *belief* that one is "in love."

On Love and Arousal: If My Heart Is Pounding, It Must Mean I Love You

The Roman poet Ovid suggested that young men (his interests were admittedly sexist) might open their ladies' hearts by taking them to the gory gladiator contests. The women could attribute the pounding of their hearts and the butterflies in their stomachs to the nearness of their dates, and conclude that they were inspired by them. Despite the saying, love does not seem to be "blind"—just a bit nearsighted. Research does suggest that strong arousal in the presence of a reasonably attractive person may lead us to believe that we are experiencing desire (Istvan & Griffitt, 1978). But if the person is decidedly *un*attractive, we may attribute our arousal to revulsion or disgust (White et al., 1981).

Let us consider a couple of experiments that studied the effects of body arousal on feelings of passion. In one study, male college students rated the attractiveness of *Playboy* nudes (Valins, 1966). Each rater was wired so that he could monitor his own heartbeat (he believed) through a microphone and earphone set. Heart sounds accelerated in frequency when certain slides were being shown. In general, subjects rated models as more attractive when the heartbeats were more rapid.

There was one catch. Valins had doctored the feedback arrangement so that raters were *not* listening to their own heartbeat. Instead, they were hearing heartbeats that were accelerated or slowed down for randomly selected

QUESTIONNAIRE

The Love Scale

Are you in love?

The following love scale was developed at Northeastern University in Boston. To compare your own score (or scores, if you have been busy) with those of Northeastern University students, simply think of your dating partner or partners and fill out the scale with each of them in mind. Then compare your scores to those at the end of the chapter.

Directions: Circle the number that best shows how true or false the items are for you according to this code:

7 = definitely true	3 = somewhat false
6 = rather true	2 = rather false
5 = somewhat true	1 = definitely false
4 = not sure, or equally true and false	

1. I look forward to being with _____ a great deal.

definitely false 1   2   3   4   5   6   7 definitely true

2. I find _____ to be sexually exciting.

definitely false 1   2   3   4   5   6   7 definitely true

3. _____ has fewer faults than most people.

definitely false 1   2   3   4   5   6   7 definitely true

4. I would do anything I could for _____.

definitely false 1   2   3   4   5   6   7 definitely true

5. _____ is very attractive to me.

definitely false 1   2   3   4   5   6   7 definitely true

6. I like to share my feelings with _____.

definitely false 1   2   3   4   5   6   7 definitely true

7. Doing things is more fun when _____ and I do them together.

definitely false 1   2   3   4   5   6   7 definitely true

8. I like to have _____ all to myself.

definitely false 1   2   3   4   5   6   7 definitely true

9. I would feel horrible if anything bad happened to _____.

definitely false 1   2   3   4   5   6   7 definitely true

10. I think about _____ very often.

definitely false 1   2   3   4   5   6   7 definitely true

11. It is very important that _____ cares for me.

definitely false 1   2   3   4   5   6   7 definitely true

12. I am most content when I am with _____.

definitely false 1   2   3   4   5   6   7 definitely true

13. It is difficult for me to stay away from _____ for very long.

definitely false 1   2   3   4   5   6   7 definitely true

14. I care about _____ a great deal.

definitely false 1   2   3   4   5   6   7 definitely true

Total Score for Love Scale: _____

models. The men may have attributed what they believed to be their own hearts racing to the slide being shown. As a consequence, perhaps they believed that this woman *must* be particularly appealing to them.

Rapid heartbeat, of course, does not only signify passion. It is a sign of arousal of the sympathetic division of the autonomic nervous system. Does heightening sympathetic arousal increase feelings of sexual attraction? Was Ovid right? Perhaps he was, according to a Canadian study with male subjects (Dutton & Aron, 1974).

This study got a rise out of subjects—a rise of 230 feet, to be precise. Some subjects were interviewed by a woman on a spindly bridge that swayed high above the rocky canyon of the Capilano River in Vancouver—and presumably heightened their sympathetic arousal, perhaps, in some cases, by inducing fear. In this unlikely setting they answered questions and wrote stories about pictures whose meanings could be interpreted in various ways. The men also received the phone number of the interviewer, supposedly in case they wished to learn more about the study. But the experimenters were setting the stage to determine whether the experimental treatment induced men to call the interviewers for dates later on. Other subjects were interviewed by the same woman on a lower and apparently safer bridge. Subjects who had gotten high—230 feet high, that is—wrote picture-based stories that contained more sexual content. They also phoned their female interviewer more frequently afterward.

Wait, you say? Perhaps the height of the bridge, and not the female interviewer, was responsible for the sexual content of the stories and the subsequent telephone calls? The investigators anticipated the possibility of such an objection, and so they arranged for another group of male subjects to be interviewed on the two bridges by men. Subjects interviewed by men wrote stories devoid of sexual content and made few calls afterward, regardless of the bridge on which they had been interviewed. And so the presence of the woman was required. Dutton and Aron reasoned that the male subjects interviewed by men could not attribute their arousal, which apparently stemmed from the height of the spindly bridge, to sexual desire. But men interviewed by a woman could attribute their physiological responses to her presence. In this way, feelings of arousal induced by height may have taken on the flavor of passion.

Many sources of stimulation can heighten our levels of arousal, and heightened arousal may just lead us to respond more positively to members of the opposite sex. And so, a horror movie or a roller-coaster ride might just stimulate your date's passion. If you believe that we should not be giving out this information, feel free not to act on it.

Romantic versus Companionate Love: Is Romantic Love Any Basis for a Marriage?

According to the American ideal, when people come of age they will find their perfect match, fall in love, get married, and live happily ever after. In the next chapter we shall see that the high divorce rate sheds some doubt on this fantasy. But for the moment, let us confine ourselves to asking whether romantic love provides a sound basis for marriage.

There is cause for skepticism. Romantic love frequently assails us in a flash. Then it may dissipate somewhat as our involvement with the loved one grows. Some philosophers and social critics have argued that romantic love is but a "passing fancy"; marriage, therefore, must be a firm legal institution for the rearing of children and the transmission of wealth from one generation to another. And so it is unwise to base marriage on romantic love. From this perspective, marriage is a sober instrument of social stability whereas love, after all, is *l'amour!* In many instances throughout Western history, it was assumed that husbands would take mistresses or visit prostitutes. In a few

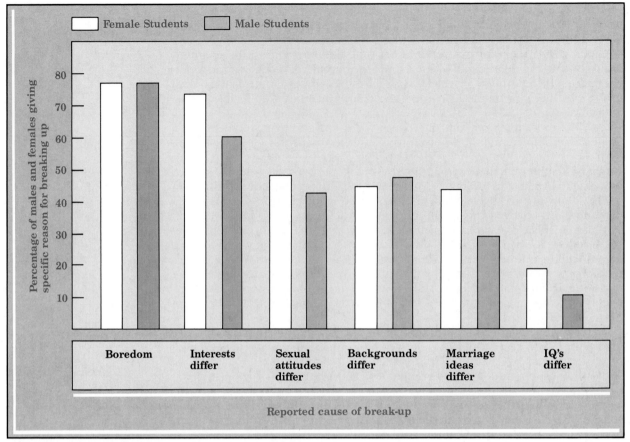

FIGURE 13.3   What Happens When Reality Sets In?

Researchers followed some 200 dating couples for a two-year period, during which more than half of them broke up. Boredom was a major reason given—romantic, passionate love apparently cooled as time went on. But the couples who broke up also reported the gradual discovery of many differences in opinion, interests, and abilities. If a relationship is to last, perhaps companionate love—which is based on mutual respect and accurate knowledge of one's partner—must wax as the fires of passion wane. (Based on data from Hill, Rubin, & Peplau, 1976).

cases, wives have also been expected to take lovers, especially among the aristocratic upper classes.

A study by Hill and colleagues (1976) appears to support some of the skepticism concerning the durability of romantic love. The researchers followed 200 college couples over a two-year period, during which more than half broke up. Figure 13.3 suggests that the reasons for the breaks, and they can be summarized as a combination of boredom and recognition of dissimilarities, two factors also found important in breakups by Byrne and Murnen (1987). Byrne and Murnen (1987) also note that these two factors give rise to a third factor—change in reciprocal evaluations. All in all, early idealized romantic passions give way to objective recognition of differences in attitudes and interests.

Berscheid and Walster (1978) suggest that people are more likely to maintain their relationship once the romance begins to fade if they have developed **companionate love.** Companionate love requires trust, loyalty,

Companionate love. A type of love that is less intense than romantic love. It is based on sharing, mutual respect, and willingness to sacrifice.

Loneliness
Why are so many people lonely? For lots of reasons, including lack of social skills, lack of interest in others, and lack of empathy; expectation of social failure; cynicism about human nature; and the self-defeating belief that there's nothing they can do about it.

sharing of feelings, mutual respect and appreciation, lack of hypercriticality, and willingness to sacrifice. Companionate love is based on genuine knowledge of the other person, not idealization.

If companionate love blooms, a relationship can survive the fading of extremes of passion. At this point a couple can work together to meet each other's sexual as well as companionate needs. Skills can substitute for the excitement of novelty.

All in all, it sounds a bit like friendship.

Loneliness. A negative feeling state characterized by a sense of painful isolation from other people.

■ Loneliness

All the lonely people,
Where do they all come from?
"Eleanor Rigby," a Beatles song

All the Lonely People
Sexual attraction was only one reason that Candy and Stretch entered into their troubled relationship. Another was **loneliness.** Being lonely is not the

same thing as being alone. Loneliness is a feeling state in which we sense ourselves as painfully isolated or cut off from other people. Being alone is a physical fact, and people with many close friends choose to be alone from time to time so that they can study, work, or just reflect on their feelings about being in the world.

People who are lonely, as compared to people who are not, show behavior patterns such as the following: They spend more time by themselves; are more likely to eat dinner alone and spend weekends alone; engage in fewer social activities and are unlikely to be dating (Russell, 1982; Russell et al., 1980). Lonely people may report having as many friends as people who are not lonely, but upon closer examination, their friendships are relatively superficial. For example, they are not very likely to share confidences with their friends, and sometimes their "friends" are surprised to learn that lonely people consider them as friends (Williams & Solano, 1983). Loneliness tends to reach a peak during adolescence, when most of us begin to replace close links to our parents with peer relationships.

It is no secret that loneliness is linked to feelings of depression. But now studies by Janice Kiecolt-Glaser and Ronald Glaser of men in their first year following separation or divorce suggest that loneliness is also associated with suppressed immune-system functioning (Lear, 1987).

Where Do They All Come From? Causes of Loneliness
The causes of loneliness are many and complex. Lonely people tend to have several of the following characteristics:

▣ Q U E S T I O N N A I R E ▣

The UCLA Loneliness Scale

What about you? Are you socially connected or lonely much of the time? Following is a 10-item version of the UCLA Loneliness Scale, which is widely used in research on this painful personal and social problem. Answer the items according to this code:

1 = Never
2 = Rarely
3 = Sometimes
4 = Often

After you have written a number from 1 to 4 to indicate your response to each item, turn to the answer key at the end of the chapter.

1. How often do you feel unhappy doing so many things alone?
2. How often do you feel you have nobody to talk to?
3. How often do you feel you cannot tolerate being so alone?
4. How often do you feel as if nobody really understands you?
5. How often do you find yourself waiting for people to call or write?
6. How often do you feel completely alone?
7. How often do you feel you are unable to reach out and communicate with those around you?
8. How often do you feel starved for company?
9. How often do you feel it is difficult for you to make friends?
10. How often do you feel shut out and excluded by others?

1. Lack of social skills. They are insensitive to the feelings of others, do not know how to make friends, and how to cope with disagreements (Baron & Byrne, 1987; Rubin, 1982).
2. Lack of interest in other people (Cutrona, 1982).
3. Lack of empathy (Lear, 1987).
4. High self-criticism concerning social behavior and expectation of failure in dealing with other people (Jones et al., 1981; Learn, 1987; Schultz & Moore, 1984).
5. Failure to disclose information about themselves to potential friends (Berg & Peplau, 1982; Solano et al., 1982).
6. Cynicism about human nature.
7. Demanding too much too soon, as characterized by misperception of other people as cold and unfriendly in the early stages of developing a relationship (Lear, 1987).
8. Pessimism about life in general.
9. External locus of control (Jones, 1982).

Coping with Loneliness

Psychologists have found that cognitive and behavioral methods are helpful with lonely people. Cognitive therapy methods attempt to combat feelings of pessimism, general cynicism about human nature ("Yes, many people are selfish and not worth knowing, but if we assume that everyone is like that, how can we develop fulfilling relationships?"), and fear of failure in social relationships (Young, 1982).

The behavior-therapy methods of assertiveness training and social-skills training help lonely people develop ways of initiating conversations, talking on the telephone, giving and receiving compliments, and handling disagreements without being submissive or aggressive (Rathus, 1978; Rook & Peplau, 1982). You can refresh yourself on assertiveness training by reviewing Chapter 5, and in the next chapter we'll have some suggestions for enhancing date-seeking skills.

Walter and Siebert's Suggestions   Tim Walter and Al Siebert also suggest a number of measures that can be taken to make friends and combat loneliness:

1. *Make frequent social contacts.* Join committees for student-body activities. Engage in intramural sports. Join social-action groups, such as Greenpeace. Join a club such as the psychology club, ski club, or photography club. Get on the school newspaper staff.
2. *Be assertive.* Express opinions. Smile and say "Hi" to interesting-looking people. Sit down next to people at the cafeteria, not in a corner by yourself.
3. *Become a good listener.* Ask people how they're "doing" and what they think about classes or events of the day. Then *listen* to them. Be reasonably tolerant of divergent opinions; no two people are exactly alike. Maintain eye contact and a friendly face.
4. *Let people get to know you.* Try exchanging opinions and talking about your interests. Sure, you'll "turn off" some people—we all do—but how else can you learn whether you have something in common?
5. *Fight fair.* Now and then a friend will disappoint you and you'll want to tell him or her about it, but do so fairly. Begin by asking your friend if it's okay to be honest about something. Then say, "I feel upset because you . . ." Ask if your friend realized that his or her behavior got you upset. Work together to figure out a way to avoid repetition. End by thanking your friend for solving the problem with you.
6. *Tell yourself that you're worthy of friends.* None of us is perfect. Each of us has

a unique pattern of traits and insights, and you'll connect with more people than you might expect. Give them a chance.

7. *Go to the counseling center.* Thousands of students are lonely and don't know exactly what to do. Some know what to do but haven't quite got the courage. College counseling centers are familiar with the problem and a valuable resource (Walter & Siebert, 1987, pp. 165–171).

In this chapter we have discussed interpersonal attraction—the force that initiates social contact. In the next chapter we follow the development of these social contacts into intimate relationships, particularly as they concern marriage and alternate styles of life.

■ Summary

1. **What is attraction?** Attraction is an attitude of liking (positive attraction) or disliking (negative attraction). Attraction involves good or bad affective responses, approach or avoidance behavior, and positive or negative evaluations.

2. **What traits contribute to physical attractiveness in our culture?** In our society, slenderness is found attractive in both sexes. Tallness is found attractive in men, but not in women. When we meet new people of the opposite sex, our first impressions focus on their clothing, figures, and faces, although men give the figure more priority than women do. Smiling enhances attractiveness.

3. **What are the stereotypes concerning attractive people?** There is an assumption that good things come in pretty packages. Physically attractive people are assumed to be more successful and well adjusted, but they are also perceived as more vain, self-centered, and given to extramarital affairs. Attractive people are less likely to be judged guilty of crimes. Attractive people have greater social skills. Research suggests that we expect attractive people to show greater social skills and that we elicit skillful behavior from them.

4. **How do attractive people interact socially?** Attractive men have more social interactions with women, but fewer with men than their less attractive peers. Attractive men and women are more likely to date and attend parties than less attractive peers and are more likely to find these activities satisfying.

5. **What is the role of attitudinal similarity in interpersonal attraction?** Experimental "Coke dates" reveal that we are most attracted to people who are physically attractive and who share our attitudes.

6. **What is the matching hypothesis?** But, in keeping with the matching hypothesis, we are more likely to ask out and marry people who are similar to ourselves in attractiveness—largely because of fear of rejection. Examination of lonely hearts ads suggests that people are frequently willing to swap good looks for financial security.

7. **What is the role of complementarity?** Other research on attraction suggests that we are sometimes attracted to people who play complementary roles, but it is also possible that complementarity is formed as relationships progress.

8. **What is the role of reciprocity?** We tend to reciprocate feelings of attraction that are expressed by others.

9. **What is the role of propinquity?** Nearness, or propinquity, increases the likelihood that attraction will develop.

10. **What is the Romeo-and-Juliet effect?** Parental opposition fans the flames of attraction during the early stage of a relationship, but may sow seeds of mistrust.

11. **How do our moods influence feelings of attraction?** Generally positive emotions increase feelings of attraction, and vice versa.
12. **What is the effect of playing "hard to get"?** We are most attracted to people who are generally hard to get, but who have "eyes" for us only.
13. **What roles do friends play in our lives?** We share activities, interests, and confidences with friends.
14. **What qualities are sought in friends?** We seek loyalty, social support, and generally positive traits, such as frankness and intelligence.
15. **What kinds of love are there?** There are several styles of love, including passionate (eros), storgic (affectionate), ludic (game-playing), pragmatic (practical), manic (possessive), and agapic (selfless) styles.
16. **What is passionate, or romantic, love?** Romantic love is a positive, intense emotion that develops in a culture that idealizes the concept. It involves arousal, presence of a person who is attractive to us, and some reason to label the arousal love.
17. **What is the role of arousal in perceptions of love?** We think of ourselves as being in love when we experience physical arousal in the presence (actual or fantasized) of another person and have some reason to label that arousal love. Experiments support the view that feelings of attraction are enhanced when we experience higher levels of physiological arousal and can attribute them to the presence of an attractive person.
18. **What factors contribute to loneliness?** Factors such as lack of social skills, fear of social rejection, cynicism about human nature, and general pessimism contribute to loneliness.
19. **What can we do to cope with loneliness?** In order to combat loneliness we can challenge our pessimism and our beliefs about other people. We can also develop social skills. In addition, we can join groups, express our ideas, become good listeners, and, when necessary, "fight fair."

■ TRUTH OR FICTION REVISITED

Beauty is in the eye of the beholder. False. Although there are individual differences, most of us have adopted cultural standards for beauty, such as preferring slenderness to obesity.

Tallness is an attractive feature in men, but not in women. True, generally speaking. Tallness is associated with social dominance, and many males are uncomfortable when they must literally "look up" to women.

College men prefer college women to be thinner than the women expect. False. College men actually prefer women to be a bit heavier than women feel they ought to be.

People are perceived as more attractive when they are smiling. True—so "put on a happy face."

Physical attractiveness is the most important trait we seek in our partners for long-term, meaningful relationships. Not according to the Nevid study. Nevid's subjects rated honesty as more important.

During telephone conversations attractive people are more likely than unattractive people to be rated as likable and socially skillful by the person to whom they are talking—even though they cannot be seen. True. On the average, attractive people display more competent social behavior than less attractive people do.

"Opposites attract": We are more likely to be attracted to people who disagree with our attitudes than to people who share them. False. We are usually more attracted to people who agree with our attitudes.

Juries are less likely to find attractive individuals guilty of burglary or of cheating on an exam. True. "Good things" are expected to "come in pretty packages."

The most sought-after quality in a friend is warmth. False. According to the *Psychology Today* survey, loyalty ranks higher.

It is possible to be in love with someone who is not also a friend. True. But when passion fades, the relationship might suffer.

Romantic love is found around the world. False. Romantic love doesn't make the entire world go 'round; it is found only in cultures that idealize the concept.

Male college students are more likely than females to play games in their love relationships—for example, to keep lovers a bit up in the air and to misrepresent their genuine level of commitment. True.

College students consider selflessness to be one attribute of love. True. It is assumed that we would place the needs of loved ones before our own.

Taking a date to a horror film or for a roller coaster ride may stimulate feelings of passion. True. Exciting experiences raise our level of arousal, and a heightened level of arousal can then be attributed to—or at least rub off on—an attractive companion.

Many lonely people report that they have as many friends as people who are not lonely do. True. But upon closer examination, these "friendships" seem relatively superficial.

Many people are lonely because they fear being rejected in social relationships. True. Lowering the odds of rejection by enhancing social skills is one way of coping with loneliness.

■ Key for the Love Scale

The Love Scale was validated with a sample of 220 undergraduates, aged 19–24 (mean age = 21), from Northeastern University. Students were asked to indicate whether they were "absolutely in love," "probably in love," "not sure," "probably not in love," or "definitely not in love" with a person they were dating. Then they answered the items on the Love Scale with the same person in mind.

Table 13.1 shows the mean score for each category. Mean scores for men and women in each of the five categories did not differ, so they were lumped together. If your Love-Scale score for your date is 84, it may be that your feelings lie somewhere in between those of Northeastern University students who claimed that they were "probably in love" and "absolutely in love."

Be warned: A number of students broke into arguments after taking the Love Scale—their "love" for one another differed by a few points! Please do not take the scale so seriously. Such scales are fun, but they will not hold up in court as grounds for divorce. Rely on your feelings, not on your scores.

TABLE 13.1 Love-Scale Scores of Northeastern University Students

Condition	N*	Mean Score
Absolutely in love	56	89
Probably in love	45	80
Not sure	36	77
Probably not in love	40	68
Definitely not in love	43	59

*N = Number of students.

■ Key for the UCLA Loneliness Scale— Ten-Question Version

Add your responses to each of the ten items to attain your total score. Lear (1987) suggests that for respondents who attain a score of 30 or above, loneliness might be a risk factor to their well-being. Students who are concerned about their scores may wish to consider discussing them with their instructors.

Communication and Intimate Relationships: A Guide on How to Get from Here to There

14

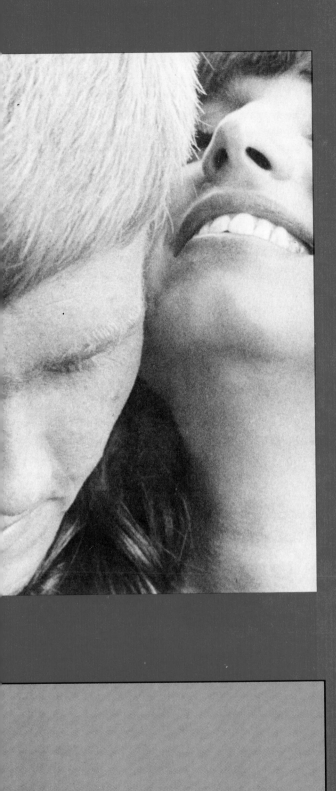

Small talk is a clumsy way to begin a new relationship.

Rapid self-disclosure of intimate information is the best way to deepen a new relationship.

We are less likely to try to iron out the wrinkles in our relationships when new partners are available to us.

Marriage is losing its popularity as a style of life.

In the ancient Hebrew and Greek civilizations, wives were viewed as their husbands' property.

Singles are more satisfied with their lives than married people are.

Couples who were engaged for at least three years before getting married have happier marriages than couples who were engaged for only a year.

Sexual problems are the single most powerful predictor of general marital dissatisfaction.

Mothers are more satisfied with their marriages than women without children are.

Disagreement is destructive to a marriage.

The most effective way of handling criticism from a marital partner is to be critical yourself.

Being single has become a more common U.S. life-style over the past few decades.

Single people are "swingers."

Cohabiting men are less likely to hold jobs than their married counterparts.

Cohabiting college students are rebellious.

"One, two. One, two." Great opening line? In the film *Play It Again, Sam,* Woody Allen plays the role of Allan Felix, a social *klutz* who has just been divorced. Diane Keaton plays his platonic friend Linda. At a bar one evening with Linda and her husband, Allan Felix spots a woman on the dance floor who is so attractive that he wishes that he could have her children.

The thing to do, Linda prompts, is to start to dance, then dance over to the woman and "Say something." With a bit more prodding, Linda starts Allan dancing. It's so simple to dance, she tells him. He need only keep time. "One, two, one, two," she says.

"One, two," Allan repeats. Linda shoves him off to his dream woman to "say something."

Hesitantly, Allan dances up to her. After a moment of working up his courage, he says, "One, two. One, two, one, two." He is ignored and he finds his way back to Linda.

"Allan, try something more meaningful," Linda implores.

Once more, Allan dances nervously back toward his ideal woman. He stammers, "Three, four, three, four."

"*Speak* to her, Allan," Linda insists.

He dances up to her again and tries, "You interested in dancing at all?"

"Get lost, creep," she replies.

Allan dances rapidly back to Linda. "What'd she say?" Linda asks.

"She'd rather not," he shrugs.

So much for "One, two, one, two," and, for that matter, "Three, four, three, four." Striking up a relationship requires some social skills, and, as we shall see, those first few conversational steps can be big ones. In this chapter we first explore stages in the development of **intimate relationships.** Then we discuss the institution of marriage, which remains the goal for most Americans, and the sources of marital satisfaction and dissatisfaction. We examine various ways of enhancing intimate relationships, including improving communication skills. Finally, we examine some alternatives to marriage, including the popular life-styles of singlehood and cohabitation.

■ Stages in Relationships

Relationships, like people, can be thought of as undergoing stages of development. Prior to the development of a relationship, according to Levinger (1980), we have a condition of **zero contact,** in which we are unaware of each other's existence. Once we become aware of one another, our relationships can develop through five stages. During each stage positive factors influence us to build or maintain the relationship. Negative factors influence us not to build, or to dissolve, the relationship.

Initial Attraction

Initial attraction occurs when people become aware of one another. Positive factors at this time include repeated meetings (propinquity), positive emotions, and personality factors such as the **need for affiliation.** Negative factors include lack of propinquity, negative emotions, and low need for affiliation.

Our impressions of another person are mostly visual during the stage of initial attraction, although we may overhear the other person in conversation, or hear others talking about the person. We go from zero contact to initial attraction when we spot a new person across a crowded lunchroom, when we enter a class with new students, or when someone takes a job in a nearby office. We may purposefully go from zero contact to initial attraction through computer matchups or blind dates, but most often we meet other people by accident. And the greatest promoter of such accidents is propinquity.

A Canadian study found that single adults most often meet other singles by means of introduction by a mutual acquaintance (92%), at parties (90%),

Intimate relationship. A relationship characterized by sharing of inmost feelings. The term *physical intimacy* implies a sexual relationship.

Zero contact. According to Levinger, the condition prior to initial attraction, when people are not aware of each other.

Initial attraction. The first stage of a relationship, according to Levinger.

Need for affiliation. The need to have friends and belong to groups.

"One, Two. One, Two." In this scene from the film *Play It Again, Sam,* Woody Allen, playing the socially awkward Allan Felix, attempts to initiate a relationship. Unfortunately, his small talk is off the mark, and according to the matching hypothesis, he and the object of his feelings do not quite seem made for each other.

at work (82%), and during leisure activities, such as sports and hobbies (80%) (Austrom & Hanel, 1985). Meeting people at work or at leisure pastimes was most likely to lead to a romantic relationship. Singles clubs (27%), church groups (26%), classified ads (20%), and dating services (10%) were much less likely methods for meeting.

Building a Relationship

After initial attraction comes the stage of **building a relationship.** Positive factors in building a relationship include matching physical attractiveness (see discussion of the **matching hypothesis** in Chapter 13), attitudinal similarity, and reciprocal positive evaluations. Negative factors—factors that might discourage us from trying to build a relationship—include nonequivalent physical attractiveness, attitudinal dissimilarity, and reciprocal negative evaluations.

Not-So-Small Talk: An Audition for Building a Relationship   Early in the stage of building a relationship, we experiment with **surface contact:** We seek common ground (e.g., attitudinal similarity, overlap of interests), and we test our feelings of attraction. At this time, the decision as to whether or not to pursue the relationship may well be made on the basis of **small talk.** Small talk is a superficial sort of conversation that provides an exchange of superficial information, but stresses breadth of topic coverage rather than in-depth discussion.

Knapp refers to small talk as an "audition for friendship" (1978, p. 112). At a cocktail party, people may flit about from person to person exchanging small talk, but now and then common ground is found and people begin to pair off.

The "Opening Line": How Do You Get Things Started?   One type of small talk is the greeting, or opening line. Greetings are usually preceded by eye contact. Reciprocation of your eye contact may mean that the other person is willing to be approached. Avoidance of eye contact may mean that he or she is not willing, but it can also be a sign of shyness. In any event, if you would like to venture from initial attraction to surface contact, try a smile and some eye contact. When the eye contact is reciprocated, choose an opening line. Since this line can be important, you will probably want to say something more useful than "One, two, one, two."

Knapp (1978, pp. 108–109) lists a variety of greetings, or opening lines. Here are some of them:

Verbal salutes, such as "Good morning"
Personal inquiries, such as "How are you doing?" (more often pronounced, "How yuh doin'?")
Compliments, such as "You're extremely attractive"
References to your mutual surroundings, such as "What do you think of that painting?" or "This is a nice apartment house, isn't it?"
Reference to people or events outside the immediate setting, such as "How do you like this weather we've been having?"
References to the other person's behavior, such as "I couldn't help noticing you were sitting alone," or "I see you out on this track every Sunday morning"
References to your own behavior, or to yourself, such as "Hi, my name is Allan Felix" (you may wish to use your own name, of course)

The simple salute "Hi" or "Hello" is very useful. A friendly glance followed by a cheerful hello ought to give you some idea as to whether the attraction you feel is reciprocated. If the hello is returned with a friendly smile and inviting eye contact, follow it up with another greeting, such as a reference to your surroundings, the other person's behavior, or your name.

How do you go about building a relationship?

Exchanging "Name, Rank, and Serial Number" Early exchanges are likely to include name, occupation, marital status, and hometown (Berger & Calabrese, 1975). This has been referred to as exchanging "name, rank, and serial number." Each person is seeking a sociological profile of the other in hope that discovery of common ground will provide a basis for pursuing a conversation. An unspoken rule seems to be at work: "If I provide you with some information about myself, you will reciprocate by giving me an equal amount of information about yourself. Or . . . 'I'll tell you my hometown if you tell me yours'" (Knapp, 1978, p. 114). If the person you approach does not follow this rule, it may mean that he or she is not interested. But it could also be that he or she doesn't "know the rules" or that you are being awkward or disclosing too much too soon and turning the other person off.

Small talk may sound "phony," but premature self-disclosure of personal information may repel the other person (Rubin, 1975).

Self-Disclosure: You Tell Me and I'll Tell You . . . Carefully Opening up, or **self-disclosure,** is central to building intimate relationships. But when you meet someone for the first time, how much is it safe to disclose? If you hold back completely, you may seem disinterested or as if you're hiding something. But if you tell a new acquaintance that your hemorrhoids have been acting up, you are being too intimate too soon.

Research warns us against disclosing certain types of information too rapidly. In one study, **confederates** of the experimenters (Wortman et al., 1976) engaged in ten-minute conversations with subjects. Some confederates were "early disclosers." They shared intimate information early in the conversations. "Late disclosers" revealed the same information but toward the end of the conversation. Subjects rated early disclosers as less mature, less secure, less well adjusted, and more phony than the late disclosers. Subjects wished to pursue relationships with late disclosers but not early disclosers. In general, people who are considered well adjusted or mentally healthy disclose much about themselves but manage to keep a lid on information that could be self-damaging or prematurely revealing (Cozby, 1973).

Still, the tendency in recent years, perhaps as a result of the sexual revolution of the 1960s and 1970s, has been to disclose intimate information early (Altman & Taylor, 1973; Rands & Levinger, 1979). Young adults may be rebelling against what they perceive as the phoniness and stodginess of their elders. Moreover, popular group processes, such as the encounter group (see Chapter 9), have encouraged instant intimacy. In one study of couples who had been dating for an average of eight months, more than half had told their partners all about their previous sexual relationships (Rubin et al., 1980). A third had opened up about even those things they were most ashamed of.

We cannot with certainty define what it is "safe" to disclose early and what should be kept under wraps. But a Chicago experiment by Berger and his colleagues (1976) may provide some clues. They showed a list of 150 statements to 200 suburbanites who sorted them into groups (see Table 14.1) according to when they should be revealed during a two-hour conversation with a stranger. Note that only superficial information was disclosed during the first 15-minute segment. Expression of preferences did not begin until the second 15-minute period. Some topics were never broached.

Mutuality: When the "We," Not the "I's," Have It If small talk and self-disclosure are mutually rewarding, a couple may develop feelings of liking or love. If attraction and the establishment of common ground cause the couple to think of themselves as "we"—no longer as two "I's" touching at the surface only—they have reached what Levinger refers to as a condition of **mutuality.**

Self-disclosure. Revealing information about oneself.

Confederate. A person in league with the researcher who pretends to be a subject in an experiment.

Mutuality. According to Levinger, a phase of a relationship in which two people think of themselves as "we."

WHAT DO YOU SAY NOW?

How to Improve Date-Seeking Skills

All right, now you're aware that your Mr. or Ms. Right exists. What do you do about it? How do you get him or her to go out with you?

In this "What Do You Say Now?" segment, we focus on enhancing date-seeking skills. Psychologists have found that we may enhance social skills, such as date-seeking skills, through *successive approximations*. That is, we engage in a series of tasks of graded difficulty. We fine-tune our skills and gain confidence at each level. As suggested in the context of assertiveness training (see Chapter 5), we may try out some skills through "behavior rehearsal" with friends. Friends can role-play the person we would like to ask out and provide candid "feedback" about our effectiveness.

In the following excerpt from *Behavior Therapy*, we suggest a series of graded tasks that can be practiced by readers who want to sharpen their date-seeking skills:

Easy Practice Level Select a person of the opposite sex with whom you are friendly, but one whom you have no desire to date. Practice making small talk about the weather, about new films that have come into town, television shows, concerts, museum shows, political events, and personal hobbies.

Select a person you might have some interest in dating. Smile when you pass this person at work, school, or elsewhere, and say "Hi." Engage in this activity with other people of both sexes to increase your skills at greeting others.

Speak into your mirror, using behavior rehearsal and role playing. Pretend you are in the process of sitting next to the person you would like to date, say, at lunch or in the laundry room. Say "Hello" with a broad smile and introduce yourself. Work on the smile until it looks inviting and genuine. Make some comment about the food or the setting—the cafeteria, the office, whatever. Use a family member or confidant to obtain feedback about the effectiveness of the smile, your tone of voice, posture, and choice of words.

Medium Practice Level Sit down next to the person you want to date and engage him or her in small talk. If you are in a classroom, talk about a homework assignment, the seating arrangement, or the instructor (be kind). If you are at work, talk about the building or some recent interesting event in the neighborhood. Ask your intended date how he or she feels about the situation. If you are at some group such as Parents Without Partners, tell the other person that you are there for the first time and ask for advice on how to relate to the group.

Engage in small talk about the weather and local events. Channel the conversation into an exchange of personal information. Give your "name, rank, and serial number"—who you are, your major field or your occupation, where you're from, why or how you came to the school or company. The other person is likely to reciprocate and provide equivalent information. Ask how he or she feels about the class, place of business, city, hometown, etc.

Behaviorally rehearse asking the person out before your mirror, a family member, or a confidant. You may wish to ask the person out for "a cup of coffee" or to a film. It is somewhat less threatening to ask someone out to a gathering at which "some of us will be getting together." Or you may rehearse asking the person to accompany you to a cultural event, such as an exhibition at a museum or a concert—it's "sort of" a date, but also less anxiety inducing.

Target Behavior Level Ask the person out on a date in a manner consistent with your behavior rehearsal. If the person says he or she has a previous engagement or can't make it, you may wish to say something like, "That's too bad," or "I'm sorry you can't make it," and add something like, "Perhaps another time." You should be able to get a feeling for whether the person you asked out was just seeking an excuse or has a genuine interest in you and, as claimed, could not in fact accept the specific invitation.

Before asking the date out again, pay attention to his or her apparent comfort level when you return to small talk on a couple of occasions. If there is still a chance, the person should smile and return your eye contact. The other person may also offer you an invitation. In any event, if you are turned down twice, do not ask a third time. And don't catastrophize the refusal. Look up. Note that the roof hasn't fallen in. The birds are still chirping in the trees. You are still paying taxes. Then give someone else a chance to appreciate your fine qualities.

Source: Adapted from Rathus and Nevid, 1977, pp. 114–115.

Continuation

Once a relationship has been built, it enters the stage of **continuation**. Factors that contribute to the continuation of a relationship (i.e., positive factors) include looking for ways to enhance variety and maintain interest (e.g., will-

Continuation. The third stage of a relationship, according to Levinger.

TABLE 14.1   Time Segments during Which Certain Disclosures Were Made during a Two-Hour Conversation with a Stranger

Segment 1: 0–15 Minutes
1. I'm a volunteer at a local hospital.
2. I'm from New York.
3. My son is a first-year student at Penn State.
4. I have a dog, three cats, and a parakeet.

Segment 2: 15–30 Minutes
5. I've been skiing only once.
6. I like hunting for antiques.
7. The Chicago Bears are a lousy football team.
8. My favorite movie of all time is *M.A.S.H.*

Segment 3: 30–45 Minutes
9. I wish I knew more about politics.
10. The sight of blood makes me sick.
11. I am a Republican.
12. I read my horoscope every day and follow it faithfully.
13. I don't like men with long hair.

Segment 4: 45–60 Minutes
14. I think singles bars are a disgrace
15. I'll go out of my way to avoid hurting someone.
16. The trouble with America is that the average guy gets ripped off by the big corporation.
17. I think a woman has the right to decide whether or not she wants to have children.
18. I don't believe in capital punishment.
19. The United States should pull out of the United Nations.
20. I have trouble falling asleep.

Segment 5: 60–75 Minutes
21. The only way to handle radicals is with force.
22. I'm a very emotional person.
23. Most men are insecure—at least the ones that I've dated.
24. I don't believe in evolution.

Segment 6: 75–90 Minutes
25. I don't make friends easily.
26. I think I'm losing my hair.
27. I don't believe that there is an afterlife, but I'm not really sure.
28. I hate lying in bed at night, listening to the clock tick.
29. I'm 45 pounds overweight.
30. My mother-in-law really dislikes me.
31. I have an ugly nose.

Segment 7: 90–105 Minutes
32. I have a violent temper.
33. My wife makes too many demands upon me.
34. People always make fun of how fat I am.
35. I dress to please men and to excite them.
36. I wish I were single again.

Segment 8: 105–120 Minutes
37. Sometimes I'm afraid I won't be able to control myself.
38. Sometimes I think I hate myself.
39. I wonder why people stare at me wherever I go.
40. I think sex is dirty.
41. My husband and I stay together for the sake of the children.

Statements Remaining Undisclosed
42. I had my first sexual experience when I was 21.
43. My wife is having an affair with my best friend.
44. I make $17,000 a year.
45. My son was arrested last night for possession of marijuana.
46. I think my teenage daughter is pregnant.
47. We got married earlier than we'd planned because I was pregnant.

What do you disclose during a conversation with a stranger, and when do you disclose it? People who disclose too much too soon tend to be perceived as immature, insecure, poorly adjusted, and phony.
Source: Adapted from Berger et al., 1976, pp. 34–39.

ingness to experiment with social activities and sexual practices), showing evidence of continuing positive evaluation (e.g., Valentine's Day cards), absence of jealousy, perceived **equity** (e.g., a fair distribution of homemaking, child-rearing, and bread-winning chores), and mutual overall satisfaction. Negative factors at this stage include boredom (e.g., falling into a rut), showing evidence of negative evaluation (e.g., arguing, ignoring or forgetting anniversaries and other important dates), jealousy, perceived inequity (e.g., one partner desires a traditional distribution of chores, whereas the other partner prefers a nontraditional distribution), and mutual dissatisfaction.

Equity. Fairness, justice.

Jealous. Resentfully suspicious of a rival or of the influence of a rival.

Jealousy   About 54 percent of adults describe themselves as **jealous** (Pines & Aronson, 1983). Possessiveness is a related concept that can also make a relationship stressful (Pinto & Hollandsworth, 1984). Highly jealous people

Deterioration. The fourth stage of a relationship, according to Levinger.

Ending. The fifth stage of a relationship, according to Levinger.

are frequently dependent. They may also harbor feelings of inadequacy and report concerns about lack of sexual exclusiveness (White, 1981). (With the advent of AIDS, of course, sexual exclusivity reflects more than concern about how well one will measure up to one's partner's past lovers!) Feelings of jealousy make a relationship less rewarding and lower the individual's self-esteem (Mathes et al., 1985).

Unfortunately many lovers—including many college students—play jealousy games. They tell their partners about their attraction to other people, they flirt openly, and even make up stories to spur their partners to pay them more attention or to test the relationship (White, 1980). Another motive for game playing is revenge for a partner's infidelity.

Equity Equity basically involves feelings that one is getting as much from the relationship as one is giving to the relationship. As noted in Chapter 13, we will make great sacrifices for people whom we love, but as a relationship continues over the years, the "accumulation of too much debt" makes the relationship lopsided and unwieldy. Even if the relationship is maintained, there are likely to resentments that may be expressed openly or indirectly, as in loss of interest in sexual relations. Dating relationships and marriages are more stable when each partner feels that the relationship is equitable (Utne et al., 1984).

Deterioration

Deterioration is the fourth stage in the development of relationships—certainly not a stage that is desirable or inevitable. Positive factors that can prevent deterioration from occurring include investing time and effort in the relationship, working at improving the relationship, and being patient—that is, giving the relationship time for improvement. Negative factors that can advance deterioration include lack of investment of time and effort in the relationship, deciding to end the relationship, or simply allowing deterioration to continue unchecked. According to Levinger (1980), deterioration begins when either or both partners perceive the relationship as less desirable or worthwhile that it had once been.

Active and Passive Responses to a Deteriorating Relationship

When partners perceive a relationship to be deteriorating, they respond in active or passive ways (Rusbult et al., 1986; Rusbult & Zembrodt, 1983). Active ways of responding include taking action that might improve the relationship (e.g., enhancing communication skills, negotiating differences, getting professional help) or deciding to end the relationship. Passive responses are essentially characterized by waiting or doing nothing—that is, by sitting back and waiting for the problems in the relationship to resolve themselves or to worsen to the point where the relationship ends.

As in coping with other sources of stress, we encourage readers to take an active approach to coping with deteriorating relationships. That is, don't just allow things to happen to you. Make a decision to work to improve things, and if improvement appears to be impossible, consider the possibility of dissolving the relationship. Later in the chapter we shall see that it is irrational (and harmful to a relationship) to believe that ideal relationships need not be worked on. No two of us are matched perfectly. Unless one member of the pair is a doormat, conflicts are bound to emerge. When they do, it is helpful to work to resolve them rather than to let them continue indefinitely or to pretend that they do not exist.

Ending

The **ending** of a relationship is the final, or fifth, of Levinger's stages. As with deterioration, it is not inevitable that relationships end. There are a number of factors that can help prevent a deteriorating relationship from ending:

presence of some sources of rewards and satisfaction in the relationship, commitment to continue the relationship, and expectation that the relationship will ultimately work out well. Recall that our **self-efficacy expectations** affect how hard we will work to attain our goals: When we believe that our efforts to save a relationship are likely to meet with success, we will work harder at the relationship. A couple of other positive factors also increase the likelihood that a relationship will be saved: Each partner has already made a heavy investment in the relationship, and alternative partners are not readily available (Rusbult, 1980, 1983; Rusbult et al., 1982).

On the other hand, relationships are likely to come to an end when negative forces such as the following are in sway: There is little satisfaction in the relationship. Alternative partners are available. The partners are not committed to maintaining the relationship, and they expect it to fail. We have a way of living up to our negative expectations as well as our positive expectations.

Of course, the end of a relationship is not always a bad thing. When the partners are incompatible (dissimilar) in basic ways, and when sincere efforts to save the relationship have failed, ending the relationship may provide both partners with the opportunity to build satisfying relationships with other people. One of the reasons that we suggest taking an active approach to coping with deteriorating relationships is that they are more likely to be dissolved before marriage takes place—or when the partners are still young and have not yet established a family. As a consequence, fewer people are likely to "get hurt," and each person is more likely to attract a new, more compatible partner.

■ Marriage

The poets have been in less-than-perfect agreement about the institution of marriage:

> It is a truth universally acknowledged, that a single man in possession of a good fortune must be in want of a wife.
>
> Jane Austen

> The joys of marriage are the heaven on earth,
> Life's paradise, . . . the soul's quiet,
> Sinews of concord, earthly immortality,
> Eternity of pleasures; no restoratives
> Like to a constant woman.
>
> John Ford

> Marriage is nothing but a civil contract.
>
> John Selden

> Marriage is like life in this—that it is a field of battle, and not a bed of roses.
> Robert Louis Stevenson

> Marriage has many pains, but celibacy has no pleasures.

> It is so far from being natural for a man and woman to live in a state of marriage that we find all the motives which they have for remaining in that connection, and the restraints which civilized society imposes to prevent separation, are hardly sufficient to keep them together.
>
> Samuel Johnson

Marriage has a long and varied history. In the **patriarchy** of the ancient Hebrews, men dominated the important aspects of life. The man of the house could take concubines or additional wives. He had the right to choose wives for his sons. He alone could initiate divorce. While he could dally, his wife had to maintain her virtue scrupulously. Failure to bear children was one

Self-efficacy expectations. Our beliefs that we can bring about desired ends through our own efforts.

Patriarchy. A form of family or community rule by the eldest male.

Chattel. A movable piece of personal property, such as furniture.

Homogamy. The principle of like marrying like.

ground for divorce. The wife was considered part of her husband's property— **chattel.**

In ancient Greece, women were also viewed as the property of men. Their purposes were to care for the household and bear children. Rarely did men see them as suitable companions. During the Golden Age of Greece, men frequently turned to high-class prostitutes or male friends for recreational sex and sophisticated conversation.

The Romans also had a powerful patriarchy in which children could be sold into slavery and marriages were arranged for financial or political gain. At one point in history, women gained some freedom of choice in marriage. But when military demands required a population increase, the Emperor Augustus decreed that women who remained unmarried or childless by the age of 20 could be fined.

In these three cultures the patriarchies eventually weakened and women became reconceptualized as companions, not mere chattel. It even became the consensus that women could profit from education. But contemporary ideas, such as the notion that women have a right to seek personal fulfillment through careers that are unrelated to their husbands' needs, would have been unthinkable.

Though varied in purpose and function, marriage remains our most common life-style. More than 96 percent of us eventually get married (Goldenberg & Goldenberg, 1980). About 63 percent of adult men and 57 percent of adult women are currently married and live with their spouses.

Why Do We Get Married?

Throughout Western history, marriage has helped people to adjust to personal and social needs. Marriage regulates and legitimizes sexual relations. Marriage creates a home life and provides an institution for the financial support and socialization of children. Marriage provides a means of determining—or at least assuming—that a woman's children have been fathered by her husband. And so marriage also permits the orderly transmission of wealth from one generation to another, and from one family to another.

Notions such as romantic love, equality, and the radical concept that men, like women, should aspire to the ideal of faithfulness are recent additions to the structure of marriage. Today, with the high number of people who believe that sex is acceptable within the bounds of an affectionate relationship, the desire to engage in sexual intercourse is less likely to motivate marriage. But marriage still offers a sense of emotional and psychological security—as the poet John Ford wrote, a "constant woman" or a constant man, someone with whom to share feelings, experiences, and goals. Love is a major motive: In one study, 86 percent of the men and 80 percent of the women reported that they would not get married without love (Campbell & Berscheid, 1976). Among the highly educated, intimacy and companionship are central motives (Long Laws & Schwartz, 1977).

To Whom Do We Get Married? Are Marriages Made in Heaven or in the Neighborhood?

Our parents usually no longer arrange our marriages, even if they still encourage us to date the charming son or daughter of that solid couple at the church. We tend to marry people to whom we are attracted. As suggested in Chapter 13, they are usually similar to us in physical attractiveness and hold similar attitudes on major issues. They also seem likely to meet our material, sexual, and psychological needs.

The concept of like marrying like is termed **homogamy.** In the U.S.A., we only rarely get married to people from different races or from outside our socioeconomic class (Eckland, 1980). According to Reiss (1980), 99.7 percent of white husbands are married to white wives, and 99.2 percent of black

☐ A CLOSER LOOK

The Marriage Contract: A Way of Clarifying Your Marital Expectations to Your Spouse

In recent years, many couples have taken to writing informal marriage contracts as a way of clarifying what they expect from their unions (Garrett, 1982). Marriage contracts of this kind are not legally binding, but they can help prevent people from entering nuptials with "blinders on."

Marriage contracts offer couples a chance to spell out their marital values and goals. If they desire a traditional marriage in which the husband acts as breadwinner while the wife cooks, cleans, and raises the kids, they can so specify. If they desire a marriage in which each partner has equal right to pursue personal fulfillment through careers, or through extramarital relationships, this, too, can be specified. By discussing who will do what before they get married, couples gain insight into potential sources of conflict and have a greater opportunity to resolve them—or to reevaluate the wisdom of maintaining present marital plans. Garrett suggests including the following items in the marriage contract:

1. Whether the wife will take her husband's surname, or retain her maiden name, or whether both will use a hyphenated last name
2. How household tasks will be allocated and who will be responsible for what everyday activities—such as cleaning, washing, cooking, minor home repairs, and so forth
3. Whether or not the couple will have children, and if so, how many and at what time in the marital life cycle
4. What type(s) of contraception to use and who will take the responsibility for birth control measures
5. How child care responsibilities will be divided between the husband and wife, as well as the child-rearing techniques they will employ in raising their children
6. Whether they will rent or buy a place to live, and whether residential decisions will accommodate the husband's or wife's career plans (will the husband, for example, be willing to move to another city so that the wife may take advantage of a better job offer?)
7. How the breadwinner functions will be divided, who will control the family finances, and how economic decisions will be made
8. How in-law relations will be handled, and whether vacations will be spent visiting relatives
9. What proportion of leisure activities will be spent apart from the spouse and what leisure activites will be spent together
10. How their sexual relations will be arranged and whether fidelity will be preserved
11. How they will go about changing specific parts of their marital contract as the marriage progresses*

Sound like a tall job? It is. Some critics note that couples entering marriage at an early age are not in a position to foresee all the consequences of their current ideas. Rigid adherence to contractual specifications may hamper rather than promote marital adjustment in such cases. Couples, they assert, must be free to change their minds about certain issues, and to outgrow some of the declarations of youth.

We agree. Perhaps, however, some use can be made of a document along these lines. For example, a marriage "contract" of this sort may be viewed as a record of who was thinking what, and when—not as a straitjacket. Such a contract may later on be referred to in the spirit of explaining *why* one partner now has certain expectations of the other; in a free society, we cannot, and should not, demand absolute compliance. None of us need feel bound forever by ill-conceived or impractical declarations from an early age. But it may be useful to have a record of our early expectations, especially when they so strongly influence the adjustment of another person.

*Source: Garrett, 1982, pp. 133–134.

husbands are married to black wives. Ninety-four percent of married couples are both of the same religion. We are even similar to our mates in height, eye color, intelligence, and personality traits (Buss, 1984; Lesnik-Oberstein & Cohen, 1984; Rubin, 1973).

We also follow a principle of age homogamy, with husbands two to three years older than their wives, on the average. Age homogamy may reflect the fact that we tend to get married soon after achieving adulthood, and that we select partners, such as classmates, with whom we have been in proximity. People who are getting remarried, or marrying for the first time at later ages, are less likely to marry partners so close in age (Leslie & Leslie, 1977).

By and large, however, we seem to be attracted to and to get married to the boy or girl (almost) next door in a quite predictable manner. Marriages seem to be made in the neighborhood—not in heaven.

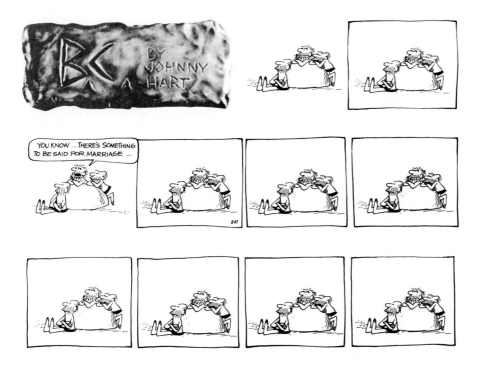

Marital Satisfaction: Is Everybody Happy?

How well do we adjust to marriage? Are married people happier than singles? How well do we adjust to children? Are parents happier than child-free couples? In this section we first define the so-called dimensions of marital satisfaction that researchers consider in their conclusions. Then we consider a number of surveys on marital satisfaction.

Factors Contributing to Marital Satisfaction   What factors contribute to a happy, well-adjusted marriage? Several studies show that communication ability is a prime factor (Banmen & Vogel, 1985; Cleek & Pearson, 1985; Floyd & Markman, 1984). Good patterns of communication among couples planning marriage are excellent predictors of marital happiness five and a half years after vows are taken (Markman, 1981). Later in the chapter we shall describe a number of ways of improving communication skills.

Other factors that contribute to marital happiness include spending focused time together (as during courtship), shared values, and flexibility (Klagsbrun, 1985). Physical intimacy, emotional closeness, and empathy also help (Tolstedt & Stokes, 1983; Zimmer, 1983).

Snyder (1979) constructed a questionnaire concerning areas of marital distress (see Table 14.2), and found that four of them consistently predicted overall marital satisfaction: *affective communication,* or amount of affection and understanding expressed by one's spouse; *problem-solving communication,* or ability to resolve disagreements; *sexual dissatisfaction,* or discord concerning the frequency and quality of sexual relations; and *disagreement about finances,* or fighting over money management. The expression of affection and capacity to resolve problems were consistently more important to a marriage than problems in child rearing, a history of family distress in the family of origin, and sex.

The Campbell Survey   In a survey of life satisfaction among 2,164 randomly selected Americans, Angus Campbell (1975) found that most saw their

■ Q U E S T I O N N A I R E ■

Do You Endorse a Traditional or a Liberal Marital Role?

What do you believe? Should the woman cook and clean, or should housework be shared? Should the man be the breadwinner, or should each couple define their own roles? Are you traditional or nontraditional in your views on marital roles for men and women?

The following items permit you to indicate the degree to which you endorse traditional roles for men and women in marriage. Answer each one by circling the letters (AS, AM, DM, or DS), according to the code given below. Then turn to the key at the end of the chapter to find out whether you tend to be traditional or non-traditional in your views. (Ignore the numbers beneath the codes for the time being.) Your may also be interested in seeing whether the answers of your date or your spouse show some agreement with your own.

AS = Agree Strongly
AM = Agree Mildly
DM = Disagree Mildly
DS = Disagree Strongly

1. A wife should respond to her husband's sexual overtures even when she is not interested.

AS	AM	DM	DS
4	3	2	1

2. In general, the father should have greater authority than the mother in the bringing up of children.

AS	AM	DM	DS
4	3	2	1

3. Only when the wife works should the husband help with housework.

AS	AM	DM	DS
4	3	2	1

TABLE 14.2   Factors Contributing to Marital Distress and Sample Questionnaire Items Used in Their Measurement

1. *Global Distress.* "My marriage has been disappointing in several ways."

2. *Affective Communication.* "I'm not sure my spouse has ever really loved me."

3. *Problem-Solving Communication.* "My spouse and I seem to be able to go for days sometimes without settling our differences."

4. *Time Together.* "My spouse and I don't have much in common to talk about."

5. *Disagreement about Finances.* "My spouse buys too many things without consulting me first."

6. *Sexual Dissatisfaction.* "My spouse sometimes shows too little enthusiasm for sex."

7. *Role Orientation.* "A wife should not have to give up her job when it interferes with her husband's career."

8. *Family History of Distress.* "I was very anxious as a young person to get away from my family."

9. *Dissatisfaction with Children.* "My children rarely seem to care how I feel about things."

10. *Conflict over Child Rearing.* "My spouse doesn't assume his (her) fair share of taking care of the children.

Source: Snyder, 1979, p. 816.

4. Husbands and wives should be equal partners in planning the family budget.

AS	AM	DM	DS
4	3	2	1

5. In marriage, the husband should make the major decisions.

AS	AM	DM	DS
4	3	2	1

6. If both husband and wife agree that sexual fidelity isn't important, there's no reason why both shouldn't have extramarital affairs if they want to.

AS	AM	DM	DS
4	3	2	1

7. If a child gets sick and his wife works, the husband should be just as willing as she to stay home from work and take care of that child.

AS	AM	DM	DS
4	3	2	1

8. In general, men should leave the housework to women.

AS	AM	DM	DS
4	3	2	1

9. Married women should keep their money and spend it as they please.

AS	AM	DM	DS
4	3	2	1

10. In the family, both of the spouses ought to have as much say on important matters.

AS	AM	DM	DS
4	3	2	1

Source: Karen Oppenheim Mason, with the assistance of Daniel R. Denison and Anita J. Schacht. *Sex-Role Attitude Items and Scales from U.S. Sample Surveys*. Rockville, MD: National Institute of Mental Health, 1975, pp. 16–19.

lives as worthwhile, hopeful, interesting, and full. Some interesting differences emerged between married couples and singles, between child-free couples and parents.

Married people reported greater life satisfaction than single, widowed, or divorced people. Younger married women without children were the most satisfied group. When children came along, stress increased and life satisfaction generally dropped off. Many couples with young children reported difficulty adjusting to being "tied down," but happiness rebounded for couples with older children, especially children of college age. They again experienced some freedom.

Campbell found no serious signs of regret among those who decided not to have children. Child-free married men over 30 were happier than most other groups. Child-free married women were somewhat less happy than their mates, but about as happy as mothers.*

We cannot infer that marriage *causes* happiness from the Campbell data. It may also be that happier people choose to marry. Still, these findings suggest that the institution of marriage is alive and well, even for couples who choose not to have children.

*Remember that these relationships hold for women who *choose* not to have children. Women who want children, but who cannot have them, report a great deal of frustration.

The* Ladies' Home Journal *Survey   The *Ladies Home Journal* recently ran a survey to answer questions such as:

"What do today's women want from their husbands and marriage?"

"What are they getting?"

"What has happened to their marriages over the last tumultuous decade?"

"Why do some marriages grow stronger and others fail?" (Schultz, 1980, p. 90)

Over 30,000 *Journal* readers responded, and the results were analyzed by psychologists Phillip Shaver and Debra Olds of New York University and research analyst Cathy Pullis. The median respondent age was 32.5. Fifty-nine percent worked outside the home. Eighty-nine percent were married, and 74 percent had children. Most were middle-of-the-road in religion and politics. Two of three had been graduated from or had attended college. The survey respondents were better educated and more affluent than the average American woman, but, as a group, they may be very similar to women readers of this book. For this reason, the survey is instructive.

A major finding is that 75 percent of these women rated their marriages as good or very good, and most expected them to get better over the next five years. Still, 54 percent had considered divorce at one time or another. The major sources of marital dissatisfaction were poor communication and lack of money, with about 33 percent of the sample reporting each. Other marital problems included differences in personal interests (20 percent), sexual dissatisfaction (20 percent), conflicts over friends or relatives (16 percent), and conflicts over children (13 percent).

As in the Campbell study, child-free women (65 percent) were more likely to report being happy than mothers (55 percent). Table 14.3 shows other responses suggestive of better overall adjustment among child-free women. It was also found that women aged 16–20 who gave birth were less happy than women who had had children later and who were probably better prepared for them. Women with children under the age of six or in their teens reported the greatest stress. Despite these differences, 53 percent of the respondents reported that they would feel "incomplete as a woman" if they did not have a child.

The *Journal* study reinforces the importance of companionate love once the flames of passion burn low. Half the women reported that sexual attraction was a high priority when they married. Thirty-six percent reported that physical appearance was important then, and 41 percent noted that they were influenced by communication ability. If they had it to do over, their priorities would change. Now only 34 percent would be swayed by sexual attraction, and 18 percent by physical appearance. But 69 percent would now look for communication ability.

The *Journal* study also finds that women who have abandoned traditional sex-role stereotypes report greater marital and general life satisfaction than

TABLE 14.3   Comparison of Child-Free Women and Mothers as Reported in the *Ladies' Home Journal* Study

Factor	Child-Free Women	Mothers
Optimism about the future	85%	75%
Feeling in control of their lives	62	50
Tiring easily	43	49
Often feeling irritable or angry	31	41
Losing interest in sex frequently	28	34
Happiness with sex lives	84	74
Satisfaction with marriage	72	57

Source: Schultz, 1980, pp. 91, 146.

TABLE 14.4   **Comparison of Psychologically Androgynous and Traditional Women as Reported in the *Ladies' Home Journal* Study**

Factor	Psychologically Androgynous Women	Traditionally Oriented Woman
Satisfied with their lives	82%	46%
Feeling in control of their lives	98	82
Feeling husband loves her equally	78	54
Feeling responsible for the way that things "turn out"	84	70
Optimism about the future	95	73
Feeling worthless	9	32
Feeling sad or depressed	25	50

Source: Schultz, 1980, pp. 152–153.

traditionally oriented women (see Table 14.4). These women are **psychologically androgynous.** They

> have eroded, and in some ways destroyed, the arbitrary division between what has long been considered the "male" and "female" personality. They . . . are assertive yet vulnerable, independent yet communicative, gentle yet self-confident . . . . In contrast, the woman who has a greater number of traditional "feminine" personality traits . . . has centered her life on her children and her partner, even if she has a job outside the home (Schultz, 1980).

Although 54 percent of the entire sample had considered divorce, 61 percent of traditional women had done so, as compared to 29 percent of psychologically androgynous women. All in all, the *Journal* claims that the happiest marriages involved the union of psychologically androgynous women and psychologically androgynous men.

The New "Hite Report": Has Marriage Taken a Drubbing During the 1980s?   In 1987, Shere Hite published her most recent survey under the title *Women and Love, A Cultural Revolution in Progress.* If we were to take her findings at face value, we would have to conclude that domestic bliss has taken a drubbing since the reports of Campbell (1975) and *The Ladies' Home Journal* (Schultz, 1980).

Based on survey responses from 4,500 U.S. Women, Hite reported the following complaints:

98 percent wanted more "verbal closeness" with their partners
95 percent complained of "emotional and psychological harrassment" from their partners
92 percent said that men show "condescending, judgmental attitudes" when they communicate with them
87 percent said that their "deepest emotional relationship" was with a female friend
80 percent said that they had to fight for their rights within their relationships
79 percent said they are reevaluating whether they should make such an investment in their love relationship
77 percent said they were most angry about the fact that their men did not listen to them
71 percent said they have given up trying to induce their partners to communicate their feelings

A heavy indictment, indeed? If we were to credit this report, we might be ready to sound the death knell for male–female relationships in the U.S.A. However, as noted in Chapter 1, this latest Hite report, like her two earlier reports (Hite, 1976, 1981), is guilty of biased sampling. Hite mailed 100,000 questionnaires to women's groups throughout the U.S.A., and received only 4,500 responses. As noted by June Reinisch, a psychologist at Indiana University's Kinsey Institute, "Unhappy people are more willing to answer these questions than happy people" (Wallis, 1987, p. 69). In other words, if you have "an axe to grind," you're more likely to seize any opportunity to express your views. And by sending her questionnaires to women's groups, Hite limited her survey to people that Regina Herzog of the University of Michigan's Institute for Social Research refers to as "joiners" (Wallis, 1987, p. 71). In sum, Hite's sample consists of women's group members who are discontent with their partners.

Hite's latest research debacle does not sound the death knell for the institution of marriage. We are pleased to be able to report that in a 1987 Harris poll of 3,000 Americans (Harris, 1988), *selected at random,* 89 percent of the respondents, male and female, reported that their relationship with their partner was generally satisfying!

■ Ways of Coping with Marital Conflict: How to Survive Once the Honeymoon Is Over

As the glow of the honeymoon fades into the sunset of the Poconos or the Caribbean island paradise, couples face the challenge of adjusting to the state of matrimony.

Marital conflicts inevitably arise—over things like money, communication, personal interests, sex, in-laws, friends, and children. If couples have not written out a personal marriage contract (and most do not), they are also faced with the chore of deciding who does what. In traditional marriages, responsibilities are delegated according to sex-role stereotypes. The wife cooks, cleans, and diapers. The husband earns the bread and adjusts the carburetor. In nontraditional marriages, chores are usually shared or negotiated, especially when the wife also works (Atkinson & Huston, 1984). However, there is friction when a nontraditional woman gets married to a traditional man (Booth & Edwards, 1985; Wallis, 1987).

Is Marriage the Perfect, Less-Than-Perfect State? Despite all its problems, marriage remains the preferred style of life for Americans. Factors that affect overall marital satisfaction include expression of affection and understanding, ability to resolve disagreements, sexual satisfaction, and agreement or disagreement over management of money.

The following list is just a sampling of the various risks that engender conflict and beset the stability of marriages (Booth & Edwards, 1985; Kornblum, 1988; McGoldrick & Carter, 1982):

Meeting "on the rebound"

Living too close to, or too distant from, the families of origin

Differences in race, religion, education, or social class

Dependence on one or both families of origin for money, shelter, or emotional support

Marriage before the couple know each other for six months, or after an engagement of more than three years

Marital instability in either family of origin

Pregnancy prior to, or during the first year of, marriage

Insensitivity to the partner's sexual needs

Discomfort with the role of husband or wife

Disputes over the division of labor

When problems such as these lead to conflict, the following suggestions may be of help.

Challenge Irrational Expectations

All couples disagree now and then. However, some people irrationally expect that their marriages should be perfect and assume that perfect couples never disagree (Epstein et al., 1979; Overturf, 1976). They assume that disagreement about in-laws, children, or sexual activities means that they do not love each other or that their marriage is on the rocks. People with distressed marriages are even more likely to believe that any disagreement is destructive, that their partners should be able to read their minds (and know what they want), that their partners cannot change, that they must be perfect sexual partners, and that men and women differ dramatically in personality and needs (Eidelson & Epstein, 1982).

Here is a sampling of irrational beliefs that increase marital distress:

"My spouse doesn't love me if he/she doesn't support me at all times"

"People who love one another don't raise their voices"

"It's awful if a disagreement isn't resolved immediately"

"If my spouse really cared about my anxiety/depression/ulcer/exam, he/she wouldn't be acting this way"

"My spouse has that annoying habit just to bug me"

"If my spouse truly loved me, he/she would know what I want"

Such beliefs magnify differences and heighten marital stress instead of helping to relieve it. The last belief is extremely harmful. We may assume that people who really care for us will know what pleases or displeases us, even when we don't tell them. But other people cannot read our minds, and we should be open and direct about our feelings and preferences (Jacobson, 1984).

Negotiate Differences

In order to effectively negotiate differences about household responsibilities, leisure time preferences, and so on, each spouse must be willing to share the power in the relationship (Scanzoni & Polonko, 1980). If a marriage "gets off on the wrong foot," with one spouse dominating the other, the discrepancy in bargaining power may hamper all future negotiations. The disadvantaged spouse may not be heard, resentments may build, and the relationship may eventually dissolve.

One strategy for averting a discrepancy in bargaining power is to list day-to-day responsibilities. Then each spouse can scale them according to their desirability. Chris and Dana ranked the chores shown in Table 14.5 by using this code:

Exchange contracting. A conflict-resolution method in which each member of a couple agrees to change his or her behavior in exchange for the partner's making of an equivalent change in behavior.

TABLE 14.5   Chris and Dana's Rankings of Marital Chores

Chore	Chris's Ranking	Dana's Ranking
Washing dishes	3	1
Cooking	1	4
Vacuuming	2	3
Cleaning the bathroom	1	3
Maintaining the automobile	3	5
Paying the bills	5	3

5 = most desirable
4 = desirable
3 = not sure, mixed feelings
2 = undesirable
1 = Are you kidding? Get lost!

Chris wound up washing the dishes and paying the bills. Dana did the cooking and toyed with the car. They agreed to alternate vacuuming and cleaning the bathroom—specifying a schedule for them so that they wouldn't procrastinate and eventually explode, "It's your turn!" Both had careers, so the breadwinning responsibility was divided evenly.

Make a Contract for Exchanging New Behaviors
In **exchange contracting,** you and your partner identify specific behaviors that you would like to see changed, and you offer to modify some of your own disturbing behavior patterns in exchange (Knox, 1971). A sample contract:

CHRIS: I agree to talk to you at the dinner table rather than watch the news on TV if you, in turn, help me type my business reports one evening a week.

DANA: I agree never to insult your mother if you, in return, absolutely refuse to discuss our sexual behavior with her.

Increase Pleasurable Marital Interactions
Satisfied couples tend to display higher rates of pleasurable behavior toward one another. One spouse also tends to reciprocate the pleasurable behavior shown by the other (Birchler et al., 1975; Robinson & Price, 1980; Weiss, 1978). So, consider the behaviors listed in Table 14.6 and try to be sure that you are using them, or similar behaviors, at home.

Unfortunately, couples experiencing problems tend to underestimate the pleasurable behaviors shown by their spouses (Robinson & Price, 1980). It may be because poorly adjusted couples may have come to expect the worst from one another, and either to ignore or not to "believe" efforts to change. If your partner has been trying to bring more pleasure into your life, it might help to show some appreciation. And if you have been trying to bring pleasure to your partner, and it has gone unnoticed, it might not hurt to say something

TABLE 14.6   Types of Pleasurable Behaviors Shown in Marriage

Paying attention, listening
Agreeing with your spouse (that is, when you do agree)
Showing approval when pleased by your spouse
Positive physical interactions such as touching and hugging
Showing concern
Showing humor; laughing and smiling
Compromising on disagreements
Complying with reasonable requests

WHAT DO YOU SAY NOW?

Delivering Criticism

You can't believe it! You've been waiting for a an important business call, and it came. There's only one hitch: Your partner was home at the time—you were out—and your partner's not sure *who* called. If only your partner would be more responsible and write down messages!

You can't let it go this time. You're bound and determined to say something. But what?

What do you say now? Note some possible responses in the spaces provided, and then see the following for some suggestions.

1. _____
   _____

2. _____
   _____

3. _____
   _____

As noted in the text, delivering criticism is tricky. Your goal should be to modify your partner's behavior without arousing extremes of anger or guilt. Consider these guidelines:

1. Be specific to communicate what *behavior* disturbs you. Don't insult your partner's personality. Say something like, "Please write down messages for me," not, "You're totally irresponsible."
2. Express dissatisfaction in terms of your own feelings. Say, "You know, it *upsets me* when something that's important to me gets lost, or misplaced," not, *"You* never think about anybody but yourself."
3. Keep complaints to the present. Say, "This was a very important phone call." It may not be helpful to say, "Last summer you didn't write that message from the computer company and as a result I didn't get the job."
4. Phrase the criticism positively, and combine it with a concrete request. Say something like, "You know, you're usually very considerate. When I need help, I always feel free to ask for it. Now I'm asking for help when I get a phone call. Will you please write down the message for me?"

like, "Hey! Look at me! I'm agreeing with you; I think you're pretty smart; and I'm smiling!"

Now let us turn our attention to one of the best ways of resolving conflicts in relationships: improving communication skills.

■ Improving Communication Skills

How do you learn about your partner's needs? How do you let your partner know about your own needs? How do you criticize someone you love? How do you accept criticism and maintain your self-esteem? How do you say no? How do you get by impasses?

All these questions focus on the need for communication. Snyder (1979) found that poor affective and problem-solving communication are two of the important factors that interfere with marital satisfaction (see Table 14.2). Moreover, people who are dissatisfied with their partners usually list difficulties in communication as one of the major rubs (e.g., Hite, 1987; Schultz, 1980).

Some of us are better communicators than others, perhaps because we are more sensitive to others' needs, or perhaps we had the advantage of observing good communicators in our own homes. However, communication is a skill, one that can be learned. Learning takes time and work, but if you are willing, the following guidelines may be of help (Crooks & Baur, 1987; Gottman et al., 1976; McKay et al., 1983):

How to Get Started

One of the trickiest aspects of communicating is getting started.

Listening to your partner is an essential part of communicating. Listening skills include "active listening," paraphrasing, reinforcement of one's partner, and—like person-centered therapists—showing unconditional positive regard.

Talk about Talking   One possibility is to begin by talking about talking. That is, explain to your partner that it is hard to talk about your conflicts. Perhaps you can refer to some of the things that have happened in the past when you tried to resolve conflicts.

Request Permission to Raise a Topic   You can also ask permission to bring up a topic. You can say something like, "Something's been on my mind. Is this a good time to bring it up?" Or try, "I need to get something off my chest, but I really don't know how to start. Will you help me?"

How to Listen

Listening to your partner is an essential part of communicating. Moreover, by being a good listener, you suggest ways that your partner can behave in listening to you.

Engage in Active Listening   First, engage in **active listening.** Don't stare off into space when your partner is talking or offer an occasional, begrudging "mm-hmm" while you're watching TV. In active listening, you maintain eye contact with your partner. You change your facial expression in a demonstration of **empathy** for his or her feelings. Nod your head as appropriate, and ask helpful questions such as, "Could you give me an example of what you mean?" or, "How did you feel about that?"

Use Paraphrasing   In **paraphrasing** you recast what your partner is saying to show that you understand. For instance, if your partner says, "Last night it really bugged me when I wanted to talk about the movie but you were on the phone," you might say something like, "It seemed that I should have known that you wanted to talk about the movie?" or, "It seems that I'm talking more to other people than to you?"

Reinforce Your Partner for Communicating   Even if you don't agree with what your partner said, you can genuinely say something like, "I'm glad you told me how you really feel about that," or, "Look, even if I don't always

Active listening. Ways of listening that help the speaker to open up and clearly express his or her views.

Empathy. The ability to share or to understand another person's feelings; viewing a situation from the frame of reference of another person.

Paraphrasing. Restating or recasting what has been said by another person.

Open-ended question. A question that allows an elaborated, rather than specific, answer.

agree with you, I care about you and I always want you to tell me what you're thinking."

Use Unconditional Positive Regard   Keep in mind the concept of unconditional positive regard, which is used by person-centered therapists (see Chapter 9). When you disagree with your partner, do so in a way that shows that you still value your partner as a person. In other words, say something like, "I love you very much, but it bugs me when you . . ." rather than, "You're rotten for doing . . ."

How to Learn about Your Partner's Needs
Listening is essential to learning about your partner's needs, but sometimes you need to do more than listen.

Ask Questions Designed to Draw Your Partner Out   Questions can either suggest a limited range of answers or be **open-ended.** The following "yes-or-no" questions require a specific response:

"Do you think I spend too much time on the phone with my sister?"
"Does it bother you that I wait until we're ready to go to bed before loading the dishwasher?"
"Do you think I don't value your opinions about cars?"

Yes-or-no questions can provide a concrete piece of information. However, open-ended questions encourage exploration of broader issues. For example,

"What do you like best about the way we make love?" or, "What bothers you about the way we make love?"
"What are your feelings about where we live?"
"How would you like to change things with us?"
"What do you think of me as a father/mother?"

If your partner finds such questions too general, you can offer an example, or you can say something like, "Do you think we're living in an ideal situation? If you had your preferences, how would you change things?"

Use Self-Disclosure   Try self-disclosure, not only because you communicate your own ideas and feelings in this way, but also because you invite reciprocation. For example, if you want to know whether your partner is concerned about your relationship with your parents, you can say something like, "You know, I have to admit that I get concerned when you call your folks from work. I get the feeling that there are things that you want to talk about with them but not have me know about . . ."

Give Your Partner Permission to Say Something That Might Be Upsetting to You   Tell your partner to level with you about a troublesome issue. Say that you realize that it might be clumsy to talk about it, but you promise to try to listen carefully without getting too upset. Consider limiting communication to, say, one difficult issue per conversation. When the entire emotional dam bursts, the chore of "mopping up" can be overwhelming.

How to Make Requests

Take Responsibility for What Happens to You   The first step in making requests is internal—that is, taking responsibility for the things that happen to you. If you want your partner to change behavior, you have to be willing to request the change. Then, if your partner refuses to change, you have to take responsibility for how you will cope with the impasse.

Be Specific   It might be useless to say, "Be nicer to me," because your partner might not recognize the abrasive nature of his or her behavior and not know what you mean. It can be more useful to say something like, "Please don't cut me off in the middle of a sentence," or, "Hey, you! Give me a smile!"

Use "I" Talk   Also, make use of the word *I* where appropriate. "I would appreciate it if you would take out the garbage tonight" might get better results than "Do you think the garbage needs to be taken out?" Similarly, "I like you to kiss me more when we're making love" might be more effective than "Jamie told me about an article that said that kissing makes sex more enjoyable."

How to Deliver Criticism

There is skill involved in effectively delivering criticism. Your goal should be to modify your partner's behavior without reducing him or her to a quivering mass of fear or guilt.

Evaluate Your Motives   First of all, evaluate your motives honestly. Do you want to change behavior or just to punish your partner? If you want to punish your partner, you might as well be crude and insulting, but if you want to resolve conflicts try a more diplomatic approach.

Pick a Good Time and Place   Express complaints privately—not in front of the neighbors, in-laws, or children. Your spouse has a right to be angry when you express intimate thoughts and feelings in public places. When you make private thoughts public, you cause resentment and cut off communication. If you're not sure that this is a good time and place, try asking permission. Say something like, "Something is on my mind. Is this a good time to bring it up?"

Be Specific   As in making requests, be specific when making complaints. By being specific, you will communicate what *behavior* disturbs you. Avoid insulting your partner's personality. Say, "Please throw your underwear in the hamper," not, "You're a disgusting slob." It is easier (and less threatening) to change problem behavior than to try to overhaul personality traits.

Express Dissatisfaction in Terms of Your Own Feelings   This is more effective than attacking the other person (Rogers, 1972). Say, "You know, it *upsets me* that you don't seem to be paying attention to what I'm saying," not, "*You're* always off in your own damn world. You never cared about anybody else and never will."

Keep Complaints to the Present   Forget who did what to whom last summer. It may also be counterproductive to say, "Every time I call my mother there's a fight afterwards!" Bringing up the past muddles the current issue and heightens feelings of anger.

Try to Phrase the Criticism Positively   Try to phrase criticism positively, and combine it with a specific request. For example, say "I love it when you kiss me. Please kiss me more often while we're making love," rather than, "You never kiss me when we're in bed and I'm sick of it." Or say, "You really make my life much easier when you help me with the dishes. How about a hand tonight?" rather than, "Would it really compromise your self-image as Mr. Macho if you gave me a hand with the dishes tonight?"

How to Receive Criticism

Taking criticism on the job, at home, anywhere, isn't easy. It's helpful to recognize that you might not be perfect and to be prepared for occasional

Validate. To confirm the logic, or the reasons behind, an expressed point of view.

Incubate. In problem solving, standing back from a problem so that one can consider the elements of the problem from new perspectives.

criticism. Your objectives in receiving criticism should be to learn about your partner's concerns, keep lines of communication open, and find, or negotiate, ways of changing the troublesome behavior. On the other hand, you should not feel that you must take verbal abuse, and you should speak up if the criticism exceeds acceptable boundaries. For example, if your partner says, "You know, you're pretty damned obnoxious," you might say something like, "Say, how about telling me what I did that's troubling you and forgetting the character assassination?" In this way, you are also making a request that your partner be specific.

Ask Clarifying Questions   Another way to help your partner be specific is to ask clarifying questions. If your partner criticizes you for spending so much time with your parents, you might ask something like, "Is it that I'm spending too much time with them, or do you feel they're having too much influence with me?"

Paraphrase the Criticism   As with being a good listener in general, paraphrase the criticism to show that you understand it.

Acknowledge the Criticism   Acknowledge the criticism even if you do not agree with it by saying something like, "I hear you," or "I can understand that you're upset that I've been investing so much time in the job lately."

Acknowledge your mistake, if you have made a mistake. If you do not believe that you have, express your genuine feelings, using "I" statements and being as specific as possible.

Negotiate Differences   Unless you feel that your partner is completely in the wrong, perhaps you can seek ways to negotiate your differences. Say something like, "Would it help if I . . . ?"

How to Cope with Impasses

When we are learning to improve our communication skills, we may arrive at the erroneous idea that all of the world's problems, including our own, could be resolved if people would only make the effort of communicating with each other. Communication helps, but it is not the whole story. Sometimes people have deep, meaningful differences. Although they may have good communication skills, they now and then arrive at an impasse. When you and your partner do arrive at an impasse, the following suggestions may be of some use.

Try to See the Situation from Your Partner's Perspective   Maybe you can honestly say something like, "I don't agree with you, but I can see where you're coming from." In this way you **validate** your partner's feelings and, often, decrease the tension between you.

Seek Validating Information   Say something like, "I'm trying, but I honestly can't understand why you feel this way. Can you help me understand?"

Take a Break   When we arrive at an impasse in solving a problem, allowing the problem to **incubate** frequently helps (Rathus, 1987). Allow each other's points of view to incubate, and perhaps a solution will dawn on one of you a bit later. You can also schedule a concrete time for a follow-up discussion so that the problem is not swept under the rug.

Tolerate Differentness   Recognize that each of you is a unique individual and that you cannot agree on everything. As Virginia Satir notes in her approach to family therapy (see Chapter 9), families function better when members tolerate each other's differentness. By and large, when we have a solid

■ WHAT DO YOU SAY NOW?

Receiving Criticism

You're having dinner one evening when your partner surprises you with, "You've got to do something about your hair." You're threatened and peeved, but you stop and think before answering.

What do you say now? Note some possible responses in the spaces provided, and then see the following for some suggestions.

1. _____

2. _____

3. _____

Although delivering criticism is tricky, taking criticism can be even more difficult. As noted in the text, your objectives should be to learn about your partner's concerns, keep your lines of communication open, and find ways of changing the troublesome behavior. Here are some ideas for responding to "You've got to do something about your hair."

1. When we deliver criticism, it helps to be aware of our motives. In receiving criticism, it helps to be aware of the motives of others. Is your partner's concern limited to your hair, or is this criticism only the opening salvo of a war that's about to erupt? When

you're not sure, you can help your partner be specific by asking clarifying questions. For example, "Could you tell me exactly what you mean?" or, "My hair?"

2. As with being a good listener in general, you can acknowledge the criticism even if you do not agree with it by saying something like, "I hear you," or "I know you're not thrilled with this style, but it's impossible to control when it gets longer."

3. If you have been letting your hair go because you've been busy, you can accept the criticism by saying something like, "I know. It was my day/week to tidy up and I blew it."

4. You can follow acceptance of criticism (as in response #3) with a request for help. For example, "Do you suppose you'd be willing to look over the styles with me so that we can settle on something we both can live with?"

5. If none of these responses work, it is possible that your partner has a **hidden agenda** and is using the remark about your hair as an opening. You can then try something like, "I'm trying to find ways to help the situation, but they don't seem to be working. Is there something else on your mind?"

6. Notice that we have *not* seized the opportunity to retaliate with something like, "You're worried about my hair? What about your teeth and that beach ball you're trying to hide under your shirt?" Although it can be tempting to retaliate, we're assuming that it might be better for the relationship, and for you in the long run, to try to resolve conflict, not heighten conflict.

sense of ego identity (of who we are and what we stand for), we are more likely to be able to tolerate differentness in others.

Agree to Disagree Recognize that we can survive as individuals and as partners even when some conflicts remain unresolved. You can "agree to disagree" and maintain self-respect and respect for one another.

Hidden agenda. A concealed group of issues that a person would like to express in a discussion but is reluctant to raise directly.

■ Divorce

Unfortunately, not all marital differences can be resolved. In 1920, about one marriage in seven ended in divorce. By 1960 this figure had risen to one in four. People today are more likely than ever before to demand continued happiness and feelings of love in their marriages. The women's movement, the relaxation of legal restrictions against divorce, and increased mobility have all interacted to yield a divorce rate of from about 33 to 40 percent. Couples aged 25–29 are most likely to get divorced, and couples over 65 are least likely to get divorced (U.S. Bureau of the Census, 1980). From 40 to 50 percent of the children born in recent years will live at least for a while in a single-parent family (Glick & Norton, 1978; Plateris, 1978).

The Cost of Divorce Divorce usually has financial and emotional repercussions. When a household splits in two, the resources may not extend far enough to maintain the former standard of living for both partners. The divorced woman who has not pursued a career may find herself competing for work with younger, more experienced people. The divorced man may not be able to manage alimony and child support and also establish a new home of his own.

Adjustment to divorce may be more difficult than adjustment to death of a spouse. When a spouse dies, legalities are minimal. But divorce often seems to require legal conflict, reams of documents, and interminable waiting periods. (The innovative approach of **divorce mediation,** in which the couple are guided through the decisions required by divorce in a cooperative spirit rather than as adversaries, may help reduce some of the stresses of the process [Schwebel et al., 1982].) When someone dies, the rest of the family remains intact. After a divorce, children and others may choose up sides and assign blame. For the parent who does not attain custody, divorce signals major changes in the parental role as well as in the marital role. After a death, people receive "compassionate leave" from work and are expected to be less productive for a while. After a divorce, they are commonly criticized. Death is final, but divorced people may nourish "what ifs?" and vacillate in their emotions.

People who are separated and divorced have the highest rates of mental and physical illness in the population (Bloom et al., 1978; Vernbrugge, 1979). For several years after divorce, people are subject to greater stress and feel that they can exert less control over their lives (Doherty, 1983). Feelings of failure as a spouse and parent, loneliness, and uncertainty about the future prompt feelings of depression. The incidence of divorce is linked closely to the suicide rate (Stack, 1980).

The hardest aspect of divorce may be separating psychologically from "the personality and the influence of the ex-spouse—to wash that man right out of your hair" (Bohannan, 1970, p. 53). Severing links to the past and becoming a whole, autonomous person once more—or, for the traditional women, perhaps for the first time—can be the greatest challenge but also the most constructive aspect of adjustment to divorce.

■ Alternate Styles of Life

Although marriage remains the ideal for most Americans, some choose not to get married. In this section we explore two alternatives to marriage, remaining single and cohabitating.

The Singles Scene: Swinging, Lonely, or All of the Above?

In recent years there has been a dramatic increase in the numbers of young adults who are single. According to the 1985 edition of *Current Population Reports,* 23.4 percent of U.S. households consisted of a single adult. In 1984 about two men in three aged 20–24 were single, along with one woman in two of the same age group (as compared to 55 percent of men and 36 percent of women in these age groups in 1970).

Several factors contribute to these figures. First, people are getting married at somewhat later ages (Kornblum, 1988). Second, more people are going on for advanced education (Glick & Norton, 1979). Third, many women are placing career objectives ahead of marriage (Current Population Reports, 1985).

But today, many young people no longer simply view **singlehood** as a stage of life that precedes marriage. Career women, for example, are no longer financially dependent on men, and so a number of them have chosen to remain single. In any event, many young adults report that they are single by choice, and they view singlehood as an alternative, open-ended life-style (Austrom & Hanel, 1985).

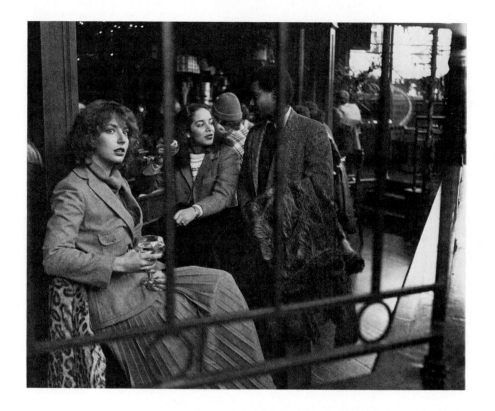

The Singles Scene
For some, the singles scene is exciting; for others, it is stressful and depressing. Today many people no longer see "singlehood" as merely a stage of life that precedes marriage. They choose to remain single.

There is no single "singles scene." Singlehood is highly varied in intention and in the style of daily life. For some, to be sure, it does mean singles bars and a string of one-night affairs. There are also singles apartment complexes, some of which permit nude sunbathing and swimming. Children and married couples not allowed, thank you.

Other single people limit sex to affectionate relationships only, and to partners they have known for some time. Many of them are simply delaying marriage until they find Mr. or Ms. Right (Stein, 1981). Some of them achieve emotional and psychological security through a network of intimate relationships with friends.

Many so-called swinging singles do not want to be "trapped" with a single partner. They fear boredom, obstacles to mobility and self-development, and sexual frustration (Stein, 1980). They opt for many dating and sex partners for the sake of novel sexual stimulation, the personal growth that can be attained through meeting many people, and the maintenance of independence and freedom.

Yet many single people find that singlehood is not always as free as it seems. Some complain that employers and coworkers view them with skepticism and are reluctant to place them in positions of trust. Their families may see them as selfish, as failures, or as sexually loose. Many single women complain that once they have entered their middle 20s, men are less willing to accept a "No" at the end of a date (Marin, 1983). They find that men assume that they are no longer virgins and that their only motives for saying no are to play games or to snare them into marriage. And many young adults have become disillusioned with frequent casual sexual involvements. The singles bar provokes anxieties and feelings of alienation as well as providing opportunities for sexual experience (Allon & Fishel, 1979; Simenauer & Carroll, 1982).

In Chapter 11 we saw that the goals and values that seem so rock solid in the 20s are often shaken in the 30s. The singles scene, too, can pall. In their late 20s and 30s, many singles decide that they would prefer to get

© King Features Syndicate, Inc., 1977.

married and have children. For women, of course, the "biological clock" for having children is felt to be running out during the 30s. But some people, men and women alike, choose to remain single for a lifetime.

Singlehood is an example of a "nontraditional" life style. During the "Swinging 60s" and the 1970s, many Americans experimented with other nontraditional life styles, such as **open marriage** (O'Neill & O'Neill, 1972), **group marriage** (Constantine & Constantine, 1973), and **communes** (Estellachild, 1972; Conover, 1975). Today, open and group marriage and communes, while still in existence here and there, have something of a nostalgic ring to them. But another nontraditional life style, cohabitation, remains widely practiced.

Cohabitation: "There's Nothing That I Wouldn't Do If You Would Be My POSSLQ"

There's Nothing That I Wouldn't Do If You Would Be My POSSLQ is the name of a book by CBS newsperson Charles Osgood (1981). *POSSLQ?* That's the unromantic abbreviation for "Person of Opposite Sex Sharing Living Quarters"—the official term used for cohabiters by the U.S. Bureau of the Census.

Cohabitation once was referred to as "living in sin," but today it is more likely to simply be called "living together." Cohabitation is an intimate relationship in which—pardon us—POSSLQ's (pronounced POSS-'l-cues?) live more or less as though they are married, but without legal sanction. There has been a profound increase in the number of cohabiting couples, from about half a million couples in 1970 to about a million couples during the 1980s (Current Population Reports, 1985). Thus, nearly 2 million Americans have chosen cohabitation as their style of life, and children live in about 24 percent of these households (Glick & Spanier, 1980).

Why do people cohabit rather than get married? For many reasons. Cohabitation is an alternative to the loneliness that can accompany living by oneself. Some love each other deeply but do not feel ready to get married. Some wish to test their relationship, or to learn to adjust to one another before getting married. By cohabiting rather than getting married, some individuals continue to receive public assistance (social security or welfare checks) or, among college students, parental support. And a few cohabiters, of course, are out to irk their parents—but this motive is *not* a sizable contributor to the statistics on cohabitation (Macklin, 1974).

Although some people cohabit as a "trial run" for marriage, cohabiters who later get married run the same risks for divorce as noncohabiters (Jacques & Chason, 1979; Newcomb & Bentler, 1980). In fact, as noted in Chapter 1, a recent Swedish study found that couples who cohabited before getting married were *more* likely to get divorced than couples who had not previously cohabited (*New York Times*, 1987). Consistent with the findings of the Swedish study, a U.S. report found that cohabitation was associated with poorer communication during marriage (from the wife's perspective), and with lower overall satisfaction for both marriage partners (DeMaris & Leslie, 1984).

TABLE 14.7 **Employment Status of Cohabiting and Married Adults, According to Sex and Age (in percents)**

Employment Status	Never-Married Cohabiting Persons		Married, Living with Spouse	
	Under 35	35–54	Under 35	35–54
MEN				
Employed	71.2	76.9	91.8	91.6
Unemployed or not in labor force	28.8	23.1	8.2	8.4
WOMEN				
Employed	67.8	95.5	43.9	47.7
Unemployed or not in labor force	32.2	4.5	56.1	52.3

Source: Glick and Spanier, 1980, p. 24.

Some Facts on Cohabiting versus Married Couples   How do cohabiting couples differ from married couples? First, never-married cohabiters are better educated (Glick & Spanier, 1980). Only 29 percent of married women continue their education past high school, but 53 percent of cohabiting women have attended college. Thirteen percent of married women are college graduates, as compared with 22 percent of cohabiting women. For men, the educational discrepancies are smaller: 46 percent of cohabiting men continue their education past high school, as compared with 41 percent of married men. About half these numbers in each group have graduated from college.

Cohabiting couples are more urbanized than marrieds. Some half of them live in metropolitan areas with populations of over 1 million. Only 37 percent of married couples live in communities as large.

Cohabiters also differ from married couples in employment status (see Table 14.7). Up through the age of 54, cohabiting men are more likely than married men to be unemployed, or not in the labor force. For many younger cohabiting men, this difference reflects the pursuit of advanced education. But for other cohabiting men, a nontraditional approach to life extends to attitudes toward work as well as attitudes toward marriage. For women, the statistics are reversed (Table 14.7). Cohabiting women are more likely than their married counterparts to be employed. For women, perhaps, the nontraditional behaviors of cohabitation and pursuing a career also cluster together.

Living Together on Campus   In the early 1960s, a female Columbia University student was discovered to be cohabiting with her boyfriend off campus. There was so much adverse publicity that she was forced to withdraw from the university.

But since then cohabitation has become a popular life-style for students. Some estimate that as many as one in three will cohabit at some time during his or her college career (Henslin, 1980). Many factors have contributed to this revolution, including availability of birth control methods, decreased emphasis on the importance of virginity, relaxed college housing regulations, and, probably, the perception that "everyone's doing it."

Who are the cohabiters? Eleanor Macklin (1974) found that cohabiting students generally came from stable homes, and their grades were equal to those of students who maintained separate dwellings. Bower and Christopherson (1977) found that 96 percent of the cohabiters surveyed at 14 state universities looked forward to eventual marriage. Cohabiters frequently—but not necessarily—plan to marry the person with whom they are living (Macklin, 1980), although they plan to become married a bit later than do noncohabiting peers. For some, in fact, cohabitation is perceived as a new phase in the courtship process (Henslin, 1980). Although cohabitation may be a nontraditional life-style, the division of labor in these households most frequently breaks down along traditional lines, with women doing the cooking and cleaning, and men the repairs (Stafford et al., 1977).

Most cohabiters in the Macklin survey thought that their parents would disapprove, but only 7 percent believed that cohabitation was morally wrong. Moreover, half the students who did *not* cohabit did not cite moralistic reasons. They were more inclined to report that they had not yet found the right person, or that their boyfriends or girlfriends lived too far away to make cohabitation practical.

Ninety-six percent of the cohabiting students surveyed by Macklin (1974) rated their sexual relationship as satisfying. Ninety percent considered the arrangement pleasurable and successful—a normal, contemporary life-style that evolved from the desire to share an intimate, affectionate relationship.

But cohabitation, like other life-styles, has its problems. Most cohabiters surveyed by Macklin tried to conceal their living arrangements from their parents. Fifty-seven percent were jealous of their partners' involvements with other people or activities. Sixty-two percent felt "overinvolved" with their partners and somewhat isolated from others. Forty-nine percent felt trapped at times. Sixty-two percent had experienced fear of pregnancy. Seventy-one percent had encountered conflicting desires for frequency of sexual activity, and 62 percent of the women had encountered occasional difficulty reaching orgasm. The percentages might differ somewhat, but all in all the problem list sounds a bit like that of young married couples undergoing a period of adjustment.

Despite experiments such as cohabitation, most Americans remain committed to marriage as the ideal intimate relationship. Many of us seem to evaluate marriage in much the same way that Winston Churchill viewed democracy as a form of government. It's flawed, frustrating, and just plain awful—but it's preferable for most people when compared to the alternatives.

■ Summary

1. **What is an intimate relationship?** In an intimate relationship, people share their inmost thoughts and feelings.
2. **What are Levinger's stages in the development of a relationship?** According to Levinger, relationships undergo a five-stage developmental sequence from initial attraction to building a relationship, continuation, deterioration, and ending. Relationships need not advance beyond any one of these stages.
3. **What is small talk, and how does it affect the development of relationships?** Small talk is a broad exploration for common ground that permits us to decide whether we wish to advance the relationship beyond surface contact.
4. **What is self-disclosure, and how does it affect the development of relationships?** Self-disclosure is the revelation of personal information. Self-disclosure invites reciprocity and can foster intimacy. However, overly rapid, premature self-disclosure has been linked to maladjustment and phoniness and tends to repel people.
5. **Why do people get married?** Historically, most marriages were patriarchies that provided an institution for legitimizing sexual relations and rearing children, and a channel for the transmission of wealth from one generation to another, or one family to another. Marriages were once arranged, frequently for financial or political gain. Today's marriages are usually based on attraction and love and the desires for emotional and psychological intimacy and security.
6. **To whom do we get married?** Most marriages are homogamous. We tend to marry people similar in race, religion, social class, even eye color and intelligence.

7. **How satisfied are married couples?** According to Campbell, married people are generally more satisfied with their lives than singles. Young, married, child-free women seem happiest. Women without children do not seem less happy than mothers. Most women respondents to a survey of *Ladies' Home Journal* readers reported that their marriages were strong, but 54 percent had considered divorce at some time. Hite recently reported that U.S. women are "fed up" with the way they are treated by men, but Hite's sampling method was invalid.

8. **What factors affect marital satisfaction?** Snyder found four factors that consistently predict overall marital satisfaction: affective communication, problem-solving communication, sexual satisfaction, and agreement about finances. Lack of money and poor communication were the greatest contributors to marital dissatisfaction in the *Ladies' Home Journal* survey, with sexual problems and in-law troubles following.

9. **How can we cope with marital conflict?** A number of suggestions are made for coping with marital conflicts: challenging irrational expectations (such as the myth that people with good marriages do not disagree), negotiating differences, being specific about complaints (complaining about behavior, not personalities), contracting to exchange desired behaviors, and increasing pleasurable marital interactions.

10. **What factors are involved in communication skills?** Good communication includes (active) listening, learning about your partner's needs, making requests, delivering and receiving criticism effectively, and finding ways of coping with impasses.

11. **How many marriages end in divorce?** From 33 to 40 percent of marriages end in divorce. Divorced people usually encounter a great deal of stress and show some decline in mental and physical health.

12. **Why do people remain single?** Many people remain single today. Some singles simply have not yet found the right marital partner, but others prefer sexual variety and wish to avoid making a commitment to another person.

13. **What is the single life-style like?** It varies. Some singles date many different partners; others practice serial monogamy. Still others remain celibate.

14. **What is cohabitation?** Cohabitation is living together without being married. There are nearly one million cohabiting couples in the U.S.

15. **How do cohabitors differ from married people?** Never-married, cohabiting women are better educated than their married peers, and more likely to be employed. Never-married, cohabiting men are less likely than their married peers to be employed, which frequently reflects the seeking of an advanced education among young cohabiting men. About one college student in three will cohabit during his or her college career. Most cohabiting students come from stable families and expect to get married someday, but not necessarily to their current partners. Most cohabiting students earn grades on a par with those who live alone, and they do not see their behavior as immoral. Cohabiting students tend to encounter jealousies and other adjustment problems that sound rather similar to those of young marrieds.

16. **Does cohabitation prior to marriage enhance the likelihood of being well adjusted in marriage?** Apparently not. Some recent studies have found that cohabiters are actually more likely than noncohabiters to get divorced after they get married.

■ TRUTH OR FICTION REVISITED

Small talk is a clumsy way to begin a new relationship. False. Small talk can be a skillful search for common ground.

Rapid self-disclosure of intimate information is the best way to deepen a new relationship. False. People who rapidly disclose intimate information are seen as maladjusted and phony. Timely disclosure is the key.

We are less likely to try to iron out the wrinkles in our relationships when new partners are available to us. True. When new partners are available, we are not likely to be so strongly motivated to work out our problems with our current partners.

Marriage is losing its popularity as a style of life. False. Well over 90 percent of us eventually get married.

In the ancient Hebrew and Greek civilizations, wives were viewed as their husbands' property. True. The notion that husbands and wives are equals is a recent development.

Singles are more satisfied with their lives than married people are. False.

Couples who were engaged for at least three years before getting married have happier marriages than couples who were engaged for only a year. False. It appears that couples who put off marriage for that long often have misgivings or conflicts that continue to harm the relationship.

Sexual problems are the single most powerful predictor of general marital dissatisfaction. False. Poor communication, inability to resolve problems, and financial woes seem to be more prominent sources of dissatisfaction.

Mothers are more satisfied with their marriages than women without children are. False. Wives without children are usually happier, unless they want to have children but cannot.

Disagreement is destructive to a marriage. False. This is one of the irrational beliefs that can imperil marital adjustment.

The most effective way of handling criticism from a marital partner is to be critical yourself. False. Retaliation heightens tensions and conflicts.

Being single has become a more common U.S. life-style over the past few decades. True, but mostly because people are delaying marriage somewhat, not because marriage has gone out of style.

Single people are "swingers." Not necessarily. Single people follow a number of different kinds of styles of life.

Cohabiting men are less likely to hold jobs than their married counterparts. True. In some cases this is because cohabiting men are pursuing advanced education.

Cohabiting college students are rebellious. False. Most of them come from stable families, earn decent grades, and plan to get married someday.

■ Scoring Key for Questionnaire on Endorsement of Traditional or Liberal Marital Roles

Below each of the scoring codes (AS, AM, DM, and DS) there is a number. Underline the numbers beneath each of your answers. Then add the underlined numbers to obtain your total score.

The total score can vary from 10 to 40. A score of 10–20 shows moderate to high traditionalism concerning marital roles, while a score of 30–40 shows moderate to high liberalism. A score between 20 and 30 suggests that you are a middle-of-the-roader.

Your endorsement of a traditional or a liberal marital role is not a matter of right or wrong. However, if you and your potential or actual spouse endorse significantly different marital roles, there may be role conflict ahead. It may be worthwhile to have a frank talk with your partner about your goals and values to determine whether the two of you have major disagreements and are willing to work to resolve them.

Sexual Behavior: Perspectives, Patterns, Pleasures, and Problems

15

Masturbation can cause mental illness.

Most women have entertained fantasies about imaginary lovers while engaging in sexual relations with their husbands.

Most of today's sophisticated young people see nothing wrong with an occasional extramarital fling.

Women, but not men, have a sex organ whose only known function is the sensing of sexual pleasure.

Nontraditional women suffer less from premenstrual distress than their traditionalist sisters do.

Homosexuals choose to be homosexual.

Homosexuals suffer from hormonal imbalances.

Pornographic films cause crimes of violence against women.

A healthy woman can successfully resist a rapist if she really wants to.

Only women can have multiple orgasms.

Most sexual dysfunctions stem from physical problems.

Painful early sexual experiences can lead to sexual dysfunctions in adulthood.

Gonorrhea and syphilis may be contracted by using toilet seats in public restrooms.

If the symptoms of sexually transmitted diseases go away by themselves, medical treatment is usually unnecessary.

Only homosexual males and intravenous drug abusers are at real risk for contracting AIDS.

■ Human Sexual Behavior in Perspective: A Tale of Two Cultures

Offshore from the misty coasts of Ireland lies the small island of Inis Beag. From the air it is a green jewel, warm and inviting. At ground level, things are somewhat different.

For example, the residents of Inis Beag do not believe that women experience sexual climax, or **orgasm.** The woman who chances to find pleasure in sex is considered deviant (Messenger, 1971). Premarital sex is all but unknown. Women engage in **coitus** in order to conceive children and to appease their husbands' "animalistic" cravings. But they need not worry about being called on for frequent performances since the men of Inis Beag believe, erroneously, that sex saps their strength. Sex on Inis Beag is carried out in the dark—literally and figuratively, and with the nightclothes on. The man lies on top in the so-called missionary position. In accord with local concepts of masculinity, he ejaculates as fast as he can. Then he rolls over and falls asleep.

If Inis Beag does not sound like your cup of tea, you may find the atmosphere of Mangaia more congenial. Mangaia is a Polynesian pearl of an island, lifting languidly from the blue waters of the Pacific. It is on the other side of the world from Inis Beag—in more ways than one.

From an early age, Mangaian children are encouraged to get in touch with their sexuality through **masturbation** (Marshall, 1971). Mangaian adolescents are expected to engage in coitus. They may be found on secluded beaches or beneath the listing fronds of palms, diligently practicing techniques learned from village elders.

Mangaian women are expected to reach orgasm several times before their partners do. Young men want their partners to reach orgasm and compete to see who is more effective at bringing young women to multiple orgasms.

The residents of Inis Beag and Mangaia have similar anatomic features, but vastly different attitudes toward sex. Their attitudes influence their patterns of sexual behavior and the pleasure they find—or do not find—in sex. Like eating, sexual activity is a natural function. Yet no other natural function has found such varied expression. No other natural function has been influenced so strongly by religious and moral beliefs, by cultural tradition, folklore, and superstition.

Throughout much of Western history, sexual behavior has been viewed as indecent or sinful. Many people feel guilty about sexual activity, and many find no pleasure in sex. Others, who viewed themselves as the children of the "sexual revolution" of the 1960s and 1970s, frequently worried about whether they had grown free enough in their sexual activity.

In this chapter we first explore patterns of sexual behavior in a changing world. We shall see that since the end of World War II, there has been a revolution in our sexual behavior and attitudes. We examine sexual anatomy and response and see that women and men may be more alike in their sexual response than you may have thought. We discuss the issues of homosexuality, pornography, and rape. We consider sexual dysfunctions and their treatment. Finally we examine sexually transmitted diseases, their treatment and prevention.

■ U.S. Sexual Behavior in Perspective: A Tale of Three Generations

Sexual practices not only differ widely from culture to culture. They have also differed widely in the United States from person to person and from generation to generation. In this section we consider the so-called sexual revolution and survey U.S. sexual practices since the end of World War II.

Orgasm. The climax of sexual arousal, characterized by pleasure, involuntary contraction of muscles in the genital region, and the release of sexual tension.

Coitus. (pronounced CO-it-us or co-EET-us). Sexual intercourse.

Masturbation. Self-stimulation of the sexual organs.

The "Woodstock Generation"
The sexual revolution reached its height in the 1960s and early 1970s and was tied into the political liberalism of the day. What happened to sexual attitudes and behavior patterns during the 1980s?

The Three R's: Repression, Revolution, and Reaction

Prior to World War II, and for 10 or 15 years afterward, sexual behavior patterns in the United States were repressed by today's standards. By and large it was expected that women would be virgins when they got married, although there was a sexual **double standard** that was more permissive toward men. Men, that is, were expected to have "sown their wild oats."

Double standard. The view that men are entitled to sexual pleasure and premarital coitus, but women are not.

Sex was by and large assumed to be more pleasurable for men than women, and this assumption was a self-fulfilling prophecy. That is, couples did not usually work together to find ways of enhancing sexual pleasure. We were not as backward as Inis Baeg, but by and large, what married couples got from sex they got from it. What they didn't get from sex they might have dreamed about, but usually they didn't talk about it.

A Pendulum Swing . . .   A sexual revolution took place during the 1960s and 1970s that changed sexual behavior in the United States in very basic ways. People became more open about their sexual feelings and needs. Masters and Johnson (1966) published research findings that showed that women could reach orgasm just as men could; in fact, women could have multiple orgasms with proper sexual stimulation. The incidence of premarital sex increased dramatically, and some people took up "recreational sex." For many people interpersonal relations were turned upside down as sex was separated from romance and commitment.

The sexual revolution seems to have been part of a broader Human Potential Movement, which focused on getting in touch with, and expressing, our genuine feelings. The sexual revolution also seems to have been tied into the political liberalism of the day, which gave a voice to groups who had previously been denied political expression. The Human Potential Movement adopted the humanistic views of Maslow and Rogers that we should find, and place our trust in, our true feelings. The motto of the sexual revolution, for some, was a derivation of Maslow and Rogers' views: They were expressed tongue-in-cheek by Bob Newhart, who played a psychologist in television's *Bob Newhart Show* of the 1970s: "If it feels right, go with it."

Sexual practices within marriage changed just as dramatically, as we shall see in the following pages.

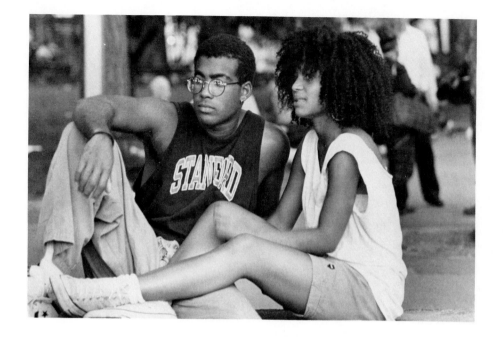

Today's young adults are generally more conservative than those of the 1960s. They tend to give their choice of partners more thought and are generally more cautious in their sexual behavior. On the other hand, many of them feel free to talk about their sexual needs and feelings.

And Back?   Today it seems that political and religious conservatism, in combination with fears of sexually transmitted diseases—particularly herpes and AIDS, has reversed some of the revolutionary trends (Baron & Byrne, 1987). The incidence of premarital sex appears to have declined over the 1980s. According to recent reports by the U.S. Bureau of the Census, there has even been a slight decline in the number of cohabiting couples. For these reasons, we can say that since the war years there have been three generations of sexual attitudes and behavior patterns: the generation of the 1940s and 1950s, the generation of the 1960s and 1970s, and the current generation, which began in the early 1980s.

During the 1960s there was a strong pendulum swing toward sexual liberalism, and, it would appear, during the past few years there has been something of a swing back. Whether our sexual behavior patterns will return to those of the days of Kinsey, whether they will stabilize somewhere in the middle, or whether we will experience another surge toward liberalism we cannot say.

Let us now turn our attention to what our sexual behavior was like in the postwar years and during the "swinging 60s," and let us also see if we can get an impression of what it is like today.

Patterns of Sexual Behavior

In the late 1940s and 1950s the publication of a pair of scientific surveys of American sexual behavior shocked the nation. The "Kinsey reports" (Kinsey et al., 1948, 1953), which described the sexual behavior of 5,300 men and 5,940 women, contained no foul language or suggestive imagery. Yet they created such a stir that a congressional committee charged that they undermined the moral fiber of the country (Gebhard, 1976). As a nation, we had not yet learned to discuss sex openly.

More recent sex surveys (e.g., Hite, 1976; Hunt, 1974; Tavris & Sadd, 1977; Wolfe, 1981) have stirred little public concern. Comparisons of sexual behavior over the generations must rely on the Kinsey reports and more recent surveys, yet they all have their shortcomings (Rathus, 1983). Kinsey's sample underrepresented blacks, the elderly, the poorly educated, southern-

Sex researcher Alfred Kinsey.

ers, and westerners. Kinsey's subjects were all interviewed by men, which may have had an inhibitory effect on women respondents. Morton Hunt's (1974) sample of 982 men and 1,044 women was drawn from phone listings in representative communities. But only about 20 percent of those contacted agreed to participate. Hunt's sample is thus likely to be a relatively open and frank group of volunteers. More recent studies also rely on volunteers.

Despite their limitations, these surveys and others provide some insight into the sexual practices of the American population. In this section we have a look at American attitudes toward, and practice of, masturbation, petting, premarital sex, and marital and extramarital sex since the 1940s and 1950s.

Masturbation

> In solitude he pollutes himself, and with his own hand blights all his prospects for both this world and the next. Even after being solemnly warned, he will often continue this worse than beastly practice, deliberately forfeiting his right to health and happiness for a moment's mad sensuality.
>
> J. W. Kellogg, M.D., *Plain Facts for Old and Young,* 1882.

This portrayal of the masturbator by one of the fathers of American breakfast cereals was typical for its day. Epilepsy, cancer, heart attacks, insanity, sterility, itching, warts—despite the lack of a shred of evidence, all were considered the lot of the masturbator. Kellogg, by the way, warned that certain foods, especially alcohol and coffee, might excite the sex organs. He recommended "unstimulating" grains instead. In case the issue comes up at a cocktail party, you are now an expert on the origins of corn flakes.

Ignorance is not restricted to the olden days. A mid-1970s sample of college students (Abramson & Mosher, 1975) showed that they thought masturbation could be harmful. Each of 312 men interviewed by Masters and Johnson (1966) believed that "excessive" masturbation could lead to a mental disorder. Ironically, none believed that his own level of masturbation exceeded the danger point.

Despite widespread though groundless fears, most people have masturbated. Men report greater **incidence** of masturbation than women. Kinsey and his colleagues (1948, 1953) and Hunt (1974) found that nearly all adult males and about two-thirds of adult women surveyed had masturbated. A survey of college students (Miller & Lief, 1976) reported a **cumulative incidence** of 97 percent for males and 78 percent for females. Religious devoutness seems to inhibit masturbation. But Hunt found that even among regular churchgoers, 92 percent of the men and 51 percent of the women have masturbated.

Men and women report using fantasies such as those listed in Table 15.1 to increase sexual arousal when they masturbate.

Incidence. The extent of the occurrence of an event.

Cumulative incidence. The accumulated extent of the occurrence of an event over time.

TABLE 15.1   Masturbation Fantasies Reported in the Hunt Study

Fantasy	Incidence of Fantasy (Percents)	
	Men	*Women*
Having intercourse with a loved person	75	80
Having intercourse with strangers	47	21
Having intercourse with more than one person of the opposite sex at the same time	33	18
Doing sexual things you would never do in reality	19	28
Being forced to have sex	10	19
Forcing someone to have sex	13	3
Having sex with someone of the same sex	7	11

Source of data: Hunt (1974), pp. 91–93.

Misinformation about masturbation persists, but among Hunt's 18- to 24-year-olds, only 14 to 15 percent said that masturbation was wrong. However, nearly one in three of respondents aged 55 and above said that it was wrong. These older subjects were in their 20s during Kinsey's surveys. Perhaps most Americans would now agree with Woody Allen's observation: He could not knock masturbation, since it meant having sex with someone he loved.

Contemporary scholars of sexual behavior agree that masturbation is neither physically nor mentally harmful. But people who believe that masturbation is harmful, wrong, or sinful may experience anxiety if they masturbate or consider masturbation.

Petting   **Petting** is touch or massage of another person's breasts or genitals. Some writers include **fellatio** and **cunnilingus** as forms of petting, whereas others consider them separately. Petting can be used to provide pleasure or reach orgasm. When used to heighten sexual arousal as a prelude to coitus, petting is called **foreplay**.

Many adolescents and young adults use petting as a halfway measure between sexual abstinence and coitus. It allows people to express affection and experience sexual excitement while avoiding pregnancy and maintaining virginity. Kinsey found petting nearly universal among male adolescents. For college men who delayed getting married, petting became a major sexual outlet for many years. Petting was also common among females, especially those who delayed marriage. Ninety-four percent of women who remained single at age 20 had petted (Kinsey et al., 1953). Hunt (1974) found petting nearly universal among adolescents in the 1970s. But Hunt's subjects began petting at younger ages than Kinsey's. They were less likely than Kinsey's subjects to use petting as a prolonged adjustment to the single life, since premarital coitus had become more common.

Premarital Intercourse   The incidence of premarital coitus in Kinsey's day clearly reflected the sexual double standard that sexual activity is more acceptable for men than women. By age 20, 77 percent of the single men in Kinsey's sample, but only 20 percent of the single women, had engaged in premarital intercourse. By age 25, 83 percent of the single men and 33 percent of single women had done so.

Table 15.2 shows that the incidence of premarital intercourse had exploded for young singles interviewed by Hunt, especially women. Results of a number of surveys suggest that the percentage of sexually active, unmarried, female college undergraduates may have peaked during the 1970s (Baron & Byrne, 1987; Gerrard, 1986). According to Gerrard (1986), less than 40 percent of female college undergraduates were sexually active during the early 1980s, as compared to about 50 percent five years earlier. But even during the height of the sexual revolution, Americans in large numbers had never climbed aboard the bandwagon of recreational sex. Fifty-four percent of the women in the Hunt study who had engaged in premarital coitus had done so with one partner only—typically the man they wished to marry. So had 48

Petting. Touching the breasts or genitals of another in order to enhance sexual arousal.

Fellatio. Oral stimulation of the male genitals.

Cunnilingus. Oral stimulation of the female genitals.

Foreplay. Petting that serves as a prelude to coitus.

TABLE 15.2   Incidence of Premarital Intercourse among Different Age Groups (Percents)

	Age Group				
	18–24	*25–34*	*35–44*	*45–54*	*55 and over*
Men	95	92	86	89	84
Women	81	65	41	36	31

Source: Hunt (1974), p. 150.

Contraceptive. Acting to prevent conception, or fertilization of an ovum.

percent of a sample of 532 12- to 17-year-old girls who visited a **contraceptive** clinic (Reichelt, 1979).

Hunt reports that many people who abstain from premarital coitus do so for moral or religious reasons; or because of fear of being caught, of pregnancy, or of disease. There are recent suggestions that the advent of AIDS has induced many unmarried people to be more cautious in their selection of partners (*Glamour,* 1988; Schulte, 1986; Wallis, 1987). For example, a young male patron of a Manhattan singles bar reported that, "You think twice. If sex is too easy, I just won't take it" (Wallis, 1987, p. 51). Of single women responding to a recent *Glamour Magazine* (1988) survey, 71 percent (up from 47 percent one year earlier!) said they had become more cautious because of AIDS; 11 percent have become celibate; 21 percent insist on using a condom, and 22 percent have become monogamous. *Glamour* readers do not represent the entire single female population, of course, but the patterns of change noted in the magazine's surveys over the years appear to reflect wider trends.

But it might be premature to conclude that conservatism and fear of AIDS have brought the sexual revolution to a crashing finale. For one thing, people appear to remain more willing to talk about their sexual needs and feelings than they were in Kinsey's day—and openness about sex is one aspect of the sexual revolution. For another, many people continue to engage in premarital intercourse. However, young adults appear to be giving the issue more thought, to be somewhat more selective in their choice of partners, and somewhat more likely to take precautions that might prevent the spread of disease.

Marital Sex   Since Kinsey's day the marital bed has become a stage with more varied parts for the players. Kinsey's samples generally restricted coitus to the man-on-top, or missionary, position. Only one-third of the sample had also used the female-superior (woman-on-top) position, but this percentage doubled with the Hunt study. Today the rear (vaginal) entry, side-by-side, and sitting positions have become spices commonly included in the sexual diet.

Kinsey and Hunt found that college-educated couples are more likely to use oral sex than couples with high-school educations. But oral sex has become popular in recent years and the great majority of young couples practice both fellatio and cunnilingus (Blumstein & Schwartz, 1983; Hunt, 1974).

In the past it was often assumed that the "virile" man ejaculated quickly during intercourse. Most of the men in Kinsey's (1948) sample reached orgasm within two minutes after beginning coitus, many within 10 to 20 seconds. But women usually take longer to reach orgasm. This message may have been successfully communicated in more recent years, because Hunt's sample reported an average duration of coitus of about 10 minutes. Younger couples engaged in coitus for even longer periods. This is a major change brought about by the sexual revolution that remains in full sway today.

Couples today also engage in sexual intercourse more frequently than in Kinsey's day. Couples in their 20s and 30s now engage in intercourse two or three times a week, on the average (Pietropinto & Simenauer, 1979; Hunt, 1974; Trussel & Westoff, 1980). As in Kinsey's day, the frequency of intercourse tends to decline gradually as the age of the couple advances.

It is common for men and women to heighten their sexual excitement during marital intercourse with sexual fantasy. Some worry that they are being disloyal, but there is no evidence that these fantasies lead to unfaithfulness or loss of interest in one's mate. Sixty-five percent of a sample of married women from an affluent New York suburb reported using sexual fantasies during coitus (Hariton & Singer, 1974). The most common fantasy, reported by 56 percent, was of "an imaginary romantic lover." Other common fantasies included reliving another sexual experience (52 percent), doing something "forbidden" (50 percent), being overpowered (49 percent), making love in another setting (47 percent), and group sex (47 percent).

Numerous researchers (e.g., Blumstein & Schwartz, 1983; Hunt, 1974) have also found links between the quality of the overall marital relationship and the satisfaction received from sexual relations. In particular, women who can talk about their sexual feelings and needs with their husbands find sex more enjoyable (Banmen & Vogel, 1985; Tavris & Sadd, 1977). Marital coitus does not take place in an emotional vacuum—the closer the relationship, the more enjoyable the sex. Sexual pleasure may contribute to feelings of closeness, just as closeness may render sex more enjoyable.

Extramarital Sex   Married people become involved in affairs for many reasons—such as breaking the routine of a confining marriage (Ellis, 1977), proving to themselves that they are still attractive (McCranie, 1979), and expressing hostility toward a mate (Prosen & Martin, 1979). Most of the women who reported affairs to Lynn Atwater (1982) stated that curiosity and the desire for growth were more powerful motives than marital dissatisfaction. However, the sexual revolution has not changed attitudes toward **extramarital sex.** The great majority of Americans disapprove of it. Eighty to 98 percent of Hunt's subjects, 85 percent of respondents to the *Ladies' Home Journal* survey (Schultz, 1980), and 89 percent of the *Glamour* magazine (1988) survey express the view that extramarital sex is wrong.

The Kinsey and Hunt studies found the incidence of extramarital sex to be about 50 percent for men and 20 percent for women aged 25 and above. About 20 percent of the *Ladies' Home Journal* readers (Schultz, 1980) also had affairs. The relatively liberal respondents to the *Redbook* survey (Tavris & Sadd, 1977) reported a 29 percent incidence of affairs. The *Redbook* survey found a significant link between work status and affairs. Twenty-four percent of all housewives in their late 30s, as compared with 53 percent of working women in the same age group, had had affairs. Traditionalists might seize upon this statistic as another reason that wives should stay at home. But working men are also likely to be more prone to affairs than "househusbands." Would men accept such a finding as a reason for them to remain in the home?

In "swinging," or **comarital sex,** husband and wife participate jointly in extramarital encounters with another couple or at swinging parties. Despite its capacity to make headlines, swinging seems rare. Only about two percent of Hunt's couples had "swung," and many of these only once. Studies suggest that swingers predominantly come from the middle or upper-middle class and are above average in income and education (Jenks, 1985). Many swingers preserve marital stability by prohibiting emotional involvement with swinging partners (Bartell, 1970).

Interestingly, Hunt found that people who had affairs usually found sex with their mates more pleasurable than sex with their lovers. Marital partners may lose a bit of novelty over the years, but perhaps relations with them take place at a more leisurely pace or they are more likely to know of their mates' sexual needs. In any event, the majority of Americans still report not having extramarital affairs.

■ The Biological Basis of Sex

Although we may consider ourselves reasonably sophisticated about sexual matters, it's astonishing how little we know about the biological basis of sex. Up through the age of 5, about half of us continue to think that babies come from mothers' "tummies"—and many of the rest of us come up with ideas not far removed from delivery by the stork (Rathus, 1988). Most children do

Extramarital sex. Sexual activity of married persons with other than the marital partner.

Comarital sex. Joint participation of a married couple in extramarital sex.

not know the correct names for their sex organs (Rathus, 1983). And what about adults? How many male readers know that women have different orifices for urination and sexual intercourse? How many readers, male and female, know that the penis—sometimes referred to by the slang terms "boner" or "muscle"—contains neither bone nor muscle?

We begin this section by surveying some of the details of female and male sexual anatomy. Then we consider the roles of sex hormones in sexual behavior and describe what happens to us as we become sexually aroused and reach orgasm.

Female Sexual Anatomy

The external female genital organs are called the **vulva,** from the Latin for "covering." The vulva is also known as the **pudendum,** from "something to be ashamed of"—a clear reflection of some ancient Mediterranean sexism. The vulva has several parts (see the bottom part of Figure 15.1): the mons veneris, clitoris, major and minor lips, and vaginal opening. Females urinate through the **urethral** (pronounced you-WREATH-r'l) opening.

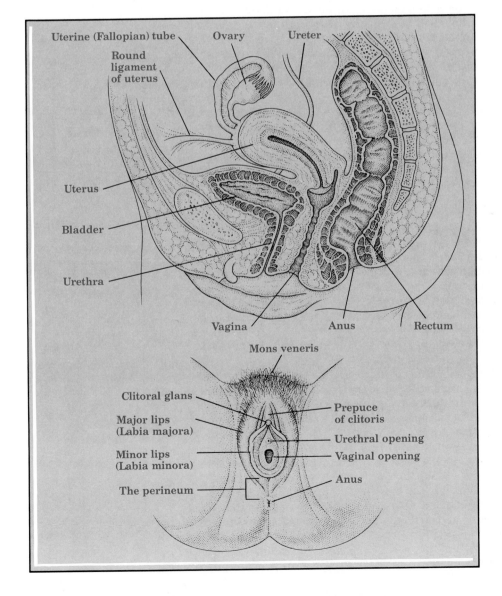

FIGURE 15.1 Female Sexual Anatomy

The above drawing is a cross section of the internal reproductive organs of the female. The drawing below is an external view of the vulva.

The **mons veneris** (Latin for "hill of love") is a fatty cushion that lies above the pubic bone and is covered with short, curly pubic hair. The mons and pubic hair cushion the woman during sexual intercourse, or coitus. The woman's most sensitive sex organ, the **clitoris** (from the Greek for "hill"), lies below the mons and above the urethral opening. The only known function of the clitoris is to receive and transmit pleasurable sensations.

During sexual arousal, the clitoris becomes engorged with blood and expands. The clitoris has a shaft and a tip, or **glans.** The glans is the more sensitive of the two and may become irritated if approached too early during foreplay, or by prolonged stimulation. Women usually masturbate by stroking the clitoral shaft (Hite, 1976).

Two layers of fatty tissue, the outer or **major lips** and the inner or **minor lips,** line the entrance to the vagina. The outer lips are covered with hair and are less sensitive to touch than the smooth, pinkish inner lips.

The woman's internal sexual and reproductive organs consist of the vagina, cervix, fallopian tubes, and ovaries (see the top part of Figure 15.1). The tubelike vagina contains the penis during intercourse. At rest the vagina is a flattened tube three to five inches in length. When aroused, it can lengthen by several inches and dilate (widen) to a diameter of about two inches. Contrary to myth, a large penis is not required to "fill" the vagina in order for a woman to experience sexual pleasure. The vagina expands as needed. The pelvic muscles that surround the vagina may also be contracted during coitus to heighten sensation. The outer third of the vagina is highly sensitive to touch. The inner two-thirds may be so insensitive that minor surgery can be performed without an anesthetic (Barbach, 1975).

When a woman is sexually aroused, the vaginal walls produce moisture that serves as lubrication for intercourse. Coitus can be painful for non-aroused, nonlubricated women. In our culture, adequate arousal usually stems from sexual attraction, positive feelings like liking and loving, fantasies, and foreplay. Excessive anxieties concerning sex or a particular partner may inhibit sexual arousal—for either sex.

High in the vagina is a small opening called the **cervix** (Latin for "neck") that connects that vagina to the uterus. Strawlike fallopian tubes lead from the uterus to the abdominal cavity. Ovaries, which produce ova and the hormones estrogen and progesterone, lie near the uterus and the fallopian tubes. When an ovum is relased from an ovary, it normally finds its way into the nearby fallopian tube (although we do not know *how* it does so) and makes its way to the uterus. Conception usually takes place in the tube, but the embryo normally becomes implanted and grows in the uterus, as we shall see in Chapter 16. During labor the cervix dilates, and the baby passes through the cervix and distended vagina.

Male Sexual Anatomy

The major male sex organs consist of the penis, testes (or testicles), scrotum, and the series of ducts, canals, and glands that store and transport sperm and produce **semen,** which is the fluid that carries the sperm during ejaculation. Whereas the female vulva has been viewed historically as "something to be ashamed of," the male sex organs were prized in ancient Greece and Rome. Greeks and Romans wore phallic-shaped trinkets, and the Greeks held their testes when offering testimony, in the same way that we swear on a Bible. *Testimony* and *testicle* both derive from the Greek *testis,* meaning "witness." Given this tradition of masculine pride, it is not surprising that Sigmund Freud believed that girls were riddled with penis envy. In recent years we have made strides in recognizing and challenging the sexism that treats female sexuality with disrespect.

The **testes** produce sperm and the male sex hormone testosterone. The **scrotum** allows the testes to hang away from the body because sperm require

---

Mons veneris. The mound of fatty tissue that covers the joint of the pubic bones and cushions the female during coitus.

Clitoris. The female sex organ whose only known function is the reception and transmission of sensations of sexual pleasure.

Glans. Tip or head.

Major lips. Large folds of skin that run along the sides of the vulva. (In Latin, *labia majora.*)

Minor lips. Folds of skin that lie within the major lips and enclose the urethral and vaginal openings. (In Latin, *labia minora.*)

Cervix. The lower part of the uterus that opens into the vagina.

Semen. The whitish fluid that carries sperm. Also called "the ejaculate."

Testes. Male reproductive organs that produce sperm cells and male sex hormones. Also called *testicles.*

Scrotum. A pouch of loose skin that houses the testes.

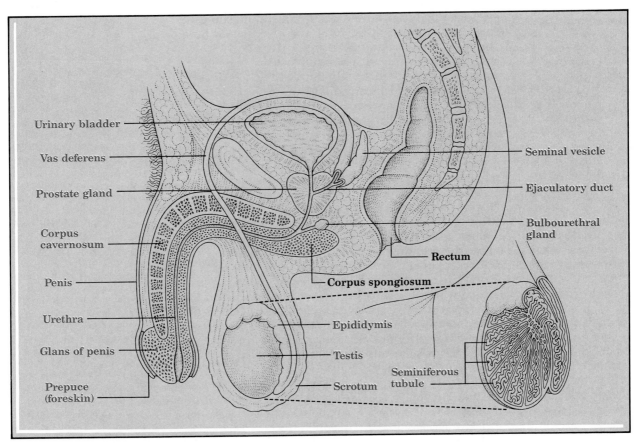

FIGURE 15.2   Male Sexual Anatomy
A cross section of the internal and external reproductive organs of the male.

a lower-than-body temperature. Sperm travel through ducts and canals up over the bladder and back down to the ejaculatory duct (see Figure 15.2), which empties into the male's urethra. In females, the urethral opening and the orifice for intercourse are different, but in males they are one and the same. Although the urethra of the male transports urine as well as sperm, a valve shuts off the bladder during ejaculation so that sperm and urine do not mix. Several glands, including the prostate, produce semen. Semen transports, activates, and nourishes sperm, enhancing their ability to swim and fertilize the ovum.

Contrary to myth, there is no evidence that ejaculation saps the strength and should be avoided on the eve of an athletic contest. The late baseball manager Casey Stengel once remarked that it was not sex on the eve of a big game that wore out his athletes. Rather, it was the loss of sleep from hunting for a sex partner.

The penis consists mainly of loose erectile tissue. Like the clitoris, the penis has a shaft and tip, or glans, that is highly sensitive to sexual stimulation, especially on the underside. Within three to eight seconds following sexual stimulation, blood will rush reflexively into caverns within the penis, just as blood engorges the clitoris during sexual stimulation. Engorgement with blood—not bone, not muscle—produces erection.

Erections are found in newborn infants and 90-year-old men. Males usually attain erection every 90 to 100 minutes while sleeping, especially during rapid-eye-movement (REM) sleep, which is associated with dreaming.

They may last 30 to 40 minutes and, contrary to another myth, erections do not reflect the need to urinate.

Vive la Différence or Vive la Similarité?

In Chapter 3 we first brought up the question as to how the sexes differ and how they are alike. The biological sex differences between men and women are obvious. The similarities are less obvious, but they are just as pervasive.

The similarities between the sexual structures of men and women are derived from the fact that they develop from the same embryonic structures. A 5-week-old male embryo is identical to a 5-week-old female in its sexual structures. But within a week or two the genetic code (XY for a male and XX for a female) asserts itself, and the structures begin to differentiate.

The penis and the clitoral glans develop from the same embryonic material and are comparable in function. Each becomes engorged with blood and swells in response to sexual stimulation, and each is exquisitely sensitive to touch. (They differ in that the penis also transports body fluids, whereas the clitoris does not.) The testes and the ovaries also develop from the same embryonic material. Each produces germ cells (sperm and ova) and sex hormones. The scrotum and vaginal lips derive from the same embryonic material and appear to be equally sensitive to sexual stimulation (although the testes, within the scrotal sac, are easily hurt by heavy touches, whereas the muscular tissue behind the vaginal lips is not so sensitive).

And so, the degree to which male and female sex organs are different or alike depends on one's point of view. Most of us are pleased to focus on the differences, of course.

Effects of Sex Hormones

Sex hormones promote biological sexual differentiation, regulate the menstrual cycle, and have organizing effects and activating effects on sexual behavior.

Hormonal Regulation of the Menstrual Cycle The ovaries produce **estrogen** and **progesterone.** Estrogen is a generic name for several female sex hormones that lead to development of female reproductive capacity and secondary sex characteristics, such as accumulation of fat in the breasts and the hips. Progesterone also has multiple functions. It stimulates growth of the female reproductive organs and maintains pregnancy. The levels of estrogen and progesterone vary markedly and regulate the menstrual cycle. Following **menstruation**—the monthly sloughing off of the inner lining of the uterus—estrogen levels increase, leading to the ripening of an ovum (egg cell) and the growth of the **endometrium,** or inner lining of the uterus. **Ovulation** occurs—that is, the ovum is released by the ovary—halfway through the menstrual cycle, when estrogens reach peak blood levels. Then, in response to secretion of progesterone, the inner lining of the uterus thickens, gaining the capacity to support an embryo if fertilization should occur. If the ovum is not fertilized, estrogen and progesterone levels drop suddenly, triggering menstruation once more.

Organizing and Activating Effects of Sex Hormones Sexual behavior among many lower animals is almost completely governed by hormones (Crews & Moore, 1986). They predispose lower animals toward masculine or feminine mating patterns (an **organizing effect**). Hormones also influence the sex drive and facilitate sexual response (**activating effects**).

Consider the influences of sex hormones on the mating behavior of rats. Male rats who have been castrated at birth—and thus deprived of **testosterone**—make no effort to mate as adults. But when they receive *female* sex hormones in adulthood, they become receptive to the sexual advances of other males and assume female mating stances (Harris & Levine, 1965). Male rats

Estrogen. A generic term for several female sex hormones that foster growth of female sex characteristics and regulate the menstrual cycle.

Progesterone. A female sex hormone that promotes growth of the sex organs, helps maintain pregnancy, and is also involved in regulation of the menstrual cycle.

Menstruation. The monthly shedding of the inner lining of the uterus by women who are not pregnant.

Endometrium. The tissue forming the inner lining of the uterus.

Ovulation. The release of an ovum from an ovary.

Organizing effects. The directional effects of sex hormones—e.g., along stereotypical masculine or feminine lines.

Activating effects. The arousal-producing effects of sex hormones that increase the likelihood of dominant sexual responses.

Testosterone. A male hormone that promotes development of male sexual characteristics and has activating effects on sexual arousal.

who are castrated in adulthood do not engage in sexual activity. But if they receive injections of testosterone, which replaces the testosterone that would have been secreted by their own testes, they resume stereotypical male sexual behavior patterns.

The sex organs of female rodents exposed to large doses of testosterone in the uterus (which occurs naturally when they share the uterus with many brothers; or artificially, as a result of hormone injections) become masculinized in appearance. Such females are also predisposed toward masculine mating behaviors. If they are given additional testosterone as adults, they attempt to mount other females about as often as males do (Goy & Goldfoot, 1975). Prenatal testosterone might have "organized" the brains of these females in the masculine direction, predisposing them toward masculine sexual behaviors in adulthood. Testosterone in adulthood would then "activate" the masculine behavior patterns.

Testosterone is also important in the behavior of human males. Men who are castrated or given drugs that decrease the amount of androgens in the blood stream ("antiandrogens") usually show gradual loss of sexual desire and of the capacities for erection and orgasm. Still, many castrated men remain sexually active for years, suggesting that for many people fantasies, memories, and other cognitive stimuli are as important as hormones in sexual motivation. Beyond minimal levels, there is no clear link between testosterone level and sexual arousal. For example, sleeping men are *not* more likely to have erections during surges in the testosterone level (Schiavi et al., 1977).

Female mice, rats, cats, and dogs are receptive to males only during **estrus,** when female sex hormones are plentiful. But women are sexually responsive during all phases of the menstrual cycle, even during menstruation itself, when hormone levels are low, and even after **menopause.** Androgens influence female as well as male sexual response (Davidson et al., 1985; Sherwin et al., 1985). Women whose adrenal glands and ovaries have been removed (so that they no longer produce androgens) may gradually lose sexual interest and the capacity for sexual response. An active and enjoyable sexual history seems to ward off loss of sexual capacity, suggestive of the importance of cognitive and experiential factors in human sexual motivation.

The message is that sex hormones do play a role in human sexual behavior, but that our sexual behavior is far from mechanical. Sex hormones initially promote the development of our sex organs, and as adults, we may need certain minimal levels of sex hormones in order to become sexually aroused. However, psychological factors also influence our sexual behavior. In human sexuality, biology apparently is not destiny.

Women and PMS: Does Premenstrual Syndrome Doom Women to Misery?

In Peru it's called a "visit from Uncle Pepé." In American Samoa, "the boogie man is coming." In Columbia it's "Little Red Riding Hood." The French may exclaim, "The English are coming" (Logan, 1978). These are some of the expressions used around the world to refer to menstruation. They reflect expectations that women are doomed to irritability and tension at that time of the month—two symptoms of **premenstrual syndrome,** or PMS.

The hormones estrogen and progesterone regulate the menstrual cycle (Rathus, 1983), and many have assumed that PMS may be attributed to "raging hormones." What is the extent of PMS? *Do* women show behavioral and emotional problems prior to and during menstruation? What are the roles of hormones and cultural expectations in PMS?

Bardwick (1971; Ivey & Bardwick, 1968) found women's moods to be most positive at time of ovulation. About 30 percent of women do report greater anxiety, depression, and fatigue for several days prior to menstruation (Laube, 1985). Physical symptoms include fluid retention ("bloating"), breast

Estrus. The periodic sexual excitement of many female mammals, during which they can conceive and are receptive to the sexual advances of males.

Menopause. The cessation of menstruation.

Premenstrual syndrome. A cluster of physical and psychological symptoms that afflict some women prior to menstruation. Abbreviated *PMS.*

tenderness, and heightened appetite, with a craving for sweets (Abraham, 1981). Dalton (1972, 1980) reported that women are more likely to commit crimes or suicide, to call in sick at work, and to develop physical and emotional problems before or during menstruation. Dalton (1968) also reported that the grades of English schoolgirls decline during the eight-day period prior to and including menstruation. But investigators in the United States have found no decline in academic performance at this time (Bernstein, 1977; Rodin, 1976; Sommer, 1972, 1973).

There is evidence showing a link between hormone levels and mood in women. Paige (1971) compared women whose hormone levels were maintained at fairly even levels by birth-control pills to women whose hormone levels varied naturally throughout the cycle. Women whose levels fluctuated showed somewhat greater anxiety and hostility prior to and during menstruation. However, in contrast to Dalton's reports, they did not commit crimes or wind up on mental wards. Other studies suggest that even among women who report PMS the symptoms are most often mild, although a small percentage may have symptoms strong enough to interfere with their functioning (Keye, 1983).

Women with PMS may be responding to negative cultural attitudes toward menstruation as well as to physical symptoms (Brooks-Gunn & Ruble, 1980; Sherif, 1980). In some societies, expectations of foul temper have consigned women to isolated living quarters (Paige, 1977). The historical view of menstruation as a time of pollution (Fisher, 1980) may heighten women's sensitivity to internal sensations at this time of the month, as well as heighten concern about discreet disposal of the menstrual flow. Women who do not share highly traditionalist cultural attitudes—including attitudes that menstruation is debilitating—are less likely to show mood changes during the different phases of the menstrual cycle (Paige, 1973). Fortunately, young Americans are less likely than their parents to believe that menstruation pollutes. They are also less inclined to restrict their activities at this time of the month (Paige, 1978).

However, some hormonal changes at time of menstruation can cause real pain. For instance, hormones called **prostaglandins** cause uterine contractions. Most contractions go unnoticed, but strong, repeated contractions are uncomfortable in themselves and may also deprive the uterus temporarily of oxygen, another source of pain (American College of Obstetricians and Gynecologists, 1985). In such cases, prostaglandin-inhibiting drugs, such as Motrin and Indocin, help a number of women (Owen, 1984). Other women report being helped by regular exercise and proper nutrition, including low-fat diets and dietary supplements, particularly B vitamins and minerals such as calcium and magnesium. Stress-management techniques such as relaxation training and seeking social support are also sometimes of help.

In sum,

1. Hormonal changes may induce some mood shifts in women, but most often these shifts are minor.
2. The evidence that women show serious performance deficits or criminal behavior prior to and during menstruation is unreliable.
3. Traditionalist views of (perfectly harmless) menstrual flow as polluting tend to contribute to any problems women encounter.
4. Some women encounter excessive menstrual discomfort, like severe cramping, and require medical treatment.

The Sexual-Response Cycle

During the 1960s William Masters and Virginia Johnson became renowned for their research in human sexual response and **sexual dysfunctions.** They disdained the standard questionnaire and interview approaches to sex re-

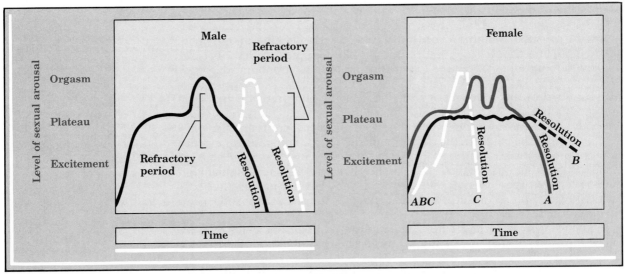

FIGURE 15.3   The Male and Female Sexual Response Cycles

The pattern of male sexual response shows that men undergo a refractory period following orgasm during which they are not responsive to further sexual stimulation. But they may be restimulated to orgasm after sufficient time passes. Pattern A, for women, shows that women may be restimulated to orgasms in quick succession (multiple orgasms). In Pattern B, a woman has been highly excited for a protracted period, but has not reached orgasm. Eventually her excitement subsides. In Pattern C, a woman quickly reaches orgasm and her excitement also rapidly subsides. Men may also experience patterns B and C. Source: Masters and Johnson (1966).

search. Instead, they arranged for volunteers to engage in sexual activity in the laboratory while their physiological responses were monitored.

Masters and Johnson (1966) found that sexual stimulation leads to many types of responses. Two of them are largely reflexive: **myotonia,** or muscle tension, and **vasocongestion,** or the flow of arterial blood into the genitals and other parts of the body, such as the breasts. These responses, and others, can be described in terms of a **sexual-response cycle** that applies to both men and women. The four phases of this cycle are the excitement, plateau, orgasm, and resolution phases (Figure 15.3).

The Excitement Phase   The **excitement phase** is the first phase of physiological response to sexual stimulation. The heart rate, blood pressure, and respiration rate increase. In the male, blood vessels in chambers of loose tissue within the penis dilate reflexively to allow blood to flow in, resulting in erection.

In the female, the breasts swell and the nipples become erect. Blood engorges the genital region and the clitoris expands. The inner part of the vagina lengthens and dilates. Within ten seconds to half a minute, vaginal lubrication reflexively appears. A **sex flush,** or mottling of the skin, may appear late in this phase.

The Plateau Phase   The **plateau phase** describes a heightening of sexual arousal that prepares the body for orgasm. The heart rate, blood pressure, and respiration rate continue to rise. In the man, further engorgement causes the ridge around the head of the penis to turn deep purple. The testes increase in size and elevate in order to allow a full ejaculation.

Myotonia. Muscle tension.

Vasocongestion. Accumulation (congestion) of blood, particularly in the genital region.

Sexual response cycle. A four-phase process that describes response to sexual stimulation in males and females.

Excitement phase. The first phase of the sexual response cycle, characterized by erection in the man, and by vaginal lubrication and clitoral swelling in the woman.

Sex flush. A reddish hue on body surfaces that is caused by vasocongestion.

Plateau phase. An advanced state of sexual arousal that precedes orgasm.

In the woman, the outer vagina becomes so engorged that its diameter is reduced about one-third. Engorgement of the area around the clitoris causes the clitoris to "withdraw" beneath a fold of skin called the clitoral hood. Further swelling of the breasts causes the nipples to appear to have become smaller, although they have not. The sex flush becomes pronounced.

The Orgasm Phase   During orgasm, breathing, blood pressure, and heart rate reach a peak, and there are involuntary muscle contractions throughout the body. In the man, muscles at the base of the penis contract and expel semen through the penis. In the woman, muscles surrounding the outer third of the vagina contract rhythmically. Most authorities agree that there is no female ejaculation, just vaginal lubrication.* For both sexes the initial contractions are most intense and spaced at about 0.8-second intervals (five contractions every four seconds). Subsequent contractions are weaker and spaced farther apart.

Following orgasm, men enter a **refractory period** during which they are unresponsive to further sexual stimulation, although some men are capable of reaching orgasm twice before sexual arousal subsides. Women can experience numerous or **multiple orgasms,** as many as 50 in rapid succession. This capacity has given some women the feeling that they ought not be satisfied with only one—the flip side of the old myth that sexual pleasure is meant for men only. In sex, as in other areas of life, our oughts and shoulds often place arbitrary demands on us that evoke anxiety and feelings of inadequacy.

Orgasm is a reflex. We can set the stage for it by receiving adequate sexual stimulation of a physical and cognitive nature (by focusing on the attractiveness of our partner, erotic fantasies, and so forth), but we cannot force or will an orgasm to happen. Efforts to force orgasm can be counterproductive, as we shall see in our discussion of the sexual dysfunctions.

The Resolution Phase   After an orgasm that is not followed by additional sexual stimulation, a **resolution phase** occurs in which the body gradually returns to its resting state. The heart rate, blood pressure, and respiration rate all return to normal levels. Blood that has engorged the genitals is dispelled from this region throughout the body.

If a lengthy plateau phase is not followed by orgasm (as in pattern B in Figure 15.3), genital engorgement may take longer to dissipate, leading to pelvic tension or discomfort in both men and women.

Sexual Response and the Aging

"Just because there's snow on the roof doesn't mean there's no fire in the furnace"—so goes the saying. Yet, for various reasons, we may think of sex as for young people only. It may be difficult for us to imagine our parents engaged in sexual activity; we may not understand why the elderly would be attracted to one another; and we may link sex with reproduction (Rathus, 1983). Research has shown that we tend to underestimate the frequency of our parents' lovemaking by a good 50 percent (Zeiss, 1982).

Despite the stereotypes, Kinsey and his colleagues (1948) found that half of the men aged 75 in his sample achieved erections regularly. Masters and Johnson (1966) found women at this age capable of multiple orgasms.

Some changes do occur with advancing age. By age 50 or so, men may require increased sexual stimulation to achieve erection and may not be able to reattain erection for from 8 to 24 hours after ejaculation (Kaplan & Sager, 1971). But from the woman's perspective, her mate may become a more effective lover. It may take older men longer to ejaculate, and so the couple

Refractory period. A period of time following orgasm during which the male is not responsive to further sexual stimulation.

Multiple orgasms. The experiencing of additional orgasms because of sexual stimulation during the resolution stage. Two or more orgasms in rapid succession.

Resolution phase. The final phase of the sexual response cycle, during which bodily functions gradually return to their prearoused state.

*See Ladas and her colleagues (1982) for a divergent view.

may be able to prolong intercourse. Many men continue to have intercourse into their 80s, but some lose the ability to attain erection. This falloff may stem from decreased production of testosterone and health problems, but can also reflect psychological factors, such as loss of interest in one's sex partner.

Along with menopause, women may experience vaginal dryness and loss of vaginal elasticity, reflecting decreased estrogen production. This condition may be corrected through use of artificial lubrication or estrogen-replacement therapy (ERT). However, as noted in Chapter 11, ERT is controversial because prolonged use has been linked to cancer. Menopause signals the end of a woman's reproductive capacity, but not of her sexual capacity. Women in their 80s can reach orgasm. Men and women with positive sexual attitudes can enjoy sexual activity for a lifetime.

■ Issues in Human Sexuality

Many of us are intrigued or mystified by certain patterns of sexual behavior, certain issues in human sexuality. One of these is homosexuality. It is difficult for many heterosexuals to imagine how people can be erotically aroused by members of their own sex. It may be of interest that many homosexuals are equally mystified by the erotic interests of heterosexuals, but, of course, the overwhelming majority of us are heterosexual. And so, one of the issues we explore is why some people are aroused by members of their own sex, and not by members of the opposite sex.

Many questions are also raised by pornography and forcible rape. What, many of us wonder, are the effects of ponography? Does pornography trigger violence in unstable people? What about the effects on stable individuals? And why do men rape women? Is it because no woman is willing to engage in sexual activity with them? Apparently not, as we shall see.

Homosexuality

Homosexuality, or a homosexual orientation, is an erotic response to members of one's own sex. Sexual activity with members of one's own sex is not in itself evidence of homosexuality. It may reflect limited sexual opportunities or even ritualistic cultural practices, as in the case of the New Guinean Sambian people. American adolescent boys may masturbate one another while fantasizing about girls. Men in prisons may similarly turn to each other as sexual outlets. Sambian male youths engage exclusively in homosexual practices with older males, since it is believed that they must drink "men's milk" to achieve the fierce manhood of the head hunter (Money, 1987). But their behavior turns exclusively **heterosexual** once they reach marrying age.

Kinsey and his colleagues (1948, 1953) estimated that as many as 37 percent of the men and 13 percent of the women in his sample had had at least one homosexual *encounter,* but only about 4 percent of his male subjects and 1 to 3 percent of his female subjects reported a homosexual *orientation.* About 2 percent of the men and 1 percent of the women in Hunt's (1974) survey reported a homosexual orientation.

Origins of Homosexuality The origins of homosexuality are complex and controversial. Developmentally speaking, about two gay males in three report "gender nonconformity" as children. That is, they preferred "girls' toys" and playing wth girls to transportation toys, guns, and rough-and-tumble play—preferences that frequently led to their being called "sissies" (Adams & Chiodo, 1983; Bell et al., 1981; Green, 1987). On the other hand, about one in three homosexuals show gender conformity. There have even been homosexuals among the ranks of professional football players. Let us consider a number of psychological and biological theories concerning the origins of homosexuality.

Homosexuality. The sexual orientation characterized by preference for sexual activity and the formation of romantic relationships with members of one's own sex.

Heterosexual. A person whose sexual orientation is characterized by preference for sexual activity and the formation of romantic relationships with members of the opposite sex.

Concordance. Agreement.

Proband. The family member first studied or tested.

Psychodynamic theory ties homosexuality into identification with male or female figures. Identification, in turn, is related to resolution of the Oedipus and Electra complexes, as discussed in Chapter 2. In men faulty resolution of the Oedipus complex would stem from a "classic pattern" in which there is a "close-binding" mother and a "detached-hostile" father. Boys reared in such a family environment would identify with their mothers and not their fathers. But psychodynamic theory has been criticized because many gay males have had excellent relationships with both parents. Too, the childhoods of many heterosexuals fit the "classic pattern."

From a learning-theory point of view, as set forth by Kinsey and others, early reinforcement of sexual behavior (as by orgasm achieved through interaction with members of one's own sex) can influence one's sexual orientation. But many gay males and lesbians are aware of their orientations before they have overt sexual contacts (Bell et al., 1981), so we cannot attribute their orientations to early reinforcement of sexual behavior by persons of the same sex. Nor can we point to the power of observational learning. In a society that denigrates homosexuality, children are unlikely to develop the expectancy that homosexual behavior will be reinforcing for them. In other words, they are unlikely to strive to imitate homosexual models. And remember the Sambian youth: Even repeated homosexual experiences do not sway them from their eventual exclusive heterosexuality.

Biological theories focus on genetic and hormonal factors. It was once thought that homosexuality might be fully genetically transmitted. Kallmann (1952) found a 100 percent **concordance** rate for homosexuality among the **probands** of 40 identical twin pairs. However, more recent studies have found much lower concordance rates (Eckert et al., 1986; Ellis & Ames, 1987; McConaghy & Blaszczynski, 1980). Although genetic factors may partly determine sexual orientation, psychologist John Money of Johns Hopkins University, who has specialized in sexual behavior, concludes that homosexuality is "not under the direct governance of chromosomes and genes" (1987, p. 384).

Since sex hormones influence the mating behavior of lower animals, it has been wondered whether gay males might be deficient in testosterone, whereas lesbians might have lower-than-normal levels of estrogen and higher-than-normal levels of androgens in their bloodstreams. However, homosexuality has not been reliably linked to current (adult) levels of male or female sex hormones (Feder, 1984).

Still, there are a number of current hypotheses concerning possible links between hormones and sexual orientation. For example, there are some indications that homosexuals may be more responsive to the presence of small amounts of hormones of the opposite sex that we all produce, even though they do not possess more of these hormones (Gladue et al., 1984).

Another possibility concerns the possible prenatal effects of sex hormones. Prenatal sex hormones can "masculinize" or "feminize" the brains of laboratory animals in the ways that they direct the development of certain brain structures, as noted in Chapter 3. It is possible that the brains of some gay males have been prenatally feminized and that the brains of some lesbians have been prenatally masculinized (Money, 1987). Even so, Money argues that prenatal hormonal influences would not induce a "robotlike" sexual orientation in humans, and that socialization—or early learning experiences— would probably also play a role.

The causes of human homosexuality are mysterious and complex. The current status of the research suggests that they might involve genetic factors—which, in turn, influence the secretion of prenatal hormones—and postnatal socialization experiences. But the precise ways in which these influences interact have so far eluded detection.

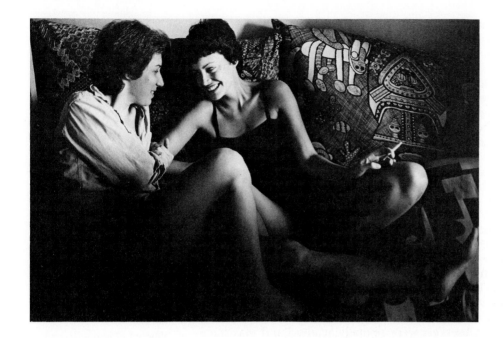

Research shows that lesbians are about as well-adjusted as heterosexual women. Bell and Weinberg found that the adjustment of gay males is tied to their life-styles. Homosexual "close couples," who live as if they are married, appear as well-adjusted as married people.

Adjustment of Homosexuals   Despite the slings and arrows of an often outraged society, it seems that homosexuals are about as well adjusted as heterosexuals. Saghir and Robins (1973) could not distinguish gay males from heterosexuals in terms of anxiety, depression, and psychosomatic complaints like headaches and ulcers. Adelman (1977) found that professionally employed lesbians were somewhat more socially isolated than professional heterosexual women, but could not otherwise be differentiated. Other studies find no more anxiety, tension, and depression among lesbians than among heterosexual females. Siegelman (1978, 1979) concludes that the similarities between lesbians and heterosexual women outweigh the differences.

Bell and Weinberg (1978) found that the adjustment of San Francisco homosexuals was linked to their life-styles. Homosexual "close couples" who live as if they are married appear as well adjusted as married people. Homosexuals who lead other life-styles show various levels of adjustment. Older homosexuals who live by themselves and have few if any sexual contacts were poorly adjusted (as are many heterosexuals who lead a similar life-style).

Homosexuality and AIDS   During the past few years it has been learned that homosexuals, particularly promiscuous males, are at high risk for being infected by the **AIDS** virus. In fact, early reports on AIDS erroneously viewed the disease as unlikely to strike the heterosexual population. One risk factor may be a form of sexual expression that is more common among gay males than heterosexuals—anal intercourse. Anal intercourse can abrade rectal tissue (and penile tissue), providing a convenient port of entry for the virus into the bloodstream, and the AIDS virus may also directly infect cells in the rectal lining. As of this writing, it has not been demonstrated that oral sex or mutual masturbation leads to infection by the AIDS virus, although these possible avenues of infection cannot be lightly dismissed (Kaplan, 1987), as we shall see later in the chapter. In any event, many gay males who in earlier years had frequent "unprotected" sexual encounters with strangers have adjusted to the threat of AIDS by using condoms in oral sex, avoiding anal sex, limiting sexual contacts to one partner or to a few well-known partners, and relying

AIDS. Acronym for acquired immune deficiency syndrome. A disorder of the immune system caused by a virus and characterized by suppression of the immune response, leaving the body prey to opportunistic diseases.

more on masturbation (Centers for Disease Control, 1985b; Lourea et al., 1986; Schechter et al., 1984).

Pornography

Since the late 1960s, when the Supreme Court ruled that prohibiting **explicit** sexual materials violated freedom of expression, **pornography** has been a boom industry in the United States. Some people complain that the availability of pornography has led to a breakdown in moral standards. Women's groups have argued that pornography inspires crimes of violence against women. In this section we review research bearing on two important questions concerning pornography: What are the effects of pornography? Does pornography inspire antisocial behavior?

What Are the Effects of Pornography?

In the 1960s, Congress created a presidential Commission on Obscenity and Pornography to review research on pornography and conduct its own studies. The commission concluded that married couples exposed to pornography reported feeling sexually aroused but were not motivated to try observed sexual activities that were "deviant" for them (Abelson et al., 1970). More recent studies with participants ranging from middle-aged couples to college students have attained similar results (Brown et al., 1976; Hatfield et al., 1978; Heiby & Becker, 1980; Herrell, 1975; Schmidt et al., 1973). Observers were sexually aroused and may have been motivated to masturbate or engage in sexual activity with their usual sex partners. But they did not lose self-control or become notably distressed or disturbed.

In a more recent study, undergraduates of both sexes were exposed to six pornographic films a week over a six-week period (Zillmann & Bryant, 1983). Generally speaking, the students became **habituated** to pornography, as shown by lessened sexual response to new pornographic films by the end of the study. The films included examples of **sadomasochism** and sex with animals, and by the end of the study, the students also showed less revulsion to these activities. Overexposure to deviant sex can apparently **desensitize** the viewer.

It is folklore that men are most sexually responsive to explicit, "hard-core" sexual materials and fantasies. Women, however, are considered more romantic, and thus more likely to be sexually aroused by affectionate, "soft-core" themes. But psychologist Julia Heiman (1975) found that **hard-core** erotica is not for men only. She played audiotapes with romantic or sexually explicit content while college students' responses were measured by the **penile strain gauge** and the **vaginal photoplethysmograph.** She found that explicit sex, with or without romantic trappings, was sexually arousing to both women and men.

Does Pornography Inspire Crimes of Violence Against Women?

In recent years **feminists** and others have argued that pornography degrades women and supports stereotypes of women as submissive to the needs of men (Blakely, 1985). They have charged that materials that depict sexual and other types of violence against women encourages male viewers to abuse women. Experiments appear to support their concerns, even though normal men and women are usually more sexually aroused by films that portray affectionate coitus than by films showing sex with aggression (Malamuth, 1981).

In one study (Donnerstein, 1980), 120 college men were either provoked or treated neutrally by a male or female confederate of the experimenter. Subjects were then shown neutral, erotic, or aggressive-erotic films. In the last film, a man forced himself into a woman's home and raped her. Subjects were then given the opportunity to be aggressive against the male or female confederate of the experimenter through a fake electric-shock apparatus. The

---

Explicit. Frank, revealing; leaving nothing implied or to the imagination.

Pornography. Explicit, uncensored portrayals of sexual activity that are intended to excite the observer sexually.

Habituation. A process during which one's response to a stimulus decreases because of continued exposure.

Sadomasochism. Activities involving attainment of gratification by the inflicting and the receiving of pain and humiliation.

Desensitize. To cause to lose sensitivity to a stimulus.

Hard-core. Unyielding, unqualified; suggestive of explicit sex in the absence of a romantic context.

Penile strain gauge. An instrument that measures the size of erection and provides an index of sexual arousal in the male.

Vaginal photoplethysmograph. An instrument that measures sexual arousal in women as a function of vaginal blood pressure.

Feminists. People (of both sexes) who seek social change and legislation to reverse discrimination against women and to otherwise advance the concerns of women.

measure of aggression was the intensity of the shock chosen. As expected, provoked subjects selected higher shock levels. But even nonprovoked men shown aggressive-erotic films showed greater aggression toward women confederates. And provoked men who were shown aggressive-erotic films chose the highest shock levels against women.

Another study (Malamuth et al., 1980) found that college men and women usually reported greater sexual response to a story about mutually desired sex than to a story about rape. But in variations of the study, Malamuth and his colleagues portrayed the rape victim as experiencing an involuntary orgasm, with or without pain. The addition of the involuntary orgasm raised students' self-reports of sexual arousal to levels that equaled the response to mutually desired sex. Women subjects were most responsive when the woman in the story did not have pain, but men were most aroused when she did. The researchers speculate that the woman's orgasm legitimized the violence. Thus, sexual response in the observers was **disinhibited.** The story may have reinforced the cultural myth that some women need to be dominated and will be "turned on" by an overpowering man. Exposure to aggressive-erotic films may increase violence, even among normal college men (Donnerstein & Linz, 1984).

The Attorney General's Commission Report A review of such research by the Attorney General's Commission on Pornography concluded, in 1986, that explicit sexual materials are a cause of violence against women. A follow-up workshop organized by Surgeon General C. Everett Koop (1987) made three points about depictions of sexual *aggression:* (1) "Pornography that portrays sexual aggression as pleasurable to the victim increases the acceptance of the use of coercion in sexual relations"; (2) "Acceptance of coercive sexuality appears to be related to sexual aggression"; and (3) "In laboratory studies measuring short-term effects, exposure to violent pornography increases punitive behavior toward women" (p. 945).

A Critique of the Attorney General's Commission Report As noted by Donnerstein and Linz (1987), the Attorney General's Report (1986) misses the point because commission members *did not separate the effects of explicit sexual materials from those of violent materials.* There is still no evidence that explicit sexual materials *in the absence of violence* stimulate antisocial behavior. Donnerstein and Linz assert that "It is not sex, but violence that is an obscenity in our society" (1986, p. 56). The same critique can be made of Koop's (1987) remarks; that is, they do not distinguish between pornography and violent pornography. As a matter of fact, the only statement that Koop's (1987) workshop could agree on concerning the effects of nonviolent pornography on adults is that "Prolonged use of pornography increases beliefs that less common sexual practices are more common" (p. 945).

The Bottom Line . . . In sum, if legislation were to be considered to answer the legitimate concerns of women who argue against the availability of *violent* pornography, it might be that the Swedish approach of outlawing portrayals of *violence* rather than sexual behavior per se would be more on target. Curtailment of *nonviolent* pornography would have be be based purely on moral grounds; scientific methods have failed to demonstrate that it has a harmful impact upon adults. Interestingly, only a minority of Americans would support legislation to make explicit erotic materials illegal, but about 75 percent of us would outlaw pornography that combines sex with violence (Harris, 1988).

But any legislation that would curtail the production or sale of pornographic materials might impede freedom of expression. Such legislation could be found in conflict with the First Amendment and therefore unconstitutional

Forcible rape. Sexual interaction with a person against that person's will.

(Blakely, 1985). Even the feminist community is split on the issue of banning pornography. Some feminist writers, such as Kate Millett, argue that "We're better off hanging tight to the First Amendment so that we have freedom of speech" (Press et al., 1985). Moreover, Linz, Donnerstein, and Penrod (1987) argue that educational programs might be able to decrease many of the negative effects of sexual violence in the media. The question of what, if anything, should and can be done about pornography is a controversial issue that is likely to remain with us for some time to come. As the debate rages on, it might be useful to separate moral issues from scientific issues, and moral judgments from scientific findings.

Forcible Rape

Forcible rape is the seeking of sexual gratification against the will of another person. There are more than 90,000 reported cases of rape in the United States each year (Allgeier & Allgeier, 1984). Since it has been estimated that only one rape in five is reported, it may be that as many as 450,000 rapes actually take place.

Alarming Statistics on Campus   Nine percent of a sample of 6,159 women reported that they had given in to sexual intercourse as a result of threats or physical force (Koss et al., 1987). Up to 2 million instances of forced sex may occur within marriage each year, although women are not likely to define forced sex by their husbands as rape.

If we add to these figures instances in which women are subjected to forced kissing and petting, the numbers grow more alarming. For example, nearly 70 percent of 282 women in one college sample had been assaulted (usually by dates and friends) at some time since entering college (Kanin & Parcell, 1977). At a major university, 40 percent of 201 male students surveyed admitted to using force to unfasten a woman's clothing, and 13 percent reported that they had forced a woman to engage in sexual intercourse (Rapaport & Burkhart, 1984). Forty-four percent of the college women in the Koss study (Koss et al., 1987) reported that they had "given in to sex play" because of a "man's continual arguments and pressure."

Why Do Men Rape Women?   Why do men coerce women into sexual activity? Many social scientists argue that sexual motivation often has little to do with it. Rape, they argue, is more often a man's way of expressing anger toward, or power over, women (e.g., Groth & Birnbaum, 1979). In fact, many rapists have long records as violent offenders (Amir, 1971). With some rapists, violence also appears to enhance sexual arousal, so that they are motivated to combine sex with aggression (Quinsey et al., 1984).

Does Our Culture Socialize Men into Becoming Rapists?   Many social critics also assert that our culture socializes men into becoming rapists (Burt, 1980). Males, who are often reinforced for aggressive and competitive behavior, could be said to be asserting culturally expected dominance over women. Sexually coercive college males, as a group, are more likely to believe that aggression is a legitimate form of behavior than are noncoercive college males (Rapaport & Burkhart, 1984).

Are Women Socialized into Becoming Victims?   Women, on the other hand, may be socialized into the victim role. The stereotypical feminine role encourages passivity, nurturance, warmth, and cooperation. Women are often taught to sacrifice for their families and not to raise their voices. Thus a woman may be totally unprepared to cope with an assailant. She may lack aggressive skills and believe that violence is inappropriate for women. Mary Beth Myers and her colleagues (1984) found that rape victims are less dominant and self-assertive than nonvictims—that is, their behavior is more consistent with what society expects of women. Victimization is not a random process, and women who appear vulnerable are apparently more likely than others to be attacked (Myers et al., 1985).

Rape Myths   Many people, including professionals who work with rapists and victims, believe a number of myths about rape. These include "Only bad girls get raped," "Any healthy woman can resist a rapist if she wants to," and "Women only cry rape when they've been jilted or have something to cover up" (Burt, 1980, p. 217). These myths tend to deny the impact of the assault and also to place blame on the victim rather than her assailant. They contribute to a social climate that is too often one of leniency toward rapists and hostility toward victims.

Rape Prevention: Shout "Fire!" Not "Rape!"   In *The New Our Bodies, Ourselves,* The Boston Women's Health Book Collective (1984) lists a number of suggestions that women can use to lower the likelihood of rape:

Establish signals and arrangements with other women in an apartment building or neighborhood
List only first initials in the telephone directory or on the mailbox
Use dead-bolt locks
Keep windows locked and obtain iron grids for first-floor windows
Keep entrances and doorways brightly lit
Have keys ready for the front door or the car
Do not walk alone in the dark
Avoid deserted areas
Never allow a strange man into your apartment or home without checking his credentials
Drive with the car windows up and the door locked
Check the rear seat of the car before entering
Avoid living in an unsafe building
Do not pick up hitchhikers (including women)
Do not talk to strange men in the street
Shout "Fire!" not "Rape!" People crowd around fires but avoid scenes of violence

■ Sexual Dysfunctions and Sex Therapy

Many of us will be troubled by a sexual dysfunction at some time or other. Masters and Johnson (1970) estimated that at least half the marriages in this nation are sexually dysfunctional. The incidence of sexual dysfunctions may be higher among single people since singles are less likely to feel secure in their sexual relationships and to be familiar with their partner's sexual needs.

Types of Sexual Dysfunctions

The sexual dysfunctions that we shall discuss are labeled as follows in the DSM–III–R (American Psychiatric Association, 1987): *hypoactive sexual desire disorder, female sexual arousal disorder, male erectile disorder, inhibited orgasm, premature ejaculation, dyspareunia,* and *vaginismus.*

In **hypoactive sexual desire disorder,** the person shows lack of interest in sexual activity and frequently reports an absence of sexual fantasies. The diagnosis exists because of the assumption that sexual fantasies and interests are normal response patterns that may be blocked by anxiety or other factors.

In the female, as noted earlier, sexual arousal is characterized by a lubricating of the vaginal walls that makes entry by the penis possible. Sexual arousal in the male is characterized by erection of the penis. Almost all women

Hypoactive sexual desire disorder. A sexual dysfunction characterized by lack of interest in sexual activity.

The incidence of rape has reached alarming proportions on campus, and many college women are becoming educated about things that they can do to protect themselves.

■ QUESTIONNAIRE ■

Cultural Myths That Create a Climate That Supports Rape

Martha Burt (1980) has compiled a number of statements concerning rape. Read each of them and indicate whether you believe it to be true or false by circling the T or the F. Then turn to the key at the end of the chapter to learn of the implications of your answers.

T F **1.** A woman who goes to the home or apartment of a man on their first date implies that she is willing to have sex.

T F **2.** Any female can get raped.

T F **3.** One reason that women falsely report a rape is that they frequently have a need to call attention to themselves.

T F **4.** Any healthy woman can successfully resist a rapist if she really wants to.

T F **5.** When women go around braless or wearing short skirts and tight tops, they are just asking for trouble.

T F **6.** In the majority of rapes, the victim is promiscuous or has a bad reputation.

T F **7.** If a girl engages in necking or petting and she lets things get out of hand, it is her own fault if her partner forces sex on her.

T F **8.** Women who get raped while hitchhiking get what they deserve.

T F **9.** A woman who is stuck-up and thinks she is too good to talk to guys on the street deserves to be taught a lesson.

T F **10.** Many women have an unconscious wish to be raped, and may then unconsciously set up a situation in which they are likely to be attacked.

T F **11.** If a woman gets drunk at a party and has intercourse with a man she's just met there, she should be considered "fair game" to other males at the party who want to have sex with her too, whether she wants to or not.

T F **12.** Many women who report a rape are lying because they are angry and want to get back at the man they accuse.

T F **13.** Many, if not most, rapes are merely invented by women who discovered they were pregnant and wanted to protect their reputation.

---

now and then have difficulty becoming or remaining lubricated. Almost all men have occasional difficulty attaining erection or maintaining an erection through intercourse. The diagnoses of **female sexual arousal disorder** and **male erectile disorder** are used when these problems are persistent or recurrent.

In **inhibited orgasm,** the man or woman, although sexually excited, is persistently delayed in reaching orgasm or does not reach orgasm at all. Inhibited orgasm is more common among women than men. In some cases, an individual can reach orgasm without difficulty while engaging in sexual relations with one partner, but not with another.

In **premature ejaculation** the male persistently ejaculates with minimal sexual stimulation, too soon to permit his partner or himself to enjoy sexual relations fully.

Female sexual arousal disorder. A sexual dysfunction characterized by difficulty in becoming sexually aroused, as defined by vaginal lubrication, or sustaining arousal long enough to engage in satisfying sexual relations.

Male erectile disorder. A sexual dysfunction characterized by difficulty in becoming sexually aroused, as defined by achieving erection, or in sustaining arousal long enough to engage in satisfying sexual relations.

In **dyspareunia,** sexual intercourse is associated with recurrent pain in the genital region. **Vaginismus** is involuntary spasm of the muscles surrounding the vagina, making sexual intercourse painful or impossible.

Causes of Sexual Dysfunctions

Perhaps 10 to 20 percent of sexual dysfunctions stem from disease. Hypoactive sexual desire, for example, can reflect diabetes and diseases of the heart and lungs. Fatigue can dampen sexual desire and inhibit orgasm. But incidents of such sexual dysfunction will be isolated unless we attach too much meaning to them and become overly concerned about future sexual performance. Depressants such as alcohol, narcotics, and tranquilizers can also impair sexual response. Physical factors can interact with psychological factors. For instance, dyspareunia can heighten anxiety, and extremes of anxiety can dampen sexual arousal.

Old-fashioned stereotypes suggest that although men may find sex pleasurable, sex is a duty for women. Women who share these sex-negative attitudes may not be fully aware of their sexual potentials. Too, they may be so anxious about sex that the attitudes become a self-fulfilling prophecy. Men, too, may be handicapped by misinformation and sexual taboos.

Physically or psychologically painful sexual experiences can cause future sexual response to be blocked by anxiety. Rape victims may encounter sexual adjustment problems such as vaginismus or inhibited orgasm. Masters and Johnson (1970) report cases of men with erectile problems who have had anxiety-evoking encounters with prostitutes.

As noted earlier, a sexual relationship is usually no better than other aspects of the relationship or marriage (Perlman & Abramson, 1982). Communication problems are linked to general marital dissatisfaction. Couples who have problems expressing their sexual desires are at a disadvantage in teaching their partners how to provide pleasure.

Sexual competencies, like other competencies, are based on knowledge and skill, and competencies are based largely on learning. We learn what makes us and others feel good through trial and error, talking and reading about sex, and, perhaps, by watching sex films. Many people do not acquire sexual competencies because of lack of knowledge and experimentation—even within marriage.

Albert Ellis (1977) and other cognitive psychologists point out that irrational beliefs and attitudes contribute to sexual dysfunctions. If we believe that we need others' approval at all times, we may catastrophize the importance of one disappointing sexual episode. If we demand that each sexual encounter be perfect, we set ourselves up for inevitable failure.

In most cases of sexual dysfunction, the physical and psychological factors we have outlined lead to yet another psychological factor—**performance anxiety,** or fear of whether we shall be able to perform sexually. People with performance anxiety may focus on recollections of past failures and expectations of another disaster, rather than lose themselves in their erotic sensations and fantasies (Barlow, 1986). Performance anxiety can make it difficult for a man to attain erection, yet spur him to ejaculate prematurely. Performance anxiety can also prevent a woman from becoming adequately lubricated or can contribute to vaginismus.

Sex therapy programs foster sexual competencies by enhancing sexual knowledge and encouraging sexual experimentation under circumstances in which performance anxiety is unlikely to be aroused.

Sex Therapy

When Kinsey was making his surveys of sexual behavior in the 1940s, there was no effective treatment for the sexual dysfunctions. But a number of treat-

Inhibited orgasm. A sexual dysfunction in which one has difficulty reaching orgasm, although one has become sexually aroused.

Premature ejaculation. Ejaculation that occurs prior to the couple's desires.

Dyspareunia. Painful coitus.

Vaginismus. Involuntary contraction of the muscles surrounding the vagina which makes entry difficult or impossible.

Performance anxiety. Fear concerning whether one will be able to perform adequately.

ments based on the social-learning model, collectively called **sex therapy,** have been developed during the past two decades. Sex therapists assume that sexual dysfunctions can be treated by directly modifying the problem behavior that occurs in the bedroom. Treatment of most dysfunctions is enhanced by the cooperation of a patient sex partner, so it may be necessary to work on the couple's relationship before sex therapy is undertaken.

Sex therapy focuses on (1) reducing performance anxiety; (2) changing self-defeating expectations; and (3) fostering sexual skills or behavioral competencies. Both sex partners are frequently involved in therapy, although, as we shall see, individual treatment may be preferable in some cases. The sex therapists, often a male and female therapy team, educate the couple and guide them through a series of homework assignments. Masters and Johnson have a standard two-week treatment format that they use with couples who live in residence at their clinic during this period. However, most therapists do not require clients to live at the clinic. And in many instances "bibliotherapy"—or treatment of problems through self-help manuals—has also been of help (e.g., Dodge et al., 1982).

Let us have a look at a sample of the techniques that have been effective in treating arousal and erectile disorders, premature ejaculation, and inhibited orgasm.

Arousal and Erectile Disorders   In sex therapy, women who have trouble becoming lubricated and men with problems in achieving erection learn that they need not "do" anything to become sexually aroused. They need only receive sexual stimulation under relaxed circumstances, so that anxiety does not inhibit their natural reflexes.

In order to reduce performance anxiety, the partners engage in contacts that do not demand lubrication or erection. They may start with **sensate-focus exercises** in which they massage one another without touching the genitals. Each partner learns to "pleasure" the other and to "be pleasured" by receiving and giving verbal instructions and guiding the other's hands. Communication skills as well as sexual skills are thus acquired. After a couple of sessions, sensate focus extends to the genitals. When the person achieves sexual excitement, the couple does not immediately attempt coitus, since this might recreate performance anxiety. Once excitement is attained reliably, the couple engages in a graduated series of sexual activities, culminating in intercourse.

Masters and Johnson (1970) report that this technique resulted in a "reversal" of erectile disorders in men in about 72 percent of the couples they treated. But it should be noted that Masters and Johnson have been criticized for their evaluation of the effectiveness of their treatments. Their shortcomings include (1) failure to operationally define degrees of improvement in clients; and (2) inadequate follow-up of treated clients to determine whether treatment "reversals" remain reversed (Adams, 1980; Zilbergeld & Evans, 1980).

Premature Ejaculation   Sensate-focus exercises are also often used in treatment of premature ejaculation so that couples will learn to give and receive pleasure under relaxed, rather than sexually demanding, circumstances. Then, when the couple is ready to begin sexual interaction, Masters and Johnson (1970) teach them the "squeeze technique," in which the tip of the penis is squeezed when the man feels he is about to ejaculate. This method, which can be learned only through personal instruction by sex therapists, prevents ejaculation. Gradually the man learns to prolong coitus without ejaculating. Masters and Johnson report this technique successful with 182 of 196 men treated.

Sex therapy. Actually, a number of cognitive and behavioral methods that seek to reverse sexual dysfunctions by reducing performance anxiety, reversing defeatist expectations, and fostering sexual competencies.

Sensate-focus exercises. Guided exercises in which sex partners give and receive physical pleasure.

In 1956, urologist James Semans suggested a simpler method called the "stop-and-go" technique, in which a man simply suspends sexual stimulation whenever he feels he is about to ejaculate. With this method, too, the man learns gradually to prolong sexual stimulation without ejaculating.

Inhibited Orgasm in the Female   Women who have never experienced orgasm often harbor beliefs that sex is dirty and may have been taught never to touch themselves. They are anxious about their sexuality, and have not had the chance to learn, through trial and error, what types of sexual stimulation will excite them and bring them to climax.

Masters and Johnson have treated women with inhibited orgasm by working with the couples involved, but other sex therapists suggest that it is preferable to use masturbation (Andersen, 1981; Barbach, 1975; Heiman & LoPiccolo, 1987; McMullen & Rosen, 1979). Masturbation provides women with a chance to learn about their own bodies and to give themselves pleasure without depending on a sex partner. Masturbation programs instruct women about their own sexual anatomy and encourage them to experiment with self-caresses at their own pace. They learn gradually to bring themselves to orgasm as pleasure helps countercondition sexual anxiety. Once women can masturbate to orgasm, additional treatment can facilitate orgasm with a partner.

When inhibited orgasm reflects a woman's relationship with or feelings about her sex partner, treatment requires dealing with the couple—if the woman chooses to maintain the relationship. Masters and Johnson again begin with sensate-focus exercises to decrease performance anxiety, open communication channels, and enhance the couple's sexual skills. During genital massage and then coitus, the woman guides her partner in the caresses and movements that she finds sexually exciting. Psychologically, the woman's taking charge helps free her from traditional stereotypes of the passive female and grants her permission to enjoy sex. Masters and Johnson (1970) report that the dysfunctions of 81 percent of 183 women treated for this problem were reversed.

Sex therapists tend to agree that success rates for treating these problems would be enhanced if everyone they worked with were fully committed to change. This observation applies to every area of life. Aren't we generally more successful at those undertakings to which we are fully committed—whether we're talking about giving up smoking, improving our marriages, or going after a graduate degree?

■ Sexually Transmitted Diseases

Sexually transmitted diseases (STD's) are epidemic, yet, as shown by the remarks of one young woman, it can be clumsy to protect oneself:

> It's one thing to talk about "being responsible about STD" and a much harder thing to do it at the very moment. It's just plain hard to say to someone I am feeling very erotic with, "Oh, yes, before we go any further, can we have a conversation about STD?" It's hard to imagine murmuring into someone's ear at a time of passion, "Would you mind slipping on this condom or using this cream just in case one of us has STD?" Yet it seems awkward to bring it up beforehand, if it's not yet clear between us that we want to make love with one another (*The New Our Bodies, Ourselves*, 1984, p. 267).

Because of the difficulties in discussing STD's with dates, some people admit that they "wing it" (Wallis, 1987). That is, they just assume that a dating partner does not have an STD, or they hope for the best—even in the age of AIDS. But as noted earlier, 71 percent of the single women responding to the *Glamour* magazine (1988) survey reported that they had become more cautious about sex because of AIDS—up from 47 percent in the previous year.

Although AIDS has deeply embedded itself in our consciousness in the past few years, there are a number of other STD's that are also of concern, or ought to be—including gonorrhea, syphilis, and herpes. In this section we discuss the causes and courses of a number of STD's, and we explore behavior patterns that influence the risk of contracting them. In the case of the AIDS virus, which has so far eluded medical efforts to develop a vaccine or a cure, prevention is the only real weapon we have (Kaplan, 1987). For that reason, a major focus of this section will be on safe(r) sex—"safe(r)" rather than "safe" because when we engage in sexual activity with another person, there are few guarantees. Let us consider these STD's more closely.

Gonorrhea

Gonorrhea is the most common STD in the United States, with nearly 2 million new cases per year reported by the Centers for Disease Control (1985a). Gonorrhea is caused by the *Neisseria gonorrhoeae* bacterium and generally spread by vaginal, oral, or anal intercourse.

Symptoms among males include a penile discharge that begins about 3 to 5 days after infection. At first the discharge is clear, but within a day it turns yellow to yellow-green, thickens, and becomes puslike. The urethra becomes inflamed and urination is accompanied by a burning sensation.

One of the tragedies of gonorrhea is that most women do not experience symptoms in the early stages of the disease. For this reason they are likely to go untreated. But when left untreated, gonorrhea spreads through the genital and urinary systems of both sexes, leading to fertility and other problems. Gonorrhea is one cause of **pelvic inflammatory disease** (PID) in women, which is symptomized by painful, irregular periods; pain in the lower abdomen; headaches; nausea; and fever.

Gonorrhea is diagnosed from samples of discharges and is treated (and almost always cured) by antibiotics such as penicillin. In recent years strains of gonorrhea have appeared that are resistant to penicillin, but they are usually cured by higher doses of penicillin or by other antibiotics.

Syphilis

Syphilis afflicts about 100,000 U.S. residents each year and is caused by the *Treponema pallidum* bacterium. Like gonorrhea, syphilis is transmitted by genital, oral, or anal contact with an infected person.

Syphilis undergoes four phases of development. The first, or primary, stage is characterized by formation of a painless chancre (a hard, round, ulcerlike lesion with raised edges) that appears at the site of infection two to four weeks after contact. The chancre will disappear within a few weeks, but if untreated syphilis will continue to work under the skin. The secondary stage begins a few weeks to a few months later and is symptomized by a skin rash, consisting of painless, reddish raised bumps that darken after a while and burst, oozing a discharge. There can also be sores in the mouth, painful swelling of joints, a sore throat, headaches, and fever, so that a sufferer may assume that he or she has "the flu." These symptoms also disappear, and then syphilis enters the latent stage and may lie dormant for from 1 to 40 years. Some people eventually encounter the final, or tertiary, stage of the disease, which can cause large ulcers and damage the cardiovascular and central nervous systems. The painter Paul Gauguin died from tertiary syphilis.

Because the symptoms of the first two stages of syphilis inevitably disappear, victims are tempted to pretend that they are no longer in danger and to avoid seeing a doctor. This is unfortunate because syphilis can be diagnosed by a simple blood test (called a "VDRL") and eradicated by penicillin. If you

Pelvic inflammatory disease. Inflammation of the woman's abdominal region that is caused by pathogens such as the gonorrhea bacterium and that is characterized by fever, local pain, and, frequently, fertility problems. Abbreviated *PID*.

have had suspicious symptoms and they have disappeared, get a VDRL. Syphilis can be treated at any stage of development.

Herpes

There are a number of kinds of herpes, and each is caused by a variant of the *Herpes simplex* virus. The most common type is the HSV-1 virus, which is usually limited to nongenital areas and causes "cold sores" or "fever blisters" on the lips or in the mouth. The HSV-2 virus causes genital herpes, or painful blisters and sores on and around the genitals. HSV-1 can also infect the genitals, and HSV-2 the mouth—particularly when there is oral–genital contact.

In 1986 the Centers for Disease control reported that about 100 million Americans had been infected by the HSV-1 virus and that nearly 10 million had genital herpes. The HSV-1 virus is easily spread by kissing, drinking from the same cup, sharing towels, and so forth. The HSV-2 virus is usually only spead by sexual intercourse and oral and anal sex.

Genital herpes is symptomized by reddish, painful bumps, or papules, in the genital region. These papules then turn into small, painful blisters filled with infectious fluid. The blisters become pus-filled and rupture. A person may also have muscle aches, headaches, swollen lymph nodes, fever, burning urination, and, in the case of women, a vaginal discharge. The blisters crust over and heal in 10 to 16 days, but 30 to 70 percent of victims have recurrent episodes. Genital herpes is most contagious when the individual is showing symptoms, but it can also be transmitted between episodes (Centers for Disease Control, 1985; Mertz et al., 1985).

Women appear to be in greater danger than men from genital herpes. Whereas men usually have only the discomfort to contend with, some infected women develop cervical cancer. Women may also infect babies with genital herpes during childbirth, which can damage or kill them (Sweet, 1985). Babies at risk can be born by Caeserean section.

Genital herpes is diagnosed visually during an eruption of the disorder or by a sample of fluid taken from the base of a sore. At this time there is no cure for herpes, but the drug acyclovir and some newer drugs appear to offer symptom relief. Loose clothing, warm baths, and aspirin may also be of help.

Acquired Immune Deficiency Syndrome (AIDS)

AIDS, like herpes, is caused by a virus. The AIDS virus has had different names over the years, but the medical community appears to be settling on human immunodeficiency virus, or HIV (Kaplan, 1987). HIV, which we shall refer to as the AIDS virus, is transmitted by heterosexual vaginal intercourse, anal intercourse, sharing contaminated hypodermic needles (as when a group of people "shoots up" a drug), transfusions of contaminated blood, and childbirth (Frumkin & Leonard, 1987; Kaplan, 1987; Kolata, 1988). As of this writing it has not been demonstrated that the AIDS virus is transmitted by oral-genital sex because victims who have engaged in oral-genital sex have also engaged in other sexual activities that are known to transmit the AIDS virus. Nor has it yet been shown that the virus can be spread by kissing, but small amounts of the virus have been found in the saliva of victims. Therefore, deep or "French" kissing might pose a threat, whereas a "dry" kiss on the cheek, as used in a greeting, probably does not. The virus can probably be transmitted by breast-feeding.

The noted sexologist Helen Singer Kaplan (1987), who directs the Human Sexuality Program at the Cornell University Medical Center, expresses concern that the AIDS virus may infect an individual any time it comes into contact with a mucus membrane, such as the inside of the mouth or the areolas of the breasts (the dark rings that surround the nipples), or any time it breaches a crack in the skin, such as a tiny abrasion or cut. We would like to be able to think of Kaplan's position as "extremist," but given the deadly nature of the virus, her view is worth consideration. As of this writing, there is no evidence that using public toilets, holding or hugging an infected person, living in the same house, or going to the same school transmits the virus.

The AIDS virus has an affinity for, and kills, white blood cells called **T-helper lymphocytes,** or T4 lymphocytes, that are found in the immune system. T-helper lymphocytes are the cells that recognize pathogens and "instruct" other white blood cells—called **B lymphocytes**—to make antibodies. As a result of depletion of T-helper lymphocytes, the body is left vulnerable to various "opportunistic diseases." These are diseases that do not stand much of a chance of developing in persons whose immune systems are intact.

To date the AIDS virus has infected fewer people than the gonorrhea and syphilis bacteria and the genital herpes virus. However, the AIDS virus has been of more concern because it may be fatal to all people who develop full-blown cases of the disease. As of today, about 5 percent of those who have been infected have developed full-blown cases. Frankly, the medical community has not yet reached a consensus as to what percentage of those infected will ultimately develop AIDS, or as to what the upper boundaries of the incubation period might be. In other words, we don't know how long an infected person can go before developing AIDS.

An infected person who goes on to develop AIDS frequently comes down with a mononucleosislike illness anywhere from a week to several months after infection. Symptoms include fever, fatigue, and swollen glands. There may also be headaches, nausea, and a rash. These symptoms usually disappear within days or weeks. Some weeks or months later the person may develop **AIDS-related complex,** or ARC, which is characterized by swollen lymph glands. Weeks or months afterward, the person may develop the full-blown case, which is characterized by fatigue, fever, weight loss, swollen glands, and diarrhea. Opportunistic infections may now take hold, such as various kinds of cancer (Kaposi's sarcoma, a cancer of the blood cells, has been seen in many gay males who contract AIDS) and a kind of pneumonia (*PCP*) that is characterized by coughing and shortness of breath.

Since AIDS is of such concern, it might be helpful to point out those who are at greatest risk for contracting the disease (Frumkin & Leonard, 1987; Kaplan, 1987):

1. Gay males: The San Francisco and New York gay communities have been particularly hard hit (Boffey, 1988). The Federal Centers for Disease Control reported that in 1988 about 65 percent of cases of AIDS were among homosexual or bisexual males (*New York Times,* 1988).
2. Intravenous (IV) drug abusers: about 17 percent of cases.
3. Sex partners of IV drug abusers.
4. Babies born to sex partners of IV drug abusers.
5. Prostitutes—particularly in the New York–New Jersey metropolitan area and Miami.
6. Men who visit prostitutes, particularly in the above areas.
7. Sex partners of men who visit infected prostitutes.
8. People receiving transfusions of blood—for example, surgery patients and hemophiliacs. However, this avenue of infection has become increasingly unlikely because of the awareness of the medical community that blood supplies may be contaminated.

Although people on this list may be at greatest risk, others cannot assume that they have nothing to worry about (Kaplan, 1987).

Infection by the AIDS virus is diagnosed by blood tests that show antibodies to the virus or the virus itself. As of this writing, tests that show the presence of the virus itself are under development; existing tests are more likely to reveal the presence of antibodies. It can take a number of months

T-helper lymphocytes. The white blood cells of the immune system that recognize invading pathogens. Also called *T4-helper lymphocytes.*

B lymphocytes. The white blood cells of the immune system that produce antibodies.

AIDS-related complex. A stage in the development of AIDS characterized mainly by swollen glands.

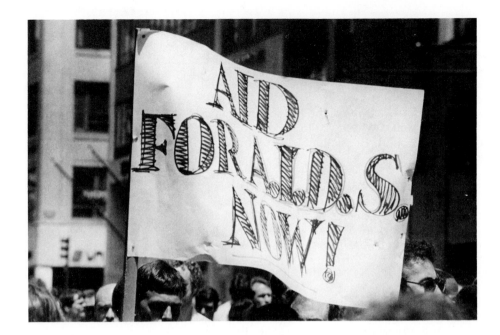

AIDS victims and other concerned individuals regularly petition government agencies to devote more resources to AIDS research and to caring for those who have contracted the disease.

after infection for antibodies to develop, and so repeated tests may be in order. Also, presence of HIV antibodies is not proof that one is infected with the virus itself; some babies, for example, apparently acquire antibodies from the bloodstreams of infected mothers without being infected by the virus. This may sound confusing, but the bottom line is this: If you have a couple of negative blood tests a few months apart, and do not engage in high-risk behavior between the tests, you're unlikely to be infected.

Unfortunately, there is not yet a vaccine for the AIDS virus or a cure for AIDS, and, as of this writing, the outlook for a breakthrough is not encouraging (Kolata, 1988). A number of antiviral drugs are under investigation, singly and in combination. However, these drugs can have severe side effects and the results are mixed at best. For these reasons, the only logical way to cope with AIDS is *prevention,* as we shall see in the section on safe(r) sex.

Other Sexually Transmitted Diseases

There are a number of other STD's that it is useful to know about. We can mention a few of them, but readers are advised to consult health or human sexuality textbooks, their physicians, or their college or university counseling or health centers for more information.

A yeast infection, or *moniliasis,* is caused by a fungus. Symptoms include vaginal irritation and a white, cheesy vaginal discharge. The condition can be cured by vaginal creams or suppositories.

Trichomoniasis, or "trich," is caused by a protozoan (a one-celled animal). Symptoms include irritation of the vulva and a white or yellow vaginal discharge with an unpleasant odor. It is treated with metronidazole (brand name Flagyl) in both sexes.

Chlamydia is caused by a bacterium. In men there is burning urination and a discharge; the testes may feel heavy and the scrotum sore. In women, chlamydia can cause PID and disrupt menstrual periods. It is treated by antibiotics such as tetracycline and erythromycin.

Pubic lice, or "crabs," are body lice that can be spread by bringing pubic hair into contact or sharing bedding or clothing. Lice cause itching and can be seen with the naked eye. They are killed by gamma benzene hexachloride (brand name Kwell) or A-200 pyrinate.

Genital, or venereal, warts are caused by a virus. On dry skin areas warts are hard and yellow-gray; on moist areas, soft and pinkish. Warts can be burned off (by a doctor!), vaporized, frozen, surgically removed, or treated with podophyllin.

Now that we have seen a number of the things that can happen when we contract STD's, perhaps it will seem that the best way to cope with STD's is not to contract them in the first place. With that is mind, let us turn our attention to methods of prevention.

Safe(r) Sex in the Age of AIDS

STD's and their prevention are not the most pleasant things to talk about. As Helen Singer Kaplan notes in the beginning of her book about AIDS, she is used to telling people things like "Enjoy, it's okay to have sexual feelings . . . Sex is a natural function . . . Sex is not dirty or harmful . . . Don't give your kids sexual hangups!" (1987, p. 11).

It's still okay to have sexual feelings, and sex is still a natural function. Unfortunately, the bacteria, viruses, and other pathogens that give rise to STD's are also natural functions—that is, they occur naturally in our world and their biological effects on us are well understood. Because of these pathogens sex is sometimes harmful. And, although we don't want to give our children, or our readers, "sexual hangups," it is wise to consider a number of precautions that decrease the risk of contracting STD's.

Here, then, are a number of things that can be done. Some of them are relatively easy to do; others take more "courage." Some of them are more important than others. They will make sex in the age of AIDS safer; nobody can guarantee that you will be absolutely safe:

1. *Be selective.* Engage in sexual activity only with people whom you have gotten to know and who do not belong to the high-risk groups for AIDS.

TABLE 15.3   Sexual Transmission of AIDS: Degrees of Risk

1. *No Risks:* Celibacy, no sex at all. *100% safe.*

2. *Ultrasafe Sex.* No touching each other. *100% safe.* Talking sexy; sharing your sexual fantasies, sharing erotica; telephone sex.

3. *Safe Sex: Dry Sex: No exchanged body fluids. Probably 100% safe.* Caressing the dry parts of each other's bodies; masturbating in each other's presence but no physical contact.

4. *Low-Risk Sex: No mingling of infected body fluids. Probably not 100% safe but close.* Stimulation of each other's genitalia to orgasm without mingling of body fluids; vaginal, anal, or oral sex using a condom* with a partner you have every reason to believe is not infected but whose AIDS status you are not certain of. (But watch out, these exciting experiences entail the danger of your being "swept away" by your passion into an unsafe sexual act.)

5. *High-Risk Sex: 10% to 30% possibility of infection* if he is a carrier. Vaginal or anal intercourse using condoms, with a high-risk male, or with a male who might have been exposed, or with a stranger whose exposure history you do not know. Oral sex with this kind of man could be just as risky.

6. *Suicidal Sex: 50% to 85% probability that you might become infected with the AIDS virus if this is repeated, but you can catch AIDS on a single exposure.* Unprotected vaginal, anal, or oral intercourse with a high-risk male or with a stranger, or with a known carrier.

Source: H. S. Kaplan. (1987). *The Real Truth about Women and AIDS.* Simon & Schuster/Fireside, p. 77.
*Heiman and LoPiccolo (1987) note that the condom should be made from latex rubber. Ask the pharmacist or read the package.

WHAT DO YOU SAY NOW?

Making Sex Safe(r) in the Age of AIDS

You've gone out with Chris a few times and you're keenly attracted. Chris is attractive, bright, witty, shares some of your attitudes, and, all in all, is a powerful turn-on. Now the evening is winding down. You've been cuddling and you're getting involved in other things—and you think you know where it's all heading.

Something clicks in your mind! You realize that as wonderful as Chris is, you don't know every place Chris has "been." As healthy as Chris looks and acts, you don't know what's swimming around in Chris's bloodstream either.

What do you say now? How do you protect yourself without turning Chris off? Write some possible responses in the spaces provided, and then check below for some ideas.

1. _____
   _____

2. _____
   _____

3. _____
   _____

Ah, the clumsiness! If you ask about STD's it is sort of making a verbal commitment to have sexual relations, and perhaps you're not exactly sure that's what your partner intends. And even if it's clear that's where you're heading, will you seem too straightforward? Will you kill the romance? The spontaneity of the moment? Sure you might—life has its risks. But which is riskier: an awkward moment or being infected with a fatal illness? Let's put it another way: Are you *really* willing to die for sex? Given that few verbal responses are perfect, here are some things you can try:

1. Ask good-naturedly, "Do you have anything to tell me?" This question is open-ended, and if Chris is as bright as you think, Chris might very well take the hint and tell you what you need to know.

2. If Chris answers "I love you," be happy about it. You could respond with something like, "I'm crazy about you, too." A minute later, add "Do you have anything *else* to tell me?"

3. If Chris says, "Like what?" you can beat around the bush one more time and say something like, "Well, I'm sure you weren't waiting for me all your life locked in a closet. I don't know everywhere you've been . . ."

4. If you're uncomfortable with that, or if you want to be more straightforward, you can say something like, "As far as I know I'm perfectly healthy. Have there been any problems with you I should know about?" Saying that you are healthy invites reciprocity in self-disclosure.

5. Once Chris has expressed unawareness of being infected by any STD's, you might pursue it by mentioning your ideas about prevention. You can say something like, "I've brought something and I'd like to use it . . ." (referring to a condom).

6. Or you can say something like "I know this is a bit clumsy" (you are assertively expressing a feeling and asking permission to pursue a clumsy topic; Chris is likely to respond something like "That's okay" or "Don't worry—what is it?"), "but the world isn't as safe as it used to be, and I think we should talk about what we're going to do."

The point in all this is that your partner hasn't been living in a remote cave. Your partner is also aware of the dangers of STD's, especially of AIDS, and ought to be working with you to make things safe and unpressured. If your partner is pressing for unsafe sex and is inconsiderate of your feelings and concerns, you need to reassess whether you really want to be with this person. We think you can do better.

Table 15.3 is taken from Kaplan's book of advice about AIDS and is directed toward women, but male readers can adapt it easily enough.

2. *Inspect your partner's genitals.* While engaging in foreplay, it might be possible to visually examine your partner's genitals for blisters, discharges, chancres, rashes, warts, and lice. An unpleasant odor should be taken as a warning sign.

3. *Wash your genitals before and after contact.* Washing beforehand helps protect your partner, and washing promply afterward with soap and water helps remove some pathogens. Urinating afterward might be of some help, particularly to men, since the acidity of urine can kill some pathogens in the urethra.

4. *Use spermicides.* Spermicides are marketed as birth-control devices, but many creams, foams, and jellies kill pathogens as well as sperm (Centers for Disease Control, 1985a; Lourea et al, 1986). Check with a pharmacist.

5. *Use condoms.* Condoms are highly effective when properly used because they protect the man from vaginal (or other) body fluids and prevent semen from entering the woman. Condoms are particularly effective in preventing gonorrhea, syphilis, and AIDS (Conant et al., 1986). Heiman and LoPiccolo (1987) note, however, that only condoms made from latex rubber prevent transmission of the AIDS virus. Combining condoms with spermicides is still more effective.

6. *Consult a physician about medication.* It can be helpful to use antibiotics after unprotected sex to guard against certain infections, but remember that medication will not protect you from herpes or AIDS. Also, routine use of antibiotics may do nothing more than make them less effective for you when you really need them.

7. *Have regular medical checkups.* These include blood tests. In this way you may learn about and be able to treat certain disorders whose symptoms you had not noticed. But again, this method is to no avail against herpes and AIDS.

8. *When in doubt, stop.* If you're not sure that what you're about to do is safe, don't do it. Get some expert advice first.

By taking reasonable precautions, you ought to be able to "enjoy" the "natural function" of sex, prevent sex from being "harmful," and avoid too many "hangups" about STD's.

■ Summary

1. **Do sexual practices vary from culture to culture?** A great deal! For example, sexual behavior is greatly restricted on Inis Beag, whereas the natives of Mangaia enjoy varied sexual practices at a relatively young age.

2. **What is, or was, the "sexual revolution"?** The sexual revolution came into being during the 1960s. It was linked to political liberalism and the Human Potential Movement and had a couple of foci. One was an explosion in the incidence of premarital sex; another was the liberation of female sexuality—recognition that women can have (and are entitled to have) as much sexual pleasure as men.

3. **Where do things stand now?** It's difficult to say, but it seems that the incidence of premarital sex has decreased today, while women's sexual awareness has been retained.

4. **What are the prominent patterns of sexual behavior in the United States today?** Masturbation is almost universal among males, and the majority of females masturbate. Petting is nearly universal among both sexes, especially when marriage is delayed. As marriage is delayed, the frequency of premarital coitus also increases. Most young married couples engage in coitus two or three times a week and practice oral sex as well. Extramarital sex is generally disapproved of.

5. **How are female and male sexual anatomy alike?** The penis and clitoris, for example, are both highly sensitive to sexual stimulation and become engorged with blood when excited. The testes and ovaries both produce germ cells (sperm and ova) and sex hormones (testosterone and estrogen).

6. **What are the effects of sex hormones?** Sex hormones promote biological sexual differentiation, regulate the menstrual cycle, and have organizing (directional) and activating (motivational) effects on sexual behavior. In lower animals, sex is controlled largely by hormones and pheromones. In more intelligent species, psychological factors are more important.

7. **What is PMS, and how many women does it affect?** Premenstrual syndrome is a combination of psychological (e.g., mood changes) and physical symptoms (e.g., bloating, cramping) that afflicts about 30 percent of

women for a few days prior to, and during, menstruation. In most cases, the symptoms are mild.

8. **What is the sexual-response cycle?** For both sexes, the sexual response cycle consists of four phases: excitement, plateau, orgasm, and resolution. The excitement phase is marked by erection and vaginal lubrication, and increases in the heart and respiration rates and blood pressure. The plateau phase prepares the body for orgasm. Orgasm is characterized by pleasure and the release of sexual tensions. In both sexes, there are involuntary muscle contractions in the genitals and elsewhere, and semen is expelled in the male. In the resolution phase, the body returns gradually to its resting state.

9. **What are the effects of aging on sexual behavior?** The aged have sexual relations less frequently than young adults, although children underestimate the incidence and extent of their parents' sexual activities. Aging can lead to some sexual problems, but generally speaking psychological factors remain more important than physical factors in sexuality throughout the later years.

10. **Why are some people homosexual?** We don't really know. Purely psychological theories run aground. The most promising hypotheses point to roles for genetic factors, prenatal hormonal influences, and socialization. Homosexual episodes do not necessarily reflect a homosexual orientation. Homosexuals are generally as well adjusted as heterosexuals, although homosexuals who lead different life-styles show different levels of adjustment.

11. **What are the effects of pornography?** Pornography appears to sexually arouse women as well as men, but there is no reliable evidence that pornography contributes to antisocial behavior. However, recent experiments suggest that aggressive-erotic (rape) films may lead to increased aggression by men toward women.

12. **Why do people commit rape?** Rape appears to be motivated more by anger and the desire to exercise power over women than by sexual needs. Social critics argue that our culture socializes men into becoming rapists, and women into assuming the victim role.

13. **What are sexual dysfunctions?** Sexual dysfunctions are problems in becoming sexually aroused or reaching orgasm. Dysfunctions include hypoactive sexual desire, female sexual arousal disorder, male erectile disorder, inhibited orgasm, premature ejaculation, dyspareunia, and vaginismus.

14. **What are the causes of sexual dysfunctions?** Sexual dysfunctions now and then reflect physical factors, such as disease, but most reflect psychosocial factors such as traditional sex-negative beliefs, psychosexual trauma, troubled relationships, lack of sexual skills, and irrational beliefs. Any of these may lead to performance anxiety, which compounds sexual problems.

15. **What is sex therapy?** Sex therapy is based largely on the social-learning model. It deals with the sexual dysfunctions through brief treatment programs that reduce performance anxiety, challenge irrational expectations and beliefs, and impart sexual competencies. Many programs involve a dysfunctional couple in sensate-focus exercises, but these programs are quite varied.

16. **What are sexually transmitted diseases (STD's)?** STD's are diseases that are transmitted by sexual contact, although some of them (e.g., AIDS, pubic lice) can be transmitted in other ways as well.

17. **What causes STD's?** A variety of pathogens. For example, gonorrhea and syphilis are caused by bacteria, and herpes and AIDS are caused by viruses.

18. **Can STD's be cured?** Most of them can. For example, gonorrhea and syphilis are cured by antibiotics. Unfortunately, there is no cure for herpes or AIDS.

19. **What's the story on AIDS?** AIDS (acquired immune deficiency syndrome) is caused by a virus that kills white blood cells in the immune system, leaving the body prey to opportunistic diseases, such as kinds of cancer and pneumonia. AIDS is transmitted by heterosexual and homosexual sexual activity, by sharing contaminated hypodermic needles, and by other methods of transferring infected blood, as through transfusions and childbirth.

20. **Is AIDS always fatal?** AIDS may be fatal to all those who develop full-blown cases of the disease. As of today, 1 to 2 million Americans have been infected, and only about 5 percent have developed full-blown cases. We don't know how many of the infected will eventually develop full-blown cases.

21. **What's the best thing to do about AIDS?** Prevent it. Avoid risky behavior patterns—e.g., casual sex, unprotected sex, sharing needles. And help educate others about AIDS.

■ TRUTH OR FICTION REVISITED

Masturbation can cause mental illness. False, but a person who is morally opposed to masturbation and who masturbates might feel anxious or guilty about it.

Most women have entertained fantasies about imaginary lovers while engaging in sexual relations with their husbands. True, according to research by Hariton and Singer. Sexual fantasies are quite normal.

Most of today's sophisticated young people see nothing wrong with an occasional extramarital fling. False. Most Americans disapprove of extramarital sex.

Women, but not men, have a sex organ whose only known function is the sensing of sexual pleasure. True—the clitoris.

Nontraditional women suffer less from premenstrual distress than their traditionalist sisters do. True. The liberated are less likely to share the myth that menstruation is a time of pollution and distress.

Homosexuals choose to be homosexual. False. We discover our sexual orientations at early ages, and choice has nothing to do with it.

Homosexuals suffer from hormonal imbalances. Not as adults—but it is possible that homosexuality is linked to prenatal hormonal influences.

Pornographic films cause crimes of violence against women. False. Films that depict violence toward women—whether or not they also contain explicit sexual content—appear to encourage violent behavior.

A healthy woman can successfully resist a rapist is she really wants to. False. This is one of many myths that, according to social critics, create a climate that is supportive of rape.

Only women can have multiple orgasms. Not necessarily—now and then a young male does. But women in general are capable of multiple orgasms, in late adulthood as well as at younger ages.

Most sexual dysfunctions stem from physical problems. False. Most sexual dysfunctions stem from psychological factors such as sex-negative attitudes, lack of sexual skills, and performance anxiety.

Painful early sexual experiences can lead to sexual dysfunctions in adulthood. True. Early experiences help shape our expectations.

Gonorrhea and syphilis may be contracted by using toilet seats in public restrooms. False. Neither can AIDS.

If the symptoms of sexually transmitted diseases go away by themselves, medical treatment is usually unnecessary. False. The symptoms of gonorrhea and syphilis go away—for a while—but the diseases continue to work under the skin.

Only homosexual males and intravenous drug abusers are at real risk for contracting AIDS. False. These groups account for the majority of victims, but no group can be guaranteed as safe.

■ Scoring Key for the Myths-That-Support-Rape Questionnaire

Item number 2 is true. The rest are false. But our concerns over your responses do not simply address their accuracy. The issue is whether you endorse cultural beliefs that tend to contribute to rape. For example, if you believe that women harbor unconscious desires to be raped, you may also tend to believe that rape victims "get what they have coming to them" and your sympathies may actually lie with the assailant.

Having and Rearing Children

16

Fertilization takes place in the uterus.

It is not possible to learn the sex of one's child prior to birth.

"Yuppies" are more likely than nonprofessionals to develop fertility problems.

Developing embryos have been successfully transferred from the womb of one woman to the womb of another.

You can predetermine the sex of your child.

Pregnant women who smoke risk having children who are low in birth weight.

Sickle-cell anemia is most prevalent among blacks.

Soon after birth, babies are slapped on the buttocks to clear passageways for air and stimulate independent breathing.

The way the umbilical cord is cut determines whether a child will have an "inny" or an "outy" for a "belly button."

Women who give birth by the Lamaze method do not have pain.

Most hospitals exclude fathers from the birth process.

It is essential for parents to have extended early contact with their babies if adequate bonding is to take place.

Children with strict parents are more likely to become competent.

Breast-feeding and bottle-feeding are equally healthful.

Women cannot become pregnant while they are breast-feeding.

Divorce is more stressful for young children than for adolescents.

Parents who have been victims of child abuse are more likely to abuse their own children.

Children placed in day care become less attached to their mothers.

On a summerlike day in October, Deborah and her husband Mitch rush out to their jobs as usual. While Deborah, a buyer for a New York department store, is arranging for dresses from the Chicago manufacturer to arrive in time for the spring line, a very different drama is unfolding in her body. Hormones are causing a follicle (egg container) in one of her ovaries to rupture and release an egg cell, or ovum. Deborah, like other women, possessed from birth all the egg cells she would ever have. How this ovum was selected for development and release this month is unknown. But for a day or so following **ovulation,** Deborah will be capable of becoming pregnant.

When it is released, the ovum begins a slow journey down a 4-inch-long **fallopian tube** to the **uterus.** It is within this tube that one of Mitch's sperm cells will unite with it.

Like many other couples, Deborah and Mitch engaged in sexual intercourse the previous night. But unlike most other couples, their timing and methodology were preplanned. Deborah had used a nonprescription kit bought in a drug store to predict when she would ovulate. She had been chemically analyzing her urine for the presence of **luteinizing hormone.** Luteinizing hormone surges about one to two days prior to ovulation, and the results placed this day at the center of the period of time when Deborah was likely to conceive.

When Deborah and Mitch made love, he ejaculated hundreds of millions of sperm, with about equal numbers of Y and X sex chromosomes. By the time of conception only a few thousand had survived the journey to the fallopian tubes. Several bombarded the ovum, attempting to penetrate. Only one succeeded. It carried a Y sex chromosome. When a Y-bearing sperm unites with an ovum, all of which contain X sex chromosomes, the couple will conceive a boy. When an X-bearing sperm fertilizes the ovum, a girl is conceived. The fertilized ovum, or **zygote,** is 1/175th of an inch long—a tiny stage for the drama yet to unfold.

The genetic material from Mitch's sperm cell combines with that in Deborah's egg cell. Deborah is 37 years old, and in four months she will have an amniocentesis to check for Down syndrome in the fetus, a chromosomal disorder that occurs more frequently among the children of couples in their 30s and 40s. Amniocentesis also provides information about the sex of the unborn child. And so, months before their son is born, Deborah and Mitch will start thinking about boys' names and prepare their nursery for a boy.

In this chapter, we focus on a number of issues concerning having and rearing children. First is the central question of whether or not to have children. We shall see that educated people these days are choosing whether to have children, not just having them as a matter of course, and we shall note some of their reasons for having, and for not having, children. Then we consider the not-so-simple matter of conception, and we see how contemporary couples cope with infertility problems. We follow prenatal development and see how parents can make that crucial period as healthful as possible for the embryo and fetus. We explore the psychological, biological, and political issues concerning childbirth and focus on ways in which women can exercise control over their own bodies throughout the process. We report research concerning the patterns of child rearing that are associated with competence in children. Finally, we examine a selection of issues in child rearing that will be of use to readers: breast-feeding versus bottle-feeding, effects of divorce on children, child abuse, and day care. The two "What Do You Say Now?" features in the chapter are chosen for their timeliness: "Selecting an Obstetrician" and "Selecting a Day-Care Center."

Ovulation. The releasing of an ovum from an ovary.

Fallopian tube. A tube that conducts ova from an ovary to the uterus.

Uterus. The hollow organ within females in which the embryo and fetus develop.

Luteinizing hormone. A hormone produced by the pituitary gland that causes ovulation.

Zygote. A fertilized ovum.

■ Children: To Have or Not to Have

Once upon a time marriage was equated with children. It was traditional for people to get married and, in what Hare-Mustin and Broderick (1979) refer to as the "motherhood mandate," it was traditional for women to bear at least two children and to rear them properly. In short, married women who could bear children usually did (Faux, 1984).

Today, this tradition—the motherhood mandate—as so many others, has to some degree broken down. More than ever, people see themselves as having the right to *choose* whether or not they will have children. Today from 10 to 25 percent of U.S. women do not want children (Cook et al., 1982; Gerson et al., 1984; Notman & Nadelson, 1982). U.S. couples are now also having fewer children than in the past—only 1.8 per couple (McFalls, 1983).

Women who report their own childhoods to have been filled with happiness and maternal love are more likely to want children of their own than are women whose memories are not so pleasant (Gerson, 1980, 1984). Level of education and sex-role attitudes also play important roles. Women who do not have children are more likely to be white, urban, and highly educated than those who do (Faux, 1984). Child-free women, black and white, are more likely to hold nontraditional, feminist beliefs than women with children (Bram, 1984; Gerson, 1984; Scott & Morgan, 1983).

For women who choose not to have children, the tenor of the times seems reasonably supportive. In a survey of college students by Hare-Mustin and Broderick (1979), only 12 percent considered the decision against having children unnatural or selfish. Only 9 percent of the respondents in one recent survey endorsed this view (Knaub et al., 1983).

Research on child-free women supports the view that children are not mandatory for women's fulfillment. Young married women without children report greater marital and general life satisfaction than do their counterparts with children (Doherty & Jackson, 1982; Gerson et al., 1984). The same finding holds for middle-aged women. Only widows with grown children appear to be more satisfied with their lives and to feel less isolated than their child-free counterparts (Beckman & Houser, 1982; Houser et al., 1984). The corollary here may be that it is erroneous for women to assume that having children will solve their problems or ensure their happiness (Baruch et al., 1983).

Keep in mind that the above findings on life satisfaction generally apply to couples who have *chosen* not to have children. For couples who want children but cannot have them, few situations are more frustrating.

What are some of the considerations involved in choosing to have, or not to have, children? Researchers have found several for each choice. Note that there are a number of pros and cons that will not impress you as good or valid reasons. They are included because other people have offered them. Ultimately you must be the judge. It's your life, and your choice.

Reasons to Have Children

Researchers (Berelson, 1979; Campbell et al., 1982; Daniels & Weingarten, 1982; Hoffman & Manis, 1978) have compiled the following reasons for having children:

1. *Personal Experience.* Having children is a unique experience. To many people, no other experience compares with having the opportunity to love them, to experience their love, to help shape their lives, and to watch them develop.
2. *Personal Pleasure.* There is fun and pleasure in playing with children, taking them to the zoo and the circus, and viewing the world through their fresh, innocent eyes.
3. *Personal Extension.* Children carry on our genetic heritage, and some of our own wishes and dreams, beyond the confines of our own mortality. We name them after ourselves or our families, and see them as extensions of ourselves. We identify with their successes.
4. *Relationship.* Parents have the opportunity to establish extremely close bonds with their children.

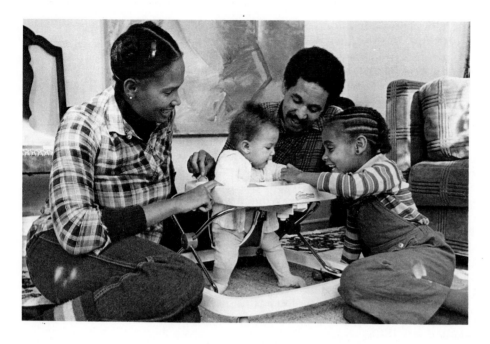

There are many reasons for having children, including the personal experience of children and the pleasure that can be derived from interacting with them. But some couples choose not to have children because children can interfere with one's personal freedom and because of the belief that the world is already heavily populated.

5. *Personal Status.* Within our culture, parents are afforded respect *just because* they are parents. Consider the commandment: "Honor thy Father and thy Mother."
6. *Personal Competence.* Parenthood is a challenge. Competence in the social roles of mother and father is a potential source of gratification to people who cannot match this competence in their vocational or other social roles.
7. *Personal Responsibility.* Parents have the opportunity to be responsible for the welfare and education of their children.
8. *Personal Power.* The power that parents hold over their children is gratifying to some people.
9. *Moral Worth.* Some people feel that having children provides the opportunity for a moral, selfless act in which they place the needs of others—their children—ahead of their own.

Reasons Not to Have Children

Researchers (Benedek & Vaughn, 1982; Bernard, 1975; Campbell et al., 1982; McFalls, 1983; Sunday & Lewin, 1985) have compiled the following reasons for which many couples choose not to have children:

1. *Strain on Resources.* The world is overpopulated and it is wrong to place additional strain on limited resources.
2. *Increase in Overpopulation.* More children will only geometrically increase the problem of overpopulation.
3. *Choice, Not Mandate.* Motherhood should be a choice, not a mandate.
4. *Time Together.* Child-free couples can spend more time together and develop a more intimate relationship.
5. *Freedom.* Children can interfere with plans for leisure time, education, and vocational advancement. Child-free couples are more able to live spontaneously, to go where they please and do as they please.
6. *Other Children.* People can enjoy other than their own children. Adoption is a possibility.
7. *Dual Careers.* Members of child-free couples may both pursue meaningful careers without distraction.
8. *Financial Security.* Children are a financial burden, especially considering the cost of a college education.

9. *Community Welfare.* Child-free couples have a greater opportunity to become involved in civic concerns and community organizations.
10. *Difficulty.* Parenthood is demanding. It requires sacrifice of time, money, and energy, and not everyone makes a good parent.
11. *Irrevocable Decision.* Once you have children, the decision cannot be changed.
12. *Failure.* Some people fear that they will not be good parents.
13. *Danger.* The world is a dangerous place, with the threats, for example, of crime and nuclear war. It is better not to bring children into such a world.

The decision to have or not to have children is a personal one—one of the most important decisions we make. Let us now follow what happens during the earliest days of development.

■ Conception

Conception is the culmination of a fantastic voyage in which one of several hundred thousand ova produced by the woman unites with one of several hundred *billion* sperm produced by the man. Each month one egg (occasionally more than one) is released from its ovarian follicle about midway during the menstrual cycle and enters a nearby fallopian tube. Each ovum contains 23 chromosomes, one of which is an X sex chromosome.

The sperm cells that approach the egg secrete an enzyme that briefly thins the gelatinous layer that surrounds the egg, allowing one sperm to enter. The chromosomes from the sperm cell line up across from the corresponding chromosomes in the egg cell to form 23 new pairs with a unique set of genetic instructions.

Coping with Infertility

For couples who want children, few problems are more frustrating than inability to conceive. Physicians are usually not concerned until couples who are trying to conceive have not done so for six months. The term *infertility* is usually not applied until the couple has not conceived for a year.

At least 10 to 15 percent of U.S. couples are infertile (Francoeur, 1985). In about four of ten cases, the problem lies with the man. In the other six, it lies with the woman.

Male Fertility Problems   Fertility problems in the male include (1) a low sperm count, (2) low sperm **motility,** (3) infectious diseases, and (4) direct trauma to the testes (Rathus, 1983). Low (or zero) sperm count is the most common problem with men.

Artificial Insemination   In some cases, multiple ejaculations of men with low sperm counts have been collected and quick-frozen. The sperm have then been injected into the woman's uterus at time of ovulation. This is one **artificial insemination** procedure. Sperm may also be collected from men with low sperm motility and injected into their partners' uteruses.

Female Fertility Problems   Women may encounter infertility because of (1) lack of ovulation, (2) infections, (3) endometriosis, and (4) obstructions or malfunctions of the reproductive tract (Rathus, 1983).

The most frequent problem, failure to ovulate, may stem from causes such as hormonal irregularities, malnutrition, and stress. "Fertility" drugs such as clomiphene and pergonal contain hormones that help regulate ovulation. They have also been linked to multiple births. Local infections such as **pelvic inflammatory disease** (PID) may impede passage of sperm or ova through the fallopian tubes and elsewhere. Antibiotics are sometimes helpful.

Conception. The combining of the genetic material of a sperm cell and an ovum, creating a zygote.

Motility. Self-propulsion.

Artificial insemination. Injection of sperm into the uterus in order to fertilize an ovum.

Pelvic inflammatory disease. Any of a number of diseases that infect the abdominal region, impairing fertility. Abbreviated PID.

Endometriosis   Endometriosis can block the fallopian tubes and also worsens the "climate" for conception for reasons that are not well understood. Endometriosis has been dubbed the "yuppies' disease" because its effects are cumulative and experienced most strongly by women who have postponed bearing children. Hormone treatments and surgery are sometimes successful in reducing endometriosis to the point where women can conceive.

A number of recent methods have been developed to help women with blocked fallopian tubes and related problems bear children.

In Vitro Fertilization   Louise Brown, the world's first "test-tube baby," was born in England in 1978 after having been conceived by means of **in vitro fertilization** (IVF). In this method, ova are surgically removed from the mother's ovary and allowed to ripen in a laboratory dish. Then they are fertilized by the father's sperm. The fertilized egg is injected into the mother's uterus and becomes implanted in the uterine wall.

Donor IVF   A variation known as *donor* IVF can be used when the mother-to-be does not produce ova. In donor IVF, an ovum from another woman is fertilized and injected into the uterus of the mother-to-be (Lutjen et al., 1984).

Embryonic Transfer   A related method under study for women who do not produce ova is termed **embryonic transfer.** A volunteer is artificially inseminated by the infertile woman's partner. After five days the embryo is removed from the volunteer and placed within the uterus of the mother-to-be, where it becomes implanted in the uterine wall and is carried to term (Bustillo et al., 1984). At this time, the in-vitro and transfer methods remain costly and are considered experimental.

Surrogate Mothers   **Surrogate mothers** have become increasingly used in recent years for women who are infertile. The surrogate mother is artifically inseminated by the husband of the infertile woman and carries the baby to term. The surrogate signs a contract to give the baby to the father and his wife. As with artificial insemination by a donor, the baby carries the genes of one parent.

Superficially, surrogate motherhood might seem the mirror image of the technique in which a fertile woman is artificially inseminated with the sperm of a donor. But many psychological and social issues are raised. For one thing, sperm donors usually do not know the identity of the women who have received their sperm. Nor do they observe their children developing within the mothers-to-be. However, surrogate mothers are involved in the entire process of prenatal development. They can become attached to their unborn children, and turning them over to other women once they are born can instill a devastating sense of loss. For this reason, some surrogate mothers have refused to part with their babies. Court cases have resulted, as with the famous "Baby M" case.

Just as new technologies are enhancing the chances for infertile couples to become parents, new methods seem to be leading to the day when we can preselect the sex of our children. In sex preselection, too, there are major social and ethical issues.

Preselecting the Sex of Your Child: Fantasy or Reality?

What would happen if we could select the sex of our children? Would we predominantly select boys or girls? Would it all balance out in the end?

According to a survey of 5,981 women, most women who would make a choice would select boys for their first children, but then balance the family with girls (Westoff & Rindfuss, 1974). Assuming that each woman in the study

Endometriosis. Inflammation of endometrial tissue (that forms the inner lining of the uterus) sloughed off into the abdominal cavity rather than out of the body during menstruation. A disease characterized by abdominal pain and impairment of fertility.

In vitro fertilization. Fertilization of an ovum in a laboratory dish.

Embryonic transfer. The transfer of a 5-day-old embryo from the uterus of one woman to that of another.

Surrogate mother. A woman who is artificially inseminated and carries to term a child who is then given to the father and his wife.

Germinal stage. The period of development between conception and the implantation of the embryo in the uterine wall.

Period of the ovum. Another term for *germinal stage*.

had two or more children, boys would still outnumber girls by a large margin. But only 39 percent of the women surveyed would select the sex of their child. Forty-seven percent would not, and 14 percent were not sure. In nations as culturally dissimilar as China, most parents would still prefer to have boys (Jiao et al., 1986).

Shettles' Approach   Sperm bearing the Y sex chromosome are smaller than those bearing the X sex chromosome, and they are faster swimmers. But sperm with the X sex chromosome are more durable. From these assumptions, Shettles (1984) derives the following strategies for selecting the sex of one's children.

In order to optimize the chances of having a boy, (1) the man should abstain from ejaculating for several days prior to his partner's time of ovulation; (2) the couple should engage in sexual intercourse on the day of ovulation; (3) the man should be penetrating deeply at time of ejaculation; and (4) the woman can make the vagina more hospitable to Y-bearing sperm by douching beforehand with two tablespoons of baking soda per quart of warm water. This will lower vaginal acidity.

In order to optimize the chances of having a girl, (1) the couple should engage in sexual intercourse about two days (or slightly more) before ovulation; (2) the woman can make the vagina *less* hospitable to Y-bearing sperm by douching with two tablespoons of vinegar per quart of warm water to raise vaginal acidity before intercourse; (3) the woman should avoid orgasm on the (debatable) assumption that orgasm facilitates the journey of sperm; and (4) the man should ejaculate with shallow penetration.

A combination of these methods has been asserted to result in the conception of a child of the desired sex in about 80 percent of cases (Kogan, 1973), but many professionals consider these figures to be exaggerated (Harlap, 1979; Karp, 1980; Simcock, 1985). The suggestions that rely on the relatively faster swimming of Y-bearing sperm are probably more useful than those that involve douching with vinegar or baking soda (Wallis, 1984).

Other preselection strategies are based on methods for separating X- and Y-bearing sperm.

Social critics brand sex-preselection technology as "stupendously sexist" (Powledge, 1981), even though many couples would use these methods to try to conceive daughters. The methods, if widely used, would see a dramatic increase in the proportion of boys.

■ Prenatal Development

During the months following conception, the single cell formed by the union of sperm and egg will multiply—becoming two, then four, then eight, and so on. Tissues, organs, and structures will form that gradually take the unmistakable shape of a human being. By the time a fetus is ready to be born, it will contain hundreds of billions of cells—more cells than there are stars in the Milky Way galaxy.

The Stages of Prenatal Development

Prenatal development is divided into three periods: the germinal stage (approximately the first two weeks), the embryonic stage (the first two months), and the fetal stage. It is also common to speak of prenatal development as lasting for three trimesters of three months each.

The Germinal Stage   The period from conception to implantation is called the **germinal stage** or the **period of the ovum.** Prior to implantation, the baby is nourished solely by the yolk of the original egg cell, and it does not gain in mass. It can gain in mass only from outside nourishment, which it will obtain once implanted in the uterine wall. Implantation is sometimes accompanied by perfectly normal bleeding as threadlike structures from the baby rupture the small blood vessels that line the uterus at this time of the menstrual cycle. But bleeding can also be a sign of miscarriage, and so it concerns many women who want to become pregnant.

The Embryonic Stage

The **embryonic stage** lasts from implantation until about the eighth week of development. During this stage, the major body organ systems differentiate. Development follows two general trends—**cephalocaudal** (Latin for from "head to tail"), as you can note from the apparently oversized heads of embryos and fetuses at various stages of prenatal development (Figure 16.1), and **proximodistal** (Latin for from "near to far"). The relatively early maturation of the brain and the major organ systems allows them to participate in the nourishment and further development of the unborn child.

Hormones and Prenatal Sexual Differentiation

At about five to six weeks, when the embryo is only a quarter to a half an inch long, nondescript sex organs have been formed. By about the seventh week following conception, the genetic code (XY or XX) begins to assert itself, leading to changes in the internal and external sex organs. If a Y sex chromosome is present, testes will form and begin to produce **androgens** that prompt further masculinization of the sexual organs. In the absence of male sex hormones, the embryo will develop female sex organs.

The Amniotic Sac

The unborn child—embryo and fetus—develops within an **amniotic sac,** a protective environment in the mother's uterus. The sac is surrounded by a clear membrane and contains **amniotic fluid,** in which the developing child is suspended. Amniotic fluid serves as a "shock absorber," preventing the child from being damaged by the mother's movements. It also helps maintain an even temperature.

The Placenta

The **placenta** is a mass of tissue that permits the embryo (and, later on, the fetus) to exchange nutrients and wastes with the mother. The placenta is unique in origin; it grows from material supplied both by mother and embryo. The fetus is connected to the placenta by the **umbilical cord.** The mother is connected to the placenta by the system of blood vessels in the uterine wall.

The circulatory systems of mother and unborn child do not mix. A membrane in the placenta permits only certain substances to pass through. Oxygen and nutrients are passed from the mother to the embryo. Carbon dioxide and other wastes are passed from the child to the mother, where they are removed by the mother's lungs and kidneys. Unfortunately, a number of other substances can pass through the placenta. They include some microscopic disease organisms—such as those that cause syphilis and German measles—and some drugs, including aspirin, narcotics, alcohol, and tranquilizers.

Ultimately, the placenta passes from the woman's body after the child is delivered. For this reason it is also called the "afterbirth."

The Fetal Stage

The fetus begins to turn and respond to external stimulation at about the ninth or tenth week. By the end of the first trimester, the major organ systems have been formed (Arms & Camp, 1987).

The second trimester is characterized by further maturation of fetal organ systems and dramatic gains in size. Toward the end of the second trimester, fetuses are nearing the **age of viability.** Still, only about one baby in ten born at the end of the second trimester who weighs less than two pounds will survive, even with expert medical care (Katchadourian, 1985).

Embryonic stage. The stage of prenatal development that lasts from implantation through the eighth week, characterized by the development of the major organ systems.

Cephalocaudal. From head to tail.

Proximodistal. From the inner part (or axis) of the body outward.

Androgens. Male sex hormones.

Amniotic sac. The sac containing the fetus.

Amniotic fluid. Fluid within the amniotic sac that suspends and protects the fetus.

Placenta. An organ connected to the fetus by the umbilical cord. The placenta serves as a relay station between mother and fetus for exchange of nutrients and wastes.

Umbilical cord. A tube that connects that fetus to the placenta.

Age of viability. The age at which a fetus can sustain independent life.

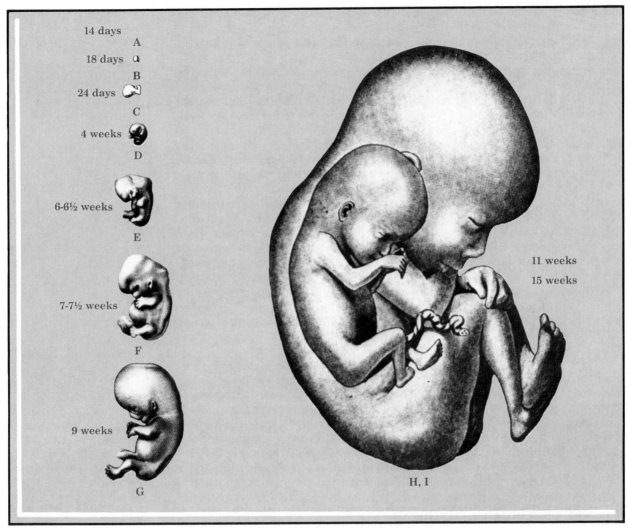

14 days A
18 days B
24 days C
4 weeks D
6-6½ weeks E
7-7½ weeks F
9 weeks G
11 weeks
15 weeks
H, I

FIGURE 16.1 Human Embryos and Fetuses Drawn at Their Actual Sizes

During the third trimester, the heart and lungs become capable of sustaining independent life. The fetus gains about 5 1/2 pounds and doubles in length. Newborn boys average about 7 1/2 pounds and newborn girls about 7 pounds.

Effects of Environmental Influences

Scientific advances have helped us chronicle the details of prenatal development and made us keenly aware of the types of things that can go wrong. Fortunately, they have also alerted us to what we can do to prevent many of these problems. In this section we consider some of the environmental factors that have an impact on our prenatal development: maternal diet, maternal disorders, Rh incompatibility, drugs, smoking, and parental age.

Maternal Diet It is widely believed that fetuses "take what they need" from their mothers, even at the expense of their mothers' nutritional needs. If it were true, pregnant women would not have to be concerned about their diets. But maternal malnutrition, especially during the last trimester when the fetus makes dramatic gains in weight, has been linked to low birth weights and heightened infant mortality (Salkind & Haskins, 1982; Winick, 1981).

Pregnant women require the following food elements in order to maintain themselves and to give birth to healthy babies: protein, most heavily concentrated in meat, fish, poultry, eggs, beans, milk, and cheese; vitamin A, found in milk and vegetables (especially carrots and sweet potatoes); vitamin B, found in vegetables, wheat germ, whole grain breads, and liver; vitamin C, found in citrus fruits; vitamin D, derived from sunshine, fish-liver oil, and vitamin-D-fortified milk; vitamin E, found in whole grains, some vegetables, eggs, and peanuts; folic acid, found in leafy green vegetables; iron, concentrated heavily in meat—especially liver, egg yolks, fish, and raisins; the trace minerals zinc and cobalt, found in seafood; calcium, found in milk and stone-ground grains; and, yes, calories. It should be noted that women who are allergic to some of these foods, or who find them distasteful, can usually find substitutes. Women who eat a well-rounded diet usually do not require food supplements, but most doctors recommend vitamin and mineral supplements to be on the safe side. However, "megavitamins" should probably be avoided, as we shall see below.

Women normally gain 20 to 25 pounds during pregnancy because of the growth of the placenta, amniotic fluid, and the fetus itself. Overweight women may gain less, and slender women may gain 30 pounds or so (Winick, 1981). Regular weight gains are most desirable.

Maternal Disorders   Environmental agents that harm the developing embryo or fetus are referred to as **teratogens,** from the Greek *teras,* meaning "monster." They include drugs such as thalidomide and alcohol, Rh-positive antibodies, metals such as lead and mercury, radiation, excessive hormones, and pathogens. Many pathogens cannot pass through the placenta and infect the embryo, but extremely small organisms, such as those responsible for syphilis, mumps, chicken pox, and measles, can. Pregnant women may also incur disorders such as toxemia that are not passed on to the child but affect the child by altering the maternal environment.

Critical Periods of Vulnerability   Because of the timing of the development of body organs and tissues, there is a timespan, or **critical period,** during which exposure to a particular teratogen is most harmful. For example, the heart develops rapidly during the third to fifth weeks, and as you can see in Figure 16.2, it is most vulnerable during that time. The arms and legs are most vulnerable from the fourth through eighth weeks. Since the major organ systems differentiate by the end of the eighth week, the embryo is generally more vulnerable to teratogens than the fetus.

Let us now consider the effects of alcohol and cigarettes. Effects of other teratogens are summarized in Table 16.1.

Alcohol   Heavy maternal use of alcohol has been associated with death of the fetus and neonate, malformations, and a variety of growth deficiencies (Streissguth et al., 1980). Forty percent or more of the children of severe alcoholics have **fetal alcohol syndrome,** or *FAS* (Jones, 1975). Mothers who drink at least 5 drinks on one occasion and 45 drinks a month are significantly more likely to deliver children with FAS than light drinkers or nondrinkers (Rosett & Sander, 1979). FAS infants are often undersized, with smaller-than-average brains. There are distinct facial features, including widely spaced eyes, a flattened nose, and an underdeveloped upper jaw. There may be mental retardation, lack of coordination, limb deformities, and heart problems (Adickes & Shuman, 1981). FAS babies suck less well than normal babies, are short for their weight, and tend not to catch up (Hollestedt et al., 1983).

Teratogen. An agent that gives rise to abnormalities in the embryo or fetus.

Critical period. A period during which an embryo is particularly vulnerable to a certain teratogen.

Fetal alcohol syndrome. A cluster of symptoms shown by children of women who drink during certain stages of pregnancy, including characteristic facial features and developmental delays. Abbreviated FAS.

An Exercise Class for Pregnant Women
Years ago the rule of thumb was that pregnant women were not to exert themselves. Today it is recognized that exercise during pregnancy is healthful. Exercise promotes cardiovascular fitness and muscle strength, both of which are assets during childbirth—and, of course, at other times.

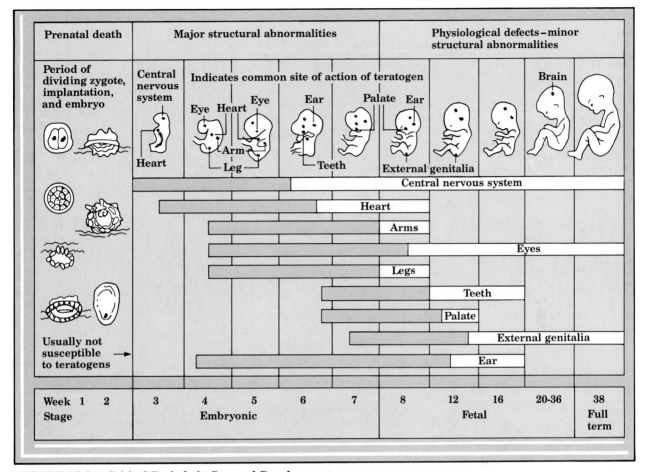

FIGURE 16.2   **Critical Periods in Prenatal Development**
The developing child is most vulnerable to teratogens during the embryonic period, when the organ systems are forming. The periods of greatest vulnerability for organ systems are shown in grey. Periods of lesser vulnerability are shown in white.

FAS and other birth problems have also been found among children of women who drank only one to two ounces of alcohol a day during the embryonic stage (Barr et al., 1984; Hanson et al., 1978; Harlap & Shiono, 1979; Streissguth et al., 1984). The critical period for the development of FAS facial features covers the third and fourth weeks of prenatal development, when the head is starting to take shape. This early in pregnancy, the mother may not realize that she is pregnant. She may simply think that she is "late," and many factors, including stress, can delay menstruation. Many women have light bleeding at implantation, too, and it is possible to confuse this "spotting" with menstruation. The message is this: Women who drink until pregnancy is confirmed may be waiting too long.

The safest course for a pregnant woman is to abstain from alcohol. If she does drink, drinking small amounts of alcohol seems less risky than drinking larger amounts, *but there is no guaranteed safe minimum.* It also makes sense for women who are trying to become pregnant—or who are not taking precautions against becoming pregnant—to assume that they may be conceiving a child any month, and to modify their drinking habits accordingly.

Smoking Cigarettes   Nicotine and carbon monoxide, two of the ingredients of cigarette smoke, are transmitted to the fetus. The effects of nicotine

TABLE 16.1 Possible Effects on the Fetus of Certain Agents during Pregnancy

Agent	Possible Effect
Accutane	Malformation, stillbirth
Alcohol	Mental retardation, addiction, hyperactivity, undersize
Aspirin (large doses)	Respiratory problems, bleeding
Bendectin	Cleft palate? heart deformities?
Caffeine (coffee, many soft drinks, chocolate, etc.)	Stimulates fetus; other effects uncertain
Cigarettes	Undersize, premature delivery, fetal death
Cocaine	Spontaneous abortion, neurological problems
Diethystilbestrol (DES)	Cancer of the cervix or testes
Heavy metals (lead, mercury)	Hyperactivity, mental retardation, stillbirth
Heavy sedation during labor	Brain damage, asphyxiation
Heroin, morphine, other narcotics	Addiction, undersize
Marijuana	Early delivery? Neurological problems? Birth defects?
Paint fumes (substantial exposure)	Mental retardation
PCB, dioxin, other insecticides and herbicides	Under study (possible stillbirth)
Progestin	Masculinization of female embryos, heightened aggressiveness?
Rubella (German measles)	Mental retardation, nerve damage impairing vision and hearing
Streptomycin	Deafness
Tetracycline	Yellow teeth, deformed bones
Thalidomide	Deformed or missing limbs
Vitamin A (large doses)	Cleft palate, eye damage
Vitamin D (large doses)	Mental retardation
X rays	Malformation of organs

Many agents have been found harmful to the fetus, or are strongly implicated in fetal damage. Pregnant women should consult their physicians about their diets, vitamin supplements, and use of any drugs—including nonprescription drugs.

are uncertain, but carbon monoxide decreases the amount of oxygen available to the unborn child. Insufficient oxygen, or **anoxia,** has been linked to mental retardation, learning disorders, and a host of behavioral problems.

Anoxia. Deprivation of oxygen.

Women who smoke during pregnancy are likely to deliver babies who weigh less than women who do not smoke (Linn et al., 1982; Nieberg et al., 1985). Birth weight is related to infant mortality, and women who smoke during pregnancy are also more likely to have stillbirths (Naeye, 1978), or to deliver babies who die soon afterward. Combined maternal drinking and smoking place the child at greater risk for low birthweight than either practice alone (Wright et al., 1983). Maternal smoking may also have negative long-term effects on academic performance (Landesman-Dwyer & Emanuel, 1979; Naeye & Peters, 1984; Streissguth et al., 1984).

Paternal smoking may also hold dangers. Men who smoke are more likely than nonsmokers to produce abnormal sperm. Evans (1981) found that men who smoke have children with higher rates of birth defects and infant mortality.

Parental Age From a biological vantage point, there is little doubt that the 20s are the ideal time for women to bear children. Women in their middle teens and younger, and women in their late 30s and beyond show dramatically greater incidences of miscarriage, birth defects, prematurity, and infant mortality.

There is also evidence that women's fertility declines after age 30 (Schwartz & Mayaux, 1982). All these negatives are dismaying for the career woman who wants to delay marriage and childbearing. Psychologically, many women, like many men, feel that they are only "coming into their own" as persons in their 30s, after they have had a chance to assess their effectiveness in, and feelings about, the world of business. It seems cruel that the biological clock can be running out when the outlook remains youthful. On the other hand, many women do bear children successfully in their 30s and beyond. We cannot ignore statistics if we are to make rational decisions, but it is comforting to know that we are people and not probabilities.

Effects of Chromosomal and Genetic Abnormalities

A number of diseases reflect chromosomal or genetic abnormalities. Some genetic abnormalities, such as phenylketonuria, are caused by a single pair of genes; others are caused by combinations of genes. A number of chromosomal and genetic abnormalities are summarized in Table 16.2.

Genetic Counseling and Prenatal Testing

In an effort to help parents avert predictable tragedies, **genetic counseling** has become widely offered. In this procedure, information about a couple's genetic backgrounds is compiled to determine the possibility that their union

TABLE 16.2   Some Chromosomal and Genetic Abnormalities

Cystic fibrosis	A genetic disease in which the pancreas and lungs become clogged with mucus, impairing the processes of respiration and digestion.
Down syndrome	A condition characterized by a third chromosome on the 21st pair in which the child shows a characteristic fold of skin over the eye and mental retardation. Risk increases as parents increase in age.
Hemophilia	A sex-linked disorder in which the blood fails to clot properly.
Huntington's chorea	A fatal neurological disorder with onset in middle adulthood.
Neural-tube defects	Disorders of the brain or spine, such as *anencephaly,* in which part of the brain is missing, and *spina bifida,* in which part of the spine is exposed or missing. Anencephaly is fatal shortly after birth, but some spina bifida victims survive for a number of years, albeit with severe handicaps.
Phenylketonuria	A disorder in which children cannot metabolize phenylalanine, which builds up in the form of phenylpyruvic acid and causes mental retardation. Diagnosed at birth and controlled by diet.
Retinoblastoma	A form of blindness caused by a dominant gene.
Sickle-cell anemia	A blood disorder that mostly afflicts blacks and obstructs small blood vessels, decreasing their capacity to carry oxygen, and heightening the risk of occasionally fatal injections.
Tay-Sachs disease	A fatal neurological disorder that afflicts Jews of European origin.

may result in genetically defective children. Some couples whose natural children would be at high risk for genetic diseases elect to adopt.

Amniocentesis   Pregnant women may also confirm the presence of certain genetic and chromosomal abnormalities in their children through **amniocentesis,** a procedure carried out about 15 weeks after conception (Figure 16.3). Fluid is withdrawn from the amniotic sac (also called the "bag of waters") containing the fetus. Sloughed-off fetal cells are grown in a culture and examined for genetic abnormalities.

Amniocentesis is commonly carried out with women who become pregnant past the age of 35, because the chances of Down syndrome increase dramatically as women approach or pass the age of 40 (Abrams & Bennet, 1981). But women carrying the children of aging fathers may also wish to have amniocentesis since one in four cases of Down syndrome have been linked to abnormal cell division in sperm (Holmes, 1978). Amniocentesis can detect the presence of sickle-cell anemia, Tay-Sachs disease, spina bifida, muscular dystrophy, and Rh incompatibility in the fetus.

Amniocentesis also permits parents to learn the sex of their unborn child through examination of the 23rd pair of chromosomes. But amniocentesis carries some risks, and it is unwise to have the procedure done solely for this purpose. If you were having amniocentesis, would you want to know the sex of your unborn child, or would you prefer to wait?

Ultrasound   Another common method of prenatal testing is the use of **ultrasound** to form a picture of the fetus. The picture is referred to as a *sonogram.* "Ultrasound" is so high in pitch that it cannot be detected by the human ear. However, it can be "bounced off" the unborn child in the same way that radar is bounced off objects in order to form a "picture" of the object.

Ultrasound is used with amniocentesis to determine the position of the fetus. Ultrasound is also used to locate fetal structures when intrauterine transfusions are necessary for the survival of the unborn child in Rh disease.

Chorionic Villi Sampling   **Chorionic villi sampling** (CVS) is similar to amniocentesis. CVS is carried out during the seventh or eighth week of pregnancy. A small tube is inserted through the vagina into the uterus, and pieces of material from the outer membrane that contains the amniotic sac are snipped off. Results are available within days. CVS is used in the place of amniocentesis but is riskier and not so widely used.

Blood Tests   The presence of a variety of disorders can be detected by testing the blood of the parents. For instance, the recessive genes causing sickle-cell anemia and Tay-Sachs disease can be detected from analysis of blood samples. If both parents carry genes for these disorders, their presence in the fetus can be confirmed by amniocentesis or CVS.

■ Childbirth

During the last few weeks of her pregnancy, Deborah continued to, as she put it, "drag myself into work. I wasn't just going to sit home all day watching *As the World Turns* like a dunce." Your first author has (secretly) watched *As the World Turns* since Dr. Bob Hughes was a little boy, and so he ignored that part of what Deborah said. (Your second author does not watch soap operas.) She added, "But since I was so exhausted by the time I got to the office, I sat behind my desk like—well—half a dunce. I also couldn't get my mind off the pregnancy—what it was going to be like when I finally delivered Jason, or, I should say, when he finally delivered me. I'd had the amniocentesis, but I

Amniocentesis. A procedure for drawing and examining fetal cells sloughed off into amniotic fluid in order to determine the presence of various disorders.

Ultrasound. Sound waves too high in pitch to be sensed by the human ear.

Chorionic villi sampling. A method for detecting genetic abnormalities that samples the membrane enveloping the amniotic sac and fetus.

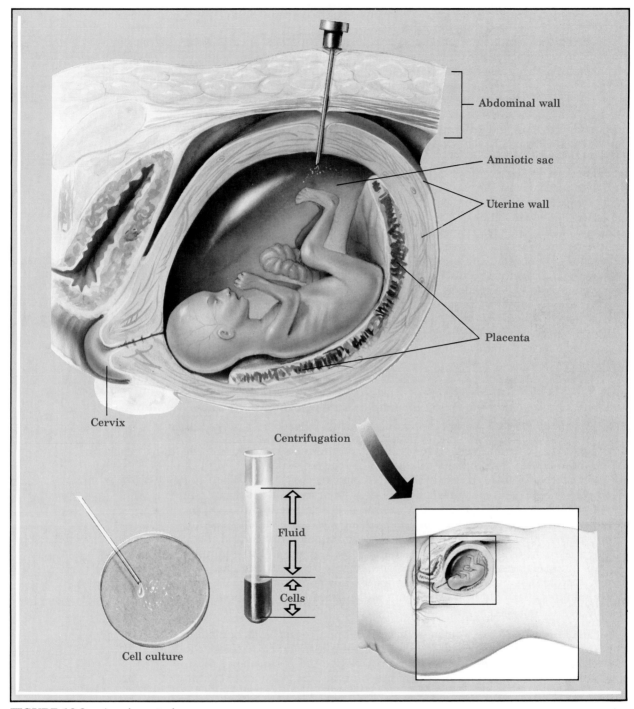

Abdominal wall

Amniotic sac

Uterine wall

Placenta

Cervix

Centrifugation

Fluid

Cells

Cell culture

FIGURE 16.3   Amniocentesis

This modern method for examining the genetic material sloughed off by a fetus into amniotic fluid allows the prenatal identification of certain genetic and chromosomal abnormalities. Amniocentesis also allows parents to learn the sex of their unborn child. Would you want to know?

was still hoping and praying everything would be normal with him. And it was just so darned* hard to get around.

During the last weeks of pregnancy it is normal, especially for first-time mothers, to worry about the mechanics of delivery and whether the child will be normal. As they near full **term,** women become increasingly heavy and, literally, "bent out of shape." It may require a feat of balance and ingenuity to get up from a chair or out of bed. Sitting behind a steering wheel—and still reaching the wheel—becomes a challenge of life. Muscle tension from supporting the fetus and other intrauterine material may cause backaches. At this time many women have the feeling that their pregnancies will never come to an end.

They do, of course. Or else this book would not have been written.

The mechanisms that initiate and maintain labor are not fully understood, but the first step might be secretion of hormones by the fetus. Perhaps the fetus chemically signals the mother when it is mature enough to sustain independent life. The fetal hormones would act by stimulating the placenta and the uterus to secrete prostaglandins. Prostaglandins, in turn, cause labor contractions by exciting the muscles of the uterus. Later during labor the pituitary gland releases **oxytocin,** a hormone that stimulates contractions strong enough to expel the baby.

Now let us consider the stages of childbirth, methods of childbirth, and some of the problems that can attend childbirth. In our discussion we shall refer to the many things that women can do to moderate the impact of stress, such as enhancing predictability, exercising control, and receiving social support.

The Stages of Childbirth

Childbirth begins with the onset of regular uterine contractions and is described in three stages.

The First Stage In the first stage of childbirth, uterine contractions cause the cervix to become **effaced** and **dilated** so that the baby may pass. Most of the pain of childbirth is caused by the stretching of the cervix. When the cervix dilates easily and quickly, there may be little or no pain at all.

The first stage may last from a few minutes to a couple of days. Twelve to 24 hours is about average for a first pregnancy. Later pregnancies require about half this time. The initial contractions are not usually very painful. They may be spaced 15 to 20 minutes apart and last from 45 seconds to a minute.

As time elapses, contractions become more frequent, regular, and strong. A woman is usually informed to go the hospital when they are four to five minutes apart. She will usually not be admitted to a labor room until the end of the first stage.

"Prepping" If the woman is to be "prepped"—that is, if her pubic hair is to be shaved—it takes place now. The prep is intended to lower the chances of infection during delivery and to facilitate the performance of an **episiotomy** (described below). A woman may now also be given an enema in order to prevent an involuntary bowel movement during contractions of labor. However, many women find prepping and enemas degrading and seek obstetricians who do not perform them routinely. The medical necessity of these procedures has been questioned (Hahn & Paige, 1980).

The Second Stage The woman may be taken to a delivery room for the second stage of childbirth, which begins when the baby first appears at the opening of the birth canal. The second stage is shorter than the first stage, lasting from a few minutes to a few hours, and ending with the birth of the baby.

*This word has been modified in order to maintain the decorum of a college textbook.

With each contraction in the second stage, the skin surrounding the birth canal stretches farther, and the baby is pushed farther along. When the baby's head starts to emerge from the birth canal, it is said to have *crowned*. Typically, the baby then fully emerges within a few minutes.

Only a couple of decades ago the husband was systematically excluded from the delivery room, and he was pictured, stereotypically, as pacing up and down awaiting news of the birth of his child. Today, however, the husband is more likely than not to participate in the birth process (May & Perrin, 1985).

The Episiotomy   When the baby's head has crowned, the obstetrician, nurse, or midwife may perform an **episiotomy.** Most women do not feel the incision because pressure from the baby's emerging head tends to numb the area. The episiotomy, like prepping and the enema, is controversial and is not practiced in Europe. The incision may cause itching and, in some cases, stabbing pain as it heals. Discomfort from an episiotomy may interfere with sexual relations for several months following delivery. Still, most physicians argue that an episiotomy is preferable to random tearing when they see that the tissue of the **perineum** is becoming severely effaced.

In the New World   The baby's passageway to the outside world is at best a tight fit. For this reason, the shape of the baby's head and facial features may be distended. The head may be molded (elongated), the nose may be flattened—as though our new arrival had been involved in a vicious prize fight—and the ears may be bent. Parents are frequently concerned about whether things will return to their proper shapes, but usually they do.

Once the baby's head emerges from the mother's body, mucus is usually aspirated from its mouth by suction, so that the passageway for breathing will not be obstructed. Aspiration is frequently repeated when the baby is fully delivered. Because of the use of suction, the baby is no longer routinely held upside down to help expel mucus. There is also no need for the baby to be slapped on the buttocks to stimulate independent breathing, as we see in so many old films.

Once the baby is breathing adequately on its own, the umbilical cord, through which it had received oxygen from the mother, is clamped and severed. The stump will dry and fall off. Whether the child will have an "inny" or an "outy" has nothing to do with the expertise or cosmetic preferences of the obstetrician.

The baby may then be taken by a nurse, so that various procedures can be performed while the mother is in the third stage of labor. Now the baby is usually given a plastic identification bracelet and footprinted. Drops of silver nitrate or an antibiotic ointment (erythromycin) are put into the baby's eyes to prevent gonorrheal infection. The newborn may also receive an injection of Vitamin K to ensure that the baby's blood will clot normally in case of bleeding.

The Third Stage   During the third or *placental* stage of childbirth, which may last from a few minutes to an hour or more, the placenta separates from the uterine wall and is expelled along with fetal membranes. There may be some bleeding, and the uterus begins the process of contracting to a smaller size. The attending physician sews the episiotomy and any tears in the perineum.

Methods of Childbirth

Until this century, childbirth typically was an intimate home procedure involving the mother, a **midwife,** family, and friends. In our culture today it is most often a hospital procedure performed by a physician who uses surgical instruments and anesthetics to help protect mother and child from infection,

Episiotomy. A surgical incision in the perineum that widens the vaginal opening, preventing random tearing during childbirth.

Perineum. The area between the female's genital region and the anus.

Midwife. A woman who helps other women in childbirth.

complications, and pain. While the use of modern medicine has saved lives, it has also made childbearing more impersonal. Social critics argue that it has, to a large degree, wrested control over their own bodies from women and, through drugs, denied them the experience of giving birth.

In this section we consider a number of contemporary methods for facilitating childbirth.

Medicated Childbirth

In sorrow thou shalt bring forth children.

—Genesis 3:16

The Bible suggests that the ancients saw suffering during childbirth as a woman's lot. But today, some anesthesia is used in more than 90 percent of U.S. deliveries.

General anesthesia affects the entire body by putting the woman to sleep. Sodium pentothal, a barbiturate, is frequently used and injected into the vein of the arm. Tranquilizers such as Valium and Librium and orally taken barbiturates are not anesthetics, but they reduce anxiety, which can compound the stress produced by pain. Narcotics such as Demerol also blunt perception of pain.

General anesthetics, tranquilizers, and narcotics decrease the strength of uterine contractions during delivery and, by crossing the placental membrane, lower the overall responsiveness of the baby. They have an immediate effect on the child, and the higher the dosage, the greater their impact.

The major question is whether these anesthetics have long-term effects on the child. Evidence is mixed. Some studies show no long-term effects. Others suggest that children whose mothers received heavy doses of anesthetics during delivery lag in their motor development and cognitive functioning at the ages of 1 year and beyond (Brackbill, 1976, 1979; Goldstein et al., 1976). But there is little suggestion that these effects are severe.

Regional anesthetics, or **local anesthetics**—also referred to as "blocks"— attempt to deaden the pain of childbirth without depressing the mother's central nervous system or putting her to sleep. For these reasons it has also been hoped that they would also have less impact on the baby. But local anesthesia does decrease the strength and lower the activity levels of babies, at least during the hours following birth (Lester et al., 1982; Murray et al., 1981; Scanlon et al., 1974). Again, we are not aware of serious long-term effects.

It should also be noted that women who have general anesthesia and are unconscious throughout childbirth have more negative feelings about childbirth and the baby than women using any other method. Women who receive spinal or other "blocks" have relatively more positive feelings about childbirth and their babies, but they feel detached from the childbirth process (Leifer, 1980).

Natural Childbirth   Partly as a reaction against the use of anesthetics, English obstetrician Grantly Dick-Read endorsed **natural childbirth** in his 1932 book, *Childbirth Without Fear.* Dick-Read argued that women's labor pains were heightened by their fear of the unknown and resultant muscle tensions. Dick-Read presaged modern practices by educating women about the biological aspects of reproduction and delivery, by encouraging physical fitness, and by teaching them breathing exercises and relaxation.

Prepared Childbirth: The Lamaze Method   The French obstetrician Fernand Lamaze (1981) visited the Soviet Union in 1951 and found that many Russian women appeared to bear babies without anesthetics or pain. Lamaze took back to Western Europe with him the techniques of the Russian women,

General anesthesia. The process of eliminating pain by putting the person to sleep.

Local anesthetic. A method that reduces pain in an area of the body.

Natural childbirth. Dick-Read's method of childbirth in which women use no anesthesia and are educated about childbirth and strategies for coping with discomfort.

■ WHAT DO YOU SAY NOW?

Selecting an Obstetrician

Congratulations! You're pregnant. You are about to have one of the most stimulating experiences of your life. But pregnancy is also stressful physically and because it carries with it a number of life changes. One of the things that you need to do very soon to make things more healthful and less stressful for you and for your baby is to select an obstetrician. Many women are informed about obstetricians by friends and relatives. Others, especially women in a new location, rely on the phonebook.

In either case, there are some things you will want to know about the obstetrician and some questions that you will need to ask. Many of them concern the degree to which the obstetrician will allow you to be in control of your own childbirth. Write down some of the things you would be interested in asking in the spaces below, and then see the following material for some suggestions.

1. _____
   _____

2. _____
   _____

3. _____
   _____

1. As in consulting any helping professional, you might be interested in inquiring about the obstetrician's academic credentials and experience. Degrees, licenses, and certificates about residencies should be clearly posted. If they are not, you might want to ask why they are not. Now get going on your other questions. Ask a lot of them; you're going to be bursting with questions over the next several months, and if your obstetrician does not handle them well now,

you would be in for a long, uncomfortable haul with him or her.

2. You might want to ask what kinds of problems the obstetrician runs into most often and how he or she handles them. This is an indirect way of inquiring about frequency of Caesareans, for example, and you never know what "bombshells" will be dropped when you ask an open-ended question.

3. Of course, you can follow up by asking directly, "What percentage of your deliveries are Caesareans?" Remember that 20 percent seems to be the national average these days. If you lean in the direction of not wanting a C-section unless absolutely necessary, you can also ask something like, "I've been reading that too many Caesareans are done these days. What do you think?"

4. Ask something like, "What are your attitudes toward medication?" You'll quickly get a sense of whether the obstetrician is open-minded about medication and willing to follow your lead.

5. Ask something like, "What do you see as the role of the father during childbirth?" You'll quickly learn whether the obstetrician's attitudes coincide with your own.

6. You may also want to ask questions about the obstetrician's beliefs concerning routine testing, weight gains, vitamin supplements, use of amniocentesis or ultrasound, and a whole range of issues. Each will give you an opportunity to determine how the obstetrician is relating to you as a person as well as to obtain specific information.

7. Finally, this is not something to say, but it is essential: See how the obstetrician handles you during the initial examination. You should have the feeling that you are being handled gently, respectfully, and competently. If you're not sure, try some comparison shopping. It's your body and your child, and you have the right to gather enough information so that you are confident you are making the right choice.

and during the 1950s they were brought to the U.S.A. as the **Lamaze method,** or *prepared childbirth*. In essence, Lamaze argues that women can learn to *dissociate* uterine contractions from pain and fear by associating *other* responses with contractions. Women can be taught to think of pleasant images such as beach scenes during delivery. They can also lessen pain through breathing and relaxation exercises.

A woman attends Lamaze classes accompanied by a "coach." The coach is the person—usually the father—who will aid her in the delivery room by timing contractions, offering moral support, and coaching her in patterns of breathing and relaxation. During each contraction, the woman breathes in a specific, rehearsed manner. She is taught how to relax muscle groups throughout her body, then how to contract a single muscle while others remain at ease. The rationale is that during labor she will be able, upon cue, to keep other muscles relaxed while the uterus contracts. In this way she will conserve energy, minimize tension and pain, and feel less anxiety. Too, mus-

Lamaze method. A childbirth method in which women are educated about childbirth, learn to relax and breathe in patterns that conserve energy and lessen pain, and have a coach (usually the father) present during childbirth. Also termed *prepared childbirth*.

cles that will be used during delivery, such as leg muscles, are strengthened through exercise.

The woman is also educated about childbirth and given an agenda of things to do during delivery. The father is integrated into the process, and it has been reported that the marital relationship is strengthened and the woman feels less alone during delivery as a result (Dooker, 1980; Wideman & Singer, 1984). The father as well as the mother take pride in "their" accomplishment of childbirth (Bing, 1983). It also seems that women report less pain and request less medication when their husbands are present (Henneborn & Cogan, 1975).

The Lamaze method appears to have considerably decreased the stress of childbirth for many women. Women using the method have generally positive feelings about childbirth and about their babies (Leifer, 1980). Still, they usually report some pain and often request anesthetics. How, then, does the Lamaze method help? Perhaps it is in part because women enhance their self-esteem by taking charge of their own delivery (Dooker, 1980; May & Perrin, 1985). They become knowledgeable about childbirth and perceive themselves as the central actors in the process, not as passive victims who need the guidance of the doctor. The breathing and relaxation exercises do not fully eradicate pain, but they give the woman coping strategies and something else to focus on.

"Birth without Violence": The Leboyer Method

Natural and prepared methods of childbirth address the comfort of the mother. In *Birth Without Violence,* French physician Frederick LeBoyer (1975) advocates another form of reaction against the institutionalization of childbearing: He focuses on gently easing the infant into the world.

In the **Leboyer method,** or *gentle birth,* the physician or midwife eases the baby along the birth canal, with fingers under its armpits. Traditional hospital delivery rooms are noisy, harshly lit places where babies are separated from their mothers after birth. Leboyer tames the hospital setting by lowering the lighting and instructing attendants to keep their voices hushed. After birth, the baby is placed on its mother's warm abdomen and is held by her until it breathes strongly on its own. Only then is the umbilical cord cut. Next, the baby is given a warm bath—frequently by the father (Berezin, 1980). When it opens its eyes and flexes its limbs, it is returned to the mother for cuddling and suckling.

There is little research on the Leboyer method. One study compared babies delivered by the Leboyer method to babies delivered by other means (Nelson et al., 1980). No differences were found in the responsiveness of the babies nor in the health of the babies or their mothers. At eight-month followups the mothers reported that they *thought* that the Leboyer method had helped their children, even though their views were not supported by objective evidence. Perhaps the Leboyer method is a potent "sugar pill," or placebo. We should also note that many contemporary hospital delivery rooms have been modified along lines suggested by Leboyer, and that babies are usually given to their mothers as soon as a few important routines have been carried out.

Caesarean Section

In a **Caesarean section,** the baby is delivered by surgery rather than through the vagina. In this procedure, by which Julius Caesar is said to have been delivered, incisions are made in the abdomen and the uterus, and the baby is removed. The incisions are sewn, and in most cases the mother is capable of walking about on the same day, although there is discomfort. In previous years, the incisions left visible scars, but today "C-sections" tend to be performed near the top line of the pubic hair. This "bikini cut" is all but invisible.

Leboyer method. A childbirth method that focuses on gently easing the neonate into the world. Also termed *gentle childbirth.*

Caesarean section. A method of childbirth in which the neonate is delivered through a surgical incision in the abdomen.

The C-section is becoming more common. It is used in about 20 percent of U.S. childbirths today, as compared with 10.4 percent in 1975 and 17 percent in 1980 (Clark & Witherspoon, 1984; Gleicher, 1984). It is most likely to be used when normal delivery is expected to be difficult or threatening to the mother or the child. Difficult deliveries can occur when the mother is weak or fatigued, the baby is very large, or the baby is in the **breech position** or the **transverse position.**

Anesthetics make C-sections pain-free, but women who receive them run a higher risk of infection than women who deliver vaginally, and recovery is prolonged. Psychologically, C-sections can be depressing. Women often take pride in childbirth as something only they can do, and C-section can cause women to see themselves as failures. Research has not uncovered any notable long-term differences between children who are born vaginally or by C-section.

The Postpartum Period

The weeks following delivery are called the **postpartum period.** The first few days of postpartum are frequently happy ones. The long wait is over. The discomforts (and fear) of labor are done with. In the great majority of cases the baby is normal, and the mother may be pleased that she is getting her "figure back." However, some women feel a great deal of depression at this time. In this section we discuss two issues concerning the postpartum period: maternal depression and "bonding."

Maternal Depression   Women may encounter one of two types of depression during the postpartum period: maternity blues or postartum depression.

Maternity Blues   The first type of depression is less severe. It is called **maternity blues,** and it is experienced by 50 to 80 percent of new mothers (Hopkins et al., 1984; Stein, 1982). The maternity blues are characterized by sadness, crying, anxiety and tension, irritability, and anger. Fortunately, they only last for about two days.

Great hormonal changes follow delivery and may play a role. Estrogen and progesterone levels drop off, while prolactin and oxytocin are secreted to facilitate breast-feeding. Oxytocin also stimulates uterine contractions and reduces bleeding.

Maternity blues are also more common following a first pregnancy, and

Breech position. A feet-downward position in which the fetus's backside first enters the birth canal.

Transverse position. A position in which the fetus lies crosswise across the opening to the birth canal.

Postpartum period. The period that immediately follows childbirth.

Maternity blues. Crying and feelings of sadness, anxiety and tension, irritability, and anger that half or more of women experience for a couple of days or so after childbirth.

▨ A CLOSER LOOK

A Family-Centered Approach to Childbirth

In recent years, childbirth has been becoming more family-centered, as opposed to hospital- or doctor-centered. In her book *The Psychology of Women,* Margaret Matlin (1987) of the State University of New York at Geneseo summarizes some of the trends toward family-centered childbirth:

1. Labor is not artificially induced simply because it is more convenient for the physician.
2. The motive for doing a Caesarean section in a given case is seriously considered.
3. Women are allowed to take an upright (sitting) position during delivery, rather than the flat-on-the-table, feet-in-the-stirrups approach.
4. Birth practices that have little or no health benefits—such as *routine* enema, shaving of the genital area, forbidding the consumption of food, and episiotomy—are reconsidered.
5. Routine use of anesthetics is reconsidered.
6. A supportive family member or friend is present.
7. Alternative physical locations for childbirth are explored.
8. Siblings are permitted to share in the birth of the new baby, and they are carefully prepared for the event.

they may reflect adjustment problems. After all, new mothers are frequently overwhelmed by their new responsibilities and the changes that are about to take place in their daily lives. New fathers might feel "paternity blues" but for the fact that the child-rearing chores usually fall squarely on the shoulders of the mother.

Postpartum Depression   About 10 to 15 percent of women have severe feelings of depression that last for several weeks following delivery (Cutrona & Troutman, 1986; Hopkins et al., 1984; O'Hara et al., 1984). These feelings are termed **postpartum depression,** and they are characterized by extreme sadness, apathy, despair, feelings of worthlessness, difficulty concentrating, and physical symptoms such as headaches and digestive problems.

Postpartum depression may reflect physiological and psychological factors. The hormonal changes in maternity blues may also be linked to postpartum depression. Moreover, women who encounter postpartum depression are more likely to have had depressive episodes prior to and during pregnancy, suggesting that they may be physiologically or psychologically predisposed toward depression (O'Hara et al., 1984). But women who encounter postpartum depression are under greater stress than women who do not. Postpartum depression, like maternity blues, may be heightened by concerns about maternal adequacy and the changes that will occur in personal and family life (Gansberg & Mostel, 1984; Hoffnung, 1984). Years of new responsibility lie ahead. For better or worse, life will never be the same. Some women, of course, may feel depressed because they did not want or plan for the baby. Women who feel helpless and guilty are more likely than others to encounter prolonged depressive episodes related to such issues (Cutrona, 1983).

Infants with difficult temperaments may also contribute to postpartum depression. Their intense emotional reactions, prolonged and vigorous crying episodes, and irregular sleeping and eating patterns are stressful in and of themselves. They also place a severe strain on the mother's sense of competence (Cutrona & Troutman, 1986). A network of social support is helpful to the mother at this time. Unfortunately, if she is isolated in the home, and if relatives live far away, such support may be hard to come by, and depression may persist.

Bonding   In recent years the notion that the first hours of postpartum provide a special opportunity for **bonding** between parents and newborns has spread into the culture—largely because of a study by physicians John Kennell and Marshall Klaus and their colleagues (Kennell et al., 1974). Kennell and Klaus held the belief that the first few hours after birth present a "maternal-sensitive" period during which the mother is particularly disposed, largely because of hormone levels, to form a bond with her baby. The researchers recruited 28 mothers and their full-term babies for the study. Most of the women were unwed, impoverished, and poorly educated.

Half the women were randomly assigned to standard hospital procedure, in which their babies were whisked away to the nursery shortly after birth. Throughout the remainder of the hospital stay, the babies visited with their mothers for half-hour periods at feeding time. The other group of mothers spent a half-hour with their neonates within three hours after birth. They spent five hours a day with their infants for the remainder of the stay. The hospital staff encouraged and reassured the group of mothers who had extended contact.

Follow-ups over a two-year period suggested that extended contact had enormous benefits for the mothers and children (Klaus & Kennell, 1976). Extended-contact mothers were more likely than controls to cuddle their ba-

Postpartum depression. More severe, prolonged depression that afflicts 10 to 15 percent of women after childbirth, and is characterized by sadness, apathy, feelings of worthlessness, difficulty concentrating, and physical symptoms.

Bonding. The process of creating feelings of attachment (bonds of affection) between parent and child.

Rooming-in. A practice in which the neonate remains with the mother in the hospital room throughout their stay.

bies, pick them up and soothe them when they cried, enjoy their presence, and worry about them in their absence. At 1 year of age, the extended-contact infants outscored controls on measures of physical and intellectual development. The advantages extended into the second year. Extended-contact mothers had more interaction with their infants. They were warmer, more encouraging, and less likely to give commands.

Since this landmark study, similar research has been carried out with subjects drawn from different social classes in various countries around the world. Most studies confirm the finding that extended early contact leads to better parent–child relationships and superior development, at least on a short-term basis (Goldberg, 1983; Thomson & Kramer, 1984). Studies on the effects of early extended father contact with newborns have shown comparable results. Extended-contact fathers engage in more face-to-face interaction with their infants several months afterward (Keller et al., 1981; Rodhölm, 1981).

But these studies are fraught with methodological problems (Chess & Thomas, 1982; Goldberg, 1983; Lamb, 1982; Myers, 1984; Svejda et al., 1980; Thomson & Kramer, 1984). For one thing, sample size was generally limited. For another, the definition of "extended early contact" varied considerably from study to study. In the Rodhölm (1981) study, for example, fathers in the extended-contact group held their newborns for *ten minutes* after birth, whereas controls caught only a glimpse of their children. Compare this to the five hours a day in the Kennell and Klaus study.

The most telling criticism is that we cannot sort out the effects of extended contact from those that stem from parents' knowledge that they were in a "special" group. Not only did mothers in the Kennell and Klaus study receive extra time with their babies, but the hospital staff showed active interest in them and gave them encouragement and support. Did their infants fare better because of superior "bonding," or because the hospital staff taught them that their relationships with their children were special and instructed them as to how to hold their babies, play with them, and care for them? Because of such criticisms as these, even Kennell and Klaus (1984) have toned down their views in their more recent writings. They now view the hours after birth as just one element in a complex and prolonged bonding process.

Regardless of the validity of these studies, awareness of the possible importance of early parent–child contact has revolutionized U.S. hospital policies. In 1983, when the first author's daughter Jordan was born in Princeton, New Jersey, her 2-year-old sister Allyn and he were encouraged to be with her at certain hours of the day for "bonding time." What a difference from Margaret Matlin's experience:

> When my oldest daughter was born in 1970, a nurse yelled at me for unwrapping her from her blanket-cocoon, and I contemplated hiding her under my bedsheets to prolong our visit beyond the specified 30 minutes. **Rooming-in** reminds everyone that the baby belongs to the mother, and not to the hospital (Matlin, 1987, p. 377).

Of course the first hours are "special." There has been a major life change for parents and siblings, and a new person has (literally) emerged upon the scene, with all the potential physical and emotional strengths and weaknesses to which we all fall heir. But research is not compelling that these hours are critical, or that failure to "form bonds" during this time will result in a second-rate parent–child relationship (Korsch, 1983). There are countless millions of fine parent–child relationships in which the parents were denied these early hours with their children (Rutter, 1981).

The message for parents may well be to relax and not worry about how well their "bonding" with their neonate is going. Still, like chicken soup, a little extra contact probably won't hurt.

■ Rearing Competent Children: How to Be an Authoritative Parent

One of the purposes of this book has been to enhance readers' competence in coping with the challenges of their lives. Research by University of California psychologist Diana Baumrind suggests that we, as parents, may also be able to foster what Baumrind calls **instrumental competence** in our children.

Instrumentally competent children are generally energetic and friendly. They are capable of manipulating their environments to achieve desired effects. Compared to other children, they tend to show self-reliance and independence, high levels of activity, maturity in the formation of goals and achievement orientation, cooperativeness and assertiveness in social relationships, and exploratory behavior.

In her search for the patterns of child rearing that might lead to instrumental competence, Baumrind (1968, 1973; Lamb & Baumrind, 1978) studied four areas of parental behavior: the extent of efforts to influence the behavior of the child; demands for the child to achieve high levels of intellectual, emotional, and social skills; communications ability; and parental warmth and involvement.

In her research, Baumrind found five patterns of child rearing: authoritative, authoritarian, permissive, nonconformist, and harmonious.

Authoritative Parents   The parents of the most instrumentally competent children were rated as high in all four areas of behavior (see Table 16.3). They made strong efforts to control their children (that is, were highly restrictive) and they made strong maturity demands. However, their restrictiveness and demands were accompanied by ability to reason with their children and by strong support and feelings of love. The parents of the most competent children expected a lot. But they also explained why and supported their children. Baumrind labeled these parents **authoritative** to suggest that they knew very clearly what they wanted, but that they were also loving and respectful of their children's points of view.

Authoritarian Parents   **Authoritarian** parents, by contrast, tend to look upon obedience as a virtue to be pursued for its own sake. Authoritarian parents believe in strict guidelines for determining what is right and wrong. They demand that their children accept these guidelines without question.

Instrumental competence. Ability to manipulate the environment to achieve desired effects.

Authoritative. Descriptive of parents who demand mature behavior, reason with their children, and provide love and encouragement.

Authoritarian. Descriptive of parents who demand obedience for its own sake.

TABLE 16.3   Baumrind's Patterns of Parenting

	Parental Behavior Patterns			
Parental Style	Restrictiveness	Demands for Mature Behavior	Communications Ability	Warmth and Support
Authoritarian	High (Physical punishments)	Moderate	Low	Low
Authoritative	High (Reasoning)	High	High	High
Permissive	Low (Lax)	Low	Low	High
Noncomformist	Low (Purposeful)	Moderate	Moderate	High
Harmonious	?	High	High	High

According to Baumrind, the children of authoritative parents show the greatest instrumental competence, while the children of permissive parents are the least mature.

Like authoritative parents, they are controlling. Unlike authoritative parents, their enforcement methods rely on coercion. Moreover, authoritarian parents communicate poorly with their children. They do not respect their children's points of view, and they are cold and rejecting.

In Baumrind's research, the children of authoritarian parents also developed some degree of independence, although other researchers have found them to be less competent socially and academically than children of authoritative parents (Maccoby & Martin, 1983). Children of authoritarian parents also tend to be conflicted and irritable. They are less friendly and spontaneous in their social interactions (Maccoby & Martin, 1983). Perhaps they have learned to be cautious in relating to others.

Permissive versus Nonconformist Parents Baumrind found two types of parents who were permissive as opposed to restrictive. She labeled one type "permissive" and the other "nonconformist." **Permissive** parents, as their label suggests, were rated low in their attempts to control their children and in their demands for mature behavior. Their brand of permissiveness also tended to cluster with high nurturance (warmth and support) but poor communication ability. The children, in short, were loved and accepted. However, they and their parents did not understand each other very well, and they did pretty much as they wished.

The **nonconformist** parents were also permissive in many ways. But the parents Baumrind labeled "permissive" tended to be disorganized and easygoing. Nonconformist parents, by contrast, were intellectually committed to allowing their children the freedom to develop their own abilities and points of view. Nonconformist parents actually had very high expectations for their children, which they communicated to them. Permissive parents, by contrast, were less involved.

It is not surprising, then, that the children of permissive and nonconformist parents show major differences. By and large, the children of permissive parents seem the least responsible and mature. They are frequently impulsive, moody, and aggressive. As infants they seem insecure in their relationships with their parents (Egeland & Sroufe, 1981). In adolescence, lack of parental monitoring is often linked to delinquency and poor academic performance (Loeb et al., 1980; Martin, 1981; Patterson, 1982; Pulkkinen, 1982).

The *sons* of nonconformist parents show a good deal of independence and a high achievement orientation, according to Baumrind. The daughters of nonconformist parents, however, are similar to those of authoritarian and permissive parents: They have little ambition and are somewhat withdrawn and dependent. We are at a loss to account for this sex difference. Perhaps nonconformist parents somehow impart an activist orientation to their sons, but not to their daughters.

Harmonious Parents A fifth group of parents was characterized by Baumrind as harmonious. Harmonious parents were high in their demands for mature behavior, their communication ability, and their warmth and support. However, since their children lived up to their expectations and little family friction was generated, there was no basis for rating their restrictiveness.

Baumrind's research does not prove that certain child-rearing patterns *cause* the outcomes described. Children also come into the world with predispositions toward developing their own personality traits. It could be that authoritativeness and instrumental competence tend to go together for genetic reasons. On the other hand, Baumrind's research suggests that we can make an effort to avoid some of the pitfalls of being authoritarian or overly permissive.

Permissive. Descriptive of parents who do not make demands of, or attempt to control, their children.

Nonconformist. Descriptive of parents who are committed to allowing their children the freedom to develop their own abilities and points of view.

And so it seems that we can offer a tentative prescription for promoting competence in children:

1. Be reasonably restrictive. Don't allow your children to "run wild." But exert control by using reasoning rather than force.

2. Do not hesitate to demand mature behavior, although these demands must be tempered by knowledge of what your child *can* do at a given stage of development.

3. Always explain why you make certain demands to your children. At an early age, the explanation can be simple: "That hurts!" or "You're breaking things that are important to Mommy and Daddy!" The point is to help your child develop a sense of values that he or she can use to form judgments and self-regulate behavior.

4. Frequently express love and caring—use lots of hugs and kisses. Show strong approval of your child's achievements (playing independently for a few minutes at the age of 2 is an achievement).

There are three limitations to these suggestions. First, research has not been carried out that shows that following these suggestions makes a difference. All we have is correlational evidence at this point.

Second, it may not be possible for parents who are authoritarian, permissive, or nonconformist to adopt these behavior patterns. They may "go against the grain."

Third, these suggestions are not value-neutral; they assume that fostering competence in children will be a high priority with readers. Nonconformist people, for example, may assume that it would be better to foster alternative values, such as lack of interest in getting ahead in a competitive society.

The choices are yours. But Baumrind's research may be of more than descriptive value.

■ Issues in Child Rearing

There are too many issues to elaborate upon in any single book, much less part of one chapter. But in this section we focus upon four issues that are of concern to today's parents. First, since most of the women reading this book will be career women, they are likely to be interested in the research on breast-feeding versus bottle-feeding. The incidence of divorce remains high, and for that reason our second topic concerns the effects of divorce on children. Child abuse, sad to say, is also widespread, and so child abuse must be our third topic. Again, because women reading this book are likely to be career-oriented, they (and their husbands) will want to know something about day care. And so our fourth topic concerns the effects of day care and—that all-important decision-making process—how to select a day-care center.

Breast-Feeding versus Bottle-Feeding: Does It Make a Difference?

The decision as to whether or not to breast-feed is not taken lightly by most parents. There are a number of concerns about the relative physical and psychological merits of breast- and bottle-feeding of infants. There are also political issues in that breast-feeding is associated with the stereotypical feminine role, and many mothers therefore ask themselves what breast- or bottle-feeding will "mean" for them as women.

Why do women formula- or bottle-feed their children? Personal preferences concerning life-styles and financial pressures prompt many new mothers to remain in the work force. Some parents prefer to share child-feeding responsibilities, and the father is equipped to hold a bottle. Other women simply find bottle-feeding more convenient and trouble-free (Manstead et al., 1983).

Today slightly over half of U.S. women breast-feed their children (Martinez & Krieger, 1985). White women are significantly more likely than black or Hispanic-American women to breast-feed (Fetterly & Graubard, 1984; Rassin et al., 1984). The percentage of breast-feeding mothers was higher early in the century, when formulas were less well-perfected and difficult to prepare. The percentage was somewhat lower a couple of decades ago, when formula-feeding became convenient and was believed just as healthful as breast-feeding.

Mother's Milk: The Ultimate Fast Food?   Mother's milk has been referred to as the ultimate fast food and as the perfect health food (Eiger & Olds, 1986). Mother's milk is superior to cow's milk or formula in its balance of nutrients (Alemi et al., 1981; Sadowitz & Oski, 1983). It contains more vitamins A and C and more iron than cow's milk. Breast milk is also served at the right temperature. Breast milk contains antibodies that help infants fend off diseases which the mother has had, or against which the mother has been inoculated, such as tetanus, chicken pox, typhoid, and small pox (Ogra & Greene, 1982). It helps prevent respiratory infections, helps prevent allergies, and is (almost always) free from infectious agents (Forman et al., 1984; Jelliffe & Jelliffe, 1983). Breast-feeding even seems to help the muscle tissue of the uterus to tighten up following delivery (Matlin, 1987). By and large, women who choose to breast-feed frequently offer the reason that breast-feeding will be better for their babies (Newton, 1971). Is it?

In attempting to answer this extremely important question, we must first note that long-term comparisons of breast-fed and bottle-fed U.S. children show few, if any, significant differences in the ultimate welfare of the children (Schmitt, 1970). However, breast-fed babies do seem to have somewhat fewer allergies, fewer digestive upsets (Larsen & Homer, 1978), and fewer infections of the respiratory system and gastrointestinal tract (Marano, 1979). On the other hand, alcohol, many drugs taken by the mother, and environmental hazards such as PCB are passed along to their babies through breast milk. So breast milk may not always be so pure as it would seem.

The Selection Factor   Most studies concerning differences in feeding practices include children whose parents have *chosen* to breast- or bottle-feed. It may be that mothers who choose to breast-feed differ from mothers who elect to bottle-feed, and that these differences rather than the breast- or bottle-feeding account for differences in the mother–child relationship or in the welfare of the children. For example, one study found that mothers who breast-fed their babies spent more time holding and rocking them (Newton, 1979). Another reported that babies who are breast-fed on demand seem more secure (Newton, 1972). It is unlikely that these findings can be attributed to breast-feeding itself. Mothers who choose to breast-feed, and to breast-feed on demand, might seek closer relationships with their infants (Manstead et al., 1983).

In one of the few experiments on breast-feeding, mothers alternately breast- and bottle-fed their children. It was found that bottle-feeding was somewhat more stressful and anxiety-evoking because of its relative inconvenience, suggesting that bottle-feeding may introduce an element of stress into the mother–child relationship (Modahl & Newton, 1979). But it must be emphasized that the women in the experiment were alternating breast- and bottle-feeding, a practice that is rare in everyday life and carries stresses of its own.

In sum, breast-feeding appears to have some health benefits for children in terms of antibodies and decreased likelihood of allergic reactions. However, these differences are minor and the great majority of bottle-fed children thrive. The current state of the evidence suggests that women are probably well-advised to choose whether to breast- or bottle-feed on the basis of financial considerations or personal preferences, and not to be overly concerned about the long-term effects of their decisions on the physical or psychological development of their infants.

One more thing: Breast-feeding delays resumption of normal menstrual cycles, thus decreasing the likelihood that a nursing mother will become pregnant during the first few months after delivery (Short, 1984), but in no way assuring it. Nursing is unreliable as a birth-control method, and nursing mothers who wish to avoid pregnancy should not assume that they are "safe."

The Children of Divorce

Divorce requires many adjustments for children as well as for parents. In addition to the miseries of the divorce itself, divorce involves a multitude of life changes.

Divorce turns the children's world topsy turvy. The simple things that had been taken for granted are no longer simple: Eating meals and going on trips with both parents, curling up with either parent to read a book or watch television, kissing both parents at bedtime come to an end. Divorced parents must support two households, not one. And so, children of divorce most often suffer downward movement in socioeconomic status. If the downward movement is not severe, it may require minor adjustments and loss of but a few privileges. But more than half of the children younger than 18 who live in father-absent homes must scrape by below the poverty level (Weiraub & Wolf, 1983). In severe cases, the downward trend can mean moving from a house into a cramped apartment, or from a more desirable to a less desirable neighborhood. With moving may come the switching of schools, and children may have to begin to relate to other children who share unfamiliar backgrounds and values. Divorce in families where the mother had stayed in the home may suddenly require her to rejoin the work force and place her children in day care. Such women typically suffer the stresses of task overload, as well as the other problems divorce entails (Hetherington et al., 1982).

One of the major conflicts between parents is differences in child-rearing practices. Children of parents who get a divorce have frequently heard them arguing about how they should be reared. Adolescents may understand that the differences reside in the parents. Young children, however, may focus on their own conflicts with their parents and blame themselves for the family upheaval. Younger children also tend to be more fearful of the unknown than adolescents are. Adolescents have had more of an opportunity to learn that they can exert some control over what happens to them (Kurdek et al., 1981; Wallerstein & Kelly, 1974, 1975).

About 90 percent of the children of divorce live with their mothers (Salkind, 1983). Fathers usually see their children frequently during the first months after the divorce, but visitation often drops precipitously later on (Clingempeel & Repucci, 1982). Also, about two-thirds of fathers do not keep up with their child-support payments, exacerbating the family's downward trend in socioeconomic status.

Given all this outer and inner turmoil, it is not surprising that children of divorce show a number of behavior problems. In a longitudinal study run by E. Mavis Hetherington and her colleagues (1975, 1982, 1983), the adjustment of children who were 4 years old at the time of the divorce was assessed at intervals of two months and one and two years. On the basis of behavioral observations at home and school, personality tests, and interviews, it was found that both boys and girls showed disturbances that increased over the course of the first year. However, by the time two years had passed, much of the disturbance had decreased. There were some sex differences. Boys showed greater behavioral disturbances than girls, as manifested by conduct disorders in school and increased anxiety and dependence. Boys and girls regained much of their equilibrium after two years, and the girls by and large could not be distinguished from girls from intact families.

Researchers attribute children's problems not only to the divorce, but also to a decline in the quality of parenting that frequently follows. The organization of family life tends to deteriorate after divorce (Hetherington et al., 1975). The family is more likely to eat their meals "pick-up style," as opposed to sitting down together. Children are less likely to get to school on time or to get to sleep at a regular hour. It is also more difficult for single mothers to set limits and enforce restrictions on sons' behavior (Santrock et al., 1982). The Hetherington group (1977) found that divorced parents, on the whole, are significantly less likely to show the authoritative behaviors that foster instrumental competence (Table 16.3). They make fewer demands for mature behavior, decline in communication ability, and show less nurturance and warmth. Moreover, their disciplinary methods become inconsistent. Not only do their children believe that they can "get away with more," they also come to conceptualize their worlds as unstructured places. As a consequence, their anxiety levels increase.

The Effects of Father-Absence   Since most children of divorce live with their mothers, and the fathers tend not to visit regularly, many of these children grow up, to a large degree, without fathers. The effects of father-absence are usually felt more by boys than girls, especially when the father is absent during the first five years or so of a boy's life (Hetherington & Deur, 1972; Huston, 1983.) There are individual differences, but boys with absent fathers show fewer sex-typed "masculine" interests, greater dependence, and a "feminine" pattern of intellectual skills—for example, greater verbal skills than math ability.

An often-cited study by E. Mavis Hetherington (1972) shows how many teenage daughters of divorced parents respond to their fathers' absence. Hetherington's sample consisted of twelve girls whose parents had been divorced, twelve girls whose fathers had died, and twelve girls whose families were intact. She compared the girls on a battery of personality tests, interviews, and behavioral observations at a recreation center and during the interviews. The behavioral observations included such measures of "body language" as how close the girl chose to sit to the interviewer, whether she was turned toward or away from the interviewer, and whether her legs were open or crossed.

Both groups of father-absent girls showed higher anxiety levels than the girls from intact homes, but there were few other differences on the personality tests. Both groups of father-absent girls reported feelings of insecurity around male peers and adults. They also reported relatively low levels of self-esteem as compared with girls from intact homes. However, despite their insecurity, the girls whose parents had been divorced reported higher levels of heterosexual activity than did the other two groups. Girls whose mothers had been widowed reported the least heterosexual contact. Behavioral observations showed that girls whose parents had been divorced spent more time in areas of the recreation center that were populated by males (see Figure 16.4). Their "body language" during interviews by male questioners was also more open and inviting. They sat closer to the male interviewers (see Table 16.4). The daughters of the widows tended to stay away from males at the recreation center, and to distance themselves from a male interviewer with a bolt-upright posture.

Father-absence apparently contributed to feelings of insecurity around males and to low self-esteem among the daughters of divorced and widowed women. However, the two groups reacted very differently. The divorced group showed increased heterosexual interest and involvement, while the widowed group distanced themselves from males. Perhaps the divorced group

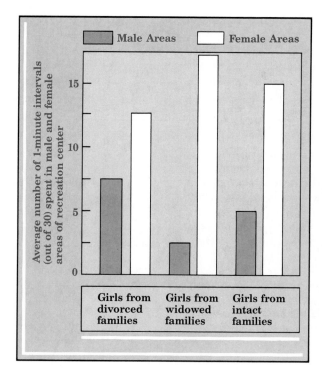

FIGURE 16.4   Behavior of Daughters of Divorced, Widowed, and Married Women in the Hetherington Study

As a group, daughters of divorced women tended to spend the most time in male areas of the recreation center.

felt rejected by their fathers' departures and were attempting to prove to themselves that they could stimulate and maintain the interest of males. The mothers who had been divorced reported the most conflict with their daughters. Daughters of divorced women were most likely to be punished for sexual activity.

In sum, father-absence alone was not responsible for the results of the Hetherington study. Group differences among the adolescent girls were linked to the reasons for father-absence. When fathers appear voluntarily to leave daughters, the girls' self-esteem and security can plummet. The girls may attempt to reconstruct their self-concepts by demonstrating that they can indeed gain the interest of men.

When Fathers Have Custody   In about 10 percent of divorces, fathers have custody of their children. Men are not usually socialized into developing parenting skills, and, as a result, sole responsibility for parenting can be overwhelming, at least at first. However, as a group, divorced fathers tend to

TABLE 16.4   Chairs Selected by Girls Interviewed by Men in the Hetherington Study

Position of Chair Selected	Number of Girls Who Selected Chair		
	Daughters of Divorced Mothers	*Daughters of Widowed Mothers*	*Daughters from Intact Homes*
Closest to interviewer	8	0	1
Across from interviewer	3	2	8
Farthest from interviewer	1	10	3

Data adapted from Hetherington, 1972, p. 317, Table 3.

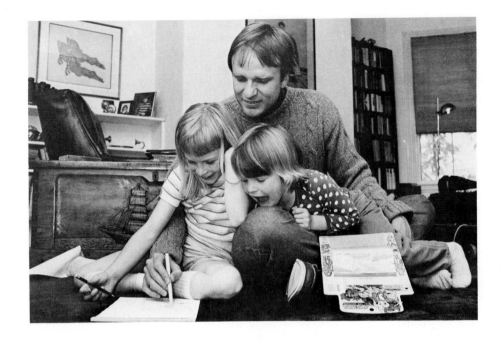

What happens when fathers have custody of the children? Sole responsibility for child-rearing can be overwhelming, at least at first, for men (as for anyone). Fathers with custody, like working mothers, frequently find it difficult to coordinate their work schedules with their children's schedules. All in all, divorced fathers report the same kinds of parenting problems encountered by divorced mothers.

report the same types of parenting problems encountered by divorced mothers. They also tend to be about as successful.

One of the most common problems for fathers who have custody is coordinating their work schedules with their children's schedules. Their problem is akin to that of divorced women who must remain in, or return to, the work force. Day-care centers, nursery schools, scout troops, music and dance lessons, and other organized activities ease these problems somewhat for fathers as they do for mothers. Single fathers also show few problems with chores such as shopping, cooking, cleaning, and getting children to doctors' appointments.

Studies of 6- to 11-year-olds suggest that boys do somewhat better when their fathers have custody of them, but that girls do somewhat better with their mothers (Santrock & Warshak, 1979). However, traits such as authoritativeness and warmth seem to be more important than the custodian's gender in promoting children's adjustment. It also comes down to an individual issue: Which parent truly wants the children and has the emotional resources to cope with their needs?

Regardless of which parent has custody, children's adjustment to divorce is facilitated when parents maintain their commitment to the children and set aside their own disputes long enough to agree on child-rearing practices (Hetherington, 1979; Moreland & Schwebel, 1981; Wallerstein & Kelly, 1980). It is helpful for divorced parents to encourage each other to continue to play roles in their children's lives and to avoid saying negative things about each other in front of the children.

Stepparent Families Seventy to 75 percent of divorced people get remarried, usually within five years. Thirty-five percent of the children born in the 1980s can expect to spend some part of their lives in a stepfamily. And so, the effects of stepparenting are also an important issue in U.S. family life.

Most investigators have found that living in stepfamilies as opposed to nuclear families has little psychological impact (Ganong & Coleman, 1984). In fact, stepfathers may now and then attenuate the effects of father-absence for boys by providing male role models and companionship.

It also appears that stepmothers can have positive effects, particularly for stepdaughters. In a study of the effects of different kinds of stepfamilies on 9- to 12-year-olds, positive stepmother–stepchild relationships were associated with lower aggression in boys and girls and with high self-esteem in girls (Clingempeel & Segal, 1986). Frequent visits with the nonresident natural mother appeared to impair stepmother–stepdaughter relations, apparently by maintaining stepdaughter resistance to forming a relationship with the stepmother. On the other hand, stepmother–stepdaughter relationships generally improved over time.

Should Conflicted Parents Stay Together for the Sake of the Children? It is good for divorced parents to cooperate in rearing their children. Is it also better for the children for parents remain to together despite their conflicts? It depends on how the parents behave in front of the children. Children as young as 2 show distress and increased aggression in response to angry adult conflict (Cummings et al., 1985). When parents argue persistently in front of the children, the children tend to develop behavior problems akin to those of children whose parents have been divorced (Emory, 1982). When parents cannot get along, divorce followed by cooperative child rearing might actually be better for the children. As E. Mavis Hetherington notes, "Divorce is often a positive solution to destructive family functioning" (1979, p. 857).

Child Abuse

At least 625,000 children in the United States are neglected or abused every year in the home (National Center on Child Abuse and Neglect, 1982), and this figure is rising (Brown, 1983). Neglect is more common than abuse. Some children are poorly fed, poorly clothed in winter, ignored, and allowed to fend for themselves in unsafe environments. Although blatant abuse is more horrifying, more injuries, illnesses, and deaths result from neglect (Cantwell, 1980; Wolock & Horowitz, 1984).

Causes of Child Abuse A number of factors contribute to the probability that parents will abuse their children. They include situational stress; a history of child abuse in at least one of the parent's families of origin; acceptance of violence as a way of coping with stress; failure to become attached to the children; and rigid attitudes about child rearing (Belsky, 1984; Milner et al., 1984; Rosenblum & Paully, 1984).

Parents who are exposed to more life changes are more likely to abuse their children (Justice & Justice, 1976). Unemployment seems to be a particularly predisposing life change. Child abuse increases during periods of rising unemployment (National Center on Child Abuse and Neglect, 1982; Steinberg et al., 1981).

Stress is created by crying infants themselves (Green et al., 1987; Murray, 1985). Infants who are already in pain of some kind, and relatively difficult to soothe, may ironically be more likely to be abused (Frodi, 1981, 1985). Why? Parents tend to become frustrated and irritated when their babies show prolonged signs of distress. Some frustrated parents may even "take it personally"—that is, draw the irrational conclusion that their children are crying because they do not love them (Steele & Pollock, 1974). Similarly, abusive mothers are more likely than nonabusive mothers to assume that their children's misbehavior is intentional, even when it is not (Bauer & Twentyman, 1985). Within our culture, intentional misconduct is seen as more deserving of punishment than incidental misconduct.

Sad to say, abused children show an alarming incidence of personal and social problems and abnormal behavior patterns. Maltreatment can disturb basic patterns of attachment. Abused children are less likely than nonabused age-mates to venture out to explore the world (Aber & Allen, 1987). Abused children are more likely to be depressed and aggressive than nonabused children, even at preschool ages (Hoffman-Plotkin & Twentyman, 1984; Kazdin et al., 1985). Nonabused toddlers are likely to show concern or sadness when their peers are distressed. Abused toddlers often respond to age-mates' distress with fear, anger, or physical attacks (Main & George, 1985).

Child abuse is somewhat more likely to run in families. But it must be emphasized that *the majority of children who are abused do not abuse their own children as adults.* According to psychologist Mindy Rosenberg, there is no evidence that women who were abused as children are more likely than other women to abuse their own children (Fisher, 1984). These facts are extremely important, because many victims of child abuse as adults are (unjustifiedly) concerned that they are destined to abuse their own children.

Why do *some* victims of child abuse become abusive themselves? One possibility is that their parents serve as violent role models. If children grow up observing their parents using violence as a means to cope with stress and feelings of anger, they are less likely to learn to diffuse anger through techniques such as humor, verbal expression of feelings, reasoning, or even "counting to ten."

Exposure to violence in their own homes may also lead some children to accept family violence as a norm. They may see little or nothing wrong in it. Certainly, there are any number of "justifications" they can find for violence—if they are seeking them. One is the age-old adage, "Spare the rod, spoil the child." Another is the belief that they are hurting their children "for their own good"—to discourage behavior that is likely to get them into trouble.

Still another "justification" of child abuse is the sometimes cloudy distinction between the occasional swat on the rear end and spanking or other types of repeated hitting. Child abusers may argue that all parents hit their children (which is not true) and claim not to understand why outsiders are making "such a fuss" about their private family behavior. Child abusers who come from families in which they were subjected to abuse are also more likely to have the (incorrect) perspective that "everyone does it."

What to Do   Dealing with child abuse is a frustrating issue in itself. Social agencies and courts can find it as difficult to distinguish between "normal"* hitting or spanking and abuse as many abusers do. Because of the U.S. belief that parents have the right to rear their children as they wish, police and courts have also historically tried to avoid involvement in "domestic quarrels" and "family disputes."

However, the alarming incidence of child abuse has spawned new efforts at detection and prevention. Many states require helping professionals such as psychologists and physicians to report any suspicion of child abuse. Many states legally require *anyone* who suspects child abuse to report it to authorities.

Many locales also have Child Abuse Hotlines. Their phone numbers are available from the telephone information service. Private citizens who suspect child abuse may call these numbers for advice. Parents who are having difficulty controlling aggressive impulses toward their children are encouraged to use them. Some hotlines are serviced by groups such as Parents Anonymous, who have had similar difficulties and may help callers diffuse feelings of anger in less harmful ways.

Other potentially helpful measures include increased publicizing of the dimensions of the child-abuse problem. To be sure, news and entertainment media have made efforts to do so, but the campaigns may be too infrequent. The public may also need more education about where an occasional swat on the behind ends and child abuse begins. Perhaps the format for such edu-

---

*We place this word in quotes because of our own horror at child abuse and our refusal to consider any hitting of children to be normal.

cation could be something like, "If you are doing such and such, make no mistake about it—you are abusing your child."

Finally, child abuse must be conceptualized and dealt with as a crime of violence. Whether or not child abusers happen to be victims of abuse themselves, child abusers are criminals and their children must be protected from them.

The Effects of Day Care

More than half of today's U.S. mothers spend the day on the job. This figure includes 41 percent of mothers of children less than 1 year old (Klein, 1985). The ideals of the women's movement and financial pressures are likely to increase this number. Many years ago, when U.S. residents were less mobile and there was more of an extended family life, the young children of working parents were frequently farmed out to relatives. Today, however, their care is often entrusted to day-care centers.

Between 7 and 8 million U.S. preschool children are now placed in day-care centers, and parents express many concerns about what happens to them there. In one survey, 59 percent of working mothers reported that worrying about their children's care increased their stress level (Trost, 1987). Fifty-six percent of parents reported difficulty arranging quality day care; 54 percent complained that the costs of day care were excessive; and 51 percent had problems with the location and hours of their day-care centers. One mother in four had considered quitting her job because of these stresses.

Moreover, most parents want day-care centers to provide more than the basics of food, warmth, and security. They want these centers to provide their children with intellectual stimulation, a variety of toys and games, successful peer interactions, and experience relating to adults outside the family.

What are the effects of day care on parent–child bonds of attachment? On children's social development? What factors contribute to a positive day-care experience?

How Do Day-Care Centers Influence Bonds of Attachment?   Many parents wonder whether day care will affect their children's feelings of attachment toward them. After all, the child will be spending many hours away at a "vulnerable" age. During these time periods, their needs will be met by outsiders. Also, if they had the time and money, most parents would prefer to care for their children personally. And so parents often feel some guilt about "sending away" their children and may fear that they will be "punished" by loss of love.

Whether these concerns are rational or not, studies of the effects of day care are encouraging. In their review of the literature, Jay Belsky and Laurence Steinberg (1978) concluded that day care has *not* been shown to interfere with mother–child bonds of attachment. Jerome Kagan and his colleagues (1978, 1980) followed children placed in day care and a matched group cared for in the home from 3 1/2 months to 29 months. Both groups were more "attached" to their mothers in the laboratory setting, as measured by time spent maintaining proximity and contact with them, and so day care had not measurably damaged mother–child bonds of attachment. However, the day-care children also became attached to their caregivers and preferred them to adult strangers.

The Kagan group suggest that initial enrollment in day care is less stressful for infants prior to the age of 7 months or after the age of 15 to 18 months. Many infants develop fear of strangers at about 7 months, and, for those who do, this fear tends to wane by about 15 months. And so, by following Kagan's suggestion, infants will be exposed to strangers before this fear develops or once it is on the wane.

What are the effects of day care? Children in day care tend to be more sociable than peers who are cared for in the home. However, they are also somewhat more aggressive, possibly reflecting competition for limited resources.

WHAT DO YOU SAY NOW?

Selecting a Day-Care Center

Selecting a day-care center can be an overwhelming task. Standards for day-care centers vary from locale to locale, so licensing is no guarantee of adequate care. Imagine that you must entrust your 1-year-old to a day-care center for most of the day, five days a week. Think of the questions that you would want to ask of the director of the center, and write them in the following spaces. Then see the following material for some suggestions.

1. _____

2. _____

3. _____

1. Although being licensed remains no absolute guarantee of quality, in a locale that provides licenses, a license is better than no license. Therefore, you might ask, "Is the center licensed? By what agency? What standards must be met to acquire a license?"
2. Everything else being equal, it would appear logical that caregivers can do a better job when there are fewer children in their charge. So you might say something like, "What is the ratio of children to caregivers?" Jerome Kagan and his colleagues (1978) recommend that caregivers not have more than three infants or toddlers assigned to their care. But it may also be of use to look beyond numbers. Quality is frequently more important than quantity.
3. Day-care workers are typically paid poorly. Financial frustrations lead many of the best-qualified workers to seek work in other fields (Saddler, 1987). So you might want to ask something like, "What kind of training have your caregivers been given?" The issue is, how well aware are they of children's needs and patterns of development? According to the findings of the National Day Care Study (Ruopp et al., 1979), children fare better when their caregivers have specific training in child development. Years of day-care experience and formal degrees are less important. If the administrators of a day-care center are reluctant to discuss the training and experience of their caregivers, consider another center.
4. You also want to know how safe the environment is. Do toys and swings seem to be in good condition? Are dangerous objects out of reach? Would strangers have a difficult time breaking in? Ask something like, "Have children been injured in this center?" Administrators should report previous injuries without hesitation.
5. You need to know what is served at mealtime, whether it it nutritious and appetizing, and whether *your child* will eat it. Some babies are placed in day care at 6 months or younger, and parents will need to know what formulas are used. Ask something like, "Can you show me the menu for the week? What brand tuna do you buy? Is it dark or light meat?"
6. You want to know which caregivers will be responsible for your child. What are their backgrounds? How do they seem to relate to children? Say something like, "Will you introduce me to the person who would be in charge of my child's class?" You might want to ask that person something like, "What do you do when they get into a fight?" or "What happened the last time a child was hurt?"
7. Ask something like, "Would you show me the toys, games, books, and other educational materials that the children use?"
8. Ask something like, "How well supervised are children when they use things like swings and tricycles?"

Other things you may want to consider when selecting a day-care center: Are the hours offered by the center convenient for your schedule? Is the location of the center convenient? Do you like the overall environment and "feel" of the center?

How Do Day-Care Centers Influence Social Development?   Day-care centers provide an opportunity for social experiences outside the home. This fact both delights and concerns many parents. Parents generally want their children to acquire the social skills to relate to outsiders, but they may also prefer to be the caregivers (and protectors) who oversee their children's early social interactions.

Day care seems to have positive and negative influences on children's social development. First, the positive. Infants with day-care experience are more peer-oriented and play at higher developmental levels. Day-care children are also more likely to share their toys (Belsky & Steinberg, 1978, 1979).

Adolescent boys who had been placed in day care before the age of 5 were rated high in sociability and were liked by their peers (Moore, 1975). And so day care may stimulate interest in peers and help in the formation of social skills.

Now, the negative. A number of studies have compared 3- and 4-year-olds who had been in full-time day care for several years with age-mates recently placed in day-care centers. The experienced children were more impulsive, more aggressive toward peers and adults, and more egocentric (Caldwell et al., 1970; Lay & Meyer, 1973; Schwartz et al., 1973, 1974). They were also less cooperative and showed less tolerance for frustration.

The negative characteristics found among children with extensive day-care experience suggest a common theme: Day care can promote interest in peers and the development of social skills, but children frequently do not receive the individual attention or resources they would like. Placed in a competitive situation, they become somewhat more aggressive in attempting to meet their needs.

Even if day care usually fosters impulsivity and aggressiveness, these outcomes are not inevitable. Fewer children per caregiver and more toys would reduce competition. Unfortunately, caregivers, on the average, are assigned nearly four infants aged under 18 months or nearly six toddlers aged 18 to 24 months. In many cases, they have even more. Two major obstructions stand in the way of having one caregiver for every three children, however: money and the scarceness of qualified personnel.

Still, for most children, day care has not been shown to be a negative experience. And the problems that have been noted might be alleviated by greater funding. Working parents can be encouraged that by careful shopping—and asking the right questions—they may be able to find a day-care center that will give their families the support they need in meeting one of the challenges of their lives.

■ Summary

1. **What reasons do people give for having children?** These include the opportunities to extend oneself and to enjoy one's children.
2. **What reasons do people give for not having children?** These include overpopulation, responsibility, expense, and loss of personal freedom.
3. **How does conception take place?** An ovum is released by an ovary and fertilized by a sperm cell in a fallopian tube.
4. **What kinds of fertility problems do people have?** The most common among men is insufficient sperm production, and, among women, endometriosis and blocked fallopian tubes.
5. **What are some ways of coping with fertility problems?** These include adoption, artificial insemination, and—more rarely—in vitro fertilization, embryonic transfer, and surrogate motherhood.
6. **Can you preselect the sex of your child?** Not with certainty. However, a number of methods that are based on the facts that Y-sex-chromosome-bearing sperm swim faster but are weaker than X-sex-chromosome-bearing sperm appear to offer above-chance probabilities of sex preselection.
7. **What are the stages of prenatal development?** These include the germinal stage, which ends with uterine implanation; the embryonic stage, during which the major organ systems develop; and the fetal stage (third–ninth months), characterized by maturation and dramatic gains in size.
8. **How do maternal diet and disorders, drugs, and parental age affect prenatal development?** Inadequate diets lead to lags in development, particularly motor development. Some maternal pathogens can be passed

through the placenta so that the child is given congenital disease. Maternal drinking is associated with fetal alcohol syndrome, and maternal smoking is associated with undersized babies and problems in learning. Parents of advanced ages put the child at risk for chromosomal disorders.

9. **What are some chromosomal and genetic abnormalities?** Chromosomal abnormalities include Down syndrome and sex-linked abnormalities, such as XYY and XXX syndromes. Genetic abnormalities include PKU, sickle-cell anemia, and Tay-Sachs disease.

10. **How can we find out if something is wrong with the baby before it is born?** There are a number of methods, including parental blood tests; amniocentesis, which examines sloughed off fetal cells in the amniotic fluid; and ultrasound, which can form a picture of the fetus.

11. **Does taking pain-killing medication during childbirth harm the baby?** It seems to make the baby relatively sluggish for a number of hours after birth, but no severe long-term effects have been clearly identified.

12. **What is the Lamaze method? The Leboyer method?** The Lamaze method prepares the mother and a coach for childbirth by education, relaxation exercises, and muscle-strengthening exercises. The Leboyer method brings the baby into a dimly lit, quiet room as gently as possible.

13. **What is the difference between maternity blues and postpartum depression? Are all women depressed after childbirth?** Maternity blues lasts for a couple of days and is milder than the longer-lasting postpartum depression. Each might reflect the interaction of hormonal influences and concern about the mother role. And no, these problems are not encountered by all new mothers.

14. **Do parents have to have extended early contact with their babies for proper bonding to occur?** Probably not—the studies that show advantages for extended early contact are methodologically flawed. However, there is no reason why hospital procedures should prevent parents who desire extended early contact from having it.

15. **How can parents rear competent children?** Baumrind found that parents of the most competent children make demands for mature behavior, clearly communicate their values and beliefs, give their children a great deal of love, and applaud their children's accomplishments.

16. **Does it matter whether a child is breast-fed or bottle-fed?** Most of the time it doesn't. Breast-feeding gives the child some of the mother's antibodies, helping fend off certain diseases, but children generally thrive with both methods, as long as they receive proper nutrients from the bottle.

17. **What happens to the children when the parents get a divorce?** There is usually emotional turmoil and, often, downward movement in socioeconomic status. Adolescents usually adjust better than younger children, and girls better than boys. Things are usually emotionally back to normal in about two years.

18. **Should parents stay together for the sake of the children?** Not if they're going to fight viciously in front of the children. But if they can agree on child-rearing practices and express their other disagreements in private, the children might be better off with both of them.

19. **Why do parents abuse their children?** Child abuse frequently reflects current stresses and attitudes, or personal experiences, suggestive that it is "normal" to hit one's children.

20. **What are the effects of day care?** Day care apparently doesn't interfere with parent–child bonds of attachment. Day care appears to foster social skills, but day-care children are also somewhat more aggressive than children cared for in the home—possibly because they become used to competing for limited resources.

■ TRUTH OR FICTION REVISITED

Fertilization takes place in the uterus. False. Conception usually occurs in a fallopian tube.

It is not possible to learn the sex of one's child prior to birth. False. Amniocentesis and ultrasound are two methods that provide this information.

"Yuppies" are more likely than nonprofessionals to develop fertility problems. True. They tend to postpone childbearing, and infertility problems increase with the years.

Developing embryos have been successfully transferred from the womb of one woman to the womb of another. True. Embryonic transfer is one method for coping with infertility.

You can predetermine the sex of your child. Not with certainty, but various methods seem to offer better than 50 percent chances.

Pregnant women who smoke risk having children who are low in birth weight. True. Smoking deprives the embryo and fetus of oxygen.

Sickle-cell anemia is most prevalent among blacks. True. It is also prevalent among Hispanic Americans.

Soon after birth, babies are slapped on the buttocks to clear passageways for air and stimulate independent breathing. False. The contemporary method is aspiration.

The way the umbilical cord is cut determines whether a child will have an "inny" or an "outy" for a "belly button." False. The stump of the cord dries and falls off by itself.

Women who give birth by the Lamaze method do not have pain. False. However, they may cope better and have somewhat less pain.

Most hospitals exclude fathers from the birth process. False. Today most U.S. hospitals encourage paternal participation.

It is essential for parents to have extended early contact with their babies if adequate bonding is to take place. False. The evidence supporting this view is invalid.

Children with strict parents are more likely to become competent. True. Parents who are restrictive but loving, encouraging, and communicative tend to have more competent children.

Breast-feeding and bottle-feeding are equally healthful. False. Breast-feeding comes out a bit ahead, everything else being equal. However, both methods yield thriving babies when nutrition and other health matters are attended to carefully.

Women cannot become pregnant while they are breast-feeding. False. The chances of pregnancy are lower, but breast-feeding is unreliable as a birth-control method.

Divorce is more stressful for young children than for adolescents. True. Younger children do not understand what is happening as well and haven't developed methods for coping as well as adolescents have.

Parents who have been victims of child abuse are more likely to abuse their own children. True in that for *men* there is a slight relationship between child abuse and later abusive behavior. But being a victim of child abuse clearly does not guarantee that a man will abuse his own children.

Children placed in day care become less attached to their mothers. False.

References

REFERENCES

Abbey, A. (1982). Sex differences in attributions for friendly behavior. *Journal of Personality and Social Psychology, 42,* 830–838.

Abel, E. L. (1980). Fetal alcohol syndrome: Behavioral teratology. *Psychological Bulletin, 87,* 29–50.

Abelson, H., Cohen, R., Heaton, E., & Slider, C. (1970). Public attitudes toward and experience with erotic materials. In *Technical reports of the Commission on Obscenity and Pornography,* Vol. 6. Washington, DC: U.S. Government Printing Office.

Aber, J. L., & Allen, J. P. (1987). Effects of maltreatment of young children on young children's socioemotional development: An attachment theory perspective. *Developmental Psychology, 23,* 406–414.

Abikoff, H., & Gittelman, R. (1985). The normalizing effects of methylphenidate on the classroom behavior of ADDH children. *Journal of Abnormal Child Psychology, 13,* 33–44.

Abraham, G. (1981). Premenstrual tension. *Current Problems in Obstetrics and Gynecology,* 1–39.

Abramowitz, C. V., Abramowitz, S. I., Roback, H. B., & Jackson, C. (1974). Differential effectiveness of directive and nondirective group therapies as a function of client internal-external control. *Journal of Consulting and Clinical Psychology, 42,* 849–853.

Abrams, D. B., & Wilson, G. T. (1983). Alcohol, sexual arousal, and self-control. *Journal of Personality and Social Psychology, 45,* 188–198.

Adams, G. R. (1977). Physical attractiveness research: Toward a developmental social psychology of beauty. *Human Development, 20,* 217–239.

Adams, H. E., & Chiodo, J. (1983). Sexual deviations. In H. E. Adams & P. B. Sutker (Eds.), *Comprehensive handbook of psychopathology.* New York: Plenum Publishing Co.

Adams, V. (1980). Sex therapies in perspective. *Psychology Today, 14*(8), 35–36.

Adelman, M. R. (1977). A comparison of professionally employed lesbians and heterosexual women on the MMPI. *Archives of Sexual Behavior, 6,* 193–202.

Adelson, A. (1988, March 9). Women still finding bias in engineering. *The New York Times,* p. D6.

Adickes, E., & Shuman, R. (1981). Fetal muscles and alcohol. *Journal of Pediatric Pathology.*

Adorno, T. W., Frenkel-Brunswick, E., & Levinson, D. J. (1950). *The authoritarian personality.* New York: Harper.

Agras, W. S., Southam, M. A., & Taylor, C. B. (1983). Long-term persistence of relaxation-induced blood pressure lowering during the working day. *Journal of Consulting and Clinical Psychology, 51,* 792–794.

Aiello, J. R., Baum, A., & Gormley, F. (1981). Social determinants of residential crowding stress. *Personality and Social Psychology Bulletin, 7,* 643–644.

Aiello, J. R., & Thompson, D. E. (1980). Personal space, crowding, and spatial behavior in a cultural context. In I. Altman, J. F. Wohlwill, & A. Rapoport (Eds.), *Human behavior and environment,* Vol. 4. New York: Plenum Publishing Co.

Albert, M. S. (1981). Geriatric neuropsychology. *Journal of Consulting and Clinical Psychology, 49,* 835–850.

Alexander, A. B. (1981). Asthma. In S. N. Haynes & L. Gannon (Eds.), *Psychosomatic disorders: A psychophysiological approach to etiology and treatment.* New York: Praeger Books.

Alexander, R. A., & Barrett, G. U. (1982). Equitable salary increase judgments based upon merit and nonmerit considerations: A cross-national comparison. *International Review of Applied Psychology, 31,* 443–454.

Allen, V. L., & Levine, J. M. (1971). Social support and conformity: The role of independent assessment of reality. *Journal of Experimental Social Psychology, 7,* 48–58.

Allgeier, A. A., & Byrne, D. (1973). Attraction toward the opposite sex as a determinant of physical proximity. *Journal of Social Psychology, 90,* 213–219.

Allgeier, E. R., & Allgeier, A. A. (1984). *Sexual interactions.* Lexington, MA: Heath.

Allon, N., & Fishel, D. (1979). Singles bars. In N. Allon (Ed.), *Urban life styles.* Dubuque: Brown.

Allport, G. W. (1937). *Personality: A psychological interpretation.* New York: Holt, Rinehart and Winston.

Allport, G. W. (1961). *Pattern and growth in personality.* New York: Holt, Rinehart and Winston.

Allport, G. W., & Oddbert, H. S. (1936). Trait names: A psycholexical study. *Psychological Monographs, 47,* 2–11.

Altman, I., & Taylor, D. A. (1973). *Social penetration: The development of interpersonal relationships.* New York: Holt, Rinehart and Winston.

Altman, L. K. (1988, January 12). AIDS researchers frustrated in hunt for genetic factors. *The New York Times,* p. C3.

Altman, L. K. (1988, January, 26). Cocaine's many dangers: The evidence mounts. *The New York Times,* p. C3.

Amato, P. R. (1983). Helping behavior in urban and rural environments: Field studies based on taxonomic organization of helping episodes. *Journal of Personality and Social Psychology, 45,* 571–586.

American College of Obstetricians and Gynecologists. (1985, January). *Dysmenorrhea.*

American Psychiatric Association (1987). *Diagnostic and statistical manual of the mental disorders–Third Edition -Revised.* Washington, DC: American Psychiatric Press, Inc.

American Psychological Association (1981). Ethical principles of psychologists. *American Psychologist, 36,* 633–638.

American Psychological Association (1984). Text of position on insanity defense. *APA Monitor, 15*(3), 11.

Amir, M. (1971). *Patterns in forcible rape.* Chicago: University of Chicago Press.

Amir, Y. (1976). The role of intergroup contact in change of prejudice and ethnic relations. In P. A. Katz (Ed.), *Towards the elimination of racism.* New York: Pergamon Press.

Andersen, B. L. (1981). A comparison of systematic desensitization and directed masturbation in the treatment of primary orgasmic dysfunction in females. *Journal of Consulting and Clinical Psychology, 49,* 568–570.

Anderson, D. J., Noyes, R., Jr., & Crowe, R. (1984). A comparison of panic-disorder and generalized anxiety disorder. *American Journal of Psychiatry, 141,* 572–575.

Andrews, G., & Harvey, R. (1981). Does psychotherapy benefit neurotic patients? *Archives of General Psychiatry, 38,* 1203–1208.

Aneshensel, C. S., & Huba, G. J. (1983). Depression, alcohol use, and smoking over one year: A four-wave longitudinal causal model. *Journal of Abnormal Psychology, 92,* 134–150.

Antill, J. K. (1983). Sex role complementarity versus similarity in married couples. *Journal of Personality and Social Psychology, 52,* 260–267.

Apfelbaum, M. (1978). Adaptation to changes in caloric intake. *Progress in Food and Nutritional Science, 2,* 543–559.

Archer, D., Iritani, B., Kimes, D. D., & Barrios, M. (1983). Face-ism: Five studies of sex differences in facial prominence. *Journal of Personality and Social Psychology, 45,* 725–735.

Archer, R. L., Diaz-Loving, R., Gollwitzer, P. M., Davis, M. H., & Foushee, H. C. (1981). The role of dispositional empathy and social evaluation in the empathic mediation of helping. *Journal of Personality and Social Psychology, 40,* 786–796.

Archer, R. P., & Cash, T. F. (1985). Physical attractiveness and maladjustment among psychiatric patients. *Journal of Social and Clinical Psychology, 3,* 170–180.

Argyris, C. (1972). *The applicability of organizational psychology.* Cambridge: Cambridge University Press.

Arkin, R. M., Detchon, C. S., & Maruyama, G. M. (1982). Roles of attribution, affect, and cognitive interference in test anxiety. *Journal of Personality and Social Psychology, 43,* 1111–1124.

Arms, K., & Camp, P. S. (1987). *Biology,* 3d ed. Philadelphia: Saunders College Publishing.

Asarnow, J. R., Carlson, G. A., & Guthrie, D. (1987). Coping strategies, self-perceptions, hopelessness, and perceived family environments in depressed and suicidal children. *Journal of Consulting and Clinical Psychology, 55,* 361–366.

Asch, S. E. (1952). *Social psychology.* Englewood Cliffs, NJ: Prentice-Hall.

Atchley, R. C. (1980). *The social forces in later life.* Belmont, CA: Wadsworth.

Atchley, R. C. (1985). *Social forces and aging: An introduction to social gerontology.* Belmont, CA: Wadsworth.

Atkins, C. J., Kaplan, R. M., Timms, R. M., Reinsch, S., & Lofback, K. (1984). Behavioral exercise programs in the management of chronic obstructive pulmonary disease. *Journal of Consulting and Clinical Psychology, 52,* 591–603.

Atkinson, J., & Huston, T. L. (1984). Sex role orientation and division of labor early in marriage. *Journal of Personality and Social Psychology, 46,* 330–345.

Attorney General's Commission on Pornography: Final Report. (1986, July). Washington, DC: U.S. Department of Justice.

Atwater, L. (1982). *The extramarital connection: Sex, intimacy, and identity.* New York: Irvington.

Austrom, D., & Hanel, K. (1985). Psychological issues of single life in Canada. *International Journal of Women's studies, 8,* 12–23.

Ayllon, T., & Haughton, E. (1962). Control of the behavior of schizophrenic patients by food. *Journal of the Experimental Analysis of Behavior, 5,* 343–352.

Azrin, N. H., Flores, T., & Kaplan, S. J. (1975). Job finding club: A group-assisted program for obtaining employment. *Behaviour Research and Therapy, 15,* 17–27.

Bach, G. R., & Deutsch, R. M. (1970). *Pairing.* New York: Peter H. Wyden.

Bachman, J. G., O'Malley, P. M., & Johnston, L. D. (1984). Drug use among young adults. *Journal of Personality and Social Psychology, 47,* 629–645.

Bakeman, R., Lumb, J. R., Jackson, R. E., & Smith, D. W. (1986). AIDS-risk group profiles in whites and members of minority groups. *New England Journal of Medicine, 315,* 191–192.

Baker, M. A., Berheide, C. W., Greckel, F. R., Gugin, L. C., Lipetz, M. J., & Segal, M. T. (1980). *Women today.* Monterey, CA: Brooks/Cole.

Bakwin, H. (1970, August 29). Sleepwalking in twins. *Lancet,* pp. 446–447.

Bakwin, H. (1971a). Enuresis in twins. *American Journal of Diseases of Children, 121,* 222–225.

Bakwin, H. (1971b). Nail-biting in twins. *Developmental Medicine and Child Neurology, 13,* 304–307.

Bales, J. (1986, November). New studies cite drug use dangers. *APA Monitor,* p. 26.

Ball-Rokeach, S. J., Rokeach, M., & Grube, J. W. (1984). The great American values test: Can television alter basic beliefs? *Psychology Today, 18*(11), 34–41.

Bandura, A. (1973). *Aggression: A social learning analysis.* Englewood Cliffs, NJ: Prentice-Hall.

Bandura, A. (1977). *Social learning theory.* Englewood Cliffs, NJ: Prentice-Hall.

Bandura, A. (1978). The self system in reciprocal determinism. *American Psychologist, 33,* 344–358.

Bandura, A. (1981). Self-referrant thought: A developmental analysis of self-efficacy. In J. H. Flavell & L. Ross (Eds.), *Social cognitive development: Frontiers and possible futures.* Cambridge: Cambridge University Press.

Bandura, A. (1982). Self-efficacy mechanism in human agency. *American Psychologist, 37,* 122–147.

Bandura, A. (1986). *Social foundations of thought and action: A social-cognitive theory.* Englewood Cliffs, NJ: Prentice-Hall.

Bandura, A., Blanchard, E. B., & Ritter, B. (1969). The relative efficacy of desensitization and modeling approaches for inducing behavioral, affective, and cognitive changes. *Journal of Personality and Social Psychology, 13,* 173–199.

Bandura, A., Reese, L., & Adams, N. E. (1982). Microanalysis of action and fear arousal as a function of differential levels of perceived self-efficacy. *Journal of Personality and Social Psychology, 43,* 5–21.

Bandura, A., & Rosenthal, T. L. (1966). Vicarious classical conditioning as a function of fear arousal. *Journal of Personality and Social Psychology, 3,* 54–62.

Bandura, A., Ross, S. A., & Ross, D. (1963). Imitation of film-mediated aggressive models. *Journal of Abnormal and Social Psychology, 66,* 3–11.

Bandura, A., Taylor, C. B., Williams, S. L., Medford, I. N., & Barchas, J. D. (1985). Catecholamine secretion as a function of perceived coping self-efficacy. *Journal of Consulting and Clinical Psychology, 53,* 406–414.

Bane, M. J. (1976). Marital disruption and the lives of children. *Journal of Social Issues, 32,* 103–117.

Banmen, J., & Vogel, N. (1985). The relationship between marital quality and interpersonal sexual communication. *Family Therapy, 12,* 45–58.

Barbach, L. G. (1975). *For yourself: The fulfillment of female sexuality.* Garden City, NY: Doubleday.

Barber, T. X. (1970). *LSD, marihuana, yoga, and hypnosis.* Chicago: Aldine.

Barber, T. X. (1982). Hypnosuggestive procedures in the treatment of clinical pain: Implications for theories of hypnosis and suggestive therapy. In T. Millon, C. J. Green, & R. B. Meagher, Jr. (Eds.), *Handbook of clinical health psychology.* New York: Plenum Publishing Co.

Barber, T. X. (1984). Hypnosis, deep relaxation, and active relaxation: Data, theory, and clinical applications. In R. L. Woolfolk & P. M. Lehrer (Eds.), *Principles and practice of stress management.* New York: Guilford Press.

Bardwick, J. M. (1971). *Psychology of women: A study of biocultural conflicts.* New York: Harper & Row.

Bardwick, J. M. (1980). The seasons of a woman's life. In D. G. McGuigan (Ed.), *Women's lives: New theory, research, and policy.* Ann Arbor: University of Michigan, Center for Continuing Education of Women.

Barefoot, J. C., Dahlstrom, W. G., & Williams, R. B., Jr. (1983). Rapid communication, hostility, CHD incidence, and total mortality: A 25-year follow-up study of 225 physicians. *Psychosomatic Medicine, 45,* 59–63.

Barlow, D. H. (1986). Causes of sexual dysfunction: The role of anxiety and cognitive interference. *Journal of Consulting and Clinical Psychology, 54,* 140–148.

Barlow, D. H. (1986). Behavioral conception and treatment of panic. *Psychopharmacology Bulletin, 22,* 802–806.

Barlow, D. H., Vermilyea, J., Blanchard, E. B., Vermilyea, B. B., DiNardo, P. A., & Cerny, J. A. (1985). The phenomenon of panic. *Journal of Abnormal Psychology, 94,* 291–297.

Barnes, M. L., & Buss, D. M. (1985). Sex differences in the interpersonal behavior of married couples. *Journal of Personality and Social Psychology, 48,* 654–661.

Barnett, R. C., & Baruch, G. K. (1985). Women's involvement in multiple roles and psychological distress. *Journal of Personality and Social Psychology, 49,* 135–145.

Baron, R. A.. (1971). Behavioral effects of interpersonal attraction: Compliance with requests from liked and disliked others. *Psychonomic Science, 25,* 325–326.

Baron, R. A. (1973). The "foot-in-the-door" phenomenon: Mediating effects of size of first request and sex of requester. *Bulletin of the Psychonomic Society, 2,* 113–114.

Baron, R. A. (1983). *Behavior in organizations.* Boston: Allyn and Bacon.

Baron, R. A. (1987). Effects of negative ions on interpersonal attraction. *Journal of Personality and Social Psychology, 52,* 547–553.

Baron, R. A., & Byrne, D. (1987). *Social psychology: Understanding human interaction,* 5th ed. Boston: Allyn and Bacon.

Baron, R. A., Mandel, D. R., Adams, C. A., & Griffen, L. M. (1976). Effects of social density in university residential requirements. *Journal of Personality and Social Psychology, 34,* 434–446.

Baron, R. A., Russell, G. W., & Arms, R. L. (1985). Negative ions and behavior: Impact on mood, memory, and aggression among Type A and Type B persons. *Journal of Personality and Social Psychology, 48,* 746–754.

Barr, H. M., Streissguth, A. P., Martin, D. C., & Herman, C. S. (1984). Infant size at 8 months of age: Relationship to maternal use of alcohol, nicotine, and caffeine during pregnancy. *Pediatrics, 74,* 336–341.

Barrett, N. S. (1979). Women in the job market: Occupations, earnings, and career opportunities. In R. E. Smith (Ed.), *The subtle revolution: Women at work.* Washington, DC: The Urban Institute.

Barrow, G. M., & Smith, P. A. (1983). *Aging, the individual, and society,* 2d ed. St. Paul: West.

Bar-Tal, D., & Saxe, L. (1976). Perceptions of similarly and dissimilarly physically attractive couples and individuals. *Journal of Personality and Social Psychology, 33,* 772–781.

Bartell, G. (1970). Group sex among the mid-Americans. *Journal of Sex Research, 6,* 113–130.

Baruch, G., Barnett, R., & Rivers, C. (1983). *Lifeprints.* New York: McGraw-Hill.

Basham, R. B. (1986). Scientific and practical advantages of comparative design in psychotherapy outcome research. *Journal of Consulting and Clinical Psychology, 54,* 88–94.

Basow, S. A. (1980). *Sex-role stereotypes.* Monterey, CA: Brooks/Cole.

Batson, C. D., Duncan, B. D., Ackerman, P., Buckley, T., & Birch, K. (1981). Is empathic emotion a source of altruistic motivation? *Journal of Personality and Social Psychology, 40,* 290–302.

Baucom, D. H., & Aiken, P. A. (1981). Effect of depressed mood on eating among obese and nonobese dieting and nondieting persons. *Journal of Personality and Social Psychology, 41,* 577–585.

Baucom, D. H., & Aiken, P. A. (1984). Sex role identity, marital satisfaction, and response to behavioral marital therapy. *Journal of Consulting and Clinical Psychology, 52,* 438–444.

Baucom, D. H., Besch, P. K., & Callahan, S. (1985). Relationship between testosterone concentration, sex role identity, and personality among females. *Journal of Personality and Social Psychology, 48,* 1218–1226.

Baucom, D. H., & Danker-Brown, P. (1979). Influence of sex roles on the development of learned helplessness. *Journal of Consulting and Clinical Psychology, 47,* 928–936.

Baucom, D. H., & Danker-Brown, P. (1983). Peer ratings of males and females possessing different sex role identities. *Journal of Personality Assessment, 44,* 334–343.

Baucom, D. H., & Danker-Brown, P. (1984). Sex role identity and sex stereotyped tasks in the development of learned helplessness in women. *Journal of Personality and Social Psychology, 46,* 422–430.

Bauer, W. D., & Twentyman, C. T. (1985). Abusing, neglectful, and comparison mothers' responses to child-related and non-child-related stressors. *Journal of Consulting and Clinical Psychology, 53,* 335–343.

Baum, A. (1988). Disasters, natural and otherwise. *Psychology Today, 22*(4), 57–60.

Baum, A., Deckel, A. W., & Gatchel, R. J. (1982). Environmental stress and health: Is there a relationship? In G. S. Sanders & J. Suls (Eds.), *Social psychology of health and illness.* Hillsdale, NJ: Erlbaum.

Baum, A., Fisher, J. D., & Solomon, S. (1981). Type of information, familiarity, and the reduction of crowding stress. *Journal of Personality and Social Psychology, 40,* 11–23.

Baum, A., Fleming, R., & Davidson, L. M. (1983). Natural disaster and technological catastrophe. *Environment and Behavior, 15,* 333–354.

Baum, A., Gatchel, R. J., & Schaeffer, M. A. (1983). Emotional, behavioral, and physiological effects of chronic stress at Three Mile Island. *Journal of Consulting and Clinical Psychology, 51,* 565–572.

Baum, A., & Valins, S. (1977). *Architecture and social behavior.* Hillsdale, NJ: Erlbaum.

Baum, M. J., et al. (1977). Hormonal basis of proceptivity and receptivity in female primates. *Archives of Sexual Behavior, 6,* 173–192.

Baumann, L. J., & Leventhal, H. (1985). "I can tell when my blood pressure is up, can't I?" *Health Psychology, 4,* 203–218.

Baum-Baicker, C. (1984). Treating and preventing alcohol abuse in the workplace. *American Psychologist, 39,* 454.

Baumeister, R. F. (1984). Choking under pressure: Self-consciousness and paradoxical effects of incentives on skillful performance. *Journal of Personality and Social Psychology, 46,* 610–620.

Baumeister, R. F., & Covington, M. V. (1985). Self-esteem, persuasion, and retrospective distortion of initial attitudes. *Electronic Social Psychology, 1,* 1–22.

Baumgardner, A. H., Heppner, P. P., & Arkin, R. M. (1986). Role of causal attribution in personal problem solving. *Journal of Personality and Social Psychology, 50,* 636–643.

Baumrind, D. (1972). Socialization and instrumental competence in young children. In W. W. Hartup (Ed.), *The young child: Reviews of research,* Vol. 12. Washington, DC: National Association for the Education of Young Children.

Baumrind, D. (1973). The development of instrumental competence through socialization. In A. D. Pick (Ed.), *Minnesota Symposia on Child Development,* Vol. 7. Minneapolis: University of Minnesota Press.

Baumrind, D. (1986). Sex differences in moral reasoning: Response to Walker's (1984) conclusion that there are none. *Child Development, 57,* 511–521.

Beard, R. R., & Wertheim, G. A. (1967). Behavioral impairment associated with small doses of carbon monoxide.

American Journal of Public Health, 57, 2012–2022.

Beardslee, W. R., Bemporad, J., Keller, M. B., & Klerman, G. L. (1983). Children of parents with major affective disorder: A review. *American Journal of Psychiatry, 140,* 825–832.

Beatty, W. W. (1979). Gonadal hormones and sex differences in nonreproductive behaviors in rodents: Organizational and activational influences. *Hormones and Behavior, 12,* 112–163.

Beauchamp, G. (1981). Paper presented to the Conference on the Determination of Behavior by Chemical Stimuli. Hebrew University, Jerusalem.

Beck, A. T. (1976). *Cognitive therapy and the emotional disorders.* New York: International Universities Press.

Beck, A. T. (1985). Theoretical perspectives on clinical anxiety. In A. H. Tuma, & J. D. Maser (Eds.), *Anxiety and the anxiety disorders.* Hillsdale, NJ: Erlbaum.

Beck, A. T., Rush, A. J., Show, B. F., & Emery, G. (1979). *Cognitive therapy of depression.* New York: Guilford Press.

Beck, J., Elsner, A., & Silverstein, C. (1977). Position uncertainty and the-perception of apparent movement. *Perception and psychophysics, 21,* 33–38.

Becker, M. H., & Maiman, L. A. (1980). Strategies for enhancing patient compliance. *Journal of Community Health, 6,* 113–135.

Beckham, E. E., & Leber, W. R. (1985). The comparative efficacy of psychotherapy and pharmacotherapy for depression. In E. E. Beckham & W. R. Leber (Eds.), *Handbook of depression: Treatment, assessment, and research.* Homewood, IL: Dorsey Press.

Beckman, L. J., & Houser, B. B. (1982). The consequences of childlessness on the social-psychological well-being of older women. *Journal of Gerontology, 37,* 243–250.

Beers, T. M., & Karoly, P. (1979). Cognitive strategies, expectancy, and coping style in the control of pain. *Journal of Consulting and Clinical Psychology, 47,* 179–180.

Behrman, R. E., & Vaughn, V. C., III. (1983). *Pediatrics.* Philadelphia: W. B. Saunders Co.

Bell, A. P., & Weinberg, M. S. (1978). *Homosexualities: A study of diversity among men and women.* New York: Simon and Schuster.

Bell, A. P., Weinberg, M. S., & Hammersmith, S. K. (1981). *Sexual preference: Its development in men and women.* Bloomington, IN: University of Indiana Press.

Bell, P. A. (1981). Physiological comfort, performance, and social effects of heat stress. *Journal of Social Issues, 37,* 71–94.

Bell, P. A. (1982, August). Theoretical interpretations of heat stress. Paper presented to the American Psychological Association, Washington, DC.

Bell, P. A., & Baron, R. A. (1981). Ambient temperature and human violence. In P. F. Brain & D. Benton (Eds.), *A multidisciplinary approach to aggression research.* Amsterdam: Elsevier.

Bell, P. A., & Doyle, D. P. (1983). Effects of heat and noise on helping behavior. *Psychological Reports, 53,* 955–959.

Bell, P. A., & Greene, T. C. (1982). Thermal stress: Physiological comfort, performance, and social effects of hot and cold environments. In G. W. Evans (Ed.), *Environmental stress.* London: Cambridge University Press.

Bell, R. R. (1983). *Marriage and family interaction,* 6th ed. Homewood, IL: Dorsey.

Belsky, J. (1980). Child maltreatment: An ecological integration. *American Psychologist, 35,* 320–335.

Belsky, J. (1984). The determinants of parenting: A process model. *Child Development, 55,* 83–96.

Belsky, J. (1984). *The psychology of aging: Theory, research, and practice.* Monterey, CA: Brooks/Cole.

Belsky, J., & Steinberg, L. D. (1978). The effects of day care: A critical review. *Child Development, 49,* 929–949.

Belsky, J., & Steinberg, L. D. (1979, July–August). What does research teach us about day care? A follow-up report. *Children Today,* pp. 21–26.

Belsky, J., Steinberg, L. D., & Walker, A. (1982). The ecology of day care. In M. E. Lamb (Ed.), *Nontraditional families: Parenting and child development.* Hillsdale, NJ: Erlbaum.

Bem, D. J. (1972). Self-perception theory. In L. Berkowitz (Ed.), *Advances in experimental social psychology,* Vol. 6. New York: Academic Press.

Bem, D. J. (1987). Social influence. In R. L. Atkinson, R. C. Atkinson, E. E. Smith, & E. R. Hilgard. *Introduction to psychology,* 9th ed., pp. 596–627. Orlando, FL: Harcourt Brace Jovanovich.

Bem, S. L. (1974). The measurement of psychological androgyny. *Journal of Consulting and Clinical Psychology, 42,* 151–162.

Bem, S. L. (1975). Sex role adaptability: One consequence of psychological androgyny. *Journal of Personality and Social Psychology, 31,* 634–643.

Bem, S. L. (1981). Gender schema theory: A cognitive account of sex typing. *Psychological Review, 88,* 354–364.

Bem, S. L. (1983). Gender schema theory and its implications for child development: Raising gender-aschematic children in a gender-schematic society. *Signs: Journal of Women in Culture and Society, 8,* 598–616.

Bem, S. L. (1985). Androgyny and gender schema theory: A conceptual and empirical integration. In T. B. Sonderegger (Ed.), *Nebraska symposium on motivation.* Lincoln, NE: University of Nebraska Press.

Bem, S. L., & Bem, D. J. (1973). Training the woman to know her place: The power of a nonconscious ideology. In L. S. Wrightsman & J. C. Brigham (Eds.), *Contemporary issues in social psychology,* 2d ed. Monterey, CA: Brooks/Cole.

Bem, S. L., & Lenney, E. (1976). Sex typing and the avoidance of cross-sexed behaviors. *Journal of Personality and Social Psychology, 33,* 48–54.

Bem, S. L., Martyna, W., & Watson, C. (1976). Sex typing and androgyny: Further explorations of the expressive domain. *Journal of Personality and Social Psychology, 34,* 1016–1023.

Bemis, K. M. (1978). Current approaches to the etiology and treatment of anorexia nervosa. *Psychological Bulletin, 85,* 593–617.

Benbow, C. P., & Stanley, J. C. (1980). Sex differences in mathematical ability: Fact or artifact? *Science, 210,* 1029–1031.

Benbow, C. P., & Stanley, J. C. (1983). Sex differences in mathematical reasoning ability: More facts. *Science, 210,* 1029–1030.

Benecke, W. M., & Harris, M. B. (1972). Teaching self-control of study behavior. *Behaviour Research and Therapy, 10,* 35–41.

Benedek, E., & Vaughn, R. (1982). Voluntary childlessness. In M. Kirkpatrick (Ed.), *Women's sexual experience.* New York: Plenum Publishing Co.

Bennett, D. (1985). Rogers: More intuition in therapy. *APA Monitor, 16* (10), 3.

Bennett, W. (1988, January 10). The drink-a-day lore. *The New York Times Magazine,* pp. 55–56.

Bennett, W., & Gurin, J. (1982). *The dieter's dilemma: Eating less and weighing more.* New York: Basic Books.

Bensinger, P. B. (1982, November–December). Drugs in the workplace. *Harvard Business Review,* 48–60.

Benson, H. (1975). *The relaxation response.* New York: Morrow.

Benson, H., Manzetta, B. R., & Rosner, B. (1973). Decreased systolic blood pressure in hypertensive subjects who practiced meditation. *Journal of Clinical Investigation, 52,* 8.

Benson, P. L., Karabenick, S. A., & Lerner, R. M. (1976). Pretty please: The effects of physical attractiveness, race, and sex on receiving help. *Journal of Experimental Social Psychology, 12,* 409–415.

Bentler, P. M. (1976). A typology of transsexualism: Gender identity theory and data. *Archives of Sexual Behavior, 5,* 567–584.

Berelson, B. (1979). The value of children: A taxonomical essay. In J. G. Wells (Ed.), *Current issues in marriage and the family,* 2d ed. New York: Macmillan.

Berezin, N. (1980). *The gentle birth book: A practical guide to Leboyer family-centered delivery.* New York: Pocket Books.

Berg, J. H., & Peplau, L. A. (1982). Loneliness: The relationship of self-disclosure and androgyny. *Personality and Social Psychology Bulletin, 8,* 624–630.

Berger, C. R., & Calabrese, R. J. (1975). Some explorations in initial interaction and beyond: Toward a developmental theory of interpersonal communication. *Human Communication Research, 1,* 99–112.

Berger, C. R., Gardner, R. R., Clatterbuck, G. W., & Schulman, L. S. (1976). Perceptions of information sequencing in relationship development. *Human Communication Research, 3,* 29–46.

Berger, P. A. (1978). Medical treatment of mental illness. *Science, 200,* 974–981.

Berkman, L. F., & Breslow, L. (1983). *Health and ways of living: The Alameda County Study.* New York: Oxford University Press.

Berkman, L. F., & Syme, S. L. (1979). Social networks, host resistance, and mortality: A nine-year follow-up study of Alameda County residents. *American Journal of Epidemiology, 109,* 186–204.

Berkowitz, L. (1983). Aversively stimulated aggression: Some parallels and differences in research with animals and humans. *American Psychologist, 38,* 1135–1144.

Berkowitz, L. (1987). Mood, self-awareness, and willingness to help. *Journal of Personality and Social Psychology, 52,* 721–729.

Berkowitz, W. R., Nebel, J. C., & Reitman, J. W. (1971). Height and interpersonal attraction: The 1960 mayoral election in New York City. Paper presented to the American Psychological Association, Washington, DC.

Berman, J. S., Miller, R. C., & Massman, P. J. (1985). Cognitive therapy versus systematic desensitization: Is one therapy superior? *Psychological Bulletin, 97,* 451–461.

Berndt, T. J. (1982). The features and effects of friendships in early adolescence. *Child Development, 53,* 1447–1460.

Berndt, T. J., & Perry, T. B. (1986). Children's perceptions of friendships as supportive relationships. *Developmental Psychology, 22,* 640–648.

Berne, E. (1976a). *Beyond games and scripts.* New York: Grove Press.

Berne, E. (1976b). *Games people play.* New York: Ballantine Books.

Bernstein, B. E. (1977). Effect of menstruation on academic performance among college women. *Archives of Sexual Behavior, 6,* 289–296.

Bernstein, W. M., Stephenson, B. O., Snyder, M. L., & Wicklund, R. A. (1983). Causal ambiguity and heterosexual affiliation. *Journal of Experimental Social Psychology, 19,* 78–92.

Berntzen, D., & Götestam, K. G. (1987). Effects of on-demand versus fixed-interval schedules in the treatment of chronic pain with analgesic compounds. *Journal of Consulting and Clinical Psychology, 55,* 213–217.

Berscheid, E. (1976). Theories of interpersonal attraction. In B. B. Wolman & L. R. Pomeroy (Eds.), *International encyclopaedia of neurology, psychiatry, psychoanalysis, and psychology.* New York: Springer.

Berscheid, E., Dion, K., Walster, E., & Walster, G. W. (1971). Physical attractiveness and dating choice: A test of the matching hypothesis. *Journal of Experimental Social Psychology, 7,* 173–189.

Berscheid, E., & Walster, E. (1974a). A little bit about love. In T. L. Huston (Ed.), *Foundations of interpersonal attraction.* New York: Academic Press.

Berscheid, E., & Walster, E. (1974b). Physical attractiveness. In L. Berkowitz (Ed.), *Advances in experimental social psychology,* Vol. 7. New York: Academic Press.

Berscheid, E., & Walster, E. (1978). *Interpersonal attraction.* Reading, MA: Addison-Wesley.

Berscheid, E., Walster, E., & Bohrnstedt, G. (1973). Body image, the happy American body: A survey report. *Psychology Today, 7*(6), 119–123, 126–131.

Berzins, J. I., Welling, M. A., & Wetter, R. E. (1977). The PRF ANDRO Scale: User's manual. Unpublished manuscript: University of Kentucky.

Betz, N. E., & Hackett, G. (1981). The relationships of career-related self-efficacy expectations to perceived career options in college women and men. *Journal of Counseling Psychology, 28,* 399–410.

Bickman, L., Teger, A., Gabriele, T., McLaughlin, C., Berger, M., & Sunaday, E. (1973). Dormitory density and helping behavior. *Environment and Behavior, 5,* 465–490.

Biglan, A., & Craker, D. (1982). Effects of pleasant-activities manipulation on depression. *Journal of Consulting and Clinical Psychology, 50,* 436–438.

Billings, A. G., Cronkite, R. C., & Moos, R. H. (1983). Social-environmental factors in unipolar depression: Comparisons of depressed patients and nondepressed controls. *Journal of Abnormal Psychology, 92,* 119–133.

Bing, E. D. (1983). *Dear Elizabeth Bing: We've had our baby.* New York: Pocket Books.

Biran, M., & Wilson, G. T. (1981). Treatment of phobic disorders using cognitive and exposure methods: A self-efficacy analysis. *Journal of Consulting and Clinical Psychology, 49,* 886–899.

Birch, K. (1981). Is empathic emotion a source of altruistic motivation? *Journal of Personality and Social Psychology, 40,* 290–302.

Birchler, G. R., Weiss, R. L., & Vincent, V. P. (1975). A multimethod analysis of social reinforcement exchange between maritally distressed and nondistressed spouses and stranger dyads. *Journal of Personality and Social Psychology, 31,* 349–360.

Birren, J. E. (1983). Aging in America: Roles for psychology. *American Psychologist, 38,* 298–299.

Blackburn, I. M., Bishop, S., Glen, A. I. M., Whalley, L. J., & Christie, J. E. (1981). The efficacy of cognitive therapy in depression: A treatment trial using cognitive therapy and pharmacotherapy, each alone and in combination. *British Journal of Psychiatry, 139,* 181–189.

Blackler, F. H. M., & Brown, C. A. (1978). *Job redesign and management control: Studies in British Leyland and Volvo.* New York: Praeger Books.

Blake, R. (1985). Neurohormones and sexual preference. *Psychology Today, 19*(1), 12–13.

Blakeley, M. K. (1985). Is one woman's sexuality another woman's pornography? The question behind a major legal battle. *Ms, 13*(10), 37–47, 120–123.

Blanchard, E. B., Andrasik, F., Ahles, T. A., Teders, S. J., & O'Keefe, D. M. (1980). Migraine and tension headache: A meta-analytic review. *Behavior Therapy, 11,* 613–621.

Blanchard, E. B., Andrasik, F., Neff, D. F., Arena, J. G., Ahles, T. A., Jurish, S. E., Pallmeyer, T. P., Saunders, N. L., Teders, S. J., Barron, K. D., & Rodichok, L. D. (1982). Biofeedback and relaxation training with three kinds of headache: Treatment effects and their prediction. *Journal of Consulting and Clinical Psychology, 50,* 562–575.

Blanchard, E. B., Andrasik, F., Evans, D. D., Neff, D. F., Appelbaum, K. A.,

& Rodichok, L. D. (1985). Behavioral treatment of 250 chronic headache patients: A clinical replication series. *Behavior Therapy, 16,* 308–327.

Blanchard, E. B., Andrasik, F., Guarnieri, P., Neff, D. F., & Rodichok, L. D. (1987). Two-, three-, and four-year follow-up on the self-regulatory treatment of chronic headache. *Journal of Consulting and Clinical Psychology, 55,* 257–259.

Blanchard, R., Steiner, B. W., & Clemmensen, L. H. (1985). Gender dysphoria, gender reorientation, and the clinical management of transsexualism. *Journal of Consulting and Clinical Psychology, 53,* 295–304.

Blau, F. O. (1975). Women in the labor force: An overview. In J. Freeman (Ed.), *Women: A feminist perspective.* Palo Alto, CA: Mayfield.

Blittner, M., Goldberg, J., & Merbaum, M. (1978). Cognitive self-control factors in the reduction of smoking behavior. *Behavior Therapy, 9,* 553–561.

Bloch, V., Hennevin, E., & Leconte, P. (1979). Relationship between paradoxical sleep and memory processes. In M. A. B. Braszier (Ed.), *Brain mechanisms in memory and learning: From the single neuron to man.* New York: Raven Press.

Block, J. (1983). Differential premises arising from differential socialization of the sexes: Some conjectures. *Child Development, 54,* 1335–1354.

Bloom, B. J., Asher, S. J., & White, S. W. (1978). Marital disruption as a stressor: A review and analysis. *Psychological Bulletin, 85,* 867–894.

Blumberg, S. H., & Izard, C. E. (1985). Affective and cognitive characteristics of depression in 10- and 11-year-old children. *Journal of Personality and Social Psychology, 49,* 194–202.

Blumstein, P., & Schwartz, P. (1983). *American couples.* New York: Morrow.

Bodenhausen, G. V., & Wyer, R. S. (1985). Effects of stereotypes on decision making and information-processing strategies. *Journal of Personality and Social Psychology, 48,* 267–282.

Boffey, P. M. (1988, February 14). Spread of AIDS abating, but deaths will still soar. *The New York Times,* pp. 1, 36.

Bohannan, P. (1970). The six stations of divorce. In P. Bohannan (Ed.), *Divorce and after.* Garden City, NY: Doubleday.

Bond, C. R., & McMahon, R. J. (1984). Relationships between marital distress and child behavior problems, maternal personal adjustment, maternal personality, and maternal parenting behavior. *Journal of Abnormal Psychology, 93,* 348–351.

Bonica, J. J. (1972). *Principles and prac-*

tices of obstetric analgesia and anesthesia, Vols. 1 & 2. Philadelphia: F. A. Davis.

Bonica, J. J. (Ed.) (1980). *Pain.* New York: Raven Press.

Booth, A., & Edwards, J. N. (1985). Age at marriage and marital instability. *Journal of Marriage and the Family, 47,* 67–75.

Booth-Kewley, S., & Friedman, H. S. (1987). Psychological predictors of heart disease: A quantitative review. *Psychological Bulletin, 101,* 343–362.

Borkan, G. A., Sparrow, D., Wisniewski, C., & Vokonas, P. S. (1986). Body weight and coronary heart disease risk: Patterns of risk factor change associated with long-term weight change. The Normative Aging Study. *American Journal of Epidemiology, 124,* 410–419.

Boskind-White, M., & White, W. C. (1983). *Bulimarexia: The binge/purge cycle.* New York: W. W. Norton.

Boskind-White, M., & White, W. C. (1986). Bulimarexia: A historical-sociocultural perspective. In K. D. Brownell & J. P. Foreyt (Eds.), *Handbook of eating disorders.* New York: Basic Books.

Boston Women's Health Book Collective. (1984). *The new our bodies, ourselves.* New York: Simon and Schuster.

Bower, D. W., & Christopherson, V. A. (1977). University student cohabitation: A regional comparison of selected attitudes and behavior. *Journal of Marriage and the Family, 39,* 447–452.

Brackbill, Y. (1976). Long-term effects of obstetrical anesthesia on infant autonomic function. *Developmental Psychobiology, 9,* 353–358.

Brackbill, Y. (1979). Obstetrical medication and infant behavior. In J. D. Osofsky (Ed.), *Handbook of infant development.* New York: Wiley-Interscience.

Bralove, M. (1981, December 7). Keeping work world out of family life is growing problem for two-job couples. *The Wall Street Journal,* pp. 28, 43.

Bram, S. (1984). Voluntary childless women: Traditional or nontraditional? *Sex Roles, 10,* 195–206.

Brazleton, E. B. (1970). Effects of prenatal drugs on the behavior of the neonate. *American Journal of Psychiatry, 126,* 95–100.

Brent, E., & Granberg, D. (1982). Subjective agreement with the presidential candidates of 1976 and 1980. *Journal of Personality and Social Psychology, 42,* 393–403.

Briddell, D. W., & Wilson, G. T. (1976). Effects of alcohol and expectancy set on male sexual arousal. *Journal of Abnormal Psychology, 85,* 225–234.

Bridgwater, C. A. (1982). What candor can do. *Psychology Today, 16*(5), 16.

Brigham, J. C. (1980). Limiting conditions of the "physical attractiveness stereotype": Attributions about divorce. *Journal of Research in Personality, 14,* 365–375.

Brody, J. (1988, January 14). "Type A" men fare better in heart attack study. *The New York Times,* p. B7.

Bromet, E. (1980). *Preliminary report on the mental health of Three Mile Island residents.* Pittsburgh: Western Pennsylvania Psychiatric Institute.

Bronfenbrenner, U. (1960). Freudian theories of identification and their derivatives. *Child Development, 31,* 15–40.

Brook, J. S., Lukoff, J. F., & Whiteman, M. (1980). Initiation into marihuana use. *Journal of Genetic Psychology, 137,* 133–142.

Brooks, J., Ruble, D. N., & Clarke, A. E. (1977). College women's attitudes and expectations concerning menstrual-related changes. *Psychosomatic Medicine, 39,* 288.

Brooks, V. R. (1982). Sex differences in student dominance behavior in female and male professors' classrooms. *Sex Roles, 8,* 683–690.

Brooks-Gunn, J., & Ruble, D. N. (1980). The menstrual attitude questionnaire. *Psychosomatic Medicine, 42,* 503–511.

Broverman, I. K., Vogel, S. R., Broverman, D. M., Clarkson, F. E., & Rosenkrantz, P. S. (1972). Sex role stereotypes: A current appraisal. *Journal of Social Issues, 28,* 59–78.

Brown, B. (1977). *Stress and the art of biofeedback.* New York: Harper & Row.

Brown, M., Amoroso, D., & Ware, E. (1976). Behavioral aspects of viewing pornography. *Journal of Social Psychology, 98,* 235–245.

Brown, N. A., Goulding, E. H., & Fabros. (1979). Ethanol embryotoxicity: Direct effects on mammalian embryos in vitro. *Science, 206,* 573–575.

Brown, P. L. (1987, September 14). Studying seasons of a woman's life. *The New York Times,* p. B17.

Brown, S. A. (1985). Expectancies versus background in the prediction of college drinking patterns. *Journal of Consulting and Clinical Psychology, 53,* 123–130.

Brown, S. A., Goldman, M. S., & Christiansen, B. A. (1985). Do alcohol expectancies mediate drinking patterns of adults? *Journal of Consulting and Clinical Psychology, 53,* 512–519.

Brown, S. A., Goldman, M. S., Inn, A., & Anderson, L. R. (1980). Expectations of reinforcement from alcohol. *Journal of Consulting and Clinical Psychology, 48,* 419–426.

Brown, W. A., Monti, P. M., & Corriveau, D. P. (1978). Serum testosterone and sexual activity and interest in men. *Archives of Sexual Behavior, 7,* 97–103.

Brownell, K. D. (1982). Obesity: Understanding and treating a serious, prevalent, and refractory disorder. *Journal of Consulting and Clinical Psychology, 50,* 820–840.

Brownell, K. D. (1986). In A. Toufexis, et al. (1986, January 20). Dieting: The losing game. *Time Magazine,* pp. 54–60.

Brownell, K. D. (1988). Yo-yo dieting. *Psychology Today, 22*(1), 20–23.

Brownlee-Duffeck, M., Peterson, L., Simonds, J. F., Goldstein, D., Kilo, C., & Hoette, S. (1987). The role of health beliefs in the regimen adherence and metabolic control of adolescents and adults with diabetes mellitus. *Journal of Consulting and Clinical Psychology, 55,* 139–144.

Brownmiller, S. (1975). *Against our will.* New York: Simon & Schuster.

Bruch, H. (1978). *The golden cage: The enigma of anorexia nervosa.* Cambridge, MA: Harvard University Press.

Brunson, B. I., & Matthews, K. A. (1981). The Type-A coronary-prone behavior pattern and reactions to uncontrollable stress. *Journal of Personality and Social Psychology, 40,* 906–918.

Bry, B. H. (1983). Predicting drug abuse: Review and reformulation. *International Journal of the Addictions, 18,* 223–233.

Buffone, G. W. (1980). Exercise as therapy: A closer look. *Journal of Counseling and Psychotherapy, 3,* 101–115.

Buffone, G. W. (1984). Running and depression. In M. L. Sachs & G. W. Buffone (Eds.), *Running as therapy: An integrated approach.* Lincoln, NE: University of Nebraska Press.

Bulman, R. J., & Wortman, C. B. (1977). Attribution of blame and coping in the "real world": Severe accident victims react to their lot. *Journal of Personality and Social Psychology, 35,* 351–363.

Burns, G. L., & Farina, A. (1987). Physical attractiveness and self-perception of mental disorder. *Journal of Abnormal Psychology, 96,* 161–163.

Burros, M. (1988, January 6). What Americans really eat: Nutrition can wait. *The New York Times,* pp. C1, C6.

Burt, M. R. (1980). Cultural myths and supports for rape. *Journal of Personality and Social Psychology, 38,* 217–230.

Buss, A. H. (1983). Social rewards and personality. *Journal of Personality and Social Psychology, 44,* 553–563.

Buss, A. H. (1986). *Social behavior and personality.* Hillsdale, NJ: Erlbaum.

Buss, D. M. (1984). Toward a psychology of person–environment (PE) correla-

tion: The role of spouse selection. *Journal of Personality and Social Psychology, 47,* 361–377.

Buss, D. M., & Barnes, M. (1986). Preferences in human mate selection. *Journal of Personality and Social Psychology, 50,* 559–570.

Buss, D. M., Gomes, M., Higgins, D. S., & Lauterbach, K. (1987). Tactics of manipulation. *Journal of Personality and Social Psychology, 52,* 1219–1229.

Bustillo, M. et al. (1984). Delivery of a healthy infant following nonsurgical ovum transfer. *Journal of the American Medical Association, 251,* 889.

Butler, N. R., & Goldstein, H. (1973). Smoking in pregnancy and subsequent child development. *British Medical Journal, 4,* 573–575.

Byrne, D. (1971). *The attraction paradigm.* New York: Academic Press.

Byrne, D., Baskett, G. D., & Hodges, L. (1971). Behavioral indicators of interpersonal attraction. *Journal of Applied Social Psychology, 1,* 137–149.

Byrne, D., Ervin, C. R., & Lamberth, J. (1970). Continuity between the experimental study of attraction and real-life computer dating. *Journal of Personality and Social Psychology, 16,* 157–165.

Byrne, D., & Murnen, S. (1987). Maintaining love relationships. In R. J. Sternberg & M. L. Barnes (Eds.), *The anatomy of love.* New Haven: Yale University Press.

Cadoret, R. J. (1978). Psychpathology in adopted-away offspring of biologic parents with antisocial behavior. *Archives of General Psychiatry, 35,* 176–184.

Cadoret, R. J., Cain, C. A., & Grove, W. M. (1980). Development of alcoholism in adoptees raised apart from alcoholic biologic relatives. *Archives of General Psychiatry, 37,* 561–563.

Calder, B. J., Ross, M., & Inkso, C. A. (1973). Attitude change and attitude attribution: Effects of incentive, choice, and consequences. *Journal of Personality and Social Psychology, 25,* 84–99.

Calhoun, J. B. (1962). Population density and social pathology. *Scientific American, 206,* 139–148.

Callahan-Levy, C. M., & Messé, L. A. (1979). Sex differences in allocation of pay. *Journal of Personality and Social Psychology, 37,* 443–446.

Campbell, A. (1975). The American way of mating: Marriage si, children only maybe. *Psychology Today, 8,* 37–43.

Campbell, F. L., Townes, B. D., & Beach, L. R. (1982). Motivational bases of childbearing decisions. In G. L. Fox (Ed.), *The childbearing decision.* Beverly Hills, CA: Sage.

Cannon, D. S., & Baker, T. B. (1981). Emetic and electric shock alcohol

aversion therapy. *Journal of Consulting and Clinical Psychology, 49,* 20–33.

Cannon, W. B. (1929). *Bodily changes in pain, hunger, fear, and rage.* New York: Appleton.

Cantor, P. C. (1976). Personality characteristics found among youthful female suicide attempters. *Journal of Abnormal Psychology, 85,* 324–329.

Caplan, P. J., MacPherson, G. M., & Tobin, P. (1985). Do sex-related differences in spatial abilities exist? A multilevel critique with new data. *American Psychologist, 40,* 786–799.

Carr, D. B., et al. (1981). Physical conditioning facilitates the exercise-induced secretion of beta-endorphins and beta-lipotropin in women. *New England Journal of Medicine, 305,* 560–563.

Carroll, D. (1985). *Living with dying.* New York: McGraw-Hill.

Carson, R. C., Butcher, J. N., & Coleman, J. C. (1988). *Abnormal psychology and modern life,* 8th ed. Glenview, IL: Scott, Foresman and Company.

Cartwright, R. D. (1978). *A primer on sleep and dreaming.* Reading, MA: Addison-Wesley.

Cartwright, R. D., Lloyd, S., Nelson, J. B., & Bass, S. (1983). The traditional-liberated woman dimension: Social stereotype and self-concept. *Journal of Personality and Social Psychology, 44,* 581–588.

Cash, T. F., & Kilcullen, R. N. (1985). The age of the beholder: Susceptibility to sexism and beautyism in the evaluation of managerial applicants. *Journal of Applied Social Psychology, 15,* 591–605.

Cassileth, B. R., Lusk, E. J., Miller, D. S., Brown, L. L., & Miller, C. (1985). Psychosocial correlates of survival in advanced malignant diseases. *New England Journal of Medicine, 312,* 1551–1555.

Cattell, R. B. (1965). *The scientific analysis of personality.* Baltimore: Penguin Books.

Cattell, R. B. (1973). Personality pinned down. *Psychology Today, 7,* 40–46.

Centers for Disease Control. (1985a, September). 1985 STD treatment guidelines. *Morbidity and mortality weekly report supplement.*

Centers for Disease Control. (1985b). Self-reported behavioral change among gay and bisexual men—San Francisco. *Morbidity and mortality weekly report, 34,* 613–615.

Chaiken, S., & Eagly, A. H. (1983). Communication modality as a determinant of persuasion: The role of communicator salience. *Journal of Personality and Social Psychology, 45,* 241–256.

Charry, J. M., & Hawkinshire, F. B. W., Jr. (1981). Effects of atmospheric electricity on some substrates of disordered social behavior. *Journal of Personality and Social Psychology, 41,* 185–197.

Chemers, M. M., Hays, R. B., Rhodewalt, F., & Wysocki, J. (1985). A person–environment analysis of job stress: A contingency model explanation. *Journal of Personality and Social Psychology, 49,* 628–635.

Chesler, P. (1972). *Women and madness.* Garden City, NY: Doubleday.

Chesney, M. A., & Rosenman, R. H. (Eds.) (1985). *Anger and hostility in cardiovascular and behavioral disorders.* Washington, DC: Hemisphere.

Chesno, F. A., & Kilmann, P. R. (1975). Effects of stimulation intensity on sociopathic avoidance learning. *Journal of Abnormal Psychology, 84,* 144–151.

Chess, S., & Thomas, A. (1982). Infant bonding: Mystique and reality. *American Journal of Orthopsychiatry, 52,* 213–222.

Christiansen, B. A., Goldman, M. S., & Inn, A. (1982). Development of alcohol-related expectancies in adolescence. *Journal of Consulting and Clinical Psychology, 50,* 336–344.

Clanton, G., & Downing, C. (1975). *Face to face.* New York: Dutton.

Clark, M., et al. (1985, August 12). AIDS. *Newsweek,* pp. 19–27.

Cleckley, H. (1964). *The mask of sanity.* St. Louis: Mosby.

Cleek, M., & Pearson, T. (1985). Perceived causes of divorce: An analysis of interrelationships. *Journal of Marriage and the Family, 47,* 179–183.

Cline, V. B., Croft, R. C., & Courrier, S. (1973). The desensitization of children to television violence. *Journal of Personality and Social Psychology, 27,* 360–365.

Clingempeel, W. G., & Repucci, N. D. (1982). Joint custody after divorce: Major issues and goals for research. *Psychological Bulletin, 91,* 102–127.

Clingempeel, W. G., & Segal, S. (1986). Stepparent–stepchild relationships and the psychological adjustment of children in stepmother and stepfather families. *Child Development, 57,* 474–484.

Clore, G. L., Bray, R. M., Itkin, S. N., & Murphy, P. (1978). Interracial attitudes and behavior at a summer camp. *Journal of Personality and Social Psychology, 36,* 107–116.

Clore, G. L., & Byrne. D. (1977). The process of personality interaction. In R. B. Cattell & R. M. Dreger (Eds.), *Handbook of modern personality theory.* Washington, DC: Hemisphere.

Clore, G. L., Wiggins, N. H., & Itkin, S. (1975). Gain and loss in attraction: Attributions from nonverbal behavior. *Journal of Personality and Social Psychology, 31,* 706–712.

Cohen, S., Evans, G. W., Krantz, D. S., & Stokols, D. (1980). Physiological, motivational, and cognitive effects of aircraft noise on children. *American Psychologist, 35,* 231–243.

Cohen, S., Evans, G. W., Krantz, D. S., Stokols, D., & Kelly, S. (1981). Aircraft noise and children: Longitudinal and cross-sectional evidence on adaptation to noise and the effectiveness of noise abatement. *Journal of Personality and Social Psychology, 40,* 331–345.

Cohen, S., Evans, G. W., Stokols, D., & Krantz, D. S. (1986). *Behavior, health, and environmental stress.* New York· Plenum Publishing Co.

Cohen, S., Glass, D. C., & Singer, J. E. (1973). Apartment noise, auditory discrimination, and reading ability in children. *Journal of Experimental Social Psychology, 9,* 407–422.

Cohen, S., & Lezak, A. (1977). Noise and inattentiveness to social cues. *Environment and Behavior, 9,* 559–572.

Cohen, S., & Wills, T. A. (1985). Stress, social supports and the buffering hypothesis. *Psychological Bulletin, 98,* 310–357.

Colby, C. Z., Lanzetta, J. T., & Kleck, R. E. (1977). Effects of the expression of pain on autonomic and pain tolerance response to subject-controlled pain. *Psychophysiology, 14,* 537–540.

Coleman, M., & Ganong, L. H. (1985). Love and sex role stereotypes: Do macho men and feminine women make better lovers? *Journal of Personality and Social Psychology, 49,* 170–176.

Colletta, N. D. (1978). Divorced mothers at two income levels: Stress, support, and child-rearing practices. Unpublished thesis, Cornell University.

Colligan, M. J., & Murphy, L. R. (1982). A review of mass psychogenic illness in work settings. In M. J. Colligan, J. W. Pennebaker, & L. R. Murphy (Eds.), *Mass psychogenic illness.* Hillsdale, NJ: Erlbaum.

Collins, D. L., Baum, A., & Singer, J. E. (1983). Coping with chronic stress at Three Mile Island: Psychological and biochemical evidence. *Health Psychology, 2,* 149–166.

Conant, M., et al. (1986). Condoms prevent transmission of the AIDS-associated retrovirus. *Journal of the American Medical Association, 255,* 1706.

Condiotte, M. M., & Lichtenstein, E. (1981). Self-efficacy and relapse in smoking cessation programs. *Journal of Consulting and Clinical Psychology, 49,* 648–658.

Conger, J. J., & Petersen, A. (1984). *Adolescence and youth: Psychological development in a changing world.* New York: Harper and Row.

Conley, J. J. (1984). Longitudinal consistency of adult personality: Self-reported psychological characteristics across 45 years. *Journal of Personality and Social Psychology, 47,* 1325–1333.

Conley, J. J. (1985). Longitudinal stability of personality traits: A multitrait-multimethod-multioccasion analysis. *Journal of Personality and Social Psychology, 49,* 1266–1282.

Connor, J. (1972). Olfactory control of aggressive and sexual behavior in the mouse. *Psychonomic Science, 27,* 1–3.

Conover, P. (1975). An analysis of communes with particular attention to sexual and general relations. *The Family Coordinator, 24,* 453–464.

Constantine, L., & Constantine, J. (1973). *Group marriage.* New York: Macmillan.

Conte, H. R., Plutchik, R., Wild, K. V., & Karasu, T. B. (1986). Combined psychotherapy and pharmacotherapy for depression: A systematic analysis of the evidence. *Archives of General Psychiatry, 43,* 471–479.

Cook, A. S., West, J. S., & Hamner, T. J. (1982). Changes in attitude toward parenting among college women: 1972 and 1979 samples. *Family Relations, 31,* 109–113.

Cooney, J. L., & Zeichner, A. (1985). Selective attention to negative feedback in Type A and Type B individuals. *Journal of Abnormal Psychology, 94,* 110–112.

Cooper, A. J. (1978). Neonatal olfactory bulb lesions: Influences on subsequent behavior of male mice. *Bulletin of the Psychonomic Society, 11,* 53–56.

Cooper, H. M. (1979). Statistically combining independent studies: A meta-analysis of sex differences in conformity research. *Journal of Personality and Social Psychology, 37,* 131–146.

Cooper, J. (1980). Reducing fears and increasing assertiveness: The role of dissonance reduction. *Journal of Experimental Social Psychology, 16,* 199–213.

Cooper, K. H. (1982). *The aerobics program for total well-being.* New York: Evans.

Cooper, K. H. (1985). *Running without fear: How to reduce the risks of heart attack and sudden death during aerobic exercise.* New York: Evans.

Cordes, C. (1985). Common threads found in suicide. *APA Monitor, 16*(10), 11.

Costa, P. T., Jr., & McCrae, R. R. (1984). Personality as a lifelong determinant of wellbeing. In C. Z. Malatesta & C. E. Izard (Eds.), *Emotion in adult development.* Beverly Hills: Sage Publications.

Coyne, J. C., Kessler, R. C., Tal, M., Turnbull, J., Wortman, C. B., & Greden, J. F. (1987). Living with a depressed person. *Journal of Consulting and Clinical Psychology, 55,* 347–352.

Cozby, P. C. (1973). Self-disclosure: A

literature review. *Psychological Bulletin, 79,* 73–91.

Creese, I., Burt, D. R., & Snyder, S. H. (1978). Biochemical actions of neuroleptic drugs. In L. L. Iverson, S. D. Iverson, & S. H. Snyder (Eds.), *Handbook of psychopharmacology,* Vol. 10. New York: Plenum Publishing Co.

Crews, D., & Moore, M. C. (1986). Evolution of mechanisms controlling mating behavior. *Science, 231,* 121–125.

Crick, F., & Mitchison, G. (1983). The function of dream sleep. *Nature, 304,* 111–114.

Crooks, R., & Baur, K. (1987). *Our sexuality,* 3d ed. Menlo Park, CA: Benjamin/Cummings.

Crowley, J. (1985). Cited in D. Zuckerman (1985). Retirement: R & R or risky? *Psychology Today, 19*(2), 80.

Croyle, R. T., & Cooper, J. (1983). Dissonance arousal: Physiological evidence. *Journal of Personality and Social Psychology, 45,* 782–791.

Crusco, A. H., & Wetzel, C. G. (1984). The midas touch: The effects of interpersonal touch on restaurant tipping. *Personality and Social Psychology Bulletin, 10,* 512–517.

Cummings, E. M., Iannotti, R. J., & Zahn-Waxler, C. (1985). Influence of conflict between adults on the emotions and aggression of young children. *Developmental Psychology, 21,* 495–507.

Cummings, N. A. (1979). Turning bread into stones: Our modern antimiracle. *American Psychologist, 34,* 1119–1129.

Cunningham, M. R. (1979). Weather, mood, and helping behavior. *Journal of Personality and Social Psychology, 37,* 1947–1956.

Current Population Reports. (1985). Marital status and living arrangements. U.S. Bureau of the Census: Washington, DC: U.S. Government Printing Office.

Cutrona, C. E. (1982). Transition to college: Loneliness and the process of social adjustment. In L. A. Peplau & D. Perlman (Eds.), *Loneliness: A sourcebook of current theory, research, and therapy.* New York: Wiley.

Cutrona, C. E. (1983). Causal attributions and perinatal depression. *Journal of Abnormal Psychology, 92,* 161–172.

Cutrona, C. E., & Troutman, B. R. (1986). Social support, infant temperament, and parenting self-efficacy: A mediational model of postpartum depression. *Child Development, 57,* 1507–1518.

Dalton, K. (1968). Menstruation and examinations. *Lancet, 2,* 1386–1388.

Dalton, K. (1972). *The menstrual cycle.* New York: Warner Books.

Dalton, K. (1980). Cyclical criminal acts in premenstrual syndrome. *Lancet, 2,* 1070–1071.

Damon, W. (1977). *The social world of the child.* San Francisco: Jossey-Bass.

Daniel, W. F., & Crovitz, H. F. (1983a). Acute memory impairment following electroconvulsive therapy: 1. Effects of electrical stimulus and number of treatments. *Acta Psychiatrica Scandinavica, 67,* 1–7.

Daniel, W. F., & Crovitz, H. F. (1983b). Acute memory impairment following electroconvulsive therapy: 2. Effects of electrode placement. *Acta Psychiatrica Scandinavica, 67,* 57–68.

Daniels, D., & Plomin, R. (1985). Origins of individual differences in infant shyness. *Developmental Psychology, 21,* 118–121.

Daniels, P., & Weingarten, K. (1982). *Sooner or Later: The timing of parenthood in adult lives.* New York: W. W. Norton.

Darley, J. M., & Gross, P. H. (1983). A hypothesis-confirming bias in labeling effects. *Journal of Personality and Social Psychology, 44,* 20–33.

Darley, J. M., & Latané, B. (1968). Bystander intervention in emergencies: Diffusion of responsibility. *Journal of Personality and Social Psychology, 8,* 377–383.

Darrow, W. W. (1983, November). Social and psychological aspects of Acquired Immune Deficiency Syndrome. Paper presented at the annual meeting of the Society for the Scientific Study of Sex, Chicago.

Darwin, C. A. (1872). *The expression of the emotions in man and animals.* London: J. Murray.

D'Atri, D. (1975). Psychophysiological responses to crowding. *Environment and Behavior, 1,* 237–252.

Dauber, R. B. (1984). Subliminal psychodynamic activation in depression: On the role of autonomy issues in depressed college women. *Journal of Abnormal Psychology, 93,* 9–18.

David, H. (1957). *Womanpower.* New York: Columbia University Press.

Davidson, J. M., Kwan, M., & Greenleaf, W. J. (1982). Hormonal replacement and sexuality in men. *Clinics in Endocrinology and Metabolism, 11,* 599–623.

Davidson, L. M., Baum, A., & Collins, D. L. (1982). Stress and control-related problems at Three Mile Island. *Journal of Applied Social Psychology, 12,* 349–359.

Davis, K. E. (1985). Near and dear: Friendship and love compared. *Psychology Today, 19*(2), 22–30.

Davison, G. C., & Neale, J. M. (1986). *Abnormal psychology,* 4th ed. New York: Wiley.

Dean, C. (1988, March 24). Red wine is linked to migraine. *The New York Times,* p. B6.

Deaux, K. (1976). *The behavior of men and women.* Monterey, CA: Brooks/Cole.

Deaux, K. (1984). From individual differences to social categories: Analysis of a decade's research on gender. *American Psychologist, 39,* 105–116.

DeBacker, G. et al. (1983). Behavior, stress, and psychosocial traits as risk factors. *Preventative Medicine, 12,* 32–36.

Deffenbacher, J. L., & Suinn, R. M. (1988). Systematic desensitization and the reduction of anxiety. *The Counseling Psychologist, 16*(1), 9–30.

DeGree, C. E., & Snyder, C. R. (1985). Adler's psychology (of use) today: Personal history of traumatic life events as a self-handicapping strategy. *Journal of Personality and Social Psychology, 48,* 1512–1519.

Delanoy, R. L., Merrin, J. S., & Gold, P. E. (1982). Moderation of long-term potentiation (LTP) by adrenergic agonists. *Neuroscience Abstracts, 8,* 316.

DeLongis, A., Coyne, J. C., Dakof, G., Folkman, S., & Lazarus, R. S. (1982). Relationship of daily hassles, uplifts, and major life events to health status. *Health Psychology, 1,* 119–136.

DeMaris, A., & Leslie, G. (1984). Cohabitation with the future spouse: Its influence upon marital satisfaction and communication. *Journal of Marriage and the Family, 46,* 77–84.

Dembroski, T. M., Lasater, T. M., & Ramirez, A. (1978). Communicator similarity, fear-arousing communications, and compliance with health care recommendations. *Journal of Applied Social Psychology, 8,* 254–269.

Dembroski, T. M., MacDougall, J. M., Williams, R. B., Haney, T. L., & Blumenthal, J. A. (1985). Components of Type A, hostility, and anger-in: Relationship to angroginphic findings. *Psychosomatic Medicine, 47,* 219–233.

Depue, R. A., Slater, J. F., Wolfstetter-Kausch, H., Klein, D., Goplerud, E., & Farr, D. (1981). A behavioral paradigm for identifying persons at risk for bipolar depressive disorder. *Journal of Abnormal Psychology, 90,* 381–438.

Dermer, M., & Thiel, D. L. (1975). When beauty may fail. *Journal of Personality and Social Psychology, 31,* 1168–1176.

DeRubeis, R. J. (1983, December). The cognitive-pharmacotherapy project: Study design, outcome, and clinical follow-up. Paper presented at the Association for the Advancement of Behavior Therapy, Washington, DC.

Diamond, E. L. (1982). The role of anger and hostility in essential hypertension and coronary heart disease. *Psychological Bulletin, 92,* 410–433.

Diamond, M. (1977). Human sexual development: Biological foundations for social development. In F. A. Beach (Ed.), *Human sexuality in four perspectives.* Baltimore: Johns Hopkins University Press.

Dickson, P. (1975). *The future of the workplace: The coming revolution in jobs.* New York: Weybright and Talley.

Diener, E. (1980). Deindividuation: The absence of self-awareness and self-regulation in group members. In P. Paulus (Ed.), *The psychology of group influence.* Hillsdale, NJ: Erlbaum.

Digman, J. M., & Inouye, J. (1986). Further specification of the five robust factors of personality. *Journal of Personality and Social Psychology, 50,* 116–123.

DiMatteo, M. R., & DiNicola, D. D. (1982). *Achieving patient compliance: The psychology of the medical practitioner's role.* New York: Pergamon Press.

Dimsdale, J. E., & Moss, J. (1980). Plasma catecholamines in stress and exercise. *Journal of the American Medical Association, 243,* 340–342.

DiNicola, D. D., & DiMatteo, M. R. (1984). Practitioners, patients, and compliance with medical regimens: A social psychological perspective. In A. Baum, S. E. Taylor, & J. E. Singer (Eds.), *Handbook of psychology and health: Vol. 4. Social psychological aspects of health.* Hillsdale, NJ: Erlbaum.

Dion, K. K., Berscheid, E., & Walster, E. (1972). What is beautiful is good. *Journal of Personality and Social Psychology, 24,* 285–290.

Dishman, R. K. (1982). Compliance/adherence in health-related exercise. *Health Psychology, 1,* 237–267.

Dodge, L. J. T., Glasgow, R. E., & O'Neill, H. K. (1982). Bibliotherapy in the treatment of female orgasmic dysfunction. *Journal of Consulting and Clinical Psychology, 50,* 442–443.

Doherty, W. J. (1983). Impact of divorce on locus of control orientation in adult women: A longitudinal study. *Journal of Personality and Social Psychology, 44,* 834–840.

Doherty, W. J., & Jacobson, N. S. (1982). Marriage and family. In B. B. Wolman (Ed.), *Handbook of developmental psychology.* Englewood Cliffs, NJ: Prentice-Hall.

Doherty, W. J., Schrott, H. G., Metcalf, L., & Iasiello-Vailas, L. (1983). Effects of spouse support and health beliefs on medication adherence. *Journal of Family Practice, 17,* 837–841.

Dohrenwend, B. P., & Shrout, P. E. (1985). "Hassles" in the conceptualization and measurement of life stress variables. *American Psychologist, 40,* 780–785.

Dohrenwend, B. S., Dohrenwend, B. P., Dodson, M., & Shrout, P. E. (1984). Symptoms, hassles, social supports and life events: The problem of confounded measures. *Journal of Abnormal Psychology, 93,* 222–230.

Dohrenwend, B. S., Krasnoff, L., Askenasy, A. R., & Dohrenwend, B. P. (1982). The psychiatric epidemiology research interview life events scale. In L. Goldberger & S. Breznitz (Eds.), *Handbook of stress: Theoretical and clinical aspects.* New York: Free Press.

Doll, R., & Peto, R. (1981). *The causes of cancer.* New York: Oxford University Press.

Donahoe, C. P., Jr., Lin, D. H., Kirschenbaum, D. S., & Keesey, R. E. (1984). Metabolic consequences of dieting and exercise in the treatment of obesity. *Journal of Consulting and Clinical Psychology, 52,* 827–836.

Donnerstein, E. I. (1980). Aggressive erotica and violence against women. *Journal of Personality and Social Psychology, 39,* 269–277.

Donnerstein, E. I., & Linz, D. G. (1984). Sexual violence in the media: A warning. *Psychology Today, 18*(1), 14–15.

Donnerstein, E. I., & Linz, D. G. (1986). The question of pornography. *Psychology Today, 20*(12), 56–60.

Donnerstein, E. I., & Linz, D. G. (1987). *The question of pornography.* New York: Free Press.

Donnerstein, E. I., & Wilson, D. W. (1976). Effects of noise and perceived control on ongoing and subsequent aggressive behavior. *Journal of Personality and Social Psychology, 34,* 774–781.

Dooker, M. (1980, July/August). Lamaze method of childbirth. *Nursing Research,* pp. 220–224.

Dooley, D., & Catalano, R. (1980). Economic change as a cause of behavioral disorder. *Psychological Bulletin, 87,* 450–468.

Dovidio, J. H., Evans, N., & Tyler, R. B. (1986). Racial stereotypes: The contents of their cognitive representations. *Journal of Experimental Social Psychology, 22,* 22–37.

Dowd, M. (1984, March 12). Twenty years after the murder of Kitty Genovese, the question remains: Why? *The New York Times,* pp. B1, B4.

Doyne, E. J., Chambless, D. L., & Bentler, L. E. (1983). Aerobic exercise as treatment for depression in women. *Behavior Therapy, 14,* 434–440.

Doyne, E. J., Ossip-Klein, D. J., Bowman, E. D., Osborn, K. M., McDougall-Wilson, I. B., & Neimeyer, R. A. (1987). Running versus weight lifting in the treatment of depression. *Journal of Consulting and Clinical Psychology, 55,* 748–754.

Driscoll, R., Davis, K. E., & Lipetz, M. E. (1972). Parental interference and romantic love. *Journal of Personality and Social Psychology, 24,* 1–10.

Duke, M. P., & Nowicki, S. (1972). A new measure and social learning model for interpersonal distance. *Journal of*

Experimental Research in Personality, 6, 119–132.

Dunn, H. G., et al. (1977). Maternal cigarette smoking during pregnancy and the child's subsequent development: II. Neurological and intellectual maturation to the age of 6 1/2 years. *Canadian Journal of Public Health, 68,* 43–50.

Durden-Smith, J. (1980, November/December). How to win the mating game by a nose. *Next,* pp. 85–89.

Dutton, D. G., & Aron, A. P. (1974). Some evidence for heightened sexual attraction under conditions of high anxiety. *Journal of Personality and Social Psychology, 30,* 510–517.

Dyer, E. D. (1983). *Courtship, marriage, and family: American style.* Homewood, IL: Dorsey.

Eagly, A. H. (1974). Comprehensibility of persuasive arguments as a determinant of opinion change. *Journal of Personality and Social Psychology, 29,* 758–773.

Eagly, A. H. (1978). Sex differences in influenceability. *Psychological Bulletin, 85,* 86–116.

Eagly, A. H. (1983). Gender and social influence: A social psychological analysis. *American Psychologist, 38,* 971–981.

Eagly, A. H., & Carli, L. L. (1981). Sex of researchers and sex-typed communications as determinants of sex differences in influenceability: A meta-analysis of social influence studies. *Psychological Bulletin, 90,* 1–20.

Eagly, A. H., & Steffen, V. J. (1984). Gender stereotypes stem from the distribution of men and women into social roles. *Journal of Personality and Social Psychology, 46,* 735–754.

Eagly, A. H., Wood, W., & Chaiken, S. (1978). Causal inferences about communicators and their effect on opinion change. *Journal of Personality and Social Psychology, 36,* 424–435.

Eagly, A. H., Wood, W., & Fishbaugh, L. (1981). Sex differences in conformity: Surveillance by the group as a determinant of male conformity. *Journal of Personality and Social Psychology, 40,* 384–394.

Easterbrooks, M. A., & Goldberg, W. A. (1985). Effects of early maternal employment on toddlers, mothers, and fathers. *Developmental Psychology, 21,* 774–783.

Ebbeson, E. B., & Bowers, J. B. (1974). Proportion of risky to conservative arguments in a group discussion and choice shift. *Journal of Personality and Social Psychology, 29,* 316–327.

Eckenrode, J. (1984). Impact of chronic and acute stressors on daily reports of mood. *Journal of Personality and Social Psychology, 46,* 907–918.

Eckert, E. D., Bouchard, T. J., Bohlen, J., & Heston, L. L. (1986). Homosexuality in monozygotic twins reared apart. *British Journal of Psychiatry, 148,* 421–425.

Eckhardt, M. J., Harford, T. C., Kaelber, C. T., Parker, E. S., Rosenthal, L. S., Ryback, R. S., Salmoiraghi, G. C., Vanderveen, E., & Warren, K. R. (1981). Health hazards associated with alcohol consumption. *Journal of the American Medical Association, 246,* 648–666.

Eckland, B. K. (1980). Theories of mate selection. In J. M. Henslin (Ed.), *Marriage and the family in a changing society.* New York: Free Press.

Eden, C., & Sims, D. (1981). Computerized vicarious experience: The future for management induction? *Personnel Review, 10,* 22–25.

Edwards, D. J. A. (1972). Approaching the unfamiliar: A study of human interaction differences. *Journal of Behavioral Sciences, 1,* 249–250.

Efran, M. G. (1974). The effect of physical appearance on the judgment of guilt, interpersonal attraction, and severity of recommended punishment in a simulated jury task. *Journal of Research in Personality, 8,* 45–54.

Egeland, J. A., Gerhard, D. S., Pauls, D. L., Sussex, J. N., Kidd, K. K., Allen, C. R., Hostetter, A. M., & Housman, D. E. (1987). Bipolar affective disorder linked to DNA markers on chromosome 11. *Nature, 325,* 783–787.

Ehrhardt, A. A., & Baker, S. W. (1975). Hormonal aberrations and their implications for the understanding of normal sex differentiation. In P. H. Mussen, J. J. Conger, & J. Kagan (Eds.), *Basic and contemporary issues in developmental psychology.* New York: Harper & Row.

Eibl-Eibesfeldt, I. (1974). *Love and hate: The natural history of behavior patterns.* New York: Schocken Books.

Eidelson, R. J., & Epstein, N. (1982). Cognition and relationship maladjustment: Development of a measure of dysfunctional relationship beliefs. *Journal of Consulting and Clinical Psychology, 50,* 715–720.

Eiger, M. S., & Olds, S. W. (1986). *The complete book of breast-feeding,* 2d ed. New York: Bantam Books.

Eisdorfer, C. (1983). Conceptual models of aging: The challenge of a new frontier. *American Psychologist, 38,* 197–202.

Elias, S., & Annas, G. (1986). Social policy considerations in noncoital reproduction. *Journal of the American Medical Society, 255,* 62–68.

Eliot, R. S., & Buell, J. C. (1983). The role of the central nervous system in sudden cardiac death. In T. M. Dembroski, T. Schmidt, & G. Blunchen (Eds.), *Biobehavioral bases of coronary-prone behavior.* New York: Karger.

Elkin, I., Parloff, M. B., Hadley, S. W., & Autrey, J. H. (1985). NIMH treatment of depression collaborative research program. *Archives of General Psychiatry, 42,* 305–316

Elkins, R. L. (1980). Covert sensitization treatment of alcoholism. *Addictive Behaviors, 5,* 67–89.

Ellington, J. E., Marsh, L. A., & Critelli, J. E. (1980). Personality characteristics of women with masculine names. *Journal of Social Psychology, 111,* 211–218.

Ellis, A. (1977). The basic clinical theory or rational-emotive therapy. In A. Ellis & R. Grieger (Eds.), *Handbook of rational-emotive therapy.* New York: Springer.

Ellis, A. (1985). Cognition and affect in emotional disturbance. *American Psychologist, 40,* 471–472.

Ellis, A. (1987). The impossibility of achieving consistently good mental health. *American Psychologist, 42,* 364–375.

Ellis, L., & Ames, M. A. (1987). Neurohormonal functioning and sexual orientation: A theory of homosexuality–heterosexuality. *Psychological Bulletin, 101,* 233–258.

Ellison, G. D. (1977). Animal models of psychopathology: The low-norepinephrine and low-serotonin rat. *American Psychologist, 32,* 1036–1045.

Ellsworth, P. C., Carlsmith, J. M., & Henson, A. (1972). The stare as a stimulus to flight in human subjects. *Journal of Personality and Social Psychology, 21,* 302–311.

Ellsworth, P. C., & Langer, E. J. (1976). Staring and approach: An interpretation of the stare as a nonspecific activator. *Journal of Personality and Social Psychology, 33,* 117–122.

Emery, R. E. (1982). Interpersonal conflict and the children of discord and divorce. *Psychological Bulletin, 92,* 310–330.

Epstein, L. H., & Wing, R. R. (1980). Aerobic exercise and weight. *Addictive Behaviors, 5,* 371–388.

Epstein, L. H., Wing, R. R., Koeske, R., & Valoski, A. (1984a). Effects of diet plus exercise on weight change in parents and children. *Journal of Consulting and Clinical Psychology, 52,* 429–437.

Epstein, L. H., Wing, R. R., Woodall, K., Penner, B. C., Kress, M. J., & Koeske, R. (1985). Effects of family-based behavioral treatment on obese 5- to 8-year-old children. *Behavior Therapy, 16,* 205–212.

Epstein, L. H., Woodall, K., Goreczny, A. J., Wing, R. R., & Robertson, R. J. (1984b). The modification of activity patterns and energy expenditure in obese young girls. *Behavior Therapy, 15,* 101–108.

Epstein, N., Finnegan, D., & Bythell, D. (1979). Irrational beliefs and perceptions of marital conflict. *Journal of Consulting and Clinical Psychology, 47,* 608–610.

Erikson, E. H. (1963). *Childhood and society.* New York: W. W. Norton.

Erikson, E. H. (1983). Cited in E. Hall (1983). A conversation with Erik Erikson. *Psychology Today, 17*(6), 22–30.

Eron, L. D. (1982). Parent–child interaction, television violence, and aggression of children. *American Psychologist, 37,* 197–211.

Eron, L. D. (1987). The development of aggressive behavior from the perspective of a developing behaviorism. *American Psychologist, 42,* 435–442.

Estellachild, V. (1972). Hippie communes. In J. Delora & J. Delora (Eds.), *Intimate life styles.* Pacific Palisades: Goodyear.

Evans, H. J. (1981). Abnormalities and cigarette smoking. *Lancet, 1,* 627–634.

Evans, R. I., Rozelle, R. M., Lasater, T. M., Dembroski, T. M., & Allen, B. P. (1970). Fear arousal, persuasion, and actual versus implied behavioral change: New perspective utilizing a real-life dental hygiene program. *Journal of Personality and Social Psychology, 16,* 220–227.

Exline, R. V. (1972). Visual interaction: The glances of power and preference. In J. K. Cole (Ed.), *Nebraska symposium on motivation,* Vol. 19. Lincoln, NE: University of Nebraska Press.

Eysenck, H. J. (1952). The effects of psychotherapy: An evaluation. *Journal of Consulting Psychology, 16,* 319–324.

Eysenck, H. J., & Eysenck, M. W. (1985). *Personality and individual differences.* New York: Plenum Publishing Co.

Fabian, W. D., Jr., & Fishkin, S. M. (1981). A replicated study of self-reported changes in psychological absorption with marijuana intoxication. *Journal of Abnormal Psychology, 90,* 546–553.

Fagot, B. I. (1974). Sex differences in toddlers' behavior and parental reaction. *Developmental Psychology, 10,* 554–558.

Fagot, B. I. (1978). The influence of sex of child on parental reactions to toddler children. *Child Development, 49,* 459–465.

Fagot, B. I. (1981). Male and female teachers: Do they treat boys and girls differently? *Sex Roles, 7,* 263–272.

Fagot, B. I. (1982). Adults as socializing agents. In T. M. Field (Ed.), *Review of human development.* New York: Wiley.

Fagot, B. I. (1985). Beyond the reinforcement principle: Another step toward understanding sex role development. *Developmental Psychology, 21,* 1097–1104.

Fagot, B. I. (1985). Changes in thinking

about early sex role development. *Developmental Review, 5*, 83–98.

Fairbanks, L. A., McGuire, M. T., & Harris, C. J. (1982). Nonverbal interaction of patients and therapists during psychiatric interviews. *Journal of Abnormal Psychology, 91*, 109–119.

Fallon, A. E., & Rozin, P. (1985). Sex differences in perceptions of desirable body shape. *Journal of Abnormal Psychology, 94*, 102–105.

Farber, B. A. (Ed.). (1983). *Stress and burnout in the human service professions.* Elmsford, NY: Pergamon Press.

Farber, E., & Egeland, B. (1987). *The invulnerable child.* New York: Guilford Press.

Farina, A., Burns, G. L., Austad, C., Bugglin, C. S., & Fischer, E. H. (1986). The role of physical attractiveness in the readjustment of discharged psychiatric patients. *Journal of Abnormal Psychology, 95*, 139–143.

Farmer, H. S. (1983). Career and homemaking plans for high school youth. *Journal of Counseling Psychology, 30*, 40–45.

Farthing, G. W., Venturino, M., & Brown, S. W. (1984). Suggestion and distraction in the control of pain: Test of two hypotheses. *Journal of Abnormal Psychology, 93*, 266–276.

Faust, M. S. (1977). Somatic development of adolescent girls. *Monographs of the Society for Research in Child Development, 42* (Whole No. 169).

Faux, M. (1984a). *Childless by choice.* Garden City, NY: Doubleday/Anchor Books.

Faux, M. (1984b). *Entering the job market.* New York: Monarch Press.

Fazio, R. H. (1986). How do attitudes guide behavior? In R. M. Sorrentino & E. T. Higgins (Eds.), *The handbook of motivation and cognition: Foundations of social behavior.* New York: Guilford Press.

Fazio, R. H., Chen, J., McDonel, E. C., & Sherman, S. J. (1982). Attitude accessibility, attitude-behavior consistency, and the strength of the object-evaluation association. *Journal of Experimental Social Psychology, 18*, 339–357.

Fazio, R. H., & Cooper, J. (1983). Arousal in the dissonance process. In J. T. Cacioppo & R. E. Petty (Eds.), *Social psychophysiology.* New York: Guilford Press.

Fazio, R. H., Sanbonmatsu, D. M., Powell, M. C., & Kardes, F. R. (1986). On the automatic activation of attitudes. *Journal of Personality and Social Psychology, 50*, 229–238.

Fazio, R. H., Sherman, S. J., & Herr, P. M. (1982). The feature-positive effect in the self-perception process: Does not doing matter as much as doing? *Journal of Personality and Social Psychology, 42*, 404–411.

Feder, H. H. (1984). Hormones and sexual behavior. *Annual Review of Psychology, 35*, 165–200.

Fein, G. G., Schwartz, P. M., Jacobson, S. W., & Jacobson, J. L. (1983). Environmental toxins and behavioral development: A new role for psychological research. *American Psychologist, 38*, 1188–1197.

Feingold, A. (1988). Cognitive gender differences are disappearing. *American Psychologist, 43*, 95–103.

Feist, J., & Brannon, L. (1988). *Health psychology.* Belmont, CA: Wadsworth Publishing Co.

Feldman, J. (1966). *The dissemination of health information.* Chicago: Aldine.

Felsenthal, N. (1976). *Orientations to mass communications.* Chicago: Science Research.

Feltz, D. L. (1982). Path analysis of the causal elements in Bandura's theory of self-efficacy and an anxiety-based model of avoidance behavior. *Journal of Personality and Social Psychology, 42*, 764–781.

Fenigstein, A. (1979). Does aggression cause a preference for viewing media violence? *Journal of Personality and Social Psychology, 37*, 2307–2317.

Fenigstein, A., Scheier, M. F., & Buss, A. H. (1975). Public and private self-consciousness: Assessment and theory. *Journal of Consulting and Clinical Psychology, 43*, 522–527.

Ferree, M. M. (1976). Working class jobs: Housework and paid work as sources of satisfaction. *Social Problems, 23*, 431–441.

Festinger, L. (1957). *A theory of cognitive dissonance.* Evanston, IL: Row, Peterson.

Festinger, L., & Carlsmith, J. M. (1959). Cognitive consequences of forced compliance. *Journal of Abnormal and Social Psychology, 58*, 203–210.

Fetterly, K., & Graubard, M. S. (1984). Racial and educational factors associated with breast-feeding—United States, 1969 and 1980. U.S. Centers for Disease Control: *Morbidity and Mortality Weekly Report, 33*(11), 153–154.

Fibel, B., & Hale, W. D. (1978). The generalized expectancy for success scale—A new measure. *Journal of Consulting and Clinical Psychology, 46*, 924–931.

Fielding, J. E. (1985). Smoking: Health effects and control. *New England Journal of Medicine, 313*, 491–498, 555–561.

Findley, M. J., & Cooper, H. M. (1983). Locus of control and academic achievement: A literature review. *Journal of Personality and Social Psychology, 44*, 419–427.

Fiore, J. (1980). *Global satisfaction scale.* Unpublished manuscript, University of Washington, Department of Psy-

chiatry and Behavioral Sciences, Seattle.

Fischman, J. (1987a). Getting tough. *Psychology Today, 21*(12), 26–28.

Fischman, J. (1987b). Type A on trial. *Psychology Today, 21*(2), 42–50.

Fisher, J. D., & Baum, A. (1980). Situational and arousal-based messages and the reduction of crowding stress. *Journal of Applied Social Psychology, 10*, 191–201.

Fisher, J. D., Bell, P. A., & Baum, A. (1984). *Environmental psychology,* 2d ed. New York: Holt, Rinehart and Winston.

Fisher, J. D., & Byrne, D. (1975). Too close for comfort: Sex differences in response to invasions of personal space. *Journal of Personality and Social Psychology, 32*, 15–21.

Fisher, K. (1982). Debate rages on 1973 Sobell study. *APA Monitor, 13*(11), 8–9.

Fisher, K. (1984). Family violence cycle questioned. *APA Monitor, 15*(12), 30.

Fisher, L. E. (1980). Relationships and sexuality in contexts and culture: The anthropology of eros. In B. B. Wolman & J. Money (Eds.), *Handbook of human sexuality.* Englewood Cliffs, NJ: Prentice-Hall.

Fisher, W. A., & Byrne, D. (1978). Sex differences in response to erotica: Love versus lust. *Journal of Personality and Social Psychology, 36*, 117–125.

Fiske, S. T., & Taylor, S. E. (1984). *Social cognition.* Reading, MA: Addison-Wesley.

Fitch, G. (1970). Effects of self-esteem, perceived performance, and choice of causal attribution. *Journal of Personality and Social Psychology, 16*, 311–315.

Flaherty, J. F., & Dusek, J. B. (1980). An investigation of the relationship between psychological androgyny and components of self-concept. *Journal of Personality and Social Psychology, 38*, 984–992.

Flaxman, J. (1978). Quitting smoking now or later: Gradual, abrupt, immediate, and delayed quitting. *Behavior Therapy, 9*, 260–270.

Fleming, M. Z., MacGowan, B. R., Robinson, L., Spitz, J., & Salt, P. (1982). The body image of the postoperative female-to-male transsexual. *Journal of Consulting and Clinical Psychology, 50*, 461–462.

Fleming, R., Baum, A., Gisriel, M. M., & Gatchel, R. J. (1982). Mediation of stress at Three Mile Island by social support. *Journal of Human Stress, 8*(3), 14–22.

Flippo, J. R., & Lewinsohn, P. M. (1971). Effects of failure on the self-esteem of depressed and nondepressed subjects. *Journal of Consulting and Clinical Psychology, 36*, 151.

Floderus-Myrhed, B., Pederson, N., &

Rasmuson, I. (1980). Assessment of heritability for personality based on a short form of the Eysenck Personality Inventory: A study of 12,898 twin pairs. *Behavior Genetics, 10,* 153–162.

Floyd, F. J., & Markman, H. J. (1984). An economical observational measure of couples' communication skill. *Journal of Consulting and Clinical Psychology, 52,* 97–103.

Fogel, M. L. (1980). Warning: Auto fumes may lower your kid's IQ. *Psychology Today, 14*(1), 108.

Fogelman, K. (1980). Smoking in pregnancy and subsequent development of the child. *Child Care, Health, and Development, 6,* 233–251.

Folkins, C. H., & Sime, W. E. (1981). Physical fitness training and mental health. *American Psychologist, 36,* 373–389.

Folkman, S., & Lazarus, R. S. (1985). If it changes it must be a process: Study of emotion and coping during three stages of a college examination. *Journal of Personality and Social Psychology, 48,* 150–170.

Ford, C. S., & Beach, F. A. (1951). *Patterns of sexual behavior.* New York: Harper & Row.

Foreyt, J. P. (1986). Treating the diseases of the 1980s: Eating disorders. *Contemporary Psychology, 31,* 658–660.

Forman, M. R., et al. (1984). The Pima infant feeding study: Breast feeding and gastroenteritis in the first year of life. *American Journal of Epidemiology, 119,* 335–349.

Fox, L. H. (1982). Sex differences among the mathematically gifted. Paper presented at the annual meeting of the American Association for the Advancement of Science, Washington, DC.

Fox, L. H., Brody, L., & Tobin, D. (1985). The impact of early intervention programs upon course-taking and attitudes in high school. In S. F. Chipman, L. R. Brush, & D. M. Wilson (Eds.), *Women and mathematics: Balancing the equation.* London: Erlbaum.

Fox, S. (1984). *The mirror makers.* New York: Morrow.

Foy, D. W., Nunn, L. B., & Rychtarik, R. G. (1984). Broad-spectrum behavioral treatment for chronic alcoholics: Effects of training controlled drinking skills. *Journal of Consulting and Clinical Psychology, 52,* 218–230.

Francis, D. (1984). *Will you still need me, will you still feed me, when I'm 84?* Bloomington: Indiana University Press.

Franck, K. D. (1979). Friends and strangers: The social experience of living in urban and nonurban settings. *Journal of Social Issues, 36,* 52–71.

Franck, K. D., Unseld, C. T., & Wentworth, W. E. (1974). Adaptation of the newcomer: A process of construction. Unpublished manuscript, City University of New York.

Francoeur, R. T. (1985). Reproductive technologies: New alternatives and new ethics. *SIECUS Report, 14,* 1–5.

Freedman, J. L., & Fraser, S. C. (1966). Compliance without pressure: The foot-in-the-door technique. *Journal of Personality and Social Psychology, 4,* 195–202.

Freedman, J. L., Wallington, S. A., & Bless, E. (1967). Compliance without pressure: The effect of guilt. *Journal of Personality and Social Psychology, 7,* 117–124.

Freedman, R. R., & Sattler, H. L. (1982). Physiological and psychological factors in sleep-onset insomnia. *Journal of Abnormal Psychology, 91,* 380–389.

French-Belgian Collaborative Group (1982). Ischemic heart disease and psychological patterns: Prevalence and incidence in Belgium and France. *Advances in Cardiology, 29,* 25–31.

Freud, S. (1909). Analysis of a phobia in a 5-year-old boy. In *Collected papers,* Vol. 3, trans. A. & James Strachey. New York: Basic Books, 1959.

Freud, S. (1927). A religious experience. In *Standard edition of the complete psychological works of Sigmund Freud,* Vol. 21. London: Hogarth Press, 1964.

Freud, S. (1930). *Civilization and its discontents,* trans. J. Strachey. New York: W. W. Norton, 1961.

Freud, S. (1933). New introductory lectures. In *Standard edition of the complete psychological works of Sigmund Freud,* Vol. 22. London: Hogarth Press, 1964.

Friedman, H. S., & Booth-Kewley, S. (1987). Personality, Type A behavior, and coronary heart disease: The role of emotional expression. *Journal of Personality and Social Psychology, 53,* 783–792.

Friedman, M., & Rosenman, R. H. (1974). *Type A behavior and your heart.* New York: Harper & Row.

Friedman, M., & Ulmer, D. (1984). *Treating Type A behavior and your heart.* New York: Fawcett Crest.

Friedman, M. I., & Stricker, E. M. (1976). The physiological psychology of hunger: A physiological perspective. *Psychological Review, 83,* 409–431.

Friman, P. C., & Christopherson, E. R. (1983). Behavior therapy and hyperactivity: A brief review of therapy for a big problem. *The Behavior Therapist, 6,* 175–176.

Frisch, H. L. (1977). Sex stereotypes in adult–infant play. *Child Development, 48,* 1671–1675.

Frodi, A. M. (1981). Contribution of infant characteristics to child abuse. *Journal of Mental Deficiency, 85,* 341–349.

Frodi, A. M. (1985). When empathy fails: Infant crying and child abuse. In B. M. Lester & C. F. Z. Boukydis (Eds.), *Infant crying.* New York: Plenum Publishing Co.

Frodi, A. M., Macauley, J., & Thome, P. R. (1977). Are women always less aggressive than men? A review of the experimental literature. *Psychological Bulletin, 84,* 634–660.

Fromm, E. (1956). *The art of loving.* New York: Harper & Row.

Frumkin, L., & Leonard, J. (1987). *Questions and answers on AIDS.* New York: Avon Books.

Funkenstein, D. (1955, May). The physiology of fear and anger. *Scientific American.*

Galassi, J. P. (1988). Four cognitive-behavioral approaches: Additional considerations. *The Counseling Psychologist, 16*(1), 102–105.

Galassi, J. P., Frierson, H. T., & Sharer, R. (1981). Behavior of high, moderate, and low test anxious students during an actual test situation. *Journal of Consulting and Clinical Psychology, 49,* 51–62.

Galassi, J. P., Frierson, H. T., Jr., & Siegel, R. G. (1984). Cognitions, test anxiety, and test performance: A closer look. *Journal of Consulting and Clinical Psychology, 52,* 319–320.

Galizio, M., & Hendrick, C. (1972). Effect of musical accompaniment on attitude: The guitar as a prop for persuasion. *Journal of Applied Social Psychology, 2,* 350–359.

Gallese, L. R. (1981, December 14). Women with demanding careers and children. *The Wall Street Journal.*

Ganellen, R. J., & Blaney, P. H. (1984). Hardiness and social support as moderators of the effects of life stress. *Journal of Personality and Social Psychology, 47,* 156–163.

Gansberg, J. M., & Mostel, A. P. (1984). *The second nine months.* New York: Tribeca.

Gardner, H. (1983). *Frames of mind: The theory of multiple intelligences.* New York: Basic Books.

Garfield, S. L. (1981). Psychotherapy: A 40-year appraisal. *American Psychologist, 36,* 174–183.

Garfield, S. L. (1982). Eclecticism and integration in psychotherapy. *Behavior Therapy, 13,* 610–623.

Garrett, W. R. (1982). *Seasons of marriage and family life.* New York: Holt, Rinehart and Winston.

Garwood, S. G., Cox, L., Kaplan, V., Wasserman, N., & Sulzer, J. L. (1980). Beauty is only "name deep": The effect of first-name in ratings of physical attraction. *Journal of Applied Social Psychology, 10,* 431–435.

Gastorf, J. W., & Galanos, A. N. (1983).

Patient compliance and physicians' attitude. *Family Practice Research Journal, 2,* 190–198.

Gatchel, R. J., & Proctor, J. D. (1976). Effectiveness of voluntary heart rate control in reducing speech anxiety. *Journal of Consulting and Clinical Psychology, 44,* 381–389.

Gebhard, P. H. (1976). The institute. In M. S. Weinberg (Ed.), *Sex research: Studies from the Kinsey Institute.* New York: Oxford University Press.

Geen, R. G. (1981). Behavioral and physiological reactions to observed violence: Effects of prior exposure to aggressive stimuli. *Journal of Personality and Social Psychology, 40,* 868–875.

Geer, J. T., O'Donohue, W. T., & Schorman, R. H. (1986). Sexuality. In M. G. H. Coles et al. (Eds.), *Psychophysiology: Systems, processes, and applications.* New York: Guilford Press.

Gelman, D., et al. (1985, August 12). The social fallout from an epidemic. *Newsweek,* pp. 28–29.

Gerard, H. B., Wilhelmy, R. A., & Conolley, E. S. (1968). Conformity and group size. *Journal of Personality and Social Psychology, 8,* 79–82.

Gerrard, G. (1986). Are men and women really different? In K. Kelley (Ed.), *Females, males, and sexuality.* Albany, NY: State University of New York at Albany Press.

Gerson, M. (1980). The lure of motherhood. *Psychology of Women Quarterly, 5,* 207–218.

Gerson, M. (1984). Feminism and the wish for a child. *Sex Roles, 11,* 389–399.

Gerson, M., Alpert, J. L., & Richardson, M. S. Mothering: The view from psychological research. *Signs, 9,* 434–453.

Gibson, J. L., Ivancevich, J. M., & Donnelly, J. H., Jr. (1985). *Organizations: Behavior, structure, processes.* Plano, TX: Business Publications, Inc.

Gilbert, S. J. (1981). Another look at the Milgram obedience studies: The role of the graduated series of shocks. *Personality and Social Psychology Bulletin, 7,* 690–695.

Gill, J. S., Zezulka, A. V., Shipley, M. J., Gill, S. K., & Beevers, D. G. (1986). Stroke and alcohol consumption. *New England Journal of Medicine, 315,* 1041–1046.

Gillen, B. (1981). Physical attractiveness: A determinant of two types of goodness. *Personality and Social Psychology Bulletin, 7,* 277–281.

Gilligan, C. (1982). *In a different voice.* Cambridge, MA: Harvard University Press.

Gillis, J. S., & Avis, W. E. (1980). The male-taller norm in mate selection. *Personality and Social Psychology Bulletin, 6,* 396–401.

Gilmartin, B. G. (1975). That swinging couple down the block. *Psychology Today, 8,* 54.

Ginzberg, E. (1972). Toward a theory of occupational choice: A restatement. *Vocational Guidance Quarterly, 20,* 169–176.

Gladue, B. A., Green, R., & Hellman, R. E. (1984). Neuroendocrine response to estrogen and sexual orientation. *Science, 225,* 1496–1499.

Glasgow, R. E., Klesges, R. C., Godding, P. R., & Gegelman, R. (1983). Controlled smoking, with or without carbon monoxide feedback, as an alternative for chronic smokers. *Behavior Therapy, 14,* 396–397.

Glasgow, R. E., Klesges, R. C., Godding, P. R., Vasey, M. W., & O'Neill, H. K. (1984). Evaluation of a worksite-controlled smoking program. *Journal of Consulting and Clinical Psychology, 52,* 137–138.

Glasgow, R. E., Klesges, R. C., Klesges, L. M., Vasey, M. W., & Gunnarson, D. F. (1985). Long-term effects of a controlled smoking program: A two and one-half year follow-up. *Behavior Therapy, 16,* 303–307.

Glass, D. C. (1977). *Stress and coronary-prone behavior.* Hillsdale, NJ: Erlbaum.

Glass, D. C., & Singer, J. E. (1972). *Urban stress.* New York: Academic Press.

Gleicher, N. (1984). Caeserean section rates in the United States. *Journal of the American Medical Association, 252,* 3273–3276.

Gleser, G., Green, B., & Winget, C. (1981). *Prolonged psychosocial effects of disaster: A study of Buffalo Creek.* New York: Academic Press.

Glick, P., & Norton, A. (1979). *Marrying, divorcing, and living together in the U.S. today.* Washington, DC: Population Reference Bureau.

Glick, P., & Spanier, G. B. (1980). Married and unmarried cohabitation in the United States. *Journal of Marriage and the Family, 42,* 19–30.

Goeders, N. E., & Smith, J. E. (1983). Cortical dopaminergic involvement in cocaine reinforcement. *Science, 221,* 773–775.

Gold, D., & Andres, D. (1978a). Comparisons of adolescent children with employed and nonemployed mothers. *Merrill-Palmer Quarterly, 24,* 243–254.

Gold, D., & Andres, D. (1978b). Developmental comparisons between ten-year-old children with employed and nonemployed mothers. *Child Development, 49,* 75–84.

Gold, D., & Andres, D. (1978c). Relations between maternal employment and development of nursery school children. *Canadian Journal of Behavioral Science, 10,* 116–129.

Gold, J. A., Ryckman, R. M., & Mosley, N. R. (1984). Romantic mood induction and attraction to a dissimilar other: Is love blind? *Personality and Social Psychology Bulletin, 10,* 358–368.

Goldberg, L. W. (1978). Differential attribution of trait-descriptive terms to oneself as compared to well-liked, neutral, and disliked others. *Journal of Personality and Social Psychology, 36,* 1012–1028.

Goldberg, S. (1983). Parent–infant bonding: Another look. *Child Development, 54,* 1355–1382.

Goldberg, S., & Lewis, M. (1969). Play behavior in the year-old infant: Early sex differences. *Child Development, 40,* 21–31.

Goldfoot, D. A., Essock-Vitale, S. M., Asa, C. S., Thornton, J. E., & Leshner, A. I. (1978). Anosmia in male rhesus monkeys does not alter copulatory activity with cycling females. *Science, 199,* 1095–1096.

Goldfried, M. R. (1988). Application of rational restructuring to anxiety disorders. *The Counseling Psychologist, 16*(1), 50–68.

Goldfried, M. R., Linehan, M. M., & Smith, J. L. (1978). Reduction of test anxiety through cognitive restructuring. *Journal of Consulting and Clinical Psychology, 46,* 32–39.

Goldman, W., & Lewis, P. (1977). Beautiful is good: Evidence that the physically attractive are more socially skillful. *Journal of Experimental Social Psychology, 13,* 125–130.

Goldsmith, H. H. (1983). Genetic influences on personality from infancy to adulthood. *Child Development, 54,* 331–355.

Goldsmith, J. R. (1968). Effects of air pollution on human health. In A. C. Stearn (Ed.), *Air pollution.* New York: Academic Press.

Goldstein, I. L., & Buxton, V. M. (1982). Training and human performance. In M. D. Dunnette & E. A. Fleishman (Eds.), *Human Performance and Productivity, 1,* 135–177.

Goldstein, K. M., Caputo, D. V., & Taub, H. V. (1976). The effects of perinatal complications on development at one year of age. *Child Development, 47,* 613–621.

Goldstein, M., & Davis, E. E. (1972). Race and belief: A further analysis of the social determinants of behavioral intentions. *Journal of Personality and Social Psychology, 22,* 345–355.

Goldstein, T. (1988, February 12). Women in the law aren't yet equal partners. *The New York Times,* p. B7.

Goleman, D. J. (1978). Special abilities of the sexes: Do they begin in the brain? *Psychology Today, 12*(11), 48–120.

Goleman, D. J. (1985, January 15). Pressure mounts for analysts to prove theory is scientific. *The New York Times,* pp. C1, C9.

Goleman, D. J. (1987, November 24).

Teen-age risk-taking: Rise in deaths prompts new research effort. *The New York Times,* pp. C1, C17.

Goleman, D. J., & Schwartz, G. E. (1976). Meditation as an intervention in stress reactivity. *Journal of Consulting and Clinical Psychology, 44,* 456–466.

Golub, S. (1976). The effect of premenstrual anxiety and depression on cognitive function. *Journal of Personality and Social Psychology, 34,* 99–104.

Goodheart, D. E. (1985). Some psychological effects associated with positive and negative thinking about stressful event outcomes. *Journal of Personality and Social Psychology, 48,* 216–232.

Goodwin, D. W. (1979). Alcoholism and heredity. *Archives of General Psychiatry, 36,* 57–61.

Goodwin, D. W. (1985). Alcoholism and genetics. *Archives of General Psychiatry, 42,* 171–174.

Goodwin, D. W., Schulsinger, F., Hermansen, L., Guze, S. B., & Winokur, G. A. (1973). Alcohol problems in adoptees raised apart from alcoholic biological parents. *Archives of General Psychiatry, 30,* 239–243.

Gordon, T., & Doyle, J. T. (1987). Drinking and mortality: The Albany Study. *American Journal of Epidemiology, 125,* 263–270.

Gormally, J., Sipps, G., Raphael, R., Edwin, D., & Varvil-Weld, D. (1981). The relationship between maladaptive cognitions and social anxiety. *Journal of Consulting and Clinical Psychology, 49,* 300–301.

Gotlib, I. H. (1982). Self-reinforcement and depression in interpersonal interaction: The role of performance level. *Journal of Abnormal Psychology, 91,* 3–13.

Gotlib, I. H. (1984). Depression and general psychopathology in university students. *Journal of Abnormal Psychology, 93,* 19–30.

Gottman, J., Notarius, C., Gonso, J., & Markman, H. (1976). *A couple's guide to communication.* Champaign, IL: Research Press.

Gouaux, C. (1971). Induced affective states and interpersonal attraction. *Journal of Personality and Social Psychology, 20,* 37–43.

Gould, R. (1975). Adult life stages: Growth toward self-tolerance. *Psychology Today, 8,* 74–81.

Goy, R. W., & Goldfoot, D. A. (1976). Neuroendocrinology: Animal models and problems of human sexuality. In E. A. Rubenstein et al. (Eds.), *New directions in sex research.* New York: Plenum Publishing Co.

Goy, R. W., & McEwen, B. S. (1982). *Sexual differentiation of the brain.* Cambridge, MA: MIT Press.

Granberg, D., & Brent, E. (1983). When prophecy bends: The preference–expectation link in U.S. presidential elections. *Journal of Personality and Social Psychology, 45,* 477–491.

Gray, V. R. (1984). The psychological response of the dying patient. In P. S. Chaney (Ed.), *Dealing with death and dying,* 2d ed. Springhouse, PA: International Communications.

Graziano, W., Brothen, T., & Berscheid, E. (1978). Height and attraction: Do men and women see eye-to-eye? *Journal of Personality, 46,* 128–145.

Green, B. L., Grace, M. C., Lindy, J. D., Titchener, J. L., & Lindy, J. G. (1983). Levels of functional impairment following a civilian disaster: The Beverly Hills Supper Club fire. *Journal of Consulting and Clinical Psychology, 51,* 573–580.

Green, J. A., Jones, L. E., & Gustafson, G. E. (1987). Perception of cries by parents and nonparents: Relation to cry acoustics. *Developmental Psychology, 23,* 370–382.

Green, R. (1987). *The "sissy boy syndrome" and the development of homosexuality.* New Haven: Yale University Press.

Green, S. K., Buchanan, D. R., & Heuer, S. K. (1984). Winners, losers, and choosers: A field investigation of dating initiation. *Personality and Social Psychology Bulletin, 10,* 502–511.

Greenbaum, P., & Rosenfeld, H. M. (1978). Patterns of avoidance in response to interpersonal staring and proximity: Effects of bystanders on drivers at a traffic intersection. *Journal of Personality and Social Psychology, 36,* 575–587.

Greenberg, R., Pearlman, C., Schwartz, W. R., & Grossman, H. Y. (1983). Memory, emotion, and REM sleep. *Journal of Abnormal Psychology, 92,* 378–381.

Greene, J. (1982). The gambling trap. *Psychology Today, 16*(9), 50–55.

Greenhouse, L. (1981, March 22). Equal pay debate now shifts to a far wider concept. *The New York Times,* Section 4, p. 20.

Greist, J. H. (1984). Exercise in the treatment of depression. *Coping with mental stress: The potential and limits of exercise intervention.* Washington, DC: National Institute of Mental Health.

Griffen, J. H. (1960). *Black like me.* Boston: Houghton Mifflin.

Grinspoon, L. (1987, July 28). Cancer patients should get marijuana. *The New York Times,* p. A23.

Grossman, K., Thane, K., & Grossman, K. E. (1981). Maternal tactual contact of the newborn after various postpartum conditions of mother–infant contact. *Developmental Psychology, 17,* 158–169.

Groth, A. N., & Birnbaum, H. J. (1979). *Men who rape.* New York: Plenum Publishing Co.

Grünbaum, A. (1985). Cited in Goleman, D. J. (1985, January 15). Pressure mounts for analyst to prove theory is scientific. *The New York Times,* pp. C1, C9.

Grush, J. E. (1980). The impact of candidate expenditures, regionality, and prior outcomes on the 1976 Democratic presidential primaries. *Journal of Personality and Social Psychology, 38,* 337–347.

Grush, J. E., & Yehl, J. G. (1979). Marital roles, sex differences, and interpersonal attraction. *Journal of Personality and Social Psychology, 37,* 116–123.

Hackett, T. P., & Cassem, N. H. (1970). Psychological reactions to life-threatening illness: Acute myocardial infarction. In H. S. Abram (Ed.), *Psychological aspects of stress.* Springfield, IL: Charles C. Thomas.

Hahn, S. R., & Paige, K. E. (1980). American birth practices: A critical review. In J. E. Parsons (Ed.), *The psychology of sex differences.* New York: McGraw-Hill.

Haley, J. (1987). *Problem-solving therapy,* 2d ed. San Francisco: Jossey-Bass.

Hall, C. S. (1966). *The meaning of dreams.* New York: McGraw-Hill.

Hall, C. S. (1984). "A ubiquitous sex difference in dreams" revisited. *Journal of Personality and Social Psychology, 46,* 1109–1117.

Hall, E. T. (1968). Proxemics. *Current Anthropology, 9,* 83–107.

Hall, J. A., & Braunwald, K. G. (1981). Gender cues in conversation. *Journal of Personality and Social Psychology, 40,* 99–100.

Hall, J. A., & Taylor, M. C. (1985). Psychological androgyny and the masculinity-femininity interaction. *Journal of Personality and Social Psychology, 49,* 429–435.

Hall, R. G., Sachs, D. P. L., Hall, S. M., & Benowitz, N. L. (1984). Two-year efficacy and safety of rapid smoking therapy in patients with cardiac and pulmonary disease. *Journal of Consulting and Clinical Psychology, 52,* 574–581.

Hall, S. M., Rugg, D., Tunstall, C., & Jones, R. T. (1984). Preventing relapse to cigarette smoking by behavioral skill training. *Journal of Consulting and Clinical Psychology, 52,* 372–382.

Hall, S. M., Tunstall, C., Rugg, D., Jones, R. T., & Benowitz, N. (1985). Nicotine gum and behavioral treatment in smoking cessation. *Journal of Consulting and Clinical Psychology, 53,* 256–258.

Halmi, K. A., Eckert, E., LaDu, T. J., & Cohen, J. (1986). Treatment efficacy of cyproheptadine and amitriptyline. *Archives of General Psychiatry, 43,* 177–181.

Hamm, N. M., Baum, M. R., & Nikels, K. W. (1975). Effects of race and exposure on judgments of interpersonal favorability. *Journal of Experimental Social Psychology, 11,* 14–24.

Hammen, C., & Mayol, A. (1982). Depression and cognitive characteristics of stressful life-event types. *Journal of Abnormal Psychology, 91,* 165–174.

Hansen, G. O. (1975). Meeting house challenges: Involvement—the elderly. In *Housing issues.* Lincoln, NE: University of Nebraska Press.

Hanson, J. W., Streissguth, A. P., & Smith, D. W. (1978). The effects of moderate alcohol consumption during pregnancy on growth and morphogenesis. *The Journal of Pediatrics, 92,* 457–460.

Harackiewicz, J. M., Sansone, C., Blair, L. W., Epstein, J. A., & Manderlink, G. (1987). Attributional processes in behavior change and maintenance: Smoking cessation and continued abstinence. *Journal of Consulting and Clinical Psychology, 55,* 372–378.

Harbeson, G. E. (1971). *Choice and challenge for the American woman,* revised ed. Cambridge, MA: Schenckman.

Harburg, E., Erfurt, J. C., Hauenstein, L. S., Chape, C., Schull, W. J., & Schork, M. A. (1973). Socioecological stress, suppressed hostility, skin color, and black-white male blood pressure: Detroit. *Psychosomatic Medicine, 35,* 276–296.

Harder, D. W., Gift, T. E., Strauss, J. S., Ritzler, B. A., & Kokes, R. F. (1981). Life events and two-year outcome in schizophrenia. *Journal of Consulting and Clinical Psychology, 49,* 619–626.

Hardy-Brown, K., & Plomin, R. (1985). Infant communicative development: Evidence from adoptive and biological families for genetic and environmental influences on rate differences. *Developmental Psychology, 21,* 378–385.

Hare-Mustin, R. (1983). An appraisal of the relationship between women and psychotherapy: 80 years after the case of Dora. *American Psychologist, 38,* 593–601.

Hare-Mustin, R., & Broderick, P. C. (1979). The myth of motherhood: A study of attitudes toward motherhood. *Psychology of Women Quarterly, 4,* 114–128.

Hariton, E. B., & Singer, J. L. (1974). Women's sexual fantasies during sexual intercourse: Normative and theoretical implications. *Journal of Consulting and Clinical Psychology, 42,* 313–322.

Harlap, S. (1979). Gender of infants conceived on different days of the menstrual cycle. *New England Journal of Medicine, 300,* 1445–1448.

Harlap, S., & Shiono, P. H. (1980). Alcohol, smoking, and incidence of spontaneous abortions in the first and second trimester. *Lancet, 2,* 173–176.

Harris, D. K., & Cole, W. E. (1980). *Sociology of aging.* Boston: Houghton Mifflin.

Harris, G. W., & Levine, S. (1965). Sexual differentiation of the brain and its experimental control. *Journal of Physiology, 181,* 379–400.

Harris, L. (1988). *Inside America.* New York: Vintage.

Harris, M. B., Harris, R. J., & Bochner, S. (1982). Fat, four-eyed, and female: Stereotypes of obesity, glasses, and gender. *Journal of Applied Social Psychology, 12,* 503–516.

Harris, T. A. (1967). *I'm OK—You're OK.* New York: Harper & Row.

Harrison, A. A., & Saeed, L. (1977). Let's make a deal: An analysis of revelations and stipulations in lonely hearts advertisements. *Journal of Personality and Social Psychology, 35,* 257–264.

Hartmann, E. L. (1973). *The functions of sleep.* New Haven, CT: Yale University Press.

Hartmann, E. L. (1981). The strangest sleep disorder. *Psychology Today, 15*(4), 14–18.

Hartmann, E. L., & Stern, W. C. (1972). Desynchronized sleep deprivation: Learning deficit and its reversal by increased catecholamines. *Physiology and Behavior, 8,* 585–587.

Hartmann, M. A. (1976). A descriptive study of the language of men and women born in Maine around 1900 as it reflects the LaKoff hypothesis in "Language and woman's place." In B. L. Dubois & I. Chouch (Eds.), *The sociology of the languages of American women.* San Antonio: Trinity University Press.

Hartz, A. J., Rupley, D. C., & Rimm, A. A. (1984). The association of girth measurements with disease in 32,856 women. *American Journal of Epidemiology, 119,* 71–80.

Harvey, J. H., Ickes, W. J., & KIdd, R. F. (Eds.) (1976). *New directions in attributional research,* Vol. 1. Hillsdale, NJ: Erlbaum.

Harvey, J. H., Ickes, W. J., & Kidd, R. F. (Eds.) (1978). *New directions in attributional research,* Vol. 2. Hillsdale, NJ: Erlbaum.

Harvey, J. R. (1978). Diaphragmatic breathing: A practical technique for breath control. *The Behavior Therapist, 1*(2), 13–14.

Hass, R. G., & Linder, D. E. (1972). Counterargument availability and the effects of message structure on persuasion. *Journal of Personality and Social Psychology, 23,* 219–233.

Hassett, J. (1978). Sex and smell. *Psychology Today, 12*(10), 40–42, 45.

Hatfield, E. (1983). What do women and men want from love and sex? In E. R. Allgeier & N. B. McCormick (Eds.), *Changing boundaries: Gender roles and sexual behavior.* Palo Alto, CA: Mayfield.

Hatfield, E., & Sprecher, S. (1986). *Mirror, mirror . . . The importance of looks in everyday life.* Albany, NY: State University of New York at Albany Press.

Hatfield, E., Sprecher, S., & Traupman, J. (1978). Men's and women's reactions to sexually explicit films: A serendipitous finding. *Archives of sexual behavior, 6,* 583–592.

Havighurst, R. J. (1972). *Developmental tasks and education,* 3d ed. New York: McKay.

Haynes, R. B. (1976). A critical review of the determinants of patient compliance with therapeutic regimens. In D. L. Sackett & R. B. Haynes (Eds.), *Compliance with therapeutic regimens.* Baltimore: Johns Hopkins University Press.

Haynes, R. B. (1979). Determinants of compliance: The disease and the mechanics of treatment. In R. B. Haynes, D. W. Taylor, & D. L. Sackett (Eds.), *Compliance in health care.* Baltimore: Johns Hopkins University Press.

Haynes, S. G., Feinleib, M., & Eaker, E. D. (1983). Type A behavior and the ten-year incidence of coronary heart disease in the Framingham heart study. In R. H. Rosenman (Ed.), *Psychosomatic risk factors and coronary heart disease.* Berne: Hans Huber.

Haynes, S. G., Feinleib, M., & Kannel, W. B. (1980). The relationship of psychosocial factors to coronary heart disease in the Framingham study: III. Eight-year incidence of coronary heart disease. *American Journal of Epidemiology, 111,* 37–58.

Haynes, S. N., Adams, A., & Franzen, M. (1981). The effects of presleep stress on sleep-onset insomnia. *Journal of Abnormal Psychology, 90,* 601–606.

Haynes, S. N. Follingstad, D. R., & McGowan, W. T. (1974). Insomnia: Sleep patterns and anxiety level. *Journal of Psychosomatic Research, 18,* 69–74.

Haynes, S. N., Sides, H., & Lockwood, G. (1977). Relaxation instructions and frontalis electromyographic feedback intervention with sleep-onset insomnia. *Behavior Therapy, 8,* 644–652.

Haynes, S. N., Woodward, S., Moran, R., & Alexander, D. (1974). Relaxation treatment of insomnia. *Behavior Therapy, 5,* 555–558.

Hays, R. B. (1984). The development and maintenance of friendship. *Journal of Social and Personal Relationships, 1,* 75–98.

Heaton, R. K., & Victor, R. G. (1976). Personality characteristics associated with psychedelic flashbacks in natural and experimental settings. *Journal of Abnormal Psychology, 85,* 83–90.

Heiby, E., & Becker, J. D. (1980). Effect of filmed modeling on the self-reported frequency of masturbation. *Archives of Sexual Behavior, 9,* 115–122.

Heiman, J. R. (1975). The physiology of erotica: Women's sexual arousal. *Psychology Today, 9,* 90–94.

Heiman, J. R., & LoPiccolo, J. (1987). *Becoming orgasmic,* 2d ed. Englewood Cliffs, NJ: Prentice-Hall.

Heingartner, A., & Hall, J. V. (1974). Affective consequences in adults and children of repeated exposure to auditory stimuli. *Journal of Personality and Social Psychology, 29,* 719–723.

Helmreich, R. L., Spence, J. T., & Holahan, C. J. (1979). Psychological androgyny and sex-role flexibility: A test of two hypotheses. *Journal of Personality and Social Psychology, 37,* 1631–1644.

Helson, R., & Moane, G. (1987). Personality change in women from college to midlife. *Journal of Personality and Social Psychology, 53,* 176–186.

Hemstone, M., & Jaspars, J. (1982). Explanations for racial discrimination: The effects of group decision on intergroup attributions. *European Journal of Social Psychology, 12,* 1–16.

Hendin, D. (1984). *Death as a fact of life.* New York: W. W. Norton.

Hendrick, C., & Hendrick, S. (1986). A theory and method of love. *Journal of Personality and Social Psychology, 50,* 392–402.

Hendrick, C. D., Wells, K. S., & Faletti, M. V. (1982). Social and emotional effects of geographical relocation on elderly retirees. *Journal of Personality and Social Psychology, 42,* 951–962.

Hendrick, J., & Hendrick, C. D. (1977). *Aging in mass society: Myths and realities.* Cambridge, MA: Winthrop.

Hendrick, S., Hendrick, C., Slapion-Foote, M. J., & Foote, F. H. (1985). Gender differences in sexual attitudes. *Journal of Personality and Social Psychology, 48,* 1630–1642.

Hennigan, K. M., Cook, T. D., & Gruder, C. L. (1982). Cognitive tuning set, source credibility, and the temporal persistence of attitude change. *Journal of Personality and Social Psychology, 42,* 412–425.

Hennigan, K. M., DelRosario, M. L., Heath, L., Cook, T. D., Wharton, J. D., & Calder, B. J. (1982). Impact of the introduction of television on crime in the United States. *Journal of Personality and Social Psychology, 42,* 461–477.

Hensley, W. E. (1981). The effects of attire, location, and sex on aiding behavior: A similarity explanation. *Journal of Nonverbal Behavior, 6,* 3–11.

Henslin, J. M. (1980). *Marriage and family in a changing society.* New York: Free Press.

Hersen, M., Bellack, A. S., Himmelhoch, J. M., & Thase, M. E. (1984). Effect of social skill training, amitriptyline, and psychotherapy in unipolar depressed women. *Behavior Therapy, 15,* 21–40.

Heston, L. L. (1966). Psychiatric disorders in foster-home-reared children of schizophrenic mothers. *British Journal of Psychiatry, 112,* 819–825.

Hetherington, E. M. (1972). Effects of father absence on personality development in adolescent daughters. *Developmental Psychology, 7,* 313–326.

Hetherington, E. M. (1979). Divorce: A child's perspective. *American Psychologist, 34,* 851–858.

Hetherington, E. M., Camara, K. A., & Featherman, D. L. (1983). Achievement and intellectual functioning of children from one-parent households. In J. Spence (Ed.), *Achievement and achievement motives.* San Francisco: Freeman.

Hetherington, E. M., Cox, M., & Cox, R. (1975). Beyond father absence: Conceptualization of effects of divorce. Paper presented at the meeting of the Society for Research in Child Development, Denver.

Hetherington, E. M., Cox, M., & Cox, R. (1977). The aftermath of divorce. In J. H. Stevens, Jr., & M. Matthews (Eds.), Mother–child, father–child relations. Washington, DC: National Association for the Education of Young Children.

Hetherington, E. M., Cox, M., & Cox, R. (1982). Effects of divorce on parents and children. In M. E. Lamb (Ed.), *Nontraditional families: Parenting and child development.* Hillsdale, NJ: Erlbaum.

Hetherington, E. M., & Duer, J. (1972). The effects of father absence on child development. In W. W. Hartup (Ed.), *The young child: Review of research,* Vol. 2. Washington, DC: National Association for the Development of Young Children.

Heuch, I., Kvale, G., Jacobsen, B. K., & Bjelke, E. (1983). Use of alcohol, tobacco and coffee, and risk of pancreatic cancer. *British Journal of Cancer, 48,* 637–643.

Hilgard, E. R. (1977). *Divided consciousness: Multiple controls in human thought and action.* New York: Wiley-Interscience.

Hilgard, E. R. (1978). Hypnosis and pain. In R. A. Sternbach (Ed.), *The psychology of pain.* New York: Raven Press.

Hill, C. (1987). Affiliation motivation: People who need people . . . but in different ways. *Journal of Personality and Social Psychology, 52,* 1008–1018.

Hill, C., Rubin, Z., & Peplau, L. A. (1976). Breakups before marriage: The end of 103 affairs. *Journal of Social Issues, 32,* 147–168.

Hinds, M. D. (1988, January 16). Coping with self-help books. *The New York Times,* p. 33.

Hinds, M. W., Kolonel, L. N., Hankin, J. H., & Lee, J. (1984). Dietary vitamin A, carotene, vitamin C and risk of lung cancer in Hawaii. *American Journal of Epidemiology, 119,* 227–237.

Hinshaw, S. P., Henker, B., & Whalen, C. K. (1984). Cognitive-behavioral and pharmacologic interventions for hyperactive boys: Comparative and combined effects. *Journal of Consulting and Clinical Psychology, 52,* 739–749.

Hite, S. (1976). *The Hite report: A nationwide study on female sexuality.* New York: Macmillan.

Hite, S. (1981). *The Hite report on male sexuality.* New York: Knopf.

Hite, S. (1987). *Women and love, a cultural revolution in progress.* New York: Knopf.

Hittleman, J. N., O'Donohue, N., Zilkha, S., & Parekh, A. (1980). Mother–infant assessment of the LeBoyer "nonviolent" method of childbirth. Paper presented to the meeting of the American Psychological Association, Montreal.

Hobson, J. A., & McCarley, R. W. (1977). The brain as a dream state generator: An activation-synthesis hypothesis of the dream process. *American Journal of Psychiatry, 134,* 1335–1348.

Hofferth, S. L., & Moore, K. A. (1979). Women's employment and marriage. In R. E. Smith (Ed.), *The subtle revolution: Women at work.* Washington, DC: The Urban Institute.

Hoffman, L. W. (1985, August). Work, family, and the child. Master lecture presented at the meeting of the American Psychological Association, Los Angeles.

Hoffman, L. W., & Manis, J. D. (1978). Influences of children on marital interaction and parental satisfaction and dissatisfaction. In R. M. Lerner & G. B. Spanier (Eds.), *Child Influences on marital and family interaction.* New York: Academic Press.

Hoffman, M. L. (1981). Is altruism part of human nature? *Journal of Personality and Social Psychology, 40,* 121–137.

Hoffmann-Plotkin, D., & Twentyman, C. T. (1984). A multimodal assessment of behavioral and cognitive deficits in abused and neglected preschoolers. *Child Development, 55,* 794–802.

Hoffnung, M. (1984). Motherhood: Contemporary conflict for women. In J. Freeman (Ed.), *Women: A feminist perspective,* 3d ed. Palo Alto: Mayfield.

Holahan, C. J. (1986). Environmental psychology. In M. R. Rosensweig &

L. W. Porter (Eds.), *Annual Review of Psychology, 37,* 381–407.

Holahan, C. J., & Moos, R. H. (1985). Life stress and health: Personality, coping, and family support in stress resistance. *Journal of Personality and Social Psychology, 49,* 739–747.

Holden, C. (1982). Hospices. In S. H. Zarit (Ed.), *Readings in aging and death,* 2d ed. New York: Harper & Row.

Holland, J. L. (1975). *Vocational preference inventory.* Palo Alto, CA: Consulting Psychologists Press.

Hollenbeck, A. R., et al. (1984). Labor and delivery medication influences parent–infant interaction in the first postpartum month. *Infant Behavior and Development, 7,* 201–209.

Hollestedt, C., et al. (1983). Outcome of pregnancy in women treated at an alcohol clinic. *Acta Psychiatrica Scandinavica, 67,* 236–248.

Hollingshead, A. B., & Redlich, F. C. (1958). *Social class and mental illness: A community study.* New York: Wiley.

Hollon, S., & Beck, A. T. (1986). Research on cognitive therapies. In S. L. Garfield & A. E. Bergin (Eds.), *Handbook of psychotherapy and behavior change,* 3d ed. New York: Wiley.

Holmes, D. S. (1984). Meditation and somatic arousal reduction: A review of the experimental evidence. *American Psychologist, 39,* 1–10.

Holmes, D. S. (1985). To meditate or to simply rest, that is the question: A response to the comments of Shapiro. *American Psychologist, 40,* 722–725.

Holmes, D. S., McGilley, B. M., & Houston, B. K. (1984). Task-related arousal of Type A and Type B persons: Level of challenge and response specificity. *Journal of Personality and Social Psychology, 46,* 1322–1327.

Holmes, D. S., Solomon, S., & Cappo, B. M., & Greenberg, J. L. (1983). Effects of transcendental meditation versus resting on physiological and subjective arousal. *Journal of Personality and Social Psychology, 44,* 1244–1252.

Holmes, D. S., & Will, M. J. (1985). Expression of interpersonal aggression by angered and nonangered persons with the Type A and Type B behavior patterns. *Journal of Personality and Social Psychology, 48,* 723–727.

Holmes, T. H., & Rahe, R. H. (1967). The social readjustment rating scale. *Journal of Psychosomatic Research, 11,* 213–218.

Holroyd, K. A., Westbrook, T., Wolf, M., & Badhorn, E. (1978). Performance, cognition, and physiological responding in test anxiety. *Journal of Abnormal Psychology, 87,* 442–451.

Horn, D. (1973, December). *Smoker's self-*

testing kit, I & II. Washington, DC: U.S. DHEW (CDC), 75-8716.

Holt, R. R. (1982). Occupational stress. In L. Goldberger & S. Brenitz (Eds.), *Handbook of stress.* New York: Free Press.

Honts, C., Hodes, R., & Raskin, D. (1985). *Journal of Applied Psychology, 70*(1).

Hook, E. (1981). Rates of chromosome abnormalities at different maternal ages. *Obstetrics and Gynecology, 61,* 282–284.

Horn, J. M. (1983). The Texas adoption project: Adopted children and their intellectual resemblance to biological and adoptive parents. *Child Development, 54,* 268–275.

Horney, K. (1967). *Feminine psychology.* New York: W. W. Norton.

Horton, E. S. (1974). The role of exercise in the prevention and treatment of obesity. In G. A. Bray (Ed.), *Obesity in perspective.* Washington, DC: U.S. Government Printing Office.

Horvath, T. (1981). Physical attractiveness: The influence of selected torso parameters. *Archives of Sexual Behavior, 10,* 21–24.

House, J. S. (1981). *Work stress and social support.* Reading, MA: Addison-Wesley.

House, J. S. (1984). Barriers to work stress: I. Social support. In W. D. Gentry, H. Benson, & C. deWolff (Eds.), *Behavioral medicine: Work, stress, and health.* The Hague: Nijhoff.

House, J. S., Robbins, C., & Metzner, H. L. (1982). The association of social relationships and activities with mortality: Prospective evidence from the Tecumseh Community Health Study. *American Journal of Epidemiology, 116,* 123–140.

Householder, J., Hatcher, R., Burns, W., & Chasnoff, I. (1982). Infants born to narcotic-addicted mothers. *Psychological Bulletin, 92,* 453–468.

Houts, P. S., Miller, R. W., Tokuhata, G. K., & Ham, K. S. (1980, April 8). *Health-related behavioral impact of the Three Mile Island nuclear incident.* Report submitted to the TMI Advisory Panel on Health Research Studies of the Pennsylvania Department of Health, Part I.

Howard, J. A., Blumstein, P., & Schwartz, P. (1987). Social or evolutionary theories: Some observations on preferences in mate selection. *Journal of Personality and Social Psychology, 53,* 194–200.

Howard, J. L., Liptzin, M. B., & Reifler, C. B. (1973). Is pornography a problem? *Journal of Social Issues, 29,* 133–145.

Howard, K. I., Kopta, S. M., Krause, M. S., & Orlinsky, D. E. (1986). The dose-effect relationship in psycho-

therapy. *American Psychologist, 41,* 159–164.

Howes, M. J., Hokanson, J. E., & Loewenstein, D. A. (1985). Induction to depressive affect after prolonged exposure to a mildly depressed individual. *Journal of Personality and Social Psychology, 49,* 1110–1113.

Hsu, L. K. G. (1986). The treatment of anorexia nervosa. *American Journal of Psychiatry, 143,* 573–581.

Hudson Institute. (1988). *Workforce 2000.* Indianapolis: Hudson Institute.

Huesmann, L. R., Eron, L. D., Klein, R., Brice, P., & Fischer, P. (1983). Mitigating the imitation of aggressive behaviors by changing children's attitudes about media violence. *Journal of Personality and Social Psychology, 44,* 899–910.

Hugdahl, K., & Ohman, A. (1977). Effects of instruction on acquisition and extinction of electrodermal response to fear-relevant stimuli. *Journal of Experimental Psychology: Human Learning and Memory, 3,* 608–618.

Hughes, P. L., Wells, L. A., Cunningham, C. J., & Ilstrup, D. M. (1986). Treating bulimia with desipramine. *Archives of General Psychiatry, 43,* 182–186.

Hull, J. G. (1981). A self-awareness model of the causes and effects of alcohol consumption. *Journal of Abnormal Psychology, 90,* 586–600.

Hull, J. G., Levenson, R. W., Young, R. D., & Sher, K. J. (1983). Self-awareness-reducing effects of alcohol consumption. *Journal of Personality and Social Psychology, 44,* 461–473.

Hull, J. G., Van Treuren, R. R., & Virnelli, S. (1987). Hardiness and health: A critique and alternative approach. *Journal of Personality and Social Psychology, 53,* 518–530.

Humphrey, F. G. (1975). Changing roles for women: Implications for marriage counselors. *Journal of Marriage and Family Counseling, 1,* 219–227.

Hunt, G. M., & Azrin, N. H. (1973). A community-reinforcement approach to alcoholism. *Behaviour Research and Therapy, 11,* 91–104.

Hunt, M. (1974). *Sexual behavior in the 1970s.* Chicago: Playboy Press.

Hunter, J. E., & Schmidt, F. L. (1983). Quantifying the effects of psychological interventions on employee job performance and work-force productivity. *American Psychologist, 38,* 473–478.

Huston, A. C. (1983). Sex-typing. In P. H. Mussen (Ed.), *Handbook of child psychology, Vol. 4: Socialization, personality, and social development.* New York: Wiley.

Hutchings, B., & Mednick, S. A. (1974). Registered criminality in the adoptive and biological parents of registered male adoptees. In S. A. Mednick, F. Schulsinger, J. Higgins, & B. Bell (Eds.), *Genetics, environment, and psychopathology.* New York: Elsevier.

Huxley, A. (1939). *Brave new world.* New York: Harper & Row.

Hyde, J. S. (1981). How large are cognitive gender differences? *American Psychologist, 36,* 892–901.

Insko, C. A. (1985). Balance theory, the Jordan paradigm, and the Wiest tetrahedron. In L. Berkowitz (Ed.), *Advances in experimental social psychology.* New York: Academic Press.

Israel, A. C., Stolmaker, L., & Andrian, C. A. G. (1985). The effects of training parents in general child management skills on a behavioral weight loss program for children. *Behavior Therapy, 16,* 169–180.

Istvan, J., & Griffitt, W. (1978). Emotional arousal and sexual attraction. Unpublished manuscript, Kansas State University.

Ivancevich, J. M., & Matteson, M. T. (1980). *Stress and work: A managerial perspective.* Glenview, IL: Scott, Foresman.

Ivey, M. E., & Bardwick, J. M. (1968). Patterns of affective fluctuation in the menstrual cycle. *Psychosomatic Medicine, 30,* 336–345.

Jacklin, C. N., & Maccoby, E. E. (1983). Issues of gender differentiation. In M. D. Levine, et al. (Eds.), *Developmental-behavioral pediatrics.* Philadelphia: W. B. Saunders.

Jacobs, T. J., & Charles, E. (1980). Life events and the occurrence of cancer in children. *Psychosomatic Medicine, 42,* 11–24.

Jacobson, E. (1938). *Progressive relaxation.* Chicago: University of Chicago Press.

Jacobson, N. S. (1984). A component analysis of behavioral marital therapy: The relative effectiveness of behavior exchange and communication/problem-solving training. *Journal of Consulting and Clinical Psychology, 52,* 295–305.

Jacques, J., & Chason, K. (1979). Cohabitation: Its impact on marital success. *Family Coordinator, 28,* 35–39.

Jaffe, H. W., Bregman, D. J., & Selik, R. M. (1983). Acquired immune deficiency syndrome in the United States. *Journal of Infectious Diseases, 148,* 339–345.

Jahoda, M. (1981). Work, employment, and underemployment: Values, theories, and approaches in social research. *American Psychologist, 36,* 184–191.

Jamison, K. K., & Akiskal, H. S. (1983). Medication compliance in patients with bipolar disorder. *Psychiatric Clinics of North America, 6,* 175–192.

Janda, L. H., & O'Grady, E. E. (1980). Development of a sex anxiety inventory. *Journal of Consulting and Clinical Psychology, 48,* 169–175.

Janicak, P. G., Davis, J. M., Gibbons, R. D., Ericksen, S., Chang, S., & Gallagher, P. (1985). Efficacy of ECT: A meta-analysis. *American Journal of Psychiatry, 142,* 297–302.

Janis, I. L., Kaye, D., & Kirschner, P. (1965). Facilitating effects of "eating while reading" on responsiveness to persuasive communications. *Journal of Personality and Social Psychology, 1,* 181–186.

Janis, I. L., & Mann, L. (1977). *Decision-making.* New York: Free Press.

Janis, I. L., & Wheeler, D. (1978). Thinking clearly about career choices. *Psychology Today, 12*(12), 66–76, 121–122.

Jankowitz, A. D. (1987). Whatever became of George Kelly? Applications and implications. *American Psychologist, 42,* 481–487.

Janowitz, H. D., & Grossman, M. I. (1949). Effects of variations in nutritive density on intake of food in dogs and cats. *American Journal of Physiology, 158,* 184–193.

Jelliffe, D. B., & Jelliffe, E. F. P. (1983). Recent scientific knowledge concerning breastfeeding. *Rev. Epidem. et Sante. Publ., 31,* 367–373.

Jellison, J. M., & Green, J. (1981). A self-presentation approach to the fundamental attribution error: The norm of internality. *Journal of Personality and Social Psychology, 40,* 643–649.

Jellison, J. M., & Oliver, D. F. (1983). Attitude similarity and attraction: An impression management approach. *Personality and Social Psychology Bulletin, 9,* 111–115.

Jemmott, J. B., Borysenko, J. Z., Borysenko, M., McClelland, D. C., Chapman, R., Meyer, D., & Benson, H. (1983). Academic stress, power motivation, and decrease in secretion rate of salivary secretory immunoglobin A. *Lancet, 1,* 1400–1402.

Jenks, R. (1985). Swinging: A replication and test of a theory. *The Journal of Sex Research, 21,* 199–210.

Jennings, J., Geis, F. L., & Brown, J. (1980). Influence of television commercials on women's self-confidence and independent judgment. *Journal of Personality and Social Psychology, 38,* 203–210.

Jiao, S., Ji, G., & Jing, Q. (1986). Comparative study of behavioral qualities of only children and sibling children. *Child Development, 57,* 357–361.

Johns, M. W., Masterson, J. P., & Bruce, D. W. (1971). Relationship between sleep habits, adrenocortical activity, and personality. *Psychosomatic Medicine, 33,* 499–507.

Johnson, J. T., & Judd, C. M. (1983). Overlooking the incongruent: Categorization biases in the identification of political statements. *Journal of Personality and Social Psychology, 45,* 978–996.

Johnson, S. M., & White, G. (1971). Self-observation as an agent of behavioral change. *Behavior Therapy, 2,* 488–497.

Johnston, L. D., & Bachman, J. G., & O'Malley, P. M. (1982). Student drug use, attitudes, and beliefs, 1975–1982. DHHS Publication No. ADM 82-1260. Washington, DC: National Institute on Drug Abuse.

Jones, E. (1961). *The life and work of Sigmund Freud.* New York: Basic Books.

Jones, K. L. (1975). The fetal alcohol syndrome. In R. D. Harbison (Ed.), *Perinatal addiction.* New York: Halsted.

Jones, M. (1975). Community care for chronic mental patients: The need for a reassessment. *Hospital and Community Psychiatry, 26,* 94–98.

Jones, M. C. (1924). Elimination of children's fears. *Journal of Experimental Psychology, 7,* 381–390.

Jones, W. H. (1982). Loneliness and social behavior. In L. A. Peplau & D. Perlman (Eds.), *Loneliness: A sourcebook of current theory, research, and therapy.* New York: Wiley.

Jones, W. H., Freeman, J. A., & Goswick, R. A. (1981). The persistence of loneliness: Self and other determinants. *Journal of Personality, 49,* 27–48.

Joos, S. K., Pollitt, E., Mueller, W. H., & Albright, D. L. (1983). The Bacon Chow study: Maternal nutritional supplementation and infant behavioral development. *Child Development, 54,* 669–676.

Julien, R. M. (1986). *A primer of drug action,* 2d ed. San Francisco: Freeman.

Jung, C. G. (1964). *Man and his symbols.* Garden City, NY: Doubleday.

Jus, A., Pineau, R., Lachance, R., Pelchat, G., Jus, K., Pires, P., & Villeneuve, R. (1976). Epidemiology of tardive dyskinesia. *Diseases of the Nervous System, 37,* 210–214.

Justice, B., & Justice, R. (1976). *The abusing family.* New York: Human Sciences Press.

Kagan, J. (1964). Acquisition and significance of sex-typing and sex-role identity. In M. L. Hoffman & L. W. Hoffman (Eds.), *Review of child development research,* Vol. 1. New York: Russell Sage.

Kagan, J. (1984). *The nature of the child.* New York: Basic Books.

Kagan, J., Kearsley, R. B., & Zelazo, P. R. (1980). *Infancy: Its place in human development.* Cambridge, MA: Harvard University Press.

Kahn, E. (1985). Heinz Kohut and Carl

Rogers: A timely comparison. *American Psychologist, 40,* 893–904.

Kahn, S., Zimmerman, G., Csikszentmihalyi, M., & Getzels, J. W. (1985). Relations between identity in young adulthood and intimacy at midlife. *Journal of Personality and Social Psychology, 49,* 1316–1322.

Kalish, R. A. (1985). *Death, grief, and caring relationships,* 2d ed. Monterey, CA: Brooks/Cole.

Kalish, R. A., & Reynolds, D. K. (1976). *Death and ethnicity: A psycho-cultural study.* Los Angeles: University of Southern California Press.

Kallmann, F. J. (1952). Comparative twin study on the genetic aspects of male homosexuality. *Journal of Nervous and Mental Disease, 115,* 283–298.

Kamens, L. (1980). Cognitive and attribution factors in sleep-onset insomnia. Unpublished doctoral dissertation, Southern Illinois University at Carbondale.

Kandel, D. B. (1980). Drug and drinking behavior among youth. *Annual Review of Sociology, 6,* 235–285.

Kandel, D. B., Davies, M., Kraus, D., & Yamaguchi, K. (1986). The consequences in young adulthood of adolescent drug involvement. *Archives of General Psychiatry, 43,* 746–754.

Kanfer, F., & Goldfoot, D. (1966). Self-control and tolerance of noxious stimulation. *Psychological Reports, 18,* 79–85.

Kanin, E. J., & Parcell, S. R. (1977). Sexual aggression: A second look at the offended female. *Archives of Sexual Behavior, 6,* 67–76.

Kanin, G. (1978). *It takes a long time to become young.* Garden City, NY: Doubleday.

Kanner, A. D., Coyne, J. C., Schaefer, C., & Lazarus, R. S. (1981). Comparison of two modes of stress measurement: Daily hassles and uplifts versus major life events. *Journal of Behavioral Medicine, 4,* 1–39.

Kaplan, A. S., & Woodside, D. B. (1987). Biological aspects of anorexia nervosa and bulimia nervosa. *Journal of Consulting and Clinical Psychology, 55,* 645–653.

Kaplan, H. R. (1978). *Lottery winners.* New York: Harper & Row.

Kaplan, H. S. (1987). *The real truth about women and AIDS.* New York: Simon & Schuster/Fireside.

Kaplan, H. S., & Sager, C. J. (1971). Sexual patterns at different ages. *Medical Aspects of Human Sexuality, 5*(6), 10–23.

Kaplan, R. M., & Singer, R. D. (1976). Television violence and viewer aggression: A reexamination of the evidence. *Journal of Social Issues, 32,* 35–70.

Karabenick, S. A., & Meisels, M. (1972).

Effects of performance evaluation on interpersonal distance. *Journal of Personality, 40,* 275–286.

Karacan, I. (1978). Advances in the psychophysiological evaluation of male erectile impotence. In J. LoPiccolo & L. LoPiccolo (Eds.), *Handbook of Sex Therapy.* New York: Plenum Publishing Co.

Karlin, R. A., McFarland, D., Aiello, J. R., & Epstein, Y. M. (1976). Normative mediation of reactions to crowding. *Environmental Psychology and Non-Verbal Behavior, 1,* 30–40.

Karp, L. (1980). The arguable propriety of preconceptual sex determination. *American Journal of Medical Genetics, 6,* 185–187.

Kastenbaum, R. (1977). *Death, society, and human behavior.* St. Louis: Mosby.

Katchadourian, H. A. (1985). *Fundamentals of human sexuality.* New York: Holt, Rinehart and Winston.

Katzell, R. A., & Guzzo, R. A. (1983). Psychological approaches to productivity improvement. *American Psychologist, 38,* 468–472.

Kavale, K. (1982). The efficacy of stimulant drug treatment for hyperactivity: A meta-analysis. *Journal of Learning Disabilities, 15,* 280–289.

Kazdin, A. E., Moser, J., Colbus, D., & Bell, R. (1985). Depressive symptoms among physically abused and psychiatrically disturbed children. *Journal of Abnormal Psychology, 94,* 298–307.

Kazdin, A. E., & Wilcoxin, L. A. (1976). Systematic desensitization and nonspecific treatment effects: A methodological evaluation. *Psychological Bulletin, 83,* 729–758.

Keating, C. F., Mazur, A., Segall, M. H., Cysneiros, P. G., Divale, W. T., Kiecolt-Glaser, J. K., Glaser, R., Williger, D., Stout, J., Messick, G., Sheppard, S., Ricker, D., Romisher, S. C., Briner, W., Bonnell, G., & Donnerberg, R. (1985). Psychosocial enhancement of immunocompetence in a geriatric population. *Health Psychology, 4,* 25–41.

Keefe, F. J., Caldwell, D. S., Queen, K. T., Gil, K. M., Martinez, S., Crisson, J. E., Ogden, W., & Nunley, J. (1987). Pain coping strategies in osteoarthritis patients. *Journal of Consulting and Clinical Psychology, 55,* 208–212.

Keesey, R. E. (1980). A set-point analysis of the regulation of body weight. In A. J. Stunkard (Ed.), *Obesity.* Philadelphia: W. B. Saunders Co.

Keesey, R. E., & Powley, T. L. (1975). Hypothalmic regulation of body weight. *American Scientist, 63,* 558–565.

Kelly, G. A. (1955). *The psychology of personal constructs,* Vols. 1 & 2. New York: W. W. Norton.

Kelly, G. A. (1958). Man's construction of his alternatives. In G. Lindzey (Ed.), *Assessment of human motives.* New York: Holt, Rinehart and Winston.

Kendall, P. C., & Norton-Ford, J. D. (1982). Therapy outcome research methods. In P. C. Kendall & J. N. Butcher (Eds.), *Handbook of research methods in clinical psychology.* New York: Wiley.

Kennedy, D. T., & Stephan, W. G. (1977). The effects of cooperation and competition on ingroup–outgroup bias. *Journal of Applied Social Psychology, 7,* 115–130.

Kennell, J. H., Jerauld, R., Wolfe, H., Chesler, D., Kreger, N., McAlpine, W., Steffa, M., & Klaus, M. H. (1974). Maternal behavior one year after early and extended post-partum contact. *Developmental Medicine and Child Neurology, 16,* 172–179.

Kennell, J. H., & Klaus, M. H. (1984). Mother–infant bonding: Weighing the evidence. *Developmental Review, 4,* 275–282.

Kenrick, D. T., & Gutierres, S. F. (1980). Contrast effects and judgments of physical attractiveness. *Journal of Personality and Social Psychology, 38,* 131–140.

Kenrick, D. T., & MacFarlane, S. W. (1986). Ambient temperature and horn honking: A field study of the heat/aggression relationship. *Environment and Behavior, 18,* 179–191.

Kerpelman, J. P., & Himmelfarb, S. (1971). Partial reinforcement effects in attitude acquisition and counter-conditioning. *Journal of Personality and Social Psychology, 19,* 301–305.

Kesey, K. (1962). *One flew over the cuckoo's nest.* New York: Viking.

Keuthen, M. (1980). Subjective probability estimation and somatic structures in phobic individuals. Unpublished manuscript, State University of New York at Stony Brook.

Keverne, E. B. (1977). Pheromones and sexual behavior. In J. Money & H. Musaph (Eds.), *Handbook of sexology.* Amsterdam: Excerpta Medica.

Keye, W. R. (1983). Update: Premenstrual syndrome. *Endocrine and Fertility Forum, 6*(4), 1–3.

Keyes, D. (1982). *The minds of Billy Milligan.* New York: Bantam Books.

Kiecolt-Glaser, J. K., Speicher, C. E., Holliday, J. E., & Glaser, R. (1984). Stress and the transformation of lymphocytes in Epstein-Barr virus. *Journal of Behavioral Medicine, 7,* 1–12.

Kilbride, J. E., Komin, S., Leahy, P., Thurman, B., & Wirsing, R. (1981). Culture and the perception of social dominance from facial expression. *Journal of Personality and Social Psychology, 40,* 615–626.

Kimmel, D. C. (1974). *Adulthood and ag-*

ing: An interdisciplinary developmental view. New York: Wiley.

Kinsey, A. C., Pomeroy, W. B., & Martin, C. E. (1948). Sexual behavior in the human male. Philadelphia: W. B. Saunders Co.

Kinsey, A. C., Pomeroy, W. B., Martin, C. E., & Gebhard, P. H. (1953). Sexual behavior in the human female. Philadelphia: W. B. Saunders Co.

Kinzel, A. S. (1970). Body buffer zone in violent prisoners. American Journal of Psychiatry, 127, 59–64.

Klagsbrun, G. (1985). Married people: Staying together in the age of divorce. New York: Bantam Books.

Klass, P. (1988, April 10). Are women better doctors? New York Times Magazine, pp. 32–35, 46–48, 96–97.

Klatsky, A. L., Freidman, G. D., & Siegelaub, A. B. (1981). Alcohol and mortality: A ten-year Kaiser-Permanente experience. Annals of Internal Medicine, 95, 139–145.

Klaus, M. H., & Kennell, J. H. (1976). Maternal–infant bonding. St. Louis: Mosby.

Klaus, M. H., & Kennell, J. H. (1978). In J. H. Stevens, Jr. & M. Mathews (Eds.), Mother/child, father/child relationships. Washington, DC: National Association for the Education of Young Children.

Klein, D. F., & Rabkin, J. G. (1984). Specificity and strategy in psychotherapy research and practice. In R. L. Spitzer & J. R. W. Williams (Eds.), Psychotherapy research: Where are we and where should we go? New York: Guilford Press.

Klein, D. N., & Depue, R. A. (1985). Obsessional personality traits and risk for bipolar affective disorder: An offspring study. Journal of Abnormal Psychology, 94, 291–297.

Klein, D. N., Depue, R. A., & Slater, J. F. (1985). Cyclothymia in the adolescent offspring of parents with bipolar affective disorder. Journal of Abnormal Psychology, 94, 115–127.

Klein, M. H., Greist, J. H., Gurman, A. S., Neimeyer, R. A., Lesser, D. P., Bushnell, N. J., & Smith, R. E. (1985). A comparative outcome study of group psychotherapy versus exercise treatments for depression. International Journal of Mental Health, 13, 148–175.

Klein, R. P. (1985). Caregiving arrangements by employed women with children under 1 year of age. Developmental Psychology, 21, 403–406.

Kleinke, C. L. (1977). Compliance to requests made by gazing and touching experimenters in field settings. Journal of Experimental Social Psychology, 13, 218–223.

Kleinke, C. L., & Staneski, R. A. (1980). First impressions of female bust size.

Journal of Social Psychology, 110, 123–134.

Kleinke, C. L., & Walton, J. H. (1982). Influence of reinforced smiling on affective responses in an interview. Journal of Personality and Social Psychology, 42, 557–565.

Knapp, M. L. (1978). Nonverbal communication in human interaction. New York: Holt, Rinehart and Winston.

Knapp, M. L. (1978). Social intercourse: From greeting to goodbye. Boston: Allyn & Bacon.

Knaub, P. K., Eversoll, D. B., & Voss, J. H. (1983). Is parenthood a desirable adult role? An assessment of attitudes held by contemporary adult women. Sex Roles, 9, 355–362.

Knowlton, W. A., Jr., & Mitchell, T. R. (1980). Effects of causal attributions on a supervisor's evaluation of subordinate performance. Journal of Applied Psychology, 65, 459–466.

Knox, D. (1971). Marriage happiness: A behavioral approach to counseling. Champaign, IL: Research Press.

Kobasa, S. C. (1979). Stressful life events, personality, and health: An inquiry into hardiness. Journal of Personality and Social Psychology, 37, 1–11.

Kobasa, S. C. (1985). Personality and health: Specifying and strengthening the conceptual links. In P. Shaver (Ed.), Self, situations, and social behavior. Beverly Hills: Sage Press.

Kobasa, S. C., Maddi, S. R., & Kahn, S. (1982). Hardiness and health: A prospective study. Journal of Personality and Social Psychology, 42, 168–177.

Kobasa, S. C., Maddi, S. R., & Zola, M. A. (1983). Type A and hardiness. Journal of Behavioral Medicine, 6, 41–51.

Kobasa, S. C., & Puccetti, M. C. (1983). Personality and social resources in stress resistance. Journal of Personality and Social Psychology, 45, 839–850.

Kogan, B. A. (1973). Human sexual expression. New York: Harcourt Brace Jovanovich.

Kohen, W., & Paul, G. L. (1976). Current trends and recommended changes in extended care placements of mental patients: The Illinois system as a case in point. Schizophrenia Bulletin, 2, 575–594.

Kohlberg, L. (1966). A cognitive-developmental analysis of children's sex-role concepts and attitudes. In E. E. Maccoby (Ed.), The development of sex differences. Stanford, CA: Stanford University Press.

Kohlberg, L. (1969). Stages in the development of moral thought and action. New York: Holt, Rinehart and Winston.

Kohlberg, L. (1981). The philosophy of moral development: Moral stages and the idea of justice. New York: Harper & Row.

Kohn, P. M., Barnes, G. E., & Hoffman, F. M. (1979). Drug-use history and

experience seeking among adult male correctional inmates. Journal of Consulting and Clinical Psychology, 47, 708–715.

Kolata, G. (1985). Down syndrome–Alzheimer's linked. Science, 230, 1152–1153.

Kolata, G. (1987, September 22). Tests of fetuses rise sharply amid doubts. The New York Times, pp. C1, C10.

Kolata, G. (1987, November 10). Alcoholism: Genetic links grow clearer. The New York Times, pp. C1, C2.

Kolata, G. (1988, February 16). Recent setbacks stirring doubts about search for AIDS vaccine. The New York Times, pp. 1, C13.

Kolata, G. (1988, March 21). Latest study disputes link of breast cancer to alcohol. The New York Times, p. A14.

Kolata, G. (1988, March 22). Fatal strategy of AIDS virus grows clearer. The New York Times, pp. C1, C11.

Kolko, D. J., & Rickard-Figueroa, J. L. (1985). Effects of video games on the adverse corollaries of chemotherapy in pediatric oncology patients: A single-case analysis. Journal of Consulting and Clinical Psychology, 53, 223–228.

Komacki, J., & Dore-Boyce, K. (1978). Self-recording: Its effects on individuals high and low in motivation. Behavior Therapy, 9, 65–72.

Konner, M. (1988, January 17). Caffeine high. The New York Times Magazine, pp. 47–48.

Koocher, G. P. (1971). Swimming, competence, and personality change. Journal of Personality and Social Psychology, 18, 275–278.

Koop, C. E. (1987). Report of the surgeon general's workshop on pornography and public health. American Psychologist, 42, 944–945.

Koop, C. E. (1987). Cited in, Koop urges AIDS test before getting pregnant. The New York Times, March 25, 1987, p. B4.

Kornblum, W. (1988). Sociology in a changing world. New York: Holt, Rinehart and Winston.

Koss, M. P., Butcher, J. L., & Strupp, H. H. (1986). Brief psychotherapy methods in clinical research. Journal of Consulting and Clinical Psychology, 54, 60–67.

Koss, M. P., Gidycz, C. A., & Wisniewski, N. (1987). The scope of rape: Incidence and prevalence of sexual aggression and victimization in a national sample of higher education students. Journal of Consulting and Clinical Psychology, 55, 162–170.

Kramsch, D. M., et al. (1981). Reduction of coronary atherosclerosis by moderate conditioning exercise in monkeys on an atherogenic diet. New England Journal of Medicine, 305, 1483–1489.

Krantz, D. S., Grunberg, N. E., & Baum,

A. (1985). Health psychology. *Annual Review of Psychology, 36,* 349–383.

Krech, D., Crutchfield, R. S., & Ballachey, E. L. (1962). *Individual in society.* New York: McGraw-Hill.

Krieger, D. T. (1983). Brain peptides: What, where, and why? *Science, 222,* 975–985.

Kromhout, D., Bosschieter, E. B., & de Lezenne Coulander, C. (1985). The inverse relation between fish consumption and 20-year mortality from coronary heart disease. *New England Journal of Medicine, 312,* 1205–1209.

Kübler-Ross, E. (1969). *On death and dying.* New York: Macmillan.

Kübler-Ross, E., & Magno, J. B. (1983). *Hospice.* Santa Fe, NM: Bear.

Kuntzleman, C. T. (1978). *Rating the exercises.* New York: Morrow.

Kurdek, A., Blisk, D., & Siesky, A. E. (1981). Correlates of children's long-term adjustment to their parents' divorce. *Developmental Psychology, 17,* 565–579.

Ladas, A. K., Whipple, B., & Perry, J. D. (1982). *The G spot and other recent discoveries about human sexuality.* New York: Holt, Rinehart and Winston.

Lahey, B. B., & Drabman, R. S. (1981). Behavior modification in the classroom. In W. E. Craighead, A. E. Kazdin, & M. J. Mahoney (Eds.), *Behavior modification: Principles, issues and applications,* 2d ed. Boston: Houghton Mifflin.

Lamaze, F. (1981). *Painless childbirth.* New York: Simon & Schuster.

Lamb, M. E. (1981). The development of father–infant relationships. In M. E. Lamb (Ed.), *The role of the father in child development.* New York: Wiley.

Lamb, M. E. (1982). Early contact and maternal–infant bonding: One decade later. *Pediatrics, 70,* 763–768.

Lamb, M. E., & Baumrind, D. (1978). Socialization and personality development in the preschool years. In M. E. Lamb (Ed.), *Social and personality development.* New York: Holt, Rinehart and Winston.

Lamb, M. E., Easterbrooks, M. A., & Holden, G. W. (1980). Reinforcement and punishment among preschoolers: Characteristics, effects, and correlates. *Child Development, 51,* 1230–1236.

Lamb, M. E., & Roopnarine, J. L. (1979). Peer influences on sex-role development in preschoolers. *Child Development, 50,* 1219–1222.

Lambert, B. (1987, December 13). New York City maps deadly pattern of AIDS. *The New York Times,* pp. 1, 58.

Lambert, M. J., Shapiro, D. A., & Bergin, A. E. (1986). The effectiveness of psychotherapy. In S. L. Garfield & A. E. Bergin (Eds.), *Handbook of psychotherapy and behavior change,* 3d ed. New York: Wiley.

Landesman-Dwyer, S., & Emanuel, I. (1979). Smoking during pregnancy. *Teratology, 19,* 119–126.

Landy, D., & Sigall, H. (1974). Beauty is talent: Task evaluation as a function of the performer's physical attractiveness. *Journal of Personality and Social Psychology, 30,* 299–304.

Landy, F. J. (1985). *Psychology of work behavior.* Homewood, IL: Dorsey Press.

Landy, F. J., & Farr, J. L. (1983). *The measurement of work performance: Methods, theory, and applications.* New York: Academic Press.

Lang, A. R., Goeckner, D. J., Adesso, V. J., & Marlatt, G. A. (1975). Effects of alcohol on aggression in male social drinkers. *Journal of Abnormal Psychology, 84,* 508–518.

Lang, A. R., Searles, J., Lauerman, R., & Adesso, V. J. (1980). Expectancy, alcohol, and sex guilt as determinants of interest in and reaction to sexual stimuli. *Journal of Abnormal Psychology, 89,* 644–653.

Langer, E. J., Bashner, R. S., & Chanowitz, B. (1985). Decreasing prejudice by increasing discrimination. *Journal of Personality and Social Psychology, 49,* 113–120.

Langer, E. J., Rodin, J., Beck, P., Weinan, C., & Spitzer, L. (1979). Environmental determinants of memory improvement in late adulthood. *Journal of Personality and Social Psychology, 37,* 2003–2013.

Langer, E. J., & Saegert, S. (1977). Crowding and cognitive control. *Journal of Personality and Social Psychology, 35,* 175–182.

Langford, H. G., et al. (1985). Dietary therapy slows the return of hypertension after stopping prolonged medication. *Journal of the American Medical Association, 253,* 657–664.

Lansky, D., & Wilson, G. T. (1981). Alcohol, expectations, and sexual arousal. *Journal of Abnormal Psychology, 90,* 35–45.

Larsen, J. (1984). Cited in, Sad news for the happy hour. *Newsweek,* March 19, 1984, p. 67.

Latané, B., & Dabbs, J. M. (1975). Sex, group size, and helping in three cities. *Sociometry, 38,* 180–194.

Latané, B., & Nida, S. (1981). Ten years of research on group size and helping. *Psychological Bulletin, 89,* 308–324.

Lau, R. R., & Hartman, K. A. (1983). Common sense representations of common illnesses. *Health Psychology, 2,* 167–185.

Lau, R. R., & Russell, D. (1980). Attributions in the sports pages. *Journal of Personality and Social Psychology, 39,* 29–38.

Laube, D. (1985). Premenstrual syndrome. *The Female Patient, 6,* 50–61.

Laudenslager, M. L., Ryan, S. M., Drugan, R. C., Hyson, R. L., & Maier, S. F. (1983). Coping and immunosuppression: Inescapable but not escapable shock suppresses lymphocyte proliferation. *Science, 221,* 568–570.

Lavrakas, P. J. (1975, May). Female preferences for male physiques. Paper presented at the Midwestern Psychological Association, Chicago.

Lavrakas, P. J. (1982). Fear of crime and behavior restriction in urban and suburban neighborhoods. *Population and Environment, 5,* 242–264.

Lawler, E. E., III. (1985, January/February). Quality circles after the fad. *Harvard Business Review,* pp. 65–71.

Lazarus, R. S. (1984). Puzzles in the study of daily hassles. *Journal of Behavioral Medicine, 7,* 375–389.

Lazarus, R. S. (1984). The trivialization of distress. In B. L. Hammonds & C. J. Scheirer (Eds.), *Psychology and health: The master lecture series.* Washington, DC: American Psychological Association.

Lazarus, R. S., DeLongis, A., Folkman, S., & Gruen, R. (1985). Stress and adaptational outcomes: The problem of confounded measures. *American Psychologist, 40,* 770–779.

Lazarus, R. S., & Folkman, S. (1984). *Stress, appraisal, and coping.* New York: Springer.

LeBon, G. (1895). *The crowd.* New York: Viking, 1960.

LeBow, M. D., Goldberg, P. S., & Collins, A. (1977). Eating behavior of overweight and nonoverweight persons in the natural environment. *Journal of Consulting and Clinical Psychology, 45,* 1204–1205.

Leboyer, F. (1975). *Birth without violence.* New York: Knopf.

Lee, T., & Seeman, P. (1977). Dopamine receptors in normal and schizophrenic human brains. *Proceedings of the Society of Neurosciences, 3,* 443.

Lefcourt, H. M., & Martin, R. A. (1986). *Humor and life stress: Antidote to adversity.* New York: Springer.

Lefcourt, H. M., Miller, R. S., Ware, E. E., & Sherk, D. (1981). Locus of control as a modifier of the relationship between stressors and moods. *Journal of Personality and Social Psychology, 41,* 357–369.

Leiblum, S., & Ersner-Hershfield, R. (1977). Sexual enhancement groups for dysfunctional women: An evaluation. *Journal of Sex and Marital Therapy, 3,* 139–152.

Leibowitz, S. F. (1986). Brain monoamines and peptides: Role in the control of eating behavior. *Federation Proceedings, 45,* 599–615.

Leifer, M. (1980). *Psychological effects of motherhood: A study of first pregnancy.* New York: Praeger.

Leonard, C. V. (1974). Depression and

suicidality. *Journal of Consulting and Clinical Psychology, 42,* 98–104.

Leonard, C. V. (1977). The MMPI as a suicide predictor. *Journal of Consulting and Clinical Psychology, 45,* 367–377.

Lerner, R. M., & Gellert, E. (1969). Body build identification, preference, and aversion in children. *Developmental Psychology, 1,* 456–462.

Leslie, G. H., & Gellert, E. (1977). *Marriage in a changing world.* New York: Wiley.

Lesnik-Oberstein, M., & Cohen, L. (1984). Cognitive style, sensation seeking, and assortive mating. *Journal of Personality and Social Psychology, 46,* 112–117.

Lester, B. M., Als, H., & Brazelton, T. B. (1982). Regional obstetric anesthesia and newborn behavior: A reanalysis toward synergistic effects. *Child Development, 53,* 687–692.

Leventhal, H., Meyer, D., & Nerenz, D. R. (1980). The commonsense representation of illness danger. In S. Rachman (Ed.), *Medical psychology,* Vol. 2. New York: Pergamon Press.

Leventhal, H., Nerenz, D. R., & Steele, D. J. (1984). Illness representations and coping with health threats. In A. Baum, S. E. Taylor, & J. E. Singer (Eds.), *Handbook of psychology and health: Vol. 4. Social psychological aspects of health.* Hillsdale, NJ: Erlbaum.

Leventhal, H., Watts, J. C., & Paogano, F. (1967). Effects of fear and instructions on how to cope with danger. *Journal of Personality and Social Psychology, 6,* 313–321.

Levinger, G. (1980). Toward the analysis of close relationships. *Journal of Experimental Social Psychology, 16,* 510–544.

Levinson, D. J., Darrow, C. N., Klein, E. B., Levinson, M. H., & McKee, B. (1978). *The seasons of a man's life.* New York: Knopf.

Levitt, R. A. (1981). *Physiological psychology.* New York: Holt, Rinehart and Winston.

Levy, J. (1985). Right brain, left brain: Fact and fiction. *Psychology Today, 19*(5), 38–44.

Levy, S. M. (1985). *Behavior and cancer: Life-style and psychosocial factors in the initiation and progression of cancer.* San Francisco: Jossey-Bass.

Levy, S. M., Herberman, R. B., Maluish, A. M., Schlien, B., & Lippman, M. (1985). Prognostic risk assessment in primary breast cancer by behavioral and immunological parameters. *Health Psychology, 4,* 99–113.

Lewinsohn, P. M. (1975). The behavioral study and treatment of depression. In M. Hersen, R. M. Eisler, & P. M. Miller (Eds.), *Progress in behavior modification,* Vol. 1. New York: Academic Press.

Lewinsohn, P. M., & Amenson, C. S. (1978). Some relations between pleasant and unpleasant mood-related events and depression. *Journal of Abnormal Psychology, 87,* 644–654.

Lewinsohn, P. M., & Graf, M. (1973). Pleasant activities and depression. *Journal of Consulting and Clinical Psychology, 41,* 261–268.

Lewinsohn, P. M., & Libet, J. (1972). Pleasant events, activity schedules, and depression. *Journal of Abnormal Psychology, 79,* 291–295.

Lewis, J., Baddeley, A. D., Bonham, K. G., & Lovett, D. (1970). Traffic pollution and mental efficiency. *Nature, 225,* 96.

Lichtenstein, E. (1982). The smoking problem: A behavioral perspective. *Journal of Consulting and Clinical Psychology, 50,* 804–819.

Lichtenstein, E., & Glasgow, R. E. (1977). Rapid smoking: Side effects and safeguards. *Journal of Consulting and Clinical Psychology, 45,* 815–821.

Lick, J. R., & Heffler, D. (1977). Relaxation training and attention placebo in the treatment of severe insomnia. *Journal of Consulting and Clinical Psychology, 45,* 153–161.

Lieberman, M. A., Yalom, I. D., & Miles, M. (1973). *Encounter groups: First facts.* New York: Basic Books.

Ling, G. S. F., MacLeod, J. M., Lee, S., Lockhart, S. H., & Pasternak, G. W. (1984). Separation of morphine analgesia from physical dependence. *Science, 226,* 462–464.

Linn, S., et al. (1982). Coffee and pregnancy. *New England Journal of Medicine, 306,* 141–145.

Linz, D., Donnerstein, E., & Penrod, S. (1987). The findings and recommendations of the Attorney General's Commission on Pornography. *American Psychologist, 42,* 946–953.

Lipinski, D. P., Black, J. L., Nelson, R. O., & Ciminero, A. R. (1975). Influence of motivational variables on the reactivity and reliability of self-recording. *Journal of Consulting and Clinical Psychology, 43,* 637–646.

Lipsky, M., Kassinove, H., & Miller, N. (1980). Effects of rational-emotive therapy, rational role reversal, and rational-emotive imagery on the emotional adjustment of community-mental-health-center patients. *Journal of Consulting and Clinical Psychology, 48,* 366–374.

Lipton, D. N., McDonel, E. C., & McFall, R. M. (1987). Heterosocial perception in rapists. *Journal of Consulting and Clinical Psychology, 55,* 17–21.

Lloyd, C., Alexander, A. A., Rice, D. G., & Greenfield, N. S. (1980). Life events as predictors of academic performance. *Journal of Human Stress, 6,* 15–25.

Lochman, J. E. (1987). Self- and peer perceptions and attributional biases of aggressive and nonaggressive boys in dyadic interactions. *Journal of Consulting and Clinical Psychology, 55,* 404–410.

Loeb, R. B., Horst, L., & Horton, P. J. (1980). Family interaction patterns associated with self-esteem in preadolescent girls and boys. *Merrill-Palmer Quarterly, 26,* 203–217.

Loehlin, J. C., Willerman, L., & Horn, J. M. (1982). Personality resemblances between unwed mothers and their adopted-away offspring. *Journal of Personality and Social Psychology, 42,* 1089–1099.

Logan, D. D. (1978, August). Variations on "the curse": Menstrual euphemisms in other countries. Paper presented to the American Psychological Association, Toronto.

Logue, J. N., Hansen, F., & Struening, E. (1979). Emotional and physical distress following Hurricane Agnes in the Wyoming Valley of Pennsylvania. *Public Health Reports, 94,* 495–502.

Lohr, J. M., & Staats, A. (1973). Attitude conditioning in Sino-Tibetan languages. *Journal of Personality and Social Psychology, 26,* 196–200.

Long, B. C. (1984). Aerobic conditioning and stress inoculation: A comparison of stress-management interventions. *Cognitive Therapy and Research, 8,* 517–542.

Long Laws, J., & Schwartz, P. (1977). *Sexual scripts.* Hinsdale, IL: Dryden Press.

LoPiccolo, J., Heiman, J. R., Hogan, D. R., & Roberts, C. W. (1985). Effectiveness of single therapists versus cotherapy teams in sex therapy. *Journal of Consulting and Clinical Psychology, 53,* 287–294.

LoPiccolo, J., & Stock, W. E. (1986). Treatment of sexual dysfunction. *Journal of Consulting and Clinical Psychology, 54,* 158–167.

Lott, B. (1981). A feminist critique of androgyny: Toward the elimination of gender attributions for learned behavior. In C. Mayo & N. M. Henley (Eds.), *Gender and nonverbal behavior.* New York: Springer.

Lott, B. (1985). The potential enhancement of social/personality psychology through feminist research and vice versa. *American Psychologist, 40,* 155–164.

Lourea, D., Rila, M., & Taylor, C. (1986). Sex in the age of AIDS. Paper presented to the Western Region Conference of the Society for the Scientific Study of Sex, Scottsdale, AZ.

Lowenthal, M. F., & Haven, C. (1981). Interaction and adaptation: Intimacy as a critical variable. In L. D. Steinberg (Ed.), *The life cycle.* New York: Columbia University Press.

Lubin, B., Larsen, R. M., Matarazzo, J. D., & Seever, M. (1985). Psychological test usage patterns in five professional settings. *American Psychologist, 40,* 857–861.

Lublin, J. S. (1984, March 8). Couples working different shifts take on new duties and pressures. *The Wall Street Journal,* p. 33.

Luborsky, L., & DeRubeis, R. J. (1984). The use of psychotherapy treatment manuals: A small revolution in psychotherapy research style. *Clinical Psychology Review, 4,* 5–15.

Luborsky, L., & Spence, D. P. (1971). Quantitative research on psychoanalytic therapy. In A. E. Bergin & S. L. Garfield (Eds.), *Handbook of psychotherapy and behavior change: An empirical analysis.* New York: Wiley.

Luchins, A. S. (1957). Primacy-recency in impression formation. In C. I. Hovland (Ed.), *The order of presentation in persuasion.* New Haven, CT: Yale University Press.

Luparello, T. J., McFadden, E. R., Lyons, H. A., & Bleecker, E. R. (1971). Psychologic factors and bronchial asthma. *New York State Journal of Medicine, 71,* 2161–2165.

Lutjen, P., et al. (1984). The establishment and maintenance of pregnancy using in vitro fertilization and embryo donation in a patient with primary ovarian failure. *Nature, 307,* 174–175.

Lykken, D. T. (1982). Fearlessness: Its carefree charm and deadly risks. *Psychology Today, 16*(9), 20–28.

Lyons, J. S., Rosen, A. J., & Dysken, M. W. (1985). Behavioral effects of tricyclic drugs in depressed patients. *Journal of Consulting and Clinical Psychology, 53,* 17–24.

Maccoby, E. E., & Jacklin, C. N. (1974). *The psychology of sex differences.* Stanford, CA: Stanford University Press.

Maccoby, E. E., & Jacklin, C. N. (1980). Sex differences in aggression: A rejoinder and reprise. *Child Development, 51,* 964–980.

Maccoby, E. E., & Martin, J. A. (1983). Socialization in the context of the family: Parent–child interaction. In P. H. Mussen (Ed.), *Handbook of child psychology, Vol. 4: Socialization, personality, and social development.* New York: Wiley.

Macfarlane, A. (1977). *The psychology of childbirth.* Cambridge, MA: Harvard University Press.

Machlowitz, M. (1980). *Workaholics: Living with them, working with them.* Reading, MA: Addison-Wesley.

Mackay, A. V. P., Iversen, L. L., Rossor, M., Spokes, E., Arregio, A., Crease, I., & Snyder, S. H. (1982). Increased brain dopamine and dopamine receptors in schizophrenia. *Archives of General Psychiatry, 39,* 991–997.

Macklin, E. D. (1974). Cohabitation in college: Going very steady. *Psychology Today, 8*(11), 53–59.

Macklin, E. D. (1978). Nonmarital heterosexual cohabitation: A review of the recent literature. *Marriage and Family Review, 1,* 1–12.

Macklin, E. D. (1980). Nonmarital heterosexual cohabitation. In A. Skolnick & J. H. Skolnick (Eds.), *Family in transition,* 3d ed. Boston: Little, Brown.

Maddi, S. R. (1980). *Personality theories: A comparative analysis.* Homewood, IL: Dorsey Press.

Maddi, S. R., & Kobasa, S. C. (1984). *The hardy executive: Health under stress.* Homewood, IL: Dow Jones–Irwin.

Mahoney, M. J. (1980). *Abnormal psychology.* New York: Harper & Row.

Main, M., & George, C. (1985). Responses of abused and disadvantaged toddlers to distress in agemates: A study in the day care setting. *Developmental Psychology, 21,* 407–412.

Maital, S. (1982). The tax-evasion virus. *Psychology Today, 16*(3), 74–78.

Malamuth, N. M. (1981). Rape fantasies as a function of exposure to violent sexual stimuli. *Archives of Sexual Behavior, 10,* 33–48.

Malamuth, N. M., Heim, N., & Feshbach, S. (1980). Sexual responsiveness of college students to rape depictions: Inhibitory or disinhibitory effects. *Journal of Personality and Social Psychology, 38,* 399–408.

Malatesta, V. J., Sutker, P. B., & Treiber, F. A. (1981). Sensation seeking and chronic public drunkenness. *Journal of Consulting and Clinical Psychology, 49,* 292–284.

Mandler, G. (1984). *Mind and body: The psychology of emotion and stress.* New York: W. W. Norton.

Mann, L. (1981). The baiting crowd in episodes of threatened suicide. *Journal of Personality and Social Psychology, 41,* 703–709.

Mann, L., Newton, J. W., & Innes, J. M. (1982). A test between deindividuation and emergent norm theories of crowd aggression. *Journal of Personality and Social Psychology, 42,* 260–272.

Manning, M. M., & Wright, T. L. (1983). Self-efficacy expectancies, outcome expectancies, and the persistence of pain control in childbirth. *Journal of Personality and Social Psychology, 45,* 421–431.

Manucia, G. K., Baumann, D. J., & Cialdini, R. B. (1984). Mood influences on helping: Direct effects or side effects? *Journal of Personality and Social Psychology, 46,* 357–364.

Marano, H. (1979). Breast-feeding. New evidence: It's far more than nutrition. *Medical World News, 20,* 62–78.

Marcus, M. G. (1976). The power of a name. *Psychology Today, 10*(5), 75–76, 108.

Marcus, T. L., & Corsini, D. A. (1978). Parental expectations of preschool children as related to child gender and socioeconomic status. *Child Development, 49,* 243–246.

Marin, P. (1983). A revolution's broken promises. *Psychology Today, 17*(7), 50–57.

Markman, H. J. (1981). Prediction of marital distress: A five-year follow-up. *Journal of Consulting and Clinical Psychology, 49,* 760–762.

Marks, G., Miller, N., & Maruyama, G. (1981). Effect of targets' physical attractiveness on assumption of similarity. *Journal of Personality and Social Psychology, 41,* 198–206.

Marks, I. M. (1982). Toward an empirical clinical science: Behavioral psychotherapy in the 1980s. *Behavior Therapy, 13,* 63–81.

Marks, M. L. (1986). The question of quality circles. *Psychology Today, 20*(3), 36–38, 42, 44, 46.

Marks, P. A., & Monroe, L. J. (1976). Correlates of adolescent poor sleepers. *Journal of Abnormal Psychology, 85,* 243–246.

Marlatt, G. A. (1985). Controlled drinking: The controversy rages on. *American Psychologist, 40,* 374–375.

Marlatt, G. A., & Gordon, J. R. (1980). Determinants of relapse: Implications for the maintenance of behavior change. In P. O. Davidson & S. M. Davidson (Eds.), *Behavioral medicine: Changing health lifestyles.* New York: Brunner/Mazel.

Marlatt, G. A., & Rohsenow, D. J. (1981). The think-drink effect. *Psychology Today, 15*(12), 60–69.

Marshall, D. D. (1971). Sexual behavior on Mangaia. In D. S. Marshall & R. C. Suggs (Eds.), *Human sexual behavior: Variations in the ethnographic spectrum.* New York: Basic Books.

Marston, A. R., London, P., Cohen, N., & Cooper, L. M. (1977). In vivo observation of the eating behavior of obese and nonobese subjects. *Journal of Consulting and Clinical Psychology, 45,* 335–336.

Martelli, M. F., Auerbach, S. M., Alexander, J., & Mercuri, L. G. (1987). Stress management in the health care setting: Matching interventions with patient coping styles. *Journal of Consulting and Clinical Psychology, 55,* 201–207.

Martin, C. L. (1987). A ratio measure of sex stereotyping. *Journal of Personality and Social Psychology, 52,* 489–499.

Martin, R. A., Kuiper, N. A., Olinger,

L. J., & Dobbin, J. (1987). Is stress always bad? Telic versus paratelic dominance as a stress-moderating variable. *Journal of Personality and Social Psychology, 53,* 970–982.

Martin, R. A., & Lefcourt, H. M. (1983). Sense of humor as a moderator of the relation between stressors and moods. *Journal of Personality and Social Psychology, 45,* 1313–1324.

Martinez, G. A., & Krieger, F. W. (1985). The 1984 milk-feeding patterns in the United States. *Pediatrics, 76,* 1004–1008.

Maruyama, G., & Miller, N. (1975). *Physical attractiveness and classroom acceptance.* Social Science Research Institute Report No. 75–2, University of Southern California.

Maslach, C. (1976, September). Burned out. *Human Behavior, 5,* 16–22.

Maslow, A. H. (1963). The need to know and the fear of knowing. *Journal of General Psychology, 68,* 111–124.

Maslow, A. H. (1970). *Motivation and personality,* 2d ed. New York: Harper & Row.

Maslow, A. H. (1971). *The farther reaches of human nature.* New York: Viking.

Masters, W. H., & Johnson, V. E. (1966). *Human sexual response.* Boston: Little, Brown.

Masters, W. H., & Johnson, V. E. (1970). *Human sexual inadequacy.* Boston: Little, Brown.

Masters, W. H., Johnson, V. E., & Kolodny, R. C. (1985). *Human sexuality,* 2d ed. Boston: Little, Brown.

Matefy, R. (1980). Role-playing theory of psychedelic flashbacks. *Journal of Consulting and Clinical Psychology, 48,* 551–553.

Mathes, E. W., Adams, H. E., & Davies, R. M. (1985). Jealousy: Loss of relationship rewards, loss of self-esteem, depression, anxiety, and anger. *Journal of Personality and Social Psychology, 48,* 1552–1561.

Matlin, M. (1987). *The psychology of women.* New York: Holt, Rinehart and Winston.

Matteson, M. T., & Ivancevich, J. M. (1987). *Controlling work stress.* San Francisco: Jossey-Bass.

Matthews, K. A., Krantz, D. S., Dembroski, T. M., & MacDougall, J. M. (1982). Unique and common variance in structured interview and Jenkins Activity Survey measures of the Type A behavior pattern. *Journal of Personality and Social Psychology, 42,* 303–313.

Maugh, T. H. (1982). Marijuana "justifies serious concern." *Science, 215,* 1488–1489.

May, J. L., & Hamilton, P. A. (1980). Effects of musically evoked affect on women's interpersonal attraction toward and perceptual judgments of physical attractiveness of men. *Motivation and Emotion, 4,* 217–228.

May, K. A., & Perrin, S. P. (1985). Prelude: Pregnancy and birth. In S. M. H. Hanson & F. W. Bozett (Eds.), *Dimensions of fatherhood.* Beverly Hills: Sage.

McBurney, D. H., Levine, J. M., & Cavanaugh, P. H. (1977). Psychophysical and social ratings of human body odor. *Personality and Social Psychology Bulletin, 3,* 135–138.

McCann, I. L., & Holmes, D. S. (1984). Influence of aerobic exercise on depression. *Journal of Personality and Social Psychology, 46,* 1142–1147.

McCaul, K. D., & Haugvedt, C. (1982). Attention, distraction, and cold-pressor pain. *Journal of Personality and Social Psychology, 43,* 154–162.

McConaghy, M. J. (1979). Gender permanence and the genital basis of gender: Stages in the development of constancy of gender. *Child Development, 50,* 1223–1226.

McConaghy, N., & Blaszczynski, A. (1980). A pair of monozygotic twins discordant for homosexuality: Sex-dimorphic behavior and penile volume responses. *Archives of Sexual Behavior, 9,* 123–12.

McCrady, B. S. (1985). Comments on the controlled drinking controversy. *American Psychologist, 40,* 370–371.

McCranie, E. J. (1979). How life crises affect the sexuality of middle-aged men. *Medical Aspects of Human Sexuality, 13*(7), 61–75.

McDavid, W. J., & Harari, H. (1966). Stereotyping of names and popularity of grade-school children. *Child Development, 37,* 453–459.

McFalls, J. A. (1983). Where have all the children gone? The future of reproduction in the United States. In O. Pocs (Ed.), *Human sexuality, 83/84.* Guilford, CT: Dushkin.

McGoldrick, M., & Carter, E. A. (1982). *The family life cycle in normal family processes.* London: Guilford Press.

McGregor, D. (1960). *The human side of enterprise.* New York: McGraw-Hill.

McIntyre, K. O., Lichtenstein, E., & Mermelstein, R. J. (1983). Self-efficacy and relapse in smoking cessation: A replication and extension. *Journal of Consulting and Clinical Psychology, 51,* 632–633.

McKay, M., Davis, M., & Fanning, P. (1983). *Messages: The communication book.* Oakland, CA: New Harbinger.

McKenna, J. F., Oritt, P. L., & Wolff, H. K. (1981). Occupational stress as a predictor in the turnover decision. *Journal of Human Stress, 7*(12), 12–17.

McMullen, S., & Rosen, R. C. (1979). Self-administered masturbation training in the treatment of primary orgasmic dysfunction. *Journal of Con-*

sulting and Clinical Psychology, 47, 912–918.

McNamara, M. L. L., & Bahr, H. M. (1980). The dimensionality of marital role satisfaction. *Journal of Marriage and the Family, 42,* 45–54.

Mechanic, D. (1978). *Medical sociology.* New York: Free Press.

Mednick, S. A. (1985). Crime in the family tree. *Psychology Today, 19*(3), 58–61.

Mehrabian, A., & Weinstein, L. (1985). Temperament characteristics of suicide attempters. *Journal of Consulting and Clinical Psychology, 53,* 544–546.

Meichenbaum, D. H. (1976). Toward a cognitive theory of self-control. In G. Schwartz & D. Shapiro (Eds.), *Consciousness and self-regulation: Advances in research.* New York: Plenum Publishing Co.

Meichenbaum, D. H. (1977). *Cognitive behavior modification: An integrative approach.* New York: Plenum Publishing Co.

Meichenbaum, D. H., & Butler, L. (1980). Toward a conceptual model for the treatment of test anxiety: Implications for research and treatment. In I. G. Sarason (Ed.), *Test anxiety: Theory, research, and application.* Hillsdale, NJ: Erlbaum.

Meichenbaum, D. H., & Deffenbacher, J. L. (1988). Stress inoculation training. *The Counseling Psychologist, 16*(1), 69–90.

Meichenbaum, D. H., & Jaremko, M. E. (Eds.) (1983). *Stress reduction and prevention.* New York: Plenum Publishing Co.

Meikle, S., Peitchinis, J. A., & Pearce, K. (1985). *Teenage sexuality.* San Diego: College-Hill Press.

Mellstrom, M., Jr., Cicala, G. A., & Zuckerman, M. (1976). General versus specific trait anxiety measures in the prediction of fear of snakes, heights, and darkness. *Journal of Consulting and Clinical Psychology, 44,* 83–91.

Melzack, R. (1973). *The puzzle of pain.* New York: Basic Books.

Melzack, R. (1980). Psychological aspects of pain. In J. J. Bonica (Ed.), *Pain.* New York: Raven Press.

Meredith, N. (1984). The gay dilemma. *Psychology Today, 18*(1), 56–62.

Mertz, G., et al. (1985). Frequency of acquisition of first-episode genital infection with herpes simplex virus from symptomatic and asymptomatic source contacts. *Sexually transmitted diseases, 12,* 33–39.

Messenger, J. C. (1971). Sex and repression in an Irish folk community. I. D. S. Marshall & R. C. Suggs, *Human sexual behavior: Variations in the ethnographic spectrum.* New York: Basic Books.

Mewborn, C. R., & Rogers, R. W. (1979).

Effects of reassuring and threatening components of fear appraisals of physiological and verbal measures of emotion and attitudes. *Journal of Experimental Social Psychology, 15,* 242–253.

Meyer, D., Leventhal, H., & Gutman, M. (1985). Common-sense models of illness: The example of hypertension. *Health Psychology, 4,* 115–135.

Meyer, J. P., & Pepper, S. (1977). Need compatibility and marital adjustment in young married couples. *Journal of Personality and Social Psychology, 35,* 331–342.

Meyers, J. K., et al. (1984). Six-month prevalence of psychiatric disorders in three communities. *Archives of General Psychiatry, 41,* 959–967.

Michael, R. P., Keverne, E. B., & Bonsall, R. W. (1971). Pheromones: Isolation of male sex attractants from a female primate. *Science, 172,* 964–966.

Mider, P. A. (1984). Failures in alcoholism and drug dependence prevention and learning from the past. *American Psychologist, 39,* 183.

Milam, J. R., & Ketcham, K. (1981). *Under the influence: A guide to the myths and realities of alcoholism.* Seattle: Madrove Publishers.

Milgram, S. (1963). Behavioral study of obedience. *Journal of Abnormal and Social Psychology, 67,* 371–378.

Milgram, S. (1970). The experience of living in cities. *Science, 167,* 1461–1468.

Milgram, S. (1974). *Obedience to authority.* New York: Harper & Row.

Milgram, S. (1977). *The individual in a social world.* Reading, MA: Addison-Wesley.

Miller, I. W., Klee, S. H., & Norman, W. H. (1982). Depressed and nondepressed inpatients' cognitions of hypothetical events, experimental tasks, and stressful life events. *Journal of Abnormal Psychology, 91,* 78–81.

Miller, N. E. (1969). Learning of visceral and glandular responses. *Science, 163,* 434–445.

Miller, N. E. (1985), Rx: Biofeedback. *Psychology Today, 19*(2), 54–59.

Miller, N. E., & Dollard, J. (1941). *Social learning and imitation.* New Haven, CT: Yale University Press.

Miller, P. M., & Mastria, M. A. (1977). *Alternatives to alcohol abuse: A social learning model.* Champaign, IL: Research Press.

Miller, S. M. (1975). Effects of maternal employment on sex-role perception, interests, and self-esteem in kindergarten girls. *Developmental Psychology, 11,* 405–406.

Miller, S. M. (1980). Why having control reduces stress: If I can stop the roller coaster I don't want to get off. In J. Garber & M. E. P. Seligman (Eds.),

Human helplessness: Theory and research. New York: Academic Press.

Miller, S. M., Lack, E. R., & Asroff, S. (1985). Preference for control and the coronary-prone behavior pattern. *Journal of Personality and Social Psychology, 49,* 492–499.

Miller, W. R. (1982). Treating problem drinkers: What works? *The Behavior Therapist, 5*(1), 15–18.

Miller, W. R., & Hester, R. K. (1980). Treating the problem drinker. In W. R. Miller (Ed.), *The addictive behaviors.* New York: Pergamon Press.

Miller, W. R., & Munoz, R. F. (1983). *How to control your drinking,* 2d ed. Albuquerque: University of New Mexico Press.

Millette, B., & Hawkins, J. (1983). *The passage through menopause.* Reston, VA: Reston Publishing.

Mills, J., & Harvey, J. (1972). Opinion change as a function of when information about the communicator is received and whether he is attractive or expert. *Journal of Personality and Social Psychology, 21,* 52–55.

Milner, J. S., Gold, R. G., Ayoub, C., & Jacewitz, M. M. (1984). Predictive validity of the child abuse potential inventory. *Journal of Consulting and Clinical Psychology, 52,* 879–884.

Mirsky, I. A. (1958). Physiologic, psychologic, and social determinants in the etiology of duodenal ulcer. *American Journal of Digestive Diseases, 3,* 285–315.

Mischel, W. (1977). On the future of personality measurement. *American Psychologist, 32,* 246–254.

Mischel, W. (1986). *Introduction to personality,* 4th ed. New York: Holt, Rinehart and Winston.

Mitchell, J. E., & Eckert, E. D. (1987). Scope and significance of eating disorders. *Journal of Consulting and Clinical Psychology, 55,* 628–634.

Mittelmark, M. B., et al. (1987). Predicting experimentation with cigarettes: The Childhood Antecedents of Smoking Study. *American Journal of Public Health, 77,* 206–208.

Moe, J. L., Nacoste, R. W., & Insko, C. A. (1981). Belief versus race as determinants of discrimination: A study of Southern adolescents in 1966 and 1979. *Journal of Personality and Social Psychology, 41,* 1031–1050.

Modahl, C., & Newton, N. (1979). Mood state differences between breast- and bottle-feeding mothers. In L. Carenza & L. Zichella (Eds.), *Emotion and reproduction.* New York: Academic Press.

Moine, D. J. (1984). Going for the gold in the selling game. *Psychology Today, 18*(3), 36–44.

Molinoff, D. (1977, May 22). Life with

father. *New York Times Magazine,* pp. 12–17.

Money, J. (1974). Prenatal hormones and posthormonal socialization in gender identity differentiation. In J. K. Cole & R. Dienstbier (Eds.), *Nebraska Symposium on Motivation.* Lincoln, NE: University of Nebraska Press.

Money, J. (1977). Human hermaphroditism. In F. A. Beach (Ed.), *Human sexuality in four perspectives.* Baltimore, MD: The Johns Hopkins University Press.

Money, J. (1980). *Love and love sickness.* Baltimore, MD: The Johns Hopkins University Press.

Money, J. (1987). Sin, sickness, or status? Homosexual gender identity and psychoneuroendocrinology. *American Psychologist, 42,* 384–399.

Money, J., & Ehrhardt, A. (1972). *Man and woman, boy and girl.* Baltimore, MD: The Johns Hopkins University Press.

Monmaney, T., et al. (1988, January 18). Heredity and drinking: How strong is the link? *Newsweek,* pp. 66–67.

Monroe, L. J., & Marks, P. A. (1977). MMPI differences between adolescent poor and good sleepers. *Journal of Consulting and Clinical Psychology, 45,* 151–152.

Monroe, S. M. (1982). Life events and disorder: Event-symptom associations and the course of disorder. *Journal of Abnormal Psychology, 91,* 14–24.

Monroe, S. M. (1983). Major and minor life events as predictors of psychological distress: Further issues and findings. *Journal of Behavioral Medicine, 6,* 189–205.

Moolgavkar, S. H. (1983). A model for human carcinogenesis: Hereditary cancers and premalignant lesions. In R. G. Crispen (Ed.), *Cancer: Etiology and prevention.* New York: Elsevier Biomedical.

Moon, J. R., & Eisler, R. M. (1983). Anger control: An experimental comparison of three behavioral treatments. *Behavior Therapy, 14,* 493–505.

Moore, J. E., & Chaney, E. F. (1985). Outpatient group treatment of chronic pain: Effects of spouse involvement. *Journal of Consulting and Clinical Psychology, 53,* 325–334.

Moore, K. A., & Hofferth, S. L. (1979). Women and their children. In R. E. Smith (Ed.), *The subtle revolution: Women at work.* Washington, DC: The Urban Institute.

Moore, T. (1975). Exclusive early mothering and its alternatives: The outcome to adolescence. *Scandinavian Journal of Psychology, 16,* 255–272.

Moos, R. (1968). The development of the Menstrual Distress Questionnaire. *Psychosomatic Medicine, 30,* 853.

Moreland, J., & Schwebel, A. (1981). A gender role transcendent perspective on fathering. *The Counseling Psychology, 9*(4), 45–54.

Moreland, R. L., & Zajonc, R. B. (1982). Exposure effects in person perception: Familiarity, similarity, and attraction. *Journal of Experimental Social Psychology, 18,* 395–415.

Moriarty, T. (1975). Crimes, commitment, and the responsive bystander: Two field experiments. *Journal of Personality and Social Psychology, 31,* 370–376.

Morin, C. M., & Azrin, N. H. (1987). Stimulus control and imagery training in treating sleep-maintenance insomnia. *Journal of Consulting and Clinical Psychology, 55,* 260–262.

Morokoff, P. J. (1985). Effects of sex guilt, repression, sexual "arousability," and sexual experience on female sexual arousal during erotica and fantasy. *Journal of Personality and Social Psychology, 49,* 177–187.

Morris, J. N., et al. (1953). Coronary heart disease and physical activity of work. *Lancet, 2,* 1053–1057, 1111–1120.

Morris, N. M., & Udry, J. R. (1978). Pheromonal influences on human sexual behavior: An experimental search. *Journal of Biosocial Science, 10,* 147–157.

Morris, W. N., Miller, R. S., & Spangenberg, S. (1977). The effects of dissenter position and task difficulty on conformity and response conflict. *Journal of Personality, 45,* 251–256.

Moscovici, S. (1985). Social influence and conformity. In G. Lindzey & E. Aronson (Eds.), *Handbook of social psychology,* Vol. 2. New York: Random House.

Motowidlo, S. T. (1982). Sex role orientation and behavior in a work setting. *Journal of Personality and Social Psychology, 42,* 935–945.

Mueser, K. T., Grau, B. W., Sussman, S., & Rosen, A. J. (1984). You're only as pretty as you feel: Facial expression as a determinant of physical attractiveness. *Journal of Personality and Social Psychology, 46,* 469–478.

Mullen, B., Futrell, D., Stairs, D., Tice, D., Baumeister, R. F., Dawson, K., Riordan, C., Radloff, C., Kennedy, J., & Rosenfeld, P. (1987). Newscasters' facial expressions and voting behavior of viewers: Can a smile elect a president? *Journal of Personality and Social Psychology, 53,* 1988, in press.

Murphy, G. E., Simons, A. D., Wetzel, R. D., & Lustman, P. J. (1984). Cognitive therapy and pharmacotherapy: Singly and together in the treatment of depression. *Archives of General Psychiatry, 41,* 33–41.

Murray, A. D. (1985). Aversiveness is in the mind of the beholder. In B. M. Lester & C. F. Z. Boukydis (Eds.), *Infant crying.* New York: Plenum Publishing Co.

Murray, A. D., Dolby, R. M., Nation, R. L., & Thomas, D. B. (1981). Effects of epidural anesthesia on newborns and their mothers. *Child Development, 52,* 71–82.

Murstein, B. I. (1972). Physical attractiveness and marital choice. *Journal of Personality and Social Psychology, 22,* 8–12.

Murstein, B. I., & Christy, P. (1976). Physical attractiveness and marital adjustment in middle-aged couples. *Journal of Personality and Social Psychology, 34,* 537–542.

Musante, L., MacDougall, J. M., Dembroski, T. M., & Van Horn, A. E. (1983). Component analysis of the Type A coronary-prone behavior pattern in male and female college students. *Journal of Personality and Social Psychology, 45,* 1104–1117.

Myers, A. M., & Gonda, G. (1982). Utility of the masculinity–femininity construct: Comparison of traditional and androgyny approaches. *Journal of Personality and Social Psychology, 43,* 514–523.

Myers, B. J. (1984). Mother–infant bonding: The status of this critical period hypothesis. *Developmental Review, 4,* 283–288.

Myers, M. B., Templer, D. I., & Brown, R. (1984). Coping ability of women who become victims of rape. *Journal of Consulting and Clinical Psychology, 52,* 73–78.

Myers, M. B., Templer, D. I., & Brown, R. (1985). Reply to Wieder on rape victims: Vulnerability does not imply responsibility. *Journal of Consulting and Clinical Psychology, 53,* 431.

Naeye, R. L. (1978). Relationship of cigarette smoking to congenital anomalies and perinatal death. *American Journal of Pathology, 90,* 269–293.

Naeye, R. L., & Peters, E. C. (1984). Mental development of children whose mothers smoked during pregnancy. *Obstetrics and Gynecology, 64,* 601.

Naffziger, C. C., & Naffziger, K. (1974). Development of sex role stereotypes. *Family Coordinator, 23,* 251–258.

Nahemow, L., & Lawton, M. P. (1975). Similarity and propinquity in a friendship formation. *Journal of Personality and Social Psychology, 32,* 205–213.

Narayanan, V. K., & Nath, R. (1982). A field test of some attitudinal and behavioral consequences of flexitime. *Journal of Applied Psychology, 67,* 214–218.

National Academy of Sciences (1981). *The effect on human health from long-term exposure to noise* (Report of Working Group 81). Washington, DC: National Academy Press.

National Center on Child Abuse and Neglect Report (1982, January–February). *Children Today,* pp. 27–28.

National Institute of Mental Health (1985). *Electroconvulsive therapy: Consensus Development Conference statement.* Bethesda, MD: U.S. Department of Health and Human Services.

National Institutes of Health (1985). *National cancer program: 1983–1984 director's report and annual plan, FY 1986–1990* (NIH Publication No. 85-2765). Washington, DC: U.S. Government Printing Office.

Nelson, N., et al. (1980). A randomized clinical trial of the Leboyer approach to childbirth. *New England Journal of Medicine, 302,* 655–660.

Neugarten, B. (1971). Grow old with me, the best is yet to be. *Psychology Today, 5*(5), 45–49.

Neugarten, B. (1982). Understanding psychological man. *Psychology Today, 16*(5), 54–55.

Neuringer, C. (1982). Affect configurations and changes in women who threaten suicide following a crisis. *Journal of Consulting and Clinical Psychology, 50,* 182–186.

Nevid, J. S. (1984). Sex differences in factors of romantic attraction. *Sex Roles, 11*(5/6), 401–411.

Nevid, J. S., & Rathus, S. A. (1978). Multivariate and normative data pertaining to the RAS with the college population. *Behavior Therapy, 9,* 675.

Newberne, P. M., & Suphakarn, V. (1983). Nutrition and cancer: A review, with emphasis on the role of vitamins C and E and selenium. *Nutrition and Cancer, 5,* 107–119.

Newcomb, M., & Bentler, P. (1980). Assessment of personality and demographic aspects of cohabitation and marital success. *Journal of Personality Development, 4,* 11–24.

Newcomb, T. M. (1971). Dyadic balance as a source of clues about interpersonal attraction. In B. I. Murstein (Ed.), *Theories of attraction and love.* New York: Springer.

Newcomb, T. M. (1981). Heiderian balance as a group phenomenon. *Journal of Personality and Social Psychology, 40,* 862–867.

Newcombe, N., & Arnkoff, D. B. (1979). Effects of speech style and sex of speaker on person perception. *Journal of Personality and Social Psychology, 37,* 1293–1303.

Newcombe, N., & Bandura, M. M. (1983). The effect of age at puberty on spatial ability in girls: A question of mechanism. *Developmental Psychology, 19,* 215–224.

Newcombe, N., Bandura, M. M., & Taylor, D. G. (1983). Sex differences in spatial ability and spatial activity. *Sex Roles, 9,* 377–386.

Newman, J., & McCauley, C. (1977). Eye contact with strangers in city, suburb, and small town. *Environment and Behavior, 9,* 547–558.

Newmark, C. S., Frerking, R. A., Cook, L., & Newmark, L. (1973). Endorsement of Ellis's irrational beliefs as a function of psychopathology. *Journal of Clinical Psychology, 29,* 300–302.

Newton, N. (1971). Psychologic differences between breast and bottle feeding. *American Journal of Clinical Nutrition, 24,* 993–1004.

Newton, N. (1972). Battle between breast and bottle. *Psychology Today, 6,* 68–70, 88–89.

Newton, N. (1979). Key psychological issues in human lactation. In L. R. Waletzky (Ed.), *Symposium on human lactation.* Rockville, MD: DHEW Publication No. HSA 79-5107.

New York Times, The (1985, May 12). Poll finds many women seek marriage plus jobs. *The New York Times,* p. 19.

New York Times, The (1987, September 14). For now, Compaq isn't rushing to follow I.B.M. *The New York Times,* pp. D1, D8.

New York Times, The (1987, November 1). Smoking vs. life expectancy. *The New York Times.*

New York Times, The (1987, December 7). Divorce may be the price of living together first. *The New York Times,* p. A25.

New York Times, The (1988, January 17). AIDS antibodies in New York infants. *The New York Times,* Section 4, p. 6.

New York Times, The (1988, February 20). AIDS risk articles criticized. *The New York Times,* p. 9.

Nezu, A. M., & Ronan, G. F. (1985). Life stress, current problems, problem solving, and depressive symptoms: An integrative model. *Journal of Consulting and Clinical Psychology, 53,* 693–697.

Nias, D. K. B. (1979). Marital choice: Matching or complementation? In M. Cook & G. Wilson (Eds.), *Love and attraction.* New York: Pergamon Press.

Nicassio, P., & Bootzin, R. (1974). A comparison of progressive relaxation and autogenic training as treatments for insomnia. *Journal of Abnormal Psychology, 83,* 253–260.

Nicholson, R. A., & Berman, J. S. (1983). Is follow-up necessary in evaluating psychotherapy? *Psychological Bulletin, 93,* 261–278.

Nieberg, P., et al. (1985). The fetal tobacco syndrome. *Journal of the American Medical Association, 253,* 2998–2999.

Nisbett, R. E., & Ross, L. (1980). *Human inference: Strategies and shortcomings of social judgment.* Englewood Cliffs, NJ: Prentice-Hall.

Nolan, J. D. (1968). Self-control procedures in the modification of smoking behavior. *Journal of Consulting and Clinical Psychology, 32,* 92–93.

Noller, P., Law, H., & Comrey, A. L. (1987). Cattell, Comrey, & Eysenck personality factors compared: More evidence for the five robust factors? *Journal of Personality and Social Psychology, 53,* 775–782.

Norton, G. R., Harrison, B., Hauch, J., & Rhodes, L. (1985). Characteristics of people with infrequent panic attacks. *Journal of Abnormal Psychology, 94,* 216–221.

Notman, M. T., & Nadelson, C. C. (1982). Changing views of the relationship between femininity and reproduction. In C. C. Nadelson & M. T. Notman (Eds.), *The woman patient,* Vol. 2. New York: Plenum Publishing Co.

Novaco, R. (1974). A treatment program for the management of anger through cognitive and relaxation controls. Doctoral dissertation, Indiana University.

Novaco, R. (1977). A stress inoculation approach to anger management in the training of law enforcement officers. *American Journal of Community Psychology, 5,* 327–346.

Nussbaum, M., et al. (1985). Follow-up investigation of patients with anorexia nervosa. *The Journal of Pediatrics, 106,* 835–840.

O'Gra, P. L., & Greene, H. L. (1982). Human milk and breast feeding: An update on the state of the art. *Pediatric Research, 16,* 266–271.

O'Grady, K. E. (1982). Sex, physical attractiveness, and perceived risk for mental illness. *Journal of Personality and Social Psychology, 43,* 1064–1071.

O'Hara, M. W., Neunaber, D. J., & Zekoski, E. M. (1984). Prospective study of postpartum depression: Prevalence, course, and predictive factors. *Journal of Abnormal Psychology, 93,* 158–171.

Ohman, A., Fredrikson, M., Hugdahl, K., & Rimmo, P. (1976). The premise of equipotentiality in human classical conditioning: Conditioned electrodermal responses to potentially phobic stimuli. *Journal of Experimental Psychology: General, 105,* 313–337.

Okun, B. F. (1984). *Working with adults: Individual, family, and career development.* Monterey, CA: Brooks/Cole.

Olson, R. P., Ganley, R., Devine, D. T., & Dorsey, G. (1981). Long-term effects of behavior versus insight-oriented therapy with inpatient alcoholics. *Journal of Consulting and Clinical Psychology, 49,* 866–877.

O'Malley, M. N., & Becker, L. A. (1984).

Removing the egocentric bias: The relevance of distress cues to evaluation of fairness. *Personality and Social Psychology Bulletin, 10,* 235–242.

O'Neill, N., & O'Neill, G. (1972). *Open marriage.* New York: Evans.

Opstad, P. K., Ekanger, R., Nummestad, M., & Raabe, N. (1978). Performance, mood and clinical symptoms in men exposed to prolonged, severe physical work and sleep deprivation. *Aviation, Space and Environmental Medicine, 49,* 1065–1073.

Orme-Johnson, D. (1973). Autonomic stability and transcendental meditation. *Psychosomatic Medicine, 35,* 341–349.

Ortega, D. F., & Pipal, J. E. (1984). Challenge seeking and the Type A coronary-prone behavior pattern. *Journal of Personality and Social Psychology, 46,* 1328–1334.

Orthener, D. K., Brown, T., & Ferguson, D. (1976). Single-parent fatherhood: An emerging family life style. *Family Coordinator, 25,* 429–437.

O'Sullivan, M., Ekman, P., Friesen, W., & Scherer, K. (1985). What you say and how you say it: The contribution of speech quality and voice content to judgments of others. *Journal of Personality and Social Psychology, 48,* 54–62.

Ouchi, W. (1981). *Theory Z: How American business can meet the Japanese challenge.* Reading, MA: Addison-Wesley.

Overturf, J. (1976). Marital therapy: Toleration of differentness: *Journal of Marriage and the Family, 2,* 235–241.

Owen, P. (1984). Prostaglandin synthetase inhibitors in the treatment of primary dysmenorrhea: Outcome trials reviewed. *American Journal of Obstetrics and Gynecology, 148,* 96–103.

Paffenbarger, R. S., Jr. (1972). Factors predisposing to fatal stroke in longshoremen. *Preventive Medicine, 1,* 522–527.

Paffenbarger, R. S., Jr., et al. (1978). Physical activity as an index of heart attack risk in college alumni. *American Journal of Epidemiology, 108,* 161–175.

Paffenbarger, R. S., Jr., et al. (1984). A natural history of athleticism and cardiovascular health. *Journal of the American Medical Association, 252,* 491–495.

Paffenbarger, R. S., Jr., et al. (1986). Physical activity, all-cause mortality, and longevity of college alumni. *New England Journal of Medicine, 314,* 605–613.

Page, R. A. (1977). Noise and helping behavior. *Environment and Behavior, 9,* 311–334.

Pagel, M., & Becker, J. (1987). Depressive thinking and depression: Relations with personality and social resources. *Journal of Personality and Social Psychology, 52,* 1043–1052.

Paige, K. E. (1971). Effects of oral contraceptives on affective fluctuations associated with the menstrual cycle. *Psychosomatic Medicine, 33,* 515–537.

Paige, K. E. (1973). Women learn to sing the menstrual blues. *Psychology, Today, 7,* 41.

Paige, K. E. (1977). Sexual pollution: Reproductive sex taboos in American society. *Journal of Social Issues, 33,* 144.

Paige, K. E. (1978). The declining taboo against menstrual sex. *Psychology Today, 12*(7), 50–51.

Palmer, D. L., & Kalin, R. (1985). Dogmatic responses to belief dissimilarity in the "bogus stranger" paradigm. *Journal of Personality and Social Psychology, 48,* 171–179.

Pantin, H. M., & Carver, C. S. (1982). Induced competence and the bystander effect. *Journal of Applied Social Psychology, 12,* 100–111.

Pardine, P., & Napoli, A. (1983). Physiological reactivity and recent life-stress experience. *Journal of Consulting and Clinical Psychology, 51,* 467–469.

Park, B., & Rothbart, M. (1982). Perception of outgroup homogeneity and levels of social categorization: Memory for the subordinate attributes of in-group and out-group members. *Journal of Personality and Social Psychology, 42,* 1051–1068.

Parkes, C. M., & Weiss, R. S. (1983). *Recovery from bereavement.* New York: Basic Books.

Parlee, M. B. (1979). The friendship bond: *Psychology Today's* survey report on friendship in America. *Psychology Today, 13*(4), 43–54, 113.

Parloff, M. B. (1986). Placebo controls in psychotherapy research: A sine qua non or a placebo for research problems? *Journal of Consulting and Clinical Psychology, 54,* 79–87.

Parloff, M. B., Waskow, I. E., & Wolfe, B. E. (1978). Research on therapist variables in relation to process and outcome. In S. L. Garfield & A. E. Bergin (Eds.), *Handbook of psychotherapy and behavior change,* 2d ed. New York: Wiley.

Parron, D. L., Solomon, F., & Jenkins, C. D. (Eds.) (1982). *Behavior, health risks, and social disadvantage.* Washington, DC: National Academy Press.

Parsons, T. (1978). *Action theory and the human condition.* New York: Free Press.

Patsiokas, A. T., Clum, G. A., & Luscomb, R. C. (1980). Cognitive characteristics of suicide attempters. *Journal of Consulting and Clinical Psychology, 47,* 478–484.

Patterson, G. R. (1982). *Coercive family processes.* Eugene, OR: Castilia Press.

Pattison, E. M. (1977). *The experience of dying.* Englewood Cliffs, NJ: Prentice-Hall.

Paul, G. L. (1969a). Outcome of systematic desensitization II: Controlled investigations of individual treatment, technique variations, and current status. In C. M. Franks (Ed.), *Behavior therapy: Appraisal and status.* New York: McGraw-Hill.

Paul, G. L. (1969b). Physiological effects of relaxation training and hypnotic suggestion. *Journal of Abnormal Psychology, 74,* 425–437.

Paulus, P. B. (1979). Crowding. In P. B. Paulus (Ed.), *Psychology of group influence.* Hillsdale, NJ: Erlbaum.

Paulus, P. B., Cox, V., McCain, G., & Chandler, J. (1975). Some effects of crowding in a prison environment. *Journal of Applied Social Psychology, 5,* 86–91.

Paulus, P. B., & Matthews, R. (1980). Crowding, attribution, and task performance. *Basic and Applied Social Psychology, 1,* 3–13.

Paulus, P. B., McCain, G., & Cox, V. (1978). Death rates, psychiatric commitments, blood pressure, and perceived crowding as a function of institutional crowding. *Environmental Psychology and Nonverbal Behavior, 3,* 107–116.

Pavlov, I. (1927). *Conditioned reflexes.* London: Oxford University Press.

Pearl, D., Bouthilet, L., & Lazar, J. (Eds.) (1982). *Television and behavior: Ten years of scientific progress and implications for the eighties,* Vols. 1 & 2. Washington, DC: U.S. Government Printing Office.

Pearlin, L. I., & Johnson, J. S. (1977). Marital status, life strains, and depression. *American Sociological Review, 42,* 704–715.

Pearlman, C. A., and Greenberg, R. (1973). Posttrial REM sleep: A critical period for consolidation of shuttlebox avoidance. *Animal Learning and Behavior, 1,* 49–51.

Pearlman, K., Schmidt, F. L., & Hunter, J. E. (1980). Test of a new model of validity generalization: Results for job proficiency and training criteria in clerical occupations. *Journal of Applied Psychology, 65,* 373–406.

Peck, R. C. (1968). Psychological developments in the second half of life. In B. L. Neugarten (Ed.), *Middle age and aging.* Chicago: University of Chicago Press.

Peele, S. (1984). The cultural context of psychological approaches to alcoholism: Can we control the effects of alcohol? *American Psychologist, 39,* 1337–1351.

Pelham, W. E. (1983). The effects of psychostimulants on academic achieve-

ment in hyperactive and learning-disabled children. *Thalamus, 3,* 1–49.

Pell, S., & Fayerweather, W. E. (1985). Trends in the incidence of myocardial infarction and in associated mortality and morbidity in a large employed population, 1957–1983. *New England Journal of Medicine, 312,* 1005–1011.

Pempus, E., Sawaya, C., & Cooper, R. E. (1975). "Don't fence me in": Personal space depends on architectural enclosure. Paper presented at the American Psychological Association, Chicago.

Pendery, M. L., Maltzman, I. M., & West, L. J. (1982). Controlled drinking by alcoholics? New findings and a re-evaluation of a major affirmative study. *Science, 217,* 169–174.

Pennebaker, J. W., & Skelton, J. A. (1981). Selective monitoring of physical sensations. *Journal of Personality and Social Psychology, 41,* 213–223.

Peplau, L. A., & Perlman, D. (1982). Perspectives on loneliness. In L. A. Peplau & D. Perlman (Eds.), *Loneliness: A sourcebook of current theory, research, and therapy.* New York: Wiley.

Perkins, D. (1982). The assessment of stress using life events scales. In L. Goldberger & S. Brenitz (Eds.), *Handbook of stress: Theoretical and clinical aspects.* New York: Free Press.

Perlman, B., & Hartman, A. (1982). Burnout: Summary and future research. *Human Relations, 35,* 283–305.

Perlman, S. D., & Abramson, P. R. (1982). Sexual satisfaction among married and cohabiting individuals. *Journal of Consulting and Clinical Psychology, 50,* 458–460.

Perls, F. S. (1971). *Gestalt therapy verbatim.* New York: Bantam Books.

Perri, M. G., Richards, C. S., & Schultheis, K. R. (1977). Behavioral self-control and smoking reduction: A study of self-initiated attempts to reduce smoking. *Behavior Therapy, 8,* 360–365.

Perry, D. G., & Bussey, K. (1979). The social learning theory of sex differences: Imitation is alive and well. *Journal of Personality and Social Psychology, 37,* 1699–1712.

Peterson, C., Schwartz, S. M., & Seligman, M. E. P. (1981). Self-blame and depressive symptoms. *Journal of Personality and Social Psychology, 41,* 253–259.

Peto, R., Doll, R., Buckley, J. D., & Spron, M. B. (1981). Can dietary beta-carotene materially reduce human cancer rates? *Nature, 290,* 201–208.

Pettingale, K. W., Morris, T., Greer, S., & Haybittle, J. L. (1985). Mental attitudes to cancer: An additional prognostic factor. *Lancet, 1,* 750.

Petty, R. E., & Cacioppo, J. T. (1986). The elaboration-likelihood model of persuasion. In L. Berkowitz (Ed.), *Advances in experimental social psychology,* Vol. 19. New York: Academic Press.

Peyser, H. (1982). Stress and alcohol. In L. Goldberger & S. Brenitz (Eds.), *Handbook of stress: Theoretical and clinical aspects.* New York: Free Press.

Pietropinto, A., & Simenauer, J. (1979). *Husbands and wives.* New York: Times Books.

Pine, C. J. (1985). Anxiety and eating behavior in obese and nonobese American Indians and White Americans. *Journal of Personality and Social Psychology, 49,* 774–780.

Pines, A., & Aronson, E. (1983). Antecedents, correlates, and consequences of sexual jealousy. *Journal of Personality, 51,* 108–136.

Pinto, R. P., & Hollandsworth, J. G., Jr. (1984). A measure of possessiveness in intimate relationships. *Journal of Social and Clinical Psychology, 2,* 273–279.

Pliner, P., Hart, H., Kohl, J., & Saari, D. (1974). Compliance without pressure: Some further data on the foot-in-the-door technique. *Journal of Experimental Social Psychology, 10,* 17–22.

Plomin, R. (1982). Quoted in M. Pines (1982, June 29). Behavior and heredity: Links for specific traits are growing stronger. *The New York Times,* pp. C1–C2.

Plomin, R., & DeFries, J. C. (1980). Genetics and intelligence: Recent data. *Intelligence, 4,* 15–24.

Polivy, J., & Herman, C. P. (1985). Dieting and binging: A causal analysis. *American Psychologist, 40,* 193–201.

Polivy, J., & Herman, C. P. (1987). Diagnosis and treatment of normal eating. *Journal of Consulting and Clinical Psychology, 55,* 635–644.

Pollock, M. L., Wilmore, J. H., & Fox, S. M., III. (1978). *Health and fitness through physical activity.* New York: Wiley.

Pomazal, R. J., & Clore, G. L. (1973). Helping on the highway: The effects of dependency and sex. *Journal of Applied Social Psychology, 3,* 150–164.

Popham, R. E., Schmidt, W., & Israelstam, S. (1984). Heavy alcohol consumption and physical health problems: A review of the epidemiologic evidence. In R. G. Smart et al. (Eds.), *Research advances in alcohol and drug problems,* Vol. 8. New York: Plenum Publishing Co.

Popper, K. (1985). Cited in Goleman (1985).

Porter, N., Geis, F. L., Cooper, E., & Newman, E. (1985). Androgyny and leadership in mixed-sex groups. *Journal of Personality and Social Psychology, 49,* 808–823.

Powell, D. H., & Driscoll, P. F. (1973). Middle-class professionals face unemployment. *Society, 10*(2), 18–26.

Powledge, T. M. (1981). Unnatural selection. In H. B. Holmes et al. (Eds.), *The custom-made child? Women-centered perspectives.* Clifton, NJ: Humana Press.

Powley, T. L. (1977). The ventromedial hypothalamic syndrome, satiety, and a cephalic phase hypothesis. *Psychological Review, 84,* 89–126.

Premack, D. (1970). Mechanisms of self-control. In W. A. Hunt (Ed.), *Learning mechanisms in smoking.* Chicago: Aldine.

Press, A., Namuth, T., Agrest, S., Gander, M., Lubenow, G. C., Reese, M., Friendly, D. T., & McDaniel, A. (1985, March 18). The war against pornography. *Newsweek,* pp. 58–66.

Prewett, M. J., van Allen, P. K., & Milner, J. S. (1978). Multiple electroconvulsive shocks and feeding and drinking behavior in the rat. *Bulletin of the Psychonomic Society, 12,* 137–139.

Price, D. D., Rafii, A., & Wakins, L. R., & Buckingham, B. (1984). A psychophysical analysis of acupuncture analgesia. *Pain, 19,* 27–42.

Qualls, P. J., & Sheehan, P. W. (1981). Imagery encouragement, absorption capacity, and relaxation during electromyographic feedback. *Journal of Personality and Social Psychology, 41,* 370–379.

Quattrone, G. A. (1982). Overattribution and unit formation: When behavior engulfs the person. *Journal of Personality and Social Psychology, 42,* 593–607.

Quinn, S. (1987). *A mind of her own: The life of Karen Horney.* New York: Summit Books.

Quinsey, V. L., Chaplin, T. C., & Upfold, D. (1984). Sexual arousal to nonsexual violence and sadomasochistic themes among rapists and non-sex-offenders. *Journal of Consulting and Clinical Psychology, 52,* 651–657.

Rabkin, J. G. (1980). Stressful life events and schizophrenia: A review of the literature. *Psychological Bulletin, 87,* 408–425.

Rada, R. T., & Kellner, R. (1979). Drug treatment in alcoholism. In J., Davis & D. J. Greenblatt (Eds.), *Recent developments in psychopharmacology.* New York: Grune & Stratton.

Radin, N. (1982). Primary caregiving and role-sharing behaviors. In M. E. Lamb (Ed.), *Nontraditional families: Parenting and child development.* Hillsdale, NJ: Erlbaum.

Raether, H. C., & Slater, R. C. (1977). Immediate postdeath activities in the United States. In H. Feifel (Ed.), *New meanings of death.* New York: McGraw-Hill.

Rapoport, K., & Burkhart, B. R. (1984). Personality and attitudinal characteristics of sexually coercive college males. *Journal of Abnormal Psychology, 93,* 216–221.

Raps, C. S., Peterson, C., Reinhard, K. E., Abramson, L. Y., & Seligman, M. E. P. (1982). Attributional style among depressed patients. *Journal of Abnormal Psychology, 91,* 102–108.

Rasmussen, K. J. V. (1931). *The Netsilik Eskimos: Social life and spiritual culture.* Copenhagen: Gylendal.

Rassin, D. K., et al. (1984). Incidence of breast-feeding in a low socioeconomic group of mothers in the United States: Ethnic patterns. *Pediatrics, 73,* 132–137.

Rathus, S. A. (1973a). A 30-item schedule for assessing assertive behavior. *Behavior Therapy, 4,* 398–406.

Rathus, S. A. (1973b). Motoric, autonomic, and cognitive reciprocal inhibition of a case of hysterical bronchial asthma. *Adolescence, 8,* 29–32.

Rathus, S. A. (1978). Assertiveness training: Rationales, procedures, and controversies. In J. M. Whiteley & J. V. Flowers (Eds.), *Approaches to assertion training.* Monterey, CA: Brooks/Cole.

Rathus, S. A. (1983). *Human sexuality.* New York: Holt, Rinehart and Winston.

Rathus, S. A. (1988). *Understanding child development.* New York: Holt, Rinehart and Winston.

Rathus, S. A. (1989). *Essentials of psychology,* 2d ed. New York: Holt, Rinehart and Winston.

Rathus, S. A., & Nevid, J. S. (1977). *Behavior therapy.* Garden City, NY: Doubleday.

Rebok, G. (1987). *Life-span cognitive development.* New York: Holt, Rinehart and Winston.

Redd, W. H., Jacobsen, P. B., Die-Trill, M., Dermatis, H., McEvoy, M., & Holland, J. C. (1987). Cognitive/attentional distraction in the control of conditioned nausea in pediatric cancer patients receiving chemotherapy. *Journal of Consulting and Clinical Psychology, 55,* 391–395.

Reddy, D. M., Baum, A., Fleming, R., & Aiello, J. R. (1981). Mediation of social density by coalition formation. *Journal of Applied Social Psychology, 11,* 529–537.

Reeder, G. D. (1982). Let's give the fundamental attribution error another chance. *Journal of Personality and Social Psychology, 43,* 341–344.

Reeder, G. D., Henderson, D. J., & Sullivan, J. J. (1982). From dispositions to behaviors: The flip side of attribution. *Journal of Research in Personality, 16,* 355–375.

Reeder, G. D., & Spores, J. M. (1983). The attribution of morality. *Journal of Personality and Social Psychology, 44,* 736–745.

Regan, D. T., Williams, M., & Sparling, S. (1972). Voluntary expiation of guilt: A field experiment. *Journal of Personality and Social Psychology, 24,* 42–45.

Rehm, L. P. (1978). Mood, pleasant events, and unpleasant events. *Journal of Consulting and Clinical Psychology, 46,* 854–859.

Reich, J. W., & Zautra, A. (1981). Life events and personal causation: Some relationships with satisfaction and distress. *Journal of Personality and Social Psychology, 41,* 1002–1012.

Reichelt, P. A. (1979). Coital and contraceptive behavior of female adolescents. *Archives of Sexual Behavior, 8,* 159–172.

Reinke, B. J., Holmes, D. S., & Harris, R. L. (1985). The timing of psychosocial changes in women's lives. *Journal of Personality and Social Psychology, 48,* 1353–1364.

Reis, H. T., Nezlek, J., & Wheeler, L. (1980). Physical attractiveness in social interaction. *Journal of Personality and Social Psychology, 38,* 604–617.

Reis, H. T., Senchak, M., & Solomon, B. (1985). Sex differences in the intimacy of social interaction. *Journal of Personality and Social Psychology, 48,* 1205–1217.

Reis, H. T., Wheeler, L., Spiegel, N., Kernis, M. H., Nezlek, J., & Perri, M. (1982). Physical attractiveness in social interaction: II. Why does appearance affect social experience? *Journal of Personality and Social Psychology, 43,* 979–996.

Reiss, I. L. (1980). *Family systems in America,* 3d ed. New York: Holt, Rinehart and Winston.

Renwick, P. A., & Lawler, E. E. (1978). What do you really want from your job? *Psychology Today, 11*(12), 53–65.

Rhodewalt, F., & Agustsdottir, S. (1984). On the relationship of hardiness to the Type A behavior pattern: Perception of life events versus coping with life events. *Journal of Research in Personality, 18,* 212–223.

Rice, B. (1985). Why am I in this job? *Psychology Today, 19*(1), 54–59.

Richardson, D. C., Bernstein, S., & Taylor, S. P. (1979). The effect of situational contingencies on female retaliative behavior. *Journal of Personality and Social Psychology, 37,* 2044–2048.

Richardson, S. (1972). Ecology of malnutrition. In Pan American Health Organization Scientific Publication No. 251, *Nutrition, the nervous system and behavior.*

Richman, D. R., O'Brien, R. M., & Dickinson, A. M. (1980, August). Comparison of cognitive and behavioral techniques for job finding. Paper presented to the American Psychological Association, Montreal.

Richter, C. P. (1957). On the phenomenon of sudden death in animals and man. *Psychosomatic Medicine, 19,* 191–198.

Riggio, R. E., & Woll, S. B. (1984). The role of nonverbal cues and physical attractiveness in the selection of dating partners. *Journal of Social and Personal Relationships, 1,* 347–357.

Riley, V. (1981). Psychoneuroendocrine influences on immunocompetence and neoplasia. *Science, 212,* 1100–1109.

Rizley, R. (1978). Depression and distortion in the attribution of causality. *Journal of Abnormal Psychology, 87,* 32–48.

Roberts, A. H. (1969). Self-control procedures in the modification of smoking behavior: A replication. *Psychological Reports, 24,* 675–676.

Robinson, E. A., & Price, M. G. (1980). Pleasurable behavior in marital interaction: An observational study. *Journal of Consulting and Clinical Psychology, 48,* 117–118.

Robinson, F. P. (1970). *Effective study,* 4th ed. New York: Harper & Row.

Robinson, M. H., & Robinson, B. (1979). By dawn's early light: Matutinal mating in a neotropical mantid. *Science, 205,* 825–826.

Rodhölm, M. (1981). Effects of father–infant postpartum contact on their interaction three months after birth. *Early Human Development, 5,* 79–86.

Rodin, J. (1976). Menstruation, reattribution, and competence. *Journal of Personality and Social Psychology, 33,* 345.

Rodin, J., & Langer, E. J. (1977). Long-term effects of a control-relevant intervention with the institutionalized aged. *Journal of Personality and Social Psychology, 35,* 897–902.

Rodin, J., & Slochower, J. (1976). Externality in the obese: The effects of environmental responsiveness on weight. *Journal of Personality and Social Psychology, 33,* 338–344.

Rogan, H. (1984a, October 29). Women executives feel that men both aid and hinder their careers. *The Wall Street Journal,* pp. 35, 59.

Rogan, H. (1984b, October 30). Executive women find it difficult to balance demands of job, home. *The Wall Street Journal,* pp. 35, 55.

Rogers, C. R. (1951). *Client-centered therapy.* Boston: Houghton Mifflin.

Rogers, C. R. (1959). A theory of therapy, personality and interpersonal relationships, as developed in the client-centered framework. In S. Koch (Ed.), *Psychology: A study of science,* Vol. 3. New York: McGraw-Hill.

Rogers, C. R. (1963). The actualizing tendency in relationship to "motives" and to consciousness. In M. R. Jones (Ed.), *Nebraska symposium on motivation.* Lincoln, NE: University of Nebraska Press.

Rogers, C. R. (1972). *Becoming partners: Marriage and its alternatives.* New York: Delacorte Press.

Rogers, C. R. (1974). In retrospect: 46 years. *American Psychologist, 29,* 115–123.

Rogers, C. R. (1985). Cited in S. Cunningham (1985). Humanists celebrate gains, goals. *APA Monitor, 16*(5), 16, 18.

Rogers, C. R., & Dymond, R. F. (Eds.) (1954). *Psychotherapy and personality change.* Chicago: University of Chicago Press.

Rogers, M. F. (1985). AIDS in children: A review of the clinical, epidemiological and public health aspects. *Pediatric Infectious Disease, 4,* 230–236.

Rogers, R. (1987). APA's position on the insanity defense: Empiricism versus emotionalism. *American Psychologist, 42,* 840–848.

Rogers, R. W. (1983). Preventive health psychology: An interface of social and clinical psychology. *Journal of Social and Clinical Psychology, 1,* 120–127.

Rogers, R. W., & Deckner, C. W. (1975). Effects of fear appeals and physiological arousal upon emotions, attitudes, and cigarette smoking. *Journal of Personality and Social Psychology, 32,* 222–230.

Rogers, R. W., & Prentice-Dunn, S. (1981). Deindividuation and anger-mediated interracial aggression: Unmasking regressive racism. *Journal of Personality and Social Psychology, 41,* 63–73.

Rohsenow, D. J. (1983). Drinking habits and expectancies about alcohol's effects for self versus others. *Journal of Consulting and ClinicalPsychology, 51,* 752–756.

Rollin, B. E. (1985). The moral status of research animals in psychology. *American Psychologist, 40,* 920–926.

Ronen, S. (1981). *Flexible working hours.* New York: McGraw-Hill.

Rook, K. S., & Dooley, D. (1985). Applying social support research: Theoretical problems and future directions. *Journal of Social Issues, 41,* 5–28.

Rook, K. S., & Peplau, L. A. (1982). Perspectives on helping the lonely. In L. A. Peplau & D. Perlman (Eds.), *Loneliness: A sourcebook of current theory, research, and therapy.* New York: Wiley.

Roper Poll (1984). *Psychology Today, 18*(1), 17.

Rose, R. M. (1975). Testosterone, aggression, and homosexuality: A review of the literature and implications for future research. In E. J. Sachar (Ed.), *Topics in psychoendocrinology.* New York: Grune & Stratton.

Rosen, G. M., Glasgow, R. E., & Barrera, M., Jr. (1976). A controlled study to assess the efficacy of totally self-administered systematic desensitization. *Journal of Consulting and Clinical Psychology, 44,* 208–217.

Rosenbaum, M., & Hadari, D. (1985). Personal efficacy, external locus of control, and perceived contingency of parental reinforcement among depressed, paranoid, and normal subjects. *Journal of Personality and Social Psychology, 49,* 539–547.

Rosenberg, M. S., & Repucci, N. D. (1985). Primary prevention of child abuse. *Journal of Consulting and Clinical Psychology, 53,* 576–585.

Rosenblum, L. A., & Paully, G. S. (1984). The effects of varying environmental demands on maternal and infant behavior. *Child Development, 55,* 305–314.

Rosenhan, D. L., Salovey, P., & Hargis, K. (1981). The joys of helping. *Journal of Personality and Social Psychology, 40,* 899–905.

Rosenstock, I. M., & Kirscht, J. P. (1979). Why people seek health care. In G. C. Stone, F. Cohen, & N. E. Adler (Eds.), *Health psychology: A handbook.* San Francisco: Jossey-Bass.

Rosett, H. L., & Sander, L. W. (1979). Effects of maternal drinking on neonatal morphology and state regulation. In J. D. Osofsky (Ed.), *Handbook of infant development.* New York: Wiley-Interscience.

Roskies, E., Seraganian, P., Oseasohn, R., Hanley, J. A., Collu, R., Martin, N., & Smilga, C. (1986). The Montreal Type A Intervention Project: Major findings. *Health Psychology, 5,* 45–69.

Rotter, J. B. (1966). Generalized expectancies for internal versus external locus of control of reinforcement. *Psychological Monographs, 80*(609).

Rotter, J. B. (1971). External control and internal control. *Psychology Today, 5,* 37–42, 58–59.

Rotter, J. B. (1972). Beliefs, social attitudes, and behavior: A social learning analysis. In J. B. Rotter, J. E. Chance, & E. J. Phares (Eds.), *Applications of a social learning theory of personality.* New York: Holt, Rinehart and Winston.

Rotter, J. B. (1975). Some problems and misconceptions related to the construct of internal versus external control of reinforcement. *Journal of Con-*

sulting and Clinical Psychology, 43, 56–67.

Rotton, J., & Frey, J. (1985). Air pollution, weather, and violent crimes: Concomitant time-series analysis of archival data. *Journal of Personality and Social Psychology, 49,* 1207–1220.

Rotton, J., Barry, T., Frey, J., & Soler, E. (1978). Air pollution and interpersonal attraction. *Journal of Applied Social Psychology, 8,* 57–71.

Rotton, J., Frey, J., Barry, T., & Fitzpatrick, M. (1979). The air pollution experience and interpersonal aggression. *Journal of Applied Social Psychology, 9,* 397–412.

Roueche, B. (1980). *The medical detectives.* New York: Truman Talley.

Rounsaville, B. J., Chevron, E. S., Prusoff, B. A., Elkin, I., Imber, S., Sotsky, S., & Watkins, J. (1987). The relation between specific and general dimensions of the psychotherapy process in interpersonal psychotherapy of depression. *Journal of Consulting and Clinical Psychology, 55,* 379–384.

Rubin, Z. (1970). Measurement of romantic love. *Journal of Personality and Social Psychology, 16,* 265–273.

Rubin, Z. (1973). *Liking and loving.* New York: Holt, Rinehart and Winston.

Rubin, Z. (1975). Disclosing oneself to a stranger: Reciprocity and its limits. *Journal of Experimental Social Psychology, 11,* 233–260.

Rubin, Z. (1982). Children without friends. In L. A. Peplau & D. Perlman (Eds.), *Loneliness: A sourcebook of current theory, research, and therapy.* New York: Wiley.

Rubin, Z., Hill, C. T., Peplau, L. A., & Dunkel-Schetter, C. (1980). Self-disclosure in dating couples: Sex role and ethic of openness. *Journal of Marriage and the Family, 42,* 305–317.

Rubinstein, E. A. (1983). Television and behavior: Research conclusions of the 1982 NIMH report and their policy implications. *American Psychologist, 38,* 820–825.

Ruderman, A. J. (1985). Dysphoric mood and overeating: A test of restraint theory's disinhibition hypothesis. *Journal of Abnormal Psychology, 94,* 78–85.

Ruiz, P., & Ruiz, P. P. (1983). Treatment compliance among Hispanics. *Journal of Operational Psychiatry, 14,* 112–114.

Ruopp, R. (1979). *Children at the center.* Cambridge, MA: Abt Associates.

Rusbult, C. E. (1980). Commitment and satisfaction in romantic associations: A test of the investment model. *Journal of Experimental Social Psychology, 16,* 172–186.

Rusbult, C. E. (1983). A longitudinal test of the investment model. *Journal of*

Personality and Social Psychology, 45, 101–117.

Rusbult, C. E., Johnson, D. J., & Morrow, G. D. (1986). Impact of couple patterns of problem solving on distress and nondistress in dating relationships. *Journal of Personality and Social Psychology, 50,* 744–753.

Rusbult, C. E., Musante, L., & Soloman, M. (1982). The effects of clarity of decision rule and favorability of verdict on satisfaction with resolution of conflicts. *Journal of Applied Psychology, 12,* 304–317.

Rusbult, C. E., & Zembrodt, I. M. (1983). Responses to dissatisfaction in romantic involvements: A multidimensional scaling analysis. *Journal of Experimental Social Psychology, 19,* 274–293.

Rush, A. J., Khatami, M., & Beck, A. T. (1975). Cognitive and behavior therapy in chronic depression. *Behavior Therapy, 6,* 398–404.

Rush, A. J., Beck, A. T., Kovacs, M., Weissenberger, J., & Hollon, S. D. (1982). Comparison of the effects of cognitive therapy and pharmacotherapy on hopelessness and self-concept. *American Journal of Psychiatry, 139,* 862–866.

Rush, D., et al. (1980). *Diet in pregnancy: A randomized controlled trial of nutritional supplements.* New York: Liss.

Russell, D. (1982). The measurement of loneliness. In L. A. Peplau & D. Perlman (Eds.), *Loneliness: A sourcebook of current theory, research, and therapy.* New York: Wiley.

Russell, D., Peplau, L. A., & Cutrona, C. E. (1980). The revised UCLA Loneliness Scale: Concurrent and discriminant validity evidence. *Journal of Personality and Social Psychology, 39,* 472–480.

Rüstemli, A. (1986). Male and female personal space needs and escape reactions under intrusion: A Turkish sample. *International Journal of Psychology.*

Rutkowski, G. K., Gruder, C. L., & Romer, D. (1983). Group cohesiveness, social norms, and bystander intervention. *Journal of Personality and Social Psychology, 44,* 545–552.

Sackeim, H. A. (1985). The case for ECT. *Psychology Today, 19*(6), 36–40.

Sackeim, H. A., Portnoy, S., Neeley, P., Steif, B. L., Decina, P., & Malitz, S. (1985). Cognitive consequences of low dosage ECT. In S. Malitz & H. A. Sackeim (Eds.), *Electroconvulsive therapy: Clinical and basic research issues.* New York: Annals of the New York Academy of Science.

Sackett, D. L., & Snow, J. C. (1979). The magnitude of compliance and noncompliance. In R. B. Haynes, D. W. Taylor, & D. L. Sackett (Eds.), *Compli-*

ance in health care. Baltimore: Johns Hopkins University Press.

Sadalla, E. K., Kenrick, D. T., & Vershure, B. (1987). Dominance and heterosexual attraction. *Journal of Personality and Social Psychology, 52,* 730–738.

Saddler, J. (1987, February 12). Low pay, high turnover plague day-care industry. *Wall Street Journal,* p. 27.

Sadker, M., & Sadker, D. (1985). Sexism in the schoolroom of the 1980s. *Psychology Today, 19*(3), 54–57.

Sadowitz, P. D., & Oski, F. A. (1983). Iron status and infant feeding practices in an urban ambulatory center. *Pediatrics, 72,* 33–36.

Saegert, S. C., & Hart, R. (1976). The development of sex differences in the environmental competence of children. In P. Burnett (Ed.), *Women in society.* Chicago: Maaroufa Press.

Saegert, S. C., & Jellison, J. M. (1970). Effects of initial level of response competition and frequency of exposure to liking and exploratory behavior. *Journal of Personality and Social Psychology, 16,* 553–558.

Safer, M. A. (1980). Attributing evil to the subject, not the situation: Student reactions to Milgram's film on obedience. *Personality and Social Psychology Bulletin, 6,* 205–209.

Saghir, M. T., & Robins, E. (1973). *Male and female homosexuality: A comprehensive investigation.* Baltimore: Williams & Wilkins.

Salkind, N. J. (1983). The father–child post divorce relationship and child support. In J. Cassely (Ed.), *The parental child-support obligation.* Lexington, MA: Lexington Books.

Sanchez-Craig, M., Annis, H. M., Bornet, A. R., & MacDonald, K. R. (1984). Random assignment to abstinence or controlled drinking: Evaluation of a cognitive-behavioral program for problem drinkers. *Journal of Consulting and Clinical Psychology, 52,* 390–403.

Sanders, B., & Soares, M. P. (1986). Sexual maturation and spatial ability in college students. *Developmental Psychology, 22,* 199–203.

Sanders, B., Soares, M. P., & D'Aquila, J. M. (1982). The sex difference on one test of spatial visualization: A nontrivial difference. *Child Development, 53,* 1106–1110.

Santee, R. T., & Maslach, C. (1982). To agree or not to agree: Personal dissent amid social pressure to conform. *Journal of Personality and Social Psychology, 42,* 690–700.

Santrock, J. W. (1970). Paternal absence, sex typing, and identification. *Developmental Psychology, 2,* 264–272.

Santrock, J. W., & Warshak, R. A. (1979).

Father custody and social development in boys and girls. *Journal of Social Issues, 35*(4), 112–125.

Santrock, J. W., Warshak, R. A., Lindbergh, C., & Meadows, L. (1982). Children's and parents' observed social behavior in stepfather families. *Child Development, 53,* 472–480.

Sarason, I. G. (1984). Stress, anxiety, and cognitive interference: Reactions to tests. *Journal of Personality and Social Psychology, 46,* 929–938.

Sarbin, T. R., & Nucci, L. P. (1973). Self-reconstitution processes: A proposal for reorganizing the conduct of confirmed smokers. *Journal of Abnormal Psychology, 81,* 182–195.

Sarrell, L. J., & Sarrell, P. M. (1984). *Sexual turning points.* New York: Macmillan.

Satir, V. (1967). *Conjoint family therapy.* Palo Alto, CA: Science and Behavior Books.

Satow, K. L. (1975). Social approval and helping. *Journal of Experimental Social Psychology, 11,* 501–509.

Saunders, C. (1984). St. Christopher's hospice. In E. S. Shneidman (Ed.), *Death: Current perspectives,* 3d ed. Palo Alto, CA: Mayfield.

Sawrey, W. L., Conger, J. J., & Turrell, E. S. (1956). An experimental investigation of the role of psychological factors in the production of gastric ulcers in rats. *Journal of Comparative and Physiological Psychology, 49,* 457–461.

Sawrey, W. L., & Weisz, J. D. (1956). An experimental method of producing gastric ulcers. *Journal of Comparative and Physiological Psychology, 49,* 269–270.

Scanlon, J. W., Brown, W. V., Jr., Weiss, J. B., & Alper, M. H. (1974). Neurobehavioral responses of newborn infants after maternal epidural anesthesia. *Anesthesiology, 40,* 121–128.

Scanzoni, J., & Polonko, K. (1980). A conceptual approach to explicit marital negotiation. *Journal of Marriage and the Family, 42,* 31–44.

Scarr, S., & Kidd, K. K. (1983). Developmental behavior genetics. In M. Haith & J. J. Campos (Eds.), *Handbook of child psychology.* New York: Wiley.

Scarr, S., Webber, P. L., Weinberg, R. A., & Wittig, M. A. (1981). Personality resemblance among adolescents and their parents in biologically related and adoptive families. *Journal of Personality and Social Psychology, 41,* 885–898.

Scarr, S., & Weinberg, R. A. (1983). The Minnesota adoption studies: Genetic differences and malleability. *Child Development, 54,* 260–267.

Schachter, S. (1971). Some extraordinary facts about obese humans and rats. *American Psychologist, 26,* 129–144.

Schachter, S. (1977). Nicotine regulation in heavy and light smokers. *Journal of Experimental Psychology: General, 106,* 5–12.

Schachter, S. (1982). Recidivism and self-cure of smoking and obesity. *American Psychologist, 37,* 436–444.

Schachter, S., & Gross, L. P. (1968). Manipulated time and eating behavior. *Journal of Personality and Social Psychology, 10,* 98–106.

Schachter, S., Kozlowski, L. T., & Silverstein, B. (1977). Effects of urinary pH on cigarette smoking. *Journal of Experimental Psychology: General, 106,* 13–19.

Schachter, S., & Latané, B. (1964). Crime, cognition, and the autonomic nervous system. In D. Levine (Ed.), *Nebraska symposium on motivation.* Lincoln, NE: University of Nebraska Press.

Schachter, S., & Rodin, J. (1974). *Obese humans and rats.* Washington, DC: Erlbaum/Halsted.

Schaeffer, J., Andrysiak, T., & Ungerleider, J. T. (1981). Cognition and long-term use of ganja (cannabis). *Science, 213,* 465–466.

Schaeffer, M., & Baum, A. (1982, August). *Consistency of stress response at Three Mile Island.* Paper presented to the American Psychological Association.

Schechter, M., et al. (1984, June 9). Changes in sexual behavior and fear of AIDS. *Lancet,* p. 1293.

Schiavi, R. C., et al. (1977). Luteinizing hormone and testosterone during nocturnal sleep: Relation to penile tumescent cycles. *Archives of Sexual Behavior, 6,* 97–104.

Schiedel, D. G., & Marcia, J. E. (1985). Ego identity, intimacy, sex-role orientation, and gender. *Developmental Psychology, 21,* 149–160.

Schifter, D. E., & Ajzen, I. (1985). Intention, perceived control, and weight loss: An application of the theory of planned behavior. *Journal of Personality and Social Psychology, 49,* 843–851.

Schindler, B. A. (1985). Stress, affective disorders, and immune function. *Medical Clinics of North America, 69,* 585–597.

Schindler, G. L. (1979). *Testosterone concentration, personality patterns, and occupational choice in women.* Unpublished doctoral dissertation: University of Houston.

Schmauk, F. J. (1970). Punishment, arousal, and avoidance learning in sociopaths. *Journal of Abnormal Psychology, 76,* 443–453.

Schmeck, H. M., Jr. (1987, December 29). New light on the chemistry of dreams. *The New York Times,* pp. C1, C12.

Schmidt, F. L., Hunter, J. E., & Pearlman, K. (1981). Task differences as moderators of aptitude test validity in selection: A red herring. *Journal of Applied Psychology, 66,* 161–185.

Schmitt, M. H. (1970, July). Superiority of breast-feeding: Fact or fancy? *American Journal of Nursing,* pp. 1488–1493.

Schneidman, B., & McGuire, L. (1976). Group therapy for nonorgasmic women: Two age levels. *Archives of Sexual Behavior, 5,* 239–247.

Schotte, D. E., & Clum, G. A. (1982). Suicide ideation in a college population: A test of a model. *Journal of Consulting and Clinical Psychology, 50,* 690–696.

Schotte, D. E., & Clum, G. A. (1987). Problem-solving skills in suicidal psychiatric patients. *Journal of Consulting and Clinical Psychology, 55,* 49–54.

Schroeder, M. L., Schroeder, K. G., & Hare, R. D. (1983). Generalizability of a checklist for assessment of psychopathy. *Journal of Consulting and Clinical Psychology, 51,* 511–516.

Schuckit, M. A. (1987). Biological vulnerability to alcoholism. *Journal of Consulting and Clinical Psychology, 55,* 301–309.

Schulsinger, F. (1972). Psychopathy: Heredity and environment. *International Journal of Mental Health, 1,* 190–206.

Schulte, L. (1986). The new dating game. *New York, 19*(9), 92–94, 96, 98, 103–104, 106.

Schultz, D. P. (1978). *Psychology and industry today.* New York: Macmillan.

Schultz, J. H. (1982). Inflation's challenge to aged income security. *Gerontologist, 22*(2), 115–116.

Schultz, N. R., Jr., & Moore, D. W. (1984). Loneliness: Correlates, attributions, and coping among older adults. *Personality and Social Psychology Bulletin, 10,* 67–77.

Schultz, T. (1980, June). Does marriage give today's women what they really want? *Ladies' Home Journal,* pp. 89–91, 146–155.

Schwartz, D., & Mayaux, F. (1982). Female fecundity as a function of age. *New England Journal of Medicine, 306,* 404–406.

Schwartz, J. C., Strickland, R. G., & Krolick, G. (1974). Infant day care: Behavioral effects at preschool age. *Developmental Psychology, 10,* 502–506.

Schwartz, L. M., Foa, U. G., & Foa, E. B. (1983). Multichannel nonverbal communication: Evidence for combinatory rules. *Journal of Personality and Social Psychology, 45,* 274–281.

Schwartz, R. M. (1982). Cognitive behavior modification: A conceptual review. *Clinical Psychology Review, 2,* 267–293.

Schwartz, R. M., & Gottman, J. M. (1976). Toward a task analysis of assertive behavior. *Journal of Consulting and Clinical Psychology, 44,* 910–920.

Schwebel, A. I., Moreland, J., Steinkohl, R., Lentz, S., & Stewart, J. (1982). Research-based intervention with divorced families. *Personnel and Guidance Journal, 60,* 523–528.

Scott, W. J., & Morgan, C. S. (1983). An analysis of factors affecting traditional family expectations and perceptions of ideal fertility. *Sex Roles, 9,* 901–914.

Scovern, A. W., & Kilmann, P. R. (1980). Status of electroconvulsive therapy: A review of the outcome literature. *Psychological Bulletin, 87,* 260–303.

Sears, R. R., Maccoby, E. E., & Levin, H. (1957). *Patterns of child rearing.* New York: Harper & Row.

Seer, P. (1979). Psychological control of essential hypertension: Review of the literature and methodological critique. *Psychological Bulletin, 86,* 1015–1043.

Segal, M. W. (1974). Alphabet and attraction: An unobtrusive measure of the effect of propinquity in the field setting. *Journal of Personality and Social Psychology, 30,* 654–657.

Seidman, A. (1978). *Working women.* Boulder, CO: Westview Press.

Seligman, M. E. P. (1973). Fall into helplessness. *Psychology Today, 7,* 43–48.

Seligman, M. E. P., Abramson, L. Y., Semmel, A., & von Baeyer, C. (1979). Depressive attributional style. *Journal of Abnormal Psychology, 88,* 242–247.

Seligman, M. E. P., Kaslow, N. J., Alloy, L. B., Peterson, C., Tanenbaum, R. L., & Abramson, L. Y. (1984). Attributional style and depressive symptoms among children. *Journal of Abnormal Psychology, 93,* 235–238.

Seligman, M. E. P., & Rosenhan, D. L. (1984). *Abnormal psychology.* New York: W. W. Norton.

Selye, H. (1976). *The stress of life,* rev. ed. New York: McGraw-Hill.

Selye, H. (1980). The stress concept today. In I. L. Kutash, L. B. Schlesinger, et al. (Eds.), *Handbook on stress and anxiety.* San Francisco: Jossey-Bass.

Semans, J. (1956). Premature ejaculation: A new approach. *Southern Medical Journal, 49,* 353–358.

Senneker, P., & Hendrick, C. (1983). Androgyny and helping behavior. *Journal of Personality and Social Psychology, 45,* 916–925.

Serbin, L. A., Conner, J. M., Burchardt, C. J., & Citron, C. C. (1979). Effects of peer presence on sex typing of children's play behavior. *Journal of Experimental Child Psychology, 27,* 303–309.

Serlin, E. (1980). Emptying the nest: Women in the launching stage. In D. G. McGuigan (Ed.), *Women's lives: New theory, research, and policy.* Ann Arbor: University of Michigan, Center for Continuing Education of Women.

Serrill, M. S. (1987, February 16). In the grip of the scourge. *Newsweek,* pp. 58–59.

Shadish, W. R., Hickman, D., & Arrick, M. C. (1981). Psychological problems of spinal injury patients: Emotional distress as a function of time and locus of control. *Journal of Consulting and Clinical Psychology, 49,* 297.

Shanteau, J., & Nagy, G. (1979). Probability of acceptance in dating choice. *Journal of Personality and Social Psychology, 37,* 522–533.

Shapiro, D. (1985). Clinical use of meditation as a self-regulation strategy: Comments on Holmes' conclusions and implications. *American Psychologist, 40,* 719–722.

Shapiro, D., & Goldstein, I. B. (1982). Behavioral perspectives on hypertension. *Journal of Consulting and Clinical Psychology, 50,* 841–859.

Shapiro, D. A., & Shapiro, D. (1982). Meta-analysis of comparative therapy outcome studies: A replication and refinement. *Psychological Bulletin, 92,* 581–594.

Shaw, E. D., Stokes, P. E., Mann, J. J., & Manevitz, A. Z. A. (1987). Effects of lithium carbonate on the memory and motor speed of bipolar patients. *Journal of Abnormal Psychology, 96,* 64–69.

Shaw, J. S. (1982). Psychological androgyny and stressful life events. *Journal of Personality and Social Psychology, 43,* 145–153.

Shaywitz, S., Cohen, D., & Shaywitz, B. (1980). Behavior and learning difficulties in children of normal intelligence born to alcoholic mothers. *The Journal of Pediatrics, 96,* 978–982.

Sheehy, G. (1976). *Passages: Predictable crises of adult life.* New York: Dutton.

Sheehy, G. (1981). *Pathfinders.* New York: Morrow.

Shekelle, R. B., et al. (1983). Hostility, risk of coronary heart disease, and mortality. *Psychosomatic Medicine, 45,* 109–114.

Shekelle, R. B., et al. (1985). The MRFIT behavior pattern study: II. Type A behavior and incidence of coronary heart disease. *American Journal of Epidemiology, 122,* 559–570.

Sherfey, M. J. (1973). *The nature and evolution of female sexuality.* New York: Vintage.

Sherif, C. W. (1980). A social psychological perspective on the menstrual cycle. In J. E. Parsons (Ed.), *The psychobiology of sex differences and sex roles.* New York: McGraw-Hill, Hemisphere.

Sherif, M. (1966). *In common predicament: Social psychology of intergroup conflict and cooperation.* Boston: Houghton Mifflin.

Shertzer, B. (1985). *Career planning,* 3d ed. Boston: Houghton Mifflin.

Sherwin, B. B., Gelfand, M. M., & Brender, W. (1985). Androgen enhances sexual motivation in females: A prospective crossover study of sex steroid medication in the surgical menopause. *Psychosomatic Medicine, 47,* 339–351.

Sherwin, R., & Sherry, C. (1985). Campus sexual norms and dating relationships: A trend analysis. *Journal of Sex Research, 21,* 258–274.

Shettles, L. B. (1972, June). Predetermining children's sex. *Medical Aspects of Human Sexuality,* p. 172.

Shiffman, S. (1982). Relapse following smoking cessation: A situational analysis. *Journal of Consulting and Clinical Psychology, 50,* 71–86.

Shiffman, S. (1984). Coping with temptations to smoke. *Journal of Consulting and Clinical Psychology, 52,* 261–267.

Shinn, M., Rosario, M., Morch, H., & Chestnut, D. E. (1984). Coping with job stress and burnout in the human services. *Journal of Personality and Social Psychology, 46,* 864–876.

Shipley, R. H. (1981). Maintenance of smoking cessation: Effect of follow-up letters, smoking motivation, muscle tension, and health locus of control. *Journal of Consulting and Clinical Psychology, 49,* 982–984.

Shipley, R. H., Butt, J. H., Horwitz, B., & Farbry, J. E. (1978). Preparation for a stressful medical procedure: Effect of amount of stimulus preexposure and coping style. *Journal of Consulting and Clinical Psychology, 46,* 499–507.

Shneidman, E. S. (Ed.) (1984). *Death: Current perspectives,* 3d ed. Palo Alto, CA: Mayfield.

Short, R. V. (1984). Breast feeding. *Scientific American, 250*(4), 35–41.

Shotland, R. L., & Heinold, W. D. (1985). Bystander response to arterial bleeding: Helping skills, the decision-making process, and differentiating the helping response. *Journal of Personality and Social Psychology, 49,* 347–356.

Shreve, A. (1982, November 2). Careers and the lure of motherhood. *The New York Times Magazine,* pp. 38–56.

Siegelman, M. (1972). Adjustments of male homosexuals and heterosexuals. *Archives of Sexual Behavior, 1,* 9–25.

Siegelman, M. (1978). Psychological adjustment of homosexual and heterosexual men: A cross-national replication. *Archives of Sexual Behavior, 7,* 1–11.

Siegelman, M. (1979). Adjustment of homosexual and heterosexual women: A cross-national replication. *Archives of Sexual Behavior, 8,* 121–126.

Silverstein, B. (1982). Cigarette smoking, nicotine addiction, and relaxation. *Journal of Personality and Social Psychology, 42,* 946–950.

Silverstein, B., Koslowski, L. T., & Schachter, S. (1977). Social life, cigarette smoking, and urinary pH. *Journal of Experimental Psychology: General, 106,* 20–23.

Simcock, B. (1985). Sons and daughters—a sex preselection study. *Medical Journal of Australia, 142,* 541–542.

Simenauer, J., & Carroll, D. (1982). *Singles: The new Americans.* New York: Simon & Schuster.

Simone, C. B. (1983). *Cancer and nutrition.* New York: McGraw-Hill.

Simons, A. D., McGowan, C. R., Epstein, L. H., Kupfer, D. J., & Robertson, R. J. (1985). Exercise as a treatment for depression: An update. *Clinical Psychology Review, 5,* 553–568.

Simons, A. D., Murphy, G. E., Levine, J. L., & Wetzel, R. D. (1986). Cognitive therapy and pharmacotherapy for depression: Sustained improvement over one year. *Archives of General Psychiatry, 43,* 43–48.

Singer, D. G. (1983). A time to reexamine the role of television in our lives. *American Psychologist, 38,* 815–816.

Sirota, A. D., Schwartz, G. E., & Shapiro, D. (1976). Voluntary control of human heart rate: Effect of reaction to aversive stimulation: A replication and extension. *Journal of Abnormal Psychology, 85,* 473–477.

Siscovick, D. S., et al. (1982). Physical activity and primary cardiac arrest. *Journal of the American Medical Association, 248,* 3113–3117.

Siscovick, D. S., et al. (1984). The incidence of primary cardiac arrest during vigorous exercise. *New England Journal of Medicine, 311,* 874–877.

Sistrunk, F., & McDavid, J. W. (1971). Sex variable in conforming behavior. *Journal of Personality and Social Psychology, 17,* 200–207.

Skalka, P. (1984). *The American Medical Association guide to health and well-being after fifty.* New York: Random House.

Skinner, B. F. (1938). *The behavior of organisms: An experimental analysis.* New York: Appleton.

Skinner, B. F. (1948). *Walden Two.* New York: Macmillan.

Skinner, B. F. (1972). *Beyond freedom and dignity.* New York: Knopf.

Skinner, B. F. (1979). *The shaping of a behaviorist.* New York: Knopf.

Skinner, B. F. (1983). Intellectual self-management in old age. *American Psychologist, 38,* 239–244.

Skinner, B. F. (1987). Whatever happened to psychology as the science of behavior? *American Psychologist, 42,* 780–786.

Slater, E., & Haber, J. D. (1984). Adolescent adjustment following divorce as a function of familial conflict. *Journal of Consulting and Clinical Psychology, 52,* 920–921.

Slater, E., & Shields, J. (1969). Genetic aspects of anxiety. In M. H. Luder (Ed.), *Studies of anxiety.* Ashford, England: Headley Brothers.

Slater, J., & Depue, R. A. (1981). The contribution of environmental events and social support to serious suicide attempts in primary depressive disorder. *Journal of Abnormal Psychology, 90,* 275–285.

Sloane, B. (1983). Health care: Physical and mental. In D. S. Woodruff & J. E. Birren (Eds.), *Aging: Scientific perspectives and social issues.* Monterey, CA: Brooks/Cole.

Smedley, J. W., & Bayton, J. A. (1978). Evaluative race-class stereotypes by race and perceived class of subjects. *Journal of Personality and Social Psychology, 36,* 530–535.

Smith, A., & Stansfeld, S. (1986). Aircraft noise exposure, noise sensitivity, and everyday errors. *Environment and Behavior, 18,* 214–226.

Smith, D. (1982). Trends in counseling and psychotherapy. *American Psychologist, 37,* 802–809.

Smith, G. F., & Dorfman, D. (1975). The effect of stimulus uncertainty on the relationship between frequency of exposure and liking. *Journal of Personality and Social Psychology, 31,* 150–155.

Smith, M. L., & Glass, G. V. (1977). Meta-analysis of psychotherapy outcome studies. *American Psychologist, 32,* 752–760.

Smith, M. L., Glass, G. V., & Miller, T. I. (1980). *The benefits of psychotherapy.* Baltimore, MD: The Johns Hopkins University Press.

Smith, R. E. (1979). The movement of women into the labor force. In R. E. Smith (Ed.), *The subtle revolution: Women at work.* Washington, DC: The Urban Institute.

Smith, R. E., & Winokur, G. (1983). Affective disorders. In R. E. Tarter (Ed.), *The child at psychiatric risk.* New York: Oxford University Press.

Smith, T. W. (1983). Change in irrational beliefs and the outcome of rational-emotive psychotherapy. *Journal of Consulting and Clinical Psychology, 51,* 156–157.

Smith, T. W., Snyder, C. R., & Handelsman, M. M. (1982). On the self-serving function of an academic wooden leg: Test anxiety as a self-handicapping strategy. *Journal of Personality and Social Psychology, 42,* 314–321.

Smith, T. W., Snyder, C. R., & Perkins,

S. C. (1983). The self-serving function of hypochondriacal complaints: Physical symptoms as self-handicapping strategies. *Journal of Personality and Social Psychology, 44,* 787–797.

Smith, U. (1985, January). American Heart Association Science Writers Forum presentation. Monterey, CA.

Snyder, D. (1979). Multidimensional assessment of marital satisfaction. *Journal of Marriage and the Family, 41,* 813–823.

Snyder, M., & Cunningham, M. R. (1975). To comply or not to comply: Testing the self-perception explanation of the foot-in-the-door phenomenon. *Journal of Personality and Social Psychology, 31,* 64–67.

Snyder, M., & DeBono, G. (1985). Appeals to image and claims about quality: Understanding the psychology of advertising. *Journal of Personality and Social Psychology, 49,* 586–597.

Snyder, M., Grether, J., & Keller, K. (1974). Staring and compliance: A field experiment on hitchhiking. *Journal of Applied Social Psychology, 4,* 165–170.

Snyder, M., Tanke, E. D., & Berscheid, E. (1977). Social perception and interpersonal behavior: On the self-fulfilling nature of social stereotypes. *Journal of Personality and Social Psychology, 35,* 656–666.

Snyder, S. H. (1977). Opiate receptors and internal opiates. *Scientific American, 236,* 44–56.

Snyder, S. H. (1980). *Biological aspects of mental disorder.* New York: Oxford University Press.

Snyder, S. H. (1984). Drug and neurotransmitter receptors in the brain. *Science, 224,* 22–31.

Sobell, M. B., & Sobell, L. C. (1973). Alcoholics treated by individualized behavior therapy: One year treatment outcomes. *Behaviour Research and Therapy, 11,* 599–618.

Sobell, M. B., & Sobell, L. C. (1976). Second year treatment outcome of alcoholics treated by individualized behavior therapy: Results. *Behaviour Research and Therapy, 14,* 195–215.

Sobell, M. B., & Sobell, L. C. (1984). The aftermath of heresy: A response to Pendery et al.'s critique of "Individualized behavior therapy for alcoholics." *Behaviour Research and Therapy, 22,* 413–440.

Solano, C. H., Batten, P. G., & Parish, E. A. (1982). Loneliness and patterns of self-disclosure. *Journal of Personality and Social Psychology, 43,* 524–531.

Sommer, B. (1972). Menstrual cycle changes and intellectual performance. *Psychosomatic Medicine, 34,* 263–269.

Sommer, B. (1973). The effects of menstruation on cognitive and perceptual motor behavior: A review. *Psychosomatic Medicine, 35,* 515–534.

Sommer, R. (1969). *Personal space.* Englewood Cliffs, NJ: Prentice-Hall.

Sommers, D., & Eck, A. (1977, January). Occupational mobility in the American labor force. *Monthly Labor Review,* pp. 3–19.

Sonstroem, R. J. (1984). Exercise and self-esteem. *Exercise and Sport Sciences Reviews, 12,* 123–155.

Sorlie, P., Gordon, T., & Kannel, W. B. (1980). Body build and mortality— The Framingham Study. *Journal of the American Medical Association, 243,* 1828–1831.

Spanos, N. P., McNeil, C., Gwynn, M. I., & Stam, H. J. (1984). Effects of suggestion and distraction on reported pain in subjects high and low on hypnotic suggestibility. *Journal of Abnormal Psychology, 93,* 277–284.

Spanos, N. P., Weekes, J. R., & Bertrand, L. D. (1985). Multiple personality: A social psychological perspective. *Journal of Abnormal Psychology, 94,* 362–376.

Spence, J. T., Helmreich, R., & Stapp, J. (1975). Ratings of self and peers on sex-role attributes and their relation to self-esteem and concepts of masculinity and femininity. *Journal of Personality and Social Psychology, 32,* 29–39.

Spielberger, C. D., Johnson, E. H., Russell, S. F., Crane, R. S., Jacobs, G. A., & Worden, T. J. (1985). In M. A. Chesney & R. H. Rosenman (Eds.), *Anger and hostility in cardiovascular and behavioral disorders.* New York: Hemisphere/McGraw-Hill.

Squire, L. R. (1977). ECT and memory loss. *American Journal of Psychiatry, 134,* 997–1001.

Squire, L. R., & Slater, P. C. (1978). Bilateral and unilateral ECT: Effects on verbal and nonverbal memory. *American Journal of Psychiatry, 135,* 1316–1320.

Stack, S. (1980). The effects of marital dissolution on suicide. *Journal of Marriage and the Family, 42,* 83–92.

Stafford, R., Backman, E., & Dibona, P. (1977). The division of labor among cohabiting and married couples. *Journal of Marriage and the Family, 34,* 43–59.

Stalonas, P. M., & Kirschenbaum, D. S. (1985). Behavioral treatments for obesity: Eating habits revisited. *Behavior Therapy, 16,* 1–14.

Stamler, J. (1985a). Coronary heart disease: Doing the "right things." *New England Journal of Medicine, 312,* 1053–1055.

Stamler, J. (1985b). The marked decline in coronary heart disease mortality rates in the United States, 1968–1981: Summary of findings and possible explanations. *Cardiology, 72,* 11–12.

Stamler, J., Wentworth, D., & Neaton, J. D. (1986). Is the relationship between serum cholesterol and risk of premature death from coronary heart disease continuous and graded? Findings in 356,222 primary screenees of the Multiple Risk Factor Intervention Trial (MRFIT). *Journal of the American Medical Association, 256,* 2823–2828.

Staub, E., Tursky, B., & Schwartz, G. (1971). Self-control and predictability: Their effects on reactions to aversive stimulation. *Journal of Personality and Social Psychology, 18,* 157–162.

Steck, L., Levitan, D., McLane, D., & Kelley, H. H. (1982). Care, need, and conceptions of love. *Journal of Personality and Social Psychology, 43,* 481–491.

Steele, B. F., & Pollock, C. B. (1974). A psychiatric study of parents who abuse infants and small children. In R. E. Helfer & C. H. Kempe (Eds.), *The battered child,* 2d ed. Chicago: University of Chicago Press.

Steele, C. M., & Southwick, L. L. (1985). Alcohol and social behavior I: The psychology of drunken excess. *Journal of Personality and Social Psychology, 48,* 18–34.

Steele, C. M., Southwick, L. L., & Critchlow, B. (1981). Dissonance and alcohol: Drinking your troubles away. *Journal of Personality and Social Psychology, 41,* 831–846.

Stehr, P. A., Glonginger, M. F., Kuller, L. H., Marsh, G. M., Radford, E. P., & Weinberg, G. B. (1985). Dietary vitamin A deficiencies and stomach cancer. *American Journal of Epidemiology, 121,* 65–70.

Stein, G. (1982). The maternity blues. In I. F. Brockington & R. Kumar (Eds.), *Motherhood and mental illness.* London: Academic Press.

Stein, P. J. (1980). Singlehood: An alternative to marriage. In J. M. Henslin (Ed.), *Marriage and the family in a changing society.* New York: Free Press.

Stein, P. J. (1981). *Single life: Unmarried adults in social context.* New York: St. Martin's Press.

Steinberg, L. D., Catalano, R., & Dooley, D. (1981). Economic antecedents of child abuse and neglect. Paper presented to the meeting of the Society for Research in Child Development, Boston.

Steinmetz, J. L., Lewinsohn, P. M., & Antonuccio, D. O. (1983). Prediction of individual outcome in a group intervention for depression. *Journal of Consulting and Clinical Psychology, 51,* 331–337.

Stephan, C. W., & Langlois, J. H. (1984). Baby beautiful: Adult attributions of infant competence as a function of infant attractiveness. *Child Development, 55,* 576–585.

Stephan, W. G. (1978). School desegregation: An evaluation of predictions made in *Brown v. Board of Education. Psychological Bulletin, 85,* 217–238.

Stephan, W. G., & Rosenfield, D. (1978). Effects of desegregation on racial attitudes. *Journal of Personality and Social Psychology, 36,* 795–804.

Stericker, A., & LeVesconte, S. (1982). Effect of brief training on sex-related differences in visual-spatial skill. *Journal of Personality and Social Psychology, 43,* 1018–1029.

Sternberg, R. J., & Grajek, S. (1984). The nature of love. *Journal of Personality and Social Psychology, 47,* 312–329.

Stewart, V., & Stewart, A. (1982). *Business applications of repertory grid.* London: McGraw-Hill.

Stier, D. S., & Hall, J. A. (1984). Gender differences in touch: An empirical and theoretical review. *Journal of Personality and Social Psychology, 47,* 440–459.

Stillman, M. J. (1977). Women's health beliefs about cancer and breast self-examination. *Nursing Research, 26,* 121–127.

Stipp, D. (1987, May 7). Breast-cancer risk may increase 40% with moderate alcohol use, studies say. *The Wall Street Journal,* p. 34.

Stokols, D., & Novaco, R. (1981). Transportation and well-being: An ecological perspective. In J. F. Wohlwill & P. B. Everett (Eds.), *Transportation and behavior.* New York: Plenum Publishing Co.

Stone, A. A., & Neale, J. M. (1984). Effects of severe daily events on mood. *Journal of Personality and Social Psychology, 46,* 137–144.

Stone, K., Grimes, D., & Magder, L. (1986). Primary prevention of sexually transmitted diseases: A primer for clinicians. *Journal of the American Medical Association, 255,* 1763–1766.

Storandt, M. (1983). Psychology's response to the graying of America. *American Psychologist, 38,* 323–326.

Storms, M. D. (1980). Theories of sexual orientation. *Journal of Personality and Social Psychology, 38,* 783–792.

Strahan, R. F. (1981). Time urgency, Type A behavior, and effect strength. *Journal of Consulting and Clinical Psychology, 49,* 134.

Strauss, M. A., Gelles, R., & Steinmetz, S. (1979). *Behind closed doors: A survey of family violence in America.* Garden City, NY: Doubleday.

Streissguth, A. P., Barr, H. M., & Martin, D. C. (1983). Maternal alcohol use and neonatal habituation assessed with the Brazelton scale. *Child Development, 54,* 1109–1118.

Streissguth, A. P., Landesman-Dwyer, S., Martin, J. C., & Smith, D. W. (1980). Teratogenic effects of alcohol in humans and laboratory animals. *Science, 209,* 353–361.

Streissguth, A. P., Martin, D. C., Barr, H. M., Sandman, B. M., Kirchner, G. L., & Darby, B. L. (1984). Interuterine alcohol and nicotine exposure: Attention and reaction time in 4-year-old children. *Developmental Psychology, 20,* 533–541.

Stretch, R. H. (1986). Posttraumatic stress disorder among Vietnam and Vietnam-era veterans. In C. R. Figley (Ed.), *Trauma and its wake: Vol. 2. Traumatic stress theory, research, and intervention.* New York: Brunner/Mazel.

Stretch, R. H. (1987). Posttraumatic stress disorder among U.S. army reservists: Reply to Nezu and Carnevale. *Journal of Consulting and Clinical Psychology, 55,* 272–273.

Strober, M. (1986). Anorexia nervosa: History and psychological concepts. In K. D. Brownell & J. P. Foreyt (Eds.), *Handbook of eating disorders.* New York: Basic Books.

Strom, J. C., & Buck, R. W. (1979). Staring and participants' sex: Physiological and subjective reactions. *Personality and Social Psychology Bulletin, 5,* 114–117.

Strube, M. J., & Werner, C. (1985). Relinquishment of control and the Type A behavior pattern. *Journal of Personality and Social Psychology, 48,* 688–701.

Stuart, R. B. (1978). *Act thin, stay thin.* New York: Norton.

Stuckey, M. F., McGhee, P. E., & Bell, N. J. (1982). Parent–child interaction: The influence of maternal employment. *Developmental Psychology, 18,* 635–644.

Stunkard, A. J. (1959). Obesity and the denial of hunger. *Psychosomatic Medicine, 1,* 281–289.

Stunkard, A. J., Sorensen, T. I. A., Hanis, C., Teasdale, T. W., Chakraborty, R., Schull, W. J., & Schulsinger, F. (1986). An adoption study of human obesity. *New England Journal of Medicine, 314,* 193, 198.

Suinn, R. M. (1976). How to break the vicious cycle of stress. *Psychology Today, 10,* 59–60.

Suinn, R. M. (1982). Intervention with Type A behaviors. *Journal of Consulting and Clinical Psychology, 50,* 933–949.

Suinn, R. M., & Deffenbacher, J. L. (1988). Anxiety management training. *The Counseling Psychologist, 16*(1), 31–49.

Suler, J. R. (1985). Meditation and somatic arousal: A comment on Holmes's review. *American Psychologist, 40,* 717.

Sullivan, W. (1988, February 16). New studies link exercise to delays in menstruation—and less cancer. *The New York Times,* p. C3.

Sunday, S., & Lewin, M. (1985). Integrating nuclear issues into the psychology curriculum. Paper presented at the meeting of the Eastern Psychological Association.

Super, D. E. (1957). *The psychology of careers.* New York: Harper & Row.

Super, D. E., & Hall, D. T. (1978). Career development: Exploration and planning. In M. R. Rosenzweig & L. W. Porter (Eds.), *Annual Review of Psychology, 29.* Palo Alto, CA: Annual Reviews.

Sussman, N. M., & Rosenfeld, H. M. (1982). Influence of culture, language, and sex on conversational distance. *Journal of Personality and Social Psychology, 42,* 66–74.

Sutton-Smith, B., & Rosenberg, B. G. (1970). *The sibling.* New York: Holt, Rinehart and Winston.

Svejda, M. J., Campos, J. J., & Emde, R. N. (1980). Mother–infant "bonding": Failure to generalize. *Child Development, 51,* 775–779.

Swank, C. (1982). Phased retirement: The European corporate experience. *Aging International, 9*(2), 10–15.

Sweeney, P. D., & Gruber, K. L. (1984). Selective exposure: Voter information preferences and the Watergate affair. *Journal of Personality and Social Psychology, 46,* 1208–1221.

Sweet, R. (1985). Chlamydia, group B streptococcus, and herpes in pregnancy. *Birth, 12,* 17–24.

Swensen, C. H. (1983). A respectable old age. *American Psychologist, 38,* 327–334.

Symons, D. (1979). *The evolution of human sexuality.* New York: Oxford University Press.

Szmukler, G. I., & Russell, G. F. M. (1986). Outcome and prognosis of anorexia nervosa. In K. D. Brownell & J. P. Foreyt (Eds.), *Handbook of eating disorders.* New York: Basic Books.

Talbott, E., et al. (1985). Occupational noise exposure, noise-induced hearing loss, and the epidemiology of high blood pressure. *American Journal of Epidemiology, 121,* 501–514.

Tasto, D. L., & Hinkle, J. E. (1973). Muscle relaxation treatment for tension headaches. *Behaviour Research and Therapy, 11,* 347–350.

Tavris, C. (1976). Women: Work isn't always the answer. *Psychology Today, 10*(4), 78.

Tavris, C., & Sadd, S. (1977). *The Redbook report on female sexuality.* New York: Delacorte.

Taylor, C. B., Farquhar, J. W., Nelson,

E., & Agras, D. (1977). Relaxation therapy and high blood pressure. *Archives of General Psychiatry, 34,* 339–343.

Taylor, S. E. (1983). Adjustment to threatening events: A theory of cognitive adaptation. *American Psychologist, 38,* 1161–1173.

Taylor, S. P., & Epstein, S. (1967). Aggression as a function of the interaction of the sex of the aggressor and the sex of the victim. *Journal of Personality, 35,* 474–486.

Teders, S. J., Blanchard, E. B., Andrasik, F., Jurish, S. E., Neff, D. F., & Arena, J. G. (1984). Relaxation training for tension headache: Comparative efficacy and cost-effectiveness of a minimal-therapist-contact versus a therapist-delivered procedure. *Behavior Therapy, 15,* 59–70.

Télégdy, G. (1977). Prenatal androgenization of primates and humans. In J. Money & H. Musaph (Eds.), *Handbook of sexology.* Amsterdam: Excerpta Medica.

Tessman, L. H. (1978). *Children of parting parents.* New York: Aronson.

Tetlock, P. E. (1983). Accountability and complexity of thought. *Journal of Personality and Social Psychology, 45,* 74–83.

Thigpen, C. H., & Cleckley, H. M. (1984). On the incidence of multiple personality disorder. *International Journal of Clinical and Experimental Hypnosis, 32,* 63–66.

Thoits, P. A. (1983). Dimensions of life events as influences upon the genesis of psychological distress and associated conditions: An evaluation and synthesis of the literature. In H. B. Kaplan (Ed.), *Psychosocial stress: Trends in theory and research.* New York: Academic Press.

Thomas, G. C., Batson, C. D., & Coke, J. S. (1981). Do good samaritans discourage helpfulness? *Journal of Personality and Social Psychology, 40,* 194–200.

Thomas, M. H., Horton, R. W., Lippincott, E. C., & Drabman, R. S. (1977). Desensitization to portrayals of real-life aggression as a function of exposure to television violence. *Journal of Personality and Social Psychology, 35,* 450–458.

Thompson, P. D. (1982). Cardiovascular hazards of physical activity. *Exercise and Sport Sciences Reviews, 10,* 208–235.

Thompson, W. C., Cowan, C. L., & Rosenhan, D. L. (1980). Focus of attention mediates the impact of negative affect on altruism. *Journal of Personality and Social Psychology, 38,* 291–300.

Thomson, M. E., & Kramer, M. S. (1984). Methodologic standards for controlled clinical trials of early contact and maternal–infant behavior. *Pediatrics, 73,* 294–300.

Tice, D. M., & Baumeiser, R. F. (1985). Masculinity inhibits helping in emergencies: Personality does predict the bystander effect. *Journal of Personality and Social Psychology, 49,* 420–428.

Titchener, J., & Kapp, F. I. (1976). Family and character change at Buffalo Creek. *American Journal of Psychiatry, 133,* 295–299.

Tobias, S. (1982). Sexist equations. *Psychology Today, 16*(1), 14–17.

Tolstedt, B., & Stokes, J. (1983). Relation of verbal, affective, and physical intimacy to marital satisfaction. *Journal of Counseling Psychology, 30,* 573–580.

Torgersen, S. (1983). Genetic factors in anxiety disorders. *Archives of General Psychiatry, 40,* 1085–1089.

Toufexis, A. (1981, July 27). Coping with Eve's curse. *Time Magazine,* p. 59.

Toufexis, A. (1982, March 8). Report from the surgeon general. *Time Magazine,* pp. 72–73.

Toufexis, A., Garcia, C., & Kalb, B. (1986, January 20). Dieting: The losing game. *Time Magazine,* pp. 54–60.

Touhey, J. C. (1972). Comparison of two dimensions of attitude similarity on heterosexual attraction. *Journal of Personality and Social Psychology, 23,* 8–10.

Touhey, J. C. (1974). Effects of additional women professionals on ratings of occupational prestige and desirability. *Journal of Personality and Social Psychology, 29,* 86–89.

Trost, C. (1987, February 12). Child-care center at Virginia firm boosts worker morale and loyalty. *Wall Street Journal,* p. 27.

Trussell, J., & Westoff, C. (1980). Contraceptive practice and trends in coital frequency. *Family Planning Perspectives, 12,* 246–249.

Tryon, R. C. (1940). Genetic differences in maze learning in rats. *Yearbook of the National Society for Studies in Education, 39,* 111–119.

Tucker, J. A., Vuchinich, R. E., & Sobell, M. B. (1981). Alcohol consumption as a self-handicapping strategy. *Journal of Abnormal Psychology, 90,* 220–230.

Turk, D. C., Meichenbaum, D., & Genest, M. (1983). *Pain and behavioral medicine: A cognitive behavioral perspective.* New York: Guilford Press.

Turkington, C. (1983). Drugs found to block dopamine receptors. *APA Monitor, 14,* 11.

Turkington, C. (1984). Hormones in rats found to control sexual behavior. *APA Monitor, 15*(11), 40–41.

Turkington, C. (1987). Alzheimer's and aluminum. *APA Monitor, 18*(1), 13–14.

Turner, J. A., & Chapman, C. R. (1982a). Psychological interventions for chronic pain: A critical review: I. Relaxation training and biofeedback. *Pain, 12,* 1–21.

Turner, J. A., & Chapman, C. R. (1982b). Psychological interventions for chronic pain: A critical review: II. Operant conditioning, hypnosis, and cognitive-behavior therapy. *Pain, 12,* 23–46.

Turner, J. S., & Helms. D. B. (1987). *Lifespan development,* 3d ed. New York: Holt, Rinehart and Winston.

Turner, R. H., & Killian, L. M. (1972). *Collective behavior.* Englewood Cliffs, NJ: Prentice-Hall.

Turner, S. M. (1987). Psychopathology in the offspring of anxiety disorders patients. *Journal of Consulting and Clinical Psychology, 55,* 229–235.

Tzuriel, D. (1984). Sex role typing and ego identity in Israeli, oriental, and western adolescents. *Journal of Personality and Social Psychology, 46,* 440–457.

Udry, J. R. (1971). *The social context of marriage.* Philadelphia: Lippincott.

Udry, J. R. (1980). Changes in the frequency of marital intercourse from panel data. *Archives of Sexual Behavior, 9,* 319–326.

Udry, J. R., & Morris, N. M. (1978). Relative contribution of male and female age to frequency of marital intercourse. *Social Biology, 25,* 128–134.

Ugwuegbu, D. C. E. (1979). Racial and evidential factors in juror attribution of legal responsibility. *Journal of Experimental Social Psychology, 15,* 133–146.

Ullman, C. (1982). Cognitive and emotional antecedents of religious conversion. *Journal of Personality and Social Psychology, 43,* 183–192.

Umberson, D., & Hughes, M. (1984, August). The impact of physical attractiveness on achievement and psychological well-being. Paper presented at the meeting of the American Sociological Association, San Antonio.

Underwood, B., & Moore, B. S. (1981). Sources of behavioral consistency. *Journal of Personality and Social Psychology, 40,* 780–785.

Unger, R. K., Hilderbrand, M., & Madar, T. (1982). Physical attractiveness and assumptions about social deviance: Some sex-by-sex comparisons. *Personality and Social Psychology Bulletin, 8,* 293–301.

U.S. Bureau of the Census. (1985). *Statistical abstract of the United States,* 105th ed. Washington, DC: U.S. Government Printing Office.

U.S. Department of Health, Education, and Welfare. (1979). *Smoking and health: A report of the Surgeon General.* (DHEW Publication No. 79-50066).

Washington, DC: U.S. Government Printing Office.

U.S. Department of Health and Human Services (1984). *The 1984 report of the Joint National Committee on Detection, Evaluation, and Treatment of High Blood Pressure.* (DHHS Publication No. NIH: 84-1088). Washington, DC: U.S. Government Printing Office.

U.S. Riot Commission (1968). *Report of the National Advisory Commission on Civil Disorders.* New York: Bantam Books.

Vaillant, G. E. (1982). *The natural history of alcoholism.* Cambridge, MA: Harvard University Press.

Vaillant, G. E., & Milofsky, E. S. (1982). The etiology of alcoholism. *American Psychologist, 37,* 494–503.

Valins, S. (1966). Cognitive effects of false heart-rate feedback. *Journal of Personality and Social Psychology, 4,* 400–408.

Vallis, M., McCabe, S. B., & Shaw, B. F. (1986, June). The relationships between therapist skill in cognitive therapy and general therapy skill. Paper presented to the Society for Psychotherapy Research, Wellesley, MA.

Van der Pligt, J., & Eiser, J. R. (1983). Actors' and observers' attributions, self-serving bias, and positivity bias. *European Journal of Social Psychology, 13,* 95–104.

Van Dyke, C., & Byck, R. (1982). Cocaine. *Scientific American, 44*(3), 128–141.

Velicer, W. F., DiClemente, C. C., Prochaska, J. O., & Brandenburg, N. (1985). Decisional balance measure for predicting smoking status. *Journal of Personality and Social Psychology, 48,* 1279–1289.

Vernbrugge, L. M. (1979). Marital status and health. *Journal of Marriage and the Family, 41,* 267–285.

Vernbrugge, L. M. (1983). Multiple roles and physical health of women and men. *Journal of Health and Social Behavior, 24,* 16–30.

Vestre, N. D. (1984). Irrational beliefs and self-reported depressed mood. *Journal of Abnormal Psychology, 93,* 239–241.

Visintainer, M. A., Volpicelli, J. R., & Seligman, M. E. P. (1982). Tumor rejection in rats after inescapable or escapable shock. *Science, 216*(23), 437–439.

Waber, D. P., Mann, M. B., Merola, J., & Moylan, P. M. (1985). Physical maturation rate and cognitive performance in early adolescence: A longitudinal examination. *Developmental Psychology, 21,* 666–681.

Wachtel, P. L. (1982). What can dynamic therapies contribute to behavior therapy? *Behavior Therapy, 13,* 594–609.

Waldholz, M. (1985, July 22). Breakthroughs in prenatal testing give hope to high-risk couples. *The Wall Street Journal,* p. 21.

Walker, A. M., Rablen, R. A., & Rogers, C. R. (1960). Development of a scale to measure process changes in psychotherapy. *Journal of Clinical Psychology, 16,* 79–85.

Walker, B. B. (1983). Treating stomach disorders: Can we reinstate regulatory processes? In W. E. Whitehead & R. Holzl (Eds.), *Psychophysiology of the gastrointestinal tract.* New York: Plenum Publishing Co.

Walker, W. B., & Franzini, L. R. (1985). Low-risk aversive group treatments, physiological feedback, and booster treatments for smoking cessation. *Behavior Therapy, 16,* 263–274.

Wallace, J. (1985). The alcoholism controversy. *American Psychologist, 40,* 372–373.

Wallerstein, J. S., & Kelly, J. B. (1974). The effects of parental divorce: The adolescent experience. In A. Koupernik (Ed.), *The child in his family: Children at psychiatric risk,* Vol. 3. New York: Wiley.

Wallerstein, J. S., & Kelly, J. B. (1975). The effects of parental divorce: Experience of the preschool child. *Journal of the American Academy of Child Psychiatry, 14,* 600–616.

Wallerstein, J. S., & Kelly, J. B. (1982). *Surviving the breakup: How children and parents cope with divorce.* New York: Basic Books.

Wallington, S. A. (1973). Consequences of transgression: Self-punishment and depression. *Journal of Personality and Social Psychology, 29,* 1–7.

Wallis, C. (1984, August 27). Can science pick a child's sex? Doctors challenge new methods of granting an ancient wish. *Time Magazine,* p. 59.

Wallis, C. (1987, February 16). The big chill: Fear of AIDS. *Time Magazine,* pp. 50–56.

Wallis, C. (1987, October 12). Back off, buddy: A new Hite report stirs up a furor over sex and love in the '80s. *Time Magazine,* pp. 68–73.

Wallston, B. (1973). The effects of maternal employment on children. *Child Psychology, 14,* 81–95.

Wallston, B. S., & Wallston, K. A. (1984). Social psychological models of health behavior: An examination and integration. In A. Baum, S. E. Taylor, & J. E. Singer (Eds.), *Handbook of psychology and health: Vol. 4. Social psychological aspects of health.* Hillsdale, NJ: Erlbaum.

Walsh, B. T., et al. (1984). Treatment of bulimia with phenelzine: A double-blind, placebo-controlled study. *Archives of General Psychiatry, 41,* 1105–1109.

Walsh, R. N., et al. (1981). The menstrual cycle, sex and academic performance. *Archives of General Psychiatry, 38,* 219–221.

Walstedt, J. J., Geis, F. L., & Brown, V. Influence of television commercials on women's self-confidence and independent judgment. *Journal of Personality and Social Psychology, 38,* 203–210.

Walster, E., Aronson, E., & Abrahams, D. (1966a). On increasing the persuasiveness of a low prestige communicator. *Journal of Experimental Social Psychology, 2,* 325–342.

Walster, E., Aronson, E., Abrahams, D., & Rottman, L. (1966b). Importance of physical attractiveness in dating behavior. *Journal of Personality and Social Psychology, 4,* 508–516.

Walster, E., & Walster, G. W. (1978). *A new look at love.* Reading, MA: Addison-Wesley.

Walster, E., Walster, G. W., Piliavin, J., & Schmidt, L. (1973). "Playing hard to get": Understanding an elusive phenomenon. *Journal of Personality and Social Psychology, 26,* 113–121.

Walter, T., & Siebert, A. (1987). *Student success: How to succeed in college and still have time for your friends,* 4th ed. New York: Holt, Rinehart and Winston.

Walton, S. (1985). Girls and science: The gap remains. *Psychology Today, 19*(6), 14.

Wang, P., Springen, K., Schmitz, T., & Bruno, M. (1987, October 12). A cure for stress? *Newsweek,* pp. 64–65.

Watson, J. B. (1924). *Behaviorism.* New York: Norton.

Watson, J. B., & Rayner, R. (1920). Conditioned emotional reactions. *Journal of Experimental Psychology, 3,* 1–14.

Watt, N. F., Grubb, T. W., & Erlenmeyer-Kimling, L. (1982). Social, emotional, and intellectual behavior among children at high risk for schizophrenia. *Journal of Consulting and Clinical Psychology, 50,* 171–181.

Weber, R., & Crocker, J. (1983). Cognitive processes in the revision of stereotypic beliefs. *Journal of Personality and Social Psychology, 45,* 961–977.

Wechsler, D. (1975). Intelligence defined and undefined: A relativistic appraisal. *American Psychologist, 30,* 135–139.

Weil, G., & Goldfried, M. R. (1973). Treatment of insomnia in an eleven-year-old child through self-relaxation. *Behavior Therapy, 4,* 282–294.

Weinberg, J., & Levine, S. (1980). Psychobiology of coping in animals: The effects of predictability. In S. Levine & H. Ursin (Eds.), *Coping and health.* New York: Plenum Publishing Co.

Weinberg, R. S., Yukelson, S., & Jackson, A. (1980). Effect of public and private efficacy expectations on competitive performance. *Journal of Sport Psychology, 2,* 340–349.

Weinberg, S. L., & Richardson, M. S. (1981). Dimensions of stress in early parenting. *Journal of Consulting and Clinical Psychology, 49,* 688–693.

Weiner, H., Thaler, M., Rieser, M. F., & Mirsky, I. A. (1957). Relation of specific psychological characteristics to rate of gastric secretion. *Psychosomatic Medicine, 17,* 1–10.

Weiner, M. J., & Wright, F. E. (1973). Effects of undergoing arbitrary discrimination upon subsequent attitudes toward a minority group. *Journal of Applied Social Psychology, 3,* 94–102.

Weinraub, M., & Wolf, B. M. (1983). Effects of stress and social supports on mother–child interactions in single- and two-parent families. *Child Development, 54,* 1297–1311.

Weinstein, M. S. (1980). *Health in the city: Environmental and behavioral influences.* New York: Pergamon Press.

Weinstein, N. D. (1980). Unrealistic optimism about future life events. *Journal of Personality and Social Psychology, 39,* 806–820.

Weinstein, N. D. (1984). Why it won't happen to me: Perceptions of risk factors and susceptibility. *Health Psychology, 3,* 431–457.

Weiss, J. M. (1972). Psychological factors in stress and disease. *Scientific American, 226*(6), 104–113.

Weiss, J. M., Glazer, H. I., & Pohorecky, L. A. (1976). Coping behavior and neurochemical changes: An alternative explanation for the original "learned helplessness" experiments. In G. Serban & A. Kling (Eds.), *Animal models of human psychobiology.* New York: Plenum Publishing Co.

Weiss, R. L. (1978). The conceptualization of marriage from a behavioral perspective. In T. Paolino & B. McGrady (Eds.), *Marriage and marital therapy.* New York: Brunner/Mazel.

Weissman, M., Klerman, C., Prusoff, B., Sholomkas, D., & Padin, N. (1981). Depressed outpatients. Results one year after treatment with drugs and/or interpersonal psychotherapy. *Archives of General Psychology, 18,* 51–55.

Wender, P. H., Rosenthal, R., Kety, S., Schulsinger, F., & Weiner, J. (1974). Cross-fostering: A research strategy for clarifying the role of genetic and experiential factors in the etiology of schizophrenia. *Archives of General Psychiatry, 30,* 121–128.

Werner, C. M., Brown, B. B., & Damron, G. (1981). Territorial marking in a game arcade. *Journal of Personality and Social Psychology, 41,* 1094–1104.

West, M. A. (1985). Meditation and somatic arousal reduction. *American Psychologist, 40,* 717–719.

Westoff, C. R., & Rindfuss, R. R. (1974). Sex preselection in the United States: Some implications. *Science, 184,* 633–636.

Wexler, D. A., & Butler, J. M. (1976). Therapist modification of client expressiveness in client-centered therapy. *Journal of Consulting and Clinical Psychology, 44,* 261–265.

Whalen, C. K., Kenker, B., Swanson, J. M., Granger, D., Kliewer, W., & Spencer, J. (1987). Natural social behaviors in hyperactive children: Dose effects of methylphenidate. *Journal of Consulting and Clinical Psychology, 55,* 187–193.

Wheeler, L., Deci, L., Reis, H., & Zuckerman, M. (1978). *Interpersonal influence.* Boston: Allyn & Bacon.

Whitcher, S. J., & Fisher, J. D. (1979). Multidimensional reaction to therapeutic touch in a hospital setting. *Journal of Personality and Social Psychology, 37,* 87–96.

White, G. L. (1980). Inducing jealousy: A power perspective. *Personality and Social Psychology Bulletin, 6,* 222–227.

White, G. L. (1981). Some correlates of romantic jealousy. *Journal of Personality, 49,* 129–146.

White, G. L., Fishbein, S., & Rutstein, J. (1981). Passionate love and the misattribution of arousal. *Journal of Personality and Social Psychology, 41,* 56–62.

White, L., & Tursky, B. (Eds.). (1982). *Clinical biofeedback: Efficacy and mechanisms.* New York: Guilford Press.

White, M. (1975). Interpersonal distance as affected by room size, status, and sex. *Journal of Social Psychology, 95,* 241–249.

Whitehead, W. E., & Bosmajian, L. S. (1982). Behavioral medicine approaches to gastrointestinal disorders. *Journal of Consulting and Clinical Psychology, 50,* 972–983.

Whitley, B. E., Jr. (1983). Sex role orientation and self-esteem: A critical meta-analysis. *Journal of Personality and Social Psychology, 44,* 765–788.

Whyte, W. W. (1956). *The organization man.* New York: Simon & Schuster.

Wideman, M. V., & Singer, J. F. (1984). The role of psychological mechanisms in preparation for childbirth. *American Psychologist, 34,* 1357–1371.

Wiens, A. N., & Menustik, C. E. (1983). Treatment outcome and patient characteristics in an aversion therapy program for alcoholism. *American Psychologist, 38,* 1089–1096.

Wiggins, J. S., Wiggins, N., & Conger, J. C. (1968). Correlates of heterosexual somatic preference. *Journal of Personality and Social Psychology, 10,* 82–90.

Wilcox, B. L. (1981). Social support, life stress, and psychological adjustment.

American Journal of Community Psychology, 9(4), 371–386.

Wilcoxon, L. A., Shrader, S. L., & Sherif, C. W. (1976). Daily self-reports on activities, life events, moods, and somatic changes during the menstrual cycle. *Psychosomatic Medicine, 38,* 399.

Wilder, D. A. (1977). Perception of groups, size of opposition, and social influence. *Journal of Experimental Social Psychology, 13,* 253–268.

Wilder, D. A., & Thompson, J. E. (1980). Intergroup contact with independent manipulations of in-group and out-group interaction. *Journal of Personality and Social Psychology, 38,* 589–603.

Williams, J. G., & Solano, C. H. (1983). The social reality of feeling lonely: Friendship and reciprocation. *Personality and Social Psychology Bulletin, 9,* 237–242.

Williams, J. H. (1980). Sexuality in marriage. in B. B. Wolman & J. Money (Eds.), *Handbook of human sexuality.* Englewood Cliffs, NJ: Prentice-Hall.

Williams, K. (1986, February 7). The role of appraisal salience in the performance evaluation process. Paper presented at a colloquium, State University of New York at Albany.

Williams, R. M., Goldman, M. S., & Williams, D. L. (1981). Expectancy and pharmacological effects of alcohol on human cognitive and motor performance: The compensation for alcohol effect. *Journal of Abnormal Psychology, 90,* 267–270.

Wilson, G. T. (1982). Psychotherapy process and procedure: The behavioral mandate. *Behavior Therapy, 13,* 291–312.

Wilson, G. T. (1987). Cognitive studies in alcoholism. *Journal of Consulting and Clinical Psychology, 55,* 325–331.

Wilson, G. T., & Lawson, D. M. (1978). Expectancies, alcohol, and sexual arousal in women. *Journal of Abnormal Psychology, 87,* 609–616.

Wilson, G. T., Leaf, R. C., & Nathan, P. E. (1975). The aversive control of excessive alcohol consumption by chronic alcoholics in the laboratory setting. *Journal of Applied Behavior Analysis, 8,* 13–26.

Wilson, T. D., & Linville, P. W. (1982). Improving the performance of college freshmen: Attribution therapy revisited. *Journal of Personality and Social Psychology, 42,* 367–376.

Wing, R. R., Epstein, L. H., & Shapira, B. (1982). The effect of increasing initial weight loss with the Scarsdale diet on subsequent weight loss in a behavioral treatment program. *Journal of Consulting and Clinical Psychology, 50,* 446–447.

Wingard, D. L., Berkman, L. F., & Brand, R. J. (1982). A multivariate analysis of health-related practices: A nine-year mortality follow-up of the Alameda County Study. *American Journal of Epidemiology, 116,* 765–775.

Witkin, H. A., Mednick, S. A., Schulsinger, F., Bakkestrom, E., Christiansen, K. O., Goodenough, D. R., Hirschhorn, K., Lundsteen, C., Owen, D. R., Philip, J., Rubin, D. B., & Stocking, M. (1976). Criminality in XYY and XXY men. *Science, 193,* 547–555.

Wittig, M. A. (1985). Metatheoretical dilemmas in the psychology of gender. *American Psychologist, 40,* 800–811.

Wolfe, J. L., & Fodor, I. G. (1975). A cognitive/behavioral approach to modifying assertive behavior in women. *The Counseling Psychologist, 5*(4), 45–52.

Wolfe, L. (1981). *The Cosmo report.* New York: Arbor House.

Wolinsky, J. (1982). Responsibility can delay aging. *APA Monitor, 13*(3), 14, 41.

Wolpe, J. (1958). *Psychotherapy by reciprocal inhibition.* Stanford, CA: Stanford University Press.

Wolpe, J. (1973). *The practice of behavior therapy.* New York: Pergamon Press.

Wolpe, J. (1985). Existential problems and behavior therapy. *The Behavior Therapist, 8*(7), 126–127.

Wolpe, J., & Lazarus, A. A. (1966). *Behavior therapy techniques.* New York: Pergamon Press.

Wolpe, J., & Rachman, S. (1960). Psychoanalytic "evidence": A critique based on Freud's case of Little Hans. *Journal of Nervous and Mental Disease, 131,* 135–147.

Wood, W. (1982). Retrieval of attitude-relevant information from memory: Effects on susceptibility to persuasion and on intrinsic motivation. *Journal of Personality and Social Psychology, 42,* 798–810.

Wood, W., & Eagly, A. H. (1981). Steps in the positive analysis of causal attributions and message comprehension. *Journal of Personality and Social Psychology, 40,* 246–259.

Woolfolk, R. L., & McNulty, T. F. (1983). Relaxation treatment for insomnia: A component analysis. *Journal of Consulting and Clinical Psychology, 51,* 495–503.

Worchel, S., Andreoli, V. A., & Folger, R. (1977). Intergroup cooperation and intergroup attraction: The effect of previous interaction and outcome of combined effort. *Journal of Experimental Social Psychology, 13,* 131–140.

Wortman, C. B., Adesman, P., Herman, E., & Greenberg, P. (1976). Self-disclosure: An attributional perspective. *Journal of Personality and Social Psychology, 33,* 184–191.

Wright, J. C., & Huston, A. C. (1983). A matter of form: Potentials of television for young viewers. *American Psychologist, 38,* 835–843.

Wright, L. (1988). The Type A behavior pattern and coronary artery disease: Quest for the active ingredients and the elusive mechanism. *American Psychologist, 43,* 2–14.

Wu, C., & Shaffer, C. R. (1987). Susceptibility to persuasive appeals as a function of source credibility and prior experience with the attitude object. *Journal of Personality and Social Psychology, 52,* 677–688.

Yankelovich, D. (1981). New rules in American life: Searching for self-fulfillment in a world turned upside down. *Psychology Today, 15*(4), 35–91.

Yarnold, P. R., & Grimm, L. G. (1982). Time urgency among coronary-prone individuals. *Journal of Abnormal Psychology, 91,* 175–177.

Yarnold, P. R., Mueser, K. T., & Grimm, L. G. (1985). Interpersonal dominance of Type A's in group discussion. *Journal of Abnormal Psychology, 94,* 233–236.

Yogev, S., & Vierra, A. (1983). The state of motherhood among professional women. *Sex Roles, 9,* 391–397.

Youkilis, H. D., & Bootzin, R. R. (1981). A psychophysiological perspective on the etiology and treatment of insomnia. In S. N. Haynes & L. R. Gannon (Eds.), *Psychosomatic disorders.* New York: Praeger.

Young, J. E. (1982). Loneliness, depression, and cognitive therapy. In L. A. Peplau & D. Perlman (Eds.), *Loneliness: A sourcebook of current theory, research, and therapy.* New York: Wiley.

Zaiden, J. (1982). Psychodynamic therapy: Clinical applications. In A. J. Rush(Ed.), *Short-term psychotherapies for depression.* New York: Guilford Press.

Zajonc, R. B. (1968). Attitudinal effects of mere exposure. *Journal of Personality and Social Psychology, Monograph Supplement 2, 9,* 1–27.

Zamansky, H. S., & Bartis, S. P. (1985). The dissociation of an experience. *Journal of Abnormal Psychology, 94,* 243–248.

Zarski, J. J. (1984). Hassles and health: A replication. *Health Psychology, 3,* 243–251.

Zatz, S., & Chassin, L. (1985). Cognitions of test-anxious children under naturalistic test-taking conditions. *Journal of Consulting and Clinical Psychology, 53,* 393–401.

Zeiss, A. M. (1982). Expectations for aging on sexuality in parents and average married couples. *Journal of Sex Research, 82,* 47–57.

Zilbergeld, B., & Evans, M. (1980). The inadequacy of Masters and Johnson. *Psychology Today, 14*(8), 29–34, 47–53.

Zillmann, D., & Bryant, J. (1983). Effects of massive exposure to pornography. In N. M. Malamuth & E. Donnerstein (Eds.), *Pornography and sexual aggression.* New York: Academic Press.

Zimbardo, P. G. (1969). The human choice: Individuation, reason, and order versus deindividuation, impulse, and chaos. In W. J. Arnold & D. Levine (Eds.), *Nebraska symposium on motivation,* Vol. 17. Lincoln, NE: University of Nebraska Press.

Zimbardo, P. G., Ebbeson, E. B., & Maslach, C. (1977). *Influencing attitudes and changing behavior.* Reading, MA: Addison-Wesley.

Zimmer, D. (1983). Interaction patterns and communication skills in sexually distressed, maritally distressed, and normal couples: Two experimental studies. *Journal of Sex and Marital Therapy, 9,* 251–265.

Zuckerman, M. (1974). The sensation-seeking motive. In B. Maher (Ed.), *Progress in Experimental Personality Research, 7.* New York: Academic Press.

Zuckerman, M. (1980). Sensation seeking. In H. London & J. Exner (Eds.), *Dimensions of personality.* New York: Wiley.

Zuckerman, M., Eysenck, S., & Eysenck, H. J. (1978). Sensation seeking in England and America: Cross-cultural, age, and sex comparisons. *Journal of Consulting and Clinical Psychology, 46,* 139–149.

Zuckerman, M., Miserandino, M., & Bernieri, F. (1983). Civil inattention exists—in elevators. *Personality and Social Psychology Bulletin, 9,* 578–586.

Zuger, B. (1976). Monozygotic twins discordant for homosexuality: Report of a pair and significance of the phenomenon. *Comprehensive Psychiatry, 17,* 661–669.

Zweigenhaft, R. L. (1970). Signature size: A key to status awareness. *Journal of Social Psychology, 81,* 49–54.

Zweigenhaft, R. L. (1975). Name styles in America and name styles in New Zealand. *Journal of Social Psychology, 97,* 289–290.

Zweigenhaft, R. L. (1977). The other side of unusual names. *Journal of Social Psychology, 103,* 291–302.

Zweigenhaft, R. L., Hayes, K. N., & Haagen, C. H. (1980). The psychological impact of names. *Journal of Social Psychology, 110,* 203–210.

Zyazema, N. Z. (1984). Toward better patient drug compliance and comprehension: A challenge to medical and pharmaceutical services in Zimbabwe. *Social Science and Medicine, 18,* 551–554.

ACKNOWLEDGMENTS

For permission to use copyrighted materials the authors thank the following:

Chapter 1
Pages 26–27. The Social-Desirability Scale. From D. P. Crowne and D. A. Marlowe. A new scale of social desirability independent of pathology. *Journal of Consulting Psychology* 24 (1960):351. Copyright 1960 by the American Psychological Association. Reprinted by permission.

Chapter 2
Page 45. Erik Erikson's Stages of Psychosocial Development. Adapted from *Childhood and Society,* 2nd ed., by Erik H. Erikson, by permission of W. W. Norton & Company, Inc. Copyright 1950, © 1963 by W. W. Norton & Company, Inc. Copyright renewed 1978 by Erik H. Erikson.

Page 64. The Expectancy for Success Scale. From B. Fibel and W. B. Hale. The generalized expectancy for success scale. *Journal of Consulting and Clinical Psychology* 46 (1978):931. Copyright 1978 by the American Psychological Association. Reprinted by permission of the publisher.

Chapter 3
Page 82. Table 3.1: Stereotypical Sex-Role Traits. Adapted from Inge K. Broverman. Sex-role stereotypes: A current appraisal. *Journal of Social Issues* 28 (1972), 2:63.

Chapter 4
Pages 131 and 146. Questionnaire and results of *Psychology Today* survey on body image. From E. Bersheid, E. Walster, and G. Bohrnsteds. Body image: The happy American body. *Psychology Today,* November 1973. Reprinted with permission from *Psychology Today* magazine, copyright © 1973 PT Partners, L. P.

Chapter 6
Pages 184–186. Social Readjustment Rating Scale. From Peggy Blake, Robert Fry, and Michael Pesjack, *Self-assessment and behavior change manual* (New York: Random House, 1984), pp. 43–47.

Chapter 8
Pages 282–283. The Temple Fear Survey Inventory. From Philip R. Braun and David J. Reynolds. A factor analysis of a 100-item fear survey inventory. *Behavior Research and Therapy* 7 (1969):399–402.

Chapter 10
Pages 355–357. Relaxation instructions reprinted with permission from Joseph Wolpe and Arnold Lazarus, *Behavior Therapy Techniques* (New York: Pergamon, 1966), pp. 177–180.

Pages 359–361. Three lists adapted/extracted from Meyer Friedman and Diane Ulmer, *Treating Type A Behavior and Your Heart.* Copyright © 1984 by Meyer Friedman. Reprinted by permission of Alfred A. Knopf, Inc.

Chapter 11
Pages 400, 405, and 412. Havighurst's developmental tasks for young adulthood, middle adulthood, and late adulthood. From *Developmental Tasks and Education,* 3d ed., by Robert J. Havighurst. Copyright © 1972 by Longman Inc. All rights reserved.

Chapter 14
Page 498. Items from marriage contract. From W. R. Garrett, *Seasons of Marriage and Family Life* (New York: Holt, Rinehart and Winston, 1982), pp. 133–134.

Page 500. Table 14.2 From D. Snyder, Multidimensional assessment of marital satisfaction. *Journal of Marriage and the Family* 41 (1979):816. Copyrighted 1979 by the National Council on Family Relations, St. Paul, Minnesota. Reprinted by permission.

Pages 502–503. Tables 14.3 and 14.4. From Terri Schultz Brooks, Does marriage give today's women what they really want? *Ladies' Home Journal,* June 1980, pp. 89–91. 146–155. Copyright © 1980, Meredith Corporation. All Rights Reserved. Reprinted from *Ladies' Home Journal* magazine with permission of the author.

Page 516. Table 14.7. From P. Glick and G. B. Spanier. Married and unmarried cohabitation in the U.S. *Journal of Marriage and the Family* 42 (1980):24. Copyrighted 1980 by the National Council on Family Relations, St. Paul, Minnesota. Reprinted by permission.

Chapter 15
Page 525. Table 15.1. From M. Hunt, *Behavior in the 1970s* (Chicago: Playboy, 1974), pp. 91–95.

Page 526. Table 15.2. From Hunt, p. 150.

Page 543. List of actions to lower likelihood of rape. From Boston Women's Health Book Collective, *The New Our Bodies, Ourselves* (New York: Simon & Schuster, 1984).

Page 552. Table 15.3. H. S. Kaplan, *The Real Truth about Women and AIDS* (New York: Simon & Schuster, 1987), p. 77.

Page 544. Cultural Myths That Create a Climate That Supports Rape. From Martha Burt, Cultural myths and supports for rape. *Journal PSP* 38 (1980):217–230. Copyright 1980 by the American Psychological Association. Reprinted by permission of the publisher.

Photo Credits
3: © Coletti, Stock, Boston. 7: Carey/The Image Works. 9: © Cannefax, EKM-Nepenthe, 18: Lejeune, Stock, Boston. 20: Spratt/The Image Works. 25: Delevingne, Stock, Boston. 31: © 1982, Wood, Taurus. 37: © Gonthier/The Image Works. 40: Sigmund Freud, Ltd. 41: Bodin, Stock, Boston. 44: Courtesy of the Association for the Advancement of Psychoanalysis of the Karen Horney Psychoanalytic Institute and Center. 47: © Fitzgerald, The Picture Cube. 51: Carey/The Image Works. 52: Times Newspapers, Ltd. 54: Bettmann Archive. 56: top: Bettmann Archive; bottom: Thaves, © 1974 by NEA, Inc. 58: Heyman, Archive Pictures. 62: Courtesy of Dr. Albert Bandura. 67: © Grecco, Stock, Boston. 70: Courtesy of Carl Rogers. 71: © Sobol, Stock, Boston. 79: © Higgins, jr., Photo Researchers. 85: © 1981, Wood, Taurus. 86: Barnes, Southern Light. 93: Courtesy of Dr. Albert Bandura. 94: © Stanley Milgram. 96 left: © Siluk, EKM-Nepenthe; right: © Crews/The Image Works. 104: Stock, Boston. 117: © 1983, Baratz, The Picture Cube. 123: Gans/The Image Works. 129: Antman, Stock, Boston. 130: "B.C." by permission of Johnny Hart and Field Enterprises, Inc. 132: © 1982, Menzel, Stock, Boston. 142: © Gans/The Image Works. 149: © Wells/The Image Works. 151: © Fritz, Jeroboam. 157 left and right: AP/Wide World. 160: © Stanley Milgram, 164: William Vandivert. 174: © Hammid, Photo Researchers. 181: © 1985, Joel Gordon. 183: © Nettis, Photo Researchers. 189: Focus on Sports. 193: © Parker, Photo Researchers. 195: © Roy Morsch. 197: © Robert Eckert/EKM/Nepenthe. 202: © McHugh, Photo Researchers. 203: © 1983 Randy O'Rourke. 215: © 1985 Cliff Moore/Taurus Photos. 231:

Indexes

■ Name Index

■ Subject Index

Page numbers in **boldface** indicate terms defined in the marginal glossary.

The Virago Book of
Women and
The Great War
1914-18